Revel™ for *Literature and the Writing Process*

REVEL™ is Pearson's newest way of delivering our respected content. Fully digital and highly engaging, REVEL™ offers an immersive learning experience designed for the way today's students read, think, and learn. Enlivening course content with media interactives and assessments, REVEL™ empowers educators to increase engagement with the course and to connect better with students.

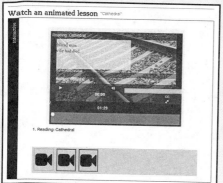

Video and Rich Multimedia Content

Videos, audio recordings, animations, and multimedia instruction provide context that enables students to engage with the text in a more meaningful way.

Interactive Readings and Exercises

Students explore readings through interactive texts. Robust annotation tools allow students to take notes, and post-reading assignments let instructors monitor their students' completion of readings before class begins.

Integrated Writing Assignments

Minimal-stakes, low-stakes, and high-stakes writing tasks allow students multiple opportunities to interact with the ideas presented in the reading assignments, ensuring that they come to class better prepared.

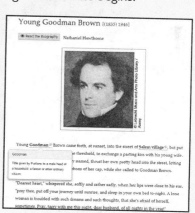

LITERATURE
and the
WRITING PROCESS

Eleventh Edition

Elizabeth McMahan
Illinois State University

Robert Funk
Eastern Illinois University

New!
2016
MLA
Updates

Susan X Day
University of Houston

Linda S. Coleman
Eastern Illinois University

PEARSON

Boston   Columbus   Indianapolis   New York   San Francisco
Amsterdam   Cape Town   Dubai   London   Madrid   Milan   Munich   Paris   Montréal
Toronto   Delhi   Mexico City   São Paulo   Sydney   Hong Kong   Seoul
Singapore   Taipei   Tokyo

Senior Acquistion Editor: Brad Potthoff
Senior Development Editor: Anne Stameshkin
Editorial Assistant: Caitlin Ghegan
Product Marketing Manager: Nicholas T. Bolt
Field Marketing Manager: Joyce Nilsen
Program Manager: Katharine Glynn
Project Manager: Denise Phillip Grant
Project Coordination, Text Design, and
    Electronic Page Makeup: Integra
    Software Services

Design Lead: Beth Paquin
Cover Designer: Studio Montage/Melissa
    Welch
Cover Image: TAlex/Fotolia
Senior Manufacturing Buyer:
    Roy L. Pickering, Jr.
Printer/Binder: R.R. Donnelley/
    Crawfordsville
Cover Printer: Phoenix Color/
    Hagerstown

Credits and acknowledgments borrowed from other sources and reproduced, with permission, in this textbook appear on the appropriate page within text and on pages 982–87.

Unless otherwise indicated herein, any third-party trademarks that may appear in this work are the property of their respective owners and any references to third-party trademarks, logos, or other trade dress are for demonstrative or descriptive purposes only. Such references are not intended to imply any sponsorship, endorsement, authorization, or promotion of Pearson's products by the owners of such marks, or any relationship between the owner and Pearson Education, Inc., or its affiliates, authors, licensees, or distributors.

Library of Congress Cataloging-in-Publication Data
McMahan, Elizabeth.
    Literature and the writing process/Elizabeth McMahan, Robert Funk, Susan X Day, Linda S. Coleman.—Eleventh edition.
        pages cm
    Includes indexes.
    ISBN 978-0-13-411790-4—ISBN 0-13-411790-5
    1. College readers.   2. English language—Rhetoric.   3. Report writing—Problems, exercises, etc.   4. Literature—Collections.   I. Funk, Robert.   II. Day, Susan.
III. Coleman, Linda S.   IV. Title.
    PE1417.M45 2015
    808'.0427—dc23
                                                                                    2015030097

1   17

www.pearsonhighered.com

Student Edition ISBN 10:   0-13-467875-3
Student Edition ISBN 13: 978-0-13-467875-7
    A la Carte ISBN 10:   0-13-470314-6
    A la Carte ISBN 13: 978-0-13-470314-5

For our dear friend and co-author Betty McMahan,
whose love of literature and exuberant laugh continue to inspire us.

Contents

PART I Composing: An Overview   1

1 The Prewriting Process   2

2 The Writing Process   17

PART II Writing About Short Fiction

6   How Do I Read Short Fiction?

7   Writing About Structure

**12   Critical Casebook: Joyce Carol Oates's
"Where Are You Going, Where Have You Been?"**   193

13   Anthology of Short Fiction   210

24   Paired Poems for Comparison   571

Contents by Genre

Drama

Thematic Table of Contents

Male and Female

Comedy and Satire

Preface

This book grew out of our long-standing interest in the possibilities of integrating the study of literature with the practice of composition. Many of our students have learned to write perceptively and well using literature as their subject matter. Great literature is always thought-provoking, always new. Why not utilize it to sharpen critical thinking and improve writing skills? Toward that end, we have combined an introduction-to-literature anthology with detailed instruction in the writing process.

Our Purpose

Literature and the Writing Process, Eleventh Edition, presents literary selections as materials for students to read, analyze, and write about. Our careful integration of rhetorical instruction with the critical study of literature guides students through the allied processes of analytical reading and argumentative writing. As a result, students learn how to write essays about the major features that are involved in interpreting short stories, poems, and plays.

New to This Edition

As always, we have been guided by the advice of our reviewers in revising this edition. Here is a list of the major additions and changes in the Eleventh Edition:

- *New Part And Chapter: Part V: Critical Approaches to Literature* begins with a concise survey of the primary systems for interpreting literature and concludes with a **new multi-genre Critical Casebook: Writing about Culture and Identity (Chapter 35).** The casebook contains seven short stories, nine poems, and two plays that deal with issues of race, class, gender, ethnicity, beliefs, and cultural values. The questions for writing and discussion in the casebook encourage students to examine their own thoughts and feelings on these topics.
- *New Feature: MultiModal Projects* supplement and extend the writing ideas in the literary chapters, casebooks, and portfolios. These twenty-three assignments, which appear throughout the text, direct students to read, interpret, analyze, and compose in modes that go beyond text on the page, exploring digital, audio, visual, and creative modes. Students are prompted to engage with words, numbers, images, graphics, animations, music, and more.

- *New Portfoilo of four stories about "singular" women* invites discussions of the ways women are characterized in fiction, encouraging comparisons across time and location.
- *Updated coverage of MLA style,* including its use in student work, reflects extensive changes from the 2016 *MLA Handbook.*
- *Making Connections prompts* are now available for all the selections in the anthologies, casebooks, and portfolios, inviting synthesis among selections.
- *New critical commentaries* for works such as Langston Hughes's poems and *The Glass Menagerie* have been added.
- *Updated sections* have been included on reflective and argumentative writing and additional suggestions for doing researched writing, as well as discussion of additional forms, such as the prose poem.
- *New works include* short stories by Arna Bontemps, Sarah Orne Jewett, James Joyce, Katherine Mansfield, H. H. Munro, Celeste Ng, and Eudora Welty; poems by Richard Blanco, Gregory Djanikian, Amy Lowell, Mina Loy, Edgar Lee Masters, Lisel Mueller, Frank O'Hara, Christina Rossetti, David Shumate, Alfred Lord Tennyson, David Wagoner, William Wordsworth, James Wright, and Mitsuye Yamada; and plays by Hernik Ibsen and Alice Childress.

Our Organization

The book is divided into five main parts:

- **Part I Composing: An Overview** provides a thorough introduction to the recursive composing process as it applies to writing about literature. This part contains individual chapters on prewriting, writing (drafting), writing convincing arguments, and rewriting. Part I also includes a chapter on researched writing, which offers instruction in planning, researching, and documenting a paper with secondary sources, along with an updated description of the MLA Style for citing and crediting these sources.
- **Part II Writing About Short Fiction** begins with a brief introduction on how to read short stories, followed by five chapters on writing about the individual elements of fiction: structure, imagery and symbolism, point of view, setting and atmosphere, and theme. Each chapter focuses on a story that clearly illustrates the literary technique to be studied. This part also contains a critical casebook on the story "Where Are You Going, Where Have You Been?" by Joyce Carol Oates, an anthology of seventeen short stories, and three portfolios of stories: science fiction, singular women, and humor and satire.
- **Part III Writing About Poetry** begins with a brief chapter on reading poetry, followed by three chapters on writing about key elements in poetry: persona and tone, poetic language, and poetic form. Poems that illustrate the literary concepts under discussion are reprinted within the chapter. This part also contains a casebook on the poetry of Langston Hughes; a color insert that contains reproductions of six paintings with corresponding poems that respond to and comment on the art; an anthology of seventy-eight poems; a group of twelve paired poems for comparison; and three portfolios of poems—about work, war, and humor/satire.

- **Part IV Writing About Drama** begins with an introductory chapter on how to read a play, followed by two chapters on writing about issues of structure and character in drama. Each chapter focuses on a particular play, and the chapter on character includes a critical casebook about Amanda in Tennessee Williams's *The Glass Menagerie*. This part also contains an anthology of three classic plays and a portfolio of two humorous and satirical plays.

- **Part V Critical Approaches to Literature** contains a brief summary of eight major systems for analyzing and interpreting fiction, poetry, and drama—and concludes with a multi-genre casebook for reading and writing about eighteen literary works that explore the themes of culture and identity.

These five parts are supplemented by a Glossary of Literary and Rhetorical Terms.

Student and Professional Writing Samples

These twelve examples of critical writing demonstrate how to analyze and argue about literature:

- The complete composing protocol that a student followed in developing her interpretation of James Joyce's "Eveline," including samples of prewriting, drafting, post-draft outlining, revising, editing, and the final draft (Chapters 1, 2, and 4).

- A student paper illustrating the use of claims, evidence, and reasoning in arguing an interpretation of Dagoberto Gilb's "Love in L.A." (Chapter 3).

- An expanded and documented version of the student paper on "Eveline" (Chapter 5).

- A documented published article on Kate Chopin's depiction of marriage in "Desireé's Baby" (Chapter 5).

- The second and final drafts of a student paper on symbolism in Shirley Jackson's "The Lottery" (Chapter 8).

- A documented student paper comparing "The Ones Who Walk Away from Omelas" by Ursula Le Guin with "Speech Sounds" by Octavia Butler (in the Portfolio of Science Fiction Stories, Chapter 14).

- A new personal-reflection essay on persona and tone in "The Nymph's Reply to the Shepherd" by Sir Walter Raleigh (Chapter 18).

- The second and final drafts of a student paper on imagery in John Donne's "A Valediction: Forbidding Mourning" (Chapter 19).

- A documented student paper on form and meaning in Robert Frost's "The Silken Tent" (Chapter 20).

- A published article on the elements of poetic form in Robert Hayden's "Those Winter Sundays" (Chapter 20).

- A student's personal reflection on Anne Sexton's "The Starry Night" (Chapter 22, The Art of Poetry).

- A student paper on the gender conflict in Sophocles's *Antigone* (Chapter 29).

Instructor's Manual

The Instructor's Manual for *Literature and the Writing Process*, 11/e (ISBN 0-13-415109-7), offers myriad teaching suggestions, activities, resources for teaching literature, and guidance on using reading journals. Supporting materials for each reading include an overview and possible responses to connected assignments. The instructor's manual is available online.

Revel

REVEL™ is Pearson's newest way of delivering our respected content. Fully digital and highly engaging, REVEL offers an immersive learning experience designed for the way today's students read, think, and learn. Enlivening course content with media interactives and assessments, REVEL empowers educators to increase engagement with the course, and to better connect with students.

REVEL™ for ***Literature and the Writing Process*** offers an enhanced digital anthology that seamlessly integrates literature and composition into one multi-purpose, flexible online environment. Careful integration of rhetorical instruction with the critical study of literature guides students through the allied processes of analytical reading and argumentative writing. Accompanied by pedagogical apparatus and multimedia resources to facilitate teaching and learning, ***Literature and the Writing Process*** enables students to enjoy, understand, and learn from imaginative literature.

Our Appreciation

We are grateful to the reviewers whose comments and suggestions helped us craft this Eleventh Edition: Joan Steele Bruckwicki, Tyler Junior College; Jan Czarnecki, Bluefield State College; Adam Floridia, Middlesex Community College; Julie Kraft, Cowley County Community College; Terence McNulty, Middlesex Community College; Wade Skinner, Tyler Junior College.

Many thanks to our former editor Joe Terry (VP and Editor-in-Chief of College Foundations); to our development editor, Anne Stameshkin, who gave us invaluable advice and contributions in producing this new edition; to editorial assistant Caitlin Ghegan for all of her help along the way; to our tireless permissions editor, Joseph Croscup; and to our first-rate production team, including our project manager, Denise Phillip Grant; and to the media team (including Julia Pomann and Elizabeth

Bravo) that is working hard to adapt this book for digital, interactive use. Also thanks to our marketing manager, Nick Bolt.

To Bill Weber, undying appreciation for his inspiration, support, and comfort.

ROBERT FUNK
SUSAN X DAY
LINDA S. COLEMAN

PART I Composing: An Overview

This text serves a dual purpose: to enable you to enjoy, understand, and learn from imaginative literature; and to help you to write clearly, intelligently, and correctly about what you have learned. Our instruction is designed to guide you through the interrelated processes of analytical reading and critical writing. Part I begins with the prewriting process and then shows you how to follow through to the completion of a finished essay about a literary work. In this section we also offer a separate chapter on how to use the elements of argument in writing about literature, and we conclude with detailed instruction on how to incorporate secondary sources into your writing.

1 The Prewriting Process

Chapter Preview

Your study of writing, as we approach it in this book, will focus on the composing process: prewriting, writing, rewriting, and editing. The first part of the text takes you through each stage, explaining one way of putting together a paper on James Joyce's "Eveline." The following parts, which include more short stories, plus poems and plays, contain further advice for understanding and writing about these various kinds of literature.

We realize, of course, that our chronological explanation of the stages in the writing process is not entirely true to experience; most of us juggle at least two steps at a time when we write. But we have adopted a linear, step-by-step presentation in order to explain and illustrate the key components of the process thoroughly and clearly. By the end of this chapter on the prewriting process, you will be able to

- Define *audience awareness*.
- Identify the main purposes for writing.
- Explain the key steps in critical reading: *analysis, inference, synthesis, evaluation*.
- Demonstrate four important techniques for discovering ideas: *self-questioning, freewriting, problem solving, clustering*.
- Define the terms *theme* and *thesis*.
- Evaluate the effectiveness of a thesis statement.

Reading for Writing

To prepare for your study of the stages of writing an essay about a literary topic, find a comfortable spot and read the following short story.

James Joyce   1882–1941

James Joyce rejected his Irish Catholic heritage and left his homeland at age twenty. Though an expatriate most of his adult life, Joyce wrote almost exclusively about his native Dublin. His first book, *Dubliners* (1914), was a series of sharply drawn vignettes based on his experiences in Ireland, the homeland he later described as "a sow that eats its own farrow." His novel *Ulysses* (1933) was banned for a time in the United States because of its coarse language and frank treatment of sexuality; it is now often ranked as the greatest novel of the twentieth century.

Eveline

She sat at the window watching the evening invade the avenue. Her head was leaned against the window curtains and in her nostrils was the odour of dusty cretonne. She was tired.

Few people passed. The man out of the last house passed on his way home; she heard his footsteps clacking along the concrete pavement and afterwards crunching on the cinder path before the new red houses. One time there used to be a field there in which they used to play every evening with other people's children. Then a man from Belfast bought the field and built houses in it—not like their little brown houses but bright brick houses with shining roofs. The children of the avenue used to play together in that field—the Devines, the Waters, the Dunns, little Keogh the cripple, she and her brothers and sisters. Ernest, however, never played: he was too grown up. Her father used often to hunt them in out of the field with his blackthorn stick; but usually little Keogh used to keep nix and call out when he saw her father coming. Still they seemed to have been rather happy then. Her father was not so bad then; and besides, her mother was alive. That was a long time ago; she and her brothers and sisters were all grown up; her mother was dead. Tizzie Dunn was dead, too, and the Waters had gone back to England. Everything changes. Now she was going to go away like the others, to leave her home.

Home! She looked round the room, reviewing all its familiar objects which she had dusted once a week for so many years, wondering where on earth all the dust came from. Perhaps she would never see again those familiar objects from which she had never dreamed of being divided. And yet during all those years she had never found out the name of the priest whose yellowing photograph hung on the wall above the broken harmonium beside the coloured print of the promises made to Blessed Margaret Mary Alacoque. He had been a school friend of her father. Whenever he showed the photograph to a visitor her father used to pass it with a casual word:

"He is in Melbourne now."

She had consented to go away, to leave her home. Was that wise? She tried to weigh each side of the question. In her home anyway she had shelter and food; she had those whom she had known all her life about her. Of course she had to work hard, both in the house and at business. What would they say of her in the Stores when they found out that she had run away with a fellow? Say she was a fool, perhaps; and her place would be filled up by advertisement. Miss Gavan would be glad. She had always had an edge on her, especially whenever there were people listening.

"Miss Hill, don't you see these ladies are waiting?"

"Look lively, Miss Hill, please."

She would not cry many tears at leaving the Stores.

But in her new home, in a distant unknown country, it would not be like that. Then she would be married—she, Eveline. People would treat her with respect then. She would not be treated as her mother had been. Even now, though she was over nineteen, she sometimes felt herself in danger of her father's violence. She knew it was that that had given her the palpitations. When they were growing up he had never gone for her, like he used to go for Harry and Ernest, because she was a girl; but latterly he had begun to threaten her and say what he would do to her only for her dead mother's sake. And now she had nobody to

A late nineteenth-century photo of Fade Street in Dublin, which conveys a sense of the neighborhood where Eveline grew up.

protect her. Ernest was dead and Harry, who was in the church decorating business, was nearly always down somewhere in the country. Besides, the invariable squabble for money on Saturday nights had begun to weary her unspeakably. She always gave her entire wages—seven shillings—and Harry always sent up what he could but the trouble was to get any money from her father. He said she used to squander the money, that she had no head, that he wasn't going to give her his hard-earned money to throw about the streets, and much more, for he was usually fairly bad on Saturday night. In the end he would give her the money and ask her had she any intention of buying Sunday's dinner. Then she had to rush out as quickly as she could and do her marketing, holding her black leather purse tightly in her hand as she elbowed her way through the crowds and returning home late under her load of provisions. She had hard work to keep the house together and to see that the two young children who had been left to her charge went to school regularly and got their meals regularly. It was hard work—a hard life—but now that she was about to leave it she did not find it a wholly undesirable life.

She was about to explore another life with Frank. Frank was very kind, manly, 10
open-hearted. She was to go away with him by the night-boat to be his wife and to live with him in Buenos Ayres where he had a home waiting for her. How well she remembered the first time she had seen him; he was lodging in a house on the main road where she used to visit. It seemed a few weeks ago. He was standing at the gate, his peaked cap pushed back on his head and his hair tumbled

forward over a face of bronze. Then they had come to know each other. He used to meet her outside the Stores every evening and see her home. He took her to see *The Bohemian Girl* and she felt elated as she sat in an unaccustomed part of the theatre with him. He was awfully fond of music and sang a little. People knew that they were courting and, when he sang about the lass that loves a sailor, she always felt pleasantly confused. He used to call her Poppens out of fun. First of all it had been an excitement for her to have a fellow and then she had begun to like him. He had tales of distant countries. He had started as a deck boy at a pound a month on a ship of the Allan Line going out to Canada. He told her the names of the ships he had been on and the names of the different services. He had sailed through the Straits of Magellan and he told her stories of the terrible Patagonians. He had fallen on his feet in Buenos Ayres, he said, and had come over to the old country just for a holiday. Of course, her father had found out the affair and had forbidden her to have anything to say to him.

"I know these sailor chaps," he said.

One day he had quarrelled with Frank and after that she had to meet her lover secretly.

The evening deepened in the avenue. The white of two letters in her lap grew indistinct. One was to Harry; the other was to her father. Ernest had been her favourite but she liked Harry too. Her father was becoming old lately, she noticed; he would miss her. Sometimes he could be very nice. Not long before, when she had been laid up for a day, he had read her out a ghost story and made toast for her at the fire. Another day, when their mother was alive, they had all gone for a picnic to the Hill of Howth. She remembered her father putting on her mother's bonnet to make the children laugh.

Her time was running out but she continued to sit by the window, leaning her head against the window curtain, inhaling the odour of dusty cretonne. Down far in the avenue she could hear a street organ playing. She knew the air. Strange that it should come that very night to remind her of the promise to her mother, her promise to keep the home together as long as she could. She remembered the last night of her mother's illness; she was again in the close dark room at the other side of the hall and outside she heard a melancholy air of Italy. The organ-player had been ordered to go away and given sixpence. She remembered her father strutting back into the sickroom saying:

"Damned Italians! coming over here!"

As she mused the pitiful vision of her mother's life laid its spell on the very quick of her being—that life of commonplace sacrifices closing in final craziness. She trembled as she heard again her mother's voice saying constantly with foolish insistence:

"Derevaun Seraun! Derevaun Seraun!"[1]

She stood up in a sudden impulse of terror. Escape! She must escape! Frank would save her. He would give her life, perhaps love, too. But she wanted to live. Why should she be unhappy? She had a right to happiness. Frank would take her in his arms, fold her in his arms. He would save her.

She stood among the swaying crowd in the station at the North Wall. He held her hand and she knew that he was speaking to her, saying something about the passage over and over again. The station was full of soldiers with brown

15

---

[1]"The end of pleasure is pain!"

baggages. Through the wide doors of the sheds she caught a glimpse of the black mass of the boat, lying in beside the quay wall, with illumined portholes. She answered nothing. She felt her cheek pale and cold and, out of a maze of distress, she prayed to God to direct her, to show her what was her duty. The boat blew a long mournful whistle into the mist. If she went, tomorrow she would be on the sea with Frank, steaming towards Buenos Ayres. This passage had been booked. Could she still draw back after all he had done for her? Her distress awoke a nausea in her body and she kept moving her lips in silent fervent prayer.

A bell clanged upon her heart. She felt him seize her hand: 20
"Come!"

All the seas of the world tumbled about her heart. He was drawing her into them: he would drown her. She gripped with both hands at the iron railing.

"Come!"

No! No! No! It was impossible. Her hands clutched the iron in frenzy. Amid the seas she sent a cry of anguish.

"Eveline! Evvy!"   25

He rushed beyond the barrier and called to her to follow. He was shouted at to go on but he still called to her. She set her white face to him, passive, like a helpless animal. Her eyes gave him no sign of love or farewell or recognition.

(1914)

◇◇◇◇◇◇◇◇◇◇◇◇◇◇◇◇◇◇◇◇◇◇◇

Now that your reading of Joyce's story has given you material to mull over, you should consider some questions that good writers think about as they prepare to write. Granted, experienced writers might go over some of these *prewriting* matters almost unconsciously—and perhaps *as* they write instead of before. But in order to explain how to get the process going for you, we will present these considerations one by one.

Who Are My Readers?

Unless you are writing a journal or a diary for your own satisfaction, your writing always has an *audience*—the person or group of people who will read it. You need to keep this audience in mind as you plan what to say and as you choose the best way to express your ideas.

Analyze the Audience

No doubt you already have considerable audience awareness. You would never write a job application letter using the latest in-group slang, nor would you normally correspond with your dear Aunt Minnie in impersonal formal English. Writing for diverse groups about whom you know little is more difficult than writing for a specific audience whom you know well. In this class, for instance, you will be writing for your fellow students and for your instructor, a mixed group sorted together by a computer registration system. Although they are diverse, they do share some characteristics. For one thing, when you begin to write a paper about "Eveline," you know that your audience has read the story;

thus, you need not summarize the plot. Also, the people in your audience are college-educated (or becoming so); therefore, you need not avoid difficult words like *epitome, eclectic,* or *protean* if they are the appropriate choices. Other shared qualities will become apparent as you get to know your classmates and your instructor.

Prewriting Exercise: Considering Audience

Compose a brief letter persuading Eveline that she should (or should not) leave Frank. Your argumentative tactics, your attitude, and even your word choice must be affected by what you know about Eveline from reading the story—her essential timidity, her insecurity, her self-doubt, her capacity for self-deception. Take all this into account as you present your argument for or against leaving Frank.

Then, write briefly to her bullying father explaining to him why his dutiful daughter has deserted him (assuming she has gone).

Finally, write Frank a short letter explaining why Eveline will not be going away with him (assuming she stays in Dublin).

Be prepared to discuss with the class specific ways in which your letters are different when you change your audience. Read at least one other student's letters to see how another writer handled the tasks.

Why Am I Writing?

Every kind of writing, even a grocery list, has a purpose. You seldom sit down to write without some aim in mind, and this purpose affects your whole approach to writing. The immediate response to the question "Why am I writing?" may be that your teacher or your employer asked you to. But that answer will not help you understand the reasons that make writing worth doing—and worth reading.

Reasons for Writing

Sometimes you may write in order *to express* your own feelings, as in a diary or a love letter. More frequently, though, you will be writing for several other people, and the response you want from these prospective readers will determine your purpose. If, for instance, you want your audience to be amused by your writing (as in an informal essay or friendly letter), your purpose is *to entertain.* If you want your readers to gain some knowledge from your writing (say, how to get to your house from the airport), then you are writing *to inform.* If you want your readers to agree with an opinion or to accept an idea (as in a letter to the editor or an advertisement), then you are writing *to persuade.* Of course, these aims overlap—as do most things in the writing process—but usually one purpose predominates.

Most of your writing in this course, as in real life, will be an argument one way or another. Your purpose is often to convince your reader to agree with the points you are making. Logical ideas set down in clear, interesting writing should prove convincing and keep your readers reading.

Prewriting Exercises: Thinking about Audience and Purpose

In writing the three letters to various characters, you have already noticed how audience and purpose can change the way you think and write about "Eveline." After studying the four writing suggestions that follow, reread the story. You may discover that you have more ideas and feelings about it than you first imagined. Thinking about prospective readers and determining your purpose will help you understand your own views and reactions better.

1. If your purpose is *to express* your personal response:
   Write down your feelings about Eveline in a journal entry or in a brief note to a close friend. Do you sympathize with Eveline? Pity her? Does she irritate you or make you angry? Be as forthright as you can.

2. If your purpose is *to inform* someone else:
   Write a brief summary (less than one hundred words) of "Eveline" for a fellow student who wants to know if the story is worth reading. Write a slightly longer summary for your instructor (or someone else who has read the story) who wants to know if you have grasped its important points.
   Which summary was easier to write? What purposes besides providing information were involved in each summary?

3. If your purpose is *to entertain* yourself or your readers:
   How would you rewrite the ending of "Eveline" to make it more positive or romantic—to make it appeal to a wider audience? Would such an ending be consistent with the earlier parts of the story? Would it be true to human experience?

4. If your purpose is *to persuade* your readers:
   The author tells us that Eveline held two letters in her lap, but we do not know their contents. Write your version of one of them. Try to construe from evidence in the story what Eveline would have said to convince her father or her brother that she had good reasons for going away with Frank. How would she persuade them to forgive her? Consider also what other purposes Eveline would try to achieve in each of these letters.

What Ideas Should I Use?

Understanding literature involves learning what questions to ask yourself as you read. To deepen your comprehension and develop ideas for writing, you need to examine the work carefully and think critically about its component parts.

Reading and Thinking Critically

Critical reading and thinking involves several overlapping procedures: analysis, inference, synthesis, and evaluation. The word *critical* does not mean "disapproving" or "faultfinding" in this context; it means thorough, thoughtful, inquisitive, and logically demanding. As a critical reader you want to discover meanings and relationships that you might otherwise miss in uncritical, superficial reading.

- *Analysis* involves examining the parts or elements of a work, the better to understand it.
- *Inference* entails drawing conclusions about a work based on your analysis. When you infer, you explore the implications of various elements (such as plot, characterization, structure, tone) and interpret their meaning.
- *Synthesis* is the process of putting your analysis and inferences together into a new, more informed understanding of the work. You create this new understanding by making connections, identifying patterns, and drawing conclusions.
- *Evaluation* means defending the judgments you have made about a work's meaning, significance, or quality.

Chapters 6, 17, and 28—"How Do I Read Short Fiction?" "How Do I Read Poetry?" and "How Do I Read a Play?"—provide specific suggestions and questions to guide you in analyzing, making inferences, synthesizing, and evaluating literary works. Here are some suggestions and questions from those chapters, along with their critical reading basis.

Example of Questions Inviting Analysis

What is the central conflict of the play? Does the play contain any secondary conflicts (subplots)? How do they relate to the main conflict?

Example of Questions That Require Inferences

Who is the main character? Does this person's character change during the course of the story? Do you feel sympathetic toward the main character? What sort of person is she or he?

Example of Questions Involving Synthesis

What is the theme (the central idea) of this poem? Can you state it in a single sentence?

Example of Evaluation Questions

Which of the poems conveys the horrors of war most effectively? Why?

Discovering and Developing Ideas

You read critically to derive meaning from a work, and you continue to think critically as you go about discovering ideas to write about. This discovery process, called **invention**, is more effective if you employ one of the following techniques designed to help you analyze literary works and generate ideas about them.

Self-Questioning

These are the kinds of questions you might ask yourself when studying a work of literature: questions about characters, their circumstances, their motives and conflicts, their fears and expectations, their relations with other characters; questions about the setting in which the story takes place; questions about any repeated details that seem significant; questions about the meaning and value of actions and events.

Exercise: Self-Questioning

Write out your responses to these questions about "Eveline" and keep them handy as you formulate your essay.

1. What is Eveline's home life like?
2. How does she expect her new life to be different?
3. Do you think this expectation is realistic?
4. Why is the word *dust* mentioned so often?
5. List all the concrete details you can find that describe Eveline's home.
6. How old is Eveline? Is her age important for any reason?
7. What sort of person is her father? What kind of "bad way" is he in on Saturday nights?
8. How does Eveline feel about her father?
9. What sort of person was Eveline's mother? What happened to her? Does Eveline identify with her mother in any way?
10. How does Eveline feel about her dead mother?
11. What do you think her mother meant when she kept repeating "the end of pleasure is pain"? Why would she say this? Was she really crazy—or only worn down?
12. What does Eveline's father mean when he tells her, "I know these sailor chaps"? What possible reasons could he have for trying to break up Eveline's romance?
13. What sort of person is Frank? What does Eveline actually know about him?
14. Has Eveline romanticized Frank in any way? Is her father's objection to him perhaps justified?
15. What is Eveline's duty to her father? What promise did she make to her dying mother?
16. What is her duty to herself? Does she really believe she has a "right to happiness"? Why or why not?
17. How does Eveline feel about leaving her brother?
18. In what ways is Eveline "like a helpless animal"? What is she afraid of?
19. Why do you think her eyes give Frank "no sign of love or farewell or recognition"?
20. Do you think Eveline made the right decision? Why or why not?

During the invention stage, you want to turn up as many ideas as possible. Later, after choosing a focus for your paper, such as characterization or theme, you will select those story details that you will be discussing when developing your argument. Even though you narrow your focus, you still need to consider other elements of the story—imagery, symbolism, setting, point of view—as these elements serve to reveal character or theme.

Directed Freewriting

Many people find that they can best bring ideas to the surface by writing freely, with no restrictions about correctness. When you engage in *freewriting* in order to "free" ideas from your subconscious mind, you should think of a pertinent question and just start writing.

Exercise: Directed Freewriting

Consider this question: "Why does Eveline stay with her abusive father?" As you think, start writing. Set down everything that comes to mind; do not concern yourself with spelling, word choice, or punctuation. You are writing for your own benefit, attempting to discover everything about Eveline's decision that you have in mind after reading and thinking about the story.

After writing for ten minutes (or after you run out of ideas), stop and read over what you have said. Underline any idea that might serve as the focus for a paper. Put stars or asterisks in the margin beside any ideas that sound useful as support for your interpretation. On page 12 you can see an example of freewriting by a student responding to this same question.

If you find freewriting a good method for generating ideas, you may want to go through the process again. This time write down a statement that you underlined in your first freewriting as a possible approach for your paper. Let's say you decide to focus (as our student did) on the idea that Eveline's sense of insecurity causes her to remain with her father. Put that sentence at the top of a fresh sheet of paper and begin writing. Continue recording your thoughts until you either run out of ideas or run out of time (fifteen minutes is usually enough). Then read over your freewriting, underlining or putting stars by any ideas that you think would be good support to include in your paper.

Problem Solving

Another method of generating material for a paper involves *problem solving*. Consider some part of the work that you feel you need to understand better and pose yourself a problem, like the following:

Sample Student Prewriting: Directed Freewriting

Why does Eveline stay? She feels a sense of duty - to her mother (dying wish/promise) ✱ Father old, lonely, needs her to keep house. She needs to be _loved_, feel she belongs. ✱ Naturally she's afraid to leave home for the first time - and go so far away. She's ✱ _insecure_. But she's 19 - must want to test her wings, have a better life than her poor mother's. She's suffocating there in all that dust! Frank offers freedom + romance - and _fun_. She thinks she likes him, may even love him - but not sure. Her father has warned her about Frank. And how ✱ much does she actually know about him? What if he's all promises, promises - and then deserts her halfway around the world? Maybe her father's right! How does she ✱ feel about her parents? She knows her mother's life was miserable + she died a pitiful death. She fears her father (who ✱ must have caused a lot of her mom's misery + hardship) But E. has a _strong sense of duty._ And does love her father, despite his faults.

Exercise: Problem Solving

Explain the ending of the story so that it is understandable and believable.

As you seek a solution, ask yourself more questions.

- Why does Eveline refuse to leave her pinched, narrow life with her father and the younger children?
- Is there anything about the way she was brought up that makes this action seem reasonable, perhaps inevitable?
- Would her life have been different if she had been born male instead of female? What happened to her brothers, for instance?
- Does her religion have any bearing on her decision?

Write down all the reasons you can find to help explain why Eveline does not leave home. Do any of these reasons shed light on the overall meaning of the story? Do you now perhaps see a meaningful point you could develop into an essay?

Clustering

Another useful way of getting ideas out of your head and down on paper involves *clustering*. Begin with a blank sheet of paper. In the center, write a crucial question about the story that you want to investigate, and circle the words. Then, draw a line out from that circle, write an idea or a question related to the central idea, and circle that. Spiraling out from that circle, add and circle any further associations that you can make. Continue drawing lines from the center, like spokes radiating from a wheel, and record any other ideas or questions that are related. When you finish, you will have a cluster of related ideas resembling the student example on page 14, which explores the question "Why does Eveline decide to stay with her father?"

Clustering works just fine with statements, as well as with questions. If you think you might want to write a paper focusing on the characterization of Eveline, you could just write her name in the center of the page and begin recording all that you know about her. Your first ring of circles might include father, mother, siblings, house, church, job, Frank, lifestyle, personality—and spiral out from there.

You can see that this technique works well for exploring any aspect of a work. As you progress through this course, you may decide to write in the middle of the page *point of view, setting, imagery,* or whatever element you think might serve as a meaningful focus for your paper.

What Point Should I Make?

Besides providing a thorough understanding of the story, these prewriting activities serve to stir up ideas for a ***thesis***—the controlling idea for your paper—and to help you discover evidence to support convincingly the observations you will make in developing that thesis.

Sample Student Prewriting: Clustering

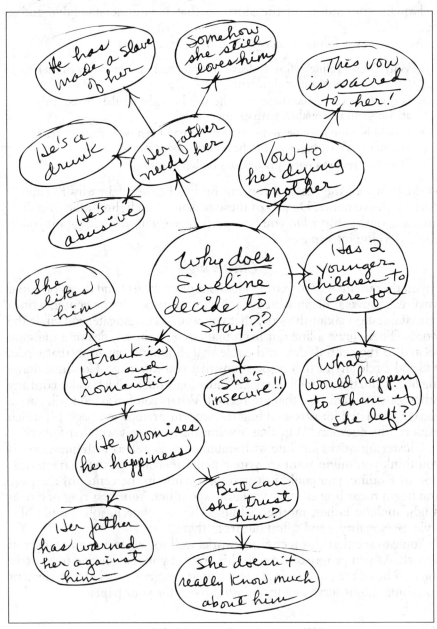

He has made a slave of her

Somehow she still loves him.

This vow is sacred to her!

He's a drunk

Her father needs her

Vow to her dying mother

He's abusive

Why does Eveline decide to stay??

She likes him

Frank is fun and romantic

She's insecure!!

Has 2 younger children to care for

What would happen to them if she left?

He promises her happiness

But can she trust him?

Her father has warned her against him—

She doesn't really know much about him

Relating a Part to the Whole

One bit of advice that will help you write meaningful literary papers is the following:

> Devise a thesis that makes its point by relating some aspect of the work to the meaning of the whole—that is, to its theme.

Our questions so far have led you to approach Joyce's story by analyzing character and plot. But writing a simple character sketch (in which you discuss what sort of person Eveline is) would not produce a satisfactory critical paper. You need to go beyond that one-dimensional approach and make your essay say something about the story itself. In short, you must argue that your analysis of her character relates to the theme.

Finding the Theme

You may have learned that the ***theme*** of a work is the moral. In a sense that is true, but a moral suggests a neatly stated, preachy comment on some vice or virtue, whereas a literary theme will seldom be so pat and should never sound preachy. In order to discover theme you need to decide what you have learned from reading the story. What did the author reveal about the behavior of human beings, about the conduct of society? Rather than looking for a moral, look for some insight into the human condition.

Sometimes you may have a theme in mind but be unable to express it except in a cliché. You could, for instance, see the theme of "Eveline" as an acceptance of the old adage "Better the devil you know than the devil you don't." Although this idea is acceptable as a theme, a clearer statement would relate the concept more closely to the story, as follows:

> In "Eveline," Joyce focuses on the painful choices a young woman faces concerning her desire for a better life, her duty to her family, and her fear of leaving home.

Certainly her character—the kind of person she is—relates directly to this theme. If, for instance, Eveline had been a willful, disobedient child who grew up into a rebellious, irresponsible young woman, the outcome of the story would surely be different.

The problem is thus to find a thesis that will allow you to argue that Eveline's upbringing has conditioned her for the inevitable failure of nerve, the return to servitude and security, the relinquishing of hopes and dreams.

Stating the Thesis

A good thesis statement should be a *complete sentence* that clearly conveys the point you plan to support in your argument. Notice the difference between a *topic*, which is not a complete sentence, and a *thesis*, which is.

Topic	A characterization of Eveline
Thesis	Joyce's characterization of Eveline as a dutiful daughter enables us to discover why she makes her strange decision at the end.
Topic	The role of the church in "Eveline"
Thesis	The role of the Catholic church is crucial in shaping Eveline's personality and in helping us understand why she sacrifices herself for her family.
Topic	Dust as a symbol in "Eveline"
Thesis	Joyce's use of dust as a controlling symbol in "Eveline" reinforces our understanding of this young woman's dreary, suffocating, arid life.

Your thesis sentence should be broad enough to include all the ideas that are necessary as evidence but narrow enough to make a precise statement of your main point and focus your thoughts. If your thesis is too broad—as, for example, "Joyce's characterization of Eveline is extremely well drawn"—you may end up skimming the surface, never providing a meaningful interpretation of the work. A thesis evaluating the excellence of Joyce's character development needs to connect this point with the whole story. Notice that the previous overly broad thesis is unsatisfactory for another reason: it fails to make a real point.

A better thesis for a paper on "Eveline" might be stated in any of the following ways:

Eveline's Catholic upbringing as a dutiful daughter makes impossible her hopes for a happier life.

If Eveline had been born male instead of female, she might have escaped her unhappy home life, as her brother did.

Eveline, "trapped like a helpless animal" by her promise to her dying mother, is morally unable to break her vow and flee her miserable home to seek a new life for herself.

Having been thoroughly beaten down by her brutal, domineering father, Eveline lacks the self-confidence to flee in search of her own life.

Most of the ideas and details you need to support any of these thesis statements will appear in the freewriting or clustering that you have already completed. In the next chapter, we will suggest some ways in which you might arrange this material in the paper itself.

2 The Writing Process

Chapter Preview

Now that you have examined your reactions to "Eveline," collected your ideas, and formulated a thesis sentence, you are ready to organize this material into a workable arrangement for writing. By the end of this chapter, you will be able to

- Describe the three parts of a traditional essay.
- Identify the elements of good argument: *claims, evidence, reasoning, refutation*.
- Explain the conventional plan for presenting an argument.
- Understand the process of using details to develop claims and ideas.
- Differentiate between *critical comments* and *plot details*.
- Identify the characteristics of a successful introduction.
- Explain the strategies for composing an effective conclusion.

How Should I Organize My Ideas?

A traditional but effective format includes three parts: the beginning (the introduction), the middle (the body), and the end (the conclusion). This simple plan will serve for almost any piece of writing.

The *beginning* of the paper has two main functions: to engage your readers' interest and to let them know what point you expect to make. The *middle* portion of your paper develops and supports the main point with details, examples, reasons, and explanations that make the general thesis more specific and more understandable. The *end* of the paper returns your readers to the main point by spotlighting the general idea you want them to accept after reading your essay. Later in the chapter, we will offer you more specific suggestions about how to begin and end a paper effectively. For now, we want to wrestle with the problem of organizing the body—or the middle part—of your paper about "Eveline."

Arguing Your Interpretation

If you want your readers to accept your interpretation of "Eveline," you have to convince them that your point of view is valid. In other words, an interpretation is an argument, and you can organize your essay according to the standard features of argumentative writing.

The Elements of Good Argument

Claims, evidence, reasoning, and *refutation* are the building blocks of effective **argument**; you need to understand and use them in order to write persuasively. Knowing how these elements work together will also help you organize your thoughts more effectively.

Claims The "engine" that propels any argument is its *claim*. In various kinds of writing, claims are also called propositions, premises, conclusions, hypotheses, or recommendations. In literary criticism, a claim is usually called a *thesis*, the term we use in this book. The sample thesis "Eveline lacks courage to flee from her domineering father and to seek her own happiness" makes a claim about the title character; it also implies that explaining her behavior is a meaningful way to interpret the story as a whole. The primary claim is usually broken down into several secondary claims, or *topic sentences*, that justify and explain the main thesis.

Evidence Evidence tells your readers how you arrived at your interpretation and shows them what your claims are based on. Most of the evidence in literary argument will come from within the reading—details and examples from the work itself. In some cases, evidence can come from your own experience; for example, your observation that people often fear the unknown might support an analysis of Eveline's motivation. Some of your evidence may also come from outside the text; for example, you might use information about the situation of Catholic working-class women in Ireland in the early 1900s and connect it to Eveline's decisions.

Reasoning The thinking process you use to connect the evidence to your claims is called *reasoning*. Sometimes the point or validity of the evidence is obvious, but more often than not you need to explain how you arrived at your interpretation. For example, you can identify words and phrases from the story that indicate Eveline is afraid of her father, but you probably should explain how you arrived at that conclusion and why you think this fear could extend to all men, including Frank. This way, your reader can share your line of reasoning.

Refutation Arguments always assume that other points of view are possible. In literary criticism, the case for your interpretation will be strengthened if you treat other possible readings with respect and understanding. Acknowledging and responding to these other views is called *refutation*. There is no best place to refute opposing opinions. Sometimes you will want to bring up other interpretations early and deal with them right away. Another approach is to anticipate objections as you argue your own interpretation point by point. Many writers add a refutation section after they have presented the evidence and reasoning on their own side. Wherever you include the refutation, your goal is to show why other interpretations are faulty or inaccurate or limited. Often, you will be able to present contrasting evidence or alternate reasoning to reveal both the weakness of another view and the strength of your own position.

Building an Effective Argument

Presenting a conventional argument involves five tasks.

1. Introduce the subject you are going to write about—for example, Eveline's decision not to go with Frank—and supply some context for your approach.
2. State your main point or thesis. This is your *claim*.
3. Provide *evidence* and *reasoning* to support your claims. This will be the longest part of your argument; each secondary claim will probably take a paragraph or more to develop.
4. Respond to opposing viewpoints. This is called the *refutation*.
5. Sum up your argument by reminding your readers of your thesis and the strength of your evidence.

Writers often alter this conventional order of tasks, especially steps 3 and 4. For example, in the sample student essay at the end of Chapter 4, the author considers several possible answers to her thesis question before presenting her main claim in the last two paragraphs. In other words, the writer rejects, or refutes, other interpretations before advancing her own.

Following are two brief plans for a literary argument based on one of our sample thesis statements. The first plan states the thesis, or claim, and indicates the subpoints that will become topic sentences for several paragraphs of development and support.

1. *Beginning:* Eveline lacks courage to flee from her domineering father and to seek her own happiness.
2. *Middle:* Evidence of Eveline's lack of courage can be seen in the following:
   —her passivity as a female who lacks the resources and imagination to challenge her traditional role
   —her physical fear of her father, perhaps generalized to all men
   —her reverence for her mother's memory and the promise she made to keep the family together
3. *End:* Eveline exemplifies how a woman may be trapped by passivity, fear, and obligations.

The second plan organizes the middle of an argument on the same thesis by stating the topic sentences as fears that contribute to Eveline's lack of courage. These topic sentences act as secondary claims that support and explain the main interpretation.

2. *Middle:* Eveline's lack of courage is illustrated in these ways:
   —She is afraid to go against her religious beliefs.
   —She is afraid something will happen to her father if she leaves him.
   —She is afraid her mother's memory will continue to haunt her.
   —She is afraid Frank will treat her as her father treated her mother.

By writing out the subpoints, you provide yourself with a plan to follow in writing the paragraphs that will make up the main part (the body) of your essay. Try using the following checklist when arguing an interpretation.

Checklist for Arguing an Interpretation

1. Make sure your interpretation is reasonable and consistent.
2. Express your interpretation in a clear thesis statement.
3. Write an introduction that states your thesis and indicates briefly how you intend to support it.
4. Place the key claims of your argument in topic sentences.
5. Present your claims in a clearly defined, logical order.
6. Provide plenty of specific evidence to back up your interpretive claims.
7. Make explicit the links between your interpretation and the evidence you provide.
8. Avoid getting bogged down in mere summary.
9. Anticipate objections to your interpretation and address them in your paper.
10. Write a conclusion that recaps your argument and highlights the significance of your interpretation.

Arranging the Ideas

As you write the middle section of your argument, you will have to decide which point to take up first and which ones to use later in the development of your main claim. Ordinarily, you can arrange your secondary claims in two ways: logical order or chronological order.

Logical order involves arranging ideas in a way that will appeal to your readers' intelligence and good sense. Many writers begin with a less crucial idea and work up to their most important one. The logic behind this arrangement is based on the assumption that since your final point is the one your readers are most likely to remember, it should also be your strongest point.

In the second plan for writing just presented to you for a paper on "Eveline," the topic sentences about fears are arranged according to the increasing strength of Eveline's feelings. The plan starts with a general point about religion, moves to more specific fears about leaving her father and remembering her mother, and concludes with an insight into what could happen in her life with Frank. The last idea is particularly appropriate, because it sums up the previous two points by relating Eveline's anxiety about Frank to her feelings about her parents' relationship.

Chronological order, which is based on time, involves writing about events in the order in which they occur. Most narratives, such as short stories and novels, use a chronological approach. Because you will be writing about literature, your organization for a paper could simply follow the chronology of the work under consideration. If you do this, be sure that your essay clearly reflects a critical thinking process, or your paper will seem like a mere plot summary.

Developing with Details

The balance between your interpretive points and the details you use to support them is critical. If your argument goes too far in the interpretive direction, it sounds too abstract, personal, and unconvincing. If it goes too far in listing details, it seems as though you are summarizing the work rather than analyzing it. Let us look further into maintaining an effective balance.

Within your argument, you will make several critical generalizations relating to your main point. These are the topic sentences that bolster the thesis. Remember to state each generalization clearly and to support each one with enough specific references to the story to be convincing. Sort through the observations that you made in your prewriting, and select those that relate to the topic sentences in your plan. The following example shows how a writer uses specific details and brief quotations from the story to develop the idea stated in the topic sentence:

Eveline lacks courage to seek a life of her own because she fears that her father will not be able to cope if she leaves him. Her anxiety is heightened as she recalls that she and her brothers and sisters are grown up and that her mother is dead. If she leaves, her father will be all alone. She realizes that he is "usually fairly bad on a Saturday night" and recognizes that his drinking problem will not get any better after she leaves. Also she has noticed that "Her father was becoming old lately" and she assumes that "he would miss her." As a dutiful daughter, Eveline seems to feel that going away with Frank means abandoning her aging father, and that may be why she has written a letter to him—to ease the blow of her departure and to soothe her own conscience.

Questions for Consideration

In the preceding example, is there adequate support for the topic sentence? What story details has the writer cited to develop the main point? What other details could be used? Where does the writer bring in personal opinion or interpretation? Do you think the interpretation is reasonable?

Maintaining a Critical Focus

The placement of your analytical content affects how a reader perceives your argument. Even with a solid interpretation, your paper could still sound like a plot summary if you imbed your critical insights in the middle of paragraphs. In order to achieve a sharp critical focus, the topic sentences (usually the first one of each paragraph in the body of the paper) should be critical observations supporting or relating to your thesis. In academic writing, placing the topic sentences at the beginnings of paragraphs helps your instructor to follow your thinking. You should, in each paragraph, use the plot details to support or prove the critical generalization in the topic sentence.

Distinguishing Critical Comments from Plot Details

The difference between a critical comment and a plot detail or poetry detail is illustrated in these sample sentences:

Plot detail	Jackson's story opens on a balmy summer day.
Critical comment	By setting her story on a balmy summer day, Jackson creates a false sense of well-being.
Plot detail	"Seventeen Syllables" begins with a communication problem between the teenager Rosie and her mother.
Critical comment	The first scene, a communication breakdown between the teenager Rosie and her mother, introduces the conflict between first- and second-generation immigrants to the United States.
Poetry detail	Blanco's poem "América" contains a number of Spanish words and phrases mixed in with the English.
Critical comment	Blanco sprinkles Spanish words and phrases throughout "América" to underscore the clash of cultures that he is describing in this poem.

(Notice that authors can be referred to by their last names: "Jackson" is Shirley Jackson and "Blanco" is Richard Blanco.)

Plot detail	While looking for some quilt patches to take to Mrs. Wright in jail, the women in *Trifles* find the dead canary that Mr. Wright apparently killed.
Critical comment	Knowing how important the canary and its bright voice were to Mrs. Wright, the women understand her motive for murder.
Combined	In searching for some way to cheer up Mrs. Wright while she is in jail, the women in *Trifles* discover the dead bird and reveal a motive that the men in the play have overlooked.

How Should I Begin?

Your introduction is crucial to the effectiveness of your essay—and often proves to be the most difficult to write. Try to think of this part as challenging (rather than merely hard to do), and you may find yourself rising to new heights of accomplishment.

Postpone If Nothing Comes

Remember that you do not have to write your introduction first just because it appears first in the finished essay. As long as you have your thesis clearly in mind (or clearly written out on your planning sheet), you can start right in on the body of the paper. Once you begin generating material, you may suddenly perceive an idea that will serve nicely as a beginning. Or if you postpone your introduction until the next day, your subconscious mind may provide you with the perfect opening. You may find that some of your best ideas come to you in the shower.

Write an Appealing Opening

Work especially hard on your opening sentence. You want to engage the interest of your readers immediately. If you begin like this,

"Eveline" is a very interesting short story by James Joyce.

no one other than your loving mother is likely to read any further unless paid to. You should mention the author and title somewhere in your introduction (even though both may appear in your title). But try also to incorporate something specific in that first sentence. You might want to focus your readers' attention on an incident that you consider significant.

In his short story "Eveline," James Joyce portrays a young woman paralyzed by the need to make a decision that will change the course of her life.

Or you could start this way:

In James Joyce's "Eveline," we see a tired young woman accustomed to the "odour of dusty cretonne" trying to muster courage to exchange her dreary existence for the unknown excitements of life with a "sailor chap" in exotic Buenos Ayres.

Or you might try this:

In the closing lines of James Joyce's "Eveline," the young woman of the title stands "passive, like a helpless animal," watching her dreams of romance and excitement fade into the mist.

State the Thesis

Even more important than an arresting opening sentence is the need to let your readers know somewhere in the introductory paragraph what the paper is going to be about. But try to avoid stating your main point too bluntly.

> I am going to show that Eveline stays home with her domineering father because she lacks courage to go with Frank.

Beginning the thesis with "I am going to show" is stylistically ineffective because that part is understood—any thesis at all could begin with those words. They waste the first few words of the sentence, words that should be full of meaning. Instead, describe the direction of your thought, the case that you will present within your essay, using vivid language. Your thesis should sound more like this:

> Having been thoroughly beaten down by her brutal, domineering father, Eveline lacks the courage to go with Frank in search of her own happiness.

That sentence includes some psychologically powerful words—*beaten down, brutal, domineering, courage,* and *happiness*—which invite a reader to continue.

If you combine your thesis with a general statement about the story, you should produce a worthwhile introduction for a short paper.

> In James Joyce's "Eveline," we see a tired young woman accustomed to the "odour of dusty cretonne" trying to muster courage to exchange her dreary existence for the unknown excitements of life with a "sailor chap" in exotic Buenos Ayres. But having been thoroughly beaten down by her brutal father, Eveline lacks the courage to go with Frank in search of her own happiness.

How Should I End?

Your conclusion is just as important as your introduction—perhaps even more so. You want to leave your readers feeling satisfied that you have written something worth reading, that their time has not been wasted. Do not give them a chance to ask, "Well, so what?" at the end.

Relate the Discussion to Theme

Impress your readers with the value of your discussion by reinforcing in the conclusion how your analysis illuminates the theme, or meaning, of the work. This process may involve echoing your thesis statement from the introduction. But take care to avoid simply repeating what you said at the beginning. Your conclusion should offer a clear expression of how your discussion relates to the theme of the story.

Postpone or Write Ahead

Conclusions, like introductions, do not necessarily have to be written when you come to them. If you should get some additional insight concerning the theme as you work on composing the main part of the paper, take a minute to jot down the idea so that you can later incorporate this insight into your ending. Or you could stop right then, write the final paragraph, and put it aside until you come to it. Chances are that you may change this conclusion later, but having something to work with is an enormous help—especially if you are getting tired.

Write an Emphatic Final Sentence

No matter how exhausted you are when you compose your final paragraph, do not risk ruining the effect of your entire essay by letting your conclusion trail off at the end with a limp last sentence. Regardless of the brilliance of your argument, your readers are going to feel let down if you end like this:

> All in all, I think "Eveline" was a fine story, and I think anyone would enjoy reading it and maybe even learn something from it.

One student's final paper on "Eveline" (which you will read in its entirety in Chapter 4) closes briefly, yet effectively:

Afraid of failing on her own, Eveline retreats into the familiar, telling herself that life with father cannot be as frightening as a risky, unknown life with Frank. So strong is her fear of failure that it overrides her fear of her father. She seems to decide that a predictable—if dreary and abused—life is better than a life without security or pattern.

Composing the First Draft

At this point you should be ready to compose the first draft of your essay on "Eveline." You have completed the prewriting activities, devised a working thesis statement, arranged your main supporting points, and selected plenty of details to use for development. You may even have written some of your introduction and conclusion. Now is the time to move beyond these preliminary stages and write a complete draft of your paper.

Pausing to Rescan

You may have been told to get your first draft down on paper as quickly as possible and then, once it is completed, to revise it. This is probably not bad advice if you suffer from writer's block, but recent studies show that most skilled writers go about it in a different way. Experienced writers tend to pause frequently as they compose—to scan and perhaps reword what they have just written; to think about what to say next; to make additions, substitutions, or deletions; to be sure a sentence says what they want it to say.

If you tend to write headlong without pausing once you begin, perhaps you should try to slow down. Mina Shaughnessy, a noted composition expert, speaks of "the messy process that leads to clarity" in writing. This messy process involves pausing and thinking and reviewing in order to write well.

Quoting from Your Sources

The Modern Language Association (MLA) has set a standard way to credit a source when you quote material in an essay. If you are using only a single *primary* source—the work of literature under discussion—you cite in parentheses after the quotation the page (or pages) on which you found that material.

> Eveline admits that hers is "a hard life," yet decides "now that she was about to leave it she did not find it a wholly undesirable life" (5).

If you are using more than one primary source, you need to include the author's last name in the parentheses—with only a single blank space separating it from the page number—unless you mention the author's name in the text of your paper.

> At the end of the story Eveline is "like a helpless animal" (Joyce 7), and Hulga at the end is similarly helpless, "left sitting on the straw in the dusty sunlight" (O'Connor 130).

(*Note:* If you are using library sources, the situation becomes more complicated. Consult Chapter 5 for complete instruction in writing researched papers.)

The Source Citation   Even if you are citing only your primary source, let your readers know what it is. If you use direct quotations, you will include page numbers in your paper, and readers need to know which book those page numbers come from. On a separate page at the end of your essay, center the title (Work Cited or Works Cited) at the top. Using double spacing, provide complete publication information for your source or sources. The Work Cited entry for a paper on "Eveline" using the current edition of this text would look like this:

> Joyce, James. "Eveline." *Literature and the Writing Process.* Ed.
> Robert Funk, et al. 11th ed. Boston: Pearson, 2017. 2–6. Print.

Notice the *hanging* indention. Indent all lines after the first line five spaces. Use an abbreviated form of the publisher's name—just *Pearson*, not *Pearson Education, Inc.* If you are using more than one source, alphabetize the entries by their authors' last names.

Sample Student Paper: First Draft

The paper that follows is the first draft of an essay on "Eveline" written by Wendy Dennison, a student at Illinois State University. The directed freewriting for this paper appears on page 3 in Chapter 1. The comments, suggestions, and questions in the margin were made electronically by Wendy's instructor.

Dennison 1

Wendy Dennison

English 102

January 23, 2009

For Fear of Failing Alone

    Eveline, the title character of Joyce's short story, is given that once-in-a-lifetime chance—to leave her old life to begin a new one. But she rejects the offer Fate—or God—makes, preferring instead to settle back down into the dusty, abusive life she has led. Why does she not go away with Frank? The obvious responses—duty to her mother's dying wish, the love of her father, the love of her home—do not quite ring true, for Eveline owes little or nothing to her parents or her home. In fact, leaving seems a much more logical choice. So why does Eveline really stay behind? She is afraid of failure.

    What does Eveline really owe her mother? Her "promise…that she keep the home together as long as she could" (6) was unfairly given. It was unfair of her mother to ask such a thing of her, as it prevents her from having a life of her own. It is very likely that Eveline will never marry and leave her father as long as he is alive, for she will always recall that promise. Why stay for this?

    Why should we be surprised that Eveline might wish to leave her father? An abusive drunk, he has taken advantage of her promise to her mother. She is forced to keep house for him, yet must beg from him money with which to do so. He practically accuses her of stealing, claiming, "she used to squander the money, that she had no head, that he wasn't going to give her his hard-earned

Comment: Mention title of story here.

Comment: Isn't it Frank?

Comment: Do you want to give away your conclusion?

Comment: This paragraph could use more details

Comment: Too many rhetorical questions?

Comment: Good intro of quotation

Dennison 2

money to throw about the streets... " (5). A bully, he has scared her with threats of beatings, giving her "palpitations" (4). Eveline realizes that with her brothers gone, there is "nobody to protect her" (4) from her father's rage. Why would she ever want to stay with a man of whom she is terribly afraid? She did remember happy moments with him when the family went on picnics and he was jolly and played with the children.

> **Comment**
> Good use of header—follow MLA guidelines from the very first draft—you'll be glad later.

> **Comment**
> Good support from story.

Eveline's home life is so unhealthy that she would be wise to leave it all behind. For all that she does, she still does not feel quite a part of everything. For example, she knows nothing about the picture of the priest, not even his name. The dustiness of the house, of which Joyce reminds us periodically, is suggestive of the pervading dirtiness and squalor of her daily life. It is significant also that she often thinks about her unpleasant, unhappy job. Her home is clearly not conducive to happiness. So why does she stay there?

> **Comment**
> Does this detail fit here?

> **Comment**
> Why is this important?

> **Comment**
> Best word?

> **Comment**
> Does this fit?

> **Comment**
> Combine sentences?

The only reason why Eveline would stay in Irelnad is the fact that she is desperately afraid of failing on her own. If she leaves the familiar, no matter how unpleasant, she risks failure. "She was about to explore another life with Frank" (5). The word "explore" is significant here, as it brings to mind uncertainty and risk, two factors that Eveline is not prepared to deal with. She admits that hers "was a hard life," yet thinks, "now that she was about to leave it she did not find it a wholly undesirable life" (5). When she sits in the growing darkness—the threat of her father returning from work—with the letters in her lap, Eveline calls up a couple of good memories to calm her fears, effectively helping to convince herself to stay home.

> **Comment**
> Check whole paper for typos.

> **Comment**
> Good!

> **Comment**
> Rephrase to avoid tense shift.

> **Comment**
> Sentence okay?

Dennison 3

Afraid of failing on her own, Eveline retreats into the familiar, convincing herself that life with father cannot be as frightening as a risky life with Frank. "Why should she be unhappy? She had a right to happiness" (6) Indeed, Eveline decides that a predictable— if abusive and unhealthy—life is better than one without direction or pattern.

> **Comment**
> Is this the best detail to use here?

> **Comment**
> Well done, Wendy! You have a good thesis and specific support from the story. But please outline this draft to be sure the material is tightly unified. For example, is there an idea that unifies your claims about Eveline's state of mind?

Dennison 4

Work Cited

Joyce, James. "Eveline," in <u>Literature and the Writing Process.</u> By Elizabeth McMahan, Susan X Day, and Robert Funk. NJ: Prentice Hall, 2008. Pages 3–7.

> **Comment**
> Wrong form for Work Cited. Check the MLA style.

3 Writing a Convincing Argument

Chapter Preview

You can write about literary works in several ways. You can record your reactions and explore how the work affects you personally; you can describe the work for others who might want to read it; you can evaluate the work and tell why you liked or disliked it. But the customary way to write about a literary work is to *interpret* it. Interpreting is also one of the most challenging ways to write about literature. The goal of this chapter is to show you how to develop your opinions about literature and shape them into clear, convincing essays that explain what a literary work means. By the end of this chapter, you will be able to

- Recognize the connection between *arguing* and *interpreting*.
- Identify and apply the key steps in arguing an interpretation: *identifying issues, making claims, using evidence, using reasoning,* and *answering opposing views*.
- Explain the *inductive approach* to making an argument.
- Describe the use of *counterargument* and *comparative argument*.

Interpreting and Arguing

When you interpret a story or poem or play, you say to other readers, "This is how I read this work; this is what I think it means." Because literary texts are often complex and seldom obvious, you can assume that other readers will not necessarily interpret a work in the same way you do. So, in addition to explaining the meaning, you will also have to convince your audience that your reading is reasonable and well founded. In other words, you will be *arguing* for your interpretation.

Presenting your interpretation as an argument will focus your writing and require you to look more carefully and closely at the literary selection. An effective way to mount an argument for your interpretation is to begin with these two steps:

- Identify an **issue** about the work that you want to discuss.
- Formulate a **claim** that takes a position on the issue.

Identifying Issues

An issue is a subject or problem that people argue about. Many issues about a literary work relate to its *theme*. When you interpret a story or play or poem, you are actually explaining its theme—and arguing for your understanding of that theme. You'll remember in Chapter 1 we offered this advice: "Devise a thesis that makes its point by relating some aspect of the work to the meaning of the whole—that is, to its theme." This strategy of identifying an issue and making a claim about it will help you to write a meaningful literary paper.

A good way to identify an issue is to see it as a question with no obvious or clear answer. In Chapter 1, we recommended that you ask yourself questions as you are reading. This self-questioning will not only generate material to consider using as evidence, but it will also help you to locate the issues in a literary work. For her essay on "Fear of Failure in Joyce's 'Eveline'" (pages 65–67), Wendy Dennison identified this key issue:

> Why does Eveline not go away with Frank when the opportunity seems so attractive?

The issue that Wendy identified is a *major issue*, a question asked by most readers of the story and one that has a number of answers.

There are, of course, other questions that readers ask about "Eveline." Several came out in our prewriting exercises in Chapter 1:

- What is the significance of Eveline's promise to her mother?
- Would Eveline's life have been different if she had been born male?
- What role does religion play in Eveline's decision?
- How realistic is Eveline's romance with Frank?
- Why does the author mention "dust" so often in the story?

These issues are interesting and important, but individually they are *minor issues* that relate to just one part of the story. Identifying a broader issue, however, would make it possible to include some of them as part of a more complete interpretation of the story's themes:

> How did social custom and her religious upbringing condition Eveline to abandon her hopes and dreams for a better life?

The specific issues of gender, religion, and Eveline's promise to her mother could then be used to answer this larger question.

The issues, of course, are quite different in various works of literature, but in working toward a claim, the process remains the same. In preparing to write about Dagoberto Gilb's short story "Love in L.A.," for instance, Brian Carter used the self-questioning approach to identify a couple of issues that he thought would direct him to a convincing interpretation:

- What is the nature of the "love" referred to in the title?
- Who is fooled by Jake's lies?
- What purpose does fantasy serve for Jake?

(You will read Gilb's story and Carter's paper about it at the end of this chapter.)

Making Claims

Once you have identified the issue that will be the center of your interpretation, you are ready to make a claim about that issue. If you stated the issue as a question, then your claim will be an answer to that question. Wendy Dennison answered her issue question with this claim:

> Afraid of failing on her own, Eveline retreats into the familiar, telling herself that life with her father cannot be as frightening as a risky, unknown life with Frank.

Working out an answer to your issue question may require several drafts, and you will probably refine and revise your claim as you are putting your interpretation together.

An effective claim will make a clear, significant assertion about the way you interpret the work's theme. It can also provide a concise preview of the way you are going to develop your case. For example, the issue question about the influence of custom and religion might be answered with this claim:

> Religious and social traditions have trapped Eveline: her Catholic upbringing, her responsibilities as a dutiful daughter, and her promise to her dying mother make it impossible for her to imagine leaving home and seeking a new life for herself.

The answers to issue questions about "Love in L.A." might produce these claims:

> The "love" that exists in L.A., according to this story, is superficial, materialistic, and self-centered.

> Jake consciously adapts his performance to fool and manipulate his audience, but he doesn't succeed with Mariana.

> Jake's fantasies allow him to avoid the truth: he isn't going anywhere.

If you think a claim is the same as a thesis statement, you're right. The term *claim* makes it clear that you are taking a stand about the meaning of a work and that you will back up your interpretation with **evidence** and **reasoning**.

Using Evidence

As we pointed out in Chapter 2, the evidence in a literary argument tells your audience where you got the ideas for your interpretation. The most important evidence will come from the literary work itself: facts, details, descriptions, incidents, key terms, and phrases. Direct quotations provide clear evidence that your claims are grounded in the text, but you'll want to be smart about quoting from the literary work. Presumably, your audience has already read the story or poem or play; you need only remind them of passages that support your interpretation. You also have to think about when to summarize and how to use a brief summary to advance your claims. You can summarize an incident or scene to help establish a point or observation—and then explain or interpret that point—but long summaries will detract from your argument. The following example uses material from the story to support a claim that religion plays a role in Eveline's decision. The supporting evidence is highlighted and labeled:

> Eveline's Catholic upbringing is established early in the story. As **she looks around the room, surveying the "familiar objects from which she had never dreamed of being divided" (4)**, Eveline takes special note of two items: **an old photograph of the priest who had been a friend of her father's** and **a colored print of the promises made to Blessed Margaret Mary Alacoque**. Then, in the story's final scene, as **she stands in the station, waiting to board the boat**, Eveline **"prayed to God to direct her, to show her what was her duty"** and **"kept moving her lips in silent fervent prayer" (7)**.

summary and quotation
specific details
summary
quotations

Brian Carter supported his claim about the "web of falsehoods" Jake weaves for Mariana by listing examples:

> His car has **fake license plates**; he has **no insurance**; he has no intention of paying for his mistake. He claims to have **glamorous occupations**, despite driving **a decrepit '58 Buick**.

specific details

You may also be asked to use evidence from outside the literary work. You might wonder, for instance, why James Joyce mentioned the promises made to Blessed Margaret Mary Alacoque. Information about those promises might be useful in developing and supporting a claim about Eveline's religious upbringing. The process of finding and using evidence in sources outside a literary work is covered in detail in Chapter 5.

Obviously, the more evidence you have, the more convincing your interpretation will be. But facts, details, and quotations by themselves do not make an argument. You have to explain how you are using this evidence to support your interpretation.

Using Reasoning

As we pointed out in Chapter 2, "the thinking process you use to connect the evidence to your claims is called *reasoning*." You'll want to give the *reasons* for drawing your conclusions about a work's meaning. In this excerpt from her essay, Wendy Dennison explained the reasoning behind her claim that Eveline's main problem is fear of the unknown (the explanations are highlighted in bold type):

> **If she leaves the familiar, no matter how unpleasant, she risks failure.** "She was about to explore another life with Frank" (5), we are told, in faraway Buenos Ayres. **The word** explore **is significant, as it brings to mind uncertainty and risk, two factors that Eveline is not prepared to deal with.** She admits that hers is "a hard life," yet she thinks that "now that she was about to leave it she did not find it a wholly undesirable life" (5). When she sits in the growing darkness with the letters in her lap, Eveline calls up a couple of good memories—of her father being jolly once on a picnic, of his kindness once when she was sick. **We see her trying to calm her fears, trying to convince herself that her home life is more bearable than it is.**

You can see a clear pattern in the six sentences of this paragraph:

—Make a claim (sentence 1).
—Quote some evidence from the story (sentence 2).
—Interpret the meaning of the evidence (sentence 3).
—Bring up some more evidence (sentences 4 and 5).
—Explain how the evidence supports the claim in the first sentence (sentence 6).

This pattern of stating claims, citing evidence, explaining the evidence, making another (related) claim, and citing more evidence is used time and again in developing an interpretation.

Here's another example that combines evidence and interpretive explanations to support a claim about Eveline's decision. The explanations are highlighted in bold type:

> **Religion plays an important role in shaping Eveline's decision not to leave with Frank.** As she sits by the window, looking at the "familiar objects" that she "had dusted once a week for so many years" (4), she notices a faded photograph of a priest who had once been a school friend of her father. But the priest is in Melbourne now, **having left Eveline's father just as she is planning to do.** Next to the photo is "a coloured print of the promises made to Blessed Margaret Mary Alacoque," **a symbol of devotion to home and family in the Catholic Church.**

> Margaret Mary Alacoque had a vision in which Jesus promised to bless any home where Alacoque's picture is exhibited, **a promise that parallels the one that Eveline made to her dying mother to "keep the home together as long as she could" (6). The photo and the print indicate how Eveline is tied to her parents; they also remind her of the traditional obligations of a good Catholic daughter. Their religious associations only increase the guilt she feels about trying to make a life for herself.**

In his final paragraph about "Love in L.A.", Brian Carter used reasoning to explain why Jake's character is so transparently foolish:

> We all laugh at such a clown, and it makes us comfortable to know that *we* aren't like Jake. Perhaps, though, while we are off guard, Gilb intends to plant a nagging thought that we *are*—just a little.

Answering Opposing Views

As we explained in Chapter 2, your interpretation will be strengthened if you anticipate and respond to other readings of the work, a process sometimes referred to as *refutation* or *rebuttal*. By definition, your claims are arguable, so you can expect that other readers will not always agree with the way you interpret the evidence. As you plan and draft your interpretation, make a list of all the opposing views you can think of. You can get help from friends and classmates who have also read the literary work. Anticipating other possible readings should cause you to reexamine why and how you arrived at your own point of view. Such a reconsideration will almost certainly help you to refine and deepen your interpretation.

Some writers answer opposing views in a separate section, sometimes immediately after the introduction as a bridge to rest of the essay. Other writers save their refutations until after they have presented their own case. A particularly effective strategy is to handle opposing views point by point as you argue at the same time for your claims, as Wendy Dennison did when weighing the importance of Eveline's promise to her dying mother:

> But surely her promise to "keep the home together as long as she could" (6) was given under extreme circumstances. It was unjust of her mother to ask such a sacrifice of her, and Eveline is aware of the unfairness.... Surely that promise cannot be the only reason she stays.

Brian Carter led into his main claim about "Love in L.A." by including an opposing interpretation of Jake:

> Some readers might find Jake too obvious and predictable to be interesting. But his character is drawn large and clueless to make a point.

Wherever you place your response to different readings, your goal is to explain why these views are faulty or incomplete. At the very least you want to show that your reading is just as valid and compelling.

Organizing Your Argument

The conventional structure for arguing your interpretation should include five elements, usually presented in this order:

1. The issue (subject)
2. Your claim about the issue (thesis)
3. The evidence that supports your claim (facts, details, quotations)
4. The reasoning that connects the evidence to your claim (explanations)
5. Your refutation of opposing views (explanations and counterevidence)

As you saw in the examples in this chapter, writers frequently combine elements 3, 4, and 5 (evidence, reasoning, and refutation).

In Chapter 2, we showed you how to arrange the steps for arguing the claim that "Eveline lacks courage to flee from her domineering father and to seek her own happiness" (see page 19). The approach we illustrated in that example is called *inductive reasoning*. It is perhaps the most common way of arguing an interpretation. But you can also arrange your arguments in other ways; two common ones are the *counterargument* and the *comparative argument*.

Using the Inductive Approach

An inductive argument moves from specific examples and observations to a general conclusion. It parallels the process you go through when reading a piece of literature: you notice details and points, words and phrases, comments and actions, which add up to your understanding of what the work means. When you reread in order to write about the work, you look even more closely for specifics to confirm your initial reactions, raise possible questions, and build an interpretation. With this accumulation of specific evidence, you can then identify the issues you want to write about and the claims you want to make about those issues.

In planning an inductive argument, you start with your major claim (thesis) and then list the minor claims that support your interpretation. Here is an example:

Major claim: Eveline doesn't leave with Frank because she subconsciously suspects that he will not really "save her" and "give her life."

Minor claims:

1. Eveline doesn't really know much about Frank.
2. She may recognize that what he has told her is more fiction than fact.
3. She has firsthand knowledge of the duplicity men are capable of.
4. The ending seems to confirm her suspicions.

If you were to flesh out these claims with specific details and explanations, you would be prepared to write a draft.

Major claim: Eveline doesn't leave with Frank because she subconsciously suspects that he will not really "save her" and "give her life." Her doubts and suspicions make it impossible for her to overcome the power of family and religion.

Minor claims:

1. Eveline doesn't really know much about Frank.
   —met only "a few weeks ago"
   —"They had come to know each other"—vague and unclear
   —no last name
2. She may recognize that what he has told her is more fiction than fact, too good to be true.
   —exotic "tales of distant countries" and "terrible Patagonians"
   —why the "pleasantly confused" feeling when he sang "about the lass that loves a sailor"?
   —claims he "had fallen on his feet" in Buenos Ayres: vague and without specific content
   —romantic promise of a "home he has waiting for her"
   —father's suspicions: "I know these sailor chaps"
3. She has firsthand knowledge of the duplicity of men.
   —father sometimes nice and thoughtful
   —but also a violent drunk who abused his wife and threatens Eveline
   —would Frank treat her the same way?
4. The ending seems to confirm her suspicions.
   —thought he "would take her in his arms, fold her in his arms"
   —instead he "seize[ed]" her hand and called to her
   —he "rushed beyond the barrier and called to her to follow"—but he did not come back

The inductive plan of Brian Carter's essay would look like this:

Major claim: Through presenting a clownishly self-glorifying character, "Love in L.A." leads the reader to think about the illusions of personal glory in his or her own life.

Minor claims:

1. The metaphor of the cars going nowhere is central: Jake is stuck, with no destination in life, though the situation might appear otherwise.
2. Jake tells plenty of lies about the quality of his life, but doesn't fool Mariana.
3. Jake's failure with Mariana gives him only the slightest self-doubt, and then he returns to his fantasy world.
4. While we are amused at the situation and ridiculing Jake's excesses, our defenses are down, and we remember our own self-inflating fantasies.

Making a Counterargument

You can anticipate how other readers might interpret a work and organize your own interpretation as a point-by-point refutation of those other possible views. This approach is effective for tackling especially complex or controversial selections and for clearing up common misunderstandings. Wendy Dennison, for example, defines her major claim by suggesting how other people might answer the issue (Why does Eveline fail to leave with Frank?) and by talking back to them. After dealing with several other readings of Eveline's motives, Wendy is ready to make the case for her own interpretation.

Arguing through Comparison

Another way to argue an interpretation is to use comparisons. Setting two works or two interpretations side-by-side permits you to use one of them to throw light on the other. Comparison involves looking at similarities; contrast directs attention to differences. But you can combine the two by showing how things that seem to be alike are really different, or vice versa.

The comparison/contrast method follows the notion that we can find out what something *is* by discovering what it is *not*. You can begin by establishing the basis for the comparison (the similarities) and then move on to the features that set the two works apart (the differences). For example, in comparing Dagoberto Gilb's "Love in L.A." (page 43) with John Updike's "A & P" (page 358), you might start by noting that both stories feature a brash, disaffected young man who unsuccessfully tries to impress an attractive young woman. You could then argue that the endings reveal a significant contrast: Jake remains pretty much unenlightened and unchanged, while Sammy realizes he has perhaps made a life-altering decision.

You could also develop an interpretation that shows how two seemingly different characters are alike in several key ways. For example, you could contrast Eveline with Elisa, the main character in John Steinbeck's "The Chrysanthemums" (page 375), pointing out the differences in their age, marital status, personality, attitude toward work, and interaction with the men in their families. After describing their differences, you could then point out two surprising and significant similarities: each woman gets a glimpse of an attractive new life from a charming stranger, but neither one has the courage to break away from her domestic trap.

Organizing a Comparison/Contrast   There are two standard ways of arranging the material in a comparison/contrast. One way is to make all your points about one work first and then to do the same for the second work. You could group all the pertinent details about Eveline in one block, followed by the contrasting points about Elisa in a second block.

This method is relatively easy to handle and works perfectly for showing how things have changed—or, in the case of Eveline and Elisa, have *not* changed. The two stories were written twenty-five years apart and deal with women of very different means and temperament, yet both end up defeated in their effort to find happiness and fulfillment. Eveline is paralyzed "like a helpless animal," and Elisa is "crying weakly—like an old woman."

A second approach involves subdividing your major claim into specific points and explaining how each point relates to one work (or character) and then to the other. This method allows you to emphasize the primary points of comparison (or contrast). But the point-by-point organization can disintegrate into little more than a list of similarities and differences if you fail to relate the points to a unifying claim.

Here is a sample plan for an interlocking comparison of the stories "A & P" and "Love in L.A.," focusing on the main characters, Jake and Sammy. The comparison supports the claim that both young men are slackers but that only Sammy appears ready to grow up and move on.

1. Life/work situation
   —Jake: unemployed; main accomplishment is keeping his old car clean and running
   —Sammy: stuck in a dead-end job, taking orders from a boss he doesn't like and being careful not to upset his parents

2. Character and personality
   —Jake: fantasizes mainly about cars; concerned only with showiness and appearances, not with honesty and ethics

  —Sammy: lively, frustrated, judgmental; builds up his low self-esteem
  by denigrating and stereotyping customers and co-workers

3. Interaction with women

  —Jake: tries to charm and impress Mariana, who is way out of his
  league; gets her phone number (which may be phony), but
  can tell that she really doesn't buy his act

  —Sammy: critical and sexist, but very taken with Queenie, mainly
  because she's aloof and clearly unattainable; quits his job
  to impress her, but she takes no notice

4. Final realization

  —Jake: unfazed and carefree; resumes driving and fantasizing about
  his dream car

  —Sammy: sticks to his decision to quit, but realizes "how hard the
  world was going to be to me hereafter"

Sample Student Paper: An Argument

In the following essay, student Brian Carter argues for his interpretation of the story "Love in L.A." by Dagoberto Gilb. You can read the story at the end of this chapter on pages 43–45. The main character, Jake, dominates the story and provides the focus for Brian's major claim, which argues for a carefully designed effect on the story's readers. The marginal notes identify key features and strategies in building this argument.

Brian Carter

Professor Day

English 102A

14 October 2008

Lying in L.A.

Dagoberto Gilb's misleading title "Love in L.A." sets
the stage for this short, humorous story involving a fender
bender on a crowded Los Angeles freeway. This story is
not about love, certainly not in the traditional sense of
the word, nor is it about a minor car accident; it is about
something more profound: our highly prized illusion of
personal good fortune and the fantasies and lies we use
to maintain that illusion. The story establishes its central
metaphor in the first sentence with the phrase "motionless
traffic" (432). The automobile is supposed to be one of
our main keys to personal freedom, providing the means
to a destination—but not in this case. We are introduced
to the main character, Jake, while he is mentally creating a
detailed fantasy about his quest for the ultimate lifestyle,
achieved through upgrading his automobile. An FM
radio, a velvet interior, heating and cooling systems—such
luxuries would, of course, lead him to the promised land
of "necklaced ladies in satin gowns, misty and sexy like a
tequila ad" (432).

Reality snaps Jake out of his fantasy world when
he hits the car in front of him. Unfortunately, Jake's
capacity for self-delusion thrusts him into another
equally ridiculous fantasyland, this time played out in the
real world. In his interactions with Mariana, the victim
of his carelessness, we learn that Jake's self-concept is
built on lies, presumably distilled from endless practice

Comment
Major claim

Comment
Minor claim

Comment
Evidence: details,
quotation

Comment
Minor claim

Carter 2

at imagining what his life should be at this stage of development. He clumsily tries to woo Mariana with a web of falsehoods. His car has fake license plates; he has no insurance; he has no intention of paying for his mistake. He claims to have glamorous occupations, despite driving a decrepit '58 Buick. Mariana is young, lives with her immigrant parents, drives the car her dad bought her, but nonetheless is more worldly-wise than Jake and views him with suspicion. Although Jake interprets her polite smiles as promising, Mariana isn't buying any of his lines, clearly wanting to get the whole accident information exchange over with as soon as possible. Her skepticism about Jake is revealed when she pulls up behind him and writes down the license plate numbers on his car before leaving (434).

Comment
Evidence: details

Comment
Evidence: reasoning

Gilb draws the character of Jake quite broadly as a self-deluded fool, although Jake does seem to have a fleeting moment of awareness when he takes "a moment or two to feel both proud and sad" about his interaction with Mariana (434). Perhaps his repeatedly failing efforts to set up a date crack his fantasy shell. However, he immediately repairs it: "His sense of freedom swelled as he drove into the now moving street traffic" (434). Some readers might find Jake too obvious and predictable to be interesting. But his character is drawn large and clueless to make a point. We all laugh at such a clown, and it makes us comfortable to know that *we* aren't like Jake. Perhaps, though, while we are off guard, Gilb intends to plant a nagging thought that we *are*—just a little. Haven't most of us been stuck in a traffic jam, imagining some unearned luxuries that would change our lives, oblivious to the fact that we aren't going anywhere?

Comment
Minor claim

Comment
Evidence: quotation

Comment
Refutation

Comment
Major claim:
conclusion

Carter 3

Work Cited

Gilb, Dagoberto. "Love in L.A." *Literature and the Writing Process*, edited by Elizabeth McMahan, et al., 8th ed., Prentice Hall, 2007, pp. 432-34.

Dagoberto Gilb   1950–

Dagoberto Gilb was born in Los Angeles, the son of an undocumented immigrant Mexican mother and a Spanish-speaking Anglo father from East Los Angeles. He put himself through college, earning a B.A. and an M.A. in philosophy. He then spent sixteen years as a construction worker, taking time off every few months to write. His collection of stories, *The Magic of Blood* (1993), made him, according to one critic, "the voice of labor and unionism, once even as a headliner alongside legendary folk singer Pete Seeger." Gilb is currently a professor and writer-in-residence at the University of Houston-Victoria.

Love in L.A.

Jake slouched in a clot of near motionless traffic, in the peculiar gray of concrete, smog, and early morning beneath the overpass of the Hollywood Freeway on Alvarado Street. He didn't really mind because he knew how much worse it could be trying to make a left onto the onramp. He certainly didn't do that every day of his life, and he'd assure anyone who'd ask that he never would either. A steady occupation had its advantages and he couldn't deny thinking about that too. He needed an FM radio in something better than this '58 Buick he drove. It would have crushed velvet interior with electric controls for the L.A. summer, a nice warm heater and defroster for the winter drives at the beach, a cruise control for those longer trips, mellow speakers front and rear of course, windows that hum closed, snuffing out that nasty exterior noise of freeways. The fact was that he'd probably have to change his whole style. Exotic colognes, plush, dark nightclubs, mai tais and daiquiris, necklaced ladies in satin gowns, misty and sexy like in a tequila ad. Jake could imagine lots of possibilities when he let himself, but none that ended up with him pressed onto a stalled freeway.

Jake was thinking about this freedom of his so much that when he glimpsed its green light he just went ahead and stared bye-bye to the steadily employed. When he turned his head the same direction his windshield faced, it was maybe one second too late. He pounced the brake pedal and steered the front wheels away from the tiny brake lights but the smack was unavoidable. Just one second sooner and it would only have been close. One second more and he'd be crawling up the Toyota's trunk. As it was, it seemed like only a harmless smack, much less solid than the one against his back bumper.

Jake considered driving past the Toyota but was afraid the traffic ahead would make it too difficult. As he pulled up against the curb a few car lengths ahead, it occurred to him that the traffic might have helped him get away too. He slammed the car door twice to make sure it was closed fully and to give himself another second more, then toured front and rear of his Buick for damage on or near the bumpers. Not an impressionable scratch even in the chrome. He perked up. Though the car's beauty was secondary to its ability to start and move, the body and paint were clean except for a few minor dings. This stood out as one of his few clear-cut accomplishments over the years.

Before he spoke to the driver of the Toyota, whose looks he could see might present him with an added complication, he signaled to the driver of the car that hit him, still in his car and stopped behind the Toyota, and waved his hands and shook his head to let the man know there was no problem as far as he was concerned. The driver waved back and started his engine.

"It didn't even scratch my paint," Jake told her in that way of his. "So how 5 you doin'? Any damage to the car? I'm kinda hoping so, just so it takes a little more time and we can talk some. Or else you can give me your phone number now and I won't have to lay my regular b. s. on you to get it later."

He took her smile as a good sign and relaxed. He inhaled her scent like it was clean air and straightened out his less than new but not unhip clothes.

"You've got Florida plates. You look like you must be Cuban."

"My parents are from Venezuela."

"My name's Jake." He held out his hand.

"Mariana." 10

They shook hands like she'd never done it before in her life.

"I really am sorry about hitting you like that." He sounded genuine. He fondled the wide dimple near the cracked taillight. "It's amazing how easy it is to put a dent in these new cars. They're so soft they might replace waterbeds soon." Jake was confused about how to proceed with this. So much seemed so unlikely, but there was always possibility. "So maybe we should go out to breakfast somewhere and talk it over."

"I don't eat breakfast."

"Some coffee then."

"Thanks, but I really can't." 15

"You're not married, are you? Not that that would matter that much to me. I'm an open-minded kinda guy."

She was smiling. "I have to get to work."

"That sounds boring."

"I better get your driver's license," she said.

Jake nodded, disappointed. "One little problem," he said. "I didn't bring it. 20 I just forgot it this morning. I'm a musician," he exaggerated greatly, "and, well, I dunno, I left my wallet in the pants I was wearing last night. If you have some paper and a pen I'll give you my address and all that."

He followed her to the glove compartment side of her car.

"What if we don't report it to the insurance companies? I'll just get it fixed for you."

"I don't think my dad would let me do that."

"Your dad? It's not your car?"

"He bought it for me. And I live at home." 25

"Right." She was slipping away from him. He went back around to the back of her new Toyota and looked over the damage again. There was the trunk lid, the bumper, a rear panel, a taillight.

"You do have insurance?" she asked, suspicious, as she came around the back of the car.

"Oh yeah," he lied.

"I guess you better write the name of that down too."

He made up a last name and address and wrote down the name of an insur-   30
ance company an old girlfriend once belonged to. He considered giving a real phone number but went against that idea and made one up.

"I act too," he lied to enhance the effect more. "Been in a couple of movies." She smiled like a fan.

"So how about your phone number?" He was rebounding maturely. She gave it to him.

"Mariana, you are beautiful," he said in his most sincere voice.   35

"Call me," she said timidly.

Jake beamed. "We'll see you, Mariana," he said holding out his hand. Her hand felt so warm and soft he felt like he'd been kissed.

Back in his car he took a moment or two to feel both proud and sad about his performance. Then he watched the rear view mirror as Mariana pulled up behind him. She was writing down the license plate numbers on his Buick, ones that he'd taken off a junk because the ones that belonged to his had expired so long ago. He turned the ignition key and revved the big engine and clicked into drive. His sense of freedom swelled as he drove into the now moving street traffic, though he couldn't stop the thought about that FM stereo radio and crushed velvet interior and the new car smell that would even make it better.

(1993)

Making Connections

1. Compare Jake with the father in Ron Hansen's story "My Kid's Dog" (page 367). Which character do you find more unprincipled? Why? Construct an argument that supports your position.

2. Compare and contrast the encounter between Jake and Mariana with the one between Betty and Bill in the play *Sure Thing* by David Ives (page 883).

4 The Rewriting Process

Chapter Preview

You are probably relieved and pleased that you have completed the first draft of your essay. A large portion of your work is finished. But do not be in a rush to print out a final version yet. You need first to do a careful revision of your paper. By the end of this chapter, you will be able to

- Define *revision* and explain its importance.
- Identify the guidelines for giving and using productive *feedback*.
- Describe the practice of outlining and reviewing a first draft.
- Explain and apply two principles for arranging ideas: *logic* and *emphasis*.
- Summarize the steps for improving the *flow* of your prose.
- Evaluate the need to combine sentences for *conciseness*.
- Identify ways to increase *emphasis* and *variety*.
- Name several methods for improving *word choice* and *tone*.
- List four pointers for successful *proofreading*.

What Is Revision?

Revision involves more than just tidying your prose. The process of correcting your spelling, punctuation, and mechanics is called *editing*, but your paper is not ready for that yet. First you need *re-vision*, seeing again, to discover ways to make your writing better. Schedule your time so that you are able to lay the rough draft aside at least overnight before attempting to revise. While a draft is still warm from the writing, you cannot look at it objectively. And looking at it objectively is the basis of revision.

As you examine your cooled-down essay, you may even see that while you were writing, your main claim shifted somewhat. Sometimes writers discover what they actually want to say while trying to write something different. For example, one student argued in the first draft of a paper on Flannery O'Connor's story "A Good Man Is Hard to Find" that the characters are all self-deceived. As she reread her draft, she noticed that she had focused almost entirely on the grandmother and her family, but had written very little about the Misfit. After some reflection—and another reading of the story—she decided to change her major claim to argue that the Misfit, who is a serial killer, is the least self-deceived character in the story. By exploring this new insight, the student discovered several related ideas that she had previously overlooked and was thus able to develop a stronger, more sophisticated interpretation.

That student was able to get some distance from her own writing, to look at it as another reader might. In revising, *look at your paper from the reader's point of view.* What questions might a reader want to ask you? These must be anticipated in the paper, because you will not be around to answer them. One of the best ways to get another reader's perspective is to enlist the help of peer reviewers.

Getting Feedback: Peer Review

Writers routinely seek the help of potential readers to find out what is working and what is not working in their drafts. Even professional writers ask for suggestions from editors, reviewers, teachers, and friends. Someone else can often see places where you *thought* you were being clear but were actually filling in details only in your head, not on the page.

The ideal people to help you evaluate your first draft are the members of your own writing class. They will be familiar with the assignment and will understand why you are writing the paper and for whom. Here are some guidelines to follow when asking for help with your revision.

1. *Specify the kind of help you want.* If you already know that the spelling needs to be checked, ask your readers to ignore those errors and focus on other elements in the draft. If you want suggestions about the thesis or the introduction or the tone or the organization or the examples, then ask questions about those features.

2. *Ask productive questions.* Be sure to pose questions that require more than a yes or no answer. Ask readers to tell you in detail what *they* see. You can use the questions in the Peer Evaluation Checklist (page 48) to help you solicit feedback.

3. *Don't get defensive.* Listen carefully to what your reviewers say; don't argue with them. If something confused them, it confused them. You want to see the writing through their eyes, not browbeat them into seeing it the way you do.

4. *Make your own decisions.* Remember that this is your paper; you are responsible for accepting or rejecting the feedback you get. If you don't agree with the suggestions, then don't follow them. But also keep in mind that your peer reviewers are likely to be more objective about your writing than you are.

Revising in Peer Groups

In many writing classes, students work together on their papers. Meeting in small groups, they read copies of each other's drafts and respond to them. Sometimes, students post their drafts on a classroom management system or by e-mail. If your instructor doesn't arrange

Peer Evaluation Checklist for Revision

The following questions are designed to address the typical concerns in arguing a literary interpretation. They will help you evaluate your own or another student's first draft.

1. Does the paper meet the assignment? What is the major claim? Does the whole paper relate to this claim? Is the claim interesting or too predictable?

2. Is the interpretation argued clearly and consistently? Make a note of any sentences or paragraphs that you had to reread. Make a note of any words or phrases that you found confusing.

3. Is the argument well organized? Is it logical? Is there perhaps a better order for the major points of the argument? Are there any paragraphs or points that do not seem to belong?

4. Is there enough material to make the interpretation clear and convincing? Does it need further details or examples? Make a note of places you would like to see more details or examples. Write questions to help the writer add details. For example, if the essay says, "Eveline did not much like her father," you could ask, "Exactly how did she feel about him?"

5. Are all the quotations from the story accurate? Do they appear within quotation marks?

6. Does the opening capture the reader's attention and make the major claim of the paper clear? Does the conclusion provide an intelligent, satisfactory ending for the argument?

for peer review, try to get several readers' reactions to your drafts. You can meet together outside of class or use a form of online collaboartion through Skype, Google Hangout, Facetime, or similar process.

Working in peer review groups gives you a chance to write for readers other than the teacher. You increase your audience awareness, get immediate feedback on your drafts, and have a chance to discuss them with someone who doesn't have the power of a grade over you.

But it takes skill to be an honest and critical reader of someone else's writing. When giving feedback, whether in groups or one-on-one, you should observe certain ground rules to ensure that your responses are productive and helpful.

- Remember that drafts are works in progress which writers intend to develop and improve. You are acting as an informed, interested reader who has questions and suggestions for improvement.
- Pay attention to *what* the other writers are saying, just as you hope they'll pay attention to what you are saying. In other words, focus on content first.

- Avoid the extremes of saying that everything is wonderful or finding fault with every detail. Instead, give thoughtful, sympathetic responses—the kind of feedback that you would like to receive.
- Talk about the writing, not about the writer. If you notice errors, feel free to mention them, but concentrate on responding and suggesting rather than correcting the writer.

Once you have gathered reactions and suggestions from your peer reviewers—and perhaps from your instructor, too—you are ready to begin rewriting. The rest of this chapter will guide you through the specifics of revising and editing.

What Should I Add or Take Out?

Revising is hard work, and you may wonder just where and how to start. If you have not been following a plan carefully worked out before you began writing, you should begin the revising process by outlining your first draft.

Outlining After the First Draft

To be sure that your discussion is unified and complete—that is, to discover whether anything needs to be taken out or added—you should briefly outline your rough draft. It may seem odd to make an outline *after* you have written the paper, but listing your main ideas and supporting details will enable you to review your essay quickly and easily. You can examine its skeleton and decide whether everything fits together properly. This step in the revising process is *essential* if you have written the first draft without an outline or a detailed plan.

Making the Outline

An outline, whether done before or after the first draft, allows you to check for sufficient and logical development of ideas as well as for unity throughout the essay. Your introductory paragraph should contain your thesis, perhaps stated in a general way but stated clearly enough to let your readers know what your focus is. Here is one way to construct an after-writing outline:

1. Take a separate sheet of paper and write your thesis statement at the top.
2. Add the topic sentences stating the main ideas of your paragraphs, along with the supporting points in each one.

Your final paragraph should draw a conclusion concerning the thesis—a conclusion that relates the material in the body of the paper to the theme or purpose of the literary work.

Checking the Outline

Check your outline this way:

1. Make sure that the idea in every topic sentence is a significant critical observation relating directly to your thesis.
2. If not, revise the topic sentence until it clearly supports your thesis— or else delete the whole paragraph.

Just as the topic sentence of each paragraph should relate to the thesis of the paper, every piece of supporting evidence in the paragraph should relate to its topic sentence. So, next check the organization within each paragraph this way:

3. In each body paragraph, examine your supporting details to be sure that each relates directly to the topic sentence.
4. Make sure that none of your points repeats an idea included elsewhere (unless you are repeating for emphasis). Eliminate any careless repetition.
5. Decide whether your support is adequate. Think about whether you have included the most convincing details and whether you have enough of them.
6. If you decide you do not have sufficient support for a topic sentence, you need to rethink the point in order to expand it, or consider omitting the paragraph if the ideas are not essential. Sometimes you can combine the material from two paragraphs into a single new one having a broader topic sentence.

Sample Student Work: After-Writing Outline

Because one peer reader of Wendy Dennison's paper on "Eveline" noticed that a couple of examples might be out of place, Wendy outlined her first draft. Here is her after-writing outline. (Her draft appeared in Chapter 2.)

1. Introduction
   —Eveline refuses to leave with Frank because she fears failure (thesis)
2. Her deathbed promise to her mother was unfair.
   —unfair to ask Eveline to give up her own life
3. She has good reasons to want to leave her father.
   —he's a drunk, takes advantage of the promise
   —he's stingy
   —he abuses her verbally
   —he's a bully, might actually beat her
   —he was sometimes fun in past, played at picnics
4. Her home life is so unhealthy she should leave.
   —doesn't feel a part of everything (picture of priest)
   —dust in house = dirtiness, squalor of her life
   —thinks of leaving and remembers her dreary job

5. Her only reason for staying is that she's afraid.
   —leaving the familiar could mean failure
   —quotation: "about to explore" suggests uncertainty
   —life is hard, so she thinks of good memories to convince herself
     to stay
6. She retreats into the familiar to avoid risk.
   —feels she has a right to happiness
   —decides a predictable life is better than one without direction and
     pattern (conclusion)

Examining the Sample Outline

If you examine Wendy's outline carefully, you can see a few problems.

Paragraph 2	Wendy needs more material about why the promise to her dying mother was unfair.
Paragraph 3	The last point, about "fun in past," does not relate to the topic sentence for the paragraph, which focuses on "good reasons to want to leave."
Paragraph 4	The last point, about Eveline's job, does not relate to the topic sentence for the paragraph, which focuses on Eveline's "unhealthy" home life.
Paragraph 5	The last point, about Eveline's "good memories," provides a good place to move the example about "fun in past" from paragraph 3.
Paragraph 6	The first point, about Eveline's "right to happiness," does not relate to the topic sentence, which focuses on Eveline's retreat "into the familiar," but could well be moved to paragraph 2 to support the topic sentence idea that her death bed promise was unfair.

In the final draft of Wendy's paper, which appears on pages 65–67, you will see how she took care of the problems revealed by her outline.

Outlining Exercise

For practice in checking the relevance and organization of ideas, outline the following paragraph in the way we just described, putting the topic sentence at the top of the page, and then listing each supporting idea.

Eveline lacks courage to seek a life of her own because she fears that her father will not be able to cope if she leaves him. Her anxiety is heightened as she recalls that she and her brothers and sisters are grown up and that her mother is dead. If she leaves, her father will soon be all alone. She realizes that he is "usually fairly bad on a Saturday night" (5) and recognizes that his drinking problem will not get any better after she leaves. Also she has noticed that "Her father was becoming old lately" and assumes that "he would miss her" (6). As a dutiful daughter, Eveline seems to feel that going away with Frank means abandoning her aging father, and that may be why she has written a letter to him—to ease the blow of her departure and to soothe her own conscience.

Next, examine your outline. Do you see any irrelevant points? Can you think of any important ideas or details that have been omitted from the paragraph? Are the points arranged in an effective order? Would another arrangement be better?

Now look at the following outline and see whether it matches yours.

Topic sentence: Eveline fears her father will not be able to manage if she leaves him.

1. Eveline thinks about his loneliness—children grown, wife dead.
2. She fears his drinking problem worsening.
3. She worries that he is becoming old lately.
4. She assumes "he would miss her."
5. She writes letter to ease the blow.

Your outline may not come out exactly like this one, but the main idea is to be sure you have included all of the supporting details.

Here are some observations to consider for a revision of the sample paragraph, based on the outline of its major points:

1. Point 1 could be expanded to include details about the neighbors who have died (Tizzie Dunn) and moved away (the Waters family).
2. An earlier draft of the paragraph included the point about Eveline's promise to her mother, but it was dropped as being irrelevant to the topic sentence. Do you agree?
3. The paragraph's supporting points appear in the same order as they do in the story. Is this chronological organization effective? Would some logical order be better?

What Should I Rearrange?

A crucial part of revision involves giving some thought to the order of your paragraphs and the order of the supporting details within them. The order in which they came to your mind is not necessarily the best. Luckily, rearranging is fairly easy once you have an after-writing outline.

Many writers use cutting and pasting on the computer to experiment with various arrangements of their ideas, reading different versions and deciding which order is most effective. They rearrange paragraphs and even sentences. For instance, sometimes the last sentence you write in a paragraph turns out to be a good topic sentence and should be moved to the beginning. Sometimes the paragraph you write at the essay's end would work better as the introduction to the paper.

If you experiment this way, save each version under a different file name (eve1, eve2, eve3, for example), so that your computer retains all the choices you have created. Otherwise, each new version may over-write the old one, and you will lose pieces you may want later.

The two principles you need to use in considering how well your points are arranged are *logic* and *emphasis*. Both principles allow you to arrange ideas in a certain sequence. The following questions will help you devise an appropriate arrangement.

1. Should I arrange the paragraphs and details in my essay in the same order in which they appear in the work I am analyzing?

If you are writing a paragraph supporting the topic that Eveline is timid, you might collect details from throughout the story. You could then put those details in the same order as they appear in the story.

2. Should I organize the descriptions in terms of space?

In a paper examining the significance of the objects in Eveline's home, you might take up these objects as though presented in a tour around the room. Other descriptions may be arranged from near to far, from outside to inside, from small to large.

3. Should I arrange my main points along a scale of value, of power, of weight, or of forcefulness? Could I use an arrangement of
    —negative to positive?
    —universal to individual?
    —most influential to least influential?
    —general to specific?
    —least impressive to most impressive?

You can arrange your ideas in either direction along any of these scales— negative to positive or positive to negative, for instance. It is usually effective to place the most emphatic point last in any essay. If you are writing about several of Eveline's reasons for not going with Frank, and you believe that the most influential reason is her promise to her dying mother, you would include that idea in the last paragraph of the body of your paper, opening with a transition like this:

> Though her timidity in general and her fear of her father in particular affect Eveline's final decision, her promise to her mother is the most powerful influence.

The strongest-point rule is just a guideline, of course. Try to arrange your ideas in a way your readers will find effective.

Does It Flow?

The best way to examine the flow (the *coherence*) of your prose is to read it aloud. Recording your essays on tape and playing them back enables you to hear with some objectivity how your writing sounds. You might also entice a friend to read your paper aloud to you. Whatever method you use, listen for choppiness or abruptness. Your ideas should be arranged in a clear sequence that is easy to follow. Will your readers experience any confusion when a new idea comes up? If so, you

need stronger connections between sentences or between paragraphs—
transitions that indicate how one idea is related to the next.

For example, when you see the words *for example*, you know what to
expect. When you see *furthermore* opening a paragraph, your mind gets
ready for some addition to the previous point. By contrast, when you see
phrases like *on the other hand* or *by contrast*, you are prepared for something different from the previous point.

These clearly transitional phrases can be supplemented by more subtle *echo transitions*. This technique repeats or echoes a word, phrase, or
idea from the last sentence of one paragraph to provide the transition at
the beginning of the next. Here is an example, beginning with the closing of a paragraph and showing the transition to the next:

> ...Throughout the story, the husband's word is considered law, and the
> wife barely dares to question it.
>
> *This unequal marriage* fits perfectly into the historical period of the
> setting....

The words *this unequal marriage* echo the inequality described in the previous paragraph.

Another technique that increases coherence in writing is the repetition of key terms and structures. In the paragraphs you have been reading, the key terms are forms of the words *transition, echo, refer, technique,*
and *repeat*. In the paragraph that began "For example," you may have
noticed how the phrase *when you see* was repeated to guide you through
the succession of examples.

In short, here are the techniques for achieving coherence.

1. A clearly sequenced flow of ideas
2. Transitional terms (a handy list follows.)
3. Echo transitions
4. Repetition of key terms
5. Repetition of parallel sentence structures

A Revising Checklist to help you review all the important aspects of
the revising process appears on the next page.

Once you are satisfied that your ideas proceed smoothly, consider the
possibility of combining sentences to avoid needless repetition of words
and to eliminate choppiness. You may also decide to combine sentences
to achieve emphasis and variety. Probably you can discover many ways to
improve your sentences.

Transitional Terms for All Occasions

To Continue to a New Point
next, second, third, besides, further, finally

To Make an Addition to a Point
too, moreover, in addition, for example, such as, that is, as an illustration, for instance, furthermore

To Show Cause and Effect
therefore, consequently, as a result, accordingly, then, thus, so, hence

To Show Contrast
but, still, on the other hand, nevertheless, however, conversely, notwithstanding, yet

To Show Similarity
too, similarly, in the same way, likewise, also

To Emphasize or Restate
again, namely, in other words, finally, especially, without doubt, indeed, in short, in brief, primarily, chiefly, as a matter of fact, no doubt

To Conclude a Point
finally, in conclusion, to summarize, to sum up, in sum

Revising Checklist

1. Is my thesis idea intelligent and clearly stated?
2. Is my argument logically and effectively organized? Does the main idea of every paragraph relate directly to the thesis?
3. Are the paragraphs fully developed, with plenty of specific examples or illustrations to support the topic sentences?
4. Do the ideas flow coherently? Are the transitions easy to follow?
5. Have I accomplished my purpose? Does the paper make the point I set out to prove?

What Is Editing?

During revision, you focused on making your paper organized, well developed, and coherent. In the editing stage, you should concentrate on improving your sentences and refining your use of language.

Combining for Conciseness

If you find that you are sometimes repeating the same word without meaning to, you may eliminate the problem by combining sentences. For instance, you might have written something like this:

> Twain savagely attacks conformity in the scene where the villagers stone the woman. The woman is suspected of being a witch.

Because the repetition of *the woman* serves no useful purpose, the two statements can be more effectively phrased in a single sentence.

> In a scene showing the villagers stoning a woman suspected of being a witch, Twain savagely attacks conformity.

When you combine sentences in this way, you take the main idea from one sentence and tuck it, usually as a modifier of some sort, within another sentence. We can illustrate the process in reverse to help you see more clearly what the technique involves. Notice that the following sentence contains two simple statements:

> Theodore, who did not wish to throw a stone, was horrified by the cruelty.

The two main ideas in that sentence are these:

> Theodore was horrified by the cruelty.
> Theodore did not wish to throw a stone.

You can recombine those sentences in various ways, depending on which idea you choose to emphasize.

> Horrified by the cruelty, Theodore did not wish to throw a stone.
> Not wishing to throw a stone, Theodore was horrified by the cruelty.

Sentence combining not only eliminates wordiness but also adds variety and focus. The various combinations provide numerous stylistic choices.

Sentence-Combining Exercise

The following sentences, all written by students, include needless repetition and wordiness that can be eliminated by sentence combining. Decide which idea in each pair of sentences should be emphasized, and put that idea in the main (independent) clause. You will, of course, need to change, add, or omit words as you work to improve these sentences, but try not to leave out any significant ideas.

1. The second common stereotype is the dark lady. Usually the dark lady stereotype symbolizes sexual temptation.
2. Kate Chopin wrote a short story called "The Storm." As the title of the story suggests, it is about a rainstorm and shows how people respond to the storm.

3. Emily Dickinson's poetry is sometimes elliptical. It is thus sometimes difficult for readers to get even the literal meaning of her poems.

4. There are three major things to consider in understanding Goodman Brown's character. These things include what the author tells us about Brown, what Brown himself says and does, and how other people respond to him.

5. Most of the incidents that inspire Walter Mitty's fantasies have humorous connotations associated with them. These can be broken down into basically two groups, the first one being his desire to be in charge of a situation.

Rearranging for Emphasis and Variety

When you rewrite to gain emphasis and variety, you will probably restructure sentences as well as combine them. In fact, you may find yourself occasionally dividing a sentence for easier reading or to produce a short, emphatic sentence. The following are some techniques to help you in polishing your sentence structure.

Varying the Pattern

The usual way of forming sentences in English is to begin with the subject, follow with the verb, and add a complement (something that completes the verb), like this:

Walter Mitty is not a brave person.

Any time you depart from this expected pattern, you gain variety and some degree of emphasis. Notice the difference.

A brave person Walter Mitty is not.

Here are other variations that you may want to try.

A Dash at the End: Twain found constant fault with humanity—with what he called "the damned human race."

An Interrupter Set Off by Dashes or Commas: Twain considered humanity in general—"the damned human race"—inferior to the so-called lower animals.

A Modifier at the Beginning: Although he loved individual human beings, Twain professed to loathe what he called "the damned human race."

A Short-Short Sentence: Because most of the sentences you will write are moderately long, you gain considerable emphasis when you follow a sentence of normal length with an extremely short one.

Plagiarizing, which means borrowing the words or ideas of another writer without giving proper credit, is a serious infraction. Do not do it.

Deliberate Repetition: Just a few pages ago, we cautioned you to combine sentences rather than to repeat words needlessly. That caution still holds. But repeating words for emphasis is a different matter. Purposeful repetition can produce effective and emphatic sentences.

Twain believed that organized religion was folly, a folly to be ridiculed discreetly.

One cannot talk well, study well, or write well if one cannot think well.

That last sentence (modeled after one written by Virginia Woolf) repeats the same grammatical structure as well as the same words to achieve a powerful effect.

Exercise on Style

Rewrite the following ordinary sentences to achieve greater emphasis, variety, and conciseness.

1. Edith Wharton was born into a rich, upper-class family, but she was not even allowed to have paper on which to write when she was a child.
2. Her governesses never taught her how to organize ideas in writing, so when she decided to write a book on the decoration of houses, she had to ask her friend Walter Berry to help her write it.
3. She married Teddy Wharton when she was twenty-three years old, and he always carried a one-thousand-dollar bill in case she wanted anything.
4. Her good friend Henry James gave her advice to help her improve her novels, yet her novels invariably sold far more copies than James's did.
5. She was awarded the Legion of Honor, which is the highest award given by the French government, following World War I for her refugee relief activities.

Which Words Should I Change?

You may have a good thesis and convincing, detailed support for it—but your writing *style* can make the difference between a dull, boring presentation and a rich, engaging one.

Check Your Verbs

After examining the construction of your sentences, look at the specific language you have used. Read through the rough draft and underline the verbs. Look for forms of these useful but well-worn words:

is (are, was, were, etc.)	go	has
get	come	move
do	make	use

Consider substituting a different verb, one that presents a type of image—visual or otherwise—to your readers. For example, this sentence is grammatically correct but dull:

> Eveline does her work with reluctance.

Searching for a more precise verb than *does*, you might write

> Eveline reluctantly plods through her work.

Plods suggests a picture of poor Eveline with slumped shoulders and slow steps, dragging through the day.

Occasionally you can pick up a lively word from somewhere else in a limp sentence and convert it into the main verb.

> Eveline is unable to leave her home because she is trapped by a promise to her dead mother.

Trapped is an arresting word in that sentence, and you could shift it to an earlier position to good effect.

> A promise to her dead mother traps Eveline in her miserable home.

This revision also cuts unnecessary words out of the first version.

Use Active Voice Most of the Time

Although the passive voice sometimes offers the best way to construct a sentence, the habitual use of the passive sprinkles your prose with colorless helping verbs, like *is* and *was*. If a sentence is in passive voice, the subject does *not* perform the action implied by the verb.

> The paper was written by Janet, Jo's roommate.
> The assignment was given poorly.
> Her roommate's efforts were hindered by a lack of understanding.

The paper, the assignment, and the roommate's efforts did *not* carry out the writing, the giving, or the hindering. In active voice, the subjects of the sentences are the doers or the causes of the action.

> Jo's roommate, Janet, wrote the paper.
> The teacher gave the assignment poorly.
> Lack of understanding hindered her roommate's efforts.

Use Passive Voice If Appropriate

Sometimes, of course, you may have a good reason for writing in the passive voice. For example, you may want to give a certain word the important position of subject even though it is not the agent of the action. In the sentence

Sensory details are emphasized in this paragraph.

the *details* are the key point. The writer of the paragraph (the agent of the action) is not important enough even to be included. In active voice, the key term would be pushed to the middle of the sentence, a much weaker position.

The writer emphasizes sensory details in this paragraph.

Clearly, you need not shun the passive, but if any of your sentences sound stilted or awkward, check to see if the passive voice may be the culprit.

Exercise on Passive Voice

Change passive voice to active in the following sentences. Feel free to add, delete, or change words.

1. Antigone is treated brutally by Creon because of her struggle to achieve justice.
2. Creon was not convinced by her tirade against his unbending authority.
3. Conflict between male and female was portrayed in the play by the author.
4. If even a small point is won against a tyrant by society, considerable benefit may be experienced.
5. The tragedy is caused by the ironbound authority exercised by Creon.

Feel the Words

Words have emotional meanings (*connotations*) as well as direct dictionary meanings (*denotations*). You may be invited to a get-together, a soiree, a social gathering, a blowout, a blast, a reception, a bash, or a do, and although all are words for parties, the connotations tell you whether to wear jeans or feathers, whether to bring a case of cheap beer or a bottle of expensive wine.

In writing, take into account the emotional content of the words you use. One of our favorite essays, "The Discus Thrower," opens with this sentence:

I spy on my patients.

The word *spy* immediately captures the imagination with its connotations of intrigue and mystery and its slight flavor of deception. "I watch my patients when they don't know it" is still an interesting sentence because of its denotative content, but essayist Richard Selzer's version commands emotional as well as intellectual engagement.

We are not encouraging you to puff up your prose with strings of adverbs and adjectives; indeed, a single emotionally charged word in a simple sentence can be quite powerful.

Exercise on Word Choice

Rewrite the following sentences using livelier words and cutting unnecessary words.

1. The first sentence of "A Good Man Is Hard to Find" is a foreshadowing of what happens to the grandmother at the end of the story.
2. The conversations between members of the family show that they are not the idealized American family on vacation but are self-absorbed and ignorant.
3. There are many instances of lying, untruths, and self-deception in the story.
4. Three men come up to the family after their car accident, but they are strange in their clothing and actions, and they are not there to help.
5. Each character has his or her own way of saying things, a manner of speech which is often amusing in a dark kind of way.

Attend to Tone

Tone—the reflection of a writer's attitude—is usually described in terms of emotion: serious, solemn, satirical, humorous, sly, mournful, expectant, and so on. Although most writing about literature calls for a plain, direct tone, other attitudes can be conveyed. Negative book reviews, for instance, sometimes have a sarcastic tone. A writer unsympathetic to Eveline might describe her as "a spineless drudge who enjoys her oppression," whereas a sympathetic reader might state that Eveline is "a pitiful victim of a brutal home life." Someone who wants to remain neutral could describe Eveline as "a young woman trapped by duty and her own fears." These variations in tone, conveyed by word choice, reflect the writers' differing attitudes toward what is being discussed.

Once you establish a tone, you should stick with it. A humorous or sarcastic section set unexpectedly in a straightforward, direct essay will distract or disconcert your readers. Be sure to set your tone in the first paragraph; then your readers will unconsciously adjust their expectations about the rest of the paper.

Use Formal Language

The nature of your audience will also determine the level of usage for your writing. Essays for college classes usually require *formal language*, a style that takes a serious or neutral tone and avoids such *informal usage* as most contractions, slang, and sentence fragments, even intentional ones.

Even one shift from formal usage to informal usage can distract your readers:

Eveline fully intends to leave with Frank, but she gets hung up at the point of departure.

The words *hung up* are surprisingly slangy in the context of a literary essay. An alternative that stays at the same usage level might read this way:

Eveline fully intends to leave with Frank, but she becomes paralyzed at the point of departure

Formal writing often involves a third-person approach.

One can sympathize with Eveline, at the same time regretting her weakness.
The reader sympathizes with Eveline,...

Most people today consider the use of first-person plural (*we, us, our, ours*) quite acceptable in formal papers.

We sympathize with Eveline,...
Eveline gains our sympathy,...

A growing number of people think the use of the first-person singular (*I, me, my, mine*) is also acceptable in formal writing.

I sympathize with Eveline,...
Eveline gains my sympathy,...

But avoid the informal second person, *you*. Do *not* write, "You can see that Eveline is caught in a terrible bind."

What Is Proofreading?

Proofreading is the last step in preparing your final draft. After you have improved your sentences and refined your word choices, you must force yourself to read the paper one last time to pick up any careless mistakes or typographical errors. Jessica Mitford rightly says that "failure to proofread is like preparing a magnificent dinner and forgetting to set the table."

Try Reading It Backward

To avoid getting so interested in what you have written that you don't see your errors, read your sentences from the last one on the page to the first, that is, from the bottom to the top. Because your ideas will lack continuity in reverse order, you stand a better chance of keeping your attention focused on each sentence *as* a sentence. Be sure that every word is correctly spelled, that each sentence is complete and correctly punctuated. Be sure to run your spelling checker and to think over its suggestions, which may be imperfect. Don't automatically accept whatever appears, or you may end up using *slyly* when you meant *slightly*!

Look for Your Typical Errors

If you know that you often have problems with certain elements of punctuation or *diction* be on guard for these particular errors as you examine each sentence.

1. Make sure that each sentence really is a sentence, not some fragment—especially those beginning with *because, since, which, that, although, as, when,* or *what*, and those beginning with words ending in *ing*.
2. Make sure that independent clauses joined by *indeed, moreover, however, nevertheless, thus,* and *hence* have a semicolon before those words, not just a comma.
3. Make sure that every modifying phrase or clause is close to the word it modifies.
4. If you know you have a problem with spelling, check every word and look up all questionable ones. Run your spelling checker, and verify that its suggestions are really the words you want.
5. Be alert for words that you know you consistently get wrong. If you are aware that you sometimes confuse words that sound alike (*it's/its, your/you're, there/their/they're, effect/affect*), check the accuracy of your usage. Remember that your spelling checker will not help you here.

If you are not sure how to correct the errors just mentioned, consult a handbook (your instructor may assign one) or a reliable online resource like the Purdue OWL: https://owl.english.purdue.edu/owl/). You will also find a handy Proofreading Checklist on page 64.

Read the Paper Aloud

In an earlier section, we recommended reading your paper aloud as a means of checking coherence. It's a good idea to read it aloud again to catch words left out or carelessly repeated.

Find a Friend to Help

If you have a literate friend who will help you proofread your paper, you are in luck. Ask this kind person to point out errors and to let you know whether your thesis is made plain at the beginning, whether every sentence is clear, and whether the paper as a whole makes sense. You risk having to do further revising if any of your friend's responses prove negative, but try to be grateful for the help. You want to turn in a paper you can be proud of.

Relying on someone else to do your proofreading, though, is unwise. There will be writing situations in college that preclude your bringing

Proofreading Checklist

1. Have I mixed up any of these easily confused words?

its/it's	their/they're/there	lie/lay
effect/affect	suppose/supposed	our/are
your/you're	woman/women	use/used
to/too/two	prejudice/prejudiced	then/than
who's/whose	accept/except	cite/site

2. Have I put an apostrophe appropriately in each of my possessive nouns?
3. Have I carelessly repeated any word?
4. Have I carelessly left any words out?
5. Have I omitted the first or final letter from any words?
6. Have I used the proper punctuation at the end of every sentence?
7. Have I spelled every word correctly?

a friend to help (e.g., essay examinations and in-class essays). Learn to find and correct your own errors so you will not risk failure when you go it alone.

Sample Student Paper: Final Draft

The following is the final draft of Wendy Dennison's paper on "Eveline." This finished version contains changes she made to correct problems revealed by her after-writing outline as well as content she added in response to her instructor's comments. The paper also includes editing changes she made to achieve precision in word choice and to increase the effectiveness of each individual sentence.

Wendy Dennison

Professor McMahan

English 102

6 February 2009

Fear of Failure in Joyce's "Eveline"

In his short story "Eveline," James Joyce gives the protagonist an exciting chance to leave her old life and begin a new one. But she rejects this offer that Frank—or Fate—makes, preferring instead to settle back into the dreary life she has known all along. Why does she not go away with Frank when the opportunity seems so attractive? We need to examine Eveline's timid personality in order to discover the answer.

Since Eveline has been raised a Catholic, we know she would not take her promise to her dying mother lightly. But surely her promise to "keep the home together as long as she could" was given under extreme circumstances (6). It was unjust of her mother to ask such a sacrifice of her, and Eveline is aware of the unfairness: "Why should she be unhappy? She had a right to happiness" (6). We know that Eveline will always be haunted by that promise, but we do not expect her to give up her chance for a life of her own in order to be a dutiful daughter. Surely that promise cannot be the only reason she stays.

We certainly should not be surprised that Eveline might wish to leave her abusive father. A hot-tempered heavy drinker, he has taken advantage of his daughter's promise to her mother. She is forced to keep house for him, yet must beg for money to feed the family. He practically accuses her of stealing, claiming that "she used to squander the money, that she had no head, that he wasn't going to give her his hard-earned money to throw about the streets" (4-5). He has so frightened her with threats of beatings that she has "palpitations" (4). Eveline realizes that with her brothers gone, there is "nobody to protect her" from her father's rage (4). Her father has treated Eveline badly and may abuse her even worse in the future. To leave him would obviously be in her best interest, yet something keeps her there.

Eveline's home life is so unhealthy that we feel she would be wise to leave. Despite all the chores she performs, she still does not feel entirely at home in her father's house. For example, she knows nothing about the picture of the priest, not even his name, yet the portrait seems quite important to her father (4). The dustiness of the house, of which Joyce reminds us periodically, suggests the pervasive dreariness of her daily life as she looks around "wondering where on earth all the dust came from" (4). Since her home is clearly not conducive to happiness, why does she stay there?

Eveline's situation reflects the unhappy restrictions of conventional sex roles. Through guilt and threats of hellfire, Catholicism enforces dutiful daughterhood. And as a young woman, Eveline is subordinate, passive, and powerless, both at work and in the home, especially with no males to support or protect her. Finally, her father's traditionally masculine lack of expressiveness makes her daily life dreary.

The main reason Eveline would remain in Ireland is that she is desperately afraid of the unknown. If she leaves the familiar, no matter how unpleasant, she risks failure. "She was about to explore another life with Frank" (5), we are told, in faraway Buenos Ayres. The word *explore* is significant, as it brings to mind uncertainty and risk, two factors that Eveline is not prepared to deal with. She admits that hers is "a hard life," yet thinks that "now that she was about to leave it she did not find it a wholly undesirable life" (5). When she sits in the growing darkness with the letters in her lap, Eveline calls up a couple of good memories—of her father being jolly once on a picnic, of his kindness once when she was sick. We see her trying to calm her fears, trying to convince herself that her home life is more bearable than it is.

Dennison 3

Afraid of failing on her own, Eveline retreats into the familiar, telling herself that life with father cannot be as frightening as a risky, unknown life with Frank. Furthermore, she may suspect that her power-less role as a woman will not really change, even in Buenos Ayres—it may not be "another life" at all (5). So strong is her fear of the unknown that it overrides her fear of her father. She seems to decide that a predictable—if dreary and abused—life is better than a life that may only compound her burdens.

Dennison 4

Work Cited

Joyce, James. "Eveline." *Literature and the Writing Process*, edited by Elizabeth McMahan, et al., 8th ed., Prentice Hall, 2008, pp. 3-7.

5 Researched Writing

At some point you may be asked to write a literary paper that doesn't draw entirely on your own understanding and judgments. In other words, you will have to do some *research*. When writing a researched paper about litera-ture, you begin, as always, with a *primary source*—the story, poem, or play the paper is about—but you expand the range of your coverage to include *secondary sources*—critical, biographical, historical, and cultural documents that support your interpretation of the primary work (or works). By the end of this chapter, you will be able to

• Describe five ways secondary sources can help you write about literature.
• Identify the major tools for accessing secondary sources: *the online catalog, indexes and databases,* and *the Internet.*
• List several ways to evaluate online sources.
• Define three methods for recording and processing source materials.
• Distinguish among *summaries, paraphrases,* and *quotations.*
• Explain how to incorporate *quotations* and *paraphrases* into your writing without committing *plagiarism.*
• Name and describe the standard features for formatting a researched paper.
• Understand how to present *in-text citations* and prepare a *list of works cited* according to the MLA documentation style.

Using Library Sources in Your Writing

Most student writers consult secondary sources to help them explain, develop, and strengthen their ideas and opinions. That's what Wendy Dennison did with her essay "Fear of Failure in Joyce's 'Eveline' " (see pages 65–67 in the previous chapter). Although Wendy had worked out her own arguments for why Eveline did not go away with Frank, she and her instructor thought it would be enlightening to see what other readers thought. So Wendy went to the library to find material by critics who had published their interpretations of "Eveline," especially about the ending of the story. After reading and taking notes from a number of books and articles, Wendy revised her paper by incorporating comments from several critics into her discussion. The revised, documented version of her essay appears on pages 84–87.

Although not everyone produces a finished paper before doing research, some writers do prepare a first draft before looking at secondary sources. Others consult secondary materials to help them decide on a topic. Another common strategy is to use the ideas of others as a platform for an interpretation, first summarizing several views and then presenting a different interpretation, a synthesizing conclusion, or an analysis of their conflicting points of view.

Secondary sources can help you in a number of different ways to develop an essay about literature:

- *Analyzing the features of a single work.* Why does E. E. Cummings disregard traditional form and punctuation in his poetry? How does the chorus function in *Antigone*?
- *Exploring connections between a work and the author's life.* What personal incident inspired John Donne to write "A Valediction: Forbidding Mourning"? How autobiographical is Anne Sexton's "You All Know the Story of the Other Woman"?
- *Assessing the impact of social, historical, or cultural backgrounds on a work.* In "Barn Burning," why is Abner Snopes infuriated when a well-dressed black servant scolds him at the entrance of a white landowner's palatial home?
- *Understanding the political or artistic objectives of a work.* In what ways can Luis Valdez's play *Los Vendidos* be seen as a drama of social protest? How well does "The Cask of Amontillado" illustrate Poe's theory about achieving "a certain unique or single effect" in a short story?
- *Comparing themes or characters in several works.* How do the mother-daughter relationships in stories by Tillie Olsen, Hisaye Yamamoto, Andre Dubus, and Joyce Carol Oates illustrate different kinds of maternal-filial bonding? What attitudes toward sports are expressed in Housman's "To an Athlete Dying Young," Updike's "Ex-Basketball Player," and Hirsch's "Execution"?

You will find ideas for researched writing in the questions that follow most of the literary selections in this book.

Conducting Your Research

The prewriting you do for a documented paper is similar to the prewriting you would do for any literary essay. You still need to consider your audience, determine your purpose, discover and develop your ideas, and decide what point you want to make. The techniques and advice presented in Chapter 1 will help you with these tasks. But the next steps will be different, perhaps even new to you. First and foremost, you have to track down relevant secondary sources, a challenging procedure that involves libraries, computer terminals, and stacks of papers and index cards. The following sections will guide you through this process.

Locating Sources

More than likely you will conduct your search for sources on a computer. Most college libraries offer workshops to help students locate materials, conduct searches, use online databases, and navigate the Internet. If these courses are not required, take them anyway—you could save yourself hours of aimless wandering. Your library's information desk will provide you with schedules of these valuable sessions.

Using the Online Catalog

Most libraries today list their holdings in a computerized *online public access catalog* (OPAC). The opening screen of the OPAC at the library Wendy Dennison used shows that she can search for books, journals and magazines, and other items owned by her library and by other libraries in the state. In electronic databases, such as InfoTrac and EBSCO, you can usually search for sources by author, title, and publication year and also by subject or *keywords*.

Subject searches focus only on the source's contents and yield more limited, precise results. They work best when the *descriptors* (subject headings) conform to a database's directory of terms. For your library's catalog, the directory is the *Library of Congress Subject Headings (LCSH)*, which is available in printed form in the reference room. *Keyword searches* look through the entire database and are not dependent on preset subject headings. If you know your exact subject, you will want to begin with a subject search. A keyword search, on the other hand, is a good place to limit and refine your subject and discover specific descriptors. Remember that computers are unforgiving about spelling and typing errors. When your results are not what you expected, check the accuracy of the search terms you used.

To begin her search of the online catalog, Wendy typed in the LSCH heading "Joyce, James, 1882–1941" and selected "subject" in the "search by" menu. The results showed more than seventy entries, most of which contained sublistings for specific titles. In other words, her library owns hundreds of books and other materials about James Joyce. Wendy refined her search by adding "Dubliners" (the title of the collection that contains "Eveline") to her descriptor; she found that her library had eight books on this topic. She saw which ones were available and where they were located in the library. Wendy also browsed a number of items under the subheading "criticism and interpretation" and took down information about books that appeared to deal with Joyce's early works. She felt she had plenty of material to begin her review of critical opinions about the motivations of Eveline.

Using Indexes and Databases

Even though you might find valuable material in books to use in documenting your ideas and critical judgments, your paper will not be well researched unless you also find articles and reviews relevant to your topic. These sources are now available electronically through online databases and text archives that your library subscribes to. The library homepage that Wendy was using allowed her to move from the online catalog to a list of searchable indexes, bibliographies, and other electronic reference tools.

The reference librarian recommended that Wendy look first in the *MLA International Bibliography*, which is the best choice for finding peer-reviewed articles about authors and their works. When Wendy typed "Eveline" in the "find" box of the MLA search page, she got 132 hits. The display also prompted her to refine her results by subject and gave her several words and phrases to add to her search term. Each citation included the article title, the name of the journal, and the volume, date, and page numbers; it also supplied the call number for any publications in her library. Many of the entries contained a brief summary of the article's content, and several included the full text of the article. She could also send the data to herself by email.

Wendy browsed through these findings and printed the citations for several articles that looked promising. Because the library did not own several of the periodicals, the librarian suggested requesting copies of the articles through an interlibrary loan, but that would take several days. Another option was to consult a full-text database, such as *JSTOR (Journal Storage Project)* or *ProjectMUSE*, to see if the articles were available there. Wendy discovered two promising articles in *JSTOR* and printed them out.

These were just some of the electronic tools that Wendy used to search for possible secondary sources. The following list includes other generally available indexes and databases for researching literary topics. You need to find out which ones are available at your library and how to use them.

- Contemporary Authors
- Dictionary of Literary Biography Complete Online
- Gale Literature Online
- Humanities International Complete
- Internet Public Library (ipl2) Literary Criticism Collection
- Literary Criticism Online

Using the Internet

You can locate additional resources using any one of several different search engines—such as Google, Yahoo!, and Bing—that catalog websites in directories and allow you to conduct keyword searches.

You can also join electronic communities called *newsgroups*, through which members exchange information about a common interest or affiliation by posting questions and answers to online sites. Or you can become a member of an Internet discussion group, frequently called a *listserv*, whose subscribers use e-mail to converse on a particular subject. You will find e-mail discussion groups to join at Google Groups (http://groups.google.com), Yahoo! Groups (http://groups.yahoo.com), and Tile.net (www.tile.net/lists).

If you need additional information, you can visit one of these helpful reference sites:

- *Internet Public Library*   www.ipl.org/div/litcrit/guide.html
- *Matisse's Glossary*   www.matisse.net/files/glossary.html
  of Internet Terms

Evaluating Online Sources

Although many online sources are informative and valuable, determining their credibility can be challenging. With scholarly books and journal articles, you can consider the information credible because it has been reviewed and edited; the authors are often recognized authorities, and their claims are documented. But anyone can create and publish a website or join a newsgroup. So when you use information from an electronic source, you want to be confident that it is reliable and that it comes from someone with the appropriate authority. Here are some guidelines for evaluating online materials:

- *Look for credentials.* What do you know about the people supplying the information? What's the basis of their expertise? Is the source also available in an established, conventional printed form?
- *Track down affiliations.* Who sponsors the online site? Is it a reputable group that you can easily identify? Is the information influenced by commercial or political sponsorship? Does the site include links to other resources?
- *Analyze motives.* What purpose does the site serve? Many online postings are trying to buy or sell something; others are promoting a favorite cause. These don't usually make good sources for research.
- *Consider currency and stability.* Is the material updated regularly? Is there an archive for older information?
- *Confirm your information.* Can you find other sources to verify what you've found online? Ideally, you want to have several different kinds of sources to achieve a credible balance of research material.

For more details about evaluating online sources, you can visit one of these sites:

- *Five Criteria For Evaluationg Web Pages*, a concise set of questions for assessing the authority, objectivity, currency, and coverage of online documents. From Cornell University Library at http://onlinuris.library .cornell.edu/ref/research/webcrit.html
- *Evaluating Web Pages: Techniques to Apply & Questions to Ask*, an online tutorial from the UC Berkeley Library, at http://www.lib.berkeley.edu /TeachingLib/Guides/Internet/Evaluate.html

Finally, check with your instructor to determine the types of resources considered appropriate for your specific assignment.

Using Reference Works in Print

As you can see, the library's computers provide an overwhelming number of sources and service options. You will have to spend some time with these data systems to find out how they work and how useful they are for your research. Most libraries still hold much of this and additional useful reference material in print. The *MLA International Bibliography*, for example, continues to be issued in book form. Your library probably has print versions of many indexes and guides to articles on literature. So if the computer terminals are crowded or not working, or if you simply want some peace and quiet while researching, the reference librarian can tell you where on the shelves these books are kept. You are likely to run across valuable material on shelves near the books you seek, an advantage to this often neglected ambulatory research system.

Working with Sources

Once you have located the books and articles you want to read and assimilate, you can begin reading, taking notes, and synthesizing the material.

Taking Notes

Many researchers use note cards for keeping track of the facts and opinions they find. If you decide to use cards, work out some system for recording information. Here are some suggestions:

1. Fill out a bibliography card every time you consult a new source, and record all the details necessary for citing this source in your paper, including where to find the source again. Then put the author's last name, an abbreviated title, and the page number or numbers on all the note cards you use for this source.
2. Write only one idea or point on each card. This allows you to shuffle the cards as you figure out the precise organization of your paper.
3. Put subject headings on the cards—one or two words in the upper right-hand corner to tell you what each note is about.
4. Summarize the ideas in your own words. If you think you might want to quote directly from the source, copy the author's exact words and enclose them in quotation marks.

There are many free notes applications such as *Evernote* available for computers, tablets, and mobile devices (most of which sync among devices), or you can purchase software for a note card system. You can use electronic notes or note cards just as you would use index cards: title each card by topic, and then type your notes onto the card or file.

Using a Research Notebook

Another option is a double-entry research notebook where you summarize and analyze readings all in one location.

1. Divide a notebook or computer page vertically down the middle.
2. On the left side of the page, summarize your reading of the source material, and write down the complete bibliographic data and any URLs. Any exact words or phrases need to be placed within quotation marks.
3. On the right side of the page, comment on your sources, noting their importance to your topic and their relationship to other sources.

The response side of the divided notebook shows the evolution of your thinking, lets you articulate questions that arise as you read and process information, and guides you toward a thesis for your paper. The system also helps you to avoid the cut-and-paste style of research writing because it encourages synthesis and analysis throughout the process. Finally, this record of your thoughts helps to identify which ideas are your own and which you picked up along the way—a key distinction that safeguards against inadvertent plagiarism and allows you to claim your own thoughts with confidence.

On page 75, you can see an example of a student's notes on the article "Eveline and the Blessed Margaret Mary Alacoque" by Donald Torchiana. In the left column, the student summarizes the key points in his own words and includes a couple of direct quotations from the article. In the right column, the student records his thoughts and reactions to the article.

Using the Printout/Photocopy Option

If the time you can spend in the library is limited, you might want to print out an online article or photocopy portions of books in order to have these materials available to study at your convenience. In fact, you might find it easier to take notes from a printout than from a computer screen. You can underline or highlight key ideas, even color-coding these highlighted passages to fit different subtopics in your paper. You can also write comments or cross-references to other sources in the margins. It's a good idea to put the information from printouts and photocopies on note cards or into your research notebook. This procedure forces you to summarize the material in your own words and makes it much easier to sort the separate items into categories.

Summarizing, Paraphrasing, and Quoting

In most of your notes, you will be summarizing or paraphrasing your source materials, rather than quoting the author's exact words. In a *summary* you condense the main point of an argument or passage

Sample Student Entry in a Divided-Page Notebook

Notes	Responses
Source: Torchiana, p. 70	
Torchiana says about Margaret Mary Alacoque that: —as a child she lost a parent and was treated like a servant by relatives who raised her. —at age 10, refused an offer of marriage —entered convent at age 24 —met hostility from the rest of sisters —performed menial tasks, took care of young children —Quotation: "Virtually addicted to suffering, she was corrected more than once for her singular notions or her clumsiness and slowness." —had a vision of Christ at age 26	Parallels with Eveline seem clear, but what do they mean? What's Joyce suggesting? The influence of Eveline's Catholic upbringing, for sure. Her destiny to be some kind of martyr? The first vision could be like her first glimpse of Frank. How old was Eveline when she met Frank? If he's her savior, then why not go with him? Or does she think she needs to stay and be a "sacrificial victim"? To whom? Surely not her father.
p. 71 —told she had been chosen to be the instrument by which Christ's love would be made known —The Lord took her heart and put it within His own, then returned it to her breast —had a number of visions; in one she was told she would be a "sacrificial victim for the lack of charity among her sister communicants." —but her vision of the Sacred Heart spread	Is Eveline "addicted to suffering"? Could be. Is she comfortable with this role? This idea seems similar to Brandabur's view of Eveline. Her promise to her dying mother seems related to this role. But it's a warning to Eveline, one she seems to recognize. Do the critics read too much into this? Margaret Mary is mentioned only once in the story.

in your own words. A summary is useful when you want to capture the gist of an idea without including the background or supporting details. Compare these sentences from an article about "Eveline" with the summary that follows it.

> **Original** "Joyce indicates why Eveline will not, in fact, be able to escape. Paralysis will win because she is not worthy to defeat it. Her inertia is revealed by the excessive value she places on the routine satisfactions of her present existence, and on the pathetically small indications of affection which her father has been prepared to give" (Hart 50).

> **Summary** Eveline won't be able to leave because she's too attached to her father and to the familiarity of her everyday life, according to Clive Hart (50).

In a *paraphrase* you restate comments and ideas from a source, using approximately the same number of words as the original. Although written in your own words and style, a good paraphrase will reflect the author's idea, tone, and point of view more clearly than a summary does. Here's a paraphrase of the passage from Clive Hart's article:

> Hart argues that Joyce shows us that Eveline is incapable of leaving home. That she doesn't have the strength of character to break away can be seen in her desperate attachment to the comforts of a familiar life, as well as to her father's meager expressions of love (50).

You will also find comments and observations that are so well expressed that you want to use the original wording rather than summarize or paraphrase it. Be sure to record the exact words of the original quotation, as well as the numbers of the pages on which they appear. Here is an example:

> Critic Clive Hart observes that Eveline's father "used to hunt Eveline and her companions in from their play" by "wielding his blackthorn stick like an angry god" (49).

Devising a Working Outline

As you are reading and taking notes, you should also be thinking about the organization of your points and ideas. Chances are the best arrangement won't emerge until you are fairly well along with your research—possibly not until you have finished it. But as you collect more and more notes, leaf through your cards or printouts occasionally to see if you can arrange them into three or four main categories to form the major claims in your argument or analysis. The sooner you can get a plan worked out, the more efficient your research becomes. You can see exactly what you are looking for and avoid wasting time on sources that would prove irrelevant or redundant. (See pages 19 and 37–38 for examples of working outlines.)

Writing a First Draft

As we pointed out at the beginning of this chapter, some people write a preliminary draft before beginning their research, especially if they are eager to get their arguments written down before they forget them. If you use this method, you should devise a thesis, assemble your evidence from the primary source, order your ideas, and write a first draft, following the procedures discussed in Chapter 2. Then you can go to the library, as Wendy did, to locate and read a number of pertinent secondary sources and incorporate ideas from this reading into your paper at appropriate places.

On the other hand, if you are not sure about your topic or your approach, you can go to the library, locate some relevant secondary sources, and study them carefully. Then return to the primary source and begin the discovery process again, using freewriting or questioning or problem solving to refine your topic, devise a major claim, and generate ideas. You may have to do further research as you work through your interpretation, but that's all part of the recursive nature of writing.

Organizing Your Notes

Once you have a clearly focused thesis, go back and read through your note cards. Using the headings that you put on the cards, group the ones with similar ideas together in stacks. If you photocopied most or all of your sources, write headings on the first page of each photocopy and sort the articles that way. Then consult your working plan or rough outline, and arrange the stacks in the order that the headings appear there. As you write, the necessary information will be in front of you, ready to be incorporated into the first draft of your paper.

If your stacks of cards don't follow the outline but lie there in a confused, overlapping mess, all is not lost. You can still bring order out of chaos. Here are a few methods:

1. *Tinker with your outline.* It may seem like a step backward, but now that you have new information from your research, the whole topic may look different. Look at the main headings and change any that don't seem to fit; add others that you have good material for but overlooked when you made the working outline.

2. *Put your note cards into different groupings.* This process may suggest an organizing strategy that you wouldn't think of any other way.

3. *Set your notes aside and begin writing*— even if you begin in the middle of a thought. Force yourself, as in freewriting, to keep going, even if your paper seems repetitive, disorganized, and sketchy. Eventually, the writing will begin to take shape, giving you an idea about where to start your first draft.

4. *Find a key article on the topic, and examine its structure.* You may be able to find an organizational scheme that will work for your paper.

5. *Explain your ideas to a friend who agrees to ask questions along the way.* Tape-record your discussion, and see whether it suggests a sensible order of exposition.

Using Quotations and Paraphrases

You want to be judicious in using the material you have gathered from secondary sources. In general, depend most upon your own interpretations of the primary material, use paraphrasing to introduce ideas gleaned through research, and turn to direct quotations of secondary sources only when the wording is especially original or powerful, saving that technique for special effect. Your main goal is to argue *your* thesis or advance *your* interpretation, not simply to paste together other people's thoughts and words. Don't just sprinkle your discussion with quotations and paraphrases; work them into your analysis and explain how they support your claims. Take a look at this example from a paper about "The Lottery":

> The author reveals the savagery that is hidden just beneath the surface of seemingly civilized exteriors. This duality of human nature is exhibited through the characterization and actions of the villagers. As Cleanth Brooks and Robert Penn Warren point out, "The cruel stoning is carried out by 'decent' citizens who in many other respects show themselves kind and thoughtful" (130). When it was time for the scapegoat to be murdered, Mrs. Delacroix, who earlier had made neighborly conversation with the victim, was one of the first to pick up a stone.

As you can see, the student writer backed up her observation about the duality of human nature with a direct quotation from a secondary source. She then used a detail from the primary source to nail down the point.

Integrating Sources

Whether you are quoting directly or simply paraphrasing someone else's ideas and observations, you should always give credit in the text of your paper to the person from whom you are borrowing. The MLA documentation style requires you to cite all sources *within* the paper. These in-text citations contain three important parts:

1. an introduction of the source, telling your reader that material from some authority is coming up, who or what the source is, and what the person's credentials are, if you know them;
2. the material from the source, quoted or paraphrased; and
3. the parenthetical documentation, which tells your reader that your use of the source is over and gives the page number for the source of that particular material.

More details about in-text citations are given in the explanation of the MLA documentation style at the end of this chapter (pages 90–97).

If you want your paper to read smoothly, pay particular attention to the way you introduce quotations and paraphrases. You need a ready supply of introductory phrases to slide the source material in gracefully—phrases like "As LeSeure discovered," "Professor Weber notes," and "According to Dr. Carter." These attributions help your readers to evaluate the source material as they read it and to distinguish source material from your remarks about it. Here are some more models for you to go by:

> As critic Lawrence Stone explains, daughters in Shakespeare's England were "often unwanted and might be regarded as no more than a tiresome drain on the economic resources of the family" (112).

> According to biographer Joan Givner, the failure of Porter's personal relationship with Josephson caused a temporary inability to write (221).

> D. G. Gillham remarks that the "male 'worm' " and "female 'rose' " in "The Sick Rose" have Freudian significance and "give rise in the speaker to half-hidden feelings of indecency, guilt, and fear so easily associated with sexual experience" (11).

> Prospero's suite in "The Masque of the Red Death" has been described by Kermit Vanderbilt as "a metaphor of nature and mortality" (382).

> "A beautiful virgin walled off from an imperfect world," Rachel Brownstein points out, "is the central figure in romance" (35).

Block Quotations

Most supporting quotations need not be more than a few lines long. But you may occasionally find a longer passage that emphatically reinforces an important claim and cannot be excerpted or paraphrased without distortion or loss of meaning. This kind of passage may state the message so effectively that you want your reader to see the original wording. If such a quotation runs longer than three lines of poetry or four lines of prose, set it off from your text by starting on a new line, indenting the entire passage a half inch from the left margin, and double spacing above, below, and within the quoted material. Do not add quotation marks (the indention marks the passage as a quotation). Any quotation marks within the passage remain double.

> Ursula K. LeGuin was inspired to write "The Ones Who Walk Away from Omelas" by this quotation from the philosopher William James:
>
> > If…millions kept permanently happy on the one simple condition that a certain lost soul on the far-off edge of things should lead a life of lonely torture, what…would make us immediately feel, even though an impulse arose within us to clutch at the happiness so offered, how hideous a thing would be its enjoyment when deliberately accepted as the fruit of such a bargain? (148)

The ellipsis dots in the preceding quotation show that the writer of the paper did shorten the passage by leaving out some words in the original version. Notice that the parenthetical page reference is not part of the direct quotation, and that it appears after the end punctuation instead of before it.

Quoting from Primary Sources

The advice for handling quotations from secondary sources also applies to quoted material from primary sources: keep quoted passages brief; use them as support for your own observations, and don't rely on a quotation to make a point for you; integrate quotations smoothly and grammatically into your own sentences; vary the way you introduce the quotations. In her essay on "Eveline," Wendy Dennison provided these models:

> Eveline realizes that with her brothers gone, there is "nobody to protect her" (5).
>
> "She was about to explore another life with Frank" (Joyce 4), we are told, in faraway Buenos Ayres.

You will also need to cite the work you are quoting from so that your readers know exactly which passage you are referring to and where it is located. For short stories and novels, give the author's last name and the page number in the parenthetical citation. The author's name may be omitted if you mention it in your paper or if authorship is clear from context.

> We are told that Jake "took a moment or two to feel both proud and sad about his performance" (Gilb 56).
>
> The narrator of Gilb's story tells us that Jake "took a moment or two to feel both proud and sad about his performance" (56).

For poems, line numbers alone are usually sufficient to identify the source—provided that the author and title are given in your essay.

> The speaker's assertion that "Something there is that doesn't love a wall, / That wants it down" (35–36) represents one side of Frost's theme.

You do not need to include the word *line* or *lines* or its abbreviation in the parenthetical citation. When citing a play, give the act and scene numbers (without abbreviations), plus the line numbers if the work is in verse.

> In *Othello*, Iago's striking comment, "What you know, you know. / From this time forth I will never speak a word" (5.2.299–300), serves as a philosophic closure.

The numbers separated by periods mean "act 5, scene 2, lines 299 through 300." In plays that are not written in verse, you may simply cite page numbers, as you would with a quotation from a short story.

> Jim's role in the play is best described by Tom, who calls him "an emissary from a world of reality" and the "long-delayed but always expected something that we live for" (771).

Avoiding Plagiarism

Research is a kind of conversation among writers, their sources, and others interested in the topic. One of the challenges for writers, then, is to clearly define their part in this broader conversation both accurately and ethically. The core principle here is *respect*: for the person whose ideas you are employing, for your own voice and credibility, and for your readers.

The failure to give proper credit to your sources is called ***plagiarism***. It usually involves carelessly—or, far worse, deliberately—presenting the words or ideas of another writer as your own. Most universities have strict policies on academic dishonesty that require sanctions ranging from failing a paper, to assigning a failing grade for the course, to dismissal from the university.

You can avoid this dishonesty by using a moderate amount of care in taking notes. Put quotation marks around any passages, even brief phrases, that you copy word for word. Circle the quotation marks in red or highlight the quoted material in some way, as a reminder to give credit to the source.

You must also avoid the original wording if you decide to paraphrase your sources, rather than quoting directly. Changing a few words or rearranging the phrases is not enough: such close paraphrasing is still considered plagiarism. The following examples may help you to see the difference between plagiarism and paraphrasing:

Original Passage: "The interest of the story lies not in the events, but in the reasons for Eveline's failure to accept the offer of salvation" (Hart 48).

Plagiarism: One critic notes that the story's main interest is not in its events but in the reasons why Eveline fails to accept Frank's offer of salvation.

Plagiarism: Most readers are interested not in the events of "Eveline" but in the reasons for the protagonist's failure to accept her salvation.

Paraphrase: As Clive Hart notes, we are interested not in what happens in the story but in why Eveline doesn't take the chance to save herself (48).

Combined Paraphrase and Direct Quotation: Hart notes that the main interest for the reader "lies not in the events" but in "Eveline's failure to accept the offer of salvation" (48).

Direct Quotation: "The interest of the story lies not in the events," critic Clive Hart claims, "but in the reasons for Eveline's failure to accept the offer of salvation" (48).

As you use your secondary sources, remember that no one wants to do the hard work of creating ideas and shaping an appropriate language only to have someone else take credit for it.

Rewriting and Editing

Many people who do researched writing make no attempt to work in direct quotations or provide complete citations in the first draft because pausing to do so interrupts the flow of their ideas. They just jot down the name of the person who has provided the information or idea; they go back later to fill in page numbers and integrate exact quotations as they revise their first draft. Putting self-stick notes on pages of sources you intend to use will help you find the precise material later.

Documenting Your Sources

Various academic disciplines use different documentation styles. Because you are writing about literature, the appropriate one for you to follow is the Modern Language Association style. Sample entries illustrating the MLA format appear at the end of this chapter. You may also use as a model the documentation included in the sample research papers that follow on pages 84–87 or the one on pages 671–73.

Revising the Draft

Because a research paper entails the extra demands of incorporating other people's ideas and acknowledging these sources, you will want to take special care in rewriting your early drafts. The checklist for revising and editing researched writing on page 83, will help you to turn your draft into a successful essay.

Formatting Your Paper

The document format recommended by the *MLA Handbook* is fairly simple. But individual course requirements may vary from the MLA design, so check with your instructor before you begin preparing your final copy. Here are some features to examine:

Margins. Provide margins of one inch at the top, bottom, and both sides of the page.

Spacing and indentions. Double-space throughout, including quotations and entries in the list of works cited. Indent paragraphs one-half inch or five spaces. Long prose quotations (more than four lines) and quotations of more than three lines of poetry should be double-spaced and indented a half inch (approximately five spaces) from the left margin.

Page numbers. Number all pages, beginning on the first page. Put the numbers in the upper-right-hand corner about one-half inch from the top. Place your last name before the page number in case the pages later become separated. Note the correct page numbering on the sample student paper, which follows.

Heading. The MLA does not require a separate title page. If your instructor asks you to use one, follow the format he or she provides. Otherwise, give your name and the date, plus any other information requested by your instructor (such as the title and number of the course), on the first page of

Checklist for Revising and Editing Researched Writing

Check the Usual Things

1. Be sure the introduction states your thesis (see pages 16, 23–24).
2. Be sure each paragraph is unified, coherent, and directly related to your thesis (see pages 49–50, 53–54).
3. Be sure that the transitions between paragraphs are clear and effective (see page 55).
4. Be sure your conclusion reinforces your main argument (see page 25).

Check the Special Things

1. Be sure that you have introduced direct quotations gracefully, using the name and, if appropriate, the title or occupation of the person quoted.
2. Be sure each citation is accurate.
3. Be sure that paraphrases are in your own words and that sources are clearly acknowledged.
4. Be sure that you have not relied too heavily on a single source.
5. Be sure that you have written most of the paper yourself; you need to examine, analyze, or explain the material, not just splice together a lot of quotations and paraphrases.
6. Be sure to separate quotations with some comment of your own.
7. Be sure to italicize the titles of books and magazines; put quotation marks around the titles of articles, stories, poems, and chapters in books.

your text. Place this heading an inch from the top of the page, aligned with the left margin. Note the heading on the sample student paper.

Title. Double-space after the heading and center the title of your paper. Do *not* underline or place your title in quotation marks, and do not set it in large type or capitalize all the letters. Do capitalize the first and last words and all other words *except* articles (*a, an, the*), prepositions, coordinating conjunctions, and the *to* in infinitives. Double-space between your title and the first line of text.

Textual headings. If you use headings within your paper to guide readers through the discussion, keep them as short as possible and make them specific to the material that follows. Do not boldface, italicize, or use bigger type or all capitals for these headings.

Sample Student Paper in MLA Style

The following is the documented version of the essay that Wendy Dennison wrote about "Eveline." See pages 65–67 for the undocumented version.

Wendy Dennison

Professor McMahan

English 102

11 March 2009

Fear of Failure in Joyce's "Eveline"

In his short story "Eveline," James Joyce gives the protagonist an exciting chance to leave her old life and begin a new one. But she rejects this offer that Frank—or Fate—makes, preferring instead to settle back into the dreary life she has known all along. Why does she not go away with Frank when the opportunity seems so attractive? One critic, Magda de Tolentino, says "Nothing but family bonds hold her back" (74). Another critic thinks Eveline is "imprisoned" in her passive, feminine role of housekeeper (Ingersoll 4), while another calls her "a meaningless sacrificial victim for a religious community lacking charity" (Torchiana 75). Some commentators think she's afraid of marrying Frank. Professor Edward Brandabur, for example, claims Eveline "is ever conscious of the effects on her mother of a brutal marriage" (63), and Professor Thomas Dilworth maintains that "her mother's marriage to her father must subconsciously condition her anticipation of married life" (458).

Obviously many factors affect Eveline and influence her decision not to go with Frank. But in the last analysis, I think, we need to examine Eveline's own character, especially her timid personality, to discover the answer to our question. For, as Professor Warren Beck has pointed out, "Eveline is not simply timid; she is racked by inner conflict, finally to the point of distraction" (113).

Since Eveline has been raised a Catholic, we know she would not take her promise to her dying mother lightly. But surely her promise to "keep the home together as long as she could" was given under extreme circumstances (Joyce 6). It was unjust of her mother to ask such a sacrifice of her, and Eveline is aware of the unfairness: "Why should she be unhappy? She had a right to happiness" (6). We know that Eveline will always be haunted by that promise, but we do not expect her to give up her chance for a life of her own in order to be a dutiful daughter. Surely that promise cannot be the only reason she stays.

    We certainly should not be surprised that Eveline might wish to leave her abusive father. A hot-tempered heavy drinker, he has taken advantage of his daughter's promise to her mother. She is forced to keep house for him, yet must beg for money to feed the family. He practically accuses her of stealing, claiming that "she used to squander the money, that she had no head, that he wasn't going to give her his hard-earned money to throw about the streets" (5). He has so frightened her with threats of beatings that she has "palpitations" (4). Eveline realizes that with her brothers gone, there is "nobody to protect her" from her father's rage (5). Her father has treated Eveline badly and may abuse her even worse in the future. On the other hand, as Professor Ingersoll points out, Eveline's father offers "the comfort and security of the familiar" and as he grows older will probably be "less likely to have the strength to abuse her, as he did her mother" (3). Yes, getting away from her father would be in her best interests, but something keeps her there.

    Eveline's home life is so unhealthy that we feel she would be wise to leave. Despite all the chores she performs, she still does not feel entirely at home in her father's house. For example, she knows nothing about the picture of the priest (Joyce 4), not even his name, yet the portrait seems quite important to her father. The dustiness of the house, of which Joyce reminds us periodically, suggests the pervasive dreariness of her daily life as she looks around "wondering where on earth all the dust came from" (4). Critic Clive Hart sums up her condition this way:

> Eveline has memories of a happier, freer past which contrasts both with the tedium of the present and with the uncertainty of the future.... The evenings, which used to be a time for play, are now one of drudgery, and even in childhood it was evident that happiness was something transient. (49)

Since her home is clearly not conducive to happiness, why does she stay there?

Dennison 3

Eveline's situation reflects the unhappy restrictions of conventional sex roles. Through guilt and threats of hellfire, Catholicism enforces dutiful daughterhood. And as a young woman, Eveline is subordinate, passive, and powerless, both at work and in the home, especially with no males to support or protect her. Finally, her father's traditionally masculine lack of expressiveness makes her daily life dreary.

The main reason Eveline would remain in Ireland is that she is desperately afraid of the unknown. If she leaves the familiar, no matter how unpleasant, she risks failure. "She was about to explore another life with Frank," we are told, in faraway Buenos Ayres (Joyce 5). The word *explore* is significant, as it brings to mind uncertainty and risk, two factors that Eveline is not prepared to deal with. She admits that hers is "a hard life," yet thinks that "now that she was about to leave it she did not find it a wholly undesirable life" (5). According to Professor Hart, Eveline is psychologically incapable of breaking away, and it shows in "the excessive value she places on the routine satisfactions of her present existence, and on the pathetically small indications of affection which her father has been prepared to give" (50). When she sits in the growing darkness with the letters in her lap, Eveline calls up a couple of good memories—of her father being jolly once on a picnic, of his kindness once when she was sick (Joyce 6). We see her trying to calm her fears, trying to convince herself that her home life is more bearable than it is. But, as Martin Dolch points out, "Change is already beyond her capacity and fills her with a crazy fear which mistakes salvation for destruction" (99).

Afraid of failing on her own, Eveline retreats into the familiar, telling herself that life with father cannot be as frightening as a risky, unknown life with Frank. Furthermore, she may suspect that her powerless role as a woman will not really change, even in Buenos Ayres—it may not be "another life" at all (5). So strong is her fear of the unknown that it overrides her fear of her father. She seems to decide that a predictable—if dreary and abused—life is better than a life that may only compound her burdens.

Dennison 5

Works Cited

Beck, Warren. *Joyce's* Dubliners: *Substance, Vision, and Art*. Duke UP, 1969.

Brandabur, Edward. *A Scrupulous Meanness: A Study of Joyce's Early Work*. U of Illinois P, 1971.

de Tolentino, Magda. "Family Bonds and Bondage within the Family: A Study of Family Ties in Clarice Lipsector and James Joyce." *Modern Language Studies*, vol. 18, no. 2, 1998, pp. 73-78. *JSTOR*, doi: 10.2307/3194767.

Dilworth, Thomas. "The Numina of Joyce's 'Eveline.'" *Studies in Short Fiction*, vol. 15, no. 4, 1978, pp. 456-58. *Academic Search Complete*, ebscohost.com.central.ezproxy.cuny.edu:2048/AN=7125692.

Dolch, Martin. "Eveline." *James Joyce's* Dubliners: *A Critical Handbook*, edited by James R. Baker and Thomas F. Staley, Wadsworth Publishing, 1969, pp. 96-101.

Hart, Clive. "Eveline." *James Joyce's* Dubliners: *Critical Essays*, edited by Clive Hart, Viking Press, 1969, pp. 48-52.

Ingersoll, Earl G. "The Stigma of Femininity in James Joyce's 'Eveline' and 'The Boarding House.'" *Studies in Short Fiction*, vol. 30, no. 40, 1993, pp. 501-10. *Academic OneFile*, go.galegroup.com/ps=AONE&sw=asid=1c961389911ff1f3a1af05246fec09d4.

Joyce, James. "Eveline." *Literature and the Writing Process*, edited by Elizabeth McMahan, et al., 8th ed., Prentice Hall, 2007, pp. 3-7.

Torchiana, Donald T. *Backgrounds for Joyce's* Dubliners. Routledge Press, 1986.

Sample Published Article

The following is an edited version of "Nature's Decoy: Kate Chopin's Presentation of Women and Marriage in Her Short Fiction" by Professor Elizabeth McMahan. It originally appeared in *Turn-of-the-Century Women* in 1985. You can use this article as a model for introducing and documenting direct quotations from the primary source (Chopin's story) as well as from secondary sources (published works about Chopin and the story) following the MLA style. The story appears in this textbook on pages 902–906.

Kate Chopin's Presentation of Marriage in "Désirée's Baby"

Written before the turn of the twentieth century, Kate Chopin's short works convey attitudes toward marriage and its effects upon women. Chopin depicts marriage almost always as restricting the female's individuality. Seldom does she show males suffering in the toils of an unfortunate union. She is most often concerned with the devastating effect of marriage on the woman's sense of self. We learn much about how late nineteenth-century patriarchal society encouraged the sweet submissiveness of women in marriage.

The tragic heroine of "Désirée's Baby" has married for love. Yet Chopin suggests in this story that such total devotion to a mate can prove disastrous for a woman. Désirée's love is so selfless that when her husband "frowned she trembled, but loved him. When he smiled, she asked no greater blessing of God" (175). For a time Désirée basks in her husband's love, but after their child is born, she notices "a strange, an awful change in [his] manner, which she dared not ask him to explain" (175). Everyone on the plantation except Désirée has already perceived that the child has Negro blood. Since Désirée was a foundling, adopted as a toddler by her aristocratic parents, her husband Armand concludes that Désirée is "not white" (177).

Like Browning's Duke who faults his last duchess for ranking his "gift of a nine-hundred-years-old name / With anybody's gift," Armand Aubigny cares greatly about his family name, "one of the oldest and proudest in Louisiana" (174). Before anyone suspected that the baby was of mixed race, Désirée had told her adopted mother, "Oh, Armand is the proudest father in the parish, I believe, chiefly because it is a boy to bear his name..." (175). Armand, after rejecting both Désirée and the baby, ceases to love her "because of the unconscious injury she has brought upon his home and his name" (177). In a typically ironic surprise ending, Chopin reveals that it is not Désirée but Armand who "belongs to the race that is cursed with the brand of slavery" (178).

The knowledge comes too late to save "the gentle Désirée." Since she has no concept of herself as a person apart from her husband, she considers her life not worth living after he shuns her. Although her mother begs, "Come home to Valmondé; back to your mother who loves you. Come with your child" (177), Désirée cannot. As Professor Cynthia Griffin Wolff observes, "When Armand's love slips into cruelty..., Désirée loses her own tenuous grasp on the balance of life" (83). She takes the little one in her arms and walks "across a deserted field, where the stubble bruised her tender feet so delicately shod, and tore her thin gown to shreds" (177).

The scene in the deserted field focuses on two powerful images. First, the imagery suggests death—"It was an October afternoon; the sun was just sinking" (177). October brings the end of summer's living vegetation, here coupled with the literal dying of the light as the sun sinks beneath the horizon. Second, the imagery suggests Désirée's innocence—her gown is white; the setting sun brings a "golden gleam" to her brown hair. White is, of course, an archetypal symbol of innocence, and the gold in her hair suggests her Caucasian heritage. Like Hamlet's Ophelia, she vanishes "among the reeds and willows that grew thick along the banks of the deep, sluggish bayou; and she did not come back again" (177).

Kate Chopin's view of marriage for women is considerably jaundiced. Yet she herself appears to have been quite happily married. Her earliest biographer, Daniel Rankin, reports that she and her husband enjoyed a felicitous union (107). Even Per Seyersted, in his thorough appraisal of Chopin's life and work, could find no evidence to contradict this report. When Oscar Chopin succumbed to swamp fever, Kate, at age thirty, was left a widow with six children. Only after Oscar's death did she begin to write. We can only speculate, of course, but something—perhaps the influence of Ibsen whom we know she read—enabled her to perceive that women as well as men can have a genuine need for self-determination.

Today a woman who is lucky in her choice of a husband can have both—marriage and self-direction. But in Chopin's fictional world that option does not exist. As Barbara Solomon says, Kate Chopin was indeed "a woman much ahead of her time" (xxvii).

Works Cited

Chopin, Kate. "Désirée's Baby." Solomon, pp. 173-78.

Rankin, Daniel. *Kate Chopin and Her Creole Stories.* U of Pennsylvania P, 1932.

Seyersted, Per. *Kate Chopin: A Critical Biography.* Louisiana State UP, 1969.

Solomon, Barbara H. Introduction. The Awakening *and Selected Stories of Kate Chopin*, edited by Barbara H. Solomon, Signet Books, 1976, pp. vii-xxvii.

Wolff, Cynthia Griffin. "Kate Chopin and the Fiction of Limits: 'Désirée's Baby.'" *Southern Literary Journal*, vol. 10, no. 2, 1978, pp. 123-33.

EXPLANATION OF THE MLA DOCUMENTATION STYLE

The documentation style of the Modern Language Association (MLA)—used in English, foreign languages and some other humanities—requires that source citations be given in the text of the paper rather than in footnotes or endnotes. This in-text style of documentation involves parenthetical references.

Throughout this section, all titles of independently published works—books, plays, magazines, journals, websites[1], online databases, television and radio programs, films, and works of art—are italicized. Titles of stories, articles, songs, and other shorter works included in larger publications are punctuated with quotation marks and not italicized.

In-Text Citations

A. You will usually introduce the cited material, whether quoted or paraphrased, by mentioning the name of the author in your lead-in and giving the page number (or numbers) in parentheses. Put the parenthetical reference near the cited material, but preserve the flow of your writing by placing the citation where a pause would naturally occur, preferably at the end of the sentence, as in this example:

> Edmund Wilson tells us that the author of *Uncle Tom's Cabin* felt "the book had been written by God" (5).

B. Your readers can identify this source by consulting your Works Cited at the end of your paper. The entry for the source cited above would appear like this one:

> Wilson, Edmund. *Patriotic Gore: Studies in the Literature of the American Civil War.* Oxford UP, 1966.

C. If you do not mention the author in your lead-in, include his or her last name in parentheses along with the page number, without an intervening comma, like this:

> One of the great all-time best-sellers, *Uncle Tom's Cabin* sold over 300,000 copies in America and more than 2 million copies world wide (Wilson 3).

D. If you refer to one of two or more works by the same author, put a comma after the author's last name and include a shortened title in the parenthetical reference.

> (Pinker, *Stuff* 95).

E. If you are using a source written or edited by more than two people, use only the name of the first person listed, followed by "et al." (meaning "and others") in your lead-in.

---

[1]The MLA prefers the spelling *Web site* (not *website*) within your papers and lists of works cited.

Blair et al. observe that the fine arts were almost ignored by colonial writers (21).

Because *et* means "and," it isn't an abbreviation and therefore doesn't need a period.

F. If you have to quote indirectly—something from another source not available to you—use "qtd. in" (for "quoted in") in your parenthetical reference. This example refers to a book written by Donald Johanson and Maitland Edey:

Richard Leakey's wife, Maeve, told the paleoanthropologist David Johanson, "We heard all about your bones on the radio last night" (qtd. in Johanson and Edey 162).

Note: It is always best to track down the original source, in case it has not been quoted precisely. You may also find even better material for your purposes in the original.

Preparing the List of Works Cited

On a separate page at the end of the paper, alphabetize your Works Cited list for all sources mentioned in your paper. Format the list according to these rules:

- Center the heading Works Cited at the top of the page.
- Arrange your sources in alphabetical order by the last name of the author. If the author is not given in the source, alphabetize the source by the first main word in the title (excluding *A, An,* or *The*).
- Double-space the entire list, both within and between entries.
- Use hanging indention: put the first line of each entry flush with the left margin, and indent any subsequent lines in the entry one-half inch.
- In both titles and subtitles, capitalize all words *except* articles (*a, an, the*), prepositions, coordinating conjunctions, and the *to* in infinitives; however, if one of these word types is the first word in a title or subtitle, capitalize it.
- Use the abbreviation *p.* or *pp.* before page references:

Kinsley, Michael. "Continental Divide." *Time*, 7 July 1997, pp. 89-91.

- Spell publishers' names in full, excluding corporate words like *Company* or *Corporation*, but including book-related words like *Press, Books,* or *Publishing*. University presses are an exception; use the abbreviation *U* for *University* and *P* for *Press*. For instance, U of Illinois P or Oxford UP. See sample entries 1 through 12.
- Use lowercase roman numerals (ii, xiv) for citing page numbers from a preface, introduction, or table of contents; use uppercase roman numerals in names of monarchs (Elizabeth II).
- Abbreviate months and titles of magazines as shown in the sample entries.
- Leave one space after all concluding punctuation marks.

Sample Entries for a List of Works Cited

The following models will help you write works-cited entries for most of the sources you will use. If you use a source not illustrated in these examples, refer to the more extensive list of sample entries found in the *MLA Handbook*, 8th ed., consult the frequently updated *MLA Style Center* (style.mla.org), or ask your instructor for guidance.

While your works-cited entries may span sources from a variety of media, the MLA emphasizes that most entries are made up of similar components: author, title, title of "container" (the larger location, such as a journal, database, website, or anthology in which an article or other selection is found), other contributors (editors, translators, performers, etc.), edition or version, volume and/or issue number, publisher, date published, and the location (the page numbers for a print source, or the URL or doi for an online source). The sample entries on the following pages provide examples.

Citing Print Publications

Books

1. **Book by one author**

   Mizejewski, Linda. *Divine Decadence: Fascism, Female Spectacle, and the Makings of Sally Bowles.* Princeton UP, 1992.

2. **Two or more books by the same author**

   Pinker, Steven. *The Language Instinct: How the Mind Creates Language.* William Morrow, 1994.

   ---. *The Stuff of Thought: Language as a Window into Human Nature.* Viking Press, 2007.

   [Give the author's name in the first entry only. Thereafter, use three hyphens in place of the author's name, followed by a period and the title.]

3. **Book by two authors**

   Anderson, Terry, and Donald Leal. *Free Market Environmentalism.* Westview Press, 1991.

   [Notice that only the first author's name is in reversed order.]

4. Book by three or more authors

Medhurst, Martin J., et al. *Cold War Rhetoric: Strategy, Metaphor, and Ideology.* Greenwood Press, 1990.

[The phrase *et al.* is an abbreviation for *et alii,* meaning "and others." Because *et* is the whole Latin word for *and,* don't put a period after it.]

5. Book with an editor

Gallegos, Bee, editor. *English: Our Official Language?* H. W. Wilson, 1994.

[When the entry begins with the editor's name, put a comma and the description "editor" after the person's name. For a book with two or more editors, use "editors."]

6. Book with an author and an editor

Vidal, Gore. *The Selected Essays of Gore Vidal.* Edited by Jay Parini, Doubleday, 2008.

7. Essay or article in a collection, casebook, or critical edition.

Geist, Stanley. "Portraits from a Family Album: *Daisy Miller.*" *James's Daisy Miller,* edited by William T. Stafford, Scribner's, 1963, pp. 131–33.

[If an italicized title contains another title that should be italicized, leave the inner title without italics.]

Matthews, James H. "Frank O'Connor." 1976. *Contemporary Literary Criticism,* edited by Dedria Bryfonski and Laurie Harris, vol. 14, Gale Publishers, 1983, pp. 399-402.

[If your source has been published before and its original publication date is relevant, include this date immediately after the source's title.]

8. Introduction, preface, or forward

Danticat, Edwidge. Introduction. *Wide Sargasso Sea,* by Jean Rhys, W. W. Norton, 2016, pp. vi-x.

9. **Work in an anthology**

Butler, Octavia. "Bloodchild." *The Norton Anthology of African American Literature*, edited by Henry Louis Gates Jr. and Nellie Y. McKay, W. W. Norton, 1997, pp. 2480-94.

10. **Article in a reference work (unsigned and signed)**

"Vietnam War." *The Columbia Encyclopedia*, 6th ed., 2007.

Van Doren, Carl. "Samuel Langhorne Clemens." *The Dictionary of American Biography*, 1958.

[For widely used reference books, do not give full publication information. List only the edition and the year of publication. Include a page reference only if the work is not organized alphabetically.]

11. **Later (second or subsequent) edition**

Harmon, William, and Hugh Holman. *A Handbook to Literature*. 11th ed., Prentice Hall, 2008.

12. **A translated book**

Cirlot, J. E. *A Dictionary of Symbols*. Translated by Jack Sage, 2nd ed., Philosophical Library, 1976.

Periodicals

13. **Article in a scholarly journal**

Haque, Danielle, "The Postsecular Turn and Muslim American Literature." *American Literature*, vol. 86, 2014, pp. 799-829.

Hoagland, Tony. "12 Things I Know about that Life of Poetry." *Gulf Coast*, vol. 27, no. 1, 2015, pp. 48-53.

[Give the volume number and the issue number, when available, for all journals. Use the abbreviations *vol.* for volume and *no.* for issue, as shown in the examples.]

14. **Article from a monthly or bimonthly magazine**

Schweitzer, Leah. "The Keeper of Pages." *Poets and Writers*, Nov./Dec. 2014, p. 11.

15. **Article from a weekly or biweekly magazine**

Wood, James. "Look Again: The Stories of Edith Pearlman." *The New Yorker*, 23 Feb. 2015, pp. 176-77.

16. **Newspaper article**

> Levine, Mark. "Books Talk Back." *The New York Times*, 9 Nov. 2014,
> p. BR23.

17. **Review of a book or movie**

> Mohutsiwa, Siyanda. Review of *When Rain Clouds Gather*, by Bessie
> Head. *Tin House*, vol. 16, no. 3, pp. 130-32.

> Franick, Darren. "A Viking's Tale." Review of *Vikings*, performance by
> Katheryn Winnick, *Entertainment Weekly*, 27 Feb. 2015, pp. 56–57.

Citing Online Publications

When an online source has an assigned DOI (digital object identifier), include this information as its location; see the first example under 18. If your source does not have a DOI, provide a permalink or stable URL instead; see the second example under 18. Always place a period after the DOI or URL. If you think the URL is unstable and will be hard to locate again, include the date that you accessed the site in your citation.

Online Periodicals

18. **Articles from online databases**
    If you retrieve source material from a full-text database, you need to indicate the name of that database. You will probably use a service to which your library subscribes, such as Academic Search Premier, JSTOR, Expanded Academic ASAP, ProQuest, Project Muse, Galenet, LexisNexis. Most of the items in these databases were previously published in print, so give the print information first. If possible, give the inclusive page numbers or, when pagination is not continuous, the first page number and a plus sign; close the print information with a period. Then add information about your second container, the database where you located the article. Usually this includes the name of the database (italicized) followed by a comma and a DOI (if available) or a permalink URL provided for the source (if there is no DOI), followed by a period. Here are examples of entries for periodical publications retrieved from online databases:

> Hammer, Langdon. "Plath's Lives." *Representations*, no. 75, 2001,
> pp. 61-88. *JSTOR*, doi: 10.2307/3176069.

> Parascandola, Louis J. "Love and Sex in a Totalitarian Society: An
> Exploration of Ha Jin and George Orwell." *Studies in the Humanities*,
> vol. 33, no. 1, 2005, pp. 38+. *Literature Resource Center*,
> go.galegroup.com/ps/i.do?p=LitRC&sw=GALE%7CA151544981&
> it=r&asid=740d98144aa3ef104fdc6b74a73ebbd6.

19. **Articles published independently online**

> For articles that are available on independent websites—as opposed to articles accessed from an aggregate database—include the site's publisher/sponsor after the site's name only if the publisher differs significantly from the site's name and its creator(s). Here are sample entries for online articles:

> Borroff, Marie. "Another Look at Robert Frost's 'Birches.'" *Literary*
> > *Imagination Online*, vol. 7, 2005, litimag.oxfordjournals.org/
> > content/7/1/69.extract.

> Fairley, Wendy W. "My Mother's Affair with F. Scott Fitzgerald."
> > *Salon*, 15 Mar. 2015, www.salon.com/2015/03/14/my_
> > mothers_affair_with_f_scott_fitzgerald_how_it_made_me_the_
> > person_and_the_reader_i_am_today/.

> "Vietnam Veterans Memorial." *Encyclopaedia Britannica*
> > *Online*, 2016, www.britannica.com/topic/
> > Vietnam-Veterans-Memorial.

> Keller, Julia. "New Hope for Do-Nothing Nobodies: A Guy
> > Named Sam Johnson." *Chicago Tribune*, 19 Oct. 2008,
> > articles.chicagotribune.com/2008-10-19/news/0810170103_
> > 1_biography-peter-martin-wide-world.

Other Online Sources

20. **An entire website**

> *Celestial Timepiece: A Joyce Carol Oates Patchwork*. Edited by Randy
> > Souther, Gleeson Library, U of San Francisco, 2016,
> > celestialtimepiece.com/. Accessed 15 Mar. 2016.

21. **Part of a website**

> Nelson, Cary. "Japanese American Concentration Camp Haiku."
> > *Modern American Poetry*. Dept. of English, U of Illinois,
> > Urbana-Champaign, www.english.illinois.edu/maps/poets/g_l/
> > haiku/haiku.htm. Accessed 1 Oct. 2016.

> [When there is no date assigned to a site or page, provide the date you accessed the source after the URL. See the examples above.]

Citing Other Common Sources

Regardless of the source type, be sure to include enough information to permit an interested reader to locate your original source. Be sure to arrange this information in a logical fashion, following as much as possible the order and punctuation of the core elements, as shown in the previous entries. To be safe, consult your instructor for suggestions about documenting unusual material.

22. A podcast

"Ron Chernow: Rockstar Biographer." *The Room Where It's Happening*,

   hosted by Travon Free and Mike Drucker, season 1, episode 3,

   29 Aug. 2016, Earwolf, www.earwolf.com/episode/

   ron-chernow-rockstar-biographer/.

23. Sound recording

Welty, Eudora, author and performer. "Why I Live at the P. O." 1956.

   Essential Welty, directed by Ward Botsford, unabridged ed.,

   Caedmon, 2006.

24. Film or video (streaming)

Ex Machina. Written and directed by Alex Garland, performances

   by Alicia Vikander and Domhnall Gleeson, Universal Studios,

   2015. *Amazon Prime*, www.amazon.com/dp/B00VWPQNJ4/

   ref=dv_web_wtls_list_pr_5.

[When citing a program or film viewed through a streaming service, treat that service as you would a database housing an article—as a second container. Italicize the name (*Netflix, Hulu, Amazon Prime*, etc.) and follow with a URL if streamed online. If streamed through an app, include version information. If downloaded, include the service (such as iTunes).]

PART II Writing About Short Fiction

This section, focusing on the short story, covers the literary and rhetorical elements that you need to understand in order to write effectively about short fiction.

6 How Do I Read Short Fiction?

Chapter Preview

As noted author Joyce Carol Oates has observed, short fiction can be difficult to understand "because it demands compression; each sentence must contribute to the effect of the whole. Its strategy is not to include an excess of detail but to exclude, to select, to focus as sharply as possible." In order to grasp the full meaning of a story, you need to read it more than once and allow some time between readings to mull the story over in your mind. Your initial reading can be purely for pleasure, but subsequent readings should involve careful and deliberate study of all the elements that combine to produce a unified whole. By the end of this chapter, you will be able to

- Identify major points of narrative structure: *plot, conflict, climax, flashbacks.*
- Define *point of view* and *setting.*
- Explain the elements of *characterization.*
- Name specialized literary techniques: *foils, irony, foreshadowing, images, motifs,* and *symbols.*
- Define *theme* and explain its importance.
- Use critical questions when reading and writing about short fiction.

Notice the Structure

During the second reading, notice the way the story is structured. The action (that is, what happens) is called the ***plot*** and is usually spurred by some ***conflict*** involving the main character (the ***protagonist***). Except in some modern works, most short stories have a clear beginning, middle, and end during which the conflict producing the action becomes increasingly intense, building to a ***climax*** that sometimes resolves the conflict and sometimes simply concludes it—often in catastrophe. Do not expect many happy endings in serious fiction. A somber conclusion is more likely.

Usually stories proceed in regular chronological order following a time sequence similar to that in real life. But occasionally an author employs ***flashbacks***—stopping the forward action to recount an episode that happened in the past—in order to supply necessary background material or to maintain suspense. For example, in James Joyce's "Eveline," the flashbacks about the title character's family life and her romance with Frank, which interrupt the basic chronology of the story, give key information that helps to explain her final, fateful decision. And when the family in Flannery O'Conner's "A Good Man Is Hard to Find" stops for lunch, the scene in the restaurant not only delays the story's violent conclusion but also adds details that prepare us for that outcome.

Consider Point of View and Setting

Sometimes the **point of view**—the position from which an author chooses to relate a story—can be crucial to the effectiveness, even to the understanding, of short fiction. In Alice Walker's "Everyday Use," we are given the mother's views and feelings about her two quite different daughters. In other stories, the point of view provides access to the thoughts and feelings of more than one character. In Nathaniel Hawthorne's "Birthmark," for example, an all-seeing, all-knowing or *omniscient* narrator provides access to the thoughts and feelings of all the major characters in the story. Ernest Hemingway, in "Hills like White Elephants," chooses to let his characters tell the story themselves through conversation. This *objective* (sometimes called *dramatic*) point of view is revealed by a glance at the pages, which consist primarily of dialogue. Some authors select one character to tell the story firsthand, but these first-person narrators can play quite different roles. In "I Stand Here Ironing," Tillie Olsen creates a strong sense of believability by presenting the reflections running through a mother's mind as she recalls her difficulties in raising a daughter with too little money and no husband to help. In Raymond Carver's "What We Talk About When We Talk About Love," the first-person narrator is essentially an observer, a peripheral character who reports the conversation between Mel and Terry but is not himself the focus of it. The narrator of "The Lesson" by Toni Cade Bambara acts as a "hostile witness" to the scenes and events she encounters, resisting the hard truths about class and oppression that she, and the reader, must finally acknowledge.

The **setting** of a story, like the point of view, is sometimes important, sometimes not. In many of the stories included in this anthology, setting plays a role of some consequence. For instance, John Steinbeck opens "The Chrysanthemums" with this description:

> The high gray-flannel fog of winter closed off the Salinas Valley from the sky and from all the rest of the world. On every side it sat like a lid on the mountains and made of the great valley a closed pot.

The isolation of the valley by the fog suggests the isolation of Elisa Allen, whose energies and experiences are restricted by her living on the ranch. As you study a short story, give some thought to the setting. Could the events just as well take place somewhere else? Or does the setting seem to play an integral part? How does its time period affect the story? Does the setting in some way add to the meaning of the work?

Study the Characters

Focusing on *characterization* often proves a fruitful approach to analyzing and writing about a short story or a play. Wendy Dennison adopts this strategy in her paper on "Eveline" (pages 64–67). You'll notice, if you look again at Wendy's paper, that she examines several other key elements to gain a thorough understanding of the title character. She discusses the setting because Eveline's dreary life is influenced by the drabness of her surroundings. She considers the plot and finds Eveline's paralysis at the end tied directly to her characterization as a timid, duty-bound daughter. She examines the imagery and finds that the religious images underscore Eveline's devout nature while, at the same time, the pervasive dust shrouds her barren existence. All of these elements combine to reveal Joyce's theme of a young woman's life sadly circumscribed by her submission to duty, family, and church.

As you reread a story, pay special attention to those passages in quotation marks that characters speak to each other. You can begin to determine characterization from these exchanges, just as you come to know real people partly by what they say. As you form an understanding of a character, notice what other people in the story say about that person and how they respond to that person, as well as what the author reveals of that person's thoughts and past behavior. Because fiction often allows us access to what the characters are thinking (as well as doing), we can sometimes know fictional persons better than we do our closest friends and family members. Sometimes, we can be certain of a character's motivation for behaving in a certain way; at other times, motivation becomes one of the elements to be determined before we can fully appreciate the work.

In Hawthorne's "The Birthmark," in order to understand why Dr. Aylmer is willing to risk his young wife's life, we need to examine his motives and behavior. In doing so, we discover that his faith in science leads to his overweening desire to create perfection—to establish (without success, of course) that science can control and improve on nature. And in Tim O'Brien's "The Things They Carried," we see that the author uses the details of what the men carried with them to take us into their minds—to reveal their motivations and define their personalities.

Foils

A *foil* is a minor character whose role sharpens our understanding of a major character by providing a contrast. Although far more common in drama than in the short story, foils can also prove useful in the analysis of works of fiction.

In Andre Dubus's "The Fat Girl," the title character's isolation and dissatisfaction are made clear by the presence and actions of her thin school friends, Joan, Marjorie, and Carrie. In "A & P," John Updike uses two minor characters to highlight why the story's narrator, Sammy, decides to quit his job. Stoksie, the fellow checker, prefigures what

Sammy might become if he stays at the A & P; and Lengel, the store manager, represents the authority figure Sammy is rebelling against.

After you have read a fictional work, ask yourself why the author included the minor characters. What role do they serve in the work as a whole? Often the role of a minor character will provide an appropriate focus for writing an analysis of a short story, a novel, or a play.

Look for Specialized Literary Techniques

As you study a story on second reading, you may notice irony and foreshadowing that you missed the first time through. Since *irony* involves an upsetting of expectations—having the opposite happen from what would be usual—you sometimes need to know the outcome of an action in order to detect the full extent of the irony. *Foreshadowing* works the same way: you may not be aware of these hints of future happenings until the happenings finally occur. But when you go through a story again, both irony and foreshadowing become easily apparent and contribute to the meaning and effectiveness.

Be alert also for *images*—for words and phrases that put a picture in your mind. These images increase the enjoyment of reading fiction and, if deliberately repeated, can become *motifs* that emphasize some important element in the story and thus convey meaning. The numerous images of the protagonist's active hands and fluttering fingers in Sherwood Anderson's "Hands" establish an impression of Wing Biddlebaum's fragile, panicky nature. If a repeated image gathers significant meaning, it then becomes a *symbol*—to be clearly related to the theme or central argument of the story. Biddlebaum's nervous hands symbolize the fear and repression that restrict his existence, just as the changes in light and the shifting pattern of the wallpaper in Charlotte Perkins Gilman's "The Yellow Wallpaper" signify the steady deterioration of the narrator's mental condition.

Examine the Title

The title may in some way point toward or be related to the meaning. T. Coraghessan Boyle's title "The Love of My Life" evokes the story's conflict between common sense and the blinding power of romantic love. Sometimes, the title identifies a story's controlling symbol, as in John Steinbeck's "The Chrysanthemums" and Katherine Anne Porter's "The Grave." A title may also suggest tone: the playful parody of romantic expectations in Margaret Atwood's "Happy Endings" is captured in the title.

Investigate the Author's Life and Times

Sometimes biographical and background information can be illuminating. For instance, knowing Hawthorne's attitude toward original sin enriches a reading of "The Birthmark," just as some knowledge of the

Catholic faith can explain the circumstances that influence the young woman's decision in Joyce's "Eveline." Knowing what life was like for poor Americans during the Great Depression of the 1930s helps to clarify the forces that drive the protagonist in Tillie Olsen's "I Stand Here Ironing," and knowing that Charlotte Perkins Gilman wrote "The Yellow Wallpaper" after having a nervous breakdown and leaving her first husband and child to live alone in California provides a strong basis for analyzing the desperate tone and point of view of that story.

Continue Questioning to Discover Theme

Your entire study of these various elements of fiction should lead to an understanding of the meaning, or *theme*, of the story. You need to ponder everything about a short story in order to discover its theme. Keep asking yourself questions until you come up with some meaningful observation about human behavior or the conduct of society. The critical questions for reading on page 105 will guide you in exploring any story and perhaps spark that essential insight that leads to understanding.

Critical Questions for Reading the Short Story

Before planning an analysis of any of the selections in the anthology of short stories, write out the answers to the following questions to be sure you understand the piece and to help you generate material for your paper.

1. Who is the main character? Does this person's character change during the course of the story? Do you feel sympathetic toward the main character? What sort of person is she or he? Does this character have a foil?

2. What pattern or structure is there to the development of the plot? Can you describe the way the events are organized? Is the structure significant to the meaning?

3. Does surprise play an important role in the plot? Is there foreshadowing? Does the author use flashbacks?

4. Is anything about the story ironic?

5. Is there any symbolism in the story? How does the author make you aware of symbolic actions, people, or objects?

6. What is the setting—the time and location? How important are these elements in the story? Could it be set in another time or place just as well? Is the setting significant to the meaning?

7. Describe the atmosphere of the story, if it is important. How does the author create this atmosphere?

8. Who narrates the story? Is the narrator reliable? What effect does the point of view have on your understanding of the story? What would be gained or lost if the story were told from a different point of view (for example, by another character)?

9. How does the title relate to the other elements in the story and to the overall meaning?

10. What is the theme of the story? Can you state it in a single sentence? How is this theme carried out?

11. Does the author's style of writing affect your interpretation of the story? If so, how would you describe the style? For example, is it conversational or formal? Familiar or unfamiliar? Simple or ornate? Ironic or satiric?

7 Writing About Structure

Chapter Preview

When you focus on structure in discussing a literary work, you are examining the way the parts fit together to form a unified meaning. Examining the structure often proves an excellent means to understand a short story, novel, poem, or play and also provides a good way to approach a written literary analysis. By the end of this chapter, you will be able to

- Define *plot* and its key components, *conflict* and *resolution*.
- Recognize *patterns* of contrast and repetition, and describe their significance.
- Identify the relationship between structure and theme.
- Explain the process for effectively integrating quotations into your writing.

What Is Structure?

Most works of literature have an underlying pattern that serves as a framework or **structure**. You are familiar with the way plays are divided into acts and scenes, identified with numerals in the script, and marked in a stage production by the opening and closing of the curtain. The structure of television drama is often marked by commercial breaks. (For a discussion of dramatic structure, see Chapter 29, "Writing About Dramatic Structure.") Poems also have a visible structure, being divided into lines and stanzas. Sometimes poetic structure is complex and arbitrary, involving a certain number of lines, an established meter, and a fixed rhyme scheme. (See Chapter 20, "Writing About Poetic Form.") Novels, as you know, are divided into chapters, usually numbered and often titled, but sometimes not. Some short stories have no visible structure at all, but many do: they have space breaks indicating the divisions. Occasionally in stories (like Zora Neale Hurston's "Spunk") and often in novellas, these sections are numbered.

In **narrative** works like novels and short stories, the plot itself is the main structural element, but these works also contain underlying structural features. Although not visible like chapter divisions or space breaks, the underlying structure serves an integral function just as a skeleton does in providing support for the body. Discovering, examining, and understanding these underlying structures will involve delving beneath the surface to discover the meaning of the work.

How Do I Discover Structure?

First, consider the **plot**. What is the central conflict and how is it resolved? Do the events in the story move in a straight line from the beginning of the conflict to its resolution? Or are there interruptions and digressions? Are there flashbacks? Is time manipulated in any other way? If so, why? For instance, the time shifts in Louise Erdrich's "The Red Convertible" set readers up to eventually realize the terrible irony in the narrator's opening remarks.

If the story has any visible structural features, such as space between sections, try to figure out why they are there. Do they divide scenes? Do they indicate time shifts?

Look next for patterns, especially for contrasts and for repetitions. In "The Things They Carried," the story included in this chapter, Tim O'Brien alternates descriptions of the physical burdens of the soldiers with descriptions of the inner, psychological burdens they carry with them. The story also involves repetitions of key events told from different vantage points and with different amounts of detail.

Look always at beginnings and endings. "The Things They Carried" begins with the romantic fantasies of the main character, Jimmy Cross, which contrast sharply with the same character's fantasies of leadership at the end of the story. How did this change in character happen?

When analyzing any work of literature, don't forget to consider the title. Does it have any relationship to the plot? Sometimes the title touches on the central conflict or an important idea, thus focusing our attention on the structure of the story and reinforcing our understanding of the theme.

Looking at Structure

With our discussion of structure in mind, read Tim O'Brien's "The Things They Carried," which follows, and try to determine how the parts work together to convey the meaning of the story.

Tim O'Brien   1946–

Tim O'Brien was born in Austin, Minnesota. After graduating *summa cum laude* from Macalester College and doing graduate work at Harvard, he was drafted into the army and served in Vietnam, where he was promoted to sergeant and received the Purple Heart. "Good stories," he told an interviewer, "deal with our moral struggles, our uncertainties, our dreams, our blunders, our contradictions, our endless quest for understanding. Good stories do not resolve the mysteries of the human spirit but rather describe and expand upon those mysteries."

The Things They Carried

First Lieutenant Jimmy Cross carried letters from a girl named Martha, a junior at Mount Sebastian College in New Jersey. They were not love letters, but Lieutenant Cross was hoping, so he kept them folded in plastic at the bottom of his rucksack. In the late afternoon, after a day's march, he would dig his foxhole, wash his hands under a canteen, unwrap the letters, hold them with the tips of his fingers, and spend the last hour of light pretending. He would imagine romantic camping trips into the White Mountains in New Hampshire. He would sometimes taste the envelope flaps, knowing her tongue had been there. More than anything, he wanted Martha to love him as he loved her, but the letters were mostly chatty, elusive on the matter of love. She was a virgin, he was almost sure. She was an English major at Mount Sebastian, and she wrote beautifully about her professors and roommates and midterm exams, about her respect for Chaucer and her great affection for Virginia Woolf. She often quoted lines of poetry; she never mentioned the war, except to say, Jimmy, take care of yourself. The letters weighed ten ounces. They were signed "Love, Martha," but Lieutenant Cross understood that "Love" was only a way of signing and did not mean what he sometimes pretended it meant. At dusk, he would carefully return the letters to his rucksack. Slowly, a bit distracted, he would get up and move among his men, checking the perimeter, then at full dark he would return to his hole and watch the night and wonder if Martha was a virgin.

The things they carried were largely determined by necessity. Among the necessities or near necessities were P-38 can openers, pocket knives, heat tabs, wrist watches, dog tags, mosquito repellant, chewing gum, candy, cigarettes, salt tablets, packets of Kool-Aid, lighters, matches, sewing kits, Military Payment Certificates, C rations, and two or three canteens of water. Together, these items weighed between fifteen and twenty pounds, depending upon a man's habits or rate of metabolism. Henry Dobbins, who was a big man, carried extra rations; he was especially fond of canned peaches in heavy syrup over pound cake. Dave Jensen, who practiced field hygiene, carried a toothbrush, dental floss, and several hotel-size bars of soap he'd stolen on R & R in Sydney, Australia. Ted Lavender, who was scared, carried tranquilizers until he was shot in the head outside the village of Than Khe in mid-April. By necessity, and because it was SOP,[1] they all carried steel helmets that weighed five pounds including the liner and camouflage cover. They carried the standard fatigue jackets and trousers. Very few carried underwear. On their feet they carried jungle boots—2.1 pounds—and Dave Jensen carried three pairs of socks and a can of Dr. Scholl's foot powder as a precaution against trench foot. Until he was shot, Ted Lavender carried six or seven ounces of premium dope, which for him was a necessity. Mitchell Sanders, the RTO,[2] carried condoms. Norman Bowker carried a diary. Rat Kiley carried comic books. Kiowa, a devout Baptist, carried an illustrated New Testament that had been presented to him by his father, who taught Sunday school in Oklahoma City, Oklahoma. As a hedge against bad times, however, Kiowa also carried his grandmother's distrust of the white man, his grandfather's old hunting hatchet. Necessity dictated. Because the land was

---

[1] Standard operating procedure.
[2] Radio and telephone operator.

mined and booby-trapped, it was SOP for each man to carry a steel-centered, nylon-covered flak jacket, which weighed 6.7 pounds, but which on hot days seemed much heavier. Because you could die so quickly, each man carried at least one large compress bandage, usually in the helmet band for easy access. Because the nights were cold, and because the monsoons were wet, each carried a green plastic poncho that could be used as a raincoat or ground sheet or make-shift tent. With its quilted liner, the poncho weighed almost two pounds, but it was worth every ounce. In April, for instance, when Ted Lavender was shot, they used his poncho to wrap him up, then to carry him across the paddy, then to lift him into the chopper that took him away.

They were called legs or grunts.

To carry something was to "hump" it, as when Lieutenant Jimmy Cross humped his love for Martha up the hills and through the swamps. In its intransitive form, "to hump" meant "to walk," or "to march," but it implied burdens far beyond the intransitive.

Almost everyone humped photographs. In his wallet, Lieutenant Cross carried two photographs of Martha. The first was a Kodachrome snapshot signed "Love," though he knew better. She stood against a brick wall. Her eyes were gray and neutral, her lips slightly open as she stared straight-on at the camera. At night, sometimes, Lieutenant Cross wondered who had taken the picture, because he knew she had boyfriends, because he loved her so much, and because he could see the shadow of the picture taker spreading out against the brick wall. The second photograph had been clipped from the 1968 Mount Sebastian yearbook. It was an action shot—women's volleyball—and Martha was bent horizontal to the floor, reaching, the palms of her hands in sharp focus, the tongue taut, the expression frank and competitive. There was no visible sweat. She wore white gym shorts. Her legs, he thought, were almost certainly the legs of a virgin, dry and without hair, the left knee cocked and carrying her entire weight, which was just over one hundred pounds. Lieutenant Cross remembered touching that left knee. A dark theater, he remembered, and the movie was *Bonnie and Clyde*, and Martha wore a tweed skirt, and during the final scene, when he touched her knee, she turned and looked at him in a sad, sober way that made him pull his hand back, but he would always remember the feel of the tweed skirt and the knee beneath it and the sound of the gunfire that killed Bonnie and Clyde, how embarrassing it was, how slow and oppressive. He remembered kissing her good night at the dorm door. Right then, he thought, he should've done something brave. He should've carried her up the stairs to her room and tied her to the bed and touched that left knee all night long. He should've risked it. Whenever he looked at the photographs, he thought of new things he should've done.

What they carried was partly a function of rank, partly of field specialty.

As a first lieutenant and platoon leader, Jimmy Cross carried a compass, maps, code books, binoculars, and a .45-caliber pistol that weighed 2.9 pounds fully loaded. He carried a strobe light and the responsibility for the lives of his men.

As an RTO, Mitchell Sanders carried the PRC-25 radio, a killer, twenty-six pounds with its battery.

As a medic, Rat Kiley carried a canvas satchel filled with morphine and plasma and malaria tablets and surgical tape and comic books and all the things a medic must carry, including M & M's for especially bad wounds, for a total weight of nearly twenty pounds.

As a big man, therefore a machine gunner, Henry Dobbins carried the M-60,   10 which weighed twenty-three pounds unloaded, but which was almost always loaded. In addition, Dobbins carried between ten and fifteen pounds of ammunition draped in belts across his chest and shoulders.

As PFCs or Spec 4s, most of them were common grunts and carried the standard M-16 gas-operated assault rifle. The weapon weighed 7.5 pounds unloaded, 8.2 pounds with its full twenty-round magazine. Depending on numerous factors, such as topography and psychology, the rifleman carried anywhere from twelve to twenty magazines, usually in cloth bandoliers, adding on another 8.4 pounds at minimum, fourteen pounds at maximum. When it was available, they also carried M-16 maintenance gear—rods and steel brushes and swabs and tubes of LSA oil—all of which weighed about a pound. Among the grunts, some carried the M-79 grenade launcher, 5.9 pounds unloaded, a reasonably light weapon except for the ammunition, which was heavy. A single round weighed ten ounces. The typical load was twenty-five rounds. But Ted Lavender, who was scared, carried thirty-four rounds when he was shot and killed outside Than Khe, and he went down under an exceptional burden, more than twenty pounds of ammunition, plus the flak jacket and helmet and rations and water and toilet paper and tranquilizers and all the rest, plus the unweighed fear. He was dead weight. There was no twitching or flopping. Kiowa, who saw it happen, said it was like watching a rock fall, or a big sandbag or something—just boom, then down—not like the movies where the dead guy rolls around and does fancy spins and goes ass over teakettle—not like that, Kiowa said, the poor bastard just flat-fuck fell. Boom. Down. Nothing else. It was a bright morning in mid-April. Lieutenant Cross felt the pain. He blamed himself. They stripped off Lavender's canteens and ammo, all the heavy things, and Rat Kiley said the obvious, the guy's dead, and Mitchell Sanders used his radio to report one U.S. KIA[3] and to request a chopper. Then they wrapped Lavender in his poncho. They carried him out to a dry paddy, established security, and sat smoking the dead man's dope until the chopper came. Lieutenant Cross kept to himself. He pictured Martha's smooth young face, thinking he loved her more than anything, more than his men, and now Ted Lavender was dead because he loved her so much and could not stop thinking about her. When the dust-off[4] arrived, they carried Lavender aboard. Afterward they burned Than Khe. They marched until dusk, then dug their holes, and that night Kiowa kept explaining how you had to be there, how fast it was, how the poor guy just dropped like so much concrete. Boom-down, he said. Like cement.

In addition to the three standard weapons—the M-60, M-16, and M-79—they carried whatever presented itself, or whatever seemed appropriate as a means of killing or staying alive. They carried catch-as-catch-can. At various times, in various situations, they carried M-14s and CAR-15s and Swedish Ks and grease guns and captured AK-47s and Chi-Coms and RPGs and Simonov carbines and black-market Uzis and .38-caliber Smith & Wesson handguns and 66 mm LAWs and shotguns and silencers and blackjacks and bayonets and C-4 plastic explosives. Lee Strunk carried a slingshot; a weapon of last resort, he called it. Mitchell

---

[3]Killed in action.
[4]Helicopter.

Sanders carried brass knuckles. Kiowa carried his grandfather's feathered hatchet. Every third or fourth man carried a Claymore antipersonnel mine—3.5 pounds with its firing device. They all carried fragmentation grenades—fourteen ounces each. They all carried at least one M-18 colored smoke grenade—twenty-four ounces. Some carried CS or tear-gas grenades. Some carried white-phosphorus grenades. They carried all they could bear, and then some, including a silent awe for the terrible power of the things they carried.

In the first week of April, before Lavender died, Lieutenant Jimmy Cross received a good-luck charm from Martha. It was a simple pebble, an ounce at most. Smooth to the touch, it was a milky-white color with flecks of orange and violet, oval-shaped, like a miniature egg. In the accompanying letter, Martha wrote that she had found the pebble on the Jersey shoreline, precisely where the land touched water at high tide, where things came together but also separated. It was this separate-but-together quality, she wrote, that had inspired her to pick up the pebble and to carry it in her breast pocket for several days, where it seemed weightless, and then to send it through the mail, by air, as a token of her truest feelings for him. Lieutenant Cross found this romantic. But he wondered what her truest feelings were, exactly, and what she meant by separate-but-together. He wondered how the tides and waves had come into play on that afternoon along the Jersey shoreline when Martha saw the pebble and bent down to rescue it from geology. He imagined bare feet. Martha was a poet, with the poet's sensibilities, and her feet would be brown and bare, the toenails unpainted, the eyes chilly and somber like the ocean in March, and though it was painful, he wondered who had been with her that afternoon. He imagined a pair of shadows moving along the strip of sand where things came together but also separated. It was phantom jealousy, he knew, but he couldn't help himself. He loved her so much. On the march, through the hot days of early April, he carried the pebble in his mouth, turning it with his tongue, tasting sea salts and moisture. His mind wandered. He had difficulty keeping his attention on the war. On occasion he would yell at his men to spread out the column, to keep their eyes open, but then he would slip away into daydreams, just pretending, walking barefoot along the Jersey shore, with Martha, carrying nothing. He would feel himself rising. Sun and waves and gentle winds, all love and lightness.

What they carried varied by mission.

When a mission took them to the mountains, they carried mosquito netting, machetes, canvas tarps, and extra bug juice.

If a mission seemed especially hazardous, or if it involved a place they knew to be bad, they carried everything they could. In certain heavily mined AOs,[5] where the land was dense with Toe Poppers and Bouncing Betties, they took turns humping a twenty-eight-pound mine detector. With its headphones and big sensing plate, the equipment was a stress on the lower back and shoulders, awkward to handle, often useless because of the shrapnel in the earth, but they carried it anyway, partly for safety, partly for the illusion of safety.

On ambush, or other night missions, they carried peculiar little odds and ends. Kiowa always took along his New Testament and a pair of moccasins for silence. Dave Jensen carried night-sight vitamins high in carotin. Lee Strunk

15

---

[5]Areas of operations.

carried his slingshot; ammo, he claimed, would never be a problem. Rat Kiley carried brandy and M & M's. Until he was shot, Ted Lavender carried the starlight scope, which weighed 6.3 pounds with its aluminum carrying case. Henry Dobbins carried his girlfriend's pantyhose wrapped around his neck as a comforter. They all carried ghosts. When dark came, they would move out single file across the meadows and paddies to their ambush coordinates, where they would quietly set up the Claymores and lie down and spend the night waiting.

Other missions were more complicated and required special equipment. In mid-April, it was their mission to search out and destroy the elaborate tunnel complexes in the Than Khe area south of Chu Lai. To blow the tunnels, they carried one-pound blocks of pentrite high explosives, four blocks to a man, sixty-eight pounds in all. They carried wiring, detonators, and battery-powered clackers. Dave Jensen carried earplugs. Most often, before blowing the tunnels, they were ordered by higher command to search them, which was considered bad news, but by and large they just shrugged and carried out orders. Because he was a big man, Henry Dobbins was excused from tunnel duty. The others would draw numbers. Before Lavender died there were seventeen men in the platoon, and whoever drew the number seventeen would strip off his gear and crawl in head first with a flashlight and Lieutenant Cross's .45-caliber pistol. The rest of them would fan out as security. They would sit down or kneel, not facing the hole, listening to the ground beneath them, imagining cobwebs and ghosts, whatever was down there—the tunnel walls squeezing in—how the flashlight seemed impossibly heavy in the hand and how it was tunnel vision in the very strictest sense, compression in all ways, even time, and how you had to wiggle in—ass and elbows—a swallowed-up feeling—and how you found yourself worrying about odd things—will your flashlight go dead? Do rats carry rabies? If you screamed, how far would the sound carry? Would your buddies hear it? Would they have the courage to drag you out? In some respects, though not many, the waiting was worse than the tunnel itself. Imagination was a killer.

On April 16, when Lee Strunk drew the number seventeen, he laughed and muttered something and went down quickly. The morning was hot and very still. Not good, Kiowa said. He looked at the tunnel opening, then out across a dry paddy toward the village of Than Khe. Nothing moved. No clouds or birds or people. As they waited, the men smoked and drank Kool-Aid, not talking much, feeling sympathy for Lee Strunk but also feeling the luck of the draw. You win some, you lose some, said Mitchell Sanders, and sometimes you settle for a rain check. It was a tired line and no one laughed.

Henry Dobbins ate a tropical chocolate bar. Ted Lavender popped a tranquilizer and went off to pee.   20

After five minutes, Lieutenant Jimmy Cross moved to the tunnel, leaned down, and examined the darkness. Trouble, he thought—a cave-in maybe. And then suddenly, without willing it, he was thinking about Martha. The stresses and fractures, the quick collapse, the two of them buried alive under all that weight. Dense, crushing love. Kneeling, watching the hole, he tried to concentrate on Lee Strunk and the war, all the dangers, but his love was too much for him, he felt paralyzed, he wanted to sleep inside her lungs and breathe her blood and be smothered. He wanted her to be a virgin and not a virgin, all at once. He wanted to know her. Intimate secrets—why poetry? Why so sad? Why the grayness in her eyes? Why so alone? Not lonely, just alone—riding her bike across campus or sitting off by herself in the cafeteria. Even dancing, she danced alone—and it was the aloneness that filled him with love. He remembered telling her that one evening. How she nodded and looked away. And how, later, when he kissed her, she received the kiss without returning it, her eyes wide open, not afraid, not a virgin's eyes, just flat and uninvolved.

Lieutenant Cross gazed at the tunnel. But he was not there. He was buried with Martha under the white sand at the Jersey shore. They were pressed together, and the pebble in his mouth was her tongue. He was smiling. Vaguely, he was aware of how quiet the day was, the sullen paddies, yet he could not bring himself to worry about matters of security. He was beyond that. He was just a kid at war, in love. He was twenty-two years old. He couldn't help it.

A few moments later Lee Strunk crawled out of the tunnel. He came up grinning, filthy but alive. Lieutenant Cross nodded and closed his eyes while the others clapped Strunk on the back and made jokes about rising from the dead.

Worms, Rat Kiley said. Right out of the grave. Fuckin' zombie.

The men laughed. They all felt great relief.   25

Spook City, said Mitchell Sanders.

Lee Strunk made a funny ghost sound, a kind of moaning, yet very happy and right then, when Strunk made that high happy moaning sound, when he went *Ahhooooo*, right then Ted Lavender was shot in the head on his way back from peeing. He lay with his mouth open. The teeth were broken. There was a swollen black bruise under his left eye. The cheekbone was gone. Oh shit, Rat Kiley said, the guy's dead. The guy's dead, he kept saying, which seemed profound—the guy's dead. I mean really.

The things they carried were determined to some extent by superstition. Lieutenant Cross carried his good-luck pebble. Dave Jensen carried a rabbit's foot. Norman Bowker, otherwise a very gentle person, carried a thumb that had been presented to him as a gift by Mitchell Sanders. The thumb was dark brown, rubbery to the touch, and weighed four ounces at most. It had been cut from a VC[6] corpse, a boy of fifteen or sixteen. They'd found him at the bottom of an irrigation ditch, badly burned, flies in his mouth and eyes. The boy wore black shorts and sandals. At the time of his death he had been carrying a pouch of rice, a rifle, and three magazines of ammunition.

You want my opinion, Mitchell Sanders said, there's a definite moral here.

He put his hand on the dead boy's wrist. He was quiet for a time, as if count-   30
ing a pulse, then he patted the stomach, almost affectionately, and used Kiowa's hunting hatchet to remove the thumb.

Henry Dobbins asked what the moral was.

Moral?

You know. *Moral.*

Sanders wrapped the thumb in toilet paper and handed it across to Norman Bowker. There was no blood. Smiling, he kicked the boy's head, watched the flies scatter, and said, It's like with that old TV show—Paladin. Have gun, will travel.

Henry Dobbins thought about it.   35

Yeah, well, he finally said. I don't see no moral.

There it *is*, man.

Fuck off.

---

[6]Vietcong, the North Vietnam army.

Soldiers in Vietnam on patrol

They carried USO stationery and pencils and pens. They carried Sterno, safety pins, trip flares, signal flares, spools of wire, razor blades, chewing tobacco, liberated joss sticks and statuettes of the smiling Buddha, candles, grease pencils, *The Stars and Stripes*,[7] fingernail clippers, Psy Ops[8] leaflets, bush hats, bolos, and much more. Twice a week, when the resupply choppers came in, they carried hot chow in green Mermite cans and large canvas bags filled with iced beer and soda pop. They carried plastic water containers, each with a two-gallon capacity. Mitchell Sanders carried a set of starched tiger fatigues for special occasions. Henry Dobbins carried Black Flag insecticide. Dave Jensen carried empty sandbags that could be filled at night for added protection. Lee Strunk carried tanning lotion. Some things they carried in common. Taking turns, they carried the big PRC-77 scrambler radio, which weighed thirty pounds with its battery. They shared the weight of memory. They took up what others could no longer bear. Often, they carried each other, the wounded or weak. They carried infections. They carried chess sets, basketballs, Vietnamese-English dictionaries, insignia of rank, Bronze Stars and Purple Hearts, plastic cards imprinted with the Code of Conduct. They carried diseases, among them malaria and dysentery. They carried lice and ringworm and leeches and paddy algae and various rots and molds. They carried the land itself—Vietnam, the place, the soil—a powdery orange-red dust that covered their boots and fatigues and faces. They carried the sky. The whole atmosphere, they carried it, the humidity, the monsoons, the stink of fungus and decay, all of it, they carried gravity. They moved like mules. By daylight they took sniper fire, at night they were mortared, but it was not battle, it was just the endless march, village to village, without purpose, nothing won

---

[7]Official overseas military newspaper.
[8]Psychological operations.

or lost. They marched for the sake of the march. They plodded along slowly, dumbly, leaning forward against the heat, unthinking, all blood and bone, simple grunts, soldiering with their legs, toiling up the hills and down into the paddies and across the rivers and up again and down, just humping, one step and then the next and then another, but no volition, no will, because it was automatic, it was anatomy, and the war was entirely a matter of posture and carriage, the hump was everything, a kind of inertia, a kind of emptiness, a dullness of desire and intellect and conscience and hope and human sensibility. Their principles were in their feet. Their calculations were biological. They had no sense of strategy or mission. They searched the villages without knowing what to look for, not caring, kicking over jars of rice, frisking children and old men, blowing tunnels, sometimes setting fires and sometimes not, then forming up and moving on to the next village, then other villages, where it would always be the same. They carried their own lives. The pressures were enormous. In the heat of early afternoon, they would remove their helmets and flak jackets, walking bare, which was dangerous but which helped ease the strain. They would often discard things along the route of march. Purely for comfort, they would throw away rations, blow their Claymores and grenades, no matter, because by nightfall the resupply choppers would arrive with more of the same, then a day or two later still more, fresh watermelons and crates of ammunition and sunglasses and woolen sweaters—the resources were stunning—sparklers for the Fourth of July, colored eggs for Easter. It was the great American war chest—the fruits of science, the smokestacks, the canneries, the arsenals at Hartford, the Minnesota forests, the machine shops, the vast fields of corn and wheat—they carried like freight trains; they carried it on their backs and shoulders—and for all the ambiguities of Vietnam, all the mysteries and unknowns, there was at least the single abiding certainty that they would never be at a loss for things to carry.

After the chopper took Lavender away, Lieutenant Jimmy Cross led his men   40 into the village of Than Khe. They burned everything. They shot chickens and dogs, they trashed the village well, they called in artillery and watched the wreckage, then they marched for several hours through the hot afternoon, and then at dusk, while Kiowa explained how Lavender died, Lieutenant Cross found himself trembling.

He tried not to cry. With his entrenching tool, which weighed five pounds, he began digging a hole in the earth.

He felt shame. He hated himself. He had loved Martha more than his men, and as a consequence Lavender was now dead, and this was something he would have to carry like a stone in his stomach for the rest of the war.

All he could do was dig. He used his entrenching tool like an ax, slashing, feeling both love and hate, and then later, when it was full dark, he sat at the bottom of his foxhole and wept. It went on for a long while. In part, he was grieving for Ted Lavender, but mostly it was for Martha, and for himself, because she belonged to another world, which was not quite real, and because she was a junior at Mount Sebastian College in New Jersey, a poet and a virgin and uninvolved, and because he realized she did not love him and never would.

Like cement, Kiowa whispered in the dark. I swear to God—boom-down. Not a word.

I've heard this, said Norman Bowker.   45

A pisser, you know? Still zipping himself up. Zapped while zipping.

All right, fine. That's enough.

Yeah, but you had to see it, the guy just—

I *heard*, man. Cement. So why not shut the fuck *up?*

Kiowa shook his head sadly and glanced over at the hole where Lieutenant 50
Jimmy Cross sat watching the night. The air was thick and wet. A warm, dense
fog had settled over the paddies and there was the stillness that precedes rain.

After a time Kiowa sighed.

One thing for sure, he said. The Lieutenant's in some deep hurt. I mean that
crying jag—the way he was carrying on—it wasn't fake or anything, it was real
heavy-duty hurt. The man cares.

Sure, Norman Bowker said.

Say what you want, the man does care.

We all got problems. 55

Not Lavender.

No, I guess not, Bowker said. Do me a favor, though.

Shut up?

That's a smart Indian. Shut up.

Shrugging, Kiowa pulled off his boots. He wanted to say more, just to lighten 60
up his sleep, but instead he opened his New Testament and arranged it beneath
his head as a pillow. The fog made things seem hollow and unattached. He tried
not to think about Ted Lavender, but then he was thinking how fast it was, no
drama, down and dead, and how it was hard to feel anything except surprise.
It seemed un-Christian. He wished he could find some great sadness, or even
anger, but the emotion wasn't there and he couldn't make it happen. Mostly he
felt pleased to be alive. He liked the smell of the New Testament under his cheek,
the leather and ink and paper and glue, whatever the chemicals were. He liked
hearing the sounds of night. Even his fatigue, it felt fine, the stiff muscles and the
prickly awareness of his own body, a floating feeling. He enjoyed not being dead.
Lying there, Kiowa admired Lieutenant Jimmy Cross's capacity for grief. He
wanted to share the man's pain, he wanted to care as Jimmy Cross cared. And yet
when he closed his eyes, all he could think was Boom-down, and all he could feel
was the pleasure of having his boots off and the fog curling in around him and
the damp soil and the Bible smells and the plush comfort of night.

After a moment Norman Bowker sat up in the dark.

What the hell, he said. You want to talk, *talk.* Tell it to me.

Forget it.

No, man, go on. One thing I hate, it's a silent Indian.

For the most part they carried themselves with poise, a kind of dignity. Now 65
and then, however, there were times of panic, when they squealed or wanted to
squeal but couldn't, when they twitched and made moaning sounds and covered
their heads and said Dear Jesus and flopped around on the earth and fired their
weapons blindly and cringed and sobbed and begged for the noise to stop and
went wild and made stupid promises to themselves and to God and to their mothers and fathers, hoping not to die. In different ways, it happened to all of them.
Afterward, when the firing ended, they would blink and peek up. They would
touch their bodies, feeling shame, then quickly hiding it. They would force themselves to stand. As if in slow motion, frame by frame, the world would take on the
old logic—absolute silence, then the wind, then sunlight, then voices. It was the
burden of being alive. Awkwardly, the men would reassemble themselves, first in
private, then in groups, becoming soldiers again. They would repair the leaks in
their eyes. They would check for casualties, call in dust-offs, light cigarettes, try

to smile, clear their throats and spit and begin cleaning their weapons. After a time someone would shake his head and say, No lie, I almost shit my pants, and someone else would laugh, which meant it was bad, yes, but the guy had obviously not shit his pants, it wasn't that bad, and in any case nobody would ever do such a thing and then go ahead and talk about it. They would squint into the dense, oppressive sunlight. For a few moments, perhaps, they would fall silent, lighting a joint and tracking its passage from man to man, inhaling, holding in the humiliation. Scary stuff, one of them might say. But then someone else would grin or flick his eyebrows and say, Roger-dodger, almost cut me a new asshole, *almost*.

There were numerous such poses. Some carried themselves with a sort of wistful resignation, others with pride or stiff soldierly discipline or good humor or macho zeal. They were afraid of dying but they were even more afraid to show it. They found jokes to tell.

They used a hard vocabulary to contain the terrible softness. *Greased*, they'd say. *Offed, lit up, zapped while zipping*. It wasn't cruelty, just stage presence. They were actors and the war came at them in 3-D. When someone died, it wasn't quite dying, because in a curious way it seemed scripted, and because they had their lines mostly memorized, irony mixed with tragedy, and because they called it by other names, as if to encyst and destroy the reality of death itself. They kicked corpses. They cut off thumbs. They talked grunt lingo. They told stories about Ted Lavender's supply of tranquilizers, how the poor guy didn't feel a thing, how incredibly tranquil he was.

There's a moral here, said Mitchell Sanders.

They were waiting for Lavender's chopper, smoking the dead man's dope. 70

The moral's pretty obvious, Sanders said, and winked. Stay away from drugs. No joke, they'll ruin your day every time.

Cute, said Henry Dobbins.

Mind-blower, get it? Talk about wiggy—nothing left, just blood and brains.

They made themselves laugh.

There it is, they'd say, over and over, as if the repetition itself were an act of 75 poise, a balance between crazy and almost crazy, knowing without going. There it is, which meant be cool, let it ride, because oh yeah, man, you can't change what can't be changed, there it is, there it absolutely and positively and fucking well *is*.

They were tough.

They carried all the emotional baggage of men who might die. Grief, terror, love, longing—these were intangibles, but the intangibles had their own mass and specific gravity, they had tangible weight. They carried shameful memories. They carried the common secret of cowardice barely restrained, the instinct to run or freeze or hide, and in many respects this was the heaviest burden of all, for it could never be put down, it required perfect balance and perfect posture. They carried their reputations. They carried the soldier's greatest fear, which was the fear of blushing. Men killed, and died, because they were embarrassed not to. It was what had brought them to the war in the first place, nothing positive, no dreams of glory or honor, just to avoid the blush of dishonor. They died so as not to die of embarrassment. They crawled into tunnels and walked point and advanced under fire. Each morning, despite the unknowns, they made their legs move. They endured. They kept humping. They did not submit to the obvious alternative, which was simply to close the eyes and fall. So easy, really. Go limp and tumble to the ground and let the muscles unwind and not speak and not budge until your buddies picked you up and lifted you into the chopper that would roar and dip its nose and carry you off to the world. A mere matter of falling, yet no one ever fell. It was not courage, exactly; the object was not valor. Rather, they were too frightened to be cowards.

By and large they carried these things inside, maintaining the masks of composure. They sneered at sick call. They spoke bitterly about guys who had found release by shooting off their own toes or fingers. Pussies, they'd say. Candyasses. It was fierce, mocking talk, with only a trace of envy or awe, but even so, the image played itself out behind their eyes.

They imagined the muzzle against flesh. They imagined the quick, sweet pain, then the evacuation to Japan, then a hospital with warm beds and cute geisha nurses.

They dreamed of freedom birds.   80

At night, on guard, staring into the dark, they were carried away by jumbo jets. They felt the rush of takeoff. *Gone!* they yelled. And then velocity, wings and engines, a smiling stewardess—but it was more than a plane, it was a real bird, a big sleek silver bird with feathers and talons and high screeching. They were flying. The weights fell off, there was nothing to bear. They laughed and held on tight, feeling the cold slap of wind and altitude, soaring, thinking *It's over, I'm gone!*—they were naked, they were light and free—it was all lightness, bright and fast and buoyant, light as light, a helium buzz in the brain, a giddy bubbling in the lungs as they were taken up over the clouds and the war, beyond duty, beyond gravity and mortification and global entanglements—*Sin loi!*[9] they yelled, *I'm sorry, motherfuckers, but I'm out of it, I'm goofed, I'm on a space cruise, I'm gone!*—and it was a restful, disencumbered sensation, just riding the light waves, sailing that big silver freedom bird over the mountains and oceans, over America, over the farms and great sleeping cities and cemeteries and highways and the golden arches of McDonald's. It was flight, a kind of fleeing, a kind of falling, falling higher and higher, spinning off the edge of the earth and beyond the sun and through the vast, silent vacuum where there were no burdens and where everything weighed exactly nothing. *Gone!* they screamed, *I'm sorry but I'm gone!* And so at night, not quite dreaming, they gave themselves over to lightness, they were carried, they were purely borne.

On the morning after Ted Lavender died, First Lieutenant Jimmy Cross crouched at the bottom of his foxhole and burned Martha's letters. Then he burned the two photographs. There was a steady rain falling, which made it difficult, but he used heat tabs and Sterno to build a small fire, screening it with his body, holding the photographs over the tight blue flame with the tips of his fingers.

He realized it was only a gesture. Stupid, he thought. Sentimental, too, but mostly just stupid.

Lavender was dead. You couldn't burn the blame.

Besides, the letters were in his head. And even now, without photographs,   85 Lieutenant Cross could see Martha playing volleyball in her white gym shorts and yellow T-shirt. He could see her moving in the rain.

When the fire died out, Lieutenant Cross pulled his poncho over his shoulders and ate breakfast from a can.

There was no great mystery, he decided.

In those burned letters Martha had never mentioned the war, except to say, Jimmy, take care of yourself. She wasn't involved. She signed the letters "Love," but it wasn't love, and all the fine lines and technicalities did not matter.

---

[9]"Sorry about that"

The morning came up wet and blurry. Everything seemed part of everything else, the fog and Martha and the deepening rain.

It was a war, after all. 90

Half smiling, Lieutenant Jimmy Cross took out his maps. He shook his head hard, as if to clear it, then bent forward and began planning the day's march. In ten minutes, or maybe twenty, he would rouse the men and they would pack up and head west, where the maps showed the country to be green and inviting. They would do what they had always done. The rain might add some weight, but otherwise it would be one more day layered upon all the other days.

He was realistic about it. There was that new hardness in his stomach.

No more fantasies, he told himself.

Henceforth, when he thought about Martha, it would be only to think that she belonged elsewhere. He would shut down the daydreams. This was not Mount Sebastian, it was another world, where there were no pretty poems or midterm exams, a place where men died because of carelessness and gross stupidity. Kiowa was right. Boom-down, and you were dead, never partly dead.

Briefly, in the rain, Lieutenant Cross saw Martha's gray eyes gazing back at him. 95

He understood.

It was very sad, he thought. The things men carried inside. The things men did or felt they had to do.

He almost nodded at her, but didn't.

Instead he went back to his maps. He was now determined to perform his duties firmly and without negligence. It wouldn't help Lavender, he knew that, but from this point on he would comport himself as a soldier. He would dispose of his good-luck pebble. Swallow it, maybe, or use Lee Strunk's slingshot, or just drop it along the trail. On the march he would impose strict field discipline. He would be careful to send out flank security, to prevent straggling or bunching up, to keep his troops moving at the proper pace and at the proper interval. He would insist on clean weapons. He would confiscate the remainder of Lavender's dope. Later in the day, perhaps, he would call the men together and speak to them plainly. He would accept the blame for what had happened to Ted Lavender. He would be a man about it. He would look them in the eyes, keeping his chin level, and he would issue the new SOPs in a calm, impersonal tone of voice, an officer's voice, leaving no room for argument or discussion. Commencing immediately, he'd tell them, they would no longer abandon equipment along the route of march. They would police up their acts. They would get their shit together, and keep it together, and maintain it neatly and in good working order.

He would not tolerate laxity. He would show strength, distancing himself. 100

Among the men there would be grumbling, of course, and maybe worse, because their days would seem longer and their loads heavier, but Lieutenant Cross reminded himself that his obligation was not to be loved but to lead. He would dispense with love; it was not now a factor. And if anyone quarreled or complained, he would simply tighten his lips and arrange his shoulders in the correct command posture. He might give a curt little nod. Or he might not. He might just shrug and say Carry on, then they would saddle up and form into a column and move out toward the villages of Than Khe.

(1986)

◇◇◇◇◇◇◇◇◇◇◇◇◇◇◇◇◇◇◇◇◇◇◇◇◇

The Writing Process
Prewriting

Before you can begin to write about structure, you must first determine the underlying patterns that serve as a framework for the story.

Exercise: Finding Patterns

Read the following questions; then carefully reread the story. Write down your answers to the questions.

1. How does each part of the story relate to the title, "The Things They Carried"?
2. What visible structure is evident, separating the parts of the story?
3. How many different time periods are described in the story? Make a list of the main events that are described. Then organize the list according to time order.
4. Trace the Martha story line that is woven through the tale. What is the reality of the relationship between Jimmy Cross and Martha? What evidence are you looking at when you guess at this reality?
5. What do we know about each soldier in the story? How do we accumulate knowledge about each one? On the other hand, what is left out of our knowledge about each soldier, information that you might have expected? If O'Brien had written some scenes from each soldier's past as a civilian, how would that change the story? Why do you think he generally avoids these scenes?
6. Why is the death of Ted Lavender important to your understanding of the story? How many times is Lavender's death retold? How is it different in the various retellings?

Writing

Once you understand some of the structural elements of the story, you need to choose a framework within which you can effectively present your observations—that is, a structure for your own paper.

Exercise: Grouping Details

Write a sentence that explains something about the author's selection of scenes, themes, or events to include repeatedly through the story. Next, discuss which details in the story support your explanations. For example, if you mentioned that the scenes involving Martha relate to the crucial change undergone by Jimmy Cross, supporting details would include the following:

- the content of the letters from Martha
- the photographs of Martha
- the lucky pebble

- descriptions of his encounters with Martha at home
- his fantasies of what might have happened or what might happen in the future with Martha
- episodes of daydreaming about Martha
- the burning of the letters and photographs

Relating Details to Theme

An accurate description of a pattern in the story and a convincing list of supporting details will be crucial to any essay about structure. But you also need to work out a thesis—a major claim that relates the structure to the overall impact or meaning of the work. For example, an essay about the structure of "The Things They Carried" might make this claim:

> Jimmy Cross's recurring thoughts about Martha throughout the story create a picture of him as a romantic, self-deceiving, sensitive young man, a character he himself rejects in the end with the symbolic burning of her letters and photographs.

Ideas for Writing

Ideas for Reflective Writing

1. In "The Things They Carried," physical objects take on extra significance as part of each soldier's kit. Are there any items in your life that have extra significance because they are associated with a certain period of time? What do you carry with you almost every day? What could we tell about you by looking through your backpack, handbag, wallet, or pockets? Write about how certain objects in your life could be interpreted.

2. In this story, Jimmy Cross builds an elaborate fantasy surrounding Martha, and sometimes he is quite aware that it's a fantasy. Write about a daydream or fantasy that you have created with some small grounding in real life.

Ideas for Critical Writing

The following claims relate structure to meaning. Adopt one of them, revise one, or create your own for arguing an interpretation of "The Things They Carried."

1. The soldiers' situation is illuminated in "The Things They Carried" by words and details referring to different kinds of weight and lightness.

2. CRITICAL APPROACHES: For this topic, review the summary of "formalism" in Chapter 34, Critical Approaches for Interpreting Literature, and use a close-reading approach. Once an event or topic is introduced

in "The Things They Carried," it accumulates more meaning each time it reoccurs. This process involves the reader in the construction of a coherent story about each event.

3. The narrator of "The Things They Carried" continually slips out of his concrete cataloguing of physical objects and wanders into the realm of psychological burdens, suggesting that Jimmy Cross will not be able to live up to his resolves at the end of the story.

Ideas for Researched Writing

1. "The Things They Carried" is the first story in a collection by Tim O'Brien, also titled *The Things They Carried*. Find out more about the whole book and how the story you have read fits into it. What is interesting about the structure of this collection of Vietnam stories?

2. What kind of critical reception did O'Brien's story receive? Find a number of reviews and analyses of the story, and write an essay summarizing the reactions and interpretations.

MultiModal Project

Blank linear spaces separate this story into ten parts. Give each part a title that fits it. Then create a chart or diagram that illustrates the story's structure. To see models of ways to diagram stories, do a Google image search for "story structure diagram." Compare your titles and your diagram with others in your class, and discuss your choices.

Rewriting

Our advice in this section focuses on problems involved in quoting when writing about a literary work.

Integrating Quotations Gracefully

In any literary essay you will need quotations from the text of the work you are examining. In fact, when you revise your essay, always consider adding more specific evidence straight from the text. This evidence will help your readers understand the general points you make and will show what inspired your thoughts. Quoting directly also serves as a self-check; by finding specific support in the work, you confirm that your ideas are, indeed, grounded in the text and not in your fancy.

Be sure that you enclose these borrowings in quotation marks as you gracefully introduce them into your own sentences. And be sure that your own language leads grammatically into the language you are quoting. For example:

O'Brien describes the soldiers' inner experience as "a dullness of desire and intellect and conscience and hope and human sensibility."

At the close of the story, Cross imagines himself giving "a curt little nod" in his new role as a man in command.

Although the narrator claims that "the things they [the soldiers] carried were largely determined by necessity," for some men these necessities included such items as a diary, comic books, and marijuana.

That last example shows how you may add your own words to explain a possibly confusing word in a quotation: use brackets.

Exercise: Integrating Quotations

Here, we reprint a passage from "The Things They Carried." To practice integrating quotations, try your hand at using parts of the passage in sentences of your own.

1. Write a sentence that uses a phrase you quote directly as an example of a general point you make about the characters, events, or setting of the story.
2. Write a sentence that relates a detail to a theme of the story, using some exact quotation from the passage.

They used a hard vocabulary to contain the terrible softness. *Greased*, they'd say. *Offed, lit up, zapped while zipping.* It wasn't cruelty, just stage presence. They were actors and the war came at them in 3-D. When someone died, it wasn't quite dying, because in a curious way it seemed scripted, and because they had their lines mostly memorized, irony mixed with tragedy, and because they called it by other names, as if to encyst and destroy the reality of death itself.

8 Writing About Imagery and Symbolism

Chapter Preview

Imagery and symbolism, two of the most important elements of serious imaginative literature, provide rich sources of insight. The interpretive skills necessary to detect and understand them can be developed with practice. Because the meaning or theme of a literary work is often reinforced through imagery and symbolism, you can effectively devote an entire paper to an examination of a key symbol or a pattern of imagery. By the end of this chapter, you will be able to

* Identify and define *images, symbols* (including *phallic* and *yonic*), and *archetypes.*
* Describe how to recognize and interpret symbols.
* Explain the characteristics of a *workable thesis statement.*
* Name several ways to create an effective *introduction.*

What Are Images?

Images are words, sometimes phrases, that appeal to the senses and often put a picture in your mind. Literary critics classify images roughly into several categories.

Visual	images of sight ("future days strung together like pearls in a rosary"—Mary E. Wilkins Freeman)
Auditory	images of sound ("the loud, iron clanking of the lift machinery"—John Cheever)
Gustatory	images of taste ("the acrid, metallic taste of gunfire"—Alberto Moravia)
Kinetic	images of motion (a thought "bumping like a helium balloon at the ceiling of the brain"—Sandra Cisneros)
Thermal	images of temperature ("the blueblack cold" of early morning—Robert Hayden)
Tactile	images of feeling ("the ache of marriage throbs in the teeth"—Denise Levertov)

Such images enrich our pleasure in reading and, if deliberately repeated, can become *motifs*, or patterns of imagery, that illuminate some element of the story. The images of clothing in Katherine Anne Porter's "The Grave" form a significant motif, one that shows how the main character, Miranda, is beginning to mature, that she's tired of being a tomboy and wants to try on the trappings of traditional female attire. In Chopin's "Désirée's Baby," the repeated images of whiteness serve to reinforce the innocence and purity of the unjustly accused Désirée.

What Are Symbols?

If a repeated image gathers significant meaning and seems to stand for something more than itself, it then becomes a *symbol*. In Louise Erdrich's "The Red Convertible," the old Oldsmobile symbolizes the changing relationship between the narrator and his brother. The repeated mention of dust in Joyce's "Eveline" settles into our consciousness as symbolizing the dreariness of the title character's daily life, just as dust settles on all surfaces in an unkempt house. In Kate Chopin's "The Story of an Hour," Mrs. Mallard gazes out her window at "the tops of trees that were all aquiver with the new spring life. The delicious breath of rain was in the air." Those images of spring and rain represent the prospect of a vibrant new life that is awakening in Mrs. Mallard's subconscious mind.

Because spring rains literally bring renewed life to the earth, water is used in the baptismal service in church to signify rebirth. Thus, in literature, we associate water with a vigorous, living spirit and its opposite—dryness, dust, aridity—with the death of the human spirit or the decay of moral values.

Archetypal Symbols

Some symbols, like the water and dust, are considered *archetypal* or universal—supposedly conveying a similar meaning in all cultures from the time of earliest civilizations. The circle, for instance, is an ancient symbol of wholeness or perfection; the sea has for centuries symbolized the voyage through life. Colors are often symbolic, like the crimson of the mark on Georgiana's cheek in Hawthorne's "The Birthmark." Occasionally a symbol can convey diametrically opposing meanings, depending on its context. For instance, white in our culture often stands for purity, as in bridal gowns; but Herman Melville makes the white whale in *Moby Dick* a symbol of evil incarnate, as Frost does with the "dimpled spider, fat and white" in his poem "Design." Both of those images also convey the often hidden, deceptive nature of evil. And black, frequently linked with death and evil, has many positive associations, such as a Black Belt in Judo; a cup of strong coffee; or the robes of a priest, judge, or graduate.

Phallic and Yonic Symbols

Two important and commonly employed symbols are associated with human sexuality. A *phallic symbol* suggests the potency of the male (as does The Misfit's gun in Flannery O'Connor's "A Good Man Is Hard to Find") or the force of male dominance in a patriarchal society (as do the stone pillar in Kate Chopin's "Désirée's Baby" and the father's "black-thorn stick" in James Joyce's "Eveline").

A *yonic symbol* suggests the fecundity of the female and the allure of female sexuality. Common yonic symbols are caves, pots, rooms, full-blown roses—round or concave objects resembling the shape of the primary sex organs of women. If you think fruit, then bananas are phallic and apples are yonic. Remember, though, that these objects will not always be charged with sexual significance. You must be sure that context supports a reasonable association with sexuality. Even Freud supposedly said that sometimes a cigar is just a cigar.

How Will I Recognize Symbols?

How can you tell if an image, a character, or an action carries symbolic meaning? The context suggests the significance. The title is often an important clue, as are repetition and placement in the story. John Steinbeck's "The Chrysanthemums" clearly intends the title flowers to be a central symbol, and as a yonic image, the connection to Elisa, the female protagonist, is obvious. But symbols in literature rarely have a single, unambiguous meaning. At first the flowers reflect Elisa's strengths and abilities, but when you learn more about her and watch her interact with the men in the story, the symbolic meanings expand and become more complex. You might think, as some readers do, that the flowers represent a strong woman's frustrations and disappointments in a male-dominated culture. Or you might conclude that the chrysanthemums stand for the children Elisa never had.

Reference Works on Symbols

You can also consult several sources that allow you to look up words to discover their symbolic implications. Your library should have copies of the following works in the humanities reference section or online:

- Cirlot, J. E. *A Dictionary of Symbols*
- Cooper, J. C. *An Illustrated Encyclopaedia of Traditional Symbols*
- Frazer, Sir James. *The Golden Bough*
- Olderr, Steven. *Symbolism: A Comprehensive Dictionary*
- Walker, Barbara. *The Woman's Encyclopedia of Myths and Secrets*

Looking at Images and Symbols

Recognizing images and symbols and responding to them sensitively are requirements for an informed reading of serious fiction. Read the following story by Shirley Jackson and see if you are aware, on first reading, of her use of symbolic imagery.

Shirley Jackson 1919–1965

Shirley Jackson did not receive attention as a writer until 1948, when the *New Yorker* published "The Lottery," a story that she wrote in just two hours. The magazine was flooded with letters, almost all of them wanting to know what the story meant. While Jackson is best known for her tales of supernatural terror, she also wrote about "the perpetual pandemonium and the constant crises" of her family life. "I can't persuade myself that writing is honest work," she once remarked. "It's great fun and I love it. For one thing, it's the only way I can get to sit down."

The Lottery

The morning of June 27th was clear and sunny, with the fresh warmth of a full-summer day; the flowers were blossoming profusely and the grass was richly green. The people of the village began to gather in the square, between the post office and the bank, around ten o'clock; in some towns there were so many people that the lottery took two days and had to be started on June 26th, but in this village, where there were only about three hundred people, the whole lottery took less than two hours, so it could begin at ten o'clock in the morning and still be through in time to allow the villagers to get home for noon dinner.

The children assembled first, of course. School was recently over for the summer, and the feeling of liberty sat uneasily on most of them; they tended to gather together quietly for a while before they broke into boisterous play, and their talk was still of the classroom and the teacher, of books and reprimands. Bobby Martin had already stuffed his pockets full of stones, and the other boys soon followed his example, selecting the smoothest and roundest stones; Bobby and Harry Jones and Dickie Delacroix—the villagers pronounced his name "Dellacroy"—eventually made a great pile of stones in one corner of the square and guarded it against the raids of the other boys. The girls stood aside, talking among themselves, looking over their shoulders at the boys, and the very small children rolled in the dust or clung to the hands of their older brothers or sisters.

Soon the men began to gather, surveying their own children, speaking of planting and rain, tractors and taxes. They stood together, away from the pile of stones in the corner, and their jokes were quiet and they smiled rather than laughed. The women, wearing faded house dresses and sweaters, came shortly after their menfolk. They greeted one another and exchanged bits of gossip as they went to join their husbands. Soon the women, standing by their husbands, began to call to their children, and the children came reluctantly, having to be called four or five times. Bobby Martin ducked under his mother's grasping hand and ran, laughing, back to the pile of stones. His father spoke up sharply, and Bobby came quickly and took his place between his father and his oldest brother.

The lottery was conducted—as were the square dances, the teen-age club, the Halloween program—by Mr. Summers, who had time and energy to devote to civic activities. He was a round-faced, jovial man and he ran the coal business, and people were sorry for him, because he had no children and his wife was a scold. When he arrived in the square, carrying the black wooden box, there was a murmur of conversation among the villagers, and he waved and called, "Little late today, folks." The postmaster, Mr. Graves, followed him, carrying a three-legged stool, and the stool was put in the center of the square and Mr. Summers set the black box down on it. The villagers kept their distance, leaving a space between themselves and the stool, and when Mr. Summers said, "Some of you fellows want to give me a hand?" there was a hesitation before two men, Mr. Martin and his oldest son, Baxter, came forward to hold the box steady on the stool while Mr. Summers stirred up the paper inside it.

The original paraphernalia for the lottery had been lost long ago, and the   5
black box now resting on the stool had been put into use even before Old Man Warner, the oldest man in town, was born. Mr. Summers spoke frequently to the villagers about making a new box, but no one liked to upset even as much tradition as was represented by the black box. There was a story that the present box had been made with some pieces of the box that had preceded it, the one that had been constructed when the first people settled down to make a village here. Every year, after the lottery, Mr. Summers began talking again about a new box, but every year the subject was allowed to fade off without anything's being done. The black box grew shabbier each year; by now it was no longer completely black but splintered badly along one side to show the original wood color, and in some places faded or stained.

Mr. Martin and his oldest son, Baxter, held the black box securely on the stool until Mr. Summers had stirred the papers thoroughly with his hand. Because so much of the ritual had been forgotten or discarded, Mr. Summers had been successful in having slips of paper substituted for the chips of wood that had been used for generations. Chips of wood, Mr. Summers had argued, had been all very well when the village was tiny, but now that the population was more than three hundred and likely to keep on growing, it was necessary to use something that would fit more easily into the black box. The night before the lottery, Mr. Summers and Mr. Graves made up the slips of paper and put them in the box, and it was then taken to the safe of Mr. Summers's coal company and locked up until Mr. Summers was ready to take it to the square next morning. The rest of the year, the box was put away, sometimes one place, sometimes another; it had spent one year in Mr. Graves's barn and another year underfoot in the post office, and sometimes it was set on a shelf in the Martin grocery and left there.

There was a great deal of fussing to be done before Mr. Summers declared the lottery open. There were the lists to make up—of heads of families, heads of households in each family, members of each household in each family. There was the proper swearing-in of Mr. Summers by the postmaster, as the official of the lottery; at one time, some people remembered, there had been a recital of some sort, performed by the official of the lottery, a perfunctory, tuneless chant that had been rattled off duly each year; some people believed that the official of the lottery used to stand just so when he said or sang it, others believed that he was supposed to walk among the people, but years and years ago this part of the ritual had been allowed to lapse. There had been, also, a ritual salute, which the official of the lottery had had to use in addressing each person who came up to draw from the box, but this also had changed with time, until now it was felt necessary only for the official to speak to each person approaching. Mr. Summers was very good at all this; in his clean white shirt and blue jeans, with one hand resting carelessly on the black box, he seemed very proper and important as he talked interminably to Mr. Graves and the Martins.

Just as Mr. Summers finally left off talking and turned to the assembled villagers, Mrs. Hutchinson came hurriedly along the path to the square, her sweater thrown over her shoulders, and slid into place in the back of the crowd.

"Clean forgot what day it was," she said to Mrs. Delacroix, who stood next to her, and they both laughed softly. "Thought my old man was out back stacking wood," Mrs. Hutchinson went on, "and then I looked out the window and the kids were gone, and then I remembered it was the twenty-seventh and came a-running." She dried her hands on her apron, and Mrs. Delacroix said, "You're in time, though. They're still talking away up there."

Mrs. Hutchinson craned her neck to see through the crowd and found her husband and children standing near the front. She tapped Mrs. Delacroix on the arm as a farewell and began to make her way through the crowd. The people separated good-humoredly to let her through; two or three people said, in voices just loud enough to be heard across the crowd, "Here comes your Missus, Hutchinson," and "Bill, she made it after all." Mrs. Hutchinson reached her husband, and Mr. Summers, who had been waiting, said cheerfully, "Thought we were going to have to get on without you, Tessie." Mrs. Hutchinson said, grinning, "Wouldn't have me leave m'dishes in the sink, now, would you, Joe?," and soft laughter ran through the crowd as the people stirred back into position after Mrs. Hutchinson's arrival.

"Well, now," Mr. Summers said soberly, "guess we better get started, get this   10
over with, so's we can go back to work. Anybody ain't here?"

"Dunbar," several people said. "Dunbar, Dunbar."

Mr. Summers consulted his list. "Clyde Dunbar," he said. "That's right. He's broke his leg, hasn't he? Who's drawing for him?"

"Me, I guess," a woman said, and Mr. Summers turned to look at her. "Wife draws for her husband," Mr. Summers said. "Don't you have a grown boy to do it for you, Janey?" Although Mr. Summers and everyone else in the village knew the answer perfectly well, it was the business of the official of the lottery to ask such questions formally. Mr. Summers waited with an expression of polite interest while Mrs. Dunbar answered.

"Horace's not but sixteen yet," Mrs. Dunbar said regretfully. "Guess I gotta fill in for the old man this year."

"Right," Mr. Summers said. He made a note on the list he was holding. Then   15
he asked, "Watson boy drawing this year?"

A tall boy in the crowd raised his hand. "Here," he said. "I'm drawing for m' mother and me." He blinked his eyes nervously and ducked his head as several voices in the crowd said things like "Good fellow, Jack," and "Glad to see your mother's got a man to do it."

"Well," Mr. Summers said, "guess that's everyone. Old Man Warner make it?"

"Here," a voice said, and Mr. Summers nodded.

A sudden hush fell on the crowd as Mr. Summers cleared his throat and looked at the list. "All ready?" he called. "Now, I'll read the names—heads of families first—and the men come up and take a paper out of the box. Keep the paper folded in your hand without looking at it until everyone has had a turn. Everything clear?"

The people had done it so many times that they only half listened to the direc-   20
tions; most of them were quiet, wetting their lips, not looking around. Then Mr. Summers raised one hand high and said, "Adams." A man disengaged himself from the crowd and came forward. "Hi, Steve," Mr. Summers said, and Mr. Adams said, "Hi, Joe." They grinned at one another humorlessly and nervously. Then Mr. Adams reached into the black box and took out a folded paper. He held it

firmly by one corner as he turned and went hastily back to his place in the crowd, where he stood a little apart from his family, not looking down at his hand.

"Allen." Mr. Summers said. "Anderson....Bentham."

"Seems like there's no time at all between lotteries any more," Mrs. Delacroix said to Mrs. Graves in the back row. "Seems like we got through with the last one only last week."

"Time sure goes fast," Mrs. Graves said.

"Clark....Delacroix."

"There goes my old man," Mrs. Delacroix said. She held her breath while   25
her husband went forward.

"Dunbar," Mr. Summers said, and Mrs. Dunbar went steadily to the box while one of the women said, "Go on, Janey," and another said, "There she goes."

"We're next," Mrs. Graves said. She watched while Mr. Graves came around from the side of the box, greeted Mr. Summers gravely, and selected a slip of paper from the box. By now, all through the crowd there were men holding the small folded papers in their large hands, turning them over and over nervously. Mrs. Dunbar and her two sons stood together, Mrs. Dunbar holding the slip of paper.

"Harburt....Hutchinson."

"Get up there, Bill," Mrs. Hutchinson said, and the people near her laughed.

"Jones."   30

"They do say," Mr. Adams said to Old Man Warner, who stood next to him, "that over in the north village they're talking of giving up the lottery."

Old Man Warner snorted. "Pack of crazy fools," he said. "Listening to the young folks, nothing's good enough for *them*. Next thing you know, they'll be wanting to go back to living in caves, nobody work any more, live *that* way for a while. Used to be a saying about 'Lottery in June, corn be heavy soon.' First thing you know, we'd all be eating stewed chickweed and acorns. There's *always* been a lottery," he added petulantly. "Bad enough to see young Joe Summers up there joking with everybody."

"Some places have already quit lotteries," Mrs. Adams said.

"Nothing but trouble in *that*," Old Man Warner said stoutly. "Pack of young fools."

"Martin." And Bobby Martin watched his father go forward. "Overdyke....   35
Percy."

"I wish they'd hurry," Mrs. Dunbar said to her oldest son. "I wish they'd hurry."

"They're almost through," her son said.

"You get ready to run tell Dad," Mrs. Dunbar said.

Mr. Summers called his own name and then stepped forward precisely and selected a slip from the box. Then he called, "Warner."

"Seventy-seventh year I been in the lottery," Old Man Warner said as he   40
went through the crowd. "Seventy-seventh time."

"Watson." The tall boy came awkwardly through the crowd. Someone said, "Don't be nervous, Jack," and Mr. Summers said, "Take your time, son."

"Zanini."

After that, there was a long pause, a breathless pause, until Mr. Summers, holding his slip of paper in the air, said, "All right, fellows." For a minute, no one moved, and then all the slips of paper were opened. Suddenly, all the women began to speak at once, saying, "Who is it?," "Who's got it?," "Is it the Dunbars?," "Is it the Watsons?" Then the voices began to say, "It's Hutchinson. It's Bill," "Bill Hutchinson's got it."

"Go tell your father," Mrs. Dunbar said to her older son.

People began to look around to see the Hutchinsons. Bill Hutchinson   45
was standing quiet, staring down at the paper in his hand. Suddenly, Tessie Hutchinson shouted to Mr. Summers, "You didn't give him time enough to take any paper he wanted. I saw you. It wasn't fair!"

"Be a good sport, Tessie," Mrs. Delacroix called, and Mrs. Graves said, "All of us took the same chance."

"Shut up, Tessie," Bill Hutchinson said.

"Well, everyone," Mr. Summers said, "that was done pretty fast, and now we've got to be hurrying a little more to get it done in time." He consulted his next list. "Bill," he said, "you draw for the Hutchinson family. You got any other households in the Hutchinsons?"

"There's Don and Eva," Mrs. Hutchinson yelled. "Make *them* take their chance!"

"Daughters draw with their husbands' families, Tessie," Mr. Summers said   50
gently. "You know that as well as anyone else."

"It wasn't *fair*," Tessie said.

"I guess not, Joe," Bill Hutchinson said regretfully. "My daughter draws with her husband's family, that's only fair. And I've got no other family except the kids."

"Then, as far as drawing for families is concerned, it's you," Mr. Summers said in explanation, "and as far as drawing for households is concerned, that's you, too. Right?"

"Right," Bill Hutchinson said.

"How many kids, Bill?" Mr. Summers asked formally.   55

"Three," Bill Hutchinson said. "There's Bill, Jr., and Nancy, and little Dave. And Tessie and me."

"All right, then," Mr. Summers said. "Harry, you got their tickets back?"

Mr. Graves nodded and held up the slips of paper. "Put them in the box, then," Mr. Summers directed. "Take Bill's and put it in."

"I think we ought to start over," Mrs. Hutchinson said, as quietly as she could. "I tell you it wasn't *fair*. You didn't give him time enough to choose. *Every*body saw that."

Mr. Graves had selected the five slips and put them in the box, and he   60
dropped all the papers but those onto the ground, where the breeze caught them and lifted them off.

"Listen, everybody," Mrs. Hutchinson was saying to the people around her.

"Ready, Bill?" Mr. Summers asked, and Bill Hutchinson, with one quick glance around at his wife and children, nodded.

"Remember," Mr. Summers said, "take the slips and keep them folded until each person has taken one. Harry, you help little Dave." Mr. Graves took the hand of the little boy, who came willingly with him up to the box. "Take a paper out of the box, Davy," Mr. Summers said. Davy put his hand into the box and laughed. "Take just *one* paper," Mr. Summers said. "Harry, you hold it for him." Mr. Graves took the child's hand and removed the folded paper from the tight fist and held it while little Dave stood next to him and looked up at him wonderingly.

"Nancy, next," Mr. Summers said. Nancy was twelve, and her school friends breathed heavily as she went forward, switching her skirt, and took a slip daintily from the box. "Bill, Jr.," Mr. Summers said, and Billy, his face red and his feet over-large, nearly knocked the box over as he got a paper out. "Tessie," Mr. Summers said. She hesitated for a minute, looking around defiantly, and then set her lips and went up to the box. She snatched a paper out and held it behind her.

"Bill," Mr. Summers said, and Bill Hutchinson reached into the box and felt 65
around, bringing his hand out at last with the slip of paper in it.

The crowd was quiet. A girl whispered, "I hope it's not Nancy," and the sound of the whisper reached the edges of the crowd.

"It's not the way it used to be," Old Man Warner said clearly. "People ain't the way they used to be."

"All right," Mr. Summers said. "Open the papers. Harry, you open little Dave's."

Mr. Graves opened the slip of paper and there was a general sigh through the crowd as he held it up and everyone could see that it was blank. Nancy and Bill, Jr., opened theirs at the same time, and both beamed and laughed, turning around to the crowd and holding their slips of paper above their heads.

"Tessie," Mr. Summers said. There was a pause, and then Mr. Summers 70
looked at Bill Hutchinson, and Bill unfolded his paper and showed it. It was blank.

"It's Tessie," Mr. Summers said, and his voice was hushed. "Show us her paper, Bill."

Bill Hutchinson went over to his wife and forced the slip of paper out of her hand. It had a black spot on it, the black spot Mr. Summers had made the night before with the heavy pencil in the coal-company office. Bill Hutchinson held it up, and there was a stir in the crowd.

"All right, folks," Mr. Summers said. "Let's finish quickly."

Although the villagers had forgotten the ritual and lost the original black box, they still remembered to use stones. The pile of stones the boys had made earlier was ready; there were stones on the ground with the blowing scraps of paper that had come out of the box. Mrs. Delacroix selected a stone so large she had to pick it up with both hands and turned to Mrs. Dunbar. "Come on," she said. "Hurry up."

Mrs. Dunbar had small stones in both hands, and she said, gasping for 75
breath, "I can't run at all. You'll have to go ahead and I'll catch up with you."

The children had stones already, and someone gave little Davy Hutchinson a few pebbles.

Tessie Hutchinson was in the center of a cleared space by now, and she held her hands out desperately as the villagers moved in on her. "It isn't fair," she said. A stone hit her on the side of the head.

Old Man Warner was saying, "Come on, come on, everyone." Steve Adams was in the front of the crowd of villagers, with Mrs. Graves beside him.

"It isn't fair, it isn't right," Mrs. Hutchinson screamed, and then they were upon her.

(1948)

The Writing Process

Prewriting

Since much of the imagery in "The Lottery" carries symbolic significance, we will focus on symbolism as the topic for writing here. Symbols in fiction are not difficult to recognize. Usually an author will give a symbol particular emphasis by mentioning it repeatedly (like the dust in "Eveline"). A crucial symbol will sometimes be placed in the story's opening or ending.

Interpreting Symbols

Shirley Jackson directs our attention to the lottery by making it the title of her story. She also gives us abundant detail about this traditional ritual. We know the exact date and time, how the lottery is conducted, who draws and in what order, what the box and the slips of paper look like, and so forth. Clearly the lottery is the story's central symbol as well as its title. The meaning of the lottery is the meaning of "The Lottery."

Exercise: Interpreting Symbols

Here are some points and questions to consider as you read the story a second time and try to work out your interpretation of its symbolism. Write out your answers, and if possible, share your responses with a small group of classmates.

1. Social psychologists observe that every group develops its own outcast or misfit, who is blamed for all sorts of group malfunctions and woes. Have you observed this dynamic in your own work, school, church, or family groups?

2. We are told a lot about the lottery, but not its exact purpose. Do the townspeople know? Is this omission significant? Intentional?

3. Why is much of the history of the lottery and the black box uncertain and vague? Why does Mr. Summers have to ask a question that he and everybody else already know the answer to?

4. The box used in the lottery is mentioned almost thirty times in the story—more than ten times in the phrase the black box. Why does the author emphasize this object and its color so strongly?

5. The stones are mentioned five times near the beginning of the story and then five or six times more at the end. Why is their presence so important? What are the historical/biblical associations of a "stoning"? Do they apply in this situation?

6. Which characters seem to stand for particular ideas or views? What about Old Man Warner? Look at his speeches and comments throughout the story. Tessie Hutchinson also gets a lot of attention, of course. What is ironic about her being the chosen victim? Does her last name have any significance for you? If not, look up *Hutchinson* in a good encyclopedia.

Writing

The key to a successful essay is a good ***thesis***—the *claim* (or *premise* or *hypothesis* or *recommendation*) that you will argue in your interpretation. Before you get too far in your writing, try to state your thesis in a single sentence.

Producing a Workable Thesis

A useful thesis should narrow the topic to an idea you can cover within your word limit. It should indicate the direction of your thinking—what you intend to say about that idea. Be sure to state your thesis in a complete sentence that indicates how you will successfully argue your claim. The following exercise provides examples.

Exercise: Thesis Statements

The numbered thesis statements lack a clear claim. Figure out how each one can be revised to include an argument for an interpretation of the story; then write an improved version. Here is an example of the kind of revisions we hope you will produce.

No claim   Shirley Jackson's "The Lottery" contains a number of significant symbols.

Improved   In "The Lottery" Shirley Jackson uses simple objects—a box, some stones, some slips of paper—to symbolize the narrow-mindedness and brutality that result from superstitious thinking.

1. Shirley Jackson's "The Lottery" is a compelling story about scapegoats.
2. The ritual of the lottery itself serves as a symbol in Shirley Jackson's story.
3. The setting of Shirley Jackson's "The Lottery" is an important element in contributing to the effectiveness of the story.
4. The characters function symbolically in Shirley Jackson's "The Lottery."
5. Shirley Jackson's "The Lottery" reveals a great deal about society and human nature.

Ideas for Writing

Ideas for Reflective Writing

1. What is Shirley Jackson saying about traditional rituals in "The Lottery"? Think of some ritual in our present society that you think ought to be dropped—or at least reconsidered and modified—and write an essay arguing your viewpoint. Consider, for example, proms, weddings, Christmas gift exchanges, dating conventions, beauty pageants, boxing matches, funeral services, graduation ceremonies, or fraternity/sorority pledging.

2. Many readers have remarked on the hypnotic power and emotional impact of this story. Did you experience a similar reaction? Do you think the author manipulated your feelings in any way?

Ideas for Critical Writing

1. Look up the word *scapegoat* in a desk-sized or online dictionary; then look at the entry in the print or online version of *Encyclopaedia Britannica*, which will give you some historical examples of the use of scapegoats. Formulate a claim that relates the symbolism of "The Lottery" to the practice of scapegoating.

2. Write an essay focusing on the symbolism of the characters in "The Lottery," especially Tessie Hutchinson, Old Man Warner, Bill Hutchinson, Mr. Graves, and Mr. Summers. Or consider the role of the children in the story. What do they symbolize? Conclude your argument by relating your observations to the story's theme.

3. CRITICAL APPROACHES: Review the reader response approach to literary interpretation (pages 898–99). Write an essay arguing that the symbolism in "The Lottery" can be interpreted in several different ways. Before you begin, you might ask several people to read the story and tell you what the symbols mean to them. Also read the student paper on "The Lottery" starting on page 138 as you gather material for your essay.

Ideas for Researched Writing

1. When "The Lottery" first appeared in the *New Yorker* on June 28, 1948, it was greeted with great consternation. So many subscribers wrote in seeking enlightenment or expressing outrage that Jackson responded to the deluge of mail with an essay entitled "Biography of a Story." Find out more about the initial reactions to "The Lottery," and read Jackson's response. Then write an essay arguing why you think the story generated such anger and was so widely misinterpreted.

2. Do some research on scapegoats. Write an essay claiming that scapegoats play a useful role in society, using examples from history, current events, novels, films, and your own experience. Or, if you prefer, argue the opposite—that scapegoating is so cruel and senseless that it must be condemned and eliminated.

MultiModal Project

Prepare and perform a *group interpretation* of "The Lottery." Group interpretation is an activity that allows readers to interpret and perform a piece of literature without memorizing lines or using costumes, makeup, props, and scenery. The presentation usually involves a narrator and a chorus or ensemble who supply the exposition and transitions from the story. Readers who play the parts of individual characters are usually part of the chorus. You may have to cut some of the text, but do not add or rewrite anything. You can also use background music to enhance the presentation. Look for examples of group interpretation performances on YouTube.

Rewriting

As you revise your first draft, try to improve it in every way possible. Our advice at this point involves ideas for improving your introduction.

Sharpening the Introduction

Look at your introductory paragraph. Does it give your readers a clear idea of the topic and purpose? Will it arouse curiosity and interest, as well as lead into your subject?

One strategy for catching the attention of your readers involves using a pertinent quotation.

> "The less there is to justify a traditional custom," wrote Mark Twain, "the harder it is to get rid of it." This comment accurately describes the situation that Shirley Jackson presents in "The Lottery." Her story illustrates how ignorance and superstition become instilled in human society and lead to unnecessary violence.

Another relevant quotation for this introduction might be Gathorne Cranbrook's observation that "The tradition of preserving traditions became a tradition." Useful quotations like these are available in library and online sources such as *Bartlett's Familiar Quotations*.

You can also take an arresting or tantalizing quotation from the story itself. Tessie Hutchinson's final scream, "It isn't fair, it isn't right," or Old Man Warner's "There's *always* been a lottery" might serve as an effective opening for an essay on this story.

Another strategy is to pose a startling question, like this:

> Why would the people in a quiet, peaceful village publicly murder one of their neighbors every summer? This is the shocking question that Shirley Jackson forces us to consider in her symbolic story "The Lottery."

Or you can combine some suspense with a *brief* overview of the story.

> The weather is sunny and clear. The residents of a peaceful village have gathered for an important annual event. They smile and chat with one another, while the children scurry about in play. Then someone brings out a black box, and the ordinary people of this ordinary town begin the process of choosing which one of their neighbors they are going to stone to death this summer. This shocking turn of events is the premise for Shirley Jackson's story about the fear and violence that lie beneath the placid surface of human societies. The story is called "The Lottery."

Another way to introduce a critical essay is to use interesting details about the author or the story's background that relate to the focus of your essay.

> In June 1948 the *New Yorker* magazine published "The Lottery," a story by Shirley Jackson. Within days the magazine began to receive a flood of telephone calls and letters, more than for any other piece of fiction it had ever published. Almost all of those who wrote were outraged or bewildered—sometimes both. Why did this story prompt such reactions? Why does it still shock readers? The answer may lie in the story's strong symbolic representation of the pointless violence and casual inhumanity that exist in all our lives.

Whatever approach you choose, keep the reader in mind. Think about reading an essay yourself. What do you expect from the introduction? Remember that the reader forms an important first impression from your opening paragraph.

Sample Student Paper on Symbolism: Second and Final Drafts

On the following left-hand pages appears the uncorrected second draft of an essay written by Todd Hageman, a student at Eastern Illinois University. On the right-hand pages you will see Todd's finished version. The questions in the margins of the final version ask you to consider the changes Todd made when he revised the paper.

Sample Student Paper: Second Draft

Todd Hageman

English 102

March 2, 2005

Symbollism in The Lottery

Shirley Jackson's "The Lottery" uses subtle symbollism along with inconngruities to exemplify the loss of significance of some rituals & traditions, and supersitions and flaws of human nature. The first incongruity used is the day the story takes place, June 27th. Jackson paints a picture of a nice, sunny summer day in a small "Anytown, USA." While Jackson paints this picture, though, the reader feels an uneasy mood and senses something is going to happen. Jackson does this by using the words "hesitant" and "reluctant" to describe the crowd while they "smile at jokes instead of laugh" (78).

The next, and one of the biggest symbols used in the story, is the box—the black box to be more exact. The box is mentioned repeatedly to bring significance to it, although the reader isn't sure why until toward the end of the story. As the lottery symbolizes tradition, the box symbolizes the lottery.

Mr. Summers, the lottery official, tells about getting a new box every year, but the talk seems to "fade off." The box was described as "faded," "splintered," and "grew shabbyier each year" (79).

Sample Student Paper: Final Draft

Todd Hageman

Professor Funk

English 102

9 March 2005

> **Comment**
> Why did Todd make the changes that he did in this opening sentence?

Symbolism in "The Lottery"

In "The Lottery" Shirley Jackson uses subtle symbolism to exemplify the emptiness of some rituals and traditions, as well as to illustrate several flaws of human nature. She begins with an incongruity in the setting on the day the story takes place, June 27. Jackson paints a picture of a sunny summer day in a small "Anytown, USA." While Jackson introduces this pleasant setting, though, the reader feels uneasy and senses that something bad is going to happen. Jackson creates this tension by using the words "hesitant" and "reluctant" to describe the crowd and by mentioning that they "smiled rather than laughed" at jokes (78).

> **Comment**
> Why did Todd delete the second part of his thesis statement (regarding "incongruities")?

> **Comment**
> Why did he change "Jackson does this..." to "Jackson creates this tension ..."?

> **Comment**
> Why did he change the quotation?

The controlling symbol in the story is the box—the black box suggestive of death. The box is mentioned repeatedly to increase its significance, although the reader is not sure why the author stresses its importance until toward the end of the story. As the lottery symbolizes empty tradition, the box symbolizes the lottery itself.

> **Comment**
> How did he improve the opening sentence of this paragraph?

Mr. Summers, the lottery official, speaks about getting a new box every year, but his talk seems to "fade off." The box is described as "faded," "splintered," and growing "shabbier

> **Comment**
> Why did Todd change this quotation from "grew shabbier each year"?

Second Draft

Hageman 2

The condition of the box symbolize the tradition of the lottery, and the need for a new box symbolizes the need for a new tradition.

There is a need for a new tradition because the lottery itself had lost its significance. Parts of the original lottery ritual had been allowed to lapse, and other parts, such as the salute of the official had "changed with the times" (79). The lottery had lapsed and changed so much from the original lottery that the people really didn't know why they were going through it any more. Probably the only reason they were going through it was the intellectual argument used by Old Man Warner, who said, "There's always been a lottery" (81). When Mr. Warner is informed that some places have stopped the lottery, he comes back with such wit as "Nothing but trouble in that," and "pack of young fools." (81). The latter idea expressed brings out the idea that all change is bad and the young are the ones who make changes.

It is generally aknowledged that the preceeding statement is false, leaving Mr. Warner on thin ice from which to argue. I think the author shows the uselessness of the lottery through Mr. Warner's ignorance.

Human nature is shown very clearliy through Tessie in the story. Tessie shows up late at the lottery very lackadaisical and in a joking mood before she was picked. She even gave her husband an extra

Final Draft

each year" (79). The worn-out condition of the box symbolizes the tradition of the lottery, while the need for a new box symbolizes the need for a new tradition, but the townspeople fail to see the need for change.

> **Comment**
> Why did Todd add this last comment?

There is a need for a new tradition because the lottery itself has lost its significance. Parts of the original lottery ritual have been allowed to lapse, and other parts, such as the salute of the official, have "changed with time" (79). The lottery has lapsed and changed so much from the original that the people really do not know why they are going through it anymore. Probably the only reason they continue is solemnly stated by Old Man Warner: "There's *always* been a lottery" (81). When Mr. Warner is informed that some places have stopped the lottery, he comes back with such meaningless arguments as "Nothing but trouble in *that*" and "Pack of young fools" (81). He simply believes that all change is bad and that the young are the ones who make changes.

> **Comment**
> Why did he eliminate the sarcasm directed at Old Man Warner?

> **Comment**
> Can you think of another way to revise the stilted, wordy language of Todd's original statement, "It is generally acknowledged that the preceding statement is false ..."?

Most people would disagree, for Mr. Warner has little evidence to support his ideas. I think the author emphasizes the uselessness of the lottery through Mr. Warner's ignorant defense of it.

The selfishness in human nature is shown clearly in the story through Tessie. She shows up late at the lottery, lackadaisically joking with her neighbors before she is picked. She even

> **Comment**
> How does the addition of the word "selfishness" in the opening sentence improve this whole paragraph?

Second Draft

nudge as he went to draw. When Tessie found out one of her family would be chosen, her mood changed rather quickly, screaming "unfair!" She even wanted her two daughters to take their chances; which she knew was wrong. Her "friends" around her showed their flaws by saying, "Be a good sport," and "We all took the same chance," and not showing a bit of pity (82). Tessie's kids also showed no pity, as they opened their blank pieces of paper, they were described as "beaming and laughing" (83) with the crowd, even though they knew it was going to be Mom or Dad picked. The final part of human nature exemplified was when Tessie drew the black dot. Every time she said, "It isn't fair," the following sentence was always her getting hit with a stone, almost as punishment for saying it. The stones seem to be saying, "You thought it was fair until you were picked; now take your medicine."

The story has one key sentence which puts the whole theme in a nutshell: "Although the villagers had forgotten the ritual and lost the original box, they still remembered to use stones"(83). Through the symbollism being used, the sentence can be translated into a theme for the story. The ritual had changed with the times and lost the original purpose, but people still remember to look out for themselves. Every time a villager threw a stone, he was probably thinking, "Better you than me."

A final thought could be about the slips of paper and what they symbolized. Jackson mentioned

Final Draft

Hageman 3

gives her husband an encouraging nudge as he goes to draw. When Tessie finds out one of her family will be chosen, her mood changes quickly, and she screams, "It wasn't fair!" (82). She even wants her married daughter and son-in-law to take their chances along with her, which hardly suggests mother love. Her "friends" around her show their lack of pity by saying, "Be a good sport" and "All of us took the same chance!" (82). Tessie's children also show no sympathy. As they open their blank pieces of paper, they are described as beaming and laughing with the crowd, even though they know one of their parents is going to be picked. Human cruelty is also exemplified after Tessie draws the black dot. Both times she cries, "It isn't fair" (83), she gets hit with a stone, almost as punishment for objecting.

> **Comment**
> How did Todd improve his argument about the ill-treatment of Tessie?

> **Comment**
> Would you have used a period in revising the comma splice, as he did? Or would you have used a semicolon? Why or why not?

The slips of paper also serve a symbolic purpose. Jackson mentions that the unused papers dropped to the ground "where the breeze caught them and lifted them off" (82). The papers could symbolize the people who have been sacrificed through the lottery. The village people make use of both the papers and the sacrificed people, then discard them as trash.

> **Comment**
> Why did Todd move his final paragraph to this position?

The story has one key sentence which captures the whole theme: "Although the villagers had forgotten the ritual and lost the original black box, they still remembered to use stones" (83).

> **Comment**
> Why did Todd replace the phrase "in a nutshell"?

Second Draft

Hageman 4

that the unused papers were dropped to the ground "where the breeze caught them and lifted them off" (82). The papers could be meant to symbolize the people who had been sacrificed through the lottery. The village people had used both the papers and the sacrificed people and had discarded them as trash.

Hageman 5

Work Cited

Shirley Jackson, "The Lottery," in *Literature and the Writing Process*, Prentice Hall, Inc.: 2005. 78–83.

Final Draft

Considering the symbolism in the story, the sentence can be translated into a theme. Although the ritual had changed with the times and lost the original purpose, people still remember to look out for themselves. Every time the villagers threw a stone, they were probably thinking, "Better you than me." Jackson dramatizes for us the harm done by ignorance which causes people to cling to outworn rituals. She also shows the selfishness and cruelty that lie just beneath the civilized surface of human behavior.

> **Comment**
> How do these last two sentences that he added improve the paper?

Work Cited

Jackson, Shirley. "The Lottery." *Literature and the Writing Process*,
    edited by Elizabeth McMahan, et al., 7th ed., Prentice Hall,
    2005, pp. 83-89.

> **Comment**
> What corrections did Todd make in his Work Cited entry?

9 Writing About Point of View

Chapter Preview

Learning about point of view in fiction will help you to understand how the author has shaped what you know and how you feel about the events in a story. When the point of view is distinctive or unusual, you may want to focus your written analysis on the narrator or on the significance of the writer's choice of narrative focus. By the end of this chapter, you will be able to

- Define *narrator* and *point of view.*
- Describe these primary points of view: *omniscient, limited omniscient, first-person, unreliable,* and *objective.*
- Explain how point of view affects other elements of fiction, especially *theme.*
- Name several ways to improve a paper's *conclusion.*

What Is Point of View?

In identifying **point of view**, you decide who tells the story—that is, whose thoughts and feelings the reader has access to. The storyteller, called the **narrator**, is a creation of the author and should not be confused with the author. In the following passage from "Everyday Use," Alice Walker takes the reader into the private world of her narrator's fantasy:

> Sometimes I dream a dream in which Dee and I are suddenly brought together on a TV program of this sort. Out of a dark and soft-seated limousine I am ushered into a bright room filled with many people.

In John Updike's story "A & P," the narrator's distinctive voice is established in the opening lines:

> In walks these three girls in nothing but bathing suits. I'm in the third checkout slot, with my back to the door, so I don't see them until they're over by the bread.

But in the opening of "The Lottery," we are not conscious of a narrator at all:

> The morning of June 27th was clear and sunny, with the fresh warmth of a full-summer day; the flowers were blossoming profusely and the grass was richly green.

Describing Point of View

There are several systems for labeling the point of view in a work of literature. They classify the stance and the identity of the person who reports the action—that is, the person whose eyes and mind become ours as we read the story.

In actuality, a great many points of view are possible, and you may find some overlapping among the categories we provide here, but the following should allow you to describe all of the works included in this text.

- *Omniscient:* An all-knowing narrator, who is not a character in the story or involved in the action, freely relates many or all of the character's thoughts, feelings, and actions. In this example from Sherwood Anderson's "Hands," the omniscient narrator gives us considerable information about the main character's life and personality in a single sentence:

    > Wing Biddlebaum, forever frightened and beset by a ghostly band of doubts, did not think of himself as in any way a part of the life of the town where he had lived for twenty years.

- *Limited omniscience:* The narration is limited to the thoughts and observations of a single character. In detective fiction, for instance, we often see the plot unfold strictly from the main character's (the detective's) point of view. Sometimes our perceptions are limited to those of a minor character. In the Sherlock Holmes stories, for instance, the events are reported from the point of view of Dr. Watson, the great detective's sidekick, whose admiration and awe for Holmes's skills become ours. Raymond Carver's "What We Talk About When We Talk About Love" is another example of limited omniscience in which a minor character narrates the entire story.

- *First-Person:* The narrator recounts events in which he or she has been involved as a major participant. The narrator, identified as "I" in the story, speaks directly to us. First-person narrators often present only their side of the story. Sammy, the first-person narrator in John Updike's "A & P," gives an obviously subjective account of why he quit his job. The narrator of Tillie Olsen's "I Stand Here Ironing" appears to tell her story quite honestly and with little self-deception:

    > We were poor and could not afford for her the soil of easy growth. I was a young mother, I was a distracted mother. There were other children pushing, demanding.

- *Unreliable:* If the storyteller misrepresents the facts, the narrator is considered unreliable. An emotionally disturbed person like the murderous narrator of "The Cask of Amontillado," for instance, is not interested in giving a truthful account of his motives and actions. Poe intensifies the shock and horror of the story by letting us see into the inner workings of a sinister mind.

  Writers often use an unreliable narrator to emphasize the subjectivity of experience or to reveal the shallowness or self-absorption of the main character. Sylvia, the narrator in Toni Cade Bambara's "The Lesson," is reliable in candidly reporting her strong thoughts and words, but she is not reliable in revealing those things she cannot yet understand, a divided perspective that involves the reader in figuring out the story's lessons along with the resistant Sylvia.

- *Objective:* Here the narrator disappears and the story seems to tell itself through action and dialogue. An objective narrative does not get into the minds of the characters; it gives us only what could be recorded by a camera and a microphone.

  In reading this kind of story, we have to make judgments and draw conclusions on our own. The objective narrator may edit the tape and direct the camera, but we have to figure out why the characters behave as they do. Shirley Jackson's "The Lottery" illustrates an objective point of view: the narrator presents the events without comment; we have to determine why the actions occur and what they mean.

  Sometimes a story with an objective point of view is easily identified because it consists largely of conversation, like Hemingway's "Hills Like White Elephants." In this story no author comments appear, only a few actions and brief scenic details. Our understanding of the characters is based entirely on the conclusions we are able to infer from reading their conversation. Because of its similarity to the script of a play, this type of story can also be called a *dramatic* point of view.

Looking at Point of View

As you read Alice Walker's "Everyday Use," think about the implications of our getting only Mama's perception of the events surrounding her daughter Dee's visit.

Alice Walker   1944–

Alice Walker was born in Eatonton, Georgia, the daughter of poor sharecroppers. When playing with her brothers at age eight, she was blinded in her right eye by a BB gun pellet. After attending Spellman and Sarah Lawrence colleges, she became a civil rights activist. In 1965, she married Mel Leventhal, a Jewish civil rights lawyer; they became the first legally married interracial couple in Mississippi. She later coined the term "womanist," meaning a feminist of color. Her novel *The Color Purple* won the 1983 Pulitzer Prize and was made into a popular film.

Everyday Use

For Your Grandmama

I will wait for her in the yard that Maggie and I made so clean and wavy yesterday afternoon. A yard like this is more comfortable than most people know. It is not just a yard. It is like an extended living room. When the hard clay is swept clean as a floor and the fine sand around the edges lined with tiny, irregular grooves, anyone can come and sit and look up into the elm tree and wait for the breezes that never come inside the house.

Maggie will be nervous until after her sister goes: she will stand hopelessly in corners, homely and ashamed of the burn scars down her arms and legs, eying her sister with a mixture of envy and awe. She thinks her sister has held life always in the palm of one hand, that "no" is a word the world never learned to say to her.

You've no doubt seen those TV shows where the child who has "made it" is confronted, as a surprise, by her own mother and father, tottering in weakly from backstage. (A pleasant surprise, of course: What would they do if parent and child came on the show only to curse out and insult each other?) On TV mother and child embrace and smile into each other's faces. Sometimes the mother and father weep, the child wraps them in her arms and leans across the table to tell how she would not have made it without their help. I have seen these programs.

Sometimes I dream a dream in which Dee and I are suddenly brought together on a TV program of this sort. Out of a dark and soft-seated limousine I am ushered into a bright room filled with many people. There I meet a smiling, gray, sporty man like Johnny Carson who shakes my hand and tells me what a fine girl I have. Then we are on the stage and Dee is embracing me with tears in her eyes. She pins on my dress a large orchid, even though she has told me once that she thinks orchids are tacky flowers.

In real life I am a large, big-boned woman with rough, man-working hands. 5 In the winter I wear flannel nightgowns to bed and overalls during the day. I can kill and clean a hog as mercilessly as a man. My fat keeps me hot in zero weather. I can work outside all day, breaking ice to get water for washing; I can eat pork liver cooked over the open fire minutes after it comes steaming from the hog. One winter I knocked a bull calf straight in the brain between the eyes with a sledge hammer and had the meat hung up to chill before nightfall. But of course all this does not show on television. I am the way my daughter would want me to be: a hundred pounds lighter, my skin like an uncooked barley pancake. My hair glistens in the hot bright lights. Johnny Carson has much to do to keep up with my quick and witty tongue.

But that is a mistake. I know even before I wake up. Who ever knew a Johnson with a quick tongue? Who can even imagine me looking a strange white man in the eye? It seems to me I have talked to them always with one foot raised in flight, with my head turned in whichever way is farthest from them. Dee, though. She would always look anyone in the eye. Hesitation was no part of her nature.

"How do I look, Mama?" Maggie says, showing just enough of her thin body enveloped in pink skirt and red blouse for me to know she's there, almost hidden by the door.

"Come out into the yard," I say.

Have you ever seen a lame animal, perhaps a dog run over by some careless person rich enough to own a car, sidle up to someone who is ignorant enough to be kind to him? That is the way my Maggie walks. She has been like this, chin on chest, eyes on ground, feet in shuffle, ever since the fire that burned the other house to the ground.

Dee is lighter than Maggie, with nicer hair and a fuller figure. She's a woman   10
now, though sometimes I forget. How long ago was it that the other house burned? Ten, twelve years? Sometimes I can still hear the flames and feel Maggie's arms sticking to me, her hair smoking and her dress falling off her in little black papery flakes. Her eyes seemed stretched open, blazed open by the flames reflected in them. And Dee. I see her standing off under the sweet gum tree she used to dig gum out of; a look of concentration on her face as she watched the last dingy gray board of the house fall in toward the red-hot brick chimney. Why don't you do a dance around the ashes? I'd wanted to ask her. She had hated the house that much.

I used to think she hated Maggie, too. But that was before we raised the money, the church and me, to send her to Augusta to school. She used to read to us without pity; forcing words, lies, other folks' habits, whole lives upon us two, sitting trapped and ignorant underneath her voice. She washed us in a river of make-believe, burned us with a lot of knowledge we didn't necessarily need to know. Pressed us to her with the serious way she read, to shove us away at just the moment, like dimwits, we seemed about to understand.

A quilt in the traditional Lone Star pattern. [*Star of LeMoyne quilt* (1850–1875), Maria Washington Layfield Miller. Patchwork, cotton, 92 in × 97 in. (29.266). The Newark Museum, Newark, New Jersey/Art Resource, NY.]

Dee wanted nice things. A yellow organdy dress to wear to her graduation from high school; black pumps to match a green suit she'd made from an old suit somebody gave me. She was determined to stare down any disaster in her efforts. Her eyelids would not flicker for minutes at a time. Often I fought off the temptation to shake her. At sixteen she had a style of her own: and knew what style was.

I never had an education myself. After second grade the school was closed down. Don't ask me why: in 1927 colored asked fewer questions than they do now. Sometimes Maggie reads to me. She stumbles along good-naturedly but can't see well. She knows she is not bright. Like good looks and money, quickness passed her by. She will marry John Thomas (who has mossy teeth in an earnest face) and then I'll be free to sit here and I guess just sing church songs to myself. Although I never was a good singer. Never could carry a tune. I was always better at a man's job. I used to love to milk till I was hooked in the side in '49. Cows are soothing and slow and don't bother you, unless you try to milk them the wrong way.

I have deliberately turned my back on the house. It is three rooms, just like the one that burned, except the roof is tin; they don't make shingle roofs any more. There are no real windows, just some holes cut in the sides, like the portholes in a ship, but not round and not square, with rawhide holding the shutters up on the outside. This house is in a pasture, too, like the other one. No doubt when Dee sees it she will want to tear it down. She wrote me once that no matter where we "choose" to live, she will manage to come see us. But she will never bring her friends. Maggie and I thought about this and Maggie asked me, "Mama, when did Dee ever *have* any friends?"

She had a few. Furtive boys in pink shirts hanging about on washday after 15
school. Nervous girls who never laughed. Impressed with her they worshiped the well-turned phrase, the cute shape, the scalding humor that erupted like bubbles in lye. She read to them.

When she was courting Jimmy T she didn't have much time to pay to us, but turned all her faultfinding power on him. He *flew* to marry a cheap city girl from a family of ignorant flashy people. She hardly had time to recompose herself.

When she comes I will meet—but there they are!
Maggie attempts to make a dash for the house, in her shuffling way, but I stay her with my hand. "Come back here," I say. And she stops and tries to dig a well in the sand with her toe.

It is hard to see them clearly through the strong sun. But even the first glimpse of leg out of the car tells me it is Dee. Her feet were always neat-looking, as if God himself had shaped them with a certain style. From the other side of the car comes a short, stocky man. Hair is all over his head a foot long and hanging from his chin like a kinky mule tail. I hear Maggie suck in her breath. "Uhnnnh," is what it sounds like. Like when you see the wriggling end of a snake just in front of your foot on the road. "Uhnnnh."

Dee next. A dress down to the ground, in this hot weather. A dress so loud it 20
hurts my eyes. There are yellows and oranges enough to throw back the light of the sun. I feel my whole face warming from the heat waves it throws out. Earrings gold, too, and hanging down to her shoulders. Bracelets dangling and making noises when she moves her arm up to shake the folds of the dress out of

her armpits. The dress is loose and flows, and as she walks closer, I like it. I hear Maggie go "Uhnnnh" again. It is her sister's hair. It stands straight up like the wool on a sheep. It is black as night and around the edges are two long pigtails that rope about like small lizards disappearing behind her ears.

"Wa-su-zo-Tean-o!" she says, coming on in that gliding way the dress makes her move. The short stocky fellow with the hair to his navel is all grinning and he follows up with "Asalamalakim, my mother and sister!" He moves to hug Maggie but she falls back, right up against the back of my chair. I feel her trembling there and when I look up I see the perspiration falling off her chin.

"Don't get up," says Dee. Since I am stout it takes something of a push. You can see me trying to move a second or two before I make it. She turns, showing white heels through her sandals, and goes back to the car. Out she peeks next with a Polaroid. She stoops down quickly and lines up picture after picture of me sitting there in front of the house with Maggie cowering behind me. She never takes a shot without making sure the house is included. When a cow comes nibbling around the edge of the yard she snaps it and me and Maggie *and* the house. Then she puts the Polaroid in the back seat of the car, and comes up and kisses me on the forehead.

Meanwhile Asalamalakim is going through motions with Maggie's hand. Maggie's hand is as limp as a fish, and probably as cold, despite the sweat, and she keeps trying to pull it back. It looks like Asalamalakim wants to shake hands but wants to do it fancy. Or maybe he don't know how people shake hands. Anyhow, he soon gives up on Maggie.

"Well," I say. "Dee."

"No, Mama," she says. "Not 'Dee,' Wangero Leewanika Kemanjo!"   25

"What happened to 'Dee'?" I wanted to know.

"She's dead," Wangero said. "I couldn't bear it any longer, being named after the people who oppress me."

"You know as well as me you was named after your aunt Dicie," I said. Dicie is my sister. She named Dee. We called her "Big Dee" after Dee was born.

"But who was *she* named after?" asked Wangero.

"I guess after Grandma Dee," I said.   30

"And who was she named after?" asked Wangero.

"Her mother," I said, and saw Wangero was getting tired. "That's about as far back as I can trace it," I said. Though, in fact, I probably could have carried it back beyond the Civil War through the branches.

"Well," said Asalamalakim, "there you are."

"Uhnnnh," I heard Maggie say.

"There I was not," I said, "before 'Dicie' cropped up in our family, so why   35
should I try to trace it that far back?"

He just stood there grinning, looking down on me like somebody inspecting a Model A car. Every once in a while he and Wangero sent eye signals over my head.

"How do you pronounce this name?" I asked.

"You don't have to call me by it if you don't want to," said Wangero.

"Why shouldn't I?" I asked. "If that's what you want us to call you, we'll call you."

"I know it might sound awkward at first," said Wangero.   40

"I'll get used to it," I said. "Ream it out again."

Well, soon we got the name out of the way. Asalamalakim had a name twice as long and three times as hard. After I tripped over it two or three times he told me to just call him Hakim-a-barber. I wanted to ask him was he a barber, but I didn't really think he was, so I didn't ask.

"You must belong to those beef-cattle peoples down the road," I said. They said "Asalamalakim" when they met you, too, but they didn't shake hands. Always too busy: feeding the cattle, fixing the fences, putting up salt-lick shelters, throwing down hay. When the white folks poisoned some of the herd the men stayed up all night with rifles in their hands. I walked a mile and a half just to see the sight.

Hakim-a-barber said, "I accept some of their doctrines, but farming and raising cattle is not my style." (They didn't tell me, and I didn't ask, whether Wangero (Dee) had really gone and married him.)

We sat down to eat and right away he said he didn't eat collards and pork   45
was unclean. Wangero, though, went on through the chitlins and corn bread, the greens and everything else. She talked a blue streak over the sweet potatoes. Everything delighted her. Even the fact that we still used the benches her daddy made for the table when we couldn't afford to buy chairs.

"Oh, Mama!" she cried. Then turned to Hakim-a-barber. "I never knew how lovely these benches are. You can feel the rump prints," she said, running her hands underneath her and along the bench. Then she gave a sigh and her hand closed over Grandma Dee's butter dish. "That's it!" she said. "I knew there was something I wanted to ask you if I could have." She jumped up from the table and went over in the corner where the churn stood, the milk in it clabber by now. She looked at the churn and looked at it.

"This churn top is what I need," she said. "Didn't Uncle Buddy whittle it out of a tree you all used to have?"

"Yes," I said.

"Uh huh," she said happily. "And I want the dasher, too."

"Uncle Buddy whittle that, too?" asked the barber.   50

Dee (Wangero) looked up at me.

"Aunt Dee's first husband whittled the dash," said Maggie so low you almost couldn't hear her. "His name was Henry, but they called him Stash."

"Maggie's brain is like an elephant's," Wangero said, laughing. "I can use the churn top as a centerpiece for the alcove table," she said, sliding a plate over the churn, "and I'll think of something artistic to do with the dasher."

When she finished wrapping the dasher the handle stuck out. I took it for a moment in my hands. You didn't even have to look close to see where hands pushing the dasher up and down to make butter had left a kind of sink in the wood. In fact, there were a lot of small sinks; you could see where thumbs and fingers had sunk into the wood. It was beautiful light yellow wood, from a tree that grew in the yard where Big Dee and Stash had lived.

After dinner Dee (Wangero) went to the trunk at the foot of my bed and   55
started rifling through it. Maggie hung back in the kitchen over the dishpan. Out came Wangero with two quilts. They had been pieced by Grandma Dee and then Big Dee and me had hung them on the quilt frames on the front porch and quilted them. One was in the Lone Star pattern. The other was Walk Around the Mountain. In both of them were scraps of dresses Grandma Dee had worn fifty and more years ago. Bits and pieces of Grandpa Jarrell's Paisley shirts. And one teeny faded blue piece, about the size of a penny matchbox, that was from Great Grandpa Ezra's uniform that he wore in the Civil War.

"Mama," Wangero said sweet as a bird. "Can I have these old quilts?"

I heard something fall in the kitchen, and a minute later the kitchen door slammed.

"Why don't you take one or two of the others?" I asked. "These old things was just done by me and Big Dee from some tops your grandma pieced before she died."

"No," said Wangero. "I don't want those. They are stitched around the borders by machine."

"That'll make them last better," I said.   60

"That's not the point," said Wangero. "These are all pieces of dresses Grandma used to wear. She did all this stitching by hand. Imagine!" She held the quilts securely in her arms, stroking them.

"Some of the pieces, like those lavender ones, come from old clothes her mother handed down to her," I said, moving up to touch the quilts. Dee (Wangero) moved back just enough so that I couldn't reach the quilts. They already belonged to her.

"Imagine!" she breathed again, clutching them closely to her bosom.

"The truth is," I said, "I promised to give them quilts to Maggie, for when she marries John Thomas."

She gasped like a bee had stung her.   65

"Maggie can't appreciate these quilts!" she said. "She'd probably be backward enough to put them to everyday use."

"I reckon she would," I said. "God knows I been saving 'em for long enough with nobody using 'em. I hope she will!" I didn't want to bring up how I had offered Dee (Wangero) a quilt when she went away to college. Then she had told me they were old-fashioned, out of style.

"But they're *priceless*!" she was saying now, furiously; for she has a temper. "Maggie would put them on the bed and in five years they'd be in rags. Less than that!"

"She can always make some more," I said. "Maggie knows how to quilt."

Dee (Wangero) looked at me with hatred. "You just will not understand. The   70 point is these quilts, *these* quilts!"

"Well," I said, stumped. "What would *you* do with them?"

"Hang them," she said. As if that was the only thing you *could* do with quilts.

Maggie by now was standing in the door. I could almost hear the sound her feet made as they scraped over each other.

"She can have them, Mama," she said, like somebody used to never winning anything, or having anything reserved for her. "I can 'member Grandma Dee without the quilts."

I looked at her hard. She had filled her bottom lip with checkerberry snuff   75 and it gave her face a kind of dopey, hangdog look. It was Grandma Dee and Big Dee who taught her how to quilt herself. She stood there with her scarred hands hidden in the folds of her skirt. She looked at her sister with something like fear but she wasn't mad at her. This was Maggie's portion. This was the way she knew God to work.

When I looked at her like that something hit me in the top of my head and ran down to the soles of my feet. Just like when I'm in church and the spirit of God touches me and I get happy and shout. I did something I never had done before: hugged Maggie to me, then dragged her on into the room, snatched the quilts out of Miss Wangero's hands and dumped them into Maggie's lap. Maggie just sat there on my bed with her mouth open.

"Take one or two of the others," I said to Dee.

But she turned without a word and went out to Hakim-a-barber.

"You just don't understand," she said, as Maggie and I came out to the car.

"What don't I understand?" I wanted to know.   80

"Your heritage," she said. And then she turned to Maggie, kissed her, and said, "You ought to try to make something of yourself, too, Maggie. It's really a new day for us. But from the way you and Mama still live you'd never know it."

She put on some sunglasses that hid everything above the tip of her nose and her chin.

Maggie smiled; maybe at the sunglasses. But a real smile, not scared. After we watched the car dust settle I asked Maggie to bring me a dip of snuff. And then the two of us sat there just enjoying, until it was time to go in the house and go to bed.

(1973)

The Writing Process

Prewriting

To help you examine the point of view of "Everyday Use" and see how it affects other elements of the story, write out answers to the following questions.

Exercise: Analyzing Point of View

1. Who is telling this story? What kind of person is she? Describe her character traits, her strengths and weaknesses, and explain how you feel about her. Is it significant that she is not given a first name but is called only Mama throughout?

2. Why do you think Walker chose Mama as the narrator instead of Maggie or Dee/Wangero? How would the story be different if told from the point of view of one of the daughters?

3. Describe the character traits of Maggie and Dee/Wangero. How do you respond to them? Do you admire them, feel sorry for them, dislike them? Explain why.

4. Why does Mama include the account of the fire in her narration? Do we know how the house caught fire? Is it important to know? Does this past tragedy shed light on the characters' actions in the story?

5. What is the significance of the African names, dress, and hair styles? Why do you think Asalamalakim appears in the story?

6. Why does Dee/Wangero want the quilts? Why does Mama give them to Maggie?

7. What is the major conflict in the story? Who best understands the family's heritage? How do you know this?

8. Imagine the conversation that Maggie and Mama have after Dee/Wangero has left. Write a page or two of dialogue in which Maggie and Mama talk to each other about Dee.

Writing

Before you decide to focus your paper on point of view, you need to determine its importance in the story. An analysis of point of view may not always merit a full-length paper. For instance, an omniscient point of view, while a conventional and often effective choice for narrating a story, may not prove a fruitful subject for an essay. But an analysis of point of view will sometimes, as in "Everyday Use," reveal rich insights into the meaning of the story.

Relating Point of View to Theme

After analyzing a story from the vantage of point of view, you need to think about how all your discoveries relate to its theme—its main point, its impact, its insight into human behavior. Your essay will explain why this particular point of view is effective for this particular story. You might argue, for example, that the neutral viewpoint in "The Lottery" supports the claim that the story depicts the ordinariness of evil. By contrast, the shift in tone by the omniscient narrator of "The Ones Who Walk Away from Omelas" sets up the story's ironic theme that creating a utopia is not humanly possible.

Ideas for Writing

Ideas for Reflective Writing

1. Write a description of Mama from the point of view of either Maggie or Dee/Wangero.

2. Have you ever known someone like Mama? Write a character sketch of this person, pointing out similarities to Mama.

3. In "Everyday Use," objects take on more importance than their simple functions—the quilts and the churn, for example. Are there any items like this in your life? Which of your belongings do you think your grandchildren will value? Why? Write about how objects acquire special significance.

4. Have you ever changed your name? Have you asked people to call you by a new name—for example, changing from Billy to Bill? Do you know anyone who has? Why do people change their names? Write an essay about what our names mean to us.

Ideas for Critical Writing

Here are some possible major claims that focus on point of view. Choose one of these claims, revise one, or make up your own to develop an interpretation of "Everyday Use."

1. Each memory recorded in "Everyday Use" serves to strengthen the foil relationship between Dee/Wangero and the narrator, a contrast that flares into a clash between two notions of heritage.

2. Alice Walker uses explanatory flashbacks to Dee/Wangero's early life but excludes any depiction of her current life (even such details as whether she is married or where she lives); this character appears from nowhere, ironically suggesting her own lack of heritage or cultural tradition, a lack she is quick to perceive in others.

3. By telling the story through the eyes of Mama, Walker subtly encourages us to agree with Mama's side of the underlying argument about cultural heritage.

4. Because we as readers have access to Mama's unspoken thoughts about her daughters and Hakim-a-barber, we realize that, despite the seriousness of the story, she is a great comic narrator.

Ideas for Researched Writing

1. Look up and study the topic "black nationalism" in a reference work, such as *The African-American Encyclopedia* or *Encyclopedia of African-American Culture* (the latter is available online). Then write an essay explaining how you think this social movement from the 1960s has influenced the appearance, behavior, and attitudes of Dee/Wangero.

2. "Everyday Use" is a story about many different themes and issues. Research the various critical readings of this story, and prepare a report for your classmates that summarizes and evaluates the interpretations you found.

MultiModal Project

Select a character from "Everyday Use," and create a print advertisement or radio commercial in which this character endorses a product or service. Draw or describe the ad, and write some dialogue for the character to speak. Explain why you picked this particular product or service for the character to endorse. (Your instructor may ask you to work in pairs or small groups on this project.)

Rewriting

When you revise, do not neglect your conclusion just because it comes last. It has a psychologically important place in your paper. Ask yourself, "Does my closing restate the main idea in an obvious, repetitive way? Will readers feel let down, dropped off, cut short?" If so, consider these ways to make your ending more lively.

Techniques for Sharpening the Conclusion

1. *Description.* In concluding a discussion of the conflicts between Mama and her distasteful daughter, you might write the following:

   Thus Dee/Wangero, with her new name, her African dress, her dangling bracelets, and her braided hair, rejects the rural simplicity of her childhood culture. Sliding on her fashionable sunglasses, she leaves Mama and Maggie sitting on their porch "just enjoying" their dip of snuff, the pleasant evening, and the comfortable everydayness of their lives.

2. *A quotation from the story.* Remember that a quotation must be integrated into your own sentence, perhaps like this:

   When Maggie says, quietly, "I can 'member Grandma Dee without the quilts," we see that heritage can have a deeper meaning than co-opting churn tops as centerpieces and hand-stitched quilts as wall hangings.

3. *An echo from your introduction.* If you wrote in your opening of the clash between two black cultures in the story, you could conclude with this echo:

   Mama, pushed too far, finally proves herself a match for her sophisticated daughter, who ignores her own family heritage as she shows off her newly adopted African roots.

4. *A thought-provoking question, suggestion, or statement.*

   Were Mama and Maggie right in rejecting the unfamiliar African heritage that Dee/Wangero introduces?

   Perhaps society would generate fewer conflicts if people paid less attention to their individual ethnic and cultural background.

10 Writing About Setting and Atmosphere

Chapter Preview

Setting and atmosphere contribute to the effectiveness of short stories in various ways. Sometimes these elements assume enough importance to become the focus of a literary analysis. By the end of this chapter, you will be able to

- Define *setting, atmosphere,* and *mood.*
- Evaluate the effects of setting on a story's meaning.
- List ways to establish and check the organization of an essay.
- Describe and use *balanced sentences.*

What Are Setting and Atmosphere?

You know, of course, the meaning of *setting* in reference to a work of literature: the setting includes the location and time of the action in a story, novel, play, or poem. Sometimes setting conveys an *atmosphere*—the emotional effect of the setting and events—that contributes to the impact or to the meaning of the work. Atmosphere (or *mood*) is that feeling of horror and foreboding that Edgar Allan Poe creates when he takes his characters (and his readers) from the "supreme madness of the carnival season" down into the dank, moldering, bone-filled catacombs in search of "The Cask of Amontillado." Atmosphere can also serve to increase irony, as Shirley Jackson does in "The Lottery" by conveying the deceptive feeling of carefree summer festivity just before turning her tale abruptly toward ritual murder. Usually, though, setting and atmosphere reflect the dominant tone and theme of a work.

In deciding whether to focus on setting or atmosphere in writing a literary paper, you need to ask yourself not only how much the effect of the work would be changed if these elements were different, but also how much you have to say about them—especially what they contribute to the power of the narrative. For instance, the stalled freeway where Dagoberto Gilb's "Love in L.A." takes place seems the perfect setting for that story. We can scarcely imagine its being set as effectively anywhere else. Los Angeles, the home of Hollywood and all the fantasies of movieland, clearly molded the main character's imaginative life and inspired

159

the false surfaces of his identity. Sweaty, noisy traffic jams pervade this L.A. dweller's life, shape his aspirations, and stick him with plenty of downtime in which to embellish his daydreams. A freeway collision is a completely believable site for Jake to bump into his version of love. Concerning any story, if you ask yourself, "In what other surroundings and time could this story happen?" and find it difficult to imagine an answer, probably the setting is a worthwhile focus for a paper.

Looking at Setting and Atmosphere

As you read the following story by Tobias Wolff, consider how crucial setting and atmosphere are in contributing to the story's effect.

Tobias Wolff   1945–

Tobias Wolff, a Stanford University graduate, served four years as an army paratrooper, including a year in Vietnam, and now teaches creative writing at Stanford. "The disaster of television," he says, "has created a tremendous vacuum in our culture. I really regard it as a catastrophe. The monster in our house devours the imagination; it's a completely passive entertainment. And reading has been the first casualty, because reading is active, demanding." His memoir, *This Boy's Life* (1989), a painful reminiscence of growing up in his stepfather's home, was made into a popular film starring Robert De Niro and Leonardo DiCaprio.

Hunters in the Snow

Tub had been waiting for an hour in the falling snow. He paced the sidewalk to keep warm and stuck his head out over the curb whenever he saw lights approaching. One driver stopped for him but before Tub could wave the man on he saw the rifle on Tub's back and hit the gas. The tires spun on the ice.

The fall of snow thickened. Tub stood below the overhang of a building. Across the road the clouds whitened just above the rooftops, and the street lights went out. He shifted the rifle strap to his other shoulder. The whiteness seeped up the sky.

A truck slid around the corner, horn blaring, rear end sashaying. Tub moved to the sidewalk and held up his hand. The truck jumped the curb and kept coming, half on the street and half on the sidewalk. It wasn't slowing down at all. Tub stood for a moment, still holding up his hand, then jumped back. His rifle slipped off his shoulder and clattered on the ice, a sandwich fell out of his pocket. He ran for the steps of the building. Another sandwich and a package of cookies tumbled onto the new snow. He made the steps and looked back.

The truck had stopped several feet beyond where Tub had been standing. He picked up his sandwiches and his cookies and slung the rifle and went up to the driver's window. The driver was bent against the steering wheel, slapping his knees and drumming his feet on the floorboards. He looked like a cartoon of a person laughing, except that his eyes watched the man on the seat beside him.

"You ought to see yourself," the driver said. "He looks just like a beach ball with a hat on, doesn't he? Doesn't he, Frank?"

The man beside him smiled and looked off.　　　　　　　　　　　　　　　5

"You almost ran me down," Tub said. "You could've killed me."

"Come on, Tub," said the man beside the driver. "Be mellow. Kenny was just messing around." He opened the door and slid over to the middle of the seat.

Tub took the bolt out of his rifle and climbed in beside him. "I waited an hour," he said. "If you meant ten o'clock why didn't you say ten o'clock?"

"Tub, you haven't done anything but complain since we got here," said the man in the middle. "If you want to piss and moan all day you might as well go home and bitch at your kids. Take your pick." When Tub didn't say anything he turned to the driver. "Okay, Kenny, let's hit the road."

Some juvenile delinquents had heaved a brick through the windshield on the　10 driver's side, so the cold and snow tunneled right into the cab. The heater didn't work. They covered themselves with a couple of blankets Kenny had brought along and pulled down the muffs on their caps. Tub tried to keep his hands warm by rubbing them under the blanket but Frank made him stop.

They left Spokane and drove deep into the country, running along black lines of fences. The snow let up, but still there was no edge to the land where it met the sky. Nothing moved in the chalky fields. The cold bleached their faces and made the stubble stand out on their cheeks and along their upper lips. They stopped twice for coffee before they got to the woods where Kenny wanted to hunt.

Tub was for trying someplace different; two years in a row they'd been up and down this land and hadn't seen a thing. Frank didn't care one way or the other, he just wanted to get out of the goddamned truck. "Feel that," Frank said, slamming the door. He spread his feet and closed his eyes and leaned his head way back and breathed deeply. "Tune in on that energy."

"Another thing," Kenny said. "This is open land. Most of the land around here is posted."

"I'm cold," Tub said.

Frank breathed out. "Stop bitching, Tub. Get centered."　　　　　　　　　15

"I wasn't bitching."

"Centered," Kenny said. "Next thing you'll be wearing a nightgown, Frank. Selling flowers out at the airport."

"Kenny," Frank said, "you talk too much."

"Okay," Kenny said. "I won't say a word. Like I won't say anything about a certain babysitter."

"What babysitter?" Tub asked.　　　　　　　　　　　　　　　　　20

"That's between us," Frank said, looking at Kenny. "That's confidential. You keep your mouth shut."

Kenny laughed.

"You're asking for it," Frank said.

"Asking for what?"

"You'll see."　　　　　　　　　　　　　　　　　　　　　　25

"Hey," Tub said, "are we hunting or what?"

They started off across the field. Tub had trouble getting through the fences. Frank and Kenny could have helped him; they could have lifted up on the top wire and stepped on the bottom wire, but they didn't. They stood and watched him. There were a lot of fences and Tub was puffing when they reached the woods.

They hunted for over two hours and saw no deer, no tracks, no sign. Finally they stopped by the creek to eat. Kenny had several slices of pizza and a couple of candy bars; Frank had a sandwich, an apple, two carrots, and a square of chocolate; Tub ate one hard-boiled egg and a stick of celery.

"You ask me how I want to die today," Kenny said, "I'll tell you burn me at the stake." He turned to Tub. "You still on that diet?" He winked at Frank.

"What do you think? You think I like hard-boiled eggs?"   30

"All I can say is, it's the first diet I ever heard of where you gained weight from it."

"Who said I gained weight?"

"Oh, pardon me. I take it back. You're just wasting away before my very eyes. Isn't he, Frank?"

Frank had his fingers fanned out, tips against the bark of the stump where he'd laid his food. His knuckles were hairy. He wore a heavy wedding band and on his right pinky another gold ring with a flat face and an "F" in what looked like diamonds. He turned the ring this way and that. "Tub," he said, "you haven't seen your own balls in ten years."

Kenny doubled over laughing. He took off his hat and slapped his leg with it.   35

"What am I supposed to do?" Tub said. "It's my glands."

They left the woods and hunted along the creek. Frank and Kenny worked one bank and Tub worked the other, moving upstream. The snow was light but the drifts were deep and hard to move through. Wherever Tub looked the surface was smooth, undisturbed, and after a time he lost interest. He stopped looking for tracks and just tried to keep up with Frank and Kenny on the other side. A moment came when he realized he hadn't seen them in a long time. The breeze was moving from him to them; when it stilled he could sometimes hear Kenny laughing but that was all. He quickened his pace, breasting hard into the drifts, fighting away the snow with his knees and elbows. He heard his heart and felt the flush on his face but he never once stopped.

Tub caught up with Frank and Kenny at a bend of the creek. They were standing on a log that stretched from their bank to his. Ice had backed up behind the log. Frozen reeds stuck out, barely nodding when the air moved.

"See anything?" Frank asked.

Tub shook his head.   40

There wasn't much daylight left and they decided to head back toward the road. Frank and Kenny crossed the log and they started downstream, using the trail Tub had broken. Before they had gone very far Kenny stopped. "Look at that," he said, and pointed to some tracks going from the creek back into the woods. Tub's footprints crossed right over them. There on the bank, plain as day, were several mounds of deer sign. "What do you think that is, Tub?" Kenny kicked at it. "Walnuts on vanilla icing?"

"I guess I didn't notice."

Kenny looked at Frank.

"I was lost."

"You were lost. Big deal."   45

They followed the tracks into the woods. The deer had gone over a fence half buried in drifting snow. A no hunting sign was nailed to the top of one of the posts. Frank laughed and said the son of a bitch could read. Kenny wanted to go after him but Frank said no way, the people out here didn't mess around.

He thought maybe the farmer who owned the land would let them use it if they asked. Kenny wasn't so sure. Anyway, he figured that by the time they walked to the truck and drove up the road and doubled back it would be almost dark.

"Relax," Frank said. "You can't hurry nature. If we're meant to get that deer, we'll get it. If we're not, we won't."

They started back toward the truck. This part of the woods was mainly pine. The snow was shaded and had a glaze on it. It held up Kenny and Frank but Tub kept falling through. As he kicked forward, the edge of the crust bruised his shins. Kenny and Frank pulled ahead of him, to where he couldn't even hear their voices any more. He sat down on a stump and wiped his face. He ate both the sandwiches and half the cookies, taking his own sweet time. It was dead quiet.

When Tub crossed the last fence into the road the truck started moving. Tub had to run for it and just managed to grab hold of the tailgate and hoist himself into the bed. He lay there, panting. Kenny looked out the rear window and grinned. Tub crawled into the lee of the cab to get out of the freezing wind. He pulled his earflaps low and pushed his chin into the collar of his coat. Someone rapped on the window but Tub would not turn around.

He and Frank waited outside while Kenny went into the farmhouse to ask   50
permission. The house was old and paint was curling off the sides. The smoke streamed westward off the top of the chimney, fanning away into a thin gray plume. Above the ridge of the hills another ridge of blue clouds was rising.

"You've got a short memory," Tub said.

"What?" Frank said. He had been staring off.

"I used to stick up for you."

"Okay, so you used to stick up for me. What's eating you?"

"You shouldn't have just left me back there like that."   55

"You're a grown-up, Tub. You can take care of yourself. Anyway, if you think you're the only person with problems I can tell you that you're not."

"Is something bothering you, Frank?"

Frank kicked at a branch poking out of the snow. "Never mind," he said.

"What did Kenny mean about the babysitter?"

"Kenny talks too much," Frank said. "You just mind your own business."   60

Kenny came out of the farmhouse and gave the thumbs-up and they began walking back toward the woods. As they passed the barn a large black hound with a grizzled snout ran out and barked at them. Every time he barked he slid backwards a bit, like a cannon recoiling. Kenny got down on all fours and snarled and barked back at him, and the dog slunk away into the barn, looking over his shoulder and peeing a little as he went.

"That's an old-timer," Frank said. "A real graybeard. Fifteen years if he's a day."

"Too old," Kenny said.

Past the barn they cut off through the fields. The land was unfenced and the crust was freezing up thick and they made good time. They kept to the edge of the field until they picked up the tracks again and followed them into the woods, farther and farther back toward the hills. The trees started to blur with the shadows and the wind rose and needled their faces with the crystals it swept off the glaze. Finally they lost the tracks.

Kenny swore and threw down his hat. "This is the worst day of hunting I   65
ever had, bar none." He picked up his hat and brushed off the snow. "This will be the first season since I was fifteen I haven't got my deer."

"It isn't the deer," Frank said. "It's the hunting. There are all these forces out here and you just have to go with them."

"You go with them," Kenny said. "I came out here to get me a deer, not listen to a bunch of hippie bullshit. And if it hadn't been for dimples here I would have, too."

"That's enough," Frank said.

"And you—you're so busy thinking about that little jailbait of yours you wouldn't know a deer if you saw one."

"Drop dead," Frank said, and turned away.

Kenny and Tub followed him back across the fields. When they were coming up to the barn Kenny stopped and pointed. "I hate that post," he said. He raised his rifle and fired. It sounded like a dry branch cracking. The post splintered along its right side, up towards the top. "There," Kenny said. "It's dead."

"Knock it off," Frank said, walking ahead.

Kenny looked at Tub. He smiled. "I hate that tree," he said, and fired again. Tub hurried to catch up with Frank. He started to speak but just then the dog ran out of the barn and barked at them. "Easy, boy," Frank said.

"I hate that dog." Kenny was behind them.

"That's enough," Frank said. "You put that gun down."

Kenny fired. The bullet went in between the dog's eyes. He sank right down into the snow, his legs splayed out on each side, his yellow eyes open and staring. Except for the blood he looked like a small bearskin rug. The blood ran down the dog's muzzle into the snow.

They all looked at the dog lying there.

"What did he ever do to you?" Tub asked. "He was just barking."

Kenny turned to Tub. "I hate you."

Tub shot from the waist. Kenny jerked backward against the fence and buckled to his knees. He folded his hands across his stomach. "Look," he said. His hands were covered with blood. In the dusk his blood was more blue than red. It seemed to belong to the shadows. It didn't seem out of place. Kenny eased himself onto his back. He sighed several times, deeply. "You shot me," he said.

"I had to," Tub said. He knelt beside Kenny. "Oh God," he said. "Frank. Frank."

Frank hadn't moved since Kenny killed the dog.

"Frank!" Tub shouted.

"I was just kidding around," Kenny said. "It was a joke. Oh!" he said, and arched his back suddenly. "Oh!" he said again, and dug his heels into the snow and pushed himself along on his head for several feet. Then he stopped and lay there, rocking back and forth on his heels and head like a wrestler doing warm-up exercises.

Frank roused himself. "Kenny," he said. He bent down and put his gloved hand on Kenny's brow. "You shot him," he said to Tub.

"He made me," Tub said.

"No no no," Kenny said.

Tub was weeping from the eyes and nostrils. His whole face was wet. Frank closed his eyes, then looked down at Kenny again. "Where does it hurt?"

"Everywhere," Kenny said, "just everywhere."

"Oh God," Tub said.

"I mean where did it go in?" Frank said.

"Here." Kenny pointed at the wound in his stomach. It was welling slowly with blood.

70

75

80

85

90

"You're lucky," Frank said. "It's on the left side. It missed your appendix. If it had hit your appendix you'd really be in the soup." He turned and threw up onto the snow, holding his sides as if to keep warm.

"Are you all right?" Tub said.

"There's some aspirin in the truck," Kenny said.   95

"I'm all right," Frank said.

"We'd better call an ambulance," Tub said.

"Jesus," Frank said. "What are we going to say?"

"Exactly what happened," Tub said. "He was going to shoot me but I shot him first."

"No sir!" Kenny said. "I wasn't either!"   100

Frank patted Kenny on the arm. "Easy does it, partner." He stood. "Let's go."

Tub picked up Kenny's rifle as they walked down toward the farmhouse. "No sense leaving this around," he said. "Kenny might get ideas."

"I can tell you one thing," Frank said. "You've really done it this time. This definitely takes the cake."

They had to knock on the door twice before it was opened by a thin man with lank hair. The room behind him was filled with smoke. He squinted at them. "You get anything?" he asked.

"No," Frank said.   105

"I knew you wouldn't. That's what I told the other fellow."

"We've had an accident."

The man looked past Frank and Tub into the gloom. "Shoot your friend, did you?"

Frank nodded.

"I did," Tub said.   110

"I suppose you want to use the phone."

"If it's okay."

The man in the door looked behind him, then stepped back. Frank and Tub followed him into the house. There was a woman sitting by the stove in the middle of the room. The stove was smoking badly. She looked up and then down again at the child asleep in her lap. Her face was white and damp; strands of hair were pasted across her forehead. Tub warmed his hands over the stove while Frank went into the kitchen to call. The man who had let them in stood at the window, his hands in his pockets.

"My friend shot your dog," Tub said.

The man nodded without turning around. "I should have done it myself. I   115
just couldn't."

"He loved that dog so much," the woman said. The child squirmed and she rocked it.

"You asked him to?" Tub said. "You asked him to shoot your dog?"

"He was old and sick. Couldn't chew his food any more. I would have done it myself but I don't have a gun."

"You couldn't have anyway," the woman said. "Never in a million years."

The man shrugged.   120

Frank came out of the kitchen. "We'll have to take him ourselves. The nearest hospital is fifty miles from here and all their ambulances are out anyway."

The woman knew a shortcut but the directions were complicated and Tub had to write them down. The man told them where they could find some boards to carry Kenny on. He didn't have a flashlight but he said he would leave the porch light on.

It was dark outside. The clouds were low and heavy-looking and the wind blew in shrill gusts. There was a screen loose on the house and it banged slowly and then quickly as the wind rose again. They could hear it all the way to the barn. Frank went for the boards while Tub looked for Kenny, who was not where they had left him. Tub found him farther up the drive, lying on his stomach. "You okay?" Tub said.

"It hurts."

"Frank says it missed your appendix."   125

"I already had my appendix out."

"All right," Frank said, coming up to them. "We'll have you in a nice warm bed before you can say Jack Robinson." He put the two boards on Kenny's right side.

"Just as long as I don't have one of those male nurses," Kenny said.

"Ha ha," Frank said. "That's the spirit. Get ready, set, *over you go,*" and he rolled Kenny onto the boards. Kenny screamed and kicked his legs in the air. When he quieted down Frank and Tub lifted the boards and carried him down the drive. Tub had the back end, and with the snow blowing into his face he had trouble with his footing. Also he was tired and the man inside had forgotten to turn the porch light on. Just past the house Tub slipped and threw out his hands to catch himself. The boards fell and Kenny tumbled out and rolled to the bottom of the drive, yelling all the way. He came to rest against the right front wheel of the truck.

"You fat moron," Frank said. "You aren't good for diddly."   130

Tub grabbed Frank by the collar and backed him hard up against the fence. Frank tried to pull his hands away but Tub shook him and snapped his head back and forth and finally Frank gave up.

"What do you know about fat," Tub said. "What do you know about glands." As he spoke he kept shaking Frank. "What do you know about me."

"All right," Frank said.

"No more," Tub said.

"All right."   135

"No more talking to me like that. No more watching. No more laughing."

"Okay, Tub. I promise."

Tub let go of Frank and leaned his forehead against the fence. His arms hung straight at his sides.

"I'm sorry, Tub." Frank touched him on the shoulder. "I'll be down at the truck."

Tub stood by the fence for a while and then got the rifles off the porch.   140
Frank had rolled Kenny back onto the boards and they lifted him into the bed of the truck. Frank spread the seat blankets over him. "Warm enough?" he asked.

Kenny nodded.

"Okay. Now how does reverse work on this thing?"

"All the way to the left and up." Kenny sat up as Frank started forward to the cab. "Frank!"

"What?"

"If it sticks don't force it."   145

The truck started right away. "One thing," Frank said, "you've got to hand it to the Japanese. A very ancient, very spiritual culture and they can still make a hell of a truck." He glanced over at Tub. "Look, I'm sorry. I didn't know you felt that way, honest to God I didn't. You should have said something."

"I did."

"When? Name one time."

"A couple of hours ago."

"I guess I wasn't paying attention."   150

"That's true, Frank," Tub said. "You don't pay attention very much."

"Tub," Frank said, "what happened back there, I should have been more sympathetic. I realize that. You were going through a lot. I just want you to know it wasn't your fault. He was asking for it."

"You think so?"

"Absolutely. It was him or you. I would have done the same thing in your shoes, no question."

The wind was blowing into their faces. The snow was a moving white wall in   155
front of their lights; it swirled into the cab through the hole in the windshield and settled on them. Tub clapped his hands and shifted around to stay warm, but it didn't work.

"I'm going to have to stop," Frank said. "I can't feel my fingers."

Up ahead they saw some lights off the road. It was a tavern. Outside in the parking lot there were several jeeps and trucks. A couple of them had deer strapped across their hoods. Frank parked and they went back to Kenny. "How you doing, partner," Frank said.

"I'm cold."

"Well, don't feel like the Lone Ranger. It's worse inside, take my word for it. You should get that windshield fixed."

"Look," Tub said, "he threw the blankets off." They were lying in a heap   160
against the tailgate.

"Now look, Kenny," Frank said, "it's no use whining about being cold if you're not going to try and keep warm. You've got to do your share." He spread the blankets over Kenny and tucked them in at the corners.

"They blew off."

"Hold on to them then."

"Why are we stopping, Frank?"

"Because if me and Tub don't get warmed up we're going to freeze solid and   165
then where will you be?" He punched Kenny lightly in the arm. "So just hold your horses."

The bar was full of men in colored jackets, mostly orange. The waitress brought coffee. "Just what the doctor ordered," Frank said, cradling the steaming cup in his hand. His skin was bone white. "Tub, I've been thinking. What you said about me not paying attention, that's true."

"It's okay."

"No. I really had that coming. I guess I've just been a little too interested in old number one. I've had a lot on my mind. Not that that's any excuse."

"Forget it, Frank. I sort of lost my temper back there. I guess we're all a little on edge."

Frank shook his head. "It isn't just that."   170

"You want to talk about it?"

"Just between us, Tub?"

"Sure, Frank. Just between us."

"Tub, I think I'm going to be leaving Nancy."

"Oh, Frank. Oh, Frank." Tub sat back and shook his head.   175

Frank reached out and laid his hand on Tub's arm. "Tub, have you ever been really in love?"

"Well—"

"I mean *really* in love." He squeezed Tub's wrist. "With your whole being."

"I don't know. When you put it like that, I don't know."

"You haven't then. Nothing against you, but you'd know it if you had." Frank   180
let go of Tub's arm. "This isn't just some bit of fluff I'm talking about."

"Who is she, Frank?"

Frank paused. He looked into his empty cup. "Roxanne Brewer."

"Cliff Brewer's kid? The babysitter?"

"You can't just put people into categories like that, Tub. That's why the whole system is wrong. And that's why this country is going to hell in a rowboat."

"But she can't be more than—" Tub shook his head.   185

"Fifteen. She'll be sixteen in May." Frank smiled. "May fourth, three twenty-seven p.m. Hell, Tub, a hundred years ago she'd have been an old maid by that age. Juliet was only thirteen."

"Juliet? Juliet Miller? Jesus, Frank, she doesn't even have breasts. She doesn't even wear a top to her bathing suit. She's still collecting frogs."

"Not Juliet Miller. The real Juliet. Tub, don't you see how you're dividing people up into categories? He's an executive, she's a secretary, he's a truck driver, she's fifteen years old. Tub, this so-called babysitter, this so-called fifteen-year-old has more in her little finger than most of us have in our entire bodies. I can tell you this little lady is something special."

Tub nodded. "I know the kids like her."

"She's opened up whole worlds to me that I never knew were there."   190

"What does Nancy think about all of this?"

"She doesn't know."

"You haven't told her?"

"Not yet. It's not so easy. She's been damned good to me all these years. Then there's the kids to consider." The brightness in Frank's eyes trembled and he wiped quickly at them with the back of his hand. "I guess you think I'm a complete bastard."

"No, Frank. I don't think that."   195

"Well, you *ought* to."

"Frank, when you've got a friend it means you've always got someone on your side, no matter what. That's the way I feel about it, anyway."

"You mean that, Tub?"

"Sure I do."

Frank smiled. "You don't know how good it feels to hear you say that."   200

Kenny had tried to get out of the truck but he hadn't made it. He was jack-knifed over the tailgate, his head hanging above the bumper. They lifted him back into the bed and covered him again. He was sweating and his teeth chattered. "It hurts, Frank."

"It wouldn't hurt so much if you just stayed put. Now we're going to the hospital. Got that? Say it—I'm going to the hospital."

"I'm going to the hospital."

"Again."

"I'm going to the hospital."   205

"Now just keep saying that to yourself and before you know it we'll be there."

After they had gone a few miles Tub turned to Frank. "I just pulled a real boner," he said.

"What's that?"

"I left the directions on the table back there."

"That's okay. I remember them pretty well." 210

The snowfall lightened and the clouds began to roll back off the fields, but it was no warmer and after a time both Frank and Tub were bitten through and shaking. Frank almost didn't make it around a curve, and they decided to stop at the next roadhouse.

There was an automatic hand-dryer in the bathroom and they took turns standing in front of it, opening their jackets and shirts and letting the jet of hot air breathe across their faces and chests.

"You know," Tub said, "what you told me back there, I appreciate it. Trusting me."

Frank opened and closed his fingers in front of the nozzle. "The way I look at it, Tub, no man is an island. You've got to trust someone."

"Frank—" 215

Frank waited.

"When I said that about my glands, that wasn't true. The truth is I just shovel it in."

"Well, Tub—"

"Day and night, Frank. In the shower. On the freeway." He turned and let the air play over his back. "I've even got stuff in the paper towel machine at work."

"There's nothing wrong with your glands at all?" Frank had taken his boots 220 and socks off. He held first his right, then his left foot up to the nozzle.

"No. There never was."

"Does Alice know?" The machine went off and Frank started lacing up his boots.

"Nobody knows. That's the worst of it, Frank. Not the being fat, I never got any big kick out of being thin, but the lying. Having to lead a double life like a spy or a hit man. This sounds strange but I feel sorry for those guys, I really do. I know what they go through. Always having to think about what you say and do. Always feeling like people are watching you, trying to catch you at something. Never able to just be yourself. Like when I make a big deal about only having an orange for breakfast and then scarf all the way to work. Oreos, Mars Bars, Twinkies. Sugar Babies. Snickers." Tub glanced at Frank and looked quickly away. "Pretty disgusting, isn't it?"

"Tub. Tub." Frank shook his head. "Come on." He took Tub's arm and led him into the restaurant half of the bar. "My friend is hungry," he told the waitress. "Bring four orders of pancakes, plenty of butter and syrup."

"Frank—" 225

"Sit down."

When the dishes came Frank carved out slabs of butter and just laid them on the pancakes. Then he emptied the bottle of syrup, moving it back and forth over the plates. He leaned forward on his elbows and rested his chin in one hand. "Go on, Tub."

Tub ate several mouthfuls, then started to wipe his lips. Frank took the napkin away from him. "No wiping," he said. Tub kept at it. The syrup covered his chin; it dripped to a point like a goatee. "Weigh in, Tub," Frank said, pushing another fork across the table. "Get down to business." Tub took the fork in his left hand and lowered his head and started really chowing down. "Clean your plate," Frank said when the pancakes were gone, and Tub lifted each of the four plates and licked it clean. He sat back, trying to catch his breath.

"Beautiful," Frank said. "Are you full?"

"I'm full," Tub said. "I've never been so full." 230

Kenny's blankets were bunched up against the tailgate again.

"They must have blown off," Tub said.

"They're not doing him any good," Frank said. "We might as well get some use out of them."

Kenny mumbled. Tub bent over him. "What? Speak up."

"I'm going to the hospital," Kenny said. 235

"Attaboy," Frank said.

The blankets helped. The wind still got their faces and Frank's hands but it was much better. The fresh snow on the road and the trees sparkled under the beam of the headlight. Squares of light from farmhouse windows fell onto the blue snow in the fields.

"Frank," Tub said after a time, "you know that farmer? He told Kenny to kill the dog."

"You're kidding!" Frank leaned forward, considering. "That Kenny. What a card." He laughed and so did Tub. Tub smiled out the back window. Kenny lay with his arms folded over his stomach, moving his lips at the stars. Right overhead was the Big Dipper, and behind, hanging between Kenny's toes in the direction of the hospital, was the North Star, Pole Star, Help to Sailors. As the truck twisted through the gentle hills the star went back and forth between Kenny's boots, staying always in his sight. "I'm going to the hospital," Kenny said. But he was wrong. They had taken a different turn a long way back.

(1980)

◇◇◇◇◇◇◇◇◇◇◇◇◇◇◇◇◇◇◇◇◇◇

The Writing Process
Prewriting

As you read the story carefully a second time, pay particular attention to the descriptive passages that appeal to the senses—especially, in this story, images of snow, cold, and ice. Underline any specific words or phrases that you think contribute to the atmosphere.

Exercise: Examining the Elements of Setting

1. Write one or two paragraphs that describe Frank, Kenny, and Tub going fishing on a hundred-degree summer day. What elements of "Hunters in the Snow" would stay the same, and what would change in this altered setting?

2. Examine the first ten paragraphs of the story, when Frank and Kenny come to pick up Tub to go hunting. What do these paragraphs reveal about the three men? What can you say about their relationship after reading only the opening of the tale?

3. What features of the setting seem essential to the way "Hunters in the Snow" unfolds? In other words, how do the snow and cold determine what happens in important ways?

4. Before planning your paper, write your responses to the following questions:

   a. When you think of men going on a hunting trip, what associations come forth? Are any of these associations reflected in the story? Are any of them contradicted or undermined?

   b. How soon in the story can you distinguish among the three characters? What are some of the ways they are distinct from one another?

   c. List the indoor scenes in this basically outdoor story. What critical events or revelations happen in each of the indoor scenes?

   d. What do you make of Frank's ordering the pancakes for Tub at the roadhouse? Is it an act of acceptance, friendship, cruelty, humor, vicarious satisfaction, or what?

   e. Although women are generally off the scene, in what ways do they influence the characters?

   f. At several points in the story, you may have been shocked by what happens. What are some of these points? Why were they shocking?

Writing

Now that you have become familiar with the story, ask yourself still more questions: How can I make a statement about the function of setting in relation to theme? What, indeed, does the setting contribute to the overall effectiveness of the story? What does the atmosphere contribute? How do both relate to the meaning of the story? Do they *heighten* the theme, do they provide a unique opportunity for the events, or do they help the reader to understand what the story is about? Would a different setting change the story in important ways? As you think about answers to these questions, review your prewriting material and continue consulting the story for clues.

Discovering an Organization

As you are trying to solve the problems posed by the questions in the preceding paragraph, write down all the likely ideas that strike you. Do not trust your memory, or some of your best inspirations may slip away. Then try to think of some point you can make about the story that will allow you to use this information. Such a point will usually make a link between the setting and something else about the story: the characters, action, plot, motivation, meaning, or emotional impact. Once you have discovered an interesting point to pursue, write out this idea in a single, clear sentence. This idea will be your thesis. Then sort through the details related to setting in the story and ask yourself: How can I organize these details in support of my thesis? You might, for instance, group your material chronologically, arranging details according to the episodes in the story as they occur from morning till night. Or you might consider a logical arrangement, emphasizing each of the main characters in turn or focusing first on everything that happens outdoors and then on everything that happens indoors.

Ideas for Writing

Ideas for Reflective Writing

1. "Hunters in the Snow" takes place in a traditionally all-male setting, a hunting trip. In your experience, do people in small same-sex groups behave differently than they would in mixed-sex groups? If so, do they behave better or worse? Outside of hunting trips, what other occasions usually bring together small same-sex groups? Write a description of a same-sex occasion you have encountered. Emphasize the influence of the setting on people's behavior.

2. It would appear that Kenny, Frank, and Tub are a group of friends. What is the evidence? On the other hand, how do they behave as though they are not friends? What philosophies of friendship are spoken out loud? What philosophies are acted out among the three characters? Do you think that these philosophies are unusual or common?

Ideas for Critical Writing

1. Examine each reference to the snow and cold. What attitude toward nature is suggested by the way it is described? How is this attitude related to the view of human nature suggested by the story?

2. The weather conditions in "Hunters in the Snow" are portrayed as obscuring the true state of things and blurring perceptions such as

vision and hearing. Relate this feature of the setting to the blurring and obscuring of truth in the human arena. What lie is pivotal to each character?

3. What effect does being cold for long periods have on people? Argue for an interpretation of the story that explains how the freezing cold drives much of the action of the story.

Ideas for Researched Writing

1. CRITICAL APPROACHES: Review the historical approaches to literary interpretation (Chapter 34). Do some research on Tobias Wolff's life, and use a biographical approach to explain his choice of setting, character, and theme in "Hunters in the Snow."

2. Using the PsychLIT database or your Internet search engine, investigate contemporary thought about male friendships. Find two or three sources that give theoretical or experimental support to the depiction of male friendship in "Hunters in the Snow." How are such friendships described and explained by experts in human behavior? Write a paper that makes a claim about the characters' relationships.

MultiModal Project

You are the casting director for a dramatization (either a play or film—choose one) of "Hunters in the Snow." Prepare an audition announcement for actors who want to try out for the parts of Frank, Kenny, and Tub. Include a specific description of the physical characteristics that you are looking for. Search online for photos of actors that fit the looks you want. Also describe the nonphysical traits that are important for these characters.

Rewriting

Once you have written out your ideas, you will try to improve every element of that draft—from the overall organization to the individual sentences.

Checking Your Organization

Each paragraph should have a topic, a main point that you can summarize in a sentence. On a separate sheet of paper, list the topics of your paragraphs. When you see the bare bones of your essay this way, you can ask yourself questions about your organization.

1. Do any of the topics repeat each other? If so, think about combining them or placing them close together. If there is a fine distinction between them, go back to the essay and express the distinction clearly.

2. Is each topic fully supported? Compare the topic as stated on your outline with the paragraph in your essay. Make sure that you can see

how each sentence in the paragraph relates to the topic. Weed out sentences that only repeat the topic. Add specific details from the literary work instead.

3. Does the order of topics make sense? You might have originally written your paragraphs in the order the topics occurred to you, but that may not be the most reasonable organization for the final essay. Group similar topics together—for example, all the topics that relate setting to character should be close to each other, and so should all the topics that relate setting to theme. At the beginning of each paragraph, write a word, phrase, clause, or sentence that shows that paragraph's relationship to the paragraph before it. These transitions will help your readers know what to expect and prepare them for what comes next.

Improving the Style: Balanced Sentences

Sound organization is vital to the success of your essay; graceful style is an added gift to your reader. One stylistic plus is the balanced or parallel sentence, which puts similar ideas into similar grammatical structures, like this:

Wolff's stories are known for their *sudden, profound,* and *powerful* endings.

Good writers acknowledge the necessity of *thinking, planning, writing, revising, resting,* and then *thinking* and *revising* still further.

In the following sentence, though, the third item in the italicized series does not match. Compare it to the corrected version.

Unbalanced   The main character would not willingly give up the *carefree, extravagant,* and *drinking and staying out late* as he did when a bachelor.

Balanced   The main character would not willingly give up the *carefree, extravagant, carousing* ways of his bachelorhood.

Probably you can already handle such balancing in ordinary sentences. But pay attention during revising to make sure that all items in series are indeed balanced.

If you need an emphatic sentence for your introduction or conclusion, a good way to learn to write impressive balanced sentences is through *sentence modeling.* Many expert writers—Robert Louis Stevenson, Abraham Lincoln, Winston Churchill, Somerset Maugham—attest that they perfected their writing by studiously copying and imitating the sentences of stylists whom they admired.

Exercise: Sentence Modeling

Examine the model sentence shown below to discover its structure. How is it formed? Does it use balanced phrases, clauses, or single words? Does it include any deliberate repetition of words as well as structures? Does it build to a climax at the end? If so, how? By adding ideas of increasing importance? By establishing a pattern that gathers momentum?

Once you have discovered the structure of the model sentence, write one as nearly like it as possible *using your own words and subject matter.* Then repeat this process of imitation four more times, changing your ideas with each new sentence, like this:

Model Until the young are informed as much about the courage of pacifists as about the obedience of soldiers, they aren't educated.

—*Coleman McCarthy*

Imitation Until Americans become as interested in the speeches of candidates as in the performance of athletes, they aren't ideal citizens.

Imitation Until men are interested as much by the minds of women as by the bodies of women, they will be seen as sexist.

First copy each of the numbered sentences carefully—including the exact punctuation. Then imitate each one at least five times.

1. He sees no seams or joints or points of intersection—only irrevocable wholes.

   —*Mina Shaughnessy*

2. We made meals and changed diapers and took out the garbage and paid bills—while other people died.

   —*Ellen Goodman*

3. The refrigerator was full of sulfurous scraps, dark crusts, furry oddments.

   —*Alice Munro*

4. It is sober without being dull; massive without being oppressive.

   —*Sir Kenneth Clark*

5. Joint by joint, line by line, pill by pill, the use of illegal drugs has become a crisis for American business.

   —*Newsweek*

11 Writing About Theme

Chapter Preview

A story's theme or meaning grows out of all the elements of imaginative fiction: character, structure, symbolism, point of view, and setting. The theme is usually not an obvious moral or message, and it may be difficult to sum up succinctly. But thinking about the theme of a story and trying to state it in your own words will help you to focus your scattered reactions and to make your understanding of the author's purpose more certain. One of the pleasures of reading a good story comes from deciding what it means and why it captures your interest. By the end of this chapter, you will be able to:

* Define *theme*, and explain its importance.
* Distinguish between the *subject* of a story and its *theme*.
* Identify specific questions that lead to understanding the theme.
* Demonstrate how concrete *details* are used to support an interpretation.
* List several ways to check for and enhance *coherence*.

What Is Theme?

Theme has been defined in many ways: the central idea or thesis; the central thought; the underlying meaning, either implied or directly stated; the general insight revealed by the entire story; the central truth; the dominating idea; the abstract concept that is made concrete through representation in person, action, and image.

Because the theme involves ideas and insights, we usually state it in general terms. "Eveline," for instance, concerns the conflicts of a specific character, but the story's main idea—its theme—relates to abstract qualities like *duty* and *fear*. If someone asks what "Eveline" is *about*, we might respond with a summary of the plot, with details about the title character's encounter with Frank and her failure to go away with him. But if someone asks for the story's *theme*, we would answer with a general statement of ideas or values: "Eveline" shows how people can be trapped by fear and obligation.

It is easy to confuse *subject* with *theme*. The subject is the topic or material the story examines—love, death, war, identity, prejudice, power, human relations, growing up, and so forth. The theme is the direct or implied statement that the story makes *about* the subject. For example, the *subject* of "Everyday Use" is mother–daughter relationships, but the *theme* emerges from what the story says about Mama, Maggie, and Dee—and from an understanding of why these characters behave and interact as they do. The theme, then, is the insight that we gain from thinking about what we have read.

Looking at Theme

As you read "A Good Man Is Hard to Find" by Flannery O'Connor, think about how this story of a family trip to Florida resembles the stories of other journeys in life.

Flannery O'Connor   1925–1964

Born in Savannah, Georgia, Mary Flannery O'Connor was raised a devout Roman Catholic in the largely Protestant South. She studied sociology and English at Georgia State College for Women and was one of the first students at the University of Iowa's renowned Writers' Workshop. Her first short story appeared in 1946; five years later, she was diagnosed with lupus erythematosus, a disease that had taken her father's life. Although she published only two novels and a collection of stories during her short lifetime (another volume of stories was published posthumously), her uncanny blend of wicked humor, brutal violence, and religious concepts produced the unmistakable literary voice of one of the most important short story writers of the 20th century.

A Good Man Is Hard to Find

The dragon is by the side of the road, watching those who pass. Beware lest he devour you. We go to the Father of Souls, but it is necessary to pass by the dragon.

—St. Cyril of Jerusalem

The grandmother didn't want to go to Florida. She wanted to visit some of her connections in east Tennessee and she was seizing at every chance to change Bailey's mind. Bailey was the son she lived with, her only boy. He was sitting on the edge of his chair at the table, bent over the orange sports section of the *Journal.* "Now look here, Bailey," she said, "see here, read this," and she stood with one hand on her thin hip and the other rattling the newspaper at his bald head. "Here this fellow that calls himself The Misfit is aloose from the Federal Pen and headed toward Florida and you read here what it says he did to these people. Just you read it. I wouldn't take my children in any direction with a criminal like that aloose in it. I couldn't answer to my conscience if I did."

Bailey didn't look up from his reading so she wheeled around then and faced the children's mother, a young woman in slacks, whose face was as broad and innocent as a cabbage and was tied around with a green headkerchief that had two points on the top like a rabbit's ears. She was sitting on the sofa, feeding the baby his apricots out of a jar. "The children have been to Florida before," the old lady said. "You all ought to take them somewhere else for a change so they would see different parts of the world and be broad. They never have been to east Tennessee."

The children's mother didn't seem to hear her but the eight-year-old boy, John Wesley, a stocky child with glasses, said, "If you don't want to go to Florida, why dontcha stay at home?" He and the little girl, June Star, were reading the funny papers on the floor.

"She wouldn't stay at home to be queen for a day," June Star said without raising her yellow head.

"Yes and what would you do if this fellow, The Misfit, caught you?" the   5 grandmother asked.

"I'd smack his face," John Wesley said.

"She wouldn't stay at home for a million bucks," June Star said. "Afraid she'd miss something. She has to go everywhere we go."

"All right, Miss," the grandmother said. "Just remember that the next time you want me to curl your hair."

June Star said her hair was naturally curly.

The next morning the grandmother was the first one in the car, ready to go.   10 She had her big black valise that looked like the head of a hippopotamus in one corner, and underneath it she was hiding a basket with Pitty Sing, the cat, in it. She didn't intend for the cat to be left alone in the house for three days because he would miss her too much and she was afraid he might brush against one of the gas burners and accidentally asphyxiate himself. Her son, Bailey, didn't like to arrive at a motel with a cat.

She sat in the middle of the back seat with John Wesley and June Star on either side of her. Bailey and the children's mother and the baby sat in front and they left Atlanta at eight forty-five with the mileage on the car at 55890. The grandmother wrote this down because she thought it would be interesting to say how many miles they had been when they got back. It took them twenty minutes to reach the outskirts of the city.

The old lady settled herself comfortably, removing her white cotton gloves and putting them up with her purse on the shelf in front of the back window. The children's mother still had on slacks and still had her head tied up in a green kerchief, but the grandmother had on a navy blue straw sailor hat with a bunch of white violets on the brim and a navy blue dress with a small white dot in the print. Her collars and cuffs were white organdy trimmed with lace and at her neckline she had pinned a purple spray of cloth violets containing a sachet. In case of an accident, anyone seeing her dead on the highway would know at once that she was a lady.

She said she thought it was going to be a good day for driving, neither too hot nor too cold, and she cautioned Bailey that the speed limit was fifty-five miles an hour and that the patrolmen hid themselves behind billboards and small clumps of trees and sped out after you before you had a chance to slow down. She pointed out interesting details of the scenery: Stone Mountain; the blue granite that in some places came up to both sides of the highway; the brilliant red clay banks slightly streaked with purple; and the various crops that made rows of green lace-work on the ground. The trees were full of silver-white sunlight and the meanest of them sparkled. The children were reading comic magazines and their mother had gone back to sleep.

"Let's go through Georgia fast so we won't have to look at it much," John Wesley said.

"If I were a little boy," said the grandmother, "I wouldn't talk about my native state that way. Tennessee has the mountains and Georgia has the hills."

"Tennessee is just a hillbilly dumping ground," John Wesley said, "and Georgia is a lousy state too."

"You said it," June Star said.

"In my time," said the grandmother, folding her thin veined fingers, "children were more respectful of their native states and their parents and everything else. People did right then. Oh look at the cute little pickaninny!" she said and pointed to a Negro child standing in the door of a shack. "Wouldn't that make a picture, now?" she asked and they all turned and looked at the little Negro out of the back window. He waved.

"He didn't have any britches on," June Star said.

"He probably didn't have any," the grandmother explained. "Little niggers in the country don't have things like we do. If I could paint, I'd paint that picture," she said.

The children exchanged comic books.

The grandmother offered to hold the baby and the children's mother passed him over the front seat to her. She set him on her knee and bounced him and told him about the things they were passing. She rolled her eyes and screwed up her mouth and stuck her leathery thin face into his smooth bland one. Occasionally he gave her a faraway smile. They passed a large cotton field with five or six graves fenced in the middle of it, like a small island. "Look at the graveyard!" the grandmother said, pointing it out. "That was the old family burying ground. That belonged to the plantation."

"Where's the plantation?" John Wesley asked.

"Gone with the Wind," said the grandmother. "Ha. Ha."

When the children finished all the comic books they had brought, they opened the lunch and ate it. The grandmother ate a peanut butter sandwich and an olive and would not let the children throw the box and the paper napkins out the window. When there was nothing else to do they played a game by choosing a cloud and making the other two guess what shape it suggested. John Wesley took one the shape of a cow and June Star guessed a cow and John Wesley said, no, an automobile, and June Star said he didn't play fair, and they began to slap each other over the grandmother.

The grandmother said she would tell them a story if they would keep quiet. When she told a story, she rolled her eyes and waved her head and was very dramatic. She said once when she was a maiden lady she had been courted by a Mr. Edgar Atkins Teagarden from Jasper, Georgia. She said he was a very good-looking man and a gentleman and that he brought her a watermelon every Saturday afternoon with his initials cut in it, E. A. T. Well, one Saturday, she said, Mr. Teagarden brought the watermelon and there was nobody at home and he left it on the front porch and returned in his buggy to Jasper, but she never got the watermelon, she said, because a nigger boy ate it when he saw the initials, E. A. T.! This story tickled John Wesley's funny bone and he giggled and giggled but June Star didn't think it was any good. She said she wouldn't marry a man that just brought her a watermelon on Saturday. The grandmother said she would have done well to marry Mr. Teagarden because he was a gentleman and had bought Coca-Cola stock when it first came out and that he had died only a few years ago, a very wealthy man.

They stopped at The Tower for barbecued sandwiches. The Tower was a part stucco and part wood filling station and dance hall set in a clearing outside of Timothy. A fat man named Red Sammy Butts ran it and there were signs stuck here and there on the building and for miles up and down the highway saying, TRY RED SAMMY'S FAMOUS BARBECUE. NONE LIKE FAMOUS RED SAMMY'S! RED SAM! THE FAT BOY WITH THE HAPPY LAUGH! A VETERAN! RED SAMMY'S YOUR MAN!

Red Sammy was lying on the bare ground outside The Tower with his head under a truck while a gray monkey about a foot high, chained to a small chinaberry tree, chattered nearby. The monkey sprang back into the tree and got on the highest limb as soon as he saw the children jump out of the car and run toward him.

Inside, The Tower was a long dark room with a counter at one end and tables at the other and dancing space in the middle. They all sat down at a board table next to the nickelodeon and Red Sam's wife, a tall burnt-brown woman with hair and eyes lighter than her skin, came and took their order. The children's mother put a dime in the machine and played "The Tennessee Waltz," and the grandmother said that tune always made her want to dance. She asked Bailey if he would like to dance but he only glared at her. He didn't have a naturally sunny disposition like she did and trips made him nervous. The grandmother's brown eyes were very bright. She swayed her head from side to side and pretended she was dancing in her chair. June Star said play something she could tap to so the children's mother put in another dime and played a fast number and June Star stepped out onto the dance floor and did her tap routine.

"Ain't she cute?" Red Sam's wife said, leaning over the counter. "Would you   30
like to come be my little girl?"

"No I certainly wouldn't," June Star said. "I wouldn't live in a broken-down place like this for a million bucks!" and she ran back to the table.

"Ain't she cute?" the woman repeated, stretching her mouth politely.

"Aren't you ashamed?" hissed the grandmother.

Red Sam came in and told his wife to quit lounging on the counter and hurry up with these people's order. His khaki trousers reached just to his hip bones and his stomach hung over them like a sack of meal swaying under his shirt. He came over and sat down at a table nearby and let out a combination sigh and yodel. "You can't win," he said. "You can't win," and he wiped his sweating red face off with a gray handkerchief. "These days you don't know who to trust," he said. "Ain't that the truth?"

"People are certainly not nice like they used to be," said the grandmother.   35

"Two fellers come in here last week," Red Sammy said, "driving a Chrysler. It was a old beat-up car but it was a good one and these boys looked all right to me. Said they worked at the mill and you know I let them fellers charge the gas they bought? Now why did I do that?"

"Because you're a good man!" the grandmother said at once.

"Yes'm, I suppose so," Red Sam said as if he were struck with this answer.

His wife brought the orders, carrying the five plates all at once without a tray, two in each hand and one balanced on her arm. "It isn't a soul in this green world of God's that you can trust," she said. "And I don't count nobody out of that, not nobody," she repeated, looking at Red Sammy.

"Did you read about that criminal, The Misfit, that's escaped?" asked the   40
grandmother.

"I wouldn't be a bit surprised if he didn't attack this place right here," said the woman. "If he hears about it being here, I wouldn't be none surprised to see him. If he hears it's two cent in the cash register, I wouldn't be a tall surprised if he...."

"That'll do," Red Sam said. "Go bring these people their Co'-Colas," and the woman went off to get the rest of the order.

"A good man is hard to find," Red Sammy said. "Everything is getting terrible. I remember the day you could go off and leave your screen door unlatched. Not no more."

He and the grandmother discussed better times. The old lady said that in her opinion Europe was entirely to blame for the way things were now. She said the way Europe acted you would think we were made of money and Red Sam said it was no use talking about it, she was exactly right. The children ran outside into the white sunlight and looked at the monkey in the lacy chinaberry tree. He was busy catching fleas on himself and biting each one carefully between his teeth as if it were a delicacy.

They drove off again into the hot afternoon. The grandmother took cat naps 45 and woke up every few minutes with her own snoring. Outside of Toombsboro she woke up and recalled an old plantation that she had visited in this neighborhood once when she was a young lady. She said the house had six white columns across the front and that there was an avenue of oaks leading up to it and two little wooden trellis arbors on either side in front where you sat down with your suitor after a stroll in the garden. She recalled exactly which road to turn off to get to it. She knew that Bailey would not be willing to lose any time looking at an old house, but the more she talked about it, the more she wanted to see it once again and find out if the little twin arbors were still standing. "There was a secret panel in this house," she said craftily, not telling the truth but wishing that she were, "and the story went that all the family silver was hidden in it when Sherman came through but it was never found...."

"Hey!" John Wesley said. "Let's go see it! We'll find it! We'll poke all the woodwork and find it! Who lives there? Where do you turn off at? Hey Pop, can't we turn off there?"

"We never have seen a house with a secret panel!" June Star shrieked. "Let's go to the house with the secret panel! Hey Pop, can't we go see the house with the secret panel!"

"It's not far from here, I know," the grandmother said. "It won't take over twenty minutes."

Bailey was looking straight ahead. His jaw was as rigid as a horseshoe. "No," he said.

The children began to yell and scream that they wanted to see the house with 50 the secret panel. John Wesley kicked the back of the front seat and June Star hung over her mother's shoulder and whined desperately into her ear that they never had any fun even on their vacation, that they could never do what THEY wanted to do. The baby began to scream and John Wesley kicked the back of the seat so hard that his father could feel the blows in his kidney.

"All right!" he shouted and drew the car to a stop at the side of the road. "Will you all shut up? Will you all just shut up for one second? If you don't shut up, we won't go anywhere."

"It would be very educational for them," the grandmother murmured.

"All right," Bailey said, "but get this: this is the only time we're going to stop for anything like this. This is the one and only time."

"The dirt road that you have to turn down is about a mile back," the grandmother directed. "I marked it when we passed."

"A dirt road," Bailey groaned. 55

After they had turned around and were headed toward the dirt road, the grandmother recalled other points about the house, the beautiful glass over the front doorway and the candle-lamp in the hall. John Wesley said that the secret panel was probably in the fireplace.

"You can't go inside this house," Bailey said. "You don't know who lives there."

"While you all talk to the people in front, I'll run around behind and get in a window," John Wesley suggested.

"We'll all stay in the car," his mother said.

They turned onto the dirt road and the car raced roughly along in a swirl of 60 pink dust. The grandmother recalled the times when there were no paved roads and thirty miles was a day's journey. The dirt road was hilly and there were sudden washes in it and sharp curves on dangerous embankments. All at once they would be on a hill, looking down over the blue tops of trees for miles around, then the next minute, they would be in a red depression with the dust-coated trees looking down on them.

"This place had better turn up in a minute," Bailey said, "or I'm going to turn around."

The road looked as if no one had traveled on it for months.

"It's not much farther," the grandmother said and just as she said it, a horrible thought came to her. The thought was so embarrassing that she turned red in the face and her eyes dilated and her feet jumped up, upsetting her valise in the corner. The instant the valise moved, the newspaper top she had over the basket under it rose with a snarl and Pitty Sing, the cat, sprang onto Bailey's shoulder.

The children were thrown to the floor and their mother, clutching the baby, was thrown out the door onto the ground; the old lady was thrown into the front seat. The car turned over once and landed right-side-up in a gulch off the side of the road. Bailey remained in the driver's seat with the cat—gray-striped with a broad white face and an orange nose—clinging to his neck like a caterpillar.

As soon as the children saw they could move their arms and legs, they scram- 65 bled out of the car, shouting, "We've had an ACCIDENT!" The grandmother was curled up under the dashboard, hoping she was injured so that Bailey's wrath would not come down on her all at once. The horrible thought she had before the accident was that the house she had remembered so vividly was not in Georgia but in Tennessee.

Bailey removed the cat from his neck with both hands and flung it out the window against the side of a pine tree. Then he got out of the car and started looking for the children's mother. She was sitting against the side of the red gutted ditch, holding the screaming baby, but she only had a cut down her face and a broken shoulder. "We've had an ACCIDENT!" the children screamed in a frenzy of delight.

"But nobody's killed," June Star said with disappointment as the grandmother limped out of the car, her hat still pinned to her head but the broken front brim standing up at a jaunty angle and the violet spray hanging off the side. They all sat down in the ditch, except the children, to recover from the shock. They were all shaking.

"Maybe a car will come along," said the children's mother hoarsely.

"I believe I have injured an organ," said the grandmother, pressing her side, but no one answered her. Bailey's teeth were clattering. He had on a yellow sport shirt with bright blue parrots designed in it and his face was as yellow as the shirt. The grandmother decided that she would not mention that the house was in Tennessee.

The road was about ten feet above and they could see only the tops of the 70 trees on the other side of it. Behind the ditch they were sitting in there were more woods, tall and dark and deep. In a few minutes they saw a car some distance away on top of a hill, coming slowly as if the occupants were watching them. The grandmother stood up and waved both arms dramatically to attract their attention. The car continued to come on slowly, disappeared around a bend and appeared again, moving even slower, on top of the hill they had gone over. It was a big black battered hearse-like automobile. There were three men in it.

It came to a stop just over them and for some minutes, the driver looked down with a steady expressionless gaze to where they were sitting, and didn't speak. Then he turned his head and muttered something to the other two and they got out. One was a fat boy in black trousers and a red sweat shirt with a silver stallion embossed on the front of it. He moved around on the right side of them and stood staring, his mouth partly open in a kind of loose grin. The other had on khaki pants and a blue striped coat and a gray hat pulled down very low, hiding most of his face. He came around slowly on the left side. Neither spoke.

The driver got out of the car and stood by the side of it, looking down at them. He was an older man than the other two. His hair was just beginning to gray and he wore silver-rimmed spectacles that gave him a scholarly look. He had a long creased face and didn't have on any shirt or undershirt. He had on blue jeans that were too tight for him and was holding a black hat and a gun. The two boys also had guns.

"We've had an ACCIDENT!" the children screamed.

The grandmother had the peculiar feeling that the bespectacled man was someone she knew. His face was as familiar to her as if she had known him all her life but she could not recall who he was. He moved away from the car and began to come down the embankment, placing his feet carefully so that he wouldn't slip. He had on tan and white shoes and no socks, and his ankles were red and thin. "Good afternoon," he said. "I see you all had you a little spill."

"We turned over twice!" said the grandmother. 75

"Oncet," he corrected. "We seen it happen. Try their car and see will it run, Hiram," he said quietly to the boy with the gray hat.

"What you got that gun for?" John Wesley asked. "Whatcha gonna do with that gun?"

"Lady," the man said to the children's mother, "would you mind calling them children to sit down by you? Children make me nervous. I want all you all to sit down right together there where you're at."

"What are you telling US what to do for?" June Star asked.

Behind them the line of woods gaped like a dark open mouth. "Come here," 80 said their mother.

"Look here now," Bailey said suddenly, "we're in a predicament! We're in..."

The grandmother shrieked. She scrambled to her feet and stood staring. "You're The Misfit!" she said. "I recognized you at once!"

"Yes'm," the man said, smiling slightly as if he were pleased in spite of himself to be known, "but it would have been better for all of you, lady, if you hadn't of reckernized me."

Bailey turned his head sharply and said something to his mother that shocked even the children. The old lady began to cry and The Misfit reddened.

"Lady," he said, "don't you get upset. Sometimes a man says things he don't 85 mean. I don't reckon he meant to talk to you thataway."

"You wouldn't shoot a lady, would you?" the grandmother said and removed a clean handkerchief from her cuff and began to slap at her eyes with it.

The Misfit pointed the toe of his shoe into the ground and made a little hole and then covered it up again. "I would hate to have to," he said.

"Listen," the grandmother almost screamed, "I know you're a good man. You don't look a bit like you have common blood. I know you must come from nice people!"

"Yes mam," he said, "finest people in the world." When he smiled he showed a row of strong white teeth. "God never made a finer woman than my mother and my daddy's heart was pure gold," he said. The boy with the red sweat shirt had come around behind them and was standing with his gun at his hip. The Misfit squatted down on the ground. "Watch them children, Bobby Lee," he said. "You know they make me nervous." He looked at the six of them huddled together in front of him and he seemed to be embarrassed as if he couldn't think of anything to say. "Ain't a cloud in the sky," he remarked, looking up at it. "Don't see no sun but don't see no cloud neither."

"Yes, it's a beautiful day," said the grandmother. "Listen," she said, "you 90 shouldn't call yourself The Misfit because I know you're a good man at heart. I can just look at you and tell."

"Hush!" Bailey yelled. "Hush! Everybody shut up and let me handle this!" He was squatting in the position of a runner about to sprint forward but he didn't move.

"I pre-chate that, lady," The Misfit said and drew a little circle in the ground with the butt of his gun.

"It'll take a half a hour to fix this here car," Hiram called, looking over the raised hood of it.

"Well, first you and Bobby Lee get him and that little boy to step over yonder with you," The Misfit said, pointing to Bailey and John Wesley. "The boys want to ast you something," he said to Bailey. "Would you mind stepping back in them woods there with them?"

"Listen," Bailey began, "we're in a terrible predicament! Nobody realizes 95 what this is," and his voice cracked. His eyes were as blue and intense as the parrots in his shirt and he remained perfectly still.

The grandmother reached up to adjust her hat brim as if she were going to the woods with him but it came off in her hand. She stood staring at it and after a second she let it fall to the ground. Hiram pulled Bailey up by the arm as if he were assisting an old man. John Wesley caught hold of his father's hand and Bobby Lee followed. They went off toward the woods and just as they reached the dark edge, Bailey turned and supporting himself against a gray naked pine trunk, he shouted, "I'll be back in a minute, Mamma, wait on me!"

"Come back this instant!" his mother shrilled but they all disappeared into the woods.

"Bailey Boy!" the grandmother called in a tragic voice but she found she was looking at The Misfit squatting on the ground in front of her. "I just know you're a good man," she said desperately. "You're not a bit common!"

"Nome, I ain't a good man," The Misfit said after a second as if he had considered her statement carefully, "but I ain't the worst in the world neither. My daddy said I was a different breed of dog from my brothers and sisters. 'You know,' Daddy said, 'it's some that can live their whole life out without asking about it and it's others has to know why it is, and this boy is one of the latters. He's going to be into everything!'" He put on his black hat and looked up suddenly and then away deep into the woods as if he were embarrassed again. "I'm sorry I don't have on a shirt before you ladies," he said, hunching his shoulders slightly. "We buried our clothes that we had on when we escaped and we're just making do until we can get better. We borrowed these from some folks we met," he explained.

"That's perfectly all right," the grandmother said. "Maybe Bailey has an extra shirt in his suitcase." 100

"I'll look and see terrectly," The Misfit said.

"Where are they taking him?" the children's mother screamed.

"Daddy was a card himself," The Misfit said. "You couldn't put anything over on him. He never got in trouble with the Authorities though. Just had the knack of handling them."

"You could be honest too if you'd only try," said the grandmother. "Think how wonderful it would be to settle down and live a comfortable life and not have to think about somebody chasing you all the time."

The Misfit kept scratching in the ground with the butt of his gun as if he were thinking about it. "Yes'm, somebody is always after you," he murmured. 105

The grandmother noticed how thin his shoulder blades were just behind his hat because she was standing up looking down on him. "Do you ever pray?" she asked.

He shook his head. All she saw was the black hat wiggle between his shoulder blades. "Nome," he said.

There was a pistol shot from the woods, followed closely by another. Then silence. The old lady's head jerked around. She could hear the wind move through the tree tops like a long satisfied insuck of breath. "Bailey Boy!" she called.

"I was a gospel singer for a while," The Misfit said. "I been most everything. Been in the arm service, both land and sea, at home and abroad, been twict married, been an undertaker, been with the railroads, plowed Mother Earth, been in a tornado, seen a man burnt alive oncet," and he looked up at the children's mother and the little girl who were sitting close together, their faces white and their eyes glassy; "I even seen a woman flogged," he said.

"Pray, pray," the grandmother began, "pray, pray...." 110

"I never was a bad boy that I remember of," The Misfit said in an almost dreamy voice, "but somewheres along the line I done something wrong and got sent to the penitentiary. I was buried alive," and he looked up and held her attention to him by a steady stare.

"That's when you should have started to pray," she said. "What did you do to get sent to the penitentiary that first time?"

"Turn to the right, it was a wall," The Misfit said, looking up again at the cloudless sky. "Turn to the left, it was a wall. Look up it was a ceiling, look down it was a floor. I forget what I done, lady. I set there and set there, trying to remember what it was I done and I ain't recalled it to this day. Oncet in a while, I would think it was coming to me, but it never come."

"Maybe they put you in by mistake," the old lady said vaguely.

"Nome," he said. "It wasn't no mistake. They had the papers on me." 115

"You must have stolen something," she said.

The Misfit sneered slightly. "Nobody had nothing I wanted," he said. "It was a head-doctor at the penitentiary said what I had done was kill my daddy but I known that for a lie. My daddy died in nineteen ought nineteen of the epidemic flu and I never had a thing to do with it. He was buried in the Mount Hopewell Baptist churchyard and you can see for yourself."

"If you would pray," the old lady said, "Jesus would help you."

"That's right," The Misfit said.

"Well then, why don't you pray?" she asked trembling with delight suddenly.   120

"I don't want no hep," he said. "I'm doing all right by myself."

Bobby Lee and Hiram came ambling back from the woods. Bobby Lee was dragging a yellow shirt with bright blue parrots in it.

"Thow me that shirt, Bobby Lee," The Misfit said. The shirt came flying at him and landed on his shoulder and he put it on. The grandmother couldn't name what the shirt reminded her of. "No, lady," The Misfit said while he was buttoning it up, "I found out the crime don't matter. You can do one thing or you can do another, kill a man or take a tire off his car, because sooner or later you're going to forget what it was you done and just be punished for it."

The children's mother had begun to make heaving noises as if she couldn't get her breath. "Lady," he asked, "would you and that little girl like to step off yonder with Bobby Lee and Hiram and join your husband?"

"Yes, thank you," the mother said faintly. Her left arm dangled helplessly and   125 she was holding the baby, who had gone to sleep, in the other. "Hep that lady up, Hiram," The Misfit said as she struggled to climb out of the ditch, "and Bobby Lee, you hold onto that little girl's hand."

"I don't want to hold hands with him," June Star said. "He reminds me of a pig."

The fat boy blushed and laughed and caught her by the arm and pulled her off into the woods after Hiram and her mother.

Alone with The Misfit, the grandmother found that she had lost her voice. There was not a cloud in the sky nor any sun. There was nothing around her but woods. She wanted to tell him that he must pray. She opened and closed her mouth several times before anything came out. Finally she found herself saying, "Jesus, Jesus," meaning Jesus will help you, but the way she was saying it, it sounded as if she might be cursing.

"Yes'm," The Misfit said as if he agreed. "Jesus thown everything off balance. It was the same case with Him as with me except He hadn't committed any crime and they could prove I had committed one because they had the papers on me. Of course," he said, "they never shown me my papers. That's why I sign myself now. I said long ago, you get your signature and sign everything you do and keep a copy of it. Then you'll know what you done and you can hold up the crime to the punishment and see do they match and in the end you'll have something to prove you ain't been treated right. I call myself The Misfit," he said, "because I can't make what all I done wrong fit what all I gone through in punishment."

There was a piercing scream from the woods, followed closely by a pistol   130 report. "Does it seem right to you, lady, that one is punished a heap and another ain't punished at all?"

"Jesus!" the old lady cried. "You've got good blood! I know you wouldn't shoot a lady! I know you come from nice people! Pray! Jesus, you ought not to shoot a lady. I'll give you all the money I've got!"

"Lady," The Misfit said, looking beyond her far into the woods, "there never was a body that give the undertaker a tip."

There were two more pistol reports and the grandmother raised her head like a parched old turkey hen crying for water and called, "Bailey Boy, Bailey Boy!" as if her heart would break.

"Jesus was the only One that ever raised the dead," The Misfit continued, "and He shouldn't have done it. He thown everything off balance. If He did what He said, then it's nothing for you to do but thow away everything and follow Him, and if He didn't, then it's nothing for you to do but enjoy the few minutes you got left the best way you can—by killing somebody or burning down his house or doing some other meanness to him. No pleasure but meanness," he said and his voice had become almost a snarl.

"Maybe He didn't raise the dead," the old lady mumbled, not knowing what   135
she was saying and feeling so dizzy that she sank down in the ditch with her legs twisted under her.

"I wasn't there so I can't say He didn't," The Misfit said. "I wisht I had of been there," he said, hitting the ground with his fist. "It ain't right I wasn't there because if I had of been there I would of known. Listen lady," he said in a high voice, "if I had of been there I would of known and I wouldn't be like I am now." His voice seemed about to crack and the grandmother's head cleared for an instant. She saw the man's face twisted close to her own as if he were going to cry and she murmured, "Why you're one of my babies. You're one of my own children!" She reached out and touched him on the shoulder. The Misfit sprang back as if a snake had bitten him and shot her three times through the chest. Then he put his gun down on the ground and took off his glasses and began to clean them.

Hiram and Bobby Lee returned from the woods and stood over the ditch, looking down at the grandmother who half sat and half lay in a puddle of blood with her legs crossed under her like a child's and her face smiling up at the cloudless sky.

Without his glasses, The Misfit's eyes were red-rimmed and pale and defenseless-looking. "Take her off and thow her where you thown the others," he said, picking up the cat that was rubbing itself against his leg.

"She was a talker, wasn't she?" Bobby Lee said, sliding down the ditch with a yodel.

"She would of been a good woman," The Misfit said, "if it had been   140
somebody there to shoot her every minute of her life."

"Some fun!" Bobby Lee said.

"Shut up, Bobby Lee," The Misfit said. "It's no real pleasure in life."

(1953)

◇◇◇◇◇◇◇◇◇◇◇◇◇◇◇◇◇◇◇◇◇◇

The Writing Process

Prewriting

Understanding the theme of a piece of literature involves figuring out what the whole work means. Your prewriting task here is, as usual, to ask yourself questions that will lead to the meaning of the story you just read.

Exercise: Figuring Out the Theme

Reread "A Good Man Is Hard to Find" and formulate specific leading questions about the following elements of the story. For example, you might ask yourself, "How does the title apply to the characters in the story?" or "Do the characters' names seem appropriate? Do they describe the characters in any way? Are they straightforward or satiric?" Consider the following:

1. The title.
2. The setting, especially the descriptions of the countryside that the family travels through.
3. The characters in the story, especially their names, their physical descriptions, and their relationships with one another.
4. Any significant objects (such as the grandmother's cat, the gray monkey at the Tower restaurant, The Misfit's glasses, Bailey's yellow sport shirt with bright blue parrots on it), as well as repeated uses of language like the platitudes that the grandmother and Red Sammy Butts string together and The Misfit's peculiar statements about Jesus.
5. Any changes that you notice in the characters and their feelings toward themselves or one another.
6. Any reversals or surprises that occur.
7. Any comments or observations the narrator makes about the characters and their actions.
8. The ending.

Exercise: Stating the Theme

After writing out the answers to the questions you have set for yourself, try to sum up the theme in a complete sentence. You may need to rewrite the sentence several times until you can express the theme satisfactorily. Then state the theme in another way, using other words. Are both statements valid? Are there any secondary themes that enrich the story and add to the primary theme? Write those down, too.

Take one of the statements of theme that you have formulated, and write it at the top of a blank sheet of paper. Fill the page with freewriting about this idea, expressing as quickly as you can your thoughts and feelings about O'Connor's view of human nature.

Writing

We have emphasized that your essays should be filled with supporting details from your source. Without specific references to the literary work that you are writing about, your judgments and conclusions will be vague and unconvincing.

Choosing Supporting Details

During a close second reading of a story, pay special attention to details that have potential for symbolic meaning. Thoughtful consideration of the names, places, objects, incidents, and minor characters can guide you to a deeper understanding of the work's theme. In "A Good Man Is Hard to Find," for example, you may notice some of the trenchant descriptions of the characters' physical features: the mother's face "as broad and innocent as a cabbage"; the grandmother's "leathery thin face"; Red Sam's stomach that "hung over" his trousers "like a sack of meal swaying under his shirt"; Bailey's eyes that "were as blue and intense as the parrots in his shirt"; and The Misfit's "red-rimmed" eyes, "pale and defenseless-looking." Go through the story one more time, and put a check mark next to each description of the characters. You may also note other references to their clothes and their voices. Then try to come up with an insight that expresses the meaning of these details—perhaps something like "The characters' physical appearances reflect their spiritual failings." You now have a useful claim for your paper or for a section of it.

A list of specific examples from the story could support your thesis statement, but a simple list would probably sound mechanical and unrevealing. So, if possible, classify the details. In this case, some of the physical traits are clearly humorous (almost jocular), but others, especially those about faces and eyes, also reveal a character flaw. Quote one or two examples of each kind, and then—most important—explain their significance. In this story, the characters don't see themselves or their pathetic lives very clearly. O'Connor carries out her satirical indictment of the human condition through merciless descriptions of people's physical frailties.

Approach the following writing ideas by rereading the story with your topic in mind. Jot down any details that seem relevant. Review all your notes on the story and see what general observations you can make; then select appropriate supporting details from your list and show how they support your critical generalizations.

Ideas for Writing

Ideas for Reflective Writing

1. Did you find "A Good Man Is Hard to Find" a disturbing story? a humorous story? both? How was it different from other stories you have read or have seen on television, especially stories about families?

2. Have you ever known anyone like the grandmother? Is she like your own grandmothers? Write a character sketch (an extended description) of the grandmother, comparing her to someone you have known.

Ideas for Critical Writing

1. Flannery O'Connor claimed that the violence in her fiction has a purpose. Write an interpretation of "A Good Man Is Hard to Find" that argues for a purpose behind the violence in the story.

2. O'Connor once said, "You must believe in order to understand, not understand in order to believe." Demonstrate how The Misfit illustrates this paradox.

3. CRITICAL APPROACHES. "A Good Man Is Hard to Find" focuses, in the end, on a crucial confrontation between a woman (the grandmother) and a man (The Misfit). Review literary interpretations based on gender (Chapter 34). Write an essay that argues for or against the importance of gender in interpreting the story's central conflict. You may also want to consider other characters in developing your claims.

Ideas for Researched Writing

1. Readers have offered a number of very different answers to the question of why The Misfit shoots the grandmother when he does. Find critical commentaries that offer at least three distinct interpretations of the ending to "A Good Man Is Hard to Find." Write your own essay that evaluates, reconciles, or refutes these differing interpretations.

2. In his 1941 book, *The Mask of Sanity*, Hervey Cleckley identified sixteen characteristics of a psychopath. Look up this list on the Internet. Can you apply these identifying traits to more than one of the characters in "A Good Man Is Hard to Find"? Write an essay arguing either (a) that one or more of the characters in the story are psychopaths or (b) that none of the characters in the story are truly psychopathic. Either way, explore the relationship of the psychopathy, or lack of it, to the theme of the story.

MultiModal Project

Either alone or with a group, design a multi-page informational website for "A Good Man Is Hard to Find"; your goal is to encourage fellow students to read the story and help them interpret it. Include both text and visuals. Here are some items to consider including: a brief synopsis of the plot (without giving too much away); a list of characters with brief descriptions; quotations from the story and/or from critics about the story; images of the setting, perhaps even a map; a photo of the author; some background on the author; quotations from the author; suggestions about themes and questions to keep in mind while reading the story. Look at existing websites that you like to get ideas for how to organize and design yours—particularly the home page, which should serve as a map for readers. Use a website-creation service like Weebly to compile and create your site; such sites will allow you to copy and paste text, add images, and create links without doing coding of your own.

As an alternate to composing a website for this assignment, create a slide show about "A Good Man Is Hard to Find" using presentation software like PowerPoint or Keynote.

Rewriting

When you revise, you should make sure that your paper *flows*—that your readers can follow your ideas easily.

Achieving Coherence

The best way to make your writing *coherent*—to make it easy to follow—is to have a clear thesis and to make sure that all your subpoints pertain to that thesis. If you organize the development of your ideas carefully, your paragraphs should unfold in a logical, connected way. Continuity also evolves from thinking through your ideas completely and developing them adequately. Leaps in thought and shifts in meaning often result from too much generalization and too little development.

Exercise: Checking for Coherence

Type up or print out a clean copy of the latest draft of your essay. In the margins, write a word or phrase that labels the point or describes the function of every group of related sentences. These words and phrases are called *glosses.* (You can even use short sentences.) To help write glosses for your sentences and paragraphs, ask yourself these questions: What have I said here? How many ideas are in this passage? What does this sentence/paragraph do?

When you have finished putting glosses in the margins of your essay, go back and review the glosses. Can you see a clear sequence of points? Are there any sentences or passages that you could not write a gloss for? Is there any place where you digress or introduce an unrelated idea? Using the glosses as a guide, make revisions that will improve the coherence of your essay: fill in gaps, combine repetitive sentences, cut out irrelevant material, add transitions. (See "Transitional Terms for All Occasions," page 55.)

Editing

Here are some other ways to help you strengthen the flow and coherence of your sentences.

Repeat Words and Synonyms

Repeat key words for coherence as well as for emphasis:

I do not want to *read another gothic romance. I especially do not want to read another long gothic romance.*

If repetition is tiresome or you want more variety, use a synonym:

> It was a rare *caper*, planned to the last second. Such elaborate *heists* seem to come right from a detective novel.

Take care when using repetition. Repeated words should be important or emphatic. Do not repeat a common, limp term because you are too tired to find a synonym. Be aware, however, that synonyms are not always interchangeable; check the meaning of any word you are not sure of. The following introduction to a student paper suffers because the writer needlessly repeats the same uninteresting verb (which we have italicized):

> Shirley Jackson's "The Lottery" is a complex story that deals with a fundamental part of human psychology, the *using* of scapegoats. Scapegoats have been *used* throughout history to justify actions. Many times scapegoats are *used* to conceal human errors or prejudices. Scapegoats are, in fact, still *used* today.

Notice that the repetition of the key word *scapegoats* emphasizes the main idea of the paper. But the ineffective repetition should be revised (our substituted verbs are italicized in the following revision):

> Shirley Jackson's "The Lottery" is a complex story that deals with a fundamental *element* of human psychology—using scapegoats. Scapegoats have been *created* throughout history to justify actions. Many times they are *employed* to conceal human errors or prejudices. In fact, scapegoats still *exist* today.

Try Parallel Structure

Repeat a grammatical pattern to tie points and details together:

> In the morning Emma Bovary ate breakfast with her husband; in the afternoon she picnicked with her paramour.
>
> The play was about to end: the villain stalked off, the lovers kissed, the curtain fell, and the audience applauded wildly.

Be sure that your grammatical patterns actually are parallel. If your phrases or clauses do not follow the same structure, you will lose the good effect.

Not parallel	In "The Lottery" these characteristics include *unwillingness to change, sticking to tradition, fear of peer pressure,* and *just plain being afraid.*
Parallel	In "The Lottery" these characteristics include *unwillingness to change, enslavement to tradition, fear of peer pressure,* and *fear of the unknown.*
Not parallel	Many times scapegoats are invoked to conceal *human errors* or *the way people unfairly judge one another.*
Parallel	Many times scapegoats are used to conceal *human errors* and *prejudices.*

12 Critical Casebook: Joyce Carol Oates's *"Where Are You Going, Where Have You Been?"*

Chapter Preview

Of the more than four hundred stories that Joyce Carol Oates has published, "Where Are You Going, Where Have You Been?" continues to be the most anthologized and the most discussed. Inspired by a magazine article about a young killer in Arizona, the story was first published in 1966. Oates has described the story as "psychological realism" and a "realistic allegory," but the exact nature of its form and meaning remains a matter for debate and discussion among literary critics and general readers alike. This casebook presents the text of the story, some information about the story's origin, and excerpts from four critical interpretations.

By the end of this chapter, you will be able to:

- Analyze a short story in a critical context.
- Compare four different critical interpretations of the same work.
- Synthesize critical interpretations with your own reflections.
- Use research to write critically about fiction.

Joyce Carol Oates   1938–

Joyce Carol Oates grew up during the depression on a farm in upstate New York. She won a scholarship to Syracuse University, where she became valedictorian of her graduating class. Oates has achieved a prodigious literary output, publishing more than eighty books of fiction, poetry, drama, essays, and literary criticism. Wryly, she once suggested that her epitaph could read, "She certainly tried." Oates has said she writes about "real people in a real society," but her fiction frequently centers on the connection between violence and sexual obsession.

Where Are You Going, Where Have You Been?

For Bob Dylan [1]

Her name was Connie. She was fifteen and she had a quick, nervous giggling habit of craning her neck to glance into mirrors or checking other people's faces to make sure her own was all right. Her mother, who noticed everything and knew everything and who hadn't much reason any longer to look at her own face, always scolded Connie about it. "Stop gawking at yourself. Who are you? You think you're so pretty?" she would say. Connie would raise her eyebrows at these familiar complaints and look right through her mother, into a shadowy vision of herself as she was right at that moment: she knew she was pretty and that was everything. Her mother had been pretty once too, if you could believe those old snapshots in the album, but now her looks were gone and that was why she was always after Connie.

"Why don't you keep your room clean like your sister? How've you got your hair fixed—what the hell stinks? Hair spray? You don't see your sister using that junk."

Her sister June was twenty-four and still lived at home. She was a secretary in the high school Connie attended, and if that wasn't bad enough—with her in the same building—she was so plain and chunky and steady that Connie had to hear her praised all the time by her mother and her mother's sisters. June did this, June did that, she saved money and helped clean the house and cooked and Connie couldn't do a thing, her mind was all filled with trashy daydreams. Their father was away at work most of the time and when he came home he wanted supper and he read the newspaper at supper and after supper he went to bed. He didn't bother talking much to them, but around his bent head Connie's mother kept picking at her until Connie wished her mother was dead and she herself was dead and it was all over. "She makes me want to throw up sometimes," she complained to her friends. She had a high, breathless, amused voice that made everything she said sound a little forced, whether it was sincere or not.

There was one good thing: June went places with girl friends of hers, girls who were just as plain and steady as she, and so when Connie wanted to do that her mother had no objections. The father of Connie's best girl friend drove the girls the three miles to town and left them off at a shopping plaza so they could walk through the stores or go to a movie, and when he came to pick them up again at eleven he never bothered to ask what they had done.

They must have been familiar sights, walking around the shopping plaza in their shorts and flat ballerina slippers that always scuffed the sidewalk, with charm bracelets jingling on their thin wrists; they would lean together to whisper and laugh secretly if someone passed who amused or interested them. Connie had long dark blond hair that drew anyone's eye to it, and she wore part of it pulled up on her head and puffed out and the rest of it she let fall down her back. She wore a pull-over jersey blouse that looked one way when she was at home and another way when she was away from home. Everything about her had two sides to it, one for home and one for anywhere that was not home: her walk, which could be childlike and bobbing, or languid enough to make anyone think

5

---

[1]Bob Dylan (b. 1941), the composer, author, and singer who devised and popularized folk rock during the 1960s.

she was hearing music in her head; her mouth, which was pale and smirking most of the time, but bright and pink on these evenings out; her laugh, which was cynical and drawling at home—"Ha, ha, very funny"—but high-pitched and nervous anywhere else, like the jingling of the charms on her bracelet.

Sometimes they did go shopping or to a movie, but sometimes they went across the highway, ducking fast across the busy road, to a drive-in restaurant where older kids hung out. The restaurant was shaped like a big bottle, though squatter than a real bottle, and on its cap was a revolving figure of a grinning boy who held a hamburger aloft. One night in mid-summer they ran across, breathless with daring, and right away someone leaned out a car window and invited them over, but it was just a boy from high school they didn't like. It made them feel good to be able to ignore him. They went up through the maze of parked and cruising cars to the bright-lit, fly-infested restaurant, their faces pleased and expectant as if they were entering a sacred building that loomed up out of the night to give them what haven and blessing they yearned for. They sat at the counter and crossed their legs at the ankles, their thin shoulders rigid with excitement, and listened to the music that made everything so good: the music was always in the background, like music at a church service; it was something to depend upon.

A boy named Eddie came in to talk with them. He sat backwards on his stool, turning himself jerkily around in semi-circles and then stopping and turning again, and after a while he asked Connie if she would like something to eat. She said she would and so she tapped her friend's arm on her way out—her friend pulled her face up into a brave, droll look—and Connie said she would meet her at eleven, across the way. "I just hate to leave her like that," Connie said earnestly, but the boy said that she wouldn't be alone for long. So they went out to his car, and on the way Connie couldn't help but let her eyes wander over the windshields and faces all around her, her face gleaming with a joy that had nothing to do with Eddie or even this place; it might have been the music. She drew her shoulders up and sucked in her breath with the pure pleasure of being alive, and just at that moment she happened to glance at a face just a few feet from hers. It was a boy with shaggy black hair, in a convertible jalopy painted gold. He stared at her and then his lips widened into a grin. Connie slit her eyes at him and turned away, but she couldn't help glancing back and there he was still watching her. He wagged a finger and laughed and said, "Gonna get you, baby," and Connie turned away again without Eddie noticing anything.

She spent three hours with him, at the restaurant where they ate hamburgers and drank Cokes in wax cups that were always sweating, and then down an alley a mile or so away, and when he left her off at five to eleven only the movie house was still open at the plaza. Her girl friend was there, talking with a boy. When Connie came up, the two girls smiled at each other and Connie said, "How was the movie?" and the girl said, "*You* should know." They rode off with the girl's father, sleepy and pleased, and Connie couldn't help but look back at the darkened shopping plaza with its big empty parking lot and its signs that were faded and ghostly now, and over at the drive-in restaurant where cars were still circling tirelessly. She couldn't hear the music at this distance.

Next morning June asked her how the movie was and Connie said, "So-so."

She and that girl and occasionally another girl went out several times a week, and the rest of the time Connie spent around the house—it was summer 10 vacation—getting in her mother's way and thinking, dreaming about the boys she met. But all the boys fell back and dissolved into a single face that was not even a face, but an idea, a feeling, mixed up with the urgent insistent pounding of the music and the humid night air of July. Connie's mother kept dragging her back to the daylight by finding things for her to do or saying, suddenly, "What's this about the Pettinger girl?"

And Connie would say nervously, "Oh, her. That dope." She always drew thick clear lines between herself and such girls, and her mother was simple and kind enough to believe her. Her mother was so simple, Connie thought, that it was maybe cruel to fool her so much. Her mother went scuffling around the house in old bedroom slippers and complained over the telephone to one sister about the other, then the other called up and the two of them complained about the third one. If June's name was mentioned her mother's tone was approving, and if Connie's name was mentioned it was disapproving. This did not really mean she disliked Connie, and actually Connie thought that her mother preferred her to June just because she was prettier, but the two of them kept up a pretense of exasperation, a sense that they were tugging and struggling over something of little value to either of them. Sometimes, over coffee, they were almost friends, but something would come up—some vexation that was like a fly buzzing suddenly around their heads—and their faces went hard with contempt.

One Sunday Connie got up at eleven—none of them bothered with church—and washed her hair so that it could dry all day long in the sun. Her parents and sister were going to a barbecue at an aunt's house and Connie said no, she wasn't interested, rolling her eyes to let her mother know just what she thought of it. "Stay home alone then," her mother said sharply. Connie sat out back in a lawn chair and watched them drive away, her father quiet and bald, hunched around so that he could back the car out, her mother with a look that was still angry and not at all softened through the windshield, and in the back seat poor old June, all dressed up as if she didn't know what a barbecue was, with all the running yelling kids and the flies. Connie sat with her eyes closed in the sun, dreaming and dazed with the warmth about her as if this were a kind of love, the caresses of love, and her mind slipped over onto thoughts of the boy she had been with the night before and how nice he had been, how sweet it always was, not the way someone like June would suppose but sweet, gentle, the way it was in movies and promised in songs; and when she opened her eyes she hardly knew where she was, the back yard ran off into weeds and a fence-like line of trees and behind it the sky was perfectly blue and still. The asbestos "ranch house" that was now three years old startled her—it looked small. She shook her head as if to get awake.

It was too hot. She went inside the house and turned on the radio to drown out the quiet. She sat on the edge of her bed, barefoot, and listened for an hour and a half to a program called XYZ Sunday Jamboree, record after record of hard, fast, shrieking songs she sang along with, interspersed by exclamations from "Bobby King": "An' look here, you girls at Napoleon's—Son and Charley want you to pay real close attention to this song coming up!"

And Connie paid close attention herself, bathed in a glow of slow-pulsed joy that seemed to rise mysteriously out of the music itself and lay languidly about the airless little room, breathed in and breathed out with each gentle rise and fall of her chest.

After a while she heard a car coming up the drive. She sat up at once, startled, because it couldn't be her father so soon. The gravel kept crunching all the way 15 in from the road—the driveway was long—and Connie ran to the window. It was a car she didn't know. It was an open jalopy, painted a bright gold that caught the sunlight opaquely. Her heart began to pound and her fingers snatched at her hair, checking it, and she whispered, "Christ. Christ," wondering how bad she looked. The car came to a stop at the side door and the horn sounded four short taps, as if this were a signal Connie knew.

She went into the kitchen and approached the door slowly, then hung out the screen door, her bare toes curling down off the step. There were two boys in the car and now she recognized the driver: he had shaggy, shabby black hair that looked crazy as a wig and he was grinning at her.

"I ain't late, am I?" he said.

"Who the hell do you think you are?" Connie said.

"Toldja I'd be out, didn't I?"

"I don't even know who you are." 20

She spoke sullenly, careful to show no interest or pleasure, and he spoke in a fast, bright monotone. Connie looked past him to the other boy, taking her time. He had fair brown hair, with a lock that fell onto his forehead. His sideburns gave him a fierce, embarrassed look, but so far he hadn't even bothered to glance at her. Both boys wore sunglasses. The driver's glasses were metallic and mirrored everything in miniature.

"You wanta come for a ride?" he said.

Connie smirked and let her hair fall loose over one shoulder.

"Don'tcha like my car? New paint job," he said. "Hey."

"What?" 25

"You're cute."

She pretended to fidget, chasing flies away from the door.

"Don'tcha believe me, or what?" he said.

"Look, I don't even know who you are," Connie said in disgust.

"Hey, Ellie's got a radio, see. Mine's broke down." He lifted his friend's arm and 30 showed her the little transistor radio the boy was holding, and now Connie began to hear the music. It was the same program that was playing inside the house.

"Bobby King?" she said.

"I listen to him all the time. I think he's great."

"He's kind of great," Connie said reluctantly.

"Listen, that guy's *great*. He knows where the action is."

Connie blushed a little, because the glasses made it impossible for her to see 35 just what this boy was looking at. She couldn't decide if she liked him or if he was just a jerk, and so she dawdled in the doorway and wouldn't come down or go back inside. She said, "What's all that stuff painted on your car?"

"Can'tcha read it?" He opened the door very carefully, as if he were afraid it might fall off. He slid out just as carefully, planting his feet firmly on the ground, the tiny metallic world in his glasses slowing down like gelatine hardening and in the midst of it Connie's bright green blouse. "This here is my name to begin with," he said. ARNOLD FRIEND was written in tarlike black letters on the side, with a drawing of a round, grinning face that reminded Connie of a pumpkin, except it wore sunglasses. "I wanta introduce myself. I'm Arnold Friend and that's my real name and I'm gonna be your friend, honey, and inside the car's Ellie Oscar, he's kinda shy." Ellie brought his transistor radio up to his shoulder and balanced it there. "Now these numbers are a secret code, honey," Arnold Friend explained. He read off the numbers 33, 19, 17 and raised his eyebrows at her to see what she thought of that, but she didn't think much of it. The left rear fender had been smashed and around it was written, on the gleaming gold background: DONE BY CRAZY WOMAN DRIVER. Connie had to laugh at that. Arnold Friend was pleased at her laughter and looked up at her. "Around the other side's a lot more—you wanta come and see them?"

"No."

"Why not?"

"Why should I?"

"Don'tcha wanta see what's on the car? Don'tcha wanta go for a ride?"   40

"I don't know."

"Why not?"

"I got things to do."

"Like what?"

"Things."   45

He laughed as if she had said something funny. He slapped his thigh. He was standing in a strange way, leaning back against the car as if he were balancing himself. He wasn't tall, only an inch or so taller than she would be if she came down to him. Connie liked the way he was dressed, which was the way all of them dressed: tight faded jeans stuffed into black, scuffed boots, a belt that pulled his waist in and showed how lean he was, and a white pull-over shirt that was a little soiled and showed the hard small muscles of his arms and shoulders. He looked as if he probably did hard work, lifting and carrying things. Even his neck looked muscular. And his face was a familiar face, somehow: the jaw and chin and cheeks slightly darkened because he hadn't shaved for a day or two, and the nose long and hawklike, sniffing as if she were a treat he was going to gobble up and it was all a joke.

"Connie, you ain't telling the truth. This is your day set aside for a ride with me and you know it," he said, still laughing. The way he straightened and recovered from his fit of laughing showed that it had been all fake.

"How do you know what my name is?" she said suspiciously.

"It's Connie."

"Maybe and maybe not."   50

"I know my Connie," he said, wagging his finger. Now she remembered him even better, back at the restaurant, and her cheeks warmed at the thought of how she had sucked in her breath just at the moment she passed him—how she must have looked to him. And he had remembered her. "Ellie and I come out here especially for you," he said. "Ellie can sit in back. How about it?"

"Where?"

"Where what?"

"Where're we going?"

He looked at her. He took off the sunglasses and she saw how pale the skin   55
around his eyes was, like holes that were not in shadow but instead in light. His eyes were chips of broken glass that catch the light in an amiable way. He smiled. It was as if the idea of going for a ride somewhere, to some place, was a new idea to him.

"Just for a ride, Connie sweetheart."

"I never said my name was Connie," she said.

"But I know what it is. I know your name and all about you, lots of things," Arnold Friend said. He had not moved yet but stood still leaning back against the side of his jalopy. "I took a special interest in you, such a pretty girl, and found out all about you—like I know your parents and sister are gone somewheres and

I know where and how long they're going to be gone, and I know who you were with last night, and your best girl friend's name is Betty. Right?"

He spoke in a simple lilting voice, exactly as if he were reciting the words to a song. His smile assured her that everything was fine. In the car Ellie turned up the volume on his radio and did not bother to look around at them.

"Ellie can sit in the back seat," Arnold Friend said. He indicated his friend with a   60
casual jerk of his chin, as if Ellie did not count and she should not bother with him.

"How'd you find out all that stuff?" Connie said.

"Listen: Betty Schultz and Tony Fitch and Jimmy Pettinger and Nancy Pettinger," he said in a chant. "Raymond Stanley and Bob Hutter—"

"Do you know all those kids?"

"I know everybody."

"Look, you're kidding. You're not from around here."   65

"Sure."

"But—how come we never saw you before?"

"Sure you saw me before," he said. He looked down at his boots, as if he were a little offended. "You just don't remember."

"I guess I'd remember you," Connie said.

"Yeah?" He looked up at this, beaming. He was pleased. He began to mark   70
time with the music from Ellie's radio, tapping his fists lightly together. Connie looked away from his smile to the car, which was painted so bright it almost hurt her eyes to look at it. She looked at that name, ARNOLD FRIEND. And up at the front fender was an expression that was familiar—MAN THE FLYING SAUCERS. It was an expression kids had used the year before but didn't use this year. She looked at it for a while as if the words meant something to her that she did not yet know.

"What're you thinking about? Huh?" Arnold Friend demanded. "Not worried about your hair blowing around in the car, are you?"

"No."

"Think I maybe can't drive good?"

"How do I know?"

"You're a hard girl to handle. How come?" he said. "Don't you know I'm   75
your friend? Didn't you see me put my sign in the air when you walked by?"

"What sign?"

"My sign." And he drew an X in the air, leaning out toward her. They were maybe ten feet apart. After his hand fell back to his side the X was still in the air, almost visible. Connie let the screen door close and stood perfectly still inside it, listening to the music from her radio and the boy's blend together. She stared at Arnold Friend. He stood there so stiffly relaxed, pretending to be relaxed, with one hand idly on the door handle as if he were keeping himself up that way and had no intention of ever moving again. She recognized most things about him, the tight jeans that showed his thighs and buttocks and the greasy leather boots and the tight shirt, and even that slippery friendly smile of his, that sleepy dreamy smile that all the boys used to get across ideas they didn't want to put into words. She recognized all this and also the singsong way he talked, slightly mocking, kidding, but serious and a little melancholy, and she recognized the way he tapped one fist against the other in homage to the perpetual music behind him. But all these things did not come together.

She said suddenly, "Hey, how old are you?"

His smile faded. She could see then that he wasn't a kid, he was much older—thirty, maybe more. At this knowledge her heart began to pound faster.

"That's a crazy thing to ask. Can'tcha see I'm your own age?"   80

"Like hell you are."

"Or maybe a coupla years older. I'm eighteen."

"Eighteen?" she said doubtfully.

He grinned to reassure her and lines appeared at the corners of his mouth.
His teeth were big and white. He grinned so broadly his eyes became slits and
she saw how thick the lashes were, thick and black as if painted with a black tarlike material. Then, abruptly, he seemed to become embarrassed and looked over
his shoulder at Ellie. "*Him*, he's crazy," he said. "Ain't he a riot? He's a nut, a
real character." Ellie was still listening to the music. His sunglasses told nothing
about what he was thinking. He wore a bright orange shirt unbuttoned halfway
to show his chest, which was a pale, bluish chest and not muscular like Arnold
Friend's. His shirt collar was turned up all around and the very tips of the collar pointed out past his chin as if they were protecting him. He was pressing the
transistor radio up against his ear and sat there in a kind of daze, right in the sun.

"He's kinda strange," Connie said.   85

"Hey, she says you're kinda strange! Kinda strange!" Arnold Friend cried. He
pounded on the car to get Ellie's attention. Ellie turned for the first time and
Connie saw with shock that he wasn't a kid either—he had a fair, hairless face,
cheeks reddened slightly as if the veins grew too close to the surface of his skin,
the face of a forty-year-old baby. Connie felt a wave of dizziness rise in her at
this sight and she stared at him as if waiting for something to change the shock
of the moment, make it all right again. Ellie's lips kept shaping words, mum-
bling along with the words blasting in his ear.

"Maybe you two better go away," Connie said faintly.

"What? How come?" Arnold Friend cried. "We come out here to take you
for a ride. It's Sunday." He had the voice of the man on the radio now. It was the
same voice, Connie thought. "Don'tcha know it's Sunday all day? And honey, no
matter who you were with last night, today you're with Arnold Friend and don't
you forget it! Maybe you better step out here," he said, and this last was in a different voice. It was a little flatter, as if the heat was finally getting to him.

"No. I got things to do."

"Hey."   90

"You two better leave."

"We ain't leaving until you come with us."

"Like hell I am—"

"Connie, don't fool around with me. I mean—I mean, don't fool *around*," he
said, shaking his head. He laughed incredulously. He placed his sunglasses on
top of his head, carefully, as if he were indeed wearing a wig, and brought the
stems down behind his ears. Connie stared at him, another wave of dizziness
and fear rising in her so that for a moment he wasn't even in focus but was just a
blur standing there against his gold car, and she had the idea that he had driven
up the driveway all right but had come from nowhere before that and belonged
nowhere and that everything about him and even about the music that was so
familiar to her was only half real.

"If my father comes and sees you—"   95

"He ain't coming. He's at a barbecue."

"How do you know that?"

"Aunt Tillie's. Right now they're—uh—they're drinking. Sitting around," he
said vaguely, squinting as if he were staring all the way to town and over to Aunt

Tillie's back yard. Then the vision seemed to get clear and he nodded energetically. "Yeah. Sitting around. There's your sister in a blue dress, huh? And high heels, the poor sad bitch—nothing like you, sweetheart! And your mother's helping some fat woman with the corn, they're cleaning the corn—husking the corn—"

"What fat woman?" Connie cried.

"How do I know what fat woman. I don't know every goddamn fat woman in   100
the world!" Arnold Friend laughed.

"Oh, that's Mrs. Hornsby.... Who invited her?" Connie said. She felt a little light-headed. Her breath was coming quickly.

"She's too fat. I don't like them fat. I like them the way you are, honey," he said, smiling sleepily at her. They stared at each other for a while through the screen door. He said softly, "Now, what you're going to do is this: you're going to come out that door. You're going to sit up front with me and Ellie's going to sit in the back, the hell with Ellie, right? This isn't Ellie's date. You're my date. I'm your lover, honey."

"What? You're crazy—"

"Yes, I'm your lover. You don't know what that is but you will," he said. "I know that too. I know all about you. But look: it's real nice and you couldn't ask for nobody better than me, or more polite. I always keep my word. I'll tell you how it is, I'm always nice at first, the first time. I'll hold you so tight you won't think you have to try to get away or pretend anything because you'll know you can't. And I'll come inside you where it's all secret and you'll give in to me and you'll love me—"

"Shut up! You're crazy!" Connie said. She backed away from the door. She   105
put her hands up against her ears as if she'd heard something terrible, something not meant for her. "People don't talk like that, you're crazy," she muttered. Her heart was almost too big now for her chest and its pumping made sweat break out all over her. She looked out to see Arnold Friend pause and then take a step toward the porch, lurching. He almost fell. But, like a clever drunken man, he managed to catch his balance. He wobbled in his high boots and grabbed hold of one of the porch posts.

"Honey?" he said. "You still listening?"

"Get the hell out of here!"

"Be nice, honey. Listen."

"I'm going to call the police—"

He wobbled again and out of the side of his mouth came a fast spat curse, an   110
aside not meant for her to hear. But even this "Christ!" sounded forced. Then he began to smile again. She watched this smile come, awkward as if he were smiling from inside a mask. His whole face was a mask, she thought wildly, tanned down to his throat but then running out as if he had plastered makeup on his face but had forgotten about his throat.

"Honey—? Listen, here's how it is. I always tell the truth and I promise you this: I ain't coming in that house after you."

"You better not! I'm going to call the police if you—if you don't—"

"Honey," he said, talking right through her voice, "honey, I'm not coming in there but you are coming out here. You know why?"

She was panting. The kitchen looked like a place she had never seen before, some room she had run inside but that wasn't good enough, wasn't going to help her. The kitchen window had never had a curtain, after three years, and there were dishes in the sink for her to do—probably—and if you ran your hand across the table you'd probably feel something sticky there.

"You listening honey? Hey?" 115

"—going to call the police—"

"Soon as you touch the phone I don't need to keep my promise and can come inside. You won't want that."

She rushed forward and tried to lock the door. Her fingers were shaking. "But why lock it," Arnold Friend said gently, talking right into her face. "It's just a screen door. It's just nothing." One of his boots was at a strange angle, as if his foot wasn't in it. It pointed out to the left, bent at the ankle. "I mean, anybody can break through a screen door and glass and wood and iron or anything else if he needs to, anybody at all, and specially Arnold Friend. If the place got lit up with a fire, honey, you'd come runnin' out into my arms, right into my arms an' safe at home—like you knew I was your lover and'd stopped fooling around. I don't mind a nice shy girl but I don't like no fooling around." Part of those words were spoken with a slight rhythmic lilt, and Connie somehow recognized them—the echo of a song from last year, about a girl rushing into her boy friend's arms and coming home again—

Connie stood barefoot on the linoleum floor, staring at him. "What do you want?" she whispered.

"I want you," he said. 120

"What?"

"Seen you that night and thought, that's the one, yes sir. I never needed to look anymore."

"But my father's coming back. He's coming to get me. I had to wash my hair first—" She spoke in a dry, rapid voice, hardly raising it for him to hear.

"No, your daddy is not coming and yes, you had to wash your hair and you washed it for me. It's nice and shining and all for me. I thank you sweetheart," he said with a mock bow, but again he almost lost his balance. He had to bend and adjust his boots. Evidently his feet did not go all the way down; the boots must have been stuffed with something so that he would seem taller. Connie stared out at him and behind him at Ellie in the car, who seemed to be looking off toward Connie's right, into nothing. This Ellie said, pulling the words out of the air one after another as if he were just discovering them, "You want me to pull out the phone?"

"Shut your mouth and keep it shut," Arnold Friend said, his face red from 125 bending over or maybe from embarrassment because Connie had seen his boots. "This ain't none of your business."

"What—what are you doing? What do you want?" Connie said. "If I call the police they'll get you, they'll arrest you—"

"Promise was not to come in unless you touch that phone, and I'll keep that promise," he said. He resumed his erect position and tried to force his shoulders back. He sounded like a hero in a movie, declaring something important. But he spoke too loudly and it was as if he were speaking to someone behind Connie. "I ain't made plans for coming in that house where I don't belong but just for you to come out to me, the way you should. Don't you know who I am?"

"You're crazy," she whispered. She backed away from the door but did not want to go into another part of the house, as if this would give him permission to come through the door. "What do you...you're crazy, you.... "

"Huh? What're you saying, honey?"

Her eyes darted everywhere in the kitchen. She could not remember what it 130 was, this room.

"This is how it is, honey: you come out and we'll drive away, have a nice ride. But if you don't come out we're gonna wait till your people come home and then they're all going to get it."

"You want that telephone pulled out?" Ellie said. He held the radio away from his ear and grimaced, as if without the radio the air was too much for him.

"I toldja shut up, Ellie," Arnold Friend said, "you're deaf, get a hearing aid, right? Fix yourself up. This little girl's no trouble and's gonna be nice to me, so Ellie keep to yourself, this ain't your date—right? Don't hem in on me, don't hog, don't crush, don't bird dog, don't trail me," he said in a rapid, meaningless voice, as if he were running through all the expressions he'd learned but was no longer sure which of them was in style, then rushing on to new ones, making them up with his eyes closed. "Don't crawl under my fence, don't squeeze in my chipmunk hole, don't sniff my glue, suck my popsicle, keep your own greasy fingers on yourself!" He shaded his eyes and peered in at Connie, who was backed against the kitchen table. "Don't mind him, honey, he's just a creep. He's a dope. Right? I'm the boy for you and like I said, you come out here nice like a lady and give me your hand, and nobody else gets hurt, I mean, your nice old bald-headed daddy and your mummy and your sister in her high heels. Because listen: why bring them in this?"

"Leave me alone," Connie whispered.

"Hey, you know that old woman down the road, the one with the chickens and stuff—you know her?"   135

"She's dead!"

"Dead? What? You know her?" Arnold Friend said.

"She's dead—"

"Don't you like her?"

"She's dead—she's—she isn't here any more—"?   140

"But don't you like her, I mean, you got something against her? Some grudge or something?" Then his voice dipped as if he were conscious of a rudeness. He touched the sunglasses perched up on top of his head as if to make sure they were still there. "Now, you be a good girl."

"What are you going to do?"

"Just two things, or maybe three," Arnold Friend said. "But I promise it won't last long and you'll like me that way you get to like people you're close to. You will. It's all over for you here, so come on out. You don't want your people in any trouble, do you?"

She turned and bumped against a chair or something, hurting her leg, but she ran into the back room and picked up the telephone. Something roared in her ear, a tiny roaring, and she was so sick with fear that she could do nothing but listen to it—the telephone was clammy and very heavy and her fingers groped down to the dial but were too weak to touch it. She began to scream into the phone, into the roaring. She cried out, she cried for her mother, she felt her breath start jerking back and forth in her lungs as if it were something Arnold Friend was stabbing her with again and again with no tenderness. A noisy sorrowful wailing rose all about her and she was locked inside it the way she was locked inside this house.

After a while she could hear again. She was sitting on the floor with her wet back against the wall.   145

Arnold Friend was saying from the door, "That's a good girl. Put the phone back."

She kicked the phone away from her.

"No, honey. Pick it up. Put it back right."

She picked it up and put it back. The dial tone stopped.

"That's a good girl. Now, you come outside."   150

She was hollow with what had been fear but what was now just an emptiness. All that screaming had blasted it out of her. She sat, one leg cramped under her, and deep inside her brain was something like a pinpoint of light that kept going and would not let her relax. She thought, I'm not going to see my mother again. She thought, I'm not going to sleep in my bed again. Her bright green blouse was all wet.

Arnold Friend said, in a gentle-loud voice that was like a stage voice, "The place where you came from ain't there any more, and where you had in mind to go is cancelled out. This place you are now—inside your daddy's house—is nothing but a cardboard box I can knock down any time. You know that and always did know it. You hear me?"

She thought, I have got to think. I have to know what to do.

"We'll go out to a nice field, out in the country here where it smells so nice and it's sunny," Arnold Friend said. "I'll have my arms tight around you so you won't need to try to get away and I'll show you what love is like, what it does. The hell with this house! It looks solid all right," he said. He ran a fingernail down the screen and the noise did not make Connie shiver, as it would have the day before. "Now, put your hand on your heart, honey. Feel that? That feels solid too but we know better. Be nice to me, be sweet like you can because what else is there for a girl like you but to be sweet and pretty and give in?—and get away before her people come back?"

She felt her pounding heart. Her hand seemed to enclose it. She thought for   155
the first time in her life that it was nothing that was hers, that belonged to her, but just a pounding, living thing inside this body that wasn't really hers either.

"You don't want them to get hurt," Arnold Friend went on. "Now, get up, honey. Get up all by yourself."

She stood.

"Now, turn this way. That's right. Come over here to me—Ellie, put that away, didn't I tell you? You dope. You miserable creepy dope," Arnold Friend said. His words were not angry but only part of an incantation. The incantation was kindly. "Now, come out through the kitchen to me, honey, and let's see a smile, try it, you're a brave, sweet little girl and now they're eating corn and hot dogs cooked to bursting over an outdoor fire, and they don't know one thing about you and never did and honey, you're better than them because not a one of them would have done this for you."

Connie felt the linoleum under her feet; it was cool. She brushed her hair back out of her eyes. Arnold Friend let go of the post tentatively and opened his arms for her, his elbows pointing in toward each other and his wrists limp, to show that this was an embarrassed embrace and a little mocking, he didn't want to make her self-conscious.

She put out her hand against the screen. She watched herself push the door   160
slowly open as if she were back safe somewhere in the other doorway, watching this body and this head of long hair moving out into the sunlight where Arnold Friend waited.

"My sweet little blue-eyed girl," he said in a half-sung sigh that had nothing to do with her brown eyes but was taken up just the same by the vast sunlit reaches of the land behind him and on all sides of him—so much land that Connie had never seen before and did not recognize except to know that she was going to it.

(1966)

The Story's Origins

Oates has acknowledged that she often bases stories on newspaper head-lines: "It is the very skeletal nature of the newspaper, I think, that attracts me to it, the need it inspires in me to give flesh to such neatly and thinly-told tales." The inspiration for "Where Are You Going" was the tale of Charles Schmid, a twenty-three-year-old from Tucson who cruised teen-age hangouts, picking up girls for rides in his gold convertible. Eventually, he murdered three of them, while other teenagers served as accomplices. He was convicted of murder in 1966; his story was written up in *Life*, as well as other newsmagazines, during the winter of 1965–66. Biographer Greg Johnson describes how Oates dealt with this source material.

> In early March, Joyce had picked up a copy of *Life* magazine and begun reading an article about Charles Schmid, an Arizona serial killer of teenage girls whom the article dubbed "The Pied Piper of Tucson." Joyce immediate-ly saw material for fiction in Schmid's story, which included many grotesque elements: only five three, Schmid stuffed rags and tin cans in the bottoms of his boots to make himself appear taller. Yet Joyce had read only part of the article, not wanting "to be distracted by too much detail." With her usual impulse toward blending realism and allegory, she connected Schmid's ex-ploits to mythic legends and folk songs about "Death and the Maiden," and "the story came to me more or less in a piece." Focusing on Connie, an or-dinary teenage girl who succumbs to the demonic Arnold Friend, the story was originally titled "Death and the Maiden," but Joyce decided the title was "too pompous, too literary." After the story's first appearance, in the fall 1966 issue of *Epoch*, Joyce dedicated the story to Bob Dylan. While writing "Where Are You Going, Where Have You Been?" she had been listening to Dylan's song "It's All Over Now, Baby Blue," which struck Joyce as "haunt-ingly elegiac," similar in tone to the story she had written.
>
> *Invisible Writer: A Biography of Joyce Carol Oates,* 1998: 135.

Four Critical Interpretations

Greg Johnson interprets the story as a "feminist allegory."

> When the ironically named Arnold Friend first arrives at Connie's house, driving his sleazy gold jalopy and accompanied by a strange, ominously silent male sidekick, Connie deflects him with her usual pert sarcasms and practiced indifference. Throughout the long scene that follows, Connie's terror slowly builds. The fast-talking Arnold Friend insinuates himself into her thinking, attempting to persuade her that he's her "lover," his smooth-talking seduc-tiveness finally giving way to threats of violence against Connie's family if she doesn't surrender to his desires. Oates places Connie inside the kitchen and Arnold Friend outside with only a locked screen door between them. While Friend could enter by force at any time, Oates emphasizes the seduction, the sinister singsong of Friend's voice: a demonic outsider, he has arrived to wrest Connie from the protective confines of her family, her home, and her

own innocence. Oates makes clear that Friend represents Connie's initiation not into sex itself—she is already sexually experienced—but into sexual bondage: "I promise it won't last long," he tells her, "and you will like me the way you get to like people you're close to. You will. It's all over for you here." As feminist allegory, then, the story describes the beginning of a young and sexually attractive girl's enslavement within a conventional, male-dominated sexual relationship....

While in realistic terms, especially considering the story's source, Connie may be approaching her actual death, in allegorical terms she is dying spiritually, surrendering her autonomous selfhood to male desire and domination. Her characterization as a typical girl reaching sexual maturity suggests that her fate represents that suffered by most young women—unwillingly and in secret terror—even in America in the 1960s. As a feminist allegory, then, "Where Are You Going, Where Have You Been?" is a cautionary tale, suggesting that young women are "going" exactly where their mothers and grandmothers have already "been": into sexual bondage at the hands of a male "Friend."

Understanding Joyce Carol Oates, 1987: 101–02.

Larry Rubin argues that Connie has fallen asleep in the sun and has a dream about a composite figure that symbolizes her fear of the adult world. He discusses the references to sleep that frame the Arnold Friend episode and the nightmare quality of her inability to control the situation.

> The fact that Connie recognizes the sensual music being broadcast on Arnold's car radio as being the same as that emanating from her own in the house provides another strong clue to his real nature—that of a dream-like projection of her erotic fantasies. His music and hers, Oates tells us, blend perfectly, and indeed Arnold's voice is perceived by Connie as being the same as that of the disc jockey on the radio. Thus the protagonist's inner state of consciousness is being given physical form by her imagination.... Connie's initial response to her first view of Arnold the night before, in the shopping center, was one of intense sexual excitement; now she discovers how dangerous that excitement can be to her survival as a person. Instinctively, she recoils; but the conflict between excitement and desire, on the one hand, and fear, on the other, leaves her will paralyzed, and she cannot even dial the phone for help. Such physical paralysis in the face of oncoming danger is a phenomenon familiar to all dreamers, like being unable to run from the monster because your legs won't respond to your will.

> Finally, the rather un-devil-like tribute that Arnold pays Connie as she finally succumbs to his threats against her family and goes out of the house to him—"you're better than them [her family] because not a one of them would have done this for you"—is exactly what poor, unappreciated Connie wants to hear. She is making a noble sacrifice, and in her dream she gives herself full credit for it.

Explicator 42 (1984): 57–59.

Joyce M. Wegs contends that "Arnold is clearly a symbolic Satan."

> As is usual with Satan, he is in disguise; the distortions in his appearance and behavior suggest not only that his identity is faked but also hint at his real self.... When he introduces himself, his name too hints at his identity, for "friend" is uncomfortably close to "fiend"; his initials could well stand for Arch Fiend. The frightened Connie sees Arnold as "only half real": he "had driven up the driveway all right but had come from nowhere before that and belonged nowhere." Especially supernatural is his mysterious knowledge about her, her family, and her friends. At one point, he even seems to be able to see all the way to the barbecue which Connie's family is attending and to get a clear vision of what all the guests are doing.

Journal of Narrative Technique 5 (1975): 69–70.

But Mike Tierce and John Micheal Crafton argue for an opposite interpretation: they see Arnold as a savior or messiah figure and base their case on identifying Arnold with Bob Dylan, the popular singer to whom Oates dedicated the story.

> In the mid-sixties Bob Dylan's followers perceived him to be a messiah. According to his biographer [Anthony Scaduto], Dylan was a "rock-and-roll king." It is no wonder then that Arnold speaks with "the voice of the man on the radio," the disc jockey whose name, Bobby King, is a reference to "Bobby" Dylan, the "king" of rock-and-roll. Dylan was more than a "friend" to his listeners; he was "Christ revisited," "the prophet leading [his followers] into [a new] Consciousness." In fact, "people were making him an idol;...thousands of men and women, young and old, felt their lives entwined with his because they saw him as a mystic, a messiah who would lead them to salvation."
>
> That Oates consciously associates Arnold Friend with Bob Dylan is clearly suggested by the similarities of their physical descriptions. Arnold's "shaggy, shabby black hair that looked crazy as a wig," his "long and hawk-like" nose, his unshaven face, his "big and white" teeth, his lashes, "thick and black as if painted with a black tarlike material," and his size ("only an inch or so taller than Connie") are all characteristic of Bob Dylan....
>
> Arnold is the personification of popular music, particularly Bob Dylan's music; and as such, Connie's interaction with him is a musically induced fantasy, a kind of "magic carpet ride" in a "convertible jalopy painted gold." Rising out of Connie's radio, Arnold Friend/Bob Dylan is a magical, musical messiah; he persuades Connie to abandon her father's house. As a manifestation of her own desires, he frees her from the limitations of a fifteen-year-old girl, assisting her maturation by stripping her of her childlike vision.

Studies in Short Fiction 22 (1985): 220, 223.

Laura Dern as Connie and Treat Williams as Arnold Friend in *Smooth Talk*, the 1985 film version of "Where Are You Going, Where Have You Been?"

Topics for Discussion and Writing

1. Explain the title. Why is it in the form of a question, and why are there two parts to the question? Who does "you" refer to?

2. Who is the story's main character, Connie or Arnold Friend?

3. How do you interpret Arnold? Do you agree with what the critics say about him?

4. What do you think of the various members of Connie's family? Why has Oates limited their roles in the story?

5. Write a comparison between Connie and Eveline (see pages 2–6). Argue that these seemingly different protagonists are similar in several significant ways.

Ideas for Researched Writing

1. In 1986, Oates's story was made into a movie called *Smooth Talk*. Watch the film on DVD or through a streaming service and read several reviews of it, including the one Oates wrote for the *New York Times* (March 23, 1986). You can find links to reviews of *Smooth Talk* on IMDB and through a search of periodicals in databases via your library's website. Oates's review has been reprinted in her collection of essays *(Woman) Writer: Occasions and Opportunities* (1988). Write a

paper comparing the movie to the story. Does the film do justice to the story? Respond to Oates's claim that the film's different ending is justified.

2. Oates wrote this story more than forty years ago. How much of the story is a product of its time? Is its picture of teenage culture still accurate and relevant? Are the story's themes and ideas still relevant and meaningful? Write an essay arguing that this story is (or is not) relevant to present-day readers.

MultiModal Project

Where does Arnold take Connie, and what happens to her? Together with 2 to 3 other students, write and record a 5-minute podcast discussing either (a) a description of what happened next or (b) the mystery of not knowing what did. For inspiration, listen to the first episode of the *Serial* podcast (available for free download on iTunes, or streaming at http://serialpodcast.org/).

13 Anthology of Short Fiction

Chapter Preview

This chapter offers a wide range of short stories, some of which your instructor may assign. By exploring some or all of them, you will gain further practice as you:

- Analyze and discuss short fiction.
- Compare and contrast themes, characters, and literary techniques from a variety of authors and eras.
- Interpret, evaluate, and argue about fiction through writing assignments.

Nathaniel Hawthorne   1804–1864

Nathaniel Hawthorne ranks with the great writers of fiction in English. He wrote richly symbolic novels and tales, often involving the supernatural, yet he once declared, "I am not quite sure that I entirely comprehend my own meaning in some of these blasted allegories." The appearance of his masterpiece of hidden guilt and redemption, *The Scarlet Letter* (1850), secured his position as America's foremost romancer. His last years were troubled by the outbreak of the Civil War, and he vehemently declared himself "a man of peace."

The Birthmark

In the latter part of the last century, there lived a man of science—an eminent proficient in every branch of natural philosophy—who, not long before our story opens, had made experience of a spiritual affinity, more attractive than any chemical one. He had left his laboratory to the care of an assistant, cleared his fine countenance from the furnace-smoke, washed the stain of acids from his fingers, and persuaded a beautiful woman to become his wife. In those days, when the comparatively recent discovery of electricity, and other kindred mysteries of nature, seemed to open paths into the region of miracle, it was not unusual for the love of science to rival the love of woman, in its depth and absorbing energy. The higher intellect, the imagination, the spirit, and even the heart, might all find their congenial aliment in pursuits which, as some of their ardent votaries believed, would ascend from one step of powerful intelligence to another, until the philosopher should lay his hand on the secret of creative force, and perhaps make new worlds for himself. We know not whether Aylmer possessed this degree of faith in man's ultimate control over nature. He had devoted himself, however, too unreservedly to scientific studies, ever to be weaned from them by any second passion. His love for his young wife might prove the stronger of the two; but it could only be by intertwining itself with his love of science, and uniting the strength of the latter to its own.

Such a union accordingly took place, and was attended with truly remarkable consequences, and a deeply impressive moral. One day, very soon after their marriage, Aylmer sat gazing at his wife, with a trouble in his countenance that grew stronger, until he spoke.

"Georgiana," said he, "has it never occurred to you that the mark upon your cheek might be removed?"

"No, indeed," said she, smiling; but perceiving the seriousness of his manner, she blushed deeply. "To tell you the truth, it has been so often called a charm, that I was simple enough to imagine it might be so."

"Ah, upon another face, perhaps it might," replied her husband. "But never   5 on yours! No, dearest Georgiana, you came so nearly perfectly from the hand of Nature, that this slightest possible defect—which we hesitate whether to term a defect or a beauty—shocks me, as being the visible mark of earthly imperfection."

"Shocks you, my husband!" cried Georgiana, deeply hurt; at first reddening with momentary anger, but then bursting into tears. "Then why did you take me from my mother's side? You cannot love what shocks you!"

To explain this conversation, it must be mentioned, that, in the centre of Georgiana's left cheek, there was a singular mark, deeply interwoven, as it were, with the texture and substance of her face. In the usual state of her complexion—a healthy, though delicate bloom—the mark wore a tint of deeper crimson, which imperfectly defined its shape amid the surrounding rosiness. When she blushed, it gradually became more indistinct, and finally vanished amid the triumphant rush of blood, that bathed the whole cheek with its brilliant glow. But, if any shifting emotion caused her to turn pale, there was the mark again, a crimson stain upon the snow, in what Aylmer sometimes deemed an almost fearful distinctness. Its shape bore not a little similarity to the human hand, though of the smallest pigmy size. Georgiana's lovers were wont to say, that some fairy, at her birth-hour, had laid her tiny hand upon the infant's cheek, and left this impress there, in token of the magic endowments that were to give her such sway over all hearts. Many a desperate swain would have risked life for the privilege of pressing his lips to the mysterious hand. It must not be concealed, however, that the impression wrought by this fairy sign-manual varied exceedingly, according to the difference of temperament in the beholders. Some fastidious persons—but they were exclusively of her own sex—affirmed that the Bloody Hand, as they chose to call it, quite destroyed the effect of Georgiana's beauty, and rendered her countenance even hideous. But it would be as reasonable to say, that one of those small blue stains, which sometimes occur in the purest statuary marble, would convert the Eve of Powers to a monster. Masculine observers, if the birthmark did not heighten their admiration, contented themselves with wishing it away, that the world might possess one living specimen of ideal loveliness, without the semblance of a flaw. After his marriage—for he thought little or nothing of the matter before—Aylmer discovered that this was the case with himself.

Had she been less beautiful—if Envy's self could have found aught else to sneer at—he might have felt his affection heightened by the prettiness of this mimic hand, now vaguely portrayed, now lost, now stealing forth again, and glimmering to-and-fro with every pulse of emotion that throbbed within her heart. But, seeing her otherwise so perfect, he found this one defect grow more and more intolerable, with every moment of their united lives. It was the fatal flaw of humanity, which Nature, in one shape or another, stamps ineffaceably on all her productions, either to imply that they are temporary and finite, or that their perfection must be wrought by toil and pain. The Crimson Hand expressed the ineludible gripe, in which mortality clutches the highest and purest of earthly mould, degrading them into kindred with the lowest, and even with the very brutes, like whom their visible frames return to dust. In this manner, selecting it as the symbol of his wife's liability to sin, sorrow, decay, and death, Alymer's sombre imagination was not long in rendering the birthmark a frightful object, causing him more trouble and horror than ever Georgiana's beauty, whether of soul or sense, had given him delight.

At all the seasons which should have been their happiest, he invariably, and without intending it—nay, in spite of a purpose to the contrary—reverted to this one disastrous topic. Trifling as it at first appeared, it so connected itself with innumerable trains of thought, and modes of feeling, that it became the central point of all. With the morning twilight, Aylmer opened his eyes upon his wife's face, and recognized the symbol of imperfection; and when they sat together at the evening hearth, his eyes wandered stealthily to her cheek, and beheld, flickering with the blaze of the wood fire, the spectral Hand that wrote mortality, where he would fain have worshipped. Georgiana soon learned to shudder at his gaze. It needed but a glance, with the peculiar expression that his face often wore, to change the roses of her cheek into a deathlike paleness, amid which the Crimson Hand was brought strongly out, like a bas-relief of ruby on the whitest marble.

Late, one night, when the lights were growing dim, so as hardly to betray the stain on the poor wife's cheek, she herself, for the first time, voluntarily took up the subject.

"Do you remember, my dear Aylmer," said she, with a feeble attempt at a smile—"have you any recollection of a dream, last night, about this odious Hand?"

"None!—none whatever!" replied Aylmer, starting; but then he added in a dry, cold tone, affected for the sake of concealing the real depth of his emotion:—"I might well dream of it; for before I fell asleep, it had taken a pretty firm hold of my fancy."

"And you did dream of it," continued Georgiana, hastily; for she dreaded lest a gush of tears should interrupt what she had to say—"A terrible dream! I wonder that you can forget it. Is it possible to forget this one expression?—'It is in her heart now—we must have it out!'—Reflect, my husband; for by all means I would have you recall that dream."

The mind is in a sad note, when Sleep, the all-involving, cannot confine her spectres within the dim region of her sway, but suffers them to break forth, affrighting this actual life with secrets that perchance belong to a deeper one. Aylmer now remembered his dream. He had fancied himself with his servant Aminadab, attempting an operation for the removal of the birthmark. But the deeper went the knife, the deeper sank the Hand, until at length its tiny grasp appeared to have caught hold of Georgiana's heart; whence, however, her husband was inexorably resolved to cut or wrench it away.

10

When the dream had shaped itself perfectly in his memory, Aylmer sat in 15
his wife's presence with a guilty feeling. Truth often finds its way to the mind
close muffled in robes of sleep, and then speaks with uncompromising direct-
ness of matters in regard to which we practise an unconscious self-deception,
during our waking moments. Until now, he had not been aware of the tyranniz-
ing influence acquired by one idea over his mind, and of the lengths which he
might find in his heart to go, for the sake of giving himself peace.

"Aylmer," resumed Georgiana, solemnly, "I know not what may be the cost
to both of us, to rid me of this fatal birthmark. Perhaps its removal may cause
cureless deformity. Or, it may be, the stain goes as deep as life itself. Again, do
we know that there is a possibility, on any terms, of unclasping the firm gripe of
this little Hand, which was laid upon me before I came into the world?"

"Dearest Georgiana, I have spent much thought upon the subject," hastily interrupted Aylmer—"I am convinced of the perfect practicability of its
removal."

"If there be the remotest possibility of it," continued Georgiana, "let the
attempt be made, at whatever risk. Danger is nothing to me; for life—while this
hateful mark makes me the object of your horror and disgust—life is a burthen
which I would fling down with joy. Either remove this dreadful Hand, or take
my wretched life! You have deep science! All the world bears witness of it. You
have achieved great wonders! Cannot you remove this little, little mark, which I
cover with the tips of two small fingers? Is this beyond your power, for the sake
of your own peace, and to save your poor wife from madness?"

"Noblest—dearest—tenderest wife!" cried Aylmer, rapturously. "Doubt not
my power. I have already given this matter the deepest thought—thought which
might almost have enlightened me to create a being less perfect than yourself.
Georgiana, you have led me deeper than ever into the heart of science. I feel
myself fully competent to render this dear cheek as faultless as its fellow; and
then, most beloved, what will be my triumph, when I shall have corrected what
Nature left imperfect, in her fairest work! Even Pygmalion, when his sculptured
woman assumed life, felt not greater ecstasy than mine will be."

"It is resolved, then," said Georgiana, faintly smiling,—"And, Aylmer, spare 20
me not, though you should find the birthmark take refuge in my heart at last."

Her husband tenderly kissed her cheek—her right cheek—not that which
bore the impress of the Crimson Hand.

The next day, Aylmer apprised his wife of a plan that he had formed, whereby
he might have opportunity for the intense thought and constant watchfulness,
which the proposed operation would require; while Georgiana, likewise, would
enjoy the perfect repose essential to its success. They were to seclude themselves
in the extensive apartments occupied by Aylmer as a laboratory, and where, during his toilsome youth, he had made discoveries in the elemental powers of
nature that had roused the admiration of all the learned societies in Europe.
Seated calmly in this laboratory, the pale philosopher had investigated the
secrets of the highest cloud-region, and of the profoundest mines; he had satisfied himself of the causes that kindled and kept alive the fires of the volcano; and
had explained the mystery of fountains, and how it is that they gush forth, some
so bright and pure, and others with such rich medicinal virtues, from the dark
bosom of the earth. Here, too, at an earlier period, he had studied the wonders
of the human frame, and attempted to fathom the very process by which Nature

assimilates all her precious influences from earth and air, and from the spiritual world, to create and foster Man, her masterpiece. The latter pursuit, however, Aylmer had long laid aside, in unwilling recognition of the truth, against which all seekers sooner or later stumble, that our great creative Mother, while she amuses us with apparently working in the broadest sunshine, is yet severely careful to keep her own secrets, and, in spite of her pretended openness, shows us nothing but results. She permits us indeed, to mar, but seldom to mend, and, like a jealous patentee, on no account to make. Now, however, Aylmer resumed these half-forgotten investigations; not, of course, with such hopes or wishes as first suggested them; but because they involved much physiological truth, and lay in the path of his proposed scheme for the treatment of Georgiana.

As he led her over the threshold of the laboratory, Georgiana was cold and tremulous. Aylmer looked cheerfully into her face, with intent to reassure her, but was so startled with the intense glow of the birthmark upon the whiteness of her cheek, that he could not restrain a strong convulsive shudder. His wife fainted.

"Aminadab! Aminadab!" shouted Aylmer, stamping violently on the floor.

Forthwith, there issued from an inner apartment a man of low stature, but   25
bulky frame, with shaggy hair hanging about his visage, which was grimed with the vapors of the furnace. This personage had been Aylmer's under-worker during his whole scientific career, and was admirably fitted for that office by his great mechanical readiness, and the skill with which, while incapable of comprehending a single principle, he executed all the practical details of his master's experiments. With his vast strength, his shaggy hair, his smoky aspect, and the indescribable earthiness that incrusted him, he seemed to represent man's physical nature; while Aylmer's slender figure, and pale, intellectual face, were no less apt a type of the spiritual element.

"Throw open the door of the boudoir, Aminadab," said Aylmer, "and burn a pastille."

"Yes, master," answered Aminadab, looking intently at the lifeless form of Georgiana; and then he muttered to himself:—"If she were my wife, I'd never part with that birthmark."

When Georgiana recovered consciousness, she found herself breathing an atmosphere of penetrating fragrance, the gentle potency of which had recalled her from her deathlike faintness. The scene around her looked like enchantment. Aylmer had converted those smoky, dingy, sombre rooms, where he had spent his brightest years in recondite pursuits, into a series of beautiful apartments, not unfit to be the secluded abode of a lovely woman. The walls were hung with gorgeous curtains, which imparted the combination of grandeur and grace, that no other species of adornment can achieve; and as they fell from the ceiling to the floor, their rich and ponderous folds, concealing all angles and straight lines, appeared to shut in the scene from infinite space. For aught Georgiana knew, it might be a pavilion among the clouds. And Aylmer, excluding the sunshine, which would have interfered with his chemical processes, had supplied its place with perfumed lamps, emitting flames of various hue, but all uniting in a soft, empurpled radiance. He now knelt by his wife's side, watching her earnestly, but without alarm; for he was confident in his science, and felt that he could draw a magic circle round her, within which no evil might intrude.

"Where am I?—Ah, I remember!" said Georgiana, faintly; and she placed her hand over her cheek, to hide the terrible mark from her husband's eyes.

"Fear not, dearest!" exclaimed he. "Do not shrink from me! Believe me, 30 Georgiana, I even rejoice in this single imperfection, since it will be such rapture to remove it."

"Oh, spare me!" sadly replied his wife—"Pray do not look at it again. I never can forget that convulsive shudder."

In order to soothe Georgiana, and, as it were, to release her mind from the burthen of actual things, Aylmer now put in practice some of the light and playful secrets, which science had taught him among its profounder lore. Airy figures, absolutely bodiless ideas, and forms of unsubstantial beauty came and danced before her, imprinting their momentary footsteps on beams of light. Though she had some indistinct idea of the method of these optical phenomena, still the illusion was almost perfect enough to warrant the belief, that her husband possessed sway over the spiritual world. Then again, when she felt a wish to look forth from her seclusion, immediately, as if her thoughts were answered, the procession of external existence flitted across a screen. The scenery and the figures of actual life were perfectly represented, but with that bewitching, yet indescribable difference, which always makes a picture, an image, or a shadow, so much more attractive than the original. When wearied of this, Aylmer bade her cast her eyes upon a vessel, containing a quantity of earth. She did so, with little interest at first, but was soon startled to perceive the germ of a plant, shooting upward from the soil. Then came the slender stalk—the leaves gradually unfolded themselves—and amid them was a perfect and lovely flower.

"It is magical!" cried Georgiana, "I dare not touch it."

"Nay, pluck it," answered Aylmer, "pluck it, and inhale its brief perfume while you may. The flower will wither in a few moments, and leave nothing save its brown seed-vessels—but thence may be perpetuated a race as ephemeral as itself."

But Georgiana had no sooner touched the flower than the whole plant suf- 35 fered a blight, its leaves turning coal-black, as if by the agency of fire.

"There was too powerful a stimulus," said Aylmer thoughtfully.

To make up for this abortive experiment, he proposed to take her portrait by a scientific process of his own invention. It was to be effected by rays of light striking upon a polished plate of metal. Georgiana assented—but, on looking at the result, was affrighted to find the features of the portrait blurred and indefinable; while the minute figure of a hand appeared where the cheek should have been. Aylmer snatched the metallic plate, and threw it into a jar of corrosive acid.

Soon, however, he forgot these mortifying failures. In the intervals of study and chemical experiment, he came to her, flushed and exhausted, but seemed invigorated by her presence, and spoke in glowing language of the resources of his art. He gave a history of the long dynasty of the Alchemists, who spent so many ages in quest of the universal solvent, by which the Golden Principle might be elicted from all things vile and base. Aylmer appeared to believe that, by the plainest scientific logic, it was altogether within the limits of possibility to discover this long-sought medium; but, he added, a philosopher who should go deep enough to acquire the power, would attain too lofty a wisdom to stoop to the exercise of it. Not less singular were his opinions in regard to the Elixir Vitæ. He more than intimated, that it was his option to concoct a liquid that should prolong life for years—perhaps interminably—but that it would produce a discord in nature, which all the world, and chiefly the quaffer of the immortal nostrum, would find cause to curse.

"Aylmer, are you in earnest?" asked Georgiana, looking at him with amazement and fear; "it is terrible to possess such power, or even to dream of possessing it!"

"Oh, do not tremble, my love!" said her husband, "I would not wrong either 40 you or myself by working such inharmonious effects upon our lives. But I would have you consider how trifling, in comparison, is the skill requisite to remove this little Hand."

At the mention of the birthmark, Georgiana, as usual, shrank, as if a red-hot iron had touched her cheek.

Again Aylmer applied himself to his labors. She could hear his voice in the distant furnace-room, giving directions to Aminadab, whose harsh, uncouth, misshapen tones were audible in response, more like the grunt or growl of a brute than human speech. After hours of absence, Aylmer reappeared, and proposed that she should now examine his cabinet of chemical products, and natural treasures of the earth. Among the former he showed her a small vial, in which, he remarked, was contained a gentle yet most powerful fragrance, capable of impregnating all the breezes that blow across a kingdom. They were of inestimable value, the contents of that little vial; and, as he said so, he threw some of the perfume into the air, and filled the room with piercing and invigorating delight.

"And what is this?" asked Georgiana, pointing to a small crystal globe, containing a gold-colored liquid. "It is so beautiful to the eye, that I could imagine it the Elixir of Life."

"In one sense it is," replied Aylmer, "or rather the Elixir of Immortality. It is the most precious poison that ever was concocted in this world. By its aid, I could apportion the lifetime of any mortal at whom you might point your finger. The strength of the dose would determine whether he were to linger out years, or drop dead in the midst of a breath. No king, on his guarded throne, could keep his life, if I, in my private station, should deem that the welfare of millions justified me in depriving him of it."

"Why do you keep such a terrific drug?" inquired Georgiana in horror. 45

"Do not mistrust me, dearest!" said her husband, smiling; "its virtuous potency is yet greater than its harmful one. But, see! here is a powerful cosmetic. With a few drops of this, in a vase of water, freckles may be washed away as easily as the hands are cleansed. A stronger infusion would take the blood out of the cheek, and leave the rosiest beauty a pale ghost."

"Is it with this lotion that you intend to bathe my cheek?" asked Georgiana anxiously.

"Oh, no!" hastily replied her husband—"this is merely superficial. Your case demands a remedy that shall go deeper."

In his interviews with Georgiana, Aylmer generally made minute inquiries as to her sensations, and whether the confinement of the rooms, and the temperature of the atmosphere, agreed with her. These questions had such a particular drift, that Georgiana began to conjecture that she was already subjected to certain physical influences, either breathed in with the fragrant air, or taken with her food. She fancied, likewise—but it might be altogether fancy—that there was a stirring up of her system—a strange indefinite sensation creeping through her veins, and tingling, half painfully, half pleasurably, at her heart. Still, whenever she dared to look into the mirror, there she beheld herself, pale as a white rose, and with the crimson birthmark stamped upon her cheek. Not even Aylmer now hated it so much as she.

To dispel the tedium of the hours which her husband found it necessary to 50
devote to the processes of combination and analysis, Georgiana turned over the
volumes of his scientific library. In many dark old tomes, she met with chapters
full of romance and poetry. They were the works of the philosophers of the
middle ages, such as Albertus Magnus, Cornelius Agrippa, Paracelsus, and the
famous friar who created the prophetic Brazen Head. All these antique natural-
ists stood in advance of their centuries, yet were imbued with some of their cre-
dulity, and therefore were believed, and perhaps imagined themselves, to have
acquired from the investigation of nature a power above nature, and from physics a sway over the spiritual world. Hardly less curious and imaginative were the
early volumes of the Transactions of the Royal Society, in which the members,
knowing little of the limits of natural possibility, were continually recording
wonders, or proposing methods whereby wonders might be wrought.

But, to Georgiana, the most engrossing volume was a large folio from her
husband's own hand, in which he had recorded every experiment of his scientific career, with its original aim, the methods adopted for its development, and
its final success or failure, with the circumstances to which either event was
attributable. The book, in truth, was both the history and emblem of his ardent,
ambitious, imaginative, yet practical and laborious, life. He handled physical
details, as if there were nothing beyond them; yet spiritualized them all, and
redeemed himself from materialism, by his strong and eager aspiration towards
the infinite. In his grasp, the veriest clod of earth assumed a soul. Georgiana,
as she read, reverenced Aylmer, and loved him more profoundly than ever, but
with a less entire dependence on his judgment than heretofore. Much as he had
accomplished, she could not but observe that his most splendid successes were
almost invariably failures, if compared with the ideal at which he aimed. His
brightest diamonds were the merest pebbles, and felt to be so by himself, in
comparison with the inestimable gems which lay hidden beyond his reach. The
volume, rich with achievements that had won renown for its author, was yet as
melancholy a record as ever mortal hand had penned. It was the sad confession,
and continual exemplification, of the short-comings of the composite man—the
spirit burthened with clay and working in matter—and of the despair that assails
the higher nature, at finding itself so miserably thwarted by the earthly part.
Perhaps every man of genius, in whatever sphere, might recognize the image of
his own experience in Aylmer's journal.

So deeply did these reflections affect Georgiana, that she laid her face upon the
open volume, and burst into tears. In this situation she was found by her husband.

"It is dangerous to read in a sorcerer's books," said he, with a smile, though
his countenance was uneasy and displeased. "Georgiana, there are pages in that
volume, which I can scarcely glance over and keep my senses. Take heed lest it
prove as detrimental to you!"

"It has made me worship you more than ever," said she.

"Ah! wait for this one success," rejoined he, "then worship me if you will. I 55
shall deem myself hardly unworthy of it. But, come! I have sought you for the
luxury of your voice. Sing to me, dearest!"

So she poured out the liquid music of her voice to quench the thirst of
his spirit. He then took his leave, with a boyish exuberance of gaiety, assur-
ing her that her seclusion would endure but a little longer, and that the result
was already certain. Scarcely had he departed, when Georgiana felt irresistibly
impelled to follow him. She had forgotten to inform Aylmer of a symptom,

which, for two or three hours past, had begun to excite her attention. It was a sensation in the fatal birthmark, not painful, but which induced a restlessness throughout her system. Hastening after her husband, she intruded, for the first time, into the laboratory.

The first thing that struck her eye was the furnace, that hot and feverish worker, with the intense glow of its fire, which, by the quantities of soot clustered above it, seemed to have been burning for ages. There was a distilling apparatus in full operation. Around the room were retorts, tubes, cylinders, crucibles, and other apparatus of chemical research. An electrical machine stood ready for immediate use. The atmosphere felt oppressively close, and was tainted with gaseous odors, which had been tormented forth by the processes of science. The severe and homely simplicity of the apartment, with its naked walls and brick pavement, looked strange, accustomed as Georgiana had become to the fantastic elegance of her boudoir. But what chiefly, indeed almost solely, drew her attention, was the aspect of Aylmer himself.

He was pale as death, anxious and absorbed, and hung over the furnace as if it depended upon his utmost watchfulness whether the liquid, which it was distilling, should be the draught of immortal happiness or misery. How different from the sanguine and joyous mien that he had assumed for Georgiana's encouragement!

"Carefully now, Aminadab! Carefully, thou human machine! Carefully, thou man of clay!" muttered Aylmer, more to himself than his assistant. "Now, if there be a thought too much or too little, it is all over!"

"Hoh! hoh!" mumbled Aminadab—"look, master, look!" 60

Aylmer raised his eyes hastily, and at first reddened, then grew paler than ever, on beholding Georgiana. He rushed towards her, and seized her arm with a gripe that left the print of his fingers upon it.

"Why do you come hither? Have you no trust in your husband?" cried he impetuously. "Would you throw the blight of that fatal birthmark over my labors? It is not well done. Go, prying woman, go!"

"Nay, Aylmer," said Georgiana, with the firmness of which she possessed no stinted endowment, "it is not you that have a right to complain. You mistrust your wife! You have concealed the anxiety with which you watch the development of this experiment. Think not so unworthily of me, my husband! Tell me all the risk we run; and fear not that I shall shrink, for my share in it is far less than your own!"

"No, no, Georgiana!" said Aylmer impatiently, "it must not be."

"I submit," replied she calmly. "And, Aylmer, I shall quaff whatever draught 65 you bring me; but it will be on the same principle that would induce me to take a dose of poison, if offered by your hand."

"My noble wife," said Aylmer, deeply moved, "I knew not the height and depth of your nature, until now. Nothing shall be concealed. Know, then, that this Crimson Hand, superficial as it seems, has clutched its grasp into your being, with a strength of which I had no previous conception. I have already administered agents powerful enough to do aught except to change your entire physical system. Only one thing remains to be tried. If that fail us, we are ruined!"

"Why did you hesitate to tell me this?" asked she.

"Because, Georgiana," said Aylmer, in a low voice, "there is danger!"

"Danger? There is but one danger—that this horrible stigma shall be left upon my cheek!" cried Georgiana. "Remove it! remove it!—whatever be the cost—or we shall both go mad!"

"Heaven knows, your words are too true," said Aylmer, sadly. "And now,   70
dearest, return to your boudoir. In a little while, all will be tested."

He conducted her back, and took leave of her with a solemn tenderness,
which spoke far more than his words how much was now at stake. After his
departure, Georgiana became wrapt in musings. She considered the character
of Aylmer, and did it completer justice than at any previous moment. Her heart
exulted, while it trembled, at his honorable love, so pure and lofty that it would
accept nothing less than perfection, nor miserably make itself contented with
an earthlier nature than he had dreamed of. She felt how much more precious
was such a sentiment, than that meaner kind which would have borne with
the imperfection for her sake, and have been guilty of treason to holy love, by
degrading its perfect idea to the level of the actual. And, with her whole spirit,
she prayed, that, for a single moment, she might satisfy his highest and deepest
conception. Longer than one moment, she well knew, it could not be; for his
spirit was ever on the march—ever ascending—and each instant required something that was beyond the scope of the instant before.

The sound of her husband's footsteps aroused her. He bore a crystal goblet,
containing a liquor colorless as water, but bright enough to be the draught of
immortality. Aylmer was pale; but it seemed rather the consequence of a highly
wrought state of mind, and tension of spirit, than of fear or doubt.

"The concoction of the draught has been perfect," said he, in answer to
Georgiana's look. "Unless all my science have deceived me, it cannot fail."

"Save on your account, my dearest Aylmer," observed his wife, "I might wish
to put off this birthmark of mortality by relinquishing mortality itself, in preference to any other mode. Life is but a sad possession to those who have attained
precisely the degree of moral advancement at which I stand. Were I weaker and
blinder, it might be happiness. Were I stronger, it might be endured hopefully.
But, being what I find myself, methinks I am of all mortals the most fit to die."

"You are fit for heaven without tasting death!" replied her husband. "But why   75
do we speak of dying? The draught cannot fail. Behold its effect upon this plant!"

On the window-seat there stood a geranium, diseased with yellow blotches,
which had overspread all its leaves. Aylmer poured a small quantity of the liquid
upon the soil in which it grew. In a little time, when the roots of the plant had
taken up the moisture, the unsightly blotches began to be extinguished in a living verdure.

"There needed no proof," said Georgiana, quietly. "Give me the goblet. I
joyfully stake all upon your word."

"Drink, then, thou lofty creature!" exclaimed Aylmer, with fervid admiration.
"There is no taint of imperfection on thy spirit. Thy sensible frame, too, shall
soon be all perfect!"

She quaffed the liquid, and returned the goblet to his hand.

"It is grateful," said she, with a placid smile. "Methinks it is like water from a   80
heavenly fountain; for it contains I know not what of unobtrusive fragrance and
deliciousness. It allays feverish thirst, that had parched me for many days. Now,
dearest, let me sleep. My earthly senses are closing over my spirit, like the leaves
round the heart of a rose, at sunset."

She spoke the last words with a gentle reluctance, as if it required almost
more energy than she could command to pronounce the faint and lingering syllables. Scarcely had they loitered through her lips, ere she was lost in slumber.
Aylmer sat by her side, watching her aspect with the emotions proper to a man,

the whole value of whose existence was involved in the process now to be tested. Mingled with this mood, however, was the philosophic investigation, characteristic of the man of science. Not the minutest symptom escaped him. A heightened flush of the cheek—a slight irregularity of breath—a quiver of the eyelid—a hardly perceptible tremor through the frame—such were the details which, as the moments passed, he wrote down in his folio volume. Intense thought had set its stamp upon every previous page of that volume; but the thoughts of years were all concentrated upon the last.

While thus employed, he failed not to gaze often at the fatal Hand, and not without a shudder. Yet once, by a strange and unaccountable impulse, he pressed it with his lips. His spirit recoiled, however, in the very act, and Georgiana, out of the midst of her deep sleep, moved uneasily and murmured, as if in remonstrance. Again, Aylmer resumed his watch. Nor was it without avail. The Crimson Hand, which at first had been strongly visible upon the marble paleness of Georgiana's cheek now grew more faintly outlined. She remained not less pale than ever; but the birthmark, with every breath that came and went, lost somewhat of its former distinctness. Its presence had been awful; its departure was more awful still. Watch the stain of the rainbow fading out of the sky; and you will know how that mysterious symbol passed away.

"By Heaven, it is well nigh gone!" said Aylmer to himself, in almost irrepressible ecstasy. "I can scarcely trace it now. Success! Success! And now it is like the faintest rose-color. The slightest flush of blood across her cheek would overcome it. But she is so pale!"

He drew aside the window-curtain, and suffered the light of natural day to fall into the room, and rest upon her cheek. At the same time, he heard a gross, hoarse chuckle, which he had long known as his servant Aminadab's expression of delight.

"Ah, clod! Ah, earthly mass!" cried Aylmer, laughing in a sort of frenzy. "You have served me well! Matter and Spirit—Earth and Heaven—have both done their part in this! Laugh, thing of senses! You have earned the right to laugh." 85

These exclamations broke Georgiana's sleep. She slowly unclosed her eyes, and gazed into the mirror, which her husband had arranged for that purpose. A faint smile flitted over her lips, when she recognized how barely perceptible was now that Crimson Hand, which had once blazed forth with such disastrous brilliancy as to scare away all their happiness. But then her eyes sought Aylmer's face, with a trouble and anxiety that he could by no means account for.

"My poor Aylmer!" murmured she.

"Poor? Nay, richest! Happiest! Most favored!" exclaimed he. "My peerless bride, it is successful! You are perfect!"

"My poor Aylmer!" she repeated, with a more than human tenderness. "You have aimed loftily!—you have done nobly! Do not repent, that, with so high and pure a feeling, you have rejected the best that earth could offer. Aylmer—dearest Aylmer—I am dying!"

Alas, it was too true! The fatal Hand had grappled with the mystery of life, 90 and was the bond by which an angelic spirit kept itself in union with a mortal frame. As the last crimson tint of the birthmark—that sole token of human imperfection—faded from her cheek, the parting breath of the now perfect woman passed into the atmosphere, and her soul, lingering a moment near her husband, took its heavenward flight. Then a hoarse, chuckling laugh was heard again! Thus ever does the gross Fatality of Earth exult in its invariable triumph over the immortal essence, which, in this dim sphere of half-development, demands the completeness of a higher state. Yet, had Aylmer reached a profounder wisdom, he need not thus have flung away the happiness, which would have woven his mortal life of the self-same texture with the celestial. The momentary circumstance was too strong for him; he failed to look beyond the shadowy scope of Time, and living once for all in Eternity to find the perfect Future in the present.

(1843)

Questions for Discussion and Writing

1. This story is often seen as a partial allegory. What concepts does each of the three characters stand for? In what way is each one flawed?
2. Is it significant that the birthmark is in the shape of a hand?
3. What is the meaning of the allegory? In other words, what is Hawthorne's theme? Is it still relevant today?
4. Write an essay arguing that Georgiana is complicit in her own fate by encouraging Aylmer's folly.

Making Connections

Compare Alymer's obsession with that of Abner Snopes in Faulkner's "Barn Burning" (page 261) or the narrator of "The Yellow Wallpaper" (page 236).

◇◇◇◇◇◇◇◇◇◇◇◇◇◇◇◇◇◇◇◇◇◇◇

Edgar Allan Poe   1809–1849

Edgar Allan Poe was born in Boston to parents who were actors. His father abandoned the family, and his mother died when Poe was only two. Taken in by a wealthy tobacco merchant, he enjoyed a happy childhood in Richmond. After a brief stay at the University of Virginia, Poe married and moved to Boston, where he began publishing poetry. His foster father sent him to West Point, but he was expelled for gambling and not attending class. Divorced and working as a journalist in New York and Baltimore, he married his thirteen-year-old cousin in 1835. It was during this time that Poe began writing the tales of horror and the supernatural for which he is best known. In 1845, he published his poem "The Raven" to great success. He died four years later in Baltimore after a drinking binge.

The Cask of Amontillado

The thousand injuries of Fortunato I had borne as I best could, but when he ventured upon insult I vowed revenge. You, who so well know the nature of my soul, will not suppose, however, that I gave utterance to a threat. *At length* I would be avenged; this was a point definitely settled—but the very definitiveness with which it was resolved precluded the idea of risk. I must not only punish but punish with impunity. A wrong is unredressed when retribution overtakes its redresser. It is equally unredressed when the avenger fails to make himself felt as such to him who has done the wrong.

It must be understood that neither by word nor by deed had I given Fortunato cause to doubt my good will. I continued, as was my wont, to smile in his face, and he did not perceive that my smile *now* was at the thought of his immolation.

He had a weak point—this Fortunato—although in other regards he was a man to be respected and even feared. He prided himself on his connoisseurship in wine. Few Italians have the true virtuoso spirit. For the most part their enthusiasm is adopted to suit the time and opportunity, to practise imposture upon the British and Austrian *millionaires*. In painting and gemmary, Fortunato, like his countrymen, was a quack, but in the matter of old wines he was sincere. In this respect I did not differ from him materially;—I was skillful in the Italian vintages myself, and bought largely whenever I could.

It was about dusk, one evening during the supreme madness of the carnival season, that I encountered my friend. He accosted me with excessive warmth, for he had been drinking much. The man wore motley.[1] He had on a tight-fitting parti-striped dress, and his head was surmounted by the conical cap and bells. I was so pleased to see him that I thought I should never have done wringing his hand.

I said to him—"My dear Fortunato, you are luckily met. How remarkably   5
well you are looking to-day. But I have received a pipe[2] of what passes for Amontillado,[3] and I have my doubts."

"How?" said he. "Amontillado? A pipe? Impossible! And in the middle of the carnival!"

"I have my doubts," I replied; "and I was silly enough to pay the full Amontillado price without consulting you in the matter. You were not to be found, and I was fearful of losing a bargain."

"Amontillado!"

"I have my doubts."

"Amontillado!"   10

"And I must satisfy them."

"Amontillado!"

"As you are engaged, I am on my way to Luchesi. If any one has a critical turn it is he. He will tell me—"

"Luchesi cannot tell Amontillado from Sherry."

"And yet some fools will have it that his taste is a match for your own."   15

"Come, let us go."

"Whither?"

"To your vaults."

"My friend, no; I will not impose upon your good nature. I perceive you have an engagement. Luchesi—"

"I have no engagement;—come."   20

---

[1]A clown costume.
[2]A large wine cask.
[3]An expensive pale, dry wine.

"My friend, no. It is not the engagement, but the severe cold with which I perceive you are afflicted. The vaults are insufferably damp. They are encrusted with nitre."[4]

"Let us go, nevertheless. The cold is merely nothing. Amontillado! You have been imposed upon. And as for Luchesi, he cannot distinguish Sherry from Amontillado."

Thus speaking, Fortunato possessed himself of my arm; and putting on a mask of black silk and drawing a *roquelaire*[5] closely about my person, I suffered him to hurry me to my palazzo.

There were no attendants at home; they had absconded to make merry in honor of the time. I had told them that I should not return until the morning, and had given them explicit orders not to stir from the house. These orders were sufficient, I well knew, to insure their immediate disappearance, one and all, as soon as my back was turned.

I took from their sconces two flambeaux, and giving one to Fortunato, 25 bowed him through several suites of rooms to the archway that led into the vaults. I passed down a long and winding staircase, requesting him to be cautious as he followed. We came at length to the foot of the descent, and stood together upon the damp ground of the catacombs of the Montresors.

The gait of my friend was unsteady, and the bells upon his cap jingled as he strode.

"The pipe?" he said.

"It is farther on," said I; "but observe the white web-work which gleams from these cavern walls."

He turned towards me, and looked into my eyes with two filmy orbs that distilled the rheum of intoxication.

"Nitre?" he asked at length. 30

"Nitre," I replied. "How long have you had that cough?"

"Ugh! ugh! ugh!—ugh! ugh! ugh!—ugh! ugh! ugh!—ugh! ugh! ugh!—ugh! ugh! ugh!"

My poor friend found it impossible to reply for many minutes.

"It is nothing," he said at last.

"Come," I said, with decision, "we will go back; your health is precious. You 35 are rich, respected, admired, beloved; you are happy, as once I was. You are a man to be missed. For me it is no matter. We will go back; you will be ill, and I cannot be responsible. Besides, there is Luchesi—"

"Enough," he said; "the cough is a mere nothing; it will not kill me. I shall not die of a cough."

"True—true," I replied; "and, indeed, I had no intention of alarming you unnecessarily—but you should use all proper caution. A draught of this Medoc will defend us from the damps."

Here I knocked off the neck of a bottle which I drew from a long row of its fellows that lay upon the mould.

"Drink," I said, presenting him the wine.

He raised it to his lips with a leer. He paused and nodded to me familiarly, 40 while his bells jingled.

---

[4] Potassium nitrate, a preservative.
[5] A heavy, silk-lined cloak.

"I drink," he said, "to the buried that repose around us."

"And I to your long life."

He again took my arm, and we proceeded.

"These vaults," he said, "are extensive."

"The Montresors," I replied, "were a great and numerous family." 45

"I forget your arms."

"A huge human foot d'or,[6] in a field azure; the foot crushes a serpent rampant whose fangs are imbedded in the heel."

"And the motto?"

"*Nemo me impune lacessit.*"[7]

"Good!" he said. 50

The wine sparkled in his eyes and the bells jingled. My own fancy grew warm with the Medoc. We had passed through walls of piled bones, with casks and puncheons intermingling, into the inmost recesses of the catacombs. I paused again, and this time I made bold to seize Fortunato by an arm above the elbow.

"The nitre!" I said; "see, it increases. It hangs like moss upon the vaults. We are below the river's bed. The drops of moisture trickle among the bones. Come, we will go back ere it is too late. Your cough—"

"It is nothing," he said; "let us go on. But first, another draught of the Medoc."

I broke and reached him a flagon of De Grâve. He emptied it at a breath. His eyes flashed with a fierce light. He laughed and threw the bottle upwards with a gesticulation I did not understand.

I looked at him in surprise. He repeated the movement—a grotesque one. 55

"You do not comprehend?" he said.

"Not I," I replied.

"Then you are not of the brotherhood."

"How?"

"You are not of the masons." 60

"Yes, yes," I said; "yes, yes."

"You? Impossible! A mason?"

"A mason," I replied.

"A sign," he said.

"It is this," I answered, producing a trowel from beneath the folds of my 65 *roquelaire*.

"You jest," he exclaimed, recoiling a few paces. "But let us proceed to the Amontillado."

"Be it so," I said, replacing the tool beneath the cloak and again offering him my arm. He leaned upon it heavily. We continued our route in search of the Amontillado. We passed through a range of low arches, descended, passed on, and descending again, arrived at a deep crypt, in which the foulness of the air caused our flambeaux rather to glow than flame.

At the most remote end of the crypt there appeared another less spacious. Its walls had been lined with human remains, piled to the vault overhead, in the fashion of the great catacombs of Paris. Three sides of this interior crypt were still ornamented in this manner. From the fourth side the bones had been thrown down, and lay promiscuously[8] upon the earth, forming at one point

---

[6] Of gold.

[7] "No one attacks me without paying dearly."

[8] Mixed together.

a mound of some size. Within the wall thus exposed by the displacing of the bones, we perceived a still interior crypt or recess, in depth about four feet, in width three, in height six or seven. It seemed to have been constructed for no especial use within itself, but formed merely the interval between two of the colossal supports of the roof of the catacombs, and was backed by one of their circumscribing walls of solid granite.

It was in vain that Fortunato, uplifting his dull torch, endeavored to pry into the depths of the recess. Its termination the feeble light did not enable us to see.

"Proceed," I said; "herein is the Amontillado. As for Luchesi—"

"He is an ignoramus," interrupted my friend, as he stepped unsteadily forward, while I followed immediately at his heels. In an instant he had reached the extremity of the niche, and finding his progress arrested by the rock, stood stupidly bewildered. A moment more and I had fettered him to the granite. In its surface were two iron staples, distant from each other about two feet, horizontally. From one of these depended a short chain, from the other a padlock. Throwing the links about his waist, it was but the work of a few seconds to secure it. He was too much astounded to resist. Withdrawing the key I stepped back from the recess.

"Pass your hand," I said, "over the wall; you cannot help feeling the nitre. Indeed, it is *very* damp. Once more let me *implore* you to return. No? Then I must positively leave you. But I must first render you all the little attentions in my power."

"The Amontillado!" ejaculated my friend, not yet recovered from his astonishment.

"True," I replied; "the Amontillado."

As I said these words I busied myself among the pile of bones of which I have before spoken. Throwing them aside, I soon uncovered a quantity of building stone and mortar. With these materials and with the aid of my trowel, I began vigorously to wall up the entrance of the niche.

I had scarcely laid the first tier of the masonry when I discovered that the intoxication of Fortunato had in a great measure worn off. The earliest indication I had of this was a low moaning cry from the depth of the recess. It was *not* the cry of a drunken man. There was a long and obstinate silence. I laid the second tier, and the third, and the fourth; and then I heard the furious vibrations of the chain. The noise lasted for several minutes, during which, that I might hearken to it with the more satisfaction, I ceased my labors and sat down upon the bones. When at last the clanking subsided, I resumed the trowel, and finished without interruption the fifth, the sixth, and the seventh tier. The wall was now nearly upon a level with my breast. I again paused, and holding the flambeaux over the mason-work, threw a few feeble rays upon the figure within.

A succession of loud and shrill screams, bursting suddenly from the throat of the chained form, seemed to thrust me violently back. For a brief moment I hesitated, I trembled. Unsheathing my rapier, I began to grope with it about the recess; but the thought of an instant reassured me. I placed my hand upon the solid fabric of the catacombs, and felt satisfied. I reapproached the wall; I replied to the yells of him who clamoured. I re-echoed, I aided, I surpassed them in volume and in strength. I did this, and the clamourer grew still.

It was now midnight, and my task was drawing to a close. I had completed the eighth, the ninth, and the tenth tier. I had finished a portion of the last and the eleventh; there remained but a single stone to be fitted and plastered in. I struggled with its weight; I placed it partially in its destined position. But now there came from out the niche a low laugh that erected the hairs upon my head. It was succeeded by a sad voice, which I had difficulty in recognizing as that of the noble Fortunato. The voice said—

"Ha! ha! ha!—he! he! he!—a very good joke, indeed—an excellent jest. We will have many a rich laugh about it at the palazzo—he! he! he!—over our wine—he! he! he!"

"The Amontillado!" I said.   80

"He! he! he!—he! he! he!—yes, the Amontillado. But is it not getting late? Will not they be awaiting us at the palazzo, the Lady Fortunato and the rest? Let us be gone."

"Yes," I said, "let us be gone."

"For the love of God, Montresor!"

"Yes," I said, "for the love of God."

But to these words I hearkened in vain for a reply. I grew impatient. I called   85
aloud—

"Fortunato!"

No answer. I called again—

"Fortunato!"

No answer still. I thrust a torch through the remaining aperture and let it fall within. There came forth in return only a jingling of the bells. My heart grew sick; it was the dampness of the catacombs that made it so. I hastened to make an end of my labor. I forced the last stone into its position; I plastered it up. Against the new masonry I re-erected the old rampart of bones. For the half of a century no mortal has disturbed them. *In pace requiescat!* [9]

(1846)

Questions for Discussion and Writing

1. Why is the first-person point of view particularly well chosen?
2. Why does Poe not tell us the nature of the insult or describe any of the "thousand injuries" that the narrator suffered?
3. How does the setting contribute to the effectiveness of the story?
4. Why is Luchesi mentioned? What other examples of reverse psychology does the narrator employ?

Making Connections

How does Montresor's motive and method for revenge compare with Abner Snopes's in Faulkner's "Barn Burning" (page 261)?

---

[9]Let him rest in peace!

Sarah Orne Jewett   1849–1909

Born in South Berwick, Maine, Sarah Orne Jewett was often sick as a child, and her father, a country doctor, thought that the best medicine for her was to be outside in the fresh air. So instead of attending school, she accompanied him on his rounds among homes in rural Maine, meeting people whose lives and conversations would inspire her writing. She published her first story at the age of nineteen. For a few months each year, usually in the winter, Jewett lived in Boston with her companion Annie Fields. But the rest of the time, she stayed in Maine and did her writing in the old house where she had grown up. Jewett published twenty books, most of them collections of short stories. She said, "You must find your own quiet center of life, and write from that."

A White Heron

I

The woods were already filled with shadows one June evening, just before eight o'clock, though a bright sunset still glimmered faintly among the trunks of the trees. A little girl was driving home her cow, a plodding, dilatory, provoking creature in her behavior, but a valued companion for all that. They were going away from whatever light there was, and striking deep into the woods, but their feet were familiar with the path, and it was no matter whether their eyes could see it or not.

There was hardly a night the summer through when the old cow could be found waiting at the pasture bars; on the contrary, it was her greatest pleasure to hide herself away among the huckleberry bushes, and though she wore a loud bell she had made the discovery that if one stood perfectly still it would not ring. So Sylvia had to hunt for her until she found her, and call Co' ! Co' ! with never an answering Moo, until her childish patience was quite spent. If the creature had not given good milk and plenty of it, the case would have seemed very different to her owners. Besides, Sylvia had all the time there was, and very little use to make of it. Sometimes in pleasant weather it was a consolation to look upon the cow's pranks as an intelligent attempt to play hide and seek, and as the child had no playmates she lent herself to this amusement with a good deal of zest. Though this chase had been so long that the wary animal herself had given an unusual signal of her whereabouts, Sylvia had only laughed when she came upon Mistress Moolly at the swamp-side, and urged her affectionately homeward with a twig of birch leaves. The old cow was not inclined to wander farther, she even turned in the right direction for once as they left the pasture, and stepped along the road at a good pace. She was quite ready to be milked now, and seldom stopped to browse. Sylvia wondered what her grandmother would say because they were so late. It was a great while since she had left home at half-past five o'clock, but everybody knew the difficulty of making this errand a short one. Mrs. Tilley had chased the hornéd torment too many summer evenings herself to blame any one else for lingering, and was only thankful as she waited that she had Sylvia, nowadays, to give such valuable assistance. The good woman suspected that Sylvia loitered occasionally on her own account; there never was such a child for straying about out-of-doors since the world was

made! Everybody said that it was a good change for a little maid who had tried
to grow for eight years in a crowded manufacturing town, but, as for Sylvia herself, it seemed as if she never had been alive at all before she came to live at the
farm. She thought often with wistful compassion of a wretched geranium that
belonged to a town neighbor.

"'Afraid of folks,'" old Mrs. Tilley said to herself, with a smile, after she had
made the unlikely choice of Sylvia from her daughter's houseful of children,
and was returning to the farm. "'Afraid of folks,' they said! I guess she won't be
troubled no great with 'em up to the old place!" When they reached the door of
the lonely house and stopped to unlock it, and the cat came to purr loudly, and rub
against them, a deserted pussy, indeed, but fat with young robins, Sylvia whispered
that this was a beautiful place to live in, and she never should wish to go home.

The companions followed the shady wood-road, the cow taking slow steps
and the child very fast ones. The cow stopped long at the brook to drink, as if
the pasture were not half a swamp, and Sylvia stood still and waited, letting her
bare feet cool themselves in the shoal water, while the great twilight moths struck
softly against her. She waded on through the brook as the cow moved away, and
listened to the thrushes with a heart that beat fast with pleasure. There was a stirring in the great boughs overhead. They were full of little birds and beasts that
seemed to be wide awake, and going about their world, or else saying good-night
to each other in sleepy twitters. Sylvia herself felt sleepy as she walked along.
However, it was not much farther to the house, and the air was soft and sweet.
She was not often in the woods so late as this, and it made her feel as if she were
a part of the gray shadows and the moving leaves. She was just thinking how long
it seemed since she first came to the farm a year ago, and wondering if everything
went on in the noisy town just the same as when she was there, the thought of
the great red-faced boy who used to chase and frighten her made her hurry along
the path to escape from the shadow of the trees.

Suddenly this little woods-girl is horror-stricken to hear a clear whistle not   5
very far away. Not a bird's-whistle, which would have a sort of friendliness, but
a boy's whistle, determined, and somewhat aggressive. Sylvia left the cow to
whatever sad fate might await her, and stepped discreetly aside into the bushes,
but she was just too late. The enemy had discovered her, and called out in a very
cheerful and persuasive tone, "Halloa, little girl, how far is it to the road?" and
trembling Sylvia answered almost inaudibly, "A good ways."

She did not dare to look boldly at the tall young man, who carried a gun over
his shoulder, but she came out of her bush and again followed the cow, while he
walked alongside.

"I have been hunting for some birds," the stranger said kindly, "and I have
lost my way, and need a friend very much. Don't be afraid," he added gallantly.
"Speak up and tell me what your name is, and whether you think I can spend the
night at your house, and go out gunning early in the morning."

Sylvia was more alarmed than before. Would not her grandmother consider
her much to blame? But who could have foreseen such an accident as this? It did
not seem to be her fault, and she hung her head as if the stem of it were broken,
but managed to answer "Sylvy," with much effort when her companion again
asked her name.

Mrs. Tilley was standing in the doorway when the trio came into view. The
cow gave a loud moo by way of explanation.

"Yes, you'd better speak up for yourself, you old trial! Where'd she tucked   10
herself away this time, Sylvy?" But Sylvia kept an awed silence; she knew by
instinct that her grandmother did not comprehend the gravity of the situation.
She must be mistaking the stranger for one of the farmer-lads of the region.

The young man stood his gun beside the door, and dropped a lumpy game-
bag beside it; then he bade Mrs. Tilley good-evening, and repeated his way-
farer's story, and asked if he could have a night's lodging.

"Put me anywhere you like," he said. "I must be off early in the morning,
before day; but I am very hungry, indeed. You can give me some milk at any
rate, that's plain."

"Dear sakes, yes," responded the hostess, whose long slumbering hospitality seemed to be easily awakened. "You might fare better if you went out to the
main road a mile or so, but you're welcome to what we've got. I'll milk right off,
and you make yourself at home. You can sleep on husks or feathers," she prof-
fered graciously. "I raised them all myself. There's good pasturing for geese just
below here towards the ma'sh. Now step round and set a plate for the gentleman, Sylvy!" And Sylvia promptly stepped. She was glad to have something to
do, and she was hungry herself.

It was a surprise to find so clean and comfortable a little dwelling in this New
England wilderness. The young man had known the horrors of its most primitive housekeeping, and the dreary squalor of that level of society which does not
rebel at the companionship of hens. This was the best thrift of an old-fashioned
farmstead, though on such a small scale that it seemed like a hermitage. He listened eagerly to the old woman's quaint talk, he watched Sylvia's pale face and
shining gray eyes with ever growing enthusiasm, and insisted that this was the
best supper he had eaten for a month, and afterward the new-made friends sat
down in the door-way together while the moon came up.

Soon it would be berry-time, and Sylvia was a great help at picking. The cow   15
was a good milker, though a plaguy thing to keep track of, the hostess gossiped
frankly, adding presently that she had buried four children, so Sylvia's mother,
and a son (who might be dead) in California were all the children she had left.
"Dan, my boy, was a great hand to go gunning," she explained sadly. "I never
wanted for pa'tridges or gray squer'ls while he was to home. He's been a great
wand'rer, I expect, and he's no hand to write letters. There, I don't blame him,
I'd ha' seen the world myself if it had been so I could.

"Sylvy takes after him," the grandmother continued affectionately, after a
minute's pause. "There ain't a foot o' ground she don't know her way over, and
the wild creatures counts her one o' themselves. Squer'ls she'll tame to come an'
feed right out o' her hands, and all sorts o' birds. Last winter she got the jay-
birds to <u>bangeing</u> here, and I believe she'd 'a' scanted herself of her own meals
to have plenty to throw out amongst 'em, if I hadn't kep' watch. Anything but
crows, I tell her, I'm willin' to help support—though Dan he had a tamed one o'
them that did seem to have reason same as folks. It was round here a good spell
after he went away. Dan an' his father they didn't hitch,—but he never held up
his head ag'in after Dan had dared him an' gone off."

The guest did not notice this hint of family sorrows in his eager interest in
something else.

"So Sylvy knows all about birds, does she?" he exclaimed, as he looked round
at the little girl who sat, very demure but increasingly sleepy, in the moonlight.
"I am making a collection of birds myself. I have been at it ever since I was a boy."

(Mrs. Tilley smiled.) "There are two or three very rare ones I have been hunting for these five years. I mean to get them on my own ground if they can be found."

"Do you cage 'em up?" asked Mrs. Tilley doubtfully, in response to this enthusiastic announcement.

"Oh no, they're stuffed and preserved, dozens and dozens of them," said the ornithologist, "and I have shot or snared every one myself. I caught a glimpse of a white heron a few miles from here on Saturday, and I have followed it in this direction. They have never been found in this district at all. The little white heron, it is," and he turned again to look at Sylvia with the hope of discovering that the rare bird was one of her acquaintances. 20

But Sylvia was watching a hop-toad in the narrow footpath.

"You would know the heron if you saw it," the stranger continued eagerly. "A queer tall white bird with soft feathers and long thin legs. And it would have a nest perhaps in the top of a high tree, made of sticks, something like a hawk's nest."

Sylvia's heart gave a wild beat; she knew that strange white bird, and had once stolen softly near where it stood in some bright green swamp grass, away over at the other side of the woods. There was an open place where the sunshine always seemed strangely yellow and hot, where tall, nodding rushes grew, and her grandmother had warned her that she might sink in the soft black mud underneath and never be heard of more. Not far beyond were the salt marshes just this side the sea itself, which Sylvia wondered and dreamed much about, but never had seen, whose great voice could sometimes be heard above the noise of the woods on stormy nights.

"I can't think of anything I should like so much as to find that heron's nest," the handsome stranger was saying. "I would give ten dollars to anybody who could show it to me," he added desperately, "and I mean to spend my whole vacation hunting for it if need be. Perhaps it was only migrating, or had been chased out of its own region by some bird of prey."

Mrs. Tilley gave amazed attention to all this, but Sylvia still watched the toad, not divining, as she might have done at some calmer time, that the creature wished to get to its hole under the door-step, and was much hindered by the unusual spectators at that hour of the evening. No amount of thought, that night, could decide how many wished-for treasures the ten dollars, so lightly spoken of, would buy. 25

The next day the young sportsman hovered about the woods, and Sylvia kept him company, having lost her first fear of the friendly lad, who proved to be most kind and sympathetic. He told her many things about the birds and what they knew and where they lived and what they did with themselves. And he gave her a jack-knife, which she thought as great a treasure as if she were a desert-islander. All day long he did not once make her troubled or afraid except when he brought down some unsuspecting singing creature from its bough. Sylvia would have liked him vastly better without his gun; she could not understand why he killed the very birds he seemed to like so much. But as the day waned, Sylvia still watched the young man with loving admiration. She had never seen anybody so charming and delightful; the woman's heart, asleep in the child, was vaguely thrilled by a dream of love. Some premonition of that great power stirred and swayed these young creatures who traversed the solemn woodlands with soft-footed silent care. They stopped to listen to a bird's song; they pressed forward again eagerly, parting the branches—speaking to each other rarely and in whispers; the young man going first and Sylvia following, fascinated, a few steps behind, with her gray eyes dark with excitement.

She grieved because the longed-for white heron was elusive, but she did not lead the guest, she only followed, and there was no such thing as speaking first. The sound of her own unquestioned voice would have terrified her—it was hard enough to answer yes or no when there was need of that. At last evening began to fall, and they drove the cow home together, and Sylvia smiled with pleasure when they came to the place where she heard the whistle and was afraid only the night before.

II

Half a mile from home, at the farther edge of the woods, where the land was highest, a great pine-tree stood, the last of its generation. Whether it was left for a boundary mark, or for what reason, no one could say; the woodchoppers who had felled its mates were dead and gone long ago, and a whole forest of sturdy trees, pines and oaks and maples, had grown again. But the stately head of this old pine towered above them all and made a landmark for sea and shore miles and miles away. Sylvia knew it well. She had always believed that whoever climbed to the top of it could see the ocean; and the little girl had often laid her hand on the great rough trunk and looked up wistfully at those dark boughs that the wind always stirred, no matter how hot and still the air might be below. Now she thought of the tree with a new excitement, for why, if one climbed it at break of day, could not one see all the world, and easily discover from whence the white heron flew, and mark the place, and find the hidden nest?

What a spirit of adventure, what wild ambition! What fancied triumph and delight and glory for the later morning when she could make known the secret! It was almost too real and too great for the childish heart to bear.

All night the door of the little house stood open and the whippoorwills came and sang upon the very step. The young sportsman and his old hostess were sound asleep, but Sylvia's great design kept her broad awake and watching. She forgot to think of sleep. The short summer night seemed as long as the winter darkness, and at last when the whippoorwills ceased, and she was afraid the morning would after all come too soon, she stole out of the house and followed the pasture path through the woods, hastening toward the open ground beyond, listening with a sense of comfort and companionship to the drowsy twitter of a half-awakened bird, whose perch she had jarred in passing. Alas, if the great wave of human interest which flooded for the first time this dull little life should sweep away the satisfactions of an existence heart to heart with nature and the dumb life of the forest!

There was the huge tree asleep yet in the paling moonlight, and small and silly Sylvia began with utmost bravery to mount to the top of it, with tingling, eager blood coursing the channels of her whole frame, with her bare feet and fingers, that pinched and held like bird's claws to the monstrous ladder reaching up, up, almost to the sky itself. First she must mount the white oak tree that grew alongside, where she was almost lost among the dark branches and the green leaves heavy and wet with dew; a bird fluttered off its nest, and a red squirrel ran to and fro and scolded pettishly at the harmless housebreaker. Sylvia felt her way easily. She had often climbed there, and knew that higher still one of the oak's upper branches chafed against the pine trunk, just where its lower

30

boughs were set close together. There, when she made the dangerous pass from one tree to the other, the great enterprise would really begin.

She crept out along the swaying oak limb at last, and took the daring step across into the old pine-tree. The way was harder than she thought; she must reach far and hold fast, the sharp dry twigs caught and held her and scratched her like angry talons, the pitch made her thin little fingers clumsy and stiff as she went round and round the tree's great stem, higher and higher upward. The sparrows and robins in the woods below were beginning to wake and twitter to the dawn, yet it seemed much lighter there aloft in the pine-tree, and the child knew she must hurry if her project were to be of any use.

The tree seemed to lengthen itself out as she went up, and to reach farther and farther upward. It was like a great main-mast to the voyaging earth; it must truly have been amazed that morning through all its ponderous frame as it felt this determined spark of human spirit wending its way from higher branch to branch. Who knows how steadily the least twigs held themselves to advantage this light, weak creature on her way! The old pine must have loved his new dependent. More than all the hawks, and bats, and moths, and even the sweet voiced thrushes, was the brave, beating heart of the solitary gray-eyed child. And the tree stood still and frowned away the winds that June morning while the dawn grew bright in the east.

Sylvia's face was like a pale star, if one had seen it from the ground, when the last thorny bough was past, and she stood trembling and tired but wholly triumphant, high in the tree-top. Yes, there was the sea with the dawning sun making a golden dazzle over it, and toward that glorious east flew two hawks with slow-moving pinions. How low they looked in the air from that height when one had only seen them before far up, and dark against the blue sky. Their gray feathers were as soft as moths; they seemed only a little way from the tree, and Sylvia felt as if she too could go flying away among the clouds. Westward, the woodlands and farms reached miles and miles into the distance; here and there were church steeples, and white villages, truly it was a vast and awesome world.

The birds sang louder and louder. At last the sun came up bewilderingly bright. Sylvia could see the white sails of ships out at sea, and the clouds that were purple and rose-colored and yellow at first began to fade away. Where was the white heron's nest in the sea of green branches, and was this wonderful sight and pageant of the world the only reward for having climbed to such a giddy height? Now look down again, Sylvia, where the green marsh is set among the shining birches and dark hemlocks; there where you saw the white heron once you will see him again; look, look! a white spot of him like a single floating feather comes up from the dead hemlock and grows larger, and rises, and comes close at last, and goes by the landmark pine with steady sweep of wing and outstretched slender neck and crested head. And wait! wait! do not move a foot or a finger, little girl, do not send an arrow of light and consciousness from your two eager eyes, for the heron has perched on a pine bough not far beyond yours, and cries back to his mate on the nest and plumes his feathers for the new day!

The child gives a long sigh a minute later when a company of shouting cat-birds comes also to the tree, and vexed by their fluttering and lawlessness the solemn heron goes away. She knows his secret now, the wild, light, slender bird that floats and wavers, and goes back like an arrow presently to his home in the green world beneath. Then Sylvia, well satisfied, makes her perilous way down again, not daring to look far below the branch she stands on, ready to cry

35

sometimes because her fingers ache and her lamed feet slip. Wondering over and over again what the stranger would say to her, and what he would think when she told him how to find his way straight to the heron's nest.

"Sylvy, Sylvy!" called the busy old grandmother again and again, but nobody answered, and the small husk bed was empty and Sylvia had disappeared.

The guest waked from a dream, and remembering his day's pleasure hurried to dress himself that it might sooner begin. He was sure from the way the shy little girl looked once or twice yesterday that she had at least seen the white heron, and now she must really be made to tell. Here she comes now, paler than ever, and her worn old frock is torn and tattered, and smeared with pine pitch. The grandmother and the sportsman stand in the door together and question her, and the splendid moment has come to speak of the dead hemlock-tree by the green marsh.

But Sylvia does not speak after all, though the old grandmother fretfully rebukes her, and the young man's kind, appealing eyes are looking straight in her own. He can make them rich with money; he has promised it, and they are poor now. He is so well worth making happy, and he waits to hear the story she can tell.

No, she must keep silence! What is it that suddenly forbids her and makes   40 her dumb? Has she been nine years growing and now, when the great world for the first time puts out a hand to her, must she thrust it aside for a bird's sake? The murmur of the pine's green branches is in her ears, she remembers how the white heron came flying through the golden air and how they watched the sea and the morning together, and Sylvia cannot speak; she cannot tell the heron's secret and give its life away.

Dear loyalty, that suffered a sharp pang as the guest went away disappointed later in the day, that could have served and followed him and loved him as a dog loves! Many a night Sylvia heard the echo of his whistle haunting the pasture path as she came home with the loitering cow. She forgot even her sorrow at the sharp report of his gun and the sight of thrushes and sparrows dropping silent to the ground, their songs hushed and their pretty feathers stained and wet with blood. Were the birds better friends than their hunter might have been,—who can tell? Whatever treasures were lost to her, woodlands and summer-time, remember! Bring your gifts and graces and tell your secrets to this lonely country child!

(1886)

Questions for Discussion and Writing

1. What does the name *Sylvia* mean? Why did the author choose that name for the main character?
2. What is the significance of the young man's carrying a gun? Why does this frighten Sylvy? What sort of person is he?
3. What similarities are there between Sylvy and the white heron? What, for instance, does the color white often symbolize?
4. Sylvy's climbing the towering tree is described as it if were a quest—like the search for the holy grail or for the golden fleece. What do you think Sylvy might be unconsciously seeking?
5. Write an interpretation arguing that Sylvy saved more than the life of the bird when she refused to tell the young man where to find the white heron.

Making Connections

Compare Sylvia in this story to Sylvia in Bambara's "The Lesson" (page 924), especially in the way they confront the truths about their place in the world.

◇◇◇◇◇◇◇◇◇◇◇◇◇◇◇◇◇◇◇◇

Kate Chopin   1851–1904

Kate Chopin was born Kate O'Flaherty in St. Louis. After her father died in a train accident when she was four, she was raised by her mother, grandmother, and great-grandmother—all widows. In 1870 she married Oscar Chopin, the son of a wealthy cotton-growing family. After their marriage, they lived in New Orleans, where she had five boys and two girls, all before she was twenty-eight. When Oscar died of swamp fever in 1882, Kate returned to St. Louis, and to support her young family, began to write stories about people she had known in Louisiana. Her explorations of female sexuality and her championing of women's self-worth in her fiction were so shocking that she was denied membership in the St. Louis Literary Society.

The Story of an Hour

Knowing that Mrs. Mallard was afflicted with a heart trouble, great care was taken to break to her as gently as possible the news of her husband's death.

It was her sister Josephine who told her, in broken sentences; veiled hints that revealed in half concealing. Her husband's friend Richards was there, too, near her. It was he who had been in the newspaper office when intelligence of the railroad disaster was received, with Brently Mallard's name leading the list of "killed." He had only taken the time to assure himself of its truth by a second telegram, and had hastened to forestall any less careful, less tender friend in bearing the sad message.

She did not hear the story as many women have heard the same, with a paralyzed inability to accept its significance. She wept at once, with sudden, wild abandonment, in her sister's arms. When the storm of grief had spent itself she went away to her room alone. She would have no one follow her.

There stood, facing the open window, a comfortable, roomy armchair. Into this she sank, pressed down by a physical exhaustion that haunted her body and seemed to reach into her soul.

She could see in the open square before her house the tops of trees that were   5 all aquiver with the new spring life. The delicious breath of rain was in the air. In the street below a peddler was crying his wares. The notes of a distant song which some one was singing reached her faintly, and countless sparrows were twittering in the eaves.

There were patches of blue sky showing here and there through the clouds that had met and piled one above the other in the west facing her window.

She sat with her head thrown back upon the cushion of the chair, quite motionless, except when a sob came up into her throat and shook her, as a child who has cried itself to sleep continues to sob in its dreams.

She was young, with a fair, calm face, whose lines bespoke repression and even a certain strength. But now there was a dull stare in her eyes, whose gaze was fixed away off yonder on one of those patches of blue sky. It was not a glance of reflection, but rather indicated a suspension of intelligent thought.

There was something coming to her and she was waiting for it, fearfully. What was it? She did not know; it was too subtle and elusive to name. But she felt it, creeping out of the sky, reaching toward her through the sounds, the scents, the color that filled the air.

Now her bosom rose and fell tumultuously. She was beginning to recognize   10
this thing that was approaching to possess her, and she was striving to beat it back with her will—as powerless as her two white slender hands would have been.

When she abandoned herself a little whispered word escaped her slightly parted lips. She said it over and over under her breath: "free, free, free!" The vacant stare and the look of terror that had followed it went from her eyes. They stayed keen and bright. Her pulses beat fast, and the coursing blood warmed and relaxed every inch of her body.

She did not stop to ask if it were or were not a monstrous joy that held her. A clear and exalted perception enabled her to dismiss the suggestion as trivial.

She knew that she would weep again when she saw the kind, tender hands folded in death; the face that had never looked save with love upon her, fixed and gray and dead. But she saw beyond that bitter moment a long procession of years to come that would belong to her absolutely. And she opened and spread her arms out to them in welcome.

There would be no one to live for her during those coming years; she would live for herself. There would be no powerful will bending hers in that blind persistence with which men and women believe they have a right to impose a private will upon a fellow-creature. A kind intention or a cruel intention made the act seem no less a crime as she looked upon it in that brief moment of illumination.

And yet she had loved him—sometimes. Often she had not. What did it matter!   15
What could love, the unsolved mystery, count for in face of this possession of self-assertion which she suddenly recognized as the strongest impulse of her being!

"Free! Body and soul free!" she kept whispering.

Josephine was kneeling before the closed door with her lips to the keyhole, imploring for admission. "Louise, open the door! I beg; open the door—you will make yourself ill. What are you doing, Louise? For heaven's sake open the door."

"Go away. I am not making myself ill." No; she was drinking in a very elixir of life through that open window.

Her fancy was running riot along those days ahead of her. Spring days, and summer days, and all sorts of days that would be her own. She breathed a quick prayer that life might be long. It was only yesterday she had thought with a shudder that life might be long.

She arose at length and opened the door to her sister's importunities. There   20
was a feverish triumph in her eyes, and she carried herself unwittingly like a goddess of Victory. She clasped her sister's waist, and together they descended the stairs. Richards stood waiting for them at the bottom.

Some one was opening the front door with a latchkey. It was Brently Mallard who entered, a little travel-stained, composedly carrying his grip-sack and umbrella. He had been far from the scene of accident, and did not even know there had been one. He stood amazed at Josephine's piercing cry; at Richards' quick motion to screen him from the view of his wife.

But Richards was too late.

When the doctors came they said she had died of heart disease—of joy that kills.

(1894)

Questions for Discussion and Writing

1. What is the double meaning of Mrs. Mallard's "heart trouble," mentioned in the first line of the story?
2. Discuss the function of the imagery in paragraphs 4, 5, and 6.
3. Discuss the dual irony of the final line.
4. Write an essay arguing that Mrs. Mallard is (or is not) a sympathetic character.

Making Connections

Compare Mrs. Mallard with Elisa Allen in "The Chrysanthemums" by Steinbeck (page 375). What do these wives have in common? How do they differ?

◇◇◇◇◇◇◇◇◇◇◇◇◇◇◇◇◇◇◇◇

Charlotte Perkins Gilman   1860–1935

A leading figure in the women's movement at the turn of the 20th century, Charlotte Perkins Gilman boldly challenged conventional gender roles in her life as well as in her fiction and nonfiction. Born into a prominent family in Hartford, Connecticut (her relatives included the author Harriet Beecher Stowe), she suffered a difficult childhood and an unhappy first marriage. In 1885, after the birth of her first child, Gilman grew increasingly depressed and turned to S. Weir Mitchell, a noted physician who prescribed complete rest and isolation—a treatment that drove her, she said, "near the borderline of utter mental ruin." When she recovered, Gilman divorced her husband, gave up custody of their daughter, moved to California, and eventually remarried. Among her works are *Women and Economics* (1899), *The Man-Made World* (1911), and three utopian feminist novels, the most famous of which is *Herland*, written in 1915 but not published until 1978. Suffering from inoperable breast cancer, Gilman took her own life at age seventy-five.

The Yellow Wallpaper

It is very seldom that mere ordinary people like John and myself secure ancestral halls for the summer.

A colonial mansion, a hereditary estate, I would say a haunted house, and reach the height of romantic felicity—but that would be asking too much of fate!

Still I will proudly declare that there is something queer about it.

Else, why should it be let so cheaply? And why have stood so long untenanted?

John laughs at me, of course, but one expects that in marriage. 5

John is practical in the extreme. He has no patience with faith, an intense horror of superstition, and he scoffs openly at any talk of things not to be felt or seen and put down in figures.

John is a physician, and *perhaps*—(I would not say it to a living soul, of course, but this is dead paper and a great relief to my mind)—*perhaps* that is one reason I do not get well faster.

You see he does not believe I am sick! And what can one do?

If a physician of high standing, and one's own husband, assures friends and relatives that there is really nothing the matter with one but temporary nervous depression—a slight hysterical tendency—what is one to do?

My brother is also a physician, and also of high standing, and he says the 10 same thing.

So I take phosphates or phosphites—whichever it is—and tonics, and journeys, and air, and exercise, and am absolutely forbidden to "work" until I am well again.

Personally, I disagree with their ideas.

Personally, I believe that congenial work, with excitement and change, would do me good.

But what is one to do?

I did write for a while in spite of them; but it *does* exhaust me a good deal— 15 having to be so sly about it, or else meet with heavy opposition.

I sometimes fancy that in my condition if I had less opposition and more society and stimulus—but John says the very worst thing I can do is to think about my condition, and I confess it always makes me feel bad.

So I will let it alone and talk about the house.

The most beautiful place! It is quite alone, standing well back from the road, quite three miles from the village. It makes me think of English places that you read about, for there are hedges and walls and gates that lock, and lots of separate little houses for the gardeners and people.

There is a *delicious* garden! I never saw such a garden—large and shady, full of box-bordered paths, and lined with long grape-covered arbors with seats under them.

There were greenhouses, too, but they are all broken now. 20

There was some legal trouble, I believe, something about the heirs and coheirs; anyhow, the place has been empty for years.

That spoils my ghostliness, I am afraid, but I don't care—there is something strange about the house—I can feel it.

I even said so to John one moonlight evening, but he said what I felt was a draft, and shut the window.

I get unreasonably angry with John sometimes. I'm sure I never used to be so sensitive. I think it is due to this nervous condition.

But John says if I feel so I shall neglect proper self-control; so I take pains to 25 control myself—before him, at least, and that makes me very tired.

I don't like our room a bit. I wanted one downstairs that opened on the piazza and had roses all over the window, and such pretty old-fashioned chintz hangings! But John would not hear of it.

He said there was only one window and not room for two beds, and no near room for him if he took another.

He is very careful and loving, and hardly lets me stir without special direction.

I have a schedule prescription for each hour in the day; he takes all care from me, and so I feel basely ungrateful not to value it more.

He said we came here solely on my account, that I was to have perfect rest   30 and all the air I could get. "Your exercise depends on your strength, my dear," said he, "and your food somewhat on your appetite; but air you can absorb all the time." So we took the nursery at the top of the house.

It is a big, airy room, the whole floor nearly, with windows that look all ways, and air and sunshine galore. It was nursery first and then playroom and gymnasium, I should judge; for the windows are barred for little children, and there are rings and things in the walls.

The paint and paper look as if a boys' school had used it. It is stripped off— the paper—in great patches all around the head of my bed, about as far as I can reach, and in a great place on the other side of the room low down. I never saw a worse paper in my life.

One of those sprawling flamboyant patterns committing every artistic sin.

It is dull enough to confuse the eye in following, pronounced enough constantly to irritate and provoke study, and when you follow the lame uncertain curves for a little distance they suddenly commit suicide—plunge off at outrageous angles, destroy themselves in unheard of contradictions.

The color is repellent, almost revolting; a smoldering unclean yellow,   35 strangely faded by the slow-turning sunlight.

It is a dull yet lurid orange in some places, a sickly sulphur tint in others.

No wonder the children hated it! I should hate it myself if I had to live in this room long.

There comes John, and I must put this away—he hates to have me write a word.

We have been here two weeks, and I haven't felt like writing before, since that first day.

I am sitting by the window now, up in this atrocious nursery, and there is   40 nothing to hinder my writing as much as I please, save lack of strength.

John is away all day, and even some nights when his cases are serious.

I am glad my case is not serious!

But these nervous troubles are dreadfully depressing.

John does not know how much I really suffer. He knows there is no *reason* to suffer, and that satisfies him.

Of course it is only nervousness. It does weigh on me so not to do my duty   45 in any way!

I meant to be such a help to John, such a real rest and comfort, and here I am a comparative burden already!

Nobody would believe what an effort it is to do what little I am able—to dress and entertain, and order things.

It is fortunate Mary is so good with the baby. Such a dear baby!

And yet I *cannot* be with him, it makes me so nervous.

I suppose John never was nervous in his life. He laughs at me so about this   50 wallpaper!

At first he meant to repaper the room, but afterwards he said that I was letting it get the better of me, and that nothing was worse for a nervous patient than to give way to such fancies.

He said that after the wallpaper was changed it would be the heavy bedstead, and then the barred windows, and then that gate at the head of the stairs, and so on.

"You know the place is doing you good," he said, "and really, dear, I don't care to renovate the house just for a three months' rental."

"Then do let us go downstairs," I said, "there are such pretty rooms there."

Then he took me in his arms and called me a blessed little goose, and said   55
he would go down cellar, if I wished, and have it whitewashed into the bargain.

But he is right enough about the beds and windows and things.

It is an airy and comfortable room as any one need wish, and, of course, I would not be so silly as to make him uncomfortable just for a whim.

I'm really getting quite fond of the big room, all but that horrid paper.

Out of one window I can see the garden, those mysterious deep-shaded arbors, the riotous old-fashioned flowers, and bushes and gnarly trees.

Out of another I get a lovely view of the bay and a little private wharf belong-   60
ing to the estate. There is a beautiful shaded lane that runs down there from the house. I always fancy I see people walking in these numerous paths and arbors, but John has cautioned me not to give way to fancy in the least. He says that with my imaginative power and habit of story-making, a nervous weakness like mine is sure to lead to all manner of excited fancies, and that I ought to use my will and good sense to check the tendency. So I try.

I think sometimes that if I were only well enough to write a little it would relieve the press of ideas and rest me.

But I find I get pretty tired when I try.

It is so discouraging not to have any advice and companionship about my work. When I get really well, John says we will ask Cousin Henry and Julia down for a long visit; but he says he would as soon put fireworks in my pillowcase as to let me have those stimulating people about now.

I wish I could get well faster.

But I must not think about that. This paper looks to me as if it *knew* what a   65
vicious influence it had!

There is a recurrent spot where the pattern lolls like a broken neck and two bulbous eyes stare at you upside down.

I get positively angry with the impertinence of it and the everlastingness. Up and down and sideways they crawl, and those absurd, unblinking eyes are everywhere. There is one place where two breadths didn't match, and the eyes go all up and down the line, one a little higher than the other.

I never saw so much expression in an inanimate thing before, and we all know how much expression they have! I used to lie awake as a child and get more entertainment and terror out of blank walls and plain furniture than most children could find in a toy-store.

I remember what a kindly wink the knobs of our big, old bureau used to have, and there was one chair that always seemed like a strong friend.

I used to feel that if any of the other things looked too fierce I could always   70
hop into that chair and be safe.

The furniture in this room is no worse than inharmonious, however, for we had to bring it all from downstairs. I suppose when this was used as a playroom they had to take the nursery things out, and no wonder! I never saw such ravages as the children have made here.

The wallpaper, as I said before, is torn off in spots, and it sticketh closer than a brother—they must have had perseverance as well as hatred.

Then the floor is scratched and gouged and splintered, the plaster itself is dug out here and there, and this great heavy bed which is all we found in the room, looks as if it had been through the wars.

But I don't mind it a bit—only the paper.

There comes John's sister. Such a dear girl as she is, and so careful of me! I must not let her find me writing. 75

She is a perfect and enthusiastic housekeeper, and hopes for no better profession. I verily believe she thinks it is the writing which made me sick!

But I can write when she is out, and see her a long way off from these windows.

There is one that commands the road, a lovely shaded winding road, and one that just looks off over the country. A lovely country, too, full of great elms and velvet meadows.

This wallpaper has a kind of sub-pattern in a different shade, a particularly irritating one, for you can only see it in certain lights, and not clearly then.

But in the places where it isn't faded and where the sun is just so—I can see a strange, provoking, formless sort of figure, that seems to skulk about behind that silly and conspicuous front design. 80

There's sister on the stairs!

Well, the Fourth of July is over! The people are all gone and I am tired out. John thought it might do me good to see a little company, so we just had mother and Nellie and the children down for a week.

Of course I didn't do a thing. Jennie sees to everything now.

But it tired me all the same.

John says if I don't pick up faster he shall send me to Weir Mitchell[1] in the fall. 85

But I don't want to go there at all. I had a friend who was in his hands once, and she says he is just like John and my brother, only more so!

Besides, it is such an undertaking to go so far.

I don't feel as if it was worth while to turn my hand over for anything, and I'm getting dreadfully fretful and querulous.

I cry at nothing, and cry most of the time.

Of course I don't when John is here, or anybody else, but when I am alone. 90

And I am alone a good deal just now. John is kept in town very often by serious cases, and Jennie is good and lets me alone when I want her to.

So I walk a little in the garden or down that lovely lane, sit on the porch under the roses, and lie down up here a good deal.

I'm getting really fond of the room in spite of the wallpaper. Perhaps *because* of the wallpaper.

It dwells in my mind so!

I lie here on this great immovable bed—it is nailed down, I believe—and follow that pattern about by the hour. It is as good as gymnastics, I assure you. 95

---

[1]S. Weir Mitchell (1829–1914), a noted physician who specialized in treating neurasthenic women, attended both Charlotte Perkins Gilman and Edith Wharton when they suffered from "nerves."

I start, we'll say, at the bottom, down in the corner over there where it has not been touched, and I determine for the thousandth time that I *will* follow that pointless pattern to some sort of a conclusion.

I know a little of the principle of design, and I know this thing was not arranged on any laws of radiation, or alternation, or repetition, or symmetry, or anything else that I ever heard of.

It is repeated, of course, by the breadths, but not otherwise.

Looked at in one way each breadth stands alone, the bloated curves and flourishes—a kind of "debased Romanesque" with delirium tremens—go waddling up and down in isolated columns of fatuity.

But, on the other hand, they connect diagonally, and the sprawling outlines run off in great slanting waves of optic horror, like a lot of wallowing seaweeds in full chase.

The whole thing goes horizontally, too, at least it seems so, and I exhaust myself trying to distinguish the order of its going in that direction.

They have used a horizontal breadth for a frieze, and that adds wonderfully to the confusion.

There is one end of the room where it is almost intact, and there, when the crosslights fade and the low sun shines directly upon it, I can almost fancy radiation after all,—the interminable grotesques seem to form around a common center and rush off in headlong plunges of equal distraction.

It makes me tired to follow it. I will take a nap I guess.

I don't know why I should write this.

I don't want to.

I don't feel able.

And I know John would think it absurd. But I *must* say what I feel and think in some way—it is such a relief!

But the effort is getting to be greater than the relief.

Half the time now I am awfully lazy, and lie down ever so much.

John says I mustn't lose my strength, and has me take cod liver oil and lots of tonics and things, to say nothing of ale and wine and rare meat.

Dear John! He loves me very dearly, and hates to have me sick. I tried to have a real earnest reasonable talk with him the other day, and tell him how I wish he would let me go and make a visit to Cousin Henry and Julia.

But he said I wasn't able to go, nor able to stand it after I got there; and I did not make out a very good case for myself, for I was crying before I had finished.

It is getting to be a great effort for me to think straight. Just this nervous weakness I suppose.

And dear John gathered me up in his arms, and just carried me upstairs and laid me on the bed, and sat by me and read to me till it tired my head.

He said I was his darling and his comfort and all he had, and that I must take care of myself for his sake, and keep well.

He says no one but myself can help me out of it, that I must use my will and self-control and not let any silly fancies run away with me.

There's one comfort, the baby is well and happy, and does not have to occupy this nursery with the horrid wallpaper.

If we had not used it, that blessed child would have! What a fortunate escape! Why, I wouldn't have a child of mine, an impressionable little thing, live in such a room for worlds.

I never thought of it before, but it is lucky that John kept me here after all, I can stand it so much easier than a baby, you see.

Of course I never mention it to them any more—I am too wise—but I keep watch for it all the same. 120

There are things in that paper that nobody knows but me, or ever will.

Behind that outside pattern the dim shapes get clearer every day.

It is always the same shape, only very numerous.

And it is like a woman stooping down and creeping about behind that pattern. I don't like it a bit. I wonder—I begin to think—I wish John would take me away from here!

It is so hard to talk with John about my case, because he is so wise, and because he loves me so. 125

But I tried it last night.

It was moonlight. The moon shines in all around just as the sun does.

I hate to see it sometimes, it creeps so slowly, and always comes in by one window or another.

John was asleep and I hated to waken him, so I kept still and watched the moonlight on that undulating wallpaper till I felt creepy.

The faint figure behind seemed to shake the pattern, just as if she wanted to get out. 130

I got up softly and went to feel and see if the paper *did* move, and when I came back John was awake.

"What is it, little girl?" he said. "Don't go walking about like that—you'll get cold."

I thought it was a good time to talk so I told him that I really was not gaining here, and that I wished he would take me away.

"Why darling!" said he, "our lease will be up in three weeks, and I can't see how to leave before.

"The repairs are not done at home, and I cannot possibly leave town just now. Of course if you were in any danger, I could and would, but you really are better, dear, whether you can see it or not. I am a doctor, dear, and I know. You are gaining flesh and color, your appetite is better. I feel really much easier about you." 135

"I don't weigh a bit more," said I, "nor as much; and my appetite may be better in the evening when you are here, but it is worse in the morning when you are away!"

"Bless her little heart!" said he with a big hug, "she shall be as sick as she pleases! But now let's improve the shining hours by going to sleep, and talk about it in the morning!"

"And you won't go away?" I asked gloomily.

"Why, how can I, dear? It is only three weeks more and then we will take a nice little trip of a few days while Jennie is getting the house ready. Really, dear, you are better!"

"Better in body perhaps—" I began, and stopped short, for he sat up straight and looked at me with such a stern, reproachful look that I could not say another word. 140

"My darling," said he, "I beg of you, for my sake and for our child's sake, as well as for your own, that you will never for one instant let that idea enter your mind! There is nothing so dangerous, so fascinating, to a temperament like yours. It is a false and foolish fancy. Can you not trust me as a physician when I tell you so?"

So of course I said no more on that score, and we went to sleep before long. He thought I was asleep first, but I wasn't, and lay there for hours trying to decide whether that front pattern and the back pattern really did move together or separately.

On a pattern like this, by daylight, there is a lack of sequence, a defiance of law, that is a constant irritant to a normal mind.

The color is hideous enough, and unreliable enough, and infuriating enough, but the pattern is torturing.

You think you have mastered it, but just as you get well underway in follow- 145 ing, it turns a back-somersault and there you are. It slaps you in the face, knocks you down, and tramples upon you. It is like a bad dream.

The outside pattern is a florid arabesque, reminding one of a fungus. If you can imagine a toadstool in joints, an interminable string of toadstools, budding and sprouting in endless convolutions—why, that is something like it.

That is, sometimes!

There is one marked peculiarity about this paper, a thing nobody seems to notice but myself, and that is that it changes as the light changes.

When the sun shoots in through the east window—I always watch for that first, long, straight ray—it changes so quickly that I never can quite believe it.

That is why I watch it always. 150

By moonlight—the moon shines in all night when there is a moon—I wouldn't know it was the same paper.

At night in any kind of light, in twilight, candlelight, lamplight, and worst of all by moonlight, it becomes bars! The outside pattern I mean, and the woman behind it is as plain as can be.

I didn't realize for a long time what the thing was that showed behind, that dim sub-pattern, but now I am quite sure it is a woman.

By daylight she is subdued, quiet. I fancy it is the pattern that keeps her so still. It is so puzzling. It keeps me quiet by the hour.

I lie down ever so much now. John says it is good for me, and to sleep all I can. 155

Indeed he started the habit by making me lie down for an hour after each meal.

It is a very bad habit I am convinced, for you see I don't sleep.

And that cultivates deceit, for I don't tell them I'm awake—O, no!

The fact is I am getting a little afraid of John.

He seems very queer sometimes, and even Jennie has an inexplicable look. 160

It strikes me occasionally, just as a scientific hypothesis, that perhaps it is the paper!

I have watched John when he did not know I was looking, and come into the room suddenly on the most innocent excuses, and I've caught him several times *looking at the paper!* And Jennie too. I caught Jennie with her hand on it once.

She didn't know I was in the room, and when I asked her in a quiet, a very quiet voice, with the most restrained manner possible, what she was doing with the paper—she turned around as if she had been caught stealing, and looked quite angry—asked me why I should frighten her so!

Then she said that the paper stained everything it touched, that she had found yellow smooches on all my clothes and John's, and she wished we would be more careful!

Did not that sound innocent? But I know she was studying that pattern, and I   165
am determined that nobody shall find it out but myself!

Life is very much more exciting now than it used to be. You see I have something more to expect, to look forward to, to watch. I really do eat better, and am
more quiet than I was.

John is so pleased to see me improve! He laughed a little the other day, and
said I seemed to be flourishing in spite of my wallpaper.

I turned it off with a laugh. I had no intention of telling him it was *because* of
the wallpaper—he would make fun of me. He might even want to take me away.

I don't want to leave now until I have found it out. There is a week more, and
I think that will be enough.

I'm feeling ever so much better! I don't sleep much at night, for it is so inter-   170
esting to watch developments; but I sleep a good deal in the daytime.

In the daytime it is tiresome and perplexing.

There are always new shoots on the fungus, and new shades of yellow all over
it. I cannot keep count of them, though I have tried conscientiously.

It is the strangest yellow, that wallpaper! It makes me think of all the yellow
things I ever saw—not beautiful ones like buttercups, but old foul, bad yellow
things.

But there is something else about that paper—the smell! I noticed it the
moment we came into the room, but with so much air and sun it was not bad.
Now we have had a week of fog and rain, and whether the windows are open or
not, the smell is here.

It creeps all over the house.   175

I find it hovering in the dining-room, skulking in the parlor, hiding in the
hall, lying in wait for me on the stairs.

It gets into my hair.

Even when I go to ride, if I turn my head suddenly and surprise it—there is
that smell!

Such a peculiar odor, too! I have spent hours in trying to analyze it, to find
what it smelled like.

It is not bad—at first, and very gentle, but quite the subtlest, most enduring   180
odor I ever met.

In this damp weather it is awful, I wake up in the night and find it hanging
over me.

It used to disturb me at first. I thought seriously of burning the house—to
reach the smell.

But now I am used to it. The only thing I can think of that it is like is the *color*
of the paper! A yellow smell.

There is a very funny mark on this wall, low down, near the mopboard. A
streak that runs round the room. It goes behind every piece of furniture, except
the bed, a long, straight, even *smooch*, as if it had been rubbed over and over.

I wonder how it was done and who did it, and what they did it for. Round and   185
round and round—round and round and round—it makes me dizzy!

I really have discovered something at last.

Through watching so much at night, when it changes so, I have finally
found out.

The front pattern *does* move—and no wonder! The woman behind shakes it!

Sometimes I think there are a great many women behind, and sometimes only one, and she crawls around fast, and her crawling shakes it all over.

Then in the very bright spots she keeps still, and in the very shady spots she just takes hold of the bars and shakes them hard. 190

And she is all the time trying to climb through. But nobody could climb through that pattern—it strangles so; I think that is why it has so many heads.

They get through, and then the pattern strangles them off and turns them upside down, and makes their eyes white!

If those heads were covered or taken off it would not be half so bad.

I think that woman gets out in the daytime!

And I'll tell you why—privately—I've seen her! 195

I can see her out of every one of my windows!

It is the same woman, I know, for she is always creeping, and most women do not creep by daylight.

I see her in that long shaded lane, creeping up and down. I see her in those dark grape arbors, creeping all around the garden.

I see her on that long road under the trees, creeping along, and when a carriage comes she hides under the blackberry vines.

I don't blame her a bit. It must be very humiliating to be caught creeping by 200 daylight!

I always lock the door when I creep by daylight. I can't do it at night, for I know John would suspect something at once.

And John is so queer now, that I don't want to irritate him. I wish he would take another room! Besides, I don't want anybody to get that woman out at night but myself.

I often wonder if I could see her out of all the windows at once.

But, turn as fast as I can, I can only see out of one at one time.

And though I always see her, she *may* be able to creep faster than I can turn! 205

I have watched her sometimes away off in the open country, creeping as fast as a cloud shadow in a high wind.

If only that top pattern could be gotten off from the under one! I mean to try it, little by little.

I have found out another funny thing, but I shan't tell it this time! It does not do to trust people too much.

There are only two more days to get this paper off, and I believe John is beginning to notice. I don't like the look in his eyes.

And I heard him ask Jennie a lot of professional questions about me. She had 210 a very good report to give.

She said I slept a good deal in the daytime.

John knows I don't sleep very well at night, for all I'm so quiet!

He asked me all sorts of questions, too, and pretended to be very loving and kind.

As if I couldn't see through him!

Still, I don't wonder he acts so, sleeping under this paper for three months. 215

It only interests me, but I feel sure John and Jennie are secretly affected by it.

Hurrah! This is the last day, but it is enough. John to stay in town over night, and won't be out until this evening.

Jennie wanted to sleep with me—the sly thing! but I told her I should undoubtedly rest better for a night all alone.

That was clever, for really I wasn't alone a bit! As soon as it was moonlight and that poor thing began to crawl and shake the pattern, I got up and ran to help her.

I pulled and she shook, I shook and she pulled, and before morning we had   220
peeled off yards of that paper.

A strip about as high as my head and half around the room.

And then when the sun came and that awful pattern began to laugh at me, I declared I would finish it today!

We go away tomorrow, and they are moving all my furniture down again to leave things as they were before.

Jennie looked at the wall in amazement, but I told her merrily that I did it out of pure spite at the vicious thing.

She laughed and said she wouldn't mind doing it herself, but I must not get tired.   225

How she betrayed herself that time!

But I am here, and no person touches this paper but Me—not *alive!*

She tried to get me out of the room—it was too patent! But I said it was so quiet and empty and clean now that I believed I would lie down again and sleep all I could; and not to wake me even for dinner—I would call when I woke.

So now she is gone, and the servants are gone, and the things are gone, and there is nothing left but the great bedstead nailed down, with the canvas mattress we found on it.

We shall sleep downstairs tonight, and take the boat home tomorrow.   230

I quite enjoy the room, now it is bare again.

How those children did tear about here!

This bedstead is fairly gnawed!

But I must get to work.

I have locked the door and thrown the key down into the front path.   235

I don't want to go out, and I don't want to have anybody come in, till John comes.

I want to astonish him.

I've got a rope up here that even Jennie did not find. If that woman does get out, and tries to get away, I can tie her!

But I forgot I could not reach far without anything to stand on!

This bed will *not* move!   240

I tried to lift and push it until I was lame, and then I got so angry I bit off a little piece at one corner—but it hurt my teeth.

Then I peeled off all the paper I could reach standing on the floor. It sticks horribly and the pattern just enjoys it! All those strangled heads and bulbous eyes and waddling fungus growths just shriek with derision!

I am getting angry enough to do something desperate. To jump out of the window would be admirable exercise, but the bars are too strong even to try.

Besides I wouldn't do it. Of course not. I know well enough that a step like that is improper and might be misconstrued.

I don't like to *look* out the windows even—there are so many of those creep-   245
ing women, and they creep so fast.

I wonder if they all come out of that wallpaper as I did?

But I am securely fastened now by my well-hidden rope—you don't get *me* out in the road there!

I suppose I shall have to get back behind the pattern when it comes night, and that is hard!

It is so pleasant to be out in this great room and creep around as I please!

I don't want to go outside. I won't, even if Jennie asks me to.   250

For outside you have to creep on the ground, and everything is green instead of yellow.

But here I can creep smoothly on the floor, and my shoulder just fits in that long smooch around the wall, so I cannot lose my way.

Why there's John at the door!

It is no use, young man, you can't open it!

How he does call and pound!   255

Now he's crying for an axe.

It would be a shame to break down that beautiful door!

"John dear!" said I in the gentlest voice, "the key is down by the front steps, under a plantain leaf!"

That silenced him for a few moments.

Then he said, very quietly indeed, "Open the door, my darling!"   260

"I can't," said I. "The key is down by the front door under a plantain leaf!"

And then I said it again, several times, very gently and slowly, and said it so often that he had to go and see, and he got it of course, and came in. He stopped short by the door.

"What is the matter?" he cried. "For God's sake, what are you doing!"

I kept on creeping just the same, but I looked at him over my shoulder.

"I've got out at last," said I, "in spite of you and Jane. And I've pulled off most   265
of the paper, so you can't put me back!"

Now why should that man have fainted? But he did, and right across my path by the wall, so that I had to creep over him every time!

                                                                             (1892)

Questions for Discussion and Writing

1. Why is it fitting that the narrator's husband chooses the room he does? What purposes has the room served in the past?
2. What would the narrator like to be doing? Why can't she? Study a few of the early conversations between the narrator and her husband for evidence to support your answer.
3. What do the sunshine and the moonlight contribute to the story?
4. What are the similarities between the narrator and the woman she sees behind the wallpaper?
5. What significance can you attach to the narrator's discovery that the woman escapes and creeps around outside? Why does the narrator assert that "most women do not creep by daylight"? Is it significant that by the end of the story she sees many women creeping about the countryside?

Making Connections

Compare the husband and wife relationships in "The Yellow Wallpaper," "The Chrysanthemums" by John Steinbeck (page 375), and "The Story of an Hour" by Kate Chopin (page 234). Are the dynamics of these marriages dated or still relevant today?

James Joyce   1882–1941

James Joyce rejected his Irish Catholic heritage and left his homeland at age twenty. Though an expatriate most of his adult life, Joyce wrote almost exclusively about his native Dublin. His first book, *Dubliners* (1914), is a series of sharply drawn vignettes based on his experiences in Ireland, the homeland he later described as "a sow that eats its own farrow." His novel *Ulysses* (1933), which was banned for a time in the United States because of its coarse language and frank treatment of sexuality, is now considered one of the greatest novels of the twentieth century.

Araby

North Richmond Street, being blind, was a quiet street except at the hour when the Christian Brothers' School set the boys free. An uninhabited house of two storeys stood at the blind end, detached from its neighbours in a square ground. The other houses of the street, conscious of decent lives within them, gazed at one another with brown imperturbable faces.

The former tenant of our house, a priest, had died in the back drawing-room. Air, musty from having been long enclosed, hung in all the rooms, and the waste room behind the kitchen was littered with old useless papers. Among these I found a few paper-covered books, the pages of which were curled and damp: *The Abbot*, by Walter Scott, *The Devout Communicant*, and *The Memoirs of Vidocq*. I liked the last best because its leaves were yellow. The wild garden behind the house contained a central apple-tree and a few straggling bushes, under one of which I found the late tenant's rusty bicycle-pump. He had been a very charitable priest; in his will he had left all his money to institutions and the furniture of his house to his sister.

When the short days of winter came, dusk fell before we had well eaten our dinners. When we met in the street the houses had grown sombre. The space of sky above us was the colour of ever-changing violet and towards it the lamps of the street lifted their feeble lanterns. The cold air stung us and we played till our bodies glowed. Our shouts echoed in the silent street. The career of our play brought us through the dark muddy lanes behind the houses, where we ran the gauntlet of the rough tribes from the cottages, to the back doors of the dark dripping gardens where odours arose from the ashpits, to the dark odorous stables where a coachman smoothed and combed the horse or shook music from the buckled harness. When we returned to the street, light from the kitchen windows had filled the areas. If my uncle was seen turning the corner, we hid in the shadow until we had seen him safely housed. Or if Mangan's sister came out on the doorstep to call her brother in to his tea, we watched her from our shadow peer up and down the street. We waited to see whether she would remain or go in and, if she remained, we left our shadow and walked up to Mangan's steps resignedly. She was waiting for us, her figure defined by the light from the half-opened door. Her brother always teased her before he obeyed, and I stood by the railings looking at her. Her dress swung as she moved her body, and the soft rope of her hair tossed from side to side.

Every morning I lay on the floor in the front parlour watching her door. The blind was pulled down to within an inch of the sash so that I could not be seen. When she came out on the doorstep my heart leaped. I ran to the hall, seized my books and followed her. I kept her brown figure always in my eye and, when we came near the point at which our ways diverged, I quickened my pace and passed her. This happened morning after morning. I had never spoken to her, except for a few casual words, and yet her name was like a summons to all my foolish blood.

Her image accompanied me even in places the most hostile to romance. On Saturday evenings when my aunt went marketing I had to go to carry some of the parcels. We walked through the flaring streets, jostled by drunken men and bargaining women, amid the curses of labourers, the shrill litanies of shop-boys who stood on guard by the barrels of pigs' cheeks, the nasal chanting of street-singers, who sang a *come-all-you* about O'Donovan Rossa, or a ballad about the troubles in our native land. These noises converged in a single sensation of life for me: I imagined that I bore my chalice safely through a throng of foes. Her name sprang to my lips at moments in strange prayers and praises which I myself did not understand. My eyes were often full of tears (I could not tell why) and at times a flood from my heart seemed to pour itself out into my bosom. I thought little of the future. I did not know whether I would ever speak to her or not or, if I spoke to her, how I could tell her of my confused adoration. But my body was like a harp and her words and gestures were like fingers running upon the wires.

One evening I went into the back drawing-room in which the priest had died. It was a dark rainy evening and there was no sound in the house. Through one of the broken panes I heard the rain impinge upon the earth, the fine incessant needles of water playing in the sodden beds. Some distant lamp or lighted window gleamed below me. I was thankful that I could see so little. All my senses seemed to desire to veil themselves and, feeling that I was about to slip from them, I pressed the palms of my hands together until they trembled, murmuring: "*O love! O love!*" many times.

At last she spoke to me. When she addressed the first words to me I was so confused that I did not know what to answer. She asked me was I going to *Araby*. I forgot whether I answered yes or no. It would be a splendid bazaar; she said she would love to go.

"And why can't you?" I asked.

While she spoke she turned a silver bracelet round and round her wrist. She could not go, she said, because there would be a retreat that week in her convent. Her brother and two other boys were fighting for their caps, and I was alone at the railings. She held one of the spikes, bowing her head towards me. The light from the lamp opposite our door caught the white curve of her neck, lit up her hair that rested there and, falling, lit up the hand upon the railing. It fell over one side of her dress and caught the white border of a petticoat, just visible as she stood at ease.

"It's well for you," she said.

"If I go,' I said, 'I will bring you something."

What innumerable follies laid waste my waking and sleeping thoughts after that evening! I wished to annihilate the tedious intervening days. I chafed against the work of school. At night in my bedroom and by day in the classroom her image came between me and the page I strove to read. The syllables of the word *Araby* were called to me through the silence in which my soul luxuriated and cast an Eastern enchantment over me. I asked for leave to go to the bazaar on Saturday night. My aunt was surprised, and hoped it was not some

Freemason affair. I answered few questions in class. I watched my master's face pass from amiability to sternness; he hoped I was not beginning to idle. I could not call my wandering thoughts together. I had hardly any patience with the serious work of life which, now that it stood between me and my desire, seemed to me child's play, ugly monotonous child's play.

On Saturday morning I reminded my uncle that I wished to go to the bazaar in the evening. He was fussing at the hallstand, looking for the hat-brush, and answered me curtly:

"Yes, boy, I know."

As he was in the hall I could not go into the front parlour and lie at the window. I felt the house in bad humour and walked slowly towards the school. The air was pitilessly raw and already my heart misgave me. 15

When I came home to dinner my uncle had not yet been home. Still it was early. I sat staring at the clock for some time and, when its ticking began to irritate me, I left the room. I mounted the staircase and gained the upper part of the house. The high, cold, empty, gloomy rooms liberated me and I went from room to room singing. From the front window I saw my companions playing below in the street. Their cries reached me weakened and indistinct and, leaning my forehead against the cool glass, I looked over at the dark house where she lived. I may have stood there for an hour, seeing nothing but the brown-clad figure cast by my imagination, touched discreetly by the lamplight at the curved neck, at the hand upon the railings and at the border below the dress.

When I came downstairs again I found Mrs. Mercer sitting at the fire. She was an old, garrulous woman, a pawnbroker's widow, who collected used stamps for some pious purpose. I had to endure the gossip of the tea-table. The meal was prolonged beyond an hour and still my uncle did not come. Mrs. Mercer stood up to go: she was sorry she couldn't wait any longer, but it was after eight o'clock and she did not like to be out late, as the night air was bad for her. When she had gone I began to walk up and down the room, clenching my fists. My aunt said:

"I'm afraid you may put off your bazaar for this night of Our Lord."

At nine o'clock I heard my uncle's latchkey in the hall door. I heard him talking to himself and heard the hallstand rocking when it had received the weight of his overcoat. I could interpret these signs. When he was midway through his dinner I asked him to give me the money to go to the bazaar. He had forgotten.

"The people are in bed and after their first sleep now," he said. 20

I did not smile. My aunt said to him energetically:

"Can't you give him the money and let him go? You've kept him late enough as it is."

My uncle said he was very sorry he had forgotten. He said he believed in the old saying: "All work and no play makes Jack a dull boy." He asked me where I was going and, when I told him a second time, he asked me did I know *The Arab's Farewell to his Steed*. When I left the kitchen he was about to recite the opening lines of the piece to my aunt.

I held a florin tightly in my hand as I strode down Buckingham Street towards the station. The sight of the streets thronged with buyers and glaring with gas recalled to me the purpose of my journey. I took my seat in a third-class carriage of a deserted train. After an intolerable delay the train moved out of the station slowly. It crept onward among ruinous houses and over the twinkling river. At Westland Row Station a crowd of people pressed to the carriage doors; but the porters moved them back, saying that it was a special train for the bazaar. I remained alone in the bare carriage. In a few minutes the train drew up beside an improvised wooden platform. I passed out on to the road and saw by the lighted dial of a clock that it was ten minutes to ten. In front of me was a large building which displayed the magical name.

I could not find any sixpenny entrance and, fearing that the bazaar would be closed, I passed in quickly through a turnstile, handing a shilling to a weary-looking man. I found myself in a big hall girded at half its height by a gallery. Nearly all the stalls were closed and the greater part of the hall was in darkness. I recognized a silence like that which pervades a church after a service. I walked into the centre of the bazaar timidly. A few people were gathered about the stalls which were still open. Before a curtain, over which the words *Café Chantant* were written in coloured lamps, two men were counting money on a salver. I listened to the fall of the coins.

Remembering with difficulty why I had come, I went over to one of the stalls and examined porcelain vases and flowered tea-sets. At the door of the stall a young lady was talking and laughing with two young gentlemen. I remarked their English accents and listened vaguely to their conversation.

"O, I never said such a thing!"

"O, but you did!"

"O, but I didn't!"

"Didn't she say that?"

"Yes. I heard her."

"O, there's a... fib!"

Observing me, the young lady came over and asked me did I wish to buy anything. The tone of her voice was not encouraging; she seemed to have spoken to me out of a sense of duty. I looked humbly at the great jars that stood like eastern guards at either side of the dark entrance to the stall and murmured:

"No, thank you."

The young lady changed the position of one of the vases and went back to the two young men. They began to talk of the same subject. Once or twice the young lady glanced at me over her shoulder.

I lingered before her stall, though I knew my stay was useless, to make my interest in her wares seem the more real. Then I turned away slowly and walked down the middle of the bazaar. I allowed the two pennies to fall against the sixpence in my pocket. I heard a voice call from one end of the gallery that the light was out. The upper part of the hall was now completely dark.

Gazing up into the darkness I saw myself as a creature driven and derided by vanity; and my eyes burned with anguish and anger.

(1914)

Questions for Discussion and Writing

1. Why is the boy unnamed?
2. What details make clear that the narrator now feels differently about the events being described than he did at the time they occurred?
3. Why does the boy see himself "as a creature driven and derided by vanity," and what are the reasons for his anger and anguish?
4. Find out more about the traditions and conventions of Courtly Love, and write an essay that interprets "Araby" as a modern-day tale of Courtly Love.

Making Connections

Compare the protagonist in this story with Sammy in "A & P" by John Updike (page 358), as examples of hopeless (and hapless) romantics.

◇◇◇◇◇◇◇◇◇◇◇◇◇◇◇◇◇◇◇◇

Katherine Anne Porter 1890–1980

Katherine Anne Porter, reared on a hard-scrabble ranch in Texas by her father and her strict grandmother, finished only one year of high school because, at age sixteen, she ran away from her convent school and got married. This early marriage, like the three that followed, did not last long; she never had children. In 1918 she very nearly died during the Spanish influenza pandemic and, after her recovery, traveled widely, living for periods in Mexico and Europe. She became an agnostic during the 1930s but finally re-embraced Catholicism in the last decade of her life. During those final years, she kept her coffin upright on display as a decoration in her living room.

The Grave

The grandfather, dead for more than thirty years, had been twice disturbed in his long repose by the constancy and possessiveness of his widow. She removed his bones first to Louisiana and then to Texas as if she had set out to find her own burial place, knowing well she would never return to the places she had left. In Texas she set up a small cemetery in a corner of her first farm, and, as the family connection grew, and oddments of relations came over from Kentucky to settle, it contained at last about twenty graves. After the grandmother's death, part of her land was to be sold for the benefit of certain of her children, and the cemetery happened to lie in the part set aside for sale. It was necessary to take up the bodies and bury them again in the family plot in the big new public cemetery, where the grandmother had been buried. At last her husband was to lie beside her for eternity, as she had planned.

The family cemetery had been a pleasant small neglected garden of tangled rose bushes and ragged cedar trees and cypress, the simple flat stones rising out of uncropped sweet-smelling wild grass. The graves were lying open and empty one burning day when Miranda and her brother Paul, who often went together to hunt rabbits and doves, propped their twenty-two Winchester rifles carefully against the rail fence, climbed over and explored among the graves. She was nine years old and he was twelve.

They peered into the pits all shaped alike with such purposeful accuracy, and looking at each other with pleased adventurous eyes, they said in solemn tones: "These were graves!" trying by words to shape a special, suitable emotion in their minds, but they felt nothing except an agreeable thrill of wonder: they were seeing a new sight, doing something they had not done before. In them both there was also a small disappointment at the entire commonplaceness of the actual spectacle. Even if it had once contained a coffin for years upon years, when the coffin was gone a grave was just a hole in the ground. Miranda leaped into the pit that had held her grandfather's bones. Scratching around aimlessly and pleasurably as any young animal, she scooped up a lump of earth and weighed it in her palm. It had a pleasantly sweet, corrupt smell, being mixed with cedar needles and small leaves, and as the crumbs fell apart, she saw a silver dove no larger than a hazel nut, with spread wings and a neat fan-shaped tail. The breast had a deep round hollow in it. Turning it up to the fierce sunlight, she saw that the inside of the hollow was cut in little whorls. She scrambled out, over the pile of loose earth that had fallen back into one end of the grave, calling to Paul that she had found something, he must guess what.... His head appeared smiling over the rim of another grave. He waved a closed hand at her. "I've got something too!" They ran to compare treasures, making a game of it, so many guesses each, all wrong, and a final show-down with opened palms. Paul had found a thin wide gold ring carved with intricate flowers and leaves. Miranda was smitten at sight of the ring and wished to have it. Paul seemed more impressed by the dove. They made a trade, with some little bickering. After he had got the dove in his hand, Paul said, "Don't you know what this is? This is a screw head for a *coffin*!...I'll bet nobody else in the world has one like this!"

Miranda glanced at it without covetousness. She had the gold ring on her thumb; it fitted perfectly. "Maybe we ought to go now," she said, "maybe one of the niggers 'll see us and tell somebody." They knew the land had been sold, the cemetery was no longer theirs, and they felt like trespassers. They climbed back over the fence, slung their rifles loosely under their arms—they had been shooting at targets with various kinds of firearms since they were seven years old—and set out to look for the rabbits and doves or whatever small game might happen along. On these expeditions Miranda always followed at Paul's heels along the path, obeying instructions about handling her gun when going through fences, learning how to stand it up properly so it would not slip and fire unexpectedly; how to wait her time for a shot and not just bang away in the air without looking, spoiling shots for Paul, who really could hit things if given a chance. Now and then, in her excitement at seeing birds whizz up suddenly before her face, or a rabbit leap across her very toes, she lost her head, and almost without sighting she flung her rifle up and pulled the trigger. She hardly ever hit any sort of mark. She had no proper sense of hunting at all. Her brother would be often completely disgusted with her. "You don't care whether you get your bird or not," he said. "That's no way to hunt." Miranda could not understand his indignation. She had seen him smash his hat and yell with fury when he had missed his aim. "What I like about shooting," said Miranda, with exasperating inconsequence, "is pulling the trigger and hearing the noise."

"Then, by golly," said Paul, "whyn't you go back to the range and shoot at bulls-eyes?"

"I'd just as soon," said Miranda, "only like this, we walk around more."

"Well, you just stay behind and stop spoiling my shots," said Paul, who, when he made a kill, wanted to be certain he had made it. Miranda, who alone brought down a bird once in twenty rounds, always claimed as her own any game they got when they fired at the same moment. It was tiresome and unfair and her brother was sick of it.

"Now, the first dove we see, or the first rabbit, is mine," he told her. "And the next will be yours. Remember that and don't get smarty."

5

"What about snakes?" asked Miranda idly. "Can I have the first snake?"

Waving her thumb gently and watching her gold ring glitter, Miranda lost 10 interest in shooting. She was wearing her summer roughing outfit: dark blue overalls, a light blue shirt, a hired-man's straw hat, and thick brown sandals. Her brother had the same outfit except his was a sober hickory-nut color. Ordinarily Miranda preferred her overalls to any other dress, though it was making rather a scandal in the countryside, for the year was 1903, and in the back country the law of female decorum had teeth in it. Her father had been criticized for letting his girls dress like boys and go careering around astride barebacked horses. Big sister Maria, the really independent and fearless one, in spite of her rather affected ways, rode at a dead run with only a rope knotted around her horse's nose. It was said the motherless family was running down, with the grandmother no longer there to hold it together. It was known that she had discriminated against her son Harry in her will, and that he was in straits about money. Some of his old neighbors reflected with vicious satisfaction that now he would probably not be so stiff-necked, nor have any more high-stepping horses either. Miranda knew this, though she could not say how. She had met along the road old women of the kind who smoked corn-cob pipes, who had treated her grandmother with most sincere respect. They slanted their gummy old eyes side-ways at the granddaughter and said, "Ain't you ashamed of yoself, Missy? It's against the Scriptures to dress like that. What yo Pappy thinkin about?" Miranda, with her powerful social sense, which was like a fine set of antennae radiating from every pore of her skin, would feel ashamed because she knew well it was rude and ill-bred to shock anybody, even bad-tempered old crones, though she had faith in her father's judgment and was perfectly comfortable in the clothes. Her father had said, "They're just what you need, and they'll save your dresses for school...." This sounded quite simple and natural to her. She had been brought up in rigorous economy. Wastefulness was vulgar. It was also a sin. These were truths; she had heard them repeated many times and never once disputed.

Now the ring, shining with the serene purity of fine gold on her rather grubby thumb, turned her feelings against her overalls and sockless feet, toes sticking through the thick brown leather straps. She wanted to go back to the farmhouse, take a good cold bath, dust herself with plenty of Maria's violet talcum powder—provided Maria was not present to object, of course—put on the thinnest, most becoming dress she owned, with a big sash; and sit in a wicker chair under the trees.... These things were not all she wanted, of course; she had vague stirrings of desire for luxury and a grand way of living which could not take precise form in her imagination but were founded on family legend of past wealth and leisure. These immediate comforts were what she could have, and she wanted them at once. She lagged rather far behind Paul, and once she thought of just turning back without a word and going home. She stopped, thinking that Paul would never do that to her, and so she would have to tell him. When a rabbit leaped, she let Paul have it without dispute. He killed it with one shot.

When she came up with him, he was already kneeling, examining the wound, the rabbit trailing from his hands. "Right through the head," he said complacently, as if he had aimed for it. He took out his sharp, competent bowie knife and started to skin the body. He did it very cleanly and quickly. Uncle Jimbilly knew how to prepare the skins so that Miranda always had fur coats for her dolls, for though she never cared much for her dolls she liked seeing them in fur coats. The children knelt facing each other over the dead animal. Miranda watched admiringly while her brother stripped the skin away as if he were taking off a glove. The flayed flesh emerged dark scarlet, sleek, firm; Miranda with thumb and finger felt the long fine muscles with the silvery flat strips binding them to the joints. Brother lifted the oddly bloated belly. "Look," he said, in a low amazed voice. "It was going to have young ones."

Very carefully he slit the thin flesh from the center ribs to the flanks, and a scarlet bag appeared. He slit again and pulled the bag open, and there lay a bundle of tiny rabbits, each wrapped in a thin scarlet veil. The brother pulled these off and there they were, dark gray, their sleek wet down lying in minute even ripples, like a baby's head just washed, their unbelievably small delicate ears folded close, their little blind faces almost featureless.

Miranda said, "Oh, I want to *see*," under her breath. She looked and looked—excited but not frightened, for she was accustomed to the sight of animals killed in hunting—filled with pity and astonishment and a kind of shocked delight in the wonderful little creatures for their own sakes, they were so pretty. She touched one of them ever so carefully, "Ah, there's blood running over them," she said and began to tremble without knowing why. Yet she wanted most deeply to see and to know. Having seen, she felt at once as if she had known all along. The very memory of her former ignorance faded, she had always known just this. No one had ever told her anything outright, she had been rather unobservant of the animal life around her because she was so accustomed to animals. They seemed simply disorderly and unaccountably rude in their habits, but altogether natural and not very interesting. Her brother had spoken as if he had known about everything all along. He may have seen all this before. He had never said a word to her, but she knew now a part at least of what he knew. She understood a little of the secret, formless intuitions in her own mind and body, which had been clearing up, taking form, so gradually and so steadily she had not realized that she was learning what she had to know. Paul said cautiously, as if he were talking about something forbidden: "They were just about ready to be born." His voice dropped on the last word. "I know," said Miranda, "like kittens. I know, like babies." She was quietly and terribly agitated, standing again with her rifle under her arm, looking down at the bloody heap. "I don't want the skin," she said, "I won't have it." Paul buried the young rabbits again in their mother's body, wrapped the skin around her, carried her to a clump of sage bushes, and hid her away. He came out again at once and said to Miranda, with an eager friendliness, a confidential tone quite unusual in him, as if he were taking her into an important secret on equal terms: "Listen now. Now you listen to me, and don't ever forget. Don't you ever tell a living soul that you saw this. Don't tell a soul: Don't tell Dad because I'll get into trouble. He'll say I'm leading you into things you ought not to do. He's always saying that. So now don't you go and forget and blab out sometime the way you're always doing.... Now, that's a secret. Don't you tell."

Miranda never told, she did not even wish to tell anybody. She thought about the whole worrisome affair with confused unhappiness for a few days. Then it sank quietly into her mind and was heaped over by accumulated thousands of impressions, for nearly twenty years. One day she was picking her path among the puddles and crushed refuse of a market street in a strange city of a strange country, when without warning, plain and clear in its true colors as if she looked through a frame upon a scene that had not stirred nor changed since the moment it happened, the episode of that far-off day leaped from its burial place before her mind's eye. She was so reasonlessly horrified she halted suddenly staring, the scene before her eyes dimmed by the vision back of them. An Indian vendor had held up before her a tray of dyed sugar sweets, in the shapes of all kinds of small creatures: birds, baby chicks, baby rabbits, lambs, baby pigs. They were in gay colors and smelled of vanilla, maybe.... It was a very hot day and the smell in the market, with its piles of raw flesh and wilting flowers, was like the mingled sweetness and corruption she had smelled that other day in the empty cemetery at home: the day she had remembered always until now vaguely as the time she and her brother had found treasure in the opened graves. Instantly upon this thought the dreadful vision faded, and she saw clearly her brother, whose childhood face she had forgotten, standing again in the blazing sunshine, again twelve years old, a pleased sober smile in his eyes, turning the silver dove over and over in his hands.

(1935)

Questions for Discussion and Writing

1. One critic observes that the two children are like Adam and Eve. What similarities do you see?
2. What associations can you make with Porter's symbols of the grave, the dove, the ring, and the stillborn rabbits?
3. Why is Miranda so shaken by seeing the dead babies? Can you explain the nature of the "secret formless intuitions" being revealed to her in paragraph 14?
4. What theme or themes can you discover in this story?
5. Write an interpretation that makes a claim about the central image of the grave and its associations with several types of burial.

Making Connections

Compare the symbolism of the gold ring that Miranda wears to the implications of the "heavy" gold ring that Aunt Jennifer wears in Adrienne Rich's poem "Aunt Jennifer's Tigers" (page 557).

<><><><><><><><><><><><><><><><>

Zora Neale Hurston   1891–1960

Zora Neale Hurston grew up in Eatonville, Florida, the first incorporated all-black community in America. Her father, a Baptist preacher, was the mayor, but the family was poor. "Mama," she said, "exhorted her children at every opportunity to 'jump at de sun.' We might not land on the sun, but at least we would get off the ground." She won a scholarship to Barnard College, studied anthropology, and became a prominent member of the black cultural revival known as the Harlem Renaissance. Although a noted author and folklorist, she alienated so many people by her opposition to the civil rights movement that she died in 1960 in poverty and obscurity.

Spunk

I

A giant of a brown-skinned man sauntered up the one street of the village and out into the palmetto thickets with a small pretty woman clinging lovingly to his arm.

"Looka theah, folkses!" cried Elijah Mosley, slapping his leg gleefully. "Theah they go, big as life an' brassy as tacks."

All the loungers in the store tried to walk to the door with an air of nonchalance but with small success.

"Now pee-eople!" Walter Thomas gasped. "Will you look at 'em!"

"But that's one thing Ah likes about Spunk Banks—he ain't skeered of   5
nothin' on God's green footstool—*nothin'*! He rides that log down at saw-mill jus' like he struts 'round wid another man's wife—jus' don't give a kitty. When Tes' Miller got cut to giblets on that circle-saw, Spunk steps right up and starts ridin'. The rest of us was skeered to go near it."

A round-shouldered figure in overalls much too large came nervously in the door and the talking ceased. The men looked at each other and winked.

"Gimme some soda-water. Sass'prilla. Ah reckon," the newcomer ordered, and stood far down the counter near the open pickled pig-feet tub to drink it.

Elijah nudged Walter and turned with mock gravity to the newcomer.

"Say, Joe, how's everything up yo' way? How's yo' wife?"

Joe started and all but dropped the bottle he was holding. He swallowed sev-   10
eral times painfully and his lips trembled.

"Aw 'Lige, you oughtn't to do nothin' like that," Walter grumbled. Elijah ignored him.

"She jus' passed heah a few minutes ago goin' thata way," with a wave of his hand in the direction of the woods.

Now Joe knew his wife had passed that way. He knew that the men loung-ing in the general store had seen her; moreover, he knew that the men knew *he* knew. He stood there silent for a long moment staring blankly, with his Adam's apple twitching nervously up and down his throat. One could actually *see* the pain he was suffering, his eyes, his face, his hands, and even the dejected slump of his shoulders. He set the bottle down upon the counter. He didn't bang it, just eased it out of his hand silently and fiddled with his suspender buckle.

"Well, Ah'm goin' after her to-day. Ah'm goin' an' fetch her back, Spunk's done gone too fur."

He reached deep down into his trouser pocket and drew out a hollow ground   15
razor, large and shiny, and passed his moistened thumb back and forth over the edge.

"Talkin' like a man, Joe. 'Course that's yo' fambly affairs, but Ah like to see grit in anybody."

Joe Kanty laid down a nickel and stumbled out into the street.

Dusk crept in from the woods. Ike Clarke lit the swinging oil lamp that was almost immediately surrounded by candle-flies. The men laughed boisterously behind Joe's back as they watched him shamble woodward.

"You oughtn't to said whut you said to him, 'Lige—look how it worked him up," Walter chided.

"And Ah hope it did work him up. Tain't even decent for a man to take and   20
take like he do."

"Spunk will sho' kill him."

"Aw, Ah doan know. You never kin tell. He might turn him up an' spank him fur gettin' in the way, but Spunk wouldn't shoot no unarmed man. Dat razor he carried outa heah ain't gonna run Spunk down an' cut him, an' Joe ain't got the nerve to go to Spunk with it knowin' he totes that Army 45. He makes that break outa heah to bluff us. He's gonna hide that razor behind the first palmetto root and sneak back home to bed. Don't tell me nothin' 'bout that rabbit-foot colored man. Didn't he meet Spunk an' Lena face to face one day las' week an' mumble sumthin' to Spunk 'bout lettin' his wife alone?"

"What did Spunk say?" Walter broke in. "Ah like him fine but tain't right the way he carries on wid Lena Kanty, jus' 'cause Joe's timid 'bout fightin'."

"You wrong theah, Walter. Tain't 'cause Joe's timid at all, it's 'cause Spunk wants Lena. If Joe was a passle of wile cats Spunk would tackle the job just the same. He'd go after *anything* he wanted the same way. As Ah wuz sayin' a min-ute ago, he tole Joe right to his face that Lena was his. 'Call her and see if she'll come. A woman knows her boss an' she answers when he calls.' 'Lena, ain't I yo' husband?' Joe sorter whines out. Lena looked at him real disgusted but she don't answer and she don't move outa her tracks. Then Spunk reaches out an' takes hold of her arm an' says: 'Lena, youse mine. From now on Ah works for you an' fights for you an' Ah never wants you to look to nobody for a crumb of bread, a stitch of close or a shingle to go over yo' head, but me long as Ah live. Ah'll git the lumber foh owah house to-morrow. Go home an' git yo' things together!'

"'Thass mah house,' Lena speaks up. 'Papa gimme that.'   25

"'Well,' says Spunk, 'doan give up whut's yours, but when youse inside doan forgit youse mine, an' let no other man git outa his place wid you!'

"Lena looked up at him with her eyes so full of love that they wuz runnin' over, an' Spunk seen it an' Joe seen it too, and his lip started to tremblin' and his Adam's apple was galloping up and down his neck like a race horse. Ah bet he's wore out half a dozen Adam's apples since Spunk's been on the job with Lena. That's all he'll do. He'll be back heah after while swallowin' an' workin' his lips like he wants to say somethin' an' can't."

"But didn't he do nothin' to stop 'em?"

"Nope, not a frazzlin' thing—jus' stood there. Spunk took Lena's arm and walked off jus' like nothin' ain't happened and he stood there gazin' after them till they was outa sight. Now you know a woman don't want no man like that. I'm jus' waitin' to see whut he's goin' to say when he gits back."

II

But Joe Kanty never came back, never. The men in the store heard the sharp   30
report of a pistol somewhere distant in the palmetto thicket and soon Spunk came walking leisurely, with his big black Stetson set at the same rakish angle and Lena clinging to his arm, came walking right into the general store. Lena wept in a frightened manner.

"Well," Spunk announced calmly, "Joe came out there wid a meat axe an' made me kill him."

He sent Lena home and led the men back to Joe—crumpled and limp with his right hand still clutching his razor.

"See mah back? Mah close cut clear through. He sneaked up an' tried to kill me from the back, but Ah got him, an' got him good, first shot," Spunk said.

The men glared at Elijah, accusingly.

"Take him up an' plant him in Stony Lonesome," Spunk said in a careless 35
voice. "Ah didn't wanna shoot him but he made me do it. He's a dirty coward,
jumpin' on a man from behind."

Spunk turned on his heel and sauntered away to where he knew his love wept
in fear for him and no man stopped him. At the general store later on, they all
talked of locking him up until the sheriff should come from Orlando, but no one
did anything but talk.

A clear case of self-defense, the trial was a short one, and Spunk walked out
of the court house to freedom again. He could work again, ride the dangerous
log-carriage that fed the singing, snarling, biting circle-saw; he could stroll the
soft dark lanes with his guitar. He was free to roam the woods again; he was free
to return to Lena. He did all these things.

III

"Whut you reckon, Walt?" Elijah asked one night later, "Spunk's gittin'
ready to marry Lena!"

"Naw! Why, Joe ain't had time to git cold yit. Nohow Ah didn't figger Spunk
was the marryin' kind."

"Well, he is," rejoined Elijah. "He done moved most of Lena's things—and 40
her along wid 'em—over to the Bradley house. He's buying it. Jus' like Ah told
yo' all right in heah the night Joe was kilt. Spunk's crazy 'bout Lena. He don't
want folks to keep on talkin' 'bout her—thass reason he's rushin' so. Funny
thing 'bout that bob-cat, wan't it?"

"What bob-cat, 'Lige? Ah ain't heered 'bout none."

"Ain't cher? Well, night befo' las' as they was goin' to bed, a big black bob-
cat, black all over, you hear me, *black*, walked round and round that house and
howled like forty, an' when Spunk got his gun an' went to the winder to shoot
it, he says it stood right still an' looked him in the eye, an' howled right at him.
The thing got Spunk so nervoused up he couldn't shoot. But Spunk says twan't
no bob-cat nohow. He says it was Joe done sneaked back from Hell!"

"Humph!" sniffed Walter, "he oughter be nervous after what he done: Ah
reckon Joe come back to dare him to marry Lena, or to come out an' fight. Ah
bet he'll be back time and again, too. Known what Ah think? Joe wuz a braver
man than Spunk."

There was a general shout of derision from the group.

"Thass a fact," went on Walter. "Lookit whut he done; took a razor an' went 45
out to fight a man he knowed toted a gun an' wuz a crack shot, too; 'nother thing
he wuz skeered of Spunk, skeered plumb stiff! But he went jes' the same. It took
him a long time to get his nerve up. Tain't nothin' for Spunk to fight when he ain't
skeered of nothin'. Now, Joe's done come back to have it out wid the man that's got
all he ever had. Y'all know Joe ain't never had nothin' nor wanted nothin' besides
Lena. It musta been a h'ant 'cause ain't nobody never seen no black bob-cat."

"'Nother thing," cut in one of the men, "Spunk was cussin' a blue streak today 'cause he 'lowed dat saw wuz wobblin'—almos' got 'im once. The machinist
come, looked it over an' said it wuz alright. Spunk musta been leanin' t'wards it
some. Den he claimed somebody pushed 'im but twan't nobody close to 'im. Ah
wuz glad when knockin' off time came. I'm skeered of dat man when he gits hot.
He'd beat you full of button holes as quick as he'd look atcher."

IV

The men gathered the next evening in a different mood, no laughter. No badinage this time.

"Look, 'Lige, you goin' to set up wid Spunk?"

"Naw, Ah reckon not, Walter. Tell yuh the truth, Ah'm a li'l bit skittish. Spunk died too wicket—died cussin' he did. You know he thought he was done outa life."

"Good Lawd, who'd he think done it?"

"Joe."

"Joe Kanty? How come?"

"Walter, Ah b'leeve Ah will walk up thata way an' set. Lena would like it Ah reckon."

"But whut did he say, 'Lige?"

Elijah did not answer until they had left the lighted store and were strolling down the dark street.

"Ah wuz loadin' a wagon wid scantlin' right near the saw when Spunk fell on the carriage but 'fore Ah could git to him the saw got him in the body—awful sight. Me an' Skint Miller got him off but it was too late. Anybody could see that. The fust thing he said wuz: 'He pushed me, 'Lige—the dirty hound pushed me in the back!'—he was spittin' blood at ev'ry breath. We laid him on the sawdust pile with his face to the East so's he could die easy. He helt mah han' till the last, Walter, and said: 'It was Joe, 'Lige...the dirty sneak shoved me...he didn't dare come to mah face...but Ah'll git the son-of-a-wood louse soon's Ah get there an' make hell too hot for him...Ah felt him shove me...!' Thass how he died."

"If spirits kin fight, there's a powerful tussle goin' on somewhere ovah Jordan,[1] cause Ah b'leeve Joe's ready for Spunk an' ain't skeered any more—yas, Ah b'leeve Joe pushed 'im mahself."

They had arrived at the house. Lena's lamentations were deep and loud. She had filled the room with magnolia blossoms that gave off a heavy sweet odor. The keepers of the wake tipped about whispering in frightened tones. Everyone in the village was there, even old Jeff Kanty, Joe's father, who a few hours before would have been afraid to come within ten feet of him, stood leering triumphantly down upon the fallen giant as if his fingers had been the teeth of steel that laid him low.

The cooling board consisted of three sixteen-inch boards on saw horses, a dingy sheet was his shroud.

The women ate heartily of the funeral baked meats and wondered who would be Lena's next. The men whispered coarse conjectures between guzzles of whiskey.

(1925)

Questions for Discussion and Writing

1. What is the significance of the title? Does it perhaps have a double meaning?
2. How does the southern black dialect in the characters' conversation contribute to the effectiveness of the story?

---

[1]Crossing the River Jordan means passing into the Promised Land, here seen as the hereafter.

3. How are gender roles important in the plot?
4. How does the tone of the story change in the last two paragraphs?
5. Write an essay making a claim about the reactions of the nosy community to Spunk's behavior before and after Joe Kanty's death.

Making Connections

Compare the humor in "Spunk" with the humor in Flannery O'Connor's "A Good Man Is Hard to Find" (page 177). What do language and point of view contribute to the development of the humor?

◇◇◇◇◇◇◇◇◇◇◇◇◇◇◇◇◇◇◇◇◇◇

William Faulkner 1897–1962

William Faulker lived most of his life in Oxford, Mississippi. He never graduated from high school or college and was rejected by the U.S. army during World War I for being too short. He worked briefly at the local post office but quit, saying he refused to be "at the beck and call of every son of a bitch with two cents in his pocket." In an interview he once observed, "The writer's only responsibility is to his art. He will be completely ruthless if he is a good one…. If a writer has to rob his mother, he will not hesitate; the 'Ode on a Grecian Urn' is worth any number of old ladies." He won two Pulitzer Prizes, and in 1949 he was awarded the Nobel Prize for Literature.

Barn Burning

The store in which the Justice of the Peace's court was sitting smelled of cheese. The boy, crouched on his nail keg at the back of the crowded room, knew he smelled cheese, and more; from where he sat he could see the ranked shelves close-packed with the solid, squat, dynamic shapes of tin cans whose labels his stomach read, not from the lettering which meant nothing to his mind but from the scarlet devils and silver curve of fish—this, the cheese which he knew he smelled and the hermetic meat[1] which his intestines believed he smelled coming in intermittent gusts momentary and brief between the other constant one, the smell and sense just a little of fear because mostly of despair and grief, the old fierce pull of blood. He could not see the table where the Justice sat and before which his father and his father's enemy (*our enemy* he thought in that despair; *ourn! mine and bisn both! He's my father!*) stood, but he could hear them, the two of them that is, because his father had no word yet:

"But what proof have you, Mr. Harris?"

"I told you. The hog got into my corn. I caught it up and sent it back to him. He had no fence that would hold it. I told him so, warned him. The next time I put the hog in my pen. When he came to get it I gave him enough wire to patch

---

[1] Canned meat.

up his pen. The next time I put the hog up and kept it. I rode down to his house and saw the wire I gave him still rolled on to the spool in his yard. I told him he could have the hog when he paid me a dollar pound fee. That evening a nigger came with the dollar and got the hog. He was a strange nigger. He said, 'He say to tell you wood and hay kin burn.' I said, 'What?' 'That whut he say to tell you,' the nigger said. 'Wood and hay kin burn.' That night my barn burned. I got the stock out but I lost the barn."

"Where is the nigger? Have you got him?"

"He was a strange nigger, I tell you. I don't know what became of him."   5

"But that's not proof. Don't you see that's not proof?"

"Get that boy up here. He knows." For a moment the boy thought too that the man meant his older brother until Harris said, "Not him. The little one. The boy," and, crouching, small for his age, small and wiry like his father, in patched and faded jeans even too small for him, with straight, uncombed, brown hair and eyes gray and wild as storm scud, he saw the men between himself and the table part and become a lane of grim faces, at the end of which he saw the Justice, a shabby, collarless, graying man in spectacles, beckoning him. He felt no floor under his bare feet; he seemed to walk beneath the palpable weight of the grim turning faces. His father, stiff in his black Sunday coat donned not for the trial but for the moving, did not even look at him. *He aims for me to lie*, he thought, again with that frantic grief and despair. *And I will have to do hit.*

"What's your name, boy?" the Justice said.

"Colonel Sartoris Snopes,"[2] the boy whispered.

"Hey?" the Justice said. "Talk louder. Colonel Sartoris? I reckon anybody   10 named for Colonel Sartoris in this country can't help but tell the truth, can they?" The boy said nothing. *Enemy! Enemy!* he thought; for a moment he could not even see, could not see that the Justice's face was kindly nor discern that his voice was troubled when he spoke to the man named Harris: "Do you want me to question this boy?" But he could hear, and during those subsequent long seconds while there was absolutely no sound in the crowded little room save that of quiet and intent breathing it was as if he had swung outward at the end of a grape vine, over a ravine, and at the top of the swing had been caught in a prolonged instant of mesmerized gravity, weightless in time.

"No!" Harris said violently, explosively. "Damnation! Send him out of here!" Now time, the fluid world, rushed beneath him again, the voices coming to him again through the smell of cheese and sealed meat, the fear and despair and the old grief of blood:

"This case is closed. I can't find against you, Snopes, but I can give you advice. Leave this country and don't come back to it."

His father spoke for the first time, his voice cold and harsh, level, without emphasis: "I aim to. I don't figure to stay in a country among people who…" he said something unprintable and vile, addressed to no one.

"That'll do," the Justice said. "Take your wagon and get out of this country before dark. Case dismissed."

His father turned, and he followed the stiff black coat, the wiry figure walk-   15 ing a little stiffly from where a Confederate provost's man's[3] musket ball had

---

[2] He is named after another of Faulkner's characters, Colonel John Sartoris, a fictional Confederate hero.

[3] Military policeman.

taken him in the heel on a stolen horse thirty years ago, followed the two backs now, since his older brother had appeared from somewhere in the crowd, no taller than the father but thicker, chewing tobacco steadily, between the two lines of grim-faced men and out of the store and across the worn gallery and down the sagging steps and among the dogs and half-grown boys in the mild May dust, where as he passed a voice hissed:

"Barn burner!"

Again he could not see, whirling; there was a face in a red haze, moonlike, bigger than the full moon, the owner of it half again his size, he leaping in the red haze toward the face, feeling no blow, feeling no shock when his head struck the earth, scrabbling up and leaping again, feeling no blow this time either and tasting no blood, scrabbling up to see the other boy in full flight and himself already leaping into pursuit as his father's hand jerked him back, the harsh, cold voice speaking above him: "Go get in the wagon."

It stood in a grove of locusts and mulberries across the road. His two hulking sisters in their Sunday dresses and his mother and her sister in calico and sun-bonnets were already in it, sitting on and among the sorry residue of the dozen and more movings which even the boy could remember—the battered stove, the broken beds and chairs, the clock inlaid with mother-of-pearl, which would not run, stopped at some fourteen minutes past two o'clock of a dead and forgotten day and time, which had been his mother's dowry. She was crying, though when she saw him she drew her sleeve across her face and began to descend from the wagon. "Get back," the father said.

"He's hurt. I got to get some water and wash his…"

"Get back in the wagon," his father said. He got in too, over the tail-gate.   20
His father mounted to the seat where the older brother already sat and struck the gaunt mules two savage blows with the peeled willow, but without heat. It was not even sadistic; it was exactly that same quality which in later years would cause his descendants to over-run the engine before putting a motor car into motion, striking and reining back in the same movement. The wagon went on, the store with its quiet crowd of grimly watching men dropped behind; a curve in the road hid it. *Forever* he thought. *Maybe he's done satisfied now, now that he has*…stopping himself, not to say it aloud even to himself. His mother's hand touched his shoulder.

"Does hit hurt?" she said.

"Naw," he said. "Hit don't hurt. Lemme be."

"Can't you wipe some of the blood off before hit dries?"

"I'll wash to-night," he said. "Lemme be, I tell you."

The wagon went on. He did not know where they were going. None of them   25
ever did or ever asked, because it was always somewhere, always a house of sorts waiting for them a day or two days or even three days away. Likely his father had already arranged to make a crop on another farm before he…Again he had to stop himself. He (the father) always did. There was something about his wolflike independence and even courage when the advantage was at least neutral which impressed strangers, as if they got from his latent ra025ening ferocity not so much a sense of dependability as a feeling that his ferocious conviction in the rightness of his own actions would be of advantage to all whose interest lay with his.

That night they camped, in a grove of oaks and beeches where a spring ran. The nights were still cool and they had a fire against it, of a rail lifted from a nearby fence and cut into lengths—a small fire, neat, niggard almost, a shrewd fire; such fires were his father's habit and custom always, even in freezing weather. Older, the boy might have remarked this and wondered why not a big one; why should not a man who had not only seen the waste and extravagance of war, but who had in his blood an inherent voracious prodigality with material not his own, have burned everything in sight? Then he might have gone a step farther and thought that that was the reason: that niggard blaze was the living fruit of nights passed during those four years in the woods hiding from all men, blue or gray, with his strings of horses (captured horses, he called them). And older still, he might have divined the true reason: that the element of fire spoke to some deep mainspring of his father's being, as the element of steel or of powder spoke to other men, as the one weapon for the preservation of integrity, else breath were not worth the breathing, and hence to be regarded with respect and used with discretion.

But he did not think this now and he had seen those same niggard blazes all his life. He merely ate his supper beside it and was already half asleep over his iron plate when his father called him, and once more he followed the stiff back, the stiff and ruthless limp, up the slope and on to the starlit road where, turning, he could see his father against the stars but without face or depth—a shape black, flat, and bloodless as though cut from tin in the iron folds of the frock-coat which had not been made for him, the voice harsh like tin and without heat like tin:

"You were fixing to tell them. You would have told him." He didn't answer. His father struck him with the flat of his hand on the side of the head, hard but without heat, exactly as he had struck the two mules at the store, exactly as he would strike either of them with any stick in order to kill a horse fly, his voice still without heat or anger: "You're getting to be a man. You got to learn. You got to learn to stick to your own blood or you ain't going to have any blood to stick to you. Do you think either of them, any man there this morning, would? Don't you know all they wanted was a chance to get at me because they knew I had them beat? Eh?" Later, twenty years later, he was to tell himself, "If I had said they wanted only truth, justice, he would have hit me again." But now he said nothing. He was not crying. He just stood there. "Answer me," his father said.

"Yes," he whispered. His father turned.   30

"Get on to bed. We'll be there to-morrow."

To-morrow they were there. In the early afternoon the wagon stopped before a paintless two-room house identical almost with the dozen others it had stopped before even in the boy's ten years, and again, as on the other dozen occasions, his mother and aunt got down and began to unload the wagon, although his two sisters and his father and brother had not moved.

"Likely hit ain't fitten for hawgs," one of the sisters said.

"Nevertheless, fit it will and you'll hog it and like it," his father said. "Get out of them chairs and help your Ma unload."

The two sisters got down, big, bovine, in a flutter of cheap ribbons; one of them drew from the jumbled wagon bed a battered lantern, the other a worn broom. His father handed the reins to the older son and began to climb stiffly over the wheel. "When they get unloaded, take the team to the barn and feed them." Then he said, and at first the boy thought he was still speaking to his brother: "Come with me."

"Me?" he said.

"Yes," his father said. "You."   35

"Abner," his mother said. His father paused and looked back—the harsh level stare beneath the shaggy, graying, irascible brows.

"I reckon I'll have a word with the man that aims to begin to-morrow owning me body and soul for the next eight months."

They went back up the road. A week ago—or before last night, that is—he would have asked where they were going, but not now. His father had struck him before last night but never before had he paused afterward to explain why; it was as if the blow and the following calm, outrageous voice still rang, repercussed, divulging nothing to him save the terrible handicap of being young, the light weight of his few years, just heavy enough to prevent his soaring free of the world as it seemed to be ordered but not heavy enough to keep him footed solid in it, to resist it and try to change the course of its events.

Presently he could see the grove of oaks and cedars and the other flowering   40 trees and shrubs where the house would be, though not the house yet. They walked beside a fence massed with honeysuckle and Cherokee roses and came to a gate swinging open between two brick pillars, and now, beyond a sweep of drive, he saw the house for the first time and at that instant he forgot his father and the terror and despair both, and even when he remembered his father again (who had not stopped) the terror and despair did not return. Because, for all the twelve movings, they had sojourned until now in a poor country, a land of small farms and fields and houses, and he had never seen a house like this before. *Hit's big as a courthouse* he thought quietly, with a surge of peace and joy whose reason he could not have thought into words, being too young for that: *They are safe from him. People whose lives are a part of this peace and dignity are beyond his touch, he no more to them than a buzzing wasp: capable of stinging for a little moment but that's all; the spell of this peace and dignity rendering even the barns and stable and cribs which belong to it impervious to the puny flames he might contrive...*this, the peace and joy, ebbing for an instant as he looked again at the stiff black back, the stiff and implacable limp of the figure which was not dwarfed by the house, for the reason that it had never looked big anywhere and which now, against the serene columned backdrop, had more than ever that impervious quality of something cut ruthlessly from tin, depthless, as though, sidewise to the sun, it would cast no shadow. Watching him, the boy remarked the absolutely undeviating course which his father held and saw the stiff foot come squarely down in a pile of fresh droppings where a horse had stood in the drive and which his father could have avoided by a simple change of stride. But it ebbed only for a moment, though he could not have thought this into words either, walking on in the spell of the house, which he could even want without envy, without sorrow, certainly never with that ravening and jealous rage which unknown to him walked in the iron-like black coat before him: *Maybe he will feel it too. Maybe it will even change him now from what maybe he couldn't help but be.*

They crossed the portico. Now he could hear his father's stiff foot as it came down on the boards with clocklike finality, a sound out of all proportion to the displacement of the body it bore and which was not dwarfed either by the white door before it, as though it had attained to a sort of vicious and ravening minimum not to be dwarfed by anything—the flat, wide, black hat, the formal coat of broadcloth which had once been black but which had now that friction-glazed greenish cast of the bodies of old house flies, the lifted sleeve which was too large, the lifted hand like a curled claw. The door opened so promptly that the boy knew the Negro must have been watching them all the time, an old man with neat grizzled hair, in a linen jacket, who stood barring the door with his body, saying, "Wipe yo foots, white man, fo you come in here. Major ain't home nohow."

"Get out of my way, nigger," his father said, without heat too, flinging the door back and the Negro also and entering, his hat still on his head. And now the boy saw the prints of the stiff foot on the doorjamb and saw them appear on the pale rug behind the machinelike deliberation of the foot which seemed to bear (or transmit) twice the weight which the boy compassed. The Negro was shouting "Miss Lula! Miss Lula!" somewhere behind them, then the boy, deluged as though by a warm wave by a suave turn of carpeted stair and a pendant glitter of chandeliers and a mute gleam of gold frames, heard the swift feet and saw her too, a lady—perhaps he had never seen her like before either—in a gray, smooth gown with lace at the throat and an apron tied at the waist and the sleeves turned back, wiping cake or biscuit dough from her hands with a towel as she came up the hall, looking not at his father at all but at the tracks on the blond rug with an expression of incredulous amazement.

"I tried," the Negro cried. "I tole him to…"

"Will you please go away?" she said in a shaking voice. "Major de Spain is not at home. Will you please go away?"

His father had not spoken again. He did not speak again. He did not even look at her. He just stood stiff in the center of the rug, in his hat, the shaggy iron-gray brows twitching slightly above the pebble-colored eyes as he appeared to examine the house with brief deliberation. Then with the same deliberation he turned; the boy watched him pivot on the good leg and saw the stiff foot drag round the arc of the turning, leaving a final long and fading smear. His father never looked at it, he never once looked down at the rug. The Negro held the door. It closed behind them, upon the hysteric and indistinguishable woman-wail. His father stopped at the top of the steps and scraped his boot clean on the edge of it. At the gate he stopped again. He stood for a moment, planted stiffly on the stiff foot, looking back at the house. "Pretty and white, ain't it?" he said. "That's sweat. Nigger sweat. Maybe it ain't white enough yet to suit him. Maybe he wants to mix some white sweat with it." 45

Two hours later the boy was chopping wood behind the house within which his mother and aunt and the two sisters (the mother and aunt, not the two girls, he knew that; even at this distance and muffled by walls the flat loud voices of the two girls emanated an incorrigible idle inertia) were setting up the stove to prepare a meal, when he heard the hooves and saw the linen-clad man on a fine sorrel mare, whom he recognized even before he saw the rolled rug in front of the Negro youth following on a fat bay carriage horse—a suffused, angry face vanishing, still at full gallop, beyond the corner of the house where his father and brother were sitting in the two tilted chairs; and a moment later, almost before he could have put the axe down, he heard the hooves again and watched the sorrel mare go back out of the yard, already galloping again. Then his father began to shout one of the sisters' names, who presently emerged backward from the kitchen door dragging the rolled rug along the ground by one end while the other sister walked behind it.

"If you ain't going to tote, go on and set up the wash pot," the first said.

"You, Sarty!" the second shouted. "Set up the wash pot!" His father appeared at the door, framed against that shabbiness, as he had been against that other bland perfection, impervious to either, the mother's anxious face at his shoulder.

"Go on," the father said. "Pick it up." The two sisters stooped, broad, lethargic; stooping, they presented an incredible expanse of pale cloth and a flutter of tawdry ribbons.

"If I thought enough of a rug to have to git hit all the way from France I wouldn't keep hit where folks coming in would have to tromp on hit," the first said. They raised the rug. [50]

"Abner," the mother said. "Let me do it."

"You go back and git dinner," his father said. "I'll tend to this."

From the woodpile through the rest of the afternoon the boy watched them, the rug spread flat in the dust beside the bubbling wash-pot, the two sisters stooping over it with that profound and lethargic reluctance, while the father stood over them in turn, implacable and grim, driving them though never raising his voice again. He could smell the harsh homemade lye they were using; he saw his mother come to the door once and look toward them with an expression not anxious now but very like despair; he saw his father turn, and he fell to with the axe and saw from the corner of his eye his father raise from the ground a flattish fragment of field stone and examine it and return to the pot, and this time his mother actually spoke: "Abner. Abner. Please don't. Please, Abner."

Then he was done too. It was dusk; the whippoorwills had already begun. He could smell coffee from the room where they would presently eat the cold food remaining from the mid-afternoon meal, though when he entered the house he realized they were having coffee again probably because there was a fire on the hearth, before which the rug now lay spread over the backs of the two chairs. The tracks of his father's foot were gone. Where they had been were now long, water-cloudy scoriations resembling the sporadic course of a lilliputian[4] mowing machine.

It still hung there while they ate the cold food and then went to bed, scattered without order or claim up and down the two rooms, his mother in one bed, where his father would later lie, the older brother in the other, himself, the aunt, and the two sisters on pallets on the floor. But his father was not in bed yet. The last thing the boy remembered was the depthless, harsh silhouette of the hat and coat bending over the rug and it seemed to him that he had not even closed his eyes when the silhouette was standing over him, the fire almost dead behind it, the stiff foot prodding him awake. "Catch up the mule," his father said. [55]

When he returned with the mule his father was standing in the black door, the rolled rug over his shoulder. "Ain't you going to ride?" he said.

"No. Give me your foot."

He bent his knee into his father's hand, the wiry, surprising power flowed smoothly, rising, he rising with it, on to the mule's bare back (they had owned a saddle once; the boy could remember it though not when or where) and with the same effortlessness his father swung the rug up in front of him. Now in the starlight they retraced the afternoon's path, up the dusty road rife with honeysuckle, through the gate and up the black tunnel of the drive to the lightless house, where he sat on the mule and felt the rough warp of the rug drag across his thighs and vanish.

"Don't you want me to help?" he whispered. His father did not answer and now he heard again that stiff foot striking the hollow portico with that wooden and clocklike deliberation, that outrageous overstatement of the weight it carried. The rug, hunched, not flung (the boy could tell that even in the darkness) from his father's shoulder struck the angle of wall and floor with a sound

---

[4] Tiny people living in Lilliput in Jonathan Swift's *Gulliver Travels* (1726).

unbelievably loud, thunderous, then the foot again, unhurried and enormous; a light came on in the house and the boy sat, tense, breathing steadily and quietly and just a little fast, though the foot itself did not increase its beat at all, descending the steps now; now the boy could see him.

"Don't you want to ride now?" he whispered. "We kin both ride now," the light within the house altering now, flaring up and sinking. *He's coming down the stairs now,* he thought. He had already ridden the mule up beside the horse block; presently his father was up behind him and he doubled the reins over and slashed the mule across the neck, but before the animal could begin to trot the hard, thin arm came round him, the hard, knotted hand jerking the mule back to a walk.

In the first red rays of the sun they were in the lot, putting plow gear on the mules. This time the sorrel mare was in the lot before he heard it at all, the rider collarless and even bareheaded, trembling, speaking in a shaking voice as the woman in the house had done, his father merely looking up once before stooping again to the hame[5] he was buckling, so that the man on the mare spoke to his stooping back:

"You must realize you have ruined that rug. Wasn't there anybody here, any of your women..." he ceased, shaking, the boy watching him, the older brother leaning now in the stable door, chewing, blinking slowly and steadily at nothing apparently. "It cost a hundred dollars. But you never had a hundred dollars. You never will. So I'm going to charge you twenty bushels of corn against your crop. I'll add it in your contract and when you come to the commissary you can sign it. That won't keep Mrs. de Spain quiet but maybe it will teach you to wipe your feet off before you enter her house again."

Then he was gone. The boy looked at his father, who still had not spoken or even looked up again, who was now adjusting the logger-head[6] in the hame.

"Pap," he said. His father looked at him—the inscrutable face, the shaggy brows beneath which the gray eyes glinted coldly. Suddenly the boy went toward him, fast, stopping as suddenly. "You done the best you could!" he cried. "If he wanted hit done different why didn't he wait and tell you how? He won't git no twenty bushels! He won't git none! We'll gether hit and hide hit! I kin watch..."

"Did you put the cutter back in that straight stock[7] like I told you?"

"No, sir," he said.

"Then go do it."

That was Wednesday. During the rest of that week he worked steadily, at what was within his scope and some which was beyond it, with an industry that did not need to be driven nor even commanded twice; he had this from his mother, with the difference that some at least of what he did he liked to do, such as splitting wood with the half-size axe which his mother and aunt had earned, or saved money somehow, to present him with at Christmas. In company with the two older woman (and on one afternoon, even one of the sisters), he built pens for the shoat[8] and the cow which were a part of his father's contract with the landlord, and one afternoon, his father being absent, gone somewhere on one of the mules, he went to the field.

---

[5] Side piece of a harness.
[6] Another part of the harness.
[7] Parts of a plow.
[8] A yearling hog.

60

65

They were running a middle buster[9] now, his brother holding the plow straight while he handled the reins, and walking beside the straining mule, the rich black soil shearing cool and damp against his bare ankles, he thought *Maybe this is the end of it. Maybe even that twenty bushels that seems hard to have to pay for just a rug will be a cheap price for him to stop forever and always from being what he used to be*; thinking, dreaming now, so that his brother had to speak sharply to him to mind the mule: *Maybe he even won't collect the twenty bushels. Maybe it will all add up and balance and vanish—corn, rug, fire; the terror and grief, the being pulled two ways like between two teams of horses—gone, done with for ever and ever.*

Then it was Saturday; he looked up from beneath the mule he was harness- 70 ing and saw his father in the black coat and hat. "Not that," his father said. "The wagon gear." And then, two hours later, sitting in the wagon bed behind his father and brother on the seat, the wagon accomplished a final curve, and he saw the weathered paintless store with its tattred tobacco- and patent-medicine post- ers and the tethered wagons and saddle animals below the gallery. He mounted the gnawed steps behind his father and brother, and there again was the lane of quiet, watching faces for the three of them to walk through. He saw the man in spectacles sitting at the plank table and he did not need to be told this was a Justice of the Peace; he sent one glare of fierce, exultant, partisan defiance at the man in collar and cravat now, whom he had seen but twice before in his life, and that on a galloping horse, who now wore on his face an expression not of rage but of amazed unbelief which the boy could not have known was at the incred- ible circumstance of being sued by one of his own tenants, and came and stood against his father and cried at the Justice: "He ain't done it! He ain't burnt..."

"Go back to the wagon," his father said.

"Burnt?" the Justice said. "Do I understand this rug was burned too?"

"Does anybody here claim it was?" his father said. "Go back to the wagon." But he did not, he merely retreated to the rear of the room, crowded as that other had been, but not to sit down this time, instead, to stand pressing among the motionless bodies, listening to the voices:

"And you claim twenty bushels of corn is too high for the damage you did to the rug?"

"He brought the rug to me and said he wanted the tracks washed out of it. I 75 washed the tracks out and took the rug back to him."

"But you didn't carry the rug back to him in the same condition it was in before you made the tracks on it."

His father did not answer, and now for perhaps half a minute there was no sound at all save that of breathing, the faint, steady suspiration[10] of complete and intent listening.

"You decline to answer that, Mr. Snopes?" Again his father did not answer. "I'm going to find against you, Mr. Snopes. I'm going to find that you were responsible for the injury to Major de Spain's rug and hold you liable for it. But twenty bushels of corn seems a little high for a man in your circumstances to have to pay. Major de Spain claims it cost a hundred dollars. October corn will be worth about fifty cents. I figure that if Major de Spain can stand a ninety-five dollar loss on something he paid cash for, you can stand a five-dollar loss you haven't earned yet. I hold you in damages to Major de Spain to the amount of

[9] A plow.
[10] Long, deep breathing.

ten bushels of corn over and above your contract with him, to be paid to him out of your crop at gathering time. Court adjourned."

It had taken no time hardly, the morning was but half begun. He thought they would return home and perhaps back to the field, since they were late, far behind all other farmers. But instead his father passed on behind the wagon, merely indicating with his hand for the older brother to follow with it, and crossed the road toward the blacksmith shop opposite, pressing on after his father, overtaking him, speaking, whispering up at the harsh, calm face beneath the weathered hat: "He won't git no ten bushels neither. He won't git one. We'll..." until his father glanced for an instant down at him, the face absolutely calm, the grizzled eyebrows tangled above the cold eyes, the voice almost pleasant, almost gentle: "You think so? Well, we'll wait till October anyway."

The matter of the wagon—the setting of a spoke or two and the tightening of the tires—did not take long either, the business of the tires accomplished by driving the wagon into the spring branch behind the shop and letting it stand there, the mules nuzzling into the water from time to time, and the boy on the seat with the idle reins, looking up the slope and through the sooty tunnel of the shed where the slow hammer rang and where his father sat on an upended cypress bolt,[11] easily, either talking or listening, still sitting there when the boy brought the dripping wagon up out of the branch and halted it before the door.

"Take them on to the shade and hitch," his father said. He did so and returned. His father and the smith and a third man squatting on his heels inside the door were talking, about crops and animals; the boy, squatting too in the ammoniac dust and hoof-parings and scales of rust, heard his father tell a long and unhurried story out of the time before the birth of the older brother even when he had been a professional horsetrader. And then his father came up beside him where he stood before a tattered last year's circus poster on the other side of the store, gazing rapt and quiet at the scarlet horses, the incredible poisings and convolutions of tulle[12] and tights and the painted leers of comedians, and said, "It's time to eat."

But not at home. Squatting beside his brother against the front wall, he watched his father emerge from the store and produce from a paper sack a segment of cheese and divide it carefully and deliberately into three with his pocket knife and produce crackers from the same sack. They all three squatted on the gallery and ate, slowly, without talking; then in the store again, they drank from a tin dipper tepid water smelling of the cedar bucket and of living beech trees. And still they did not go home. It was a horse lot this time, a tall rail fence upon and along which men stood and sat and out of which one by one horses were led, to be walked and trotted and then cantered back and forth along the road while the slow swapping and buying went on and the sun began to slant westward, they—the three of them—watching and listening, the older brother with his muddy eyes and his steady, inevitable tobacco, the father commenting now and then on certain animals, to no one in particular.

It was after sundown when they reached home. They ate supper by lamplight, then, sitting on the doorstep, the boy watched the night fully accomplish, listening to the whippoorwills and the frogs, when he heard his mother's voice: "Abner! No! No! Oh, God. Oh, God. Abner!" and he rose, whirled, and saw the

80

---

[11] Short round section of a log.
[12] Sheer material used in veils and ruffles.

altered light through the door where a candle stub now burned in a bottle neck on the table and his father, still in the hat and coat, at once formal and burlesque as though dressed carefully for some shabby and ceremonial violence, emptying the reservoir of the lamp back into the five-gallon kerosene can from which it had been filled, while the mother tugged at his arm until he shifted the lamp to the other hand and flung her back, not savagely or viciously, just hard, into the wall, her hands flung out against the wall for balance, her mouth open and in her face the same quality of hopeless despair as had been in her voice. Then his father saw him standing in the door.

"Go to the barn and get that can of oil we were oiling the wagon with," he   85 said. The boy did not move. Then he could speak.

"What..." he cried. "What are you..."

"Go get that oil," his father said. "Go."

Then he was moving, running, outside the house, toward the stable: this the old habit, the old blood which he had not been permitted to choose for himself, which had been bequeathed him willy nilly and which had run for so long (and who knew where, battening on what of outrage and savagery and lust) before it came to him. *I could keep on,* he thought. *I could run on and on and never look back, never need to see his face again. Only I can't, I can't,* the rusted can in his hand now, the liquid sploshing in it as he ran back to the house and into it, into the sound of his mother's weeping in the next room, and handed the can to his father.

"Ain't you going to even send a nigger?" he cried. "At least you sent a nigger before!"

This time his father didn't strike him. The hand came even faster than the   90 blow had, the same hand which had set the can on the table with almost excruciating care flashing from the can toward him too quick for him to follow it, gripping him by the back of his shirt and on to tiptoe before he had seen it quit the can, the face stooping at him in breathless and frozen ferocity, the cold, dead voice speaking over him to the older brother who leaned against the table, chewing with that steady, curious, sidewise motion of cows:

"Empty the can into the big one and go on. I'll catch up with you."

"Better tie him up to the bedpost," the brother said.

"Do like I told you," the father said. Then the boy was moving, his bunched shirt and the hard, bony hand between his shoulder-blades, his toes just touching the floor, across the room and into the other one, past the sisters sitting with spread heavy thighs in the two chairs over the cold hearth, and to where his mother and aunt sat side by side on the bed, the aunt's arms about his mother's shoulders.

"Hold him," the father said. The aunt made a startled movement. "Not you," the father said. "Lennie. Take a hold of him. I want to see you do it." His mother took him by the wrist. "You'll hold him better than that. If he gets loose don't you know what he is going to do? He will go up yonder." He jerked his head toward the road. "Maybe I'd better tie him."

"I'll hold him," his mother whispered.   95

"See you do then." Then his father was gone, the stiff foot heavy and measured upon the boards, ceasing at last.

Then he began to struggle. His mother caught him in both arms, he jerking and wrenching at them. He would be stronger in the end, he knew that. But he had no time to wait for it. "Lemme go!" he cried. "I don't want to have to hit you!"

"Let him go!" the aunt said. "If he don't go, before God, I am going up there myself!"

"Don't you see I can't?" his mother cried. "Sarty! Sarty! No! No! Help me, Lizzie!"

Then he was free. His aunt grasped at him but it was too late. He whirled, 100 running, his mother stumbled forward on to her knees behind him, crying to the nearer sister: "Catch him, Net! Catch him!" But that was too late too, the sister (the sisters were twins, born at the same time, yet either of them now gave the impression of being, encompassing as much living meat and volume and weight as any other two of the family) not yet having begun to rise from the chair, her head, face, alone merely turned, presenting to him in the flying instant an astonishing expanse of young female features untroubled by any surprise even, wearing only an expression of bovine interest. Then he was out of the room, out of the house, in the mild dust of the starlit road and the heavy rifeness[13] of honeysuckle, the pale ribbon unspooling with terrific slowness under his running feet, reaching the gate at last and turning in, running, his heart and lungs drumming, on up the drive toward the lighted house, the lighted door. He did not knock, he burst in, sobbing for breath, incapable for the moment of speech; he saw the astonished face of the Negro in the linen jacket without knowing when the Negro had appeared.

"De Spain!" he cried, panted. "Where's..." then he saw the white man too emerging from a white door down the hall. "Barn!" he cried. "Barn!"

"What?" the white man said. "Barn?"

"Yes!" the boy cried. "Barn!"

"Catch him!" the white man shouted.

But it was too late this time too. The Negro grasped his shirt, but the entire 105 sleeve, rotten with washing, carried away, and he was out that door too and in the drive again, and had actually never ceased to run even while he was screaming into the white man's face.

Behind him the white man was shouting, "My horse! Fetch my horse!" and he thought for an instant of cutting across the park and climbing the fence into the road, but he did not know the park nor how high the vine-massed fence might be and he dared not risk it. So he ran on down the drive, blood and breath roaring; presently he was in the road again though he could not see it. He could not hear either: the galloping mare was almost upon him before he heard her, and even then he held his course, as if the very urgency of his wild grief and need must in a moment more find him wings, waiting until the ultimate instant to hurl himself aside and into the weed-choked roadside ditch as the horse thundered past and on, for an instant in furious silhouette against the stars, the tranquil early summer night sky which, even before the shape of the horse and rider vanished, stained abruptly and violently upward: a long, swirling roar incredible and soundless, blotting the stars, and he springing up and into the road again, running again, knowing it was too late yet still running even after he heard the shot and, an instant later, two shots, pausing now without knowing he had ceased to run, crying "Pap! Pap!," running again before he knew he had begun to run, stumbling, tripping over something and scrabbling up again without ceasing to run, looking backward over his shoulder at the glare as he got up, running on among the invisible trees, panting, sobbing, "Father! Father!"

At midnight he was sitting on the crest of a hill. He did not know it was midnight and he did not know how far he had come. But there was no glare behind

---

[13] Abundance.

him now and he sat now, his back toward what he had called home for four days anyhow, his face toward the dark woods which he would enter when breath was strong again, small, shaking steadily in the chill darkness, hugging himself into the remainder of his thin, rotten shirt, the grief and despair now no longer terror and fear but just grief and despair. *Father. My father,* he thought. "He was brave!" he cried suddenly, aloud but not loud, no more than a whisper: "He was! He was in the war! He was in Colonel Sartoris' cav'ry!" not knowing that his father had gone to that war a private in the fine old European sense, wearing no uniform, admitting the authority of and giving fidelity to no man or army or flag, going to war as Malbrouck[14] himself did: for booty—it meant nothing and less than nothing to him if it were enemy booty or his own.

The slow constellations wheeled on. It would be dawn and then sun-up after a while and he would be hungry. But that would be to-morrow and now he was only cold, and walking would cure that. His breathing was easier now and he decided to get up and go on, and then he found that he had been asleep because he knew it was almost dawn, the night almost over. He could tell that from the whippoorwills. They were everywhere now among the dark trees below him, constant and inflectioned and ceaseless, so that, as the instant for giving over to the day birds drew nearer and nearer, there was no interval at all between them. He got up. He was a little stiff, but walking would cure that too as it would the cold, and soon there would be the sun. He went on down the hill, toward the dark woods within which the liquid silver voices of the birds called unceasing—the rapid and urgent beating of the urgent and quiring[15] heart of the late spring night. He did not look back.

(1939)

Questions for Discussion and Writing

1. What picture of the Snopes family life can you deduce? Look at the details describing each member to help you understand the Snopes's dynamics.

2. What do blood ties mean, according to Abner? Is his own behavior consistent with these claims?

3. Sarty once refers to himself as "pulled two ways like between two teams of horses." What does he mean?

4. Though Abner often behaves and talks viciously, he is repeatedly described as unfeeling. Why do you think he lacks emotion behind his force? Explain this paradox.

5. Defend the idea that "Barn Burning" has a happy ending. For support, use as many details as you can from the last two paragraphs of the story.

Making Connections

Compare Abner Snopes to the men in Tobias Wolff's "Hunters in the Snow" (page 160), focusing especially on the themes of male vanity and violence.

---

[14] The English Duke of Malborough, accused of profiteering during Queen Anne's War (1702–13).
[15] Singing (a variant of *choir*).

Ernest Hemingway 1899–1961

Ernest Hemingway was born in Oak Park, a Chicago suburb he described as a "town of wide lawns and narrow minds." Rather than attend college, he became a newspaper reporter, a job that helped develop his spare, forceful writing style. As a volunteer ambulance driver in World War I, Hemingway was seriously wounded. He married the first of his four wives in 1921 and took her to Paris, where he worked as a foreign correspondent, wrote fiction, and became a voice of the "Lost Generation" of American expatriates. In 1954 he won the Nobel Prize for Literature. When he was sixty-two and terminally ill with cancer, he committed suicide by shooting himself with a shotgun.

Hills Like White Elephants[*]

The hills across the valley of the Ebro[1] were long and white. On this side there was no shade and no trees and the station was between two lines of rails in the sun. Close against the side of the station there was the warm shadow of the building and a curtain, made of strings of bamboo beads, hung across the open door into the bar, to keep out flies. The American and the girl with him sat at a table in the shade, outside the building. It was very hot and the express from Barcelona would come in forty minutes. It stopped at this junction for two minutes and went on to Madrid.

"What should we drink?" the girl asked. She had taken off her hat and put it on the table.

"It's pretty hot," the man said.

"Let's drink beer."

"Dos cervezas," the man said into the curtain.   5

"Big ones?" a woman asked from the doorway.

"Yes. Two big ones."

The woman brought two glasses of beer and two felt pads. She put the felt pads and the beer glasses on the table and looked at the man and the girl. The girl was looking off at the line of hills. They were white in the sun and the country was brown and dry.

"They look like white elephants," she said.

"I've never seen one," the man drank his beer.   10

"No, you wouldn't have."

"I might have," the man said. "Just because you say I wouldn't have doesn't prove anything."

The girl looked at the bead curtain. "They've painted something on it," she said. "What does it say?"

"Anis del Toro. It's a drink."

"Could we try it?"   15

The man called "Listen" through the curtain. The woman came out from the bar.

---

[*] Ernest Hemingway, "Hills Like White Elephants." Reprinted with the permission of Scribner, a Division of Simon & Schuster, Inc., from *Men Without Women* by Ernest Hemingway. Copyright 1927 by Charles Scribner's Sons. Copyright renewed 1955 by Ernest Hemingway.

[1] A river in Spain.

"Four reales."[2]

"We want two Anis del Toro."

"With water?"

"Do you want it with water?"   20

"I don't know," the girl said. "Is it good with water?"

"It's all right."

"You want them with water?" asked the woman.

"Yes, with water."

"It tastes like licorice," the girl said and put the glass down.   25

"That's the way with everything."

"Yes," said the girl. "Everything tastes of licorice. Especially all the things you've waited so long for, like absinthe."

"Oh, cut it out."

"You started it," the girl said. "I was being amused. I was having a fine time."

"Well, let's try and have a fine time."   30

"All right. I was trying. I said the mountains looked like white elephants. Wasn't that bright?"

"That was bright."

"I wanted to try this new drink. That's all we do, isn't it—look at things and try new drinks?"

"I guess so."

The girl looked across at the hills.   35

"They're lovely hills," she said. "They don't really look like white elephants. I just meant the coloring of their skin through the trees."

"Should we have another drink?"

"All right."

The warm wind blew the bead curtain against the table.

"The beer's nice and cool," the man said.   40

"It's lovely," the girl said.

"It's really an awfully simple operation, Jig," the man said. "It's not really an operation at all."

The girl looked at the ground the table legs rested on.

"I know you wouldn't mind it, Jig. It's really not anything. It's just to let the air in."

The girl did not say anything.

"I'll go with you and I'll stay with you all the time. They just let the air in and   45
then it's all perfectly natural."

"Then what will we do afterward?"

"We'll be fine afterward. Just like we were before."

"What makes you think so?"

"That's the only thing that bothers us. It's the only thing that's made us unhappy."   50

The girl looked at the bead curtain, put her hand out and took hold of two of the strings of beads.

"And you think then we'll be all right and be happy."

"I know we will. You don't have to be afraid. I've known lots of people that have done it."

"So have I," said the girl. "And afterward they were all so happy."

---

[2] Spanish coins.

"Well," the man said, "if you don't want to you don't have to. I wouldn't have   55
you do it if you didn't want to. But I know it's perfectly simple."

"And you really want to?"

"I think it's the best thing to do. But I don't want you to do it if you don't
really want to."

"And if I do it you'll be happy and things will be like they were and you'll
love me?"

"I love you now. You know I love you."

"I know. But if I do it, then it will be nice again if I say things are like white   60
elephants, and you'll like it?"

"I'll love it. I love it now but I just can't think about it. You know how I get
when I worry."

"If I do it you won't ever worry?"

"I won't worry about that because it's perfectly simple."

"Then I'll do it. Because I don't care about me."

"What do you mean?"   65

"I don't care about me."

"Well, I care about you."

"Oh, yes. But I don't care about me. And I'll do it and then everything will
be fine."

"I don't want you to do it if you feel that way."

The girl stood up and walked to the end of the station. Across, on the other   70
side, were fields of grain and trees along the banks of the Ebro. Far away,
beyond the river, were mountains. The shadow of a cloud moved across the field
of grain and she saw the river through the trees.

"And we could have all this," she said. "And we could have everything and
every day we make it more impossible."

"What did you say?"

"I said we could have everything."

"We can have everything."

"No, we can't."

"We can have the whole world."   75

"No, we can't."

"We can go everywhere."

"No, we can't. It isn't ours any more."

"It's ours."

"No, it isn't. And once they take it away, you never get it back."   80

"But they haven't taken it away."

"We'll wait and see."

"Come on back in the shade," he said. "You mustn't feel that way."

"I don't feel any way," the girl said. "I just know things."   85

"I don't want you to do anything that you don't want to do—"

"Nor that isn't good for me," she said. "I know. Could we have another beer?"

"All right. But you've got to realize—"

"I realize," the girl said. "Can't we maybe stop talking?"

They sat down at the table and the girl looked across at the hills on the dry   90
side of the valley and the man looked at her and at the table.

"You've got to realize," he said, "that I don't want you to do it if you don't
want to. I'm perfectly willing to go through with it if it means anything to you."

"Doesn't it mean anything to you? We could get along."

"Of course it does. But I don't want anybody but you. I don't want anyone else. And I know it's perfectly simple."

"Yes, you know it's perfectly simple."

"It's all right for you to say that, but I do know it." 95

"Would you do something for me now?"

"I'd do anything for you."

"Would you please please please please please please please stop talking?"

He did not say anything but looked at the bags against the wall of the station. There were labels on them from all the hotels where they had spent nights.

"But I don't want you to," he said. "I don't care anything about it." 100

"I'll scream," the girl said.

The woman came out through the curtains with two glasses of beer and put them down on the damp felt pads. "The train comes in five minutes," she said.

"What did she say?" asked the girl.

"That the train is coming in five minutes."

The girl smiled brightly at the woman, to thank her. 105

"I'd better take the bags over to the other side of the station," the man said. She smiled at him.

"All right. Then come back and we'll finish the beer."

He picked up the two heavy bags and carried them around the station to the other tracks. He looked up the tracks but could not see the train. Coming back, he walked through the barroom, where people waiting for the train were drinking. He drank an Anis at the bar and looked at the people. They were all waiting reasonably for the train. He went out through the bead curtain. She was sitting at the table and smiled at him.

"Do you feel better?" he asked.

"I feel fine," she said. "There's nothing wrong with me. I feel fine." 110

(1927)

Questions for Discussion and Writing

1. How would you describe the point of view in this story?
2. The number *two* is used ten times in the story. What is the significance of this repetition? (Note especially the two parallel train tracks and the two strings of beads that do not intersect: Do they suggest anything about the characters' lives?)
3. What is the main point or theme of the story? What is the central issue between the lovers?
4. What is a "white elephant"? Explain the story's title.
5. Write an essay in which you argue that Jig will (or will not) do what her lover wants.

Making Connections

Compare Jig to the young wife in Rosario Morales's "The Day It Happened" (page 300) or to China in T. Coraghessan Boyle's "The Love of My Life" (page 312). What similarities do you see in their ability (or lack of ability) to deal with their male lovers?

Arna Bontemps   1902–1973

Arna Bontemps was born in Louisiana, but when he was three years old his father, threatened by two white men, decided the South was no place to live. The family moved to Los Angeles, and Arna grew up in California, where he graduated from Pacific Union College. In the early 1920s, he completed graduate work at the University of Chicago and moved to New York City, where he became associated with the Harlem Renaissance. Bontemps explored his black heritage in poems, stories, novels, plays, essays, and children's literature. He also preserved much of that heritage in anthologies of folklore, slave narratives, short stories, and poetry. In addition, Bontemps held several teaching jobs before becoming librarian at Fisk University, a position he held for more than twenty years. "A Summer Tragedy," his most anthologized short story, describes an elderly couple's preparations to carry out a solemn decision.

A Summer Tragedy

Old Jeff Patton, the black share farmer, fumbled with his bow tie. His fingers trembled and the high, stiff collar pinched his throat. A fellow loses his hand for such vanities after thirty or forty years of simple life. Once a year, or maybe twice if there's a wedding among his kinfolks, he may spruce up, but generally fancy clothes do nothing but adorn the wall of the big room and feed the moths. That had been Jeff Patton's experience. He had not worn his stiff-bosomed shirt more than a dozen times in all his married life. His swallow-tailed coat lay on the bed beside him, freshly brushed and pressed, but it was as full of holes as the overalls in which he worked on weekdays. The moths had used it badly. Jeff twisted his mouth into a hideous toothless grimace as he contended with the obstinate bow. He stamped his good foot and decided to give up the struggle.

"Jennie," he called.

"What's that, Jeff?" His wife's shrunken voice came out of the adjoining room like an echo. It was hardly bigger than a whisper.

"I reckon you'll have to he'p me wid this heah bow tie, baby," he said meekly. "Dog if I can hitch it up."

Her answer was not strong enough to reach him, but presently the old woman came to the door, feeling her way with a stick. She had a wasted, dead-life appearance. Her body, as scrawny and gnarled as a string bean, seemed less than nothing in the ocean of frayed and faded petticoats that surrounded her. These hung an inch or two above the tops of her heavy unlaced shoes and showed little grotesque piles where the stockings had fallen down from her negligible legs.   5

"You oughta could do a heap mo' wid a thing like that'n me—beingst as you got yo' good sight."

"Looks like I oughta could," he admitted. "But my fingers is gone democrat on me. I get all mixed up in the looking glass an' can't tell wicha way to twist the devilish thing."

Jennie sat on the side of the bed, and old Jeff Patton got down on one knee while she tied the bow knot. It was a slow and painful ordeal for each of them in this position. Jeff's bones cracked, his knee ached, and it was only after a half dozen attempts that Jennie worked a semblance of a bow into the tie.

"I got to dress maself now," the old woman whispered. "These is ma old shoes an' stockings, and I ain't so much as unwrapped ma dress."

"Well, don't worry 'bout me no mo', baby," Jeff said. "That 'bout finishes me.   10
All I got to do now is slip on that old coat 'n ves' an' I'll be fixed to leave."

Jennie disappeared again through the dim passage into the shed room. Being blind was no handicap to her in that black hole. Jeff heard the cane placed against the wall beside the door and knew that his wife was on easy ground. He put on his coat, took a battered top hat from the bed post, and hobbled to the front door. He was ready to travel. As soon as Jennie could get on her Sunday shoes and her old black silk dress, they would start.

Outside the tiny log house, the day was warm and mellow with sunshine. A host of wasps were humming with busy excitement in the trunk of a dead sycamore. Gray squirrels were searching through the grass for hickory nuts, and blue jays were in the trees, hopping from branch to branch. Pine woods stretched away to the left like a black sea. Among them were scattered scores of log houses like Jeff's, houses of black share farmers. Cows and pigs wandered freely among the trees. There was no danger of loss. Each farmer knew his own stock and knew his neighbor's as well as he knew his neighbor's children.

Down the slope to the right were cultivated acres on which the colored folks worked. They extended to the river, more than two miles away, and they were today green with the unmade cotton crop. A tiny thread of a road, which passed directly in front of Jeff's place, ran through these green fields like a pencil mark.

Jeff, standing outside the door, with his absurd hat in his left hand, surveyed the wide scene tenderly. He had been forty-five years on these acres. He loved them with the unexplained affection that others have for the countries to which they belong.

The sun was hot on his head, his collar still pinched his throat, and the   15
Sunday clothes were intolerably hot. Jeff transferred the hat to his right hand and began fanning with it. Suddenly the whisper that was Jennie's voice came out of the shed room.

"You can bring the car round front whilst you's waitin'," it said feebly. There was a tired pause; then it added, "I'll soon be fixed to go."

"A 'right baby," Jeff answered. "I'll get it in a minute."

But he didn't move. A thought struck him that made his mouth fall open. The mention of the car brought to his mind with new intensity, the trip he and Jennie were about to take. Fear came into his eyes; excitement took his breath. Lord, Jesus!

"Jeff....O Jeff," the old woman's whisper called.

He awakened with a jolt. "Hunh, baby?"   20

"What you doin'?"

"Nuthin. Jes studyin'. I jes been turnin' things round 'n round in ma mind."

"You could be getting' the car," she said.

"Oh yes, right away, baby"

He started round the shed, limping heavily on his bad leg. There were   25
three frizzly chickens in the yard. All his other chicks had been killed or stolen recently. But the frizzly chickens had been saved somehow. That was fortunate indeed, for these curious creatures had a way of devouring "poison" from the yard and in that way protecting against conjure and black luck and spells. But even the frizzly chickens seemed now to be in a stupor. Jeff thought they had some ailment; he expected all three of them to die shortly.

The shed in which the old T-model Ford stood was only a grass roof held up by four corner poles. It had been built by tremulous hands at a time when the little rattletrap car had been regarded as a peculiar treasure. And, miraculously, despite wind and downpour, it still stood.

Jeff adjusted the crank and put his weight upon it. The engine came to life with a sputter and bang that rattled the old car from radiator to tail light. Jeff hopped into the seat and put his foot on the accelerator. The sputtering and banging increased. The rattling became more violent. That was good. It was good banging, good sputtering and rattling, and it meant that the aged car was still in running condition. She could be depended on for this trip.

Again Jeff's thought halted as if paralyzed. The suggestion of the trip fell into the machinery of his mind like a wrench. He felt dazed and weak. He swung the car out into the yard, made a half turn, and drove around to the front door. When he took his hands off the wheel, he noticed that he was trembling violently. He cut off the motor and climbed to the ground to wait for Jennie.

A few minutes later she was at the window, her voice rattling against the pane like a broken shutter.

"I'm ready, Jeff." 30

He did not answer, but limped into the house and took her by the arm. He led her slowly through the big room, down the step, and across the yard.

"You reckon I'd oughta lock the do'?" he asked softly.

They stopped and Jennie weighed the question. Finally she shook her head. "Ne' mind the do'," she said. "I don't see no cause to lock up things."

"You right," Jeff agreed. "No cause to lock up." 35

Jeff opened the door and helped his wife into the car. A quick shudder passed over him. Jesus! Again he trembled.

"How come you shaking so?" Jennie whispered.

"I don't know," he said.

"You mus' be scairt, Jeff."

"No, baby, I ain't scairt." 40

He slammed the door after her and went around to crank up again. The motor started easily. Jeff wished that it had not been so responsive. He would have liked a few more minutes in which to turn things around in his head. As it was, with Jennie chiding him about being afraid, he had to keep going. He swung the car into the little pencil-mark road and started off toward the river, driving very slowly, very cautiously.

Chugging across the green countryside, the small battered Ford seemed tiny indeed. Jeff felt a familiar excitement, a thrill, as they came down the first slope to the immense levels on which the cotton was growing. He could not help reflecting that the crops were good. He knew what that meant, too. He made forty-five of them with his own hands. It was true that he had worn out nearly a dozen mules, but that was the fault of the old man Stevenson, the owner of the land. Major Stevenson had the old notion that one mule was all a share farmer needed to work a thirty-acre plot. It was an expensive notion, the way it killed mules from overwork, but the old man held to it. Jeff thought it killed a good many share farmers as well as mules, but he had no patience with weakness in men. Women or children might be tolerated if they were puny, but a weak man was a curse. Of course, his own children—

Jeff's thought halted there. He and Jennie never mentioned their dead children any more. And naturally, he did not wish to dwell upon them in his mind. Before he knew it, some remark would slip out of his mouth and that would make Jennie feel blue. Perhaps she would cry. A woman like Jennie could not easily throw off the grief that comes from losing five grown children within two years. Even Jeff was still staggered by the blow. His memory had not been much good recently. He frequently talked to himself. And, although he had kept it a secret, he knew that his courage had left him. He was terrified by the least unfamiliar sound at night. He was reluctant to venture far from home in the daytime. And that habit of trembling when he felt fearful was now far beyond his control. Sometimes he became afraid and trembled without knowing what had frightened him. The feeling would just come over him like a chill.

The car rattled slowly over the dusty road. Jennie sat erect and silent with a little absurd hat pinned to her hair. Her useless eyes seemed very large, very white in their deep sockets. Suddenly Jeff heard her voice, and he inclined his head to catch the words.

"Is we passed Delia Moore's house yet?" she asked. 45

"Not yet," he said.

"You must be drivin' mighty slow, Jeff."

"We just as well take our time, baby."

There was a pause. A little puff of steam was coming out of the radiator of the car. Heat wavered above the hood. Delia Moore's house was nearly half a mile away. After a moment Jennie spoke again.

"You ain't really scairt, is you Jeff?" 50

"Nah, baby, I ain't scairt."

"You know how we agreed—we gotta keep on goin'."

Jewels of perspiration appeared on Jeff's forehead. His eyes rounded, blinked, became fixed on the road.

"I don't know," he said with a shiver, "I reckon it's the only thing to do."

"Hm." 55

A flock of guinea fowls, pecking in the road, were scattered by the passing car. Some of them took to their wings; others hid under the bushes. A blue jay, swaying on a leafy twig, was annoying a roadside squirrel. Jeff held an even speed till he came near Delia's place. Then he slowed down noticeably.

Delia's house was really no house at all, but an abandoned stone building converted into a dwelling. It sat near a crossroads, beneath a single black cedar tree. There Delia, a cattish old creature of Jennie's age, lived alone. She had been there for more years than anyone could remember, and long ago had won the disfavor of such women as Jennie. For in her younger days Delia had been gayer, yellower, and saucier than seemed proper in those parts. Her ways with men-folks had been dark and suspicious. And the fact that she had had as many husbands as children did not help her reputation.

"Yonder's old Delia," Jeff said as they passed.

"What she doin'?"

"Jes sittin' in the do'," he said. 60

"She see us?"

"Hm," Jeff said. "Musta did."

That relieved Jennie. It strengthened her to know that her old enemy had seen her pass in her best clothes. That would give the old she-devil something to chew her gums and fret about, Jennie thought. Wouldn't she have a fit if she didn't find out? Old evil Delia! This would be just the thing for her. It would pay her back for being so evil. It would also pay her, Jennie thought, for the way she used to grin at Jeff—long ago, when her teeth were good.

The road became smooth and red, and Jeff could tell by the smell of the air that they were nearing the river. He could see the rise where the road turned and ran along parallel to the stream. The car chugged on monotonously. After a long silent spell, Jennie leaned against Jeff and spoke.

"How many bale o' cotton you think we got standin'?" she said. Jeff wrinkled   65
his forehead as he calculated.

"'Bout twenty-five, I reckon."

"How many you make las' year?"

"Twenty-eight," he said. "How come you ask that?"

"I's jes thinkin'," Jennie said quietly.

"It don't make a speck o' difference though," Jeff reflected. "If we get much   70
or if we get little, we still gonna be in debt to old man Stevenson when he gets through counting up agin us. It's took us a long time to learn that."

Jennie was not listening to these words. She had fallen into a trancelike meditation. Her lips twitched. She chewed her gum and rubbed her gnarled hands nervously. Suddenly, she leaned forward, buried her face in the nervous hands, and burst into tears. She cried aloud in a dry cracked voice that suggested the rattle of fodder on dead stalks. She cried aloud like a child, for she had never learned to suppress a genuine sob. Her slight old frame shook heavily and seemed hardly able to sustain such violent grief.

"What's the matter, baby?" Jeff asked awkwardly. "Why you cryin' like all that?"

"I's jes thinkin'," she said.

"So you the one what's scairt now, hunh?"

"I ain't scairt, Jeff. I's jes thinkin' 'bout leavin' eve'thing like this—eve'thing   75
we been used to. It's right sad-like."

Jeff did not answer, and presently Jennie buried her face again and cried.

The sun was almost overhead. It beat down furiously on the dusty wagon-path road, on the parched roadside grass and the tiny battered car. Jeff's hands, gripping the wheel, became wet with perspiration; his forehead sparkled. Jeff's lips parted. His mouth shaped a hideous grimace. His face suggested the face of a man being burned. But the torture passed in his expression softened again.

"You mustn't cry, baby," he said to his wife. "We gotta be strong. We can't break down."

Jennie waited a few seconds, then said, "You reckon we oughta do it, Jeff? You reckon we oughta go 'head an' do it, really?"

Jeff's voice choked; his eyes blurred. He was terrified to hear Jennie say the   80
thing that had been in his mind all morning. She had egged him on when he had wanted more than anything in the world to wait, to reconsider, to think things over a little longer. Now she was getting cold feet. Actually, there was no need of thinking the question through again. It would only end in making the same painful decision once more. Jeff knew that. There was no need of fooling around longer.

"We jes as well to do like we planned," he said. "They ain't nothin' else for us now—it's the bes' thing."

Jeff thought of the handicaps, the near impossibility of making another crop with his leg bothering him more and more each week. Then there was always the chance that he would have another stroke, like the one that had made him lame. Another one might kill him. The least it could do would be to leave him helpless. Jeff gasped—Lord Jesus! He could not bear to think of being helpless, like a baby on Jennie's hands. Frail, blind Jennie.

The little pounding motor of the car worked harder and harder. The puff of steam from the cracked radiator became larger. Jeff realized that they were climbing a little rise. A moment later the road turned abruptly and he looked down upon the face of the river.

"Jeff."

"Hunh?"

"Is that the water I hear?"

"Hm. Tha's it."

"Well, which way you goin' now?"

"Down this-a way," he said. "The road runs 'long 'side o' the water a lil piece."

She waited a while calmly. Then she said, "Drive faster."

"A 'right, baby," Jeff said.

The water roared in the bed of the river. It was fifty or sixty feet below the level of the road. Between the road and the water there was a long smooth slope, sharply inclined. The slope was dry, the clay hardened by prolonged summer heat. The water below, roaring in a narrow channel, was noisy and wild.

"Jeff."

"Hunh?"

"How far you goin'?"

"Jes a lil piece down the road."

"You ain't scairt, is you, Jeff?"

"Nah, baby," he said trembling. "I ain't scairt."

"Remember how we planned it, Jeff. We gotta do it like we said. Bravelike."

"Hm."

Jeff's brain darkened. Things suddenly seemed unreal, like figures in a dream. Thoughts swam in his mind foolishly, hysterically, like little blind fish in a pool within a dense cave. They rushed again. Jeff soon became dizzy. He shuttered violently and turned to his wife.

"Jennie, I can't do it. I can't." His voice broke pitifully.

She did not appear to be listening. All the grief had gone from her face. She sat erect, her unseeing eyes wide open, strained and frightful. Her glossy black skin had become dull. She seemed as thin, as sharp and bony, as a starved bird. Now, having suffered and endured the sadness of tearing herself away from beloved things, she showed no anguish. She was absorbed with her own thoughts, and she didn't even hear Jeff's voice shouting in her ear.

Jeff said nothing more. For an instant there was light in his cavernous brain. The great chamber was, for less than a second, peopled by characters he knew and loved.

They were simple, healthy creatures, and they behaved in a manner that he could understand. They had quality. But since he had already taken leave of them long ago, the remembrance did not break his heart again. Young Jeff Patton was among them, the Jeff Patton of fifty years ago who went down to New Orleans with a crowd of country boys to the Mardi Gras doings. The gay young crowd, boys with candy-stripped shirts and rouged brown girls in noisy silks, was like a picture in his head. Yet it did not make him sad. On that very trip Slim Burns had killed Joe Beasley—the crowd had been broken up. Since then Jeff Patton's world had been the Greenbriar Plantation. If there had been other Mardi Gras carnivals, he had not heard of them. Since then there had been no time; the years had fallen on him like waves. Now he was old, worn out. Another paralytic stroke (like the one he had already suffered) would put him on his back for keeps. In that condition, with a frail blind woman to look after him, he would be worse off than if he were dead.

Suddenly Jeff's hands became steady. He actually felt brave. He slowed   105
down the motor of the car and carefully pulled off the road. Below the water of the stream boomed, a soft thunder in the deep channel. Jeff ran the car onto the clay slope, pointed it directly toward the stream, and put his foot heavily on the accelerator. The little car leaped furiously down the steep incline toward the water. The movement was nearly as swift and direct as a fall. The two old black folks, sitting quietly side by side, showed no excitement. In another instant the car hit the water and dropped immediately out of sight.

A little later it logged in the mud of a shallow place. One wheel of the crushed and upturned little Ford became visible above the rushing water.

(1933)

Questions for Discussion and Writing

1. Consider the contradictory title: How do the words "summer" and "tragedy" define and control the paradoxical mood of this story?
2. What are the main themes of this story? What is the author suggesting about the effects of social and economic forces on people's lives? Why is the couple no longer attached to the land where they have worked and lived for so many years?
3. At what point did you become aware that the old couple had decided to commit suicide? Analyze how the foreshadowing influenced your reactions to the story.
4. How do you feel at the end of the story? Write an essay about the thoughts and feelings the story aroused in you.
5. Write an obituary for Jeff and Jennie Patton.

Making Connections

Compare the couple in this story with the "old yellow pair" in Gwendolyn Brooks's poem "The Bean Eaters" (page 587) and with Mr. and Mrs. Tozzi in Katha Pollitt's "The Old Neighbors" (page 588).

◇◇◇◇◇◇◇◇◇◇◇◇◇◇◇◇◇◇◇◇◇◇

Tillie Olsen   1913–2007

Tillie Olsen was born in Omaha, Nebraska, the daughter of political refugees from the repression of Czarist Russia. In her book *Silences* (1978), Olsen explains how gender, race, and class can render people inarticulate. Her own life illustrates the problem. She began working on a novel before she was twenty, but then she married, had four children, worked, participated in union activities, and did not resume writing until the 1950s, when her youngest daughter started school. The completed novel, *Yonnondio*, was finally published in 1974. Her long story "Tell Me a Riddle" won the O. Henry Prize in 1961. Olsen has said that she felt no personal guilt as a working parent because "guilt is a word used far too sloppily, to cover up harmful situations in society that must be changed."

I Stand Here Ironing

I stand here ironing, and what you asked me moves tormented back and forth with the iron.

"I wish you would manage the time to come in and talk with me about your daughter. I'm sure you can help me understand her. She's a youngster who needs help and whom I'm deeply interested in helping."

"Who needs help?" Even if I came what good would it do? You think because I am her mother I have a key, or that in some way you could use me as a key? She has lived for nineteen years. There is all that life that has happened outside of me, beyond me.

And when is there time to remember, to sift, to weigh, to estimate, to total? I will start and there will be an interruption and I will have to gather it all together again. Or I will become engulfed with all I did or did not do, with what should have been and what cannot be helped.

She was a beautiful baby. The first and only one of our five that was beautiful   5 at birth. You do not guess how new and uneasy her tenancy in her now-loveliness. You did not know her all those years she was thought homely, or see her poring over her baby pictures, making me tell her over and over how beautiful she had been—and would be, I would tell her—and was now, to the seeing eye. But the seeing eyes were few or nonexistent. Including mine.

I nursed her. They feel that's important nowadays. I nursed all the children, but with her, with all the fierce rigidity of first motherhood, I did like the books then said. Though her cries battered me to trembling and my breasts ached with swollenness, I waited till the clock decreed.

Why do I put that first? I do not even know if it matters, or if it explains anything.

She was a beautiful baby. She blew shining bubbles of sound. She loved motion, loved light, loved color and music and textures. She would lie on the floor in her blue overalls patting the surface so hard in ecstasy her hands and feet would blur. She was a miracle to me, but when she was eight months old I had to leave her daytimes with the woman downstairs to whom she was no miracle at all, for I worked or looked for work and for Emily's father, who "could no longer endure" (he wrote in his good-by note) "sharing want with us."

I was nineteen. It was the pre-relief, pre-WPA world of the depression. I would start running as soon as I got off the streetcar, running up the stairs, the place smelling sour, and awake or asleep to startle awake, when she saw me she would break into a clogged weeping that could not be comforted, a weeping I can yet hear.

After a while I found a job hashing at night so I could be with her days, and   10 it was better. But it came to where I had to bring her to his family and leave her.

It took a long time to raise the money for her fare back. Then she got chicken pox and I had to wait longer. When she finally came, I hardly knew her, walking quick and nervous like her father, looking like her father, thin, and dressed in a shoddy red that yellowed her skin and glared at the pockmarks. All the baby loveliness gone.

She was two. Old enough for nursery school they said, and I did not know then what I know now—the fatigue of the long day, and the lacerations of group life in the kinds of nurseries that are only parking places for children.

Except that it would have made no difference if I had known. It was the only place there was. It was the only way we could be together, the only way I could hold a job.

And even without knowing, I knew. I knew the teacher that was evil because all these years it has curdled into my memory, the little boy hunched in the corner, her rasp, "why aren't you outside, because Alvin hits you? that's no reason, go out, scaredy." I knew Emily hated it even if she did not clutch and implore "don't go Mommy" like the other children, mornings.

She always had a reason why we should stay home. Momma, you look sick.   15
Momma, I feel sick. Momma, the teachers aren't there today, they're sick. Momma, we can't go, there was a fire there last night. Momma, it's a holiday today, no school, they told me.

But never a direct protest, never rebellion. I think of our others in their three-, four-year-oldness—the explosions, the tempers, the denunciations, the demands—and I feel suddenly ill. I put the iron down. What in me demanded that goodness in her? And what was the cost, the cost to her of such goodness?

The old man living in the back once said in his gentle way: "You should smile at Emily more when you look at her." What *was* in my face when I looked at her? I loved her. There were all the acts of love.

It was only with the others I remembered what he said, so that it was the face of joy, and not of care or tightness or worry I turned to them—too late for Emily. She does not smile easily, let alone almost always as her brothers and sisters do. Her face is closed and somber, but when she wants, how fluid. You must have seen it in her pantomimes, you spoke of her rare gift for comedy on the stage that rouses a laughter out of the audience so dear they applaud and applaud and do not want to let her go.

Where does it come from, that comedy? There was none of it in her when she came back to me that second time, after I had had to send her away again. She had a new daddy now to learn to love, and I think perhaps it was a better time.

Except when we left her alone nights, telling ourselves she was old enough.   20
"Can't you go some other time, Mommy, like tomorrow?" she would ask. "Will it be just a little while you'll be gone? Do you promise?"

The time we came back, the front door open, the clock on the floor in the hall. She rigid awake. "It wasn't just a little while. I didn't cry. Three times I called you, just three times, and then I ran downstairs to open the door so you could come faster. The clock talked loud, I threw it away, it scared me when it talked."

She said the clock talked loud that night I went to the hospital to have Susan. She was delirious with the fever that comes before red measles, but she was fully conscious all the week I was gone and the week after we were home when she could not come near the new baby or me.

She did not get well. She stayed skeleton thin, not wanting to eat, and night after night she had nightmares. She would call for me, and I would sleepily call back, "you're all right, darling, go to sleep, it's just a dream," and if she still called, in a sterner voice, "now go to sleep, Emily, there's nothing to hurt you." Twice, only twice, when I had to get up for Susan anyway, I went in to sit with her.

Now when it is too late (as if she would let me hold and comfort her like I 25 do the others) I get up and go to her at her moan or restless stirring. "Are you awake? Can I get you something?" And the answer is always the same: "No, I'm all right, go back to sleep, Mother."

They persuaded me at the clinic to send her away to a convalescent home in the country where "she can have the kind of food and care you can't manage for her, and you'll be free to concentrate on the new baby." They still send children to that place. I see pictures on the society page of sleek young women planning affairs to raise money for it, or dancing at the affairs, or decorating Easter eggs or filling Christmas stockings for children.

They never have a picture of the children so I do not know if they still wear those gigantic red bows and the ravaged looks on the every other Sunday when parents can come to visit "unless otherwise notified"—as we were notified the first six weeks.

Oh it is a handsome place, green lawns and tall trees and fluted flower beds. High up on the balconies of each cottage the children stand, the girls in their red bows and white dresses, the boys in white suits and giant red ties. The parents stand below shrieking up to be heard and the children shriek down to be heard, and between them the invisible wall "Not To Be Contaminated by Parental Germs or Physical Affection."

There was a tiny girl who always stood hand in hand with Emily. Her parents never came. One visit she was gone. "They moved her to Rose Cottage," Emily shouted in explanation. "They don't like you to love anybody here."

She wrote once a week, the labored writing of a seven-year-old. "I am fine. 30 How is the baby. If I write my leter nicly I will have a star. Love." There was never a star. We wrote every other day, letters she could never hold or keep but only hear read—once. "We simply do not have room for children to keep any personal possessions," they patiently explained when we pieced one Sunday's shrieking together to plead how much it would mean to Emily to keep her letters and cards.

Each visit she looked frailer. "She isn't eating," they told us.

(They had runny eggs for breakfast or mush with lumps, Emily said later, I'd hold it in my mouth and not swallow. Nothing ever tasted good, just when they had chicken.)

It took us eight months to get her released home, and only the fact that she gained back so little of her seven lost pounds convinced the social worker.

I used to try to hold and love her after she came back, but her body would stay stiff, and after a while she'd push away. She ate little. Food sickened her, and I think much of life too. Oh she had physical lightness and brightness, twinkling by on skates, bouncing like a ball up and down up and down over the jump rope, skimming over the hill; but these were momentary.

She fretted about her appearance, thin and dark and foreign-looking at a 35 time when every little girl was supposed to look or thought she should look a chubby blond replica of Shirley Temple. The doorbell sometimes rang for her, but no one seemed to come and play in the house or be a best friend. Maybe because we moved so much.

There was a boy she loved painfully through two school semesters. Months later she told me how she had taken pennies from my purse to buy him candy.

"Licorice was his favorite and I bought him some every day, but he still liked Jennifer better'n me. Why, Mommy?" The kind of question for which there is no answer.

School was a worry to her. She was not glib or quick in a world where glibness and quickness were easily confused with ability to learn. To her overworked and exasperated teachers she was an over-conscientious "slow learner" who kept trying to catch up and was absent entirely too often.

I let her be absent, though sometimes the illness was imaginary. How different from my now-strictness about attendance with the others. I wasn't working. We had a new baby, I was home anyhow. Sometimes, after Susan grew old enough, I would keep her home from school, too, to have them all together.

Mostly Emily had asthma, and her breathing, harsh and labored, would fill the house with a curiously tranquil sound. I would bring the two old dresser mirrors and her boxes of collections to her bed. She would select beads and single earrings, bottle tops and shells, dried flowers and pebbles, old postcards and scraps, all sorts of oddments; then she and Susan would play Kingdom, setting up landscapes and furniture, peopling them with action.

Those were the only times of peaceful companionship between her and Susan. I have edged away from it, that poisonous feeling between them, that terrible balancing of hurts and needs I had to do between the two, and did so badly, those earlier years.   40

Oh there are conflicts between the others too, each one human, needing, demanding, hurting, taking—but only between Emily and Susan, no, Emily toward Susan that corroding resentment. It seems so obvious on the surface, yet it is not obvious. Susan, the second child, Susan, golden and curly haired and chubby, quick and articulate and assured, everything in appearance and manner Emily was not; Susan, not able to resist Emily's precious things, losing or sometimes clumsily breaking them; Susan telling jokes and riddles to company for applause while Emily sat silent (to say to me later: that was *my* riddle, Mother, I told it to Susan); Susan, who for all the five years' difference in age was just a year behind Emily in developing physically.

I am glad for that slow physical development that widened the difference between her and her contemporaries, though she suffered over it. She was too vulnerable for that terrible world of youthful competition, of preening and parading, of constant measuring of yourself against every other, of envy: "If I had that copper hair," or "If I had that skin...." She tormented herself enough about not looking like the others, there was enough of the unsureness, the having to be conscious of words before you speak, the constant caring—what are they thinking of me? what kind of an impression am I making?—without having it all magnified unendurably by the merciless physical drives.

Ronnie is calling. He is wet and I change him. It is rare there is such a cry now. That time of motherhood is almost behind me when the ear is not one's own but must always be racked and listening for the child cry, the child call. We sit for a while and I hold him, looking out over the city spread in charcoal with its soft aisles of light. "*Shoogily*," he breathes and curls closer. I carry him back to bed, asleep. *Shoogily.* A funny word, a family word, inherited from Emily, invented by her to say: *comfort.*

In this and other ways she leaves her seal, I say aloud. And startle at my saying it. What do I mean? What did I start to gather together, to try and make coherent? I was at the terrible, growing years. War years. I do not remember them well. I was working again, there were four smaller ones now, there was no time for her. She had to help be a mother, and housekeeper, and shopper. She had to set her seal. Mornings of crisis and near hysteria trying to get lunches packed, hair combed, coats and shoes found, everyone to school or Child Care on time, the baby ready for transportation. And always the paper scribbled on by a smaller one, the book looked at by Susan then mislaid, the homework not done. Running out to that huge school where she was one, she was lost, she was a drop; suffering over her unpreparedness, stammering and unsure in her classes.

There was so little left at night after the kids were bedded down. She would   45
struggle over her books, always eating (it was in those years she developed her enormous appetite that is legendary in our family) and I would be ironing, or preparing food for the next day, or writing V-mail[1] to Bill, or tending the baby. Sometimes, to make me laugh, or out of her despair, she would imitate happenings or types at school.

I think I said once: "Why don't you do something like this in the school amateur show?" One morning she phoned me at work, hardly understandable through the weeping: "Mother, I did it. I won, I won; they gave me first prize; they clapped and clapped and wouldn't let me go."

Now suddenly she was Somebody, and as imprisoned in her difference as she had been in her anonymity.

She began to be asked to perform at other high schools, even in colleges, then at city and state-wide affairs. The first one we went to, I only recognized her that first moment when thin, shy, she almost drowned herself into the curtains. Then: Was this Emily? The control, the command, the convulsing and deadly clowning, the spell, then the roaring, stamping audience, unwilling to let this rare and precious laughter out of their lives.

Afterwards: You ought to do something about her with a gift like that—but without money or knowing how, what does one do? We have left it all to her, and the gift has as often eddied inside, clogged and clotted, as been used and growing.

She is coming. She runs up the stairs two at a time with her light graceful   50
step, and I know she is happy tonight. Whatever it was that occasioned your call did not happen today.

"Aren't you ever going to finish the ironing, Mother? Whistler painted his mother in a rocker. I'd have to paint mine standing over an ironing board." This is one of the communicative nights and she tells me everything and nothing as she fixes herself a plate of food out of the icebox.

She is so lovely. Why did you want me to come in at all? Why were you concerned? She will find her way.

She starts up the stairs to bed. "Don't get *me* up with the rest in the morning." "But I thought you were having midterms." "Oh, those," she comes back in, kisses me, and says quite lightly, "in a couple of years when we'll all be atom-dead they won't matter a bit."

She has said it before. She *believes* it. But because I have been dredging the past, and all that compounds a human being is so heavy and meaningful in me, I cannot endure it tonight.

I will never total it all. I will never come in to say: She was a child seldom   55
smiled at. Her father left me before she was a year old. I had to work away

---

[1] Victory mail; letter written to personnel in the armed forces overseas during World War II.

from her her first six years when there was work, or I sent her home and to his relatives. There were years she had care she hated. She was dark and thin and foreign-looking in a world where the prestige went to blondness and curly hair and dimples, she was slow where glibness was prized. She was a child of anxious, not proud, love. We were poor and could not afford for her the soil of easy growth. I was a young mother, I was a distracted mother. There were the other children pushing up, demanding. Her younger sister seemed all that she was not. There were years she did not want me to touch her. She kept too much in herself, her life was such she had to keep too much in herself. My wisdom came too late. She has much to her and probably little will come of it. She is a child of her age, of depression, of war, of fear.

Let her be. So all that is in her will not bloom—but in how many does it? There is still enough left to live by. Only help her to know—help make it so there is cause for her to know—that she is more than this dress on the ironing board, helpless before the iron.

(1961)

Questions for Discussion and Writing

1. The story is a monologue. What is the speaker's situation? Where is she and to whom is she talking?
2. Identify some of the conflicts in the story. Are any of them resolved?
3. How is personal responsibility portrayed in this story? To what extent is the speaker responsible for Emily's character and success in life? To what extent are circumstances responsible? To what extent is Emily herself responsible?
4. Write an essay in which you argue that this story reflects the common experiences of millions of people.
5. Rewrite the story from Emily's point of view.

Making Connections

Examine the mother–daughter relationship in this story with those in Hisaye Yamamoto's "Seventeen Syllables" (which follows) and Alice Walker's "Everyday Use" (page 149). What connections can you see among the relationships and the settings of the stories?

◇◇◇◇◇◇◇◇◇◇◇◇◇◇◇◇◇◇◇◇◇◇◇◇

Hisaye Yamamoto   1921–

Hisaye Yamamoto was born in Redondo Beach, California, the daughter of Japanese immigrants. She loved to read as a child and majored in foreign languages when she attended community college. During World War II, she and her family were forcibly interned in a relocation center in Arizona. While the family was confined, her brother Johnny, a soldier in the U.S. army, was killed in action in Italy. After returning to California, she became a housewife and mother, too busy to write much. "Most of the time I am cleaning house, or cooking or doing yard work," she once explained. "Very little time is spent writing. But if somebody told me I couldn't write, it would probably grieve me very much."

Seventeen Syllables

The first Rosie knew that her mother had taken to writing poems was one evening when she finished one and read it aloud for her daughter's approval. It was about cats, and Rosie pretended to understand it thoroughly and appreciate it no end, partly because she hesitated to disillusion her mother about the quantity and quality of Japanese she had learned in all the years now that she had been going to Japanese school every Saturday (and Wednesday, too, in the summer). Even so, her mother must have been skeptical about the depth of Rosie's understanding, because she explained afterwards about the kind of poem she was trying to write.

See, Rosie, she said, it was a *haiku*, a poem in which she must pack all her meaning into seventeen syllables only, which were divided into three lines of five, seven, and five syllables. In the one she had just read, she had tried to capture the charm of a kitten, as well as comment on the superstition that owning a cat of three colors meant good luck.

"Yes, yes, I understand. How utterly lovely," Rosie said, and her mother, either satisfied or seeing through the deception and resigned, went back to composing.

The truth was that Rosie was lazy; English lay ready on the tongue but Japanese had to be searched for and examined, and even then put forth tentatively (probably to meet with laughter). It was so much easier to say yes, yes, even when one meant no, no. Besides, this was what was in her mind to say: I was looking through one of your magazines from Japan last night, Mother, and towards the back I found some *haiku* in English that delighted me. There was one that made me giggle off and on until I fell asleep—

> It is morning, and lo!
> I lie awake, comme il faut,[1]
> sighing for some dough.

Now, how to reach her mother, how to communicate the melancholy song? 5
Rosie knew formal Japanese by fits and starts, her mother had even less English, no French. It was much more possible to say yes, yes.

It developed that her mother was writing the *haiku* for a daily newspaper, the *Mainichi Shimbun*, that was published in San Francisco. Los Angeles, to be sure, was closer to the farming community in which the Hayashi family lived and several Japanese vernaculars were printed there, but Rosie's parents said they preferred the tone of the northern paper. Once a week, the *Mainichi* would have a section devoted to *haiku*, and her mother became an extravagant contributor, taking for herself the blossoming pen name, Ume Hanazono.

So Rosie and her father lived for awhile with two women, her mother and Ume Hanazono. Her mother (Tome Hayashi by name) kept house, cooked, washed, and, along with her husband and the Carrascos, the Mexican family hired for the harvest, did her ample share of picking tomatoes out in the sweltering fields and

---

[1] In good form; proper. Pronounced *come il* fō.

boxing them in tidy strata in the cool packing shed. Ume Hanazono, who came to life after the dinner dishes were done, was an earnest, muttering stranger who often neglected speaking when spoken to and stayed busy at the parlor table as late as midnight scribbling with pencil on scratch paper or carefully copying characters on good paper with her fat, pale green Parker.

The new interest had some repercussions on the household routine. Before, Rosie had been accustomed to her parents and herself taking their hot baths early and going to bed almost immediately afterwards, unless her parents challenged each other to a game of flower cards or unless company dropped in. Now if her father wanted to play cards, he had to resort to solitaire (at which he always cheated fearlessly), and if a group of friends came over, it was bound to contain someone who was also writing *haiku*, and the small assemblage would be split in two, her father entertaining the non-literary members and her mother comparing ecstatic notes with the visiting poet.

If they went out, it was more of the same thing. But Ume Hanazono's life span, even for a poet's, was very brief—perhaps three months at most.

One night they went over to see the Hayano family in the neighboring town   10
to the west, an adventure both painful and attractive to Rosie. It was attractive because there were four Hayano girls, all lovely and each one named after a season of the year (Haru, Natsu, Aki, Fuyu), painful because something had been wrong with Mrs. Hayano ever since the birth of her first child. Rosie would sometimes watch Mrs. Hayano, reputed to have been the belle of her native village, making her way about a room, stooped, slowly shuffling, violently trembling (*always* trembling), and she would be reminded that this woman, in this same condition, had carried and given issue to three babies. She would look wonderingly at Mr. Hayano, handsome, tall, and strong, and she would look at her four pretty friends. But it was not a matter she could come to any decision about.

On this visit, however, Mrs. Hayano sat all evening in the rocker, as motionless and unobtrusive as it was possible for her to be, and Rosie found the greater part of the evening practically anaesthetic. Too, Rosie spent most of it in the girls' room, because Haru, the garrulous one, said almost as soon as the bows and other greetings were over, "Oh, you must see my new coat!"

It was a pale plaid of grey, sand, and blue, with an enormous collar, and Rosie, seeing nothing special in it, said, "Gee, how nice."

"Nice?" said Haru, indignantly. "Is that all you can say about it? It's gorgeous! And so cheap, too. Only seventeen-ninety-eight, because it was a sale. The saleslady said it was twenty-five dollars regular."

"Gee," said Rosie. Natsu, who never said much and when she said anything said it shyly, fingered the coat covetously and Haru pulled it away.

"Mine," she said, putting it on. She minced in the aisle between the two large   15
beds and smiled happily. "Let's see how your mother likes it."

She broke into the front room and the adult conversation and went to stand in front of Rosie's mother, while the rest watched from the door. Rosie's mother was properly envious. "May I inherit it when you're through with it?"

Haru, pleased, giggled and said yes, she could, but Natsu reminded gravely from the door, "You promised me, Haru."

Everyone laughed but Natsu, who shamefacedly retreated into the bedroom. Haru came in laughing, taking off the coat. "We were only kidding, Natsu," she said. "Here, you try it on now."

Migrant workers harvesting a field in central California.

After Natsu buttoned herself into the coat, inspected herself solemnly in the bureau mirror, and reluctantly shed it, Rosie, Aki, and Fuyu got their turns, and Fuyu, who was eight, drowned in it while her sisters and Rosie doubled up in amusement. They all went into the front room later, because Haru's mother quaveringly called to her to fix the tea and rice cakes and open a can of sliced peaches for everybody. Rosie noticed that her mother and Mr. Hayano were talking together at the little table—they were discussing a *haiku* that Mr. Hayano was planning to send to the *Mainichi*, while her father was sitting at one end of the sofa looking through a copy of *Life*, the new picture magazine. Occasionally, her father would comment on a photograph, holding it toward Mrs. Hayano and speaking to her as he always did—loudly, as though he thought someone such as she must surely be at least a trifle deaf also.

The five girls had their refreshments at the kitchen table, and it was while   20
Rosie was showing the sisters her trick of swallowing peach slices without chewing (she chased each slippery crescent down with a swig of tea) that her father brought his empty teacup and untouched saucer to the sink and said, "Come on, Rosie, we're going home now."

"Already?" asked Rosie.

"Work tomorrow," he said.

He sounded irritated, and Rosie, puzzled, gulped one last yellow slice and stood up to go, while the sisters began protesting, as was their wont.

"We have to get up at five-thirty," he told them, going into the front room quickly, so that they did not have their usual chance to hang onto his hands and plead for an extension of time.

Rosie, following, saw that her mother and Mr. Hayano were sipping tea and   25
still talking together, while Mrs. Hayano concentrated, quivering, on raising the

handleless Japanese cup to her lips with both her hands and lowering it back to her lap. Her father, saying nothing, went out the door, onto the bright porch, and down the steps. Her mother looked up and asked, "Where is he going?"

"Where is he going?" Rosie said. "He said we were going home now."

"Going home?" Her mother looked with embarrassment at Mr. Hayano and his absorbed wife and then forced a smile. "He must be tired," she said.

Haru was not giving up yet. "May Rosie stay overnight?" she asked, and Natsu, Aki, and Fuyu came to reinforce their sister's plea by helping her make a circle around Rosie's mother. Rosie, for once having no desire to stay, was relieved when her mother, apologizing to the perturbed Mr. and Mrs. Hayano for her father's abruptness at the same time, managed to shake her head no at the quartet, kindly but adamant, so that they broke their circle and let her go.

Rosie's father looked ahead into the windshield as the two joined him. "I'm sorry," her mother said. "You must be tired." Her father, stepping on the starter, said nothing. "You know how I get when it's *haiku*," she continued, "I forget what time it is." He only grunted.

As they rode homeward silently, Rosie, sitting between, felt a rush of hate for   30 both—for her mother for begging, for her father for denying her mother. I wish this old Ford would crash, right now, she thought, then immediately, no, no, I wish my father would laugh, but it was too late: already the vision had passed through her mind of the green pick-up crumpled in the dark against one of the mighty eucalyptus trees they were just riding past, of the three contorted, bleeding bodies, one of them hers.

Rosie ran between two patches of tomatoes, her heart working more rambunctiously than she had ever known it to. How lucky it was that Aunt Taka and Uncle Gimpachi had come tonight, though, how very lucky. Otherwise she might not have really kept her half-promise to meet Jesus Carrasco. Jesus was going to be a senior in September at the same school she went to, and his parents were the ones helping with the tomatoes this year. She and Jesus, who hardly remembered seeing each other at Cleveland High where there were so many other people and two whole grades between them, had become great friends this summer—he always had a joke for her when he periodically drove the loaded pick-up up from the fields to the shed where she was usually sorting while her mother and father did the packing, and they laughed a great deal together over infinitesimal repartee during the afternoon break for chilled watermelon or ice cream in the shade of the shed.

What she enjoyed most was racing him to see which could finish picking a double row first. He, who could work faster, would tease her by slowing down until she thought she would surely pass him this time, then speeding up furiously to leave her several sprawling vines behind. Once he had made her screech hideously by crossing over, while her back was turned, to place atop the tomatoes in her greenstained bucket a truly monstrous, pale green worm (it had looked more like an infant snake). And it was when they had finished a contest this morning, after she had pantingly pointed a green finger at the immature tomatoes evident in the lugs at the end of his row and he had returned the accusation (with justice), that he had startlingly brought up the matter of their possibly meeting outside the range of both their parents' dubious eyes.

"What for?" she had asked.

"I've got a secret I want to tell you," he said.

"Tell me now," she demanded.   35

"It won't be ready till tonight," he said.

She laughed. "Tell me tomorrow then."

"It'll be gone tomorrow," he threatened.

"Well, for seven hakes, what is it?" she had asked, more than twice, and when he had suggested that the packing shed would be an appropriate place to find out, she had cautiously answered maybe. She had not been certain she was going to keep the appointment until the arrival of mother's sister and her husband. Their coming seemed a sort of signal of permission, of grace, and she had definitely made up her mind to lie and leave as she was bowing them welcome.

So as soon as everyone appeared settled back for the evening, she announced   40
loudly that she was going to the privy outside. "I'm going to the *benjo!*" and slipped out the door. And now that she was actually on her way, her heart pumped in such an undisciplined way that she could hear it with her ears. It's because I'm running, she told herself, slowing to a walk. The shed was up ahead, one more patch away, in the middle of the fields. Its bulk, looming in the dimness, took on a sinisterness that was funny when Rosie reminded herself that it was only a wooden frame with a canvas roof and three canvas walls that made a slapping noise on breezy days.

Jesus was sitting on the narrow plank that was the sorting platform and she went around to the other side and jumped backwards to seat herself on the rim of a packing stand. "Well, tell me," she said without greeting, thinking her voice sounded reassuringly familiar.

"I saw you coming out the door," Jesus said. "I heard you running part of the way, too."

"Uh-huh," Rosie said. "Now tell me the secret."

"I was afraid you wouldn't come," he said.

Rosie delved around on the chicken-wire bottom of the stall for number two   45
tomatoes, ripe, which she was sitting beside, and came up with a left-over that felt edible. She bit into it and began sucking out the pulp and seeds. "I'm here," she pointed out.

"Rosie, are you sorry you came?"

"Sorry? What for?" she said. "You said you were going to tell me something."

"I will, I will," Jesus said, but his voice contained disappointment, and Rosie fleetingly felt the older of the two, realizing a brand-new power which vanished without category under her recognition.

"I have to go back in a minute," she said. "My aunt and uncle are here from Wintersburg. I told them I was going to the privy."

Jesus laughed. "You funny thing," he said. "You slay me!"   50

"Just because you have a bathroom *inside*," Rosie said. "Come on, tell me."

Chuckling, Jesus came around to lean on the stand facing her. They still could not see each other very clearly, but Rosie noticed that Jesus became very sober again as he took the hollow tomato from her hand and dropped it back into the stall. When he took hold of her empty hand, she could find no words to protest; her vocabulary had become distressingly constricted and she thought desperately that all that remained intact now was yes and no and oh, and even these few sounds would not easily out. Thus, kissed by Jesus, Rosie fell for the first time entirely victim to a helplessness delectable beyond speech. But the terrible, beautiful sensation lasted no more than a second, and the reality of Jesus' lips and tongue and teeth and hands made her pull away with such strength that she nearly tumbled.

Rosie stopped running as she approached the lights from the windows of home. How long since she had left? She could not guess, but gasping yet, she went to the privy in back and locked herself in. Her own breathing deafened her in the dark, close space, and she sat and waited until she could hear at last the nightly calling of the frogs and crickets. Even then, all she could think to say was oh, my, and the pressure of Jesus' face against her face would not leave.

No one had missed her in the parlor, however, and Rosie walked in and through quickly, announcing that she was next going to take a bath. "Your father's in the bathhouse," her mother said, and Rosie, in her room, recalled that she had not seen him when she entered. There had been only Aunt Taka and Uncle Gimpachi with her mother at the table, drinking tea. She got her robe and straw sandals and crossed the parlor again to go outside. Her mother was telling them about the *haiku* competition in the *Mainichi* and the poem she had entered.

Rosie met her father coming out of the bathhouse. "Are you through, Father?" she asked. "I was going to ask you to scrub my back."   55

"Scrub your own back," he said shortly, going toward the main house.

"What have I done now?" she yelled after him. She suddenly felt like doing a lot of yelling. But he did not answer, and she went into the bathhouse. Turning on the dangling light, she removed her denims and T-shirt and threw them in the big carton for dirty clothes standing next to the washing machine. Her other things she took with her into the bath compartment to wash after her bath. After she had scooped a basin of hot water from the square wooden tub, she sat on the grey cement of the floor and soaped herself at exaggerated leisure, singing "Red Sails in the Sunset" at the top of her voice and using da-da-da where she suspected her words. Then, standing up, still singing, for she was possessed by the notion that any attempt now to analyze would result in spoilage and she believed that the larger her volume the less she would be able to hear herself think, she obtained more hot water and poured it on until she was free of lather. Only then did she allow herself to step into the steaming vat, one leg first, then the remainder of her body inch by inch until the water no longer stung and she could move around at will.

She took a long time soaking, afterwards remembering to go around outside to stoke the embers of the tin-lined fireplace beneath the tub and to throw on a few more sticks so that the water might keep its heat for her mother, and when she finally returned to the parlor, she found her mother still talking *haiku* with her aunt and uncle, the three of them on another round of tea. Her father was nowhere in sight.

At Japanese school the next day (Wednesday, it was), Rosie was grave and giddy by turns. Preoccupied at her desk in the row for students on Book Eight, she made up for it at recess by performing wild mimicry for the benefit of her friend Chizuko. She held her nose and whined a witticism or two in what she considered was the manner of Fred Allen; she assumed intoxication and a British accent to go over the climax of the Rudy Vallee recording of the pub conversation about William Ewart Gladstone; she was the child Shirley Temple piping, "On the Good Ship Lollipop"; she was the gentleman soprano of the Four Inkspots trilling, "If I Didn't Care." And she felt reasonably satisfied when Chizuko wept and gasped, "Oh, Rosie, you ought to be in the movies!"

Her father came after her at noon, bringing her sandwiches of minced ham 60
and two nectarines to eat while she rode, so that she could pitch right into the
sorting when they got home. The lugs were piling up, he said, and the ripe
tomatoes in them would probably have to be taken to the cannery tomorrow
if they were not ready for the produce haulers tonight. "This heat's not doing
them any good. And we've got no time for a break today."

It *was* hot, probably the hottest day of the year, and Rosie's blouse stuck damply
to her back even under the protection of the canvas. But she worked as efficiently
as a flawless machine and kept the stalls heaped, with one part of her mind listening in to the parental murmuring about the heat and the tomatoes and with
another part planning the exact words she would say to Jesus when he drove up
with the first load of the afternoon. But when at last she saw that the pick-up was
coming, her hands went berserk and the tomatoes started falling in the wrong
stalls, and her father said, "Hey, hey! Rosie, watch what you're doing!"

"Well, I have to go to the *benjo*," she said, hiding panic.

"Go in the weeds over there," he said, only half-joking.

"Oh, Father!" she protested.

"Oh, go on home," her mother said. "We'll make out for awhile." 65

In the privy Rosie peered through a knothole toward the fields, watching as
much as she could of Jesus. Happily she thought she saw him look in the direction of the house from time to time before he finished unloading and went back
toward the patch where his mother and father worked. As she was heading for
the shed, a very presentable black car purred up the dirt driveway to the house
and its driver motioned to her. Was this the Hayashi home, he wanted to know.
She nodded. Was she a Hayashi? Yes, she said, thinking that he was a good-
looking man. He got out of the car with a huge, flat package and she saw that he
warmly wore a business suit. "I have something here for your mother then," he
said, in a more elegant Japanese than she was used to.

She told him where her mother was and he came along with her, patting his
face with an immaculate white handkerchief and saying something about the
coolness of San Francisco. To her surprised mother and father, he bowed and
introduced himself as, among other things, the *haiku* editor of the *Mainichi
Shimbun*, saying that since he had been coming as far as Los Angeles anyway, he
had decided to bring her the first prize she had won in the recent contest.

"First prize?" her mother echoed, believing and not believing, pleased and
overwhelmed. Handed the package with a bow, she bobbed her head up and
down numerous times to express her utter gratitude.

"It is nothing much," he added, "but I hope it will serve as a token of our
great appreciation for your contributions and our great admiration of your considerable talent."

"I am not worthy," she said, falling easily into his style. "It is I who should 70
make some sign of my humble thanks for being permitted to contribute."

"No, no, to the contrary," he said, bowing again.

But Rosie's mother insisted, and then saying that she knew she was being
unorthodox, she asked if she might open the package because her curiosity was
so great. Certainly she might. In fact, he would like her reaction to it, for personally, it was one of his favorite *Hiroshiges*.

Rosie thought it was a pleasant picture, which looked to have been sketched
with delicate quickness. There were pink clouds, containing some graceful
calligraphy, and a sea that was a pale blue except at the edges, containing four

sampans with indications of people in them. Pines edged the water and on the far-off beach there was a cluster of thatched huts towered over by pine-dotted mountains of grey and blue. The frame was scalloped and gilt.

After Rosie's mother pronounced it without peer and somewhat prodded her father into nodding agreement, she said Mr. Kuroda must at least have a cup of tea after coming all this way, and although Mr. Kuroda did not want to impose, he soon agreed that a cup of tea would be refreshing and went along with her to the house, carrying the picture for her.

"Ha, your mother's crazy!" Rosie's father said, and Rosie laughed uneasily   75
as she resumed judgment on the tomatoes. She had emptied six lugs when he broke into an imaginary conversation with Jesus to tell her to go and remind her mother of the tomatoes, and she went slowly.

Mr. Kuroda was in his shirtsleeves expounding some *haiku* theory as he munched a rice cake, and her mother was rapt. Abashed in the great man's presence, Rosie stood next to her mother's chair until her mother looked up inquiringly, and then she started to whisper the message, but her mother pushed her gently away and reproached, "You are not being very polite to our guest."

"Father says the tomatoes..." Rosie said aloud, smiling foolishly.

"Tell him I shall only be a minute," her mother said, speaking the language of Mr. Kuroda.

When Rosie carried the reply to her father, he did not seem to hear and she said again, "Mother says she'll be back in a minute."

"All right, all right," he nodded, and they worked again in silence. But suddenly,   80
her father uttered an incredible noise, exactly like the cork of a bottle popping, and the next Rosie knew, he was stalking angrily toward the house, almost running in fact, and she chased after him crying, "Father! Father! What are you going to do?"

He stopped long enough to order her back to the shed. "Never mind!" he shouted. "Get on with the sorting!"

And from the place in the fields where she stood, frightened and vacillating, Rosie saw her father enter the house. Soon Mr. Kuroda came out alone, putting on his coat. Mr. Kuroda got into his car and backed out down the driveway onto the highway. Next her father emerged, also alone, something in his arms (it was the picture, she realized), and, going over to the bathhouse woodpile, he threw the picture on the ground and picked up the axe. Smashing the picture, glass and all (she heard the explosion faintly), he reached over for the kerosene that was used to encourage the bath fire and poured it over the wreckage. I am dreaming, Rosie said to herself, I am dreaming, but her father, having made sure that his act of cremation was irrevocable, was even then returning to the fields.

Rosie ran past him and toward the house. What had become of her mother? She burst into the parlor and found her mother at the back window watching the dying fire. They watched together until there remained only a feeble smoke under the blazing sun. Her mother was very calm.

"Do you know why I married your father?" she said without turning.

"No," said Rosie. It was the most frightening question she had ever been   85
called upon to answer. Don't tell me now, she wanted to say, tell me tomorrow, tell me next week, don't tell me today. But she knew she would be told now, that the telling would combine with the other violence of the hot afternoon to level her life, her world to the very ground.

It was like a story out of the magazines illustrated in sepia, which she had consumed so greedily for a period until the information had somehow reached her that those wretchedly unhappy autobiographies, offered to her as the testi-monials of living men and women, were largely inventions: Her mother, at nine-teen, had come to America and married her father as an alternative to suicide.

At eighteen she had been in love with the first son of one of the well-to-do families in her village. The two had met whenever and wherever they could, secretly, because it would not have done for his family to see him favor her—her father had no money; he was a drunkard and a gambler besides. She had learned she was with child; an excellent match had already been arranged for her lover. Despised by her family, she had given premature birth to a stillborn son, who would be seventeen now. Her family did not turn her out, but she could no longer project herself in any direction without refreshing in them the memory of her indiscretion. She wrote to Aunt Taka, her favorite sister in America, threatening to kill herself if Aunt Taka would not send for her. Aunt Taka hastily arranged a marriage with a young man of whom she knew, but lately arrived from Japan, a young man of simple mind, it was said, but of kindly heart. The young man was never told why his unseen betrothed was so eager to hasten the day of meeting.

The story was told perfectly, with neither groping for words nor untoward passion. It was as though her mother had memorized it by heart, reciting it to herself so many times over that its nagging vileness had long since gone.

"I had a brother then?" Rosie asked, for this was what seemed to matter now; she would think about the other later, she assured herself, pushing back the illumination which threatened all that darkness that had hitherto been merely mysterious or even glamorous. "A half-brother?"

"Yes."

90

"I would have liked a brother," she said.

Suddenly, her mother knelt on the floor and took her by the wrists. "Rosie," she said urgently, "Promise me you will never marry!" Shocked more by the request than the revelation, Rosie stared at her mother's face. Jesus, Jesus, she called silently, not certain whether she was invoking the help of the son of the Carrascos or of God, until there returned sweetly the memory of Jesus' hand, how it had touched her and where. Still her mother waited for an answer, hold-ing her wrists so tightly that her hands were going numb. She tried to pull free. Promise, her mother whispered fiercely, promise. Yes, yes, I promise, Rosie said. But for an instant she turned away, and her mother, hearing the familiar glib agreement, released her. Oh, you, you, you, her eyes and twisted mouth said, you fool. Rosie, covering her face, began at last to cry, and the embrace and con-soling hand came much later than she expected.

(1949)

Questions for Discussion and Writing

1. What conflicts between the mother and teenaged daughter are set up in the opening section of the story? Why are these conflicts and Rosie's way of dealing with them important to the story as a whole?

2. How does Ume's talent affect her husband? How does he express his feelings about it? How does he finally end her career as a poet?

3. What does Rosie feel for Jesus? List the various feelings she has and how she deals with them. Why are these feelings important when Tome finally tells Rosie the story of her marriage?

4. What are the connections between the episodes in the story about Rosie and those about her mother?

5. Why does Rosie find that "the embrace and consoling hand came much later than she expected" at the end of the story?

Making Connections

Compare the sexual response and involvement of Rosie in "Seventeen Syllables" with that of China in T. Coraghessan Boyle's "The Love of My Life" (page 312). What saves Rosie from China's fate?

◇◇◇◇◇◇◇◇◇◇◇◇◇◇◇◇◇◇◇◇◇

Rosario Morales 1930–

Although raised in New York City, Rosario Morales spent her adult life in Puerto Rico, where she loved the beauty of the lush island but missed the freedom enjoyed by women in the mainland. She became a "Puerto Rican, Jewish, radical feminist" and complained that on the island there were "too many people nagging, harping, pushing you into line, into feminine behavior, into caution and fear, provocativeness and manipulativeness, full of predatory males who punish you for being female." Her credo is, "I am what I am. Take it or leave me alone."

The Day It Happened

The day it happened I was washing my hair. I had long hair then that went halfway down my back and I washed it once a week and rinsed it with lemon juice "to bring out the blond highlights" Mami said. Then I'd set it into pincurls that took an age to do because there was so much to wind around and around my finger. But if Mami was in a good mood, and she looked like she might be that day, she curled the back for me. I usually did all this on Saturday so I would look great for church on Sunday, and for a date Saturday night if I ever had one. ¡Ojala!

Naturally the moment when it all began I was rinsing the big soapy mess. Nosy Maria was leaning out the window drying her dark red fingernails in the breeze when Josie stepped out of our apartment house doorway with a suitcase in her hand. Maria sucked in her breath so hard the sound brought my mother, who took one look, crossed herself, or so Maria says, and started praying. Someone needed to pray for Josie. It was five o'clock and Ramón was due home any minute.

I wouldn't have known anything about any of this if Olga next door hadn't rung our doorbell and banged on the door just when Mami was too deep in prayer to hear and Maria was leaning out over the sill with her eyes bugging out. I cursed, very quietly of course, because if Mami or Papi heard me curse I'd get a slap across my face. I wrapped my sopping head in a towel and opened the door to Olga's "Oh my goodness, oh my dear. Oh honey, did you see? Look out the window this minute. I wouldn't have believed it if I hadn't seen it with my own two eyes. That poor little kid. I hate to think…" and on and on as we crossed the apartment to look out on the street.

Little Mikey from across the way was telling the rest of the kids how he'd found a taxi for Josie the minute he'd hit Southern Boulevard and how he'd hailed it and how the driver had let him ride back to Brook Street in the front seat—even though all of them had seen him arrive and step out with his back stiff with pride. Meantime Josie was back down in the street with Doña Toña from across the hall and Betty Murphy upstairs right behind her, all of them loaded down with two lamps, a typewriter and a big box of books. Doña Toña was muttering something we couldn't hear up here on the second story but it was probably either the prayer I was hearing on my right or the "…hurry oh hurry oh God he'll be here any minute are you mad girl, are you mad" that came at me from the left.

It was hard not to be scared as well as glad that Josie was packing up and leaving Ramón. They'd been married only six months but already they were in a pattern, like the Garcias down the block who did everything the same way on the same day, all year. Ramón worked late till seven every week day and five on Saturday. When he arrived he expected a good dinner to be on the table at the right temperature exactly five minutes after he walked in the door. He yelled if she didn't get it right and sometimes even if she did.

Saturday evening they went out to a party or the bar down the avenue, both of them dressed up and Ramón looking proud and cheerful for a change. Josie always looked great. She's so cute. Small and plump with long lashes on her dark eyes and, get this, naturally curly hair. She smiled a lot when she was happy but she hadn't been happy much lately and not at all since she got pregnant. I wasn't supposed to know this. God, I was almost thirteen! But Maria, who was fourteen and a half and thought she was twenty, listened in on conversations in the living room by opening the door a sliver and she told me all about it.

Saturday nights there was sure to be a fight. Either it was that Josie was "no fun, a man can't be a man with such a wet rag around." Or it was that Josie was "a tramp. Why else was that guy staring at you, eating you up with his eyes?" The first time it happened, soon after they moved in, it woke me up from a deep sleep and I was so scared I crept into Maria's bed. I'd never heard such yelling in my life. When my parents fight it's during the day and in angry whispers. It sounds like a snake convention in my parents' bedroom. That's bad enough. Maria and I get real nervous and nothing's right until they make up and talk in normal voices again. But Ramón could be heard right through the floor at two in the morning. And then he took to throwing things and then he started hitting her. The first time that happened Josie didn't go to morning mass at St. Francis and Mami went down to her apartment to see if she was sick or something. Josie came to the door with a big bruise on her face. After that Mami went to fetch her every Sunday and stayed with her if she was too ashamed to go to church.

After she found out she was pregnant Josie had talked it over with Doña Toña and Doña Toña had talked it over with Mami and by and by we all knew she was scared he would hurt the little baby growing inside of her and worried about the child growing up with Ramón for a father. He expected too much of everyone and little kids hurt so when a parent thinks whatever they do is all wrong. Ha! Tell that to Mami and Papi, will you.

I don't think there was anyone in the neighborhood on Ramón's side, not even Joe who liked to bully his wife and daughters but didn't realize he did or

Tito who talked all the time about "wearing the pants in this family." Ramón was too much, even for them. Josie was so clearly a fine person, a quiet home-body, a sweetypie. Ramón was out of his mind, that's what most of us thought. I mean you had to be to be so regularly mean to a person who adored you. And she did, at least at first. You could see it in the way she looked at him, boasted about his strength, his good job, his brains. The way she excused his temper. "He can't help himself. He doesn't mean it."

And now she was packed up and sitting in the taxi. Waiting for him to come home, I guess. That was too much for Mami and she scooted out the door with Olga, Maria, Papi, no less, and me right behind her with that soaked blue towel wrapped sloppily around my head. "Ai Mamita! Jesus, Maria y José. Jesus Maria y José," came faintly up the stairs in the front of the hurrying line. I knew Mami and I knew she meant to stand in front of Josie to protect her from that bully and, sure as shooting, Papi was going to protect Mami who was going so fast in her house slip-pers she almost fell down except that Olga gripped her hard and kept her upright.

When we streamed out the door into the small crowd that had gathered by now it was to see Ramón coming down the street with a sour look on his face. He looked up once or twice but mostly just stared at his feet as he strode up the block. He swept past us and almost into the house the way he did when he came home weary from the shipyard and the long ride home. He would have missed seeing Josie for sure, as I was praying he would, except that she called to him.

"Ramón," she said in her soft voice, stepping out of the taxi. "Ramón." He looked up and around then, took in the crowd, the taxi with a tall lamp lying on the back seat and Josie in her good suit. He stood looking at all this and especially at Josie for a long time. When he spoke it was only to Josie, as if we weren't there at all. He had to clear his throat to say "Josie?"

I was totally surprised and confused. He sounded so small, you know. So uncertain. It was Josie looked tall now and hard. If I hadn't known what I knew I would've said Josie was the bully in the family. She looked him straight in the eye and said stiffly, as if they were lines someone had given her to memorize, "I warned you. I said I would leave if you ever hit me again. I am not safe with you. Our child is not safe with you. I'm going now. I left arroz con pollo on the stove and the electric bill on the table." He didn't answer so she turned to hug Doña Toña and Mami before sitting herself back down. It was then that Ramón acted. Before I could blink he'd hurled himself at her, thrown himself on his knees and gripped her around her stockinged legs. "No! No te vayas. Tu no comprendes. Eres muy joven para comprender. Tu no puedes dejarme asi. Estamos casados para la vida. Te amo para siempre, para siempre. Josita, mi amor, no te vayas. Si te vas me mato. Te lo juro. No te puedes ir. No te puedes ir…" and on and on in a hoarse voice while Josie stood there frozen, fear on her face. There was no sound but Maria whispering occasional translations into Olga's impatient ear "Don't go." "You're too young to understand." "We're married for life." "I'll love you always." "I'll kill myself, I swear it."

It went on forever, Josie standing there, Ramón kneeling, all of us listening, tears running down my face, Josie's face, Mami's face. It was Olga who ended it, who walked up to Ramón, knelt down beside him, put an arm around him, and started talking, telling him Josie was a mother now and had to think about what was best for her baby, that it was his baby too, that he had to let her go now so she could bear a baby healthy in body and soul, that she knew he loved Josie, that his love would let him do what was best for them all. He was crying now, arguing with her while he slowly let go while he said he never could let her go, that she was his whole life, that he would die without her, while Josie kissed Toña quickly on the cheek and climbed in next to the taxi driver who sat there looking the way I probably looked, dazed, like he'd stumbled into a movie screen and couldn't get out. She had to tell him to drive off.

(1992)

Questions for Discussion and Writing

1. Why do Josie's neighbors and even her family treat her beatings as a drama to be observed rather than as an outrage that must be stopped?
2. Why is even Josie herself embarrassed by the beatings? Do you think she should be? What is her mother's attitude toward the abuse?
3. Can you make the argument that Josie would never have found the stamina to leave Ramón if she had not discovered she was pregnant? Support your claim with evidence from the story.
4. How would you describe the remarkable change that Ramón undergoes? Can you reconcile his machismo swaggering in the first part of the story with his contrite weeping at the end?
5. What do you think Morales's point is in telling this story? In other words, can you state her theme?

Making Connections

Compare the strong Elisa Allen in Steinbeck's "The Chrysanthemums" (page 375) with the weak wife in "The Day It Happened." How does each character fare at the end of her story?

◇◇◇◇◇◇◇◇◇◇◇◇◇◇◇◇◇◇◇◇

Raymond Carver 1938–1988

Raymond Carver grew up poor in Yakima, Washington. Married at nineteen and a father of two by twenty, he moved to California, worked nights, attended college, divorced, and, as he put it, "took up drinking as a serious pursuit." At age thirty-nine, though, he gave up alcohol and observed, "In this second life, this post-drinking life, I still retain a certain sense of pessimism." But he did not give up smoking, declaring himself "a cigarette with a body attached to it." Two years before dying of lung cancer at age fifty, he and his partner, the poet Tess Gallagher, were married in a Reno chapel in a ceremony he described as a "high tacky affair."

What We Talk About When We Talk About Love

My friend Mel McGinnis was talking. Mel McGinnis is a cardiologist, and sometimes that gives him the right.

The four of us were sitting around his kitchen table drinking gin. Sunlight filled the kitchen from the big window behind the sink. There were Mel and me and his second wife, Teresa—Terri, we called her—and my wife, Laura. We lived in Albuquerque then. But we were all from somewhere else.

There was an ice bucket on the table. The gin and the tonic water kept going around, and we somehow got on the subject of love. Mel thought real love was nothing less than spiritual love. He said he'd spent five years in a seminary before quitting to go to medical school. He said he still looked back on those years in the seminary as the most important years in his life.

Terri said the man she lived with before she lived with Mel loved her so much he tried to kill her. Then Terri said, "He beat me up one night. He dragged me around the living room by my ankles. He kept saying, 'I love you, I love you, you bitch.' He went on dragging me around the living room. My head kept knocking on things." Terri looked around the table. "What do you do with love like that?"

She was a bone-thin woman with a pretty face, dark eyes, and brown hair that   5
hung down her back. She liked necklaces made of turquoise, and long pendant earrings.

"My God, don't be silly. That's not love, and you know it," Mel said. "I don't know what you'd call it, but I sure know you wouldn't call it love."

"Say what you want to, but I know it was," Terri said. "It may sound crazy to you, but it's true just the same. People are different, Mel. Sure, sometimes he may have acted crazy. Okay. But he loved me. In his own way maybe, but he loved me. There was love there, Mel. Don't say there wasn't."

Mel let out his breath. He held his glass and turned to Laura and me. "The man threatened to kill me," Mel said. He finished his drink and reached for the gin bottle. "Terri's a romantic. Terri's of the kick-me-so-I'll-know-you-love-me school. Terri, hon, don't look that way." Mel reached across the table and touched Terri's cheek with his fingers. He grinned at her.

"Now he wants to make up," Terri said.

"Make up what?" Mel said. "What is there to make up? I know what I know.   10
That's all."

"How'd we get started on this subject, anyway?" Terri said. She raised her glass and drank from it. "Mel always has love on his mind," she said. "Don't you, honey?" She smiled, and I thought that was the last of it.

"I just wouldn't call Ed's behavior love. That's all I'm saying, honey," Mel said. "What about you guys?" Mel said to Laura and me. "Does that sound like love to you?"

"I'm the wrong person to ask," I said. "I didn't even know the man. I've only heard his name mentioned in passing. I wouldn't know. You'd have to know the particulars. But I think what you're saying is that love is an absolute."

Mel said, "The kind of love I'm talking about is. The kind of love I'm talking about, you don't try to kill people."

Laura said, "I don't know anything about Ed, or anything about the situation.   15
But who can judge anyone else's situation?"

I touched the back of Laura's hand. She gave me a quick smile. I picked up Laura's hand. It was warm, the nails polished, perfectly manicured. I encircled the broad wrist with my fingers, and I held her.

"When I left, he drank rat poison," Terri said. She clasped her arms with her hands. "They took him to the hospital in Santa Fe. That's where we lived then, about ten miles out. They saved his life. But his gums went crazy from it. I mean they pulled away from his teeth. After that, his teeth stood out like fangs. My God," Terri said. She waited a minute, then let go of her arms and picked up her glass.

"What people won't do!" Laura said.

"He's out of the action now," Mel said. "He's dead."

Mel handed me the saucer of limes. I took a section, squeezed it over my   20
drink, and stirred the ice cubes with my finger.

"It gets worse," Terri said. "He shot himself in the mouth. But he bungled that too. Poor Ed," she said. Terri shook her head.

"Poor Ed nothing," Mel said. "He was dangerous."

Mel was forty-five years old. He was tall and rangy with curly soft hair. His face and arms were brown from the tennis he played. When he was sober, his gestures, all his movements, were precise, very careful.

"He did love me though, Mel. Grant me that," Terri said. "That's all I'm asking. He didn't love me the way you love me. I'm not saying that. But he loved me. You can grant me that, can't you?"

"What do you mean, he bungled it?" I said.   25

Laura leaned forward with her glass. She put her elbows on the table and held her glass in both hands. She glanced from Mel to Terri and waited with a look of bewilderment on her open face, as if amazed that such things happened to people you were friendly with.

"How'd he bungle it when he killed himself?" I said.

"I'll tell you what happened," Mel said. "He took this twenty-two pistol he'd bought to threaten Terri and me with. Oh, I'm serious, the man was always threatening. You should have seen the way we lived in those days. Like fugitives. I even bought a gun myself. Can you belive it? A guy like me? But I did. I bought one for self-defense and carried it in the glove compartment. Sometimes I'd have to leave the apartment in the middle of the night. To go to the hospital, you know? Terri and I weren't married then, and my first wife had the house and kids, the dog, everything, and Terri and I were living in this apartment here. Sometimes, as I say, I'd get a call in the middle of the night and have to go in to the hospital at two or three in the morning. It'd be dark out there in the parking lot, and I'd break into a sweat before I could even get to my car. I never knew if he was going to come up out of the shrubbery or from behind a car and start shooting. I mean, the man was crazy. He was capable of wiring a bomb, anything. He used to call my service at all hours and say he needed to talk to the doctor, and when I'd return the call, he'd say, 'Son of a bitch, your days are numbered.' Little things like that. It was scary, I'm telling you."

"I still feel sorry for him," Terri said.

"It sounds like a nightmare," Laura said. "But what exactly happened after he   30
shot himself?"

Laura is a legal secretary. We'd met in a professional capacity. Before we knew it, it was a courtship. She's thirty-five, three years younger than I am. In addition to being in love, we like each other and enjoy one another's company. She's easy to be with.

"What happened?" Laura said.

Mel said, "He shot himself in the mouth in his room. Someone heard the shot and told the manager. They came in with a passkey, saw what had happened, and called an ambulance. I happened to be there when they brought him in, alive but past recall. The man lived for three days. His head swelled up to twice the size of a normal head. I'd never seen anything like it, and I hope I never do again. Terri wanted to go in and sit with him when she found out about it. We had a fight over it. I didn't think she should see him like that. I didn't think she should see him, and I still don't."

"Who won the fight?" Laura said.

"I was in the room with him when he died," Terri said. "He never came up   35
out of it. But I sat with him. He didn't have anyone else."

"He was dangerous," Mel said. "If you call that love, you can have it."

"It was love," Terri said. "Sure, it's abnormal in most people's eyes. But he was willing to die for it. He did die for it."

"I sure as hell wouldn't call it love," Mel said. "I mean, no one knows what he did it for. I've seen a lot of suicides, and I couldn't say anyone ever knew what they did it for."

Mel put his hands behind his neck and tilted his chair back. "I'm not interested in that kind of love," he said. "If that's love, you can have it."

Terri said, "We were afraid. Mel even made a will out and wrote to his   40
brother in California who used to be a Green Beret. Mel told him who to look for if something happened to him."

Terri drank from her glass. She said, "But Mel's right—we lived like fugitives. We were afraid. Mel was, weren't you, honey? I even called the police at one point, but they were no help. They said they couldn't do anything until Ed actually did something. Isn't that a laugh?" Terri said.

She poured the last of the gin into her glass and waggled the bottle. Mel got up from the table and went to the cupboard. He took down another bottle.

"Well, Nick and I know what love is," Laura said. "For us, I mean," Laura said. She bumped my knee with her knee. "You're supposed to say something now," Laura said, and turned her smile on me.

For an answer, I took Laura's hand and raised it to my lips. I made a big production out of kissing her hand. Everyone was amused.

"We're lucky," I said.   45

"You guys," Terri said. "Stop that now. You're making me sick. You're still on the honeymoon, for God's sake. You're still gaga, for crying out loud. Just wait. How long have you been together now? How long has it been? A year? Longer than a year?"

"Going on a year and a half," Laura said, flushed and smiling.

"Oh, now," Terri said. "Wait awhile."

She held her drink and gazed at Laura.

"I'm only kidding," Terri said.   50

Mel opened the gin and went around the table with the bottle.

"Here, you guys," he said. "Let's have a toast. I want to propose a toast. A toast to love. To true love," Mel said.

We touched glasses.

"To love," we said.

Outside in the backyard, one of the dogs began to bark. The leaves of the   55
aspen that leaned past the window ticked against the glass. The afternoon sun was like a presence in this room, the spacious light of ease and generosity. We could have been anywhere, somewhere enchanted. We raised our glasses

again and grinned at each other like children who had agreed on something forbidden.

"I'll tell you what real love is," Mel said. "I mean, I'll give you a good example. And then you can draw your own conclusions." He poured more gin into his glass. He added an ice cube and a sliver of lime. We waited and sipped our drinks. Laura and I touched knees again. I put a hand on her warm thigh and left it there.

"What do any of us really know about love?" Mel said. "It seems to me we're just beginners at love. We say we love each other and we do, I don't doubt it. I love Terri and Terri loves me, and you guys love each other too. You know the kind of love I'm talking about now. Physical love, that impulse that drives you to someone special, as well as love of the other person's being, his or her essence, as it were. Carnal love and, well, call it sentimental love, the day-to-day caring about the other person. But sometimes I have a hard time accounting for the fact that I must have loved my first wife too. But I did, I know I did. So I suppose I am like Terri in that regard. Terri and Ed." He thought about it and then he went on. "There was a time when I thought I loved my first wife more than life itself. But now I hate her guts. I do. How do you explain that? What happened to that love? What happened to it, is what I'd like to know. I wish someone could tell me. Then there's Ed. Okay, we're back to Ed. He loves Terri so much he tries to kill her and he winds up killing himself." Mel stopped talking and swallowed from his glass. "You guys have been together eighteen months and you love each other. It shows all over you. You glow with it. But you both loved other people before you met each other. You've both been married before, just like us. And you probably loved other people before that too, even. Terri and I have been together five years, been married for four. And the terrible thing, the terrible thing is, but the good thing too, the saving grace, you might say, is that if something happened to one of us—excuse me for saying this—but if something happened to one of us tomorrow, I think the other one, the other person, would grieve for a while, you know, but then the surviving party would go out and love again, have someone else soon enough. All this, all of this love we're talking about, it would just be a memory. Maybe not even a memory. Am I wrong? Am I way off base? Because I want you to set me straight if you think I'm wrong. I want to know. I mean, I don't know anything, and I'm the first one to admit it."

"Mel, for God's sake," Terri said. She reached out and took hold of his wrist. "Are you getting drunk? Honey? Are you drunk?"

"Honey, I'm just talking," Mel said. "All right? I don't have to be drunk to say what I think. I mean, we're all just talking, right?" Mel said. He fixed his eyes on her.

"Sweetie, I'm not criticizing," Terri said.   60

She picked up her glass.

"I'm not on call today," Mel said. "Let me remind you of that. I am not on call," he said.

"Mel, we love you," Laura said.

Mel looked at Laura. He looked at her as if he could not place her, as if she was not the woman she was.

"Love you too, Laura," Mel said. "And you, Nick, love you too. You know   65 something?" Mel said. "You guys are our pals," Mel said.

He picked up his glass.

Mel said, "I was going to tell you about something. I mean, I was going to prove a point. You see, this happened a few months ago, but it's still going on right now, and it ought to make us feel ashamed when we talk like we know what we're talking about when we talk about love."

"Come on now," Terri said. "Don't talk like you're drunk if you're not drunk."

"Just shut up for once in your life," Mel said very quietly. "Will you do me a favor and do that for a minute? So as I was saying, there's this old couple who had this car wreck out on the interstate. A kid hit them and they were all torn to shit and nobody was giving them much chance to pull through."

Terri looked at us and then back at Mel. She seemed anxious, or maybe that's   70
too strong a word.

Mel was handing the bottle around the table.

"I was on call that night," Mel said. "It was May or maybe it was June. Terri and I had just sat down to dinner when the hospital called. There'd been this thing out on the interstate. Drunk kid, teenager, plowed his dad's pickup into this camper with this old couple in it. They were up in their mid-seventies, that couple. The kid—eighteen, nineteen, something—he was DOA. Taken the steering wheel through his sternum. The old couple, they were alive, you understand. I mean, just barely. But they had everything. Multiple fractures, internal injuries, hemorrhaging, contusions, lacerations, the works, and they each of them had themselves concussions. They were in a bad way, believe me. And, of course, their age was two strikes against them. I'd say she was worse off than he was. Ruptured spleen along with everything else. Both kneecaps broken. But they'd been wearing their seatbelts and, God knows, that's what saved them for the time being."

"Folks, this is an advertisement for the National Safety Council," Terri said. "This is your spokesman, Dr. Melvin R. McGinnis, talking." Terri laughed. "Mel," she said, "sometimes you're just too much. But I love you, hon," she said.

"Honey, I love you," Mel said.

He leaned across the table. Terri met him halfway. They kissed.   75

"Terri's right," Mel said as he settled himself again. "Get those seatbelts on. But seriously, they were in some shape, those oldsters. By the time I got down there, the kid was dead, as I said. He was off in a corner, laid out on a gurney. I took one look at the old couple and told the ER nurse to get me a neurologist and an orthopedic man and a couple of surgeons down there right away."

He drank from his glass. "I'll try to keep this short," he said. "So we took the two of them up to the OR and worked like fuck on them most of the night. They had these incredible reserves, those two. You see that once in a while. So we did everything that could be done, and toward morning we're giving them a fifty-fifty chance, maybe less than that for her. So here they are, still alive the next morning. So, okay, we move them into the ICU, which is where they both kept plugging away at it for two weeks, hitting it better and better on all the scopes. So we transfer them out to their own room."

Mel stopped talking. "Here," he said, "let's drink this cheapo gin the hell up. Then we're going to dinner, right? Terri and I know a new place. That's where we'll go, to this new place we know about. But we're not going until we finish up this cut-rate, lousy gin."

Terri said, "We haven't actually eaten there yet. But it looks good. From the outside, you know."

"I like food," Mel said. "If I had it to do all over again, I'd be a chef, you   80
know? Right, Terri?" Mel said.

He laughed. He fingered the ice in his glass.

"Terri knows," he said. "Terri can tell you. But let me say this. If I could come
back again in a different life, a different time and all, you know what? I'd like
to come back as a knight. You were pretty safe wearing all that armor. It was all
right being a knight until gunpowder and muskets and pistols came along."

"Mel would like to ride a horse and carry a lance," Terri said.

"Carry a woman's scarf with you everywhere," Laura said.

"Or just a woman," Mel said.   85

"Shame on you," Laura said.

Terri said, "Suppose you came back as a serf. The serfs didn't have it so good
in those days," Terri said.

"The serfs never had it good," Mel said. "But I guess even the knights were
vessels to someone. Isn't that the way it worked? But then everyone is always
a vessel to someone. Isn't that right? Terri? But what I liked about knights,
besides their ladies, was that they had that suit of armor, you know, and they
couldn't get hurt very easy. No cars in those days, you know? No drunk teenagers to tear into your ass."

"Vassals," Terri said.

"What?" Mel said.   90

"Vassals," Terri said. "They were called vassals, not vessels."

"Vassals, vessels," Mel said, "what the fuck's the difference? You knew what
I meant anyway. All right," Mel said. "So I'm not educated. I learned my stuff.
I'm a heart surgeon, sure, but I'm just a mechanic. I go in and fuck around and I
fix things. Shit," Mel said.

"Modesty doesn't become you," Terri said.

"He's just a humble sawbones," I said. "But sometimes they suffocated in all
that armor, Mel. They'd even have heart attacks if it got too hot and they were
too tired and worn out. I read somewhere that they'd fall off their horses and
not be able to get up because they were too tired to stand with all that armor on
them. They got trampled by their own horses sometimes."

"That's terrible," Mel said. "That's a terrible thing, Nicky. I guess they'd just lay   95
there and wait until somebody came along and made a shish kebab out of them."

"Some other vessel," Terri said.

"That's right," Mel said. "Some vassal would come along and spear the bastard
in the name of love. Or whatever the fuck it was they fought over in those days."

"Same things we fight over these days," Terri said.

Laura said, "Nothing's changed."

The color was still high in Laura's cheeks. Her eyes were bright. She brought   100
her glass to her lips.

Mel poured himself another drink. He looked at the label closely as if studying a long row of numbers. Then he slowly put the bottle down on the table and
slowly reached for the tonic water.

"What about the old couple?" Laura said. "You didn't finish that story you
started."

Laura was having a hard time lighting her cigarette. Her matches kept
going out.

The sunshine inside the room was different now, changing, getting thinner. But the leaves outside the window were still shimmering, and I stared at the pattern they made on the panes and on the Formica counter. They weren't the same patterns, of course.

"What about the old couple?" I said.   105

"Older but wiser," Terri said.

Mel stared at her.

Terri said, "Go on with your story, hon. I was only kidding. Then what happened?"

"Terri, sometimes," Mel said.

"Please, Mel," Terri said. "Don't always be so serious, sweetie. Can't you take   110
a joke?"

"Where's the joke?" Mel said.

He held his glass and gazed steadily at his wife.

"What happened?" Laura said.

Mel fastened his eyes on Laura. He said, "Laura, if I didn't have Terri and if I didn't love her so much, and if Nick wasn't my best friend, I'd fall in love with you. I'd carry you off, honey," he said.

"Tell your story," Terri said. "Then we'll go to that new place, okay?"   115

"Okay," Mel said. "Where was I?" he said. He started at the table and then he began again.

"I dropped in to see each of them every day, sometimes twice a day if I was up doing other calls anyway. Casts and bandages, head to foot, the both of them. You know, you've seen it in the movies. That's just the way they looked, just like in the movies. Little eye-holes and nose-holes and mouth-holes. And she had to have her legs slung up on top of it. Well, the husband was very depressed for the longest while. Even after he found out that his wife was going to pull through, he was still very depressed. Not about the accident, though. I mean, the accident was one thing, but it wasn't everything. I'd get up to his mouth-hole, you know, and he'd say no, it wasn't the accident exactly but it was because he couldn't see her through his eye-holes. He said that was what was making him feel so bad. Can you imagine? I'm telling you, the man's heart was breaking because he couldn't turn his goddamn head and *see* his goddamn wife."

Mel looked around the table and shook his head at what he was going to say.

"I mean, it was killing the old fart just because he couldn't *look* at the fucking woman."

We all looked at Mel.   120

"Do you see what I'm saying?" he said.

Maybe we were a little drunk by then. I know it was hard keeping things in focus. The light was draining out of the room, going back through the window where it had come from. Yet nobody made a move to get up from the table to turn on the overhead light.

"Listen," Mel said. "Let's finish this fucking gin. There's about enough here for one shooter all around. Then let's go eat. Let's go to the new place."

"He's depressed," Terri said. "Mel, why don't you take a pill?"

Mel shook his head. "I've taken everything there is."   125

"We all need a pill now and then," I said.

"Some people are born needing them," Terri said.

She was using her finger to rub at something on the table. Then she stopped rubbing.

"I think I want to call my kids," Mel said. "Is that all right with everybody? I'll call my kids," he said.

Terri said, "What if Marjorie answers the phone? You guys, you've heard us 130
on the subject of Marjorie? Honey, you know you don't want to talk to Marjorie. It'll make you feel even worse."

"I don't want to talk to Marjorie," Mel said. "But I want to talk to my kids."

"There isn't a day goes by that Mel doesn't say he wishes she'd get married again. Or else die," Terri said. "For one thing," Terri said, "she's bankrupting us. Mel says it's just to spite him that she won't get married again. She has a boy-friend who lives with her and the kids, so Mel is supporting the boyfriend too."

"She's allergic to bees," Mel said. "If I'm not praying she'll get married again, I'm praying she'll get herself stung to death by a swarm of fucking bees."

"Shame on you," Laura said.

"Bzzzzzzz," Mel said, turning his fingers into bees and buzzing them at 135
Terri's throat. Then he let his hands drop all the way to his sides.

"She's vicious," Mel said. "Sometimes I think I'll go up there dressed like a bee-keeper. You know, that hat that's like a helmet with the plate that comes down over your face, the big gloves, and the padded coat? I'll knock on the door and let loose a hive of bees in the house. But first I'd make sure the kids were out, of course."

He crossed one leg over the other. It seemed to take him a lot of time to do it. Then he put both feet on the floor and leaned forward, elbows on the table, his chin cupped in his hands.

"Maybe I won't call the kids, after all. Maybe it isn't such a hot idea. Maybe we'll just go eat. How does that sound?"

"Sounds fine to me," I said. "Eat or not eat. Or keep drinking. I could head right on out into the sunset."

"What does that mean, honey?" Laura said. 140

"It just means what I said," I said. "It means I could just keep going. That's all it means."

"I could eat something myself," Laura said. "I don't think I've ever been so hungry in my life. Is there something to nibble on?"

"I'll put out some cheese and crackers," Terri said.

But Terri just sat there. She did not get up to get anything.

Mel turned his glass over. He spilled it out on the table. 145

"Gin's gone," Mel said.

Terri said, "Now what?"

I could hear my heart beating. I could hear everyone's heart. I could hear the human noise we sat there making, not one of us moving, not even when the room went dark.

(1981)

Questions for Discussion and Writing

1. What different definitions and descriptions of love come up during the con-versation? Do the characters ever get anywhere with the subject? Why or why not?

2. What distinguishes this story from other stories you have read in this course? Do you think you could recognize another Raymond Carver story? How?

3. When the narrator says of himself and Laura, "In addition to being in love, we like each other and enjoy one another's company," what is he saying about his definition of love?

4. Reread the first two paragraphs of the story. What expository information do you get in these few sentences?

5. Is this story optimistic or pessimistic about love? Write an essay arguing your answer to this question.

Making Connections

What type of love is evident at the beginning of the relationship between China and Jeremy in Boyle's "The Love of My Life" (page 312)? How about the love described in Donne's poem "A Valediction: Forbidding Mourning" (page 491) or Shakespeare's "Let Me Not to the Marriage of True Minds" (page 487)? Do these kinds of love fit any of the categories described in Carver's story?

T. Coraghessan Boyle   1948–

T. Coraghessan Boyle, born Thomas John Boyle, changed his middle name at age seventeen and explains how to pronounce it: "It's Cor-AG-hessan, accent on second syllable. As you may know, this is an old Gaelic term meaning 'Take two and call me in the morning.'" He was a radically alienated teenager but made it to college, where he "wandered into a creative writing class" and discovered that "writing was what I could do." He says now that hearing others reading or performing his stories "gives me—the disaffected, misanthropic non-player—a rush of pure joy and connection: somebody else is singing my song. I'm happy."

The Love of My Life

They wore each other like a pair of socks. He was at her house, she was at his. Everywhere they went—to the mall, to the game, to movies and shops and the classes that structured their days like a new kind of chronology—their fingers were entwined, their shoulders touching, their hips joined in the slow trium-phant sashay of love. He drove her car, slept on the couch in the family room at her parents' house, played tennis and watched football with her father on the big, thirty-six-inch TV in the kitchen. She went shopping with his mother and hers, a triumvirate of tastes, and she would have played tennis with his father, if it came to it, but his father was dead. "I love you," he told her, because he did, because there was no feeling like this, no triumph, no high—it was like being immortal and unconquerable, like floating. And a hundred times a day she said it, too: " I love you. I love you."

They were together at his house one night when the rain froze on the streets and sheathed the trees in glass. It was her idea to take a walk and feel it in their hair and on the glistening shoulders of their parkas, an other-worldly drumming of pellets flung down out of the troposphere, alien and familiar at the same time, and they glided the length of the front walk and watched the way the power lines bellied and swayed. He built a fire when they got back, while she towelled her hair and made hot chocolate laced with Jack Daniel's. They'd rented a pair of slasher movies for the ritualized comfort of them—"Teens have sex," he said, "and then they pay for it in body parts"—and the maniac had just climbed out of the heating vent, with a meat hook dangling from the recesses of his empty sleeve, when the phone rang.

It was his mother, calling from the hotel room in Boston where she was curled up—shacked up?—for the weekend with the man she'd been dating. He tried to picture her, but he couldn't. He even closed his eyes a minute, to concentrate, but there was nothing there. Was everything all right? she wanted to know. With the storm and all? No, it hadn't hit Boston yet, but she saw on the Weather Channel that it was on its way. Two seconds after he hung up—before she could even hit the Start button on the VCR—the phone rang again, and this time it was her mother. Her mother had been drinking. She was calling from the restaurant, and China could hear a clamor of voices in the background. "Just stay put," her mother shouted into the phone. "The streets are like a skating rink. Don't you even think of getting in that car."

Well, she wasn't thinking of it. She was thinking of having Jeremy to herself, all night, in the big bed in his mother's room. They'd been having sex ever since they started going together at the end of their junior year, but it was always sex in the car or sex on a blanket or the lawn, hurried sex, nothing like she wanted it to be. She kept thinking of the way it was in the movies, where the stars ambushed each other on beds the size of small planets and then did it again and again until they lay nestled in a heap of pillows and blankets, her head on his chest, his arm flung over her shoulder, the music fading away to individual notes plucked softly on a guitar and everything in the frame glowing as if it had been sprayed with liquid gold. That was how it was supposed to be. That was how it was going to be. At least for tonight.

She'd been wandering around the kitchen as she talked, dancing with the phone in an idle slow saraband, watching the frost sketch a design on the window over the sink, no sound but the soft hiss of the ice pellets on the roof, and now she pulled open the freezer door and extracted a pint box of ice cream. She was in her socks, socks so thick they were like slippers, and a pair of black leggings under an oversize sweater. Beneath her feet, the polished floorboards were as slick as the sidewalk outside, and she liked the feel of that, skating indoors in her big socks. "Uh-huh," she said into the phone. "Uh-huh. Yeah, we're watching a movie." She dug a finger into the ice cream and stuck it in her mouth.

"Come on," Jeremy called from the living room, where the maniac rippled menacingly over the Pause button. "You're going to miss the best part."

"O.K., Mom, O.K.," she said into the phone, parting words, and then she hung up. "You want ice cream?" she called, licking her finger.

Jeremy's voice came back at her, a voice in the middle range, with a congenital scratch in it, the voice of a nice guy, a very nice guy who could be the star of a TV show about nice guys: "What kind?" He had a pair of shoulders and pumped-up biceps, too, a smile that jumped from his lips to his eyes, and close-cropped hair that stood up straight off the crown of his head. And he was always singing—she loved that—his voice so true he could do any song, and there was no lyric he didn't know, even on the oldies station. She scooped ice cream and saw him in a scene from last summer, one hand draped casually over the wheel of his car, the radio throbbing, his voice raised in perfect synch with Billy Corgan's, and the night standing still at the end of a long dark street overhung with maples.

"Chocolate. Swiss-chocolate almond."

"O.K.," he said, and then he was wondering if there was any whipped cream,   10
or maybe hot fudge—he was sure his mother had a jar stashed away somewhere, *Look behind the mayonnaise on the top row*—and when she turned around he was standing in the doorway.

She kissed him—they kissed whenever they met, no matter where or when, even if one of them had just stepped out of the room, because that was love, that was the way love was—and then they took two bowls of ice cream into the living room and, with a flick of the remote, set the maniac back in motion.

It was an early spring that year, the world gone green overnight, the thermometer twice hitting the low eighties in the first week of March. Teachers were holding sessions outside. The whole school, even the halls and the cafeteria, smelled of fresh-mowed grass and the unfolding blossoms of the fruit trees in the development across the street, and students—especially seniors—were cutting class to go out to the quarry or the reservoir or to just drive the backstreets with the sunroof and the windows open wide. But not China. She was hitting the books, studying late, putting everything in its place like pegs in a board, even love, even that. Jeremy didn't get it. "Look, you've already been accepted at your first-choice school, you're going to wind up in the top ten G.P.A.-wise, and you've got four years of tests and term papers ahead of you, and grad school after that. You'll only be a high-school senior once in your life. Relax. Enjoy it. Or at least *experience* it."

He'd been accepted at Brown, his father's alma mater, and his own G.P.A. would put him in the top ten percent of their graduating class, and he was content with that, skating through his final semester, no math, no science, taking art and music, the things he'd always wanted to take but never had time for—and Lit., of course, A.P. History, and Spanish 5. "*Tú eres el amor de mi vida,*" he would tell her when they met at her locker or at lunch or when he picked her up for a movie on Saturday nights.

"*Y tú también,*" she would say, "or is it '*yo también*'?"—French was her language. "But I keep telling you it really matters to me, because I know I'll never catch Margery Yu or Christian Davenport, I mean they're a lock for val and salut, but it'll kill me if people like Kerry Sharp or Jalapy Seegrand finish ahead of me—you should know that, you of all people—"

It amazed him that she actually brought her books along when they went   15
backpacking over spring break. They'd planned the trip all winter and through the long wind tunnel that was February, packing away freeze-dried entrées, PowerBars, Gore-Tex windbreakers, and matching sweatshirts, weighing each item on a handheld scale with a dangling hook at the bottom of it. They were going up into the Catskills, to a lake he'd found on a map, and they were going to be together, without interruption, without telephones, automobiles, parents, teachers, friends, relatives, and pets, for five full days. They were going to cook over an open fire, they were going to read to each other and burrow into the double sleeping bag with the connubial zipper up the seam he'd found in his mother's closet, a relic of her own time in the lap of nature. It smelled of her,

of his mother, a vague scent of her perfume that had lingered there dormant all these years, and maybe there was the faintest whiff of his father, too, though his father had been gone so long he didn't even remember what he looked like, let alone what he might have smelled like. Five days. And it wasn't going to rain, not a drop. He didn't even bring his fishing rod, and that was love.

When the last bell rang down the curtain on Honors Math, Jeremy was waiting at the curb in his mother's Volvo station wagon, grinning up at China through the windshield while the rest of the school swept past with no thought for anything but release. There were shouts and curses, T-shirts in motion, slashing legs, horns bleating from the seniors' lot, the school buses lined up like armored vehicles awaiting the invasion—chaos, sweet chaos—and she stood there a moment to savor it. "Your mother's car?" she said, slipping in beside him and laying both arms over his shoulders to pull him to her for a kiss. He'd brought her jeans and hiking boots along, and she was going to change as they drove, no need to go home, no more circumvention and delay, a stop at McDonald's, maybe, or Burger King, and then it was the sun and the wind and the moon and the stars. Five days. Five whole days.

"Yeah," he said, in answer to her question, "my mother said she didn't want to have to worry about us breaking down in the middle of nowhere—"

"So she's got your car? She's going to sell real estate in your car?"

He just shrugged and smiled. "Free at last," he said, pitching his voice down low till it was exactly like Martin Luther King's. "Thank God Almighty, we are free at last."

It was dark by the time they got to the trailhead, and they wound up camp- 20 ing just off the road in a rocky tumble of brush, no place on earth less likely or less comfortable, but they were together, and they held each other through the damp whispering hours of the night and hardly slept at all. They made the lake by noon the next day, the trees just coming into leaf, the air sweet with the smell of the sun in the pines. She insisted on setting up the tent, just in case—it could rain, you never knew—but all he wanted to do was stretch out on a gray neoprene pad and feel the sun on his face. Eventually, they both fell asleep in the sun, and when they woke they made love right there, beneath the trees, and with the wide blue expanse of the lake giving back the blue of the sky. For dinner, it was étouffée and rice, out of the foil pouch, washed down with hot chocolate and a few squirts of red wine from Jeremy's bota bag.

The next day, the whole day through, they didn't bother with clothes at all. They couldn't swim, of course—the lake was too cold for that—but they could bask and explore and feel the breeze out of the south on their bare legs and the places where no breeze had touched before. She would remember that always, the feel of that, the intensity of her motions, the simple unrefined pleasure of living in the moment. Wood smoke. Duelling flashlights in the night. The look on Jeremy's face when he presented her with the bag of finger-size crayfish he'd spent all morning collecting.

What else? The rain, of course. It came midway through the third day, clouds the color of iron filings, the lake hammered to iron, too, and the storm that crashed through the trees and beat at their tent with a thousand angry fists. They huddled in the sleeping bag, sharing the wine and a bag of trail mix, read-ing to each other from a book of Donne's love poems (she was writing a paper for Mrs. Masterson called "Ocular Imagery in the Poetry of John Donne") and the last third of a vampire novel that weighed eighteen-point-one ounces.

And the sex. They were careful, always careful—*I will never, never be like those breeders that bring their puffed-up squalling little red-faced babies to class*, she told him, and he agreed, got adamant about it, even, until it became a running theme in their relationship, the breeders overpopulating an overpopulated world and ruining their own lives in the process—but she had forgotten to pack her pills and he had only two condoms with him, and it wasn't as if there were a drugstore around the corner.

In the fall—or the end of August, actually—they packed their cars separately and left for college, he to Providence and she to Binghamton. They were separated by three hundred miles, but there was the telephone, there was e-mail, and for the first month or so there were Saturday nights in a motel in Danbury, but that was a haul, it really was, and they both agreed that they should focus on their course work and cut back to every second or maybe third week. On the day they'd left—and no, she didn't want her parents driving her up there, she was an adult and she could take care of herself—Jeremy followed her as far as the Bear Mountain Bridge and they pulled off the road and held each other till the sun fell down into the trees. She had a poem for him, a Donne poem, the saddest thing he'd ever heard. It was something about the moon. *More than moon*, that was it, lovers parting and their tears swelling like an ocean till the girl—the woman, the female—had more power to raise the tides than the moon itself, or some such. More than moon. That's what he called her after that, because she was white and round and getting rounder, and it was no joke, and it was no term of endearment.

She was pregnant. Pregnant, they figured, since the camping trip, and it was   25
their secret, a new constant in their lives, a fact, an inescapable fact that never varied no matter how many home-pregnancy kits they went through. Baggy clothes, that was the key, all in black, cargo pants, flowing dresses, a jacket even in summer. They went to a store in the city where nobody knew them and she got a girdle, and then she went away to school in Binghamton and he went to Providence. "You've got to get rid of it," he told her in the motel room that had become a prison. "Go to a clinic," he told her for the hundredth time, and outside it was raining—or, no, it was clear and cold that night, a foretaste of winter. "I'll find the money—you know I will."

She wouldn't respond. Wouldn't even look at him. One of the *Star Wars* movies was on TV, great flat thundering planes of metal roaring across the screen, and she was just sitting there on the edge of the bed, her shoulders hunched and hair hanging limp. Someone slammed a car door—two doors in rapid succession—and a child's voice shouted, "Me! Me first!"

"China," he said. "Are you listening to me?"

"I can't," she murmured, and she was talking to her lap, to the bed, to the floor. "I'm scared. I'm so scared." There were footsteps in the room next door, ponderous and heavy, then the quick tattoo of the child's feet and a sudden thump against the wall. "I don't want anyone to know," she said.

He could have held her, could have squeezed in beside her and wrapped her in his arms, but something flared in him. He couldn't understand it. He just couldn't. "What are you thinking? Nobody'll know. He's a doctor, for Christ's sake, sworn to secrecy, the doctor-patient compact and all that. What are you going to do, keep it? Huh? Just show up for English 101 with a baby on your lap and say, 'Hi, I'm the Virgin Mary'?"

She was crying. He could see it in the way her shoulders suddenly crumpled 30
and now he could hear it, too, a soft nasal complaint that went right through
him. She lifted her face to him and held out her arms and he was there beside
her, rocking her back and forth in his arms. He could feel the heat of her face
against the hard fibre of his chest, a wetness there, fluids, her fluids. "I don't
want a doctor," she said.

And that colored everything, that simple negative: life in the dorms, roommates, bars, bullshit sessions, the smell of burning leaves and the way the light
fell across campus in great wide smoking bands just before dinner, the unofficial
skateboard club, films, lectures, pep rallies, football—none of it mattered. He
couldn't have a life. Couldn't be a freshman. Couldn't wake up in the morning and tumble into the slow steady current of the world. All he could think of
was her. Or not simply her—her and him, and what had come between them.
Because they argued now, they wrangled and fought and debated, and it was no
pleasure to see her in that motel room with the queen-size bed and the big color
TV and the soaps and shampoos they made off with as if they were treasure.
She was pig-headed, stubborn, irrational. She was spoiled, he could see that
now, spoiled by her parents and their standard of living and the socioeconomic
expectations of her class—of his class—and the promise of life as you like it, an
unscrolling vista of pleasure and acquistion. He loved her. He didn't want to
turn his back on her. He would be there for her no matter what, but why did she
have to be so stupid?

Big sweats, huge sweats, sweats that drowned and engulfed her, that was her
campus life, sweats and the dining hall. Her dorm mates didn't know her, and
so what if she was putting on weight? Everybody did. How could you shovel
down all those carbohydrates, all that sugar and grease and the puddings and
nachos and all the rest, without putting on ten or fifteen pounds the first semester alone? Half the girls in the dorm were waddling around like the Doughboy,
their faces bloated and blotched with acne, with crusting pimples and white-
heads fed on fat. So she was putting on weight. Big deal. "There's more of me to
love," she told her roommate, "and Jeremy likes it that way. And, really, he's the
only one that matters." She was careful to shower alone, in the early morning,
long before the light had begun to bump up against the windows.

On the night her water broke—it was mid-December, almost nine months,
as best as she could figure—it was raining. Raining hard. All week she'd been
having tense rasping sotto-voce debates with Jeremy on the phone—arguments,
fights—and she told him that she would die, creep out into the woods like
some animal and bleed to death, before she'd go to a hospital. "And what am I
supposed to do?" he demanded in a high childish whine, as if he were the one
who'd been knocked up, and she didn't want to hear it, she didn't.

"Do you love me?" she whispered. There was a long hesitation, a pause you
could have poured all the affirmation of the world into.

"Yes," he said finally, his voice so soft and reluctant it was like the last gasp of 35
a dying old man.

"Then you're going to have to rent the motel."

"And then what?"

"Then—I don't know." The door was open, her roommate framed there in
the hall, a burst of rock and roll coming at her like an assault. "I guess you'll
have to get a book or something."

By eight, the rain had turned to ice and every branch of every tree was coated with it, the highway littered with glistening black sticks, no moon, no stars, the tires sliding out from under her, and she felt heavy, big as a sumo wrestler, heavy and loose at the same time. She'd taken a towel from the dorm and put it under her, on the seat, but it was a mess, everything was a mess. She was cramping. Fidgeting with her hair. She tried the radio, but it was no help, nothing but songs she hated, singers that were worse. Twenty-two miles to Danbury and the first of the contractions came like a seizure, like a knife blade thrust into her spine. Her world narrowed to what the headlights would show her.

Jeremy was waiting for her at the door to the room, the light behind him a 40 pale rinse of nothing, no smile on his face, no human expression at all. They didn't kiss—they didn't even touch—and then she was on the bed, on her back, her face clenched like a fist. She heard the rattle of the sleet at the window, the murmur of TV: *I can't let you go like this,* a man protested, and she could picture him, angular and tall, a man in a hat and overcoat in a black-and-white world that might have been another planet, *I just can't.* "Are you—?" Jeremy's voice drifted into the mix, and then stalled. "Are you ready? I mean, is it time? Is it coming now?"

She said one thing then, one thing only, her voice as pinched and hollow as the sound of the wind in the gutters: "Get it out of me."

It took a moment, and then she could feel his hands fumbling with her sweats.

Later, hours later, when nothing had happened but pain, a parade of pain with drum majors and brass bands and penitents crawling on their hands and knees till the streets were stained with their blood, she cried out and cried out again. "It's like *Alien*," she gasped, "like that thing in *Alien* when it, it—"

"It's O.K.," he kept telling her, "it's O.K.," but his face betrayed him. He looked scared, looked as if he'd been drained of blood in some evil experiment in yet another movie, and a part of her wanted to be sorry for him, but another part, the part that was so commanding and fierce it overrode everything else, couldn't begin to be.

He was useless, and he knew it. He'd never been so purely sick at heart and 45 terrified in all his life, but he tried to be there for her, tried to do his best, and when the baby came out, the baby girl all slick with blood and mucus and the lumped white stuff that was like something spilled at the bottom of a garbage can, he was thinking of the ninth grade and how close he'd come to fainting while the teacher went around the room to prick their fingers one by one so they each could smear a drop of blood across a slide. He didn't faint now. But he was close to it, so close he could feel the room dodging away under his feet. And then her voice, the first intelligible thing she'd said in an hour: "Get rid of it. Just get rid of it."

Of the drive back to Binghamton he remembered nothing. Or practically nothing. They took towels from the motel and spread them across the seat of her car, he could remember that much...and the blood, how could he forget the blood? It soaked through her sweats and the towels and even the thick cotton bathmat and into the worn fabric of the seat itself. And it all came from inside her, all of it, tissue and mucus and the shining bright fluid, no end to it, as if she'd been turned inside out. He wanted to ask her about that, if that was normal, but she was asleep the minute she slid out from under his arm and dropped into the seat. If he focused, if he really concentrated, he could remember the way her head lolled against the doorframe while the engine whined and the car rocked and the slush threw a dark blanket over the windshield every time a truck shot past in the opposite direction. That and the exhaustion. He'd never been so tired, his head on a string, shoulders slumped, his arms like two pillars of concrete. And what if he'd nodded off? What if he'd gone into a skid and hurtled over an embankment into the filthy gray accumulation of the worst day of his life? What then?

She made it into the dorm under her own power, nobody even looked at her, and, no, she didn't need his help. "Call me," she whispered, and they kissed, her lips so cold it was like kissing a steak through the plastic wrap, and then he parked her car in the student lot and walked to the bus station. He made Danbury late that night, caught a ride out to the motel, and walked right through the "Do Not Disturb" sign on the door. Fifteen minutes. That was all it took. He bundled up everything, every trace, left the key in the box at the desk, and stood scraping the ice off the windshield of his car while the night opened up above him to a black glitter of sky. He never gave a thought to what lay discarded in the Dumpster out back, itself wrapped in plastic, so much meat, so much cold meat.

He was at the very pinnacle of his dream, the river dressed in its currents, the deep hole under the cutbank, and the fish like silver bullets swarming to his bait, when they woke him—when Rob woke him, Rob Greiner, his roommate, Rob with a face of crumbling stone and two policemen there at the door behind him and the roar of the dorm falling away to a whisper. And that was strange, policemen, a real anomaly in that setting, and at first—for the first thirty seconds, at least—he had no idea what they were doing there. Parking tickets? Could that be it? But then they asked him his name, just to confirm it, joined his hands together behind his back, and fitted two loops of naked metal over his wrists, and he began to understand. He saw McCaffrey and Tuttle from across the hall starting at him as if he were Jeffrey Dahmer or something, and the rest of them, all the rest, every head poking out of every door up and down the corridor, as the police led him away.

"What's all this about?" he kept saying, the cruiser nosing through the dark streets to the station house, the man at the wheel and the man beside him as incapable of speech as the seats or the wire mesh or the gleaming black dashboard that dragged them forward into the night. And then it was up the steps and into an explosion of light, more men in uniform, stand here, give me your hand, now the other one, and then the cage and the questions. Only then did he think of that thing in the garbage sack and the sound it had made—its body had made—when he flung it into the Dumpster like a sack of flour and the lid slammed down on it. He stared at the walls, and this was a movie, too. He'd never been in trouble before, never been inside a police station, but he knew his role well enough, because he'd seen it played out a thousand times on the tube: deny everything. Even as the two detectives settled in across from him at the bare wooden table in the little box of the overlit room he was telling himself just that: *Deny it, deny it all.*

The first detective leaned forward and set his hands on the table as if he'd come for a manicure. He was in his thirties, or maybe his forties, a tired-looking man with the scars of the turmoil he'd witnessed gouged into the flesh under his 50 eyes. He didn't offer a cigarette ("I don't smoke," Jeremy was prepared to say, giving them that much at least), and he didn't smile or soften his eyes. And when he spoke his voice carried no freight at all, not outrage or threat or cajolery—it was just a voice, flat and tired. "Do you know a China Berkowitz?" he said.

And she. She was in the community hospital, where the ambulance had deposited her after her roommate had called 911 in a voice that was like a bone stuck in the back of her throat, and it was raining again. Her parents were there, her mother red-eyed and sniffling, her father looking like an actor who has forgotten his lines, and there was another woman there, too, a policewoman. The policewoman sat in an orange plastic chair in the corner, dipping her head to the knitting in her lap. At first, China's mother had tried to be pleasant to the woman, but pleasant wasn't what the circumstances called for, and now she ignored her, because the very unpleasant fact was that China was being taken into custody as soon as she was released from the hospital.

For a long while no one said anything—everything had already been said, over and over, one long flood of hurt and recrimination—and the antiseptic silence of the hospital held them in its grip while the rain beat at the windows and the machines at the foot of the bed counted off numbers. From down the hall came a snatch of TV dialogue, and for a minute China opened her eyes and thought she was back in the dorm. "Honey," her mother said, raising a purgatorial face to her, "are you all right? Can I get you anything?"

"I need to—I think I need to pee."

"Why?" her father demanded, and it was the perfect non sequitur. He was up out of the chair, standing over her, his eyes liked cracked porcelain. "Why didn't you tell us, or at least tell your mother—or Dr. Fredman? Dr. Fredman, at least. He's been—he's like a family member, you know that, and he could have, or he would have…What were you *thinking*, for Christ's sake?"

Thinking? She wasn't thinking anything, not then and not now. All she   55
wanted—and she didn't care what they did to her, beat her, torture her, drag her weeping through the streets in a dirty white dress with "Baby Killer" stitched over her breast in scarlet letters—was to see Jeremy. Just that. Because what really mattered was what he was thinking.

The food at the Sarah Barnes Cooper Women's Correctional Institute was exactly what they served at the dining hall in college, heavy on the sugars, starches, and bad cholesterol, and that would have struck her as ironic if she'd been there under other circumstances—doing community outreach, say, or researching a paper for sociology class. But given the fact that she'd been locked up for more than a month now, the object of the other girls' threats, scorn, and just plain *nastiness*, given the fact that her life was ruined beyond any hope of redemption, and every newspaper in the country had her shrunken white face plastered across its front page under a headline that screamed **"MOTEL MOM,"** she didn't have much use for irony. She was scared twenty-four hours a day. Scared of the present, scared of the future, scared of the reporters waiting for the judge to set bail so that they could swarm all over her the minute she stepped out the door. She couldn't concentrate on the books and magazines her mother brought her, or even on the TV in the rec room. She sat in her room—it was a room, just like a dorm room, except that they locked you in at night—and stared at the walls, eating peanuts, M&M's, sunflower seeds by the handful, chewing for the pure animal gratification of it. She was putting on more weight, and what did it matter?

Jeremy was different. He'd lost everything—his walk, his smile, the muscles of his upper arms and shoulders. Even his hair lay flat now, as if he couldn't bother with a tube of gel and a comb. When she saw him at the arraignment, saw him for the first time since she'd climbed out of the car and limped into the dorm with the blood wet on her legs, he looked like a refugee, like a ghost. The room they were in—the courtroom—seemed to have grown up around them, walls, windows, benches, lights, and radiators already in place, along with the judge, the American flag, and the ready-made spectators. It was hot. People coughed into their fists and shuffled their feet, every sound magnified. The judge presided, his arms like bones twirled in a bag, his eyes searching and opaque as he peered over the top of his reading glasses.

China's lawyer didn't like Jeremy's lawyer, that much was evident, and the state prosecutor didn't like anybody. She watched him—Jeremy, only him—as the reporters held their collective breath and the judge read off the charges and her mother bowed her head and sobbed into the bucket of her hands. And Jeremy was watching her, too, his eyes locked on hers as if he defied them all, as if nothing mattered in the world but her, and when the judge said *First-degree murder* and *Murder by abuse or neglect* he never flinched.

She sent him a note that day—"I love you, will always love you no matter what, More than Moon"—and in the hallway, afterward, while their lawyers fended off the reporters and the bailiffs tugged impatiently at them, they had a minute, just a minute, to themselves. "What did you tell them?" he whispered. His voice was a rasp, almost a growl; she looked at him, inches away, and hardly recognized him.

"I told them it was dead."

"My lawyer—Mrs. Teagues?—she says they're saying it was alive when we, when we put it in the bag." His face was composed, but his eyes were darting like insects trapped inside his head.

"It was dead."

"It looked dead," he said, and already he was pulling away from her and some callous shit with a camera kept annihilating them with flash after flash of light, "and we certainly didn't—I mean, we didn't slap it or anything to get it breathing...."

And then the last thing he said to her, just as they were pulled apart, and it was nothing she wanted to hear, nothing that had any love in it, or even the hint of love: "You told me to get rid of it."

There was no elaborate name for the place where they were keeping him. It was known as Drum Hill Prison, period. No reform-minded notions here, no verbal gestures toward rehabilitation or behavior modification, no benefactors, mayors, or role models to lend the place their family names, but then who in his right mind would want a prison named after him anyway? At least they kept him separated from the other prisoners, the gangbangers and dope dealers and sexual predators and the like. He was no longer a freshman at Brown, not officially, but he had his books and his course notes and he tried to keep up as best he could. Still, when the screams echoed through the cell block at night and the walls dripped with the accumulated breath of eight and a half thousand terminally angry sociopaths, he had to admit it wasn't the sort of college experience he'd bargained for.

And what had he done to deserve it? He still couldn't understand. That thing in the Dumpster—and he refused to call it human, let alone a baby—was nobody's business but his and China's. That's what he'd told his attorney, Mrs.

60

65

Teagues, and his mother and her boyfriend, Howard, and he'd told them over and over again: *I didn't do anything wrong.* Even if it was alive, and it was, he knew in his heart that it was, even before the state prosecutor presented evidence of blunt-force trauma and death by asphyxiation and exposure, it didn't matter, or shouldn't have mattered. There was no baby. There was nothing but a mistake, a mistake clothed in blood and mucus. When he really thought about it, thought it through on its merits and dissected all his mother's pathetic arguments about where he'd be today if she'd felt as he did when she was pregnant herself, he hardened like a rock, like sand turning to stone under all the pressure the planet can bring to bear. Another unwanted child in an overpopulated world? They should have given him a medal.

It was the end of January before bail was set—three hundred and fifty thousand dollars his mother didn't have—and he was released to house arrest. He wore a plastic anklet that set off an alarm if he went out the door, and so did she, so did China, imprisoned like some fairy-tale princess at her parents' house. At first, she called him every day, but mostly what she did was cry— "I want to see it," she sobbed. "I want to see our daughter's *grave.*" That froze him inside. He tried to picture her—her now, China, the love of his life—and he couldn't. What did she look like? What was her face like, her nose, her hair, her eyes and breasts and the slit between her legs? He drew a blank. There was no way to summon her the way she used to be or even the way she was in court, because all he could remember was the thing that had come out of her, four limbs and the equipment of a female, shoulders rigid and eyes shut tight, as if she were a mummy in a tomb...and the breath, the shuddering long gasping rattle of a breath he could feel ringing inside her even as the black plastic bag closed over her face and the lid of the Dumpster opened like a mouth.

He was in the den, watching basketball, a drink in his hand (7UP mixed with Jack Daniel's in a ceramic mug, so no one would know he was getting shit-faced at two o'clock on a Sunday afternoon), when the phone rang. It was Sarah Teagues. "Listen, Jeremy," she said in her crisp, equitable tones, "I thought you ought to know—the Berkowitzes are filing a motion to have the case against China dropped."

His mother's voice on the portable, too loud, a blast of amplified breath and static: "On what grounds?"

"She never saw the baby, that's what they're saying. She thought she had a 70 miscarriage."

"Yeah, right," his mother said.

Sarah Teagues was right there, her voice as clear and present as his mother's. "Jeremy's the one that threw it in the Dumpster, and they're saying he acted alone. She took a polygraph test day before yesterday."

He could feel his heart pounding like it used to when he plodded up that last agonizing ridge behind the school with the cross-country team, his legs sapped, no more breath left in his body. He didn't say a word. Didn't even breathe.

"She's going to testify against him."

Outside was the world, puddles of ice clinging to the lawn under a weak 75 afternoon sun, all the trees stripped bare, the grass dead, the azalea under the window reduced to an armload of dead brown twigs. She wouldn't have wanted to go out today anyway. This was the time of year she hated most, the long interval between the holidays and spring break, when nothing grew and nothing changed—it didn't even seem to snow much anymore. What was out there for her anyway? They wouldn't let her see Jeremy, wouldn't even let her talk to him on the phone or write him anymore, and she wouldn't be able to show her face at the mall or even the movie theater without somebody shouting out her name as if she were a freak, as if she were another Monica Lewinsky or Heidi Fleiss. She wasn't China Berkowitz, honor student, not anymore—she was the punch line to a joke, a footnote to history.

She wouldn't mind going for a drive, though—that was something she missed, just following the curves out to the reservoir to watch the way the ice cupped the shore, or up to the turnout on Route 9 to look out over the river where it oozed through the mountains in a shimmering coil of light. Or to take a walk in the woods, just that. She was in her room, on her bed, posters of bands she'd outgrown staring down from the walls, her high-school books on two shelves in the corner, the closet door flung open on all the clothes she'd once wanted so desperately she could have died for each individual pair of boots or the cashmere sweaters that felt so good against her skin. At the bottom of her left leg, down there at the foot of the bed, was the anklet she wore now, the plastic anklet with the transmitter inside, no different, she supposed, than the collars they put on wolves to track them across all those miles of barren tundra or the bears sleeping in their dens. Except that hers had an alarm on it.

For a long while she just lay there gazing out the window, watching the rinsed-out sun slip down into the sky that had no more color in it than a TV tuned to an unsubscribed channel, and then she found herself picturing things the way they were an eon ago, when everything was green. She saw the azalea bush in bloom, the leaves knifing out of the trees, butterflies—or were they cabbage moths?—hovering over the flowers. Deep green. That was the color of the world. And she was remembering a night, summer before last, just after she and Jeremy started going together, the crickets thrumming, the air thick with humidity, and him singing along with the car radio, his voice so sweet and pure it was as if he'd written the song himself, just for her. And when they got to where they were going, at the end of that dark lane overhung with trees, to a place where it was private and hushed and the night fell in on itself as if it couldn't support the weight of the stars, he was as nervous as she was. She moved into his arms and they kissed, his lips groping for hers in the dark, his fingers trembling over the thin yielding silk of her blouse. He was Jeremy. He was the love of her life. And she closed her eyes and clung to him as if that were all that mattered.

(2000)

Questions for Discussion and Writing

1. How would you describe China and Jeremy at the beginning of the story—and at the end? Do you consider them to blame for what has happened to them?
2. Why is China so adamant in her refusal to deal with her pregnancy beyond simply hiding it?
3. Can you in any way justify China's telling Jeremy to "Just get rid of it" and then later agreeing to testify against him in court for getting rid of it?

4. Why does Jeremy feel he has done nothing wrong? Write an essay arguing for (or against) his position.
5. Write a continuation of the story telling what happens to China and Jeremy at the trial and what their lives are like afterward.

Making Connections

Compare the young couple's response to an unplanned pregnancy in this story with that of the couple in Hemingway's "Hills Like White Elephants" (page 274).

◇◇◇◇◇◇◇◇◇◇◇◇◇◇◇◇◇◇◇◇

Louise Erdrich 1954–

Louise Erdrich was raised as a member of the Turtle Mountain Chippewas in North Dakota with her grandfather as the tribal chief. Growing up, she worked as a farmhand, a waitress, a lifeguard, and a construction worker. After graduating from Dartmouth, she eventually married one of her professors, the writer Michael Dorris. She was having no luck getting her first novel accepted until he sent submission letters on stationery he made himself with "Michael Dorris Agency" as the letterhead. The book became a best-seller, but the couple later separated, and he committed suicide. Erdrich presently lives, writes, and owns a bookstore in Minneapolis.

The Red Convertible

Lyman Lamartine

I was the first one to drive a convertible on my reservation. And of course it was red, a red Olds. I owned that car along with my brother Henry Junior. We owned it together until his boots filled with water on a windy night and he bought out my share. Now Henry owns the whole car, and his youngest brother Lyman (that's myself), Lyman walks everywhere he goes.

How did I earn enough money to buy my share in the first place? My own talent was I could always make money. I had a touch for it, unusual in a Chippewa. From the first I was different that way, and everyone recognized it. I was the only kid they let in the American Legion Hall to shine shoes, for example, and one Christmas I sold spiritual bouquets for the mission door to door. The nuns let me keep a percentage. Once I started, it seemed the more money I made the easier the money came. Everyone encouraged it. When I was fifteen I got a job washing dishes at the Joliet Cafe, and that was where my first big break happened.

It wasn't long before I was promoted to busing tables, and then the short-order cook quit and I was hired to take her place. No sooner than you know it I was managing the Joliet. The rest is history. I went on managing. I soon became part owner, and of course there was no stopping me then. It wasn't long before the whole thing was mine.

After I'd owned the Joliet for one year, it blew over in the worst tornado ever seen around here. The whole operation was smashed to bits. A total loss.

The fryalator was up in a tree, the grill torn in half like it was paper. I was only sixteen. I had it all in my mother's name, and I lost it quick, but before I lost it I had every one of my relatives, and their relatives, to dinner, and I also bought that red Olds I mentioned, along with Henry.

The first time we saw it! I'll tell you when we first saw it. We had gotten a   5
ride to Winnipeg, and both of us had money. Don't ask me why, because we never mentioned a car or anything, we just had all our money. Mine was cash, a big bankroll from the Joliet's insurance. Henry had two checks—a week's extra pay for being laid off, and his regular check from the Jewel Bearing Plant.

We were walking down Portage anyway, seeing the sights, when we saw it. There it was, parked, large as life. Really as *if* it was alive. I thought of the word *repose*, because the car wasn't simply stopped, parked, or whatever. That car reposed, calm and gleaming, a FOR SALE sign in its left front window. Then, before we had thought it over at all, the car belonged to us and our pockets were empty. We had just enough money for gas back home.

We went places in that car, me and Henry. We took off driving all one whole summer. We started off toward the Little Knife River and Mandaree in Fort Berthold and then we found ourselves down in Wakpala somehow, and then suddenly we were over in Montana on the Rocky Boy, and yet the summer was not even half over. Some people hang on to details when they travel, but we didn't let them bother us and just lived our everyday lives here to there.

I do remember this place with willows. I remember I laid under those trees and it was comfortable. So comfortable. The branches bent down all around me like a tent or a stable. And quiet, it was quiet, even though there was a powwow close enough so I could see it going on. The air was not too still, not too windy either. When the dust rises up and hangs in the air around dancers like that, I feel good. Henry was asleep with his arms thrown wide. Later on, he woke up and we started driving again. We were somewhere in Montana, or maybe on the Blood Reserve—it could have been anywhere. Anyway it was where we met the girl.

All her hair was in buns around her ears, that's the first thing I noticed about her. She was posed alongside the road with her arm out, so we stopped. That girl was short, so short her lumber shirt looked comical on her, like a night-gown. She had jeans on and fancy moccasins and she carried a little suitcase.

"Hop on in," says Henry. So she climbs in between us.   10

"We'll take you home," I says. "Where do you live?"

"Chicken," she says.

"Where the hell's that?" I ask her.

"Alaska."

"Okay," says Henry, and we drive.   15

We got up there and never wanted to leave. The sun doesn't truly set there in summer, and the night is more a soft dusk. You might doze off, sometimes, but before you know it you're up again, like an animal in nature. You never feel like you have to sleep hard or put away the world. And things would grow up there. One day just dirt or moss, the next day flowers and long grass. The girl's name was Susy. Her family really took to us. They fed us and put us up. We had our own tent to live in by their house, and the kids would be in and out of there all day and night. They couldn't get over me and Henry being brothers, we looked so different. We told them we knew we had the same mother, anyway.

One night Susy came in to visit us. We sat around in the tent talking of this and that. The season was changing. It was getting darker by that time, and the cold was even getting just a little mean. I told her it was time for us to go. She stood up on a chair.

"You never seen my hair," Susy said.

That was true. She was standing on a chair, but still, when she unclipped her buns the hair reached all the way to the ground. Our eyes opened. You couldn't tell how much hair she had when it was rolled up so neatly. Then my brother Henry did something funny. He went up to the chair and said, "Jump on my shoulders." So she did that, and her hair reached down past his waist, and he started twirling, this way and that, so her hair was flung out from side to side.

"I always wondered what it was like to have long pretty hair," Henry says.   20
Well, we laughed. It was a funny sight, the way he did it. The next morning we got up and took leave of those people.

On to greener pastures, as they say. It was down through Spokane and across Idaho then Montana and very soon we were racing the weather right along under the Canadian border through Columbus, Des Lacs, and then were in Bottineau County and soon home. We'd made most of the trip, that summer, without putting up the car hood at all. We got home just in time.

I don't wonder that the army was so glad to get my brother that they turned him into a Marine. He was built like a brick outhouse anyway. We liked to tease him that they really wanted him for his Indian nose. He had a nose big and sharp as a hatchet, like the nose on Red Tomahawk, the Indian who killed Sitting Bull, whose profile is on signs all along the North Dakota highways. Henry went off to training camp, came home once during Christmas, then the next thing you know we got an overseas letter from him. It was 1970, and he said he was stationed up in the northern hill country. Whereabouts I did not know. He wasn't such a hot letter writer, and only got off two before the enemy caught him. I could never keep it straight, which direction those good Vietnam soldiers were from.

I wrote him back several times, even though I didn't know if those letters would get through. I kept him informed all about the car. Most of the time I had it up on blocks in the yard or half taken apart, because that long trip did a hard job on it under the hood.

I always had good luck with numbers, and never worried about the draft myself. I never even had to think about what my number was. But Henry was never lucky in the same way as me. It was at least three years before Henry came home. By then I guess the whole war was solved in the government's mind, but for him it would keep on going. In those years I'd put his car into almost perfect shape. I always thought of it as his car while he was gone, even though when he left he said, "Now it's yours," and threw me his key.

"Thanks for the extra key," I'd said. "I'll put it in your drawer just in case I   25
need it." He laughed.

When he came home, though, Henry was very different, and I'll say this: the change was no good. You could hardly expect him to change for the better, I know. But he was quiet, so quiet, and never comfortable sitting still anywhere but always up and moving around. I thought back to times we'd sat still for whole afternoons, never moving a muscle, just shifting our weight along the ground, talking to whoever sat with us, watching things. He'd always had a joke, then, too, and now you couldn't get him to laugh, or when he did it was more the sound of a man choking, a sound that stopped up the throats of other people around him. They got to leaving him alone most of the time, and I didn't blame them. It was a fact: Henry was jumpy and mean.

I'd bought a color TV set for my mom and the rest of us while Henry was away. Money still came very easy. I was sorry I'd ever bought it though, because of Henry. I was also sorry I'd bought color, because with black-and-white the pictures seem older and farther away. But what are you going to do? He sat in front of it, watching it, and that was the only time he was completely still. But it was the kind of stillness that you see in a rabbit when it freezes and before it will bolt. He was not easy. He sat in his chair gripping the armrests with all his might, as if the chair itself was moving at a high speed and if he let go at all he would rocket forward and maybe crash right through the set.

Once I was in the room watching TV with Henry and I heard his teeth click at something. I looked over, and he'd bitten through his lip. Blood was going down his chin. I tell you right then I wanted to smash that tube to pieces. I went over to it but Henry must have known what I was up to. He rushed from his chair and shoved me out of the way, against the wall. I told myself he didn't know what he was doing.

My mom came in, turned the set off real quiet, and told us she had made something for supper. So we went and sat down. There was still blood going down Henry's chin, but he didn't notice it and no one said anything, even though every time he took a bite of his bread his blood fell onto it until he was eating his own blood mixed in with the food.

While Henry was not around we talked about what was going to happen to   30
him. There were no Indian doctors on the reservation, and my mom couldn't come around to trusting the old man, Moses Pillager, because he courted her long ago and was jealous of her husbands. He might take revenge through her son. We were afraid that if we brought Henry to a regular hospital they would keep him.

"They don't fix them in those places," Mom said; "they just give them drugs."

"We wouldn't get him there in the first place," I agreed, "so let's just forget about it."

Then I thought about the car.

Henry had not even looked at the car since he'd gotten home, though like I said, it was in tip-top condition and ready to drive. I thought the car might bring the old Henry back somehow. So I bided my time and waited for my chance to interest him in the vehicle.

One night Henry was off somewhere. I took myself a hammer. I went out to   35
that car and I did a number on its underside. Whacked it up. Bent the tail pipe double. Ripped the muffler loose. By the time I was done with the car it looked worse than any typical Indian car that has been driven all its life on reservation roads, which they always say are like government promises—full of holes. It just about hurt me, I'll tell you that! I threw dirt in the carburetor and I ripped all the electric tape off the seats. I made it look just as beat up as I could. Then I sat back and waited for Henry to find it.

Still, it took him over a month. That was all right, because it was just getting warm enough, not melting, but warm enough to work outside.

"Lyman," he says, walking in one day, "that red car looks like shit."

"Well, it's old," I says. "You got to expect that."

"No way!" says Henry. "That car's a classic! But you went and ran the piss right out of it, Lyman, and you know it don't deserve that. I kept that car in A-one shape. You don't remember. You're too young. But when I left, that car was running like a watch. Now I don't even know if I can get it to start again, let alone get it anywhere near its old condition."

"Well, you try," I said, like I was getting mad, "but I say it's a piece of junk." 40

Then I walked out before he could realize I knew he'd strung together more than six words at once.

After that I thought he'd freeze himself to death working on that car. He was out there all day, and at night he rigged up a little lamp, ran a cord out the window, and had himself some light to see by while he worked. He was better than he had been before, but that's still not saying much. It was easier for him to do the things the rest of us did. He ate more slowly and didn't jump up and down during the meal to get this or that or look out the window. I put my hand in the back of the TV set, I admit, and fiddled around with it good, so that it was almost impossible now to get a clear picture. He didn't look at it very often anyway. He was always out with that car or going off to get parts for it. By the time it was really melting outside, he had it fixed.

I had been feeling down in the dumps about Henry around this time. We had always been together before. Henry and Lyman. But he was such a loner now that I didn't know how to take it. So I jumped at the chance one day when Henry seemed friendly. It's not that he smiled or anything. He just said, "Let's take that old shit-box for a spin." Just the way he said it made me think he could be coming around.

We went out to the car. It was spring. The sun was shining very bright. My only sister, Bonita, who was just eleven years old, came out and made us stand together for a picture. Henry leaned his elbow on the red car's windshield, and he took his other arm and put it over my shoulder, very carefully, as though it was heavy for him to lift and he didn't want to bring the weight down all at once.

"Smile," Bonita said, and he did. 45

That picture. I never look at it anymore. A few months ago, I don't know why, I got his picture out and tacked it on the wall. I felt good about Henry at the time, close to him. I felt good having his picture on the wall, until one night when I was looking at television. I was a little drunk and stoned. I looked up at the wall and Henry was staring at me. I don't know what it was, but his smile had changed, or maybe it was gone. All I know is I couldn't stay in the same room with that picture. I was shaking. I got up, closed the door, and went into the kitchen. A little later my friend Ray came over and we both went back into that room. We put the picture in a brown bag, folded the bag over and over tightly, then put it way back in a closet.

I still see that picture now, as if it tugs at me, whenever I pass that closet door. The picture is very clear in my mind. It was so sunny that day Henry had to squint against the glare. Or maybe the camera Bonita held flashed like a mirror, blinding him, before she snapped the picture. My face is right out in the sun, big and round. But he might have drawn back, because the shadows on his face are deep as holes. There are two shadows curved like little hooks around the ends of his smile, as if to frame it and try to keep it there—that one, first smile that looked like it might have hurt his face. He has his field jacket on and the wornin clothes he'd come back in and kept wearing ever since. After Bonita took the picture, she went into the house and we got into the car. There was a full cooler in the trunk. We started off, east, toward Pembina and the Red River because Henry said he wanted to see the high water.

The trip over there was beautiful. When everything starts changing, drying up, clearing off, you feel like your whole life is starting. Henry felt it, too. The top was down and the car hummed like a top. He'd really put it back in shape, even the tape on the seats was very carefully put down and glued back in layers. It's not that he smiled again or even joked, but his face looked to me as if it was clear, more peaceful. It looked as though he wasn't thinking of anything in particular except the bare fields and windbreaks and houses we were passing.

The river was high and full of winter trash when we got there. The sun was still out, but it was colder by the river. There were still little clumps of dirty snow here and there on the banks. The water hadn't gone over the banks yet, but it would, you could tell. It was just at its limit, hard swollen, glossy like an old gray scar. We made ourselves a fire, and we sat down and watched the current go. As I watched it I felt something squeezing inside me and tightening and trying to let go all at the same time. I knew I was not just feeling it myself; I knew I was feeling what Henry was going through at that moment. Except that I couldn't stand it, the closing and opening. I jumped to my feet. I took Henry by the shoulders and I started shaking him. "Wake up," I says, "wake up, wake up, wake up!" I didn't know what had come over me. I sat down beside him again.

His face was totally white and hard. Then it broke, like stones break all of a   50
sudden when water boils up inside them.

"I know it," he says. "I know it. I can't help it. It's no use."

We start talking. He said he knew what I'd done with the car. It was obvious it had been whacked out of shape and not just neglected. He said he wanted to give the car to me for good now, it was no use. He said he'd fixed it just to give it back and I should take it.

"No way," I says. "I don't want it."

"That's okay," he says, "you take it."

"I don't want it, though," I says back to him, and then to emphasize, just to   55
emphasize, you understand, I touch his shoulder. He slaps my hand off.

"Take that car," he says.

"No," I say. "Make me," I say, and then he grabs my jacket and rips the arm loose. That jacket is a class act, suede with tags and zippers. I push Henry backwards, off the log. He jumps up and bowls me over. We go down in a clinch and come up swinging hard, for all we're worth, with our fists. He socks my jaw so hard I feel like it swings loose. Then I'm at his rib cage and land a good one under his chin so his head snaps back. He's dazzled. He looks at me and I look at him and then his eyes are full of tears and blood and at first I think he's crying. But no, he's laughing. "Ha, ha!" he says. "Ha! Ha! Take good care of it."

"Okay," I says. "Okay, no problem. Ha! Ha!"

I can't help it, and I start laughing, too. My face feels fat and strange, and after a while I get a beer from the cooler in the trunk, and when I hand it to Henry he takes his shirt and wipes my germs off. "Hoof-and-mouth disease," he says. For some reason this cracks me up, and so we're really laughing for a while, and then we drink all the rest of the beers one by one and throw them in the river and see how far, how fast, the current takes them before they fill up and sink.

"You want to go on back?" I ask after a while. "Maybe we could snag a couple   60
nice Kashpaw girls."

He says nothing. But I can tell his mood is turning again.

"They're all crazy, the girls up here, every damn one of them."

"You're crazy too," I say, to jolly him up. "Crazy Lamartine boys!"

He looks as though he will take this wrong at first. His face twists, then clears, and he jumps up on his feet. "That's right!" he says. "Crazier 'n hell. Crazy Indians!"

I think it's the old Henry again. He throws off his jacket and starts spring- 65
ing his legs up from the knees like a fancy dancer. He's down doing something between a grass dance and a bunny hop, no kind of dance I ever saw before, but neither has anyone else on all this green growing earth. He's wild. He wants to pitch whoopee! He's up and at me and all over. All this time I'm laughing so hard, so hard my belly is getting tied up in a knot.

"Got to cool me off!" he shouts all of a sudden. Then he runs over to the river and jumps in.

There's boards and other things in the current. It's so high. No sound comes from the river after the splash he makes, so I run right over. I look around. It's getting dark. I see he's halfway across the water already, and I know he didn't swim there but the current took him. It's far. I hear his voice, though, very clearly across it.

"My boots are filling," he says.

He says this in a normal voice, like he just noticed and he doesn't know what to think of it. Then he's gone. A branch comes by. Another branch. And I go in.

By the time I get out of the river, off the snag I pulled myself onto, the sun is 70
down. I walk back to the car, turn on the high beams, and drive it up the bank. I put it in first gear and then I take my foot off the clutch. I get out, close the door, and watch it plow softly into the water. The headlights reach in as they go down, searching, still lighted even after the water swirls over the back end. I wait. The wires short out. It is all finally dark. And then there is only the water, the sound of it going and running and going and running and running.

(1984)

Questions for Discussion and Writing

1. How does the red Oldsmobile function as the story's central symbol? What changes does the car go through? How do these changes stand for what Lyman and Henry are going through?
2. Why is Lyman upset by the picture of himself and his brother? When does the picture begin to bother Lyman—before or after Henry's death? Do we know for sure? Does it make any difference?
3. Why does Lyman send the car into the river? Why are the car's lights left on?
4. Write an essay that makes a major claim about the brothers' relationship.
5. Analyze a single episode in the story (such as the visit to Alaska or Henry's watching TV), and discuss its relation to the story as a whole.

Making Connections

Analyze the narrator of this story. Is he reliable? Compare him to other first-person narrators in stories you've read [for instance, Sammy in "A & P" (page 358), Sylvia in "The Lesson" (page 924), or the mother in "I Stand Here Ironing" (page 284)].

14 A Portfolio of Science Fiction Stories

Chapter Preview

Science fiction, also called "speculative fiction," differs from other kinds of literature primarily in its use of the lessons of science and the fancies of the imagination to create characters, settings, and events that are outside known reality and experience. According to Rod Serling, the creator of *The Twilight Zone*, "Science fiction is the improbable made possible." Science fiction became an established literary genre at the end of the 19th century and the beginning of the 20th, mainly through the novels and stories of Jules Verne, Edward Bellamy, and H. G. Wells. But older canonical works of literature—*Utopia, The Tempest, The Blazing World, Gulliver's Travels, Frankenstein*—also used many of the same themes and literary devices found in modern-day science fiction.

In this chapter, you will learn to do the following:

- Apply reading and analyzing fiction to a specific genre, social science fiction.
- Compare and contrast plot, character, theme, and other literary elements among works of science fiction.
- Write about science fiction stories.

The frequently repeated subjects and motifs of science fiction include technological and biological experimentation, lost or alien cultures, space and time travel, artificial life, post-apocalyptic societies, paranormal abilities, and parallel or alternate worlds. By the 1950s, the genre had gained greater respectability in the hands of serious writers such as Ray Bradbury, Isaac Asimov, and Kurt Vonnegut, Jr., who combined futuristic narratives with concerns about technological progress and the impact of scientific advances on human behavior. These works reflect modern society's fears of nuclear energy, distrust of the military-industrial complex, worries about the environment, and changing views of gender and the family. As author Ursula Le Guin has pointed out, "Science fiction is particularly good at showing what a different society would actually be like to live in." The three stories in this portfolio fit into this subcategory of "social science fiction."

Ray Bradbury   1920–2012

Born in Waukegan, Illinois, Bradbury moved west with his family during the Depression. His formal education ended when he graduated from a Los Angeles high school in 1938, but he continued to educate himself, selling newspapers on Los Angeles street corners in the day and spending nights in the library. He sold his first science fiction story in 1941. In a long and vigorous career, Bradbury produced hundreds of short stories, novels, plays, poetry, and screenplays for TV and films; these publications range from light humor through satire to gothic horror. His first major success came in 1951 with *The Martian Chronicles*, a collection of linked stories about the human settlement of Mars; it has remained immensely popular and is considered a classic of speculative fiction. The following story is the next-to-last entry in that collection.

There Will Come Soft Rains

In the living room the voice-clock sang, *Tick-tock, seven o'clock, time to get up, time to get up, seven o'clock!* as if it were afraid that nobody would. The morning house lay empty. The clock ticked on, repeating and repeating its sounds into the emptiness. *Seven-nine, breakfast time, seven-nine!*

In the kitchen the breakfast stove gave a hissing sigh and ejected from its warm interior eight pieces of perfectly browned toast, eight eggs sunnyside up, sixteen slices of bacon, two coffees, and two cool glasses of milk.

"Today is August 4, 2026," said a second voice from the kitchen ceiling, "in the city of Allendale, California." It repeated the date three times for memory's sake. "Today is Mr. Featherstone's birthday. Today is the anniversary of Tilita's marriage. Insurance is payable, as are the water, gas, and light bills."

Somewhere in the walls, relays clicked, memory tapes glided under electric eyes.

Eight-one, tick-tock, eight-one o'clock, off to school, off to work, run, run, eight-one! 5
But no doors slammed, no carpets took the soft tread of rubber heels. It was raining outside. The weather box on the front door sang quietly: "Rain, rain, go away; rubbers, raincoats for today ..." And the rain tapped on the empty house, echoing.

Outside, the garage chimed and lifted its door to reveal the waiting car. After a long wait the door swung down again.

At eight-thirty the eggs were shriveled and the toast was like stone. An aluminum wedge scraped them into the sink, where hot water whirled them down a metal throat which digested and flushed them away to the distant sea. The dirty dishes were dropped into a hot washer and emerged twinkling dry.

Nine-fifteen, sang the clock, *time to clean.*

Out of warrens in the wall, tiny robot mice darted. The rooms were acrawl with the small cleaning animals, all rubber and metal. They thudded against chairs, whirling their mustached runners, kneading the rug nap, sucking gently at hidden dust. Then, like mysterious invaders, they popped into their burrows. Their pink electric eyes faded. The house was clean.

Ten o'clock. The sun came out from behind the rain. The house stood alone 10
in a city of rubble and ashes. This was the one house left standing. At night the ruined city gave off a radioactive glow which could be seen for miles.

Ten-fifteen. The garden sprinklers whirled up in golden founts, filling the soft morning air with scatterings of brightness. The water pelted windowpanes, running down the charred west side where the house had been burned evenly free of its white paint. The entire west face of the house was black, save for five places. Here the silhouette in paint of a man mowing a lawn. Here, as in a photograph, a woman bent to pick flowers. Still farther over, their images burned on wood in one titanic instant, a small boy, hands flung into the air; higher up, the image of a thrown ball, and opposite him a girl, hands raised to catch a ball which never came down.

The five spots of paint—the man, the woman, the children, the ball—remained. The rest was a thin charcoaled layer.

The gentle sprinkler rain filled the garden with falling light.

Until this day, how well the house had kept its peace. How carefully it had inquired, "Who goes there? What's the password?" and, getting no answer from lonely foxes and whining cats, it had shut up its windows and drawn shades in an old-maidenly preoccupation with self-protection which bordered on a mechanical paranoia.

It quivered at each sound, the house did. If a sparrow brushed a window, the shade snapped up. The bird, startled, flew off! No, not even a bird must touch the house!

The house was an altar with ten thousand attendants, big, small, servicing, attending, in choirs. But the gods had gone away, and the ritual of the religion continued senselessly, uselessly.

Twelve noon.

A dog whined, shivering, on the front porch.

The front door recognized the dog voice and opened. The dog, once huge and fleshy, but now gone to bone and covered with sores, moved in and through the house, tracking mud. Behind it whirled angry mice, angry at having to pick up mud, angry at inconvenience.

For not a leaf fragment blew under the door but what the wall panels flipped open and the copper scrap rats flashed swiftly out. The offending dust, hair, or paper, seized in miniature steel jaws, was raced back to the burrows. There, down tubes which fed into the cellar, it was dropped into the sighing vent of an incinerator which sat like evil Baal in a dark corner.

The dog ran upstairs, hysterically yelping to each door, at last realizing, as the house realized, that only silence was here.

It sniffed the air and scratched the kitchen door. Behind the door, the stove was making pancakes which filled the house with a rich baked odor and the scent of maple syrup.

The dog frothed at the mouth, lying at the door, sniffing, its eyes turned to fire. It ran wildly in circles, biting at its tail, spun in a frenzy, and died. It lay in the parlor for an hour.

Two o'clock, sang a voice.

Delicately sensing decay at last, the regiments of mice hummed out as softly as blown gray leaves in an electrical wind.

Two-fifteen.

The dog was gone.

In the cellar, the incinerator glowed suddenly and a whirl of sparks leaped up the chimney.

Two thirty-five.

Bridge tables sprouted from patio walls. Playing cards fluttered onto pads in   30
a shower of pips. Martinis manifested on an oaken bench with egg-salad sandwiches. Music played.

But the tables were silent and the cards untouched.

At four o'clock the tables folded like great butterflies back through the pan-
eled walls.

Four-thirty.
The nursery walls glowed.

Animals took shape: yellow giraffes, blue lions, pink antelopes, lilac panthers   35
cavorting in crystal substance. The walls were glass. They looked out upon color
and fantasy. Hidden films docked through well-oiled sprockets, and the walls
lived. The nursery floor was woven to resemble a crisp, cereal meadow. Over
this ran aluminum roaches and iron crickets, and in the hot still air butterflies of
delicate red tissue wavered among the sharp aroma of animal spoors! There was
the sound like a great matted yellow hive of bees within a dark bellows, the lazy
bumble of a purring lion. And there was the patter of okapi feet and the murmur
of a fresh jungle rain, like other hoofs, falling upon the summer-starched grass.
Now the walls dissolved into distances of parched weed, mile on mile, and warm
endless sky. The animals drew away into thorn brakes and water holes.

It was the children's hour.

Five o'clock. The bath filled with clear hot water.

Six, seven, eight o'clock. The dinner dishes manipulated like magic tricks, and
in the study a click. In the metal stand opposite the hearth where a fire now
blazed up warmly, a cigar popped out, half an inch of soft gray ash on it, smoking, waiting.

Nine o'clock. The beds warmed their hidden circuits, for nights were cool here.

Nine-five. A voice spoke from the study ceiling: 40
"Mrs. McClellan, which poem would you like this evening?"

The house was silent.

The voice said at last, "Since you express no preference, I shall select a poem
at random." Quiet music rose to back the voice. "Sara Teasdale. As I recall, your
favorite ….

"There will come soft rains and the smell of the ground,
And swallows circling with their shimmering sound;

And frogs in the pools singing at night,   45
And wild plum trees in tremulous white;

Robins will wear their feathery fire,
Whistling their whims on a low fence-wire;

And not one will know of the war, not one
Will care at last when it is done.

Not one would mind, neither bird nor tree,
If mankind perished utterly;

And Spring herself, when she woke at dawn
Would scarcely know that we were gone."

The fire burned on the stone hearth and the cigar fell away into a mound of   50
quiet ash on its tray. The empty chairs faced each other between the silent walls,
and the music played.

At ten o'clock the house began to die.

The wind blew. A failing tree bough crashed through the kitchen window.
Cleaning solvent, bottled, shattered over the stove. The room was ablaze in an
instant!

"Fire!" screamed a voice. The house lights flashed, water pumps shot water
from the ceilings. But the solvent spread on the linoleum, licking, eating, under
the kitchen door, while the voices took it up in chorus: "Fire, fire, fire!"

The house tried to save itself. Doors sprang tightly shut, but the windows
were broken by the heat and the wind blew and sucked upon the fire.

The house gave ground as the fire in ten billion angry sparks moved with   55
flaming ease from room to room and then up the stairs. While scurrying water
rats squeaked from the walls, pistoled their water, and ran for more. And the
wall sprays let down showers of mechanical rain.

But too late. Somewhere, sighing, a pump shrugged to a stop. The quench-
ing rain ceased. The reserve water supply which had filled baths and washed
dishes for many quiet days was gone.

The fire crackled up the stairs. It fed upon Picassos and Matisses in the upper
halls, like delicacies, baking off the oily flesh, tenderly crisping the canvases into
black shavings.

Now the fire lay in beds, stood in windows, changed the colors of drapes!

And then, reinforcements.

From attic trapdoors, blind robot faces peered down with faucet mouths   60
gushing green chemical.

The fire backed off, as even an elephant must at the sight of a dead snake.
Now there were twenty snakes whipping over the floor, killing the fire with a
clear cold venom of green froth.

But the fire was clever. It had sent flames outside the house, up through
the attic to the pumps there. An explosion! The attic brain which directed the
pumps was shattered into bronze shrapnel on the beams.

The fire rushed back into every closet and felt of the clothes hung there.

The house shuddered, oak bone on bone, its bared skeleton cringing from
the heat, its wire, its nerves revealed as if a surgeon had torn the skin off to let
the red veins and capillaries quiver in the scalded air. Help, help! Fire! Run, run!
Heat snapped mirrors like the brittle winter ice. And the voices wailed Fire, fire,
run, run, like a tragic nursery rhyme, a dozen voices, high, low, like children
dying in a forest, alone, alone. And the voices fading as the wires popped their
sheathings like hot chestnuts. One, two, three, four, five voices died.

In the nursery the jungle burned. Blue lions roared, purple giraffes bounded   65
off. The panthers ran in circles, changing color, and ten million animals, running before the fire, vanished off toward a distant steaming river ….

Ten more voices died. In the last instant under the fire avalanche, other choruses, oblivious, could be heard announcing the time, playing music, cutting the
lawn by remote-control mower, or setting an umbrella frantically out and in the
slamming and opening front door, a thousand things happening, like a clock
shop when each clock strikes the hour insanely before or after the other, a scene
of maniac confusion, yet unity; singing, screaming, a few last cleaning mice

darting bravely out to carry the horrid ashes away! And one voice, with sublime disregard for the situation, read poetry aloud in the fiery study, until all the film spools burned, until all the wires withered and the circuits cracked.

The fire burst the house and let it slam flat down, puffing out skirts of spark and smoke.

In the kitchen, an instant before the rain of fire and timber, the stove could be seen making breakfasts at a psychopathic rate, ten dozen eggs, six loaves of toast, twenty dozen bacon strips, which, eaten by fire, started the stove working again, hysterically hissing!

The crash. The attic smashing into kitchen and parlor. The parlor into cellar, cellar into sub-cellar. Deep freeze, armchair, film tapes, circuits, beds, and all like skeletons thrown in a cluttered mound deep under.

Smoke and silence. A great quantity of smoke.   70

Dawn showed faintly in the east. Among the ruins, one wall stood alone. Within the wall, a last voice said, over and over again and again, even as the sun rose to shine upon the heaped rubble and steam:

"Today is August 5, 2026, today is August 5, 2026, today is ..."

(1951)

Questions for Discussion and Writing

1. Find out more about the poem that gives this story its title. Why did Bradbury choose this poem? What is its function in the story?
2. Choose one of the following statements of the story's main theme, and argue for or against it:
   a. Humankind will be destroyed by placing too much trust in technology.
   b. Nature is a more powerful force than science.
   c. Nature is indifferent to human existence.
   Or formulate a statement of theme of your own, and develop an argument for it.
3. Look at how often Bradbury uses the words *soft* and *softly*. What is the point or purpose of this motif of images?
4. Identify and explain several situational ironies in the story.
5. "There Will Come Soft Rains" does not take place on Mars and does not contain any human characters. Why do you think Bradbury included it in a collection of linked stories about the human settlement of Mars? Why is it placed next-to-last in the collection?

◇◇◇◇◇◇◇◇◇◇◇◇◇◇◇◇◇◇◇◇◇◇

Ursula K. Le Guin   1929–

Ursula Kroeber was born and grew up in Berkeley, California, where her mother was a psychologist and her father was a professor of anthropology at the University of California. After attending Radcliffe College and doing graduate work at Columbia University, she married historian Charles Le Guin in Paris, and has lived in Portland, Oregon, since 1958. A popular and prolific author of science fiction and fantasy novels, Le Guin regards these works as "thought experiments." She often examines contemporary problems by restating them in terms of other imagined worlds. *The Left Hand of Darkness* (1969), for instance, depicts life on an androgynous planet, and *The Dispossessed* (1974) explores the possibilities for an anarchic society. Le Guin is also the author of a fantasy series for children, the *Earthsea* trilogy.

The Ones Who Walk Away from Omelas

With a clamor of bells that set the swallows soaring, the Festival of Summer came to the city. Omelas, bright-towered by the sea. The rigging of the boats in harbor sparkled with flags. In the streets between houses with red roofs and painted walls, between old moss-grown gardens and under avenues of trees, past great parks and public buildings, processions moved. Some were decorous: old people in long stiff robes of mauve and grey, grave master workmen, quiet, merry women carrying their babies and chatting as they walked. In other streets the music beat faster, a shimmering of gong and tambourine, and the people went dancing, the procession was a dance. Children dodged in and out, their high calls rising like the swallows' crossing flights over the music and the singing. All the processions wound towards the north side of the city, where on the great water-meadow called the Green Fields boys and girls, naked in the bright air, with mud-stained feet and ankles and long, lithe arms, exercised their restive horses before the race. The horses wore no gear at all but a halter without bit. Their manes were braided with streamers of silver, gold, and green. They flared their nostrils and pranced and boasted to one another; they were vastly excited, the horse being the only animal who has adopted our ceremonies as his own. Far off to the north and west the mountains stood up half encircling Omelas on her bay. The air of morning was so clear that the snow still crowning the Eighteen Peaks burned with white-gold fire across the miles of sunlit air, under the dark blue of the sky. There was just enough wind to make the banners that marked the racecourse snap and flutter now and then. In the silence of the broad green meadows one could hear the music winding through the city streets, farther and nearer and ever approaching, a cheerful faint sweetness of the air that from time to time trembled and gathered together and broke out into the great joyous clanging of the bells.

Joyous! How is one to tell about joy? How describe the citizens of Omelas?

They were not simple folk, you see, though they were happy. But we do not say the words of cheer much any more. All smiles have become archaic. Given a description such as this one tends to make certain assumptions. Given a description such as this one tends to look next for the King, mounted on a splendid stallion and surrounded by his noble knights, or perhaps in a golden litter borne by great-muscled slaves. But there was no king. They did not use swords, or keep slaves. They were not barbarians. I do not know the rules and laws of their society, but I suspect that they were singularly few. As they did without monarchy and slavery, so they also got on without the stock exchange, the advertisement, the secret police, and the bomb. Yet I repeat that these were not simple folk, not dulcet shepherds, noble savages, bland utopians. They were not less complex than us. The trouble is that we have a bad habit, encouraged by pedants and sophisticates, of considering happiness as something rather stupid. Only pain is intellectual, only evil interesting. This is the treason of the artist: a refusal to admit the banality of evil and the terrible boredom of pain. If you can't lick 'em, join 'em. If it hurts, repeat it. But to praise despair is to condemn delight, to embrace violence is to lose hold of everything else. We have almost lost hold; we can no longer describe a happy man, nor make any celebration of joy. How can I tell you about the people of Omelas? They were not naïve and happy children—though their children were, in fact, happy. They were mature, intelligent, passionate adults whose lives were not wretched. O miracle! but I wish I could describe it better. I wish I could convince you. Omelas sounds in my words like a city in a fairy tale, long ago and far away, once upon a time. Perhaps it would be best if you imagined it as your own fancy bids, assuming it will rise to the occasion, for certainly I cannot suit you all. For instance, how about technology? I think that there would be no cars or helicopters in and above the streets; this follows from the fact that the people of Omelas are happy people. Happiness is based on a just discrimination of what is necessary, what is neither necessary nor destructive, and what is destructive. In the middle category, however—that of the unnecessary but undestructive, that of comfort, luxury, exuberance, etc.—they could perfectly well have central heating, subway trains, washing machines, and all kinds of marvelous devices not yet invented here, floating light-sources, fuelless power, a cure for the common cold. Or they could have none of that: it doesn't matter. As you like it. I incline to think that people from towns up and down the coast have been coming in to Omelas during the last days before the Festival on very fast little trains and double-decked trams and that the train station of Omelas is actually the handsomest building in town, though plainer than the magnificent Farmers' Market. But even granted trains, I fear that Omelas so far strikes some of you as goody-goody. Smiles, bells, parades, horses, bleh. If so, please add an orgy. If an orgy would help, don't hesitate. Let us not, however, have temples from which issue beautiful nude priests and priestesses already half in ecstasy and ready to copulate with any man or woman, lover or stranger, who desires union with the deep godhead of the blood, although that was my first idea. But really it would be better not to have any temples in Omelas—at least, not manned temples. Religion yes, clergy no. Surely the beautiful nudes can just wander about, offering themselves like divine soufflés to the hunger of the needy and the rapture of the flesh. Let them join the processions. Let tambourines be struck above the copulations, and the glory of desire be proclaimed upon the gongs, and (a not unimportant point) let the offspring of these delightful rituals be beloved and looked after by all. One thing I know there is none of in Omelas is guilt. But what else should there be? I thought at first there were no drugs, but that is puritanical. For those who like it, the faint insistent sweetness of *drooz* may perfume the ways of the city, *drooz* which first brings a great lightness and brilliance to the mind and limbs, and then after some hours a dreamy languor and wonderful visions at last of the very arcana and inmost secrets of the Universe, as well as exciting the pleasure of sex beyond all belief; and it is not habit-forming. For more modest tastes I think there ought to be beer. What else, what else belongs in the joyous city? The sense of victory, surely, the celebration of courage. But as we did without clergy, let us do without soldiers. The joy built upon successful slaughter is not the right kind of joy; it will not do; it is fearful and it is trivial. A boundless and generous contentment, a magnanimous triumph felt not against some outer enemy but in communion with the finest and fairest in the souls of all men everywhere and the splendor of the world's summer: this is what swells the hearts of the people of Omelas, and the victory they celebrate is that of life. I really don't think many of them need to take *drooz*.

Most of the processions have reached the Green Fields by now. A marvelous smell of cooking goes forth from the red and blue tents of the provisioners. The faces of small children are amiably sticky; in the benign grey beard of a man a couple of crumbs of rich pastry are entangled. The youths and girls have mounted their horses and are beginning to group around the starting line of the course. An old woman, small, fat, and laughing, is passing out flowers from a basket, and tall young men wear her flowers in their shining hair. A child of nine or ten sits at the edge of the crowd, alone, playing on a wooden flute. People pause to listen, and they smile, but they do not speak to him, for he never ceases playing and never sees them, his dark eyes wholly rapt in the sweet, thin magic of the tune.

He finishes, and slowly lowers his hands holding the wooden flute.   5

As if that little private silence were the signal, all at once a trumpet sounds from the pavillion near the starting line: imperious, melancholy, piercing. The horses rear on their slender legs, and some of them neigh in answer. Soberfaced, the young riders stroke the horses' necks and soothe them, whispering, "Quiet, quiet, there my beauty, my hope...." They begin to form in rank along the starting line. The crowds along the racecourse are like a field of grass and flowers in the wind. The Festival of Summer has begun.

Do you believe? Do you accept the festival, the city, the joy? No? Then let me describe one more thing.

In a basement under one of the beautiful public buildings of Omelas, or perhaps in the cellar of one of its spacious private homes, there is a room. It has one locked door, and no window. A little light seeps in dustily between cracks in the boards, secondhand from a cobwebbed window somewhere across the cellar. In one corner of the little room a couple of mops, with stiff, clotted, foul-smelling heads, stand near a rusty bucket. The floor is dirt, a little damp to the touch, as cellar dirt usually is. The room is about three paces long and two wide: a mere broom closet or disused tool room. In the room a child is sitting. It could be a boy or a girl. It looks about six, but actually is nearly ten. It is feeble-minded. Perhaps it was born defective, or perhaps it has become imbecile through fear, malnutrition, and neglect. It picks its nose and occasionally fumbles vaguely with its toes or genitals, as it sits hunched in the corner farthest from the bucket and the two mops. It is afraid of the mops. It finds them horrible. It shuts its eyes, but it knows the mops are still standing there; and the door is locked; and nobody will come. The door is always locked; and nobody ever comes except that sometimes—the child has no understanding of time or interval—sometimes the door rattles terribly and opens, and a person, or several people, are there. One of them may come in and kick the child to make it stand up. The others never come close, but peer in at it with frightened, disgusted eyes. The food bowl and the water jug are hastily filled, the door is locked, the eyes disappear. The people at the door never say anything, but the child, who has not always lived in the tool room, and can remember sunlight and its mother's voice, sometimes speaks. "I will be good," it says. "Please let me out. I will be good!" They never answer. The child used to scream for help at night, and cry a good deal, but now it only makes a kind of whining, "eh-haa, eh-haa," and it speaks less and less often. It is so thin there are no calves to its legs; its belly protrudes; it lives on a half-bowl of corn meal and grease a day. It is naked. Its buttocks and thighs are a mass of festered sores, as it sits in its own excrement continually.

They all know it is there, all the people of Omelas. Some of them have come to see it, others are content merely to know it is there. They all know that it has to be there. Some of them understand why, and some do not, but they all understand that their happiness, the beauty of their city, the tenderness of their friendships, the health of their children, the wisdom of their scholars, the skill of their makers, even the abundance of their harvest and the kindly weathers of their skies, depend wholly on this child's abominable misery.

This is usually explained to children when they are between eight and twelve, whenever they seem capable of understanding; and most of those who come to see the child are young people, though often enough an adult comes, or comes back, to see the child. No matter how well the matter has been explained to them, these young spectators are always shocked and sickened at the sight. They feel disgust, which they had thought themselves superior to. They feel anger, outrage, impotence, despite all the explanations. They would like to do something for the child. But there is nothing they can do. If the child were brought up into the sunlight out of that vile place, if it were cleaned and fed and comforted, that would be a good thing, indeed; but if it were done, in that day and hour all the prosperity and beauty and delight of Omelas would wither and be destroyed. Those are the terms. To exchange all the goodness and grace of every life in Omelas for that single, small improvement: to throw away the happiness of thousands for the chance of the happiness of one: that would be to let guilt within the walls indeed.

The terms are strict and absolute; there may not even be a kind word spoken to the child.

Often the young people go home in tears, or in a tearless rage, when they have seen the child and faced this terrible paradox. They may brood over it for weeks or years. But as time goes on they begin to realize that even if the child could be released, it would not get much good of its freedom: a little vague pleasure of warmth and food, no doubt, but little more. It is too degraded and imbecile to know any real joy. It has been afraid too long ever to be free of fear. Its habits are too uncouth for it to respond to humane treatment. Indeed, after so long it would probably be wretched without walls about it to protect it, and darkness for its eyes, and its own excrement to sit in. Their tears at the bitter injustice dry when they begin to perceive the terrible justice of reality and to accept it. Yet it is their tears and anger, the trying of their generosity and the acceptance of their helplessness, which are perhaps the true source of the splendor of their lives. Theirs is no vapid, irresponsible happiness. They know that they, like the child, are not free. They know compassion. It is the existence of the child, and their knowledge of its existence, that makes possible the nobility of their architecture, the poignancy of their music, the profundity of their science. It is because of the child that they are so gentle with children. They know that if the wretched one were not there snivelling in the dark, the other one, the fluteplayer, could make no joyful music as the young riders line up in their beauty for the race in the sunlight of the first morning of summer.

Now do you believe in them? Are they not more credible? But there is one more thing to tell, and this is quite incredible.

At times one of the adolescent girls or boys who go to see the child does not go home to weep or rage, does not, in fact, go home at all. Sometimes also a man or woman much older falls silent for a day or two, and then leaves home. These people go out into the street, and walk down the street alone. They keep walking, and walk straight out of the city of Omelas, through the beautiful gates. They keep walking across the farmlands of Omelas. Each one goes alone, youth or girl, man or woman. Night falls; the traveler must pass down village streets, between the houses with yellow-lit windows, and on out into the darkness of the fields. Each alone, they go west or north, towards the mountains. They go on. They leave Omelas, they walk ahead into the darkness, and they do not come back. The place they go towards is a place even less imaginable to most of us than the city of happiness. I cannot describe it at all. It is possible that it does not exist. But they seem to know where they are going, the ones who walk away from Omelas.

(1976)

Questions for Discussion and Writing

1. Who is the narrator of this story? What opinion does the narrator have of Omelas and of those who walk away?
2. Describe the conflict in the story. Who or what are the protagonist and the antagonist?
3. Is this story a fable? If so, what moral or lesson does it teach?
4. In what ways does this story provide a critique of modern American society?
5. Write a narrative or essay from the point of view of someone who walked away from Omelas.

◇◇◇◇◇◇◇◇◇◇◇◇◇◇◇◇◇◇◇◇◇◇

Octavia E. Butler 1947–2006

Reared by her hardworking mother after her father died, Octavia Butler began writing while still a child. "I began with horse stories," she says, "because I was crazy over horses, even though I never got near one." She worked at a number of blue-collar jobs to earn her way through college. In 1969 she joined the Screen Writers' Guild Open Door Program, where she studied with Harlan Ellison. After five years, her stories began to be published. She won a MacArthur Foundation "genius" grant in 1995, the first one given to a writer of science fiction. "Writers use everything," she declares. "If it doesn't kill you, you probably wind up using it in your writing."

Speech Sounds

There was trouble aboard the Washington Boulevard bus. Rye had expected trouble sooner or later in her journey. She had put off going until loneliness and hopelessness drove her out. She believed she might have one group of relatives left alive—a brother and his two children twenty miles away in Pasadena. That was a day's journey one-way, if she were lucky. The unexpected arrival of the bus as she left her Virginia Road home had seemed to be a piece of luck—until the trouble began.

Two young men were involved in a disagreement of some kind, or, more likely, a misunderstanding. They stood in the aisle, grunting and gesturing at each other, each in his own uncertain T stance as the bus lurched over the potholes. The driver seemed to be putting some effort into keeping them off balance. Still, their gestures stopped just short of contact—mock punches, hand games of intimidation to replace lost curses.

People watched the pair, then looked at one another and made small anxious sounds. Two children whimpered.

Rye sat a few feet behind the disputants and across from the back door. She watched the two carefully, knowing the fight would begin when someone's nerve broke or someone's hand slipped or someone came to the end of his limited ability to communicate. These things could happen anytime.

One of them happened as the bus hit an especially large pothole and one   5
man, tall, thin, and sneering, was thrown into his shorter opponent.

Instantly, the shorter man drove his left fist into the disintegrating sneer. He hammered his larger opponent as though he neither had nor needed any weapon other than his left fist. He hit quickly enough, hard enough to batter his opponent down before the taller man could regain his balance or hit back even once.

People screamed or squawked in fear. Those nearby scrambled to get out of the way. Three more young men roared in excitement and gestured wildly. Then, somehow, a second dispute broke out between two of these three—probably because one inadvertently touched or hit the other.

As the second fight scattered frightened passengers, a woman shook the driver's shoulder and grunted as she gestured toward the fighting.

The driver grunted back through bared teeth. Frightened, the woman drew away.

Rye, knowing the methods of bus drivers, braced herself and held on to the   10
crossbar of the seat in front of her. When the driver hit the brakes, she was ready and the combatants were not. They fell over seats and onto screaming passengers, creating even more confusion. At least one more fight started.

The instant the bus came to a full stop, Rye was on her feet, pushing the back door. At the second push, it opened and she jumped out, holding her pack in one arm. Several other passengers followed, but some stayed on the bus. Buses were so rare and irregular now, people rode when they could, no matter what. There might not be another bus today—or tomorrow. People started walking, and if they saw a bus they flagged it down. People making intercity trips like Rye's from Los Angeles to Pasadena made plans to camp out, or risked seeking shelter with locals who might rob or murder them.

The bus did not move, but Rye moved away from it. She intended to wait until the trouble was over and get on again, but if there was shooting, she wanted the protection of a tree. Thus, she was near the curb when a battered blue Ford on the other side of the street made a U-turn and pulled up in front of the bus. Cars were rare these days—as rare as a severe shortage of fuel and of relatively unimpaired mechanics could make them. Cars that still ran were as likely to be used as weapons as they were to serve as transportation. Thus, when the driver of the Ford beckoned to Rye, she moved away warily. The driver got out—a big man, young, neatly bearded with dark, thick hair. He wore a long overcoat and a look of wariness that matched Rye's. She stood several feet from him, waiting to see what he would do. He looked at the bus, now rocking with the combat inside, then at the small cluster of passengers who had gotten off. Finally he looked at Rye again.

She returned his gaze, very much aware of the old forty-five automatic her jacket concealed. She watched his hands.

He pointed with his left hand toward the bus. The dark-tinted windows prevented him from seeing what was happening inside.

His use of the left hand interested Rye more than his obvious question. Left-handed people tended to be less impaired, more reasonable and comprehending, less driven by frustration, confusion, and anger.

She imitated his gesture, pointing toward the bus with her own left hand, then punching the air with both fists.

The man took off his coat, revealing a Los Angeles Police Department uniform complete with baton and service revolver.

Rye took another step back from him. There was no more LAPD, no more *any* large organization, governmental or private. There were neighborhood patrols and armed individuals. That was all.

The man took something from his coat pocket, then threw the coat into the car. Then he gestured Rye back, back toward the rear of the bus. He had something made of plastic in his hand. Rye did not understand what he wanted until he went to the rear door of the bus and beckoned her to stand there. She obeyed mainly out of curiosity. Cop or not, maybe he could do something to stop the stupid fighting.

He walked around the front of the bus, to the street side where the driver's window was open. There, she thought she saw him throw something into the bus. She was still trying to peer through the tinted glass when people began stumbling out the rear door, choking and weeping. Gas.

Rye caught an old woman who would have fallen, lifted two little children down when they were in danger of being knocked down and trampled. She could see the bearded man helping people at the front door. She caught a thin old man shoved out by one of the combatants. Staggered by the old man's weight, she was barely able to get out of the way as the last of the young men pushed his way out. This one, bleeding from nose and mouth, stumbled into another, and they grappled blindly, still sobbing from the gas.

The bearded man helped the bus driver out through the front door, though the driver did not seem to appreciate his help. For a moment, Rye thought there would be another fight. The bearded man stepped back and watched the driver gesture threateningly, watched him shout in wordless anger.

The bearded man stood still, made no sound, refused to respond to clearly obscene gestures. The least impaired people tended to do this—stand back unless they were physically threatened and let those with less control scream and jump around. It was as though they felt it beneath them to be as touchy as the less comprehending. This was an attitude of superiority, and that was the way people like the bus driver perceived it. Such "superiority" was frequently punished by beatings, even by death. Rye had had close calls of her own. As a result, she never went unarmed. And in this world where the only likely common language was body language, being armed was often enough. She had rarely had to draw her gun or even display it.

The bearded man's revolver was on constant display. Apparently that was enough for the bus driver. The driver spat in disgust, glared at the bearded man for a moment longer, then strode back to his gas-filled bus. He stared at it for a moment, clearly wanting to get in, but the gas was still too strong. Of the windows, only his tiny driver's window actually opened. The front door was open, but the rear door would not stay open unless someone held it. Of course, the air conditioning had failed long ago. The bus would take some time to clear. It was the driver's property, his livelihood. He had pasted old magazine pictures of items he would accept as fare on its sides. Then he would use what he collected to feed his family or to trade. If his bus did not run, he did not eat. On the other hand, if the inside of his bus was torn apart by senseless fighting, he would not eat very well either. He was apparently unable to perceive this. All he could see was that it would be some time before he could use his bus again. He shook his fist at the bearded man and shouted. There seemed to be words in his shout, but Rye could not understand them. She did not know whether this was his fault or hers. She had heard so little coherent human speech for the past three years, she was no longer certain how well she recognized it, no longer certain of the degree of her own impairment.

The bearded man sighed. He glanced toward his car, then beckoned to Rye.   25
He was ready to leave, but he wanted something from her first. No. No, he wanted her to leave with him. Risk getting into his car when, in spite of his uniform, law and order were nothing—not even words any longer.

She shook her head in a universally understood negative, but the man continued to beckon.

She waved him away. He was doing what the less impaired rarely did—drawing potentially negative attention to another of his kind. People from the bus had begun to look at her.

One of the men who had been fighting tapped another on the arm, then pointed from the bearded man to Rye, and finally held up the first two fingers of his right hand as though giving two-thirds of a Boy Scout salute. The gesture was very quick, its meaning obvious even at a distance. She had been grouped with the bearded man. Now what?

The man who had made the gesture started toward her.

She had no idea what he intended, but she stood her ground. The man was   30
half a foot taller than she was and perhaps ten years younger. She did not imagine she could outrun him. Nor did she expect anyone to help her if she needed help. The people around her were all strangers.

She gestured once—a clear indication to the man to stop. She did not intend to repeat the gesture. Fortunately, the man obeyed. He gestured obscenely and several other men laughed. Loss of verbal language had spawned a whole new set of obscene gestures. The man, with stark simplicity, had accused her of sex with the bearded man and had suggested she accommodate the other men present—beginning with him.

Rye watched him wearily. People might very well stand by and watch if he tried to rape her. They would also stand and watch her shoot him. Would he push things that far?

He did not. After a series of obscene gestures that brought him no closer to her, he turned contemptuously and walked away.

And the bearded man still waited. He had removed his service revolver, holster and all. He beckoned again, both hands empty. No doubt his gun was in the car and within easy reach, but his taking it off impressed her. Maybe he was all right. Maybe he was just alone. She had been alone herself for three years. The illness had stripped her, killing her children one by one, killing her husband, her sister, her parents.

The illness, if it was an illness, had cut even the living off from one another. 35
As it swept over the country, people hardly had time to lay blame on the Soviets
(though they were falling silent along with the rest of the world), on a new virus,
a new pollutant, radiation, divine retribution .... The illness was stroke-swift in
the way it cut people down and strokelike in some of its effects. But it was highly
specific. Language was always lost or severely impaired. It was never regained.
Often there was also paralysis, intellectual impairment, death.

Rye walked toward the bearded man, ignoring the whistling and applauding
of two of the young men and their thumbs-up signs to the bearded man. If he
had smiled at them or acknowledged them in any way, she would almost certainly have changed her mind. If she had let herself think of the possible deadly
consequences of getting into a stranger's car, she would have changed her mind.
Instead, she thought of the man who lived across the street from her. He rarely
washed since his bout with the illness. And he had gotten into the habit of uri-
nating wherever he happened to be. He had two women already—one tending
each of his large gardens. They put up with him in exchange for his protection.
He had made it clear that he wanted Rye to become his third woman.

She got into the car and the bearded man shut the door. She watched as he
walked around to the driver's door—watched for his sake because his gun was
on the seat beside her. And the bus driver and a pair of young men had come
a few steps closer. They did nothing, though, until the bearded man was in the
car. Then one of them threw a rock. Others followed his example, and as the car
drove away, several rocks bounced off harmlessly.

When the bus was some distance behind them, Rye wiped sweat from her
forehead and longed to relax. The bus would have taken her more than halfway
to Pasadena. She would have had only ten miles to walk. She wondered how far
she would have to walk now—and wondered if walking a long distance would be
her only problem.

At Figuroa and Washington, where the bus normally made a left turn, the
bearded man stopped, looked at her, and indicated that she should choose a
direction. When she directed him left and he actually turned left, she began to
relax. If he was willing to go where she directed, perhaps he was safe.

As they passed blocks of burned, abandoned buildings, empty lots, and 40
wrecked or stripped cars, he slipped a gold chain over his head and handed it
to her. The pendant attached to it was a smooth, glassy, black rock. Obsidian.
His name might be Rock or Peter or Black, but she decided to think of him
as Obsidian. Even her sometimes useless memory would retain a name like
Obsidian.

She handed him her own name symbol—a pin in the shape of a large golden
stalk of wheat. She had bought it long before the illness and the silence began.
Now she wore it, thinking it was as close as she was likely to come to Rye.
People like Obsidian who had not known her before probably thought of her
as Wheat. Not that it mattered. She would never hear her name spoken again.

Obsidian handed her pin back to her. He caught her hand as she reached for
it and rubbed his thumb over her calluses.

He stopped at First Street and asked which way again. Then, after turning
right as she had indicated, he parked near the Music Center. There, he took a
folded paper from the dashboard and unfolded it. Rye recognized it as a street
map, though the writing on it meant nothing to her. He flattened the map, took
her hand again, and put her index finger on one spot. He touched her, touched

himself, pointed toward the floor. In effect, "We are here." She knew he wanted to know where she was going. She wanted to tell him, but she shook her head sadly. She had lost reading and writing. That was her most serious impairment and her most painful. She had taught history at UCLA. She had done freelance writing. Now she could not even read her own manuscripts. She had a houseful of books that she could neither read nor bring herself to use as fuel. And she had a memory that would not bring back to her much of what she had read before.

She stared at the map, trying to calculate. She had been born in Pasadena, had lived for fifteen years in Los Angeles. Now she was near L.A. Civic Center. She knew the relative positions of the two cities, knew streets, directions, even knew to stay away from freeways, which might be blocked by wrecked cars and destroyed overpasses. She ought to know how to point out Pasadena even though she could not recognize the word.

Hesitantly, she placed her hand over a pale orange patch in the upper right   45
corner of the map. That should be right. Pasadena.

Obsidian lifted her hand and looked under it, then folded the map and put it back on the dashboard. He could read, she realized belatedly. He could probably write, too. Abruptly, she hated him—deep, bitter hatred. What did literacy mean to him—a grown man who played cops and robbers? But he was literate and she was not. She never would be. She felt sick to her stomach with hatred, frustration, and jealousy. And only a few inches from her hand was a loaded gun.

She held herself still, staring at him, almost seeing his blood. But her rage crested and ebbed and she did nothing.

Obsidian reached for her hand with hesitant familiarity. She looked at him. Her face had already revealed too much. No person still living in what was left of human society could fail to recognize that expression, that jealousy.

She closed her eyes wearily, drew a deep breath. She had experienced longing for the past, hatred of the present, growing hopelessness, purposelessness, but she had never experienced such a powerful urge to kill another person. She had left her home, finally, because she had come near to killing herself. She had found no reason to stay alive. Perhaps that was why she had gotten into Obsidian's car. She had never before done such a thing.

He touched her mouth and made chatter motions with thumb and fingers.   50
Could she speak?

She nodded and watched his milder envy come and go. Now both had admitted what it was not safe to admit, and there had been no violence. He tapped his mouth and forehead and shook his head. He did not speak or comprehend spoken language. The illness had played with them, taking away, she suspected, what each valued most.

She plucked at his sleeve, wondering why he had decided on his own to keep the LAPD alive with what he had left. He was sane enough otherwise. Why wasn't he at home raising corn, rabbits, and children? But she did not know how to ask. Then he put his hand on her thigh and she had another question to deal with.

She shook her head. Disease, pregnancy, helpless, solitary agony … no.

He massaged her thigh gently and smiled in obvious disbelief.

No one had touched her for three years. She had not wanted anyone to touch   55
her. What kind of world was this to chance bringing a child into even if the father were willing to stay and help raise it? It was too bad, though. Obsidian could not know how attractive he was to her—young, probably younger than she was, clean, asking for what he wanted rather than demanding it. But none

of that mattered. What were a few moments of pleasure measured against a life-time of consequences?

He pulled her closer to him and for a moment she let herself enjoy the close-ness. He smelled good—male and good. She pulled away reluctantly.

He sighed, reached toward the glove compartment. She stiffened, not knowing what to expect, but all he took out was a small box. The writing on it meant nothing to her. She did not understand until he broke the seal, opened the box, and took out a condom. He looked at her, and she first looked away in surprise. Then she giggled. She could not remember when she had last giggled.

He grinned, gestured toward the backseat, and she laughed aloud. Even in her teens, she had disliked backseats of cars. But she looked around at the empty streets and ruined buildings, then she got out and into the backseat. He let her put the condom on him, then seemed surprised at her eagerness.

Sometime later, they sat together, covered by his coat, unwilling to become clothed near strangers again just yet. He made rock-the-baby gestures and looked questioningly at her.

She swallowd, shook her head. She did not know how to tell him her children were dead. 60

He took her hand and drew a cross in it with his index finger, then made his baby-rocking gesture again.

She nodded, held up three fingers, then turned away, trying to shut out a sudden flood of memories. She had told herself that the children growing up now were to be pitied. They would run through the downtown canyons with no real memory of what the buildings had been or even how they had come to be. Today's children gathered books as well as wood to be burned as fuel. They ran through the streets chasing one another and hooting like chimpanzees. They had no future. They were now all they would ever be.

He put his hand on her shoulder, and she turned suddenly, fumbling for his small box, then urging him to make love to her again. He could give her forget-fulness and pleasure. Until now, nothing had been able to do that. Until now, every day had brought her closer to the time when she would do what she had left home to avoid doing: putting her gun in her mouth and pulling the trigger.

She asked Obsidian if he would come home with her, stay with her.

He looked surprised and pleased once he understood. But he did not answer 65 at once. Finally, he shook his head as she had feared he might. He was probably having too much fun playing cops and robbers and picking up women.

She dressed in silent disappointment, unable to feel any anger toward him. Perhaps he already had a wife and a home. That was likely. The illness had been harder on men than on women—had killed more men, had left male survivors more severely impaired. Men like Obsidian were rare. Women either settled for less or stayed alone. If they found an Obsidian, they did what they could to keep him. Rye suspected he had someone younger, prettier, keeping him.

He touched her while she was strapping her gun on and asked with a compli-cated series of gestures whether it was loaded.

She nodded grimly.

He patted her arm.

She asked once more if he would come home with her, this time using a dif- 70 ferent series of gestures. He had seemed hesitant. Perhaps he could be courted.

He got out and into the front seat without responding.

She took her place in front again, watching him. Now he plucked at his uniform and looked at her. She thought she was being asked something but did not know what it was.

He took off his badge, tapped it with one finger, then tapped his chest. Of course.

She took the badge from his hand and pinned her wheat stalk to it. If playing cops and robbers was his only insanity let him play. She would take him, uniform and all. It occurred to her that she might eventually lose him to someone he would meet as he had met her. But she would have him for a while.

He took the street map down again, tapped it, pointed vaguely northeast 75 toward Pasadena, then looked at her.

She shrugged, tapped his shoulder, then her own, and held up her index and second fingers tight together, just to be sure.

He grasped the two fingers and nodded. He was with her.

She took the map from him and threw it onto the dashboard. She pointed back southwest—back toward home. Now she did not have to go to Pasadena. Now she could go on having a brother there and two nephews—three right-handed males. Now she did not have to find out for certain whether she was as alone as she feared. Now she was not alone.

Obsidian took Hill Street south, then Washington west, and she leaned back, wondering what it would be like to have someone again. With what she had scavenged, what she had preserved, and what she grew, there was easily enough food for them. There was certainly room enough in a four-bedroom house. He could move his possessions in. Best of all, the animal across the street would pull back and possibly not force her to kill him.

Obsidian had drawn her closer to him, and she had put her head on his 80 shoulder when suddenly he braked hard, almost throwing her off the seat. Out of the corner of her eye, she saw that someone had run across the street in front of the car. One car on the street and someone had to run in front of it.

Straightening up, Rye saw that the runner was a woman, fleeing from an old frame house to a boarded-up storefront. She ran silently, but the man who followed her a moment later shouted what sounded like garbled words as he ran. He had something in his hand. Not a gun. A knife, perhaps.

The woman tried a door, found it locked, looked around desperately, finally snatched up a fragment of glass broken from the storefront window. With this she turned to face her pursuer. Rye thought she would be more likely to cut her own hand than to hurt anyone else with the glass.

Obsidian jumped from the car, shouting. It was the first time Rye had heard his voice—deep and hoarse from disuse. He made the same sound over and over the way some speechless people did, "Da, da, da!"

Rye got out of the car as Obsidian ran toward the couple. He had drawn his gun. Fearful, she drew her own and released the safety. She looked around to see who else might be attracted to the scene. She saw the man glance at Obsidian, then suddenly lunge at the woman. The woman jabbed his face with her glass, but he caught her arm and managed to stab her twice before Obsidian shot him.

The man doubled, then toppled, clutching his abdomen. Obsidian shouted, 85 then gestured Rye over to help the woman.

Rye moved to the woman's side, remembering that she had little more than bandages and antiseptic in her pack. But the woman was beyond help. She had been stabbed with a long, slender boning knife.

She touched Obsidian to let him know the woman was dead. He had bent to check the wounded man who lay still and also seemed dead. But as Obsidian looked around to see what Rye wanted, the man opened his eyes. Face contorted, he seized Obsidian's just-holstered revolver and fired. The bullet caught Obsidian in the temple and he collapsed.

It happened just that simply, just that fast. An instant later, Rye shot the wounded man as he was turning the gun on her.

And Rye was alone—with three corpses.

She knelt beside Obsidian, dry-eyed, frowning, trying to understand why everything had suddenly changed. Obsidian was gone. He had died and left her—like everyone else. 90

Two very small children came out of the house from which the man and woman had run—a boy and girl perhaps three years old. Holding hands, they crossed the street toward Rye. They stared at her, then edged past her and went to the dead woman. The girl shook the woman's arm as though trying to wake her.

This was too much. Rye got up, feeling sick to her stomach with grief and anger. If the children began to cry, she thought she would vomit.

They were on their own, those two kids. They were old enough to scavenge. She did not need any more grief. She did not need a stranger's children who would grow up to be hairless chimps.

She went back to the car. She could drive home, at least. She remembered how to drive.

The thought that Obsidian should be buried occurred to her before she reached the car, and she did vomit. 95

She had found and lost the man so quickly. It was as though she had been snatched from comfort and security and given a sudden, inexplicable beating. Her head would not clear. She could not think.

Somehow, she made herself go back to him, look at him. She found herself on her knees beside him with no memory of having knelt. She stroked his face, his beard. One of the children made a noise and she looked at them, at the woman who was probably their mother. The children looked back at her, obviously frightened. Perhaps it was their fear that reached her finally.

She had been about to drive away and leave them. She had almost done it, almost left two toddlers to die. Surely there had been enough dying. She would have to take the children home with her. She would not be able to live with any other decision. She looked around for a place to bury three bodies. Or two. She wondered if the murderer were the children's father. Before the silence, the police had always said some of the most dangerous calls they went out on were domestic disturbance calls. Obsidian should have known that—not that the knowledge would have kept him in the car. It would not have held her back either. She could not have watched the woman murdered and done nothing.

She dragged Obsidian toward the car. She had nothing to dig with her, and no one to guard for her while she dug. Better to take the bodies with her and bury them next to her husband and her children. Obsidian would come home with her after all.

When she had gotten him onto the floor in the back, she returned for the woman. The little girl, thin, dirty, solemn, stood up and unknowingly gave Rye a gift. As Rye began to drag the woman by her arms, the little girl screamed, "No!" 100

Rye dropped the woman and stared at the girl.

"No!" the girl repeated. She came to stand beside the woman. "Go away!" she told Rye.

"Don't talk," the little boy said to her. There was no blurring or confusing of sounds. Both children had spoken and Rye had understood. The boy looked at the dead murderer and moved further from him. He took the girl's hand. "Be quiet," he whispered.

Fluent speech! Had the woman died because she could talk and had taught her children to talk? Had she been killed by a husband's festering anger or by a stranger's jealous rage? And the children ... they must have been born after the silence. Had the disease run its course, then? Or were these children simply immune? Certainly they had had time to fall sick and silent. Rye's mind leaped ahead. What if children of three or fewer years were safe and able to learn language? What if all they needed were teachers? Teachers and protectors.

Rye glanced at the dead murderer. To her shame, she thought she could understand some of the passions that must have driven him, whomever he was. Anger, frustration, hopelessness, insane jealousy ... how many more of him were there—people willing to destroy what they could not have? 105

Obsidian had been the protector, had chosen that role for who knew what reason. Perhaps putting on an obsolete uniform and patrolling the empty streets had been what he did instead of putting a gun into his mouth. And now that there was something worth protecting, he was gone.

She had been a teacher. A good one. She had been a protector, too, though only of herself. She had kept herself alive when she had no reason to live. If the illness let these children alone, she could keep them alive.

Somehow she lifted the dead woman into her arms and placed her on the backseat of the car. The children began to cry, but she knelt on the broken pavement and whispered to them, fearful of frightening them with the harshness of her long unused voice.

"It's all right," she told them. "You're going with us, too. Come on." She lifted them both, one in each arm. They were so light. Had they been getting enough to eat?

The boy covered her mouth with his hand, but she moved her face away. "It's all right for me to talk," she told him. "As long as no one's around, it's all right." She put the boy down on the front seat of the car and he moved over without being told to, to make room for the girl. When they were both in the car, Rye leaned against the window, looking at them, seeing that they were less afraid now, that they watched her with at least as much curiosity as fear. 110

"I'm Valerie Rye," she said, savoring the words. "It's all right for you to talk to me."

(1983)

Questions for Discussion and Writing

1. What details in the first two paragraphs let readers know that the story takes place in the future following some breakdown in society?

2. Write an essay explaining how the names *Rye* and *Obsidian* suit their characters' roles and personalities?

3. How does the children's ability to speak affect the ending?

4. What is the major claim of this cautionary tale?
5. Write an essay explaining how Butler conveys the importance of language and human speech in maintaining a civil society.

Ideas for Writing: Making Connections

1. Ray Bradbury has said, "I don't try to describe the future. I try to prevent it." What condition(s) in the future does each story in this portfolio seek to prevent?
2. Argue that all three stories in the portfolio present examples of dystopias.
3. Identify the point of view for each of the three stories (see pages 146–48). Consider the character and situation of the person whose mind you are allowed into. How does the point of view help you to understand and accept the future world depicted in each story?
4. Which of these stories would make a good film? Explain and justify your choice. If you can, nominate a director for the movie or some actors to star in the major roles, and explain your choices.
5. Compare the scapegoats in "The Ones Who Walk Away from Omelas" with those in "The Lottery" (page 127).
6. Compare and contrast the fantasy elements in Le Guin's "The Ones Who Walk Away from Omelas" with those in Hawthorne's "The Birthmark" (page 210).

MultiModal Project

Reread "The Ones Who Walk Away from Omelas" (pages 336–41). Then write a narrative from the point of view of someone who walked away from Omelas. In your story, explain why you walked away and tell what happened to you afterward.

Sample Student Paper: Comparing Dystopias

In the following paper, a student compares the way that two science fiction writers project what could go wrong with social relationships in the future.

Ben Hardy

Professor Day

English 150

15 November 2011

When Social Contracts Go Bad

As members of a civilized society, most of us know there are limits on what we can say and do. Some of these limits are written down as laws, but many of them are simply understood. This set of guidelines has been called "the social contract," which *The Harper Dictionary of Modern Thought* defines as the "unwritten agreement between the members of a society to behave with reciprocal responsibility in their relationships" (Reilly 783). Two short stories, "The Ones Who Walk Away from Omelas," by Ursula Le Guin (319-23), and "Speech Sounds," by Octavia Butler (371-80), describe societies where social contracts have broken down. In Le Guin's Omelas, a joyous society's ease and wealth are held together by a single horrible outrage. In Butler's post-apocalyptic Los Angeles, the sudden loss of the ability to read, write, and speak has led to the complete breakdown of civil order.

All societies have laws governing citizens' behavior. For the most part, these are a list of actions one *cannot* do. Such laws are "singularly few" in the anything-goes society of Omelas (Le Guin 319). People are generally free to do as they please, and what they choose to do is play music, dance in festivals, enjoy lavish banquets. They also choose, through knowing inaction, to agree to the torture of a young child, ensuring the beauty of their society and its common pleasures. Their social contract is clear, but vicious.

In Butler's futuristic Los Angeles, the lack of police, clergy, and governing laws has quite a different effect. Crimes of theft, murder, and rape are rampant. Injustice abounds, but in contrast to Omelas, the lawlessness affects everyone, not just a single person. Whatever social contract there was in the past, the loss of language is the loss of the contract. Seventeenth-century philosopher Thomas Hobbes believed that people in a natural state are selfish, brutish, and egotistic (Popkin 66). Hobbes could have predicted what would happen with the breakdown of language in Los Angeles: no government at all, and no code of behavior except force.

As members of a well-running society we don't think, on an everyday basis, about what holds our civilization together. But in Omelas, citizens are fully aware of the deal they have made. They do not have to know disease or want, but they silently consent to the constant suffering of an innocent child, and having to live with this knowledge is the price they must pay. Most of them apparently learn to rationalize the choice and push it into the background of their joyful lives. By contrast, in post-plague Los Angeles, probably few people realize that it was language that enforced civil behavior, cementing agreements and negotiating disagreements, affecting everything from banning sexual assault to quibbling over seats on a bus. Both societies have their dissidents—people like Rye and Obsidian, trying to keep words alive in Los Angeles, and of course, people like the ones who walk away from Omelas.

It's unclear whether authors Le Guin and Butler view human nature as inherently good or inherently evil. Both writers have created societies where people act horribly, and neither offers a solution to the serious problem. However, neither author appears to have given up on the human race, and both offer a ray of hope to the reader. Rye sees in the children's ability to speak a possible way out of the uncivilized dystopia. She will care for them, teach them, probably at great risk. And, while no one staying in Omelas knows where the people who walk away are going, we can be relatively sure it's to a place where happiness is not built upon a child kept chained in a squalid basement.

Hardy 3

Works Cited

Butler, Octavia. "Speech Sounds." *Literature and the Writing Process*, edited by Elizabeth McMahan, et al., 9th ed., Longman, 2011, pp. 371-80.

Le Guin, Ursula. "The Ones Who Walk Away From Omelas." *Literature and the Writing Process*, edited by Elizabeth McMahan, et al., 7th ed., Prentice Hall, 2005, pp. 319-23.

Popkin, Richard, and Avrum Stroll. *Philosophy Made Simple.* Broadway Books, 1993.

Reilly, Steve. "Social Contract." *The Harper Dictionary of Modern Thought*, edited by Alan Bullock and Stephen Trombley, revised ed., Harper Collins, 1988, p. 783.

15 A Portfolio of Humorous and Satirical Stories

Chapter Preview

As the poet Billy Collins says, "If you're majoring in English, you're majoring in death." Students often agree with Collins that serious literature can be seriously depressing. This group of humorous pieces is included to offset that effect, to lighten the load, so to speak. You can approach a humorous story the same way you would any other work of literature (through plot, character, point of view, and so on), or you can analyze the comic effects employed by the author. Each selection in this portfolio is designed to be funny, using common strategies such as irony to achieve the comic intent. Another technique at work in some of the stories is a more cutting form of humor—**satire**. Through exaggeration and striking contrasts, the object of the satire (a character, a theme, a style of writing) is openly or indirectly made fun of and criticized, often with the intent to provoke some form of improvement in a custom or institution or to change the reader's thinking about that custom or institution.

In this chapter, you will learn to do the following:

- Analyze humorous and satirical stories, identifying and evaluating comic effects and satire.
- Compare and contrast different humorous stories.
- Write about stories that employ humor and satire.

H. H. Munro ("Saki")   1870–1916

The son of a military policeman in Burma, H[ector] H[ugh] Munro was raised in England by aunts after his mother died when the boy was only two years old. In 1893 he returned to Burma (today called Myanmar) for a short time to follow his father's example in the military. Ultimately, he chose to pursue writing in London. Using the pen name of Saki, Munro gained fame for his witty, sometimes macabre short stories that satirized the hypocrisy and pretensions of his era. He frequently used clever protagonists to inflict vengeance on conventional society. Although he was forty-three when World War I started, Munro enlisted and rose to the rank of lance sergeant. While taking cover in a bomb crater, he was killed by a German sniper.

The Open Window

"My aunt will be down presently, Mr. Nuttel," said a very self-possessed young lady of fifteen; "in the meantime you must try and put up with me."

Framton Nuttel endeavoured to say the correct something which should duly flatter the niece of the moment without unduly discounting the aunt that was to come. Privately he doubted more than ever whether these formal visits on a succession of total strangers would do much towards helping the nerve cure which he was supposed to be undergoing.

"I know how it will be," his sister had said when he was preparing to migrate to this rural retreat; "you will bury yourself down there and not speak to a living soul, and your nerves will be worse than ever from moping. I shall just give you letters of introduction to all the people I know there. Some of them, as far as I can remember, were quite nice."

Framton wondered whether Mrs. Sappleton, the lady to whom he was presenting one of the letters of introduction, came into the nice division.

"Do you know many of the people round here?" asked the niece, when she judged that they had had sufficient silent communion. "Hardly a soul," said Framton. "My sister was staying here, at the rectory, you know, some four years ago, and she gave me letters of introduction to some of the people here."

He made the last statement in a tone of distinct regret.

"Then you know practically nothing about my aunt?" pursued the self-possessed young lady.

"Only her name and address," admitted the caller. He was wondering whether Mrs. Sappleton was in the married or widowed state. An undefinable something about the room seemed to suggest masculine habitation.

"Her great tragedy happened just three years ago," said the child; "that would be since your sister's time."

"Her tragedy?" asked Framton; somehow in this restful country spot tragedies seemed out of place.

"You may wonder why we keep that window wide open on an October afternoon," said the niece, indicating a large French window that opened on to a lawn.

"It is quite warm for the time of the year," said Framton; "but has that window got anything to do with the tragedy?"

"Out through that window, three years ago to a day, her husband and her two young brothers went off for their day's shooting. They never came back. In crossing the moor to their favourite snipe-shooting ground they were all three engulfed in a treacherous piece of bog. It had been that dreadful wet summer, you know, and places that were safe in other years gave way suddenly without warning. Their bodies were never recovered. That was the dreadful part of it." Here the child's voice lost its self-possessed note and became falteringly human. "Poor aunt always thinks that they will come back some day, they and the little brown spaniel that was lost with them, and walk in at that window just as they used to do. That is why the window is kept open every evening till it is quite dusk. Poor dear aunt, she has often told me how they went out, her husband with his white waterproof coat over his arm, and Ronnie, her youngest brother, singing 'Bertie, why do you bound?' as he always did to tease her, because she said it got on her nerves. Do you know, sometimes on still, quiet evenings like this, I almost get a creepy feeling that they will all walk in through that window - "

She broke off with a little shudder. It was a relief to Framton when the aunt bustled into the room with a whirl of apologies for being late in making her appearance.

"I hope Vera has been amusing you?" she said.

"She has been very interesting," said Framton.

"I hope you don't mind the open window," said Mrs. Sappleton briskly; "my husband and brothers will be home directly from shooting, and they always come in this way. They've been out for snipe in the marshes to-day, so they'll make a fine mess over my poor carpets. So like you men-folk, isn't it?"

She rattled on cheerfully about the shooting and the scarcity of birds, and the prospects for duck in the winter. To Framton it was all purely horrible. He made a desperate but only partially successful effort to turn the talk on to a less ghastly topic; he was conscious that his hostess was giving him only a fragment of her attention, and her eyes were constantly straying past him to the open window and the lawn beyond. It was certainly an unfortunate coincidence that he should have paid his visit on this tragic anniversary.

"The doctors agree in ordering me complete rest, an absence of mental excitement, and avoidance of anything in the nature of violent physical exercise," announced Framton, who laboured under the tolerably wide-spread delusion that total strangers and chance acquaintances are hungry for the least detail of one's ailments and infirmities, their cause and cure. "On the matter of diet they are not so much in agreement," he continued.

"No?" said Mrs. Sappleton, in a voice which only replaced a yawn at the last moment. Then she suddenly brightened into alert attention—but not to what Framton was saying.

"Here they are at last!" she cried. "Just in time for tea, and don't they look as if they were muddy up to the eyes!"

Framton shivered slightly and turned towards the niece with a look intended to convey sympathetic comprehension. The child was staring out through the open window with dazed horror in her eyes. In a chill shock of nameless fear Framton swung round in his seat and looked in the same direction.

In the deepening twilight three figures were walking across the lawn towards the window; they all carried guns under their arms, and one of them was additionally burdened with a white coat hung over his shoulders. A tired brown spaniel kept close at their heels. Noiselessly they neared the house, and then a hoarse young voice chanted out of the dusk: "I said, Bertie, why do you bound?"

Framton grabbed wildly at his stick and hat; the hall-door, the gravel-drive, and the front gate were dimly-noted stages in his headlong retreat. A cyclist coming along the road had to run into the hedge to avoid an imminent collision.

"Here we are, my dear," said the bearer of the white mackintosh, coming in through the window; "fairly muddy, but most of it's dry. Who was that who bolted out as we came up?"

"A most extraordinary man, a Mr. Nuttel," said Mrs. Sappleton; "could only talk about his illnesses, and dashed off without a word of good-bye or apology when you arrived. One would think he had seen a ghost."

"I expect it was the spaniel," said the niece calmly; "he told me he had a horror of dogs. He was once hunted into a cemetery somewhere on the banks of the Ganges by a pack of pariah dogs, and had to spend the night in a newly dug grave with the creatures snarling and grinning and foaming just above him. Enough to make anyone lose their nerve."

Romance at short notice was her speciality.

(1914)

Questions for Discussion and Writing

1. What does the name Vera mean?

2. When did you figure out that Vera was playing a prank on Framton? The key to the story is the last line. What does "romance" mean in this context?

3. The narrator says that Framton "laboured under the tolerable wide-spread delusion that total strangers and chance acquaintances are hungry for the least detail of one's ailments and infirmities, their cause and cure." What does that line reveal about the author's attitude toward people like Framton Nuttel?

4. Many readers are entertained by Vera's virtuoso performance, even though she causes distress to another human. Others have accused Munro of creating characters that are a little too cruel. Do you sympathize with Nutttel or, like Vera, laugh at his foolishness? Write an essay that argues your position on this question.

5. Munro said he enjoyed attacking "the prigs, snobs, bores, politicians, and other self-important comedians, spiteful old women, and silly, smug young ones" that he met in the British society of the Edwardian era (1890–1916). Write an essay arguing that he accomplished his purpose in "The Open Window."

◇◇◇◇◇◇◇◇◇◇◇◇◇◇◇◇◇◇◇◇◇◇

John Updike   1932–2009

John Updike grew up in Pennsylvania, an only child who loved reading but suffered from stammering and psoriasis. He went to Harvard on a scholarship, got married during his junior year, and graduated summa cum laude in 1954. He briefly studied art at Oxford, then worked on the staff of the *New Yorker*, but after two years moved to Massachusetts. His prodigious output caused one critic to complain, "Updike can write faster than I can read." He has twice won the Pulitzer Prize, twice appeared on the cover of *Time*, and twice received the National Medal of Honor. Updike died of lung cancer in 2009 at the age of seventy-six.

A & P

In walks these three girls in nothing but bathing suits. I'm in the third checkout slot, with my back to the door, so I don't see them until they're over by the bread. The one that caught my eye first was the one in the plaid green two-piece. She was a chunky kid, with a good tan and a sweet broad soft-looking can with those two crescents of white just under it, where the sun never seems to hit, at the top of the backs of her legs. I stood there with my hand on a box of HiHo crackers trying to remember if I rang it up or not. I ring it up again and the customer starts giving me hell. She's one of these cash-register-watchers, a witch about fifty with rouge on her cheekbones and no eyebrows, and I know it made her day to trip me up. She'd been watching cash registers for fifty years and probably never seen a mistake before.

By the time I got her feathers smoothed and her goodies into a bag—she gives me a little snort in passing, if she'd been born at the right time they would have burned her over in Salem—by the time I get her on her way the girls had circled around the bread and were coming back, without a pushcart, back my way along the counters, in the aisle between the checkouts and the Special bins. They didn't even have shoes on. There was this chunky one, with the two-piece—it was bright green and the seams on the bra were still sharp and her belly was still pretty pale so I guessed she just got it (the suit)—there was this one, with one of those chubby berry-faces, the lips all bunched together under her nose, this one, and a tall one, with black hair that hadn't quite frizzed right, and one of these sunburns right across under the eyes and a chin that was too long—you know, the kind of girl other girls think is very "striking" and "attractive" but never quite makes it, as they very well know, which is why they like her so much—and then the third one, that wasn't quite so tall. She was the queen. She kind of led them, the other two peeking around and making their shoulders round. She didn't look around, not this queen, she just walked straight on slowly, on these long white prima-donna legs. She came down a little hard on her heels, as if she didn't walk in bare feet that much, putting down her heels and then letting the weight move along to her toes as if she was testing the floor with every step, putting a little deliberate extra action into it. You never know for sure how girls' minds work (do you really think it's a mind in there or just a little buzz like a bee in a glass jar?) but you got the idea she had talked the other two into coming in here with her, and now she was showing them how to do it, walk slow and hold yourself straight.

She had on a kind of dirty-pink—beige maybe, I don't know—bathing suit with a little nubble all over it and, what got me, the straps were down. They were off her shoulders looped loose around the cool tops of her arms, and I guess as a result the suit had slipped a little on her, so all around the top of the cloth there was this shining rim. If it hadn't been there you wouldn't have known there could have been anything whiter than those shoulders. With the straps pushed off, there was nothing between the top of the suit and the top of her head except just *her*, this clean bare plane of the top of her chest down from the shoulder bones like a dented sheet of metal tilted in the light. I mean, it was more than pretty.

She had a sort of oaky hair that the sun and salt had bleached, done up in a bun that was unraveling, and a kind of prim face. Walking into the A & P with your straps down, I suppose it's the only kind of face you *can* have. She held her head so high her neck, coming up out of those white shoulders, looked kind of stretched, but I didn't mind. The longer her neck was, the more of her there was.

She must have felt in the corner of her eye me and over my shoulder Stokesie in the second slot watching, but she didn't tip. Not this queen. She kept her eyes moving across the racks, and stopped, and turned so slow it made my stomach rub the inside of my apron, and buzzed to the other two, who kind of huddled against her for relief, and then they all three of them went up the

5

cat-and-dog-food-breakfast-cereal-macaroni-rice-raisins-seasonings-spreads-spaghetti-soft-drinks-crackers-and-cookies aisle. From the third slot I look straight up this aisle to the meat counter, and I watched them all the way. The fat one with the tan sort of fumbled with the cookies, but on second thought she put the package back. The sheep pushing their carts down the aisle—the girls were walking against the usual traffic (not that we have one-way signs or anything)—were pretty hilarious. You could see them, when Queenie's white shoulders dawned on them, kind of jerk, or hop, or hiccup, but their eyes snapped back to their own baskets and on they pushed. I bet you could set off dynamite in an A & P and the people would by and large keep reaching and checking oatmeal off their lists and muttering "Let me see, there was a third thing, began with A, asparagus, no, ah, yes, applesauce!" or whatever it is they do mutter. But there was no doubt, this jiggled them. A few houseslaves in pin curlers even looked around after pushing their carts past to make sure what they had seen was correct.

You know, it's one thing to have a girl in a bathing suit down on the beach, where what with the glare nobody can look at each other much anyway, and another thing in the cool of the A & P, under the fluorescent lights, against all those stacked packages, with her feet paddling along naked over our checker-board green-and-cream rubber-tile floor.

"Oh Daddy," Stokesie said beside me. "I feel so faint."

"Darling," I said. "Hold me tight." Stokesie's married, with two babies chalked up on his fuselage already, but as far as I can tell that's the only difference. He's twenty-two, and I was nineteen this April.

"Is it done?" he asks, the responsible married man finding his voice. I forgot to say he thinks he's going to be manager some sunny day, maybe in 1990 when it's called the Great Alexandrov and Petrooshki Tea Company or something.

What he meant was, our town is five miles from a beach, with a big summer colony out on the Point, but we're right in the middle of town, and the women generally put on a shirt or shorts or something before they get out of the car into the street. And anyway these are usually women with six children and varicose veins mapping their legs and nobody, including them, could care less. As I say, we're right in the middle of town, and if you stand at our front doors you can see two banks and the Congregational church and the newspaper store and three real-estate offices and about twenty-seven old freeloaders tearing up Central Street because the sewer broke again. It's not as if we're on the Cape; we're north of Boston and there's people in this town haven't seen the ocean for twenty years.

The girls had reached the meat counter and were asking McMahon something. He pointed, they pointed, and they shuffled out of sight behind a pyramid of Diet Delight peaches. All that was left for us to see was old McMahon patting his mouth and looking after them sizing up their joints. Poor kids, I began to feel sorry for them, they couldn't help it.

Now here comes the sad part of the story, at least my family says it's sad, but I don't think it's so sad myself. The store's pretty empty, it being Thursday afternoon, so there was nothing much to do except lean on the register and wait for the girls to show up again. The whole store was like a pinball machine and I didn't know which tunnel they'd come out of. After a while they come around out of the far aisle, around the light bulbs, records at discount of the Caribbean Six or Tony Martin Sings or some such gunk you wonder they waste the wax on, six-packs of

10

candy bars, and plastic toys done up in cellophane that fall apart when a kid looks at them anyway. Around they come, Queenie still leading the way, and holding a little gray jar in her hand. Slots Three through Seven are unmanned and I could see her wondering between Stokes and me, but Stokesie with his usual luck draws an old party in baggy gray pants who stumbles up with four giant cans of pineapple juice (what do these bums *do* with all that pineapple juice? I've often asked myself) so the girls come to me. Queenie puts down the jar and I take it into my fingers icy cold. Kingfish Fancy Herring Snacks in Pure Sour Cream: 49¢. Now her hands are empty, not a ring or a bracelet, bare as God made them, and I wonder where the money's coming from. Still with that prim look she lifts a folded dollar bill out of the hollow at the center of her nubbled pink top. The jar went heavy in my hand. Really, I thought that was so cute.

Then everybody's luck begins to run out. Lengel comes in from haggling with a truck full of cabbages on the lot and is about to scuttle into that door marked MANAGER behind which he hides all day when the girls touch his eye. Lengel's pretty dreary, teaches Sunday school and the rest, but he doesn't miss that much. He comes over and says, "Girls, this isn't the beach."

Queenie blushes, though maybe it's just a brush of sunburn I was noticing for the first time, now that she was so close. "My mother asked me to pick up a jar of herring snacks." Her voice kind of startled me, the way voices do when you see the people first, coming out so flat and dumb yet kind of tony, too, the way it ticked over "pick up" and "snacks." All of a sudden I slid right down her voice into her living room. Her father and the other men were standing around in ice-cream coats and bow ties and the women were in sandals picking up herring snacks on toothpicks off a big glass plate and they were all holding drinks the color of water with olives and sprigs of mint in them. When my parents have somebody over they get lemonade and if it's a real racy affair Schlitz in tall glasses with "They'll Do It Every Time" cartoons stencilled on.

"That's all right," Lengel said. "But this isn't the beach." His repeating this   15 struck me as funny, as if it had just occurred to him, and he had been thinking all these years the A & P was a great big dune and he was the head lifeguard. He didn't like my smiling—as I say he doesn't miss much—but he concentrates on giving the girls that sad Sunday-school-superintendent stare.

Queenie's blush is no sunburn now, and the plump one in plaid, that I liked better from the back—a really sweet can—pipes up, "We weren't doing any shopping. We just came in for the one thing."

"That makes no difference," Lengel tells her, and I could see from the way his eyes went that he hadn't noticed she was wearing a two-piece before. "We want you decently dressed when you come in here."

"We *are* decent," Queenie says suddenly, her lower lip pushing, getting sore now that she remembers her place, a place from which the crowd that runs the A & P must look pretty crummy. Fancy Herring Snacks flashed in her very blue eyes.

"Girls, I don't want to argue with you. After this come in here with your shoulders covered. It's our policy." He turns his back. That's policy for you. Policy is what the kingpins want. What the others want is juvenile delinquency.

All this while, the customers had been showing up with their carts but, you   20 know, sheep, seeing a scene, they had all bunched up on Stokesie, who shook open a paper bag as gently as peeling a peach, not wanting to miss a word. I could feel in the silence everybody getting nervous, most of all Lengel, who asks me, "Sammy, have you rung up their purchase?"

I thought and said "No" but it wasn't about that I was thinking. I go through the punches, 4, 9, GROC, TOT—it's more complicated than you think, and after you do it often enough, it begins to make a little song, that you hear words to, in my case "Hello (*bing*) there, you (*gung*) hap-py *pee*-pul (*splat*)!"—the *splat* being the drawer flying out. I uncrease the bill, tenderly as you may imagine, it just having come from between the two smoothest scoops of vanilla I had ever known there were, and pass a half and a penny into her narrow pink palm, and nestle the herrings in a bag and twist its neck and hand it over, all the time thinking.

The girls, and who'd blame them, are in a hurry to get out, so I say "I quit" to Lengel quick enough for them to hear, hoping they'll stop and watch me, their unsuspected hero. They keep right on going, into the electric eye; the door flies open and they flicker across the lot to their car, Queenie and Plaid and Big Tall Goony-Goony (not that as raw material she was so bad), leaving me with Lengel and a kink in his eyebrow.

"Did you say something, Sammy?"

"I said I quit."

"I thought you did."

"You didn't have to embarrass them."

"It was they who were embarrassing us."

I started to say something that came out "Fiddle-de-do." It's a saying of my grandmother's, and I know she would have been pleased.

"I don't think you know what you're saying," Lengel said.

"I know you don't," I said. "But I do."

I pull the bow at the back of my apron and start shrugging it off my shoulders. A couple of customers that had been heading for my slot begin to knock against each other, like scared pigs in a chute.

Lengel sighs and begins to look very patient and old and gray. He's been a friend of my parents for years. "Sammy, you don't want to do this to your Mom and Dad," he tells me. It's true, I don't. But it seems to me that once you begin a gesture it's fatal not to go through with it. I fold the apron, "Sammy" stitched in red on the pocket, and put it on the counter, and drop the bow tie on top of it. The bow tie is theirs, if you've ever wondered. "You'll feel this for the rest of your life," Lengel says, and I know that's true, too, but remembering how he made that pretty girl blush makes me so scrunchy inside I punch the No Sale tab and the machine whirs "pee-pul" and the drawer splats out. One advantage to this scene taking place in summer, I can follow this up with a clean exit, there's no fumbling around getting your coat and galoshes, I just saunter into the electric eye in my white shirt that my mother ironed the night before, and the door heaves itself open, and outside the sunshine is skating around on the asphalt.

I look around for my girls, but they're gone, of course. There wasn't anybody but some young married screaming with her children about some candy they didn't get by the door of a powder-blue Falcon station wagon. Looking back in the big windows, over the bags of peat moss and aluminum lawn furniture stacked on the pavement, I could see Lengel in my place in the slot, checking the sheep through. His face was dark gray and his back stiff, as if he's just had an injection of iron, and my stomach kind of fell as I felt how hard the world was going to be to me hereafter.

(1962)

Questions for Discussion and Writing

1. What is Sammy's attitude toward his job, the people he works with, and his customers? List some of his descriptions, especially the metaphors (like "I got her feathers smoothed"), that reveal these attitudes.
2. Why does Sammy quit his job? Does he have more than one reason? Why does he see it as an act of heroism? Is it?
3. As the story closes, Sammy thinks "how hard the world was going to be to me hereafter." Will it? Why or why not?
4. Why do some readers find the story offensively sexist? Write an essay arguing your position on this question.
5. Rewrite a section of the story from a different point of view: Queenie's, Lengel's, the other shoppers', or an objective position. Show how point of view makes a difference in the story's interpretation.

◇◇◇◇◇◇◇◇◇◇◇◇◇◇◇◇◇◇◇◇◇◇◇◇

Margaret Atwood   1939–

Perhaps best known for her feminist dystopian novel *The Handmaid's Tale* (1985), prize-winning novelist, poet, essayist, and activist Margaret Atwood is often described as Medusa-like, partly because of her unruly hair and the glint in her eye, but more for the intensity of her prolific literary output and political work. Although she is adamant that her first loyalty is always to her art, Atwood has served as president of PEN, an organization committed to the welfare of politically oppressed writers around the world, and has engaged in Green Party environmental politics in her native Canada. Her publisher described "Happy Endings" as intended to "reveal the logic of irrational behavior and the many textures lying beneath ordinary life."

Happy Endings

John and Mary meet.
What happens next?
If you want a happy ending, try A.

A.

John and Mary fall in love and get married. They both have worthwhile and remunerative jobs which they find stimulating and challenging. They buy a charming house. Real estate values go up. Eventually, when they can afford live-in help, they have two children, to whom they are devoted. The children turn out well. John and Mary have a stimulating and challenging sex life and worthwhile friends. They go on fun vacations together. They retire. They both have hobbies which they find stimulating and challenging. Eventually they die. This is the end of the story.

B.

Mary falls in love with John but John doesn't fall in love with Mary. He merely uses her body for selfish pleasure and ego gratification of a tepid kind. He comes to her apartment twice a week and she cooks him dinner, you'll notice that he doesn't even consider her worth the price of a dinner out, and after he's eaten dinner he fucks her and after that he falls asleep, while she does the dishes so he won't think she's untidy, having all those dirty dishes lying around, and puts on fresh lipstick so she'll look good when he wakes up, but when he wakes up he doesn't even notice, he puts on his socks and his shorts and his pants and his shirt and his tie and his shoes, the reverse order from the one in which he took them off. He doesn't take off Mary's clothes, she takes them off herself, she acts as if she's dying for it every time, not because she likes sex exactly, she doesn't, but she wants John to think she does because if they do it often enough surely he'll get used to her, he'll come to depend on her and they will get married, but John goes out the door with hardly so much as a good-night and three days later he turns up at six o'clock and they do the whole thing over again.

Mary gets run-down. Crying is bad for your face, everyone knows that and so does Mary but she can't stop. People at work notice. Her friends tell her John is a rat, a pig, a dog, he isn't good enough for her, but she can't believe it. Inside John, she thinks, is another John, who is much nicer. This other John will emerge like a butterfly from a cocoon, a Jack from a box, a pit from a prune, if the first John is only squeezed enough.

One evening John complains about the food. He has never complained about her food before. Mary is hurt.

Her friends tell her they've seen him in a restaurant with another woman,   5 whose name is Madge. It's not even Madge that finally gets to Mary: it's the restaurant. John has never taken Mary to a restaurant. Mary collects all the sleeping pills and aspirins she can find, and takes them and a half a bottle of sherry. You can see what kind of a woman she is by the fact that it's not even whiskey. She leaves a note for John. She hopes he'll discover her and get her to the hospital in time to repent and then they can get married, but this fails to happen and she dies.

John marries Madge and everything continues as in A.

C.

John, who is an older man, falls in love with Mary, and Mary, who is only twenty-two, feels sorry for him because he's worried about his hair falling out. She sleeps with him even though she's not in love with him. She met him at work. She's in love with someone called James, who is twenty-two also and not yet ready to settle down. John on the contrary settled down long ago: this is what is bothering him. John has a steady, respectable job and is getting ahead in his field, but Mary isn't impressed by him, she's impressed by James, who has a motorcycle and a fabulous record collection. But James is often away on his motorcycle, being free. Freedom isn't the same for girls, so in the meantime Mary spends Thursday evenings with John.

Thursdays are the only days John can get away.

John is married to a woman called Madge and they have two children, a charming house which they bought just before the real estate values went up, and hobbies which they find stimulating and challenging, when they have the time. John tells Mary how important she is to him, but of course he can't leave his wife because a commitment is a commitment. He goes on about this more than is necessary and Mary finds it boring, but older men can keep it up longer so on the whole she has a fairly good time.

One day James breezes in on his motorcycle with some top-grade California   10
hybrid and James and Mary get higher than you'd believe possible and they climb into bed. Everything becomes very underwater, but along comes John, who has a key to Mary's apartment. He finds them stoned and entwined. He's hardly in any position to be jealous, considering Madge, but nevertheless he's overcome with despair. Finally he's middle-aged, in two years he'll be as bald as an egg and he can't stand it. He purchases a handgun, saying he needs it for target practice—this is the thin part of the plot, but it can be dealt with later—and shoots the two of them and himself. Madge, after a suitable period of mourning, marries an understanding man called Fred and everything continues as in A, but under different names.

D.

Fred and Madge have no problems. They get along exceptionally well and are good at working out any little difficulties that may arise. But their charming house is by the seashore and one day a giant tidal wave approaches. Real estate values go down. The rest of the story is about what caused the tidal wave and how they escape from it. They do, though thousands drown, but Fred and Madge are virtuous and grateful, and continue as in A.

E.

Yes, but Fred has a bad heart. The rest of the story is about how kind and understanding they both are until Fred dies. Then Madge devotes herself to charity work until the end of A. If you like, it can be "Madge," "cancer," "guilty and confused," and "bird watching."

F.

If you think this is all too bourgeois, make John a revolutionary and Mary a counterespionage agent and see how far that gets you. Remember, this is Canada. You'll still end up with A, though in between you may get a lustful brawling saga of passionate involvement, a chronicle of our times, sort of.

You'll have to face it, the endings are the same however you slice it. Don't be deluded by any other endings, they're all fake, either deliberately fake, with malicious intent to deceive, or just motivated by excessive optimism if not by downright sentimentality.

The only authentic ending is the one provided here:

John and Mary die. John and Mary die. John and Mary die.   15

So much for endings. Beginnings are always more fun. True connoisseurs, however, are known to favor the stretch in between, since it's the hardest to do anything with.

That's about all that can be said for plots, which anyway are just one thing after another, a what and a what and a what.

Now try How and Why.

(1983)

Questions for Discussion and Writing

1. What definitions of love and the good life emerge from each version of the story? What themes can be identified when all versions are read together?

2. Why does Atwood end story B with "and everything continues as in A"? Why does she repeat the phrase, with some variation, throughout the many versions? In the end, how does this refrain contribute to your understanding of Atwood's view of the classic "happily-ever-after" story ending?

3. Why does Atwood repeat "John and Mary die. John and Mary die. John and Mary die" in section F?

4. How would you describe the tone of these phrases from story B: "you'll notice he doesn't even consider her worth the price of a dinner out" and "Crying is bad for your face, everyone knows that"? Is there a similar kind of commentary in version A? In the other versions? What accounts for any differences in tone between A and B?

5. Atwood has offered this advice on writing fiction: "Unless something has gone disastrously wrong, other people aren't that interesting to write about.... This is lesson No. 1 in narrative: Something has to happen. It can be good people to whom bad things happen, a nice person getting bitten in two by a shark or crushed by an earthquake, or their husbands run off on them. Or then it can be people of devious or shallow character getting into trouble or making trouble." Write an essay employing Atwood's claim to explain the relationship between plot and theme in "Happy Endings."

◇◇◇◇◇◇◇◇◇◇◇◇◇◇◇◇◇◇◇◇◇◇◇◇◇◇

Ron Hansen   1947–

Award-winning fiction writer Ron Hansen first received wide publicity for his novel *The Assassination of Jesse James by the Coward Robert Ford* (1983), which was made into a film starring Brad Pitt. He has written in varied literary genres—such as the western, murder mystery, and romantic novel—and religious ideas are basic to his themes (he is a deacon of the Catholic church). However, Hansen doesn't classify himself as a conventional Christian author. In an interview, he explained: "Evil is just too stark in Christian fiction. But there does exist a more nuanced view of evil in which the devil doesn't propose temptations that are easy to resist. The devil proposes temptations that seem to be good. And you find yourself going down the wrong path for all kinds of good reasons."

My Kid's Dog

My kid's dog died.

Sparky.

I hated that dog.

The feeling was mutual.

We got off on the wrong foot. Whining in his pen those first nights. My 5
squirt gun in his face and him blinking from the water. And then the holes in the yard. The so-called accidents in the house. His nose snuffling into my Brooks Brothers trousers. Him slurping my fine Pilsner beer or sneaking bites of my Dagwood sandwich when I fell asleep on the sofa. Also his inability to fetch, to take a joke, to find the humor in sudden air horns. To be dandled, roughhoused, or teased. And then the growling, the skulking, the snapping at my ankles, the hiding from me under the house, and literally thousands of abject refusals to obey. Like, *Who the hell are you?*

You'd have thought he was a cat.

When pushed to the brink I shouted, "I'll cut your face off and show it to you," and the small-brained mammal just stared at me.

But with the kids or my wife little Foo-Foo was a changeling, conning them with the tail, the prance, the peppiness, the soft chocolate eyes, the sloppy expressions of love, the easy tricks that if I performed I'd get no credit for.

Oh, we understood each other all right. I was on to him.

And then, at age ten, and none too soon, he kicked the bucket. You'd think 10
that would be it. End of story. But no, he had to get even.

Those who have tears, prepare to shed them.

I was futzing with the hinges on the front yard gate on a Saturday afternoon, my tattersall shirtsleeves rolled up and mind off in Oklahoma, when I noticed Fido in the California shade, snoozing, but for once a little wistful, too, and far more serene than he usually was in my offensive presence. I tried to surprise him with my standard patriarchal shout, but it was no go, so I walked over and prodded the little guy with my wingtip. Nothing doing. And not so much as a flutter in his oddly abstracted face. Surely this was the big sleep, I thought.

She who must be obeyed was at the mall, provisioning, so I was safe from objection or inquiry on that account. I then made an inventory of my progeny: Buzz in the collegiate East, in the realm of heart-attack tuitions, Zack in the netherworld of the surf shop, Suzy, my last kid, on her bike and somewhere with her cousin. Were I to bury Rover with due haste and dispatch I could forestall the waterworks, even convince them that he'd signed up with the circus, run afoul of Cruella DeVil—anything but died.

I got a green tarpaulin from the garage and laid it out on the front lawn where I hesitated before using my shoe to roll Spot into his funeral shroud, then dragged him back into the Victory garden where August's dying zucchini plants were in riot. With trusty spade I dug his burial place, heaped earth atop him, tamped it down with satisfying *whumps*.

I was feeling good about myself, heroic, as if, miraculously, compassion and 15
charity had invaded not only my bones but my sinewy muscle tissues. I fixed

myself a tall glass of gin and tonic and watched the first quarter of the USC football game.

And then pangs of conscience assailed me. Hadn't my investigation of said demise of Precious been rather cursory? Wouldn't I, myself, closely cross-examine a suspect whose emotions were clouded, whose nefarious wishes were well-established, whose veterinary skills were without credential? The innocence of my childhood had been spoiled with the tales of Edgar Allan Poe, so it was not difficult to conjure images of Scruffy clawing through tarpaulin and earth as he fought for one last gasp of air, air that others could more profitably use.

I trudged out to the garden with aforementioned spade and with great lumbar strain exhumed our darling lap dog. Considering the circumstances, he seemed none the worse for wear, but I did detect a marked disinclination to respire, which I took as a sign either of his inveterate stubbornness or of his having reached the Stygian shore. The latter seemed more likely. I heard in my fuddled head a line from *The Wild Bunch* when a critically injured gunman begs his outlaw gang to "Finish it!" And in the healing spirit of Hippocrates I lifted high the shovel and whanged it down on Harvey's head.

To my relief, not a whimper issued from him. I was confident he was defunct.

With care I shrouded and buried him again, committing earth to earth and dust to dust and so on, and with spritelike step conveyed myself to the kitchen where I made another gin and tonic and, in semi-prone position, settled into the game's third quarter, the fabled Trojan running attack grinding out, it would seem, another win.

I was shocked awake by the impertinence of a ringing telephone, which I, 20 with due caution, answered. It was my wife's friend, Vicki, inquiring about the pooch, for it was her assertion that Snip had fancied a taste of her son's upper calf and without invitation or permission to do so had partaken of same within the last twenty-four hours. Even while I was wondering what toxicity lurked in the child's leg and to what extent the poison was culpably responsible for our adored pet's actionable extinction, a loss we would feel for our lifetimes, Vicki insisted that I have the dog checked out by a vet to ascertain if he had rabies.

Cause of death: rabies? It seemed unlikely. Notwithstanding his surliness, there'd been no Cujoesque frothing or lunging at car windows; but my familiarity with torts has made me both careful and rather unctuous in confrontation with a plaintiff, and so I assured my wife's friend that I would accede to her request.

Off to the back yard again, my pace that of a woebegone trudge, and with aforementioned implement of agriculture I displaced the slack and loosened earth. This was getting old. With an accusatory tone I said, "You're doing this on purpose, aren't you," and I took his silence as a plea of *nolo contendere*.

My plan, of course, was to employ the Oldsmobile 88 to transport my burden to the canine's autopsy at Dr. Romo's office just a half mile away. However, upon settling into its plush front seat, it came to my attention that Zack—he who is but a sojourner on this earth—had not thought to replenish the fuel he'd used up on his trip to the Hollywood Bowl last night. The vehicle was not in a condition of plenitude. Would not ferry us farther than a block.

With Buster lying in the altogether on the driveway, not yet unsightly but no calendar page, I went into the house and found an old leather suitcase in the attic, then stuffed the mutt into the larger flapped compartment before hefting Shortcake on his final journey to those veterinary rooms he always shivered in.

I am, as I may have implied, a man of depth, perspicacity, and nearly 25 Olympian strength, but I found myself hauling my heavy and lifeless cargo to Dr. Romo's with a pronounced lack of vigor and resolve. The September afternoon was hot, the Pasadena streets were vacant, the entire world seemed to have found entertainment and surcease in ways that I had not. I was, in a word, in a sweaty snit, and after many panting and pain-filled stops, my spine in Quasimodo configuration and my right arm gradually inching longer than my left, it was all I could do not to heave the suitcase containing Wonderdog into a haulaway behind the Chinese restaurant.

But during our joint ordeal I had developed a grudging affection for our pet; he who'd been so quick to defend my kith and kin against the noise of passing trucks, who took loud notice of the squirrels outside, who held fast in the foyer, hackles raised, fearlessly barking, whenever company arrived at the front door. With him I seemed calm, masterful, and uneccentric, the Superior Man that the *I Ching* talks so much about. Without him, I thought, I might be otherwise.

I put down the suitcase to shake the ache from my fingers and subtract affliction from my back, and it was then that my final indignity came. An angel of mercy spied my plight, braked his ancient Cadillac, and got out, his facial piercings and tattoos and shoot-the-marbles eyes belying the kindness and decency of his heart as he asked, "Can I help you with that suitcase?"

"I can handle it."

"Are you sure?"

"I'm just two blocks away."   30

"What the heck's in it?" he asked.

And for some reason I said, "A family heirloom."

"Wow!" he said. "Why don't you put it in my trunk and I'll help you with it? I got nothin' better to do."

Well, I did not just fall off the turnip truck. I would have been, in other circumstances, suspicious. But I was all too aware of the weight and worthlessness of my cumbrance, and so I granted his specified offer, hoisting the deceased into the Seville and slamming down the trunk lid. And, in evidence of our fallen state, my Samaritan immediately took off without me, jeering and peeling rubber and speeding west toward Los Angeles.

I could only lift my hand in a languid wave. *So long, old sport.*   35

Our world being the location of penance and recrimination, it was only right that my last kid should pedal up to me on her bike just then and ask, "Daddy, what are you doing here?"

Waving to a guy, I thought, *who's about to become a gravedigger.*

And then I confessed. Sparky's sudden death, the burial, not the exhumation and execution attempt, but the imputation of rabies and my arduous efforts to acquit his reputation with a pilgrimage to the vet's.

Suzy took it in with sangfroid for a little while but then the lip quivered and tears spilled from her gorgeous eyes, and as I held her close she begged me to get her another dog just like Sparky. And that was Sparky's final revenge, for I said, "Okay, honey. Another dog, just like him."

(2003)

Questions for Discussion and Writing

1. What is the dog's name? Why does the narrator use so many different names? How does his slippery notion of the dog's name add to the humor of the last line?

2. List some terms you would use to describe the narrator. How does he reveal his personality? Does he understand how much he's revealing, or does he convey information accidentally in the way he tells the story? In what ways is he an older version of Sammy in Updike's "A & P" (page 358)? Find details that support your claim about his level of self-awareness.

3. What does the story suggest about middle-class suburban life in the United States? Is there a serious point as well as a humorous purpose? Reread the author's quotation in the biographical sketch preceding the story. Can you see a relationship between that quotation and this story?

4. Does the narrator of "My Kid's Dog" change? Support your answer with logical reasoning and details from the story. You might gain some insight into the question by listening to the author read this story on OxMag's Blog (oxmag.wordpress.com/tag/ron-hansen).

Ideas for Writing: Making Connections

1. Compare and contrast the main characters of the stories in this portfolio: Vera, Sammy, John and Mary, and Daddy. Discuss their similarities and differences, or adopt a central quality (like reliability, personality, motivation) as the basis for comparing them.

2. What is the point of view in each of the four stories? Do you think the choice of narrator is appropriate for each story? How would the stories change if told by a different kind of narrator? Try rewriting the opening paragraphs of "The Open Window," for example, with Vera as the first-person narrator. Or recast "A & P" into a third-person narration. Discuss the effects of these changes.

3. Choose a story and try to explain its humor. Why is it funny or entertaining? Consider tone, word choice, characters, and plot in making your explanations.

4. Which of these stories are satires? What institutions, beliefs, or human frailties are being mocked or ridiculed? What changes in attitude or behavior do the authors want to see made?

5. Flannery O'Connor's "A Good Man Is Hard to Find" (page 177) contains strong elements of humor and satire. Which of the stories in this portfolio seem most similar in tone, theme, and satirical purpose to the O'Connor story?

Multimedia Project

Prepare a stage script for dramatizing a key scene from one of the stories in this portfolio: make a diagram of the set, describe the characters, write the dialogue and the stage directions. You might also identify famous actors who would fit the roles, and explain your choices. Use your cell phone to make a video or audio recording of the dialogue being read by yourself and/or other classmates.

16 A Portfolio of Stories About Singular Women

Chapter Preview

The word *singular* can mean "exceptional" and "unusual"; it can also mean "alone" and "isolated." Each of the four stories in this portfolio focuses on a woman who can be defined as "singular" in one or more senses of the word. And each of the women deals with her singular situation in her own way. As you read, pay particular attention to the qualities that set these women apart. What makes them "singular" women? Consider, also, what part *gender* plays in determining their characters and directing their actions. The Questions for Discussion and Writing that follow each story will help you to develop your understanding and refine your interpretations.

In this chapter, you will learn to do the following:

- Analyze characters closely, with particular attention to how gender influences their characterization, choices, and actions.
- Identify what makes characters in a story "singular," examining all definitions of that word.
- Compare and contrast the characterization of different female characters across stories.
- Write about "singular" women in fiction.

Katherine Mansfield   1888–1923

At the age of nineteen, Katherine Mansfield moved from her native New Zealand to London to establish herself as a writer. Although her literary output was not voluminous, her influence on the form and development of the short story was substantial. Many writers were inspired by her technique of using small, seemingly inconsequential moments of decision, defeat, and minor triumph to reveal the psychological depths of her characters. One notable theme in Mansfield's work was the *dame seule*, the "woman alone," which was the basis for the poignancy in many of her stories. Mansfield died of complications from tuberculosis at age thirty-five.

Miss Brill

Although it was so brilliantly fine—the blue sky powdered with gold and great spots of light like white wine splashed over the Jardins Publiques—Miss Brill

371

was glad that she had decided on her fur. The air was motionless, but when you opened your mouth there was just a faint chill, like a chill from a glass of iced water before you sip, and now and again a leaf came drifting—from nowhere, from the sky. Miss Brill put up her hand and touched her fur. Dear little thing! It was nice to feel it again. She had taken it out of its box that afternoon, shaken out the moth powder, given it a good brush, and rubbed the life back into the dim little eyes. "What has been happening to me?" said the sad little eyes. Oh, how sweet it was to see them snap at her again from the red eiderdown! ... But the nose, which was of some black composition, wasn't at all firm. It must have had a knock, somehow. Never mind—a little dab of black sealing-wax when the time came—when it was absolutely necessary ... Little rogue! Yes, she really felt like that about it. Little rogue biting its tail just by her left ear. She could have taken it off and laid it on her lap and stroked it. She felt a tingling in her hands and arms, but that came from walking, she supposed. And when she breathed, something light and sad—no, not sad, exactly—something gentle seemed to move in her bosom.

There were a number of people out this afternoon, far more than last Sunday. And the band sounded louder and gayer. That was because the Season had begun. For although the band played all the year round on Sundays, out of season it was never the same. It was like some one playing with only the family to listen; it didn't care how it played if there weren't any strangers present. Wasn't the conductor wearing a new coat, too? She was sure it was new. He scraped with his foot and flapped his arms like a rooster about to crow, and the bandsmen sitting in the green rotunda blew out their cheeks and glared at the music. Now there came a little "flutey" bit—very pretty!—a little chain of bright drops. She was sure it would be repeated. It was; she lifted her head and smiled.

Only two people shared her "special" seat: a fine old man in a velvet coat, his hands clasped over a huge carved walking-stick, and a big old woman, sitting upright, with a roll of knitting on her embroidered apron. They did not speak. This was disappointing, for Miss Brill always looked forward to the conversation. She had become really quite expert, she thought, at listening as though she didn't listen, at sitting in other people's lives just for a minute while they talked round her.

She glanced, sideways, at the old couple. Perhaps they would go soon. Last Sunday, too, hadn't been as interesting as usual. An Englishman and his wife, he wearing a dreadful Panama hat and she button boots. And she'd gone on the whole time about how she ought to wear spectacles; she knew she needed them; but that it was no good getting any; they'd be sure to break and they'd never keep on. And he'd been so patient. He'd suggested everything—gold rims, the kind that curve round your ears, little pads inside the bridge. No, nothing would please her. "They'll always be sliding down my nose!" Miss Brill had wanted to shake her.

The old people sat on a bench, still as statues. Never mind, there was always 5 the crowd to watch. To and fro, in front of the flower beds and the band rotunda, the couples and groups paraded, stopped to talk, to greet, to buy a handful of flowers from the old beggar who had his tray fixed to the railings. Little children ran among them, swooping and laughing; little boys with big white silk bows under their chins, little girls, little French dolls, dressed up in velvet and lace. And sometimes a tiny staggerer came suddenly rocking into the open from under the trees, stopped, stared, as suddenly sat down "flop," until its small high-stepping mother, like a young hen, rushed scolding to its rescue. Other people sat on the benches and green chairs, but they were nearly always the same, Sunday after Sunday, and—Miss Brill had often noticed—there was something funny about nearly all of them. They were odd, silent, nearly all old, and from the way they stared they looked as though they'd just come from dark little rooms or even—even cupboards!

Behind the rotunda the slender trees with yellow leaves down drooping, and through them just a line of sea, and beyond the blue sky with gold-veined clouds.

Tum-tum-tum tiddle-um! tiddle-um! tum tiddley-um tum ta! blew the band. Two young girls in red came by and two young soldiers in blue met them, and they laughed and paired and went off arm-in-arm. Two peasant women with funny straw hats passed, gravely, leading beautiful smoke-coloured donkeys. A cold, pale nun hurried by. A beautiful woman came along and dropped her bunch of violets, and a little boy ran after to hand them to her, and she took them and threw them away as if they'd been poisoned. Dear me! Miss Brill didn't know whether to admire that or not! And now an ermine toque and a gentleman in gray met just in front of her. He was tall, stiff, dignified, and she was wearing the ermine toque she'd bought when her hair was yellow. Now everything, her hair, her face, even her eyes, was the same colour as the shabby ermine, and her hand, in its cleaned glove, lifted to dab her lips, was a tiny yellowish paw. Oh, she was so pleased to see him—delighted! She rather thought they were going to meet that afternoon. She described where she'd been—everywhere, here, there, along by the sea. The day was so charming—didn't he agree? And wouldn't he, perhaps? ... But he shook his head, lighted a cigarette, slowly breathed a great deep puff into her face, and even while she was still talking and laughing, flicked the match away and walked on. The ermine toque was alone; she smiled more brightly than ever. But even the band seemed to know what she was feeling and played more softly, played tenderly, and the drum beat, "The Brute! The Brute!" over and over. What would she do? What was going to happen now? But as Miss Brill wondered, the ermine toque turned, raised her hand as though she'd seen someone else, much nicer, just over there, and pattered away. And the band changed again and played more quickly, more gayly than ever, and the old couple on Miss Brill's seat got up and marched away, and such a funny old man with long whiskers hobbled along in time to the music and was nearly knocked over by four girls walking abreast.

Oh, how fascinating it was! How she enjoyed it! How she loved sitting here, watching it all! It was like a play. It was exactly like a play. Who could believe the sky at the back wasn't painted? But it wasn't till a little brown dog trotted on solemn and then slowly trotted off, like a little "theatre" dog, a little dog that had been drugged, that Miss Brill discovered what it was that made it so exciting. They were all on stage. They weren't only the audience, not only looking on; they were acting. Even she had a part and came every Sunday. No doubt somebody would have noticed if she hadn't been there; she was part of the performance after all. How strange she'd never thought of it like that before! And yet it explained why she made such point of starting from home at just the same time each week—so as not to be late for the performance—and it also explained why she had a queer, shy feeling at telling her English pupils how she spent her Sunday afternoons. No wonder! Miss

Brill nearly laughed out loud. She was on the stage. She thought of the old invalid gentleman to whom she read the newspaper four afternoons a week while he slept in the garden. She had got quite used to the frail head on the cotton pillow, the hollowed eyes, the open mouth and the high pinched nose. If he'd been dead she mightn't have noticed for weeks; she wouldn't have minded. But suddenly he knew he was having the paper read to him by an actress! "An actress!" The old head lifted; two points of light quivered in the old eyes. "An actress—are ye?" And Miss Brill smoothed the newspaper as though it were the manuscript of her part and said gently; "Yes, I have been an actress for a long time."

The band had been having a rest. Now they started again. And what they played was warm, sunny, yet there was just a faint chill—a something, what was it?—not sadness—no, not sadness—a something that made you want to sing. The tune lifted, lifted, the light shone; and it seemed to Miss Brill that in another moment all of them, all the whole company, would begin singing. The young ones, the laughing ones who were moving together, they would begin and the men's voices, very resolute and brave, would join them. And then she too, she too, and the others on the benches—they would come in with a kind of accompaniment—something low, that scarcely rose or fell, something so beautiful—moving.... And Miss Brill's eyes filled with tears and she looked smiling at all the other members of the company. Yes, we understand, we understand, she thought—though what they understood she didn't know.

Just at that moment a boy and girl came and sat down where the old couple had been. They were beautifully dressed; they were in love. The hero and heroine, of course, just arrived from his father's yacht. And still soundlessly singing, still with that trembling smile, Miss Brill prepared to listen.

"No, not now," said the girl. "Not here, I can't."

"But why? Because of that stupid old thing at the end there?" asked the boy. "Why does she come here at all—who wants her? Why doesn't she keep her silly old mug at home?"

"It's her fu-ur which is so funny," giggled the girl. "It's exactly like a fried whiting."

"Ah, be off with you!" said the boy in an angry whisper. Then: "Tell me, ma petite chère—"

"No, not here," said the girl. "Not *yet*."

On her way home she usually bought a slice of honeycake at the baker's. It was her Sunday treat. Sometimes there was an almond in her slice, sometimes not. It made a great difference. If there was an almond it was like carrying home a tiny present—a surprise—something that might very well not have been there. She hurried on the almond Sundays and struck the match for the kettle in quite a dashing way.

But today she passed the baker's by, climbed the stairs, went into the little dark room—her room like a cupboard—and sat down on the red eiderdown. She sat there for a long time. The box that the fur came out of was on the bed. She unclasped the necklet quickly; quickly, without looking, laid it inside. But when she put the lid on she thought she heard something crying.

(1920)

Questions for Discussion and Writing

1. The story opens and closes with scenes involving Miss Brill's fur. What is the significance of the fur?

2. What do Miss Brill's observations about the people around her tell us about her own character? Why doesn't she interact with any of these people?

3. How does Miss Brill change after overhearing the young lovers' remarks? Why do they have such an effect on her?

4. What is the "something crying" at the end of the story?

5. Why doesn't Mansfield give many details about Miss Brill's physical appearance? Why doesn't she have a first name? Write a description of Miss Brill that reveals your understanding of her personality and character. Give her an appropriate first name.

6. Write an essay responding to the claim that this is a story about a woman who is justly punished for her pride.

◇◇◇◇◇◇◇◇◇◇◇◇◇◇◇◇◇◇◇◇

John Steinbeck 1902–1968

John Steinbeck was born in Salinas, California, where he worked as a fruit-picker, hod carrier, and ranch hand. After high school graduation, he continued working at menial jobs while taking classes in marine biology at Stanford University. In 1925, he went to New York City to become a writer. He got a job as a laborer on the building of Madison Square Garden but could not get published, so he moved back to California. His early works met with little success, but *Tortilla Flat* (1935) became a best seller and received the California Commonwealth Club's Gold Medal for best novel by a California author. Steinbeck went on to write a number of highly successful novels and stories. In 1962 he was awarded the Nobel Prize for Literature.

The Chrysanthemums

The high gray-flannel fog of winter closed off the Salinas Valley from the sky and from all the rest of the world. On every side it sat like a lid on the mountains and made of the great valley a closed pot. On the broad, level land floor the gang plows bit deep and left the black earth shining like metal where the shares had cut. On the foothill ranches across the Salinas River, the yellow stubble fields seemed to be bathed in pale cold sunshine, but there was no sunshine in the valley now in December. The thick willow scrub along the river flamed with sharp and positive yellow leaves.

It was a time of quiet and of waiting. The air was cold and tender. A light wind blew up from the southwest so that the farmers were mildly hopeful of a good rain before long; but fog and rain do not go together.

Across the river, on Henry Allen's foothill ranch there was little work to be done, for the hay was cut and stored and the orchards were plowed up to receive the rain deeply when it should come. The cattle on the higher slopes were becoming shaggy and rough-coated.

Elisa Allen, working in her flower garden, looked down across the yard and saw Henry, her husband, talking to two men in business suits. The three of them stood by the tractor shed, each man with one foot on the side of the little Fordson. They smoked cigarettes and studied the machine as they talked.

Elisa watched them for a moment and then went back to her work. She was 5 thirty-five. Her face was lean and strong and her eyes were as clear as water. Her figure looked blocked and heavy in her gardening costume, a man's black hat pulled down over her eyes, clodhopper shoes, a figured print dress almost completely covered by a big corduroy apron with four big pockets to hold the snips, the trowel and scratcher, the seeds and the knife she worked with. She wore heavy leather gloves to protect her hands while she worked.

She was cutting down the old year's chrysanthemum stalks with a pair of short and powerful scissors. She looked down toward the men by the tractor shed now and then. Her face was eager and mature and handsome; even her work with the scissors was over-eager, over-powerful. The chrysanthemum stems seemed too small and easy for her energy.

She brushed a cloud of hair out of her eyes with the back of her glove, and left a smudge of earth on her cheek in doing it. Behind her stood the neat white farm house with red geraniums close-banked around it as high as the windows. It was a hard-swept looking little house, with hard-polished windows, and a clean mud-mat on the front steps.

Elisa cast another glance toward the tractor shed. The strangers were getting into their Ford coupe. She took off a glove and put her strong fingers down into the forest of new green chrysanthemum sprouts that were growing around the old roots. She spread the leaves and looked down among the close-growing stems. No aphids were there, no sowbugs or snails or cutworms. Her terrier fingers destroyed such pests before they could get started.

Elisa started at the sound of her husband's voice. He had come near quietly, and he leaned over the wire fence that protected her flower garden from cattle and dogs and chickens.

"At it again," he said. "You've got a strong new crop coming." 10

Elisa straightened her back and pulled on the gardening glove again. "Yes. They'll be strong this coming year." In her tone and on her face there was a little smugness.

"You've got a gift with things," Henry observed. "Some of those yellow chrysanthemums you had this year were ten inches across. I wish you'd work out in the orchard and raise some apples that big."

Her eyes sharpened. "Maybe I could do it, too. I've a gift with things, all right. My mother had it. She could stick anything in the ground and make it grow. She said it was having planters' hands that knew how to do it."

"Well, it sure works with flowers," he said.

"Henry, who were those men you were talking to?" 15

"Why, sure, that's what I came to tell you. They were from the Western Meat Company. I sold them those thirty head of three-year-old steers. Got nearly my own price, too."

"Good," she said. "Good for you."

"And I thought," he continued, "I thought how it's Saturday afternoon, and we might go into Salinas for dinner at a restaurant, and then to a picture show— to celebrate, you see."

"Good," she repeated. "Oh, yes. That will be good."

Henry put on his joking tone. "There's fights tonight. How'd you like to go   20
to the fights?"

"Oh, no," she said breathlessly. "No, I wouldn't like fights."

"Just fooling, Elisa. We'll go to a movie. Let's see. It's two now. I'm going to
take Scotty and bring down those steers from the hill. It'll take us maybe two
hours. We'll go in town about five and have dinner at the Cominos Hotel. Like
that?"

"Of course I'll like it. It's good to eat away from home."

"All right, then. I'll go get up a couple of horses."

She said, "I'll have plenty of time to transplant some of these sets, I guess."   25

She heard her husband calling Scotty down by the barn. And a little later she
saw the two men ride up the pale yellow hillside in search of the steers.

There was a little square sandy bed kept for rooting the chrysanthemums.
With her trowel she turned the soil over and over, and smoothed it and patted it
firm. Then she dug ten parallel trenches to receive the sets. Back at the chrysanthemum bed she pulled out the little crisp shoots, trimmed off the leaves of each
one with her scissors and laid it on a small orderly pile.

A squeak of wheels and plod of hoofs came from the road. Elisa looked up.
The country road ran along the dense bank of willows and cottonwoods that
bordered the river, and up this road came a curious vehicle, curiously drawn. It
was an old spring-wagon, with a round canvas top on it like the cover of a prairie
schooner. It was drawn by an old bay horse and a little gray-and-white burro.
A big stubble-bearded man sat between the cover flaps and drove the crawling
team. Underneath the wagon, between the hind wheels, a lean and rangy mongrel dog walked sedately. Words were painted on the canvas, in clumsy, crooked
letters. "Pots, pans, knives, sisors, lawn mores, Fixed." Two rows of articles, and
the triumphantly definitive "Fixed" below. The black paint had run down in
little sharp points beneath each letter.

Elisa, squatting on the ground, watched to see the crazy, loose-jointed wagon
pass by. But it didn't pass. It turned into the farm road in front of her house,
crooked old wheels skirling and squeaking. The rangy dog darted from between
the wheels and ran ahead. Instantly the two ranch shepherds flew out at him.
Then all three stopped, and with stiff and quivering tails, with taut straight legs,
with ambassadorial dignity, they slowly circled, sniffing daintily. The caravan
pulled up to Elisa's wire fence and stopped. Now the newcomer dog, feeling
out-numbered, lowered his tail and retired under the wagon with raised hackles
and bared teeth.

The man on the wagon seat called out, "That's a bad dog in a fight when he   30
gets started."

Elisa laughed. "I see he is. How soon does he generally get started?"

The man caught up her laughter and echoed it heartily. "Sometimes not for
weeks and weeks," he said. He climbed stiffly down, over the wheel. The horse
and the donkey drooped like unwatered flowers.

Elisa saw that he was a very big man. Although his hair and beard were graying, he did not look old. His worn black suit was wrinkled and spotted with
grease. The laughter had disappeared from his face and eyes the moment his
laughing voice ceased. His eyes were dark, and they were full of the brooding
that gets in the eyes of teamsters and of sailors. The calloused hands he rested
on the wire fence were cracked, and every crack was a black line. He took off his
battered hat.

"I'm off my general road, ma'am," he said. "Does this dirt road cut over across the river to the Los Angeles highway?"

Elisa stood up and shoved the thick scissors in her apron pocket. "Well, yes, it does, but it winds around and then fords the river. I don't think your team could pull through the sand." 35

He replied with some asperity, "It might surprise you what them beasts can pull through."

"When they get started?" she asked.

He smiled for a second. "Yes. When they get started."

"Well," said Elisa, "I think you'll save time if you go back to the Salinas road and pick up the highway there."

He drew a big finger down the chicken wire and made it sing. "I ain't in any hurry, ma'am. I go from Seattle to San Diego and back every year. Takes all my time. About six months each way. I aim to follow nice weather." 40

Elisa took off her gloves and stuffed them in the apron pocket with the scissors. She touched the under edge of her man's hat, searching for fugitive hairs. "That sounds like a nice kind of way to live," she said.

He leaned confidentially over the fence. "Maybe you noticed the writing on my wagon. I mend pots and sharpen knives and scissors. You got any of them things to do?"

"Oh, no," she said quickly. "Nothing like that." Her eyes hardened with resistance.

"Scissors is the worst thing," he explained. "Most people just ruin scissors trying to sharpen 'em, but I know how. I got a special tool. It's a little bobbit kind of thing, and patented. But it sure does the trick."

"No. My scissors are all sharp." 45

"All right, then. Take a pot," he continued earnestly, "a bent pot, or a pot with a hole. I can make it like new so you don't have to buy no new ones. That's a saving for you."

"No," she said shortly. "I tell you I have nothing like that for you to do."

His face fell to an exaggerated sadness. His voice took on a whining undertone. "I ain't had a thing to do today. Maybe I won't have no supper tonight. You see I'm off my regular road. I know folks on the highway clear from Seattle to San Diego. They save their things for me to sharpen up because they know I do it so good and save them money."

"I'm sorry," Elisa said irritably. "I haven't anything for you to do."

His eyes left her face and fell to searching the ground. They roamed about until they came to the chrysanthemum bed where she had been working. "What's them plants, ma'am?" 50

The irritation and resistance melted from Elisa's face. "Oh, those are chrysanthemums, giant whites and yellows. I raise them every year, bigger than anybody around here."

"Kind of a long-stemmed flower? Looks like a quick puff of colored smoke?" he asked.

"That's it. What a nice way to describe them."

"They smell kind of nasty till you get used to them," he said.

"It's a good bitter smell," she retorted, "not nasty at all." 55

He changed his tone quickly. "I like the smell myself."

"I had ten-inch blooms this year," she said.

The man leaned farther over the fence. "Look. I know a lady down the road a piece, has got the nicest garden you ever seen. Got nearly every kind of flower but no chrysanthemums. Last time I was mending a copper-bottom washtub for her (that's a hard job but I do it good), she said to me, 'If you ever run acrost some nice chrysanthemums I wish you'd try to get me a few seeds.' That's what she told me."

Elisa's eyes grew alert and eager. "She couldn't have known much about chrysanthemums. You *can* raise them from seed, but it's much easier to root the little sprouts you see there."

"Oh," he said. "I s'pose I can't take none to her, then."

"Why yes you can," Elisa cried. "I can put some in damp sand, and you can carry them right along with you. They'll take root in the pot if you keep them damp. And then she can transplant them."

"She'd sure like to have some, ma'am. You say they're nice ones?"

"Beautiful," she said. "Oh, beautiful." Her eyes shone. She tore off the battered hat and shook out her dark pretty hair. "I'll put them in a flower pot, and you can take them right with you. Come into the yard."

While the man came through the picket gate Elisa ran excitedly along the geranium-bordered path to the back of the house. And she returned carrying a big red flower pot. The gloves were forgotten now. She kneeled on the ground by the starting bed and dug up the sandy soil with her fingers and scooped it into the bright new flower pot. Then she picked up the little pile of shoots she had prepared. With her strong fingers she pressed them into the sand and tamped around them with her knuckles. The man stood over her. "I'll tell you what to do," she said. "You remember so you can tell the lady."

"Yes, I'll try to remember."

"Well, look. These will take root in about a month. Then she must set them out, about a foot apart in good rich earth like this, see?" She lifted a handful of dark soil for him to look at. "They'll grow fast and tall. Now remember this: In July tell her to cut them down, about eight inches from the ground."

"Before they bloom?" he asked.

"Yes, before they bloom." Her face was tight with eagerness. "They'll grow right up again. About the last of September the buds will start."

She stopped and seemed perplexed. "It's the budding that takes the most care," she said hesitantly. "I don't know how to tell you." She looked deep into his eyes, searchingly. Her mouth opened a little, and she seemed to be listening. "I'll try to tell you," she said. "Did you ever hear of planting hands?"

"Can't say I have, ma'am."

"Well, I can only tell you what it feels like. It's when you're picking off the buds you don't want. Everything goes right down into your fingertips. You watch your fingers work. They do it themselves. You can feel how it is. They pick and pick the buds. They never make a mistake. They're with the plant. Do you see? Your fingers and the plant. You can feel that, right up your arm. They know. They never make a mistake. You can feel it. When you're like that you can't do anything wrong. Do you see that? Can you understand that?"

She was kneeling on the ground looking up at him. Her breast swelled passionately.

The man's eyes narrowed. He looked away self-consciously. "Maybe I know," he said. "Sometimes in the night in the wagon there—"

Elisa's voice grew husky. She broke in on him, "I've never lived as you do, but I know what you mean. When the night is dark—why, the stars are sharp-pointed, and there's quiet. Why, you rise up and up! Every pointed star gets driven into your body. It's like that. Hot and sharp and—lovely."

Kneeling there, her hand went out toward his legs in the greasy black trou-   75
sers. Her hesitant fingers almost touched the cloth. Then her hand dropped to
the ground. She crouched low like a fawning dog.

He said, "It's nice, just like you say. Only when you don't have no dinner, it ain't."

She stood up then, very straight, and her face was ashamed. She held the
flower pot out to him and placed it gently in his arms. "Here. Put it in your
wagon, on the seat, where you can watch it. Maybe I can find something for
you to do."

At the back of the house she dug in the can pile and found two old and
battered aluminum saucepans. She carried them back and gave them to him.
"Here, maybe you can fix these."

His manner changed. He became professional. "Good as new I can fix them."
At the back of his wagon he set a little anvil, and out of an oily tool box dug
a small machine hammer. Elisa came through the gate to watch him while he
pounded out the dents in the kettles. His mouth grew sure and knowing. At a
difficult part of the work he sucked his underlip.

"You sleep right in the wagon?" Elisa asked.   80

"Right in the wagon, ma'am. Rain or shine I'm dry as a cow in there."

"It must be nice," she said. "It must be very nice. I wish women could do such
things."

"It ain't the right kind of life for a woman."

Her upper lip raised a little, showing her teeth. "How do you know? How
can you tell?" she said.

"I don't know, ma'am," he protested. "Of course I don't know. Now here's   85
your kettles, done. You don't have to buy no new ones."

"How much?"

"Oh, fifty cents'll do. I keep my prices down and my work good. That's why I
have all them satisfied customers up and down the highway."

Elisa brought him a fifty-cent piece from the house and dropped it in his
hand. "You might be surprised to have a rival some time. I can sharpen scissors,
too. And I can beat the dents out of little pots. I could show you what a woman
might do."

He put his hammer back in the oily box and shoved the little anvil out of
sight. "It would be a lonely life for a woman, ma'am, and a scary life, too, with
animals creeping under the wagon all night." He climbed over the singletree,
steadying himself with a hand on the burro's white rump. He settled himself in
the seat, picked up the lines. "Thank you kindly, ma'am," he said. "I'll do like
you told me; I'll go back and catch the Salinas road."

"Mind," she called, "if you're long in getting there, keep the sand damp."   90

"Sand, ma'am?...Sand? Oh, sure. You mean around the chrysanthemums. Sure
I will." He clucked his tongue. The beasts leaned luxuriously into their collars.
The mongrel dog took his place between the back wheels. The wagon turned
and crawled out the entrance road and back the way it had come, along the river.

Elisa stood in front of her wire fence watching the slow progress of the caravan. Her shoulders were straight, her head thrown back, her eyes half-closed,
so that the scene came vaguely into them. Her lips moved silently, forming the
words "Good-bye—good-bye." Then she whispered, "That's a bright direction.
There's a glowing there." The sound of her whisper startled her. She shook herself free and looked about to see whether anyone had been listening. Only the

dogs had heard. They lifted their heads toward her from their sleeping in the dust, and then stretched out their chins and settled asleep again. Elisa turned and ran hurriedly into the house.

In the kitchen she reached behind the stove and felt the water tank. It was full of hot water from the noonday cooking. In the bathroom she tore off her soiled clothes and flung them into the corner. And then she scrubbed herself with a little block of pumice, legs and thighs, loins and chest and arms, until her skin was scratched and red. When she had dried herself she stood in front of a mirror in her bedroom and looked at her body. She tightened her stomach and threw out her chest. She turned and looked over her shoulder at her back.

After a while she began to dress slowly. She put on her newest underclothing and her nicest stockings and the dress which was the symbol of her prettiness. She worked carefully on her hair, penciled her eyebrows and rouged her lips.

Before she was finished she heard the little thunder of hoofs and the shouts of Henry and his helper as they drove the red steers into the corral. She heard the gate bang shut and set herself for Henry's arrival. 95

His steps sounded on the porch. He entered the house calling, "Elisa, where are you?"

"In my room, dressing. I'm not ready. There's hot water for your bath. Hurry up. It's getting late."

When she heard him splashing in the tub, Elisa laid his dark suit on the bed, and shirt and socks and tie beside it. She stood his polished shoes on the floor beside the bed. Then she went to the porch and sat primly and stiffly down. She looked toward the river road where the willow-line was still yellow with frosted leaves so that under the high gray fog they seemed a thin band of sunshine. This was the only color in the gray afternoon. She sat unmoving for a long time. Her eyes blinked rarely.

Henry came banging out of the door, shoving his tie inside his vest as he came. Elisa stiffened and her face grew tight. Henry stopped short and looked at her. "Why—why, Elisa. You look so nice!"

"Nice? You think I look nice? What do you mean by 'nice'?" 100

Henry blundered on. "I don't know. I mean you look different, strong and happy."

"I am strong? Yes, strong. What do you mean 'strong'?"

He looked bewildered. "You're playing some kind of a game," he said helplessly. "It's a kind of a play. You look strong enough to break a calf over your knee, happy enough to eat it like a watermelon."

For a second she lost her rigidity. "Henry! Don't talk like that. You didn't know what you said." She grew complete again. "I'm strong," she boasted. "I never knew before how strong."

Henry looked down toward the tractor shed, and when he brought his eyes back to her, they were his own again. "I'll get out the car. You can put on your coat while I'm starting." 105

Elisa went into the house. She heard him drive to the gate and idle down his motor, and then she took a long time to put on her hat. She pulled it here and pressed it there. When Henry turned the motor off she slipped into her coat and went out.

The little roadster bounced along on the dirt road by the river, raising the birds and driving the rabbits into the brush. Two cranes flapped heavily over the willow-line and dropped into the riverbed.

Far ahead on the road Elisa saw a dark speck. She knew.

She tried not to look as they passed it, but her eyes would not obey. She whispered to herself sadly, "He might have thrown them off the road. That wouldn't have been much trouble, not very much. But he kept the pot," she explained. "He had to keep the pot. That's why he couldn't get them off the road."

The roadster turned a bend and she saw the caravan ahead. She swung full 110 around toward her husband so she could not see the little covered wagon and the mismatched team as the car passed them.

In a moment it was over. The thing was done. She did not look back.

She said loudly, to be heard above the motor, "It will be good, tonight, a good dinner."

"Now you're changed again," Henry complained. He took one hand from the wheel and patted her knee. "I ought to take you in to dinner oftener. It would be good for both of us. We get so heavy out on the ranch."

"Henry," she asked, "could we have wine at dinner?"

"Sure we could. Say! That will be fine." 115

She was silent for a while; then she said, "Henry, at those prize fights, do the men hurt each other very much?"

"Sometimes a little, not often. Why?"

"Well, I've read how they break noses, and blood runs down their chests. I've read how the fighting gloves get heavy and soggy with blood."

He looked around at her. "What's the matter, Elisa? I didn't know you read things like that." He brought the car to a stop, then turned to the right over the Salinas River bridge.

"Do any women ever go to the fights?" she asked. 120

"Oh, sure, some. What's the matter, Elisa? Do you want to go? I don't think you'd like it, but I'll take you if you really want to go."

She relaxed limply in the seat. "Oh, no. No. I don't want to go. I'm sure I don't." Her face was turned away from him. "It will be enough if we can have wine. It will be plenty." She turned up her coat collar so he could not see that she was crying weakly—like an old woman.

(1938)

Questions for Discussion and Writing

1. The chrysanthemums are clearly a symbol. What do they represent? Write an essay that makes a claim about the symbolism of the chrysanthemums.

2. How does the description of the setting at the beginning relate to the condition of Elisa's life?

3. Discuss the interactions between Elisa and the two males in the story. How do the men manipulate her? How does she try to manipulate them?

4. Why is Elisa interested in the prize fights? Why does she ask, "Do the men hurt each other very much?"

5. How do you think Elisa would respond to the "Wife's Chart" on page 383? In what ways does Steinbeck's characterization of Elisa act as a rebuttal to the values articulated in the chart?

MARITAL RATING SCALE

WIFE'S CHART

George W. Crane, Ph.D., M.D.

(copyright 1939)

In computing the score, check the various items under DEMERITS which fit the wife, and add the total. Each item counts as one point unless specifically weighted as in parentheses. Then check the items under MERITS which apply; now subtract the DEMERIT score from the MERIT score. The result is the wife's raw score. Interpret it according to this table:

RAW SCORES	INTERPRETATION
0–24	Very Poor (Failures)
25–41	Poor
42–58	Average
59–75	Superior
76 and up	Very Superior

DEMERITS		MERITS	
1. Slow in coming to bed—delays til husband is almost asleep.		1. A good hostess—even to unexpected guests.	
2. Doesn't like children. (5)		2. Has supper on time.	
3. Fails to sew on buttons or clean socks regularly.		3. Can carry on interesting conversation.	
4. Wears soiled or ragged dresses and aprons around the house.		4. Can play a musical instrument, as piano, violin, etc.	
5. Wears red nail polish.		5. Dresses for breakfast.	
6. Often late for appointments. (5)		6. Neat housekeeper—tidy and clean.	
7. Seams in hose often crooked.		7. Personally puts children to bed.	
8. Goes to bed with curlers on her hair or much face cream.		8. Never goes to bed angry, always makes up first . (5)	
9. Puts her cold feet on husband at night to warm them.		9. Asks husband's opinion regarding important decisions and purchases.	
10. Is a back seat driver.		10. Good sense of humor—jolly and gay.	
11. Flirts with other men at parties or in restaurants. (5)		11. Religious—sends children to church or Sunday school and goes herself. (10)	
12. Is suspicious and jealous. (5)		12. Lets husband sleep late on Sunday and holidays.	

During the period of this story, women were often asked in popular magazines to review their performance as wives using scales like this one.

Eudora Welty 1909–2001

Eudora Welty, one of America's most distinguished writers of fiction, was born in Jackson, Mississippi, and attended the University of Wisconsin and Columbia University. Returning to Jackson in 1932, she worked for a radio station and several newspapers; she also traveled throughout Mississippi for the Works Project Administration, interviewing and photographing people from all walks of life—experiences she would later draw on in her fiction. Welty was the kind of artist, as author Carol Shields put it, who made great literature "out of the humble clay of home." Her awards include three O. Henry Prizes, a Pulitzer Prize (for *The Optimist's Daughter*, 1972), and the Howells Medal (for her *Collected Stories*, 1980). The e-mail program Eudora, used by millions of people, was named in honor of Welty.

A Worn Path

It was December—a bright frozen day in the early morning. Far out in the country there was an old Negro woman with her head tied in a red rag, coming along a path through the pinewoods. Her name was Phoenix Jackson. She was very old and small and she walked slowly in the dark pine shadows, moving a little from side to side in her steps, with the balanced heaviness and lightness of a pendulum in a grandfather clock. She carried a thin, small cane made from an umbrella, and with this she kept tapping the frozen earth in front of her. This made a grave and persistent noise in the still air, that seemed meditative like the chirping of a solitary little bird.

She wore a dark striped dress reaching down to her shoe tops, and an equally long apron of bleached sugar sacks, with a full pocket: all neat and tidy, but every time she took a step she might have fallen over her shoelaces, which dragged from her unlaced shoes. She looked straight ahead. Her eyes were blue with age. Her skin had a pattern all its own of numberless branching wrinkles and as though a whole little tree stood in the middle of her forehead, but a golden color ran underneath, and the two knobs of her cheeks were illumined by a yellow burning under the dark. Under the red rag her hair came down on her neck in the frailest of ringlets, still black, and with an odor like copper.

Now and then there was a quivering in the thicket. Old Phoenix said, "Out of my way, all you foxes, owls, beetles, jack rabbits, coons and wild animals!...Keep out from under these feet, little bob-whites....Keep the big wild hogs out of my path. Don't let none of those come running my direction. I got a long way." Under her small black-freckled hand her cane, limber as a buggy whip, would switch at the brush as if to rouse up any hiding things.

On she went. The woods were deep and still. The sun made the pine needles almost too bright to look at, up where the wind rocked. The cones dropped as light as feathers. Down in the hollow was the mourning dove—it was not too late for him.

The path ran up a hill. "Seem like there is chains about my feet, time I get this far," she said, in the voice of argument old people keep to use with themselves. "Something always take a hold of me on this hill—pleads I should stay."   5

After she got to the top she turned and gave a full, severe look behind her where she had come. "Up through pines," she said at length. "Now down through oaks."

Her eyes opened their widest, and she started down gently. But before she got to the bottom of the hill a bush caught her dress.

Her fingers were busy and intent, but her skirts were full and long, so that before she could pull them free in one place they were caught in another. It was not possible to allow the dress to tear. "I in the thorny bush," she said. "Thorns, you doing your appointed work. Never want to let folks pass, no sir. Old eyes thought you was a pretty little *green* bush."

Finally, trembling all over, she stood free, and after a moment dared to stoop for her cane.

"Sun so high!" she cried, leaning back and looking, while the thick tears went   10
over her eyes. "The time getting all gone here."

At the foot of this hill was a place where a log was laid across the creek.

"Now comes the trial," said Phoenix.

Putting her right foot out, she mounted the log and shut her eyes. Lifting her skirt, leveling her cane fiercely before her, like a festival figure in some parade, she began to march across. Then she opened her eyes and she was safe on the other side.

"I wasn't as old as I thought," she said.

But she sat down to rest. She spread her skirts on the bank around her and   15
folded her hands over her knees. Up above her was a tree in a pearly cloud of mistletoe. She did not dare to close her eyes, and when a little boy brought her a plate with a slice of marble-cake on it she spoke to him. "That would be acceptable," she said. But when she went to take it there was just her own hand in the air.

So she left that tree, and had to go through a barbed-wire fence. There she had to creep and crawl, spreading her knees and stretching her fingers like a baby trying to climb the steps. But she talked loudly to herself: she could not let her dress be torn now, so late in the day, and she could not pay for having her arm or her leg sawed off if she got caught fast where she was.

At last she was safe through the fence and risen up out in the clearing. Big dead trees, like black men with one arm, were standing in the purple stalks of the withered cotton field. There sat a buzzard.

"Who you watching?"

In the furrow she made her way along.

"Glad this not the season for bulls," she said, looking sideways, "and the   20
good Lord made his snakes to curl up and sleep in the winter. A pleasure I don't see no two-headed snake coming around that tree, where it come once. It took a while to get by him, back in the summer."

She passed through the old cotton and went into a field of dead corn. It whispered and shook and was taller than her head. "Through the maze now," she said, for there was no path.

Then there was something tall, black, and skinny there, moving before her.

At first she took it for a man. It could have been a man dancing in the field. But she stood still and listened, and it did not make a sound. It was as silent as a ghost.

"Ghost," she said sharply, "who be you the ghost of? For I have heard of nary death close by."

But there was no answer—only the ragged dancing in the wind.   25

She shut her eyes, reached out her hand, and touched a sleeve. She found a coat and inside that an emptiness, cold as ice.

"You scarecrow," she said. Her face lighted. "I ought to be shut up for good," she said with laughter. "My senses is gone. I too old. I the oldest people I ever know. Dance, old scarecrow," she said, "while I dancing with you."

She kicked her foot over the furrow, and with mouth drawn down, shook her head once or twice in a little strutting way. Some husks blew down and whirled in streamers about her skirts.

Then she went on, parting her way from side to side with the cane, through the whispering field. At last she came to the end, to a wagon track where the silver grass blew between the red ruts. The quail were walking around like pullets, seeming all dainty and unseen. 30

"Walk pretty," she said. "This the easy place. This the easy going."

She followed the track, swaying through the quiet bare fields, through the little strings of trees silver in their dead leaves, past cabins silver from weather, with the doors and windows boarded shut, all like old women under a spell sitting there. "I walking in their sleep," she said, nodding her head vigorously.

In a ravine she went where a spring was silently flowing through a hollow log. Old Phoenix bent and drank. "Sweet-gum makes the water sweet," she said, and drank more. "Nobody know who made this well, for it was here when I was born."

The track crossed a swampy part where the moss hung as white as lace from every limb. "Sleep on, alligators, and blow your bubbles." Then the track went into the road.

Deep, deep the road went down between the high green-colored banks. Overhead the live-oaks met, and it was as dark as a cave.

A black dog with a lolling tongue came up out of the weeds by the ditch. She was meditating, and not ready, and when he came at her she only hit him a little with her cane. Over she went in the ditch, like a little puff of milkweed. 35

Down there, her senses drifted away. A dream visited her, and she reached her hand up, but nothing reached down and gave her a pull. So she lay there and presently went to talking. "Old woman," she said to herself, "that black dog come up out of the weeds to stall you off, and now there he sitting on his fine tail, smiling at you."

A white man finally came along and found her—a hunter, a young man, with his dog on a chain.

"Well, Granny!" he laughed. "What are you doing there?"

"Lying on my back like a June-bug waiting to be turned over, mister," she said, reaching up her hand.

He lifted her up, gave her a swing in the air, and set her down. "Anything broken, Granny?" 40

"No sir, them old dead weeds is springy enough," said Phoenix, when she had got her breath. "I thank you for your trouble."

"Where do you live, Granny?" he asked, while the two dogs were growling at each other.

"Away back yonder, sir, behind the ridge. You can't even see it from here."

"On your way home?"

"No sir, I going to town." 45

"Why, that's too far! That's as far as I walk when I come out myself, and I get something for my trouble." He patted the stuffed bag he carried, and there hung down a little closed claw. It was one of the bob-whites, with its beak hooked bitterly to show it was dead. "Now you go on home, Granny!"

"I bound to go to town, mister," said Phoenix. "The time come around."

He gave another laugh, filling the whole landscape. "I know you old colored people! Wouldn't miss going to town to see Santa Claus!"

But something held old Phoenix very still. The deep lines in her face went into a fierce and different radiation. Without warning, she had seen with her own eyes a flashing nickel fall out of the man's pocket onto the ground.

"How old are you, Granny?" he was saying.   50

"There is no telling, mister," she said, "no telling."

Then she gave a little cry and clapped her hands and said, "Git on away from here, dog! Look! Look at that dog!" She laughed as if in admiration. "He ain't scared of nobody. He a big black dog." She whispered, "Sic him!"

"Watch me get rid of that cur," said the man. "Sic him, Pete! Sic him!"

Phoenix heard the dogs fighting, and heard the man running and throwing sticks. She even heard a gunshot. But she was slowly bending forward by that time, further and further forward, the lids stretched down over her eyes, as if she were doing this in her sleep. Her chin was lowered almost to her knees. The yellow palm of her hand came out from the fold of her apron. Her fingers slid down and along the ground under the piece of money with the grace and care they would have in lifting an egg from under a setting hen. Then she slowly straightened up, she stood erect, and the nickel was in her apron pocket. A bird flew by. Her lips moved. "God watching me the whole time. I come to stealing."

The man came back, and his own dog panted about them. "Well, I scared   55
him off that time," he said, and then he laughed and lifted his gun and pointed it at Phoenix.

She stood straight and faced him.

"Doesn't the gun scare you?" he said, still pointing it.

"No, sir, I seen plenty go off closer by, in my day, and for less than what I done," she said, holding utterly still.

He smiled, and shouldered the gun. "Well, Granny," he said, "you must be a hundred years old, and scared of nothing. I'd give you a dime if I had any money with me. But you take my advice and stay home, and nothing will happen to you."

"I bound to go on my way, mister," said Phoenix. She inclined her head in   60
the red rag. Then they went in different directions, but she could hear the gun shooting again and again over the hill.

She walked on. The shadows hung from the oak trees to the road like curtains. Then she smelled wood-smoke, and smelled the river, and she saw a steeple and the cabins on their steep steps. Dozens of little black children whirled around her. There ahead was Natchez shining. Bells were ringing. She walked on.

In the paved city it was Christmas time. There were red and green electric lights strung and crisscrossed everywhere, and all turned on in the daytime. Old Phoenix would have been lost if she had not distrusted her eyesight and depended on her feet to know where to take her.

She paused quietly on the sidewalk where people were passing by. A lady came along in the crowd, carrying an armful of red-, green- and silver-wrapped presents; she gave off perfume like the red roses in hot summer, and Phoenix stopped her.

"Please, missy, will you lace up my shoe?" She held up her foot.

"What do you want, Grandma?"   65

"See my shoe," said Phoenix. "Do all right for out in the country, but wouldn't look right to go in a big building."

"Stand still then, Grandma," said the lady. She put her packages down on the sidewalk beside her and laced and tied both shoes tightly.

"Can't lace 'em with a cane," said Phoenix. "Thank you, missy. I doesn't mind asking a nice lady to tie up my shoe, when I gets out on the street."

Moving slowly and from side to side, she went into the big building, and into a tower of steps, where she walked up and around and around until her feet knew to stop.

She entered a door, and there she saw nailed up on the wall the document that had been stamped with the gold seal and framed in the gold frame, which matched the dream that was hung up in her head. 70

"Here I be," she said. There was a fixed and ceremonial stiffness over her body.

"A charity case, I suppose," said an attendant who sat at the desk before her.

But Phoenix only looked above her head. There was sweat on her face, the wrinkles in her skin shone like a bright net.

"Speak up, Grandma," the woman said. "What's your name? We must have your history, you know. Have you been here before? What seems to be the trouble with you?"

Old Phoenix only gave a twitch to her face as if a fly were bothering her. 75

"Are you deaf?" cried the attendant.

But then the nurse came in.

"Oh, that's just old Aunt Phoenix," she said. "She doesn't come for herself— she has a little grandson. She makes these trips just as regular as clockwork. She lives away back off the Old Natchez Trace." She bent down. "Well, Aunt Phoenix, why don't you just take a seat? We won't keep you standing after your long trip." She pointed.

The old woman sat down, bolt upright in the chair.

"Now, how is the boy?" asked the nurse. 80

Old Phoenix did not speak.

"I said, how is the boy?"

But Phoenix only waited and stared straight ahead, her face very solemn and withdrawn into rigidity.

"Is his throat any better?" asked the nurse. "Aunt Phoenix, don't you hear me? Is your grandson's throat any better since the last time you came for the medicine?"

With her hands on her knees, the old woman waited, silent, erect and motionless, just as if she were in armor. 85

"You mustn't take up our time this way, Aunt Phoenix," the nurse said. "Tell us quickly about your grandson, and get it over. He isn't dead, is he?"

At last there came a flicker and then a flame of comprehension across her face, and she spoke.

"My grandson. It was my memory had left me. There I sat and forgot why I made my long trip."

"Forgot?" The nurse frowned. "After you came so far?"

Then Phoenix was like an old woman begging a dignified forgiveness for waking up frightened in the night. "I never did go to school, I was too old at the Surrender," she said in a soft voice. "I'm an old woman without an education. It was my memory fail me. My little grandson, he is just the same, and I forgot it in the coming." 90

"Throat never heals, does it?" said the nurse, speaking in a loud, sure voice to old Phoenix. By now she had a card with something written on it, a little list. "Yes. Swallowed lye. When was it?—January—two, three years ago—"

Phoenix spoke unasked now. "No, missy, he not dead, he just the same. Every little while his throat begin to close up again, and he not able to swallow. He not get his breath. He not able to help himself. So the time come around, and I go on another trip for the soothing medicine."

"All right. The doctor said as long as you came to get it, you could have it," said the nurse. "But it's an obstinate case."

"My little grandson, he sit up there in the house all wrapped up, waiting by himself," Phoenix went on. "We is the only two left in the world. He suffer and it don't seem to put him back at all. He got a sweet look. He going to last. He wear a little patch quilt and peep out holding his mouth open like a little bird. I remembers so plain now. I not going to forget him again, no, the whole enduring time. I could tell him from all the others in creation."

"All right." The nurse was trying to hush her now. She brought her a bottle   95
of medicine. "Charity," she said, making a check mark in a book.

Old Phoenix held the bottle close to her eyes, and then carefully put it into her pocket.

"I thank you," she said.

"It's Christmas time, Grandma," said the attendant. "Could I give you a few pennies out of my purse?"

"Five pennies is a nickel," said Phoenix stiffly.

"Here's a nickel," said the attendant.   100

Phoenix rose carefully and held out her hand. She received the nickel and then fished the other nickel out of her pocket and laid it beside the new one. She stared at her palm closely, with her head on one side.

Then she gave a tap with her cane on the floor.

"This is what come to me to do," she said. "I going to the store and buy my child a little windmill they sells, made out of paper. He going to find it hard to believe there such a thing in the world. I'll march myself back where he waiting, holding it straight up in this hand."

She lifted her free hand, gave a little nod, turned around, and walked out of the doctor's office. Then her slow step began on the stairs, going down.

(1941)

Questions for Discussion and Writing

1. Discuss the mythic and religious parallels in the story, including the title, Phoenix's name, the journey described in the story, and the references to the Christmas season in which the story takes place.

2. How would you describe Phoenix's responses to the white people she encounters? What do these brief meetings suggest about her? About the people she meets?

3. What is the story really about? Write an essay in which you argue for the story's "most important theme" (in your opinion).

4. Why do some readers think Phoenix's grandson is already dead? Would the story be altered in a major way if this were true?

5. Welty once remarked that Phoenix's victory comes when she sees the doctor's diploma "nailed up on the wall." Can you explain how this moment is the climax of the story? What is different about what happens before this moment and what happens after?

◇◇◇◇◇◇◇◇◇◇◇◇◇◇◇◇◇◇◇◇

Katherine Min   1959–

Born in Champaign, Illinois, Katherine Min studied at both Amherst College and the Columbia School of Journalism before entering a career in writing and teaching. Currently a faculty member at the University of North Carolina at Asheville, Min has placed her work in a number of prestigious journals, including *TriQuarterly*, *Ploughshares*, and *The Threepenny Review*. Her short story "Eyelids" was included in *The Best American Short Stories of 1997*, and she received a Pushcart Prize the following year for "Courting a Monk." When asked about becoming a writer, Min responded, "I was, I'm afraid, an incorrigible liar when I was a child. The truth just didn't hold appeal for me.... From such ignoble beginnings, one has no choice but to become a fiction writer—or a felon, I suppose." The brief story that follows opens Min's first novel, *Secondhand World* (2006).

Secondhand World

My name is Isadora Myung Hee Sohn and I am eighteen years old. I was recently ninety-five days in a pediatric burn unit at Tri-State Medical Center, in Albany, New York, being treated for second- and third-degree burns on my legs, complicated by a recurring bacterial infection. The same fire that injured me killed my parents, Hae Kyoung Chung and Tae Mun Sohn, on June 11, 1976, at approximately 3:20 A.M.

It's very isolating to recover from a severe burn injury. The pain requires a great deal of attention and inward focus. While your skin tissue rages and dies, you try and put yourself as far away as possible mentally, to take refuge in small, retrievable thoughts. Nursery rhymes are sometimes useful, as are television theme songs and knock-knock jokes.

Here's a riddle. A jumbo jet takes off from New York en route to Vancouver with 246 people on board. There's a massive snowstorm, visibility worsens, passengers pray and panic. The pilot loses control, and the plane ends up doing a nosedive on the border of the United States and Canada. The weather is so bad it takes the rescue helicopters two days to get to the remote crash site in the mountains. When they finally manage to land, amid the snow and the wreckage, they're confronted with a terrible dilemma. Since the plane crashed exactly on the boundary line separating the two countries, the recovering authorities don't know whether to bury the survivors in Canada or the United States.

It took me a while to get it. The trick is knowing where to focus. There's so much clamor and confusion—the plane, the storm, the panic—that you're easily thrown off. You end up overlooking what you should have noticed right away.

The fact is that survivors aren't buried. They keep walking around. They go through the varied motions of normalcy, trying to forget the screams, the shudder of the fuselage, the sound of crumpling metal. The frozen wait among the dead for rescue.

(2006)

Questions for Discussion and Writing

1. At what point did you understand Isadora's riddle? Explain how it helps you to grasp the theme of the story.
2. "I am a short story writer by temperament. I like perfection, transcendence, moments." How does Min's description of her craft affect you as a reader of her story?
3. Reread the first paragraph of the story, and discuss Isadora's motives for including the kind and level of detail in her self-description. Consider, as well, why she phrases the second sentence of the paragraph as she does. Who uses phrases such as "was recently ninety-five days in a pediatric burn unit" or "complicated by a recurring bacterial infection"?
4. Write an essay describing your strategies for dealing with pain and loss. You might want to focus on an experience when these coping skills were tested. How do your strategies compare with Isadora's?

Ideas for Writing: Making Connections

1. Set up a scale for ranking the women in the four stories of this portfolio: Miss Brill, Elisa Allen, Phoenix Jackson, and Isadora Myung Hee Sohn. It could be something like "least admirable to most admirable," "strongest to weakest," or "most passive to most active." Write a brief paragraph to explain your placement of each character on your scale.
2. Compare how the women in these stories cope with their situations. Which do you think is most successful?
3. What part does gender play in the lives of the women in these stories? How might things be different for them if they were men?
4. Write an essay comparing "Miss Brill" to "Eveline" (page 2). What themes do these stories have in common? What differences do you see?
5. Compare Elisa Allen to wives in other stories in this book—particularly to Tome Hayashi in "Seventeen Syllables" (page 290), as well as to the young wife in "The Day It Happened" (page 300) and the narrator of "I Stand Here Ironing" (page 285).

MultiModal Project

In *Spoon River Anthology*, Edgar Lee Masters composed a collection of epitaphs, spoken as monologues by the deceased inhabitants of a fictional small town. In these brief poems, the speakers expressed their feelings about their lives, including both their joys and their complaints. For examples, see "Lucinda Matlock" and "Margaret Fuller Slack" on pages 519–21. Write a monologue for at least two of the women in the stories in this portfolio. They don't have to be poems, but they should be written in the first person. (You can find additional examples by searching for *Spoon River Anthology* online.)

PART III

Writing About
Poetry

The language of poetry is even more compressed than the language of the short story. You need to give yourself willingly to the understanding of poetry. The pleasure of reading it derives from the beauty of the language—the delight of the sounds and the images—as well as the power of the emotion and the depth of the insights conveyed. Poetry may seem difficult, but it can also be intensely rewarding.

17 How Do I Read Poetry?

Chapter Preview

In order to enjoy discovering the meaning of poetry, you must approach it with a positive attitude—a willingness to understand. Poetry invites your creative participation. More than any other form of literature, poetry allows you as reader to inform its meaning as you bring your own knowledge and experience to bear in interpreting images, motifs, and symbols. By the end of this chapter, you will be able to

- Explain the value of reading poetry aloud.
- Define *paraphrasing*, and explain how it helps in discovering the *literal meaning* of a poem.
- Identify key questions for making *associations* and discovering meaning.
- Define *allusions* and *archetype*.
- Use critical questions when interpreting and writing about poetry.

Get the Literal Meaning First: Paraphrase

Begin by reading the poem out loud—or at least by sounding the words aloud in your mind. Rhyme and rhythm work in subtle ways to emphasize key words and clarify meaning. As you reread, go slowly, paying careful attention to every word, looking up any that are unclear, and examining any difficult lines again and again. Reading aloud will force you to decide how to interpret the words and phrases.

You want to be sure that you understand the literal meaning. Because one of the delights of poetry stems from the unusual ways in which poets put words together, you may sometimes need to straighten out the syntax. For instance, Thomas Hardy writes

> And why unblooms the best hope ever sown?

The usual way of expressing that question would be something like this:

> And why does the best hope ever sown not bloom?

Occasionally you may need to fill in words that the poet has deliberately omitted through ellipsis. When Walt Whitman writes

> But I with mournful tread,
> Walk the deck my Captain lies,
> Fallen cold and dead,

we can tell that he means "the deck on which my Captain lies, / Fallen cold and dead."

Pay close attention to punctuation; it can provide clues to meaning. But do not be distressed if you discover that poets (like Emily Dickinson and Stevie Smith) sometimes use punctuation in strange ways or (like E. E. Cummings) not at all. Along with the deliberate fracturing of syntax, this unusual use of punctuation comes under the heading of poetic license.

Always you must look up any words that you do not know—as well as any familiar words that fail to make complete sense in the context. When you read this line from Whitman:

> Passing the apple-tree blows of white and pink in the orchards,

the word "blows" seems a strange choice. If you consult your dictionary, you will discover an unusual definition of blows: "masses of blossoms," a meaning which fits exactly.

Make Associations for Meaning

Once you understand the literal meaning of a poem, you can begin to expand that meaning into an interpretation. As you do so, keep asking yourself questions: Who is the speaker? Who is being addressed? What is the message? What do the images contribute? What do the symbols suggest? How does it all fit together?

When, for instance, Emily Dickinson in the following lines envisions "Rowing in Eden," how do you respond to this image?

> Rowing in Eden—
> Ah, the Sea!
> Might I but moor—Tonight—
> In Thee!

Can she mean *literally* rowing in Eden? Not unless you picture a lake in the Garden, which is, of course, a possibility. What do you associate with Eden? Complete bliss? Surely. Innocence, perhaps—the innocence of

Adam and Eve before the Fall? Or their lustful sensuality after the Fall? Given the opening lines of the poem,

> Wild Nights—Wild Nights!
> Were I with thee
> Wild Nights should be
> Our luxury!

one fitting response might be that "Rowing in Eden" suggests paddling through sexual innocence in a far from chaste anticipation of reaching the port of ecstasy: to "moor—Tonight— / In Thee!"

Sometimes poems, like stories and plays, contain *allusions* (indirect references to famous persons, events, places, or to other works of literature) that add to the meaning. Some allusions are fairly easy to perceive. When Eliot's Prufrock, in his famous love song, observes

> No! I am not Prince Hamlet, nor was meant to be,

we know that he declines to compare himself with Shakespeare's Hamlet, a character who also had difficulty taking decisive action. Some allusions, though, are more subtle. You need to know these lines from Ernest Dowson:

> Last night, ah, yesternight, betwixt her lips and mine,
> There fell thy shadow, Cynara!

in order to catch the allusion to them in Eliot's "The Hollow Men":

> Between the motion
> And the act
> Falls the shadow.

Many allusions you can simply look up. If you are puzzled by Swinburne's line

> Thou has conquered, O pale Galilean,

your dictionary will identify the Galilean as Jesus Christ. For less well-known figures or events, you may need to consult a dictionary of biblical characters, a dictionary of classical mythology, or a good encyclopedia.

Other valuable reference tools are Sir James Frazer's *The Golden Bough*, which discusses preclassical myth, magic, and religion, and Cirlot's *A Dictionary of Symbols*, which traces through mythology and world literature the significance of various **archetypes**, i.e. universal symbols—the sea, the seasons, colors, numbers, islands, serpents, and a host of others.

Thus, learning to understand poetry—like learning to understand any imaginative literature—involves asking yourself questions and then speculating and researching until you come up with satisfying answers. The box below will give you a starting list of questions.

Critical Questions for Reading Poetry

Before planning an analysis of any selection in the anthology of poetry, write out your answers to the following questions to confirm your understanding of the poem and to generate material for the paper.

1. Can you paraphrase the poem if necessary?
2. Who is the speaker in the poem? How would you describe this persona?
3. What is the speaker's tone? Which words reveal this tone? Is the poem perhaps ironic?
4. What heavily connotative words are used? What words have unusual or special meanings? Are any words or phrases repeated? If so, why? Which words do you need to look up?
5. What images does the poet use? How do the images relate to one another? Do these images form a unified pattern (a motif) throughout the poem? Is there a central, controlling image?
6. What figures of speech are used? How do they contribute to the tone and meaning of the poem?
7. Are there any symbols? What do they mean? Are they universal symbols, or do they arise from the particular context of this poem?
8. Is the occasion for or the setting of the poem important in understanding its meaning? If so, why?
9. What is the theme (the central idea) of this poem? Can you state it in a single sentence?
10. How important is the role of metrics (sound effects), such as rhyme and rhythm? How do they affect tone and meaning?
11. How important is the contribution of form, such as rhyme scheme and line arrangement? How does the form influence the overall effect of the poem?

18 Writing About Persona and Tone

Chapter Preview

Tone, which can be important in analyzing a short story, is crucial to the interpretation of poetry. Persona is closely related to tone. In order to identify persona and determine tone, you need (as usual) to ask yourself questions about the poem. By the end of this chapter you will be able to

- Define *persona*, and explain its importance for understanding a poem.
- Identify and illustrate *verbal irony*.
- List adjectives for describing tone.
- Identify and use questions for determining tone.
- Demonstrate the process for developing a major claim based on persona and tone.
- Distinguish between *explication* and *analysis*.
- Summarize the key conventions for quoting poetry in an essay.

Who Is Speaking?

A good question to begin with is this: Who is the speaker in the poem? Often the most obvious answer seems to be "The poet," especially if the poem is written in the first person. When Emily Dickinson begins

> This is my letter to the world
> That never wrote to me—

we can be fairly sure that she is writing in her own voice—that the poem itself is her "letter to the world." But poets often adopt a ***persona***; that is, they speak through the voice of a character they have created. Stevie Smith, herself a middle-aged woman, adopts a persona of a different age and of the opposite sex in these lines:

> An old man of seventy-three
> I lay with my young bride in my arms....

Thomas Hardy in "The Ruined Maid" (on page 402) composes a dramatic monologue with a dual persona (or two personae), two young women who converse throughout the poem. The speaker in Auden's "The Unknown Citizen" (on page 403) is apparently a spokesperson for the bureaucracy—but most certainly is not Auden himself. Thus, in order to be strictly accurate, you should avoid "The poet says…" and use instead "The speaker in the poem says…" or "The persona in the poem says…."

What Is Tone?

After deciding who the speaker is, your next question might be "What is the tone of this poetic voice?" *Tone* in poetry is essentially the same as in fiction, drama, or expository prose: the attitude of the writer toward the subject matter of the work—the poem, story, play, or essay. And tone in a piece of writing is always similar to tone of voice in speaking. If a friend finds you on the verge of tears and comments, "You certainly look cheerful today," her tone of voice—as well as the absurdity of the statement—lets you know that your friend is using *verbal irony*; that is, she means the opposite of what she says.

Recognizing Verbal Irony

Because verbal irony involves a reversal of meaning, it is the most important tone to recognize. To miss the irony is to miss the meaning in many cases. When Stephen Crane begins a poem

> Do not weep, maiden, for war is kind,

an alert reader will catch the ironic tone at once from the word *kind*, which war definitely is not. But irony can at times be much more subtle. Sometimes you need to put together a number of verbal clues in order to perceive the irony. W. H. Auden's poem "The Unknown Citizen," which appears in this chapter, is such a poem. Gradually as you read, you realize that the tribute being paid to this model worker (identified by number rather than name) is not the eulogy you are led to expect but an ironic commentary on the regimented society that molded the man. By the time you reach the last two lines, the irony has become apparent. (For a discussion of other types of irony that appear in drama and fiction, but not often in poetry, look up *irony* in the Glossary.)

Describing Tone

One of the chief problems in identifying tone involves finding exactly the right word or words to describe it. Even after you have detected that a work's tone is ironic, you may need to decide whether the irony is gentle or bitter, or whether it is light or scathing in tone. Remember that you are trying to identify the tone of the poetic voice, just as you would identify the tone of anyone speaking to you.

You need a number of adjectives at your command to pinpoint tone. As you analyze poetic tone, keep the following terms in mind to see whether any may prove useful: *humorous, joyous, playful, light, hopeful, brisk, lyrical, admiring, celebratory, laudatory, expectant, wistful, sad, mournful, dreary, tragic, elegiac, solemn, somber, poignant, earnest, blasé, disillusioned, straightforward, curt, hostile, sarcastic, cynical, ambivalent, ambiguous.*

Looking at Persona and Tone

Read the following five poems for pleasure. Then, as you read through them again slowly and carefully, pay attention to the persona and try to identify the tone of this speaker's voice. Is the speaker angry, frightened, astonished, admiring? Or perhaps sincere, sarcastic, humorous, deceptive?

Theodore Roethke   1908–1963

Born in Saginaw, Michigan, Theodore Roethke was strongly influenced by his father, Otto, and his father's brother, stern German immigrants who co-owned a twenty-five-acre greenhouse complex. Much of the poet's childhood and adolescence was spent working there, as reflected by the images of nature and growth that pervade his poetry. In 1923, when Theodore was only fifteen, his uncle committed suicide and his father died from cancer. While an undergraduate at the University of Michigan, Roethke decided to pursue both poetry and teaching. He was awarded the Pulitzer Prize for poetry in 1953.

My Papa's Waltz

The whiskey on your breath
Could make a small boy dizzy;
But I hung on like death:
Such waltzing was not easy.

We romped until the pans   5
Slid from the kitchen shelf;
My mother's countenance
Could not unfrown itself.

The hand that held my wrist
Was battered on one knuckle;   10
At every step you missed
My right ear scraped a buckle.

You beat time on my head
With a palm caked hard by dirt,
Then waltzed me off to bed   15
Still clinging to your shirt.

(1948)

W. D. Ehrhart   1948–

W(illiam) D(aniel) Ehrhart was born and raised in Pennsylvania. He enlisted in the U.S. Marine Corps at the age of seventeen and served for three years, including thirteen months in Vietnam. His poetry first appeared in *Winning Hearts and Minds: War Poems by Vietnam Veterans* (1972), an anthology published by Vietnam Veterans Against the War. He has since written more than fifteen books of poetry and prose and edited a number of anthologies. Although the Vietnam War figures prominently in much of Erhart's work, his poems cover a wide range of topics: the death of a friend, memories of a grandmother, respect for nature, and dismay with the human condition. He cites his wife and his daughter as major sources of inspiration.

Sins of the Father

Today my child came home from school in tears.
A classmate taunted her about her clothes,
and the other kids joined in, enough of them
to make her feel as if the fault was hers,
as if she can't fit in no matter what.   5
A decent child, lovely, bright, considerate.
It breaks my heart. It makes me want someone
to pay. It makes me think—O Christ, it makes
me think of things I haven't thought about
in years. How we nicknamed Barbara Hoffman   10
"Barn," walked behind her through the halls and mooed
like cows. We kept this up for years, and not
for any reason I could tell you now
or even then except that it was fun.
Or seemed like fun. The nights that Barbara   15
must have cried herself to sleep, the days
she must have dreaded getting up for school.
Or Suzanne Heider. We called her "Spider."
And we were certain Gareth Schultz was queer
and let him know it. Now there's nothing I   20
can do but stand outside my daughter's door
listening to her cry herself to sleep.

(2010)

Thomas Hardy   1840–1928

An architect in London, Thomas Hardy first became interested in literature at age thirty, when he began to write novels. Among the sixteen he produced, the best-known are *The Return of the Native* (1878) and *Tess of the D'Urbervilles* (1891). When his novel *Jude the Obscure* (1895) was called immoral for criticizing marriage, Hardy became so angry that he wrote nothing but poetry for the rest of his life. Many modern poets, including W. H. Auden, Philip Larkin, and Dylan Thomas, were influenced by Hardy's use of irony and spoken language.

The Ruined Maid

"O 'Melia, my dear, this does everything crown!
Who could have supposed I should meet you in Town?
And whence such fair garments, such prosperi-ty?"—
"O didn't you know I'd been ruined?" said she.

—"You left us in tatters, without shoes or socks,   5
Tired of digging potatoes, and spudding up docks;
And now you've gay bracelets and bright feathers three!"—
"Yes: that's how we dress when we're ruined," said she.

—"At home in the barton° you said 'thee' and 'thou,'
And 'thik oon,' and 'theas oon,' and 't'other'; but now   10
Your talking quite fits 'ee for high compa-ny!"—
"Some polish is gained with one's ruin," said she.

—"Your hands were like paws then, your face blue and bleak,
But now I'm bewitched by your delicate cheek,
And your little gloves fit as on any la-dy!"—   15
"We never do work when we're ruined," said she.

—"You used to call home-life a hag-ridden dream,
And you'd sigh, and you'd sock,° but at present you seem
To know not of megrims° or melancho-ly!"—
"True. One's pretty lively when ruined," said she.   20

—"I wish I had feathers, a fine sweeping gown,
And a delicate face, and could strut about Town!"—
"My dear—a raw country girl, such as you be,
Cannot quite expect that. You ain't ruined," said she.

(1866)

---

9 **barton** Farmyard.   18 **sock** Moan.   19 **megrims** Sadness.

W. H. Auden 1907–1973

Although born and raised in England, W(ystan) H(ugh) Auden became a U.S. citizen in 1946. An extremely talented poet, he was the major literary voice of the 1930s, an "age of anxiety" that faced world war and global depression. Influenced by Freud, Auden often wrote about human guilt and fear, but he also celebrated the power of love to overcome anxiety. His volume of poetry *The Age of Anxiety* (1947) won the Pulitzer Prize. Auden also collaborated on verse plays and wrote librettos for operas.

The Unknown Citizen

(To JS/07/M/378
This Marble Monument
Is Erected by the State)

He was found by the Bureau of Statistics to be
One against whom there was no official complaint,
And all the reports on his conduct agree
That, in the modern sense of an old-fashioned word, he was a saint,
For in everything he did he served the Greater Community.   5
Except for the War till the day he retired
He worked in a factory and never got fired,
But satisfied his employers, Fudge Motors Inc.
Yet he wasn't a scab or odd in his views,
For his Union reports that he paid his dues,   10
(Our report on his Union shows it was sound)
And our Social Psychology workers found
That he was popular with his mates and liked a drink.
The Press are convinced that he bought a paper every day
And that his reactions to advertisements were normal in every way.   15
Policies taken out in his name prove that he was fully insured,
And his Health-card shows he was once in hospital but left it cured.
Both Producers Research and High-Grade Living declare
He was fully sensible to the advantages of the Installment Plan
And had everything necessary to the Modern Man,   20
A phonograph, a radio, a car and a frigidaire.
Our researchers into Public Opinion are content
That he held the proper opinions for the time of year;
When there was peace, he was for peace; when there was war, he went.
He was married and added five children to the population,   25
Which our Eugenist says was the right number for a parent of
    his generation,
And our teachers report that he never interfered with their education.
Was he free? Was he happy? The question is absurd:
Had anything been wrong, we should certainly have heard.

(1940)

Edmund Waller 1606–1687

Edmund Waller was an English poet and a wealthy member of Parliament. In 1643 he was arrested for his part in a plot to turn London over to the exiled king, Charles I. By betraying his co-conspirations and by making lavish bribes, Waller avoided death. His smooth, graceful verses were extremely popular and included both love poems and tributes to important public figures of the day.

Go, Lovely Rose

Go, lovely Rose,
Tell her that wastes her time and me,
   that now she knows,
When I resemble her to thee,
How sweet and fair she seems to be.   5

Tell her that's young,
And shuns to have her graces spied,
   that had'st thou sprung
In deserts where no men abide,
Thou must have uncommended died.   10

Small is the worth
Of beauty from the light retir'd:
   Bid her come forth,
Suffer herself to be desir'd,
And not blush so to be admir'd.   15

Then die, that she
The common fate of all things rare
   May read in thee,
How small a part of time they share,
That are so wondrous sweet and fair.   20

(1645)

The Writing Process

Prewriting

As you search for a fuller understanding of a poem and for a possible writing thesis, remember to keep rereading the poem (or at least pertinent parts of it). The questions you pose for yourself will become easier to answer and your responses more enlightened.

Asking Questions About the Speaker in "My Papa's Waltz"

If a poem lends itself to an approach through persona or tone, you will, of course, find something unusual or perhaps puzzling about the speaker or the poetic voice. Consider Theodore Roethke's "My Papa's Waltz," which you just read. Ask yourself first "Who is the speaker?" You know from line 2: "a small boy." But the past tense verbs suggest that the boy may be grown now, remembering a childhood experience. Sometimes this adult perspective requires additional consideration.

Exercise: How to Determine Tone

Ask yourself "What is the speaker's attitude toward his father?" The boy's feelings about his father become the crucial issue in determining the tone of the poem. You need to look carefully at details and word choice to discover your answer.

1. Try to recapture your own childhood perspective on some interaction with adults: being kissed and hugged by relatives, encountering an adult who acted oddly, relating to your first schoolteacher, meeting a babysitter. Was it fun? Were you uncomfortable? Write a description of the experience that includes only your point of view as a child.

2. Is it pleasant or unpleasant to be made dizzy from the smell of whiskey on someone's breath?

3. Does it sound like fun to hang on "like death"?

4. How does it change the usually pleasant experience of waltzing to call it "not easy"?

5. What sort of "romping" would be necessary to cause pans to slide from a shelf?

6. Is it unusual to hold your dancing partner by the wrist? How is this different from being held by the hand?

7. Would it be enjoyable or painful to have your ear scraped repeatedly by a buckle?

8. Would you like or resent having someone "beat time" on your head with a hard, dirty hand?

9. If the father is gripping the boy's wrist with one hand and thumping his head with the other, does this explain why the boy must hang on for dear life?

10. What other line in the poem does the last line echo?

If your answers to the questions in the previous exercise lead you to conclude that this waltzing was not fun for the boy, then you could describe the tone as ironic (because of the discrepancy between the pleasant idea of the waltz and the boy's unpleasant experience). You could, possibly, describe the tone as detached, because the boy gives no clear indication of his feelings. We have to deduce them from details in the poem. You could even describe the tone as reminiscent, but this term is too general to indicate the meaning carried by the tone.

We all bring our own experience to bear in interpreting a poem. What you should be careful about is allowing your personal experience to carry too much weight in your response. If, for instance, you had an abusive father, you might so strongly identify with the boy's discomfort that you would call the tone resentful. On the other hand, if you enjoyed a loving relationship with your father, you might well find, as does X. J. Kennedy, "the speaker's attitude toward his father warmly affectionate" and take this recollection of childhood to be a happy one. Kennedy cites as evidence "the rollicking rhythms of the poem; the playfulness of a rhyme like *dizzy* and *easy*; the joyful suggestions of the words *waltz, waltzing,* and *romped.*" He suggests that a reader who sees the tone as resentful fails "to visualize this scene in all its comedy, with kitchen pans falling and the father happily using his son's head for a drum." Kennedy also feels in the last line the suggestion of "the boy *still clinging* with persistent love."[1]

Devising a Thesis

Since your prewriting questioning has been directed toward discovering the attitude of the speaker in the poem, you could formulate a thesis that allows you to argue for the need to understand the persona in order to perceive the tone of the poem. Of course, the way you interpret the poem will determine the way you state your thesis. You could write a convincing paper on any one of the following claims:

> The tone of Roethke's "My Papa's Waltz" reveals the speaker's ambivalent feelings toward his father.

> The tone of Roethke's "My Papa's Waltz" subtly conveys the speaker's resentment toward his father.

> The speaker's affection for his father is effectively captured in the tone of Roethke's "My Papa's Waltz."

If you wrote on the first claim, you would focus on the conflicting evidence suggesting that the boy is delighted by his father's attention

---

[1] *An Introduction to Poetry*, 4th ed. (Boston: Little, Brown, 1971), 10.

but frightened by the coercion of the dance. If you wrote on the second claim, you would cite evidence of the boy's discomfort and argue that the "waltz" in the title and the rollicking meter are thus clearly ironic. If you wrote on the last claim, you would emphasize the sprightly meter and playful rhymes, which present the dance as a frisky romp and show that the boy is having a splendid time.

Exercise: Considering the Speaker in "The Sins of the Father"

1. Do you think the author and the speaker are the same person? How can you tell?
2. What is the speaker's main concern at the beginning of the poem? Describe his feelings. What is the tone of the opening lines?
3. At what point does the speaker have an **epiphany**, or realization? What is his major concern after this point? How does the tone change? When does the tone change again?
4. The speaker says "It makes me want someone / to pay" (7–8). By the end of the poem who does he think should pay?
5. The speaker says "there's nothing I / can do but stand outside my daughter's door / listening to her cry herself to sleep" (20–22). Do you agree? What would you do if something like this happened to your child (or to a sibling or a good friend)?
6. What is the significance of the title? (It comes from a verse in the Bible, which is also quoted in a Shakespearean play.) How does its meaning help to explain the speaker's changing emotions? Does he blame himself in some way for what happened to his daughter?

Exercise: Describing the Tone in "The Ruined Maid"

You can see by now that speaker and tone are all but impossible to separate. In order to get at the tone of Hardy's poem, write out responses to the following questions and be prepared to discuss the tone in class.

1. Who are the two speakers in this poem?
2. What does the term *maid* mean in the title? Look it up in your dictionary if you are not sure.
3. What different meanings does your dictionary give for *ruined?* Which one applies in the poem?
4. How does the ruined maid probably make her living? What details suggest this?
5. Describe how the tone of the country maid's speeches changes during the course of the poem.
6. What tone does the ruined maid use in addressing her former friend?
7. How does the final line undercut the ruined maiden's boast that she gained "polish" with her ruin?
8. What is Hardy's tone—that is, the tone of the poem itself?

Developing a Thesis

If you are going to write on tone in "The Ruined Maid," you might devise a major claim focusing on the way we, as readers, discover the irony in the poem. Your claim could read something like this:

> In Hardy's poem the discrepancy between the supposedly "ruined" woman's present condition and her previous wretched state reveals the ironic tone.

If you wanted, instead, to write about the dual personae in the poem, you might think about how they function—to figure out why Hardy chose to present the poem through two speakers instead of the usual one. Perhaps he chose this technique because the two voices enable him to convey his theme convincingly. You might invent a claim along these lines:

> Hardy employs dual personae in "The Ruined Maid" to convince us that prostitution, long considered "a fate worse than death," is actually much preferable to grinding poverty.

In each paper, although your focus would be different, the evidence you use in presenting the contrast would be essentially the same.

Exercise: Describing the Tone in "The Unknown Citizen"

1. "The Unknown Citizen" begins with the citizen's epitaph. In a five- to ten-line poem, write your own epitaph as it might appear if you died in the next year. Think about what you would like to emphasize and what you prefer to downplay. Would you try to get a message across to people who read your gravestone?
2. How is the "he" being referred to in the poem identified in the italicized epigraph?
3. Who is the speaker in the poem? Why does the speaker use *our* and *we* instead of *my* and *I*?
4. Is *Fudge Motors Inc.* a serious name for a corporation? What is the effect of rhyming *Inc.* (line 8) with *drink* (line 13)?
5. Why does Auden capitalize so many words and phrases that normally would not be capitalized (like *Greater Community*, *Installment Plan*, *Modern Man*, and *Public Opinion*)?
6. What is the attitude of the poetic voice toward the Unknown Citizen? What is Auden's attitude toward the Unknown Citizen? What is Auden's attitude toward the speaker in the poem?
7. What, then, is the tone of the poem?

Formulating a Thesis

If you were going to write on tone in Auden's "The Unknown Citizen," you would focus on the features of the poem that reveal that tone— beginning or ending perhaps with the epigraph in which he is referred to as a number, not a name. You might frame a claim something like this:

> Auden's sharply ironic tone reveals to us that the Unknown Citizen is being honored not for his accomplishments but for being a model of conformity to the policies of the state.

As you develop this claim, you can focus on the discrepancies you recognize between the solemn praise offered by the speaker and your recognition of these qualities as far from admirable.

Exercise: Determining Tone in "Go, Lovely Rose"

1. What has happened between the speaker and the woman before the poem was written?
2. Why does he choose a rose to carry his message?
3. What does *uncommended* mean in line 10?
4. Can you detect a tone slightly different in lines 2 and 7 from the speaker's admiring tone in the poem as a whole?
5. How do you respond to his telling the rose to die so that the woman may be reminded of how quickly her beauty will also die?
6. Does the title "Song," as the poem is sometimes called, convey any hint about the tone?
7. How would you describe the tone of this poem?

Writing

Because you may find poetry more difficult to write about than short stories, first be sure that you understand the poem. If the poem is difficult, write a complete *paraphrase* in which you straighten out the word order and replace any unfamiliar words or phrases with everyday language. Yes, you damage the poem when you paraphrase it, but the poem will survive.

After you are sure you have a firm grasp on the literal level, you can then begin to examine the images, make associations, and flesh out the meanings that will eventually lead you to an interpretation of the poem. By this time, you should have generated sufficient material to write about the work. The writing process is essentially the same as it is for analyzing a short story.

Explicating and Analyzing

In explicating a poem, you proceed carefully through the text, interpreting it, usually, line by line. Because of the attention to detail, *explication* is best suited to writing about a short poem or a key section of a longer work. As an explicator you may look at any or all elements of the poem—tone, persona, images, symbolism, metrics—as you discuss the way these elements function together to form the poem. Although you may paraphrase an occasional line, your explication will be concerned mainly with revealing hidden meanings in the poem. Probably most of your class discussions involve a kind of informal explication of poems, stories, or plays.

A written explication is easy to organize: you start with the first line and work straight through the poem. But explicating well requires a discerning eye. You have to make numerous decisions about what to comment on and how far to pursue a point, and you also have to pull various strands together in the end to arrive at a conclusion involving a statement of the theme or purpose of the poem. This approach, if poorly handled, can be a mechanical task, but if well done, explication can prove a rewarding way to examine a rich and complex work.

A written *analysis* involves explication but differs by focusing on some element of the poem and examining how that element (tone, persona, imagery, symbolism, metrics) contributes to an understanding of the meaning or purpose of the whole. You can see that an analysis is more challenging to write because you must exercise more options in selecting and organizing your material. Your instructor will let you know if it matters which type of paper you compose.

Ideas For Writing

Ideas for Reflective Writing

1. Were you ever frightened or hurt as a child, like the boy in Roethke's poem, by being handled too roughly by an adult? Describe the experience, explaining not only how you felt but also what you now think the adult's motives might have been.

2. Write an ironic or humorous response to Christopher Marlowe's "The Passionate Shepherd to His Love" (pages 571–72) or compose the woman's reply to Andrew Marvell's "To His Coy Mistress" (pages 492–93).

3. Do you know anyone well who is a conformist, a person very much like Auden's Unknown Citizen? If so, write an updated ironic tribute to the type of person who always goes along with the crowd. Write your satirical praise as a speech, an essay, or a poem.

Ideas for Critical Writing

1. Choose one of the sample claims included in the "Prewriting" section of this chapter and write an essay defending that claim.

2. Both "My Papa's Waltz" (page 400) by Theodore Roethke and "Piano" by D. H. Lawrence (page 532) concern the childhood experience of a young boy. Study both poems until you are sure you understand them; then compare or contrast their tones.

3. Explain the situational irony in Ehrhart's "Sins of the Father." Consider using the idea suggested by the poem's title in your analysis.

4. Argue that the satire of "The Unknown Citizen" depends on Auden's use of a detached narrator.

5. CRITICAL APPROACHES: Review the formalist approach to literary interpretation (page 895). Using evidence only from within "Go, Lovely Rose," explain the reasoning the narrator is presenting. What is his goal? What comparisons does he encourage the reader ("her") to make between herself and the rose? What point of argument is developed in each stanza?

Ideas for Researched Writing

1. To discover more about tone, consult reference works such as *A Handbook to Literature*, the *New Princeton Encyclopedia of Poetry and Poetics*, or the online *Glossary of Poetic Terms* at www.poeticbyway .com/glossary.html. Apply what you learn in an essay analyzing the tone of Lisel Mueller's "Losing My Sight" (pages 551–52).
2. Investigate the difference of opinion about the tone of "My Papa's Waltz." Locate at least three different interpretations, and write an essay in which you respond to and evaluate these views.

MultiModal Project

Set one or two of the poems in this chapter to music, and create an audio or video recording using a phone, computer, or tablet. If you are not musically inclined, then choose the video option: do an oral reading of the poem or poems, selecting background music and visuals to go with your reading.

Editing

In this section we will explain a few conventions that you should observe in writing about poetry. If you have often written papers analyzing poetry, you probably incorporate these small but useful bits of mechanical usage automatically. If not, take time during the revising or editing stage to get them right.

Quoting Poetry in Essays

The following are the main conventions to observe when quoting poetry in writing:

Inserting Slash Marks When quoting only a couple of lines, use a slash mark to indicate the end of each line (except the last).

Whitman similarly describes the soul's position in the universe in these lines: "And you O my soul where you stand, / Surrounded, detached, in measureless oceans of space" (6–7).

Citing Line Numbers Cite line numbers in parentheses after the quotation marks and before the period when quoting complete lines, as in the previous example. When quoting only a phrase, cite the line number immediately after closing the quotation marks, even if your sentence continues.

> In the italicized portion of the poem, the bird sings a carol in praise of "lovely and soothing death" (135) to help the persona overcome his grief.

Using Ellipsis Dots   To show omissions when quoting poetry, use three dots, just as you would if quoting prose.

> The poet's sympathies are not for the living but for the dead: "They themselves were fully at rest..../ The living remain'd and suffer'd..." (181–82).

Using Square Brackets   If you need to change a word, a capital letter, or some punctuation within the line or lines you quote, enclose the changed letter or mark of punctuation in square brackets (not parentheses).

> The persona brings visions of the varying beauty of the entire country "[t]o adorn the burial-house of him [he] love[s]" (80).

Remember that you do not have to quote complete lines. Rather than clutter your sentence with three sets of brackets, you could quote only the telling phrase in that line.

> The persona brings visions of the varying beauty of the entire country to "adorn the burial-house" (80) of the one he loves.

Quoting Multiple Lines   If you are quoting more than two or three lines, indent ten spaces and omit the quotation marks (since the indention tells your readers that the material is quoted).

> After describing the carnage of war dead, the persona realizes that his sympathies have been misplaced:
>
> > They themselves were fully at rest, they suffer'd not,
> > The living remain'd and suffer'd, the mother suffer'd,
> > And the wife and the child and the musing comrade suffer'd
> > And the armies that remain'd suffer'd. (181–84)

The indented material should still be double-spaced (unless your instructor asks you to single-space the lines).

Sample Student Paper: Persona and Tone

The following student paper is a reflection on Sir Walter Raleigh's poem "The Nymph's Reply to the Shepherd" and is included here to generate class discussion about interpreting tone and persona. Read the poem, and its companion "The Passionate Shepherd to His Love" by Christopher Marlowe, which appear on pages 571–72, and decide whether you agree with the writer's claims about the two poems.

Morris Richards

Professor Funk

English 1092

12 October 2008

Time Passes and So Does Love

In Greek and Latin mythology a "nymph" is a minor deity in the shape of a young woman who lives in forests, meadows, mountains, and water. The word can also refer to a young girl, especially one who inspires lustful thoughts. But the speaker in Sir Walter Raleigh's poem "The Nymph's Reply to the Shepherd" (572) doesn't seem to fit these definitions. Raleigh's speaker is clearly older, wiser, and quite real, especially when contrasted with Marlowe's "Passionate Shepherd" (571). This difference in the speakers of these companion poems also creates a clear contrast in tone, a tone that is seldom heard in a Renaissance love poem.

The romantic enticements that the shepherd offers don't stand up to the nymph's pragmatic realism about life and love. She begins by questioning the "truth in every shepherd's tongue." She does not believe there can be much substance in the fleeting words of a poet, and dismisses them as "pretty pleasures" to be enjoyed and forgotten like the moment in which they pass. It's important, I think, to notice that the nymph focuses on the shepherd's words and doesn't reveal her own feelings for him. Could it be that she uses her doubts about his promises as a way to avoid telling him that she just doesn't care for him?

In pointing out the illusory nature of the charming enticements that Marlowe's shepherd has offered her, Raleigh's nymph uses words that are very different from her ardent suitor's. While the shepherd speaks of "Melodious birds," "fragrant posies," "buckles of the purest gold," "coral clasps and amber studs," the nymph counters with "sorrow's fall," "wayward winter," "reason rotten," and "cares to come." This frank appraisal of poetic language is similar to Shakespeare's treatment of the popular metaphors of the day in his sonnet "My Mistress' Eyes Are Nothing Like the Sun" (488). In his poem Shakespeare rejects the fanciful, artificial comparisons in favor of

Richards 2

realistic descriptions of his beloved, suggesting that the exaggerated conceits are false and inappropriate. Raleigh's nymph expresses a similar distrust of the shepherd's "honey tongue."

The nymph speaks with a skepticism that seems to come from experience and maturity. She knows that men lie, weather turns bad, flowers and young women fade and wither, just as gowns, skirts, and posies do. And she wonders what will happen when her beauty has left her. Will he stay around? Or is he just a "honey tongue" who will leave her with sorrow and a heart of bitterness when the "rivers rage" and the "rocks grow cold" and the birds stop singing?

The allusion to Philomel who "becometh dumb" introduces an ominous note about the possible consequences of excessive love and unchecked sexual passion. According to the Latin poet Ovid, Philomel (or Philomela) was raped by her brother-in-law, who tore out her tongue so she couldn't accuse him. The gods later turned her into a nightingale. We probably shouldn't make too much of this brief reference, but it may suggest that Raleigh's nymph has not only been dumped before but was also treated badly by a former lover. In any case, she is certainly cautious about accepting the shepherd's promises.

Analyzing the Student's Reflection

After rereading the two poems, write your reactions to the preceding student paper. (Or, if you prefer, write your own interpretation of the tone and persona of "The Nymph's Reply to the Shepherd.") The following questions may help you:

1. Do you agree with the student about the speaker's attitude toward the shepherd and his "honey tongue"? Do you think she's being fair toward him and his intentions?
2. What do you think of the student's assessment of the language that the speaker uses?
3. Do you think the nymph is more experienced and mature than the shepherd?
4. What do you think of the student's speculations about the nymph's past experiences with lovers?
5. Does the last stanza offer a more positive interpretation than the student allows for?

19 Writing About Poetic Language

Chapter Preview

In no other form of literature are words so important as in poetry. As you study the language of poetry—its freshness, precision, and beauty—you can learn ways in which to use words effectively in your own prose writing. By the end of this chapter, you will be able to

- Differentiate between *connotation* and *denotation*.
- Define and identify *metaphors, similes,* and *personification*.
- Explain *imagery* and *symbolism*.
- Define *paradox* and *oxymoron*.
- Analyze the poetic language of poems.
- Describe the process of *comparing* and *contrasting*.
- Identify questions to find and replace vacant words.

What Do the Words Suggest?

What do the words of a poem suggest? Your sensitivity to poetic language will be enhanced if you learn the meaning of a few terms in literary criticism. (The important term *allusion* is defined on page 396.)

Connotation and Denotation

Many single words carry a rich load of meaning, both denotative and connotative. The **denotation** of a word is the definition you will find in the dictionary. The **connotation** of a word is the emotional overtone you may feel when encountering the term. Consider the word *mother.* Most people would respond positively with feelings of warmth, security, and love associated with bedtime stories, a warm lap, and fresh apple pies. So, when Stephen Crane includes the word in these moving lines:

> Mother whose heart hung humble as a button
> On the bright splendid shroud of your son,
> Do not weep.
> War is kind,

the connotations of the word *mother* probably account for part of our emotional response.

415

Figures of Speech

The most common figures of speech—metaphor, simile, and personification—appear in our everyday language. You might say, if you keep forgetting things, "My mind is a sieve," creating a metaphor. Or you might note, "That dog looks like a dust mop without a handle," making a simile. Or you might complain, "My computer can't spell worth a darn," using personification. Of course, poets use figures of speech that are much fresher and more imaginative than the kind most of us employ—one of the cardinal reasons for considering them poets.

Metaphor and Simile

A *metaphor* is an imaginative comparison that makes use of the connotative values of words. When Shakespeare writes to a young lover, "Thy eternal summer shall not fade," he is comparing youth to the joys of summertime. In "Dulce et Decorum Est" (pages 606–07), a compelling antiwar poem, Wilfred Owen uses the metaphors "drunk with fatigue," "blood-shod," "like old beggars under sacks," "coughing like hags," "flound'ring like a man in fire or lime," and "his hanging face, like a devil's sick of sin." The last four of these singularly grim comparisons would usually be called *similes* because they include the connective *like*, but you can also find similes that use *as* and other explicitly comparative words. In fact, many people use the broader term *metaphor* to refer to any figure of speech that involves a comparison.

A metaphor goes beyond descriptive detail by making an association that can *only* be imaginary, one that is impossible in reality. A person's life does not have seasons except in a metaphorical way; nor do people really become intoxicated with fatigue. However, the mental stretch these comparisons demand is part of their power. "Drunk with fatigue" makes many imaginative associations: the tired soldiers have lost their ability to think straight; they are staggering along about to fall over; they are not physiologically alert. In the poem, it is this state that makes one of them unable to don his mask quickly when a chlorine gas bomb strikes. His reaction time is fatally impaired, just like a drunk's. You can see how the metaphor packs in meaning and guides our response to the poem's narrative.

These metaphorical ideas—life having seasons or people feeling drunk with fatigue—are not difficult to grasp, because they resonate with our own experiences. Some critics would say that the best metaphors demand a more intellectual leap, having a shocking or puzzling aspect. An example from "Dulce et Decorum Est" might be the description of the soldiers' hurry to grab their gas masks as "an ecstasy of fumbling." We usually associate "ecstasy" with happiness, yet this cannot be the meaning here. We are forced to think beyond the obvious, to the features of ecstasy that do apply—intensity, overpowering emotion, lack of thought, lack of conscious control. The student paper beginning on page 426 explicates several such unusual metaphors in John Donne's "A Valediction: Forbidding Mourning."

In this chapter, the poem "In the Long Hall" (page 421) provides an example of an *extended metaphor*. An extended metaphor is exactly what it sounds like: an imaginative comparison worked out through several lines or perhaps even an entire poem, accruing meaning as it goes along. In this case, your understanding of the poem hinges on your understanding of the metaphor it develops.

Personification

"Daylight is nobody's friend," writes Anne Sexton in a metaphor that compares daylight to a friend. More exactly it is a *personification*, because it makes a nonhuman thing sound like a human being. T. S. Eliot uses personification when he writes "the afternoon, the evening, sleeps so peacefully," as does Andrew Marvell in "Fate with jealous eyes does see."

Imagery

Perhaps personification is so widely used in poetry because it gives us a clear image of something otherwise vague or abstract, like daylight or fate. *Imagery* is the term we use to speak of these sensory impressions literature gives us. Robert Frost, in a famous poem, describes a sleigh driver "stopping here / To watch his woods fill up with snow," providing a visual image that most readers find easy to picture. In the same poem, Frost gives us an apt auditory image: "The only other sound's the sweep / Of easy wind and downy flake." And Langston Hughes infuses strong images of taste and odor into the similes of his famous poem "Harlem (A Dream Deferred)": "Does it stink like rotten meat? / Or crust and sugar over— / like a syrupy sweet?" (page 460).

Symbol

A *symbol* is an image that becomes so suggestive that it takes on much more meaning than its descriptive value. Poems are often constructed around a controlling image that gathers meaning and becomes a symbol, like the spider and its web in Walt Whitman's "A Noiseless Patient Spider" (page 419) or the automobile accident in Karl Shapiro's "Auto Wreck" (page 543). The connotations of the words, the repetition, the placement, and the relationship with the rest of the poem help identify an image as a symbol. For instance, the concrete description of the wreck in Shapiro's poem leads to abstract speculation about the sudden and arbitrary nature of death. And the image of the cherry tree in A. E. Housman's poem "Loveliest of Trees" (page 516) becomes a symbol of aging and the brevity of life. (You should also review the discussion of images and symbols in fiction, pages 124–26.)

Paradox

Sometimes a poet will arrest the reader's attention by composing a *paradox*—a phrase or statement that seems contradictory or absurd on its surface but may actually turn out to be true or well founded. John Donne, for example, concluded his poem "Death Be Not Proud" (page 489) with the paradoxical declaration "Death, thou shalt die!" To understand a paradox, the reader needs to discover the sense that underlies the paradox. In this case, Donne was assuming that a shared belief in life after death would make his meaning clear to the readers of his holy sonnets. John Keats achieved a similar effect when he wrote "Heard melodies are sweet, but those unheard / Are sweeter" (page 501), a paradoxical theme at the center of "Ode on a Grecian Urn."

Oxymoron

Another figure of speech that appears occasionally in both poetry and prose is an *oxymoron*, an extreme paradox in which two words having opposite meanings are juxtaposed, as in "deafening silence" or "elaborately simple."

Looking at Poetic Language

The six poems you are about to study exemplify elements of poetic language. As you read them over several times, identify figures of speech, imagery, symbol, and paradox.

Mary Oliver   1935–

Born in Maple Heights, Ohio, Mary Oliver attended Ohio State University and Vassar College but did not earn a degree. She also worked for a time as a teenager with the sister of Edna St. Vincent Millay, studying the papers of a poet whose influence is apparent in Oliver's early lyrics. Oliver's many volumes of poetry have been met with wide critical acclaim, including the Pulitzer Prize–winning *American Primitive* (1983), from which "August" is taken. The collection celebrates the natural world and the rewards of solitude in nature. When asked about her work, Oliver has said, "I consider myself kind of a reporter—one who uses words that are more like music and that have a choreography."

August

When the blackberries hang
swollen in the woods, in the brambles
nobody owns, I spend

all day among the high
branches, reaching   5
my ripped arms, thinking

of nothing, cramming
the black honey of summer
into my mouth; all day my body

accepts what it is. In the dark   10
creeks that run by there is
this thick paw of my life darting among

the black bells, the leaves; there is
this happy tongue.
                                            (1983)

Walt Whitman   1819–1892

Born on an impoverished farm in Long Island, Whitman moved with his family
to Brooklyn, where he worked for many years as a printer, teacher, journalist, and
carpenter. In 1855, he published his own book of poetry, *Leaves of Grass*, a collection of twelve long poems, which he expanded and revised throughout his life. His
work as a volunteer nurse in the Civil War inspired his next collection of poems,
Drum Taps (1865). Whitman's bold experiments with free verse and his celebration
of human sexuality shocked his contemporaries—but liberated American poetry and
influenced generations of modern poets.

A Noiseless Patient Spider

A noiseless patient spider,
I mark'd where on a little promontory it stood isolated,
Mark'd how to explore the vacant vast surrounding,
It launched forth filament, filament, filament, out of itself,
Ever unreeling them, ever tirelessly speeding them.   5

And you O my soul where you stand,
Surrounded, detached, in measureless oceans of space,
Ceaselessly musing, venturing, throwing, seeking
    the spheres to connect them,
Till the bridge you will need be form'd, till the ductile anchor hold,
Till the gossamer thread you fling catch somewhere,   10
    O my soul.
                                            (1881)

William Shakespeare 1564–1616

See page 730 for a biographical note about this author.

Shall I Compare Thee to a Summer's Day?

Shall I compare thee to a summer's day?
Thou art more lovely and more temperate:
Rough winds do shake the darling buds of May,
And summer's lease hath all too short a date:
Sometimes too hot the eye of heaven shines,   5
And often is his gold complexion dimmed;
And every fair from fair sometimes declines,
By chance or nature's changing course untrimmed;
But thy eternal summer shall not fade,
Nor lose possession of that fair thou ow'st;   10
Nor shall death brag thou wander'st in his shade,
When in eternal lines to time thou grow'st:
So long as men can breathe, or eyes can see,
So long lives this, and this gives life to thee.

(1609)

Kay Ryan 1945–

While a student at UCLA, Kay Ryan was denied membership in the university poetry club. In 2004 she was awarded the $100,000 Ruth Lilly Poetry Prize and in 2008 was named Poet Laureate of the United States. "All of us want instant success," she says. "I'm glad I was on a sort of slow drip." A lifetime Californian, she lives in Marin County with her partner, Carol Adair, and has taught remedial English at the College of Marin for thirty years.

Turtle

Who would be a turtle who could help it?
A barely mobile hard roll, a four-oared helmet,
She can ill afford the chances she must take
In rowing toward the grasses that she eats.
Her track is graceless, like dragging   5
A packing-case places, and almost any slope
Defeats her modest hopes. Even being practical,
She's often stuck up to the axle on her way
To something edible. With everything optimal,
She skirts the ditch which would convert   10
Her shell into a serving dish. She lives

Below luck-level, never imagining some lottery
Will change her load of pottery to wings.
Her only levity is patience,
The sport of truly chastened things.   15

(1994)

Hayden Carruth   1921–2008

Hayden Carruth, who held a master's degree from the University of Chicago, spent eighteen months in his thirties in what he called "the loony bin," recovering from agoraphobia so severe that for five years he huddled in the attic of his parents' house, barely able to write—"like squeezing old glue out of the tube." Eventually he moved to Vermont, where he scraped out a hard living—chopping wood, smoking pigs, and typing manuscripts for a dollar a page. Married four times, he declared, "The women in my life got me through." He won the National Book Award in 1996 for his collection *Scrambled Eggs & Whiskey*.

In the Long Hall

On his knees he was weaving a tapestry
which was unraveling behind him. At first
he didn't mind it; the work was flawed,
loose ends, broken threads, a pattern
he could not control; but as his skill   5
improved he began to resent the way
his tapestry was undoing itself.
He resolved not to look back
but to keep going ahead, as he did
successfully for a long time. Still   10
later, however, he began to notice
that the part of the tapestry in front
of him was unraveling too; threads
he had just knotted became loose.
He tied them again. But before long   15
he could not keep up, his hands
were too slow, his fingers too weak.
The unraveling in front pushed
him toward the unraveling in back
until he found himself isolated   20
on a small part of the tapestry whose
pattern he could not see because
it was beneath his own body. He spun
this way and that. He worked as fast as
he could with trembling fingers   25
in futility, in frenzy, in despair.

(1978)

Donald Hall 1928–

Donald Hall was born in Connecticut and educated at Exeter Academy and at Harvard and Oxford universities. He met and married the poet Jane Kenyon in 1972, and the couple moved to Eagle Pond Farm in rural New Hampshire, where Hall remains affiliated with Bennington College. In 1989, he was diagnosed with colon cancer and given a slim chance of surviving five years. In 1994 Kenyon developed leukemia and died within fifteen months. Hall's collection *Without: Poems* (1998) focuses on her illness and death. In 2006, he was named Poet Laureate of the United States.

My Son My Executioner

My son, my executioner,
   I take you in my arms,
Quiet and small and just astir,
   And whom my body warms.

Sweet death, small son, our instrument   5
   Of immortality,
Your cries and hungers document
   Our bodily decay.

We twenty-five and twenty-two,
   Who seemed to live forever,   10
Observe enduring life in you
   And start to die together.

                   (1955)

Father holding his son, who looks nothing like an executioner.

The Writing Process

Prewriting

The following exercises will help you analyze the use of language in the poems that you just read in preparation for writing a paper focusing on that approach.

Exercise: Examining Poetic Language

1. Why could one say that "Shall I Compare Thee to a Summer's Day?" presents contrast rather than comparison?

2. In a group of classmates, attempt to write a companion poem to "Shall I Compare Thee to a Summer's Day?" using instead the extended metaphor "Shall I compare thee to a winter's day?" Try to use connotative language.

3. What is the main comparison made in "A Noiseless Patient Spider"? What is personified? Using a thesaurus, paraphrase the poem, substituting near synonyms for some of the original words. Comment on the differences in meaning and tone you create. (Imagine, for example, if the spider "launched forth string, string, string, out of itself.")

4. "August" and "Turtle" contain a number of figures of speech. Identify as many as you can. Which ones do you find fresh and effective? Which ones are less successful in your opinion?

5. What metaphor is developed through "In the Long Hall"? It may help you to fill in the blank: "_____ is like weaving a tapestry." Within this metaphor, what do changes in the process of weaving mean?

6. Explain the paradox that is central to "My Son My Executioner."

Writing

Poetic language is one of the richest veins of material for writing. You could, for example, analyze the role of nature imagery in "Turtle," in "Shall I Compare Thee to a Summer's Day?" or in "A Noiseless Patient Spider." Or you could examine the cumulative effect of the extended metaphor in "In the Long Hall."

Comparing and Contrasting

Noticing similarities and differences between poems will sharpen your sensitivity to each of them. If you listed all the words in the short poem "My Son My Executioner" and scrambled them and then listed all the words in "Turtle" and scrambled them, putting the two lists side by side, you might see for the first time that "Turtle" has few words longer than two syllables, that it has few abstract terms, and that in contrast with "My Son My Executioner" it has few words that convey emotion. Taking the comparison further, you might say that "Turtle" focuses on creating a strong, sensual image while "My Son My Executioner" focuses on expression of ideas and feelings.

The following writing assignments suggest some meaningful comparisons to explore. You might want to review the suggestions for organizing a comparison, which you'll find in Chapter 3, pp. 38–40.

Ideas For Writing

Ideas for Reflective Writing

1. Whitman's poem comparing the explorations of the spider to the searchings of his soul makes the totally abstract idea of the soul's search for meaning clear and concrete. Think of some abstraction that you might want to explain to a five-year-old child—something like gentleness, aggression, wisdom, slyness, or perseverance. Then think of an appropriate animal or insect to illustrate the quality, and write a poem or a fable to show the child why the quality is good or bad. Remember to keep your vocabulary simple and your lines or sentences short.

2. Who is the "he," the weaver, in "In the Long Hall"? Write an essay explaining whether "he" is everyone, a certain type of person, or a specific character created by Carruth. Be specific about how you came to your conclusion.

3. Write a detailed description of an animal, using personification and metaphors the way Kay Ryan does in her poem "Turtle."

Ideas for Critical Writing

1. In your study of literature and in your everyday life, you have come across many metaphors and similes for the life span (for example, the idea that life is a journey). Explain the extended metaphor in "In the Long Hall" in terms of similarities to and differences from other figures of speech that describe the life span.

2. Write an essay explaining how the sense imagery and metaphors in "August" prepare the reader for the meaning of "this happy tongue" at the end of the poem.

3. Interpret the symbol of the spider in "Design" (page 527) and in "A Noiseless Patient Spider" (page 419).

4. Compare and contrast the nature imagery in Shakespeare's Sonnet 18 ("Shall I Compare Thee to a Summer's Day?" on page 420) and Sonnet 73 ("That Time of Year Thou Mayst in Me Behold" on page 488).

5. CRITICAL APPROACHES: Review the psychological approach to interpreting literature (Chapter 34). Read D. H. Lawrence's "Piano" (page 532), looking for clues to the narrator's conscious and unconscious motivations, defenses, inner conflicts, and symbolic representations. Write an explication of the poem from a psychological point of view.

Ideas for Researched Writing

1. In the early twentieth century, a prominent group of poets developed an identity as *imagists*, dedicated to concrete, concentrated poetic language. The movement was called *imagism*. Several of these poets are represented in the poetry anthology in this text.

Consult reference works and article databases for information about this movement and its followers. Write a paper explaining the principles of the movement, using examples from imagist poets.

2. When asked whether she was happiest when walking in the woods or sitting at her desk, Mary Oliver responded, "Probably walking in the woods, because I do feel like I vanish and become part of the natural world, which for whatever reason has always felt safe to me. But my mind is more invested when I'm working on a poem at my desk, and that's fun. In order to be good, you have to really love the work of it." Select one of the poets in this chapter and research that person's writing process and how it fits into his or her everyday life.

MultiModal Project

William Blake illustrated and printed the pages for many of his poems. See the illustrated page for "The Sick Rose" on page 496. Create an illustrated page or poster for one of the poems in this chapter. If you can't draw, search for images online and choose one that's particularly fitting to use. Your instructor may ask you to write a statement that explains how the illustration you created or found relates to the poem.

Rewriting: Style

After looking so closely at poetic language, you should have a grasp of how important every word is to the total effect of a piece of writing.

Choosing Vivid, Descriptive Terms

Dudley Randall's "To the Mercy Killers" (page 547) draws its strength almost exclusively from the vividness of its language. He describes himself as "a clot, an aching clench, / a stub, a stump, a butt, a scab, a knob, / a screaming pain, a putrefying stench." While your expository prose should not be quite so packed with arresting terminology, it can probably be improved by some attention to descriptive wording. Look at several of your back papers from this class. See whether you can identify your favorite vacant words. Do you always express positive evaluations with *nice* or *beautiful*? Do you usually intensify an adjective with the word *very*? Do you refer to everything from ideas to irises as *things*? And do you describe anything that causes a faint stir in your being as *interesting*, causing you to come up with vapid sentences like "This beautiful poem is full of very interesting things"? If so, you need to find livelier, more exact terms.

Sample Student Paper: Poetic Language

Here are the second and final drafts of an Eastern Illinois University student's essay analyzing the love imagery in Donne's "A Valediction: Forbidding Mourning" (pages 491–92).

Sample Student Paper: Second Draft

Weaver 1

Sonya Weaver

Professor Funk

English 1002

April 3 2008

Images of a Love

The speaker in John Donne's poem "A Valediction: Forbidding Mourning" is an unromantic man who is sternly forbidding his wife to be sorrowful at his parting. This description is not true of course, but it is the way the *punct.* speaker might be perceived if all comparisons, contrasts, and images were taken out of the poem. In order to appreciate the beauty of this poem and interpret it *wordy* *sentence* correctly, it is necessary to take a close look at each image or comparison.

The first comparison we come to likens the speaker's parting to the quiet and easy death of virtuous men. The speaker paints a picture of a virtuous or upright man who, because he does not fear it, is passing peacefully into death. His deathbed is surrounded by his friends who are having trouble deciding if he has actually passed away or if he is still quietly breathing. The speaker says that his departure from his wife should be just as calm. He says, "let us melt" (5) which implies slowly and easily parting without any noise or tears. He explains that showing great emotion would expose their love to *vague* *reference* the common people and he does not want this because *best word* *choice?* he believes their love is special, and that exposure would lower their love.

Weaver 2

The speaker next contrasts their love to the love of
common people. He states that common people notice
earthquakes, but not trepidations or tremblings that take
place among the stars. He is illustrating that common
people's love is earthly, but that their love is heavenly.

*misleading
reference?*

He goes on to say that "sublunary" (13) or earthly lovers
cannot be apart from each other because when they are,
they lose their love because it is only physical. He claims

*needs
rephrasing*

that he and his wife are not like this. He feels that their

*weak
reference*

love (his and his wife's) is spiritual and refined and that it
is so great that it is above their understanding ("ourselves
know not what it is" [18]). They do not have to worry

rephrase

about their spouse being unfaithful, as earthly lovers do,
because their love is not just physical.

Next the speaker compares the malleability of gold
to the distance that their souls can stretch (21–24). The
speaker says that temporary separation should not be

*maybe
expand
with other
associations
of gold*

viewed as a break. He believes that even though they may
be many miles apart, they are still one. He claims their

clarify

souls can expand over distances equal to the malleability
of gold or 250 square feet. This is a truly beautiful image.

The last image is another very beautiful one. It
compares their two souls to twin compasses (25–36). The
speaker believes that if their souls are two (instead of one),
they are still linked to each other, as are the parts of a
compass. He likens his wife to the foot in the center. She
makes no attempt on her own to move. She does so only if
he does. She is also like the center foot in that if he leaves,
she leans after him and then becomes upright when he
returns home as does the center foot of a compass when
the outer foot is at a distance drawing a circle. He says
that there will be times when he must leave but that he

Weaver 3

will always return to her even as a compass returns to its starting point upon completion of a circle.

Without its images, this poem would be nothing more than a husband prohibiting his wife from being sad at his departure. However, Donne's images transform this rough message into a beautiful and romantic love poem. Images are important! *Weak closing line*

Be sure to add Work Cited (on a separate page).
This is a good second draft showing sensitivity to the images.
I have marked a few places where your style needs more clarity
and grace as well as one paragraph that could be expanded.

Sample Student Paper: Final Draft

Sonya Weaver

Professor Funk

English 1002

10 April 2008

Images of a Love

The speaker in John Donne's poem "A Valediction: Forbidding Mourning" is an unromantic man who is sternly forbidding his love to be sorrowful at his parting. This description is not true, of course, but it is the way the speaker might be perceived if all comparisons, contrasts, and images were taken out of the poem. In order to appreciate the beauty of this poem and interpret it accurately, each image or comparison must be closely analyzed.

The first comparison we come to likens the speaker's parting to the quiet and easy death of virtuous men. The speaker paints a picture of a virtuous or upright man who, because he does not fear it, is passing peacefully into death. His deathbed is surrounded by his friends, who are having trouble deciding if he has actually passed away or if he is still quietly breathing. The speaker suggests that his departure from his wife should be just as calm. He says, "let us melt" (5), which implies slow and easy movement, without any clamor or sobbing. He explains that showing great emotion would display their love to the common people, and he does not want this display because he believes it would make their special love seem common.

The speaker next contrasts their special love to common love. He states that common people notice earthquakes, but not trepidations or tremblings that take place among the stars. He is illustrating that common people's love is earthly, but that the love between him and his wife is heavenly. He goes on to say that "sublunary" (13) or earthly lovers mourn physical separation because their love is limited to the physical realm. He claims that he and his wife are not thus limited. Their love is so spiritual and refined that it is even beyond their own understanding ("ourselves know not what it is" [18]). They do not have to worry about unfaithfulness, as earthly lovers do, because their love is not merely defined by the physical.

    Next the speaker compares their love to the rare, precious, and beautiful metal gold (21–24). The comparison suggests not only that their love shares these three qualities, but also that it shares gold's malleability. An ounce of gold can be spread thin enough to cover 250 square feet. The speaker compares this span to the distance that their souls can stretch. The speaker says that temporary separation should not be viewed as a break. He believes that even though they may be many miles apart, they are still one, like a continuous sheet of spread gold—an unusual and expressive image.

    The last image is another quite eloquent one. It compares their two souls to twin compasses (25–36). The speaker believes that if their souls are two (instead of one), they are still linked to each other, as are the parts of a drafting compass. He likens his wife to the foot in the center. She makes no attempt on her own to move but does so only if he does. She is also like the center foot in that if he leaves, she leans after him and then becomes upright when he returns home, behaving like the center foot of a compass when the outer foot draws a circle and

Weaver 3

then folds into the center. He says that there will be times

when he must leave but that he will always return to

her even as a compass returns to its starting point upon

completion of a circle.

Without its images, this poem would be nothing

more than a husband's prohibiting his wife from being sad

at his departure. However, Donne's often extraordinary

images transform this austere message into a beautiful

and romantic love poem.

Weaver 4

Work Cited

Donne, John. "A Valediction: Forbidding Mourning." *Literature and the Writing Process*, edited by Elizabeth McMahan, et al., 8th ed., Prentice Hall, 2007, p. 427.

Exercise: Comparison

Now that you have read both drafts, go over them again, making point-by-point comparisons. Notice that the writer went beyond the instructor's specific suggestions in her final revision. Write your response to the following topics, and be prepared to discuss your findings in class.

1. Identify five cases in which the writer made changes in word choice (diction). Using a dictionary, explain the rationale for the changes.
2. Identify two sentences that have been significantly changed. Explain the reasons for the changes.
3. Closely analyze all the alterations in the third paragraph of the essay.

20 Writing About Poetic Form

Chapter Preview

When we say that poetry has *form*, we mean it has design or structure. All poems have some kind of form. Many elements go into making the forms of poetry, but they all involve arranging the words in patterns. Sometimes sound controls the pattern; sometimes the number of words or the length of the lines determines the form. By the end of this chapter, you will be able to

- Define and explain *rhythm* and *rhyme*.
- Identify the primary patterns of poetic *meter: iambic, trochaic, anapestic,* and *dactylic*.
- Define *alliteration, assonance,* and *consonance*.
- Distinguish between *closed-form* and *open-form* poems.
- Describe the common forms of English poetry: *couplets, quatrains, sonnets, free verse,* and *concrete*.
- Explain the process of relating poetic form to meaning.
- List and analyze five sources of word confusion: *inexact synonyms, homophones, imprecise adjectives, malapropisms, inappropriate connotations*.

What Are the Forms of Poetry?

Poetic forms can be divided into those that use sound effects (rhythm, rhyme), those that involve the length and organization of lines (stanza), and those that artistically manipulate word order (syntax).

Rhythm and Rhyme

Sound effects are produced by organized repetition. Stressing or accenting words and syllables produces *rhythm*; repeating similar sounds in an effective scheme produces *rhyme*. Both effects intensify the meaning of a poem, arouse interest, and give pleasure. Once we notice a pattern of sound we expect it to continue, and this expectation makes us more attentive to subtleties in the entire poem.

Rhythm can affect us powerfully. We respond almost automatically to the beat of a drum, the thumping of our heart, the pulsing of an engine. Poetic rhythm, usually more subtle, is created by repeating stresses and pauses. Rhythm conveys no verbal meaning itself, but when used skillfully it reinforces the meaning and tone of a poem. Consider how Theodore Roethke captures the raucous spirit of "My Papa's Waltz" in the recurring three-stress rhythm of these lines.

> We rómped untíl the páns
> Slíd from the kítchen shélf;
>
> Then wáltzed me óff to béd
> Still clínging tó your shírt.

For more details about the rhythms of poetry, see the following box.

Rhythm and Meter in Poetry

When the rhythm has a regular pattern—that is, when the stress recurs at regular intervals—the result is ***meter***. Not all poems are metered, but many are written in one dominant pattern.

Number of Feet　Poetic meter is measured in feet, units of stressed and unstressed syllables. A line of poetry may be written in monometer (having one foot), dimeter (two feet), trimeter (three feet), tetrameter (four feet), pentameter (five feet), hexameter (six feet), and so on.

Kinds of Feet　The syllables in a line can occur in regular patterns. The most common pattern for poetry written in English is *iambic*, an unstressed syllable (˘) followed by a stressed one (´). This line is written in iambic pentameter; it has five iambic feet:

My mis | tress' eyes | are no | thing like | the sun

Three other meters are of some importance in English poetry.

Trochaic (a stressed syllable followed by an unstressed one):

Tell me | not in | mourn ful | num bers

Anapestic (two unstressed syllables followed by a stressed one):

'Twas the night | be fore Christ | mas and all | through the house

Dactylic (a stressed syllable followed by two unstressed ones):

Hig gle dy | pig gle dy | Pres i dent | Jeff er son

Rhyme, a recurring pattern of similar sounds, also enhances tone and meaning. Because rhymed language is special language, it helps to set poetry apart from ordinary expression and calls attention to the sense, feeling, and tone of the words. Rhyme also gives a certain pleasure to the reader by fulfilling the expectation of the sound patterns. Rhyme, which usually depends on sound, not spelling, occurs when accented syllables contain the same or a similar vowel sound with identical consonant sounds following the vowel: *right* and *bite*, *knuckle* and *buckle*. Rhymes are commonly used at regular intervals within a poem, often at the ends of lines:

> Yet he wasn't a scab or odd in his views,
> For his Union reports that he paid his dues.

Alliteration, Assonance, and Consonance

Closely allied to rhyme are other verbal devices that depend on the correspondence of sounds. *Alliteration* is the repetition of consonant sounds either at the beginning of words or in stressed syllables: "The Soul selects her own Society—" or "Nature's first green is gold, / Her hardest hue to hold." *Assonance* is the repetition of similar vowel sounds that are not followed by identical consonant sounds: *grave* and *gain*, *shine* and *bright*. *Consonance* is a kind of half-rhyme in which the consonants are parallel but the vowels change: *blade* and *blood*, *flash* and *flesh*. Alliteration, assonance, and consonance are likely to be used occasionally and not in regular, recurring patterns; but these devices of sound do focus our attention and affect the tone, melody, and tempo of poetic expression.

Exercise: Poetic Form

Listen to a favorite popular song and copy down the lyrics (you may have to listen several times). Now arrange the lines on the page as you think they would be printed. What patterns of rhythm and sound do you see? Did you notice them before you wrote the words down and arranged the lines? Does the lineation (the arrangement into lines of poetry) help make the meaning any clearer? If possible, compare your written version with one from the album liner or an online lyrics site.

Stanzas: Closed and Open Forms

In the past, almost all poems were written in *closed form*: poetry with lines of equal length arranged in fixed patterns of stress and rhyme. Although these elements of form are still much in evidence today, modern poets prefer the greater freedom of *open-form poetry*, which uses lines of varying length and avoids prescribed patterns of rhyme or rhythm.

Closed forms give definition and shape to poetic expression. *Rhyme schemes* and *stanza patterns* demand the careful arrangement of words and lines into units of meaning that guide both writer and reader in understanding poetry.

Couplets and Quatrains Stanzas can be created on the basis of the number of lines, the length of the lines, the pattern of stressed syllables (the meter), and the rhyme scheme (the order in which rhymed words recur). The simplest stanza form is the *couplet*: two rhymed lines, usually of equal length and similar meter. W. H. Auden's "The Unknown Citizen" (page 403) is written in rhyming couplets, although the lines vary in length and sometimes in rhythm. The most common stanza in English poetry is the *quatrain*, a group of four lines with any number of rhyme schemes. "The Ruined Maid" (page 402) is composed of six quatrains in which the lines rhyme as couplets (critics indicate this pattern of rhyme with letters: *a a b b*). The same rhyme scheme and stanza form are used in "Aunt Jennifer's Tigers" (page 557), while the quatrains of "My Papa's Waltz" (page 400) employ an alternating rhyme pattern (*a b a b*). Longer stanza patterns are used, of course, but the quatrain and the couplet remain the basic components of closed-form poetry.

Sonnets The fixed form that has been used most frequently by the greatest variety of notable poets in England and America is the *sonnet*. Originated in Italy in the fourteenth century, the sonnet became a staple of English poetry in the sixteenth century and has continued to attract practitioners ever since.

The form of the sonnet is firmly fixed: fourteen lines, with ten syllables per line, arranged in a set rhyme scheme. The *Shakespearean sonnet* uses the rhyme scheme most common for sonnets in English: *a b a b, c d c d, e f e f, g g*. You will notice the rhyme scheme falls into three quatrains and an ending couplet, with a total of seven rhymes. "Shall I Compare Thee to a Summer's Day?" (page 420) and "That Time of Year Thou Mayst in Me Behold" (page 488) are splendid examples of Shakespeare's mastery of the sonnet (he wrote 154 of them) and illustrate why this traditional verse form continues to entice and stir both poets and readers. Dudley Randall's "To the Mercy Killers" (page 547) is an intriguing example of a modern Shakespearean sonnet.

The Italian sonnet, not very common in English poetry, uses fewer rhymes (five) and has only two groupings of lines, the first eight called the *octave* and the last six the *sestet*. Robert Frost created a chilling Italian sonnet in "Design" (page 527).

Free Verse A poem written in *free verse* or *open form* generally has no rhyme scheme and no basic meter for the entire selection. Rhyme and rhythm do occur, of course, but not in the fixed patterns that are required of stanzas and sonnets. Many readers think that open-form poetry is easy to write, but that is not the case. Only careless poetry is easy to write, and even closed forms can be sloppily written. Open forms demand their own special arrangements; without the fixed patterns of traditional forms to guide them, modern poets must discover these structures on their own.

Walt Whitman's "A Noiseless Patient Spider" (page 419) demonstrates how open form still uses sound and rhythm to create tone, enhance meaning, and guide the responses of the reader.

Poetic Syntax

Rhyme, rhythm, and stanza are not the only resources of form available to poets. Writers can also manipulate the way the words are arranged into sentences. For instance, the short, staccato sentences of "We Real Cool" (page 437) impress us in a way entirely different from the effect of the intricate expression of "The Silken Tent" (page 439), which is a single sentence stretching over fourteen lines. Words in English sentences must be arranged in fairly standard patterns. If we reverse the order of "John struck the ball" to "The ball struck John," the words take on a new meaning altogether. As with stanza form and rhyme scheme, poets can either stick with the rigidity of English sentence structure (syntax) or try to achieve unusual effects through inversion. E. E. Cummings, for example, forces his readers to pay close attention to the line "anyone lived in a pretty how town" by rearranging the words in an unexpected way. (In the standard pattern of an exclamation, the line would read "How pretty a town anyone lived in!")

Visual Poetry

Someone once defined poetry as "lines of words that don't go all the way to the margin." But for a ***prose poem*** that's not true. As the name implies, prose poetry is printed in blocks and paragraphs instead of stanzas or lines. The poetic characteristics of a prose poem can be seen in its rhythmic phrasing, ***internal rhyme***, patterns of sound (like alliteration or assonance), and intensive use of figurative language.

Concrete poetry, on the other hand, makes extensive use of line breaks and spatial arrangements. A mix of conventional poetry and graphic art, a concrete poem takes on the shape of its subject. Some famous examples include George Herbert's "Easter Wings," which looks like a pair of wings on the page, and John Hollander's "Swan and Shadow," which arranges the words and lines to create the outline of a swan and its reflection in the water. You will find examples of concrete or visual poetry through the ages at http://www.webexhibits.org/poetry/explore_21_visual_examples.html.

Looking at the Forms of Poetry

The following poems illustrate many of the variations of sound and organization that we have just discussed. As you read these poems, be alert for the special effects that the poets create with rhythm, rhyme, stanza form, and syntax. You may have to read some selections several times to appreciate how thoroughly form and meaning work together.

Gwendolyn Brooks 1917–2000

Gwendolyn Brooks once confessed that as a child she "was very ill-adjusted. I couldn't skate, I was never a good rope-jumper, and I can remember thinking I must be a very inferior kind of child since I couldn't play jacks." Although she grew up as a middle-class African American, in her poetry Brooks identified with the poor blacks of Chicago (where she spent most of her life) and the simplicity of her poetic voice successfully conveys the meager circumstance of her subjects. In 1950 she became the first black woman to win the Pulitzer Prize.

We Real Cool

The Pool Players
Seven at the Golden Shovel

We real cool. We
Left school. We

Lurk late. We
Strike straight. We

Sing sin. We   5
Thin gin. We

Jazz June. We
Die soon.

                            (1960)

Looking cool shooting pool at the local hangout.

A. E. Housman   1859–1936

After failing his finals at Oxford, A(lfred) E(dward) Housman became a clerk in the London Patent Office. An extremely capable scholar, he published several studies of classical authors and was eventually appointed a professor of Latin at London University and then at Cambridge University. Housman's own poetry, admired for its exquisite simplicity and penetrating feeling, often deals with the tragedy of doomed youth. His poetic works include *A Shropshire Lad* (1896) and *Last Poems* (1922).

Eight O'Clock

He stood, and heard the steeple
  Sprinkle the quarters on the morning town.
One, two, three, four, to market-place and people
  It tossed them down.

Strapped, noosed, nighing his hour,   5
  He stood and counted them and cursed his luck;
And then the clock collected in the tower
  Its strength, and struck.

                      (1922)

E. E. Cummings   1894–1962

Born in Cambridge, Massachusetts, E(dward) E(stlin) Cummings is perhaps best known for his eccentric antipathy toward capital letters—a style copied by many poetry students. His volumes of poetry include *Tulips and Chimneys* (1923) and *95 Poems* (1958). During World War I, Cummings served as an ambulance driver in France and was mistakenly committed to a French prison camp for three months, an experience he recounted in the prose journal *The Enormous Room* (1922).

anyone lived in a pretty how town

anyone lived in a pretty how town
(with up so floating many bells down)
spring summer autumn winter
he sang his didn't he danced his did.

Women and men (both little and small)   5
cared for anyone not at all
they sowed their isn't they reaped their same
sun moon stars rain

children guessed (but only a few
and down they forgot as up they grew   10

autumn winter spring summer)
that noone loved him more by more

when by now and tree by leaf
she laughed his joy she cried his grief
bird by snow and stir by still   15
anyone's any was all to her

someones married their everyones
laughed their cryings and did their dance
(sleep wake hope and then) they
said their nevers they slept their dream   20

stars rain sun moon
(and only the snow can begin to explain
how children are apt to forget to remember
with up so floating many bells down)

one day anyone died i guess   25
(and noone stooped to kiss his face)
busy folk buried them side by side
little by little and was by was

all by all and deep by deep
and more by more they dream their sleep   30
noone and anyone earth by april
wish by spirit and if by yes.

Women and men (both dong and ding)
summer autumn winter spring
reaped their sowing and went their came   35
sun moon stars rain

                                             (1940)

Robert Frost   1874–1963

One of the most popular and honored of American poets, Robert Frost was born in San Francisco, but as a young boy his family moved east, and much of his work reflects a love of the New England landscape. Before gaining success as a poet, Frost worked as a teacher, a chicken farmer, and a handyman. His poems are characterized by colloquial, restrained language that implies messages rather than openly stating them. Frost was awarded four Pulitzer Prizes for his poetry.

The Silken Tent

She is as in a field a silken tent
At midday when the sunny summer breeze
Has dried the dew and all its ropes relent,

So that in guys it gently sways at ease,
And its supporting central cedar pole,   5
That is its pinnacle to heavenward
And signifies the sureness of the soul,
Seems to owe naught to any single cord,
But strictly held by none, is loosely bound
By countless silken ties of love and thought   10
To everything on earth the compass round,
And only by one's going slightly taut
In the capriciousness of summer air
Is of the slightest bondage made aware.

(1943)

Billy Collins 1941–

Born in New York City, William James (Billy) Collins has lived there ever since. His father is an electrician, his mother a nurse. Selected as Poet Laureate of the United States in 2000, he served two terms. He has managed to combine critical approval with unprecedented popular success: his last three collections of poems have broken sales records for poetry. "Usually," he says, "I try to create a hospitable tone at the beginning of the poem. Stepping from the title to the first lines is like stepping into a canoe. A lot of things can go wrong."

Sonnet

All we need is fourteen lines, well thirteen now,
and after this one just a dozen
to launch a little ship on love's storm-tossed seas,
then only ten more left like rows of beans.
How easily it goes unless you get Elizabethan   5
and insist the iambic bongos must be played
and rhymes positioned at the ends of lines,
one for every station of the cross.
But hang on here while we make the turn
into the final six where all will be resolved,   10
where longing and heartache will find an end,
where Laura will tell Petrarch to put down his pen,
take off those crazy medieval tights,
blow out the lights, and come at last to bed.

(1999)

David Shumate 1950–

A native Midwesterner, David Shumate lives in central Indiana, where he is the Poet-in-Residence at Marian University. His work is frequently featured on National Public Radio's *The Writer's Almanac* and has been included in the anthology *Good Poems for Hard Times*. Shumate says the "prose poem teeters precariously between prose and poetry because of its heavier reliance on narrative on the one hand and its use of all other lyrical elements, save the line break, on the other hand." He has published three volumes of prose poems.

A Hundred Years from Now

I'm sorry I won't be around a hundred years from now. I'd like to see how it all turns out. What language most of you are speaking. What country is swaggering across the globe. I'm curious to know if your medicines cure what ails us now. And how intelligent your children are as they parachute down through the womb. Have you invented new vegetables? Have you trained spiders to do your bidding? Have baseball and opera merged into one melodic sport? A hundred years…. My grandfather lived almost that long. The doctor who came to the farmhouse to deliver him arrived in a horse-drawn carriage. Do you still have horses?

(2013)

Roger McGough 1937–

Award-winning poet, playwright, broadcaster, and children's author, Roger McGough has been one of the most successful poets in England for more than thirty years. His 1960s poems captured the verve and irreverence of that era. McGough has always used his wit to undermine the sad disappointments of life.

40	Love
middle	aged
couple	playing
ten	nis
when	the
game	ends
and	they
go	home
the	net
will	still
be	be-
tween	them

(1971)

The Writing Process
Prewriting

Writing about poetic form is challenging. Because it is impossible to separate form from meaning, you must be sure that you understand what a poem says before you try to analyze how its formal characteristics contribute to your understanding and appreciation. In completing the following exercises, you should read the poems aloud, if possible, and reread the difficult passages a number of times before you decide on your answers.

Exercise: Experimenting with Poetic Forms

1. Examine "We Real Cool" by Gwendolyn Brooks (page 437). How would you describe the rhythm of this poem? How does the rhythm affect your perception of the speakers (the "We" of the poem)? Why are all the sentences in the last four stanzas only three words long? What is the effect of placing the subject of those sentences ("We") at the ends of the lines?

2. Look at the alliteration in "Eight O'Clock" by A. E. Housman (page 438). What events or feelings are emphasized by alliteration? How do other elements of form—rhyme, stress, stanza, pattern—influence the tone and point of the brief drama described in the poem? Write an objective account of the events in "Eight O'Clock." What did you have to leave out of your account?

3. Study the rhyme schemes and line variations of the following poems, all of which are written in quatrains:

   —"Eight O'Clock" (page 438)
   —"My Son My Executioner" (page 422)
   —"anyone lived in a pretty how town" (pages 438–39)
   —"Piano" (page 532)
   —"A Valediction: Forbidding Mourning" (pages 491–92)

   In which of the poems do the stanza divisions indicate a change of time or a shift in thought? Do any of the poets disregard the stanza patterns? Try to decide why all of these poets used quatrains.

4. Rewrite the following lines—from "The Unknown Citizen" and "anyone lived in a pretty how town"—putting them in the word order you would expect them to follow in ordinary speech:

   > For in everything he did he served the Greater Community.

   > Except for the War till the day he retired
   > He worked in a factory....

   > anyone lived in a pretty how town
   > (with up so floating many bells down)

   > Women and men (both little and small)
   > cared for anyone not at all

5. Do you think "A Hundred Years from Now" (page 441) is poetry? What are its poetic qualities? Try rearranging the prose to make it look like a poem on the page. Where would you break the lines?

Writing

Because rhythm, rhyme, syntax, and stanza convey no meaning in themselves, you probably will not write an entire essay on form alone. Instead you can use what you have learned about poetic form to help you analyze and interpret a poem (or poems) with greater understanding and confidence.

Relating Form to Meaning

You can use observations about form to confirm and develop your ideas about the meaning or theme of a poem. Looking at a poem's formal characteristics will help you to answer such important questions as these: What is the tone? Is the speaker being ironic? What are the key words and images? And how does the main idea advance through the poem?

Specifically, elements of form offer clues like these:

1. Close, obvious rhyme often indicates a comic or ironic tone. Subtle rhymes support more serious tones.
2. Heavy stress can be humorous, but it can also suggest anger, defiance, strength, or fear.
3. Alliteration can be humorous, but it can also be chillingly serious; it serves to provide emphasis by slowing the reading of the line.
4. Assonance can provide a rich, solemn effect, a certain grandeur perhaps, or even a sensuous effect.
5. Rhythm and repetition emphasize key words.
6. Stanzas and rhyme schemes mark out patterns of thought and can serve as guides to development of theme.
7. Important images are often underscored with rhyme and stress.
8. Inverted or unusual syntax calls attention to complex ideas.
9. Various elements of form can be used to indicate a change in speaker or a shift in thought or tone.
10. Typographical effects can call attention to significant feelings or ideas.

This list does not exhaust the possibilities, but it should alert you to the various ways that form relates to thought and meaning in poetry.

Ideas for Writing

Ideas for Expressive Writing

1. Write an original haiku. A *haiku* is a rhymeless Japanese poem. Its form is based on syllables: seventeen syllables usually arranged in three lines, often following a pattern of five, seven, and five. Haiku written in English, however, do not always follow the original Japanese syllable pattern and may even be rhymed. Because of their

brevity, haiku compress their expression by focusing on images and letting the closely observed details suggest the feelings and meanings. The following haiku, translated from Japanese originals and some written in English, provide a variety of models for you to follow.

> The piercing chill I feel:
> my dead wife's comb, in our bedroom,
> under my heel...
> —Taniguchi Buson (trans. Harold G. Henderson)

> When looking for spring
> trust only the daffodil
> never the groundhog.
>
> —W. V. Weber

> the old woman holds
> lilac buds
> to her good ear—
>
> —Raymond Roseliep

> Heat-lightning streak—
> through darkness pierces
> the heron's shriek.
>
> —Matsuo Basho

Notice that the images in these haiku convey strong sensory experiences implying a great deal more than a mere description would suggest.

2. Turn "anyone lived in a pretty how town" into a prose narrative. Straighten out the syntax and supply details to fill in the story. Discuss what is lost and what is gained by recasting the poem this way.

Ideas for Critical Writing

1. Explain how rhythm, repetition, and rhyme affect the tone and meaning in "We Real Cool" and "Eight O'Clock." Are the effects the same in both poems?

2. CRITICAL APPROACHES: Review the discussion of the deconstructionists' approach to interpreting literature (page 899). Then analyze the poem "Sonnet" explaining how Billy Collins deconstructs the form and purposes of a traditional sonnet at the same time he uses them. Is the poem a parody or a clever treatment of the conventional form—or both?

3. Compare one of Shakespeare's sonnets (page 420 or pages 486–89) with a modern sonnet, such as Frost's "Design" (page 527) or Randall's "To the Mercy Killers" (page 547). Why do the modern poems *not* seem like sonnets? Pay close attention to the syntax and the way the rhyme scheme subdivides each poem.

4. Explain how the spacing and the arrangement of words contribute to the tone and meaning of "40------Love" (page 441). You probably need to find out what "40-love" means in tennis.

Ideas for Researched Writing

1. What is a *villanelle* or a *sestina* or a *cinquain*? Examine the rules for writing one of these closed forms of poetry and read a number of examples. Consult a reference work such as *The New Princeton Encyclopedia of Poetry*, *The Poetry Dictionary*, or *The Teachers & Writers Handbook of Poetic Forms*. Using illustrative examples, write a paper in which you describe the form to an audience of classmates and general readers.

2. Research the phenomenon of *slam poetry*. What happens at these events? What kinds of poetry do they produce? You might include the *spoken word movement*, which is a spinoff of slam poetry, in your investigation.

MultiModal Project

Write a concrete poem. Decide on a topic (an object, an activity, or an emotion), then imagine how to make the appearance of the words on the page reflect what they mean. For example, if you were writing about running or driving, you might runthewordstogetherlikethis to suggest speed, or you could arrange the letters in the word *staircase* so they actually climb up the page. You can vary the typeface or color to represent different ways to emphasize the words, such as bold face to suggest anger or all capitals to indicated loudness. Use the search term "Images of famous concrete poems" to find examples online.

Rewriting: Style

As a writer, you must choose your words carefully. Many English words are to some extent synonymous, even interchangeable, but often the distinctions between synonyms are as important as their similarities. "The difference between the right word and the almost right word," said Mark Twain, "is the difference between lightning and the lightning bug." When you revise your essay, focus on the accuracy and precision of the words you use.

Finding the Exact Word

You must take care that both the denotations and the connotations of the words you use are the ones you intend. You do not want to write *heroics* when you really mean *heroism*. You do not want to "*expose* three main topics" when you really intend to *explore* them. The following are some problem areas to consider as you look at the words you have used in your essay.

1. **Distinguish among synonyms.**

   Exact writing demands that you choose among different shades of meaning. Although *feeling* and *sensation* are synonyms, they are certainly not interchangeable. Neither are *funny* and *laughable* or *famous* and *notorious*. Consult your dictionary for help in choosing the word that says exactly what you mean.

   ## Exercise: Differentiating Words

   Explain the differences in meaning among the following groups of words and phrases:

   a. a *renowned* politician, a *famous* politician, a *notorious* politician
   b. an *indifferent* parent, a *detached* parent, an *unconcerned* parent
   c. to *condone* an action, to *excuse* an action, to *forgive* an action
   d. *pilfer, steal, rob, burglarize, loot, ransack*
   e. an *apparent* error, a *visible* error, an *egregious* error

2. **Watch out for words with similar sound or spelling.**

   Homophones (words that have the same pronunciation but different meanings and different spellings) are sometimes a source of confusion. The student who wrote that a song conveyed the composer's "piece of mind" let the sound of the word override her knowledge of spelling and meaning. Words that are similar in sound and spelling can also be confusing. If you are not careful, you can easily confuse *eminent* with *imminent* or write *quiet* when you mean *quite*.

   ## Exercise: Distinguishing Homophones

   Explain the difference in meaning in the following pairs of words:

   a. *apprise, appraise*
   b. *anecdote, antidote*
   c. *elicit, illicit*
   d. *martial, marital*
   e. *statue, statute*
   f. *human, humane*
   g. *lose, loose*
   h. *idol, idle*
   i. *accept, except*
   j. *simple, simplistic*
   k. *beside, besides*
   l. *weather, whether*
   m. *incidence, incident*
   n. *angle, angel*

3. **Choose the precise adjective form.**

   Many words have two or more adjective forms: a *questioning* remark is not the same as a *questionable* remark. As with homophones and other words that sound alike, do not let the similarity in spelling and pronunciation mislead you.

   ## Exercise: Recognizing Connotations

   Point out the connotative differences in meaning in the following pairs of adjectives.

   a. an *intelligible* essay, an *intelligent* essay
   b. a *hateful* sibling, a *hated* sibling

c. a *likely* roommate, a *likable* roommate
d. an *informed* speaker, an *informative* speaker
e. a *workable* thesis, a *working* thesis

4. **Watch out for malapropisms.**

Misused words are often unintentionally funny. These humorous confusions and near misses are called *malapropisms*. You may get a laugh from your readers if you write "My car insurance collapsed last week," but you will not be impressing them with your command of the language.

Exercise: Correcting Malapropisms

In the following sentences, what do you think the writer probably meant to say?

a. He has only a *supercilious* knowledge of the subject.
b. She was the *pineapple* of perfection.
c. They burned the *refuge*.
d. He passed his civil service *eliminations*.
e. They are in for a *shrewd* awakening.

5. **Be sure the words fit the context.**

Sentences can be disconcerting if all the words do not have the same emotional associations. For instance, "The thief brandished his gun and angrily requested the money" is confusing because *brandished* and *angrily* suggest a different emotion from *requested*. A better word choice would be "*demanded* the money."

Exercise: Editing for Context

Explain why the italicized words are inappropriate in the following sentences. What words would you use as replacements?

a. Her *stubbornness* in the face of danger saved our lives.
b. The use of violence to obtain a goal is too *poignantly* barbaric for most people to *sympathize* with.
c. The mob shouted in *displeasure*.

Sample Student Paper on Poetic Form

The following paper, written by a student at Eastern Illinois University, advances several claims about Robert Frost's use of the sonnet form in "The Silken Tent" (pages 439–40).

Elizabeth Curvey

Professor Coleman

English 1003

12 December 2011

Consistency of Character and Form in

"The Silken Tent"

The speaker in Robert Frost's poem "The Silken Tent" compares a woman he admires to a flexible shelter. In an extended metaphor, he conveys two distinct impressions: the soft femininity of a delicate fabric (silk) and the protective toughness of a tent. The speaker admires his subject, the woman, for being feminine and strong at the same time; but it is her seamless, genuine character that inspires his praise most. This inspiration is expressed in both the content and the form of the poem.

Frost's speaker uses detailed descriptions of the tent to illustrate the personality traits that he most admires. The woman's poise and self-confidence are first conveyed in the description of the tent's movements: "it gently sways at ease" (4), without rigidity. And the depiction of the tent's "supporting central cedar pole" (5) seems to stress the woman's pride and integrity. By comparing the woman's soul to a "pinnacle"—a sharp, straight, upright object—that points "heavenward" (6-7), the speaker reinforces his admiration of her firmness of character.

The admiration is intensified by the speaker's realization that everything the woman has and stands for is her own creation from materials in the world around her. This notion is expressed in the line "Seems to owe naught to any single cord" (8), a remark that implies that the woman is self-sustaining, not relying on someone else for her esteem. Yet the woman's self-confidence has not made her insensitive to others. She is connected "By countless silken ties of love and thought / To everything on earth the compass round" (10–11). The speaker suggests that the woman is capable of loving generously because she is self-assured.

Perhaps the most significant compliment comes in the last three lines of the poem, where the speaker comments on the woman's temperament:

And only by one's going slightly taut

In the capriciousness of summer air

Is of the slightest bondage made aware. (12–14) Using the image of a summer breeze to suggest the tugs of change, the speaker indicates that the woman handles her obligations with ease and composure. As Professor Modecai Marcus explains, "the slightness of the bondage shows that the woman's tender dutifulness responds not to compulsion but to loving necessity" (167).

The form of "The Silken Tent" is a traditional Shakespearean sonnet: three quatrains with *abab, cdcd, efef* rhyme schemes, followed by a *gg* couplet. In the conventional sonnet, each quatrain expresses its own statement, topic, or question. Usually, the couplet wraps up all the quatrains with a concluding comment (Harmon 519). However, in "The Silken Tent" the thoughts and observations are not divided up into the conventional units set out by the patterns of rhyme. The quatrains do not end with terminal punctuation: periods, semicolons, question marks, or colons. Instead, the whole poem comprises one long sentence. So the logic flows smoothly from one section into the next—for example, the last three lines (quoted above) are a logical unit, not the last two lines.

Curvey 3

Professor Judith Oster sums up the overall effect in this way:

> The single sentence construction provides, even more firmly than the sonnet form, a unified tightness which corresponds to the tightness of the single image and the tightness of the ropes controlling the very existence of the silken structure. (187)

The continuity and inner logic of the sonnet reflect the speaker's appraisal of the woman, as being both conventional and unique, a person with a wholeness and unity all her own. Though influenced by the demands of custom, she remains splendidly herself.

Curvey 4

Works Cited

Frost, Robert. "The Silken Tent." *Literature and the Writing Process*, edited by Elizabeth McMahan et al., 9th ed., Longman, 2011, p. 510.

Harmon, William, and Hugh Holman. "Sonnet." *A Handbook to Literature*, 11th ed., Prentice Hall, 2009.

Marcus, Mordecai. *The Poems of Robert Frost: An Explication*. G.K. Hall, 1991.

Oster, Judith. *Toward Robert Frost: The Reader and the Poet*. U of Georgia P, 1991.

Sample Published Essay: Poetic Form

David Huddle's essay—"The 'Banked Fire' of Robert Hayden's 'Those Winter Sundays'"—on the following pages is an example of a published essay on poetic form. (Hayden's poem appears on page 584.)

David Huddle

The "Banked Fire" of Robert Hayden's "Those Winter Sundays"

For twenty years I've been teaching Robert Hayden's most frequently anthologized poem to undergraduate poetry-writing students. By "teach," I mean that from our textbook I read the poem aloud in the classroom, I ask one of the students to read it aloud, I make some observations about it, I invite the students to make some observations about it, then we talk about it a while longer. Usually to wrap up the discussion, I'll read the poem through once more. Occasions for such teaching come up about half a dozen times a year, and so let's say that during my life I've been privileged to read this poem aloud approximately 240 times. "Those Winter Sundays" has withstood my assault upon it. It remains a poem I look forward to reading and discussing in my classroom. The poem remains alive to me, so that for hours and sometimes days after it visits my classroom, I'm hearing its lines in my mind's ear.

Though a fourteen-liner, "Those Winter Sundays" is only loosely a sonnet. Its stanzas are five, four, and five lines long. There are rhymes and near-rhymes, but no rhyme scheme. The poem's lines probably average about eight syllables. There are only three strictly iambic lines: the fourth, the eighth, and (significantly) the fourteenth.

It's a poem that's powerfully informed by the sonnet form; it's a poem that "feels like" a sonnet—it has the density and gravity of a sonnet—which is to say that in its appearance on the page, in its diction and syntax, in its tone, cadence, and argumentative strategy, "Those Winter Sundays" presents the credentials of a work of literary art in the tradition of English letters. But it's also a poem that has gone its own way, a definite departure from that most conventional of all the poetic forms of English and American verse.

The abstract issue of this poem's sonnethood is of less value to my beginning poets than the tangible matter of the sounds the poem makes, especially those *k*-sounding words of the first eleven lines that one comes to associate with discomfort: "clothes...blueblack cold...cracked...ached... weekday...banked...thanked...wake...cold...breaking...call... chronic...cold." What's missing from the final three lines? The *k* sounds have been driven from the poem, as the father has "driven out the cold" from the house. The sounds that have replaced those *k* sounds are the *o* sounds of "good... shoes...know...know...love...lonely offices." The poem lets us associate the *o* sounds with love and loneliness. Sonically the poem tells the same story the poem narrates for us. The noise of this poem moves us through its emotional journey from discomfort to lonely love. If ever there was a poem that could teach a beginning poet the viability of the element of sound-crafting, it is "Those Winter Sundays."

Quote its first two words, and a great many poets and English teachers will be able to finish the first line (if not the whole poem) from memory. Somewhat remarkably, the poem's thesis—that the office of love can be relentless, thankless, and more than a little mysterious—resides in that initially odd-sounding

two-word beginning, "Sundays too." The rest of the line—
the rest of the independent clause—is ordinary. Nowhere
else in Anglo-American literature does the word too carry
the weight it carries in "Those Winter Sundays."

Not as immediately apparent as its opening words
but very nearly as important to the poem's overall strategy
is the two-sentence engineering of the first stanza.
Because they will appreciate it more if they discover it
for themselves, I often maneuver Socratically to have my
students describe the poem's first two sentences: long and
complex, followed by short and simple. It almost always
seems to me worthwhile to ask, "Why didn't Hayden
begin his poem this way: 'No one ever thanked my father
for getting up early on Sundays, too'? Wouldn't that be a
more direct and hospitable way to bring the reader into
the poem?" After I've taken my students that far, they are
quick to see how that ordinary five-word unit, "No one
ever thanked him," gains meaning and emotion, weight,
and force, from the elaborate preparation given it by the
thirty-two-word "Sundays too" first sentence.

So much depends on "No one ever thanked him" that
it requires the narrative enhancement of the first four and
a half lines. It is the crux of the poem. What is this poem
about? It is about a son's remorse over never thanking his
father not only for what he did for him but also for how (he
now realizes) he felt about him. And what is the poem if not
an elegantly fashioned, permanent expression of gratitude?

"Those Winter Sundays" tells a story, or it describes a
circumstance, of father-son conflict, and it even makes some
excuses for the son's "Speaking indifferently" to the father:
there was a good deal of anger between them; "chronic
angers of that house" suggests that the circumstances were
complicated somewhat beyond the usual and ordinary

conflict between fathers and sons. Of the father, we know that he labored outdoors with his hands. Of the son, we know that he was, in the classic manner of youth, heedless of the ways in which his father served him.

Though the evidence of his "labor" is visible in every stanza of this poem, the father himself is somewhere else. We don't see him. He is in some other room of the house than the one where our speaker is. That absence suggests the emotional distance between the father and the son as well as the current absence, through death, of the father on the occasion of this utterance. It's easy enough to imagine this poem as a graveside meditation, an elegy, and a rather impassioned one at that, "What did I know, what did I know?"

The grinding of past against present gives the poem its urgency. The story is being told with such clarity, thoughtfulness, and apparent calm that we are surprised by the outburst of the repeated question of the thirteenth line. The fourteenth line returns to a tone of tranquillity. Its diction is formal, even arch, and its phrasing suggests an extremely considered conclusion; the fourteenth line is the answer to a drastic rephrasing of the original question: *What is the precise name of what as a youth I was incapable of perceiving but that as a life-examining adult, I now suddenly understand?*

I tell my students that they may someday need this poem, they may someday be walking along downtown and find themselves asking aloud, "What did I know, what did I know?" But what I mean to suggest to them is that Hayden has made them the gift of this final phrase like a package that in ten years' time they may open and find immensely valuable: "love's austere and lonely offices." Like "the banked fires" his father made, Hayden has made a poem that will be of value to readers often years after they've first read it.

(1996)

21 Critical Casebook: The Poetry of Langston Hughes

Chapter Preview

A leading figure in the Harlem Renaissance of the 1920s and 30s, Langston Hughes celebrated African American culture in many literary genres. But he is best known for his "jazz poetry," a then-new poetic form that combines the musical rhythms of jazz with the blues and black "street talk." This casebook presents a representative selection of Hughes's poetry along with biographical information and critical commentary. By the end of the chapter you will be able to

- Identify and define the place of Langston Hughes in the Harlem Renaissance.
- Analyze and interpret Hughes's poetry.
- Synthesize critics' comments with your own judgments about Hughes's poems.
- Write critically about Hughes's poetry, especially its musical and biographical elements.

Langston Hughes: A Brief Biography

Langston Hughes was born in Joplin, Missouri, in 1902 and spent his youth in the Midwest. He went to grade school in Lawrence, Kansas, where he lived with his grandmother after his parents divorced. At the time, Lawrence's population of 12,000 was 20 percent African American. His father, a businessman, had moved to Mexico, where his mixed race (both grandfathers being white) was not a social barrier. After his mother remarried, Langston joined her to go to high school in Cleveland, Ohio. At a progressive, racially mixed school, he was class poet and published stories in the school magazine. He graduated in 1920 and went to Mexico in an attempt to reunite with his father. The emotional bond did not flourish. However, the Mexican experience was formative, particularly the culture's straightforward acceptance of his brown skin, and Hughes had links to the Hispanic literary world throughout his life. His most famous poem, "The Negro Speaks of Rivers," was written on the train to Mexico in 1921.

Such a background ensured that matters of skin color and class were ingrained in Hughes's consciousness. After one unhappy year at Columbia University, he embarked on a series of world travels as a sea-man and menial worker in Africa and Europe. The various attitudes toward race and class became obvious to Hughes, and he endorsed a gut socialism and the primitivism popular in the 1920s and 1930s, which viewed dark-skinned people as more directly in touch with nature and emotional wisdom than others were. Hughes returned to finish school in the United States at the nation's first black college, Lincoln University in Pennsylvania, graduating in 1929. Meanwhile, he had become a noted poet through publishing in small literary and left-wing magazines.

Hughes's life was enriched by artistic innovations in New York's Harlem during this same period. He visited the city frequently to enjoy the theater, dance, music, and sociability of blacks from the South and the Caribbean who had moved to the district and created the Harlem Renaissance. Hughes was entranced by the jazz and blues of the era, as well as the diversity among people of color he found in Harlem and in

Langston Hughes, a leading figure of the Harlem Renaissance in the 1920s and 1930s, who celebrated the vitality of African American culture in many genres. (Schomburg Center, The New York Public Library. Astor, Lenox and Tilden Foundations/Art Resource, NY.)

the wider world. At Harlem clubs, he listened to music performed by Duke Ellington, Charlie Mingus, Count Basie, Bessie Smith, and Louis Armstrong, and echoes of their musical style can be heard in recordings of Hughes reading his own poetry.

Besides poetry, Hughes wrote short stories, novels, two autobiographies, newspaper columns, children's books, anthologies of African-American literature, plays, musicals, operettas, and translations of Spanish and French poetry. He maintained political activism through efforts such as composing poems and a play to protest the racist treatment of the Scottsboro Boys in Alabama, nine young black males wrongfully convicted of raping two white women in 1931. Because of his socialist opinions, the McCarthy committee investigating U.S. communists called him to testify in 1953, and under pressure Hughes essentially disowned his early writings. From then on, he avoided blatantly socialist messages in his publications until his final book of poetry, *The Panther and the Lash*, which came out after his death in 1967. During the second half of his life, Hughes nurtured the talents of many other African American writers and gained international admiration. Although a very public figure, Hughes was circumspect about private matters, and almost nothing is known about his intimate relationships with others.

Langston Hughes died alone in New York City after surgery for prostate cancer, in 1967.

The Negro Speaks of Rivers

(To W. E. B. Du Bois)

I've known rivers:
I've known rivers ancient as the world and older than the
    flow of human blood in human veins.

My soul has grown deep like the rivers.

I bathed in the Euphrates when dawns were young.
I built my hut near the Congo and it lulled me to sleep.   5
I looked upon the Nile and raised the pyramids above it.
I heard the singing of the Mississippi when Abe Lincoln
    went down to New Orleans, and I've seen its muddy
    bosom turn all golden in the sunset.

I've known rivers:
Ancient, dusky rivers.

My soul has grown deep like the rivers.   10

(1921)

Mother to Son

Well, son, I'll tell you:
Life for me ain't been no crystal stair.
It's had tacks in it,
And splinters,
And boards torn up,   5
And places with no carpet on the floor—
Bare.
But all the time
I'se been a-climbin' on,
And reachin' landin's,   10
And turnin' corners,
And sometimes goin' in the dark
Where there ain't been no light.
So boy, don't you turn back.
Don't you set down on the steps   15
'Cause you finds it's kinder hard.
Don't you fall now—
For I'se still goin', honey,
I'se still climbin',
And life for me ain't been no crystal stair.   20
                    (1922)

The Weary Blues

Droning a drowsy syncopated tune,
Rocking back and forth to a mellow croon,
    I heard a Negro play.
Down on Lenox Avenue the other night
By the pale dull pallor of an old gas light   5
    He did a lazy sway...
    He did a lazy sway...
To the tune o' those Weary Blues.
With his ebony hands on each ivory key
He made that poor piano moan with melody.   10
    O Blues!
Swaying to and fro on his rickety stool
He played the sad raggy tune like a musical fool.
    Sweet Blues!
Coming from a black man's soul!   15
    O Blues!
In a deep song voice with a melancholy tone
I heard that Negro sing, that old piano moan—
    "Ain't got nobody in all this world,
        Aint' got nobody but ma self.   20
        I's gwine to quit ma frownin'
        And put ma troubles on the shelf."

Thump, thump, thump went his foot on the floor
He played a few chords then he sang some more—
    "I got the Weary Blues 25
      And I can't be satisfied.
      Got the Weary Blues
      And can't be satisfied—
      I ain't happy no mo'
      And I wish that I had died." 30
And far into the night he crooned that tune.
The stars went out and so did the moon.
The singer stopped playing and went to bed
While the Weary Blues echoed through his head.
He slept like a rock or a man that's dead. 35

               (1925)

Saturday Night

    Play it once.
    O, play some more.
    Charlie is a gambler
    An' Sadie is a whore.
      A glass o' whiskey 5
      An' a glass o' gin:
      Strut, Mr. Charlie,
      Till de dawn comes in.
    Pawn yo' gold watch
    An' diamond ring. 10
    Git a quart o' licker,
    Let's shake dat thing!
      Skee-de-dad! De-dad!
      Doo-doo-doo!
      Won't be nothin' left 15
      When de worms git through
      An' you's a long time
      Dead
      When you is
      Dead, too. 20
      So beat dat drum, boy!
      Shout dat song:
      Shake 'em up an' shake 'em up
      All night long.
      Hey! Hey! 25
    Ho...Hum!
    Do it, Mr. Charlie,
    Till de red dawn come.

          (1927)

Harlem (A Dream Deferred)

What happens to a dream deferred?

Does it dry up
like a raisin in the sun?
Or fester like a sore—
And then run?   5
Does it stink like rotten meat?
Or crust and sugar over—
like a syrupy sweet?

Maybe it just sags
like a heavy load.   10

Or does it explode?

(1951)

Theme for English B

The instructor said,

Go home and write
a page tonight.
And let that page come out of you—
Then, it will be true.   5

I wonder if it's that simple?
I am twenty-two, colored, born in Winston-Salem.
I went to school there, then Durham, then here
to this college on the hill above Harlem.
I am the only colored student in my class.   10
The steps from the hill lead down into Harlem,
through a park, then I cross St. Nicholas,
Eighth Avenue, Seventh, and I come to the Y,
the Harlem Branch Y, where I take the elevator
up to my room, sit down, and write this page: 15
It's not easy to know what is true for you or me
at twenty-two, my age. But I guess I'm what
I feel and see and hear, Harlem, I hear you:
hear you, hear me—we two—you, me, talk on this page.
(I hear New York, too.) Me—who?   20
Well, I like to eat, sleep, drink, and be in love.
I like to work, read, learn, and understand life.
I like a pipe for a Christmas present,

or records—Bessie,° bop,° or Bach.
I guess being colored doesn't make me *not* like   25
the same things other folks like who are other races.
So will my page be colored that I write?
Being me, it will not be white.
But it will be
a part of you, instructor.   30
You are white—
yet a part of me, as I am a part of you.
That's American.
Sometimes perhaps you don't want to be a part of me.
Nor do I often want to be a part of you.   35
But we are, that's true!
I guess you learn from me—
although you're older—and white—
and somewhat more free.

This is my page for English B.   40
                                         (1951)

---

24 Bessie (Smith, 1894–1937), African American blues singer.   **bop** A kind of jazz; also called be-bop.

Questions for Discussion: Considering the Poems

1. Think about why a river is an apt metaphor for a human soul. Then consider Hughes's choice of specific rivers to mention in the poem "The Negro Speaks of Rivers." What makes each river appropriate to the poem's theme?

2. What is the extended metaphor in "Mother to Son"? Who is the speaker, and what has her life been like? What would a "crystal stair" life be like?

3. How would you describe the mood of "The Weary Blues"? Harold Bloom wrote that "the piano player brims with pathos and joy." Can you see these emotions in the poem, or was Bloom reading too much into it?

4. Recall your first response to reading "Saturday Night." Countee Cullen, another leading poet of the Harlem Renaissance, criticized Hughes's zeal for poems like this one, saying, "I wonder if jazz poems really belong to that dignified company, that select and austere circle of high literary expression which we call poetry." Do you agree with Cullen?

5. Examine the similes Hughes employs to evoke the effects of the "dream deferred." How is each simile different from the others, in terms of how it would be manifested in the real world? For example, what would be the difference between a *sagging* society and an *exploding* one?

6. In "Theme for English B," the belief that what comes out of a person is, by its very nature, "true" sounds strange to the student. The contrast between the English teacher's assumptions and the student writer's is clear. What different ways of describing himself truly does the student writer attempt? Are they satisfactory, in your opinion?

7. Compare and contrast the narrators in "Harlem (A Dream Deferred)," "Theme for English B," and "The Negro Speaks of Rivers." How does Hughes vary the persona in each poem? How does his choice of persona affect your response and understanding of the poem?

Critical Commentaries

Arnold Rampersad, "On the Persona in 'The Negro Speaks of Rivers'"

[T]he persona moves steadily from dimly starred personal memory ("I've known rivers") toward a rendezvous with modern history (Lincoln going down the Mississippi and seeing the horror of slavery that, according to legend, would make him one day free the slaves). The death wish, benign but suffusing, of its images of rivers older than human blood, of souls grown as deep as these rivers, gives way steadily to the alerting, ennobling vision whose final effect gleams in the evocation of the Mississippi's "muddy bosom" turning at last "all golden in the sunset." Personal anguish has been alchemized by the poet into a gracious meditation on his race, whose despised ("muddy") culture and history, irradiated by the poet's vision, changes within the poem from mud into gold. This is a classic example of the essential process of creativity in Hughes.

The Southern Review, vol. 21, no. 3, 1985, pp. 703-704.

Margaret Larkin, "A Poet for the People"

Ever since I first heard Langston Hughes read his verse, I am continually wanting to liken his poems to those of Bobby Burns. Burns caught three things in his poems: dialect, speech cadence, and character of the people, so that he seems more Scotch than all of bonnie Scotland. It is a poet's true business to distill this pure essence of life, more potent by far than life ever turns out to be, even for poets. I think that Hughes is doing for the Negro race what Burns did for the Scotch—squeezing out the beauty and rich warmth of a noble people into enduring poetry.

In hearing a group of young poets reading their new poems to each other recently, I was struck with their common tendency to intricacy, mysticism, and preoccupation with brilliant technique. Their poems are competent and beautiful, and the antithesis of simple. To any but other poets, skilled in the craft, they are probably as completely mysterious as though in a foreign tongue. The machine age and the consequent decline of the arts has driven many poets and artists into the philosophy that art is the precious possession of the few initiate. Poets now write for the appreciation of other poets, painters are scornful of all but painters, even music, most popular of all the arts, is losing the common touch. Perhaps this is an inevitable development. Yet the people perish. Beauty is not an outworn ideal, for they still search for it on Fourteenth Street. While the poets and artists hoard up beauty for themselves and each other, philosophizing upon the "aristocracy of art," some few prophets are calling for art to come out of rich men's closets and become the "proletarian art" of all the people.

Perhaps Langston Hughes does not relish the title of Proletarian Poet, but he deserves it just the same. "Railroad Avenue," "Brass Spitoons," "Prize Fighter," "Elevator Boy," "Porter," "Saturday Night," and the songs from the Georgia Roads, all have their roots deep in the lives of workers. They give voice to the philosophy of men of the people, more rugged, more beautiful, better food for poetry, than the philosophy of the "middle classes."

This is a valuable example for all poets of what can be done with simple technique and "every day" subjects, but it is particularly valuable, I believe, for other Negro poets. Booker T. Washington's adjuration to "educate yourself" has sunk too deep in the Race philosophy. As in all American life, there is a strong urge to escape life's problems by reaching another station. "The life of a professional man must surely be happier than that of a factory worker," America reasons. "A teacher must surely find greater satisfaction than a farmer." Poets, influenced by this group sentiment, want to write about "nicer" emotions.

Opportunity: Journal of Negro Life, vol. 5, 1927, pp. 84-85.

Karen Jackson Ford, "Do Right to Write Right: Langston Hughes's Aesthetics of Simplicity"

The one thing most readers of twentieth-century American poetry can say about Langston Hughes is that he has known rivers. "The Negro Speaks of Rivers" has become memorable for its lofty, oratorical tone, mythic scope, and powerful rhythmic repetitions.

> I've known rivers:
> I've known rivers ancient as the world and older than
> the flow of human blood in human veins.

But however beautiful its cadences, the poem is remembered primarily because it is Hughes's most frequently anthologized work. The fact is, "The Negro Speaks of Rivers" is one of Hughes's most uncharacteristic poems, and yet it has defined his reputation, along with a small but constant selection of other poems included in anthologies....

The repression of the great bulk of Hughes's poems is the result of chronic critical scorn for their simplicity. Throughout his long career, but especially after his first two volumes of poetry (readers were at first willing to assume that a youthful poet might grow to be more complex), his books received their harshest reviews for a variety of "flaws" that all originate in an aesthetics of simplicity. From his first book, *The Weary Blues* (1926), to his last one, *The Panther and the Lash* (1967), the reviews invoke a litany of faults: the poems are superficial, infantile, silly, small, unpoetic, common, jejune, iterative, and, of course, simple. Even his admirers reluctantly conclude that Hughes's poetics failed. Saunders Redding flatly opposes simplicity and artfulness. "While Hughes's rejection of his own growth shows an admirable loyalty to his self-commitment as the poet of the 'simple, Negro common-folk'...it does a disservice to his art." James Baldwin, who recognizes the potential of simplicity as an artistic principle, faults the poems for "tak[ing] refuge...in a fake simplicity in order to avoid the very difficult simplicity of the experience."

Despite a lifetime of critical disappointments, then, Hughes remained loyal to the aesthetic program he had outlined in 1926 in his decisive poetic treatise, "The Negro Artist and the Racial Mountain." There he had predicted that the common people would "give to this world its truly great Negro artist, the one who is not afraid to be himself," a poet who would explore the "great field of unused [folk] material ready for his art" and recognize that this source would provide "sufficient matter to furnish a black artist with a lifetime of creative work." This is clearly a portrait of the poet Hughes would become, and he maintained his fidelity to this ideal at great cost to his literary reputation.

Twentieth Century Literature, vol. 38, no. 4, 1992, pp. 436-37.

Peter Townsend, "Jazz and Langston Hughes's Poetry"

Hughes's engagement with jazz was close and long-lived, from his "Weary Blues" of 1926 up to the time of his death in 1967. Jazz crops naturally out of the landscape of Hughes's poetry, which is largely that of the black communities of Harlem and Chicago, and it remains fluid in its significance....

Hughes responded with particular sympathy to jazz of the bebop period, which he saw as having great political significance. *Montage of a Dream Deferred*, published in 1951, is one of Hughes's most substantial sequences of poems, and it is shot through with references to jazz. His editorial note to the sequence explains the stylistic influence of bebop on its composition:

> This poem on contemporary Harlem, like bebop, is marked by conflicting changes, sudden nuances, sharp and impudent interjections, and passages

sometimes in the manner of the jam session, sometimes the popular song, punctuated by the riffs, runs, breaks and distortions of the music of a community in transition....

Bebop affected the forms of Hughes's poetry at the higher architectural levels, dictating the structural rhythm of longer works like "Dream Deferred," but otherwise he employed a small range of simple verse forms that originate in earlier styles of black music. A particular favourite was a two-stress line rhymed in quatrains, derived from spirituals, and he also frequently used a looser form drawn from the 12-bar blues. The first of these Hughes was able to use with remarkable flexibility, considering its brevity. The form is often used for aphoristic effect.

Jazz in American Culture, 2001, pp. 126–28.

Langston Hughes, *"Harlem Rent Parties"*

Then [in the early thirties] it was that house-rent parties began to flourish—and not always to raise the rent either. But, as often as not, to have a get-together of one's own, where you could do the black-bottom with no stranger behind you trying to do it, too. Non-theatrical, non-intellectual Harlem was an unwilling victim of its own vogue. It didn't like to be stared at by white folks. But perhaps the downtowners never knew this—for the cabaret owners, the entertainers, and the speakeasy proprietors treated them fine—as long as they paid.

The Saturday night rent parties that I attended were often more amusing than any night club, in small apartments where God knows who lived—because the guests seldom did—but where the piano would often be augmented by a guitar, or an odd cornet, or somebody with a pair of drums walking in off the street. And where awful bootleg whiskey and good fried fish or steaming chitterling were sold at very low prices. And the dancing and singing and impromptu entertaining went on until dawn came in at the windows.

These parties, often termed whist parties or dances, were usually announced by brightly colored cards stuck in the grille of apartment house elevators. Some of the cards were highly entertaining in themselves:

We got yellow girls, we've got black and tan
Will you have a good time? - YEAH MAN !

𝕬 𝖘𝖔𝖈𝖎𝖆𝖑 𝖂𝖍𝖎𝖘𝖙 𝖕𝖆𝖗𝖙𝖞
—GIVEN BY—
MARY WINSTON

147 West 145th Street   Apt. 5

SATURDAY EVE., MARCH 19th, 1932

GOOD MUSIC   **REFRESHMENTS**

Almost every Saturday night when I was in Harlem I went to a house-rent party. I wrote lots of poems about house-rent parties, and ate thereat many a fried fish and pig's foot—with liquid refreshments on the side. I met ladies' maids and truck drivers, laundry workers and shoe shine boys, seamstresses and porters. I can still hear their laughter in my ears, hear the soft slow music, and feel the floor shaking as the dancers danced.

The Big Sea, 1940, pp. 228–30.

Ideas for Writing About Langston Hughes

1. From reading about Hughes's life, and from the commentaries excerpted here, write an essay making claims about where he got his material and why he chose this subject matter. Use examples from the works you have read. Include a discussion of how it differed from the conventional subject matter of poetry in the early twentieth century.

2. Write an essay responding to various negative criticisms of Hughes's poetry. When you first read the selections by Hughes reprinted here, did you see the same flaws as those reported in the commentaries? Do you think that Hughes's critics had valid literary points, or were they driven by political concerns, or a combination of both?

3. Music is a prominent element in Hughes's poetry. Write an essay in which you develop an argument about the musical features in the poems. Be sure to discuss how music and poetry are interconnected in general.

Ideas for Researched Writing

1. Some of the writers that Langston Hughes acknowledged as influences were Paul Dunbar, W. E. B. DuBois, Richard Wright, James Baldwin, Walt Whitman, and Carl Sandburg. Look up information on these writers. Biographies of Hughes often remark on their influence. Write an essay explaining what it was about each of these writers that affected Langston Hughes.

2. For a weekly newspaper column, Hughes wrote a series of fictional editorials from the point of view of Jesse B. Semple, a black workingman who lived in Harlem. This folksy character related humorous moral tales about the social, political, and economic disparities in the United States. Read a number of these columns, which were later collected in book form, and compare them to Hughes's poems. What similarities in content, tone, theme, and form do you see? What differences are there?

MultiModal Project

Langston Hughes made a number of recordings reading his own poems. Compile a playlist or list of links featuring these recordings; try to find one for each of the six poems in this casebook. Play your compilation for the class, and discuss how hearing Hughes's readings affects your understanding and appreciation of his poetry.

22 The Art of Poetry

Chapter Preview

Writers frequently find inspiration in what they see—the beauty of nature, the energy of a city street, the image of an odd stranger, or the message of a work of art. Each writer's interpretation of a work of art is highly individual because each of us sees through the lens of our own experience. In her poem "American Literature," Lisel Mueller describes this process of poetic interpretation as writers ponder the paintings of Edward Hopper.

By the end of this chapter, you will be able to

- Analyze poems that are based on works of fine art.
- Compare poems with the visual art that inspired them, evaluating how their words capture that art.
- Write responsively and reflectively about both poetry and art.
- Conduct research about poetry based on art.

Poetic Interpretations of Art

Lisel Mueller   1924–

American Literature

Poets and storytellers
move into the vacancies
Edward Hopper left them.
They settle down in blank spaces,
where the light has been scoured and bleached   5
skull-white, and nothing grows
except absence. Where something is missing,
the man a woman waits for,
or furniture in a room
stripped like a hospital bed   10
after the patient has died.

Such bereft interiors
are just what they've been looking for,
the writers, who come with their baggage
of dowsing rods and dog-eared books,   15
their uneasy family photographs,
their lumpy beds, their predilection
for starting fires in empty rooms.

(1996)

Before you read each poem in this section, look closely at the repro-
duction of the work of art that goes with it, and write down words and
phrases that describe your response to the art. Then you can see how
your response compares to the poems we have selected.

Edward Hopper (American, 1882–1967), *Nighthawks*, 1942.

[*Nighthawks* (1942), Edward Hopper. Oil on canvas, 84.1 × 152.4 cm. Friends of American Art Collection, 1942.51/The Art Institute of Chicago. Photography Copyright © 2012 The Art Institute of Chicago.]

Samuel Yellen 1906–1983

Nighthawks

The place is the corner of Empty and Bleak,
The time is night's most desolate hour,
The scene is Al's Coffee Cup or the Hamburger Tower,
The persons in this drama do not speak.

We who peer through that curve of plate glass   5
Count three nighthawks seated there—patrons of life:
The counterman will be with you in a jiff,
The thick white mugs were never meant for demitasse.

The single man whose hunched back we see
Once put a gun to his head in Russian roulette,   10
Whirled the chamber, pulled the trigger, won the bet,
And now lives out his *x* years' guarantee.

And facing us, the two central characters
Have finished their coffee, and have lit
A contemplative cigarette;   15
His hand lies close, but not touching hers.

Not long ago together in a darkened room,
Mouth burned mouth, flesh beat and ground
On ravaged flesh, and yet they found
No local habitation and no name.   20

Oh, are we not lucky to be none of these!
We can look on with complacent eye:
Our satisfactions satisfy,
Our pleasures, our pleasures please.

(1951)

Susan Ludvigson   1942–

Inventing My Parents

After Edward Hopper's Nighthawks *(1942)*

They sit in the bright cafe
discussing Hemingway, and how
this war will change them.
Sinclair Lewis' name comes up,
and Kay Boyle's, and then Fitzgerald's.   5
They disagree about the American Dream.
My mother, her bare arms
silver under fluorescent lights,
says she imagines it a hawk
flying over, its shadow sweeping   10
every town. Their coffee's getting cold
but they hardly notice. My mother's face
is lit by ideas. My father's gestures
are a Frenchman's. When he concedes
a point, he shrugs, an elaborate lift   15
of the shoulders, his hands and smile
declaring an open mind.

I am five months old, at home with a sitter
this August night, when the air outside
is warm as a bath. They decide,   20
though the car is parked nearby,
to walk the few blocks home, savoring
the fragrant night, their being alone together.
As they go out the door, he's reciting
Donne's "Canonization": "For God's sake   25
hold your tongue, and let me love,"
and she's laughing, light
as summer rain when it begins.

                                            (1992)

Pieter Brueghel the Elder (c. 1525–1569), *Landscape with the Fall of Icarus*, c. 1554–1555.

[*Landscape with the Fall of Icarus* (c. 1555), Pieter Bruegel the Elder. Oil on canvas, 73.5 × 112 cm. Musees Royaux des Beaux-Arts de Belgique, Brussels, Belgium/Giraudon/The Bridgeman Art Library.]

W. H. Auden   1907–1973

Musée des Beaux Arts

About suffering they were never wrong,
The Old Masters: how well they understood
Its human position; how it takes place
While someone else is eating or opening a window or just
   walking dully along;
How, when the aged are reverently, passionately waiting   5
For the miraculous birth, there always must be
Children who did not specially want it to happen, skating
On a pond at the edge of the wood:
They never forgot
That even the dreadful martyrdom must run its course   10
Anyhow in a corner, some untidy spot
Where the dogs go on with their doggy life and the torturer's horse
Scratches its innocent behind on a tree.

In Brueghel's *Icarus*, for instance: how everything turns away
Quite leisurely from the disaster; the ploughman may   15
Have heard the splash, the forsaken cry,
But for him it was not an important failure; the sun shone
As it had to on the white legs disappearing into the green
Water; and the expensive delicate ship that must have seen
Something amazing, a boy falling out of the sky,   20
Had somewhere to get to and sailed calmly on.

                                  (1940)

Paolo Uccello (1397–1475)
St. George and the Dragon, 1470.

[*St. George and the Dragon* (c. 1470),
Paolo Uccello. Oil on canvas/National
Gallery, London, UK/The Bridgeman
Art Library.]

U. A. Fanthorpe   1929–2009

Not My Best Side

I

Not my best side, I'm afraid.
The artist didn't give me a chance to
Pose properly, and as you can see,
Poor chap, he had this obsession with
Triangles, so he left off two of my   5
Feet. I didn't comment at the time
(What, after all, are two feet
To a monster?) but afterwards
I was sorry for the bad publicity.
Why, I said to myself, should my conqueror   10
Be so ostentatiously beardless, and ride
A horse with a deformed neck and square hoofs?
Why should my victim be so
Unattractive as to be inedible,
And why should she have me literally   15
On a string? I don't mind dying
Ritually, since I always rise again,
But I should have liked a little more blood
To show they were taking me seriously.

II

It's hard for a girl to be sure if   20
She wants to be rescued. I mean, I quite
Took to the dragon. It's nice to be
Liked, if you know what I mean. He was
So nicely physical, with his claws
And lovely green skin, and that sexy tail,   25
And the way he looked at me,
He made me feel he was all ready to

Eat me. And any girl enjoys that.
So when this boy turned up, wearing
  machinery,
On a really dangerous horse, to be honest   30
I didn't much fancy him. I mean,
What was he like underneath the hardware?
He might have acne, blackheads or even
Bad breath for all I could tell, but the dragon—
Well, you could see all his equipment   35
At a glance. Still, what could I do?
The dragon got himself beaten by the boy,
And a girl's got to think of her future.

III

I have diplomas in Dragon
Management and Virgin Reclamation.   40
My horse is the latest model, with
Automatic transmission and built-in
Obsolescence. My spear is custom-built,
And my prototype armour
Still on the secret list. You can't   45
Do better than me at the moment.
I'm qualified and equipped to the
Eyebrow. So why be difficult?
Don't you want to be killed and/or rescued
In the most contemporary way? Don't   50
You want to carry out the roles
That sociology and myth have designed for you?
Don't you realize that, by being choosy,
You are endangering job prospects
In the spear- and horse-building industries? 55
What, in any case, does it matter what
You want? You're in my way.

(1989)

Vincent van Gogh
(1853–1890), *The Starry
Night*, 1889

[*The Starry Night* (1889),
Vincent Van Gogh. Oil
on canvas, 29 × 36 1/4.
(472.1941). The Museum
of Modern Art, New York.
Acquired through the Lillie
P. Bliss Bequest/Digital
Image copyright © 2008
The Museum of Modern
Art/Licensed by SCALA/
Art Resource, NY.]

Anne Sexton   1928–1974

The Starry Night

*"That does not keep me from having a terrible need of—shall I say
the word—religion. Then I go out at night to paint the stars."*
— Vincent van Gogh in a letter to his brother

The town does not exist
except where one black-haired tree slips
up like a drowned woman into the hot sky.
The town is silent. The night boils with eleven stars
Oh starry starry night! This is how   5
I want to die.

It moves. They are all alive.
Even the moon bulges in its orange irons
to push children, like a god, from its eye.
The old unseen serpent swallows up the stars.   10
Oh starry starry night! This is how
I want to die:

into that rushing beast of the night,
sucked up by that great dragon, to split
from my life with no flag,   15
no belly,
no cry.

(1961)

Henri Matisse (1869–1954) *The Red Studio*, 1911.

[*The Red Studio* (1911), Henri Matisse. Oil on canvas, 71 1/4 in. × 7 ft. 2 1/4 in. (181 × 219.1 cm). The Museum of Modern Art, New York. Mrs. Simon Guggenheim Fund/Photograph copyright © 2004 The Museum of Modern Art/Licensed by SCALA/Art Resource, NY/Copyright © 2012 Succession H. Matisse/Artists Rights Society (ARS), New York.]

W. D. Snodgrass   1926–2009
Matisse: "The Red Studio"

There is no one here.
But the objects: they are real. It is not
As if he had stepped out or moved away;
There is no other room and no
Returning. Your foot or finger would pass   5
Through, as into unreflecting water
Red with clay, or into fire.
Still, the objects: they are real. It is
As if he had stood
Still in the bare center of this floor,   10

His mind turned in in concentrated fury,
Till he sank
Like a great beast sinking into sands
Slowly, and did not look up.
His own room drank him.   15
What else could generate this
Terra cotta raging through the floor and walls,
Through chests, chairs, the table and the clock,
Till all environments of living are
Transformed to energy—   20
Crude, definitive and gay.
And so gave birth to objects that are real.
How slowly they took shape, his children, here,
Grew solid and remain:
The crayons; these statues; the clear brandybowl;   25
The ashtray where a girl sleeps, curling among
    flowers;
This flask of tall glass, green, where a vine begins
Whose bines circle the other girl brown as a
    cypress knee.
Then, pictures, emerging on the walls:
Bathers; a landscape; a still life with a vase;   30
To the left, a golden blonde, lain in magentas with flowers
    scattering like stars;
Opposite, top right, these terra cotta women, living, in
    their world of living's colors;
Between, but yearning toward them, the sailor on his red
    cafe chair, dark blue, self-absorbed.
These stay, exact,
Within the belly of these walls that burn,   35
That must hum like the domed electric web
Within which, at the carnival, small cars bump
    and turn,
Toward which, for strength, they reach their
    iron hands:
Like the heavens' walls of flame that the old magi
    could see;
Or those ethereal clouds of energy   40
From which all constellations form,
Within whose love they turn.
They stand here real and ultimate.
But there is no one here.

(1967)

◇◇◇◇◇◇◇◇◇◇◇◇◇◇◇◇◇◇◇◇◇◇◇◇◇

Kitagawa Utamaro (1754–1806), *Two Women Fixing Their Hair*, from the series *Daily Life of Women*, 1794–1795.

[*Two Women Fixing their Hair* (1794–95), Kitagawa Utamaro. From the series, *Daily Life of Women*. Nishiki-e print, oban format, 38.0 × 25.2 cm. Musee des Arts Asiatiques-Guimet, Paris/Photo by Harry Brejat, RMN-Grand Palais/Art Resource, NY.]

Cathy Song 1952–
Beauty and Sadness

for Kitagawa Utamaro

He drew hundreds of women
in studies unfolding
like flowers from a fan.
Teahouse waitresses, actresses,
geishas, courtesans and maids.   5
They arranged themselves
before this quick, nimble man
whose invisible presence
one feels in these prints
is as delicate   10
as the skinlike paper
he used to transfer
and retain their fleeting loveliness.

Crouching like cats,
they purred amid the layers of kimono   15
swirling around them
as though they were bathing
in a mountain pool with irises
growing in the silken sunlit water.
Or poised like porcelain vases,   20
slender, erect and tall; their heavy
brocaded hair was piled high
with sandalwood combs and blossom sprigs
poking out like antennae.
They resembled beautiful iridescent
    insects,   25
creatures from a floating world.

Utamaro absorbed these women of Edo
in their moments of melancholy.
He captured the wisp of shadows,
the half-draped body   30
emerging from a bath; whatever
skin was exposed
was powdered white as snow.
A private space disclosed.
Portraying another girl   35
catching a glimpse of her own vulnerable
face in the mirror, he transposed
the trembling plum lips
like a drop of blood
soaking up the white expanse of paper. 40

At times, indifferent to his inconsolable
eye, the women drifted
through the soft gray feathered light,
maintaining stillness, the moments in
    between.
Like the dusty ash-winged moths   45
that cling to the screens in summer
and that the Japanese venerate
as ancestors reincarnated;
Utamaro graced these women with
    immortality
in the thousand sheaves of prints   50
fluttering into the reverent hands of keepers:
the dwarfed and bespectacled painter
holding up to a square of sunlight
what he had carried home beneath his coat
one afternoon in winter.   55

                                   (1983)

The Art of Poetry

Questions for Discussion

American Literature by Lisel Mueller   [p. 467]

The daughter of two teachers, Lisel Mueller grew up in Hamburg, Germany, during the rise of Adolf Hitler. Fearing that their anti-Fascist beliefs would result in persecution (her father had been arrested once), the family fled the country when Mueller was fifteen, settling in Evansville, Indiana, where her father became a professor at the University of Evansville. Influenced early by the poetry of Carl Sandburg, Muller writes in a familiar, easy-to-understand style, but her poems are deceptively intricate and often layered with meaning. Her collection *Alive Together* won the 1997 Pulitzer Prize for poetry.

1. List the set of images related to Hopper's paintings. Look on the Internet or at an art collection for Hopper paintings besides *Nighthawks*. Do you see the types of images Mueller describes?
2. What images are related to the poets and storytellers in the poem? Explain what each image denotes. For example, what do dog-eared books and lumpy beds suggest to you? Why might you carry those into a new apartment? What is the function of a dowsing-rod? How do the poets' and storytellers' images contrast with the Hopper images?

Nighthawks by Samuel Yellen   [p. 469]

Born in Lithuania, Yellen attended college in the United States and settled permanently in Bloomington, Indiana, where he was an English professor at Indiana University. Besides many books of poems, Yellen wrote *American Labor Struggles* (1936), the story of ten significant union movements. Several of his poems have been set to music.

1. Which details in the poem best capture the tone of the painting?
2. What does having once played Russian roulette suggest about the man with the hunched shoulders?
3. Is the last stanza ironic? Argue your response.

Inventing My Parents by Susan Ludvigson   [p. 470]

Writing poetry in both open and closed forms, Susan Ludvigson is renowned for giving voice to an astonishing range of characters in her works: rural women in Wisconsin with dark secrets, little girls playing house, the mistress of sculptor Auguste Rodin, a young man attempting suicide in the Paris Metro, a Japanese film crew building a sand castle. When Ludvigson was a child, her father owned two restaurants in a small town in Wisconsin, and images from that period may influence the poem here.

1. Explain how Ludvigson's envisioning of the painting creates a different tone from the stark one presented in Yellen's poem.
2. What do the details of the couple's conversation reveal about the kind of people the parents are?
3. What adjectives would you choose to describe the mother? Which might you choose to describe the father? Explain the reasoning behind your choices.
4. Why do Yellen and Ludvigson interpret Hopper's painting differently? What personal meanings do they seem to discover in the art? Which response is closer to yours?

Musée des Beaux Arts by W. H. Auden   [p. 471]

See page 403 for a biographical note about this poet.

1. What are the two kinds of events contrasted in this poem?
2. What examples does Auden give of suffering that goes unnoticed in life?
3. Look up the myth of Icarus in an encyclopedia or other reference work. What comments about the human condition or human nature does the story deal with? Does the poem make the same point or a different one? Use details from both the story and poem as evidence of similarity or difference.
4. Compare this poem with Frost's " 'Out, Out—' " (p. 525). What does each poem say about the attitudes of people toward the suffering of others? Are these poems cynical, ironic, disillusioned, truthful? Provide details from the poems to support your points.

Not My Best Side by U. A. Fanthorpe   [p. 472]

A British poet who published her first book of verse at the age of fifty, Fanthorpe earlier made her living as an English teacher and then as a hospital ward clerk. These occupations no doubt lent the dark humor and appreciation of quirky individualism that characterize her unsentimental poetry. Fanthorpe rarely writes about herself, saying, "The people I want to write about are, on the whole, the ones whom nobody notices, whose voices aren't heard. I'm interested in neglected places, and in the boundaries of language, the language of small children, the inarticulate and the mentally confused."

1. When you first read this poem, at what point did you realize it was humorous? What made you realize this? What makes the poem funny?
2. The poem has three stanzas, each with a different speaker. Which character in the painting is speaking in each stanza? What kind of person is each one? What are the main goals of each speaker? If you

were going to make the poem into a movie, what actor would you cast in each role? Explain the reasoning behind your choices.

3. Look up the story of St. George and the Dragon, the topic of Uccello's painting. Relate details of the story to details in the poem. How are they similar and different? What different main points do they make?

4. Review the forms of poetry (Chapter 20) and identify the form of "Not My Best Side." Argue that this is the most suitable form for the poem.

The Starry Night by Anne Sexton   [p. 473]

Instead of attending college, Anne Sexton eloped at nineteen, became a housewife and mother, and worked briefly as a fashion model. She suffered her first nervous breakdown when she was twenty-eight, and for the rest of her life, she was "in and out of mental institutions, on and off psychiatric drugs." Her psychiatrist suggested writing poetry as therapy. She did, and her highly introspective poetry won her a wide and loyal audience. Sexton once wrote that poetry "should be a shock to the senses. It should hurt." Her collection of poems *Live or Die* (1966) won a Pulitzer Prize. She committed suicide at age forty-six.

1. Both van Gogh and Sexton, suffering from depression, sought death, and both spent periods when they lived only for their creative arts. How are these states of mind reflected in Sexton's "The Starry Night"? Use details from the poem to argue your point.

2. The epigraph is from a letter of van Gogh's to his brother. Such letters are main sources for van Gogh's biographers. Describe the connection between the quotation and the poem.

3. In what ways does Sexton's poem *not* describe or evoke van Gogh's painting?

The Red Studio by W. D. Snodgrass   [pp. 474–75]

Some of W. D. Snodgrass's most well-known poetry is filled with references to the wives and children from his three marriages. Though Snodgrass is usually named as a founder of the highly personal, self-examining confessional movement in poetry, he does not like the label himself. One of his decidedly nonconfessional books, *The Fuehrer Bunker*, consists of poems spoken by men and women in Hitler's bunker in 1945. One critic wrote of Snodgrass that he "has identified himself with exquisite suffering and guilt and with all those who barely manage to exist on the edge of life."

1. Throughout this poem, the artist (Henri Matisse) is "not here," but the objects in his studio are real. Look at the poem in terms of the artist's relationship to his work. What is this relationship like? Can you guess what has happened to the artist, at least in the poet's opinion? Use words and phrases from the poem as evidence for your claim.

2. Look at www.artchive.com for images of Matisse's paintings. Can you recognize any of them in the painting and the poem? Can you connect Matisse's other paintings to "The Red Studio" in style or content? Give some examples that demonstrate the connection you see.

3. In *The Shock of the New*, a book about modern art, Robert Hughes wrote about Matisse: "His studio was a world within the world: a place of equilibrium that, for sixty continuous years, produced images of comfort, refuge, and balanced satisfaction." Does your impression of the painting agree with Hughes's description? Do you think that the poet Snodgrass would agree with Hughes's description? Point out specific details from the painting and poem to support your claims.

4. Can you think of a specific room or setting that you strongly associate with your identity, your activities, or your creations? Consider how you would present this place in a painting or in words. See whether this activity helps you understand the painting and poem "The Red Studio."

Beauty and Sadness by Cathy Song   [p. 476]

Cathy Song grew up in Hawaii, the daughter of Chinese and Korean Americans. As a young girl, she wished to become a songwriter like Joan Baez or Joni Mitchell, but she turned her attention to writing poetry while in high school. She won a prestigious award in 1982 for her book *Picture Bride*, where the subject matter clearly reflected her Asian American heritage. "Two Women Fixing Their Hair" appeared in that volume. However, Song's themes and content have broadened since that time, and her poetry today is known for its treatment of universal topics: love, death, motherhood, family, and aging.

1. In the first stanza, the speaker remarks on the "fleeting loveliness" of the women. What images and comparisons reinforce this idea in the rest of the poem?

2. What do the women look like in each stanza? How well does the poet's description match the visual art? Find other reproductions of drawings by Kitagawa Utamaro. Does Song's description fit these drawings too? Use details from the poem and drawings to support your ideas about the accuracy of Song's description.

3. What does the title mean? Why are the women sad? What is the connection between their sadness and their beauty?

4. Line 34 speaks of "A private space disclosed." What does this line mean?

5. Why does Song tell us that Utamaro was a "dwarfed and bespectacled painter"? Why does she wait until late in the poem to give these details? Use logical reasoning to explain your idea.

6. Look up information about Kitagawa Utamaro. Does what you learned help you to understand the poem? Explain by relating biographical material to the poem and the drawing or drawings.

Poetry and Art: Ideas for Writing

1. According to Lisel Mueller (p. 467), why are the Hopper paintings just what the poets and storytellers have been looking for? What relationship between real-life settings and poetic interpretations of them is suggested by Mueller's poem? Use details from the poem as evidence of this relationship.

2. Explain how Mueller's last image in particular brings together Hopper's rooms and the work of the writer. Think of the various nonliteral meanings of "starting fires." How do those relate to writing poetry? Use logical reasoning to support your ideas.

3. Compose your own backstory for the three nighthawks in Hopper's painting (p. 469).

4. Compare Samuel Yellen's handling of the three characters sketched in his poem (p. 469) with John Updike's presentation of the down-and-out Flick Webb in "Ex-Basketball Player" (pp. 591–92).

5. How does the depiction of the sexual relationship of the couple in Yellen's poem differ from that suggested in Susan Ludvigson's version (p. 470)? Use details from the poems to argue your point.

6. Does Ludvigson's poem change the way you view Edward Hopper's *Nighthawks*? Or does the painting still seem to present the bleak café and alienated patrons seen by Yellen? Consider the title that Hopper chose.

7. What point does W. H. Auden (p. 471) make about the visual arrangement of Brueghel's painting? Does he make an accurate interpretation of the artwork? Devise a claim for your own reaction to the painting.

8. Find out trends and styles in Italian painting in the fifteenth century, when Uccello created *St. George and the Dragon* (p. 472). Point out how the painting reflects these trends and styles. Does the poem allude to any of these? Give examples.

9. Choose Hopper's *Nighthawks* (p. 469) or Utamaro's *Two Women Fixing Their Hair* (p. 476), paintings reproduced in this section. Write a humorous poem using the points of view of people in the paintings, as U. A. Fanthorpe did in "Not My Best Side" (p. 472).

10. Review the types of poetic language in Chapter 19. Discuss the imagery, metaphor and simile, and connotations in Anne Sexton's "The Starry Night" (p. 473). Tie the poetic language to a main point about the poem's meaning.

11. If possible, find a bigger and clearer image of van Gogh's *The Starry Night* (see www.vangoghgallery.com, for instance). What ideas and feelings emerge as you study the painting? How do your responses compare to Sexton's? Write a brief paper exploring what might account for the similarities and differences.

12. Write your own paragraph or poem responding to *The Starry Night* or to another van Gogh painting. Then reflect upon your

experience looking at the painting as subject matter for writing. Did the effort to write about it change your thoughts or perceptions of the visual art?

13. W. D. Snodgrass closes his poem (pp. 474–75) with three metaphors for the walls of Matisse's studio: the "domed electric web" of a carnival ride, the magi's "wall of flame," and "ethereal clouds of energy" that are the source of all things. Follow up on these comparisons and what they mean by doing some research. Then explain how they illuminate Snodgrass's interpretation of *The Red Studio*.

14. Paraphrase the last stanza of Cathy Song's poem (p. 476). What claim is the poet making about the artist and his mission? Relate details from the stanza to this claim.

15. Write your own response to Kitagawa Utamaro's drawing (p. 476). If possible, try to make a claim or create an interpretation of the drawing different from Song's.

MultiModal Project

Work with a small group of fellow students to put together a video presentation entitled "Versions of Icarus." Include both poems and paintings that have interpreted the myth of Icarus. Structure your program like a documentary you might find on PBS, HBO, or the History Channel. In addition to Pieter Brueghel (page 471), artists who used the Icarus myth in their paintings include H. J. Draper, Jacob Peter Gowy, and Marc Chagall. A number of poets have written about Icarus: W. H. Auden (page 471), William Carlos Williams, Alan Devenish, Anne Sexton, Edward Field, Muriel Rukeyser, Carol Ann Duffy, Wendy Shaffer, Jack Gilbert, and P. K. Page.

Sample Student Paper: Reflection on Poetry and Art

The following personal reflection was written by a student at Eastern Illinois University. She was responding to this prompt: If possible, find a bigger and clearer image of van Gogh's *The Starry Night*. When you look at the painting, is your point of view similar to Sexton's? Why or why not?

Jamie Olson

Professor Coleman

English 1092

10 January 2012

Starry Night: Two Readings

While experts recognize Vincent Van Gogh's *Starry Night* as a
brilliant work of art, there is something else that makes it so well loved
by the general public. It projects a spark, a burst of life that makes a
statement to the world. Almost every kid in America recognizes the
painting—the swirls in the sky, the tiny town on the dark horizon, and the
distinctive textured brush strokes—but not many of us truly look at the
scene's personality.

To me, the sky is like a creature, dancing and twisting and twirling
while the town sleeps below. The sky is a late-night club, with flashing
lights, and the stars are dancers covered in sequins. But all of this
splendor, boldly displayed in the sky, goes unnoticed below. There is a
sense of mystery. This beautiful scene is flowing over the town, but no one
knows about it. The secret in the sky, like a gentle beast, hides during the
day, but at night, under the cover of darkness, it springs into the open
space, into its playground. As a viewer, I feel as if I am hiding behind an
old twisted tree, seeing a previously undiscovered spectacle for the first
time.

Anne Sexton's poem about Van Gogh's painting expresses a reaction
to the work that is very different from mine. Sexton begins the poem
by focusing on the town and the tree in the foreground of the painting.
Although Sexton and I agree on the peacefulness of the town, she ends
the first stanza with the phrase "this is how I want to die," a line that is
repeated throughout the poem. She contrasts the silence of the town with
the boldness of the sky and describes the scene among the stars as being
like a creature. To her, it is snake-like, a dragon, and a menacing beast that
dominates the sky. In the last stanza, she describes again how she wishes
to die, to separate from her earthly body and become a part of the being
in the sky, without an allegiance to a flag, without hunger, and without

pain. The most interesting feature of this poem is the negative imagery that menaces and frightens. Despite using the words "drowned," "boils," "serpent swallows," "rushing beast," "bulges," "sucked up," and "split," the speaker isn't adversely affected; instead, she marvels at the sight in front of her, confessing that this is the place where she wants to die.

Looking at this painting can be an adventure. It can take you to a completely different world for a few brief moments, and not everyone goes to the same place. I saw a place of magic and wonder that is unknown to the rest of the town. Anne Sexton also saw an undiscovered scene, but she described it as a frightening, humbling experience—and imagined the scene as her final resting place. Despite Sexton's and my different responses to the painting's imagery, together we appreciate the beauty and importance of this iconic work of art.

Making Connections

Write your own interpretation of Van Gogh's *Starry Night*. Include how your response to the imagery compares to Anne Sexton's and Jamie Olson's.

23 Anthology of Poetry

Chapter Preview

You will find in this chapter a wide selection of poems, arranged chrono-logically. The accompanying questions will guide you in interpreting them. In this chapter you will gain a greater understanding of poetry, as you

- Interpret and discuss poems from many different authors and eras.
- Compare themes, techniques, and forms among selections.
- Write explications and analyses of poems.

Thomas Wyatt 1503–1542

Like many of his peers, Thomas Wyatt wrote poems of great charm and wit while pursuing a career as a politician and diplomat. He was rumored to have been Anne Boleyn's lover before she married King Henry VIII. On a diplomatic mission to Italy, he became acquainted with the poetry of Petrarch and, as a result, was one of the first poets to compose sonnets in English.

They Flee from Me

They flee from me, that sometime did me seek,
With naked foot, stalking in my chamber:
I have seen them gentle, tame, and meek,
That now are wild, and do not remember
That sometime they put themselves in danger   5
To take bread at my hand; and now they range,
Busily seeking with a continual change.

Thankèd be fortune, it hath been otherwise
Twenty times better; but once, in special,
In thin array, after a pleasant guise,   10
When her loose gown from her shoulders did fall,
And she me caught in her arms long and small,
Therewithal sweetly did me kiss,
And softly said, "Dear heart, how like you this?"

It was no dream; I lay broad waking.   15
But all is turned, thorough my gentleness,
Into a strange fashion of forsaking;

And I have leave to go of her goodness,
And she also to use new-fangleness.
But since that I so kindely am served,   20
I would fain know what she hath deserved.
                              (ca. 1535)

Questions for Discussion and Writing

1. What is the speaker's attitude toward the special woman of stanzas 2 and 3? Why does she stand out from the others?
2. Describe in your own words what happens in the second stanza. Why does the woman do what she does? How would you describe her?
3. What does the speaker suggest is the cause of his abandonment?
4. Write a character sketch of the speaker, paying particular attention to his views about love and women.

Making Connections

Compare the complaint of the lover in this poem with the ones expressed in "To His Coy Mistress" (page 492) and "Go, Lovely Rose" (page 404).

◇◇◇◇◇◇◇◇◇◇◇◇◇◇◇◇◇◇◇◇◇◇

William Shakespeare   1564–1616

See page 730 for a biographical note about this author.

When in Disgrace with Fortune and Men's Eyes

When, in disgrace with fortune and men's eyes,
I all alone beweep my outcast state,
And trouble deaf heaven with my bootless° cries,
And look upon myself, and curse my fate,
Wishing me like to one more rich in hope,   5
Featured like him, like him with friends possessed,
Desiring this man's art and that man's scope,
With what I most enjoy contented least;
Yet in these thoughts myself almost despising,
Haply I think on thee—and then my state,°   10
Like to the lark at break of day arising
From sullen earth, sings hymns at heaven's gate;
For thy sweet love remembered such wealth brings
That then I scorn to change my state with kings.
                              (1609)

---

3 bootless Helpless.   **10 state** Condition.

Questions for Discussion and Writing

1. Is it believable that the mere thought of his beloved could change the speaker's whole outlook on life?
2. Summarize the speaker's state of mind before the shift that occurs in line 10.
3. How does the meaning of the poem change if the reader interprets "thee" (line 10) and "thy" (line 13) to refer to God instead of a romantic lover?

Making Connections

Compare this sonnet's portrayal of love as a solace against the harshness of the world with Matthew Arnold's expression of that same idea in "Dover Beach" (page 506).

Let Me Not to the Marriage of True Minds

Let me not to the marriage of true minds
Admit impediments. Love is not love
Which alters when it alteration finds,
Or bends with the remover to remove:
O, no! it is an ever-fixèd mark   5
That looks on tempests and is never shaken;
It is the star to every wandering bark,
Whose worth's unknown, although his height be taken.
Love's not Time's fool, though rosy lips and cheeks
Within his bending sickle's compass come;   10
Love alters not with his brief hours and weeks,
But bears it out even to the edge of doom.
If this be error and upon me proved,
I never writ, nor no man ever loved.

(1609)

Questions for Discussion and Writing

1. What familiar part of the traditional Christian marriage service is echoed in the first line?
2. Notice that the poem celebrates "the marriage of true minds," not of bodies. In a brief paragraph, summarize in your own words the nature of this kind of love.
3. What two comparisons does Shakespeare make in lines 5–8? What is the connection between "an ever-fixèd mark" and "the star"?

Making Connections

Compare the qualities of love expressed in this sonnet with those that John Donne evokes in "A Valediction: Forbidding Mourning" (page 491).

That Time of Year Thou Mayst in Me Behold

That time of year thou mayst in me behold
When yellow leaves, or none, or few, do hang
Upon those boughs which shake against the cold,
Bare ruined choirs, where late the sweet birds sang.
In me thou see'st the twilight of such day   5
As after sunset fadeth in the west,
Which by and by black night doth take away,
Death's second self that seals up all in rest.
In me thou see'st the glowing of such fire,
That on the ashes of his youth doth lie,   10
As the death-bed, whereon it must expire
Consumed with that which it was nourished by.
This thou perceiv'st, which makes thy love more strong
To love that well, which thou must leave ere long.
                                                (1609)

Questions for Discussion and Writing

1. How does the speaker portray himself in this sonnet?
2. What are the controlling metaphors in each of the quatrains? How are they related?
3. How do you explain the idea expressed in the last two lines? Why would the loved one's love grow stronger when he/she sees that the speaker is getting older?

Making Connections

How do this poem's thoughts and feelings about love and aging compare with those expressed in "Sailing to Byzantium" by William Butler Yeats (page 517)?

My Mistress' Eyes Are Nothing Like the Sun

My mistress' eyes are nothing like the sun;
Coral is far more red than her lips' red;
If snow be white, why then her breasts are dun;
If hairs be wires, black wires grow on her head.
I have seen roses damask'd, red and white,   5
But no such roses see I in her cheeks,
And in some perfumes there is more delight
Than in the breath that from my mistress reeks.
I love to hear her speak, yet well I know
That music hath a far more pleasing sound.   10
I grant I never saw a goddess go;
My mistress, when she walks, treads on the ground:

And yet, by heaven, I think my love as rare
As any she belied with false compare.

(1609)

Questions for Discussion and Writing

1. The comparisons that Shakespeare uses negatively in this sonnet were familiar enough in his time to be considered clichés even then. What is the poet's point in cataloging these overused images?
2. What is the speaker's attitude toward his mistress? Is he making fun of her? Do the "if...then" constructions help you to figure out the distinction the speaker is making between the artificial comparisons and his real-life girlfriend?
3. Paraphrase the last two lines of the poem.

Making Connections

What different attitudes toward the beloved are expressed by Shakespeare in this sonnet and in "Shall I Compare Thee to a Summer's Day?" (page 420)?

◇◇◇◇◇◇◇◇◇◇◇◇◇◇◇◇◇◇◇◇◇

John Donne 1572–1631

The first and perhaps greatest of the *metaphysical poets*, John Donne wrote erotic lyrics and cynical love poems in his youth. A politically disastrous marriage ruined his civil career, but in 1615 he converted to Anglicanism and later became dean of St. Paul's Cathedral, the most influential preacher in England. In later years, he wrote religious sonnets, elegies, epigrams, and verse letters. Donne's use of complex conceits and compressed phrasing influenced many twentieth-century poets, especially T. S. Eliot.

Death, Be Not Proud

Death, be not proud, though some have callèd thee
Mighty and dreadful, for thou art not so,
For those whom thou think'st thou dost overthrow
Die not, poor Death, nor yet canst thou kill me.
From rest and sleep, which but thy pictures be,   5
Much pleasure, then from thee much more must flow;
And soonest our best men with thee do go—
Rest of their bones and souls' delivery!
Thou'rt slave to fate, chance, kings, and desperate men,
And dost with poison, war, and sickness dwell,   10
And poppy or charms can make us sleep as well,
And better than thy stroke; why swell'st thou then?
One short sleep past, we wake eternally,
And death shall be no more: Death, thou shalt die!

(1633)

Questions for Discussion and Writing

1. What is the speaker's attitude toward Death in this poem?
2. How are paradox and personification used in this sonnet to signify a victory over Death?
3. Summarize each step in the argument that "proves" Death not to be very powerful.
4. Upon what beliefs does the success of the argument depend? In what senses are the speaker's final claims about Death not justified?

Making Connections

Compare Donne's attitude toward death with Dylan Thomas's in "Do Not Go Gentle into That Good Night" (page 549).

The Flea

Mark but this flea, and mark in this
How little that which thou deny'st me is;
Me it sucked first, and now sucks thee,
And in this flea our two bloods mingled be;
Thou know'st that this cannot be said   5
A sin, or shame, or loss of maidenhead,
    Yet this enjoys before it woo,
    And pampered swells with one blood made of two,
    And this, alas, is more than we would do.

Oh stay, three lives in one flea spare,   10
Where we almost, nay more than married, are.
This flea is you and I, and this
Our marriage bed and marriage temple is;
Though parents grudge, and you, we're met
And cloistered in these living walls of jet.   15
    Though use make you apt to kill me,
    Let not to that, self-murder added be,
    And sacrilege, three sins in killing three.

Cruel and sudden, has thou since
Purpled thy nail in blood of innocence?   20
Wherein could this flea guilty be,
Except in that drop which it sucked from thee?
Yet thou triumph'st, and say'st that thou
Find'st not thyself, nor me, the weaker now;
    'Tis true; then learn how false fears be;   25
    Just so much honor, when thou yield'st to me,
    Will waste, as this flea's death took life from thee.

(1633)

Questions for Discussion and Writing

1. What is the "little" thing the lover says the lady is denying him (line 2)? Is it really a small matter? Be sure to put the poem in the context of Elizabethan times when you answer.
2. What action is the woman about to take at the beginning of stanza two? Whose are the three lives the speaker wants to spare?
3. What is the argument that her parents might not believe but he hopes the lady will (lines 12–15)? What are the "living walls of jet"?
4. In what sense will the lady be guilty of killing both the lover and herself if she kills the flea (lines 16–18)?
5. What has happened at the beginning of stanza three? Why is the lady's nail purple?

Making Connections

How is this poem different from or similar to other poems about sex and love, such as Whitman's "Song of Myself (Section 11)" (page 505), Dickinson's "Wild Nights— Wild Nights!" (page 511), or Olds's "Sex Without Love" (page 561)?

A Valediction: Forbidding Mourning

As virtuous men pass mildly away,
    And whisper to their souls, to go,
Whilst some of their sad friends do say,
    "The breath goes now," and some say, "No,"

So let us melt, and make no noise,   5
    No tear-floods, nor sigh-tempests move,
'Twere profanation of our joys
    To tell the laity our love.

Moving of th' earth brings harms and fears,
    Men reckon what it did and meant;   10
But trepidation of the spheres,
    Though greater far, is innocent.°

Dull sublunary lovers' love
    (Whose soul is sense) cannot admit
Absence, because it doth remove   15
    Those things which elemented° it.

But we, by a love so much refined
    That our selves know not what it is,
Inter-assurèd of the mind,
    Care less, eyes, lips, and hands to miss.   20

Our two souls therefore, which are one,
    Though I must go, endure not yet
A breach, but an expansion,
    Like gold to airy thinness beat.

---

12 innocent Innocuous, harmless. **16 elemented** Composed.

> If they be two, they are two so   25
>   As stiff twin compasses are two:
> Thy soul, the fixed foot, makes no show
>   To move, but doth, if th' other do.
>
> And though it in the center sit,
>   Yet when the other far doth roam,   30
> It leans, and hearkens after it,
>   And grows erect, as that comes home.
>
> Such wilt thou be to me, who must
>   Like th' other foot, obliquely run;
> Thy firmness makes my circle just,   35
>   And makes me end, where I begun.
>   (1633)

Questions for Discussion and Writing

1. What is a "valediction"? And why does the speaker forbid mourning?
2. Explain how the simile about the passing away of virtuous men (lines 1–4) relates to the couple (in lines 5–8).
3. What distinction does the speaker make between "dull sublunary lovers" and the love that he and his beloved share?
4. According to the speaker, why will he end where he began? Can you explain his reasons?

Making Connections

In this poem and "The Flea" (page 490), Donne presents very different views of love. Analyze the differences in the speaker's intended audience, tone, and purpose.

◇◇◇◇◇◇◇◇◇◇◇◇◇◇◇◇◇◇◇◇◇

Andrew Marvell   1621–1678

Though not a Puritan himself, Andrew Marvell supported the Puritan cause in the English Civil War. He held a number of posts during the Commonwealth and was instrumental in saving John Milton from punishment after the Restoration. One of the metaphysical poets, Marvell is best known for his witty lyrics that often present a tacit debate about opposing values. He has been called "the most major minor poet" in English.

To His Coy Mistress

> Had we but world enough, and time,
> This coyness,° lady, were no crime.
> We would sit down, and think which way

---

2 **coyness** Modesty, reluctance.

To walk, and pass our long love's day.
Thou by the Indian Ganges' side   5
Shouldst rubies find; I by the tide
Of Humber° would complain. I would
Love you ten years before the Flood:
And you should if you please refuse
Till the conversion of the Jews.   10
My vegetable love should grow
Vaster than empires, and more slow.
An hundred years should go to praise
Thine eyes, and on thy forehead gaze.
Two hundred to adore each breast: 15
But thirty thousand to the rest.
An age at least to every part,
And the last age should show your heart.
For, lady, you deserve this state;
Nor would I love at lower rate.   20
    But at my back I always hear
Time's wingèd chariot hurrying near:
And yonder all before us lie
Deserts of vast eternity.
Thy beauty shall no more be found,   25
Nor, in thy marble vault, shall sound
My echoing song; then worms shall try
That long preserved virginity:
And your quaint honour turn to dust;
And into ashes all my lust.   30
The grave's a fine and private place,
But none, I think, do there embrace.
    Now therefore, while the youthful hue
Sits on thy skin like morning dew,
And while thy willing soul transpires   35
At every pore with instant fires,
Now let us sport us while we may;
And now, like amorous birds of prey,
Rather at once our time devour,
Than languish in his slow-chapped° pow'r.   40
Let us roll all our strength, and all
Our sweetness, up into one ball:
And tear our pleasures with rough strife,
Through the iron gates of life.
Thus, though we cannot make our sun
Stand still, yet we can make him run.

(1681)

---

7 Humber A river in northern England.   **40 slow-chapped** Slow chewing.

Questions for Discussion and Writing

1. What is the tone of the assertion in the first 20 lines? How does the speaker's tone change after line 20?

2. In the second stanza (lines 21–23), why is time behind the speaker and eternity in front of him?
3. What words contribute to a second change in tone (after line 32)?
4. In the 17th century, a cannonball was simply called a "ball." What is the point, then, of the description of a cannonball ripping through the gates of a fortified city?
5. What universal human concern does this poem reflect? What basic human needs might be said to motivate the speaker?

Making Connections

Edmund Waller's "Go, Lovely Rose" (page 404) is a persuasion-to-love poem similar to Marvell's. Do the entreaties in these two poems differ? Which do you think would be more likely to overcome a young woman's resistance?

◇◇◇◇◇◇◇◇◇◇◇◇◇◇◇◇◇◇◇◇◇◇

William Blake   1757–1827

William Blake was both artist and poet, though he achieved little success as either during his lifetime. Of the more than half-dozen books he wrote and illustrated, only one of them was published conventionally; his wife helped him print the rest. A mystic and visionary, Blake created his own mythology, complete with illustrations. His best-known volumes of poetry are *Songs of Innocence* (1789) and *Songs of Experience* (1794).

The Lamb

From Songs of Innocence

Little Lamb, who made thee?
Dost thou know who made thee?
Gave thee life, and bid thee feed
By the stream and o'er the mead;
Gave thee clothing of delight,   5
Softest clothing, wooly, bright;
Gave thee such a tender voice,
Making all the vales rejoice?
Little Lamb, who made thee?
Dost thou know who made thee?   10

Little Lamb, I'll tell thee,
Little Lamb, I'll tell thee:
He is callèd by thy name,
For he calls himself a Lamb.
He is meek, and he is mild;   15
He became a little child.
I a child, and thou a lamb,

We are callèd by his name.
    Little Lamb, God bless thee!
    Little Lamb, God bless thee!   20
       (1789)

Questions for Discussion and Writing

1. What symbolic meanings are conveyed by the image of the lamb?
2. What view of God and creation does this poem present?
3. How does Blake establish the Lamb as a symbol of creation?

The Tyger

From Songs of Experience

Tyger, Tyger, burning bright
In the forests of the night,
What immortal hand or eye
Could frame thy fearful symmetry?

In what distant deeps or skies   5
Burnt the fire of thine eyes?
On what wings dare he aspire?
What the hand dare seize the fire?

And what shoulder and what art
Could twist the sinews of thy heart?   10
And, when thy heart began to beat,
What dread hand? and what dread feet?

What the hammer? What the chain?
In what furnace was thy brain?
What the anvil? What dread grasp   15
Dare its deadly terrors clasp?

When the stars threw down their spears,
And watered heaven with their tears,
Did He smile his work to see?
Did He who made the lamb make thee?   20

Tyger, Tyger, burning bright
In the forests of the night,
What immortal hand or eye
Dare frame thy fearful symmetry?
               (1794)

Questions for Discussion and Writing

1. What side of creation is presented in this poem? Is the creator of the tiger the same as the creator of the lamb?
2. What Christian metaphors do you find in this poem? What mythological allusions are contained in lines 7 and 8?

3. Explain why "The Tyger" and "The Lamb" should be considered as a pair, one the reverse of the other.

4. Why does an allegedly all-powerful and beneficent creator permit evil at all?

Making Connections

Why does Blake answer his question in "The Lamb" (page 494) but not in "The Tyger"?

The Sick Rose

O Rose, thou art sick!
The invisible worm
That flies in the night,
In the howling storm,

Has found out thy bed   5
Of crimson joy,
And his dark secret love
Does thy life destroy.

(1794)

Illustrated manuscript of "The Sick Rose" from *Songs of Experience* (1794), designed and printed by Blake himself.
[*The Sick Rose* (c. 1802–08), William Blake. Plate 40 from *Songs of Innocence and of Experience* (copy R). P. 124–1950, pt 40. Etching, ink and watercolor. Fitzwilliam Museum, University of Cambridge, UK/The Bridgeman Art Library.]

Questions for Discussion and Writing

1. Are there sexual implications in the poem?
2. What do you think the rose and the worm might represent?
3. What causes the rose to be sick?
4. Write an allegorical interpretation of the poem, explaining its hidden meaning.

Making Connections

How is Blake's use of the rose unconventional? Argue your claims by comparing "The Sick Rose" to Edmund Waller's "Go, Lovely Rose" (page 404).

◇◇◇◇◇◇◇◇◇◇◇◇◇◇◇◇◇◇◇◇◇◇◇◇

William Wordsworth 1770–1850

An English poet recognized for his use of common language and his love of nature, William Wordsworth was educated at Cambridge University. He lived for a time in France, where he fathered an illegitimate daughter and experienced the French Revolution firsthand. When he returned to England, he began writing in earnest. His works include *Lyrical Ballads* (1798), *Poems in Two Volumes* (1807), and *The Excursion* (1814). A leader of English Romanticism, Wordsworth was named Poet Laureate in 1843.

The World Is Too Much with Us

The world is too much with us; late and soon,
Getting and spending, we lay waste our powers;
Little we see in Nature that is ours;
We have given our hearts away, a sordid boon!°
This Sea that bares her bosom to the moon,   5
The winds that will be howling at all hours,
And are up-gathered now like sleeping flowers,
For this, for everything, we are out of tune;
It moves us not.—Great God! I'd rather be
A Pagan suckled in a creed outworn;   10
So might I, standing on this pleasant lea,°
Have glimpses that would make me less forlorn;
Have sight of Proteus°rising from the sea;
Or hear old Triton°blow his wreathèd horn.

(1807)

---

4 boon Blessing.   **11 lea** Meadow.   **13 Proteus** A sea god who could change shape.
14 Triton A sea god whose top half was man and bottom half was fish.

Questions for Discussion and Writing

1. In what way, according to the speaker in the poem, have we "given our hearts away" (line 4)?
2. The poem is a sonnet divided into an octave and a sestet. Where does the sestet begin?
3. How is the poem unified? What is the poem's theme?

Making Connections

Contrast Wordsworth's view of the world with Matthew Arnold's in "Dover Beach" (page 506). Which one is closer to your own point of view?

I Wandered Lonely as a Cloud

I wandered lonely as a cloud
That floats on high o'er vales and hills,
When all at once I saw a crowd,
A host, of golden daffodils;
Beside the lake, beneath the trees,   5
Fluttering and dancing in the breeze.

Continuous as the stars that shine
And twinkle on the milky way,
They stretched in never-ending line
Along the margin of a bay: 10
Ten thousand saw I at a glance,
Tossing their heads in sprightly dance.

The waves beside them danced; but they
Out-did the sparkling waves in glee:
A poet could not but be gay,   15
In such a jocund company:
I gazed—and gazed—but little thought
What wealth the show to me had brought:

For oft, when on my couch I lie
In vacant or in pensive mood,   20
They flash upon that inward eye
Which is the bliss of solitude;
And then my heart with pleasure fills,
And dances with the daffodils.

(1804)

Questions for Discussion and Writing

1. How would you define the tone of this poem? How does it change?
2. What do the daffodils mean to the speaker?
3. Write a paper that examines the personification in the poem.

4. Wordsworth said that poetry springs from "emotion recollected in tranquility." How does this poem fit that definition?

Making Connections

Compare the use of flowers in this poem to the use in "The Sick Rose" by Blake (page 496).

◇◇◇◇◇◇◇◇◇◇◇◇◇◇◇◇◇◇◇◇◇◇

George Gordon, Lord Byron   1788–1824

Born in London and educated at Cambridge, George Gordon, Lord Byron, became a public figure as much for his scandalous personal life as for his irreverent, satiric poetry. Rumors about an affair with his half-sister forced him to leave England in 1816. His masterpiece is the comic epic poem *Don Juan*, begun in 1819 and still unfinished when he died in Greece from a fever he contracted while fighting for Greek independence.

She Walks in Beauty

She walks in beauty, like the night
    Of cloudless climes and starry skies;
And all that's best of dark and bright
    Meet in her aspect and her eyes:
Thus mellowed to that tender light   5
    Which Heaven to gaudy day denies.

One shade the more, one ray the less,
    Had half impaired the nameless grace
Which waves in every raven tress,
    Or softly lightens o'er her face;   10
Where thoughts serenely sweet express,
    How pure, how dear their dwelling-place.

And on that cheek, and o'er that brow,
    So soft, so calm, yet eloquent,
The smiles that win, the tints that glow,   15
    But tell of days in goodness spent,
A mind at peace with all below,
    A heart whose love is innocent!

(1814)

Questions for Discussion and Writing

1. The light image introduced in the first stanza is the foundation of the poem, but just which image of light is dominant?
2. What does the word "eloquent" refer to? In those same lines, are the smiles on the cheek and the glow on the brow? How does that description work?
3. What are the speaker's attitudes toward women and beauty?

Making Connections

Compare Byron's "She Walks in Beauty" with the depiction of a female lover in Thomas Wyatt's "They Flee from Me" (page 485).

◇◇◇◇◇◇◇◇◇◇◇◇◇◇◇◇◇◇◇◇◇◇◇◇◇◇◇◇

Percy Bysshe Shelley 1792–1822

Percy Shelley married sixteen-year-old Harriet Westbrook in 1811, the same year he was expelled from Oxford for writing a pamphlet on atheism. In 1814 he went to France with Mary Wollstonecraft, later famous for writing *Frankenstein*. The two were wed in 1816 after Harriet committed suicide. The couple then settled in Italy, where Shelley wrote some of his best lyrics, including "Ozymandias," "Ode to the West Wind," and *Adonais*.

Ozymandias

I met a traveller from an antique land
Who said: Two vast and trunkless legs of stone
Stand in the desert....Near them, on the sand,
Half sunk, a shattered visage lies, whose frown,
And wrinkled lip, and sneer of cold command,   5
Tell that its sculptor well those passions read
Which yet survive, stamped on these lifeless things,
The hand that mocked them, and the heart that fed:
And on the pedestal these words appear:
"My name is Ozymandias, king of kings: 10
Look on my works, ye Mighty, and despair!"
Nothing beside remains. Round the decay
Of that colossal wreck, boundless and bare
The lone and level sands stretch far away.

(1817)

Questions for Discussion and Writing

1. The statue that this poem is written about has been described as one of the largest in Egypt. It has this inscription: "I am Ozymandias, king of kings; if anyone wishes to know what I am and where I lie, let him surpass me in some of my exploits." Does having this information help your understanding of the poem?

2. What contrast is there between what the king said and how the statue now looks?

3. How does the final image (the "lone and level sands" stretching far away) work to reinforce the tone and theme of the poem?

Making Connections

Compare the form, tone, and content of "Ozymandias" with Claude McKay's "America" (page 937).

◇◇◇◇◇◇◇◇◇◇◇◇◇◇◇◇◇◇◇◇◇◇◇◇◇◇◇◇

John Keats 1795–1821

A major figure in the romantic period of English poetry, John Keats began writing at age eighteen and died of tuberculosis in Italy at age twenty-five, after having seen both his mother and brother die of the disease. His poems, which are rich in imagery and dignified in expression, include "Ode on a Grecian Urn," "To Autumn," and "The Eve of St. Agnes."

Ode on a Grecian Urn

Thou still unravished bride of quietness,
  Thou foster-child of silence and slow time,
Sylvan historian, who canst thus express
  A flowery tale more sweetly than our rhyme:
What leaf-fringed legend haunts about thy shape   5
Of deities or mortals, or of both,
  In Tempe° or the dales of Arcady?°
What men or gods are these? What maidens loth?
  What mad pursuit? What struggle to escape?
    What pipes and timbrels? What wild ecstasy?   10

Heard melodies are sweet, but those unheard
  Are sweeter; therefore, ye soft pipes, play on;
Not to the sensual ear, but, more endeared,
  Pipe to the spirit ditties of no tone:
Fair youth, beneath the trees, thou canst not leave   15
  Thy song, nor ever can those trees be bare;
    Bold Lover, never, never canst thou kiss,
Though winning near the goal—yet, do not grieve;
  She cannot fade, though thou hast not thy bliss,
    For ever wilt thou love, and she be fair!   20

Ah, happy, happy boughs! that cannot shed
  Your leaves, nor ever bid the spring adieu;
And, happy melodist, unwearièd,
  For ever piping songs for ever new;
More happy love! more happy, happy love!   25
For ever warm and still to be enjoyed,
  For ever panting, and for ever young;
    All breathing human passion far above,
That leaves a heart high-sorrowful and cloyed,
    A burning forehead, and a parching tongue.   30

Who are these coming to the sacrifice?
  To what green altar, O mysterious priest,
Lead'st thou that heifer lowing at the skies,
  And all her silken flanks with garlands dressed?

---

7 Tempe Valley in Thessaly, noted for its natural beauty. **Arcady** Region in Greece, a traditional setting for pastoral poetry.

What little town by river or sea shore,   35
   Or mountain-built with peaceful citadel,
     Is emptied of this folk, this pious morn?
And, little town, thy streets for evermore
   Will silent be; and not a soul to tell
     Why thou art desolate, can e'er return.   40
O Attic° shape! Fair attitude! with brede°
   Of marble men and maidens overwrought,
With forest branches and the trodden weed;
   Thou, silent form, dost tease us out of thought
As doth eternity: Cold Pastoral!   45
   When old age shall this generation waste,
     Thou shalt remain, in midst of other woe
Than ours, a friend to man, to whom thou say'st,
   "Beauty is truth, truth beauty,"—that is all
     Ye know on earth, and all ye need to know.   50
              (1819)

---

41 Attic Of Attica, thus, classic in grace and simplicity.   **brede** Design, decoration.

Questions for Discussion and Writing

1. How can unheard melodies be sweeter than heard ones?
2. Why are the figures so lucky to exist on the urn (lines 15–27)? What disadvantages do living lovers experience (lines 28–30)?
3. How is the urn a "Cold Pastoral"? How is it a "friend to man"?
4. Explain the closing line and give your reactions to this assertion about beauty and truth.

Making Connections

Compare Keats's views about art—and a specific piece of art—to what W. D. Snodgrass says on the same subject in his poem "Matisse: 'The Red Studio'" (page 474).

◇◇◇◇◇◇◇◇◇◇◇◇◇◇◇◇◇◇◇◇◇◇

Alfred, Lord Tennyson   1809–1892

One of the most popular poets in Victorian England, Tennyson showed his talents early, publishing his first volume at the age of eighteen. Encouraged to devote himself to poetry by friends at Cambridge, he was particularly close to Arthur Hallam, whose sudden death inspired the long elegy *In Memoriam* (1850). This work brought Tennyson lasting recognition; he was appointed poet laureate the year it appeared. His other works include *Idylls of the King* (1859–1885), a series of poems about King Arthur and the knights of the round table.

Ulysses

It little profits that an idle king,
By this still hearth, among these barren crags,
Match'd with an aged wife, I mete and dole
Unequal laws unto a savage race,
That hoard, and sleep, and feed, and know not me.   5
I cannot rest from travel: I will drink
Life to the lees. All times I have enjoyed
Greatly, have suffered greatly, both with those
That loved me, and alone, on shore, and when
Through scudding drifts the rainy Hyades   10
Vext the dim sea. I am become a name;
For always roaming with a hungry heart
Much have I seen and known—cities of men
And manners, climates, councils, governments,
Myself not least, but honoured of them all—   15
And drunk delight of battle with my peers,
Far on the ringing plains of windy Troy.
I am a part of all that I have met;
Yet all experience is an arch wherethrough
Gleams that untravelled world whose margin fades   20
For ever and for ever when I move.
How dull it is to pause, to make an end,
To rust unburnished, not to shine in use!
As though to breathe were life! Life piled on life
Were all too little, and of one to me   25
Little remains; but every hour is saved
From that eternal silence, something more,
A bringer of new things; and vile it were
For some three suns to store and hoard myself,
And this gray spirit yearning in desire   30
To follow knowledge like a sinking star,
Beyond the utmost bound of human thought.
      This is my son, mine own Telemachus,
To whom I leave the sceptre and the isle—
Well-loved of me, discerning to fulfill   35
This labor, by slow prudence to make mild
A rugged people, and through soft degrees
Subdue them to the useful and the good.
Most blameless is he, centered in the sphere
Of common duties, decent not to fail   40
In offices of tenderness, and pay
Meet adoration to my household gods,
When I am gone. He works his work, I mine.
      There lies the port; the vessel puffs her sail:
There gloom the dark, broad seas. My mariners,   45

Souls that have toiled, and wrought, and thought with me—
That ever with a frolic welcome took
The thunder and the sunshine, and opposed
Free hearts, free foreheads—you and I are old;
Old age hath yet his honor and his toil.   50
Death closes all; but something ere the end,
Some work of noble note, may yet be done,
Not unbecoming men that strove with Gods.
The lights begin to twinkle from the rocks;
The long day wanes; the slow moon climbs; the deep   55
Moans round with many voices. Come, my friends,
'Tis not too late to seek a newer world.
Push off, and sitting well in order smite
The sounding furrows; for my purpose holds
To sail beyond the sunset, and the baths   60
Of all the western stars, until I die.
It may be that the gulfs will wash us down;
It may be we shall touch the Happy Isles,
And see the great Achilles, whom we knew.
Though much is taken, much abides; and though   65
We are not now that strength which in old days
Moved earth and heaven, that which we are, we are—
One equal temper of heroic hearts,
Made weak by time and fate, but strong in will
To strive, to seek, to find, and not to yield.   70
                                                                    (1842)

Questions for Discussion and Writing

1. Who was Ulysses, and what had he done before the start of the poem? (Hint: *Ulysses* is the Latin name for *Odysseus*.)
2. What does Ulysses want? What is his attitude toward life in Ithaca?
3. At first the poem seems optimistic and positive. Is it? Argue your view.
4. What does Ulysses have in mind when he speaks of "Some work of noble note, may yet be done"?
5. Does this poem present an argument for how life should be lived? Write an essay defending or refuting that argument.

Making Connections

Compare this poem about the end of life to Yeats's "Sailing to Byzantium" (page 518).

◇◇◇◇◇◇◇◇◇◇◇◇◇◇◇◇◇◇◇◇◇◇

Walt Whitman 1819–1892

See page 419 for a biographical note about this author.

When I Heard the Learn'd Astronomer

When I heard the learn'd astronomer,
When the proofs, the figures, were ranged in columns before me,
When I was shown the charts and diagrams, to add, divide, and
    measure them,
When I sitting heard the astronomer where he lectured with much
    applause in the lecture-room,
How soon unaccountable I became tired and sick,   5
Till rising and gliding out I wander'd off by myself,
In the mystical moist night-air, and from time to time,
Look'd up in perfect silence at the stars.

                                  (1865)

Questions for Discussion and Writing

1. Why is the speaker in the poem unable to appreciate the astronomy lecture?
2. Whitman's lines neither rhyme nor scan, so what makes this a poem?
3. Do you think poetry and science are antithetical? Write an essay about the similarities and differences between the methods and purposes of science and poetry. Use specific poems to support your claims.

Making Connections

Compare the ideas about nature and beauty in this poem with those expressed in Keats's "Ode on a Grecian Urn" (page 501) or with Emily Dickinson's comments on faith and microscopes in "Faith Is a Fine Invention" (page 508).

Song of Myself

SECTION 11

Twenty-eight young men bathe by the shore,
Twenty-eight young men and all so friendly;
Twenty-eight years of womanly life and all so lonesome.

She owns the fine house by the rise of the bank,
She hides handsome and richly drest aft the blinds of the window.   5

Which of the young men does she like the best?
Ah the homeliest of them is beautiful to her.

Where are you off to, lady? for I see you,
You splash in the water there, yet stay stock still in your room.

Dancing and laughing along the beach came the twenty-ninth bather,   10
The rest did not see her, but she saw them and loved them.

The beards of the young men glisten'd with wet, it ran from their
    long hair,
Little streams pass'd all over their bodies.

An unseen hand also pass'd over their bodies,
It descended tremblingly from their temples and ribs.   15

The young men float on their backs, their white bellies bulge to the
    sun, they do not ask who seizes fast to them,
They do not know who puffs and declines with pendant and
    bending arch,
They do not think whom they souse with spray.

(1881)

Questions for Discussion and Writing

1. Why does the woman hide "handsome and richly drest" behind the window blinds? What sort of life do you think she leads?
2. How can the woman splash in the water and also "stay stock still" in her room?
3. What is the sexual implication of the phrase "souse with spray"? What other sexually charged language is there in these lines?
4. What does this episode imply about the sexual differences between men and women? Do you think these implications are valid?

Making Connections

How is this poem different from or similar to other poems about sex and love, such as Donne's "The Flea" (page 490), Dickinson's "Wild Nights—Wild Nights!" (page 511), or Olds's "Sex Without Love" (page 561)?

◇◇◇◇◇◇◇◇◇◇◇◇◇◇◇◇◇◇◇◇◇◇

Matthew Arnold   1822–1888

Matthew Arnold was born in Middlesex, England, studied classics at Oxford, and later taught there. He was appointed inspector of schools for England and remained at that post for thirty-five years. As a poet, Arnold took his inspiration from Greek tragedies, Keats, and Wordsworth. An eminent social and literary critic in later years, he lectured in America in 1883 and 1886.

Dover Beach

The sea is calm to-night,
The tide is full, the moon lies fair

Upon the Straits;—on the French coast, the light
Gleams, and is gone; the cliffs of England stand,
Glimmering and vast, out in the tranquil bay.   5
Come to the window, sweet is the night air!
Only, from the long line of spray
Where the sea meets the moon-blanched sand,
Listen! you hear the grating roar
Of pebbles which the waves draw back, and fling,   10
At their return, up the high strand,
Begin, and cease, and then again begin,

With tremulous cadence slow, and bring
The eternal note of sadness in.
Sophocles° long ago   15
Heard it on the Aegean, and it brought
Into his mind the turbid ebb and flow
Of human misery; we
Find also in the sound a thought,
Hearing it by this distant northern sea.   20

The Sea of Faith
Was once, too, at the full, and round earth's shore
Lay like the folds of a bright girdle furled;
But now I only hear
Its melancholy, long, withdrawing roar,   25
Retreating to the breath
Of the night-wind down the vast edges drear
And naked shingles° of the world.

Ah, love, let us be true
To one another! for the world, which seems   30
To lie before us like a land of dreams,
So various, so beautiful, so new,
Hath really neither joy, nor love, nor light,
Nor certitude, nor peace, nor help for pain;
And we are here as on a darkling° plain   35
Swept with confused alarms of struggle and flight,
Where ignorant armies clash by night.

(1867)

---

15 Sophocles In *Antigone* the Greek dramatist likens the curse of heaven to the ebb and flow of the sea.   **28 shingles** Gravel beaches.   **35 darkling** Darkened.

Questions for Discussion and Writing

1. Describe the setting of the poem. To whom is the persona speaking?
2. What could have caused the "Sea of Faith" to be retreating like the tide? Note the date of the poem.
3. What does the persona pose as a solution to the loss of religious faith?
4. Write an essay in which you argue that the images of sound and sight—or lack of sight—contribute to the effectiveness of the poem.

Making Connections

Compare Arnold's ideas about the loss of faith around the world with Emily Dickinson's comments concerning faith and microscopes in "Faith Is a Fine Invention," the next poem on this page.

◇◇◇◇◇◇◇◇◇◇◇◇◇◇◇◇◇◇◇◇◇

Emily Dickinson 1830–1886

Emily Dickinson is among the greatest of American poets. During most of her adult life, she was a recluse, confining herself to her father's home in Amherst, Massachusetts, wearing only white and shunning company. She produced more than 1,700 lyrics, which are characterized by startling imagery, ellipses, and unexpected juxtapositions. Only seven of her poems were published in her lifetime—and those without her permission. Her influence is still felt in modern poetry.

Faith Is a Fine Invention

> Faith is a fine invention
> For Gentlemen who *see*.
> But *Microscopes* are prudent—
> In an Emergency!
>
> (1860)

Questions for Discussion and Writing

1. Consider "invention" as a key word choice. What kinds of things are usually called inventions? What does the word imply about faith?
2. According to the poem, when are microscopes better tools than faith? Why might this be so? How do microscopes improve on vision?
3. Write a paragraph interpreting this poem as a satire.

Making Connections

Compare this poem to others that concern the nature and value of "faith": Arnold's "Dover Beach" (page 506) and Whitman's "When I Heard the Learn'd Astronomer" (page 505).

I'm Nobody! Who Are You?

> I'm Nobody! Who are you?
> Are you—Nobody—Too?
> Then there's a pair of us!
> Don't tell! they'd banish us—you know!

How dreary—to be—Somebody!   5
How public—like a Frog—
To tell your name—the livelong June—
To an admiring Bog!

(1861)

Questions for Discussion and Writing

1. Who are "they" in the first stanza? In what way would they "banish us"?
2. Explain the simile about the frog in the final stanza. What makes it effective?
3. What kind of person is the speaker in the poem? Do you know anyone like that? Are you perhaps a private person yourself, or are you an extrovert? Write a statement explaining why you want—or don't want—to be in the public eye.

Making Connections

Contrast the voice (or persona) in this poem with several others by Dickinson. Develop an argument about the poet's range and variety of speakers.

Much Madness Is Divinest Sense

Much Madness is divinest Sense—
To a discerning Eye—
Much Sense—the starkest Madness—
'Tis the Majority
In this, as All, prevail—   5
Assent—and you are sane—
Demur—you're straightway dangerous—
And handled with a Chain—

(ca. 1862)

Questions for Discussion and Writing

1. Can you think of an example, perhaps historical, of something that was considered madness that turned out to be the truth?
2. Can you think of something that is accepted by most people in society that you consider "madness"?
3. What does Dickinson mean by "handled with a Chain"?

Making Connections

Compare this poem's message about conformity to the theme of "The Supremes" by Cornelius Eady (page 567). Do you think the speaker of Eady's poem would agree with the views expressed in Dickinson's poem?

Because I Could Not Stop for Death

Because I could not stop for Death—
He kindly stopped for me—
The Carriage held but just Ourselves—
And Immortality—

We slowly drove—He knew no haste   5
And I had put away
My labor and my leisure too,
For His Civility—

We passed the School, where Children strove
At Recess—in the Ring—   10
We passed the Fields of Gazing Grain—
We passed the Setting Sun—

Or rather—He passed Us—
The Dews drew quivering and chill—
For only Gossamer,° my Gown   15
My Tippet°—only Tulle°—

We paused before a House that seemed
A Swelling of the Ground—
The Roof was scarcely visible—
The Cornice—in the Ground—   20

Since then—'tis Centuries—and yet
Feels shorter than the Day
I first surmised the Horses' Heads
Were toward Eternity—

(ca. 1863)

---

15 Gossamer Thin, sheer.   **16 Tippet** Short cape covering just the shoulders.   **Tulle** Soft net fabric.

Questions for Discussion and Writing

1. What is the action described in the poem? What do the images in stanza 3 suggest? What is the "House" in lines 17–20?
2. Death is personified in the poem. What sort of person is he?
3. What is the persona's attitude toward death?
4. Can you state a theme for the poem?

Making Connections

Contrast the personification of death in this poem with that in John Donne's "Death Be Not Proud" (page 489). How do they differ? Which do you find more appealing?

Some Keep the Sabbath Going to Church

Some keep the Sabbath going to Church—
I keep it, staying at Home—
With a Bobolink for a Chorister—
And an Orchard, for a Dome—

Some keep the Sabbath in Surplice— 5
I just wear my Wings—
And instead of tolling the Bell, for Church,
Our little Sexton—sings.

God preaches, a noted Clergyman—
And the sermon is never long 10
So instead of getting to Heaven, at last—
I'm going, all along.

(1864)

Questions for Discussion and Writing

1. Describe the persona in the poem.
2. How does the speaker celebrate the sabbath? Point out the contrasts with conventional religious observance.
3. What is the tone of the poem? Does it have a theme?

Making Connections

How does this poem differ from Gerard Manley Hopkins's "Pied Beauty" (page 513), which also praises the beauty of nature but with a different set of philosophical underpinnings?

Wild Nights—Wild Nights!

Wild Nights—Wild Nights!
Were I with thee
Wild Nights should be
Our luxury!

Futile—the Winds— 5
To a Heart in port—
Done with the Compass—
Done with the Chart!

Rowing in Eden—
Ah, the Sea! 10
Might I but moor—Tonight—
In Thee!

(1861)

Questions for Discussion and Writing

1. What is the speaker looking forward to in this poem?
2. What does the word *luxury* mean in line 4?
3. Paraphrase the second stanza, adding any words that may have been omitted.
4. Explain the image of "a Heart in port" in stanza 2.
5. What does the speaker long for in the last two lines?

Making Connections

How is this poem different from or similar to other poems about sex and love, such as Donne's "The Flea" (page 490), Whitman's "Song of Myself (Section 11)" (page 505), or Olds's "Sex Without Love" (page 561)?

◇◇◇◇◇◇◇◇◇◇◇◇◇◇◇◇◇◇◇◇◇◇◇

Christina Rossetti　1830–1894

　　Sometimes called the finest female poet England has yet produced, Christina Rossetti was born into a highly cultured family. Early on, she showed a lively imagination and a technical skill for poetry, and in the 1850s began contributing poetry and prose to various periodicals. A devout Anglican, Rossetti rejected two Catholic suitors rather than stray from her faith, and religious themes became a strong theme in her writing. In 1872 she was afflicted with Graves' disease and became reclusive. Her poetry often dwells on frustration and loneliness, as well as the nature of art and beauty.

In an Artist's Studio

One face looks out from all his canvasses,
One selfsame figure sits or walks or leans;
We found her hidden just behind those screens,
That mirror gave back all her loveliness.
A queen in opal or in ruby dress,　　　　　　　　　　　　5
A nameless girl in freshest summer greens,
A saint, an angel—every canvass means
The same one meaning, neither more nor less.
He feeds upon her face by day and night,
And she with true kind eyes looks back on him,　　　　10
Fair as the moon and joyful as the light:
Not wan with waiting, not with sorrow dim;
Not as she is, but was when hope shone bright;
Not as she is, but as she fills his dream.

　　　　　　　　　　　　　　(1861)

Questions for Discussion and Writing

1. Is the female in all the artist's canvases the same person? Does it make any difference if she is or is not?
2. This poem is a sonnet. What does the octave describe? And what is the message of the sestet?
3. What does the image "He feeds upon her face" suggest to you?
4. Write an essay about the idea that women are the embodiment of beauty, goodness, and self-sacrifice. Does that idealization have a down side? Argue your position on this matter.

Making Connections

How does Byron's poem "She Walks in Beauty" (page 499) typify the artistic treatment of women that Rossetti describes in this poem?

◇◇◇◇◇◇◇◇◇◇◇◇◇◇◇◇◇◇◇◇◇◇◇◇◇

Gerard Manley Hopkins   1844–1889

Gerard Manley Hopkins was a major poet who was not recognized during his lifetime. Born in Essex, England, he attended Oxford, converted to Catholicism, and became a Jesuit priest. He died of typhoid fever at age forty-four, having never published his poetry. Nearly thirty years later, a friend brought out Hopkins's *Poems* (1918), and he has since been acknowledged as a major poet.

Pied Beauty

Glory be to God for dappled things—
    For skies of couple-color as a brinded° cow;
      For rose-moles all in stipple° upon trout that swim;
Fresh-firecoal chestnut-falls;° finches' wings;
    Landscape plotted and pieced—fold, fallow, and plow;   5
      And áll trádes, their gear and tackle and trim.°

All things counter, original, spare, strange;
    Whatever is fickle, freckled (who knows how?)
      With swift, slow; sweet, sour; adazzle, dim;
He fathers-forth whose beauty is past change: 10
    Praise him.

               (1877)

---

2 brinded Striped.   **3 stipple** Small dots.   **4 chestnut-falls** Chestnuts fresh from the fire with their hulls off.   **6 trim** Tools.

Questions for Discussion and Writing

1. What words in the poem did Hopkins coin?
2. Can you describe what he means by "Landscape plotted and pieced"?
3. Why does the poet praise things made by human hands as well as things in nature?

Making Connections

Compare Hopkins's attitude toward nature with the views expressed by Robert Frost in "Design" (page 527) or by Maxine Kumin in "Woodchucks" (page 552).

Spring and Fall

To a Young Child

> Márgarét áre you gríeving
> Over Goldengrove unleaving?
> Leáves, líke the things of man, you
> With your fresh thoughts care for, can you?
> Áh! ás the heart grows older   5
> It will come to such sights colder
> By and by, nor spare a sigh
> Though worlds of wanwood°leafmeal° lie;
> And yet you *will* weep and know why.
> Now no matter, child, the name: 10
> Sórrow's spríngs áre the same.
> Nor mouth had, no nor mind, expressed
> What heart heard of, ghost° guessed:
> It ís the blight man was born for,
> It is Margaret you mourn for.   15

(1880)

---

8 wanwood Pale woods, as though bloodless. **leafmeal** Fallen leaf by leaf. **13 ghost** Spirit, soul.

Questions for Discussion and Writing

1. What does Hopkins mean in his unusual phrase "Goldengrove unleaving"? In other words, why is Margaret grieving?
2. Does the fall of the leaves suggest any other kind of fall, perhaps a metaphorical one?
3. Explain why Margaret is, in effect, mourning for herself.

Making Connections

Compare this poem about growing older and facing the prospect of death to "My Son My Executioner" by Donald Hall (page 422), "Do Not Go Gentle into That Good Night" by Dylan Thomas (page 548), or "The Leap" by James Dickey (page 550).

◇◇◇◇◇◇◇◇◇◇◇◇◇◇◇◇◇◇◇◇◇◇◇◇◇◇◇◇◇◇

A. E. Housman   1859–1936

See page 438 for a biographical note about this author.

To an Athlete Dying Young

The time you won your town the race
We chaired you through the market-place;
Man and boy stood cheering by,
And home we brought you shoulder-high.

To-day, the road all runners come,   5
Shoulder-high we bring you home,
And set you at your threshold down,
Townsman of a stiller town.

Smart lad, to slip betimes away
From fields where glory does not stay,   10
And early though the laurel grows
It withers quicker than the rose.

Eyes the shady night has shut
Cannot see the record cut,
And silence sounds no worse than cheers   15
After earth has stopped the ears.

Now you will not swell the rout
Of lads that wore their honors out,
Runners whom renown outran
And the name died before the man.   20

So set, before its echoes fade,
The fleet foot on the sill of shade,
And hold to the low lintel° up
The still-defended challenge-cup.

And round that early-laurelled° head   25
Will flock to gaze the strengthless dead,
And find unwithered on its curls
The garland briefer than a girl's.

(1896)

---

23 lintel Horizontal support above a door.   **25 laurelled** In ancient times victors were crowned with laurel wreaths.

Questions for Discussion and Writing

1. What is "the road all runners come" in line 5? What is that "stiller town" the road leads to? What is the significance of the laurel in line 11?
2. How valuable is the approbation the lad receives in the final stanza? Would it have been worth dying for?
3. What point do you think Housman is making here?

Making Connections

Compare this poem with Emily Dickinson's "Because I Could Not Stop for Death" (page 510) or with John Updike's "Ex-Basketball Player" (page 591).

Loveliest of Trees

Loveliest of trees, the cherry now
Is hung with bloom along the bough,
And stands about the woodland ride,°
Wearing white for Eastertide.

Now, of my threescore years and ten,   5
Twenty will not come again,
And take from seventy springs a score,
It only leaves me fifty more.

And since to look at things in bloom
Fifty springs are little room,   10
About the woodlands I will go
To see the cherry hung with snow.

                                                (1896)

---

3 ride Path.

Questions for Discussion and Writing

1. How old is the speaker in the poem?
2. What associations can you make with the white blossoms in the first stanza and with "snow," the last word in the poem?
3. Does the poem have a theme? If so, can you state it?

Making Connections

Compare this poem about nature and the passing of time to "Spring and Fall" by Gerard Manley Hopkins (page 514).

◇◇◇◇◇◇◇◇◇◇◇◇◇◇◇◇◇◇◇◇◇

William Butler Yeats 1865–1939

One of the most important poets of the twentieth century, William Butler Yeats was born near Dublin, attended art school for a time, but quit to devote himself to poetry, plays, and politics. He served as a senator in the Irish Free State (1922–1928), helped found the Irish National Theatre Society at the now famous Abbey Theatre, and was awarded the Nobel Prize for Literature in 1923.

The Second Coming

Turning and turning in the widening gyre°
The falcon cannot hear the falconer;
Things fall apart; the centre cannot hold;
Mere anarchy is loosed upon the world,
The blood-dimmed tide is loosed, and everywhere   5
The ceremony of innocence is drowned;
The best lack all conviction, while the worst
Are full of passionate intensity.

Surely some revelation is at hand;
Surely the Second Coming is at hand.   10
The Second Coming! Hardly are those words out
When a vast image out of *Spiritus Mundi*°
Troubles my sight: somewhere in sands of the desert
A shape with lion body and the head of a man,
A gaze blank and pitiless as the sun,   15
Is moving its slow thighs, while all about it
Reel shadows of the indignant desert birds.
The darkness drops again; but now I know
That twenty centuries of stony sleep
Were vexed to nightmare by a rocking cradle,   20
And what rough beast, its hour come round at last,
Slouches towards Bethlehem to be born?

(1921)

---

1 gyre A spiral motion, used by Yeats to suggest the cycles of history.

12 Spiritus Mundi The Soul of the World, a collective unconscious from which humans draw memories, symbols, dreams.

Questions for Discussion and Writing

1. What is the state of the world being described by the speaker in the first stanza?
2. What does the "ceremony of innocence" suggest?
3. Why does Yeats envision the "rough beast" as coming from the desert? What associations can you make with a desert?
4. Can you explain lines 19 and 20? Whose rocking cradle is it?
5. Write a brief essay explaining what the beast represents.

Making Connections

Compare this poem to "Fire and Ice" by Robert Frost (page 526).

Sailing to Byzantium°*

That is no country for old men. The young
In one another's arms, birds in the trees
—Those dying generations—at their song,
The salmon-falls, the mackerel-crowded seas,
Fish, flesh, or fowl, commend all summer long   5
Whatever is begotten, born, and dies.
Caught in that sensual music all neglect
Monuments of unaging intellect.

An agéd man is but a paltry thing,
A tattered coat upon a stick, unless   10
Soul clap its hands and sing, and louder sing
For every tatter in its mortal dress,
Nor is there singing school but studying
Monuments of its own magnificence;
And therefore I have sailed the seas and come   15
To the holy city of Byzantium.

O sages standing in God's holy fire
As in the gold mosaic of a wall,
Come from the holy fire, perne in a gyre,°
And be the singing-masters of my soul.   20
Consume my heart away; sick with desire
And fastened to a dying animal
It knows not what it is; and gather me
Into the artifice of eternity.
Once out of nature I shall never take   25
My bodily form from any natural thing,
But such a form as Grecian goldsmiths make
Of hammered gold and gold enamelling
To keep a drowsy Emperor awake;
Or set upon a golden bough to sing   30
To lords and ladies of Byzantium
Of what is past, or passing, or to come.

                                        (1928)

Title: The capital of the Byzantine Empire, the city now called Istanbul; for Yeats, a symbol of life perfected by art.

19 gyre The spiraling motion that Yeats associates with the whirling of fate; see "The Second Coming."

Questions for Discussion and Writing

1. What does the imagery in the first stanza suggest? Why does Yeats describe the young as "those dying generations"? Do you know the Renaissance meaning for the word "die"?
2. What is that "country" referred to in the first line?
3. Why does the speaker want to sail to Byzantium? Can you explain what Byzantium symbolizes? Why is it a perfect choice?
4. What is the "dying animal" in line 22 that the speaker wants to be freed from?

Making Connections

How does this poem about art compare to John Keats's "Ode on a Grecian Urn" (page 501)?

◇◇◇◇◇◇◇◇◇◇◇◇◇◇◇◇◇◇◇◇◇◇◇◇

Edgar Lee Masters   1868–1950

Born in Kansas, Edgar Lee Masters grew up on a farm near Springfield, Illinois, and became a successful Chicago lawyer before his first poems were published. Although he wrote many novels and a number of biographies of literary and public figures, Masters is known today almost entirely for his *Spoon River Anthology*, a series of two hundred short monologues spoken by the deceased inhabitants of a fictitious village. The book caused a sensation mainly because of its blunt attitude toward sex and its pointed commentary on the morals and hypocrisies of small town life. It was enormously successful. No matter what Masters published after *Spoon River*, he could never produce a rival. It was (to borrow a phrase from it) his "true epitaph, more lasting than stone."

Lucinda Matlock

I went to the dances at Chandlerville,
And played snap-out at Winchester.
One time we changed partners,
Driving home in the moonlight of middle June,
And then I found Davis.   5
We were married and lived together for seventy years,
Enjoying, working, raising the twelve children,
Eight of whom we lost
Ere I had reached the age of sixty.
I spun, I wove, I kept the house, I nursed the sick,   10
I made the garden, and for holiday
Rambled over the fields where sang the larks,
And by Spoon River gathering many a shell,
And many a flower and medicinal weed—

Shouting to the wooded hills, singing to the green valleys. 15
At ninety-six I had lived enough, that is all,
And passed to a sweet repose.
What is this I hear of sorrow and weariness,
Anger, discontent and drooping hopes?
Degenerate sons and daughters, 20
Life is too strong for you—
It takes life to love Life.

(1916)

Questions for Discussion and Writing

1. What do you think of Lucinda Matlock? Would you like to have her for a friend or neighbor? Is there anything about her that puts you off?
2. What kind of life did Lucinda live? Would you like to live as she did? Do many people live like that any more?
3. Come up with three adjectives to describe the tone of this monologue. Does it change at any point?
4. Explicate the last two lines.

Making Connections

Compare Lucinda Matlock to Aunt Jennifer in Adrienne Rich's "Aunt Jennifer's Tigers" (page 557).

◇◇◇◇◇◇◇◇◇◇◇◇◇◇◇◇◇◇◇◇◇◇◇

Margaret Fuller Slack

I would have been as great as George Eliot
But for an untoward fate.
For look at the photograph of me made by Penniwit,
Chin resting on hand, and deep-set eyes—
Gray, too, and far-searching. 5
But there was the old, old problem:
Should it be celibacy, matrimony, or unchastity?
Then John Slack, the rich druggist, wooed me,
Luring me with the promise of leisure for my novel,
And I married him, giving birth to eight children, 10
And had no time to write.
It was all over with me, anyway,
When I ran the needle in my hand
While washing the baby's things,
And died from lock-jaw, an ironical death. 15
Hear me, ambitious souls,
Sex is the curse of life!

(1916)

Questions for Discussion and Writing

1. Do you think Margaret Fuller Slack could have been a successful author? Or is she engaging in some rationalization?
2. What does "untoward" mean?
3. Why does she say dying from lock-jaw was "an ironical death"?

Making Connections

Do you think Margaret Fuller Slack and Lucinda Matlock would have been friends? Write a comparison/contrast essay about these two women and their outlook on life.

◇◇◇◇◇◇◇◇◇◇◇◇◇◇◇◇◇◇◇◇◇◇

Paul Laurence Dunbar 1872–1906

Paul Laurence Dunbar was born in Dayton, Ohio, the son of former slaves. He graduated from high school but could not afford college and worked instead as an elevator operator. He published his first two books of poetry with his own money. Following the appearance of *Lyrics of Lowly Life* (1896), he became the first African American poet to win national recognition.

We Wear the Mask

We wear the mask that grins and lies,
It hides our cheeks and shades our eyes,—
This debt we pay to human guile;
With torn and bleeding hearts we smile,
And mouth with myriad subtleties.   5

Why should the world be overwise,
In counting all our tears and sighs?
Nay, let them only see us, while
    We wear the mask.
We smile, but, O great Christ, our cries   10
To thee from tortured souls arise.
We sing, but oh the clay is vile
Beneath our feet, and long the mile;
But let the world dream otherwise,
    We wear the mask!   15

(1895)

Questions for Discussion and Writing

1. Who is speaking in the poem? Who are the "we"?
2. The poet doesn't say why the mask is necessary. Can you tell why?
3. How would you state the theme of this poem?

4. People often appear happy although they are secretly seething over some real or imagined wrong—especially people who have little power, like children, women, or the members of minority groups. If you have ever had such an experience, describe it in writing and try to explain just how the incident made you feel. How do your feelings match those expressed in Dunbar's poem?

Making Connections

Compare Dunbar's feelings about living in a racist country to those expressed by Claude McKay in "America" (page 937) and Langston Hughes in "Harlem (A Dream Deferred)" (page 460).

◇◇◇◇◇◇◇◇◇◇◇◇◇◇◇◇◇◇◇◇◇◇

Robert Frost   1874–1963

See page 439 for a biographical note about this poet.

Mending Wall

Something there is that doesn't love a wall,
That sends the frozen-ground-swell under it
And spills the upper boulders in the sun,
And makes gaps even two can pass abreast.
The work of hunters is another thing: 5
I have come after them and made repair
Where they have left not one stone on a stone,
But they would have the rabbit out of hiding,
To please the yelping dogs. The gaps I mean,
No one has seen them made or heard them made,   10
But at spring mending-time we find them there.
I let my neighbor know beyond the hill;
And on a day we meet to walk the line
And set the wall between us once again.
We keep the wall between us as we go.   15
To each the boulders that have fallen to each.
And some are loaves and some so nearly balls
We have to use a spell to make them balance:
"Stay where you are until our backs are turned!"
We wear our fingers rough with handling them.   20
Oh, just another kind of outdoor game,
One on a side. It comes to little more:
There where it is we do not need the wall:
He is all pine and I am apple orchard.
My apple trees will never get across   25
And eat the cones under his pines, I tell him.
He only says, "Good fences make good neighbors."

Spring is the mischief in me, and I wonder
If I could put a notion in his head:
"*Why* do they make good neighbors? Isn't it   30
Where there are cows? But here there are no cows.
Before I built a wall I'd ask to know
What I was walling in or walling out,
And to whom I was like to give offense.
Something there is that doesn't love a wall,   35
That wants it down." I could say "Elves" to him,
But it's not elves exactly, and I'd rather
He said it for himself. I see him there,
Bringing a stone grasped firmly by the top
In each hand, like an old-stone savage armed.   40
He moves in darkness as it seems to me,
Not of woods only and the shade of trees.
He will not go behind his father's saying,
And he likes having thought of it so well
He says again, "Good fences make good neighbors."   45

(1914)

Questions for Discussion and Writing

1. Who is the speaker in the poem? What sort of person is he or she? What sort of person is the neighbor?
2. The line "Something there is that doesn't love a wall" appears twice. Why? What does the line mean? Does it state the poem's theme?
3. How does the speaker feel about walls? About hunters?
4. Do "Good fences make good neighbors," or are they "like to give offense"? Write an essay arguing your views on this issue.

Making Connections

How do you think the neighbor in this poem might respond to the attitude toward nature expressed in Whitman's "When I Heard the Learn'd Astronomer" (page 505) or in Oliver's "August" (page 418)?

Birches

When I see birches bend to left and right
Across the lines of straighter darker trees,
I like to think some boy's been swinging them.
But swinging doesn't bend them down to stay
As ice-storms do. Often you must have seen them   5
Loaded with ice a sunny winter morning
After a rain. They click upon themselves
As the breeze rises, and turn many-colored
As the stir cracks and crazes their enamel.
Soon the sun's warmth makes them shed crystal shells   10

Shattering and avalanching on the snow-crust—
Such heaps of broken glass to sweep away
You'd think the inner dome of heaven had fallen.
They are dragged to the withered bracken by the load,
And they seem not to break; though once they are bowed   15
So low for long, they never right themselves:
You may see their trunks arching in the woods
Years afterwards, trailing their leaves on the ground
Like girls on hands and knees that throw their hair
Before them over their heads to dry in the sun.   20
But I was going to say when Truth broke in
With all her matter-of-fact about the ice-storm,
I should prefer to have some boy bend them
As he went out and in to fetch the cows—
Some boy too far from town to learn baseball,   25
Whose only play was what he found himself,
Summer or winter, and could play alone.
One by one he subdued his father's trees
By riding them down over and over again
Until he took the stiffness out of them,   30
And not one but hung limp, not one was left
For him to conquer. He learned all there was
To learn about not launching out too soon
And so not carrying the tree away
Clear to the ground. He always kept his poise   35
To the top branches, climbing carefully
With the same pains you use to fill a cup
Up to the brim, and even above the brim.
Then he flung outward, feet first, with a swish,
Kicking his way down through the air to the ground.   40
So was I once myself a swinger of birches.
And so I dream of going back to be.
It's when I'm weary of considerations,
And life is too much like a pathless wood
Where your face burns and tickles with the cobwebs   45
Broken across it, and one eye is weeping
From a twig's having lashed across it open.
I'd like to get away from earth awhile
And then come back to it and begin over.
May no fate willfully misunderstand me   50
And half grant what I wish and snatch me away
Not to return. Earth's the right place for love:
I don't know where it's likely to go better.
I'd like to go by climbing a birch tree,
And climb black branches up a snow-white trunk,   55
Toward heaven, till the tree could bear no more,
But dipped its top and set me down again.
That would be good both going and coming back.
One could do worse than be a swinger of birches.

(1916)

Questions for Discussion and Writing

1. Why does the speaker prefer to think that the birches have been bent by boys instead of by ice storms? Refer to lines 23 to 27 for his image of the boy.
2. Explain the extended comparison in lines 41 through 49.
3. Why does the speaker insist that he would want to return to earth? He says, "Earth's the right place for love." Do you agree? What does this statement imply about the speaker's philosophy of life? How do you interpret the last line in terms of how one should live?
4. Write a short essay or long poem about some childhood pleasure you wish you could sometimes recapture.

Making Connections

How does the attitude toward nature in this poem differ from the view in some other Frost poems, such as "Design" (page 527) or "Mending Wall" (page 522)?

"Out, Out—"

The buzz saw snarled and rattled in the yard
And made dust and dropped stove-length sticks of wood,
Sweet-scented stuff when the breeze drew across it.
And from there those that lifted eyes could count
Five mountain ranges one behind the other   5
Under the sunset far into Vermont.
And the saw snarled and rattled, snarled and rattled,
As it ran light, or had to bear a load.
And nothing happened: day was all but done.
Call it a day, I wish they might have said   10
To please the boy by giving him the half hour
That a boy counts so much when saved from work.
His sister stood beside them in her apron
To tell them 'Supper.' At the word, the saw,
As if to prove saws knew what supper meant,   15
Leaped out at the boy's hand, or seemed to leap—
He must have given the hand. However it was,
Neither refused the meeting. But the hand!
The boy's first outcry was a rueful laugh,
As he swung toward them holding up the hand   20
Half in appeal, but half as if to keep
The life from spilling. Then the boy saw all—
Since he was old enough to know, big boy
Doing a man's work, though a child at heart—
He saw all spoiled. 'Don't let him cut my hand off—   25
The doctor, when he comes. Don't let him, sister!'
So. But the hand was gone already.
The doctor put him in the dark of ether.
He lay and puffed his lips out with his breath.

And then—the watcher at his pulse took fright.   30
No one believed. They listened at his heart.
Little—less—nothing!—and that ended it.
No more to build on there. And they, since they
Were not the one dead, turned to their affairs.
                                                        (1916)

Questions for Discussion and Writing

1. Who is speaking this narrative poem? Why are the characters not named?
2. What does Frost achieve by personifying the saw?
3. What is the theme of the poem?
4. The title is an allusion to Shakespeare's *Macbeth*, Act 5, Scene 5, lines 23–28. Look up the passage and explain in writing how the title refers to the meaning of the poem.

Making Connections

Compare the attitude expressed in this poem toward the boy's death with the attitude toward the death of the young soldier in Tim O'Brien's "The Things They Carried" (page 107) and/or the attitude toward the death of Jane MacNaughton in James Dickey's "The Leap" (page 550).

Fire and Ice

Some say the world will end in fire,
Some say in ice.
From what I've tasted of desire
I hold with those who favor fire.
But if it had to perish twice,   5
I think I know enough of hate
To say that for destruction ice
Is also great
And would suffice.
                                                        (1923)

Questions for Discussion and Writing

1. Why does the persona associate "fire" with desire and "ice" with hate?
2. Why does he choose "fire" and "ice" as the two possible ways that the world might end?
3. How does the word "suffice" as a rhyme for "ice" affect the meaning of the poem?

Making Connections

Compare this poem to "The Second Coming" by Yeats (page 517).

Design

I found a dimpled spider, fat and white,
On a white heal-all,° holding up a moth
Like a white piece of rigid satin cloth—
Assorted characters of death and blight
Mixed ready to begin the morning right,   5
Like the ingredients of a witches' broth—
A snow-drop spider, a flower like a froth,
And dead wings carried like a paper kite.

What had that flower to do with being white,
The wayside blue and innocent heal-all?   10
What brought the kindred spider to that height,
Then steered the white moth thither in the night?
What but design of darkness to appall?—
If design govern in a thing so small.

(1936)

---

2 heal-all A low-growing plant, usually having violet-blue flowers.

Questions for Discussion and Writing

1. How does the title relate to the poem?
2. What associations do you get from the words used to describe the spider? How do you usually think of spiders?
3. What do the speaker's questions lead you to consider? What answers does the poem suggest?
4. Write an essay interpreting Frost's ironic use of white in the poem.

Making Connections

Compare the working out of the theme in this poem with that of Matthew Arnold in "Dover Beach" (page 506).

◇◇◇◇◇◇◇◇◇◇◇◇◇◇◇◇◇◇◇◇◇◇◇◇◇◇◇

Carl Sandburg   1878–1967

Carl Sandburg was born in Galesburg, Illinois, and worked as a day laborer, soldier, political activist, and journalist. These experiences provided a rich palette of poetic colors to select from, and Sandburg painted boldly in vigorous free verse. He also wrote an acclaimed six-volume biography of Abraham Lincoln.

Fog

The fog comes
on little cat feet.

It sits looking
over harbor and city
on silent haunches   5
and then moves on.
(1916)

Questions for Discussion and Writing

1. Does this poem have a theme? What do you think its purpose is?
2. Compare this poem with the fog-as-cat image in lines 15 through 23 of
   Eliot's "The Love Song of J. Alfred Prufrock" (pages 533–516). Which do
   you think puts a better picture in your mind?

Making Connections

Compare the use of imagery in this poem to the images in "Reapers" by Jean
Toomer (page 590) or "The Red Wheelbarrow" by William Carlos Williams
(page 531).

Chicago

Hog Butcher for the World,
Tool Maker, Stacker of Wheat,
Player with Railroads and the Nation's Freight Handler;
Stormy, husky, brawling,
City of the Big Shoulders: 5
They tell me you are wicked and I believe them, for I have seen
  your painted women under the gas lamps luring the farm boys.
And they tell me you are crooked and I answer: Yes, it is true I
  have seen the gunman kill and go free to kill again.
And they tell me you are brutal and my reply is: On the faces of
  women and children I have seen the marks of wanton hunger.
And having answered so I turn once more to those who sneer at this
  my city, and I give them back the sneer and say to them:
Come and show me another city with lifted head singing so proud
  to be alive and coarse and strong and cunning.   10
Flinging magnetic curses amid the toil of piling job on job, here is a tall
  bold slugger set vivid against the little soft cities;
Fierce as a dog with tongue lapping for action, cunning as a savage
  pitted against the wilderness,
    Bareheaded,
    Shoveling,
    Wrecking,   15
    Planning,
    Building, breaking, rebuilding,
Under the smoke, dust all over his mouth, laughing with white teeth,
Under the terrible burden of destiny laughing as a young man laughs,
Laughing even as an ignorant fighter laughs who has never lost a battle,   20

Bragging and laughing that under his wrist is the pulse, and under his
    ribs the heart of the people,
Laughing!
Laughing the stormy, husky, brawling laughter of Youth, half-naked,
    sweating, proud to be Hog Butcher, Tool Maker, Stacker of
    Wheat, Player with Railroads and Freight Handler to the Nation.

(1914)

Questions for Discussion and Writing

1. What are the defining characteristics of Sandburg's Chicago?
2. How does he handle the city's obvious drawbacks—its violence and brutality?
3. What makes this piece a poem? That is, what elements of poetry are functioning in this unpoetic-sounding poem?
4. Write an essay arguing for or against the effectiveness of Sandburg's personification of the city in the poem. Does it work throughout, or do you find it strained at times?

Making Connections

Compare this poem to William Blake's "London" (page 936). How do the two poems about cities differ in tone, focus, and purpose?

◇◇◇◇◇◇◇◇◇◇◇◇◇◇◇◇◇◇◇◇◇◇

Mina Loy   1882–1966

Born Mina Gertrude Lowy in London, Mina Loy was sent to art school in Munich, Germany, at the age of seventeen. She continued her studies in Paris and London, trying her hand at acting, fashion, design, drawing, and modeling. She then moved to Florence in 1906 with her first husband; in 1916, she traveled to New York, got divorced, and became the epitome of a modern bohemian woman. Her poetry was both hailed and hated by her contemporaries. Her dramatic vocabulary, difficult syntax, and scornful treatment of love can offend and perplex many readers. But few will deny the work's originality and the author's forceful intelligence. Loy prized her visual art more than her writing, claiming that she "never was a poet."

Moreover, the Moon

Face of the skies
preside
over our wonder.

Fluorescent
truant of heaven   5
draw us under.

Silver, circular corpse
your decease
infects us with unendurable ease,

touching nerve-terminals   10
to thermal icicles

Coercive as coma, frail as bloom
innuendoes of your inverse dawn
suffuse the self;
our every corpuscle become an elf.   15

Questions for Discussion and Writing

1. In what way is the moon the "Face of the skies"? a "Fluorescent truant of
   heaven"? a "Silver, circular corpse"? Try to explain these metaphors in prosaic language.
2. Why is "Moreover" the first word in the title?
3. What effects does the moon have on "us," according to the poem's speaker?
   One commentator says the moon is "oppressive," especially to women.
   Explain that interpretation, and then write your response to it.

Making Connections

Compare Loy's poem to Anne Sexton's "The Starry Night" (page 473). What
similarities can you see in both theme and tone?

◇◇◇◇◇◇◇◇◇◇◇◇◇◇◇◇◇◇◇◇◇◇◇◇

William Carlos Williams   1883–1963

William Carlos Williams spent almost his entire life as a physician in Rutherford,
New Jersey. The "inarticulate poems" that he heard in the words of his patients
inspired him to write, jotting down lines and phrases whenever he could find a
moment. Williams wrote about common objects and experiences and imbued them
with spiritual qualities. His works include *Pictures from Brueghel* (1962), which won
a Pulitzer Prize, and his masterpiece, *Paterson* (1946–1958), a poem in five volumes.

Danse Russe

If when my wife is sleeping
and the baby and Kathleen
are sleeping
and the sun is a flame-white disc
in silken mists   5
above shining trees,—
if I in my north room
dance naked, grotesquely

before my mirror
waving my shirt round my head   10
and singing softly to myself:
"I am lonely, lonely.
I was born to be lonely,
I am best so!"
If I admire my arms, my face,   15
my shoulders, flanks, buttocks
against the yellow drawn shades,—
Who shall say I am not
the happy genius of my household?
                                        (1916)

Questions for Discussion and Writing

1. What does the French phrase *Danse Russe* mean? Why do you think Williams chose that title for this poem?
2. Where is the speaker and what time is it?
3. Why is he dancing naked?

Making Connections

Compare the theme of this poem to the theme of Kate Chopin's "The Story of an Hour" (page 234).

The Red Wheelbarrow

so much depends
upon

a red wheel
barrow

glazed with rain   5
water

beside the white
chickens.
                                        (1923)

Questions for Discussion and Writing

1. Does the poem need to be interpreted, or should readers just enjoy the sharply revealed images?
2. What makes this a poem? Do you consider it a successful one?
3. Write your own "so much depends" passage or poem.

Making Connections

Contrast the images in this poem with those in another poem where the images carry the meaning, like Whitman's "A Noiseless, Patient Spider" (page 419), Sandburg's "Fog" (page 527), or Housman's "Loveliest of Trees" (page 516).

◇◇◇◇◇◇◇◇◇◇◇◇◇◇◇◇◇◇◇◇

D. H. Lawrence   1885–1930

D[avid] H[erbert] Lawrence was a celebrated British poet, novelist, essayist, and short-story writer who regarded sex, the primitive subconscious, and nature as cures for what he saw as the dehumanization of modern society. In 1912, he fell in love with a married woman who abandoned her family to live with him in exile. Lawrence's rebellion against Puritanism and social conventions led to some of the most famous censorship trials of the twentieth century: his novel *Lady Chatterly's Lover* (1928), for example, was banned as pornographic in both the United States and Britain until 1960.

Piano

Softly, in the dusk, a woman is singing to me;
Taking me back down the vista of years, till I see
A child sitting under the piano, in the boom of the tingling strings
And pressing the small, poised feet of a mother who smiles as she sings.

In spite of myself, the insidious mastery of song   5
Betrays me back, till the heart of me weeps to belong
To the old Sunday evenings at home, with winter outside
And hymns in the cozy parlour, the tinkling piano our guide.

So now it is vain for the singer to burst into clamour
With the great black piano appassionato. The glamour   10
Of childish days is upon me, my manhood is cast
Down in the flood of remembrance, I weep like a child for the past.

                                                                              (1918)

Questions for Discussion and Writing

1. Where is the speaker in the first line of the poem? In line 3?
2. Who is the woman in the first line? In line 4?
3. The speaker resists crying because in 1918 it was considered unmanly to weep. Does he try for any other reason to stem "the flood of remembrance"?

Making Connections

Compare the point of view of the young persona in "Piano" with the speaker's viewpoint in Audre Lorde's "Hanging Fire" (page 939).

<><><><><><><><><><><><><><><><>

T. S. Eliot   1888–1965

Born in St. Louis, T(homas) S(tearns) Eliot studied at Harvard and emigrated to London, where he worked as a bank clerk and as an editor. In 1927 he became a British citizen and joined the Church of England. His landmark poem *The Waste Land* (1922) influenced a generation of young poets. As a critic, he revived interest in John Donne and other metaphysical poets. In later years, he wrote verse plays, such as *Murder in the Cathedral* (1935) and *The Cocktail Party* (1950), and won the Nobel Prize for Literature in 1948.

The Love Song of J. Alfred Prufrock

> *S'io credesse che mia risposta fosse*
> *A persona che mai tornasse al mondo,*
> *Questa fiamma staria senza piu scosse.*
> *Ma perciocche giammai di questo fondo*
> *Non torno vivo alcun, s'i'odo il vero,*
> *Senze tema d'infamia ti rispondo.°*

Let us go then, you and I,
When the evening is spread out against the sky
Like a patient etherised upon a table;
Let us go, through certain half-deserted streets,
The muttering retreats   5
Of restless nights in one-night cheap hotels
And sawdust restaurants with oyster-shells:
Streets that follow like a tedious argument
Of insidious intent
To lead you to an overwhelming question…   10
Oh, do not ask, "What is it?"
Let us go and make our visit.

In the room the women come and go
Talking of Michelangelo.

The yellow fog that rubs its back upon the window-panes,   15
The yellow smoke that rubs its muzzle on the window-panes
Licked its tongue into the corners of the evening,

Epigraph: From Dante's *Inferno*—the speech of one dead and damned, Count Guido da Montefe, who thinks his hearer is also going to remain in hell; he offers to tell Dante his story: "If I thought my reply were to someone who could ever return to the world, this flame would waver no more. But since, I'm told, nobody ever escapes from this pit, I'll tell you without fear of ill fame."

Lingered upon the pools that stand in drains,
Let fall upon its back the soot that falls from chimneys,
Slipped by the terrace, made a sudden leap,   20
And seeing that it was a soft October night,
Curled once about the house, and fell asleep.

And indeed there will be time
For the yellow smoke that slides along the street
Rubbing its back upon the window-panes;   25
There will be time, there will be time
To prepare a face to meet the faces that you meet;
There will be time to murder and create,
And time for all the works and days of hands
That lift and drop a question on your plate;   30
Time for you and time for me,
And time yet for a hundred indecisions,
And for a hundred visions and revisions,
Before the taking of a toast and tea.

In the room the women come and go   35
Talking of Michelangelo.

And indeed there will be time
To wonder, "Do I dare? " and, "Do I dare?"
Time to turn back and descend the stair,
With a bald spot in the middle of my hair—   40
(They will say: "How his hair is growing thin!")
My morning coat, my collar mounting firmly to the chin,
My necktie rich and modest, but asserted by a simple pin—
(They will say: "But how his arms and legs are thin!")
Do I dare   45
Disturb the universe?
In a minute there is time
For decisions and revisions which a minute will reverse.

For I have known them all already, known them all—
Have known the evenings, mornings, afternoons,   50
I have measured out my life with coffee spoons;
I know the voices dying with a dying fall
Beneath the music from a farther room.
    So how should I presume?

And I have known the eyes already, known them all—   55
The eyes that fix you in a formulated phrase,
And when I am formulated, sprawling on a pin,
When I am pinned and wriggling on the wall,
Then how should I begin
To spit out all the butt-ends of my days and ways?   60
    And how should I presume?

And I have known the arms already, known them all—
Arms that are braceleted and white and bare
(But in the lamplight, downed with light brown hair!)

Is it perfume from a dress   65
That makes me so digress?
Arms that lie along a table, or wrap about a shawl.
    And should I then presume?
    And how should I begin?

         ....

Shall I say, I have gone at dusk through narrow streets   70
And watched the smoke that rises from the pipes
Of lonely men in shirt-sleeves, leaning out of windows?…
I should have been a pair of ragged claws
Scuttling across the floors of silent seas.

         ....

And the afternoon, the evening, sleeps so peacefully!   75
Smoothed by long fingers,
Asleep…tired…or it malingers,
Stretched on the floor, here beside you and me.
Should I, after tea and cakes and ices,
Have the strength to force the moment to its crisis?   80
But though I have wept and fasted, wept and prayed,
Though I have seen my head (grown slightly bald) brought in upon a
    platter,°
I am no prophet—and here's no great matter;
I have seen the moment of my greatness flicker,
And I have seen the eternal Footman hold my coat, and snicker,   85
And in short, I was afraid.

And would it have been worth it, after all,
After the cups, the marmalade, the tea,
Among the porcelain, among some talk of you and me,
Would it have been worth while,   90
To have bitten off the matter with a smile,
To have squeezed the universe into a ball
To roll it toward some overwhelming question,
To say: "I am Lazarus,°come from the dead,
Come back to tell you all, I shall tell you all"—   95
If one, settling a pillow by her head,
    Should say: "That is not what I meant at all;
    That is not it, at all."
And would it have been worth it, after all,
Would it have been worth while,   100
After the sunsets and the dooryards and the sprinkled streets,
After the novels, after the teacups, after the skirts that trail along the
    floor—
And this, and so much more?—
It is impossible to say just what I mean!
But as if a magic lantern threw the nerves in patterns on a screen: 105

---

82 upon a platter The head of John the Baptist was presented to Salome on a platter. See Matthew 14:1–11.
    94 Lazarus Jesus raised Lazarus from the dead. See John 11:1–41.

Would it have been worth while
If one, settling a pillow or throwing off a shawl,
And turning toward the window, should say:
"That is not it at all,
That is not what I meant, at all." 110

....

No! I am not Prince Hamlet, nor was meant to be;
Am an attendant lord, one that will do
To swell a progress, start a scene or two,
Advise the prince; no doubt, an easy tool,
Deferential, glad to be of use, 115
Politic, cautious, and meticulous;
Full of high sentence, but a bit obtuse;
At times, indeed, almost ridiculous—
Almost, at times, the Fool.

I grow old…I grow old… 120
I shall wear the bottoms of my trousers rolled.

Shall I part my hair behind? Do I dare to eat a peach?
I shall wear white flannel trousers, and walk upon the beach.
I have heard the mermaids singing, each to each.

I do not think that they will sing to me. 125

I have seen them riding seaward on the waves
Combing the white hair of the waves blown back
When the wind blows the water white and black.
We have lingered in the chambers of the sea
By sea-girls wreathed with seaweed red and brown 130
Till human voices wake us, and we drown.

(1917)

Questions for Discussion and Writing

1. Who is speaking in the poem and to whom?
2. What is the situation depicted?
3. What sort of person is J. Alfred Prufrock? Why is he so wary about going to this party? Why does he consider parting his hair behind? What does it mean to measure out one's life with coffee spoons? Why do women make him so nervous? Why does he think he should have been a crab, "Scuttling across the floors of silent seas"? Why does he exaggerate so? Is he right in deciding that he's more like Polonius than Hamlet? Why does he wonder if he dares to eat a peach? Why does he decide the mermaids will not sing to him?

Making Connections

What does J. Alfred Prufrock, the speaker in Eliot's "love song," have in common with the woman described in Walt Whitman's much shorter poem, Section 11 of "Song of Myself" (page 505)?

Edna St. Vincent Millay   1892–1950

Born in Maine and educated at Vassar, Edna St. Vincent Millay moved in 1917 to Greenwich Village and published her first book of poetry, *Renascence and Other Poems*. She won the Pulitzer Prize for *The Harp-Weaver* (1922), a collection of sonnets that deal wittily and flippantly with love. Although Millay became politically involved and used her poetry to speak out for social causes, she is known best for her poems about the bittersweet emotions of love and the brevity of life.

Oh, Oh, You Will Be Sorry for That Word!

Oh, oh, you will be sorry for that word!
Give back my book and take my kiss instead.
Was it my enemy or my friend I heard,
"What a big book for such a little head!"
Come, I will show you now my newest hat,   5
And you may watch me purse my mouth and prink!
Oh, I shall love you still, and all of that.
I never again shall tell you what I think.
I shall be sweet and crafty, soft and sly;
You will not catch me reading any more: 10
I shall be called a wife to pattern by;
And some day when you knock and push the door,
Some sane day, not too bright and not too stormy,
I shall be gone, and you may whistle for me.

(1923)

Questions for Discussion and Writing

1. Why is the speaker in the poem angry?
2. What does she plan to do in response to the insult?
3. In 1923 when the poem was written, what qualities would have been expected of "a wife to pattern by" (line 11)?

Making Connections

Compare and contrast the speaker in this poem to the wife/speaker in Linda Pastan's "Marks" (page 614) or the one in "My Ex-Husband" by Gabriel Spera (page 575). Which wife would you prefer to be or have?

First Fig

My candle burns at both ends;
    It will not last the night;
But ah, my foes, and oh, my friends—
    It gives a lovely light!

(1920)

Questions for Discussion and Writing

1. Explain the metaphor in this little poem.
2. What is the attitude of the speaker? How do you know?
3. Why is the poem called "First Fig"?

Making Connections

Compare this poem to other single-statement poems, like Dickinson's "Faith Is a Fine Invention" (page 508) or Williams's "The Red Wheelbarrow" (page 531).

<><><><><><><><><><><><><>

E. E. Cummings   1894–1962

See page 438 for a biographical note about this author.

in Just-

in Just-
spring   when the world is mud-
luscious the little
lame balloonman

whistles   far   and wee   5

and eddieandbill come
running from marbles and
piracies and it's
spring.

when the world is puddle-wonderful   10

the queer
old balloonman whistles

far   and   wee
and bettyandisbel come dancing

from hop-scotch and jump-rope and   15

it's
spring
and
        the

                goat-footed°   20
balloonMan   whistles
far
and
wee

                                (1923)

---

20 goat-footed The Greek god Pan, portrayed with the body of a man and the legs of a goat.

Questions for Discussion and Writing

1. Why are the children's names run together? What activities is each pair engaged in before heeding the balloonman's whistle? Considering your answers to these questions, what does the poem emphasize about the children?
2. What do you know about the goat-footed god Pan? If you can't place him, look him up. Why is the balloonman described as Pan-like?
3. What is the powerful whistle that makes kids come running from their play? In other words, what is calling "far and wee" to the children? The change in the typography of balloonMan in line 21 may give you a clue.

Making Connections

Compare this poem to "Spring and Fall" by Gerard Manley Hopkins (page 514). How do the two poems view the coming of spring?

pity this busy monster,manunkind

pity this busy monster,manunkind,

not.   Progress is a comfortable disease:
your victim (death and life safely beyond)

plays with the bigness of his littleness
—electrons deify one razorblade   5
into a mountainrange; lenses extend

unwish through curving wherewhen till unwish
return on its unself.
                          A world of made
is not a world of born—pity poor flesh   10

and trees,poor stars and stones, but never this
fine specimen of hypermagical

ultraomnipotence. We doctors know

a hopeless case if—listen:there's a hell
of a good universe next door; let's go   15
                    (1944)

Questions for Discussion and Writing

1. How does the speaker define "Progress"? What extended metaphor is used?
2. Paraphrase the lines "A world of made / is not a world of born." What distinction do these lines stress? Why is that distinction so important?
3. What does the poem suggest about technological advancement? Write a short essay agreeing or disagreeing with the claim.

Making Connections

How do you think the sentiments of this poem match up with those expressed by William Wordsworth in "The World Is Too Much with Us" (page 497)?

◇◇◇◇◇◇◇◇◇◇◇◇◇◇◇◇◇◇◇◇◇◇◇◇◇◇◇◇◇◇◇

Stevie Smith 1902–1971

Born Florence Margaret Smith in Hull, England, Stevie Smith worked as a secretary and occasionally as a writer and broadcaster for the BBC. She began publishing verse, which she often illustrated herself, in the 1930s but did not gain much recognition until 1962, when her *Selected Poems* appeared. Noted for her eccentricity and humor, Smith often aimed her satirical barbs at religion and made unexpected use of traditional hymns, songs, and nursery rhymes in her poems.

Not Waving but Drowning

Nobody heard him, the dead man,
But still he lay moaning:
I was much further out than you thought
And not waving but drowning.

Poor chap, he always loved larking   5
And now he's dead
It must have been too cold for him his heart gave way,
They said.

Oh, no no no, it was too cold always
(Still the dead one lay moaning)   10
I was much too far out all my life
And not waving but drowning.

(1957)

Questions for Discussion and Writing

1. Who are the two speakers in the poem? How does one misunderstand the other?
2. The lines "I was much too far out all my life /And not waving but drowning" are obviously meant to carry more than a literal meaning. What does the dead man mean?
3. In what ways might your outward demeanor be contrary to the "inner you"? Write an essay about how you or someone you know might give a false impression to others.

Making Connections

Compare this poem to another one that employs more than one speaker: "Not My Best Side" by U. A. Fanthorpe (page 472). What does each poet accomplish by using more than a single speaker (persona)? Do you think this multiple-speaker approach is equally effective in these poems?

◇◇◇◇◇◇◇◇◇◇◇◇◇◇◇◇◇◇◇◇◇◇◇

W. H. Auden   1907–1973

See page 403 for a biographical note about this author.

Funeral Blues

Stop all the clocks, cut off the telephone,
Prevent the dog from barking with a juicy bone,
Silence the pianos and with muffled drum
Bring out the coffin, let the mourners come.

Let aeroplanes circle moaning overhead
Scribbling on the sky the message He Is Dead,
Put crepe bows round the white necks of the public doves,
Let the traffic policemen wear black cotton gloves.

He was my North, my South, my East and West,
My working week and my Sunday rest,
My noon, my midnight, my talk, my song;
I thought that love would last for ever: I was wrong.

The stars are not wanted now: put out every one;
Pack up the moon and dismantle the sun;
Pour away the ocean and sweep up the wood;
For nothing now can ever come to any good.

(1936)

Questions for Discussion and Writing

1. What is the name for a poem that mourns and honors someone who has died? Is this one typical of the genre?
2. Do you think the lost lover in this poem is dead or merely departed?
3. What is the tone of the poem? What are your clues?
4. Do you think that the poem is just a parody, or do you think that Auden truly cared for his lost love? What makes you think so?
5. Write an elegy—serious or playful—about a person (or a pet) you loved and lost.

Making Connections

Compare this poem about the reaction to a death with "The Leap" by James Dickey (page 550) or to "'Out, Out—'" by Robert Frost (page 525).

◇◇◇◇◇◇◇◇◇◇◇◇◇◇◇◇◇◇◇◇◇

Elizabeth Bishop   1911–1979

Elizabeth Bishop was born in Massachusetts. Her father died when she was a baby and her mother was committed as insane when Elizabeth was five; she was raised by relatives in New England and Nova Scotia. Educated at Vassar, she lived mainly in Key West and in Brazil. Bishop's poetry, known for its understanding of the natural world, often provides meticulously detailed descriptions that focus on external reality. Her first book, *North & South*, was published in 1946; collected with her second book, *Cold Spring*, it won the 1955 Pulitzer Prize.

One Art

The art of losing isn't hard to master;
so many things seem filled with the intent
to be lost that their loss is no disaster.

Lose something every day. Accept the fluster
of lost door keys, the hour badly spent.   5
The art of losing isn't hard to master.

Then practice losing farther, losing faster:
places, and names, and where it was you meant
to travel. None of these will bring disaster.

I lost my mother's watch. And look! my last, or   10
next-to-last, of three loved houses went.
The art of losing isn't hard to master.

I lost two cities, lovely ones. And, vaster,
some realms I owned, two rivers, a continent.
I miss them, but it wasn't a disaster.   15

—Even losing you (the joking voice, a gesture
I love) I shan't have lied. It's evident
the art of losing's not too hard to master
though it may look like (*Write it!*) like disaster.
                                        (1976)

Questions for Discussion and Writing

1. What is the form of this poem? What effect does the repetition have on the tone and point of the poem?

2. What experiences does the poem relate?
3. What kinds of loss does the speaker mention?
4. Is losing an art? Is it really "easy"? How does one "master" it? Has the speaker mastered it?

Making Connections

Compare this poem to Dylan Thomas's "Do Not Go Gentle into That Good Night" (page 549), another villanelle.

◇◇◇◇◇◇◇◇◇◇◇◇◇◇◇◇◇◇◇◇◇◇

Karl Shapiro   1913–2000

Karl Shapiro believed that poems should convey not just ideas but "what ideas feel like—ideas on Sunday, thoughts on vacation." His poetry captures the authenticity of everyday experience rather than abstract philosophy. Without ever finishing a college degree, he won the Pulitzer Prize in 1944 for a collection of poems he wrote during his army service in World War II. Shapiro taught at several universities but remarked, "I have a sort of special status around English departments—I'm not really a professor, but sort of a mad guest."

Auto Wreck

Its quick soft silver bell beating, beating,
And down the dark one ruby flare
Pulsing out red light like an artery,
The ambulance at top speed floating down
Past beacons and illuminated clocks   5
Wings in a heavy curve, dips down,
And brakes speed, entering the crowd.
The doors leap open, emptying light;
Stretchers are laid out, the mangled lifted
And stowed into the little hospital.   10
Then the bell, breaking the hush, tolls once,
And the ambulance with its terrible cargo
Rocking, slightly rocking, moves away,
As the doors, an afterthought, are closed.

We are deranged, walking among the cops   15
Who sweep glass and are large and composed.
One is still making notes under the light.
One with a bucket douches ponds of blood
Into the street and gutter.
One hangs lanterns on the wrecks that cling,   20
Empty husks of locusts, to iron poles.

Our throats were tight as tourniquets,
Our feet were bound with splints, but now,
Like convalescents intimate and gauche,
We speak through sickly smiles and warn   25
With the stubborn saw of common sense,
The grim joke and the banal resolution.
The traffic moves around with care,
But we remain, touching a wound
That opens to our richest horror.   30

Already old, the question Who shall die?
Becomes unspoken Who is innocent?
For death in war is done by hands;
Suicide has cause and stillbirth, logic;
And cancer, simple as a flower, blooms.   35
But this invites the occult mind,
Cancels our physics with sneer,
And spatters all we knew of denouement
Across the expedient and wicked stones.
                                        (1942)

Questions for Discussion and Writing

1. In what ways is an auto wreck an unusual subject for a poem? In what ways is the poem a conventional one?
2. Who is the "we" in the poem? How does witnessing the auto wreck affect them?
3. Point out images that appeal to senses other than sight.

Making Connections

Compare this poem to Sharon Olds's "The Death of Marilyn Monroe" (page 562). How do the poets use reaction to a disaster as the basis for their poetic themes?

◇◇◇◇◇◇◇◇◇◇◇◇◇◇◇◇◇◇◇◇◇◇

Octavio Paz 1914–1998

The first Mexican to be awarded the Nobel Prize for Literature (1990), Octavio Paz was born in Mexico City, the son and grandson of prominent political activists. For twenty years, Paz served as a diplomat for the Mexican government with posts in New York, Paris, India, and Japan. In 1968, however, he resigned from the diplomatic service in protest against the government's violent suppression of the student demonstrations during the Olympic Games in Mexico. After that, Paz worked as an editor and publisher, founding two important magazines dedicated to the arts and politics. In 1980, he was named honorary doctor at Harvard University.

The Street

Translated by Muriel Rukeyser

A long silent street.
I walk in blackness and I stumble and fall
and rise, and I walk blind, my feet
stepping on silent stones and dry leaves.
Someone behind me also stepping on stones, leaves: 5
if I slow down, he slows;
if I run, he runs. I turn: nobody.
Everything dark and doorless.
Turning and turning among these corners
which lead forever to the street   10
where nobody waits for, nobody follows me,
where I pursue a man who stumbles
and rises and says when he sees me: nobody.

(1963)

Questions for Discussion and Writing

1. Reread the first four lines of the poem. What is familiar about this scene? How does it make you feel?
2. What are the main sensory appeals of the poem? List the words that carry this appeal.
3. Why do you think the leaves are dry rather than wet? What about the choice of the word "doorless" in line 8?

Making Connections

Consider the extended metaphors in this poem and in Hayden Carruth's "In the Long Hall" (page 421). What do the poems suggest about the meaning of life?

◇◇◇◇◇◇◇◇◇◇◇◇◇◇◇◇◇◇◇◇◇◇

Dudley Randall   1914–2000

Dudley Randall was born in Washington, D.C., and graduated from Wayne State and the University of Michigan, where he earned degrees in English and library science. In 1969 he became librarian and poet-in-residence at the University of Detroit. A pioneer in the movement to publish the work of African-American writers, Randall founded Broadside Press, one of the most influential small publishing houses in America. Collections of his work include *Cities Burning* (1968), *More to Remember* (1971), *After the Killing* (1973), and *A Litany of Friends* (1981).

Ballad of Birmingham

"Mother dear, may I go downtown
instead of out to play,
and march the streets of Birmingham
in a Freedom March today?"

"No, baby, no, you may not go,   5
for the dogs are fierce and wild,
and clubs and hoses, guns and jails
aren't good for a little child."

"But, mother, I won't be alone.
Other children will go with me,   10
and march the streets of Birmingham
to make our country free."

"No, baby, no, you may not go,
for I fear those guns will fire.
But you may go to church instead   15
and sing in the children's choir."

She has combed and brushed her night-dark hair,
and bathed rose petal sweet,
and drawn white gloves on her small brown hands,
and white shoes on her feet.   20

The mother smiled to know her child
was in the sacred place,
but that smile was the last smile
to come upon her face.

For when she heard the explosion,   25
her eyes grew wet and wild.
She raced through the street of Birmingham
calling for her child.

She clawed through bits of glass and brick,
then lifted out a shoe.   30
"O, here is the shoe my baby wore,
but, baby, where are you?"

                                        (1964)

Questions for Discussion and Writing

1. Explain the situational irony that is present in this poem.
2. Look up the conventions of a traditional ballad. Which ones does this poem employ? And how does it differ from the traditional form?
3. Find out about the actual incident that inspired this poem. How well does Randall's treatment of the events capture the emotions of the situation?
4. Try your hand at writing a ballad about a memorable event during your lifetime.

Making Connections

Occasional poetry is written to mark or commemorate some particular occasion or event. In what ways is the "Ballad of Birmingham" an "occasional poem"? How does it compare with "The Death of Marilyn Monroe" by Sharon Olds (page 562) or "Funeral Blues" by W. H. Auden (page 541)?

To the Mercy Killers

If ever mercy move you murder me,
I pray you, kindly killers, let me live.
Never conspire with death to set me free,
but let me know such life as pain can give.
Even though I be a clot, an aching clench,   5
a stub, a stump, a butt, a scab, a knob,
a screaming pain, a putrefying stench,
still let me live, so long as life shall throb.
Even though I turn such traitor to myself
as beg to die, do not accomplice me.   10
Even though I seem not human, a mute shelf
of glucose, bottled blood, machinery
to swell the lung and pump the heart—even so,
do not put out my life. Let me still glow.

                                                (1973)

Questions for Discussion and Writing

1. Point out the ironic word choice in the first two lines of the poem.
2. Why does the speaker want to be allowed to live even when enduring the horrors he describes? Do you agree with his position?
3. What is the implied comparison in the last line?
4. Write a short response in which you agree or disagree with the poem's main argument.

Making Connections

In what ways is the theme of this poem similar to the one expressed in "Do Not Go Gentle into That Good Night" by Dylan Thomas (page 549)?

◇◇◇◇◇◇◇◇◇◇◇◇◇◇◇◇◇◇◇◇◇◇◇◇

William Stafford   1914–1993

As a boy growing up in Kansas during the great depression, William Stafford helped support his family working in sugar beet fields, growing vegetables, and delivering papers. He was of a gentle nature, so during World War II he became a conscientious objector, refusing to be drafted, and spent the war years in work camps doing soil conservation, fighting fires, and building roads. After the war, he taught for many years at Lewis and Clark College in Portland, Oregon. Stafford said of his own writing, "I have woven a parachute out of everything broken."

Traveling Through the Dark

Traveling through the dark I found a deer
dead on the edge of the Wilson River road.
It is usually best to roll them into the canyon:
that road is narrow; to swerve might make more dead.
By glow of the tail-light I stumbled back of the car   5
and stood by the heap, a doe, a recent killing;
she had stiffened already, almost cold.
I dragged her off; she was large in the belly.

My fingers touching her side brought me the reason—
her side was warm; her fawn lay there waiting,   10
alive, still, never to be born.
Beside that mountain road I hesitated.
The car aimed ahead its lowered parking lights;
under the hood purred the steady engine.
I stood in the glare of the warm exhaust turning red;   15
around our group I could hear the wilderness listen.
I thought hard for us all—my only swerving—,
then pushed her over the edge into the river.

(1957)

Questions for Discussion and Writing

1. Brainstorm about possible interpretations of the poem's title.
2. Why does the speaker roll the dead deer into the canyon? Does the doe's pregnancy make any difference?
3. The poem includes vivid details about the speaker's car. How do they add to your understanding of the poem as a whole?
4. Look carefully at the last stanza. What do you think the speaker "thought hard" about? Who are "us all"? Why does he call his thought "my only swerving"?

Making Connections

How does the speaker's attitude toward the deer in this poem compare to the feelings about killing the woodchucks in Maxine Kumin's poem (page 552)?

◇◇◇◇◇◇◇◇◇◇◇◇◇◇◇◇◇◇◇◇◇◇◇

Dylan Thomas   1914–1953

Dylan Thomas was born in Wales. Shunning school to pursue a writing career, he published his first book of poetry at age twenty. Limited by his lack of a degree, he had trouble making a living as a writer, and his early life was marked by poverty and heavy drinking. Calling his poetry a "record of my struggle from darkness towards some measure of light," Thomas delighted in sound, sometimes at the expense of sense.

Do Not Go Gentle into That Good Night

Do not go gentle into that good night,
Old age should burn and rave at close of day;
Rage, rage against the dying of the light.

Though wise men at their end know dark is right,
Because their words had forked no lightning they   5
Do not go gentle into that good night.

Good men, the last wave by, crying how bright
Their frail deeds might have danced in a green bay,
Rage, rage against the dying of the light.

Wild men who caught and sang the sun in flight,   10
And learn, too late, they grieved it on its way,
Do not go gentle into that good night.

Grave men, near death, who see with blinding sight
Blind eyes could blaze like meteors and be gay,
Rage, rage against the dying of the light.   15

And you, my father, there on the sad height,
Curse, bless, me now with your fierce tears, I pray.
Do not go gentle into that good night.
Rage, rage against the dying of the light.

(1952)

Questions for Discussion and Writing

1. What do the repeated images "that good night" and "dying of the light" stand for?
2. What repeated pattern can you see in stanzas two through five? What kinds of people are described in these stanzas?
3. Explain the seeming contradiction in line 17.

Making Connections

Compare the speaker's feelings about death in this poem to the ones expressed by the speakers in Housman's "To an Athlete Dying Young" (page 515) and/or Randall's "To the Mercy Killers" (page 547).

James Dickey 1923–1997

James Dickey was born in Atlanta, played football in college, served in the Army Air Force in World War II, worked in advertising, taught at several universities, and was poet-in-residence at the University of South Carolina. Dickey's poems are usually wedded to personal incidents and project an almost demonic view of life. His several volumes of poetry include *Buckdancer's Choice* (1965), winner of the National Book Award. He also wrote the best-selling novel *Deliverance* (1970).

The Leap

The only thing I have of Jane MacNaughton
Is one instant of a dancing-class dance.
She was the fastest runner in the seventh grade,
My scrapbook says, even when boys were beginning
To be as big as the girls,   5
But I do not have her running in my mind,
Though Frances Lane is there, Agnes Fraser,
Fat Betty Lou Black in the boys-against-girls
Relays we ran at recess: she must have run

Like the other girls, with her skirts tucked up   10
So they would be like bloomers,
But I cannot tell; that part of her is gone.
What I do have is when she came,
With the hem of her skirt where it should be
For a young lady, into the annual dance   15
Of the dancing class we all hated, and with a light
Grave leap, jumped up and touched the end
Of one of the paper-ring decorations

To see if she could touch it. She could.
And reached me now as well, hanging in my mind   20
From a brown chain of brittle paper, thin
And muscular, wide-mouthed, eager to prove
Whatever it proves when you leap
In a new dress, a new womanhood, among the boys
Whom you easily left in the dust   25
Of the passionless playground. If I said I saw
In the paper where Jane MacNaughton Hill,

Mother of four, leapt to her death from a window
Of a downtown hotel, and that her body crushed-in
The top of a parked taxi, and that I held   30
Without trembling a picture of her cradled
In that papery steel as though lying in the grass,
One shoe idly off, arms folded across her breast,
I would not believe myself. I would say

The convenient thing, that it was a bad dream   35
Of maturity, to see that eternal process
Most obsessively wrong with the world
Come out of her light, earth-spurning feet
Grown heavy: would say that in the dusty heels
Of the playground some boy who did not depend   40
On speed of foot, caught and betrayed her.
Jane, stay where you are in my first mind:
It was odd in that school, at that dance.
I and the other slow-footed yokels sat in corners
Cutting rings out of drawing paper   45

Before you leapt in your new dress
And touched the end of something I began,
Above the couples struggling on the floor,
New men and women clutching at each other
And prancing foolishly as bears: hold on   50
To that ring I made for you, Jane—
My feet are nailed to the ground
By dust I swallowed thirty years ago—
While I examine my hands.

                                        (1967)

Questions for Discussion and Writing

1. What does the title of the poem mean?
2. What happens to boys and girls around seventh grade? What images show that the narrator here is aware of the significance of the time his memory reconstructs?
3. What is the "eternal process / Most obsessively wrong with the world"? What does the narrator think happened to Jane? What personal meaning does her suicide hold for him?

Making Connections

How do the speaker's feelings about Jane MacNaughton's death compare to the feelings expressed by the speaker in Auden's "Funeral Blues" (page 541)?

◇◇◇◇◇◇◇◇◇◇◇◇◇◇◇◇◇◇◇

Lisel Mueller   1924–

See page 467 for a biographical note about this poet.

Losing My Sight

I never knew that by August
the birds are practically silent,

only a twitter here and there.
Now I notice. Last spring
their noisiness taught me the difference   5
between screamers and whistlers and cooers
and O, the coloraturas.
I have already mastered
the subtlest pitches in our cat's
elegant Chinese. As the river   10
turns muddier before my eyes,
its sighs and little smacks
grow louder. Like a spy,
I pick up things indiscriminately:
the long approach of a truck,   15
car doors slammed in the dark,
the night life of animals—shrieks and hisses,
sex and plunder in the garage.
Tonight the crickets spread static
across the air, a continuous rope   20
of sound extended to me,
the perfect listener.

                                                    (1996)

Questions for Discussion and Writing

1. Why does the speaker in this poem call herself "the perfect listener"?
2. List at least five images of sound in this poem. Which ones do you find most striking and evocative?
3. How does the speaker feel about losing her sight? Do you think you would feel the same way?
4. Spend some time sitting somewhere with your eyes closed. Then write a description of the sounds you heard. You can begin by making a list of the different sounds, then turn them into a poem or poetic description, using metaphors and similes to re-create the auditory images.

Making Connections

How does Mueller's use of images in this poem compare in tone and purpose to the way Dudley Randall uses images in "To the Mercy Killers" (page 547)?

◇◇◇◇◇◇◇◇◇◇◇◇◇◇◇◇◇◇◇◇◇◇

Maxine Kumin   1925–2014

When Maxine Kumin was in college, an instructor wrote this comment about her poetry: "Say it with flowers, but for God's sake don't try to write poems." So she didn't for a long time. But in her thirties, during her third pregnancy, she took up writing poetry again. "The grit of discontent, the acute misery of early and uninformed motherhood," she said, "worked under my skin to force out the writer."

Kumin likes to write about what she calls "small overlooked things" and bring them "back to the world's attention." She won a Pulitzer Prize for *Up Country* (1972), poems inspired by her New Hampshire farm.

Woodchucks

Gassing the woodchucks didn't turn out right.
The knockout bomb from the Feed and Grain Exchange
was featured as merciful, quick at the bone
and the case we had against them was airtight,
both exits shoehorned shut with puddingstone,   5
but they had a sub-sub-basement out of range.

Next morning they turned up again, no worse
for the cyanide than we for our cigarettes
and state-store Scotch, all of us up to scratch.
They brought down the marigolds as a matter of course   10
and then took over the vegetable patch
nipping the broccoli shoots, beheading the carrots.

The food from our mouths, I said, righteously thrilling
to the feel of the .22, the bullets' neat noses.
I, a lapsed pacifist fallen from grace   15
puffed with Darwinian pieties for killing,
now drew a bead on the littlest woodchuck's face.
He died down in the everbearing roses.

Ten minutes later I dropped the mother. She
flipflopped in the air and fell, her needle teeth   20
still hooked in a leaf of early Swiss chard.
Another baby next. O one-two-three
the murderer inside me rose up hard,
the hawkeye killer came on stage forthwith.

There's one chuck left. Old wily fellow, he keeps   25
me cocked and ready day after day after day.
All night I hunt his humped-up form. I dream
I sight along the barrel in my sleep.
If only they'd all consented to die unseen
gassed underground the quiet Nazi way.   30

(1972)

Questions for Discussion and Writing

1. What kind of person is the speaker of the poem before she starts shooting woodchucks? What details let you know?
2. What side of her does the killing bring out? How is the order of the killings significant?
3. Why does the speaker assert that it would be better if the woodchucks had "consented to die unseen"?

Making Connections

Compare the attitude toward animals implied in this poem with the ones expressed in Stafford's "Traveling Through the Dark" (page 547) or Ryan's "Turtle" (page 420).

◇◇◇◇◇◇◇◇◇◇◇◇◇◇◇◇◇◇◇◇◇◇◇◇◇◇◇

Frank O'Hara   1926–1966

Francis Russell O'Hara was born in Baltimore, Maryland. While growing up, he studied to be a concert pianist. But after high school, he enlisted in the U.S. Navy and served on a destroyer during World War II. He then went to Harvard on the GI Bill, first majoring in music but changing to English. After studying comparative literature at the University of Michigan, he moved to New York, where he became associated with the city's art community. He began working at Museum of Modern Art at the front desk selling souvenirs, but eventually became an associate curator of painting and sculpture. O'Hara sought to capture the immediacy of life in his verse, which he once described as "I do this, I do that" poetry because his poems often sound like entries in a diary.

Having a Coke with You

is even more fun than going to San Sebastian, Irún, Hendaye, Biarritz, Bayonne
or being sick to my stomach on the Travesera de Gracia in Barcelona
partly because in your orange shirt you look like a better happier St. Sebastian
partly because of my love for you, partly because of your love for yoghurt
partly because of the fluorescent orange tulips around the birches   5
partly because of the secrecy our smiles take on before people and statuary
it is hard to believe when I'm with you that there can be anything as still
as solemn as unpleasantly definitive as statuary when right in front of it
in the warm New York 4 o'clock light we are drifting back and forth
between each other like a tree breathing through its spectacles   10
and the portrait show seems to have no faces in it at all, just paint
you suddenly wonder why in the world anyone ever did them
I look
at you and I would rather look at you than all the portraits in the world
except possibly for the Polish Rider occasionally and anyway it's in the Frick   15
which thank heavens you haven't gone to yet so we can go together the first
    time
and the fact that you move so beautifully more or less takes care of Futurism
just as at home I never think of the Nude Descending a Staircase or
at a rehearsal a single drawing of Leonardo or Michelangelo that used to wow me
and what good does all the research of the Impressionists do them   20
when they never got the right person to stand near the tree when the sun sank
or for that matter Marino Marini when he didn't pick the rider as carefully
as the horse

it seems they were all cheated of some marvelous experience
which is not going to go wasted on me which is why I am telling you about it   25
                                                                                                                 (1958)

Questions for Discussion and Writing

1. Suggest three adjectives to describe the tone of this poem.
2. What is unusual and unconventional about the style and form of the poem? What makes it poetry?
3. How many of the references to places and works of art do you know? Do you need to know them to understand the poem?
4. How would you feel if you were the "you" in this poem? Write a response to the speaker, either in verse or prose.
5. O'Hara said that poetry should be "between two persons instead of two pages." Write an essay discussing how this poem accomplishes that aim.

Making Connections

Compare the form and style of this poem to the poetry of E. E. Cummings (pages 538–39). Which do you prefer?

◇◇◇◇◇◇◇◇◇◇◇◇◇◇◇◇◇◇◇◇◇◇◇

David Wagoner   1926–

David Wagoner was born in Ohio, raised in Indiana, went to college in Pennsylvania and to graduate school in Indiana. In 1954 he moved to the Pacific Northwest, where he remained, first teaching at the University of Washington and then in the MFA program at the Northwest Institute of Literary Arts on Whidbey Island. Wagoner has written eighteen books of poetry and ten novels, one of which, *The Escape Artist*, was made into a movie in 1982. The natural environment of the coastal rain forest of the West Coast is the subject of much of Wagoner's poetry.

The Escaped Gorilla

When he walked out in the park that early evening
just before closing time, he didn't take
the nearest blonde in one arm and climb a tree
to wait for the camera crews. He didn't savage
anyone in uniform, upend cars   5
or beat his chest or scream, and nobody screamed
when they found him hiding behind the holly hedge
by the zoo office where he waited for someone

to take him by the hand and walk with him
around two corners and along a pathway   10
through the one door that wasn't supposed to be open

> and back to the oblong place with the hard sky
> where all of his unbreakable toys were waiting
> to be broken, with the wall he could see through,
> but not as far as the place he almost remembered,   15
> which was too far away to be anywhere.
>
> (2008)

Questions for Discussion and Writing

1. What allusion does the poet make in the first six lines? Why doesn't the go-rilla in the poem act this way? What has happened to him?
2. Why are the details of the walk, the pathway, the door, the "oblong place," and the wall included? What point do they make?
3. Where is "the place he almost remembered"? Why is it "too far away to be anywhere"?
4. In the end, how do you feel about the gorilla? Write a brief reflective essay about your understanding of the poem and your emotional reactions to it.

Making Connections

Compare the attitude toward the gorilla in this poem to the attitudes toward animals in other poems: Kumin's "Woodchucks" (page 552), Stafford's "Traveling Through the Dark" (page 547), and Ryan's "Turtle" (page 420).

◇◇◇◇◇◇◇◇◇◇◇◇◇◇◇◇◇◇◇◇◇◇

Anne Sexton   1928–1974

See page 479 for a biographical note about this poet.

You All Know the Story of the Other Woman

> It's a little Walden.
> She is private in her breathbed
> as his body takes off and flies,
> flies straight as an arrow.
> But it's a bad translation.   5
> Daylight is nobody's friend.
> God comes in like a landlord
> and flashes on his brassy lamp.
> Now she is just so-so.
> He puts his bones back on,   10
> turning the clock back an hour.
> She knows flesh, that skin balloon,
> the unbound limbs, the boards,
> the roof, the removable roof.

She is his selection, part time.   15
You know the story too! Look,
when it is over he places her,
like a phone, back on the hook.
                                                                (1967)

Questions for Discussion and Writing

1. Concentrate on the title. Do you all know the story of the other woman?
   What is "the conventional wisdom" about what happens to the other woman?
2. This poem depends on metaphors and similes for its meaning. Identify and
   explain five of them. Why does the last simile make the point unmistakable?
3. How does the man behave after he has had sex with the woman? Write a
   paraphrase of lines 6 through 14.

Making Connections

Does this poem complement or contradict Sharon Olds's "Sex Without Love"
(page 561)?

Adrienne Rich   1929–2012

Born in Baltimore, Adrienne Rich graduated from Radcliffe College in 1951,
the same year that her first book of poetry, *A Change in the World*, appeared in the
Yale Series of Younger Poets. The Vietnam War and her teaching experience with
minority youth in New York City heightened Rich's political awareness, and she
became increasingly involved in the women's movement. Her poetry collection
Diving into the Wreck (1973) won the National Book Award.

Aunt Jennifer's Tigers

Aunt Jennifer's tigers prance across a screen,
Bright topaz denizens of a world of green.
They do not fear the men beneath the tree;
They pace in sleek chivalric certainty.

Aunt Jennifer's fingers fluttering through her wool   5
Find even the ivory needle hard to pull.
The massive weight of Uncle's wedding band
Sits heavily upon Aunt Jennifer's hand.

When Aunt is dead, her terrified hands will lie
Still ringed with ordeals she was mastered by.   10
The tigers in the panel that she made
Will go on prancing, proud and unafraid.
                                                                (1951)

Questions for Discussion and Writing

1. What human traits do the tigers possess? What kind of life do they lead? What does "prancing" suggest?
2. What kind of life does Aunt Jennifer lead? How do the tigers help you to understand her plight? Why might she have chosen them for her tapestry?
3. What does Aunt Jennifer's wedding band symbolize? What is a wedding ring supposed to symbolize?
4. One critic says that the speaker in the poem is "almost callous in her disregard for Aunt's death," that the speaker cares more for the gorgeous tigers than for Aunt Jennifer. Argue your response to this interpretation.

Making Connections

How is the symbolic meaning of Aunt Jennifer's tigers related to "The Tyger" by William Blake (page 495)?

◇◇◇◇◇◇◇◇◇◇◇◇◇◇◇◇◇◇◇◇◇◇◇◇◇

Ruth Fainlight   1931–

Born in New York City, Ruth Fainlight moved to England at age fifteen and is considered a British poet. She has published thirteen collections of poems, some translated into Portuguese, French, and Spanish. In an unusual application of poetic skill, she has also written the libretti (the words) for several operas. In an interview Fainlight said, "When students or young poets proudly tell me that they do not work on their poems because they do not want to lose the first inspiration,...I try to explain that to make a poem sound simple and inevitable requires a great deal of time, thought, knowledge, and effort."

Flower Feet

Silk Shoes in the Whitworth Museum, Manchester, England

Real women's feet wore these objects
that look like toys or spectacle cases stitched
from bands of coral, jade, and apricot silk
embroidered with twined sprays of flowers.
Those hearts, tongues, crescents, and disks, leather   5
shapes an inch across, are the soles of shoes
no wider or longer than the span of my ankle.
If the feet had been cut off and the raw stumps
thrust inside the opening, surely
it could not hurt more than broken toes, twisted   10
back and bandaged tight. An old woman,
leaning on a cane outside her door
in a Chinese village, smiled to tell how

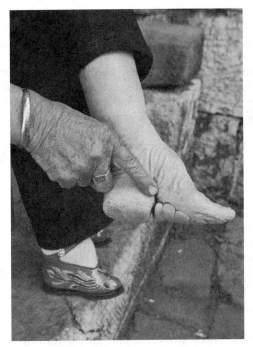

Feet were bound by breaking bones in four small toes and
forcing them to grow underneath.

she fought and cried, how when she stood on points
of pain that gnawed like fire, nurse and mother   15
praised her tottering walk on flower feet.
Her friends nodded, glad the times had changed.
Otherwise, they would have crippled their daughters.
(1989)

Questions for Discussion and Writing

1. Where is the narrator standing as she describes the shoes? Why is this setting
   important to understanding the poem?
2. Compare the imagery of the first stanza with the imagery of the second
   stanza. What contrast is emphasized by the difference in imagery?
3. What comment on the power of culture is made in the last two lines?
4. Look up historical information on Chinese foot-binding and write an informative short essay that would help other readers understand the poem.

Making Connections

How is the message of this poem similar to the point about female attractiveness
that Marge Piercy makes in "Barbie Doll" (page 560)?

Marge Piercy   1936–

Marge Piercy was born in Detroit, Michigan. Concerned with depicting and dignifying women's experiences, Piercy has been accused of politicizing her work. In the introduction to her book of poetry *Circles on the Water* (1982), she explains how her writing can be "of use" to women: "To find ourselves spoken for in art gives dignity to our pain, our anger, our lust, our losses." Among her popular novels are *Small Changes* (1973), *Woman on the Edge of Time* (1976), and *Gone to Soldiers* (1987).

Barbie Doll

This girlchild was born as usual
and presented dolls that did pee-pee
and miniature GE stoves and irons
and wee lipsticks the color of cherry candy.
Then in the magic of puberty, a classmate said: 5
You have a great big nose and fat legs.

She was healthy, tested intelligent,
possessed strong arms and back,
abundant sexual drive and manual dexterity.
She went to and fro apologizing.   10
Everyone saw a fat nose on thick legs.

She was advised to play coy,
exhorted to come on hearty,
exercise, diet, smile and wheedle.
Her good nature wore out   15
like a fan belt.
So she cut off her nose and her legs
and offered them up.

In the casket displayed on satin she lay
with the undertaker's cosmetics painted on,   20
a turned-up putty nose,
dressed in a pink and white nightie.
Doesn's she look pretty? everyone said.
Consummation at last.
To every woman a happy ending.   25

(1973)

Questions for Discussion and Writing

1. What led to the suicide in the poem? In what way is it a happy ending?
2. Why is the poem titled "Barbie Doll"? What qualities do you associate with Barbie?
3. This poem was written in 1973. Do you think its view of female socialization is still relevant today? Write a paper arguing your answer to this question.

Making Connections

Compare the issues about beauty and identity raised in this poem with those that Jane Martin explores in the play *Beauty* (page 879).

◇◇◇◇◇◇◇◇◇◇◇◇◇◇◇◇◇◇◇◇

Sharon Olds 1942–

Sharon Olds, born in San Francisco and educated at Stanford University, is the author of several books of poetry. Because of her intense focus on family and sexual relationships, she is often compared to confessional poets Sylvia Plath and Anne Sexton. Olds teaches creative writing at New York University and at the Goldwater Hospital, a facility for the physically disabled. A review of her book *The Unswept Room* (2002) calls her poetry "fiery, penetrating, and unnerving."

Sex Without Love

How do they do it, the ones who make love
without love? Beautiful as dancers,
gliding over each other like ice-skaters
over the ice, fingers hooked
inside each other's bodies, faces   5
red as steak, wine, wet as the
children at birth whose mothers are going to
give them away. How do they come to the
come to the   come to the   God   come to the
still waters, and not love   10
the one who came there with them, light
rising slowly as steam off their joined
skin? These are the true religious,
the purists, the pros, the ones who will not
accept a false Messiah, love the   15
priest instead of the God. They do not
mistake the lover for their own pleasure,
they are like great runners: they know they are alone
with the road surface, the cold, the wind,
the fit of their shoes, their over-all cardio-   20
vascular health—just factors, like the partner
in the bed, and not the truth, which is the
single body alone in the universe
against its own best time.

(1984)

Questions for Discussion and Writing

1. What other kinds of people are those who have sex without love compared with? Would you call these comparisons positive, negative, or mixed?

2. What do you think is the speaker's attitude toward people who have sex without love? What in the poem contributes to your opinion?
3. What ideas about love and sex are challenged in this poem?

Making Connections

Compare this poem with John Donne's "A Valediction: Forbidding Mourning" (page 491). How does Donne's distinction between earthly and spiritual love parallel Olds's views?

The Death of Marilyn Monroe

The ambulance men touched her cold
body, lifted it, heavy as iron,
onto the stretcher, tried to close the
mouth, closed the eyes, tied the
arms to the sides, moved a caught   5
strand of hair, as if it mattered,
saw the shape of her breasts, flattened by
gravity, under the sheet,
carried her, as if it were she,
down the steps.   10

These men were never the same. They went out
afterwards, as they always did,
for a drink or two, but they could not meet
each other's eyes.
                        Their lives took   15
a turn—one had nightmares, strange
pains, impotence, depression. One did not
like his work, his wife looked
different, his kids. Even death
seemed different to him—a place where she   20
would be waiting,

and one found himself standing at night
in the doorway to a room of sleep, listening to a
woman breathing, just an ordinary
woman   25
breathing.

                                        (1983)

Questions for Discussion and Writing

1. In the first stanza, why does the poet choose the specific physical details of Marilyn's body?
2. How would the ambulance carry her "as if it were she" (line 9)? Is it not "she"? Why would they carry her this way, knowing she is dead?

3. Why do you think the men always went out for a drink or two after their duties? What purpose did this routine serve?

4. How did the men respond to their experience? Write a paper explaining what the various responses to this unusual experience represent. In particular, consider the last man described. Why is the woman he listens to called "ordinary"?

Making Connections

Relate the themes or issues in this poem to those expressed by Marge Piercy in "Barbie Doll" (page 560). Do you think Piercy would agree with the way Olds depicts Marilyn Monroe?

◇◇◇◇◇◇◇◇◇◇◇◇◇◇◇◇◇◇◇◇◇◇

Edward Hirsch 1950–

Edward Hirsch was born in Chicago. When he was eight years old, he "wandered down to the basement of our house to pick through some of my grandfather's forgotten books" and read a verse (by Emily Bronte) that captivated him. It was the beginning of a lifelong love affair with poetry, which he explored at Grinnell College and the University of Pennsylvania, where he received a Ph.D. in folklore. His book *How to Read a Poem and Fall in Love with Poetry* was a surprise bestseller in 1999 and remains in print today.

Execution

The last time I saw my high school football coach
He had cancer stenciled into his face
Like pencil marks from the sun, like intricate
Drawings on the chalkboard, small x's and o's
That he copied down in a neat numerical hand   5
Before practice in the morning. By day's end
The board was a spiderweb of options and counters,
Blasts and sweeps, a constellation of players
Shining under his favorite word, Execution,
Underlined in the upper right-hand corner of things.   10
He believed in football like a new religion
And had perfect unquestioning faith in the fundamentals
Of blocking and tackling, the idea of warfare
Without suffering or death, the concept of teammates
Moving in harmony like the planets—and yet   15
Our awkward adolescent bodies were always canceling
The flawless beauty of Saturday afternoons in September,
Falling away from the particular grace of autumn,
The clear weather, the ideal game he imagined.
And so he drove us through punishing drills   20
On weekday afternoons, and doubled our practice time,

And challenged us to hammer him with forearms,
And devised elaborate, last-second plays—a flea-
Flicker, a triple reverse—to save us from defeat.
Almost always they worked. He despised losing　　　　　　25
And loved winning more than his own body, maybe even
More than himself. But the last time I saw him
He looked wobbly and stunned by illness,
And I remembered the game in my senior year
When we met a downstate team who loved hitting　　　　　30
More than we did, who battered us all afternoon
With a vengeance, who destroyed us with timing
And power, with deadly, impersonal authority,
Machine-like fury, perfect execution.

(1989)

Questions for Discussion and Writing

1. How does the coach feel about football? What comparisons does the speaker use to describe the coach's feelings?
2. What is the significance of the game with the downstate team (lines 29–34)? Why did the speaker remember that game the last time he saw the coach?
3. What do you think of the lines "He despised losing / And loved winning more than his own body"? What is the speaker implying?
4. What is the speaker's attitude toward his coach? Do you think he likes or admires him? Write a paper arguing your position on this issue.
5. Explain the ironies that you find in this poem. Start with the title.

Making Connections

Compare the situation of the coach in this poem with that of the dispirited young man in Updike's "Ex-Basketball Player" (page 591).

◇◇◇◇◇◇◇◇◇◇◇◇◇◇◇◇◇◇◇◇◇◇◇

Jimmy Santiago Baca　1952–

Jimmy Santiago Baca endured a family life shattered by matricide, a childhood in a state orphanage, and years in a state prison for supposed drug crimes. Baca managed to teach himself to read and write between state-ordered electroshock sessions to curb his combative nature. His poetry, especially that about prison life, has won him critical acclaim.

There Are Black

There are black guards slamming cell gates
on black men,
　　　And brown guards saying hello to brown men

with numbers on their backs,
   And white guards laughing with white cons,
   and red guards, few, say nothing
to red inmates as they walk by to chow and cells.   5

   There you have it, the little antpile...
convicts marching in straight lines, guards flying
on badged wings, permits to sting, to glut themselves
at the cost of secluding themselves from their people...
   Turning off their minds like watertaps   10
wrapped in gunnysacks that insulate the pipes
carrying the pale weak water to their hearts.

   It gets bad when you see these same guards
carrying buckets of blood out of cells,
see them puking at the smell, the people,   15
their own people slashing their wrists,
hanging themselves with belts from light outlets;
it gets bad to see them clean up the mess,
carry the blue cold body out under sheets,
and then retake their places in guard cages,
watching their people maul and mangle themselves,   20

   And over this blood-rutted land,
the sun shines, the guards talk of horses and guns,
go to the store and buy new boots,
and the longer they work here the more powerful they become,
taking on the presence of some ancient mummy,   25
down in the dungeons of prison, a mummy
that will not listen, but has a strange power
in this dark world, to be so utterly disgusting in ignorance,
and yet so proudly command so many men....

   And the convicts themselves, at the mummy's   30
feet, blood-splattered leather, at this one's feet,
they become cobras sucking life out of their brothers,
they fight for rings and money and drugs,
in this pit of pain their teeth bare fangs,
to fight for what morsels they can....   35

   And the other convicts, guilty
of nothing but their born color, guilty of being innocent,
they slowly turn to dust in the nightly winds here,
flying in the wind back to their farms and cities.
From the gash in their hearts, sand flies up spraying   40
over houses and through trees,

   look at the sand blow over this deserted place,
you are looking at them.
          (1979)

Questions for Discussion and Writing

1. What is it about the prison guards that horrifies the speaker in "There Are Black"?
2. The speaker understands what motivates the guards to keep their jobs. What are their motivations?
3. What are the two types of convicts described in stanzas five and six?
4. Do you think that this subject matter is appropriate for poetry? Why or why not?

Making Connections

Compare Baca's use of strong, vivid images to depict violence with the similar use of such imagery in "Dulce et Decorum Est" by Wilfred Owen (page 606).

◇◇◇◇◇◇◇◇◇◇◇◇◇◇◇◇◇◇

Judith Ortiz Cofer   1952–

Judith Ortiz Cofer was born in Puerto Rico; her family emigrated to the United States when she was six. This mixed heritage animates her writing, which often describes the experience of balancing two cultures in one life. Cofer wrote poetry as a graduate student and began focusing on prose in the late 1980s, publishing the novel *The Line of the Sun*, which was nominated for a 1989 Pulitzer Prize. She has also written widely published essays and a volume of stories for young adults.

Latin Women Pray

Latin women pray
In incense sweet churches
They pray in Spanish to an Anglo God
With a Jewish heritage.
And this Great White Father   5
Imperturbable in his marble pedestal
Looks down upon his brown daughters
Votive candles shining like lust
In his all seeing eyes
Unmoved by their persistent prayers.   10

Yet year after year
Before his image they kneel
Margarita Josefina Maria and Isabel
All fervently hoping
That if not omnipotent
At least he be bilingual   15

(1987)

Questions for Discussion and Writing

1. To what religion do the women belong? How can you tell?
2. List words that describe the God worshipped in the poem and words that describe the women. How are the two lists opposites? Do they contain any similarities? What other views of God may be compared with this one?
3. What are the women probably praying for "year after year"? Why do they never get it? Why do they persist?
4. Of all the ways possible to describe the reflection of votive candles in a statue's eyes, the writer chose the image "shining like lust." What does this image contribute to our understanding of the God in the poem?

Making Connections

Compare the women described in this poem with the mother in Gina Valdés's "My Mother Sews Blouses" (page 941). Does the hope of the women in either poem seem rational or helpful? Or is it delusional?

◇◇◇◇◇◇◇◇◇◇◇◇◇◇◇◇◇◇◇◇◇◇◇

Cornelius Eady   1954–

Cornelius Eady, an African-American poet, was born in Rochester, New York, currently resides in New York City, and directs the Poetry Center at the State University of New York at Stony Brook. Author of five books of poetry and winner of the Lamont Poetry Selection of the American Academy of Poets, he has been nominated for a Pulitzer Prize and has received fellowships from the Lila Wallace-Reader's Digest Foundation, the Guggenheim Foundation, and the National Endowment for the Arts.

The Supremes

We were born to be gray. We went to school,
Sat in rows, ate white bread,
Looked at the floor a lot. In the back
Of our small heads

A long scream. We did what we could,   5
And all we could do was
Turn on each other. How the fat kids suffered!
Not even being jolly could save them.

And then there were the anal retentives,
The terrified brown-noses, the desperately   10
Athletic or popular. This, of course,
Was training. At home

Our parents shook their heads and waited.
We learned of the industrial revolution,

The Supremes—Mary Wilson, Diana Ross, and Cindy Birdsong—performing in vibrant, sequined gowns.

The sectioning of the clock into pie slices.   15
We drank cokes and twiddled our thumbs. In the
Back of our minds

A long scream. We snapped butts in the showers,
Froze out shy girls on the dance floor,
Pin-pointed flaws like radar.   20
Slowly we understood: this was to be the world.

We were born insurance salesmen and secretaries,
Housewives and short order cooks,
Stock room boys and repairmen,
And it wouldn't be a bad life, they promised,   25
In a tone of voice that would force some of us
To reach in self-defense for wigs,
Lipstick,

Sequins.

(1991)

Questions for Discussion and Writing

1. What does the speaker mean when he says, "We were born to be gray"? Who is he talking about?

2. The speaker says that "all we could do was / Turn on each other" (lines 6–7). In what ways do they turn on each other? Is the speaker trying to justify this behavior?

3. Explain line 21: "Slowly we understood: this was to be the world."

4. What happens in the last two stanzas? Why do "some of us" reach for "wigs, / Lipstick, / Sequins"? What does that mean? And what is the "tone of voice" that would force them to do so? In what ways is it self-defense?

Making Connections

Compare this poem about growing up to others on the same theme: "Hanging Fire" by Audre Lorde (page 940), and "Ex-Basketball Player" by John Updike (page 591).

◇◇◇◇◇◇◇◇◇◇◇◇◇◇◇◇◇◇◇◇

Martín Espada 1957–

Martin Espada came from a family of Puerto Rican immigrants, and his many volumes of poetry reflect these origins. His writing is openly political, expressing anger at injustice and racism. The poems often tell stories from the points of view of gutsy, vivid Latino characters, such as janitors, junkies, prisoners, or mental patients. Humor and empathy infuse his depictions of these characters' struggles. Espada's third book of poetry, *Rebellion Is the Circle of a Lover's Hands*, won the 1990 PEN/ Revson Award and the Paterson Poetry Prize.

Bully

Boston, Massachusetts, 1987

In the school auditorium
the Theodore Roosevelt statue
is nostalgic
for the Spanish American War,
each fist lonely for a saber   5
or the reins of anguished horses,
or a podium to clatter with speeches
glorying in the malaria of conquest.

But now the Roosevelt school
is pronounced *Hernandez.*   10
Puerto Rico has invaded Roosevelt
with its army of Spanish-singing children
in the hallways,
brown children devouring
the stockpiles of the cafeteria,   15
children painting *Taíno* ancestors
that leap naked across murals.

Roosevelt is surrounded
by all the faces
he ever shoved in eugenic spite   20
and cursed as mongrels, skin of one race,
hair and cheekbones of another.

Once Marines tramped
from the newsreel of his imagination;

now children plot to spray graffiti   25
in parrot-brilliant colors
across the Victorian mustache
and monocle.

(1990)

Questions for Discussion and Writing

1. The poet depends on our knowing at least a few things about Teddy Roosevelt, the Spanish-American War, eugenics, and Taíno Puerto Rican ancestors. If you aren't familiar with any of this history, use an encyclopedia to fill in the gaps, and then explain how this information helps you to read the poem. Can you understand its main theme without these insights?
2. There are several surprising images in the poem, created by unexpected word combinations—for example, the linking of "lonely" and "fist," as well as "statue" and "nostalgic." Find other examples and discuss the tone created by these images.
3. There are four stanzas in the poem. Summarize the main point of each, and explain the reasons for the order in which Espada places his ideas.
4. Who is the "bully" in the poem? Why did Espada select this title? Why did he include "Boston, Massachusetts, 1987"? Write an essay in which you argue your position on these questions.

Making Connections

Compare the attitudes toward wars and war memorials expressed by Yusef Komunyakaa in "Facing It" (page 611) with those in Espada's "Bully."

24 Paired Poems for Comparison

Chapter Preview

Poets are often inspired by the work of earlier poets. This section contains six pairs of poems that respond to each other in some way. In the first pair, for example, the speaker in the second poem replies directly to the enticement made by the speaker in the first poem. In some cases the two poets present differing perspectives on the same topic. Other responses are light-hearted *parodies*—imitations that copy some features such as diction, style, or form, but change or exaggerate other features for humorous effect.

After reading this chapter, you will know how to

- Analyze the ways that poets respond, modify, and complement the work of other poets.
- Identify purpose and audience in poetry.
- Use argument and research to write about assigned pairs of poems.

Pair #1

Christopher Marlowe   1564–1593

The son of a Canterbury shoemaker, Christopher Marlowe was one of the leading poets and dramatists of his day. His major plays, which include *Tamburlaine the Great* (1587), *Dr. Faustus* (1588), and *Edward II* (1592), concern heroic figures who are brought down by their own extravagant passions. He was one of the first to use blank verse in his plays, a practice that Shakespeare perfected. Marlowe's lyric poetry is graceful and warmly sensuous. He was killed in a quarrel over a tavern bill.

The Passionate Shepherd to His Love

Come live with me and be my love,
And we will all the pleasures prove,
That valleys, groves, hills and fields,
Woods, or steepy mountain yields.

And we will sit upon the rocks,   5
And see the shepherds feed their flocks,

By shallow rivers to whose falls
Melodious birds sing madrigals.

And I will make thee beds of roses
With a thousand fragrant posies,   10
A cap of flowers, and a kirtle
Embroidered all with leaves of myrtle;

A gown made of the finest wool
Which from our pretty lambs we pull;
Fair lined slippers for the cold,   15
With buckles of the purest gold;

A belt of straw and ivy buds,
With coral clasps and amber studs:
And if these pleasures may thee move,
Come live with me and be my love.   20

The shepherds' swains shall dance and sing
For thy delight each May morning:
If these delights thy mind may move,
Then live with me and be my love.

(1600)

Questions for Discussion and Writing

1. How does the young lover vary his appeals? Is there an implication that the object of his invitation is rejecting him?
2. Does the speaker go too far ("buckles of the purest gold") and lose credibility? Or is credibility even an issue in this kind of poem?
3. By the end of the poem, how convincing do you find the Shepherd's appeal? Just how "passionate" is he?

Sir Walter Raleigh   ca. 1552–1618

Sir Walter Raleigh was an English soldier, explorer, courtier, and man of letters. A favorite of Queen Elizabeth I, he organized the colonizing expeditions to North America that ended tragically with the lost colony of Roanoke Island. Imprisoned for thirteen years in the Tower of London by James I, Raleigh was released to search for gold in South America. When he returned empty-handed, he was executed. A true court poet, he circulated his poems in manuscript; as a result, only a few have survived.

The Nymph's Reply to the Shepherd

If all the world and love were young,
And truth in every shepherd's tongue,

These pretty pleasures might me move,
To live with thee, and be thy love.

Time drives the flocks from field to fold,   5
When rivers rage, and rocks grow cold,
And Philomel becometh dumb,
The rest complains of cares to come.

The flowers do fade, and wanton fields,
To wayward winter reckoning yields: 10
A honey tongue, a heart of gall,
Is fancy's spring, but sorrow's fall.

Thy gowns, thy shoes, thy beds of roses,
Thy cap, thy kirtle, and thy posies,
Soon break, soon wither, soon forgotten: 15
In folly ripe, in reason rotten.

Thy belt of straw and ivy buds,
Thy coral clasps and amber studs,
All these in me no means can move,
To come to thee, and be thy love.   20

But could youth last, and love still breed,
Had joys no date, nor age no need,
Then these delights my mind might move
To live with thee and be thy love.

(1600)

Making Connections

1. How does the nymph counter the shepherd's pleasant pastoral images?
2. Note how the nymph mentions all of the images drawn from nature that were used in the Marlowe poem. But what does she do with them?
3. Which of the two lovers, the shepherd or the nymph, do you like better? Which approach to love do you find more attractive? Write a comparison essay in which you defend your choice.

Pair #2

Robert Browning 1812–1889

Robert Browning was an English poet who experimented with diction and rhythm as well as with psychological portraits in verse. He secretly married Elizabeth Barrett, and they moved to Italy in 1846, partly to avoid her domineering father. Browning was a master of dramatic monologues, exemplified in "My Last Duchess" and "Porphyria's Lover." After the death of his wife, Browning returned to England where he wrote what some consider his masterwork, *The Ring and the Book* (1868–1869).

My Last Duchess

Ferrara

That's my last Duchess painted on the wall,
Looking as if she were alive; I call
That piece a wonder, now: Frà Pandolf's° hands
Worked busily a day, and there she stands.
Will't please you sit and look at her? I said   5
"Frà Pandolf" by design, for never read
Strangers like you that pictured countenance,
The depth and passion of its earnest glance,
But to myself they turned (since none puts by
The curtain I have drawn for you, but I)   10
And seemed as they would ask me, if they durst,
How such a glance came there; so, not the first
Are you to turn and ask thus. Sir, 'twas not
Her husband's presence only, called that spot
Of joy into the Duchess' cheek: perhaps   15
Frà Pandolf chanced to say "Her mantle laps
Over my Lady's wrist too much," or "Paint
Must never hope to reproduce the faint
Half-flush that dies along her throat": such stuff
Was courtesy, she thought, and cause enough   20
For calling up that spot of joy. She had
A heart—how shall I say?—too soon made glad,
Too easily impressed; she liked whate'er
She looked on, and her looks went everywhere.
Sir, 'twas all one! My favor at her breast,   25
The dropping of the daylight in the West,
The bough of cherries some officious fool
Broke in the orchard for her, the white mule
She rode with round the terrace—all and each
Would draw from her alike the approving speech,   30

---

3 Frà Pandolf's A fictitious artist.

Or blush, at least. She thanked men,—good; but thanked
Somehow—I know not how—as if she ranked
My gift of a nine-hundred-years-old name
With anybody's gift. Who'd stoop to blame
This sort of trifling? Even had you skill   35
In speech—(which I have not)—to make your will
Quite clear to such an one, and say, "Just this
Or that in you disgusts me; here you miss,
Or there exceed the mark"—and if she let
Herself be lessoned so, nor plainly set   40
Her wits to yours, forsooth, and made excuse,
—E'en then would be some stooping, and I choose
Never to stoop. Oh, Sir, she smiled, no doubt,
Whene'er I passed her; but who passed without
Much the same smile? This grew; I gave commands;   45
Then all smiles stopped together. There she stands
As if alive. Will't please you rise? We'll meet
The company below, then. I repeat,
The Count your Master's known munificence
Is ample warrant that no just pretence   50
Of mine for dowry will be disallowed;
Though his fair daughter's self, as I avowed
At starting, is my object. Nay, we'll go
Together down, Sir! Notice Neptune, though,
Taming a sea-horse, thought a rarity,   55
Which Claus of Innsbruck° cast in bronze for me.
                                                              (1842)

---

56 Claus of Innsbruck Another fictitious artist.

Questions for Discussion and Writing

1. Who is speaking to whom? What is the situation?
2. According to the Duke, what were the Duchess's faults? Do you trust the speaker's account of the Duchess and her "failings"?
3. Does the Duke's carefully controlled composure slip as he relates his story about the last duchess? Or is he intentionally letting the emissary know his (the Duke's) feelings about women and wives?
4. If you were the emissary for the Count whose daughter the Duke hopes to marry, what would you report to your master?

◇◇◇◇◇◇◇◇◇◇◇◇◇◇◇◇◇◇◇◇◇◇

Gabriel Spera   1966–

Gabriel Spera is a technical writer and the director of the Aerospace Press in El Segundo, California. He was born in New York, grew up in New Jersey, and holds a B.A. from Cornell University and an M.F.A. from the University of North Carolina.

His first collection of poems, *The Standing Wave,* received the 2004 PEN Center USA Literary Award. According to one critic, Spera's poetry "distinguishes itself with intelligence, wit, impeccable technique, and openness, and it has real substance to impart."

My Ex-Husband

That's my ex-husband pictured on the shelf,
Smiling as if in love. I took it myself
With his Leica, and stuck it in that frame
We got for our wedding. Kind of a shame
To waste it on him, but what could I do?   5
(Since I haven't got a photograph of you.)
I know what's on your mind—you want to know
Whatever could have made me let him go—
He seems like any woman's perfect catch,
What with his ruddy cheeks, the thin mustache,   10
Those close-set, baggy eyes, that tilted grin.
But snapshots don't show what's beneath the skin!
He had a certain charm, charisma, style,
That passionate, earnest glance he struck, meanwhile
Whispering the sweetest things, like "Your lips   15
Are like plump rubies, eyes like diamond chips,"
Could flush the throat of any woman, not
Just mine. He knew the most romantic spots
In town, where waiters, who all knew his face,
Reserved an intimately dim-lit place   20
Half-hidden in a corner nook. Such stuff
Was all too well rehearsed, I soon enough
Found out. He had an attitude—how should
I put it—smooth, self-satisfied, too good
For the rest of the world, too easily   25
Impressed with his officious self. And he
flirted—fine! but flirted somehow a bit
Too ardently, too blatantly, as if,
If someone ever noticed, no one cared
How slobbishly he carried on affairs.   30
Who'd lower herself to put up with shit
Like that? Even if you'd the patience—which
I have not—to go and see some counsellor
And say, "My life's a living hell," or
"Everything he does disgusts, the lout!"—   35
And even if you'd somehow worked things out,
Took a long trip together, made amends,
Let things get back to normal, even then
You'd still be on the short end of the stick;
And I choose never ever to get stuck.   40
Oh, no doubt, it always made my limbs go
Woozy when he kissed me, but what bimbo

In the steno pool went without the same
Such kisses? So, I made some calls, filed some claims,
All kisses stopped together. There he grins,   45
Almost lovable. Shall we go? I'm in
The mood for Chez Pierre's, perhaps, tonight,
Though anything you'd like would be all right
As well, of course, though I'd prefer not to go
To any place with checkered tables. No,   50
We'll take my car. By the way, have I shown
You yet these lovely champagne flutes, hand blown,
Imported from Murano, Italy,
Which Claus got in the settlement for me!

(1992)

Making Connections

1. Look at this poem alongside the original, Browning's "My Last Duchess," and note the similarities. Make a list of parallels in the form and tone of the two poems. Then discuss parallels in content: what changes are made in the details of the situation?

2. What do the speakers of the poems have in common? What does the persona of "My Ex-Husband" do rather than have the spouse murdered?

3. Is there a difference in the ways you respond to the speakers? If so, how do you account for the difference?

Pair #3

Walt Whitman 1819–1892

See page 419 for a biographical note about this author.

Of the Terrible Doubt of Appearances

Of the terrible doubt of appearances,
Of the uncertainty after all, that we may be deluded,
That may-be reliance and hope are but speculations after all,
That may-be identity beyond the grave is a beautiful fable
    only,
May-be the things I perceive, the animals, plants, men, hills,
    shining and flowing waters,   5
The skies of day and night, colors, densities, forms, may-be
    these are (as doubtless they are) only apparitions, and
    the real something has yet to be known,
(How often they dart out of themselves as if to confound me
    and mock me!
How often I think neither I know, nor any man knows,
    aught of them),
May-be seeming to me what they are (as doubtless they
    indeed but seem) as from my present point of view, and
    might prove (as of course they would) nought of what
    they appear, or nought anyhow, from entirely changed
    points of view;
To me these and the like of these are curiously answer'd by
    my lovers, my dear friends,   10
When he whom I love travels with me or sits a long while
    holding me by the hand,
When the subtle air, the impalpable, the sense that words and
    reason hold not, surround us and pervade us,
Then I am charged with untold and untellable wisdom, I am
    silent, I require nothing further,
I cannot answer the question of appearances or that of
    identity beyond the grave,
But I walk or sit indifferent, I am satisfied,   15
He ahold of my hand has completely satisfied me.

                    (1860)

Questions for Discussion and Writing

1. What terrible doubts does the speaker of the poem have about appearances?
What kinds of questions does he think about when he is filled with uncertainty? Are these doubts and questions common, in your experience?

2. This poem contrasts doubt and uneasiness with satisfaction. What line makes the change from doubt to satisfaction? Where does the narrator find reassuring comfort, and why does he find it there?

3. The poem includes a very difficult line: "How often they dart out of themselves as if to confound me and mock me!" Discuss with a classmate what this line means. You might start with figuring out what the words "they" and "themselves" refer to.

◇◇◇◇◇◇◇◇◇◇◇◇◇◇◇◇◇◇◇◇◇◇◇◇

Tony Hoagland   1953–

Tony Hoagland was born in North Carolina. Unlike most widely published poets, Hoagland is known for his humorous, down-to-earth touch. In fact, he won the 2005 Mark Twain Award for his contributions to humor in American poetry. In making this award for The Poetry Foundation, Stephen Young said, "Wit and morality rarely consort these days; it's good to see them happily, often hilariously reunited in the winner's poetry."

Romantic Moment

After seeing the nature documentary we walk down Canyon Road,
into the plaza of art galleries and high-end clothing stores

where the orange trees are fragrant in the summer night
and the smooth adobe walls glow fleshlike in the dark.

It is just our second date, and we sit down on a bench,   5
holding hands, not looking at each other,

and if I were a bull penguin right now I would lean over
and vomit softly into the mouth of my beloved,

and if I were a peacock I'd flex my gluteal muscles to
erect and spread the quills of my Cinemax tail.   10

If she were a female walkingstick bug she might
insert her hypodermic probiscus directly into my neck

and inject me with a rich hormonal sedative
before attaching her egg sac to my thoracic undercarriage,

and if I were a young chimpanzee I would break off a nearby tree limb   15
and smash all the windows in the plaza jewelry stores.

And if she was a Brazilian leopard frog she would wrap her impressive
tongue three times around my right thigh and

pummel me softly against the surface of our pond
and I would know her feelings were sincere.   20

Instead we sit awhile in silence, until
she remarks that in the relative context of tortoises and iguanas,

human males seem to be actually rather expressive.
And I say that female crocodiles really don't receive

enough credit for their gentleness.   25
Then she suggests that it is time for us to go

do something personal, hidden and human.

(2010)

Questions for Discussion and Writing

1. Reread the first three stanzas of the poem. What do they lead you to expect as you continue reading? How are these expectations challenged? Try to identify the exact words that clued you in to a shift in tone, to the humorous side of this romantic poem. Identify one more shift in tone later in the poem.
2. Where are the two characters in the poem? Why are they thinking about animals? What qualities of the animals are highlighted by the details Hoagland describes?
3. How do the human characters compliment each other? What are the compliments leading up to?
4. This is not the first version of "Romantic Moment." Hoagland has been re-working it since 2006. Look up earlier versions of the poem online (you may have to find one or more versions in journals using your library's access to subscription databases: see Chapter 5), and see whether you can explain the changes he has made over the years.

Making Connections

Both "Of the Terrible Doubt of Appearances" and "Romantic Moment" could be called poems about love. Why? Support your ideas with details from the poems. Each poem includes an unromantic twist, though. What is it? What works against romance?

Pair #4

Edwin Arlington Robinson 1869–1935

Edwin Arlington Robinson was born in Tide Head, Maine. Though now considered an important poet, Robinson spent many years depending on friends for a livelihood. The publication of his narrative poem *Tristram* (1927) brought him wide recognition and some measure of financial independence. Although his verse is traditional in form, he anticipated many twentieth-century poets with his emphasis on themes of alienation and failure. His poetry won three Pulitzer Prizes—in 1921, 1924, and 1927.

Richard Cory

Whenever Richard Cory went downtown,
We people on the pavement looked at him;
He was a gentleman from sole to crown,
Clean favored, and imperially slim.

And he was always quietly arrayed, 5
And he was always human when he talked;
But still he fluttered pulses when he said,
"Good-morning," and he glittered when he walked.

And he was rich—yes, richer than a king—
And admirably schooled in every grace: 10
In fine,° we thought that he was everything
To make us wish that we were in his place.

So on we worked, and waited for the light,
And went without the meat, and cursed the bread;
And Richard Cory, one calm summer night, 15
Went home and put a bullet through his head.

(1896)

---

11 In fine In short.

Questions for Discussion and Writing

1. Who is the speaker in this poem?
2. What sort of person is Richard Cory? What does it mean to be "a gentleman from sole to crown"?
3. Trace the motif of images of royalty in the poem. What do they suggest about Richard Cory and those who admired him?

Paul Simon   1942–

Paul Simon was born in Newark, New Jersey, and attended Queens College, where he majored in English. In 1964 he teamed with Art Garfunkel to form one of the most successful singing duos in rock history, recording such hits as "Mrs. Robinson," "Bridge over Troubled Waters," and "The Sounds of Silence." The team split in 1971. Simon's solo albums include *Still Crazy After All These Years* (1975) and *Graceland* (1986). He was inducted into the Rock and Roll Hall of Fame in 1990.

Richard Cory [1]

They say that Richard Cory owns one half of this whole town
With political connections to spread his wealth around.
Born into society, a banker's only child,
He had everything a man could want: power, grace, and style.

But I work in his factory   5
And I curse the life I'm livin'
And I curse my poverty
And I wish that I could be
Oh I wish that I could be
Oh I wish that I could be   10
Richard Cory.

The papers print his picture almost everywhere he goes;
Richard Cory at the opera, Richard Cory at a show,
And the rumor of his parties and the orgies on his yacht,
Oh he surely must be happy with everything he's got.   15

But I work in his factory
And I curse the life I'm livin'
And I curse my poverty
And I wish that I could be
Oh I wish that I could be   20
Oh I wish that I could be
Richard Cory.

He freely gave to charity, he had the common touch,
And they were thankful for his patronage and they thanked him very
        much,
So my mind was filled with wonder when the evening headlines read: 25
"Richard Cory went home last night and put a bullet through his head."

But I work in his factory
And I curse the life I'm livin'
And I curse my poverty
And I wish that I could be   30
Oh I wish that I could be
Oh I wish that I could be
Richard Cory.

                                                                    (1966)

---

[1] Simon, Paul, *Richard Cory* Words and Music by Paul Simon. Copyright © 1966 Paul Simon (BMI). International Copyright Secured. All Rights Reserved.

Making Connections

1. What difference in tone do you see between the Robinson and Simon versions of "Richard Cory"? Does the difference in time of composition (1896 and 1966, respectively) account for the change?

2. Choose a different poem from the nineteenth century or early twentieth century and write a modernized version, perhaps for a rock, folk, pop, or hip-hop group to perform.

Pair #5

Robert Hayden 1913–1980

Born Asa Bundy Sheffey in Detroit, Robert Hayden was renamed by his foster parents. In the poetry of his first collection, *Heart-Shape in the Dust* (1940), he used facts about African American history that he unearthed as a researcher for the Federal Writers' Project (1936–40). Educated at Wayne State and the University of Michigan, Hayden taught at Fisk University and returned to teach at Michigan. He considered his writing "a form of prayer—a prayer for illumination, perfection."

Those Winter Sundays

Sundays too my father got up early
and put his clothes on in the blueblack cold,
then with cracked hands that ached
from labor in the weekday weather made
banked fires blaze. No one ever thanked him.   5
I'd wake and hear the cold splintering, breaking.
When the rooms were warm, he'd call,
and slowly I would rise and dress,
fearing the chronic angers of that house,

Speaking indifferently to him,   10
who had driven out the cold
and polished my good shoes as well.
What did I know, what did I know
of love's austere and lonely offices°?

(1966)

---

14 offices Duties.

Questions for Discussion and Writing

1. The speaker is clearly looking back at a pattern of life experienced as a child. What does the speaker know now that he or she didn't know then?
2. What kind of home was the speaker's? How do you know?
3. What are the various expressions of love? Which ones are "austere and lonely"?
4. What is the religious meaning of the word "office"? How does that connotation fit the use of the word in this poem?

George Bilgere 1951–

George Bilgere survived an unhappy childhood in Riverside, California. His father was a drunk, his parents divorced, then his mother died. Yet he came out of it as a basically contented individual. Dealing with the pain of his own divorce, he has said, enabled him to use more "open" language in his poetry. Billy Collins observes that the poems are "balanced between humor and seriousness, between the sadness of loss and the joy of being alive to experience it. Whenever a parade of Bilgere poems goes by, I'll be there waving my little flag."

Like Riding a Bicycle

I would like to write a poem
About how my father taught me
To ride a bicycle one soft twilight,
A poem in which he was tired
And I was scared, unable to disbelieve   5
In gravity and believe in him,
As the fireflies were coming out
And only enough light remained
For one more run, his big hand at the small
Of my back, pulling away like the gantry   10
At a missile launch, and this time, this time
I wobbled into flight, caught a balance
I would never lose, and pulled away
From him as he eased, laughing, to a stop,
A poem in which I said that even today   15
As I make some perilous adult launch,
Like pulling away from my wife
Into the fragile new balance of our life
Apart, I can still feel that steadying hand,
Still hear that strong voice telling me   20
To embrace the sweet fall forward
Into the future's blue
Equilibrium. But,

Of course, he was drunk that night,
Still wearing his white shirt   25
And tie from the office, the air around us
Sick with scotch, and the challenge
Was keeping his own balance
As he coaxed his bulk into a trot
Beside me in the hot night, sweat   30
Soaking his armpits, the eternal flame
Of his cigarette flaring as he gasped
And I fell, again and again, entangled
In my gleaming Schwinn, until
He swore and stomped off   35
Into the house to continue

Working with my mother
On their own divorce, their balance
Long gone and the hard ground already
Rising up to smite them   40
While I stayed outside in the dark,
Still falling, until at last I wobbled
Into the frail, upright delight
Of feeling sorry for myself, riding
Alone down the neighborhood's   45
Black street like the lonely western hero
I still catch myself in the act
Of performing.

And yet, having said all this,
I must also say that this summer evening   50
Is very beautiful, and I am older
Than my father ever was
As I coast the Pacific shoreline
On my old bike, the gears clicking
Like years, the wind   55
Touching me for the first time, it seems,
In a very long time,
With soft urgency all over.

                                        (2002)

Questions for Discussion and Writing

1. What is a "gantry" (line 10)? Explain why "gantry" is a perfect word choice in the poem.
2. How would you describe the boy's relationship with his father? On what specific words and phrases in the poem do you base your interpretation?
3. Why does the poet place the stanza breaks where they are? Summarize the meaning of each of the three stanzas.

Making Connections

Write an essay comparing this poem with Hayden's "Those Winter Sundays." Focus on the speaker's attitude toward his father in each poem.

Pair #6

Gwendolyn Brooks 1917–2000

See page 437 for a biographical note about this author.

The Bean Eaters

They eat beans mostly, this old yellow pair.
Dinner is a casual affair.
Plain chipware on a plain and creaking wood,
Tin flatware.

Two who are Mostly Good.   5
Two who have lived their day,
But keep on putting on their clothes
And putting things away.

And remembering…
Remembering, with twinklings and twinges,   10
As they lean over the beans in their rented back room that
    is full of beads and receipts and dolls and cloths,
    tobacco crumbs, vases and fringes.

(1945)

Questions for Discussion and Writing

1. Why is the couple eating beans? How do you know?
2. What overall impression does the list at the end of the poem give you?
3. Why does the writer include the phrase "Mostly Good"? Why aren't the people described as "Good"?
4. What is the significance of "putting on their clothes /And putting things away"?

Katha Pollitt 1949–

Essayist, poet, and journalist, Katha Pollitt was born into a half-Jewish, half-Protestant family in Brooklyn Heights, New York. Her parents were prolific readers and political activists (both had FBI surveillance files several inches thick). Following their lead, Katha Pollitt is best-known for her column "Subject to Debate" in *The Nation* magazine, where she writes about feminism, racism, abortion rights, welfare reform, and other controversial social issues. Her first collection of poetry, *Antarctic Traveler* (1982), won the National Book Critics Circle Award. About her second collection, *The Mind-Body Problem* (2009), Poet Laureate Kay Ryan wrote, "It's awfully good to have such a great-hearted poet...take on mortality's darkest themes. Again and again she finds a human-sized crack of light and squeezes us through with her."

The Old Neighbors

The weather's turned, and the old neighbors creep out
from their crammed rooms to blink in the sun, as if
surprised to find they've lived through another winter.
Though steam heat's left them pale and shrunken
like old root vegetables,   5
Mr. and Mrs. Tozzi are already
hard at work on their front-yard mini-Sicily:
a Virgin Mary birdbath, a thicket of roses,
and the only outdoor aloes in Manhattan.
It's the old immigrant story,   10
the beautiful babies
grown up into foreigners. Nothing's
turned out the way they planned
as sweethearts in the sinks of Palermo. Still,
each waves a dirt-caked hand   15
in geriatric fellowship with Stanley,
the former tattoo king of the Merchant Marine,
turning the corner with his shaggy collie,
who's hardly three but trots
arthritically in sympathy. It's only   20
the young who ask if life's worth living, not
Mrs. Sansanowitz, who for the last hour
has been inching her way down the sidewalk,
lifting and placing
her new aluminum walker as carefully   25
as a spider testing its web. On days like these,
I stand for a long time
under the wild gnarled root of the ancient wisteria,
dry twigs that in a week
will manage a feeble shower of purple blossom,   30
and I believe it: this is all there is,
all history's brought us here to our only life
to find, if anywhere,
our hanging gardens and our street of gold:
cracked stoops, geraniums, fire escapes, these old   35
stragglers basking in their bit of sun.

(2009)

Questions for Discussion and Writing

1. Who is the speaker in this poem?
2. What are aloes (line 9), and why is it unusual to find them outdoors in Manhattan? What does this detail tell you about Mr. and Mrs. Tozzi?

3. What is "the old immigrant story" (lines 10-12)?
4. In line 31, the speaker says "I believe it." What does she believe? Explicate lines 31–36; then write out your reactions to the claims expressed in these lines.

Making Connections

1. What parallels do you see between the "old yellow pair" in "The Bean Eaters" and the "old stragglers" in "The Old Neighbors"? What philosophy of life do they seem to share? Can you relate these people to anyone you know or have observed?
2. Where does most of the activity in "The Old Neighbors" take place? How does this compare to the setting of "The Bean Eaters"? Does the contrast affect the tones of the poems—and your responses?

25 A Portfolio of Poems About Work

Chapter Preview

Sigmund Freud believed that the communal life of human beings has two foundations: work and love (*Civilization and Its Discontents*, 1930). We spend about 80,000 lifetime hours at work—arguably more than forty times the hours we spend falling in and out of love, even when we're extremely lucky or unfortunate in this arena. Yet the topic of love is among the first to come to mind when we think of poetry, while the topic of work is not. It may not seem like a high-flown subject, but everyday life on the job does permeate much literature, as the poems in this portfolio illustrate.

After reading this chapter, you will know how to

- Respond to and analyze poems about work.
- Synthesize poets' views about work with your own thoughts and feelings.
- Write critically about poems that focus on work and workers.

Jean Toomer   1894–1967

Jean Toomer grew up in Washington, D.C., attended several colleges, and worked briefly as the headmaster of a Black school in Georgia. His best-known work, *Cane* (1923), combines poetry, fiction, and drama into an artistic vision of the Black American experience. Widely acclaimed for its innovative style and penetrating insights, *Cane* is one of the most important works of the Harlem Renaissance, although Toomer later disavowed any connection with that movement.

Reapers

Black reapers with the sound of steel on stones
Are sharpening scythes. I see them place the hones°
In their hip-pockets as a thing that's done,
And start their silent swinging, one by one.

Black horses drive a mower through the weeds,   5
And there, a field rat, startled, squealing bleeds,

---

2 hones Whetstone for sharpening blades.

His belly close to ground. I see the blade,
Blood-stained, continue cutting weeds and shade.
(1923)

Questions for Discussion and Writing

1. Read the poem aloud. Notice several patterns of sound. How do they relate to the picture described in the poem?
2. Does the speaker of the poem, the viewer of the scene, see life as a joyful romp, a dashing adventure, or a predetermined grind? How do you know?
3. Death is sometimes called "The Grim Reaper." Do you think Toomer had this in mind when he wrote "Reapers"? Why?

◇◇◇◇◇◇◇◇◇◇◇◇◇◇◇◇◇◇◇◇

John Updike 1932–2009

See page 358 for a biographical note about this author.

Ex-Basketball Player

Pearl Avenue runs past the high-school lot,
Bends with the trolley tracks, and stops, cut off
Before it has a chance to go two blocks,
At Colonel McComsky Plaza. Berth's Garage
Is on the corner facing west, and there,   5
Most days, you'll find Flick Webb, who helps Berth out.

Flick stands tall among the idiot pumps—
Five on a side, the old bubble-head style,°
Their rubber elbows hanging loose and low.
One's nostrils are two S's, and his eyes   10
An E and O.°And one is squat, without
A head at all—more of a football type.

Once Flick played for the high-school team, the Wizards.
He was good: in fact, the best. In '46
He bucketed three hundred ninety points,   15
A county record still. The ball loved Flick.
I saw him rack up thirty-eight or forty
In one home game. His hands were like wild birds.

He never learned a trade, he just sells gas,
Checks oil, and changes flats. Once in a while,   20

---

8 bubble-head style Gasoline pumps with round glass globes on top.
11 E and O ESSO—a major oil company in the 1940s, the time frame of the poem.

An "old bubble-head" ESSO gasoline pump.

As a gag, he dribbles an inner tube,
But most of us remember anyway.
His hands are fine and nervous on the lug wrench.
It makes no difference to the lug wrench, though.

Off work, he hangs around Mae's luncheonette.   25
Grease-gray and kind of coiled, he plays pinball,
Smokes those thin cigars, nurses lemon phosphates.
Flick seldom says a word to Mae, just nods
Beyond her face toward bright applauding tiers
Of Necco Wafers, Nibs, and Juju Beads.   30

(1958)

Questions for Discussion and Writing

1. What is the story of Flick Webb's life? How do both his first and last names fit his life story?
2. Who is the narrator (the "I") of the poem? How old is he? Where does he live?
3. Though the poem has no regular rhyme, it follows patterns. Explain the logic of the stanza breaks and line breaks.
4. What is Flick's attitude toward his work? What details reveal it? Is this attitude common among people you know? Why or why not?

Marge Piercy   1936–

See page 560 for a biographical note about this author.

To Be of Use

The people I love the best
jump into work head first
without dallying in the shallows
and swim off with sure strokes almost out of sight.
They seem to become natives of that element,   5
the black sleek heads of seals
bouncing like half submerged balls.

I love people who harness themselves, an ox to a heavy cart,
who pull like water buffalo, with massive patience,
who strain in the mud and the muck to move things forward,   10
who do what has to be done, again and again.

I want to be with people who submerge
in the task, who go into the fields to harvest
and work in a row and pass the bags along,
who stand in the line and haul in their places,   15
who are not parlor generals and field deserters
but move in a common rhythm
when the food must come in or the fire be put out.

The work of the world is common as mud.
Botched, it smears the hands, crumbles to dust.   20
But the thing worth doing well done
has a shape that satisfies, clean and evident.
Greek amphoras for wine or oil,
Hopi vases that held corn, are put in museums
but you know they were made to be used.   25
The pitcher cries for water to carry
and a person for work that is real.

(1973)

Questions for Discussion and Writing

1. In stanzas 1–3, good workers are described through extended comparisons.
   Identify the metaphor developed in each stanza: Good workers are like ....

2. In stanza 4, the poet asserts a relationship between work and art. What is
   this relationship? You might start by considering the relationship of mud,
   amphoras, and vases.

3. Write a paragraph explaining the last two lines of the poem. Besides
   logical reasoning, use at least one example from your own life in your
   explanation.

Alberto Ríos   1952–

The son of a Guatemalan father and an English mother, Alberto Ríos grew up on the American side of the city of Nogales, Arizona, on the Mexican border. Having earned an M.F.A. in creative writing at the University of Arizona, he is the author of nine books of poems, three short-story collections, and a memoir. He won the Walt Whitman Award for his poetry, which has been adapted to dance and both classical and popular music. Ríos was also featured in the documentary *Birthwrite: Growing Up Hispanic* (1989). Since 1994, he has been Regents' Professor of English at Arizona State University.

In Second Grade Miss Lee I Promised Never to Forget You and I Never Did

In a letting-go moment
Miss Lee the Teacher
Who was not married
And who the next year was not at school,
Said to us, her second grade,   5
French lovers in the morning
Keep an apple next to the bed,
Each taking a bite
On first waking, to take away
The blackish breath of the night,   10
You know the kind.
A bite and then kissing,
And kissing like that was better.

I saw her once more
When she came to sell encyclopedias.   15
I was always her favorite—
The erasers, and the way she looked at me.
I promised, but not to her face,
Never to forget
The story of the apples.   20
Miss Lee all blond hair and thin,
Like *a real movie star*
If she would have just combed herself more.
Miss Lee, I promised,
I would keep apples   25
For you.

(2002)

Questions for Discussion and Writing

1. Put together a profile of Miss Lee from the details you know about her. Why did she change jobs the next year? Compare her teaching job with her next job.

2. How old are second grade students? Why did the narrator remember forever the apple story Miss Lee told? Do you remember any single classroom incident from your grade school years? Why? Generally, what kinds of incidents stand out in a child's mind?

3. How does Ríos sustain the child's point of view in the poem? What would be different from an adult's point of view? For example, what would the point of view of the child's parents include?

◇◇◇◇◇◇◇◇◇◇◇◇◇◇◇◇◇◇◇

Dorianne Laux 1952–

Dorianne Laux worked at lowly service jobs from the age of eighteen until thirty, raising a daughter as a single mother and taking writing classes and workshops at the local college when she could. Obtaining scholarships and grants, she was able to return to school full-time and graduated with honors from Mills College in 1988. In a 2006 interview with *Southern Hum*, Laux asserted, "It seems to me that all poems are odes in one way or another. Even poems of desperation or loss are odes to human emotion and endurance, to the spirit that rages quietly on."

What I Wouldn't Do

The only job I didn't like, quit
after the first shift, was selling
subscriptions to *TV Guide* over the phone.
Before that it was fast food, all
the onion rings I could eat, handing   5
sacks of deep fried burritos through
the sliding window, the hungry hands
grabbing back. And at the laundromat,
plucking bright coins from a palm
or pressing them into one, kids   10
screaming from the bathroom and twenty
dryers on high. Cleaning houses was fine,
polishing the knick-knacks of the rich.
I liked holding the hand-blown glass bell
from Czechoslovakia up to the light,   15
the jewelled clapper swinging lazily
from side to side, its foreign,
A-minor ping. I drifted, an itinerant,
from job to job, the sanatorium
where I pureed peas and carrots   20
and stringy beets, scooped them,
like pudding, onto flesh-colored
plastic plates, or the gas station

where I dipped the ten-foot measuring stick
into the hole in the blacktop,   25
pulled it up hand over hand
into the twilight, dripping
its liquid gold, pink-tinged.
I liked the donut shop best, 3 AM,
alone in the kitchen, surrounded   30
by sugar and squat mounds of dough,
the flashing neon sign strung from wire
behind the window, gilding my white uniform
yellow, then blue, then drop-dead red.
It wasn't that I hated calling them, hour   35
after hour, stuck in a booth with a list
of strangers' names, dialing their numbers
with the eraser end of a pencil and them
saying hello. It was that moment
of expectation, before I answered back,   40
the sound of their held breath,
their disappointment when they realized
I wasn't who they thought I was,
the familiar voice, or the voice they loved
and had been waiting all day to hear.   45

                                              (1994)

Questions for Discussion and Writing

1. List the jobs the narrator describes before her telemarketing job. What do they have in common? What is similar in the way she describes each one?
2. What can you infer about the narrator by the way she describes the jobs? Why do you think she liked them all right?
3. How does the *TV Guide* job contrast with the others in the poem? Can you explain why she quit after the first shift? Does the nature of *TV Guide* play a role in the poem's meaning?
4. Write a descriptive paragraph or poem about a job you enjoyed or hated.

◇◇◇◇◇◇◇◇◇◇◇◇◇◇◇◇◇◇◇◇◇◇

Lynn Powell   1955–

Lynn Powell has written two books of poetry, but she is also well known for her nonfiction book, *Framing Innocence: A Mother's Photographs, a Prosecutor's Zeal, and a Small Town's Response*, which chronicles the legal battle that ensued when a neighbor was arrested for child pornography. Powell's poetry earned her a grant from the National Endowment for the Arts, and in accepting the award, she said: "Living in America, poets can sometimes feel lonesome and beside-the-point. Our culture, which thrives on commerce and entertainment, places little value on the slow, contemplative pleasures of poetry or on its reach for complex truths."

Acceptance Speech

The radio's replaying last night's winners
and the gratitude of the glamorous,
everyone thanking everybody for making everything
so possible, until I want to shush
the faucet, dry my hands, join in right here   5
at the cluttered podium of the sink, and thank

my mother for teaching me the true meaning of okra,
my children for putting back the growl in hunger,
my husband, *primo uomo* of dinner, for not
begrudging me this starring role—   10
without all of them, I know this soup
would not be here tonight.

And let me just add that I could not
have made it without the marrow bone, that blood-
brother to the broth, and the tomatoes   15
who opened up their hearts, and the self-effacing limas,
the blonde sorority of corn, the cayenne
and oregano who dashed in
in the nick of time.

Special thanks, as always, to the salt—   20
you know who you are—and to the knife,
who revealed the ripe beneath the rind,
the clean truth underneath the dirty peel.

—I hope I've not forgotten anyone—
oh, yes, to the celery and the parsnip,   25
those bit players only there to swell the scene,
let me just say: sometimes I know exactly how you feel.

But not tonight, not when it's all
coming to something and the heat is on and
I'm basking in another round
of blue applause.

(2003)

Questions for Discussion and Writing

1. What is the main character listening to on the radio? What is happening on the program when she begins her fantasy?
2. In this fantasy, what role does she play? What is her role in real life? Who and what are included in her thank-you speech, and why?
3. In stanza 6, what does the narrator reveal concerning her feelings about her job? Point out some contrasts between the narrator's real situation and the award winner's situation.
4. In what lines can you perceive imitations of an entertainment award winner's speech?

Stephen Cushman   1956–

The son of a literature professor and a librarian, Stephen Cushman grew up in a world of words, and he is now a literature professor at the University of Virginia. His books of poetry bear inviting titles such as *Cussing Lesson* (2002), *Blue Pajamas* (1996), and *Riffraff* (2011). He argues that poetry thrives within a prosaic life: "Although the pressures of everydayness can definitely impinge on creativity, creativity—or least mine, such as it is—cannot do without that wear-and-tear. For one thing, it's a constant source of words and phrases, as well as images and experiences. For another, it balances the excesses of self-absorption, which can be just as destructive as the excesses of worldly busyness."

Beside the Point

The sky has never won a prize.
The clouds have no careers.
The rainbow doesn't say *my work*,
thank goodness.

The rock in the creek's not so productive.   5
The mud on the bank's not too pragmatic.
There's nothing useful in the noise
the wind makes in the leaves.

Buck up now, my fellow superfluity,
and let's both be of that worthless ilk,   10
self-indulgent as shooting stars,
self-absorbed as sunsets.

Who cares if we're inconsequential?
At least we can revel, two good-for-nothings,
in our irrelevance; at least come and make   15
no difference with me.

                                                (2006)

Questions for Discussion and Writing

1. According to the narrator, what characteristics are not found in natural phenomena? List the words and phrases used to describe these features: prize, careers, and so forth.

2. In which stanza do you realize that the speaker is addressing another person? List the words and phrases he uses to describe himself and the other person: superfluity, worthless, and so forth.

3. What does the narrator want the partner to do? Compare this poem with "The Passionate Shepherd to His Love," page 571. Write a paragraph explaining what strategies of seduction are shared by narrators of these two poems.

Nancy A. Henry   1961–

Born in Chipley, Florida, Nancy A. Henry grew up in Gainesville, Florida. After graduating from college, she moved to Maine and took a law degree. Still a practicing attorney, she also teaches English at Southern Maine Community College and works as a child advocate. She lives in the western foothills of the White Mountains with her husband, who is a physicist. About her poetry, Gary Lawless writes, "These are poems from the hard world, poems from the heart, the soul, the deep interior, passing through a poet of wise intelligence, empathy and love."

People Who Take Care

People who take care of people
get paid less than anybody
people who take care of people
are not worth much
except to people who are   5
sick, old, helpless, and poor
people who take care of people
are not important to most other people
are not respected by many other people
come and go without much fuss   10
unless they don't show up
when needed
people who make more money
tell them what to do
never get shit on their hands   15
never mop vomit or wipe tears
don't stand in danger
of having plates thrown at them
sharing every cold
observing agonies   20
they cannot tell at home
people who take care of people
have a secret
that sees them through the double shift
that moves with them from room to room   25
that keeps them on the floor
sometimes they fill a hollow
no one else can fill
sometimes through the shit
and blood and tears   30
they go to a beautiful place, somewhere
those clean important people
have never been.

(2003)

Questions for Discussion and Writing

1. What is the irony conveyed by the first twelve lines of the poem?
2. Does caring for people sound like a job that should pay more? Why do you suppose it doesn't?
3. What secret do people who take care of people have?
4. Write a brief explanation of what the speaker means by that "beautiful place, somewhere / those clean important people / have never been."
5. Did you ever have a job that was hard, dirty, and ill paid? How did you feel about it? Write an argument for why you liked it or hated it.

Ideas for Writing: Making Connections

1. Identify two or three attitudes toward work illustrated in these eight poems. Develop a paragraph of explanation of each attitude using details from the poems. Close with a paragraph explaining which attitude matches your own point of view best.
2. Find one other poem in this book that fits into the general theme of work. Show how it is similar to one other poem in this portfolio and how it contrasts with a different one. Suggestions: "Those Winter Sundays" (584), "Dulce et Decorum Est" (606), "A Waitress's Instructions on Tipping" (620), "The Unknown Citizen" (403), "My Mother Sews Blouses" (941), "The Old Neighbors" (page 587), "Marks" (page 614).
3. Using the poems in the portfolio and from the list in the previous prompt, choose some poems that make a point about the traditional work of women. Write down two or three sentences that could serve as thesis statements for essays (see pages 15–16). Choose one of the statements and jot down a list of supporting details from the poems, with notes on how these details support the thesis. These notes can serve as the basis for a course paper.

MultiModal Project

The Poetry in Motion program, which was launched in New York in 1992 by the Poetry Society of America and the Metropolitan Transportation Authority (MTA), places poems in subways and public transit systems across the country. Over the years this program has put more than 200 poems or excerpts before the eyes of millions of subway riders and rail commuters. The artwork accompanying the poems is taken from sketches and drawings by contributing artists in the Art & Design program of New York.

Select two poems from this portfolio that you think would be good choices for the Poetry in Motion program, and design a poster for each of the poems. You can see a large collection of posters at http://web.mta .info/mta/aft/poetry/poetry.html.

26 A Portfolio of War Poetry

Chapter Preview

War stirs powerful feelings and has inspired an abundance of powerful poetry. Admirable emotions—courage, honor, bravery—are aroused by the excitement and passion of war. But at the same time, negative emotions—grief, anger, misery—are stoked by the senseless slaughter of war. Perhaps this emotional duality helps somewhat to explain why the eloquence and power of antiwar poems have done so little to halt humans' willingness to engage in war, despite its destruction and its staggering toll.

In this chapter, you will learn how to do the following:

- Analyze poetry about war.
- Compare poets' different representations of war.
- Compose essays using reflections on, arguments about, and research on poetry about war.

Richard Lovelace   1618–1657

A wealthy, handsome Cavalier poet and a loyal supporter of King Charles I, Richard Lovelace was twice imprisoned by the Puritan Parliament during the English Civil War. He died in poverty in a London slum. Much of Lovelace's poetry is labored and lifeless, but he did write several charming, graceful lyrics, such as "To Althea from Prison," "To Amarantha, That She Would Dishevel Her Hair," and "To Lucasta, on Going to the Wars."

To Lucasta, on Going to the Wars

Tell me not, sweet, I am unkind,
    That from the nunnery
Of thy chaste breast and quiet mind
    To war and arms I fly.

True, a new mistress now I chase,   5
    The first foe in the field;
And with stronger faith embrace
    A sword, a horse, a shield.

Yet this inconstancy is such
    As thou shalt adore;   10
I could not love thee, dear, so much,
    Loved I not honor more.

(1649)

Questions for Discussion and Writing

1. What seems to be the speaker's attitude toward war? How old do you imagine the speaker to be?
2. Who is the speaker's "new mistress"?
3. What values or virtues are contrasted in the poem?

◇◇◇◇◇◇◇◇◇◇◇◇◇◇◇◇◇◇◇◇◇◇

Stephen Crane 1871–1900

Stephen Crane was born in Newark, New Jersey, the fourteenth child of a Methodist minister who died when Crane was nine. Leaving college early, he moved to New York City, where he observed firsthand the boozers and prostitutes who inhabited the slums. Crane's first novel, *Maggie: A Girl of the Streets* (1893), drew on these observations. At age twenty-four, and with no military experience, he wrote *The Red Badge of Courage* (1895), a Civil War novel that became an American classic and made Crane famous.

War Is Kind

Do not weep, maiden, for war is kind.
Because your lover threw wild hands toward the sky
And the affrighted steed ran on alone,
Do not weep.
War is kind.   5

    Hoarse, booming drums of the regiment,
    Little souls who thirst for fight,
    These men were born to drill and die.
    The unexplained glory flies above them,
    Great is the Battle-God, great, and his Kingdom—   10
    A field where a thousand corpses lie.

Do not weep, babe, for war is kind.
Because your father tumbled in the yellow trenches,
Raged at his breast, gulped and died,
Do not weep.   15
War is kind.

    Swift blazing flag of the regiment,
    Eagle with crest of red and gold,
    These men were born to drill and die.
    Point for them the virtue of slaughter,   20
    Make plain to them the excellence of killing
    And a field where a thousand corpses lie.

Mother whose heart hung humble as a button
On the bright splendid shroud of your son,
Do not weep.   25
War is kind.

(1899)

Questions for Discussion and Writing

1. Why do you think stanzas 2 and 4 are indented?
2. Why is the flag referred to as "the unexplained glory" (line 9)?
3. What is the tone of the poem? And the theme?

◇◇◇◇◇◇◇◇◇◇◇◇◇◇◇◇◇◇◇◇◇◇◇◇

Amy Lowell   1874–1925

A member of a prominent New England family, Amy Lowell rejected her upbringing and devoted herself to modern poetry and the company of gifted women. She became the chief advocate for the Imagist Movement in poetry, which favored hard, clear imagery and rejected the sentimentality of nineteenth-century verse. Her best poems contain evocative images that recall the impressionist painters and composers she admired.

Patterns

I walk down the garden paths,
And all the daffodils
Are blowing, and the bright blue squills.
I walk down the patterned garden paths
In my stiff, brocaded gown.   5
With my powdered hair and jeweled fan,
I too am a rare
Pattern. As I wander down
The garden paths.

My dress is richly figured,   10
And the train
Makes a pink and silver stain
On the gravel, and the thrift
Of the borders.
Just a plate of current fashion,   15
Tripping by in high-heeled, ribboned shoes.
Not a softness anywhere about me,
Only whalebone and brocade.
And I sink on a seat in the shade

Of a lime tree. For my passion   20
Wars against the stiff brocade.
The daffodils and squills
Flutter in the breeze
As they please.
And I weep;   25
For the lime tree is in blossom
And one small flower has dropped upon my bosom.

And the plashing of waterdrops
In the marble fountain
Comes down the garden paths.   30
The dripping never stops.
Underneath my stiffened gown
Is the softness of a woman bathing in a marble basin,
A basin in the midst of hedges grown
So thick, she cannot see her lover hiding,   35
But she guesses he is near,
And the sliding of the water
Seems the stroking of a dear
Hand upon her.
What is Summer in a fine brocaded gown!   40
I should like to see it lying in a heap upon the ground.
All the pink and silver crumpled up on the ground.

I would be the pink and silver as I ran along the paths,
And he would stumble after,
Bewildered by my laughter.   45
I should see the sun flashing from his sword-hilt and the
    buckles on his shoes.
I would choose
To lead him in a maze along the patterned paths,
A bright and laughing maze for my heavy-booted lover,
Till he caught me in the shade,   50
And the buttons of his waistcoat bruised my body as
    he clasped me,
Aching, melting, unafraid.
With the shadows of the leaves and the sundrops,
And the plopping of the waterdrops,
All about us in the open afternoon   55
I am very like to swoon
With the weight of this brocade,
For the sun sifts through the shade.

Underneath the fallen blossom
In my bosom,   60
Is a letter I have hid.
It was brought to me this morning by a rider from the Duke.

"Madam, we regret to inform you that Lord Hartwell
Died in action Thursday sen'night."
As I read it in the white, morning sunlight,   65
The letters squirmed like snakes.
"Any answer, Madam," said my footman.
"No," I told him.
"See that the messenger takes some refreshment.
No, no answer."   70
And I walked into the garden,
Up and down the patterned paths,
In my stiff, correct brocade.
The blue and yellow flowers stood up proudly in the sun,
Each one.   75
I stood upright too,
Held rigid to the pattern
By the stiffness of my gown;
Up and down I walked,
Up and down.   80

In a month he would have been my husband.
In a month, here, underneath this lime,
We would have broke the pattern;
He for me, and I for him,
He as Colonel, I as Lady,   85
On this shady seat.
He had a whim
That sunlight carried blessing.
And I answered, "It shall be as you have said."
Now he is dead.   90

In Summer and in Winter I shall walk
Up and down
The patterned garden paths
In my stiff, brocaded gown.
The squills and daffodils   95
Will give place to pillared roses, and to asters, and to snow.
I shall go
Up and down
In my gown.
Gorgeously arrayed,   100
Boned and stayed.
And the softness of my body will be guarded from embrace
By each button, hook, and lace.
For the man who should loose me is dead,
Fighting with the Duke in Flanders,   105
In a pattern called a war.
Christ! What are patterns for?

(1916)

Questions for Discussion and Writing

1. Lowell wrote this poem during World War I and published it in 1916. Why do you think she set it in a much earlier period?
2. Can you describe the speaker? Why is her attire described in such detail?
3. How many patterns can you find in the poem? Why is war referred to as a pattern?
4. How would you answer the question in the last line? What is its tone?
5. In what ways is "Patterns" an anti-war poem?
6. Write an interpretation of the poem based on the contrasts between the grieving woman and her surroundings in the garden.

◇◇◇◇◇◇◇◇◇◇◇◇◇◇◇◇◇◇◇◇

Wilfred Owen   1893–1918

Wilfred Owen began writing poetry at the University of London. After teaching English in France for a few years, he returned to England and joined the army. Owen was wounded in 1917 and killed in action a few days before the armistice was declared in 1918. Owen's poems, published only after his death, are some of the most powerful and vivid accounts of the horrors of war to emerge from World War I.

Dulce et Decorum Est

Bent double, like old beggars under sacks,
Knock-kneed, coughing like hags, we cursed through sludge,
Till on the haunting flares we turned our backs
And towards our distant rest began to trudge.
Men marched asleep. Many had lost their boots   5
But limped on, blood-shod. All went lame; all blind;
Drunk with fatigue; deaf even to the hoots
Of tired, outstripped Five-Nines° that dropped behind.

---

8 Five-Nines Poison gas shells.

John Singer Sargent's painting *Gassed* (1918) depicts World War I soldiers blinded by mustard gas being led back to hospital tents and dressing stations. [*Gassed* (1919), John Singer Sargent. Oil on canvas, 91 in × 240 1/2 in. Imperial War Museum, London, UK/The Art Archive at Art Resource, NY.]

Gas! Gas! Quick, boys!—An ecstasy of fumbling,
Fitting the clumsy helmets just in time;   10
But someone still was yelling out and stumbling
And flound'ring like a man in fire or lime …
Dim, through the misty panes and thick green light,
As under a green sea, I saw him drowning.
In all my dreams before my helpless sight,   15
He plunges at me, guttering, choking, drowning.

If in some smothering dreams you too could pace
Behind the wagon that we flung him in,
And watch the white eyes writhing in his face,
His hanging face, like a devil's sick of sin;   20
If you could hear, at every jolt, the blood
Come gargling from the froth-corrupted lungs,
Obscene as cancer, bitter as the cud
Of vile, incurable sores on innocent tongues,—
My friend, you would not tell with such high zest   25
To children ardent for some desperate glory,
The old Lie: *Dulce et decorum est*
Pro patria mori.°

                                        (1920)

27–28 The old Lie The quotation is from the Latin poet Horace, meaning "It is sweet and fitting to die for one's country."

Questions for Discussion and Writing

1. What are "Five-Nines"? Why does the speaker describe them as "tired"?
2. To whom is this poem addressed (the "you" in the third stanza)? What is the tone of the phrase "My friend" (line 25)?
3. What is the "desperate glory" mentioned in line 26? Can you think of any examples of it from books or movies?
4. What is "the old Lie," and do people still tell it?

◇◇◇◇◇◇◇◇◇◇◇◇◇◇◇◇◇◇◇◇◇◇

Mitsuye Yamada 1923–

Mitsuye Yamada, the daughter of Japanese immigrants to the United States, was born in Japan during her mother's return visit to her native country. Yamada was raised in Seattle; but in 1942 her father was wrongfully accused of spying, and the family was incarcerated and then taken to a relocation center in Idaho. Mitsuye and her brother were allowed to leave the camp when they renounced their allegiance to Japan. In 1955 she became an American citizen and attended the University of Cincinnati, New York University, and the University of Chicago. She later taught at Cypress College in Seattle and the University of California in Irvine. She has been an activist for women's rights, and her poetry recounts her experience of internment, as well as her feelings about racial violence, discrimination, and feminist issues.

To the Lady

The one in San Francisco who asked
Why did the Japanese Americans let
the government put them in
those camps without protest?

Come to think of it I   5
    should've run off to Canada
    should've hijacked a plane to Algeria
    should've pulled myself up from my
    bra straps
    and kicked 'm in the groin   10
    should've bombed a bank
    should've tried self-immolation
    should've holed myself up in a
    woodframe house
    and let you watch me   15

May 1942, Hayward, California—A Japanese American family, tagged and waiting for the bus that will take them to an internment camp.

burn up on the six o'clock news
should've run howling down the street
naked and assaulted you at breakfast
by AP wirephoto
should've screamed bloody murder   20
like Kitty Genovese

Then
YOU would've
  come to my aid in shining armor
  laid yourself across the railroad track   25
  marched on Washington
  tattooed a Star of David on your arm
  written six million enraged
  letters to Congress

But we didn't draw the line   30
anywhere
law and order Executive Order 9066
social order moral order internal order

You let'm
I let'm   35
All are punished.

                                          (1976)

Questions for Discussion and Writing

1. Find out what Executive Order 9066 was, and speculate on how it contributed to the speaker's attitude and response to the Lady's question.
2. In essence, what is the speaker saying in the answers to the Lady's question
   (lines 5–21)? What is the tone of these answers?
3. Who was Kitty Genovese? Can you explain any of the other allusions in
   the poem—running off to Canada, hijacking a plane, bombing a bank, self-
   immolation, holing up in a house that burns up, running naked in the streets?
   How about the references in lines 24–29?
4. Explain and comment on the last three lines of the poem.

◇◇◇◇◇◇◇◇◇◇◇◇◇◇◇◇◇◇◇◇◇◇◇◇

Peg Lauber 1938–

Born and reared in Detroit, Michigan, Peg Lauber now spends summers in
Wisconsin and winters in New Orleans raising sandhill cranes. One critic says that
in her collection, *New Orleans Suite*, she "captures the river, the birds, the fish, the
snakes, the barge traffic, the strippers and prostitutes—all the sweetness and squalor,
the festivity and fever, the miracle and mayhem of the human spectacle."

Six National Guardsmen Blown Up Together

Today the six come home for good,
those who grew up together on the bayous,
like those boys in the Civil War
who enlisted together, died together,
sometimes leaving small towns   5
with no young men—
a whole generation gone. These six hunted,
fished, trapped together, but someone
tracked them, hunted them
a world away from their usual prey—   10
alligators, nutrias, crawfish, bass.

Right across the canal out front
is the Naval base's runway approach
where we'll hear or even see
the big cargo plane carrying   15
what is left of the men coming in,
rumbling and lumbering along, scaring
the brown pelican and his mate
flying low up the channel
and scattering seventeen members   20
of the Cajun Air Force,
those bigger white pelicans,
cruising, then banking away.

Only the gulls will remain
gliding around with mournful   25
screeches, appropriate requiem.
Then silence, all planes grounded
in respect for the relatives, the wives
who huddle on folding chairs, bent
weeping into their small children's hair,   30
the children frightened, weeping with them,
now understanding that their father
in that flag-draped box will not,
like a Jack, pop out
if they touch a button—   35
that nothing, nothing
will ever be the same.

(2006)

Questions for Discussion and Writing

1. Why did the poet select the title "Six National Guardsmen Blown Up Together"? How does it shape your expectations for the poem?

2. What is the setting for this poem? How many different kinds of local animals are mentioned? How does their presence affect your feelings about the people and events in the poem?

3. What do you think of the Jack-in-the-Box simile in the final lines? How effectively does it capture the events and feelings of the moment being described?

◇◇◇◇◇◇◇◇◇◇◇◇◇◇◇◇◇◇◇◇◇◇◇

Yusef Komunyakaa 1947–

Born James Willie Brown Jr., Yusef Komunyakaa was born and grew up in Bogalusa, Louisiana, just as the civil rights movement was gathering momentum. He later reclaimed the name *Komunyakaa* from his great-grandparents, who had been stowaways in a ship from Trinidad. He served in the U.S. Army in Vietnam from 1965 to 1967, and his war poems rank with the best on the subject. Komunyakaa has said, "Poetry is a kind of distilled insinuation. It's a way of expanding and talking around an idea or question. Sometimes more actually gets said through such a technique than a full-frontal assault." His collection *Neon Vernacular* won the Pulitzer Prize for poetry in 1994.

Facing It

My black face fades,
hiding inside the black granite.
I said I wouldn't,
Dammit: No tears.
I'm stone. I'm flesh.   5
My clouded reflection eyes me
like a bird of prey, the profile of night
slanted against morning. I turn
this way—the stone lets me go.
I turn that way—I'm inside   10
the Vietnam Veterans Memorial
again, depending on the light
to make a difference.
I go down the 58,002 names,
half-expecting to find   15
my own in letters like smoke.
I touch the name Andrew Johnson;
I see the booby trap's white flash.
Names shimmer on a woman's blouse
but when she walks away   20
the names stay on the wall.
Brushstrokes flash, a red bird's
wings cutting across my stare.
The sky. A plane in the sky.
A white vet's image floats   25
closer to me, then his pale eyes
look through mine. I'm a window.

He's lost his right arm
inside the stone. In the black mirror
a woman's trying to erase names: 30
No, she's brushing a boy's hair.

(1988)

The Vietnam Veterans Memorial in Washington, D. C., contains
58,325 names of the killed and missing from the Vietnam War.
The wall's mirror-like surface (polished black granite) reflects the
images of surrounding trees, lawns, monuments, and visitors.

Questions for Discussion and Writing

1. Explain the title of the poem. What is "It"?

2. Why is the speaker "half-expecting to find my own [name] in letters like
   smoke" (lines 15–16)?

3. From line 19 on, the speaker describes images he sees reflected in the Wall.
   Can you explain the choice of these particular images?

4. What is the significance of the error in perception that the speaker makes
   at the end of the poem? Why are the woman and boy present? How is their
   activity symbolic?

Ideas for Writing: Making Connections

1. Compare the speaker's attitude toward war in "To Lucasta, on Going to the Wars" with the attitudes of the speakers in at least three other poems in this portfolio.
2. Write a paper discussing the ways in which the memorial in Washington to the Vietnam War dead differs from the usual monuments honoring dead soldiers. Consider why some patriotic groups at first were offended by the monument.
3. In what ways is "To the Lady" a war poem? How does it differ from the rest of the selections in this portfolio?
4. Choose two poems that depict war's destruction of cities and landscapes, and contrast their imagery with the images in two poems depicting the destruction of human life.
5. Several poems directly or indirectly attack the causes of war. Make a list of as many of these causes as you can. Which ones seem valid to you? Which do you question?

MultiModal Project

Organize the poems in this portfolio into a poetry reading to be performed at your local coffee house or bookstore. In what order will you place the poems? How long will the reading be? How many readers do you want, and what qualities will you look for in the readers? How should they dress? What pieces of music will add to the total effect, and how will you integrate the music and the oral readings? Do you want live or recorded music? Will you design any special staging effects? Explain your reasoning about your choices in orchestrating this event.

27 A Portfolio of Humorous and Satirical Poetry

Chapter Preview

Oddly enough, many adults who claim not to enjoy poetry once loved it, in the form of nursery rhymes like this one:

> Hey, diddle, diddle,
> The cat and the fiddle,
> The cow jumped over the moon.
> The little dog laughed
> To see such sport,
> And the dish ran away with the spoon.

Though written for adults, the poems in this portfolio use many of the same tactics as "Hey Diddle Diddle" does to amuse readers. A little bit of nonsense, some unexpected combinations of familiar things, a funny shift in point of view, characters and objects performing unfeasible actions, a surprising set of incongruities, a lighthearted warmth in the tone—these are all qualities that made you giggle as a child, and you will see them in the poems to follow. But as you remember, some funny nursery rhymes lack that lighthearted tone, such as "Jack and Jill Went Up the Hill" and "Humpty Dumpty," whose characters come to no good end. And in our collection, poems appear that are also humorous in a dark, satiric way, showing a sharper intolerance for foolishness and inconsistency. We hope that through studying these poems, you regain your childhood pleasure in the genre.

After reading this chapter, you will know how to

- Analyze humorous poetry, including satire.
- Compare how and why a range of poets use humor in their poetry.
- Write about humor and satire in poems, using reflection, argument, and research.

Linda Pastan   1932–

Born in the Bronx, Linda Pastan was raised in a Jewish family. After graduating from college, she put her career on hold to get married and raise children. Ten years later she returned to poetry, publishing her first book at age thirty-nine. The poet May Sarton writes that Pastan offers "a wry unsentimental acceptance of hard truth." In a typical line, Pastan observes, "I made a list of things I have to remember and a list of things I want to forget, but I see they are the same list." Her works investigate the depths of seemingly mundane experience, using clear language and everyday metaphors.

Marks

My husband gives me an A
for last night's supper,
an incomplete for my ironing,
a B plus in bed.
My son says I am average,   5
an average mother, but if
I put my mind to it
I could improve.
My daughter believes
in Pass/Fail and tells me   10
I pass. Wait 'til they learn
I'm dropping out.

(1978)

Questions for Discussion and Writing

1. How would you describe the speaker in the poem? What is her status in the family? How do the other family members perceive her?
2. Explain the significance of the title. Make up another title that would also fit the poem.
3. What do the speaker's marks in different activities suggest about her? About the graders?
4. Did you ever feel that you were being evaluated on something that you really shouldn't be given marks for? Remember your feelings about this and relate them to the meaning of "Marks."

◇◇◇◇◇◇◇◇◇◇◇◇◇◇◇◇◇◇◇◇◇◇◇◇

Ron Koertge   1940–

Ron Koertge, an only child, grew up "fairly happy" in a comfortable home in Olney, Illinois. As a teenager, he was taken ill with rheumatic fever, which weakened his heart and left him with "a sense of the insubstantiality of my body and made me alternately tentative and foolishly bold." He had a dramatic flair and loved attention, loved to shock people, "to leave them lurching, not laughing." He did not begin writing poetry until he was in graduate school. In fact, he claims, "I didn't so much plan to be a writer. Mostly I wrote a lot. Then people started to call me a writer."

Cinderella's Diary

I miss my stepmother. What a thing to say
but it's true. The prince is so boring: four
hours to dress and then the cheering throngs.
Again. The page who holds the door is cute
enough to eat. Where is he once Mr. Charming   5
kisses my forehead goodnight?

Every morning I gaze out a casement window
at the hunters, dark men with blood on their
boots who joke and mount, their black trousers
straining, rough beards, callused hands, selfish,   10
abrupt…

Oh, dear diary—I am lost in ever after:
Those insufferable birds, someone in every
room with a lute, the queen calling me to look
at another painting of her son, this time   15
holding the transparent slipper I wish
I'd never seen.

(2007)

Questions for Discussion and Writing

1. What do people usually write in diaries? How does your answer help you understand the poem?
2. What does Koertge's Cinderella really want? Support your answer with details. What is unexpected about her desires?
3. What is the writer's attitude toward Cinderella? Explain your answer using evidence from the poem. What is *your* attitude toward this Cinderella, and why?

<><><><><><><><><><><><><><><>

Billy Collins 1941–

Born in New York City, William James (Billy) Collins has lived there ever since. His father is an electrician, his mother a nurse. Selected as Poet Laureate of the United States in 2000, he served two terms. He has managed to combine critical approval with unprecedented popular success. His last three collections of poems have broken sales records for poetry. "Usually," he says, "I try to create a hospitable tone at the beginning of a poem. Stepping from the title to the first lines is like stepping into a canoe. A lot of things can go wrong."

Introduction to Poetry

I ask them to take a poem
and hold it up to the light
like a color slide

or press an ear against its hive.

I say drop a mouse into a poem   5
and watch him probe his way out,

or walk inside the poem's room
and feel the walls for a light switch.

I want them to water-ski
across the surface of a poem   10
waving at the author's name on the shore.

But all they want to do
is tie the poem to a chair with a rope
and torture a confession out of it.

They begin beating it with a hose   15
to find out what it really means.

                                              (1988)

Questions for Discussion and Writing

1. Who is "I" in the poem? Who are "they"? Does the title help you identify who these people represent? In what two different ways could you take the title?

2. The "I" presents five metaphors as possible approaches to understanding a poem. Can you explain what type of approach each metaphor suggests? Even if not, can you identify which approach *you* usually take when studying a poem? How would you describe your usual process if you don't understand a poem right away?

3. While the "I" uses five metaphors, the "they" present only one metaphor. What is it? Why is the last metaphor humorous? Can you explain more than one reason why this metaphor for understanding a poem represents a bad approach?

◇◇◇◇◇◇◇◇◇◇◇◇◇◇◇◇◇◇◇◇◇◇◇◇

Andrea Carlisle   1944–

Andrea Carlisle is a writer and editor who lives on a houseboat in Oregon, enjoying her neighbors: beavers, muskrats, eagles, hawks, herons, and generous, eccentric humans. She has received awards for fiction and nonfiction works and has earned grateful endorsements from the many other authors she has helped. She reports that she has edited prose about "high altitude balloonists, lesbian debutantes, Alaskan midwives, Mexican healers, Swiss bank account robbers, dysfunctional families, and multiprocessing computer systems."

Emily Dickinson's To-Do List

Monday
Figure out what to wear—white dress?
Put hair in bun
Bake gingerbread for Sue
Peer out window at passersby   5
Write poem
Hide poem

Tuesday
White dress? Off-white dress?
Feed cats   10
Chat with Lavinia
Work in garden
Letter to T.W.H.

Wednesday
White dress or what?   15
Eavesdrop on visitors from behind door
Write poem
Hide poem

Thursday
Try on new white dress   20
Gardening—watch out for narrow fellows in grass!
Gingerbread, cakes, treats
Poems: Write and hide them

Friday
Embroider sash for white dress   25
Write poetry
Water flowers on windowsill
Hide everything

                                                    (1996)

Questions for Discussion and Writing

1. The denotation of the term "to-do list" is obvious. What are the connotations of the term? Read the biographical sketch of Emily Dickinson on page 508. Why is the idea of a to-do list for someone like Emily Dickinson humorous?

2. What theme runs through all the activities on Emily Dickinson's to-do list—that is, what is similar about all of her days? Is there a serious point behind their similarity?

3. Look up more information on Emily Dickinson and apply it to details of the poem. How many allusions and references to Emily Dickinson poems can you find in Carlisle's poem?

Craig Raine   1944–

Born into a working-class family in Durham, England, Craig Raine says he "wasn't a religious boy," that he "never liked God." One of his early teachers described his attempts at poetry as "pimply Dylan Thomas," but he was not deterred. "I really have a free-floating acceptance of possibilities," he later declared; "I don't think anything is unthinkable. What the poet does is as ordinary and mysterious as digesting. I question. I break life down. I impose chaos on order."

A Martian Sends a Postcard Home

Caxtons are mechanical birds with many wings
and some are treasured for their markings—

they cause the eyes to melt
or the body to shriek without pain.

I have never seen one fly, but   5
sometimes they perch on the hand.

Mist is when the sky is tired of flight
and rests its soft machine on the ground:

then the world is dim and bookish
like engravings under tissue paper.   10

Rain is when the earth is television.
It has the properites of making colours darker.

Model T is a room with the lock inside—
a key is turned to free the world

for movement, so quick there is a film   15
to watch for anything missed.

But time is tied to the wrist
or kept in a box, ticking with impatience.

In homes, a haunted apparatus sleeps,
that snores when you pick it up.   20

If the ghost cries, they carry it
to their lips and soothe it to sleep

with sounds. And yet, they wake it up
deliberately, by tickling with a finger.

Only the young are allowed to suffer   25
openly. Adults go to a punishment room

with water but nothing to eat.
They lock the door and suffer the noises

alone. No one is exempt
and everyone's pain has a different smell. 30

At night, when all the colours die,
they hide in pairs

and read about themselves—
in colour, with their eyelids shut.

(1979)

Questions for Discussion and Writing

1. Craig Raine and his fellow poet Christopher Reid were main writers in the Martian Poetry movement in the 1970s and early 1980s in England. This poetry used odd and unusual metaphors to describe things through the eyes of a Martian, as the poem printed here does. Why would things look different to a Martian than they do to an Earthling? Have you ever felt like an alien trying to understand your surroundings? Describe the situation.

2. The postcard describes a series of common objects and phenomenon. In a small group of classmates, work to explain as many of these as you can identify and why the Martian sees them the way it does. As a whole class, see whether you can identify all of the images in the postcard.

◇◇◇◇◇◇◇◇◇◇◇◇◇◇◇◇◇◇◇◇◇◇◇◇

Jan Beatty   1952–

Born in Pittsburgh, Jan Beatty, who directs the creative writing program at Carlow, a Catholic university in Pennsylvania, is in charge of their Madwomen in the Attic Writing Workshop—so named to challenge old traditions of women's writing (when these crazy ladies were kept shut away from view). One critic observes that her poems "question icons, invoke taboos, and walk the tightrope between sex and love." In April 2008 Beatty encountered difficulty at a poetry reading because her poems were considered "too sexually explicit."

A Waitress's Instructions on Tipping
or
Get the Cash Up and Don't Waste My Time

20% minimum as long as the waitress doesn't inflict bodily harm.
If you're two people at a four top, tip extra.
If you sit a long time, pay rent.
Double tips for special orders.
Always tip extra when using coupons. 5
Better yet, don't use coupons.
Never leave change instead of bills.
Never leave pennies at all.

Never hide a tip for fun.
Overtip, overtip, overtip.   10
Remember, I am somebody's mother or daughter.
Large parties *must* overtip, no separate piles of change.
If people in your party don't show up, tip *for* them.
Don't wait around for gratitude if you overtip.
Take a risk. Don't adjust your tip so your credit card total is even.   15
Don't ever, ever pull out a tipping guide in public.
If you leave 10% or less, eat at home.
If I call a taxi for you, tip me.
If I hang your coat for you, tip me.
If I get cigarettes for you, tip me.   20
Better yet, do it yourself.
If you buy a $50 bottle of wine, pull out a $10.
If I serve you one cocktail, don't hand me $.35
If you're just having coffee, leave a $5.
Don't fold a bill and hand it to me like you're a big shot.   25
Don't say, *there's a big tip in it for you if…*
Don't say, *I want to make sure you get this*, like a busboy would steal it.
Don't say, *Here, honey, this is for you.*—ever.
Don't say, *I'll make it worth your while.*
If you're miserable, there's not enough money in the world.   30

                                                                    (1995)

Questions for Discussion and Writing

1. Who is the speaker? What is her attitude toward restaurant customers?
   Quote words and phrases that show this attitude. How would you describe
   the language used in the poem?

2. Did you learn anything about being a waitress or a customer from reading
   this poem? What was it? Do you think that Jan Beatty ever held a job as a
   waitress? Why?

3. Much of the poem tells us about the customers, but the last two lines tell us
   something more about the speaker. What may we conclude about her from
   these lines?

◇◇◇◇◇◇◇◇◇◇◇◇◇◇◇◇◇◇◇◇◇◇◇

Jeanne Marie Beaumont 1954–

Jeanne Marie Beaumont, born in Springfield, Pennsylvania, spent her childhood
there in the suburbs, which she says she detested, "feeling stifled and rebellious."
Her parents, who neither encouraged nor discouraged her writing, did instill in her
"a sense of discipline." Her poetry is informed by her interest in folklore, fairy tales,
history, modernism, surrealism, theatre of the absurd, and play. A three-minute film
using the text of "Afraid So" read by Garrison Keillor has been shown in schools
and at many film festivals since appearing in January 2000.

Afraid So

Is it starting to rain?
Did the check bounce?
Are we out of coffee?
Is this going to hurt?
Could you lose your job?   5
Did the glass break?
Was the baggage misrouted?
Will this go on my record?
Are you missing much money?
Was anyone injured?   10
Is the traffic heavy?
Do I have to remove my clothes?
Will it leave a scar?
Must you go?
Will this be in the papers?   15
Is my time up already?
Are we seeing the understudy?
Will it affect my eyesight?
Did all the books burn?
Are you still smoking?   20
Is the bone broken?
Will I have to put him to sleep?
Was the car totaled?
Am I responsible for these charges?
Are you contagious?   25
Will we have to wait long?
Is the runway icy?
Was the gun loaded?
Could this cause side effects?
Do you know who betrayed you?   30
Is the wound infected?
Are we lost?
Will it get any worse?

(2004)

Questions for Discussion and Writing

1. What is the answer to all of the questions that compose the poem? When you were reading the poem, when did you realize this was true? Did this realization add to the humor? Why or why not?

2. Reread the poem looking for some logical reason for the order of the questions. Can you make sense of the organization? What is it? Give some examples to support your idea.

Peter Pereira 1959–

Born in Spokane, Washington, Peter Pereira is a family physician in Seattle and co-founder of Floating Bridge Press. His parents, who were pen pals after World War II, eventually met, fell in love, married, and raised ten kids together. As a Catholic during the restive 1960s, Pereira learned to question authority, social conventions, and Biblical constructs. "Reconsidering the Seven," he says, "is an example of such questioning." He has been happily united with his partner Dean for twenty-two years.

Reconsidering the Seven

Deadly Sins? Please—let's replace Pride
with Modesty, especially when it's false.

And thank goodness for Lust, without it
I wouldn't be here. Would you?

Envy, Greed—why not? If they lead us   5
to better ourselves, to Ambition.

And Gluttony, like a healthy belch, is a guest's
best response to being served a good meal.

I'll take Sloth over those busybodies
who can't sit still, watch a sunset   10

without yammering, or snapping a picture.
Now *that* makes me Wrathful.

                                                    (2007)

Questions for Discussion and Writing

1. What are the seven deadly sins? Where does the list come from originally?
2. Why does the speaker reconsider the seven deadly sins? What makes the reconsideration funny? Do you find the argument persuasive? Why or why not?

Ideas for Writing: Making Connections

1. Much of the humorous quality of poetry comes from its *tone*: that is, the attitude it conveys, such as in "tone of voice." Following is a list of words that can describe tone in literature. Look up any unfamiliar or vague terms in a dictionary so that you are clear on their meaning. Assign at least two of the terms to each of the poems in this portfolio. Get together with a group of classmates and discuss your choices, and report to the whole class the choices where you found most agreement.

whimsical	naive	intolerant
satiric	sympathetic	surprising
bitter	forgiving	intellectual
comical	sharp	ludicrous
warm	wistful	regretful
sad		

2. Some of our pleased reaction to poems comes from the joy of figuring out some puzzle that they present. This principle is obvious in "A Martian Sends a Postcard Home." What other poems in this portfolio involve your unraveling a puzzle of some kind? Apply this principle to at least four other poems in the portfolio, and explain what the puzzle is that had to be solved by the reader. Then do the same to two poems in the Anthology of Poetry.

MultiModal Project

> Write an imitation or response to one of the humorous poems in this portfolio.
>
> Possibilities:
>
> - a humorous verse about how a roommate or co-worker might grade you;
> - a diary entry about what happens *after* the end of a well-known story;
> - a fanciful description of how you study a poem;
> - a five-stanza poem with details from your own five-day week;
> - a postcard from a Martian that uses riddling descriptions to depict objects or behaviors that the Martian doesn't understand;
> - a list of pointed advice for customers, clients, or bosses you have worked with;
> - a poem with the title "Probably Not," "You Bet," or some other phrase that can answer all the questions you write;
> - a verse or prose poem in which you suggest the positive side of something usually negative.
>
> Share your creations with your fellow students.

PART IV Writing About Drama

Jaq. All the world's a stage,
And all the men and women merely players:
They have their exits and their entrances;
And one man in his time plays many parts,
His acts being seven ages. At first the infant
Mewling and puking in the nurse's arms.

This section, focusing on drama and including brief discussions of its beginnings and more recent developments in contemporary theater, completes our study of the major literary genres.

28 How Do I Read a Play?

Chapter Preview

A play is written to be performed. Although most drama begins with a written script, the author of a play counts on the collaboration of others—actors, directors, set designers, costumers, makeup artists, lighting and sound engineers—to translate the written words into a performance on stage or film or videotape. Unlike novelists and poets, playwrights do not necessarily expect their words to be read by the audience. By the end of this chapter, you will be able to

- Explain the differences between watching a play and reading one.
- Define *dialogue* and explain its importance.
- Describe the process of listening imaginatively to the written lines of a play.
- Summarize the advantages of reading a play over viewing one.
- Define the basic terminology of stagecraft: *proscenium, apron, upstage* and *downstage, flats, theater in the round*.
- Explain the importance of picturing movements, gestures, and setting when reading a play.
- Identify points to consider when comparing a filmed version of a play with its written script.

Listen to the Lines

The performance goal of drama does not mean that you cannot read and study a play as you would a story or a poem. Plays share many literary qualities with other types of creative writing: character, plot, structure, atmosphere, theme, symbolism, and point of view. But it is important to recognize the differences between reading a play and seeing one performed.

The major difference between reading and watching a play is that, as a reader, you do not have the actors' voices and gestures to interpret the lines and establish the characters for you. Because playwrights rely almost entirely on speeches or conversations (called *dialogue*) to define character, develop plot, and convey theme, it will be your task as a reader to listen to the lines in your mind. Read the dialogue as you would expect to hear it spoken. For example, when you read Antigone's response to Creon,

> This death of mine
> Is of no importance; but if I had left my brother
> Lying in death unburied, I should have suffered.
> Now I do not.

do you hear the assurance and passion in her voice? Or when you read Tom's farewell speech to his sister in *The Glass Menagerie*, can you detect the mixture of tenderness and regret in his words, "Oh, Laura, Laura, I tried to leave you behind me, but I am more faithful than I intended to be! ... Blow out your candles, Laura—and so goodbye ...."?

Of course, the tone of these lines is not as clear when they are taken out of context, but even these brief quotations illustrate the charged nature of language you should expect when you read a play.

You can actually read the lines out loud to yourself or enlist some fellow students to act out some scenes with you. These oral readings will force you to decide how to interpret the words. Most of the time, however, you will have to use your imagination to re-create the sound of the spoken medium. If you do get to see a performance of a play you are reading or to hear a recording of it, you will appreciate the extraordinary liveliness of dramatic literature when it is lifted from the page and provided with sound and action.

Reading a play does have some advantage over viewing a live performance. Unlike a theatergoer, a reader can stop and return to lines or speeches that seem especially complicated or meaningful. Close reading gives you the opportunity to examine and consider the playwright's exact words, which often fly by quickly, sometimes in altered form, in an actual performance.

Visualize the Scene

In addition to imagining the sound of the dialogue, you will want to picture in your mind what the stage looks like. In a traditional theater the audience sits out front while the actors perform on a raised stage separated from the viewers by a curtain and perhaps an orchestra. The arch from which the curtain hangs is called the *proscenium*; the space extending from the bottom of the curtain to the footlights is the *apron*. The stage directions (printed in italics) indicate where the playwright wants the actors to move. *Upstage* means toward the back; *downstage* means toward the apron. A traditional set, made of canvas-covered frames called *flats*, will look like a room—with one wall removed for the audience to see through. Sometimes the set will be constructed to resemble the battlements of a castle, an opening in a forest, or a lifeboat on the ocean. Occasionally the setting is only suggested: a character climbs a ladder to deliver lines supposedly from a balcony or from an upstairs room. In one modern play, the two protagonists are presented on a bare stage speaking throughout the production (with only their heads visible) from inside garbage cans.

Another kind of stage, called *theater in the round* or an *arena stage*, puts the audience in raised seats on all sides with the players performing in the round space in the middle. After the audience is seated, the lights are extinguished, and the actors enter through the same aisles used earlier by the audience. When the actors are in position, the lights come up, illuminating only the stage, and the play begins. At the end of a scene or an act, the lights go down again, signifying the fall of the curtain and allowing the actors to leave. Stagehands come on between acts or scenes, if needed, to rearrange the setting. Not all plays are suited to this intimate staging, of course, but the audience at an arena production gains an immediacy, a feeling almost of being involved in the action, that cannot be achieved in a traditional theater.

Envision the Action

Poet and playwright Ezra Pound pointed out that the "medium of drama is not words, but persons moving about on a stage using words." This observation underlines the importance of movement, gesture, and setting in the performance of a play. These nonverbal elements of the language of drama are sometimes described in the author's stage directions. Often, though, you will find the cues for gestures, movements, and facial expressions in the words themselves, just as the director and the actors do when they are preparing a script for production. For example, these lines of Othello, spoken when he has been roused from his bed by a fight among his men, suggest the physical performance that would accompany the words:

> Why, how now, ho! from whence ariseth this?
> Are we turned to Turks, and to ourselves do that
> Which heaven hath forbid the Ottomites?
> For Christian shame, put by this barbarous brawl!
> He that stirs next to carve for his own rage
> Holds his soul light; he dies upon his motion.
> Silence that dreadful bell.

Reading this speech with an actor's or director's imagination, you can see in your mind the character stride angrily into the fight scene, gesture threateningly at the men who are poised to continue the fight, and then point suddenly offstage in the direction of the clamoring alarm bell. Such a detailed reading will take time, but you will be rewarded by the fun and satisfaction of catching the full dramatic quality of the play.

In more recent years, playwrights like Jane Martin and Tennessee Williams have tried to keep artistic control over the interpretations of their works by including detailed stage directions in their scripts. The extensive production notes for Williams's *The Glass Menagerie* sometimes read like descriptions from a novel or an essay:

> The light dims out on Tom and comes up in the Wingfield living room—a delicate lemony light. It is about five on a Friday evening of late spring which comes "scattering poems in the sky" .... A fragile, unearthly prettiness has come out in Laura; she is like a piece of translucent glass touched by light, given a momentary radiance, not actual, not lasting.

With or without notes like this, your imagination will be working full time when you read a play. You will not be at the mercy of some designer's taste or the personal interpretation of a director or actor. You will be free to produce the play in the theater of your mind.

Drama on Film

Many plays are available on videotape or digital videodiscs. These include filmed versions of stage performances, such as the Laurence Olivier production of Shakespeare's *Othello*, and movies adapted from plays, such as the 1973 film adaptation of *A Doll's House* starring Anthony Hopkins and Claire Bloom. You will find that many plays in this book are on video.

You can often gain insight and special pleasure from seeing a dramatic work on film. A video production provides you with an opportunity to compare your responses to the play as you read it with your responses as you watch the video. You will also be able to think about the decisions that the film director has made. Here are some points to consider when comparing a film to the written text of a play:

- What scenes or characters, if any, have been cut? What, if anything, has been added? Why do you think these changes were made? What is their effect?
- Are the characters portrayed as you imagined they would be? Has the film changed your perception of the characters or your understanding of the plot?
- Would you have cast the same actors in these roles? If not, whom would you have chosen? What difference do you think your choices would make?
- Does the film focus your attention on certain characters or actions through such techniques as close-ups or reaction shots? What are the results of these uses of the camera?
- How is the setting different from what you imagined as you read the play? Did the filmmaker take liberties with the setting suggested by the playwright? (For example, were indoor play scenes transferred outdoors in the film?)

- Does the play transfer effectively from the page to the screen? Do you think the play is better suited to the stage?
- Does the film version clarify the play for you? Does it enhance your appreciation of the play? Can you explain why or why not?
- Do you think the playwright would be pleased with the film version? Why or why not?
- Imagine that you are directing a film version of a play that you have read. What important decisions about character, setting, and pacing of the action would you have to make? Would you cut any scenes? Would you add any new scenes? What advice would you give to the performers about their roles?

Before writing about a play or a film, be sure to respond to the critical questions that follow.

Critical Questions for Reading Plays

Before planning an analysis of any of the plays in this text, write out your answers to the following questions to be sure you understand the play and to help you generate material for your paper.

1. What is the central conflict in the play? How is it resolved?
2. Does the play contain any secondary conflicts (subplots)? How do they relate to the main conflict?
3. Does the play follow a traditional dramatic structure (see Chapter 29)? What is the climax? Is there a denouement?
4. Who is the main character or protagonist (see Chapter 29)? What sort of person is he or she? Does this protagonist have a fatal flaw? Is the protagonist a hero (see Chapter 30)?
5. Is the antagonist (the one who opposes the protagonist) a person, an environment, or a social force (see Chapter 29)? If a person, does the antagonist cause conflict intentionally?
6. Do the other characters provide exposition (background information)? Are they used as *foils* to oppose, contrast, criticize, and thus help develop the main characters?
7. What are the time and setting of the play? How important are these elements? Could the play be set just as effectively in another time or place?
8. Does the title provide any clues to an understanding of the play? If you had to give the play another title, what would it be?
9. What is the theme of the play? Can you state it in a single sentence?
10. Is the play a tragedy, a comedy, or a mixture (see Chapter 30)? Is this classification important?
11. Is the presentation realistic? Does the playwright use any special theatrical devices (such as lighting, music, costumes, distinctive or surreal settings)? If so, what effect do they have on your impression of the play?

29 Writing About Dramatic Structure

Chapter Preview

Drama is not as flexible as other forms of literature. A writer of fiction can take as much time as needed to inform the reader about character, setting, motivations, or theme. The dramatist must do everything quickly and clearly. Audiences will not sit through a tedious first act; neither can they stop the play, pick it up tomorrow, or go back to Act I to refresh their memories. Even with the technologies of film and video recording, most plays, including movies and television drama, are seen in a single, relatively brief sitting. By the end of this chapter, you will be able to

- Define the key terms in Aristotle's requirements for effective drama: *fable, argument, protagonist,* and *antagonist.*
- Describe the stages in conventional dramatic structure: *point of attack, exposition, rising action, climax, falling action,* and *denouement.*
- Analyze the structure of the play *Antigone.*
- Explain the process for developing an *argumentative thesis.*
- Identify the basic conventions for quoting from a play.
- Evaluate three types of unclear language to avoid: *Engfish, jargon,* and *abstract words.*

What Is Dramatic Structure?

More than two thousand years ago the Greek philosopher Aristotle pointed out that the most important element of drama is the *fable,* what we call the *story,* or *plot.* The fable, said Aristotle, has to have a beginning, a middle, and an end. As obvious as this observation seems, it emphasizes the dramatist's special need to engage an audience early and keep it engaged until the conclusion of the play.

Recognizing the drama's strict time limits, Aristotle set down a number of conditions for developing the fable, or plot, in a clear and interesting way. According to Aristotle, the heart of the dramatic story is the *agon,* or *argument,* and the conflict surrounding this argument creates tension and incites interest. The two sides of the conflict, the pros and

631

cons of the argument, are represented on stage by the ***protagonist*** and the ***antagonist***. The protagonist may be one person or many, and the antagonist may be a person, a group, a thing, or a force (supernatural or natural). We often call the protagonist of a play its **hero** or **heroine**, and sometimes the antagonist is also the *villain*.

The fundamental struggle between the protagonist and the antagonist is developed according to a set pattern that theater audiences have come to recognize and expect. This conventional structure can be varied, of course, but most dramatic literature contains the following components:

1. ***Point of attack:*** the starting point from which the dramatist leads the audience into the plot. A playwright can begin at the story's beginning and allow the audience to discover what is going on at the same time the characters do; or the writer can begin in the middle of things (*in medias res*), or even near the end, and gradually reveal the events that have already taken place.

2. ***Exposition:*** the revelation of facts, circumstances, and past events. The essential facts about the characters and the conflict can be established in a number of ways, from having minor characters reveal information through conversation to plunging the audience right into the action.

3. ***Rising action:*** the building of interest through complication of the conflict. In this stage, the protagonist and antagonist move steadily toward a confrontation.

4. ***Climax:*** the play's high point, the decisive showdown between protagonist and antagonist. The climax—the play's turning point—can be a single moment or a series of events, but once reached, it becomes a point of no return.

5. ***Falling action:*** the unraveling of the plot, where events fall into place and the conflict moves toward final resolution.

6. ***Denouement:*** the play's conclusion, the explanation or outcome of the action. The term *denouement* (literally an "untying") may be applied to both comedy and tragedy, but the Greeks used the word *catastrophe* for a tragic denouement, probably because it involved the death of the hero or heroine. Comedies, of course, end happily, often with a wedding.

Whatever it is called, the denouement marks the end of the play: the lovers kiss, the bodies are carried off the stage, and the audience goes home. Most dramatists employ this traditional pattern. Even when they mix in other devices, rearrange elements, and invent new ways to exhibit their materials, dramatists still establish a conflict, develop both sides of the argument, and reach a credible conclusion. After centuries of theater history, the basic structure of drama has changed very little.

Looking at Dramatic Structure

As you read *Antigone*, written in 441 B.C., notice that the play's central conflict is introduced, developed, and resolved according to the pattern we have just described.

Although written first, *Antigone* is the third and last play in the chronology of events composing Sophocles's Oedipus cycle; the first two plays are *Oedipus the King* and *Oedipus at Colonus*.

According to Greek legend, King Laius of Thebes and his descendants were doomed by the god Apollo. Warned by the Oracle of Delphi that his own son would kill him, Laius leaves the son, Oedipus, to die in the mountains. But Oedipus survives and unknowingly kills his father, whom he encounters on the road to Thebes. Oedipus solves the riddle of the Sphinx for the Thebans and becomes their king, unwittingly marrying his mother, Jocasta, the widow of Laius. Several years later, when he learns what he has done, Oedipus blinds himself and leaves Thebes. Creon, brother of Jocasta, becomes the ruler of Thebes and is entrusted with caring for Oedipus's two daughters, Antigone and Ismene. Oedipus's two sons, Polyneices and Eteocles, reject their father and struggle for power in Thebes. Polyneices is driven from the city but returns with an army; in the ensuing battle he and Eteocles kill each other, while Creon succeeds to the throne. As the play opens, Antigone and Ismene are discussing Creon's first official decree.

Sophocles   ca. 496–ca. 405 B.C.

Sophocles wrote more than 120 plays, but only 7 have survived. Born in Colonus, near Athens, he studied under Aeschylus, the master of Greek tragedy. Sophocles did not question the justice of the gods; his plays assume a divine order that humans must follow. His strong-willed protagonists end tragically because of pride and lack of self-knowledge. His works include *Oedipus the King, Antigone, Electra,* and *Ajax.*

In this scene from a modern-dress production Creon condemns Antigone, standing to the right, while the chorus sits on benches center-stage and the leader of the chorus looks on.

Antigone

Translated by David Grene

CHARACTERS

ANTIGONE	HAEMON
ISMENE	TEIRESIAS
CHORUS OF THEBAN ELDERS	A MESSENGER
CREON	EURYDICE
A SENTRY	SECOND MESSENGER

(The two sisters Antigone and Ismene meet in front of the palace gates in Thebes.)

ANTIGONE: Ismene, my dear sister,
 whose father was my father, can you think of any
 of all the evils that stem from Oedipus°
 that Zeus does not bring to pass for us, while we yet live?
 No pain, no ruin, no shame, and no dishonor   5
 but I have seen it in our mischiefs,
 yours and mine.
 And now what is the proclamation that they tell of
 made lately by the commander, publicly,
 to all the people? Do you know it? Have you heard it?   10
 Don't you notice when the evils due to enemies
 are headed towards those we love?
ISMENE: Not a word, Antigone, of those we love,
 either sweet or bitter, has come to me since the moment
 when we lost our two brothers,   15
 on one day, by their hands dealing mutual death.
 Since the Argive army fled in this past night,
 I know of nothing further, nothing
 of better fortune or of more destruction.
ANTIGONE: *I* knew it well; that is why I sent for you   20
 to come outside the palace gates
 to listen to me, privately.
ISMENE: What is it? Certainly your words
 come of dark thoughts.

---

3 the evils that stem from Oedipus: As Sophocles describes in *Oedipus the King*, the King of Thebes discovered that he had lived his life under a curse. Unknowingly, he had slain his father and married his mother. On realizing this terrible truth, Oedipus put out his own eyes and departed into exile. Now, years later, as *Antigone* opens, Antigone and Ismene, daughters of Oedipus, are recalling how their two brothers died. After the abdication of their father, the brothers had ruled Thebes together. But they fell to quarreling. When Eteocles expelled Polyneices, the latter returned with an army and attacked the city. The two brothers killed each other in combat, leaving the throne to Creon. The new king of Thebes has buried Eteocles with full honors, but, calling Polyneices a traitor, has decreed that his body shall be left to the crows—an especially terrible decree, for a rotting corpse might offend Zeus; bring down plague, blight, and barrenness upon Thebes; and prevent the soul of a dead hero from entering the Elysian Fields, abode of those favored by the gods.

ANTIGONE: Yes, indeed; for those two brothers of ours, in burial   25
    has not Creon honored the one, dishonored the other?
    Eteocles, they say he has used justly
    with lawful rites and hid him in the earth
    to have his honor among the dead men there.
    But the unhappy corpse of Polyneices   30
    he has proclaimed to all the citizens,
    they say, no man may hide
    in a grave nor mourn in funeral,
    but leave unwept, unburied, a dainty treasure
    for the birds that see him, for their feast's delight.   35
    That is what, they say, the worthy Creon
    has proclaimed for you and me—for me, I tell you—
    and he comes here to clarify to the unknowing
    his proclamation; he takes it seriously;
    for whoever breaks the edict death is prescribed,   40
    and death by stoning publicly.
    There you have it; soon you will show yourself
    as noble both in your nature and your birth,
    or yourself as base, although of noble parents.
ISMENE: If things are as you say, poor sister, how   45
    can I better them? how loose or tie the knot?
ANTIGONE: Decide if you will share the work, the deed.
ISMENE: What kind of danger is there? How far have your thoughts gone?
ANTIGONE: Here is this hand. Will you help it to lift the dead man?
ISMENE: Would you bury him, when it is forbidden the city?   50
ANTIGONE: At least he is my brother—and yours, too,
    though you deny him. *I* will not prove false to him.
ISMENE: You are so headstrong. Creon has forbidden it.
ANTIGONE: It is not for him to keep me from my own.
ISMENE: O God!   55
    Consider, sister, how our father died,
    hated and infamous; how he brought to light
    his own offenses; how he himself struck out
    the sight of his two eyes;
    his own hand was their executioner.   60
    Then, mother and wife, two names in one, did shame
    violently on her life, with twisted cords.
    Third, our two brothers, on a single day,
    poor wretches, themselves worked out their mutual doom.
    Each killed the other, hand against brother's hand.   65
    Now there are only the two of us, left behind,
    and see how miserable our end shall be
    if in the teeth of law we shall transgress
    against the sovereign's decree and power.
    You ought to realize we are only women,   70
    not meant in nature to fight against men,
    and that we are ruled, by those who are stronger,
    to obedience in this and even more painful matters.

I do indeed beg those beneath the earth
to give me their forgiveness, 75
since force constrains me,
that I shall yield in this to the authorities.
Extravagant action is not sensible.

ANTIGONE: I would not urge you now; nor if you wanted
to act would I be glad to have you with me. 80
Be as you choose to be; but for myself
I myself will bury him. It will be good
to die, so doing. I shall lie by his side,
loving him as he loved me; I shall be
a criminal—but a religious one. 85
The time in which I must please those that are dead
is longer than I must please those of this world.
For there I shall lie forever. You, if you like,
can cast dishonor on what the gods have honored.

ISMENE: I will not put dishonor on them, but 90
to act in defiance of the citizenry,
my nature does not give me means for that.

ANTIGONE: Let that be your excuse. But I will go
to heap the earth on the grave of my loved brother.

ISMENE: How I fear for you, my poor sister! 95

ANTIGONE: Do not fear for me. Make straight your own path to destiny.

ISMENE: At least do not speak of this act to anyone else;
bury him in secret; I will be silent, too.

ANTIGONE: Oh, oh, no! shout it out. I will hate you still worse
for silence—should you not proclaim it, 100
to everyone.

ISMENE: You have a warm heart for such chilly deeds.

ANTIGONE: I know I am pleasing those I should please most.

ISMENE: If you can do it. But you are in love
with the impossible. 105

ANTIGONE No. When I can no more, then I will stop.

ISMENE: It is better not to hunt the impossible
at all.

ANTIGONE: If you will talk like this I will loathe you,
and you will be adjudged an enemy— 110
justly—by the dead's decision. Let me alone
and my folly with me, to endure this terror.
No suffering of mine will be enough
to make me die ignobly.

ISMENE: Well, if you will, go on. 115
Know this; that though you are wrong to go, your friends
are right to love you.

CHORUS: Sun's beam, fairest of all
that ever till now shone
on seven-gated Thebes;
O golden eye of day, you shone 120
coming over Dirce's stream;°

---

122 **Dirce's stream**: a river near Thebes.

You drove in headlong rout
the whiteshielded man from Argos,
complete in arms;   125
his bits rang sharper
under your urging.

Polyneices brought him here
against our land, Polyneices,
roused by contentious quarrel;   130
like an eagle he flew into our country,
with many men-at-arms,
with many a helmet crowned with horsehair.
He stood above the halls, gaping with murderous lances,
encompassing the city's   135
seven-gated mouth.
But before his jaws would be sated
with our blood, before the fire,
pine fed, should capture our crown of towers,
he went hence—   140
such clamor of war stretched behind his back,
from his dragon foe, a thing he could not overcome.

For Zeus, who hates the most
the boasts of a great tongue,
saw them coming in a great tide,   145
insolent in the clang of golden armor.
The god struck him down with hurled fire,
as he strove to raise the victory cry,
now at the very winning post.

The earth rose to strike him as he fell swinging.   150
In his frantic onslaught, possessed, he breathed upon us
with blasting winds of hate.
Sometimes the great god of war was on one side,
and sometimes he struck a staggering blow on the other;
the god was a very wheel horse on the right trace.   155

At seven gates stood seven captains,
ranged equals against equals, and there left
their brazen suits of armor
to Zeus, the god of trophies.
Only those two wretches born of one father and mother   160
set their spears to win a victory on both sides;
they worked out their share in a common death.

Now Victory, whose name is great, has come
to Thebes of many chariots
with joy to answer her joy,   165
to bring forgetfulness of these wars;
let us go to all the shrines of the gods
and dance all night long.
Let Bacchus lead the dance,
shaking Thebes to trembling.   170

But here is the king of our land,
Creon, son of Menoeceus;
in our new contingencies with the gods,
he is our new ruler.
He comes to set in motion some design—   175
what design is it? Because he has proposed
the convocation of the elders.
He sent a public summons for our discussion.
CREON: Gentlemen: as for our city's fortune,
the gods have shaken her, when the great waves broke,   180
but the gods have brought her through again to safety.
For yourselves, I chose you out of all and summoned you
to come to me, partly because I knew you
as always loyal to the throne—at first,
when Laius was king, and then again   185
when Oedipus saved our city and then again
when he died and you remained with steadfast truth
to their descendants,
until they met their double fate upon one day,
striking and stricken, defiled each by a brother's murder.   190
Now here I am, holding all authority
and the throne, in virtue of kinship with the dead.

It is impossible to know any man—
I mean his soul, intelligence, and judgment—
until he shows his skill in rule and law.   195
I think that a man supreme ruler of a whole city,
if he does not reach for the best counsel for her,
but through some fear, keeps his tongue under lock and key,
him I judge the worst of any;
I have always judged so; and anyone thinking   200
another man more a friend than his own country,
I rate him nowhere. For my part, God is my witness,
who sees all, always, I would not be silent
if I saw ruin, not safety, on the way
towards my fellow citizens. I would not count   205
any enemy of my country as a friend—
because of what I know, that she it is
which gives us our security. If she sails upright
and we sail on her, friends will be ours for the making.
In the light of rules like these, I will make her greater still.   210

In consonance with this, I here proclaim
to the citizens about Oedipus' sons.
For Eteocles, who died this city's champion,
showing his valor's supremacy everywhere,
he shall be buried in his grave with every rite   215
of sanctity given to heroes under earth.
However, his brother, Polyneices, a returned exile,

who sought to burn with fire from top to bottom
his native city, and the gods of his own people;
who sought to taste the blood he shared with us,   220
and lead the rest of us to slavery—
I here proclaim to the city that this man
shall no one honor with a grave and none shall mourn.
You shall leave him without burial; you shall watch him
chewed up by birds and dogs and violated.   225
Such is my mind in the matter; never by me
shall the wicked man have precedence in honor
over the just. But he that is loyal to the state
in death, in life alike, shall have my honor.
CHORUS: Son of Menoeceus, so it is your pleasure   230
    to deal with foe and friend of this our city.
    To use any legal means lies in your power,
    both about the dead and those of us who live.
CREON: I understand, then, you will do my bidding.
CHORUS: Please lay this burden on some younger man.   235
CREON: Oh, watchers of the corpse I have already.
CHORUS: What else, then, do your commands entail?
CREON: That you should not side with those who disagree.
CHORUS: There is none so foolish as to love his own death.
CREON: Yes, indeed those are the wages, but often greed   240
    has with its hopes brought men to ruin.
SENTRY: My lord, I will never claim my shortness of breath
    is due to hurrying, nor were there wings in my feet.
    I stopped at many a lay-by in my thinking;
    I circled myself till I met myself coming back.   245
    My soul accosted me with different speeches.
    "Poor fool, yourself, why are you going somewhere
    when once you get there you will pay the piper?"
    "Well, aren't you the daring fellow! stopping again?
    and suppose Creon hears the news from someone else—   250
    don't you realize that you will smart for that?"
    I turned the whole matter over. I suppose I may say
    "I made haste slowly" and the short road became long.
    However, at last I came to a resolve:
    I must go to you; even if what I say   255
    is nothing, really, still I shall say it.
    I come here, a man with a firm clutch on the hope
    that nothing can betide him save what is fated.
CREON: What is it then that makes you so afraid?
SENTRY: No, I want first of all to tell you my side of it.   260
    I didn't do the thing; I never saw who did it.
    It would not be fair for me to get into trouble.
CREON: You hedge, and barricade the thing itself.
    Clearly you have some ugly news for me.
SENTRY: Well, you know how disasters make a man   265
    hesitate to be their messenger.

CREON: For God's sake, tell me and get out of here!

SENTRY: Yes, I *will* tell you. Someone just now
    buried the corpse and vanished. He scattered on the skin
    some thirsty dust; he did the ritual,   270
    duly, to purge the body of desecration.

CREON: What! Now who on earth could have done that?

SENTRY: I do not know. For there was there no mark
    of axe's stroke nor casting up of earth
    of any mattock; the ground was hard and dry,   275
    unbroken; there were no signs of wagon wheels.
    The doer of the deed had left no trace.
    But when the first sentry of the day pointed it out,
    there was for all of us a disagreeable
    wonder. For the body had disappeared;   280
    not in a grave, of course; but there lay upon him
    a little dust as of a hand avoiding
    the curse of violating the dead body's sanctity.
    There were no signs of any beast nor dog
    that came there; he had clearly not been torn.   285
    There was a tide of bad words at one another,
    guard taunting guard, and it might well have ended
    in blows, for there was no one there to stop it.
    Each one of us was the criminal but no one
    manifestly so; all denied knowledge of it.   290
    We were ready to take hot bars in our hands
    or walk through fire, and call on the gods with oaths
    that we had neither done it nor were privy
    to a plot with anyone, neither in planning
    nor yet in execution.   295
    At last when nothing came of all our searching,
    there was one man who spoke, made every head
    bow to the ground in fear. For we could not
    either contradict him nor yet could we see how
    if we did what he said we would come out all right.   300
    His word was that we must lay information
    about this matter to yourself; we could not cover it.
    This view prevailed and the lot of the draw chose me,
    unlucky me, to win that prize. So here
    I am. I did not want to come,   305
    and you don't want to have me. I know that.
    For no one likes the messenger of bad news.

CHORUS: My lord: I wonder, could this be God's doing?
    This is the thought that keeps on haunting me.

CREON: Stop, before your words fill even me with rage,   310
    that you should be exposed as a fool, and you so old.
    For what you say is surely insupportable
    when you say the gods took forethought for this corpse.
    Is it out of excess of honor for the man,
    for the favors that he did them, they should cover him?   315

This man who came to burn their pillared temples,
their dedicated offerings—and this land
and laws he would have scattered to the winds?
Or do you see the gods as honoring
criminals? This is not so. But what I am doing   320
now, and other things before this, some men disliked,
within this very city, and muttered against me,
secretly shaking their heads; they would not bow
justly beneath the yoke to submit to me.
I am very sure that these men hired others   325
to do this thing. I tell you the worst currency
that ever grew among mankind is money. This
sacks cities, this drives people from their homes,
this teaches and corrupts the minds of the loyal
to acts of shame. This displays   330
all kinds of evil for the use of men,
instructs in the knowledge of every impious act.
Those that have done this deed have been paid to do it,
but in the end they will pay for what they have done.

It is as sure as I still reverence Zeus—   335
know this right well—and I speak under oath—
if you and your fellows do not find this man
who with his own hand did the burial
and bring him here before me face to face,
your death alone will not be enough for me.   340
You will hang alive till you open up this outrage.
That will teach you in the days to come from what
you may draw profit—safely—from your plundering.
It's not from anything and everything
you can grow rich. You will find out   345
that ill-gotten gains ruin more than they save.
SENTRY: Have I your leave to say something—or should I
    just turn and go?
CREON: Don't you know your talk is painful enough already?
SENTRY: Is the ache in your ears or in your mind?   350
CREON: Why do you dissect the whereabouts of my pain?
SENTRY: Because it is he who did the deed who hurts
    your mind. I only hurt your ears that listen.
CREON: I am sure you have been a chatterbox since you were born.
SENTRY: All the same, I did not do this thing.   355
CREON: You might have done this, too, if you sold your soul.
SENTRY: It's a bad thing if one judges and judges wrongly.
CREON: You may talk as wittily as you like of judgment.
    Only, if you don't bring to light those men
    who have done this, you will yet come to say   360
    that your wretched gains have brought bad consequences.
SENTRY (ASIDE): It were best that he were found, but whether
    the criminal is taken or he isn't—

for that chance will decide—one thing is certain,
you'll never see me coming here again. 365
I never hoped to escape, never thought I could.
But now I have come off safe, I thank God heartily.
CHORUS: Many are the wonders, none
is more wonderful than what is man.
This it is that crosses the sea 370
with the south winds storming and the waves swelling,
breaking around him in roaring surf.
He it is again who wears away
the Earth, oldest of gods, immortal, unwearied,
as the ploughs wind across her from year to year 375
when he works her with the breed that comes from horses.

The tribe of the lighthearted birds he snares
and takes prisoner the races of savage beasts
and the brood of the fish of the sea,
with the close-spun web of nets. 380
A cunning fellow is man. His contrivances
make him master of beasts of the field
and those that move in the mountains.
So he brings the horse with the shaggy neck
to bend underneath the yoke; 385
and also the untamed mountain bull;
and speech and windswift thought
and the tempers that go with city living
he has taught himself, and how to avoid
the sharp frost, when lodging is cold 390
under the open sky
and pelting strokes of the rain.
He has a way against everything,
and he faces nothing that is to come
without contrivance. 395
Only against death
can he call on no means of escape;
but escape from hopeless diseases
he has found in the depths of his mind.
With some sort of cunning, inventive 400
beyond all expectation
he reaches sometimes evil,
and sometimes good.

If he honors the laws of earth,
and the justice of the gods he has confirmed by oath, 405
high is his city; no city
has he with whom dwells dishonor
prompted by recklessness.
He who is so, may he never
share my hearth! 410
may he never think my thoughts!

           Is this a portent sent by God?
           I cannot tell.
           I know her. How can I say
           that this is not Antigone?   415
           Unhappy girl, child of unhappy Oedipus,
           what is this?
           Surely it is not you they bring here
           as disobedient to the royal edict,
           surely not you, taken in such folly.   420
SENTRY: She is the one who did the deed;
    we took her burying him. But where is Creon?
CHORUS: He is just coming from the house, when you most need him.
CREON: What is this? What has happened that I come
    so opportunely?   425
SENTRY: My lord, there is nothing
    that a man should swear he would never do.
    Second thoughts make liars of the first resolution.
    I would have vowed it would be long enough
    before I came again, lashed hence by your threats.   430
    But since the joy that comes past hope, and against all hope,
    is like no other pleasure in extent,
    I have come here, though I break my oath in coming.
    I bring this girl here who has been captured
    giving the grace of burial to the dead man.   435
    This time no lot chose me; this was my jackpot,
    and no one else's. Now, my lord, take her
    and as you please judge her and test her; I
    am justly free and clear of all this trouble.
CREON: This girl—how did you take her and from where?   440
SENTRY: She was burying the man. Now you know all.
CREON: Do you know what you are saying? Do you mean it?
SENTRY: She is the one; I saw her burying
    the dead man you forbade the burial of.
    Now, do I speak plainly and clearly enough?   445
CREON: How was she seen? How was she caught in the act?
SENTRY: This is how it was. When we came there,
    with those dreadful threats of yours upon us,
    we brushed off all the dust that lay upon
    the dead man's body, heedfully   450
    leaving it moist and naked.
    We sat on the brow of the hill, to windward,
    that we might shun the smell of the corpse upon us.
    Each of us wakefully urged his fellow
    with torrents of abuse, not to be careless   455
    in this work of ours. So it went on,
    until in the midst of the sky the sun's bright circle
    stood still; the heat was burning. Suddenly
    a squall lifted out of the earth a storm of dust,
    a trouble in the sky. It filled the plain,   460

ruining all the foliage of the wood
that was around it. The great empty air
was filled with it. We closed our eyes, enduring
this plague sent by the gods. When at long last
we were quit of it, why, then we saw the girl.   465

She was crying out with the shrill cry
of an embittered bird
that sees its nest robbed of its nestlings
and the bed empty. So, too, when she saw
the body stripped of its cover, she burst out in groans,   470
calling terrible curses on those that had done that deed;
and with her hands immediately
brought thirsty dust to the body; from a shapely brazen
urn, held high over it, poured a triple stream
of funeral offerings; and crowned the corpse.   475
When we saw that, we rushed upon her and
caught our quarry then and there, not a bit disturbed.
We charged her with what she had done, then and the first time.
She did not deny a word of it—to my joy,
but to my pain as well. It is most pleasant   480
to have escaped oneself out of such troubles
but painful to bring into it those whom we love.
However, it is but natural for me
to count all this less than my own escape.
CREON: You there, that turn your eyes upon the ground,   485
do you confess or deny what you have done?
ANTIGONE: Yes, I confess; I will not deny my deed.
CREON (TO THE SENTRY): You take yourself off where you like.
You are free of a heavy charge.
Now, Antigone, tell me shortly and to the point,   490
did you know the proclamation against your action?
ANTIGONE: I knew it; of course I did. For it was public.
CREON: And did you dare to disobey that law?
ANTIGONE: Yes, it was not Zeus that made the proclamation;
nor did Justice, which lives with those below, enact   495
such laws as that, for mankind. I did not believe
your proclamation had such power to enable
one who will someday die to override
God's ordinances, unwritten and secure.
They are not of today and yesterday;   500
they live forever; none knows when first they were.
These are the laws whose penalties I would not
incur from the gods, through fear of any man's temper.

I know that I will die—of course I do—
even if you had not doomed me by proclamation.   505
If I shall die before my time, I count that
a profit. How can such as I, that live

among such troubles, not find a profit in death?
So for such as me, to face such a fate as this
is pain that does not count. But if I dared to leave 510
the dead man, my mother's son, dead and unburied,
that would have been real pain. The other is not.
Now, if you think me a fool to act like this,
perhaps it is a fool that judges so.
CHORUS: The savage spirit of a savage father 515
shows itself in this girl. She does not know
how to yield to trouble.
CREON: I would have you know the most fanatic spirits
fall most of all. It is the toughest iron,
baked in the fire to hardness, you may see 520
most shattered, twisted, shivered to fragments.
I know hot horses are restrained
by a small curb. For he that is his neighbor's slave cannot
be high in spirit. This girl had learned her insolence
before this, when she broke the established laws. 525
But here is still another insolence
in that she boasts of it, laughs at what she did.
I swear I am no man and she the man
if she can win this and not pay for it.
No; though she were my sister's child or closer 530
in blood than all that my hearth god acknowledges
as mine, neither she nor her sister should escape
the utmost sentence—death. For indeed I accuse her,
the sister, equally of plotting the burial.
Summon her. I saw her inside, just now, 535
crazy, distraught. When people plot
mischief in the dark, it is the mind which first
is convicted of deceit. But surely I hate indeed
the one that is caught in evil and then makes
that evil look like good. 540
ANTIGONE: Do you want anything
beyond my taking and my execution?
CREON: Oh, nothing! Once I have that I have everything.
ANTIGONE: Why do you wait, then? Nothing that you say
pleases me; God forbid it ever should. 545
So my words, too, naturally offend you.
Yet how could I win a greater share of glory
than putting my own brother in his grave?
All that are here would surely say that's true,
if fear did not lock their tongues up. A prince's power 550
is blessed in many things, not least in this,
that he can say and do whatever he likes.
CREON: You are alone among the people of Thebes
to see things in that way.
ANTIGONE: No, these do, too, 555
but keep their mouths shut for the fear of you.

CREON: Are you not ashamed to think so differently
  from them?
ANTIGONE: There is nothing shameful in honoring my brother.
CREON: Was not he that died on the other side your brother? 560
ANTIGONE: Yes, indeed, of my own blood from father and mother.
CREON: Why then do you show a grace that must be impious
  in *his* sight?
ANTIGONE: That other dead man
  would never bear you witness in what you say. 565
CREON: Yes he would, if you put him only on equality
  with one that was a desecrator.
ANTIGONE: It was his brother, not his slave, that died.
CREON: He died destroying the country the other defended.
ANTIGONE: The god of death demands these rites for both. 570
CREON: But the good man does not seek an *equal* share only,
  with the bad.
ANTIGONE: Who knows
  if in that other world this is true piety?
CREON: My enemy is still my enemy, even in death.
ANTIGONE: My nature is to join in love, not hate. 575
CREON: Go then to the world below, yourself, if you
  must love. Love *them*. When I am alive no woman shall rule.
CHORUS: Here before the gates comes Ismene
  shedding tears for the love of a brother.
  A cloud over her brow casts shame 580
  on her flushed face, as the tears wet
  her fair cheeks.
CREON: You there, who lurked in my house, viper-like—
  secretly drawing its lifeblood; I never thought
  that I was raising two sources of destruction, 585
  two rebels against my throne. Come tell me now,
  will you, too, say you bore a hand in the burial
  or will you swear that you know nothing of it?
ISMENE: I did it, yes—if she will say I did it
  I bear my share in it, bear the guilt, too. 590
ANTIGONE: Justice will not allow you what you refused
  and I will have none of your partnership.
ISMENE: But in your troubles I am not ashamed
  to sail with you the sea of suffering.
ANTIGONE: Where the act was death, the dead are witnesses. 595
  I do not love a friend who loves in words.
ISMENE: Sister, do not dishonor me, denying me
  a common death with you, a common honoring
  of the dead man.
ANTIGONE: Don't die with me, nor make your own 600
  what you have never touched. I that die am enough.
ISMENE: What life is there for me, once I have lost you?
ANTIGONE: Ask Creon; all your care was on his behalf.
ISMENE: Why do you hurt me, when you gain nothing by it?
ANTIGONE: I am hurt by my own mockery—if I mock you. 605

ISMENE: Even now—what can I do to help you still?
ANTIGONE: Save yourself; I do not grudge you your escape.
ISMENE: I cannot bear it! Not even to share your death!
ANTIGONE: Life was your choice, and death was mine.
ISMENE: You cannot say I accepted that choice in silence.   610
ANTIGONE: You were right in the eyes of one party, I in the other.
ISMENE: Well then, the fault is equally between us.
ANTIGONE: Take heart; you are alive, but my life died
    long ago, to serve the dead.
CREON: Here are two girls; I think that one of them   615
    has suddenly lost her wits—the other was always so.
ISMENE: Yes, for, my lord, the wits that they are born with
    do not stay firm for the unfortunate.
    They go astray.
CREON: Certainly yours do,
    when you share troubles with the troublemaker.   620
ISMENE: What life can be mine alone without her?
CREON: Do not
    speak of *her*. *She* isn't, anymore.
ISMENE: Will you kill your son's wife to be?
CREON: Yes, there are other fields for him to plough.
ISMENE: Not with the mutual love of him and her.   625
CREON: I hate a bad wife for a son of mine.
ANTIGONE: Dear Haemon, how your father dishonors you.
CREON: There is too much of you—and of your marriage!
CHORUS: Will you rob your son of this girl?
CREON: Death—it is death that will stop the marriage for me.   630
CHORUS: Your decision it seems is taken: she shall die.
CREON: Both you and I have decided it. No more delay.

(He turns to the servants.)

Bring her inside, you. From this time forth,
these must be women, and not free to roam.
For even the stout of heart shrink when they see   635
the approach of death close to their lives.
CHORUS: Lucky are those whose lives
        know no taste of sorrow.
        But for those whose house has been shaken by God
        there is never cessation of ruin;   640
        it steals on generation after generation
        within a breed. Even as the swell
        is driven over the dark deep
        by the fierce Thracian winds
        I see the ancient evils of Labdacus' house   645
        are heaped on the evils of the dead.
        No generation frees another, some god
        strikes them down; there is no deliverance.
        Here was the light of hope stretched
        over the last roots of Oedipus' house,   650
        and the bloody dust due to the gods below

has mowed it down—that and the folly of speech
and ruin's enchantment of the mind.

Your power, O Zeus, what sin of man can limit?
All-aging sleep does not overtake it,   655
nor the unwearied months of the gods; and you,
for whom time brings no age,
you hold the glowing brightness of Olympus.

For the future near and far,   660
and the past, this law holds good:
nothing very great
comes to the life of mortal man
without ruin to accompany it.
For Hope, widely wandering, comes to many of mankind
as a blessing,   665
but to many as the deceiver,
using light-minded lusts;
she comes to him that knows nothing
till he burns his foot in the glowing fire.
With wisdom has someone declared   670
a word of distinction:
that evil seems good to one whose mind
the god leads to ruin,
and but for the briefest moment of time
is his life outside of calamity.   675

Here is Haemon, youngest of your sons.
Does he come grieving
for the fate of his bride to be,
in agony at being cheated of his marriage?
CREON: Soon we will know that better than the prophets.   680
My son, can it be that you have not heard
of my final decision on your betrothed?
Can you have come here in your fury against your father?
Or have I your love still, no matter what I do?
HAEMON: Father, I am yours; with your excellent judgment   685
you lay the right before me, and I shall follow it.
No marriage will ever be so valued by me
as to override the goodness of your leadership.
CREON: Yes, my son, this should always be
in your very heart, that everything else   690
shall be second to your father's decision.
It is for this that fathers pray to have
obedient sons begotten in their halls,
that they may requite with ill their father's enemy
and honor his friend no less than he would himself.   695
If a man have sons that are no use to him,
what can one say of him but that he has bred
so many sorrows to himself, laughter to his enemies?
Do not, my son, banish your good sense
through pleasure in a woman, since you know   700

that the embrace grows cold
when an evil woman shares your bed and home.
What greater wound can there be than a false friend?
No. Spit on her, throw her out like an enemy,
this girl, to marry someone in Death's house.   705
I caught her openly in disobedience
alone out of all this city and I shall not make
myself a liar in the city's sight. No, I will kill her.
So let her cry if she will on the Zeus of kinship;
for if I rear those of my race and breeding   710
to be rebels, surely I will do so with those outside it.
For he who is in his household a good man
will be found a just man, too, in the city.
But he that breaches the law or does it violence
or thinks to dictate to those who govern him   715
shall never have my good word.
The man the city sets up in authority
must be obeyed in small things and in just
but also in their opposites.
I am confident such a man of whom I speak   720
will be a good ruler, and willing to be well ruled.
He will stand on his country's side, faithful and just,
in the storm of battle. There is nothing worse
than disobedience to authority.
It destroys cities, it demolishes homes;   725
it breaks and routs one's allies. Of successful lives
the most of them are saved by discipline.
So we must stand on the side of what is orderly;
we cannot give victory to a woman.
If we must accept defeat, let it be from a man;   730
we must not let people say that a woman beat us.
CHORUS: We think, if we are not victims of Time the Thief,
    that you speak intelligently of what you speak.
HAEMON: Father, the natural sense that the gods breed
    in men is surely the best of their possessions.   735
I certainly could not declare you wrong—
may I never know how to do so!—Still there might
be something useful that some other than you might think.
It is natural for me to be watchful on your behalf
concerning what all men say or do or find to blame.   740
Your face is terrible to a simple citizen;
it frightens him from words you dislike to hear.
But what *I* can hear, in the dark, are things like these:
the city mourns for this girl; they think she is dying
most wrongly and most undeservedly   745
of all womenkind, for the most glorious acts.
Here is one who would not leave her brother unburied,
a brother who had fallen in bloody conflict,
to meet his end by greedy dogs or by
the bird that chanced that way. Surely what she merits   750

is golden honor, isn't it? That's the dark rumor
that spreads in secret. Nothing I own
I value more highly, father, than your success.
What greater distinction can a son have than the glory
of a successful father, and for a father   755
the distinction of successful children?
Do not bear this single habit of mind, to think
that what you say and nothing else is true.
A man who thinks that he alone is right,
or what he says, or what he *is* himself,   760
unique, such men, when opened up, are seen
to be quite empty. For a man, though he be wise,
it is no shame to learn—learn many things,
and not maintain his views too rigidly.
You notice how by streams in wintertime   765
the trees that yield preserve their branches safely,
but those that fight the tempest perish utterly.
The man who keeps the sheet of his sail tight
and never slackens capsizes his boat
and makes the rest of his trip keel uppermost.   770
Yield something of your anger, give way a little.
If a much younger man, like me, may have
a judgment, I would say it were far better
to be one altogether wise by nature, but,
as things incline not to be so, then it is good   775
also to learn from those who advise well.
CHORUS: My lord, if he says anything to the point,
    you should learn from him, and you, too, Haemon,
    learn from your father. Both of you
    have spoken well.   780
CREON: Should we that are my age learn wisdom
    from young men such as he is?
HAEMON: Not learn injustice, certainly. If I am young,
    do not look at my years but what I do.
CREON: Is what you do to have respect for rebels?
HAEMON: I   785
    would not urge you to be scrupulous
    towards the wicked.
CREON: Is *she* not tainted by the disease of wickedness?
HAEMON: The entire people of Thebes says no to that.
CREON: Should the city tell me how I am to rule them?   790
HAEMON: Do you see what a young man's words these are of yours?
CREON: Must I rule the land by someone else's judgment
    rather than my own?
HAEMON: There is no city
    possessed by one man only.
CREON: Is not the city thought to be the ruler's?   795
HAEMON: You would be a fine dictator of a desert.
CREON: It seems this boy is on the woman's side.
HAEMON: If you are a woman—my care is all for you.

CREON: You villain, to bandy words with your own father!
HAEMON: I see your acts as mistaken and unjust.   800
CREON: Am I mistaken, reverencing my own office?
HAEMON: There is no reverence in trampling on God's honor.
CREON: Your nature is vile, in yielding to a woman.
HAEMON: You will not find me yield to what is shameful.
CREON: At least, your argument is all for her.   805
HAEMON: Yes, and for you and me—and for the gods below.
CREON: You will never marry her while her life lasts.
HAEMON: Then she must die—and dying destroy another.
CREON: Has your daring gone so far, to threaten me?
HAEMON: What threat is it to speak against empty judgments?   810
CREON: Empty of sense yourself, you will regret
    your schooling of me in sense.
HAEMON: If you were not
    my father, I would say you are insane.
CREON: You woman's slave, do not try to wheedle me.
HAEMON: You want to talk but never to hear and listen.   815
CREON: Is that so? By the heavens above you will not—
    be sure of that—get off scot-free, insulting,
    abusing me.

(He speaks to the servants.)

              You people bring out this creature,
    this hated creature, that she may die before
    his very eyes, right now, next her would-be husband.   820
HAEMON: Not at my side! Never think that! She will not
    die by my side. But you will never again
    set eyes upon my face. Go then and rage
    with such of your friends as are willing to endure it.
CHORUS: The man is gone, my lord, quick in his anger.   825
    A young man's mind is fierce when he is hurt.
CREON: Let him go, and do and think things superhuman.
    But these two girls he shall not save from death.
CHORUS: Both of them? Do you mean to kill them both?
CREON: No, not the one that didn't do anything.   830
    You are quite right there.
CHORUS: And by what form of death do you mean to kill her?
CREON: I will bring her where the path is loneliest,
    and hide her alive in a rocky cavern there.
    I'll give just enough of food as shall suffice   835
    for a bare expiation, that the city may avoid pollution.
    In that place she shall call on Hades, god of death,
    in her prayers. That god only she reveres.
    Perhaps she will win from him escape from death
    or at least in that last moment will recognize   840
    her honoring of the dead is labor lost.
CHORUS: Love undefeated in the fight,
        Love that makes havoc of possessions,
        Love who lives at night in a young girl's soft cheeks,

> Who travels over sea, or in huts in the countryside—   845
> there is no god able to escape you
> nor anyone of men, whose life is a day only,
> and whom you possess is mad.
>
> You wrench the minds of just men to injustice,
> to their disgrace; this conflict among kinsmen   850
> it is you who stirred to turmoil.
> The winner is desire. She gleaming kindles
> from the eyes of the girl good to bed.
> Love shares the throne with the great powers that rule.
> For the golden Aphrodite° holds her play there   855
> and then no one can overcome her.
>
> Here I too am borne out of the course of lawfulness
> when I see these things, and I cannot control
> the springs of my tears
> when I see Antigone making her way   860
> to her bed—but the bed
> that is rest for everyone.

ANTIGONE: You see me, you people of my country,
> as I set out on my last road of all,
> looking for the last time on this light of this sun—   865
> never again. I am alive but Hades who gives sleep to everyone
> is leading me to the shores of Acheron,°
> though I have known nothing of marriage songs
> nor the chant that brings the bride to bed.
> My husband is to be the Lord of Death.   870

CHORUS: Yes, you go to the place where the dead are hidden,
> but you go with distinction and praise.
> You have not been stricken by wasting sickness;
> you have not earned the wages of the sword;
> it was your own choice and alone among mankind   875
> you will descend, alive,
> to that world of death.

ANTIGONE: But indeed I have heard of the saddest of deaths—
> of the Phrygian stranger, daughter of Tantalus,°
> whom the rocky growth subdued, like clinging ivy.   880
> The rains never leave her, the snow never fails,
> as she wastes away. That is how men tell the story.
> From streaming eyes her tears wet the crags;
> most like to her the god brings me to rest.

CHORUS: Yes, but she was a god, and god born,   885
> and you are mortal and mortal born.
> Surely it is great renown
> for a woman that dies, that in life and death
> her lot is a lot shared with demigods.

---

855 Aphrodite: goddess of love and beauty.   **867 Acheron:** a river in Hades, domain of the dead.
879 daughter of Tantalus: Niobe, a Theban queen whose fourteen children were slain. She wept so copiously she was transformed into a stone on Mount Sipylos, and her tears became the mountain's streams.

ANTIGONE: You mock me. In the name of our fathers' gods   890
  why do you not wait till I am gone to insult me?
  Must you do it face to face?
  My city! Rich citizens of my city!
  You springs of Dirce, you holy groves of Thebes,
  famed for its chariots! I would still have you as my witnesses,   895
  with what dry-eyed friends, under what laws
  I make my way to my prison sealed like a tomb.
  Pity me. Neither among the living nor the dead
  do I have a home in common—
  neither with the living nor the dead.   900
CHORUS: You went to the extreme of daring
  and against the high throne of Justice
  you fell, my daughter, grievously.
  But perhaps it was for some ordeal of your father
  that you are paying requital.   905
ANTIGONE: You have touched the most painful of my cares—
  the pity for my father, ever reawakened,
  and the fate of all of our race, the famous Labdacids;
  the doomed self-destruction of my mother's bed
  when she slept with her own son,   910
  my father.
  What parents I was born of, God help me!
  To them I am going to share their home,
  the curse on me, too, and unmarried.
  Brother, it was a luckless marriage you made,   915
  and dying killed my life.
CHORUS: There *is* a certain reverence for piety.
  But for him in authority,
  he cannot see that authority defied;
  it is your own self-willed temper   920
  that has destroyed you.
ANTIGONE: No tears for me, no friends, no marriage. Brokenhearted
  I am led along the road ready before me.
  I shall never again be suffered
  to look on the holy eye of the day.   925
  But my fate claims no tears—
  no friend cries for me.
CREON (TO THE SERVANTS): Don't you know that weeping and wailing before death
  would never stop if one is allowed to weep and wail?
  Lead her away at once. Enfold her   930
  in that rocky tomb of hers—as I told you to.
  There leave her alone, solitary,
  to die if she so wishes
  or live a buried life in such a home;
  we are guiltless in respect of her, this girl.   935
  But living above, among the rest of us, this life
  she shall certainly lose.

ANTIGONE: Tomb, bridal chamber, prison forever
   dug in rock, it is to you I am going
   to join my people, that great number that have died,   940
   whom in their death Persephone° received.
   I am the last of them and I go down
   in the worst death of all—for I have not lived
   the due term of my life. But when I come
   to that other world my hope is strong   945
   that my coming will be welcome to my father,
   and dear to you, my mother, and dear to you,
   my brother deeply loved. For when you died,
   with my own hands I washed and dressed you all,
   and poured the lustral offerings on your graves.   950
   And now, Polyneices, it was for such care of your body
   that I have earned these wages.
   Yet those who think rightly will think I did right
   in honoring you. Had I been a mother
   of children, and my husband been dead and rotten,   955
   I would not have taken this weary task upon me
   against the will of the city. What law backs me
   when I say this? I will tell you:
   If my husband were dead, I might have had another,
   and child from another man, if I lost the first.   960
   But when father and mother both were hidden in death
   no brother's life would bloom for me again.
   That is the law under which I gave you precedence,
   my dearest brother, and that is why Creon thinks me
   wrong, even a criminal, and now takes me   965
   by the hand and leads me away,
   unbedded, without bridal, without share
   in marriage and in nurturing of children;
   as lonely as you see me; without friends;
   with fate against me I go to the vault of death   970
   while still alive. What law of God have I broken?
   Why should I still look to the gods in my misery?
   Whom should I summon as ally? For indeed
   because of piety I was called impious.
   If this proceeding is good in the gods' eyes   975
   I shall know my sin, once I have suffered.
   But if Creon and his people are the wrongdoers
   let their suffering be no worse than the injustice
   they are meting out to me.
CHORUS: It is the same blasts, the tempests of the soul,   980
   possess her.
CREON: Then for this her guards,
   who are so slow, will find themselves in trouble.

---

941 Persephone: daughter of Zeus and Demeter whom Pluto, god of the underworld, abducted to be his queen.

ANTIGONE (CRIES OUT): Oh, that word has come
 very close to death.
CREON: I will not comfort you   985
 with hope that the sentence will not be accomplished.
ANTIGONE: O my father's city, in Theban land,
 O gods that sired my race,
 I am led away, I have no more stay.
 Look on me, princes of Thebes,   990
 the last remnant of the old royal line;
 see what I suffer and who makes me suffer
 because I gave reverence to what claims reverence.
CHORUS: Danae suffered,° too, when, her beauty lost, she gave
 the light of heaven in exchange for brassbound walls,   995
 and in the tomb-like cell was she hidden and held;
 yet she was honored in her breeding, child,
 and she kept, as guardian, the seed of Zeus
 that came to her in a golden shower.
 But there is some terrible power in destiny   1000
 and neither wealth nor war
 nor tower nor black ships, beaten by the sea,
 can give escape from it.

 The hot-tempered son of Dryas,° the Edonian king,
 in fury mocked Dionysus,   1005
 who then held him in restraint
 in a rocky dungeon.
 So the terrible force and flower of his madness
 drained away. He came to know the god
 whom in frenzy he had touched with his mocking tongue,   1010
 when he would have checked the inspired women
 and the fire of Dionysus,
 when he provoked the Muses that love the lyre.

 By the black rocks, dividing the sea in two,
 are the shores of the Bosporus, Thracian Salmydessus.   1015
 There the god of war who lives near the city
 saw the terrible blinding wound
 dealt by his savage wife
 on Phineus' two sons.
 She blinded and tore with the points of her shuttle,   1020
 and her bloodied hands, those eyes
 that else would have looked on her vengefully.
 As they wasted away, they lamented

---

 994 Danae suffered: In legend, when an oracle told Acrisius, king of Argos, that his daughter
Danae would bear a son who would grow up to slay him, he locked the princess into a chamber
made of bronze, lest any man impregnate her. But Zeus, father of the gods, entered Danae's prison
in a shower of gold. The resultant child, the hero Perseus, was accidentally to fulfill the prophecy
by killing Acrisius with an ill-aimed discus throw.   **1004 son of Dryas:** King Lycurgus of Thrace,
whom Dionysus, god of wine, caused to be stricken with madness.

their unhappy fate that they were doomed
to be born of a mother cursed in her marriage. 1025
She traced her descent from the seed
of the ancient Erechtheidae.
In far-distant caves she was raised
among her father's storms, that child of Boreas,
quick as a horse, over the steep hills, 1030
a daughter of the gods.
But, my child, the long-lived Fates
bore hard upon her, too.

(Enter Teiresias, the blind prophet, led by a boy.)

TEIRESIAS: My lords of Thebes, we have come here together,
one pair of eyes serving us both. For the blind 1035
such must be the way of going, by a guide's leading.
CREON: What is the news, my old Teiresias?
TEIRESIAS: I will tell you; and you, listen to the prophet.
CREON: Never in the past have I turned from your advice.
TEIRESIAS: And so you have steered well the ship of state. 1040
CREON: I have benefited and can testify to that.
TEIRESIAS: Then realize you are on the razor edge
of danger.
CREON: What can that be? I shudder to hear those words.
TEIRESIAS: When you learn the signs recognized by my art 1045
you will understand.
I sat at my ancient place of divination
for watching the birds, where every bird finds shelter;
and I heard an unwonted voice among them;
they were horribly distressed, and screamed unmeaningly. 1050
I knew they were tearing each other murderously;
the beating of their wings was a clear sign.
I was full of fear; at once on all the altars,
as they were fully kindled, I tasted the offerings,
but the god of fire refused to burn from the sacrifice, 1055
and from the thighbones a dark stream of moisture
oozed from the embers, smoked and sputtered.
The gall bladder burst and scattered to the air
and the streaming thighbones lay exposed
from the fat wrapped round them— 1060
so much I learned from this boy here,
the fading prophecies of a rite that failed.
This boy here is my guide, as I am others'.
This is the city's sickness—and your plans are the cause of it.
For our altars and our sacrificial hearths 1065
are filled with the carrion meat of birds and dogs,
torn from the flesh of Oedipus' poor son.
So the gods will not take our prayers or sacrifice
nor yet the flame from the thighbones, and no bird

cries shrill and clear, so glutted 1070
are they with fat of the blood of the killed man.
Reflect on these things, son. All men
can make mistakes; but, once mistaken,
a man is no longer stupid nor accursed
who, having fallen on ill, tries to cure that ill, 1075
not taking a fine undeviating stand.
It is obstinacy that convicts of folly.
Yield to the dead man; do not stab him—
now he is gone—what bravery is this,
to inflict another death upon the dead? 1080
I mean you well and speak well for your good.
It is never sweeter to learn from a good counselor
than when he counsels to your benefit.
CREON: Old man, you are all archers, and I am your mark.
I must be tried by your prophecies as well. 1085
By the breed of you I have been bought and sold
and made a merchandise, for ages now.
But I tell you: make your profit from silver-gold
from Sardis and the gold from India
if you will. But this dead man you shall not hide 1090
in a grave, not though the eagles of Zeus should bear
the carrion, snatching it to the throne of Zeus itself.
Even so, I shall not so tremble at the pollution
to let you bury him.
           No, I am certain
no human has the power to pollute the gods. 1095
They fall, you old Teiresias, those men,
—so very clever—in a bad fall whenever
they eloquently speak vile words for profit.
TEIRESIAS: I wonder if there's a man who dares consider—
CREON: What do you mean? What sort of generalization 1100
is this talk of yours?
TEIRESIAS: How much the best of possessions is the ability
to listen to wise advice.
CREON: As I should imagine that the worst
injury must be native stupidity. 1105
TEIRESIAS: Now that is exactly where your mind is sick.
CREON: I do not like to answer a seer with insults.
TEIRESIAS: But you do, when you say my prophecies are lies.
CREON: Well,
the whole breed of prophets certainly loves money. 1110
TEIRESIAS: And the breed that comes from princes loves to take
advantage—base advantage.
CREON: Do you realize
you are speaking in such terms of your own prince?
TEIRESIAS: I know. But it is through me you have saved the city.
CREON: You are a wise prophet, but what you love is wrong. 1115

TEIRESIAS: You will force me to declare what should be hidden
    in my own heart.
CREON: Out with it—
    but only if your words are not for gain.
TEIRESIAS: They won't be for *your* gain—that I am sure of.
CREON: But realize you will not make a merchandise   1120
    of my decisions.
TEIRESIAS: And you must realize
    that you will not outlive many cycles more
    of this swift sun before you give in exchange
    one of your own loins bred, a corpse for a corpse,
    for you have thrust one that belongs above   1125
    below the earth, and bitterly dishonored
    a living soul by lodging her in the grave;
    while one that belonged indeed to the underworld
    gods you have kept on this earth without due share
    of rites of burial, of due funeral offerings,   1130
    a corpse unhallowed. With all of this you, Creon,
    have nothing to do, nor have the gods above.
    These acts of yours are violence, on your part.
    And in requital the avenging Spirits
    of Death itself and the gods' Furies shall   1135
    after *your* deeds, lie in ambush for you, and
    in their hands you shall be taken cruelly.
    Now, look at this and tell me I was bribed
    to say it! The delay will not be long
    before the cries of mourning in your house,   1140
    of men and women. All the cities will stir in hatred
    against you, because their sons in mangled shreds
    received their burial rites from dogs, from wild beasts
    or when some bird of the air brought a vile stink
    to each city that contained the hearths of the dead.   1145
    These are the arrows that archer-like I launched—
    you vexed me so to anger—at your heart.
    You shall not escape their sting. You, boy,
    lead me away to my house, so he may discharge
    his anger on younger men; so may he come to know   1150
    to bear a quieter tongue in his head and a better
    mind than that now he carries in him.
CHORUS: That was a terrible prophecy, my lord.
    The man has gone. Since these hairs of mine grew white
    from the black they once were, he has never spoken   1155
    a word of a lie to our city.
CREON: I know, I know.
    My mind is all bewildered. To yield is terrible.
    But by opposition to destroy my very being
    with a self-destructive curse must also be reckoned   1160
    in what is terrible.
CHORUS: You need good counsel, son of Menoeceus,
    and need to take it.

CREON: What must I do, then? Tell me; I shall agree.
CHORUS: The girl—go now and bring her up from her cave, 1165
   and for the exposed dead man, give him his burial.
CREON: That is really your advice? You would have me yield.
CHORUS: And quickly as you may, my lord. Swift harms
   sent by the gods cut off the paths of the foolish.
CREON: Oh, it is hard; I must give up what my heart 1170
   would have me do. But it is ill to fight
   against what must be.
CHORUS: Go now, and do this;
   do not give the task to others.
CREON: I will go, 1175
   just as I am. Come, servants, all of you;
   take axes in your hands; away with you
   to the place you see, there.
   For my part, since my intention is so changed,
   as I bound her myself, myself will free her. 1180
   I am afraid it may be best, in the end
   of life, to have kept the old accepted laws.
CHORUS: You of many names,° glory of the Cadmeian
      bride, breed of loud thundering Zeus;
      you who watch over famous Italy; 1185
      you who rule where all are welcome in Eleusis;
      in the sheltered plains of Deo—
      O Bacchus that dwells in Thebes,
      the mother city of Bacchanals,
      by the flowing stream of Ismenus, 1190
      in the ground sown by the fierce dragon's teeth.

      You are he on whom the murky gleam of torches glares,
      above the twin peaks of the crag
      where come the Corycean nymphs
      to worship you, the Bacchanals; 1195
      and the stream of Castalia° has seen you, too;
      and you are he that the ivy-clad
      slopes of Nisaean hills,
      and the green shore ivy-clustered,
      sent to watch over the roads of Thebes, 1200
      where the immortal Evoe° chant rings out.

1183 You of many names: Dionysus was also called Iacchos (or, by the Romans, Bacchus). He was the son of Zeus ("the Thunderer") and of Semele, daughter of Kadmos (or Cadmus), legendary founder of Thebes. "Regent of Eleusis' plain" is another name for Dionysus, honored in secret rites at Eleusis, a town northwest of Athens. "Prince of maenad Thebes" is yet another: the Maenads were women of Thebes said to worship Dionysus with wild orgiastic rites. Kadmos, so the story goes, sowed dragon's teeth in a field beside the river Ismenus. Up sprang a crop of fierce warriors who fought among themselves until only five remained. These victors became the first Thebans. **1196 Castalia:** a spring on Mount Parnassus, named for a maiden who drowned herself in it to avoid rape by the god Apollo. She became a nymph, or nature spirit, dwelling in its waters. In the temple of Delphi, at the mountain's foot, priestesses of Dionysus (the "nymphs of Iacchos") used the spring's waters in rites of purification. **1201 Evoe:** cry of the Maenads in supplicating Dionysus: "Come forth, come forth!"

It is Thebes which you honor most of all cities,
you and your mother both,
she who died by the blast of Zeus' thunderbolt.
And now when the city, with all its folk,   1205
is gripped by a violent plague,
come with healing foot, over the slopes of Parnassus,
over the moaning strait.
You lead the dance of the fire-breathing stars,
you are master of the voices of the night.   1210
True-born child of Zeus, appear,
my lord, with your Thyiad attendants,
who in frenzy all night long
dance in your house, Iacchus,
dispenser of gifts.   1215

MESSENGER: You who live by the house of Cadmus and Amphion,°
hear me. There is no condition of man's life
that stands secure. As such I would not
praise it or blame. It is chance that sets upright;
it is chance that brings down the lucky and the unlucky,   1220
each in his turn. For men, that belong to death,
there is no prophet of established things.
Once Creon was a man worthy of envy—
of my envy, at least. For he saved this city
of Thebes from her enemies, and attained   1225
the throne of the land, with all a king's power.
He guided it right. His race bloomed
with good children. But when a man forfeits joy
I do not count his life as life, but only
a life trapped in a corpse.   1230
Be rich within your house, yes greatly rich,
if so you will, and live in a prince's style.
If the gladness of these things is gone, I would not
give the shadow of smoke for the rest,
as against joy.   1235

CHORUS: What is the sorrow of our princes
of which you are the messenger?

MESSENGER: Death; and the living are guilty of their deaths.

CHORUS: But who is the murderer? Who the murdered? Tell us.

MESSENGER: Haemon is dead; the hand that shed his blood   1240
was his very own.

CHORUS: Truly his own hand? Or his father's?

MESSENGER: His own hand, in his anger
against his father for a murder.

CHORUS: Prophet, how truly you have made good your word!   1245

MESSENGER: These things are so; you may debate the rest.

1216 Amphion: a name for Thebes. Amphion, son of Zeus, had built a wall around the city by
playing so beautifully on his lyre that the charmed stones leaped into their slots.

CHORUS: Here I see Creon's wife Eurydice
    approaching. Unhappy woman!
    Does she come from the house as hearing about her son
    or has she come by chance?   1250
EURYDICE: I heard your words, all you men of Thebes, as I
    was going out to greet Pallas° with my prayers.
    I was just drawing back the bolts of the gate
    to open it when a cry struck through my ears
    telling of my household's ruin. I fell backward   1255
    in terror into the arms of my servants; I fainted.
    But tell me again, what is the story? I
    will hear it as one who is no stranger to sorrow.
MESSENGER: Dear mistress, I will tell you, for I was there,
    and I will leave out no word of the truth.   1260
    Why should I comfort you and then tomorrow
    be proved a liar? The truth is always best.

I followed your husband, at his heels, to the end of the plain
where Polyneices' body still lay unpitied,
and torn by dogs. We prayed to Hecate, goddess   1265
of the crossroads, and also to Pluto°
that they might restrain their anger and turn kind.
And him we washed with sacred lustral water
and with fresh-cut boughs we burned what was left of him
and raised a high mound of his native earth;   1270
then we set out again for the hollowed rock,
death's stone bridal chamber for the girl.
Someone then heard a voice of bitter weeping
while we were still far off, coming from that unblest room.
The man came to tell our master Creon of it.   1275
As the king drew nearer, there swarmed about him
a cry of misery but no clear words.
He groaned and in an anguished mourning voice
cried "Oh, am I a true prophet? Is this the road
that I must travel, saddest of all my wayfaring?   1280
It is my son's voice that haunts my ear. Servants,
get closer, quickly. Stand around the tomb
and look. There is a gap there where the stones
have been wrenched away; enter there, by the very mouth,
and see whether I recognize the voice of Haemon   1285
or if the gods deceive me." On the command
of our despairing master we went to look.
In the furthest part of the tomb we saw her, hanging
by her neck. She had tied a noose of muslin on it.
Haernon's hands were about her waist embracing her,   1290
while he cried for the loss of his bride gone to the dead,

1252 Pallas: Pallas Athene, goddess of wisdom, and hence an excellent source of advice.
1265–1266 Hecate . . . Pluto: two fearful divinities—the goddess of witchcraft and sorcery and
the king of Hades, underworld of the dead.

and for all his father had done, and his own sad love.
When Creon saw him he gave a bitter cry,
went in and called to him with a groan: "Poor son!
what have you done? What can you have meant?   1295
What happened to destroy you? Come out, I pray you!"
The boy glared at him with savage eyes, and then
spat in his face, without a word of answer.
He drew his double-hilted sword. As his father
ran to escape him, Haemon failed to strike him,   1300
and the poor wretch in anger at himself
leaned on his sword and drove it halfway in,
into his ribs. Then he folded the girl to him,
in his arms, while he was conscious still,
and gasping poured a sharp stream of bloody drops   1305
on her white cheeks. There they lie,
the dead upon the dead. So he has won
the pitiful fulfillment of his marriage
within death's house. In this human world he has shown
how the wrong choice in plans is for a man   1310
his greatest evil.
CHORUS: What do you make of this? My lady is gone,
   without a word of good or bad.
MESSENGER: I, too,
   am lost in wonder. I am inclined to hope
   that hearing of her son's death she could not   1315
   open her sorrow to the city, but chose rather
   within her house to lay upon her maids
   the mourning for the household grief. Her judgment
   is good; she will not make any false step.
CHORUS: I do not know. To me this over-heavy silence   1320
   seems just as dangerous as much empty wailing.
MESSENGER: I will go in and learn if in her passionate
   heart she keeps hidden some secret purpose.
   You are right; there is sometimes danger in too much silence.
CHORUS: Here comes our king himself. He bears in his hands   1325
   a memorial all too clear;
   it is a ruin of none other's making,
   purely his own if one dare to say that.
CREON: The mistakes of a blinded man
   are themselves rigid and laden with death.   1330
   You look at us the killer and the killed
   of the one blood. Oh, the awful blindness
   of those plans of mine. My son, you were so young,
   so young to die. You were freed from the bonds of life
   through no folly of your own—only through mine.   1335
CHORUS: I think you have learned justice—but too late.
CREON: Yes, I have learned it to my bitterness. At this moment
   God has sprung on my head with a vast weight
   and struck me down. He shook me in my savage ways;
   he has overturned my joy, has trampled it,   1340

underfoot. The pains men suffer
are pains indeed.
SECOND MESSENGER: My lord, you have troubles and a store besides;
some are there in your hands, but there are others
you will surely see when you come to your house.   1345
CREON: What trouble can there be beside these troubles?
SECOND MESSENGER: The queen is dead. She was indeed true mother
of the dead son. She died, poor lady,
by recent violence upon herself.
CREON: Haven of death, you can never have enough.   1350
Why, why do you destroy me?
You messenger, who have brought me bitter news,
what is this tale you tell?
It is a dead man that you kill again—
what new message of yours is this, boy?   1355
Is this new slaughter of a woman
a doom to lie on the pile of the dead?
CHORUS: You can see. It is no longer
hidden in a corner.

*(By some stage device, perhaps the so-called eccyclema,° the inside of the palace is
shown, with the body of the dead Queen.)*

CREON: Here is yet another horror   1360
for my unhappy eyes to see.
What doom still waits for me?
I have but now taken in my arms my son,
and again I look upon another dead face.
Poor mother and poor son!   1365
SECOND MESSENGER: She stood at the altar, and with keen whetted knife
she suffered her darkening eyes to close.
First she cried in agony recalling the noble fate of Megareus,°
who died before all this,
and then for the fate of this son; and in the end   1370
she cursed you for the evil you had done
in killing her sons.
CREON: I am distracted with fear. Why does not someone
strike a two-edged sword right through me?
I am dissolved in an agony of misery.   1375
SECOND MESSENGER: You were indeed accused
by her that is dead of Haemon's and of Megareus' death.
CREON: By what kind of violence did she find her end?
SECOND MESSENGER: Her own hand struck her to the entrails   1380
when she heard of her son's lamentable death.
CREON: These acts can never be made to fit another
to free me from the guilt. It was I that killed her.

1359 s.d. eccyclema: a platform on wheels pushed onto the stage to display an offstage scene.
1368 Megareus: Son of Creon and brother of Haemon, Megareus was slain in the unsuccessful
attack upon Thebes.

Poor wretch that I am, I say it is true!
Servants, lead me away, quickly, quickly.   1385
I am no more a live man than one dead.

CHORUS: What you say is for the best—if there be a best
in evil such as this. For the shortest way
is best with troubles that lie at our feet.

CREON: O, let it come, let it come,   1390
that best of fates that waits on my last day.
Surely best fate of all. Let it come, let it come!
That I may never see one more day's light!

CHORUS: These things are for the future. We must deal
with what impends. What in the future is to care for   1395
rests with those whose duty it is
to care for them.

CREON: At least, all that *I* want
is in that prayer of mine.

CHORUS: Pray for no more at all. For what is destined   1400
for us, men mortal, there is no escape.

CREON: Lead me away, a vain silly man
who killed you, son, and you, too, lady.
I did not mean to, but I did.
I do not know where to turn my eyes   1405
to look to, for support.
Everything in my hands is crossed. A most unwelcome fate
has leaped upon me.

CHORUS: Wisdom is far the chief element in happiness
and, secondly, no irreverence towards the gods.   1410
But great words of haughty men exact
in retribution blows as great
and in old age teach wisdom.   [441 B.C.]

The Writing Process

Prewriting

Now that you have read *Antigone* and have some sense of its basic
structure, read the play again carefully and write out the answers to the
questions below. Your responses will not only help you to sharpen your
understanding of dramatic structure; they will also lead you to clarify
your reactions to *Antigone*'s characters and themes.

Exercise: Analyzing Dramatic Structure

1. Think about a clash with authority that you have experienced in your
   own life. What caused the clash? How firmly did you stand your
   ground in the conflict? What were the consequences of your behavior?

2. What background is given in the opening conversation between
   Antigone and Ismene (lines 1–117)? List the main points of information that you learn from this exchange between the sisters.

3. What exposition does the Chorus provide in lines 118–178?

4. How does Sophocles use the Sentry (lines 242–367)? Does this character provide more than factual exposition?

5. What do you think the main conflict is? State it as specifically as you can in a single sentence.

6. Identify the protagonist and the antagonist. Is it fair to apply the labels *heroine* and *villain* to them?

7. Where does the climax occur? Identify the scene and describe what happens. Why do you think this is the play's turning point?

8. Does the climax seem to come early in the play? How does Sophocles maintain interest after the turning point? Did you expect such dramatic developments after the climax? Do you think Creon expected them?

9. When does the catastrophe occur? Was this outcome inevitable? Were your feelings about the outcome different the second time you read the play?

10. State what you consider the play's theme to be.

11. A *foil* is a contrasting character who sets off or helps to define another character. How is Ismene a foil to Antigone? Are there any foils to Creon?

12. Why is Eurydice included in the plot? How do you feel about her fate?

Having answered these questions about the structure of *Antigone*, devise a graph or chart that illustrates the pattern of events in the play. Make sure your graph shows the six structural components discussed on page 632.

Writing

Your understanding of the structure of *Antigone* will enable you to write more easily about the play's arguments. As you watched the conflict develop between Antigone and Creon, you undoubtedly became aware of the opposing values that these two characters represent. As one critic has observed about *Antigone*, "The characters *are* the issues, and the issues the characters."[1] It is now your turn to examine these issues and decide where you stand.

Discovering a Workable Argumentative Thesis

Argument means dispute; it implies that there are opposing sides. Any matter worth arguing will involve at least one "issue"—that is, an essential point in question or disagreement. You need not always take sides, but once you have decided what issues are involved in an argument, you can write an effective paper by taking a stand and explaining why you have chosen one side over the other.

Your approach to *Antigone* will have to take into account the controversial nature of the play's conflict. Review your responses to the prewriting questions about the disagreement and about the antagonist and protagonist. Can you identify an issue that you think is central to the

---

[1]Charles Paul Segal. "Sophocles' Praise of Man and the Conflicts of *Antigone*." *Sophocles: A Collection of Critical Essays*, edited by T. Woodward, Prentice Hall, 1966, p. 63.

play's meaning? Are there other issues involved in the conflict? Try to get the main issues stated as clearly and specifically as you can before you begin to write. The ideas for writing that follow should help you to work out the important issues of the play.

You can argue an issue in two ways. You can devise a major claim about one side of the question and present reasons and evidence to support your stand. Or you can anticipate the claims of the opposing side and show how the evidence does not support this side, indicating where the fallacies or errors lie in the opposition's reasoning. You will probably want to combine both techniques in writing about *Antigone*.

Whatever your approach, you need to study the evidence and examine the ideas on both sides for flaws in logical thinking. One way to make this examination involves listing the main arguments, pro and con, in two columns on a sheet of paper.

Creon	Antigone
Public interest outweighs private loyalties.	Eternal unwritten laws take precedence.
Polyneices made war on his own country.	All the dead deserve honor.

You can make a similar listing of speeches or lines from the play that serve as evidence for the two sides of the argument. For instance, you may want to note such revealing statements by Creon as these:

> "Whoever is chosen to govern should be obeyed."
> "If we must lose,/Let's lose to a man, at least! Is a woman stronger than we?"
> "The State is the King!"

Compare these lists and see which side has the stronger arguments and the greater amount of evidence. You can then decide which side you are going to support; you also have a convenient listing of specific ideas and quotations to use in developing your essay.

Quoting from a Play

For plays written in verse (like *Antigone* or *Othello*), you may quote a single line within your text by putting it in quotation marks and giving act, scene, and line numbers in parentheses at the end of the quoted material. Because *Antigone* is not divided into acts, give the line numbers for the quotations you use.

As the Sentry warns Creon, "It is a bad thing if one judges and judges wrongly" (357).

You may also incorporate two or three lines in this way, using a slash mark with a space on each side to separate them.

> Antigone points out to Creon that "All that are here would surely say that's true / if fear did not lock their tongues up" (549–50).

Longer quotations (more than three lines) should be indented a half inch from the margin with *no* quotation marks. Use the same line spacing both around and within the quotation.

> At first Creon is taken in by his son's words and demeanor:
> > Yes, my son, this should always be
> > In your very heart, that everything else
> > Shall be second to your father's decision.
> > It is for this that fathers pray to have
> > obedient sons begotten in their halls. (689–93)

If you quote a passage in which more than one character speaks, indent the dialogue and begin each part with the appropriate character's name, written in all capital letters. Follow the name with a period, and start the quotation.

> Creon and his son Haemon argue about the king's authority:
> > CREON. Must I rule the land by someone else's judgment
> > > Rather than my own?
> > HAEMON. There is no city
> > > Possessed by one man only.
> > CREON. Is not the city thought to be the ruler's?
> > HAEMON. You would be a fine dictator of a desert. (792–96)

For plays *not* written in verse, give act and scene or page numbers in parentheses at the end of the quoted material.

Ideas for Writing

Ideas for Reflective Writing

1. Do you see yourself as approving of or opposing the rules and norms of the society you live in? How do you support, change, or disobey these rules and norms? Write about one rule or group of related rules (for example, sex roles or parent–child relationships) that you accept or reject.

2. In modern society, what might Creon and Antigone disagree about? Write an essay explaining where the two characters would probably stand on one of today's issues.

Ideas for Critical Writing

1. Is Creon a politician concerned with imposing and maintaining order? Is Antigone an anarchist whose action will destroy that order? Or is she a private citizen determined to follow the dictates of her personal beliefs? Write an essay that interprets *Antigone* as a struggle between public policy and individual conscience, supporting the side that you think is right.

2. CRITICAL APPROACHES: Read about gender-focused approaches to interpreting literature (page 898). Can you explain the conflict between Antigone and Creon as a psychological clash between a woman and a man? Write an essay that develops a claim about the male–female opposition in the play. You may want to work Ismene, Haemon, and Eurydice into your scheme of opposing values.

Ideas for Researched Writing

1. A. R. Gurney wrote *Another Antigone* (1988), an updated version of *Antigone* in which a classics professor and a headstrong college student clash over a term paper on Sophocles. Read this modern *Antigone*, and write an essay comparing and contrasting it to the original. Some topics to consider: What problems did the modern writer encounter in changing the setting? Are the same themes developed in both versions? Are the conflicts resolved in similar ways? Compare and contrast specific scenes. You may want to read reviews of productions of *Another Antigone* to see how critics and audiences respond to it.

2. The chorus is a distinctive device of ancient Greek drama. Investigate the use and function of the Greek chorus. Then read, or re-read, *Our Town* by Thornton Wilder, and write an essay that argues that the Stage Manager in *Our Town* performs many of the same functions as the chorus in *Antigone*. Or write an essay that argues for or against the view that Tom Wingfield serves as a Greek chorus in *The Glass Menagerie*.

MultiModal Project

You are a playwright with the task of converting Louise Erdrich's "The Red Convertible" (p. 324) into a stage play. How many acts would you write? What do you think is the main conflict, and how would you suggest this conflict in your on-stage version of the story? What would you portray as the climax of the play, and in which act would you place it? Explain your reasoning about how you would structure the play. Write the stage directions and dialogue for one of the acts or scenes in your play. (If your instructor approves, you might choose a different story to dramatize.)

Rewriting

You will want to be certain that your arguments about *Antigone* are perfectly clear. Take some time to ensure that what you have written cannot be misunderstood. If you can, coax a friend or classmate into reading your first draft; ask your reader to point out sentences that do not make sense or that are unclear.

Avoiding Unclear Language

Multisyllabic words and long, involved sentences may dazzle your readers, but they can also hinder clear communication. Your first goal in writing should be to convey ideas and information. Trying to impress your readers with big words and fancy phrases may lead to one or more forms of unclear expression.

1. *Engfish:* Writing specialist Ken Macrorie uses this term to call attention to artificial language that does not represent a writer's own experience and education. Engfish is phony, pretentious, stuffy, and often impossible to decode. Writers use Engfish, it seems, when they are unsure of which attitude to take toward their subject and their audience. The student who wrote

   > Antigone's unacceptable posture toward the designated governmental powers inevitably entailed the termination of her existence,

   no doubt thought that this inflated diction was appropriate for a serious paper on a classical play. But most readers probably would prefer to see that sentence revised to read more clearly, like this one:

   > Antigone's defiance led to her death.

   In the long run, clarity will impress your readers more than Engfish ever can.

2. *Jargon:* This term applies to the specialized language used by a particular group of people. Computer operators, sociologists, teenagers, architects, hockey players, mobsters—all sorts of interest groups and professions—employ words and terms that relate only to their particular activities. The problem with jargon is that outsiders do not understand it. Writing about a "love game" or the "ad court" will be all right for an audience of tennis buffs, but you will have to change your language for more general readers. Jargon may not come up in your essay about *Antigone*, but it can creep in from other sources. For instance, the student who wrote

   > Antigone's behavior is marked by regressive reaction formation toward authoritarian figures

   was apparently influenced by the jargon of her psychology class. Unless you are writing for an audience of fellow psychoanalysts, you would do better to say the following:

   > Antigone sometimes acted like a disobedient daughter.

3. *Abstract words:* Abstract terms and general expressions do not automatically make your writing intellectual and impressive. Although

it is true that writing an argumentative essay requires using abstract ideas, your paper will be more persuasive if it is factual, concrete, and clear. Abstractions tend to be hazy and difficult to define. Words like *duty, anarchy, patriotism*, and *truth* have different meanings to different people. When writing about an abstract concept, make certain that you have a definite meaning in your own mind. If, for instance, you write that

> Antigone is a woman of honor

it is a good idea to check the dictionary to see if your understanding of the word *honor* coincides with a standard definition. *The American Heritage Dictionary* gives thirteen entries for *honor*. Which one does the above sentence convey? Would "a woman's chastity" be accurate in this context? It might be more meaningful to say

> Antigone is a woman of principle and integrity

although those words are also abstract. Try, if possible, to specify the meaning you want when using an abstract term.

> Above all, Creon is a master politician—a man of ambition intent on holding his power.

Sample Student Paper

In the following paper, Laurie Dahlberg, a student at Illinois State University, argues that the chief conflict in *Antigone* involves a power struggle between male and female. Notice how she uses and documents quoted material from the play to support her claims.

Laurie Dahlberg
Professor Day
English 102
2 Apr. 2016

"We Cannot Give Victory to a Woman":

Gender Conflict in *Antigone*

Antigone is a drama built around two basic conflicts. Beneath the more obvious conflict of the individual versus the state lies a struggle of male against female. The protagonist, Antigone, becomes a criminal by choice but a feminist by chance. The antagonist, Creon, is fighting to retain control over Antigone, not only as king over subject but also as man over woman.

Antigone knows that she has violated the king's order not to bury her brother Polyneices, but she seems not to notice that she has also violated the social code by stepping outside the boundaries of acceptable feminine behavior. Her act of defiance is courageous, self-reliant, and completely contrary to the obedience expected of women in her society. She fearlessly assures her sister, Ismene, that "It is not for [Creon] to keep me from my own" (54). It is up to Ismene, then, to point out the obvious: "You ought to realize we are only women, / not meant in nature to fight against men" (70-71). Ismene, a perfect foil for Antigone, epitomizes the good Theban woman—she is deferential, passive, and timid. Though she loves Antigone dearly, Ismene is still bound to her male masters and cannot follow her sister:

> I do indeed beg those beneath the earth
>
> to give me their forgiveness,
>
> since force constrains me,
>
> that I shall yield in this to the authorities.
>
> Extravagant action is not sensible. (74-78)

Eventually, Ismene is rewarded for her passivity when Creon spares her life.

When Antigone is arrested, King Creon expresses shock that a woman in his court has committed the crime. But his disbelief soon turns to perverse pleasure at the opportunity to punish this woman for her authority. Creon's speeches show his contempt for women: "Here are two girls; I think that one of them / has suddenly lost her wits—the other was always so" (615-16).

Antigone, however, rises above the pettiness of sexual rivalry by responding only to the conflict between king and subject. Unlike Creon, Antigone acts out of a heartfelt moral obligation, proclaiming "There is nothing shameful in honoring my brother" (559). As Antigone calmly and eloquently argues the righteousness of her action, instead of quivering with fear under Creon's threats, the king's feeling of triumph slowly turns to rage. At the close of her defense, Antigone says "Now, if you think me a fool to act like this, / perhaps it is a fool that judges so" (513-14). To which Creon angrily replies:

> This girl had learned her insolence
> before this, when she broke the established laws.
> But here is still another insolence
> in that she boasts of it, laughs at what she did.
> I swear I am no man and she the man
> If she can win this and not pay for it. (524-29)

Although Antigone's illegal act is punishable by death, it is the fact that a mere woman had defied him that enrages Creon. Her death alone will not satisfy him. He needs to master her willfulness and make her regret her arrogance. Instead of killing her, he entombs her, where she will die slowly. This method of execution, Creon says, will teach the woman a lesson:

> In that place she shall call on Hades, god of death,
> in her prayers. That god only she reveres.
> Perhaps she will win from him escape from death
> or at least in that last moment will recognize
> her honoring of the dead is labor lost. (837-41)

Dahlberg 3

The key to the king's personality is found in a comment Creon makes to Haemon when explaining why he has sentenced his son's bride-to-be to death: "we cannot give victory to a woman. / If we must accept defeat, let it be from a man; / we must not let people say that a woman beat us" (728-30). Creon refuses to listen to Haemon's defense of Antigone, calling his son a "woman's slave"; and the young man, disgusted by his father's cruelty, rejects him. This rejection makes the king even more bitter. Creon's pride has made him blind to his mistake.

Throughout the course of the play, Creon changes from a strict but competent ruler to a wildly insecure man, plagued by imaginary enemies. He has come to suspect that anyone who disagrees with him is involved in a plot against him:

> You there, who lurked in my house, viper-like—
> secretly drawing it lifeblood; I never thought
> that I was raising two sources of destruction,
> two rebels against my throne. (583-86)

Creon has mistaken Antigone's act of piety for a treasonous attempt by a power-hungry female to undermine his rule. Out of his own fear of being bested by a woman, Creon begins a chain of events which will finally destroy him, fulfilling Antigone's prediction: "But if Creon and his people are the wrongdoers/let their suffering be no worse than the injustice/they are meting out to me" (977–79).

Dahlberg 4

Work Cited

Sophocles. *Antigone*. Translated by David Grene. *Literature and the Writing Process*, edited by Elizabeth McMahan, et al., 11th ed., Pearson, 2017, pp. 634-64.

Questions for Discussion and Writing

1. Do you think this essay overemphasizes the gender issue in analyzing the conflict between Creon and Antigone? Has the author slighted or ignored more important issues?

2. Can you find any additional evidence that the author of the essay overlooked or chose not to use? Would the argument be strengthened by including Eurydice in the analysis?

3. The author says that Antigone rises above sexual rivalry in her defiant behavior. Is this view accurate? Can you cite evidence to suggest that Antigone is also caught up in the power struggle between male and female?

4. The author of the essay analyzes Creon more than Antigone. Why? Is the strategy productive? Do you agree with the conclusions about Creon's character development?

30 Writing About Character

Chapter Preview

Pondering people's characters comes quite naturally and easily. You will remember that we began our approach to literature with the study of character in the short story. Drama also provides us with carefully drawn examples of human speech and behavior. Whether the presentation is realistic or not, the characters are at the heart of the play. By the end of this chapter you will be able to

* Explain the difference between the *classic tragic hero* and the *modern tragic hero*.
* Analyze the characters in the play *The Glass Menagerie*.
* Identify several options for arranging the minor claims in critical essays.
* Describe the process for supporting claims with specific details and quotations.

What Is the Modern Hero?

In everyday life, we use the word *heroic* to describe people who save others' lives while risking their own, acts of great self-sacrifice or self-control, feats that we hold in awe. Before you read on, think of the last time you remember calling something heroic or referring to someone as a hero. Note the situation, and think about what you meant by the word. We often use it lightly—the person who supplies a much needed extension cord or an emergency ten-dollar loan may temporarily be a hero. But drama practically forces us into deeper consideration of what a hero is.

The Classical Tragic Hero

In the fourth century B.C., Aristotle described the classic concept of the tragic hero. He wrote that the hero must be someone "who is highly renowned and prosperous." Classical tragedy involves the inevitable destruction of a noble person by means of a character flaw, usually a disproportionate measure of a specific human attribute such as pride or jealousy or indecision. The Aristotelian definition implies this basic premise: there is a natural order and proportion of traits within the human being that, if violated, produces calamity. Many critics cite

Antigone's "difficult willfulness" as the explanation of her fate. Charles Segal claims that "she can assert what she is only by staking her entire being, her life. It is by this extreme defense of her beliefs that she rises to heroic and deeply tragic stature."[1]

The Modern Tragic Hero

In 1949, the famous playwright Arthur Miller described what he considered a new kind of hero. In an article titled "Tragedy and the Common Man" (*New York Times*, 27 Feb. 1949, 3.1.3.), he challenged Aristotle's idea that the hero must be a "highly renowned and prosperous" figure who has a tragic flaw. In contrast to a disorder exclusively within the personal traits of the hero, Miller's idea of the modern hero emphasizes a clash between the character and the environment, especially the social environment. He says that each person has a chosen image of self and position and that tragedy results when the character's environment denies the fulfillment of this self-concept. The hero no longer must be born into the nobility but gains stature in the action of pitting self against cosmos. The tragedy is "the disaster inherent in being torn away from our chosen image of what and who we are in this world." Feelings of displacement and indignity, then, are the driving forces for Miller's modern tragic hero. In his own play *Death of a Salesman*, the character Willy Loman imagines himself as a well-liked, successful, worldly businessman. Tragically, he is really an object of ridicule and contempt, always on the edge of poverty. Such conflicts between ideal self-image and reality occur over and over in the modern play you are about to read.

Looking at the Modern Hero

As you read for pleasure *The Glass Menagerie* by Tennessee Williams, take special note of the characters. Who is the hero? the heroine?—or are there none? Which characters do you respond positively to? Are there any to whom you respond negatively?

Tennessee Williams   1911–1983

Tennessee Williams was born Thomas Lanier Williams in Columbus, Mississippi, but grew up in St. Louis. When his mother gave him a typewriter for his eleventh birthday, he began to write—and he continued to write for the rest of his life. He dropped out of the University of Missouri, worked at a shoe company, later attended the University of Iowa, and won a grant for promising playwrights. The promise was fulfilled in 1945 with the performance of *The Glass Menagerie*. His remarkably successful career included two Pulitzer Prize–winning plays, *A Streetcar Named Desire* (1947) and *Cat on a Hot Tin Roof* (1955). Several of his plays have been made into popular and award-winning movies.

---

[1]Charles Paul Segal. "Sophocles' Praise of Man and the Conflicts of *Antigone*." *Sophocles: A Collection of Critical Essays*. Ed. T. Woodward. Englewood Cliffs, NJ: Prentice, 1966: 65.

The Glass Menagerie

Nobody, not even the rain, has such small hands.

—*E. E. Cummings*

SCENE

An Alley in St. Louis
Part I. Preparation for a Gentleman Caller
Part II. The Gentleman Calls
Time:—Now and the Past

THE CHARACTERS

AMANDA WINGFIELD, *the mother:*
A little woman of great but confused vitality clinging frantically to another time and place. Her characterization must be carefully created, not copied from type. She is not paranoiac, but her life is paranoia. There is much to admire in Amanda, and as much to love and pity as there is to laugh at. Certainly she has endurance and a kind of heroism, and though her foolishness makes her unwittingly cruel at times, there is tenderness in her slight person.

LAURA WINGFIELD, *her daughter:*
Amanda, having failed to establish contact with reality, continues to live vitally in her illusions, but Laura's situation is even graver. A childhood illness has left her crippled, one leg slightly shorter than the other, and held in a brace. This defect need not be more than suggested on the stage. Stemming from this, Laura's separation increases till she is like a piece of her own glass collection, too exquisitely fragile to move from the shelf.

TOM WINGFIELD, *her son:* And the narrator of the play. A poet with a job in a warehouse. His nature is not remorseless, but to escape from a trap he has to act without pity.

JIM O'CONNOR, *the gentleman caller:* A nice, ordinary, young man.

SCENE I

The Wingfield apartment is in the rear of the building, one of those vast hive-like conglomerations of cellular living-units that flower as warty growths in overcrowded urban centers of lower middle-class population and are symptomatic of the impulse of this largest and fundamentally enslaved section of American society to avoid fluidity and differentiation and to exist and function as one interfused mass of automatism.

The apartment faces an alley and is entered by a fire escape, a structure whose name is a touch of accidental poetic truth, for all of these huge buildings are always burning with the slow and implacable fires of human desperation. The fire escape is part of what we see—that is, the landing of it and steps descending from it.

The scene is memory and is therefore nonrealistic. Memory takes a lot of poetic license. It omits some details; others are exaggerated, according to the emotional value of the articles it touches, for memory is seated predominantly in the heart. The interior is therefore rather dim and poetic.

The original cast of the New York production of *The Glass Menagerie* (1945) with Laurette Taylor as Amanda. (Museum of the City of New York)

 At the rise of the curtain, the audience is faced with the dark, grim rear wall of the Wingfield tenement. This building is flanked on both sides by dark, narrow alleys which run into murky canyons of tangled clotheslines, garbage cans, and the sinister latticework of neighboring fire escapes. It is up and down these side alleys that exterior entrances and exits are made during the play. At the end of TOM's opening commentary, the dark tenement wall slowly becomes transparent and reveals the interior of the ground-floor Wingfield apartment.

 Nearest the audience is the living room, which also serves as a sleeping room for LAURA, the sofa unfolding to make her bed. Just beyond, separated from the living room by a wide arch or second proscenium with transparent faded portieres (or second curtain), is the dining room. In an old-fashioned whatnot in the living room are seen scores of transparent glass animals. A blown-up photograph of the father hangs on the wall of the living room, to the left of the archway. It is the face of a very handsome young man in a doughboy's First World War cap. He is gallantly smiling, ineluctably smiling, as if to say "I will be smiling forever."

 Also hanging on the wall, near the photograph, are a typewriter keyboard chart and a Gregg shorthand diagram. An upright typewriter on a small table stands beneath the charts. The audience hears and sees the opening scene in the dining room through both the transparent fourth wall of the building and the transparent gauze portieres of the dining-room arch. It is during this revealing scene that the fourth wall slowly ascends, out of sight. This transparent exterior wall is not brought down again until the very end of the play, during TOM's final speech.

The narrator is an undisguised convention of the play. He takes whatever license with dramatic convention is convenient to his purposes.

TOM *enters, dressed as a merchant sailor, and strolls across to the fire escape. There he stops and lights a cigarette. He addresses the audience.*

TOM. Yes, I have tricks in my pocket, I have things up my sleeve. But I am the opposite of a stage magician. He gives you illusion that has the appearance of truth. I give you truth in the pleasant disguise of illusion.

To begin with, I turn back time. I reverse it to that quaint period, the thirties, when the huge middle class of America was matriculating in a school for the blind. Their eyes had failed them, or they had failed their eyes, and so they were having their fingers pressed forcibly down on the fiery Braille alphabet of a dissolving economy.

In Spain there was revolution. Here there was only shouting and confusion. In Spain there was Guernica.[1] Here there were disturbances of labor, sometimes pretty violent, in otherwise peaceful cities such as Chicago, Cleveland, Saint Louis...

This is the social background of the play. [*Music begins to play.*]

The play is memory. Being a memory play, it is dimly lighted, it is sentimental, it is not realistic. In memory everything seems to happen to music. That explains the fiddle in the wings.

I am the narrator of the play, and also a character in it. The other characters are my mother, Amanda, my sister, Laura, and a gentleman caller who appears in the final scenes. He is the most realistic character in the play, being an emissary from a world of reality that we were somehow set apart from. But since I have a poet's weakness for symbols, I am using this character also as a symbol; he is the long-delayed but always expected something that we live for.

There is a fifth character in the play who doesn't appear except in this larger-than-life-size photograph over the mantel. This is our father who left us a long time ago. He was a telephone man who fell in love with long distances; he gave up his job with the telephone company and skipped the light fantastic out of town...

The last we heard of him was a picture postcard from Mazatlan, on the Pacific coast of Mexico, containing a message of two words: "Hello—Goodbye!" and no address.

I think the rest of the play will explain itself.... [AMANDA *'s voice becomes audible through the portieres.*] [*Legend on screen:* "Ou sont les neiges d'antan?"[2]] [TOM *divides the portieres and enters the dining room.* AMANDA *and* LAURA *are seated at a drop-leaf table. Eating is indicated by gestures without food or utensils.* AMANDA *faces the audience.* TOM *and* LAURA *are seated in profile. The interior is lit up softly and through the scrim we see* AMANDA *and* LAURA *seated at the table.*]

AMANDA [*calling*]. Tom?

TOM. Yes, Mother.

AMANDA. We can't say grace until you come to the table!

TOM. Coming, Mother. [*He bows slightly and withdraws, reappearing a few moments later in his place at the table.*]

---

[1]Spanish town bombed by fascists in the Spanish Civil War, 1937.

[2]"Where are the snows of yester-year?" A quotation from a poem by François Villon, fifteenth century.

AMANDA [*to her son*]. Honey, don't *push* with your *fingers*. If you have to push with something, the thing to push with is a crust of bread. And chew—chew! Animals have secretions in their stomachs which enable them to digest food without mastication, but human beings are supposed to chew their food before they swallow it down. Eat food leisurely, son, and really enjoy it. A well-cooked meal has lots of delicate flavors that have to be held in the mouth for appreciation. So chew your food and give your salivary glands a chance to function! [TOM *deliberately lays his imaginary fork down and pushes his chair back from the table.*]

TOM. I haven't enjoyed one bite of this dinner because of your constant directions on how to eat it. It's you that make me rush through meals with your hawklike attention to every bite I take. Sickening—spoils my appetite—all this discussion of—animals' secretion—salivary glands—mastication!

AMANDA [*lightly*]. Temperament like a Metropolitan star! [TOM *rises and walks toward the living room.*] You're not excused from the table.

TOM. I'm getting a cigarette.

AMANDA. You smoke too much. [LAURA *rises.*]

LAURA. I'll bring in the blanc mange. [TOM *remains standing with his cigarette by the portieres.*]

AMANDA [*rising*]. No, sister, no, sister—you be the lady this time and I'll be the darky.

LAURA. I'm already up.

AMANDA. Resume your seat, little sister—I want you to stay fresh and pretty—for gentlemen callers!

LAURA [*sitting down*]. I'm not expecting any gentlemen callers.

AMANDA [*crossing out to the kitchenette, airily*]. Sometimes they come when they are least expected! Why, I remember one Sunday afternoon in Blue Mountain— [*She enters the kitchenette.*]

TOM. I know what's coming!

LAURA. Yes. But let her tell it.

TOM. Again?

LAURA. She loves to tell it. [AMANDA *returns with a bowl of dessert.*]

AMANDA. One Sunday afternoon in Blue Mountain—your mother received— *seventeen!*—gentlemen callers! Why, sometimes there weren't chairs enough to accommodate them all. We had to send the nigger over to bring in folding chairs from the parish house.

TOM [*remaining at the portieres*]. How did you entertain those gentlemen callers?

AMANDA. I understood the art of conversation!

TOM. I bet you could talk.

AMANDA. Girls in those days knew how to talk, I can tell you.

TOM. Yes? [*Image on screen: Amanda as a girl on a porch, greeting callers.*]

AMANDA. They knew how to entertain their gentleman callers. It wasn't enough for a girl to be possessed of a pretty face and a graceful figure—although I wasn't slighted in either respect. She also needed to have a nimble wit and a tongue to meet all occasions.

TOM. What did you talk about?

AMANDA. Things of importance going on in the world! Never anything coarse or common or vulgar. [*She addresses* TOM *as though he were seated in the vacant chair at the table though he remains by the portieres. He plays this scene as though reading from a script.*] My callers were gentlemen—all! Among my callers were some of the most prominent young planters of the Mississippi Delta—planters and sons of planters! [TOM *motions for music and a spot of light on* AMANDA. *Her eyes lift, her face glows, her voice becomes rich and elegiac.*] [*Screen legend:* "Ou sont les neiges d'antan?"] There was young Champ Laughlin who later became vice-president of the Delta Planters Bank. Hadley Stevenson who was drowned in Moon Lake and left his widow one hundred and fifty thousand in Government bonds. There were the Cutrere brothers, Wesley and Bates. Bates was one of my bright particular beaux! He got in a quarrel with that wild Wainwright boy. They shot it out on the floor of Moon Lake Casino. Bates was shot through the stomach. Died in the ambulance on his way to Memphis. His widow was also well provided-for, came into eight or ten thousand acres, that's all. She married him on the rebound—never loved her—carried my picture on him the night he died! And there was that boy that every girl in the Delta had set her cap for! That beautiful, brilliant young Fitzhugh boy from Greene County!

TOM. What did he leave his widow?

AMANDA. He never married! Gracious, you talk as though all of my old admirers had turned up their toes to the daisies!

TOM. Isn't this the first you've mentioned that still survives?

AMANDA. That Fitzhugh boy went North and made a fortune—came to be known as the Wolf of Wall Street! He had the Midas touch, whatever he touched turned to gold! And I could have been Mrs. Duncan J. Fitzhugh, mind you! But—I picked your *father!*

LAURA [*rising*]. Mother, let me clear the table.

AMANDA. No, dear, you go in front and study your typewriter chart. Or practice your shorthand a little. Stay fresh and pretty!—It's almost time for our gentlemen callers to start arriving. [*She flounces girlishly toward the kitchenette.*] How many do you suppose we're going to entertain this afternoon? [TOM *throws down the paper and jumps up with a groan.*]

LAURA [*alone in the dining room*]. I don't believe we're going to receive any, Mother.

AMANDA [*reappearing, airily*]. What? No one—not one? You must be joking! [LAURA *nervously echoes her laugh. She slips in a fugitive manner through the half-open portieres and draws them gently behind her. A shaft of very clear light is thrown on her face against the faded tapestry of the curtains. Faintly the music of "The Glass Menagerie" is heard as she continues, lightly.*] Not one gentleman caller? It can't be true! There must be a flood, there must have been a tornado!

LAURA. It isn't a flood, it's not a tornado, Mother. I'm just not popular like you were in Blue Mountain.... [TOM *utters another groan.* LAURA *glances at him with a faint, apologetic smile. Her voice catches a little.*] Mother's afraid I'm going to be an old maid. [*The scene dims out with the "Glass Menagerie" music.*]

SCENE II

On the dark stage the screen is lighted with the image of blue roses. Gradually LAURA'S *figure becomes apparent and the screen goes out. The music subsides.*

LAURA *is seated in the delicate ivory chair at the small claw-foot table. She wears a dress of soft violet material for a kimono—her hair is tied back from her forehead with a ribbon. She is washing and polishing her collection of glass.* AMANDA *appears on the fire escape steps. At the sound of her ascent* LAURA *catches her breath, thrusts the bowl of ornaments away, and sets herself stiffly before the diagram of the typewriter keyboard as though it held her spellbound. Something has happened to* AMANDA. *It is written in her face as she climbs to the landing: a look that is grim and hopeless and a little absurd. She has on one of those cheap or imitation velvety-looking cloth coats with imitation fur collar. Her hat is five or six years old, one of those dreadful cloche hats that were worn in the late twenties, and she is clutching an enormous black patent-leather pocketbook with nickel clasps and initials. This is her full-dress outfit, the one she usually wears to the D.A.R.*[3] *Before entering she looks through the door. She purses her lips, opens her eyes very wide, rolls them upward and shakes her head. Then she slowly lets herself in the door. Seeing her mother's expression* LAURA *touches her lips with a nervous gesture.*

LAURA. Hello, Mother, I was—[*She makes a nervous gesture toward the chart on the wall.* AMANDA *leans against the shut door and stares at* LAURA *with a martyred look.*]

AMANDA. Deception? Deception? [*She slowly removes her hat and gloves, continuing the sweet suffering stare. She lets the hat and gloves fall on the floor—a bit of acting.*]

LAURA [*shakily*]. How was the D.A.R. meeting? [AMANDA *slowly opens her purse and removes a dainty white handkerchief which she shakes out delicately and delicately touches to her lips and nostrils.*] Didn't you go to the D.A.R. meeting, Mother?

AMANDA [*faintly, almost inaudibly*].—No. —No. [*then more forcibly*] I did not have the strength—to go to the D.A.R. In fact, I did not have the courage! I wanted to find a hole in the ground and hide myself in it forever! [*She crosses slowly to the wall and removes the diagram of the typewriter keyboard. She holds it in front of her for a second, staring at it sweetly and sorrowfully—then bites her lips and tears it in two pieces.*]

LAURA [*faintly*]. Why did you do that, Mother? [AMANDA *repeats the same procedure with the chart of the Gregg Alphabet.*] Why are you—

AMANDA. Why? Why? How old are you, Laura?

LAURA. Mother, you know my age.

AMANDA. I thought that you were an adult; it seems that I was mistaken. [*She crosses slowly to the sofa and sinks down and stares at* LAURA.]

LAURA. Please don't stare at me, Mother. [AMANDA *closes her eyes and lowers her head. There is a ten-second pause.*]

AMANDA. What are we going to do, what is going to become of us, what is the future? [*There is another pause.*]

LAURA. Has something happened, Mother? [AMANDA *draws a long breath, takes out the handkerchief again, goes through the dabbing process.*] Mother, has—something happened?

AMANDA. I'll be all right in a minute, I'm just bewildered— [*She hesitates.*]—by life...

LAURA. Mother, I wish that you would tell me what's happened!

AMANDA. As you know, I was supposed to be inducted into my office at the D.A.R. this afternoon. [*Screen image:* A swarm of typewriters.] But I stopped off at Rubicam's Business College to speak to your teachers about your having a cold and ask them what progress they thought you were making down there.

LAURA. Oh...

---

[3]The Daughters of the American Revolution.

AMANDA. I went to the typing instructor and introduced myself as your mother. She didn't know who you were. "Wingfield," she said. "We don't have any such student enrolled at the school!" I assured her she did, that you had been going to classes since early in January. "I wonder," she said, "if you could be talking about that terribly shy little girl who dropped out of school after only a few days' attendance?" "No," I said, "Laura, my daughter, has been going to school every day for the past six weeks!" "Excuse me," she said. She took the attendance book out and there was your name, unmistakably printed, and all the dates you were absent until they decided that you had dropped out of school. I still said, "No, there must have been some mistake! There must have been some mix-up in the records!" And she said, "No—I remember her perfectly now. Her hands shook so that she couldn't hit the right keys! The first time we gave a speed test, she broke down completely—was sick at the stomach and almost had to be carried into the wash room! After that morning she never showed up any more. We phoned the house but never got any answer"—While I was working at Famous-Barr, I suppose, demonstrating those—[*She indicates a brassiere with her hands.*] Oh, I felt so weak I could barely keep on my feet! I had to sit down while they got me a glass of water! Fifty dollars' tuition, all of our plans—my hopes and ambitions for you—just gone up the spout, just gone up the spout like that. [LAURA *draws a long breath and gets awkwardly to her feet. She crosses to the Victrola and winds it up.*] What are you doing?

LAURA. Oh! [*She releases the handle and returns to her seat.*]

AMANDA. Laura, where have you been going when you've gone out pretending that you were going to business college?

LAURA. I've just been going out walking.

AMANDA. That's not true.

LAURA. It is. I just went walking.

AMANDA. Walking? Walking? In winter? Deliberately courting pneumonia in that light coat? Where did you walk to, Laura?

LAURA. All sorts of places—mostly in the park.

AMANDA. Even after you'd started catching that cold?

LAURA. It was the lesser of two evils, Mother. [*Screen image:* Winter scene in a park.] I couldn't go back there. I—threw up—on the floor!

AMANDA. From half past seven till after five every day you mean to tell me you walked around in the park, because you wanted to make me think that you were still going to Rubicam's Business College?

LAURA. It wasn't as bad as it sounds. I went inside places to get warmed up.

AMANDA. Inside where?

LAURA. I went in the art museum and the bird houses at the Zoo. I visited the penguins every day! Sometimes I did without lunch and went to the movies. Lately I've been spending most of my afternoons in the Jewel Box, that big glass house where they raise the tropical flowers.

AMANDA. You did all this to deceive me, just for deception? [LAURA *looks down.*] Why?

LAURA. Mother, when you're disappointed, you get that awful suffering look on your face, like the picture of Jesus' mother in the museum!

AMANDA. Hush!

LAURA. I couldn't face it. [*There is a pause. A whisper of strings is heard. Legend on screen:* "The Crust of Humility."]

AMANDA [*hopelessly fingering the huge pocketbook*]. So what are we going to do the rest of our lives? Stay home and watch the parades go by? Amuse ourselves with the glass menagerie, darling? Eternally play those worn-out phonograph records your father left as a painful reminder of him? We won't have a business career—we've given that up because it gave us nervous indigestion! [*She laughs wearily.*] What is there left but dependency all our lives? I know so well what becomes of unmarried women who aren't prepared to occupy a position. I've seen such pitiful cases in the South—barely tolerated spinsters living upon the grudging patronage of sister's or brother's wife!—stuck away in some little mousetrap of a room—encouraged by one in-law to visit another—little birdlike women without any nest—eating the crust of humility all their life! Is that the future that we've mapped out for ourselves? I swear it's the only alternative I can think of! [*She pauses.*] It isn't a very pleasant alternative, is it? [*She pauses again.*] Of course—some girls *do marry.* [LAURA *twists her hands nervously.*] Haven't you ever liked some boy?

LAURA. Yes. I liked one once. [*She rises.*] I came across his picture a while ago.

AMANDA [*with some interest*]. He gave you his picture?

LAURA. No, it's in the yearbook.

AMANDA [*disappointed*]. Oh—a high school boy. [*Screen image:* Jim as the high school hero bearing a silver cup]

LAURA. Yes. His name was Jim. [*She lifts the heavy annual from the claw-foot table.*] Here he is in *The Pirates of Penzance.*

AMANDA [*absently*]. The what?

LAURA. The operetta the senior class put on. He had a wonderful voice and we sat across the aisle from each other Mondays, Wednesdays and Fridays in the Aud. Here he is with the silver cup for debating! See his grin?

AMANDA [*absently*]. He must have had a jolly disposition.

LAURA. He used to call me—Blue Roses. [*Screen image:* Blue roses.]

AMANDA. Why did he call you such a name as that?

LAURA. When I had that attack of pleurosis—he asked me what was the matter when I came back. I said pleurosis—he thought that I said Blue Roses! So that's what he always called me after that. Whenever he saw me, he'd holler, "Hello, Blue Roses!" I didn't care for the girl that he went out with. Emily Meisenbach. Emily was the best-dressed girl at Soldan. She never struck me, though, as being sincere...It says in the Personal Section—they're engaged. That's—six years ago! They must be married by now.

AMANDA. Girls that aren't cut out for business careers usually wind up married to some nice man. [*She gets up with a spark of revival.*] Sister, that's what you'll do! [LAURA *utters a startled, doubtful laugh. She reaches quickly for a piece of glass.*]

LAURA. But, Mother—

AMANDA. Yes? [*She goes over to the photograph.*]

LAURA [*in a tone of frightened apology*]. I'm—crippled!

AMANDA. Nonsense! Laura, I've told you never, never to use that word. Why, you're not crippled, you just have a little defect—hardly noticeable, even! When people have some slight disadvantage like that, they cultivate other things to make up for it—develop charm—and vivacity—and—*charm!* That's all you have to do! [*She turns again to the photograph.*] One thing your father had *plenty of*—was *charm!* [TOM *motions to the fiddle in the wings. The scene fades out with music.*]

SCENE III

Legend on screen: "After the fiasco—"
TOM *speaks from the fire escape landing.*

TOM. After the fiasco at Rubicam's Business College, the idea of getting a gentleman caller for Laura began to play a more and more important part in Mother's calculations. It became an obsession. Like some archetype of the universal unconscious, the image of the gentleman caller haunted our small apartment... [*Screen image:* A young man at the door of a house with flowers.] An evening at home rarely passed without some allusion to this image, this specter, this hope....Even when he wasn't mentioned, his presence hung in Mother's preoccupied look and in my sister's frightened, apologetic manner— hung like a sentence passed upon the Wingfields! Mother was a woman of action as well as words. She began to take logical steps in the planned direction. Late that winter and in the early spring—realizing that extra money would be needed to properly feather the nest and plume the bird—she conducted a vigorous campaign on the telephone, roping in subscribers to one of those magazines for matrons called *The Homemaker's Companion*, the type of journal that features the serialized sublimations of ladies of letters who think in terms of delicate cuplike breasts, slim, tapering waists, rich, creamy thighs, eyes like wood smoke in autumn, fingers that soothe and caress like strains of music, bodies as powerful as Etruscan sculpture. [*Screen image:* The cover of a glamor magazine.] [AMANDA *enters with the telephone on a long extension cord. She is spotlighted in the dim stage.*]

AMANDA. Ida Scott? This is Amanda Wingfield! We *missed* you at the D.A.R. last Monday! I said to myself: She's probably suffering with that sinus condition! How is that sinus condition? Horrors! Heaven have mercy—You're a Christian martyr, yes, that's what you are, a Christian martyr! Well, I just now happened to notice that your subscription to the *Companion*'s about to expire! Yes, it expires with the next issue, honey!—just when that wonderful new serial by Bessie Mae Hopper is getting off to such an exciting start. Oh, honey, it's something that you can't miss! You remember how *Gone with the Wind* took everybody by storm? You simply couldn't go out if you hadn't read it. All everybody *talked* was Scarlett O'Hara. Well, this is a book that critics already compare to *Gone with the Wind*. It's the *Gone with the Wind* of the post-World War generation!—What—Burning?—Oh, honey, don't let them burn, go take a look in the oven and I'll hold the wire! Heavens—I think she's hung up! [*The scene dims out.*] [*Legend on screen:* "You think I'm in love with Continental Shoemakers?"] [*Before the lights come up again, the violent voices of* TOM *and* AMANDA *are heard. They are quarreling behind the portieres. In front of them stands* LAURA *with clenched hands and panicky expression. A clear pool of light is on her figure throughout this scene.*]

TOM. What in Christ's name am I—
AMANDA [*shrilly*]. Don't you use that—
TOM. —supposed to do!
AMANDA. —expression! Not in my—
TOM. Ohhh!
AMANDA. —presence! Have you gone out of your senses?
TOM. I have, that's true, *driven* out!

AMANDA. What is the matter with you, you—big—big—IDIOT!

TOM. Look!—I've got *no thing*, no single thing—

AMANDA. Lower your voice!

TOM. —in my life here that I can call my OWN! Everything is—

AMANDA. Stop that shouting!

TOM. Yesterday you confiscated my books! You had the nerve to—

AMANDA. I took that horrible novel back to the library—yes! That hideous book by that insane Mr. Lawrence. [TOM *laughs wildly.*] I cannot control the output of diseased minds or people who cater to them—[TOM *laughs still more wildly.*] BUT I WON'T ALLOW SUCH FILTH BROUGHT INTO MY HOUSE! No, no, no, no, no!

TOM. House, house! Who pays rent on it, who makes a slave of himself to—

AMANDA [*fairly screeching*]. Don't you DARE to—

TOM. No, no, *I* mustn't say things! *I've* got to just—

AMANDA. Let me tell you—

TOM. I don't want to hear any more! [*He tears the portieres open. The dining-room area is lit with a turgid smoky red glow. Now we see* AMANDA; *her hair is in metal curlers and she is wearing a very old bathrobe, much too large for her slight figure, a relic of the faithless Mr. Wingfield. The upright typewriter now stands on the drop-leaf table, along with a wild disarray of manuscripts. The quarrel was probably precipitated by* AMANDA's *interruption of* TOM's *creative labor. A chair lies overthrown on the floor. Their gesticulating shadows are cast on the ceiling by the fiery glow.*]

AMANDA. You *will* hear more, you—

TOM. No, I won't hear more, I'm going out!

AMANDA. You come right back in—

TOM. Out, out, out! Because I'm—

AMANDA. Come back here, Tom Wingfield! I'm not through talking to you!

TOM. Oh, go—

LAURA [*desperately*].—Tom!

AMANDA. You're going to listen, and no more insolence from you! I'm at the end of my patience! [*He comes back toward her.*]

TOM. What do you think I'm at? Aren't I supposed to have any patience to reach the end of, Mother? I know, I know. It seems unimportant to you, what I'm *doing*—what I *want* to do—having a little *difference* between them. You don't think that—

AMANDA. I think you've been doing things that you're ashamed of. That's why you act like this. I don't believe that you go every night to the movies. Nobody goes to the movies night after night. Nobody in their right mind goes to the movies as often as you pretend to. People don't go to the movies at nearly midnight, and movies don't let out at two A.M. Come in stumbling. Muttering to yourself like a maniac! You get three hours' sleep and then go to work. Oh, I can picture the way you're doing down there. Moping, doping, because you're in no condition.

TOM [*wildly*]. No, I'm in no condition!

AMANDA. What right have you got to jeopardize your job? Jeopardize the security of us all? How do you think we'd manage if you were—

TOM. Listen! You think I'm crazy about the *warehouse*? [*He bends fiercely toward her slight figure.*] You think I'm in love with the Continental Shoemakers? You think I want to spend fifty-five *years* down there in that—*celotex interior!*

with—*fluorescent*—*tubes!* Look! I'd rather somebody picked up a crowbar and battered out my brains—than go back mornings! I *go!* Every time you come in yelling that Goddamn *"Rise and Shine!"* *"Rise and Shine!"* I say to myself, "How *lucky dead* people are!" But I get up. I *go!* For sixty-five dollars a month I give up all that I dream of doing and being *ever!* And you say self—*self's* all I ever think of. Why, listen, if self is what I thought of, Mother, I'd be where he is—GONE! [*He points to his father's picture.*] As far as the system of transportation reaches! [*He starts past her. She grabs his arm.*] Don't grab at me, Mother!

AMANDA. Where are you going?

TOM. I'm going to the *movies!*

AMANDA. I don't believe that lie!

[Tom *crouches toward her, overtowering her tiny figure. She backs away, gasping.*]

TOM. I'm going to opium dens! Yes, opium dens, dens of vice and criminals' hangouts, Mother. I've joined the Hogan Gang, I'm a hired assassin, I carry a tommy gun in a violin case! I run a string of cat houses in the Valley! They call me Killer, Killer Wingfield, I'm leading a double-life, a simple, honest, warehouse worker by day, by night a dynamic *czar* of the *underworld, Mother.* I go to gambling casinos, I spin away fortunes on the roulette table! I wear a patch over one eye and a false mustache, sometimes I put on green whiskers. On those occasions they call me—*El Diablo!* Oh, I could tell you many things to make you sleepless! My enemies plan to dynamite this place. They're going to blow us all sky-high some night! I'll be glad, very happy, and so will you! You'll go up, up on a broomstick, over Blue Mountain with seventeen gentlemen callers! You ugly—babbling old—*witch* ....[*He goes through a series of violent, clumsy movements, seizing his overcoat, lunging to the door, pulling it fiercely open. The women watch him, aghast. His arm catches in the sleeve of the coat as he struggles to pull it on. For a moment he is pinioned by the bulky garment. With an outraged groan he tears the coat off again, splitting the shoulder of it, and hurls it across the room. It strikes against the shelf of* LAURA's *glass collection, and there is a tinkle of shattering glass.* LAURA *cries out as if wounded.*] [*Music.*] [*Screen legend:* "The Glass Menagerie."]

LAURA [*shrilly*]. My *glass!*—menagerie ....[*She covers her face and turns away.*] [*But* AMANDA *is still stunned and stupefied by the "ugly witch" so that she barely notices this occurrence. Now she recovers her speech.*]

AMANDA [*in an awful voice*]. I won't speak to you—until you apologize! [*She crosses through the portieres and draws them together behind her.* TOM *is left with* LAURA. LAURA *clings weakly to the mantel with her face averted.* TOM *stares at her stupidly for a moment. Then he crosses to the shelf. He drops awkwardly on his knee to collect the fallen glass, glancing at* LAURA *as if he would speak but couldn't.*]

[*"The Glass Menagerie" music steals in as the scene dims out.*]

SCENE IV

The interior of the apartment is dark. There is a faint light in the alley. A deep-voiced bell in a church is tolling the hour of five.

TOM *appears at the top of the alley. After each solemn boom of the bell in the tower, he shakes a little noisemaker or rattle as if to express the tiny spasm of man in contrast to the sustained power and dignity of the Almighty. This and the unsteadiness of his advance make it evident that he has been drinking. As he climbs the few steps to the fire escape landing light steals up inside.* LAURA *appears in the front room in a nightdress. She notices that* TOM *'s bed is empty.* TOM *fishes in his pockets for his door key, removing a motley assortment of articles in this search, including a shower of movie ticket stubs and an empty bottle. At last he finds the key, but just as he is about to insert it, it slips from his fingers. He strikes a match and crouches below the door.*

TOM [*bitterly*]. One crack—and it falls through! [LAURA *opens the door.*]

LAURA. Tom! Tom, what are you doing?

TOM. Looking for a door key.

LAURA. Where have you been all this time?

TOM. I have been to the movies.

LAURA. All this time at the movies?

TOM. There was a very long program. There was a Garbo picture and a Mickey Mouse and a travelogue and a newsreel and a preview of coming attractions. And there was an organ solo and a collection for the Milk Fund—simultaneously—which ended up in a terrible fight between a fat lady and an usher!

LAURA [*innocently*]. Did you have to stay through everything?

TOM. Of course! And, oh, I forgot! There was a big stage show! The headliner on this stage show was Malvolio the Magician. He performed wonderful tricks, many of them such as pouring water back and forth between pitchers. First it turned to wine and then it turned to beer and then it turned to whiskey. I know it was whiskey it finally turned to because he needed somebody to come up out of the audience to help him, and I came up—both shows! It was Kentucky Straight Bourbon. A very generous fellow, he gave souvenirs. [*He pulls from his pocket a shimmering rainbow-colored scarf.*] He gave me this. This is his magic scarf. You can have it, Laura. You wave it over a canary cage and you get a bowl of goldfish. You wave it over the goldfish bowl and they fly away canaries....But the wonderfullest trick of all was the coffin trick. We nailed him into a coffin and he got out of the coffin without removing one nail. [*He has come inside.*] There is a trick that would come in handy for me—get me out of this two-by-four situation!

LAURA. Tom—shhh!

TOM. What're you shushing me for?

LAURA. You'll wake up Mother.

TOM. Goody, goody! Pay'er back for all those "Rise an' Shines." [*He lies down, groaning.*] You know it don't take much intelligence to get yourself into a nailed-up coffin, Laura. But who in hell ever got himself out of one without removing one nail?

   [*As if in answer, the father's grinning photograph lights up. The scene dims out.*]

   [*Immediately following, the church bell is heard striking six. At the sixth stroke the alarm clock goes off in* AMANDA*'s room, and after a few moments we hear her calling: "Rise and Shine! Rise and Shine! Laura go tell your brother to rise and shine!"*]

TOM [*sitting up slowly*]. I'll rise—but I won't shine. [*The light increases.*]

AMANDA. Laura, tell your brother his coffee is ready. [LAURA *slips into the front room.*]

LAURA. Tom—It's nearly seven. Don't make Mother nervous. [*He stares at her stupidly.*] [*beseechingly:*] Tom, speak to Mother this morning. Make up with her, apologize, speak to her!

Tom. She won't to me. It's her that started not speaking.

Laura. If you just say you're sorry she'll start speaking.

Tom. Her not speaking—is that such a tragedy?

Laura. Please—please!

Amanda [*calling from the kitchenette*]. Laura, are you going to do what I asked you to do, or do I have to get dressed and go out myself?

Laura. Going, going—soon as I get on my coat! [*She pulls on a shapeless felt hat with a nervous, jerky movement, pleadingly glancing at* Tom. *She rushes awkwardly for her coat. The coat is one of* Amanda's *inaccurately made-over, the sleeves too short for* Laura.] Butter and what else?

Amanda [*entering from the kitchenette*]. Just butter. Tell them to charge it.

Laura. Mother, they make such faces when I do that.

Amanda. Sticks and stones can break our bones, but the expression on Mr. Garfinkel's face won't harm us! Tell your brother his coffee is getting cold.

Laura [*at the door*]. Do what I asked you, will you, will you, Tom? [*He looks sullenly away.*]

Amanda. Laura, go now or just don't go at all!

Laura [*rushing out*]. Going—going! [*A second later she cries out.* Tom *springs up and crosses to the door.* Tom *opens the door.*]

Tom. Laura?

Laura. I'm all right. I slipped, but I'm all right.

Amanda [*peering anxiously after her*]. If anyone breaks a leg on those fire-escape steps, the landlord ought to be sued for every cent he possesses! [*She shuts the door. Now she remembers she isn't speaking to* Tom *and returns to the other room.*] [*As* Tom *comes listlessly for his coffee, she turns her back to him and stands rigidly facing the window on the gloomy gray vault of the areaway. Its light on her face with its aged but childish features is cruelly sharp, satirical as a Daumier print.*] [*The music of "Ave Maria" is heard softly.*] [Tom *glances sheepishly but sullenly at her averted figure and slumps at the table. The coffee is scalding hot; he sips it and gasps and spits it back in the cup. At his gasp,* Amanda *catches her breath and half turns. Then she catches herself and turns back to the window.* Tom *blows on his coffee, glancing sidewise at his mother. She clears her throat.* Tom *clears his. He starts to rise, sinks back down again, scratches his head, clears his throat again.* Amanda *coughs.* Tom *raises his cup in both hands to blow on it, his eyes staring over the rim of it at his mother for several moments. Then he slowly sets the cup down and awkwardly and hesitantly rises from the chair.*]

Tom [*hoarsely*]. Mother. I—I apologize, Mother. [Amanda *draws a quick shuddering breath. Her face works grotesquely. She breaks into childlike tears.*] I'm sorry for what I said, for everything that I said, I didn't mean it.

Amanda [*sobbingly*]. My devotion has made me a witch and so I make myself hateful to my children!

Tom. No, you *don't*.

Amanda. I worry so much, don't sleep, it makes me nervous!

Tom [*gently*]. I understand that.

Amanda. I've had to put up a solitary battle all these years. But you're my right-hand bower! Don't fall down, don't fail!

Tom [*gently*]. I try, Mother.

Amanda [*with great enthusiasm*]. Try and you will *succeed!* [*The notion makes her breathless.*] Why, you—you're just *full* of natural endowments! Both of my children—they're *unusual* children! Don't you think I know it? I'm so—*proud!*

Happy and—feel I've—so much to be thankful for but—promise me one thing, son!

Tom. What, Mother?

Amanda. Promise, son, you'll—never be a drunkard!

Tom [*turns to her grinning*]. I will never be a drunkard, Mother.

Amanda. That's what frightened me so, that you'd be drinking! Eat a bowl of Purina!

Tom. Just coffee, Mother.

Amanda. Shredded wheat biscuit?

Tom. No. No, Mother, just coffee.

Amanda. You can't put in a day's work on an empty stomach. You've got ten minutes—don't gulp! Drinking too-hot liquids makes cancer of the stomach.... Put cream in.

Tom. No, thank you.

Amanda. To cool it.

Tom. No! No, thank you, I want it black.

Amanda. I know, but it's not good for you. We have to do all that we can to build ourselves up. In these trying times we live in, all that we have to cling to is—each other.... That's why it's important to—Tom, I—I sent out your sister so I could discuss something with you. If you hadn't spoken I would have spoken to you. [*She sits down.*]

Tom [*gently*]. What is it, Mother, that you want to discuss?

Amanda. *Laura!* [Tom *puts his cup down slowly.*] [*Legend on screen:* "Laura." *Music:* "*The Glass Menagerie.*"]

Tom. —Oh.—Laura...

Amanda [*touching his sleeve*]. You know how Laura is. So quiet but—still water runs deep! She notices things and I think she—broods about them. [Tom *looks up.*] A few days ago I came in and she was crying.

Tom. What about?

Amanda. You.

Tom. Me?

Amanda. She has an idea that you're not happy here.

Tom. What gave her that idea?

Amanda. What gives her any idea? However, you do act strangely. I—I'm not criticizing, understand *that!* I know your ambitions do not lie in the warehouse, that like everybody in the whole wide world—you've had to—make sacrifices, but—Tom—Tom—life's not easy, it calls for—Spartan endurance! There's so many things in my heart that I cannot describe to you! I've never told you but I—*loved* your father....

Tom [*gently*]. I know that, Mother.

Amanda. And you—when I see you taking after his ways! Staying out late—and—well, you *had* been drinking the night you were in that—terrifying condition! Laura says that you hate the apartment and that you go out nights to get away from it! Is that true, Tom?

Tom. No. You say there's so much in your heart that you can't describe to me. That's true of me, too. There's so much in my heart that I can't describe to *you!* So let's respect each other's—

Amanda. But, why—*why*, Tom—are you always so *restless?* Where do you *go* to, nights?

Tom. I—go to the movies.

AMANDA. But, Tom, you go to the movies *entirely* too *much!*

TOM. I like a lot of adventure. [AMANDA *looks baffled, then hurt. As the familiar inquisition resumes,* TOM *becomes hard and impatient again.* AMANDA *slips back into her querulous attitude toward him.*] [*Image on screen:* A sailing vessel with Jolly Roger.]

AMANDA. Most young men find adventure in their careers.

TOM. Then most young men are not employed in a warehouse.

AMANDA. The world is full of young men employed in warehouses and offices and factories.

TOM. Do all of them find adventure in their careers?

AMANDA. They do or they do without it! Not everybody has a craze for adventure.

TOM. Man is by instinct a lover, a hunter, a fighter, and none of those instincts are given much play at the warehouse!

AMANDA. Man is by instinct! Don't quote instinct to me! Instinct is something that people have got away from! It belongs to animals! Christian adults don't want it!

TOM. What do Christian adults want, then, Mother?

AMANDA. Superior things! Things of the mind and the spirit! Only animals have to satisfy instincts! Surely your aims are somewhat higher than theirs! Than monkeys—pigs—

TOM. I reckon they're not.

AMANDA. You're joking. However, that isn't what I wanted to discuss.

TOM [*rising*]. I haven't much time.

AMANDA [*pushing his shoulders*]. Sit down.

TOM. You want me to punch in red at the warehouse, Mother?

AMANDA. You have five minutes. I want to talk about Laura. [*Screen legend:* "Plans and Provisions."]

TOM. All right! What about Laura?

AMANDA. We have to be making some plans and provisions for her. She's older than you, two years, and nothing has happened. She just drifts along doing nothing. It frightens me terribly how she just drifts along.

TOM. I guess she's the type that people call home girls.

AMANDA. There's no such type, and if there is, it's a pity! That is unless the home is hers, with a husband!

TOM. What?

AMANDA. Oh, I can see the handwriting on the wall as plain as I see the nose in front of my face! It's terrifying! More and more you remind me of your father! He was out all hours without explanation!—Then *left! Goodbye!* And me with the bag to hold. I saw that letter you got from the Merchant Marines. I know what you're dreaming of. I'm not standing here blindfolded. [*She pauses.*] Very well, then. Then *do* it! But not till there's somebody to take your place.

TOM. What do you mean?

AMANDA. I mean that as soon as Laura has got somebody to take care of her, married, a home of her own, independent—why, then you'll be free to go wherever you please, on land, on sea, whichever way the wind blows you. But until that time you've got to look out for your sister. I don't say me because I'm old and don't matter! I say for your sister because she's young and dependent. I put her in the business college—a dismal failure! Frightened her so it made her sick at the stomach. I took her over to the Young People's League at the church. Another fiasco. She spoke to nobody, nobody spoke to her. Now all she does is fool with those pieces of glass and play those worn-out records. What kind of a life is that for a girl to lead?

Tom. What can I do about it?

Amanda. Overcome selfishness! Self, self, self is all that you ever think of! [Tom *springs up and crosses to get his coat. It is ugly and bulky. He pulls on a cap with earmuffs.*] Where is your muffler? Put your wool muffler on! [*He snatches it angrily from the closet, tosses it around his neck and pulls both ends tight.*] Tom! I haven't said what I had in mind to ask you.

Tom. I'm too late to—

Amanda [*catching his arm—very importunately; then shyly*]. Down at the warehouse, aren't there some—nice young men?

Tom. No!

Amanda. There *must* be—*some* ...

Tom. Mother—[*He gestures.*]

Amanda. Find out one that's clean-living—doesn't drink and ask him out for sister!

Tom. What?

Amanda. For *sister!* To *meet!* Get *acquainted!*

Tom [*stamping to the door*]. Oh, my go-osh!

Amanda. Will you? [*He opens the door. She says, imploringly:*] Will you? [*He starts down the fire escape.*] Will you? *Will* you, dear?

Tom [*calling back*]. Yes! [Amanda *closes the door hesitantly and with a troubled but faintly hopeful expression.*] [*Screen image:* The cover of a glamor magazine.] [*The spotlight picks up* Amanda *at the phone.*]

Amanda. Ella Cartwright? This is Amanda Wingfield! How are you, honey? How is that kidney condition? [There is a five-second pause.] Horrors! [There is another pause.]You're a Christian martyr, yes, honey, that's what you are, a Christian martyr! Well, I just now happened to notice in my little red book that your subscription to the Companion has just run out! I knew that you wouldn't want to miss out on the wonderful serial starting in this new issue. It's by Bessie Mae Hopper, the first thing she's written since Honeymoon for Three. Wasn't that a strange and interesting story? Well, this one is even lovelier, I believe. It has a sophisticated, society background. It's all about the horsey set on Long Island! [*The light fades out.*]

SCENE V

Legend on the screen: "Annunciation."
Music is heard as the light slowly comes on.
It is early dusk of a spring evening. Supper has just been finished in the Wingfield apartment. Amanda and Laura, in light-colored dresses, are removing dishes from the table in the dining room, which is shadowy, their movements formalized almost as a dance or ritual, their moving forms as pale and silent as moths. Tom, in white shirt and trousers, rises from the table and crosses toward the fire escape.

Amanda [*as he passes her*]. Son, will you do me a favor?

Tom. What?

Amanda. Comb your hair! You look so pretty when your hair is combed! [Tom *slouches on the sofa with the evening paper. Its enormous headline reads: "Franco*

Triumphs."[4]] There is only one respect in which I would like you to emulate your father.

TOM. What respect is that?

AMANDA. The care he always took of his appearance. He never allowed himself to look untidy. [*He throws down the paper and crosses to the fire escape.*] Where are you going?

TOM. I'm going out to smoke.

AMANDA. You smoke too much. A pack a day at fifteen cents a pack. How much would that amount to in a month? Thirty times fifteen is how much, Tom? Figure it out and you will be astounded at what you could save. Enough to give you a night-school course in accounting at Washington U.! Just think what a wonderful thing that would be for you, son! [TOM *is unmoved by the thought.*]

TOM. I'd rather smoke. [*He steps out on the landing, letting the screen door slam.*]

AMANDA [*sharply*]. I know! That's the tragedy of it...[*Alone, she turns to look at her husband's picture.*] [*Dance music: "The World Is Waiting for the Sunrise!"*]

TOM [*to the audience*]. Across the alley from us was the Paradise Dance Hall. On evenings in spring the windows and doors were open and the music came outdoors. Sometimes the lights were turned out except for a large glass sphere that hung from the ceiling. It would turn slowly about and filter the dusk with delicate rainbow colors. Then the orchestra played a waltz or a tango, something that had a slow and sensuous rhythm. Couples would come outside, to the relative privacy of the alley. You could see them kissing behind ash pits and telephone poles. This was the compensation for lives that passed like mine, without any change or adventure. Adventure and change were imminent in this year. They were waiting around the corner for all these kids. Suspended in the mist over Berchtesgaden, caught in the folds of Chamberlain's[5] umbrella. In Spain there was Guernica! But here there was only hot swing music and liquor, dance halls, bars, and movies, and sex that hung in the gloom like a chandelier and flooded the world with brief, deceptive rainbows....All the world was waiting for bombardments! [AMANDA *turns from the picture and comes outside.*]

AMANDA [*sighing*]. A fire escape landing's a poor excuse for a porch. [*She spreads a newspaper on a step and sits down, gracefully and demurely as if she were settling into a swing on a Mississippi veranda.*] What are you looking at?

TOM. The moon.

AMANDA. Is there a moon this evening?

TOM. It's rising over Garfinkel's Delicatessen.

AMANDA. So it is! A little silver slipper of a moon. Have you made a wish on it yet?

TOM. Um-hum.

AMANDA. What did you wish for?

TOM. That's a secret.

AMANDA. A secret, huh? Well, I won't tell mine either. I will be just as mysterious as you.

TOM. I bet I can guess what yours is.

AMANDA. Is my head so transparent?

TOM. You're not a sphinx.

---

[4]Franco headed the fascist forces in the Spanish Civil War.

[5]Chamberlain was the prime minister of Great Britain from 1937 to 1940. He met with Hitler at Berchtesgaden, Germany, trying to avoid World War II.

AMANDA. No, I don't have secrets. I'll tell you what I wished for on the moon. Success and happiness for my precious children! I wish for that whenever there's a moon, and when there isn't a moon, I wish for it, too.

TOM. I thought perhaps you wished for a gentleman caller.

AMANDA. Why do you say that?

TOM. Don't you remember asking me to fetch one?

AMANDA. I remember suggesting that it would be nice for your sister if you brought home some nice young man from the warehouse. I think that I've made that suggestion more than once.

TOM. Yes, you have made it repeatedly.

AMANDA. Well?

TOM. We are going to have one.

AMANDA. *What?*

TOM. A gentleman caller! [*The annunciation is celebrated with music.*] [AMANDA *rises.*] [*Image on screen: A caller with a bouquet.*]

AMANDA. You mean you have asked some nice young man to come over?

TOM. Yep. I've asked him to dinner.

AMANDA. You really did?

TOM. I did!

AMANDA. You did, and did he—*accept?*

TOM. He did!

AMANDA. Well, well—well, well! That's—lovely!

TOM. I thought that you would be pleased.

AMANDA. It's definite then?

TOM. Very definite.

AMANDA. Soon?

TOM. Very soon.

AMANDA. For heaven's sake, stop putting on and tell me some things, will you?

TOM. What things do you want me to tell you?

AMANDA. *Naturally* I would like to know when he's *coming!*

TOM. He's coming tomorrow.

AMANDA. *Tomorrow?*

TOM. Yep. Tomorrow.

AMANDA. But, Tom!

TOM. Yes, Mother?

AMANDA. Tomorrow gives me no time!

TOM. Time for what?

AMANDA. Preparations! Why didn't you phone me at once, as soon as you asked him, the minute that he accepted? Then, don't you see, I could have been getting ready!

TOM. You don't have to make a fuss.

AMANDA. Oh, Tom, Tom, Tom, of course I have to make a fuss! I want things nice, not sloppy! Not thrown together. I'll certainly have to do some fast thinking, won't I?

TOM. I don't see why you have to think at all.

AMANDA. You just don't know. We can't have a gentleman caller in a pigsty! All my wedding silver has to be polished, the monogrammed table linen ought to be laundered! The windows have to be washed and fresh curtains put up. And how about clothes? We have to *wear* something, don't we?

TOM. Mother, this boy is no one to make a fuss over!

AMANDA. Do you realize he's the first young man we've introduced to your sister? It's terrible, dreadful, disgraceful that poor little sister has never received a single gentleman caller! Tom, come inside! [*She opens the screen door.*]

TOM. What for?

AMANDA. I want to ask you some things.

TOM. If you're going to make such a fuss, I'll call it off, I'll tell him not to come!

AMANDA. You certainly won't do anything of the kind. Nothing offends people worse than broken engagements. It simply means I'll have to work like a Turk! We won't be brilliant, but we will pass inspection. Come on inside. [TOM *follows her inside, groaning.*] Sit down.

TOM. Any particular place you would like me to sit?

AMANDA. Thank heavens I've got that new sofa! I'm also making payments on a floor lamp I'll have sent out! And put the chintz covers on, they'll brighten things up! Of course I'd hoped to have these walls re-papered....What is the young man's name?

TOM. His name is O'Connor.

AMANDA. That, of course, means fish—tomorrow is Friday! I'll have that salmon loaf—with Durkee's dressing! What does he do? He works at the warehouse?

TOM. Of course! How else would I—

AMANDA. Tom, he—doesn't drink?

TOM. Why do you ask me that?

AMANDA. Your father *did!*

TOM. Don't get started on that!

AMANDA. He *does* drink, then?

TOM. Not that I know of!

AMANDA. Make sure, be certain! The last thing I want for my daughter's a boy who drinks!

TOM. Aren't you being a little bit premature? Mr. O'Connor has not yet appeared on the scene!

AMANDA. But will tomorrow. To meet your sister, and what do I know about his character? Nothing! Old maids are better off than wives of drunkards!

TOM. Oh, my God!

AMANDA. Be still!

TOM [*leaning forward to whisper*]. Lots of fellows meet girls whom they don't marry!

AMANDA. Oh, talk sensibly, Tom—and don't be sarcastic! [*She has gotten a hairbrush.*]

TOM. What are you doing?

AMANDA. I'm brushing that cowlick down! [*She attacks his hair with the brush.*] What is this young man's position at the warehouse?

TOM [*submitting grimly to the brush and the interrogation*]. This young man's position is that of a shipping clerk, Mother.

AMANDA. Sounds to me like a fairly responsible job, the sort of a job *you* would be in if you just had more *get-up*. What is his salary? Have you any idea?

TOM. I would judge it to be approximately eighty-five dollars a month.

AMANDA. Well—not princely, but—

TOM. Twenty more than I make.

AMANDA. Yes, how well I know! But for a family man, eighty-five dollars a month is not much more than you can just get by on....

TOM. Yes, but Mr. O'Connor is not a family man.

AMANDA. He might be, mightn't he? Some time in the future?

TOM. I see. Plans and provisions.

AMANDA. You are the only young man that I know of who ignores the fact that the future becomes the present, the present the past, and the past turns into everlasting regret if you don't plan for it!

TOM. I will think that over and see what I can make of it.

AMANDA. Don't be supercilious with your mother! Tell me some more about this—what do you call him?

TOM. James D. O'Connor. The D. is for Delaney.

AMANDA. Irish on *both* sides! *Gracious!* And doesn't drink?

TOM. Shall I call him up and ask him right this minute?

AMANDA. The only way to find out about those things is to make discreet inquiries at the proper moment. When I was a girl in Blue Mountain and it was suspected that a young man drank, the girl whose attentions he had been receiving, if any girl *was*, would sometimes speak to the minister of his church, or rather her father would if her father was living, and sort of feel him out on the young man's character. That is the way such things are discreetly handled to keep a young woman from making a tragic mistake!

TOM. Then how did you happen to make a tragic mistake?

AMANDA. That innocent look of your father's had everyone fooled! He *smiled*—the world was *enchanted!* No girl can do worse than put herself at the mercy of a handsome appearance! I hope Mr. O'Connor is not too good-looking.

TOM. No, he's not too good-looking. He's covered with freckles and hasn't too much of a nose.

AMANDA. He's not right-down homely, though?

TOM. Not right-down homely. Just medium homely, I'd say.

AMANDA. Character's what to look for in a man.

TOM. That's what I've always said, Mother.

AMANDA. You've never said anything of the kind and I suspect you would never give it a thought.

TOM. Don't be so suspicious of me.

AMANDA. At least I hope he's the type that's up and coming.

TOM. I think he really goes in for self-improvement.

AMANDA. What reason have you to think so?

TOM. He goes to night school.

AMANDA [*beaming*]. Splendid! What does he do, I mean study?

TOM. Radio engineering and public speaking!

AMANDA. Then he has visions of being advanced in the world! Any young man who studies public speaking is aiming to have an executive job some day! And radio engineering? A thing for the future! Both of these facts are very illuminating. Those are the sort of things that a mother should know concerning any young man who comes to call on her daughter. Seriously or—not.

TOM. One little warning. He doesn't know about Laura. I didn't let on that we had dark ulterior motives. I just said, why don't you come and have dinner with us? He said okay and that was the whole conversation.

AMANDA. I bet it was! You're eloquent as an oyster. However, he'll know about Laura when he gets here. When he sees how lovely and sweet and pretty she is, he'll thank his lucky stars he was asked to dinner.

TOM. Mother, you mustn't expect too much of Laura.

AMANDA. What do you mean?

TOM. Laura seems all those things to you and me because she's ours and we love her. We don't even notice she's crippled any more.

AMANDA. Don't say crippled! You know that I never allow that word to be used!

TOM. But face facts, Mother. She is and—that's not all—

AMANDA. What do you mean "not all"?

TOM. Laura is very different from other girls.

AMANDA. I think the difference is all to her advantage.

TOM. Not quite all—in the eyes of others—strangers—she's terribly shy and lives in a world of her own and those things make her seem a little peculiar to people outside the house.

AMANDA. Don't say peculiar.

TOM. Face the facts. She is. [*The dance hall music changes to a tango that has a minor and somewhat ominous tone.*]

AMANDA. In what way is she peculiar—may I ask?

TOM [*gently*]. She lives in a world of her own—a world of little glass ornaments, Mother....[*He gets up.* AMANDA *remains holding the brush, looking at him, troubled.*] She plays old phonograph records and—that's about all—[*He glances at himself in the mirror and crosses to the door.*]

AMANDA [*sharply*]. Where are you going?

TOM. I'm going to the movies. [*He goes out the screen door.*]

AMANDA. Not to the movies, every night to the movies! [*She follows quickly to the screen door.*] I don't believe you always go to the movies! [*He is gone.* AMANDA *looks worriedly after him for a moment. Then vitality and optimism return and she turns from the door, crossing to the portieres.*] Laura! Laura! [LAURA *answers from the kitchenette.*]

LAURA. Yes, Mother.

AMANDA. Let those dishes go and come in front! [LAURA *appears with a dish towel.* AMANDA *speaks to her gaily.*] Laura, come here and make a wish on the moon! [*Screen image:* The Moon.]

LAURA [*entering*]. Moon—moon?

AMANDA. A little silver slipper of a moon. Look over your left shoulder, Laura, and make a wish! [LAURA *looks faintly puzzled as if called out of sleep.* AMANDA *seizes her shoulders and turns her at an angle by the door.*] Now! Now, darling, wish!

LAURA. What shall I wish for, Mother?

AMANDA [*her voice trembling and her eyes suddenly filling with tears.*] Happiness! Good fortune! [*The sound of the violin rises and the stage dims out.*]

SCENE VI

The light comes up on the fire escape landing. TOM *is leaning against the grill, smoking.* [*Screen image: The high school hero.*]

TOM. And so the following evening I brought Jim home to dinner. I had known Jim slightly in high school. In high school Jim was a hero. He had tremendous Irish good nature and vitality with the scrubbed and polished look of white chinaware. He seemed to move in a continual spotlight. He was a star in basketball, captain of the debating club, president of the senior class and the glee club and he sang the male lead in the annual light operas. He was always running or bounding, never just walking. He seemed always at the point of defeating the law of gravity. He was shooting with such velocity through his adolescence that you would logically expect him to arrive at nothing short of the White House by the time he was thirty. But Jim apparently ran into more interference after his graduation from Soldan. His speed had definitely slowed. Six years after he left high school he was holding a job that wasn't much better than mine. [*Screen image:* The Clerk.] He was the only one at the warehouse with whom I was on friendly terms. I was valuable to him as someone who could remember his former glory, who had seen him win basketball games and the silver cup in debating. He knew of my secret practice of retiring to a cabinet of the washroom to work on poems when business was slack in the warehouse. He called me Shakespeare. And while the other boys in the warehouse regarded me with suspicious hostility, Jim took a humorous attitude toward me. Gradually his attitude affected the others, their hostility wore off and they also began to smile at me as people smile at an oddly fashioned dog who trots across their path at some distance. I knew that Jim and Laura had known each other at Soldan, and I had heard Laura speak admiringly of his voice. I didn't know if Jim remembered her or not. In high school Laura had been as unobtrusive as Jim had been astonishing. If he did remember Laura, it was not as my sister, for when I asked him to dinner, he grinned and said, "You know, Shakespeare, I never thought of you as having folks!" He was about to discover that I did.... [*Legend on screen* "The accent of a coming foot."] [*The light dims out on* TOM *and comes up in the Wingfield living room—a delicate lemony light. It is about five on a Friday evening of late spring which comes "scattering poems in the sky."*] [AMANDA *has worked like a Turk in preparation for the gentleman caller. The results are astonishing. The new floor lamp with its rose silk shade is in place, a colored paper lantern conceals the broken light fixture in the ceiling, new billowing white curtains are at the windows, chintz covers are on the chairs and sofa, a pair of new sofa pillows make their initial appearance. Open boxes and tissue paper are scattered on the floor.*] [LAURA *stands in the middle of the room with lifted arms while* AMANDA *crouches before her adjusting the hem of a new dress, devout and ritualistic. The dress is colored and designed by memory. The arrangement of* LAURA'S *hair is changed; it is softer and more becoming. A fragile, unearthly prettiness has come out in* LAURA; *she is like a piece of translucent glass touched by light, given a momentary radiance, not actual, not lasting.*]

AMANDA [*impatiently*]. Why are you trembling?

LAURA. Mother, you've made me so nervous!

AMANDA. How have I made you nervous?

LAURA. By all the fuss! You make it seem so important!

AMANDA. I don't understand you, Laura. You couldn't be satisfied with just sitting home, and yet whenever I try to arrange something for you, you seem to resist it. [*She gets up.*] Now take a look at yourself. No, wait! Wait just a moment—I have an idea!

LAURA. What is it now? [AMANDA *produces two powder puffs which she wraps in handkerchiefs and stuffs in* LAURA'S *bosom.*]

LAURA. Mother, what are you doing?

AMANDA. They call them "Gay Deceivers"!

LAURA. I won't wear them!

AMANDA. You will!

LAURA. Why should I?

AMANDA. Because, to be painfully honest, your chest is flat.

LAURA. You make it seem like we were setting a trap.

AMANDA. All pretty girls are a trap, a pretty trap, and men expect them to be. [*Legend on screen:* "A pretty trap."]Now look at yourself, young lady. This is the prettiest you will ever be! [*She stands back to admire* LAURA.] I've got to fix myself now! You're going to be surprised by your mother's appearance! [AMANDA *crosses through the portieres, humming gaily.* LAURA *moves slowly to the long mirror and stares solemnly at herself. A wind blows the white curtains inward in a slow, graceful motion and with a faint, sorrowful sighing.*]

AMANDA [*from somewhere behind the portieres*]. It isn't dark enough yet. [LAURA *turns slowly before the mirror with a troubled look.*] [*Legend on screen:* "This is my sister: Celebrate her with strings!" *Music plays.*]

AMANDA [*laughing, still not visible*]. I'm going to show you something. I'm going to make a spectacular appearance!

LAURA. What is it, Mother?

AMANDA. Possess your soul in patience—you will see! Something I've resurrected from that old trunk! Styles haven't changed so terribly much after all....[*She parts the portieres.*] Now just look at your mother! [*She wears a girlish frock of yellowed voile with a blue silk sash. She carries a bunch of jonquils—the legend of her youth is nearly revived. Now she speaks feverishly:*] This is the dress in which I led the cotillion. Won the cakewalk twice at Sunset Hill, wore one Spring to the Governor's Ball in Jackson! See how I sashayed around the ballroom, Laura? [*She raises her skirt and does a mincing step around the room.*] I wore it on Sundays for my gentlemen callers! I had it on the day I met your father....I had malaria fever all that Spring. The change of climate from East Tennessee to the Delta—weakened resistance. I had a little temperature all the time—not enough to be serious—just enough to make me restless and giddy! Invitations poured in—parties all over the Delta! "Stay in bed," said Mother, "you have a fever!"—but I just wouldn't. I took quinine but kept on going, going! Evenings, dances! Afternoons, long, long rides! Picnics—lovely! So lovely, that country in May—all lacy with dogwood, literally flooded with jonquils! That was the spring I had the craze for jonquils. Jonquils became an absolute obsession. Mother said, "Honey, there's no more room for jonquils." And still I kept on bringing in more jonquils. Whenever, wherever I saw them, I'd say, "Stop! Stop! I see jonquils!" I made the young men help me gather the jonquils! It was a joke, Amanda and her jonquils! Finally there were no more vases to hold them, every available space was filled with jonquils. No vases to hold them? All right, I'll hold them myself! And then I—[*She stops in front of the picture. Music plays.*] met your father! Malaria fever and jonquils and then— this—boy....[*She switches on the rose-colored lamp.*] I hope they get here before it starts to rain. [*She crosses the room and places the jonquils in a bowl on the table.*] I gave your brother a little extra change so he and Mr. O'Connor could take the service car home.

LAURA [*with an altered look*]. What did you say his name was?

AMANDA. O'Connor.

LAURA. What is his first name?

AMANDA. I don't remember. Oh, yes, I do. It was—Jim! [LAURA *sways slightly and catches hold of a chair.*] [*Legend on screen:* "Not Jim!"]

LAURA [*faintly*]. Not—Jim!

AMANDA. Yes, that was it, it was Jim! I've never known a Jim that wasn't nice! [*The music becomes ominous.*]

LAURA. Are you sure his name is Jim O'Connor?

AMANDA. Yes. Why?

LAURA. Is he the one that Tom used to know in high school?

AMANDA. He didn't say so. I think he just got to know him at the warehouse.

LAURA. There was a Jim O'Connor we both knew in high school—[*then, with effort*] If that is the one that Tom is bringing to dinner—you'll have to excuse me, I won't come to the table.

AMANDA. What sort of nonsense is this?

LAURA. You asked me once if I'd ever liked a boy. Don't you remember I showed you this boy's picture?

AMANDA. You mean the boy you showed me in the yearbook?

LAURA. Yes, that boy.

AMANDA. Laura, Laura, were you in love with that boy?

LAURA. I don't know, Mother. All I know is I couldn't sit at the table if it was him!

AMANDA. It won't be him! It isn't the least bit likely. But whether it is or not, you will come to the table. You will not be excused.

LAURA. I'll have to be, Mother.

AMANDA. I don't intend to humor your silliness, Laura. I've had too much from you and your brother, both! So just sit down and compose yourself till they come. Tom has forgotten his key so you'll have to let them in, when they arrive.

LAURA [*panicky*]. Oh, Mother—*you* answer the door!

AMANDA [*lightly*]. I'll be in the kitchen—busy!

LAURA. Oh, Mother, please answer the door, don't make me do it!

AMANDA [*crossing into the kitchenette*]. I've got to fix the dressing for the salmon. Fuss, fuss—silliness!—over a gentleman caller! [*The door swings shut. LAURA is left alone.*] [*Legend on screen: "Terror!"*] [*She utters a low moan and turns off the lamp—sits stiffly on the edge of the sofa, knotting her fingers together.*] [*Legend on screen: "The Opening of a Door!"*] [*TOM and JIM appear on the fire escape steps and climb to the landing. Hearing their approach, LAURA rises with a panicky gesture. She retreats to the portieres. The doorbell. LAURA catches her breath and touches her throat. Low drums sound.*]

AMANDA [*calling*]. Laura, sweetheart! The door! [*LAURA stares at it without moving.*]

JIM. I think we just beat the rain.

TOM. Uh-huh. [*He rings again, nervously. JIM whistles and fishes for a cigarette.*]

AMANDA [*very, very gaily*]. Laura, that is your brother and Mr. O'Connor! Will you let them in, darling? [*LAURA crosses toward the kitchenette door.*]

LAURA [*breathlessly*]. Mother—you go to the door! [*AMANDA steps out of the kitchenette and stares furiously at LAURA. She points imperiously at the door.*]

LAURA. Please, please!

AMANDA [*in a fierce whisper*]. What is the matter with you, you silly thing?

LAURA [*desperately*]. Please, you answer it, *please!*

AMANDA. I told you I wasn't going to humor you, Laura. Why have you chosen this moment to lose your mind?

LAURA. Please, please, you go!

AMANDA. You'll have to go to the door because I can't!

LAURA [*despairingly*]. I can't either!

AMANDA. *Why?*

LAURA. I'm *sick!*

AMANDA. I'm sick, too—of your nonsense! Why can't you and your brother be normal people? Fantastic whims and behavior! [TOM *gives a long ring.*] Preposterous goings on! Can you give me one reason—[*She calls out lyrically.*] *Coming! Just one second!*—why you should be afraid to open a door? Now you answer it, Laura!

LAURA. Oh, oh, oh.... [*She returns through the portieres, darts to the Victrola, winds it frantically and turns it on.*].

AMANDA. Laura Wingfield, you march right to that door!

LAURA. *Yes*—yes, Mother! [*A faraway, scratchy rendition of "Dardanella" softens the air and gives her strength to move through it. She slips to the door and draws it cautiously open.* TOM *enters with the caller,* JIM O'CONNOR.]

TOM. Laura, this is Jim. Jim, this is my sister, Laura.

JIM [*stepping inside*]. I didn't know that Shakespeare had a sister!

LAURA [*retreating, stiff and trembling, from the door*]. How—how do you do?

JIM [*heartily, extending his hand*]. Okay! [LAURA *touches it hesitantly with hers.*] Your hand's *cold*, Laura!

LAURA. Yes, well—I've been playing the Victrola....

JIM. Must have been playing classical music on it! You ought to play a little hot swing music to warm you up!

LAURA. Excuse me—I haven't finished playing the Victrola.... [*She turns awkwardly and hurries into the front room. She pauses a second by the Victrola. Then she catches her breath and darts through the portieres like a frightened deer.*]

JIM [*grinning*]. What was the matter?

TOM. Oh—with Laura? Laura is—terribly shy.

JIM. Shy, huh? It's unusual to meet a shy girl nowadays. I don't believe you ever mentioned you had a sister.

TOM. Well, now you know. I have one. Here is the *Post Dispatch*. You want a piece of it?

JIM. Uh-huh.

TOM. What piece? The comics?

JIM. Sports! [*He glances at it.*] Ole Dizzy Dean is on his bad behavior.

TOM [*uninterested*]. Yeah? [*He lights a cigarette and goes over to the fire-escape door.*]

JIM. Where are *you* going?

TOM. I'm going out on the terrace.

JIM [*going after him*]. You know, Shakespeare—I'm going to sell you a bill of goods!

TOM. What goods?

JIM. A course I'm taking.

TOM. Huh?

JIM. In public speaking! You and me, we're not the warehouse type.

TOM. Thanks—that's good news. But what has public speaking got to do with it?

JIM. It fits you for—executive positions!

TOM. Awww.

JIM. I tell you it's done a helluva lot for me. [*Image on screen:* Executive at his desk.]

TOM. In what respect?

JIM. In every! Ask yourself what is the difference between you an' me and men in the office down front? Brains?—No!—Ability?—No! Then what? Just one little thing—

TOM. What is that one little thing?

JIM. Primarily it amounts to—social poise! Being able to square up to people and hold your own on any social level!

AMANDA [*from the kitchenette*]. Tom?

TOM. Yes, Mother?

AMANDA. Is that you and Mr. O'Connor?

TOM. Yes, Mother.

AMANDA. Well, you just make yourselves comfortable in there.

TOM. Yes, Mother.

AMANDA. Ask Mr. O'Connor if he would like to wash his hands.

JIM. Aw, no—no—thank you—I took care of that at the warehouse. Tom—

TOM. Yes?

JIM. Mr. Mendoza was speaking to me about you.

TOM. Favorably?

JIM. What do you think?

TOM. Well—

JIM. You're going to be out of a job if you don't wake up.

TOM. I am waking up—

JIM. You show no signs.

TOM. The signs are interior. [*Image on screen:* The sailing vessel with the Jolly Roger again.]

TOM. I'm planning to change. [*He leans over the fire-escape rail, speaking with quiet exhilaration. The incandescent marquees and signs of the first-run movie houses light his face from across the alley. He looks like a voyager.*] I'm right at the point of committing myself to a future that doesn't include the warehouse and Mr. Mendoza or even a night-school course in public speaking.

JIM. What are you gassing about?

TOM. I'm tired of the movies.

JIM. Movies!

TOM. Yes, movies! Look at them—[*a wave toward the marvels of Grand Avenue*] All of those glamorous people—having adventures—hogging it all, gobbling the whole thing up! You know what happens? People go to the *movies* instead of *moving!* Hollywood characters are supposed to have all the adventures for everybody in America, while everybody in America sits in a dark room and watches them have them! Yes, until there's a war. That's when adventure becomes available to the masses! *Everyone's* dish, not only Gable's! Then the people in the dark room come out of the dark room to have some adventures themselves—goody, goody! It's our turn now, to go to the South Sea Island—to make a safari—to be exotic, far-off! But I'm not patient. I don't want to wait till then. I'm tired of the *movies* and I am *about* to move!

JIM [*incredulously*]. Move?

TOM. Yes.

JIM. When?

TOM. Soon!

JIM. Where? Where? [*The music seems to answer the question, while* TOM *thinks it over. He searches in his pockets.*]

TOM. I'm starting to boil inside. I know I seem dreamy, but inside—well, I'm boiling! Whenever I pick up a shoe, I shudder a little thinking how short life is and what I am doing! Whatever that means, I know it doesn't mean shoes—except as something to wear on a traveler's feet! [*He finds what he has been searching for in his pockets and holds out a paper to* Jim.] Look—

Jim. What?

Tom. I'm a member.

Jim [*reading*]. The Union of Merchant Seamen.

Tom. I paid my dues this month, instead of the light bill.

Jim. You will regret it when they turn the lights off.

Tom. I won't be here.

Jim. How about your mother?

Tom. I'm like my father. The bastard son of a bastard! Did you notice how he's grinning in his picture in there? And he's been absent going on sixteen years!

Jim. You're just talking, you drip. How does your mother feel about it?

Tom. Shhh! Here comes Mother! Mother is not acquainted with my plans!

Amanda [*coming through the portieres*]. Where are you all?

Tom. On the terrace, Mother. [*They start inside. She advances to them.* Tom *is visibly shocked at her appearance. Even* Jim *blinks a little. He is making his first contact with girlish Southern vivacity and in spite of the night-school course in public speaking is somewhat thrown off the beam by the unexpected outlay of social charm. Certain responses are attempted by* Jim *but are swept aside by* Amanda's *gay laughter and chatter.* Tom *is embarrassed but after the first shock* Jim *reacts very warmly. He grins and chuckles, is altogether won over.*] [*Image on screen:* Amanda *as a girl.*]

Amanda [*coyly smiling, shaking her girlish ringlets*]. Well, well, well, so this is Mr. O'Connor. Introductions entirely unnecessary. I've heard so much about you from my boy. I finally said to him, Tom—good gracious!—why don't you bring this paragon to supper? I'd like to meet this nice young man at the warehouse!—instead of just hearing him sing your praises so much! I don't know why my son is so stand-offish—that's not Southern behavior! Let's sit down and—I think we could stand a little more air in here! Tom, leave the door open. I felt a nice fresh breeze a moment ago. Where has it gone to? Mmm, so warm already! And not quite summer, even. We're going to burn up when summer really gets started. However, we're having—we're having a very light supper. I think light things are better fo' this time of year. The same as light clothes are. Light clothes an' light food are what warm weather calls fo'. You know our blood gets so thick during th' winter—it takes a while fo' us to adjust ou'selves—when the season changes.... It's come so quick this year. I wasn't prepared. All of a sudden—heavens! Already summer! I ran to the trunk an' pulled out this light dress—terribly old! Historical almost! But feels so good—so good an' co-ol, y' know....

Tom. Mother—

Amanda. Yes, honey?

Tom. How about—supper?

Amanda. Honey, you go ask Sister if supper is ready! You know that Sister is in full charge of supper! Tell her you hungry boys are waiting for it. [*to* Jim] Have you met Laura?

Jim. She—

Amanda. Let you in? Oh, good, you've met already! It's rare for a girl as sweet an' pretty as Laura to be domestic! But Laura is, thank heavens, not only pretty but also very domestic. I'm not at all, I never was a bit. I never could make a thing but angel-food cake. Well, in the South we had so many servants. Gone, gone, gone. All vestiges of gracious living! Gone completely! I wasn't prepared

for what the future brought me. All of my gentlemen callers were sons of planters and so of course I assumed that I would be married to one and raise my
family on a large piece of land with plenty of servants. But man proposes—and
woman accepts the proposal! To vary that old, old saying a little bit—I married
no planter! I married a man who worked for the telephone company! That gallantly smiling gentleman over there! [*She points to the picture.*] A telephone man
who—fell in love with long-distance! Now he travels and I don't even know
where! But what am I going on for about my—tribulations? Tell me yours—I
hope you don't have any! Tom?

TOM [*returning*]. Yes, Mother?

AMANDA. Is supper nearly ready?

TOM. It looks to me like supper is on the table.

AMANDA. Let me look—[*She rises prettily and looks through the portieres.*] Oh, lovely!
But where is Sister?

TOM. Laura is not feeling well and she says that she thinks she'd better not come
to the table.

AMANDA. What? Nonsense! Laura? Oh, Laura!

LAURA [*from the kitchenette, faintly*]. Yes, Mother.

AMANDA. You really must come to the table. We won't be seated until you come to
the table! Come in, Mr. O'Connor. You sit over there, and I'll . . . . Laura? Laura Wingfield! You're keeping us waiting, honey! We can't say grace until you
come to the table! [*The kitchenette door is pushed weakly open and* LAURA *comes in.
She is obviously quite faint, her lips trembling, her eyes wide and staring. She moves
unsteadily toward the table.*] [*Screen legend: "Terror!"*] [*Outside a summer storm is
coming on abruptly. The white curtains billow inward at the windows and there is a
sorrowful murmur from the deep blue dusk.*] [LAURA *suddenly stumbles; she catches
at a chair with a faint moan.*]

TOM. Laura!

AMANDA. Laura! [*There is a clap of thunder.*] [*Screen legend: "Ah!"*] [*despairingly*]
Why, Laura, you are ill, darling! Tom, help your sister into the living room,
dear! Sit in the living room, Laura—rest on the sofa. Well! [*to* JIM *as* TOM *helps
his sister to the sofa in the living room*] Standing over the hot stove made her ill!
I told her it was just too warm this evening, but—[TOM *comes back to the table.*]
Is Laura all right now?

TOM. Yes.

AMANDA. What is that? Rain? A cool rain has come up! [*She gives* JIM *a frightened
look.*] I think we may—have grace—now . . . [TOM *looks at her stupidly.*] Tom,
honey—you say grace!

TOM. Oh . . . "For these and all thy mercies—" [*They bow their heads,* AMANDA
stealing a nervous glance at JIM. *In the living room* LAURA, *stretched on the sofa,
clenches her hand to her lips, to hold back a shuddering sob.*] "God's Holy Name be
praised—" [*The scene dims out.*]

SCENE VII

It is half an hour later. Dinner is just being finished in the dining room, LAURA *is still
huddled upon the sofa, her feet drawn under her, her head resting on a pale blue pillow, her
eyes wide and mysteriously watchful. The new floor lamp with its shade of rose-colored silk
gives a soft, becoming light to her face, bringing out the fragile, unearthly prettiness which*

usually escapes attention. From outside there is a steady murmur of rain, but it is slacken-
ing and soon stops; the air outside becomes pale and luminous as the moon breaks through
the clouds. A moment after the curtain rises, the lights in both rooms flicker and go out.

JIM. Hey, there, Mr. Light Bulb! [AMANDA *laughs nervously.*] [*Legend on screen:* "Suspension of public service."]
AMANDA. Where was Moses when the lights went out? Ha-ha. Do you know the answer to that one, Mr. O'Connor?
JIM. No, Ma'am, what's the answer?
AMANDA. In the dark! [JIM *laughs appreciatively.*] Everybody sit still. I'll light the candles. Isn't it lucky we have them on the table? Where's a match? Which of you gentlemen can provide a match?
JIM. Here.
AMANDA. Thank you, Sir.
JIM. Not at all, Ma'am!
AMANDA [*as she lights the candles*]. I guess the fuse has burnt out. Mr. O'Connor, can you tell a burnt-out fuse? I know I can't and Tom is a total loss when it comes to mechanics. [*They rise from the table and go into the kitchenette, from where their voices are heard.*] Oh, be careful you don't bump into something. We don't want our gentleman caller to break his neck. Now wouldn't that be a fine howdy-do?
JIM. Ha-ha! Where is the fuse-box?
AMANDA. Right here next to the stove. Can you see anything?
JIM. Just a minute.
AMANDA. Isn't electricity a mysterious thing? Wasn't it Benjamin Franklin who tied a key to a kite? We live in such a mysterious universe, don't we? Some people say that science clears up all the mysteries for us. In my opinion it only creates more! Have you found it yet?
JIM. No, Ma'am. All these fuses look okay to me.
AMANDA. Tom!
TOM. Yes, Mother?
AMANDA. That light bill I gave you several days ago. The one I told you we got the notices about? [*Legend on screen:* "Ha!"]
TOM. Oh—yeah.
AMANDA. You didn't neglect to pay it by any chance?
TOM. Why I—
AMANDA. Didn't! I might have known it!
JIM. Shakespeare probably wrote a poem on that light bill, Mrs. Wingfield.
AMANDA. I might have known better than to trust him with it! There's such a high price for negligence in this world!
JIM. Maybe the poem will win a ten-dollar prize.
AMANDA. We'll just have to spend the remainder of the evening in the nineteenth century, before Mr. Edison made the Mazda lamp!
JIM. Candlelight is my favorite kind of light.
AMANDA. That shows you're romantic! But that's no excuse for Tom. Well, we got through dinner. Very considerate of them to let us get through dinner before they plunged us into everlasting darkness, wasn't it, Mr. O'Connor?
JIM. Ha-ha!
AMANDA. Tom, as a penalty for your carelessness you can help me with the dishes.
JIM. Let me give you a hand.

AMANDA. Indeed you will not!

JIM. I ought to be good for something.

AMANDA. Good for something? [*Her tone is rhapsodic.*] *You?* Why, Mr. O'Connor, nobody, *nobody's* given me this much entertainment in years—as you have!

JIM. Aw, now, Mrs. Wingfield!

AMANDA. I'm not exaggerating, not one bit! But Sister is all by her lonesome. You go keep her company in the parlor! I'll give you this lovely old candelabrum that used to be on the altar at the church of the Heavenly Rest. It was melted a little out of shape when the church burnt down. Lightning struck it one spring. Gypsy Jones was holding a revival at the time and he intimated that the church was destroyed because the Episcopalians gave card parties.

JIM. Ha-ha.

AMANDA. And how about you coaxing Sister to drink a little wine? I think it would be good for her! Can you carry both at once?

JIM. Sure. I'm Superman!

AMANDA. Now, Thomas, get into this apron! [JIM *comes into the dining room, carrying the candelabrum, its candles lighted, in one hand and a glass of wine in the other. The door of the kitchenette swings closed on* AMANDA's *gay laughter; the flickering light approaches the portieres.* LAURA *sits up nervously as* JIM *enters. She can hardly speak from the almost intolerable strain of being alone with a stranger.*] [*Screen legend: "I don't suppose you remember me at all!"*] [*At first, before* JIM's *warmth overcomes her paralyzing shyness,* LAURA's *voice is thin and breathless, as though she had just run up a steep flight of stairs.* JIM's *attitude is gently humorous. While the incident is apparently unimportant, it is to* LAURA *the climax of her secret life.*]

JIM. Hello there, Laura.

LAURA [*faintly*]. Hello. [*She clears her throat.*]

JIM. How are you feeling now? Better?

LAURA. Yes. Yes, thank you.

JIM. This is for you. A little dandelion wine. [*He extends the glass toward her with extravagant gallantry.*]

LAURA. Thank you.

JIM. Drink it—but don't get drunk! [*He laughs heartily.*] [LAURA *takes the glass uncertainly; she laughs shyly.*] Where shall I set the candles?

LAURA. Oh—oh, anywhere...

JIM. How about here on the floor? Any objections?

LAURA. No.

JIM. I'll spread a newspaper under to catch the drippings. I like to sit on the floor. Mind if I do?

LAURA. Oh, no.

JIM. Give me a pillow?

LAURA. What?

JIM. A pillow!

LAURA. Oh... [*She hands him one quickly.*]

JIM. How about you? Don't you like to sit on the floor?

LAURA. Oh—yes.

JIM. Why don't you, then?

LAURA. I—will.

JIM. Take a pillow! [LAURA *does. She sits on the floor on the other side of the candelabrum.* JIM *crosses his legs and smiles engagingly at her.*] I can't hardly see you sitting way over there.

LAURA. I can—see you.

JIM. I know, but that's not fair, I'm in the limelight. [LAURA *moves her pillow closer.*] Good! Now I can see you! Comfortable?

LAURA. Yes.

JIM. So am I. Comfortable as a cow! Will you have some gum?

LAURA. No, thank you.

JIM. I think that I will indulge, with your permission. [*He musingly unwraps a stick of gum and holds it up.*] Think of the fortune made by the guy that invented the first piece of chewing gum. Amazing, huh? The Wrigley Building is one of the sights of Chicago—I saw it when I went up to the Century of Progress. Did you take in the Century of Progress?

LAURA. No, I didn't.

JIM. Well, it was quite a wonderful exposition. What impressed me most was the Hall of Science. Gives you an idea of what the future will be in America, even more wonderful than the present time is! [*There is a pause.* JIM *smiles at her.*] Your brother tells me you're shy. Is that right, Laura?

LAURA. I—don't know.

JIM. I judge you to be an old-fashioned type of girl. Well, I think that's a pretty good type to be. Hope you don't think I'm being too personal—do you?

LAURA [*hastily, out of embarrassment*]. I believe I *will* take a piece of gum, if you— don't mind. [*clearing her throat*] Mr. O'Connor, have you—kept up with your singing?

JIM. Singing? —Me?

LAURA. Yes. I remember what a beautiful voice you had.

JIM. When did you hear me sing? [LAURA *does not answer, and in the long pause which follows a man's voice is heard singing offstage.*]

VOICE:
O blow, ye winds, heigh-ho,
A-roving I will go!
   I'm off to my love
    With a boxing glove—
Ten thousand miles away!

JIM. You say you've heard me sing?

LAURA. Oh, yes! Yes, very often...I—don't suppose—you remember me—at all?

JIM [*smiling doubtfully*]. You know I have an idea I've seen you before. I had that idea as soon as you opened the door. It seemed almost like I was about to re-member your name. But the name that I started to call you—wasn't a name! And so I stopped myself before I said it.

LAURA. Wasn't it—Blue Roses?

JIM [*springing up, grinning*]. Blue Roses! My gosh, yes—Blue Roses! That's what I had on my tongue when you opened the door. Isn't it funny what tricks your memory plays? I didn't connect you with high school somehow or other. But that's where it was; it was high school. I didn't even know you were Shake-speare's sister! Gosh, I'm sorry.

LAURA. I didn't expect you to. You—barely knew me!

JIM. But we did have a speaking acquaintance, huh?

LAURA. Yes, we—spoke to each other.

JIM. When did you recognize me?

LAURA. Oh, right away!

JIM. Soon as I came in the door?

LAURA. When I heard your name I thought it was probably you. I knew that Tom used to know you a little in high school. So when you came in the door—well, then I was—sure.

JIM. Why didn't you *say* something, then?

LAURA [*breathlessly*]. I didn't know what to say, I was—too surprised!

JIM. For goodness' sakes! You know, this sure is funny!

LAURA. Yes! Yes, isn't it though...

JIM. Didn't we have a class in something together?

LAURA. Yes, we did.

JIM. What class was that?

LAURA. It was—singing—chorus!

JIM. Aw!

LAURA. I sat across the aisle from you in the Aud.

JIM. Aw.

LAURA. Mondays, Wednesdays, and Fridays.

JIM. Now I remember—you always came in late.

LAURA. Yes, it was so hard for me, getting upstairs. I had that brace on my leg—it clumped so loud!

JIM. I never heard any clumping.

LAURA [*wincing at the recollection*]. To me it sounded like—thunder!

JIM. Well, well, well, I never even noticed.

LAURA. And everybody was seated before I came in. I had to walk in front of all those people. My seat was in the back row. I had to go clumping all the way up the aisle with everyone watching!

JIM. You shouldn't have been self-conscious.

LAURA. I know, but I was. It was always such a relief when the singing started.

JIM. Aw, yes, I've placed you now! I used to call you Blue Roses. How was it that I got started calling you that?

LAURA. I was out of school a little while with pleurosis. When I came back you asked me what was the matter. I said I had pleurosis—you thought I said *Blue Roses*. That's what you always called me after that.

JIM. I hope you didn't mind.

LAURA. Oh, no—I liked it. You see, I wasn't acquainted with many—people....

JIM. As I remember you sort of stuck by yourself.

LAURA. I—I—never have had much luck at—making friends.

JIM. I don't see why you wouldn't.

LAURA. Well, I—started out badly.

JIM. You mean being—

LAURA. Yes, it sort of—stood between me—

JIM. You shouldn't have let it!

LAURA. I know, but it did and—

JIM. You were shy with people!

LAURA. I tried not to be but never could—

JIM. Overcome it?

LAURA. No, I—I never could!

JIM. I guess being shy is something you have to work out of kind of gradually.

LAURA [*sorrowfully*]. Yes—I guess it—

JIM. Takes time!

Laura. Yes—

Jim. People are not so dreadful when you know them. That's what you have to remember! And everybody has problems, not just you, but practically everybody has got some problems. You think of yourself as having the only problems, as being the only one who is disappointed. But just look around you and you will see lots of people as disappointed as you are. For instance, I hoped when I was going to high school that I would be further along at this time, six years later, than I am now. You remember that wonderful write-up I had in *The Torch?*

Laura. Yes! [*She rises and crosses to the table.*]

Jim. It said I was bound to succeed in anything I went into! [Laura *returns with the high school yearbook.*] Holy Jeez, *The Torch!* [*He accepts it reverently. They smile across the book with mutual wonder.* Laura *crouches beside him and they begin to turn the pages.* Laura's *shyness is dissolving in his warmth.*]

Laura. Here you are in *The Pirates of Penzance!*

Jim [*wistfully*]. I sang the baritone lead in that operetta.

Laura [*raptly*]. So—*beautifully!*

Jim [*protesting*]. Aw—

Laura. Yes, yes—beautifully—beautifully!

Jim. You heard me?

Laura. All three times!

Jim. No!

Laura. Yes!

Jim. All three performances?

Laura [*looking down*]. Yes.

Jim. Why?

Laura. I—wanted to ask you to—autograph my program. [*She takes the program from the back of the yearbook and shows it to him.*]

Jim. Why didn't you ask me to?

Laura. You were always surrounded by your own friends so much that I never had a chance to.

Jim. You should have just—

Laura. Well, I—thought you might think I was—

Jim. Thought I might think you was—what?

Laura. Oh—

Jim [*with reflective relish*]. I was beleaguered by females in those days.

Laura. You were terribly popular!

Jim. Yeah—

Laura. You had such a friendly way—

Jim. I was spoiled in high school.

Laura. Everybody—liked you!

Jim. Including you?

Laura. I—yes, I—did, too—[*She gently closes the book in her lap.*]

Jim. Well, well, well! Give me that program, Laura. [*She hands it to him. He signs it with a flourish.*] There you are—better late than never!

Laura. Oh, I—what a—surprise!

Jim. My signature isn't worth very much right now. But some day—maybe—it will increase in value! Being disappointed is one thing and being discouraged is something else. I am disappointed but I am not discouraged. I'm twenty-three years old. How old are you?

LAURA. I'll be twenty-four in June.

JIM. That's not old age!

LAURA. No, but—

JIM. You finished high school?

LAURA [*with difficulty*]. I didn't go back.

JIM. You mean you dropped out?

LAURA. I made bad grades in my final examinations. [*She rises and replaces the book and the program on the table. Her voice is strained.*] How is—Emily Meisenbach getting along?

JIM. Oh, that kraut-head!

LAURA. Why do you call her that?

JIM. That's what she was.

LAURA. You're not still—going with her?

JIM. I never see her.

LAURA. It said in the "Personal" section that you were—engaged!

JIM. I know, but I wasn't impressed by that—propaganda!

LAURA. It wasn't—the truth?

JIM. Only in Emily's optimistic opinion!

LAURA. Oh—[*Legend:* "What have you done since high school?"] [JIM *lights a cigarette and leans indolently back on his elbows smiling at* LAURA *with a warmth and charm which lights her inwardly with altar candles. She remains by the table, picks up a piece from the glass menagerie collection, and turns it in her hand to cover her tumult.*]

JIM [*after several reflective puffs on his cigarette*]. What have you done since high school? [*She seems not to hear him.*] Huh? [LAURA *looks up.*] I said what have you done since high school, Laura?

LAURA. Nothing much.

JIM. You must have been doing something these six long years.

LAURA. Yes.

JIM. Well, then, such as what?

LAURA. I took a business course at business college—

JIM. How did that work out?

LAURA. Well, not very—well—I had to drop out, it gave me—indigestion—[JIM *laughs gently.*]

JIM. What are you doing now?

LAURA. I don't do anything—much. Oh, please don't think I sit around doing nothing! My glass collection takes up a good deal of time. Glass is something you have to take good care of.

JIM. What did you say—about glass?

LAURA. Collection I said—I have one—[*She clears her throat and turns away again, acutely shy.*]

JIM [*abruptly*]. You know what I judge to be the trouble with you? Inferiority complex! Know what that is? That's what they call it when someone low-rates himself! I understand it because I had it, too. Although my case was not so aggravated as yours seems to be. I had it until I took up public speaking, developed my voice, and learned that I had an aptitude for science. Before that time I never thought of myself as being outstanding in any way whatsoever! Now I've never made a regular study of it, but I have a friend who says I can analyze people better than doctors that make a profession of it. I don't claim that to be necessarily true, but I can sure guess a person's psychology, Laura! [*He takes out his gum.*] Excuse me, Laura. I always take it out when the flavor is gone. I'll use this scrap of paper to wrap it in. I know how it is to get it stuck on a shoe. [*He wraps the gum in paper and puts it in his pocket.*] Yep—that's what I judge to be your principal trouble. A lack of confidence in yourself as a person. You don't have the proper amount of faith in yourself. I'm basing that fact on a number of your remarks and also on certain observations I've made. For instance that clumping you thought was so awful in high school. You say that you even dreaded to walk into class. You see what you did? You dropped out of school, you gave up an education because of a clump, which as far as I know was practically nonexistent! A little physical defect is what you have. Hardly noticeable even! Magnified thousands of times by imagination! You know what my strong advice to you is? Think of yourself as *superior* in some way!

LAURA. In what way would I think?

JIM. Why, man alive, Laura! Just look about you a little. What do you see? A world full of common people! All of 'em born and all of 'em going to die! Which of them has one-tenth of your good points! Or mine! Or anyone else's, as far as that goes—gosh! Everybody excels in some one thing. Some in many! [*He unconsciously glances at himself in the mirror.*] All you've got to do is discover in *what!* Take me, for instance. [*He adjusts his tie at the mirror.*] I'm taking a course in radio engineering at night school, Laura, on top of a fairly responsible job at the warehouse. I'm taking that course and studying public speaking.

LAURA. Ohhhh.

JIM. Because I believe in the future of television! [*turning his back to her*] I wish to be ready to go up right along with it. Therefore I'm planning to get in on the ground floor. In fact I've already made the right connections and all that remains is for the industry itself to get under way! Full steam—[*His eyes are starry.*] *Knowledge*—Zzzzzp! *Money*—Zzzzzp!—*Power!* That's the cycle democracy is built on! [*His attitude is convincingly dynamic.* LAURA *stares at him, even her shyness eclipsed in her absolute wonder. He suddenly grins.*] I guess you think I think a lot of myself!

LAURA. No—o-o-o, I—

JIM. Now how about you? Isn't there something you take more interest in than anything else?

LAURA. Well, I do—as I said—have my—glass collection—[*A peal of girlish laughter rings from the kitchenette.*]

JIM. I'm not right sure I know what you're talking about. What kind of glass is it?

LAURA. Little articles of it, they're ornaments mostly! Most of them are little animals made out of glass, the tiniest little animals in the world. Mother calls them a glass menagerie! Here's an example of one, if you'd like to see it! This one is one of the oldest. It's nearly thirteen. [*Music: "The Glass Menagerie."*] [*He stretches out his hand.*] Oh, be careful—if you breathe, it breaks!

JIM. I'd better not take it. I'm pretty clumsy with things.

LAURA. Go on, I trust you with him! [*She places the piece in his palm.*] There now—you're holding him gently! Hold him over the light, he loves the light! You see how the light shines through him!

JIM. It sure does shine!

LAURA. I shouldn't be partial, but he is my favorite one.

JIM. What kind of a thing is this one supposed to be?

LAURA. Haven't you noticed the single horn on his forehead?

JIM. A unicorn, huh?

LAURA. Mmmm-hmmm!

JIM. Unicorns—aren't they extinct in the modern world?

LAURA. I know!

JIM. Poor little fellow, he must feel sort of lonesome.

LAURA [*smiling*]. Well, if he does, he doesn't complain about it. He stays on a shelf with some horses that don't have horns and all of them seem to get along nicely together.

JIM. How do you know?

LAURA [*lightly*]. I haven't heard any arguments among them!

JIM [*grinning*]. No arguments, huh? Well, that's a pretty good sign! Where shall I set him?

LAURA. Put him on the table. They all like a change of scenery once in a while!

JIM. Well, well, well—[*He places the glass piece on the table, then raises his arms and stretches.*] Look how big my shadow is when I stretch!

LAURA. Oh, oh, yes—it stretches across the ceiling!

JIM [*crossing to the door*]. I think it's stopped raining. [*He opens the fire-escape door and the background music changes to a dance tune.*] Where does the music come from?

LAURA. From the Paradise Dance Hall across the alley.

JIM. How about cutting the rug a little, Miss Wingfield?

LAURA. Oh, I—

JIM. Or is your program filled up? Let me have a look at it. [*He grasps an imaginary card.*] Why, every dance is taken! I'll just have to scratch some out. [*Waltz music: "La Golondrina."*] Ahhh, a waltz! [*He executes some sweeping turns by himself, then holds his arms toward* LAURA.]

LAURA [*breathlessly*]. I—can't dance!

JIM. There you go, that inferiority stuff!

LAURA. I've never danced in my life!

JIM. Come on, try!

LAURA. Oh, but I'd step on you!

JIM. I'm not made out of glass.

LAURA. How—how—how do we start?

JIM. Just leave it to me. You hold your arms out a little.

LAURA. Like this?

JIM [*taking her in his arms*]. A little bit higher. Right. Now don't tighten up, that's the main thing about it—relax.

LAURA [*laughing breathlessly*]. It's hard not to.

JIM. Okay.

LAURA. I'm afraid you can't budge me.

JIM. What do you bet I can't? [*He swings her into motion.*]

LAURA. Goodness, yes, you can!

JIM. Let yourself go, now, Laura, just let yourself go.

LAURA. I'm—

JIM. Come on!

LAURA. —trying!

JIM. Not so stiff—easy does it!

LAURA. I know but I'm—

JIM. Loosen th' backbone! There now, that's a lot better.

LAURA. Am I?

JIM. Lots, lots better! [*He moves her about the room in a clumsy waltz.*]

LAURA. Oh, my!

JIM. Ha-ha!

LAURA. Oh, my goodness!

JIM. Ha-ha-ha! [*They suddenly bump into the table, and the glass piece on it falls to the floor. JIM stops the dance.*] What did we hit on?

LAURA. Table.

JIM. Did something fall off it? I think—

LAURA. Yes.

JIM. I hope that it wasn't the little glass horse with the horn!

LAURA. Yes. [*She stoops to pick it up.*]

JIM. Aw, aw, aw. Is it broken?

LAURA. Now it is just like all the other horses.

JIM. It's lost its—

LAURA. Horn! It doesn't matter. Maybe it's a blessing in disguise.

JIM. You'll never forgive me. I bet that was your favorite piece of glass.

LAURA. I don't have favorites much. It's no tragedy, Freckles. Glass breaks so easily. No matter how careful you are. The traffic jars the shelves and things fall off them.

JIM. Still I'm awfully sorry that I was the cause.

LAURA [*smiling*]. I'll just imagine he had an operation. The horn was removed to make him feel less—freakish! [*They both laugh.*] Now he will feel more at home with the other horses, the ones that don't have horns....

JIM. Ha-ha, that's very funny! [*Suddenly he is serious.*] I'm glad to see that you have a sense of humor. You know—you're—well—very different! Surprisingly different from anyone else I know! [*His voice becomes soft and hesitant with a genuine feeling.*] Do you mind me telling you that? [LAURA *is abashed beyond speech.*] I mean it in a nice way— [LAURA *nods shyly, looking away.*] You make me feel sort of—I don't know how to put it! I'm usually pretty good at expressing things, but—this is something that I don't know how to say! [LAURA *touches her throat and clears it—turns the broken unicorn in her hands. His voice becomes softer.*] Has anyone ever told you that you were pretty? [*There is a pause and the music rises slightly.* LAURA *looks up slowly, with wonder, and shakes her head.*] Well, you are! In a very different way from anyone else. And all the nicer because of the difference, too. [*His voice becomes low and husky.* LAURA *turns away, nearly faint with the novelty of her emotions.*] I wish that you were my sister. I'd teach you to have some confidence in yourself. The different people are not like other people, but being different is nothing to be ashamed of. Because other people are not such wonderful people. They're one hundred times one thousand. You're one times one! They walk all over the earth. You just stay here. They're common as—weeds, but—you—well, you're—*Blue Roses!* [*Image on screen:* Blue Roses.] [*The music changes.*]

LAURA. But blue is wrong for—roses....

JIM. It's right for you! You're—pretty!

LAURA. In what respect am I pretty?

JIM. In all respects—believe me! Your eyes—your hair—are pretty! Your hands are pretty! [*He catches hold of her hand.*] You think I'm making this up because I'm invited to dinner and have to be nice. Oh, I could do that! I could put on an act for you, Laura, and say lots of things without being very sincere. But this time I am. I'm talking to you sincerely. I happened to notice you had this inferiority complex that keeps you from feeling comfortable with people. Somebody needs to build your confidence up and make you proud instead of shy and turning away and—blushing. Somebody—ought to—*kiss* you, Laura! [*His hand slips slowly up her arm to her shoulder as the music swells tumultuously. He suddenly turns her about and kisses her on the lips. When he releases her,* LAURA *sinks on the sofa with a bright, dazed look.* JIM *backs away and fishes in his pocket for a cigarette.*] [*Legend on screen:* "Souvenir."] Stumblejohn! [*He lights the cigarette, avoiding her look. There is a peal of girlish laughter from* AMANDA *in the kitchenette.* LAURA *slowly raises and opens her hand. It still contains the little broken glass animal. She looks at it with a tender, bewildered expression.*] Stumblejohn! I shouldn't have done that—that was way off the beam. You don't smoke, do you? [*She looks up, smiling, not hearing the question. He sits beside her rather gingerly. She looks at him speechlessly—waiting. He coughs decorously and moves a little farther aside as he considers the situation and senses her feelings, dimly, with perturbation. He speaks gently.*] Would you—care for a—mint? [*She doesn't seem to hear him but her look grows brighter even.*] Peppermint? Life Saver? My pocket's a regular drugstore—wherever I go.... [*He pops a mint in his mouth. Then he gulps and decides to make a clean breast of it. He speaks slowly and gingerly.*] Laura, you know, if I had a sister like you, I'd do the same thing as Tom. I'd bring out fellows and—introduce her to them. The right type of boys—of a type to—appreciate her. Only—well—he made a mistake about me. Maybe I've got no call to be saying this. That may not have been the idea in having me over. But what if it was? There's nothing wrong about that. The only trouble is that in my case—I'm not in a situation to—do the right thing. I can't take down your number and say I'll phone. I can't call up next week and—ask for a date. I thought I had better explain the situation in case you—misunderstood it and—I hurt your feelings.... [*There is a pause. Slowly, very slowly,* LAURA'S *look changes, her eyes returning slowly from his to the glass figure in her palm.* AMANDA *utters another gay laugh in the kitchenette.*]

LAURA [*faintly*]. You—won't—call again?

JIM. No, Laura, I can't. [*He rises from the sofa.*] As I was just explaining, I've—got strings on me. Laura, I've—been going steady! I go out all the time with a girl named Betty. She's a home-girl like you, and Catholic, and Irish, and in a great many ways we—get along fine. I met her last summer on a moonlight boat trip up the river to Alton, on the *Majestic*. Well—right away from the start it was—love! [*Legend: Love!*] [LAURA *sways slightly forward and grips the arm of the sofa. He fails to notice, now enrapt in his own comfortable being.*] Being in love has made a new man of me! [*Leaning stiffly forward, clutching the arm of the sofa,* LAURA *struggles visibly with her storm. But* JIM *is oblivious; she is a long way off.*] The power of love is really pretty tremendous! Love is something that—changes the whole world, Laura! [*The storm abates a little and* LAURA *leans back. He notices her again.*] It happened that Betty's aunt took sick, she got a wire and had to go to Centralia. So Tom—when he asked me to dinner—I naturally just accepted the invitation, not knowing that you—that he—that I—[*He stops awkwardly.*] Huh—I'm a stumblejohn! [*He flops back on the sofa. The holy candles on the altar of* LAURA'S *face have been snuffed out. There is a look of almost infinite desolation.* JIM *glances at her uneasily.*] I wish that you would—say something. [*She bites her lip which was trembling and then bravely smiles. She opens her hand again on the broken glass figure. Then she gently takes his hand and raises it level with her own. She carefully places the unicorn in the palm of his hand, then pushes his fingers closed upon it.*] What are you—doing that for? You want me to have him? Laura? [*She nods.*]

LAURA. A—souvenir.... [*She rises unsteadily and crouches beside the Victrola to wind it up.*] [*Legend on screen: "Things have a way of turning out so badly!" Or image: "Gentleman caller waving goodbye—gaily."*] [*At this moment* AMANDA *rushes brightly back into the living room. She bears a pitcher of fruit punch in an old-fashioned cut-glass pitcher, and a plate of macaroons. The plate has a gold border and poppies painted on it.*]

AMANDA. Well, well, well! Isn't the air delightful after the shower? I've made you children a little liquid refreshment. [*She turns gaily to* JIM.] Jim, do you know that song about lemonade?

"Lemonade, lemonade
Made in the shade and stirred with a spade—
Good enough for any old maid!"

JIM [*uneasily*]. Ha-ha! No—I never heard it.

AMANDA. Why, Laura! You look so serious!

JIM. We were having a serious conversation.

AMANDA. Good! Now you're better acquainted!

JIM [*uncertainly*]. Ha-ha! Yes.

AMANDA. You modern young people are much more serious-minded than my generation. I was so gay as a girl!

JIM. You haven't changed, Mrs. Wingfield.

AMANDA. Tonight I'm rejuvenated! The gaiety of the occasion, Mr. O'Connor! [*She tosses her head with a peal of laughter, spilling some lemonade.*] Oooo! I'm baptizing myself!

JIM. Here—let me—

AMANDA [*setting the pitcher down*]. There now. I discovered we had some maraschino cherries. I dumped them in, juice and all!

JIM. You shouldn't have gone to that trouble, Mrs. Wingfield.

AMANDA. Trouble, trouble? Why, it was loads of fun! Didn't you hear me cutting up in the kitchen? I bet your ears were burning! I told Tom how outdone with him I was for keeping you to himself so long a time! He should have brought you over much, much sooner! Well, now that you've found your way, I want you to be a very frequent caller! Not just occasional but all the time. Oh, we're going to have a lot of gay times together! I see them coming! Mmm, just breathe that air! So fresh, and the moon's so pretty! I'll skip back out—I know where my place is when young folks are having a—serious conversation!

JIM. Oh, don't go out, Mrs. Wingfield. The fact of the matter is I've got to be going.

AMANDA. Going, now? You're joking! Why, it's only the shank of the evening, Mr. O'Connor!

JIM. Well, you know how it is.

AMANDA. You mean you're a young workingman and have to keep workingmen's hours. We'll let you off early tonight. But only on the condition that next time you stay later. What's the best night for you? Isn't Saturday night the best night for you workingmen?

JIM. I have a couple of time-clocks to punch, Mrs. Wingfield. One at morning, another one at night!

AMANDA. My, but you *are* ambitious! You work at night, too?

JIM. No, Ma'am, not work but—Betty! [*He crosses deliberately to pick up his hat. The band at the Paradise Dance Hall goes into a tender waltz.*]

AMANDA. Betty? Betty? Who's—Betty! [*There is an ominous cracking sound in the sky.*]

JIM. Oh, just a girl. The girl I go steady with! [*He smiles charmingly. The sky falls.*] [*Legend: "The Sky Falls."*]

AMANDA [*a long-drawn exhalation*]. Ohhhh ... Is it a serious romance, Mr. O'Connor?

JIM. We're going to be married the second Sunday in June.

AMANDA. Ohhhh—how nice! Tom didn't mention that you were engaged to be married.

JIM. The cat is not out of the bag at the warehouse yet. You know how they are. They call you Romeo and stuff like that. [*He stops at the oval mirror to put on his hat. He carefully shapes the brim and the crown to give a discreetly dashing effect.*] It's been a wonderful evening, Mrs. Wingfield. I guess this is what they mean by Southern hospitality.

AMANDA. It wasn't really anything at all.

JIM. I hope it don't seem like I'm rushing off. But I promised Betty I'd pick her up at the Wabash depot, an' by the time I get my jalopy down there her train'll be in. Some women are pretty upset if you keep 'em waiting.

AMANDA. Yes, I know—the tyranny of women! [*She extends her hand.*] Good-bye, Mr. O'Connor. I wish you luck—and happiness—and success! All three of them, and so does Laura! Don't you, Laura?

LAURA. Yes.

JIM [*taking* LAURA's *hand*]. Goodbye, Laura. I'm certainly going to treasure that souvenir. And don't forget the good advice I gave you. [*He raises his voice to a cheery shout.*] So long, Shakespeare! Thanks again, ladies. Good night! [*He grins and ducks jauntily out. Still bravely grimacing,* AMANDA *closes the door on the gentleman caller. Then she turns back to the room with a puzzled expression. She and* LAURA *don't dare face each other.* LAURA *crouches beside the Victrola to wind it.*]

AMANDA [*faintly*]. Things have a way of turning out so badly. I don't believe that I would play the Victrola. Well, well—well! Our gentleman caller was engaged to be married! [*She raises her voice.*] Tom!

TOM [*from the kitchenette*]. Yes, Mother?

AMANDA. Come in here a minute. I want to tell you something awfully funny.

TOM [*entering with a macaroon and a glass of the lemonade*]. Has the gentleman caller gotten away already?

AMANDA. The gentleman caller has made an early departure. What a wonderful joke you played on us!

TOM. How do you mean?

AMANDA. You didn't mention that he was engaged to be married.

TOM. Jim? Engaged?

AMANDA. That's what he just informed us.

TOM. I'll be jiggered! I didn't know about that.

AMANDA. That seems very peculiar.

TOM. What's peculiar about it?

AMANDA. Didn't you call him your best friend down at the warehouse?

TOM. He is, but how did I know?

AMANDA. It seems extremely peculiar that you wouldn't know your best friend was going to be married!

TOM. The warehouse is where I work, not where I know things about people.

AMANDA. You don't know things anywhere! You live in a dream; you manufacture illusions! [*He crosses to the door.*] Where are you going?

TOM. I'm going to the movies.

AMANDA. That's right, now that you've had us make such fools of ourselves. The effort, the preparations, all the expense! The new floor lamp, the rug, the clothes for Laura! All for what? To entertain some other girl's fiancé! Go to the movies, go! Don't think about us, a mother deserted, an unmarried sister who's crippled and has no job! Don't let anything interfere with your selfish pleasure! Just go, go, go—to the movies!

TOM. All right, I will! The more you shout about my selfishness to me the quicker I'll go, and I won't go to the movies!

AMANDA. Go, then! Go to the moon—you selfish dreamer! [TOM *smashes his glass on the floor. He plunges out on the fire escape, slamming the door. LAURA screams in fright. The dance-hall music becomes louder. TOM stands on the fire escape, gripping the rail. The moon breaks through the storm clouds, illuminating his face.*] [*Legend on screen:* "And so goodbye . . ."] [TOM'*s closing speech is timed with what is happening inside the house. We see, as though through soundproof glass, that AMANDA appears to be making a comforting speech to LAURA who is huddled upon the sofa. Now that we cannot hear the mother's speech, her silliness is gone and she has dignity and tragic beauty. LAURA's hair hides her face until, at the end of the speech, she lifts her head to smile at her mother. AMANDA's gestures are slow and graceful, almost dancelike, as she comforts her daughter. At the end of her speech she glances a moment at the father's picture—then withdraws through the portieres. At the close of TOM's speech, LAURA blows out the candles, ending the play.*]

TOM. I didn't go to the moon. I went much further—for time is the longest distance between two places. Not long after that I was fired for writing a poem on the lid of a shoe-box. I left Saint Louis. I descended the steps of this fire escape for a last time and followed, from then on, in my father's footsteps, attempting to find in motion what was lost in space. I traveled around a great deal. The cities swept about me like dead leaves, leaves that were brightly colored but torn away from the branches. I would have stopped, but I was pursued by something. It always came upon me unawares, taking me altogether by surprise. Perhaps it was a familiar bit of music. Perhaps it was only a piece of transparent glass. Perhaps I am walking along a street at night, in some strange city, before I have found companions. I pass the lighted window of a shop where perfume is sold. The window is filled with pieces of colored glass, tiny transparent bottles in delicate colors, like bits of a shattered rainbow. Then all at once my sister touches my shoulder. I turn around and look into her eyes. Oh, Laura, Laura, I tried to leave you behind me, but I am more faithful than I intended to be! I reach for a cigarette, I cross the street, I run into the movies or a bar, I buy a drink, I speak to the nearest stranger—anything that can blow your candles out! [LAURA *bends over the candles.*] For nowadays the world is lit by lightning! Blow out your candles, Laura—and so goodbye. . . . [*She blows the candles out.*]

(1944)

The Writing Process

Prewriting

Begin your study of *The Glass Menagerie* by writing about and discussing the ideas explored in the following exercise.

Exercise: Analyzing the Characters

1. One way to look at this play is as a tangle of deceptions. List five deceptions that occur in the play. Compare your list with those of others in your class. Discuss how you would rank the seriousness or harmlessness of the deceptions you have identified. Be sure to consider possible self-deceptions for each character.
2. In Scene IV, Tom says, "Man is by instinct a lover, a hunter, a fighter, and none of those instincts are given much play at the warehouse!" How does this statement fit in with Miller's concept of tragic heroism? Find statements by each of the characters that imply displacement or indignity. How is the heroism of Antigone different?
3. How is tradition important to the characters in both *Antigone* and *The Glass Menagerie*?
4. Reread Tom's closing speech. Why is he unable to leave Laura behind him?
5. Choose a character from *The Glass Menagerie* and argue that he or she is the hero. Can you argue for more than one character as a hero?

Writing

In your prewriting, you gathered a list of deceptions that you found in *The Glass Menagerie*. Looking at that list, you may come up with a thesis for an essay on the play. "Deception is an important element in *The Glass Menagerie*" is not enough even though that may be your first reaction to such a long list. You must say why deception is important. Here are some possible thesis ideas:

Though Amanda's deceptions and self-deceptions are the most obvious, every character in the play practices deception. This tempers our attitude toward her.

One of the moral questions addressed in *The Glass Menagerie* is this: Which is more damaging to the spirit, deception of others or self-deception?

In *The Glass Menagerie*, Williams presents deception on all levels of seriousness, seeming to encourage a view of humanity as suffused with lies and illusions.

Choosing a Structure

Your choice of thesis should determine how you organize your raw material—in this case, your list of examples from the prewriting activity. Perhaps your list looks something like this.

Deception

—Rubicam's Business College—Laura.
—Amanda—that Laura isn't crippled or "peculiar," that she is able to have gentleman callers, that her "unusual" children make her proud and

happy, that the Gentleman Caller will surely fall in love with Laura, that Tom has constantly praised Jim at home.

—Tom's secret plans to join the Merchant Marines.

—Whatever he does if he doesn't go to the movies.

—Pays union dues instead of light bill.

—The father was deceptively charming.

—Powder puffs (gay deceivers).

—Emily tells yearbook that she and Jim are engaged.

—Jim—will a night school course really do all he believes it will? Does he believe it? His stubborn cheerfulness and optimism. Disappointment that he hasn't gone further often concealed.

—Amanda—that Laura isn't "satisfied with just sitting home." White lie to Jim, "You know Sister is in full charge of supper!"

This unorganized jumble can be structured in several ways. For the first thesis we mentioned, you would probably sort the deceptions character by character, perhaps presenting Amanda's first and then those of the others. For the second thesis, you would separate deceptions of others from self-deceptions and devote a section of your essay to each type, closing with an evaluation of the spiritual damage done by each. For the last thesis, you would have the challenging work of arranging the list from the most trivial to the most serious so that your readers appreciate the full spectrum.

Ideas for Writing

Ideas for Reflective Writing

1. Devise a scale for ranking your responses to the four characters: Amanda, Tom, Laura, and Jim. It could be something like "least likable to most likable," "most realistic to least realistic," "most neurotic to well-adjusted," or "most passive to most active." Write a brief paragraph to explain your placement of each character on your scale.

2. Amanda's memories of her youth are strong and positive. What will Laura's memories be like? Write a first-person narrative in which an older Laura looks back at her life. How does she remember her family and the time the gentleman caller visited?

Ideas for Critical Writing

1. Expand the comparison made by Williams in the "Characters" section: Laura "is like a piece of her own glass collection, too exquisitely fragile to move from the shelf."

2. CRITICAL APPROACHES: Review the discussion of mythological and archetypal approaches to interpreting literature (pages 897–98). Then analyze the character of the gentleman caller as a mythic or archetypal figure. Is he, as Tom says, "an emissary from the world of reality…the long-delayed but always expected something that we live for"?

3. Support or refute this major claim: The father is the most important character in the play even though he never appears in person.

4. Character development and change are key elements in drama and fiction. Does Jim's visit change Laura? Devise a thesis that explains why or why not.

5. What does this play say about oddness and normality? Develop an interpretation that answers this question.

Ideas for Researched Writing

1. Tennessee Williams wrote several versions of this play before putting it in its final form. It began as a short story, "Portrait of a Girl in Glass," which was reworked into a one-act play, "If You Breathe, It Breaks! Or Portrait of a Girl in Glass." It was subsequently modified into a screenplay called *The Gentleman Caller* and then into another version of a stage play, which Williams revised extensively. He also wrote another story based on the same characters and themes as *The Glass Menagerie*: "The Resemblance between a Violin Case and a Coffin." Research the development of *The Glass Menagerie* from story to drama. How does the character of Laura change from the author's original depiction of her? Write an essay in which you describe the changes and explain their significance.

2. CRITICAL APPROACHES: Review the description of cultural criticism on page 896 as well as the issues discussed in "Exploring Cultural Themes" in Chapter 35, Critical Casebook: Writing About Culture and Identity (page 967). Write an essay in which you explain how the family dynamics in this play are understandable in terms of its time (1944). Go to the library and peruse popular magazines from this era to develop your material.

3. In real life, Williams's sister (Rose) was institutionalized for schizophrenia and underwent a lobotomy. After some exploratory research on this disease and the procedure, argue how this experience might have affected the playwright and influenced his development of Laura's character.

MultiModal Project

Using a template from an online site, create a brief storyboard of an important scene in *The Glass Menagerie*, one that captures what you think is a key theme or an essential point about a character. Include visuals and a narrative. One idea would be to use Google images to locate photos from different productions of the play. Guides to storyboarding can be found at http://multimedia.journalism.berkeley.edu/tutorials/starttofinish/storyboarding and http://digitalstorytelling.coe.uh.edu/page.cfm?id=23&cid=23&sublinkid=97.

Rewriting

The more specifically you support your statements about the work, the more credible you will be to your readers. Another crucial advantage of forcing yourself to be specific is that you will prevent yourself from straying from the printed page into the fields of your own mind, which may be rich and green but not relevant.

Developing Paragraphs Specifically

The following paragraph makes several good observations but lacks specifics:

> In many ways, Tom fulfills Arthur Miller's characterization of the modern tragic hero. His ideal image of himself is constantly frustrated both at home and at work. He feels misunderstood, a victim of indignity. He is clearly at odds with his environment.

Although these statements are true, the writer has given the reader no particular cause to believe them. The paragraph should have additional details from the play. Compare the following:

> In many ways, Tom fulfills Arthur Miller's characterization of the modern tragic hero. In the list of characters, Williams describes him as "a poet with a job in a warehouse" (677). His ideal image of himself is constantly frustrated both at home and at work. He complains, "Man is by instinct a lover, a hunter, a fighter, and none of those instincts are given much play at the warehouse!" (691). Tom feels misunderstood, a victim of indignity. He accuses Amanda, "It seems unimportant to you, what I'm *doing*—what I *want* to do—having a little *difference* between them!" (686). This is clearly a man at odds with his environment.

The references to the text of the play specifically support the writer's contentions. The exercise that follows will give you practice in finding such support.

Exercise: Providing Quotations

For each general statement, provide appropriate quotations from the play. Some of these generalizations may give you further ideas for papers.

1. Amanda is not deeply and completely self-deceived.
2. Human sexuality disturbs Amanda.
3. Characters in the play take both realistic and unrealistic action toward their goals.
4. Both times glass is broken in the play, the forces of masculinity and sexuality are involved.
5. Tom Wingfield may live as much in his imagination as Amanda and Laura do in theirs.

31 Critical Casebook: *The Glass Menagerie:* Interpreting Amanda

Chapter Preview

- Compare a range of reviewers' and critics' views about a controversial character.
- Evaluate the interpretations made by critics.
- Synthesize other critics' analyses with your own interpretation.
- Write about a play—specifically, a character—in a critical context.

Amanda Wingfield is Tennessee Williams's first great female character, and audiences and readers respond to her in very different ways. Is she, as one critic says, "the terrible old woman at the center of the play"? Or is she, as another claims, "one of the playwright's most vivid Southern belles"? Is Amanda tragic or comic? a devoted mother or a domineering matriarch? a victim or a victimizer? This brief casebook presents excerpts from published reviews and critical essays that argue for different interpretations of Amanda's character. They should help you to enjoy and understand the play more fully by providing insights, raising questions, and challenging your own responses.

Eight Critical Interpretations

Burton Rasco, Review of The Glass Menagerie

In describing the first New York production of the play, with actress Laurette Taylor as Amanda, Rasco gives a harsh reading of Amanda's character.

> She was...a simple, sanely insane, horrible Mother, pathetic and terribly human and terribly real. She succeeded in destroying every vestige of hope and beauty and joy in the lives of the two people who loved her—her son and daughter.

> She had no love for anyone except herself. She was married once to a handsome young Irishman, who was charming and beguiling—but he

722

Laurette Taylor as the original Amanda; she appeared in both the Chicago and New York productions of 1945. (Museum of the City of New York, The Burns Mantle Collection. 48.210.2075)

drank. She didn't drink. Therefore she had one up on him. Apparently she told him so many times that he was a drunkard that he drank himself to death just to get shut of her telling him that....But she kept a smiling picture of him in the death-house she created for her son and daughter; and she kept tucked away a faded tulle evening gown in which she had once danced with him. She liked to remind her miserable son and her even more miserable daughter that she had once been a pretty, gay-hearted bride of a gay blade of a drinking Irishman.

New York World Telegram, 2 April 1945, p. 8.

Durant Da Ponte, "Tennessee Williams' Gallery of Feminine Characters"

Professor Da Ponte sympathizes with Amanda, seeing her caught between the gentility of her past and the harshness of her present circumstances.

Many of the personages [Williams] has created would seem to be projections of his own disoriented personality, frightened, timid, groping, highly sensitive, somewhat neurotic dreamers who, like their creator, are unable to adjust to the harsh realities of a world of crass materialism and brute strength. Or, if they have been forced to make an adjustment, this adjustment usually hardens and distorts them, as in the case of Amanda in *The Glass Menagerie*. For certainly in many ways Amanda *has* come to terms with the real world (although in many other ways she has not). The tenement apartment overlooking the slum alley in St. Louis where she lives is very real indeed, as is the moon that comes up over Garfinkel's Delicatessen. Against this grim world with its struggle for existence (Laura's futile attempts to learn typing, Tom's $65-a-month job in a shoe company, Amanda's magazine subscriptions) is juxtaposed a remembered world of romance—Blue Mountain, where as a girl Amanda received seventeen gentleman callers on one memorable Sunday afternoon and where conversation dwelt on things of importance—"Never anything coarse or common or vulgar."

If we did not laugh at Amanda, I suspect we should cry, for there is a certain pathetic heroism in her efforts to provide for her children—her daughter, especially. A measure of her refusal to face actuality appears in her attitude toward Laura—the cotton wads she makes her stuff into her blouse ("gay deceivers" she calls them), her shrill denial that Laura is crippled.... Amanda is a curious combination of exaggerated gentility on the one hand and exasperating practicality on the other.... At times cranky and cantankerous, at times wistful and tender, at times gallant and heroic—Amanda is one of Tennessee Williams' most impressive creations.

Tennessee Studies in Literature, vol. 10, 1965, pp. 12–13.

Joseph K. Davis, "Landscapes of the Dislocated Mind"

Davis calls Amanda the "pivotal figure" in the play and holds her responsible for her children's desperate situation:

She has consistently indulged in illusions and failed completely to meet life directly; and her bitter disappointments have left her impotent, as both adult and mother. Amanda's response to life generates devastating consequences for her children, crippling them psychologically and seriously inhibiting their own quests for maturity and self-realization....

Amanda Wingfield's past not only animates but also sustains her in the present.... She is simply unable to break out of the framework of her dreamy recollections and to achieve any degree of perspective on them as real or imagined elements. She makes invidious comparisons between her former life and her current situation, and she emphatically rejects the present in favor of the past.

Tennessee Williams: A Tribute, 1977, pp. 198–99.

Marc Robinson, *"Amanda"*

Robinson says that "Amanda is a mess of contradictions," that she is "too boisterous for any easy interpretation." He argues that the "suffocating nature of her love" rises, in part, from her constant fear of being abandoned.

While Amanda says she wants to secure marriage for her daughter, she really loathes the thought of seeing Laura happier than she is; further, she wouldn't be able to stand the loneliness if Laura left home. In all situations, Amanda is practical at the same time that she is helplessly romantic. The two contrary forces vie with each other most strongly when it comes to envisioning the future. Laura may not be particularly glamorous company for Amanda, but at least she's someone who won't go unless pushed. So, for all her cajoling, Amanda never really forces change on Laura. In fact, Amanda makes a point of comforting Laura at the end of *The Glass Menagerie*, setting things aright again after Jim has revealed his engagement. It's the one place where Amanda drops her many roles and allows herself a moment of true feeling. After she wipes away Laura's tears, she glances briefly at the portrait of her absent husband. Tom, too, has now left. We can almost hear Amanda's sigh of thankfulness that her last possible companion won't be leaving just yet.

The Other American Drama, 1994, p. 37.

Karen Allen as Laura and Joanne Woodward as Amanda in the 1987 film version of *The Glass Menagerie*, directed by Paul Newman.

C. W. E. Bigsby, "Entering
The Glass Menagerie"

Bigsby uses a theatrical metaphor to explain the many sides of Amanda's character.

Early in the play Amanda is presented as an actress, self-dramatizing, self-conscious. Her first part is that of martyred mother. When she removes her hat and gloves, she does so with a theatrical gesture ("a bit of acting"). She dabs at her lips and nostrils to indicate her distress before melodramatically tearing the diagram of a typewriter keyboard to pieces. When the gentleman caller arrives for her daughter, she changes roles, dressing herself in the clothes of a young woman and becoming a Southern belle, rendered grotesque by the distance between performer and role. But at the end of the play all such pretences are abandoned. As we see but do not hear her words of comfort to her daughter, so her various roles— shrewish mother, coquettish belle, ingratiating saleswoman—are set aside. The tableau which we see as Tom delivers his final speech is one in which mother and daughter are reunited in their abandonment. "Her silliness is gone," Williams tells us. Amanda "withdraws through the portieres," retreating from the stage which Tom has summoned into being but also from the arena in which she has chosen to play out her own drama.

The Cambridge Companion to Tennessee Williams, 1997, pp. 29–30.

Chris Jones, "A Domestic Drama
of Dashed Dreams"

In his review of the 1998 production of *The Glass Menagerie* at the Steppenwolf Theater in Chicago, Jones describes a gritty, unconventional interpretation of Amanda:

Molly Regan is an unusual choice for Amanda. With an intense Irish energy and a working-class physicality, Regan downplays this character's typical obsession with gentility. Regan's nakedly open Amanda is no ersatz Blanche, weeping for finer days. She comes across rather as a selfish and rough-hewn social climber worried more about money than her daughter's happiness. Even as it challenges the play's typical romantic elements, this choice diminishes what little sympathy we might usually have for Amanda.

Variety, 11 January 1999.

Charles Isherwood, "Gritty Polish
for a Tennessee Williams Jewel"

In reviewing the 2010 New York production of *The Glass Menagerie,* critic Charles Isherwood credits Judith Ivey's natural interpretation of Amanda for drawing out "all the humor in Williams's depiction of this smothering woman without surrendering her complexity or humanity":

> Ivey excels at conveying the fear that claws insistently at Amanda's heart, the anxiety behind her admonitory lectures. The trembling rage with which she berates a cowering Laura for abandoning her typing classes is fueled by the knowledge that the $50 fee represented a sizable investment for the family, but, more important, by the collapse of her hope that the inhibited Laura will be able to fend for herself.
>
> For all her harshness, however, Ms. Ivey's Amanda is also a loving mother with a caressing hand who invests every ounce of her energy, every thought in her scheming mind, in her hopes for her children. The moments of tender truce between mother and son are all the sweeter for the real violence of the storms that have come before.

The New York Times, 25 March 2010.

Ben Brantley, "The Shape of Memory, Both Fragile and Fierce"

Calling Cherry Jones "perhaps the greatest stage actress of her generation," the critic for *The New York Times* says her interpretation is both tough and touching:

> [Ms. Jones] delivers a magnificently human performance, anchoring Amanda without the customary grotesque eccentricities. For all her florid talk of a glorious, genteel Southern youth, this Amanda is rooted in the shabby, debt-plagued present and determined to take command of it, even though the tools she uses are woefully anachronistic. Ms. Jones makes Amanda's garrulousness her survival strategy, as if talking might keep the wolf from the door—and keep her from seeing the darkness that waits to devour her family. She knows it's there; you hear that knowledge when Ms. Jones's voice sinks into cryptlike chest tones. As for that fabled scene where Amanda dons a frilly frock from her girlhood to greet Laura's gentleman caller, Ms. Jones presents it without camp or pathos. When Amanda, in that frock, describes one spinning, malaria-touched summer of her gilded youth, Ms. Jones miraculously becomes the beautiful girl who first wore that dress.

The New York Times, 14 February 2013

Responding to the Critics

1. What do you think of Amanda? Which of the critics' views do you most agree with? Which do you disagree with? Write your own analysis of Amanda's character. You might begin by reacting to one or more of the critical viewpoints you just read. You can use them as points of departure or as support for your own interpretation.

Keira Keeley as Laura and Judith Ivey as Amanda in the 2010 New York production of *The Glass Menagerie.* (Joan Marcus)

2. Enter the search term "Amanda Glass Menagerie" on YouTube or other streaming video site, and watch a number of filmed scenes. Several productions of the play are also available on DVD, perhaps at your library. (Note: Some libraries may house copies of productions that can be viewed only on their premises.) What do you think of the various interpretations of Amanda's character? Which do you prefer? How do they stack up against the performances and interpretations described in this casebook? Discuss what you watched with your classmates or write up a report.

Ideas for Researched Writing

1. Actress Laurette Taylor's interpretation of Amanda in the 1943 Chicago and New York productions of *The Glass Menagerie* is often cited as one of the chief reasons for the play's initial success. Find out as much as you can about Taylor's performance. What was so extraordinary about it? How did she interpret the role? Write a paper in which you describe Taylor's performance and explain why it contributed so much to the play's positive reception.

2. Investigate the symbolism behind the various props and costumes that are associated with Amanda: the jonquils, the moon, her husband's picture, the telephone, the "girlish frock of yellowed voile," the "fulldress outfit" that she wears to the D.A.R., and so forth. How do these items help to establish and emphasize Amanda's character?

MultiModal Project

To explore the differing interpretations of Amanda, divide into groups that will each act out or present an oral reading of the play's first scene involving Amanda, Tom, and Laura (pp. 679–81). Each group should seek to interpret Amanda in a specific, assigned way—for example, loving and gentle, overbearing and selfish, strong but caring, demanding but sensible, and so forth. Perform your readings, and then discuss them. Determine or debate which interpretation seems most valid, and why.

32 Anthology of Drama

Chapter Preview

This chapter includes three additional plays, some or all of which your instructor may assign. By exploring them, you will gain further practice as you:

- Analyze and discuss three classic plays.
- Compare different playwrights' approaches to this genre.
- Interpret, evaluate, and develop arguments about drama through writing assignments.
- Use research to write about dramatic works.

William Shakespeare   1564–1616

William Shakespeare is the most widely known author in all English literature. He was born in Stratford-on-Avon, probably attended grammar school there, and at eighteen married Anne Hathaway, who bore him three children. In 1585 or shortly thereafter, he went to London and began his apprenticeship as an actor. By 1594 he had won recognition as a poet, but it was in the theater that he made his strongest reputation. Shakespeare produced perhaps thirty-five plays in twenty-five years, including historical dramas, comedies, romances, and the great tragedies: *Hamlet* (1602), *Othello* (1604), *King Lear* (1605), and *Macbeth* (1606). His 154 sonnets are supreme examples of the form.

Othello, the Moor of Venice

THE NAMES OF THE ACTORS

OTHELLO, *the Moor.*
BRABANTIO, *a senator; father to Desdemona.*
CASSIO, *an honourable lieutenant to Othello.*
IAGO, *Othello's ancient, a villain.*
RODERIGO, *a gulled gentleman.*
DUKE OF VENICE.
SENATORS *of Venice.*
MONTANO, *governor of Cyprus.*
LODOVICO *and* GRATIANO,

kinsmen to Brabantio, two noble Venetians.
SAILORS.
CLOWN.
DESDEMONA, *daughter to Brabantio and wife to Othello.*
EMILIA, *wife to Iago*
BIANCA, *a courtezan and mistress to Cassio.*
MESSENGER, HERALD, OFFICERS, GENTLEMEN, MUSICIANS, *and* ATTENDANTS.

[SCENE: VENICE; A SEA-PORT IN CYPRUS]

ACT I

SCENE I

Venice. A street.

[*Enter* RODERIGO *and* IAGO.]

RODERIGO. Tush! never tell me; I take it much unkindly
    That thou, Iago, who hast had my purse
    As if the strings were thine, shouldst know of this.
IAGO. 'Sblood,[1] but you'll not hear me:
    If ever I did dream of such a matter,
    Abhor me.
RODERIGO. Thou told'st me thou didst hold him in thy hate.
IAGO. Despise me, if I do not. Three great ones of the city,[2]
    In personal suit to make me his lieutenant,
    Off-capp'd to him:[3] and, by the faith of man,   10
    I know my price, I am worth no worse a place:
    But he, as loving his own pride and purposes,
    Evades them, with a bombast circumstance
    Horribly stuff'd with epithets of war;
    And, in conclusion,
    Nonsuits[4] my mediators; for, "Certes," says he,
    "I have already chose my officer."
    And what was he?
    Forsooth, a great arithmetician,[5]
    One Michael Cassio, a Florentine,   20
    A fellow almost damn'd in a fair wife;[6]
    That never set a squadron in the field,
    Nor the division[7] of a battle knows
    More than a spinster; unless the bookish theoric,[8]
    Wherein the toged[9] consuls can propose[10]
    As masterly as he: mere prattle, without practice,
    Is all his soldiership. But he, sir, had th' election:
    And I, of whom his eyes had seen the proof

---

1 **'Sblood** an oath, "by God's blood."
2 **great ones of the city** Iago means to indicate his importance in the community; this is suggested also by his use of the word *worth* in line 11.
3 **him** Othello.
4 **Nonsuits** rejects.
5 **arithmetician** a man whose military knowledge was merely theoretical, based on books of tactics.
6 **A . . . wife** Cassio does not seem to be married, but his counterpart in Shakespeare's source did have a wife.
7 **division** disposition of a battle line.
8 **theoric** theory.
9 **toged** wearing the toga.
10 **propose** discuss.

James Earl Jones as Othello and Dianne Wiest as Desdemona in the 1982 Broadway production of *Othello*.

    At Rhodes, at Cyprus[11] and on other grounds
    Christian and heathen, must be be-lee'd and calm'd   30
    By debitor and creditor: this counter-caster,[12]
    He, in good time,[13] must his lieutenant be,
    And I—God bless the mark![14] —Moorship's ancient.[15]
RODERIGO. By heaven, I rather would have been his hangman.
IAGO. Why, there's no remedy; 'tis the curse of service,
    Preferment goes by letter and affection,
    And not by old gradation,[16] where each second
    Stood heir to th' first. Now, sir, be judge yourself,
    Whether I in any just term am affin'd[17]
    To love the Moor.   40
RODERIGO.   I would not follow then.
IAGO. O, sir, content you;
    I follow him to serve my turn upon him:
    We cannot all be masters, nor all masters
    Cannot be truly follow'd. You shall mark

---

    11 **Rhodes, Cyprus** islands in the Mediterranean south of Asia Minor, long subject to contention between the Venetians and the Turks.
    12 **counter-caster** a sort of bookkeeper; contemptuous term.
    13 **in good time** opportunely.
    14 **God bless the mark** anciently, a pious interjection to avert evil omens.
    15 **ancient** standardbearer, ensign.
    16 **old gradation** seniority; Iago here expresses a characteristic prejudice of professional soldiers.
    17 **affin'd** bound.

Many a duteous and knee-crooking knave,
That, doting on his own obsequious bondage,
Wears out his time, much like his master's ass,
For nought but provender, and when he's old, cashier'd:
Whip me such honest knaves. Others there are 50
Who, trimm'd in forms and visages of duty,
Keep yet their hearts attending on themselves,
And, throwing but shows of service on their lords,
Do well thrive by them and when they have lin'd their coats
Do themselves homage: these fellows have some soul;
And such a one do I profess myself. For, sir,
It is as sure as you are Roderigo,
Were I the Moor, I would not be Iago:[18]
In following him, I follow but myself;
Heaven is my judge, not I for love and duty, 60
But seeming so, for my peculiar end:
For when my outward action doth demonstrate
The native act and figure of my heart
In compliment extern,[19] 'tis not long after
But I will wear my heart upon my sleeve
For daws to peck at: I am not what I am.

RODERIGO. What a full fortune does the thick-lips[20] owe,
If he can carry 't thus!

IAGO.   Call up her father,
Rouse him: make after him, poison his delight, 70
Proclaim him in the streets, incense her kinsmen,
And, though he in a fertile climate dwell,
Plague him with flies: though that his joy be joy,
Yet throw such changes of vexation on 't,
As it may lose some colour.

RODERIGO. Here is her father's house; I'll call aloud.

IAGO. Do, with like timorous[21] accent and dire yell
As when, by night and negligence, the fire
Is spied in populous cities.

RODERIGO. What, ho, Brabantio! Signior Brabantio, ho! 80

IAGO. Awake! what, ho, Brabantio! thieves! thieves! thieves!
Look to your house, your daughter and your bags!
Thieves! thieves!

[BRABANTIO *appears above at a window.*]

BRABANTIO. What is the reason of this terrible summons?
What is the matter there?

RODERIGO. Signior, is all your family within?

IAGO. Are your doors lock'd?

BRABANTIO.   Why, wherefore ask you this?

---

18 **Were . . . Iago** Were I in the position of the Moor, I should not feel as Iago feels.
19 **compliment extern** outward civility.
20 **thick-lips** Elizabethans often applied the term Moor to Negroes.
21 **timorous** frightening.

IAGO. 'Zounds, sir, y' are robb'd; for shame, put on your gown;
    Your heart is burst, you have lost half your soul;   90
    Even now, now, very now, an old black ram
    Is tupping your white ewe. Arise, arise:
    Awake the snorting[22] citizens with the bell,
    Or else the devil will make a grandsire of you:
    Arise, I say.
BRABANTIO.   What, have you lost your wits?
RODERIGO. Most reverend signior, do you know my voice?
BRABANTIO. Not I: what are you?
RODERIGO. My name is Roderigo.
BRABANTIO.   The worser welcome: 100
    I have charg'd thee not to haunt about my doors:
    In honest plainness thou has heard me say
    My daughter is not for thee; and now, in madness,
    Being full of supper and distemp'ring draughts,
    Upon malicious bravery,[23] doest thou come
    To start[24] my quiet.
RODERIGO. Sir, sir, sir,—
BRABANTIO.   But thou must needs be sure
    My spirit and my place have in them power
    To make this bitter to thee.   110
RODERIGO.   Patience, good sir.
BRABANTIO. What tell'st thou me of robbing? this is Venice;
    My house is not a grange.[25]
RODERIGO.   Most grave Brabantio,
    In simple and pure soul I come to you.
IAGO. 'Zounds, sir, you are one of those that will not serve God, if the devil
    bid you. Because we come to do you service and you think we are ruffians,
    you'll have your daughter covered with a Barbary horse; you'll have your
    nephews[26] neigh to you; you'll have coursers for cousins and gennets[27] for
    germans.[28]   120
BRABANTIO. What profane wretch are thou?
IAGO. I am one, sir, that comes to tell you your daughter and the
    Moor are now making the beast with two backs.
BRABANTIO. Thou art a villain.
IAGO.   You are—a senator.
BRABANTIO. This thou shalt answer; I know thee, Roderigo.
RODERIGO. Sir, I will answer any thing. But, I beseech you,
    If 't be your pleasure and most wise consent,
    As partly I find it is, that your fair daughter,
    At this odd-even[29] and dull watch o' th' night,   130

---

22 **snorting** snoring.
23 **bravery** defiance, bravado.
24 **start** disrupt.
25 **grange** isolated farmhouse.
26 **nephews** grandsons.
27 **gennets** small Spanish horses.
28 **germans** near relatives.
29 **odd-even** between night and morning.

Transported, with no worse nor better guard
But with a knave of common hire, a gondolier,
To the gross clasps of a lascivious Moor,—
If this be known to you and your allowance,[30]
We then have done you bold and saucy wrongs;
But if you know not this, my manners tell me
We have your wrong rebuke. Do not believe
That, from[31] the sense of all civility,
I thus would play and trifle with your reverence:
Your daughter, if you have not given her leave,   140
I say again, hath made a gross revolt;
Tying her duty, beauty, wit and fortunes
In an extravagant[32] and wheeling[33] stranger
Of here and every where. Straight satisfy yourself:
If she be in her chamber or your house,
Let loose on me the justice of the state
For thus deluding you.
BRABANTIO.   Strike on the tinder,[34] ho!
Give me a taper! call up all my people!
This accident[35] is not unlike my dream: 150
Belief of it oppresses me already.
Light, I say! light!

                                        [*Exit above.*]

IAGO.   Farewell; for I must leave you:
It seems not meet, nor wholesome to my place,
To be produc'd—as, if I stay, I shall—
Against the Moor: for, I do know, the state,
However this may gall him with some check,[36]
Cannot with safety cast[37] him, for he's embark'd
With such loud reason to the Cyprus wars,
Which even now stand in act,[38] that, for their souls,   160
Another of his fathom[39] they have none,
To lead their business: in which regard,
Though I do hate him as I do hell-pains,
Yet, for necessity of present life,
I must show out a flag and sign of love,
Which is indeed but sign. That you shall surely find him,
Lead to the Sagittary[40] the raised search:
And there will I be with him. So, farewell.

                                        [*Exit.*]

---

30 **allowance** permission.
31 **from** contrary to.
32 **extravagant** wandering.
33 **wheeling** vagabond.
34 **tinder** charred linen kept in a metal box, and ignited by a spark from flint and steel.
35 **accident** occurrence, event.
36 **check** rebuke.
37 **cast** dismiss.
38 **stand in act** are going on.
39 **fathom** ability.
40 **Sagitarry** probably an inn.

[*Enter below* BRABANTIO, *with* SERVANTS *and torches.*]

BRABANTIO. It is too true an evil: gone she is;
    And what's to come of my despised time   170
    Is nought but bitterness. Now, Roderigo,
    Where didst thou see her? O unhappy girl!
    With the Moor, say'st thou? Who would be a father!
    How didst thou know 'twas she? O, she deceives me
    Past thought! What said she to you? Get moe[41] tapers:
    Raise all my kindred. Are they married, think you?
RODERIGO. Truly, I think they are.
BRABANTIO. O heaven! How got she out? O treason of the blood!
    Fathers, from hence trust not your daughters' minds
    By what you see them act. Is[42] there not charms   180
    By which the property[43] of youth and maidhood
    May be abus'd? Have you not read, Roderigo,
    Of some such thing?
RODERIGO.   Yes, sir, I have indeed.
BRABANTIO. Call up my brother. O, would you[44] had had her!
    Some one way, some another. Do you know
    Where we may apprehend her and the Moor?
RODERIGO. I think I can discover him, if you please
    To get good guard and go along with me.
BRABANTIO. Pray you, lead on. At every house I'll call;   190
    I may command at most. Get weapons, ho!
    And raise some special officers of night.[45]
    On, good Roderigo: I will deserve your pains.

                                      [*Exeunt.*]

SCENE II

Another street.

[*Enter* OTHELLO, IAGO, ATTENDANTS *with torches.*]

IAGO. Though in the trade of war I have slain men,
    Yet do I hold it very stuff o' th' conscience
    To do no contriv'd murder: I lack iniquity
    Sometime to do me service: nine or ten times
    I had thought t' have yerk'd[46] him here under the ribs.
OTHELLO. 'Tis better as it is.
IAGO.   Nay, but he prated,
    And spoke such scurvy and provoking terms
    Against your honour

---

41 **moe** more.
42 **Is** are.
43 **property** special quality.
44 **you** Roderigo.
45 **officers of night** police.
46 **yerk'd** stabbed.

That, with the little godliness I have,   10
I did full hard forbear him. But, I pray you, sir,
Are you fast married? Be assur'd of this,
That the magnifico[47] is much belov'd,
And hath in his effect[48] a voice potential[49]
As double[50] as the duke's: he will divorce you;
Or put upon you what restraint and grievance
The law, with all his might to enforce it on,
Will give him cable.

OTHELLO.   Let him do his spite;
My services, which I have done the signiory[51]   20
Shall out-tongue his complaints. 'Tis yet to know—
Which, when I know that boasting is an honour,
I shall promulgate—I fetch my life and being
From men of royal siege,[52] and my demerits[53]
May speak unbonneted[54] to as proud a fortune
As this that I have reach'd: for know, Iago,
But that I love the gentle Desdemona,
I would not my unhoused free condition
Put into circumscription and confine
For the sea's worth. But, look! what lights come yond?   30

IAGO. Those are the raised father and his friends:
You were best go in.

OTHELLO.   Not I; I must be found:
My parts, my title and my perfect soul[55]
Shall manifest me rightly. Is it they?

IAGO. By Janus, I think no.

[*Enter* CASSIO *and certain* OFFICERS *with torches.*]

OTHELLO. The servants of the duke, and my lieutenant.
The goodness of the night upon you, friends!
What is the news?

CASSIO.   The duke does greet you, general,   40
And he requires your haste-post-haste appearance,
Even on the instant.

OTHELLO.   What is the matter, think you?

CASSIO. Something from Cyprus, as I may divine:
It is a business of some heat: the galleys
Have sent a dozen sequent[56] messengers
This very night at one another's heels,

---

47 **magnifico** Venetian grandee (i.e., Brabantio).
48 **effect** influence.
49 **potential** powerful.
50 **double** twice as influential as most men's.
51 **signiory** Venetian government.
52 **siege** rank.
53 **demerits** deserts.
54 **unbonneted** on equal terms.
55 **perfect soul** unflawed conscience.
56 **sequent** successive.

And many of the consuls,[57] rais'd and met,
Are at the duke's already: you have been hotly call'd for;
When, being not at your lodging to be found,   50
The senate hath sent about three several[58] quests
To search you out.

OTHELLO.   'Tis well I am found by you.
I will but spend a word here in the house,
And go with you.

[*Exit.*]

CASSIO.   Ancient, what makes he here?
IAGO. 'Faith, he to-night hath boarded a land carack:[59]
If it prove lawful prize, he's made for ever.
CASSIO. I do not understand.
IAGO.   He's married.   60
CASSIO.   To who?

[*Enter* OTHELLO.]

IAGO. Marry, to—Come, captain will you?
OTHELLO.   Have with you.
CASSIO. Here comes another troop to seek for you.

[*Enter* BRABANTIO, RODERIGO, *with* OFFICERS *and torches.*]

IAGO. It is Brabantio. General, be advis'd;
He comes to bad intent.
OTHELLO.   Holla! stand there!
RODERIGO. Signoir, it is the Moor.
BRABANTIO.   Down with him, thief!   70

[*They draw on both sides.*]

IAGO. You, Roderigo! come, sir, I am for you.
OTHELLO. Keep up your bright swords, for the dew will rust them.
Good Signior, you shall more command with years
Than with your weapons.
BRABANTIO. O thou foul thief, where hast thou stow'd my daughter?
Damn'd as thou art, thou has enchanted her;
For I'll refer me to all things of sense,[60]
If she in chains of magic were not bound,
Whether a maid so tender, fair and happy,
So opposite to marriage that she shunn'd   80
The wealthy curled darlings of our nation,
Would ever have, t' incur a general mock,
Run from her guardage[61] to the sooty bosom
Of such a thing as thou, to fear, not to delight.

---

57 **consuls** senators.
58 **several** separate.
59 **carack** large merchant ship.
60 **things of sense** commonsense understandings of the natural order.
61 **guardage** guardianship.

Judge me the world, if 'tis not gross in sense[62]
That thou has practis'd on her with foul charms,
Abus'd her delicate youth with drugs or minerals[63]
That weaken motion:[64] I'll have't disputed on;[65]
'Tis probable and palpable to thinking.
I therefore apprehend and do attach thee   90
For an abuser of the world,[66] a practiser
Of arts inhibited[67] and out of warrant.
Lay hold upon him: if he do resist,
Subdue him at his peril.

OTHELLO.   Hold your hands,
Both you of my inclining,[68] and the rest:
Were it my cue to fight, I should have known it
Without a prompter. Whither will you that I go
To answer this charge?

BRABANTIO.   To prison, till fit time
Of law and course of direct session[69]   100
Call thee to answer.

OTHELLO.   What if I do obey?
How may the duke be therewith satisfied,
Whose messengers are here about my side,
Upon some present business of the state
To bring me to him?

FIRST OFFICER.   'Tis true, most worthy signior;
The duke's in council, and your noble self,
I am sure, is sent for.   110

BRABANTIO.   How! the duke in council!
In this time of night! Bring him away:
Mine's not an idle cause: the duke himself,
Or any of my brothers of the state,
Cannot but feel this wrong as 'twere their own;
For if such actions may have passage free,
Bond-slaves and pagans[70] shall our statesmen be.

                                                            [*Exeunt.*]

SCENE III

A council-chamber.

[*Enter* DUKE, SENATORS *and* OFFICERS *set at a table, with lights and* ATTENDANTS.]

DUKE. There is no composition in these news
That gives them credit.

---

62 **gross in sense** easily discernible in apprehension or perception.
63 **minerals** medicine, poison.
64 **motion** thought, reason.
65 **disputed on** argued in court by professional counsel.
66 **abuser of the world** corrupter of society.
67 **inhibited** prohibited.
68 **inclining** following, party.
69 **course of direct session** regular legal proceedings.
70 **Bond-slaves and pagans** contemptuous reference to Othello's past history.

FIRST SENATOR.   Indeed, they are disproportion'd;[71]
    My letters say a hundred and seven galleys.
DUKE. And mine, a hundred forty.
SECOND SENATOR.   And mine, two hundred:
    But though they jump[72] not on a just account,—
    As in these cases, where the aim[73] reports,
    'Tis oft with difference—yet do they all confirm
    A Turkish fleet, and bearing up to Cyprus.   10
DUKE. Nay, it is possible enough to judgment:
    I do not so secure me[74] in the error,
    But the main article[75] I do approve
    In fearful sense.
SAILOR.   [*Within*] What, ho! what, ho! what, ho!
FIRST OFFICER. A messenger from the galleys.

    [*Enter* SAILOR.]

DUKE.   Now, what's the business?
SAIL. The Turkish preparation makes for Rhodes;
    So was I bid report here to the state
    By Signior Angelo.   20
DUKE. How say you by this change?
FIRST SENATOR.   This cannot be,
    By no assay[76] of reason: 'tis a pageant,
    To keep us in false gaze. When we consider
    Th' importancy of Cyprus to the Turk,
    And let ourselves again but understand,
    That as it more concerns the Turk than Rhodes,
    So may he with more facile question[77] bear it,
    For that it stands not in such warlike brace,[78]
    But altogether lacks th' abilities   30
    That Rhodes is dress'd in: if we make thought of this,
    We must not think the Turk is so unskilful
    To leave that latest which concerns him first,
    Neglecting an attempt of ease and gain,
    To wake and wage a danger profitless.
DUKE. Nay, in all confidence, he's not for Rhodes.
FIRST OFFICER. Here is more news.

    [*Enter a* MESSENGER.]

MESSENGER. The Ottomites, reverend and gracious,
    Steering with due course toward the isle of Rhodes,
    Have there injointed them with an after fleet.   40

---

71 **disproportion'd** inconsistent.
72 **jump** agree.
73 **aim** conjecture.
74 **secure me** feel myself secure.
75 **main article** i.e., that the Turkish fleet is threatening.
76 **assay** test.
77 **more facile question** greater facility of effort.
78 **brace** state of defense.

FIRST SENATOR. Ay, so I thought. How many, as you guess?
MESSENGER. Of thirty sail: and now they do re-stem[79]
    Their backward course, bearing with frank appearance
    Their purposes toward Cyprus. Signior Montano,
    Your trusty and most valiant servitor,
    With his free duty recommends you thus,
    And prays you to believe him.
DUKE. 'Tis certain, then, for Cyprus.
    Marcus Luccicos, is not he in town?
FIRST SENATOR. He's now in Florence.   50
DUKE. Write from us to him; post-post-haste dispatch.
FIRST SENATOR. Here comes Brabantio and the valiant Moor.

    [*Enter* BRABANTIO, OTHELLO, CASSIO, IAGO, RODERIGO, *and* OFFICERS.]

DUKE. Valiant Othello, we must straight employ you
    Against the general enemy Ottoman.
    [*To* BRABANTIO.] I did not see you; welcome, gentle signior;
    We lack'd your counsel and your help to-night.
BRABANTIO. So did I yours. Good your grace, pardon me;
    Neither my place nor aught I heard of business
    Hath rais'd me from my bed, nor doth the general care
    Take hold on me, for my particular grief   60
    Is of so flood-gate and o'erbearing nature
    That it engluts[80] and swallows other sorrows
    And it is still itself.
DUKE.   Why, what's the matter?
BRABANTIO. My daughter! O, my daughter!
DUKE *and* SENATOR.   Dead?
BRABANTIO.   Ay, to me;
    She is abus'd, stol'n from me, and corrupted
    By spells and medicines bought of mountebanks;
    For nature so preposterously to err,   70
    Being not deficient, blind, or lame of sense,
    Sans witchcraft could not.
DUKE. Whoe'er he be that in this foul proceeding
    Hath thus beguil'd your daughter of herself
    And you of her, the bloody book of law
    You shall yourself read in the bitter letter
    After your own sense, yea, though our proper son
    Stood in your action.[81]
BRABANTIO.   Humbly I thank your grace.
    Here is the man, this Moor, whom now, it seems,   80
    Your special mandate for the state-affairs
    Hath hither brought.

---

79 **re-stem** steer again.
80 **engluts** engulfs.
81 **Stood . . . action** was under your accusation.

DUKE *and* SENATOR.   We are very sorry for 't.
DUKE [*To Othello.*] What, in your own part, can you say to this?
BRABANTIO. Nothing, but this is so.
OTHELLO. Most potent, grave, and reverend signiors,
    My very noble and approv'd good masters,
    That I have ta'en away this old man's daughter,
    It is most true; true, I have married her:
    The very head and front of my offending   90
    Hath this extent, no more. Rude am I in my speech,
    And little bless'd with the soft phrase of peace;
    For since these arms of mine had seven years' pith,[82]
    Till now some nine moons wasted, they have us'd
    Their dearest action in the tented field,
    And little of this great world can I speak,
    More than pertains to feats of broil and battle,
    And therefore little shall I grace my cause
    In speaking for myself. Yet, by your gracious patience,[83]
    I will a round unvarnish'd tale deliver   100
    Of my whole course of love; what drugs, what charms,
    What conjuration and what mighty magic,
    For such proceeding I am charg'd withal,
    I won his daughter.
BRABANTIO.   A maiden never bold;
    Of spirit so still and quiet, that her motion
    Blush'd at herself,[84] and she, in spite of nature,
    Of years, of country, credit, every thing,
    To fall in love with what she fear'd to look on!
    It is a judgement maim'd and most imperfect   110
    That will confess perfection so could err
    Against all rules of nature, and must be driven
    To find out practices of cunning hell,
    Why this should be. I therefore vouch[85] again
    That with some mixtures pow'rful o'er the blood,
    Or with some dram conjur'd to this effect,
    He wrought upon her.
DUKE.   To vouch this is no proof,
    Without more wider and more overt test
    Than these thin habits and poor likelihoods   120
    Of modern seeming do prefer against him.
FIRST SENATOR. But, Othello, speak:
    Did you by indirect and forced courses
    Subdue and poison this young maid's affections?
    Or came it by request and such fair question
    As soul to soul affordeth?

---

82 **pith** strength, vigor.
83 **patience** suffering, permission.
84 **motion . . . herself** inward impulses blushed at themselves.
85 **vouch** assert.

OTHELLO.   I do beseech you,
　　Send for the lady to the Sagittary,
　　And let her speak of me before her father:
　　If you do find me foul in her report,   130
　　The trust, the office I do hold of you,
　　Not only take away, but let your sentence
　　Even fall upon my life.
DUKE.   Fetch Desdemona hither.
OTHELLO. Ancient, conduct them; you best know the place.

　　　　　　　　　　　　[*Exeunt* IAGO *and* ATTENDANTS.]

　　And, till she come, as truly as to heaven
　　I do confess the vices of my blood,
　　So justly to your grave ear I'll present
　　How I did thrive in this fair lady's love,
　　And she in mine.   140
DUKE. Say it, Othello.
OTHELLO. Her father lov'd me; oft invited me;
　　Still question'd me the story of my life,
　　From year to year, the battles, sieges, fortunes,
　　That I have pass'd.
　　I ran it through, even from my boyish days,
　　To th' very moment that he bade me tell it;
　　Wherein I spake of most disastrous chances,
　　Of moving accidents by flood and field,
　　Of hair-breadth scapes i' th' imminent[86] deadly breach,   150
　　Of being taken by the insolent foe
　　And sold to slavery, of my redemption thence
　　And portance[87] in my travels' history:
　　Wherein of antres[88] vast and deserts idle,[89]
　　Rough quarries, rocks and hills whose heads touch heaven,
　　It was my hint[90] to speak,—such was the process;
　　And of the Cannibals that each other eat,[91]
　　The Anthropophagi[92] and men whose heads
　　Do grow beneath their shoulders. This to hear
　　Would Desdemona seriously incline: 160
　　But still the house-affairs would draw her thence:
　　Which ever as she could with haste dispatch,
　　She 'd come again, and with a greedy ear
　　Devour up my discourse: which I observing,
　　Took once a pliant hour, and found good means
　　To draw from her a prayer of earnest heart

---

86 **imminent** i.e., impending parts when a gap has been made in a fortification.
87 **portance** conduct.
88 **antres** caverns.
89 **idle** barren, unprofitable.
90 **hint** occasion.
91 **eat** ate.
92 **Anthropophagi** man-eaters.

That I would all my pilgrimage dilate,[93]
Whereof by parcels she had something heard,
But not intentively:[94] I did consent,
And often did beguile her of her tears,   170
When I did speak of some distressful stroke
That my youth suffer'd. My story being done,
She gave me for my pains a world of sighs:
She swore, in faith, 'twas strange, 'twas passing strange,
'Twas pitiful, 'twas wondrous pitiful:
She wish'd she had not heard it, yet she wish'd
That heaven had made her such a man: she thank'd me,
And bade me, if I had a friend that lov'd her,
I should but teach him how to tell my story,
And that would woo her. Upon this hint I spake: 180
She lov'd me for the dangers I had pass'd,
And I lov'd her that she did pity them.
This only is the witchcraft I have us'd:
Here comes the lady; let her witness it.

[*Enter* DESDEMONA, IAGO, *and* ATTENDANTS.]

DUKE. I think this tale would win my daughter too.
   Good Brabantio,
   Take up this mangled matter at the best:
   Men do their broken weapons rather use
   Than their bare hands.

BRABANTIO.   I pray you, hear her speak: 190
   If she confess that she was half the wooer,
   Destruction on my head, if my bad blame
   Light on the man! Come hither, gentle mistress:
   Do you perceive in all this noble company
   Where most you owe obedience?

DESDEMONA.   My noble father,
   I do perceive here a divided duty:[95]
   To you I am bound for life and education;
   My life and education both do learn me
   How to respect you; you are the lord of duty;   200
   I am hitherto your daughter: but here's my husband,
   And so much duty as my mother show'd
   To you, preferring you before her father,
   So much I challenge that I may profess
   Due to the Moor my lord.

BRABANTIO.   God be with you! I have done.
   Please it your grace, on to[96] the state-affairs:
   I had rather to adopt a child than get[97] it.
   Come hither, Moor:

---

93 **dilate** relate in detail.
94 **intentively** with full attention.
95 **divided duty** Desdemona recognizes that she still owes a duty to her father even after marriage.
96 **on to** i.e., proceed with.
97 **get** beget.

I here do give thee that with all my heart   210
Which, but thou hast already, with all my heart
I would keep from thee. For your sake,[98] jewel,
I am glad at soul I have no other child;
For thy escape would teach me tyranny,
To hang clogs on them. I have done, my lord.
DUKE. Let me speak like yourself,[99] and lay a sentence,[100]
Which, as a grise[101] or step, may help these lovers
Into your favour.
When remedies are past, the griefs are ended
 By seeing the worst, which late on hopes depended.   220
To mourn a mischief that is past and gone
Is the next[102] way to draw new mischief on.
What cannot be preserv'd when fortune takes,
Patience her injury a mock'ry makes.
The robb'd that smiles steals something from the thief;
He robs himself that spends a bootless grief.
BRABANTIO. So let the Turk of Cyprus us beguile;
We lost it not, so long as we can smile.
He bears the sentence well that nothing bears
But the free comfort[103] which from thence he hears,   230
But he bears both the sentence and the sorrow
That, to pay grief, must of poor patience borrow.
These sentences, to sugar, or to gall,
Being strong on both sides, are equivocal:
But words are words; I never yet did hear
That the bruis'd heart was pierced through the ear.
I humbly beseech you, proceed to th' affairs of state.
DUKE. The Turk with a most mighty preparation makes for Cyprus. Othello, the
fortitude[104] of the place is best known to you; and though we have there a
substitute of most allowed[105] sufficiency, yet opinion, a sovereign mistress   240
of effects, throws a more safer voice on you:[106] you must therefore be con-
tent to slubber[107] the gloss of your new fortunes with this more stubborn
and boisterous expedition.
OTHELLO. The tyrant custom, most grave senators,
Hath made the flinty and steel couch of war
My thrice-driven[108] bed of down: I do agnize[109]

---

98 **For your sake** on your account.
99 **like yourself** i.e., as you would, in your proper temper.
100 **sentence** maxim.
101 **grise** step.
102 **next** nearest.
103 **comfort** i.e., the consolation that it may be borne with patience.
104 **fortitude** strength.
105 **allowed** acknowledged.
106 **opinion . . . on you** public opinion, an important determiner of affairs, chooses you as the
best man.
107 **slubber** soil, sully.
108 **thrice-driven** thrice sifted.
109 **agnize** know in myself.

A natural and prompt alacrity
I find in hardness[110] and do undertake
These present wars against the Ottomites.
Most humbly therefore bending to your state,   250
I crave fit disposition for my wife,
Due reference of place and exhibition,[111]
With such accommodation and besort[112]
As levels with her breeding.

DUKE.   If you please,
Be 't at her father's.

BRABANTIO.   I'll not have it so.

OTHELLO. Nor I.

DESDEMONA. Nor I; I would not there reside,
To put my father in impatient thoughts   260
By being in his eye. Most gracious duke,
To my unfolding lend your prosperous[113] ear;
And let me find a charter[114] in your voice,
T' assist my simpleness.[115]

DUKE. What would you, Desdemona?

DESDEMONA. That I did love the Moor to live with him,
My downright violence and storm of fortunes,
May trumpet to the world: my heart's subdu'd
Even to the very quality of my lord:
I saw Othello's visage in his mind,   270
And to his honours and his valiant parts
Did I my soul and fortunes consecrate.
So that, dear lords, if I be left behind,
A moth of peace, and he go to the war,
The rites for why I love him are bereft me,
And I a heavy interim shall support
By his dear absence. Let me go with him.

OTHELLO. Let her have your voices.
Vouch with me, heaven, I therefore beg it not,
To please the palate of my appetite,   280
Nor to comply with heat—the young affects[116]
In me defunct—and proper satisfaction,
But to be free and bounteous to her mind:
And heaven defend your good souls, that you think
I will your serious and great business scant
When she is with me. No, when light-wing'd toys
Of feather'd Cupid seel[117] with wanton dullness

---

110 **hardness** hardship.
111 **exhibition** allowance.
112 **besort** suitable company.
113 **prosperous** propitious.
114 **charter** privilege.
115 **simpleness** simplicity.
116 **affects** inclinations, desires.
117 **seel** in falconry, to make blind by sewing up the eyes of the hawk in training.

My speculative and offic'd instruments,[118]
That[119] my disports[120] corrupt and taint[121] my business,
Let housewives make a skillet of my helm,   290
And all indign[122] and base adversities
Make head against my estimation![123]
DUKE. Be it as you shall privately determine,
    Either for her stay or going: th' affair cries haste,
    And speed must answer it.
FIRST SENATOR. You must away to-night.
OTHELLO.   With all my heart.
DUKE. At nine i' th' morning here we'll meet again.
    Othello, leave some officer behind,
    And he shall our commission bring to you;   300
    With such things else of quality and respect
    As doth import[124] you.
OTHELLO.   So please your grace, my ancient;
    A man he is of honesty and trust:
    To his conveyance I assign my wife,
    With what else needful your good grace shall think
    To be sent after me.
DUKE.   Let it be so.
    Good night to every one. [*To* BRABANTIO.] And, noble signior,
    If virtue no delighted[125] beauty lack,   310
    Your son-in-law is far more fair than black.
FIRST SENATOR. Adieu, brave Moor; use Desdemona well.
BRABANTIO. Look to her, Moor, if thou hast eyes to see;
    She has deceiv'd her father, and may thee.
                            [*Exeunt* DUKE, SENATORS, OFFICERS, *etc.*]
OTHELLO. My life upon her faith! Honest Iago,[126]
    My Desdemona must I leave to thee:
    I prithee, let thy wife attend on her;
    And bring them after in the best advantage.
    Come, Desdemona; I have but an hour
    Of love, of wordly matters and direction,   320
    To spend with thee: we must obey the time.
                            [*Exit with* DESDEMONA.]
RODERIGO. Iago—
IAGO. What say'st thou, noble heart?
RODERIGO. What will I do, thinkest thou?
IAGO. Why, go to bed, and sleep.

---

118 **speculative . . . instruments** ability to see and reason clearly.
119 **That** so that.
120 **disports** pastimes.
121 **taint** impair.
122 **indign** unworthy, shameful.
123 **estimation** reputation.
124 **import** concern.
125 **delighted** delightful.
126 **Honest Iago** an evidence of Iago's carefully built reputation.

Roderigo. I will incontinently[127] drown myself.

Iago. If thou dost, I shall never love thee after. Why, thou silly gentleman!

Roderigo. It is silliness to live when to live is torment; and then have we a prescription to die when death is our physician.

Iago. O villainous! I have looked upon the world for four times seven years; and
since I could distinguish betwixt a benefit and an injury, I never found
man that knew how to love himself. Ere I would say, I would drown
myself for the love of a guinea-hen, I would change my humanity with a
baboon.   330

Roderigo. What should I do? I confess it is my shame to be so fond; but it is not
in my virtue[128] to amend it.

Iago. Virtue! a fig! 'tis in ourselves that we are thus or thus. Our bodies are
our gardens, to the which our wills are gardeners; so that if we will plant
nettles, or sow lettuce, set hyssop[129] and weed up thyme, supply it with
one gender[130] of herbs, or distract it with many, either to have it sterile   340
with idleness,[131] or manured with industry, why, the power and corrigible
authority[132] of this lies in our wills. If the balance of our lives had not one
scale of reason to poise another of sensuality, the blood and baseness of
our natures would conduct us to most preposterous conclusions:[133] but we
have reason to cool our raging motions,[134] our carnal stings, our unbitted[135] lusts, whereof I take this that you call love to be a sect[136] or scion.

Roderigo. It cannot be.

Iago. It is merely a lust of the blood and a permission of the will. Come, be a man.
Drown thyself! Drown cats and blind puppies. I have professed me thy
friend and I confess me knit to thy deserving with cables of perdurable[137]   350
toughness; I could never better stead thee than now. Put money in thy
purse; follow thou the wars; defeat thy favour[138] with an usurped beard; I
say, put money in thy purse. It cannot be that Desdemona should long continue her love to the Moor,—put money in thy purse,—nor he his to her:
it was a violent commencement in her, and thou shalt see an answerable
sequestration:[139]—put but money in thy purse. These Moors are changeable
in their wills:—fill thy purse with money:—the food that to him now is as
luscious as locusts,[140] shall be to him shortly as bitter as coloquintida.[141]

---

127 **incontinently** immediately.

128 **virtue** strength.

129 **hyssop** an herb of the mint family.

130 **gender** kind.

131 **idleness** want of cultivation.

132 **corrigible authority** the power to correct.

133 **reason . . . conclusions** Iago understands the warfare between reason and sensuality, but
his ethics are totally inverted; reason works in him not good, as it should according to natural law,
but evil, which he has chosen for his good.

134 **motions** appetites.

135 **unbitted** uncontrolled.

136 **sect** cutting.

137 **perdurable** very durable.

138 **defeat thy favour** disguise and disfigure thy face.

139 **answerable sequestration** a corresponding separation or estrangement.

140 **locusts** of doubtful meaning; defined as fruit of the carob tree, as honeysuckle, and as lol-
lipops or sugar sticks.

141 **coloquintida** colocynth, or bitter apple, a purgative.

She must change for youth: when she is sated with his body, she will find the error of her choice: she must have change, she must: therefore put money in thy purse. If thou wilt needs damn thyself, do it a more delicate way than drowning. Make all the money thou canst: if sanctimony and a frail vow betwixt an erring[142] barbarian and a super-subtle Venetian be not too hard for my wits and all the tribe of hell, thou shalt enjoy her; therefore make money. A pox of drowning thyself! it is clean out of the way: seek thou rather to be hanged in compassing the joy than to be drowned and go without her.

RODERIGO. Wilt thou be fast to my hopes, if I depend on the issue?

IAGO. Thou art sure of me: —go, make money:—I have told thee often, and I re-tell thee again and again, I hate the Moor: my cause is hearted;[143] thine hath no less reason. Let us be conjunctive[144] in our revenge against him; if thou canst cuckold him, thou dost thyself a pleasure, me a sport. There are many events in the womb of time which will be delivered. Traverse![145] go, provide thy money. We will have more of this to-morrow. Adieu.

RODERIGO. Where shall we meet i' the morning?

IAGO. At my lodging.

RODERIGO. I'll be with thee betimes.

IAGO. Go to; farewell. Do you hear, Roderigo?

RODERIGO. What say you?

IAGO. No more of drowning, do you hear?

RODERIGO. I am changed. I'll go sell all my land.   [*Exit.*]

IAGO. Thus do I ever make my fool my purse;
For I mine own gain'd knowledge should profane,
If I would time expend with such a snipe,[146]
But for my sport and profit. I hate the Moor;
And it is thought abroad, that 'twixt my sheets
H' as done my office: I know not if 't be true;
But I, for mere suspicion in that kind,
Will do as if for surety. He holds me well;
The better shall my purpose work on him.
Cassio's a proper man: let me see now:
To get his place and to plume up[147] my will
In double knavery—How, how?—Let's see:—
After some time, to abuse Othello's ears
That he[148] is too familiar with his wife.
He hath a person and a smooth dispose[149]
To be suspected, fram'd to make women false.
The Moor is of a free[150] and open nature,

360

370

380

390

---

142 **erring** wandering.
143 **hearted** fixed in the heart.
144 **conjunctive** united.
145 **Traverse** go (military term).
146 **snipe** gull, fool.
147 **plume up** glorify, gratify.
148 **he** i.e., Cassio.
149 **dispose** external manner.
150 **free** frank.

That thinks men honest that but seem to be so,
And will as tenderly be led by th' nose   380
As asses are.
I have 't. It is engend'red. Hell and night
Must bring this monstrous birth to the world's light.

[*Exit.*]

ACT II

SCENE I

A Sea-port in Cyprus. An open place near the quay.

[*Enter* Montano *and two* Gentlemen.]

Montano. What from the cape can you discern at sea?
First Gentleman. Nothing at all: it is a high-wrought flood;
    I cannot, 'twixt the heaven and the main,
    Descry a sail.
Montano. Methinks the wind hath spoke aloud at land;
    A fuller blast ne'er shook our battlements:
    If it hath ruffian'd[1] so upon the sea,
    What ribs of oak, when mountains melt on them,
    Can hold the mortise?[2] What shall we hear of this?
Second Gentleman. A segregation[3] of the Turkish fleet: 10
    For do but stand upon the foaming shore,
    The chidden billow seems to pelt the clouds:
    The wind-shak'd surge, with high and monstrous mane,
    Seems to cast water on the burning bear,[4]
    And quench the guards[5] of th' ever-fixed pole:
    I never did like molestation view
    On the enchafed[6] flood.
Montano.   If that the Turkish fleet
    Be not enshelter'd and embay'd, they are drown'd;
    It is impossible they bear it out.   20

[*Enter a third* Gentleman.]

Third Gentleman. News, lads! our wars are done.
    The desperate tempest hath so bang'd the Turks,
    That their designment[7] halts: a noble ship of Venice
    Hath seen a grievous wrack and sufferance[8]
    On most part of their fleet.
Montano. How! is this true?

---

1 **ruffian'd** raged.
2 **mortise** the socket hollowed out in fitting timbers.
3 **segregation** dispersion.
4 **bear** a constellation.
5 **quench the guards** overwhelm the stars near the polestar.
6 **enchafed** angry.
7 **designment** enterprise.
8 **sufferance** disaster.

THIRD GENTLEMAN.   The ship is here put in,
    A Veronesa; Michael Cassio,
    Lieutenant to the warlike Moor Othello,
    Is come on shore: the Moor himself at sea,   30
    And is in full commission here for Cyprus.
MONTANO. I am glad on 't; 'tis a worthy governor.
THIRD GENTLEMAN. But this same Cassio, though he speak of comfort
    Touching the Turkish loss, yet he looks sadly,
    And prays the Moor be safe; for they were parted
    With foul and violent tempest.
MONTANO.   Pray heavens he be;
    For I have serv'd him, and the man commands
    Like a full⁹ soldier. Let's to the seaside, ho!
    As well to see the vessel that's come in   40
    As to throw out our eyes for brave Othello,
    Even till we make the main and th' aerial blue
    An indistinct regard.¹⁰
THIRD GENTLEMAN.   Come, let's do so;
    For every minute is expectancy
    Of more arrivance.¹¹

    [*Enter* CASSIO.]

CASSIO. Thanks, you the valiant of this warlike isle,
    That so approve the Moor! O, let the heavens
    Give him defence against the elements,
    For I have lost him on a dangerous sea.   50
MONTANO. Is he well shipp'd?
CASSIO. His bark is stoutly timber'd, and his pilot
    Of very expert and approv'd allowance;¹²
    Therefore my hopes, not surfeited to death,
    Stand in bold cure. [*A cry within.*] "A sail, a sail, a sail!"

    [*Enter a fourth* GENTLEMAN.]

CASSIO. What noise?
FOURTH GENTLEMAN. The town is empty; on the brow o' th' sea
    Stand ranks of people, and they cry "A sail!"
CASSIO. My hopes do shape him for the governor.   [*Guns heard.*]
SECOND GENTLEMAN. They do discharge their shot of courtesy: 60
    Our friends at least.
CASSIO.   I pray you, sir, go forth,
    And give us truth who 'tis that is arriv'd.
SECOND GENTLEMAN. I shall.
                                                              [*Exit.*]

MONTANO. But, good lieutenant, is your general wiv'd?
CASSIO. Most fortunately: he hath achiev'd a maid

---

9 **full** perfect.
10 **make . . . regard** cause the blue of the sea and the air to grow indistinguishable in our view.
11 **arrivance** arrival.
12 **allowance** reputation.

That paragons[13] description and wild fame;
One that excels the quirks[14] of blazoning[15] pens,
And in th' essential vesture of creation[16]
Does tire the ingener.[17]   70

[*Enter second* Gentleman.]

                                                 How now! who has put in?
Second Gentleman. 'Tis one Iago, ancient to the general.
Cassio. Has had most favourable and happy speed:
    Tempests themselves, high seas and howling winds,
    The gutter'd[18] rocks and congregated sands,—
    Traitors ensteep'd[19] to clog the guiltless keel,—
    As having sense of beauty, do omit
    Their mortal[20] natures, letting go safely by
    The divine Desdemona.
Montano.   What is she?   80
Cassio. She that I spake of, our great captain's captain,
    Left in the conduct of the bold Iago,
    Whose footing here anticipates our thoughts
    A se'nnight's[21] speed. Great Jove, Othello guard,
    And swell his sail with thine own powr'ful breath,
    That he may bless this bay with his tall ship,
    Make love's quick pants in Desdemona's arms,
    Give renew'd fire to our extincted spirits,
    And bring all Cyprus comfort!

[*Enter* Desdemona, Iago, Roderigo, *and* Emilia *with* Attendants.]

                                   O, behold,   90
    The riches of the ship is come on shore!
    You men of Cyprus, let her have your knees.
    Hail to thee, lady! and the grace of heaven,
    Before, behind thee and on every hand,
    Enwheel thee round!
Desdemona.   I thank you, valiant Cassio.
    What tidings can you tell me of my lord?
Cassio. He is not yet arriv'd: nor know I aught
    But that he's well and will be shortly here.
Desdemona. O, but I fear—How lost you company?   100
Cassio. The great contention of the sea and skies

---

13 **paragons** surpasses.
14 **quirks** witty conceits.
15 **blazoning** setting forth honorably in words.
16 **vesture of creation** the real qualities with which creation has invested her.
17 **ingener** inventor, praiser.
18 **gutter'd** jagged, trenched.
19 **ensteep'd** lying under water.
20 **mortal** deadly.
21 **se'nnight's** week's.

Parted our fellowship—But, hark! a sail.
[*Within*] "A sail, a sail!" [*Guns heard.*]
SECOND GENTLEMAN. They give their greeting to the citadel:
    This likewise is a friend.
CASSIO.   See for the news.
                                      [*Exit* GENTLEMAN.]
    Good ancient, you are welcome. [*To* EMILIA.] Welcome, mistress:
    Let it not gall your patience, good Iago,
    That I extend my manners; 'tis my breeding
    That gives me this bold show of courtesy.   [*Kissing her.*]   110
IAGO. Sir, would she give you so much of her lips
    As of her tongue she oft bestows on me,
    You would have enough.
DESDEMONA.   Alas, she has no speech.
IAGO. In faith, too much;
    I find it still, when I have list to sleep:
    Marry, before your ladyship, I grant,
    She puts her tongue a little in her heart,
    And chides with thinking.
EMILIA. You have little cause to say so.   120
IAGO. Come on, come on; you are pictures out of doors,
    Bells in your parlours, wild-cats in your kitchens,
    Saints in your injuries, devils being offended,
    Players in your housewifery, and housewives[22] in your beds.
DESDEMONA. O, fie upon thee, slanderer!
IAGO. Nay, it is true, or else I am a Turk:
    You rise to play and go to bed to work.
EMILIA. You shall not write my praise.
IAGO.   No, let me not.
DESDEMONA. What wouldst thou write of me, if thou shouldst praise me?   130
IAGO. O gentle lady, do not put me to 't;
    For I am nothing, if not critical.[23]
DESDEMONA. Come on, assay. There's one gone to the harbour?
IAGO. Ay, madam.
DESDEMONA. I am not merry; but I do beguile
    The thing I am, by seeming otherwise.
    Come, how wouldst thou praise me?
IAGO. I am about it; but indeed my invention
    Comes from my pate as birdlime[24] does from frieze;[25]
    It plucks out brains and all: but my Muse labours,   140
    And thus she is deliver'd.
    If she be fair and wise, fairness and wit,
    The one's for use, the other useth it.
DESDEMONA. Well praised! How if she be black and witty?
IAGO. If she be black, and thereto have a wit,

---

22 **housewives** hussies.
23 **critical** censorious.
24 **birdlime** sticky substance smeared on twigs to catch small birds.
25 **frieze** coarse woolen cloth.

She'll find a white[26] that shall her blackness fit.

DESDEMONA. Worse and worse.

EMILIA. How if fair and foolish?

IAGO. She never yet was foolish that was fair;
    For even her folly help'd her to an heir.   150

DESDEMONA. These are old fond[27] paradoxes to make fools laugh i' the alehouse.
    What miserable praise hast thou for her that's foul and foolish?

IAGO. There's none so foul and foolish thereunto,
    But does foul pranks which fair and wise ones do.

DESDEMONA. O heavy ignorance! thou praisest the worst best. But what praise
    couldst thou bestow on a deserving woman indeed, one that, in the authority
    of her merit, did justly put on the vouch[28] of her malice itself?

IAGO. She that was ever fair and never proud,
    Had tongue at will and yet was never loud,
    Never lack'd gold and yet went never gay,   160
    Fled from her wish and yet said "Now I may,"
    She that being ang'red, her revenge being nigh,
    Bade her wrong stay and her displeasure fly,
    She that in wisdom never was so frail
    To change the cod's head for the salmon's tail,[29]
    She that could think and ne'er disclose her mind,
    See suitors following and not look behind,
    She was a wight, if ever such wight were,—

DESDEMONA. To do what?

IAGO. To suckle fools and chronicle small beer.[30]   170

DESDEMONA. O most lame and impotent conclusion! Do not learn of him, Emilia,
    though he be thy husband. How say you, Cassio? Is he not a most profane
    and liberal[31] counsellor?

CASSIO. He speaks home,[32] madam: you may relish him more in the soldier than
    in the scholar.

IAGO [*Aside*]. He takes her by the palm: ay, well said, whisper: with as little a web
    as this will I ensnare as great a fly as Cassio. Ay, smile upon her, do; I will
    gyve[33] thee in thine own courtship.[34] You say true; 'tis so, indeed: if such
    tricks as these strip you out of your lieutenantry, it had been better you had
    not kissed your three fingers[35] so oft, which now again you are most apt   180
    to play the sir[36] in. Very good; well kissed! an excellent courtesy! 'tis so,
    indeed. Yet again your fingers to your lips? would they were clyster-pipes[37]
    for your sake. [*Trumpet within.*] The Moor! I know his trumpet.

---

26 **white** a fair person, with a wordplay on *wight*.
27 **fond** foolish.
28 **put on the vouch** compel the approval.
29 **To change . . . tail** to exchange a delicacy for mere refuse.
30 **chronicle small beer** keep petty household accounts.
31 **liberal** licentious.
32 **speaks home** i.e., without reserve.
33 **gyve** fetter, shackle.
34 **courtship** courtesy.
35 **kissed your three fingers** he kisses his own hand as a token of reverence.
36 **the sir** i.e., the fine gentleman.
37 **clyster-pipes** tubes used for enemas.

CASSIO. 'Tis truly so.
DESDEMONA. Let's meet him and receive him.
CASSIO. Lo, where he comes!

[*Enter* OTHELLO *and* ATTENDANTS.]

OTHELLO. O my fair warrior!
DESDEMONA.   My dear Othello!
OTHELLO. It gives me wonder great as my content
    To see you here before me. O my soul's joy!   190
    If after every tempest comes such calms,
    May the winds blow till they have waken'd death!
    And let the labouring bark climb hills of seas
    Olympus-high and duck again as low
    As hell 's from heaven! If it were now to die,
    'Twere now to be most happy; for, I fear,
    My soul hath her content so absolute
    That not another comfort like to this
    Succeeds in unknown fate.
DESDEMONA.   The heavens forbid   200
    But that our loves and comforts should increase,
    Even as our days do grow!
OTHELLO.   Amen to that, sweet powers!
    I cannot speak enough of this content;
    It stops me here; it is too much of joy:
    And this, and this, the greatest discords be [*Kissing her.*]
    That e'er our hearts shall make!
IAGO.   [*Aside.*] O, you are well tun'd now!
    But I'll set down the pegs[38] that make this music,
    As honest as I am.   210
OTHELLO.   Come, let us to the castle.
    News, friends; our wars are done, the Turks are drowned.
    How does my old acquaintance of this isle?
    Honey, you shall be well desir'd in Cyprus;
    I have found great love amongst them. O my sweet,
    I prattle out of fashion, and I dote
    In mine own comforts. I prithee, good Iago,
    Go to the bay and disembark my coffers:
    Bring thou the master to the citadel;
    He is a good one, and his worthiness   220
    Does challenge much respect. Come, Desdemona,
    Once more, well met at Cyprus.

[*Exeunt* OTHELLO *and* DESDEMONA
and all but IAGO *and* RODERIGO.]

IAGO [*To an* ATTENDANT]. Do thou meet me presently at the harbour. [*To* RODERIGO].
    Come hither. If thou be'st valiant,—as, they say, base men being in love have
    then a nobility in their natures more than is native to them,—list me. The
    lieutenant tonight watches on the court of guard.[39] I must tell thee this—
    Desdemona is directly in love with him.

---

38 **set down the pegs** lower the pitch of the strings, i.e., disturb the harmony.
39 **court of guard** guardhouse.

RODERIGO. With him! why 'tis not possible.

IAGO. Lay thy finger thus, and let thy soul be instructed. Mark me with what violence she first loved the Moor, but for bragging and telling her fantastical 230
lies: and will she love him still for prating? Let not thy discreet heart think
it. Her eye must be fed; and what delight shall she have to look on the
devil? When the blood is made dull with the act of sport, there should be,
again to inflame it and to give satiety a fresh appetite, loveliness in favour,
sympathy in years, manners and beauties; all which the Moor is defective
in: now, for want of these required conveniences, her delicate tenderness
will find itself abused, begin to heave the gorge, disrelish and abhor the
Moor; very nature will instruct her in it and compel her to some second
choice. Now, sir, this granted,—as it is a most pregnant and unforced
position—who stands so eminent in the degree of this fortune as Cassio 240
does? a knave very voluble; no further conscionable[40] than in putting on
the mere form of civil and humane seeming, for the better compassing of
his salt[41] and most hidden loose affection? why, none; why, none: a slipper[42] and subtle knave, a finder of occasions, that has an eye can stamp and
counterfeit advantages, though true advantage never present itself; a devilish knave. Besides, the knave is handsome, young, and hath all those requisites in him that folly and green minds look after: a pestilent complete
knave; and the woman hath found him already.

RODERIGO. I cannot believe that in her; she's full of most blessed condition.

IAGO. Blessed fig's-end! the wine she drinks is made of grapes: if she had been 250
blessed, she would never have loved the Moor. Blessed pudding! Didst
thou not see her paddle with the palm of his hand? didst not mark that?

RODERIGO. Yes, that I did; but that was but courtesy.

IAGO. Lechery, by his hand; an index and obscure prologue to the history
of lust and foul thoughts. They met so near with their lips that their
breaths embraced together. Villainous thoughts, Roderigo! when these
mutualities so marshall the way, hard at hand comes the master and
main exercise, the incorporate conclusion. Pish! But, sir, be you ruled
by me: I have brought you from Venice. Watch you to-night; for the
command, I'll lay't upon you. Cassio knows you not. I'll not be far from 260
you: do you find some occasion to anger Cassio, either by speaking too
loud, or tainting[43] his discipline; or from what other course you please,
which the time shall more favourably minister.

RODERIGO. Well.

IAGO. Sir, he is rash and very sudden in choler, and haply may strike at you: provoke
him, that he may; for even out of that will I cause these of Cyprus to mutiny;
whose qualification[44] shall come into no true taste again but by the displanting of Cassio. So shall you have a shorter journey to your desires by the
means I shall then have to prefer them; and the impediment most profitably
removed, without the which there were no expectation of our prosperity. 270

RODERIGO. I will do this, if I can bring it to any opportunity.

---

40 **conscionable** conscientious.
41 **salt** licentious.
42 **slipper** slippery.
43 **tainting** disparaging.
44 **qualification** appeasement.

IAGO. I warrant thee. Meet me by and by[45] at the citadel: I must fetch his necessaries ashore. Farewell.
RODERIGO. Adieu.

[*Exit.*]

IAGO. That Cassio loves her, I do well believe 't;
That she loves him, 'tis apt[46] and of great credit:[47]
The Moor, howbeit that I endure him not,
Is of a constant, loving, noble nature,
And I dare think he'll prove to Desdemona
A most dear husband. Now, I do love her too;   280
Not out of absolute lust, though peradventure
I stand accountant for as great a sin,
But partly led to diet my revenge,
For that I do suspect the lusty Moor
Hath leap'd into my seat; the thought whereof
Doth, like a poisonous mineral, gnaw my inards;
And nothing can or shall content my soul
Till I am even'd with him, wife for wife,
Or failing so, yet that I put the Moor
At least into a jealousy so strong   290
That judgement cannot cure. Which thing to do,
If this poor trash[48] of Venice, whom I trace[49]
For his quick hunting, stand the putting on,[50]
I'll have our Michael Cassio on the hip,[51]
Abuse him to the Moor in the rank garb—
For I fear Cassio with my night-cap too—
Make the Moor thank me, love me and reward me,
For making him egregiously an ass
And practicing upon his peace and quiet
Even to madness. 'Tis here, but yet confus'd: 300
Knavery's plain face is never seen till us'd.

[*Exit.*]

SCENE II

A street.

[*Enter Othello's* HERALD *with a proclamation.*]

HERALD. It is Othello's pleasure, our noble and valiant general, that, upon certain tidings now arrived, importing the mere perdition[52] of the Turkish
fleet, every man put himself into triumph; some to dance, some to make
bonfires, each man to what sport and revels his addiction leads him: for,

---

45 **by and by** immediately.
46 **apt** probable.
47 **credit** credibility.
48 **trash** worthless thing (Roderigo).
49 **trash** train.
50 **putting on** incitement to quarrel.
51 **on the hip** at my mercy (wrestling term).
52 **mere perdition** complete destruction.

besides these beneficial news, it is the celebration of his nuptial. So much was his pleasure should be proclaimed. All offices[53] are open, and there is full liberty of feasting from this present hour of five till the bell have told eleven. Heaven bless the isle of Cyprus and our general Othello!

[*Exit.*]

SCENE III

A hall in the castle.

[*Enter* OTHELLO, DESDEMONA, CASSIO, *and* ATTENDANTS.]

OTHELLO. Good Michael, look you to the guard to-night:
　　Let's teach ourselves that honourable stop,[54]
　　Not to outsport discretion.
CASSIO. Iago hath direction what to do;
　　But, notwithstanding, with my personal eye
　　Will I look to 't.
OTHELLO. 　　　　　Iago is most honest.
　　Michael, goodnight: to-morrow with your earliest
　　Let me have speech with you. [*To* DESDEMONA.] Come, my dear love,
　　The purchase made, the fruits are to ensue;　　　　　　　　　　　　　　10
　　That profit's yet to come 'tween me and you.
　　Good night.

[*Exit* OTHELLO, *with* DESDEMONA
and ATTENDANTS.]

[*Enter* IAGO.]

CASSIO. Welcome, Iago; we must to the watch.
IAGO. Not this hour, lieutenant; 'tis not yet ten o' the clock. Our general cast[55] us thus early for the love of his Desdemona; who let us not therefore blame: he hath not yet made wanton the night with her; and she is sport for Jove.
CASSIO. She's a most exquisite lady.
IAGO. And, I'll warrant her, full of game.
CASSIO. Indeed, she's a most fresh and delicate creature.
IAGO. What an eye she has! Methinks it sounds a parley of provocation.　　　　20
CASSIO. An inviting eye; and yet methinks right modest.
IAGO. And when she speaks, is it not an alarum to love?
CASSIO. She is indeed perfection.
IAGO. Well, happiness to their sheets! Come, lieutenant, I have a stoup[56] of wine; and here without are a brace of Cyprus gallants that would fain have a measure to the health of black Othello.
CASSIO. Not to-night, good Iago: I have very poor and unhappy brains for drinking: I could well wish courtesy would invent some other custom of entertainment.
IAGO. O, they are our friends, but one cup: I'll drink for you.　　　　　　30

---

53 **offices** rooms where food and drink were kept.
54 **stop** restraint.
55 **cast** dismissed.
56 **stoup** measure of liquor, two quarts.

CASSIO. I have drunk but one cup tonight, and that was craftily qualified[57] too,
and, behold, what innovation[58] it makes here:[59] I am unfortunate in the
infirmity, and dare not task my weakness with any more.

IAGO. What, man! 'tis a night of revels: the gallants desire it.

CASSIO. Where are they?

IAGO. Here at the door; I pray you, call them in.

CASSIO. I'll do 't; but it dislikes me.   [*Exit.*]

IAGO. If I can fasten but one cup upon him,
    With that which he hath drunk to-night already,
    He'll be as full of quarrel and offence   40
    As my young mistress' dog. Now, my sick fool Roderigo,
    Whom love hath turn'd almost the wrong side out,
    To Desdemona hath to-night carous'd
    Potations pottle-deep;[60] and he's to watch:
    Three lads of Cyprus, noble swelling spirits,
    That hold their honours in a wary distance,[61]
    The very elements[62] of this warlike isle,
    Have I to-night fluster'd with flowing cups,
    And they watch[63] too. Now, 'mongst this flock of drunkards,
    Am I to put our Cassio in some action   50
    That may offend the isle.—But here they come:

[*Enter* CASSIO, MONTANO, *and* GENTLEMEN; SERVANTS *following with wine.*]

    If consequence do but approve[64] my dream,
    My boat sails freely, both with wind and stream.

CASSIO. 'Fore God, they have given me a rouse[65] already.

MONTANO. Good faith, a little one; not past a pint, as I am a soldier.

IAGO. Some wine, ho!
    [*Sings.*] And let me the canakin[66] clink, clink;
        And let me the canakin clink
            A soldier's a man;
            A life's but a span;   60
        Why, then, let a soldier drink.
    Some wine, boys!

CASSIO. 'Fore God, an excellent song.

IAGO. I learned it in England, where, indeed, they are most potent in pot-
ting your Dane, your German, and your swag-bellied Hollander—Drink,
ho!—are nothing to your English.

CASSIO. Is your Englishman so expert in his drinking?

---

57 **qualified** diluted.
58 **innovation** disturbance.
59 **here** i.e., in Cassio's head.
60 **pottle-deep** to the bottom of the tankard.
61 **hold . . . distance** i.e., are extremely sensitive of their honor.
62 **very elements** true representatives.
63 **watch** are members of the guard.
64 **approve** confirm.
65 **rouse** full draft of liquor.
66 **canakin** small drinking vessel.

IAGO. Why, he drinks you, with facility, your Dane dead drunk; he sweats not to overthrow your Almain;[67] he gives your Hollander a vomit, ere the next pottle can be filled.   70

CASSIO. To the health of our general!

MONTANO. I am for it, lieutenant; and I'll do you justice.[68]

IAGO. O sweet England! [*Sings.*]

    King Stephen was a worthy peer,
        His breeches cost him but a crown;
        He held them sixpence all too dear,
    With that he call'd the tailor lown.[69]

    He was a wight of high renown,
        And thou art but of low degree:
    'Tis pride that pulls the country down;   80
        Then take thine auld cloak about thee.

    Some wine, ho!

CASSIO. Why, this is a more exquisite song than the other.

IAGO. Will you hear 't again?

CASSIO. No; for I hold him to be unworthy of his place that does those things. Well, God's above all; and there be souls must be saved, and there be souls must not be saved.

IAGO. It's true, good lieutenant.

CASSIO. For mine own part,—no offence to the general, nor any man of quality,—I hope to be saved.   90

IAGO. And so do I too, lieutenant.

CASSIO. Ay, but, by your leave, not before me; the lieutenant is to be saved before the ancient. Let's have no more of this; let's to our affairs.—God forgive us our sins!—Gentlemen, let's look to our business. Do not think, gentlemen, I am drunk: this is my ancient; this is my right hand, and this is my left: I am not drunk now: I can stand well enough, and speak well enough.

ALL. Excellent well.

CASSIO. Why, very well then; you must not think then that I am drunk.   [*Exit.*]

MONTANO. To th' platform, masters; come, let's set the watch.   100

IAGO. You see this fellow that is gone before;

    He's soldier fit to stand by Caesar
    And give direction and do but see his vice;
    'Tis to his virtue a just equinox,[70]
    The one as long as th' other 'tis pity of him.
    I fear the trust Othello puts him in,
    On some odd time of his infirmity,
    Will shake this island.

MONTANO.   But is he often thus?

IAGO. 'Tis evermore the prologue to his sleep: 110

---

67 **Almain** German.

68 **I'll . . . justice** i.e., drink as much as you.

69 **lown** lout, loon.

70 **equinox** equal length of days and nights; used figuratively to mean "counterpart."

He'll watch the horologe[71] a double set,[72]
If drink rock not his cradle.
MONTANO.   It were well
The general were put in mind of it.
Perhaps he sees it not; or his good nature
Prizes the virtue that appears in Cassio,
And looks not on his evils: is not this true?

[*Enter* RODERIGO.]

IAGO [*Aside to him*]. How now, Roderigo!
I pray you, after the lieutenant; go.

                                                        [*Exit* RODERIGO.]

MONTANO. And 'tis great pity that the noble Moor   120
Should hazard such a place as his own second
With one of an ingraft[73] infirmity:
It were an honest action to say
So to the Moor.
IAGO.   Not I, for this fair island:
I do love Cassio well; and would do much
To cure him of this evil—But, hark! what noise?
[*Cry within:* "Help! help!"]

[*Enter* CASSIO, *pursing* RODERIGO.]

CASSIO. 'Zounds, you rogue! you rascal!
MONTANO.   What's the matter, lieutenant?   130
CASSIO. A knave teach me my duty!
I'll beat the knave into a twiggen[74] bottle.
RODERIGO. Beat me!
CASSIO.   Dost thou prate, rogue?   [*Striking* RODERIGO.]
MONTANO.   Nay, good lieutenant; [*Staying him.*]
I pray you, sir, hold your hand.
CASSIO.   Let me go, sir,
Or I'll knock you o'er the mazzard.[75]
MONTANO.   Come, come, you're drunk.
CASSIO. Drunk!   [*They fight.*]   140
IAGO [*aside to* RODERIGO]. Away, I say; go out, and cry a mutiny.

                                                        [*Exit* RODERIGO.]

Nay, good lieutenant,—God's will, gentlemen;—
Help, ho!—Lieutenant,—sir,—Montano,—sir,—
Help, masters!—Here's a goodly watch indeed!   [*Bell rings.*]
Who's that which rings the bell?—Diablo,[76] ho!
The town will rise:[77] God's will, lieutenant, hold!
You'll be asham'd for ever.

[*Enter* OTHELLO *and* ATTENDANTS.]

---

71 **horologe** clock.
72 **double set** twice around.
73 **ingraft** ingrafted, inveterate.
74 **twiggen** covered with woven twigs.
75 **mazzard** head.
76 **Diablo** the devil.
77 **rise** grow riotous.

OTHELLO. What is the matter here?

MONTANO. 'Zounds, I bleed still; I am hurt to th' death.
He dies! [*Thrusts at* CASSIO.]

OTHELLO. Hold, for your lives! 150

IAGO. Hold, ho! Lieutenant,—sir,—Montano,—gentlemen,—
Have you forgot all sense of place and duty?
Hold! the general speaks to you; hold, for shame!

OTHELLO. Why, how now, ho! from whence ariseth this?
Are we turn'd Turks[78] and to ourselves do that
Which heaven hath forbid the Ottomites?
For Christian shame, put by this barbarous brawl:
He that stirs next to carve for[79] his own rage
Holds his soul light; he dies upon his motion.
Silence that dreadful bell: it frights the isle 160
From her propriety.[80] What is the matter, masters?
Honest Iago, that looks dead with grieving,
Speak, who began this? on thy love, I charge thee.

IAGO. I do not know: friends all but now, even now,
In quarter,[81] and in terms like bride and groom
Devesting them for bed; and then, but now—
As if some planet had unwitted men—
Swords out, and tilting one at other's breast,
In opposition bloody. I cannot speak
Any beginning to this peevish odds;[82] 170
And would in action glorious I had lost
Those legs that brought me to a part of it!

OTHELLO. How comes it, Michael, you are thus forgot?

CASSIO. I pray you, pardon me; I cannot speak.

OTHELLO. Worthy Montano, you were wont be civil;
The gravity and stillness of your youth
The world hath noted, and your name is great
In mouths of wisest censure.[83] What's the matter,
That you unlace[84] your reputation thus
And spend your rich opinion for the name 180
Of a night-brawler? Give me answer to it.

MONTANO. Worthy Othello, I am hurt to danger:
Your officer, Iago, can inform you,—
While I spare speech, which something now offends me,—
Of all that I do know: nor know I aught
By me that's said or done amiss this night;
Unless self-charity be sometimes a vice,
And to defend ourselves it be a sin
When violence assails us.

---

78 **turn'd Turks** changed completely for the worse; proverbial.
79 **carve for** indulge.
80 **propriety** proper state or condition.
81 **In quarter** on terms.
82 **peevish odds** childish quarrel.
83 **censure** judgment.
84 **unlace** degrade.

OTHELLO.   Now, by heaven,   190
 My blood begins my safer guides to rule;
 And passion, having my best judgment collied,[85]
 Assays to lead the way: if I once stir,
 Or do but lift this arm, the best of you
 Shall sink in my rebuke. Give me to know
 How this foul rout began, who set it on;
 And he that is approv'd in[86] this offence,
 Though he had twinn'd with me, both at a birth,
 Shall lose me. What! in a town of war,
 Yet wild, the people's hearts brimful of fear,   200
 To manage private and domestic quarrel,
 In night, and on the court and guard[87] of safety!
 'Tis monstrous. Iago, who began 't?
MONTANO [*to* IAGO]. If partially affin'd,[88] or leagu'd in office,
 Thou dost deliver more or less than truth,
 Thou art no soldier.
IAGO.   Touch me not so near:
 I had rather have this tongue cut from my mouth
 Than it should do offense to Michael Cassio;
 Yet, I persuade myself, to speak the truth   210
 Shall nothing wrong him. Thus it is, general.
 Montano and myself being in speech,
 There comes a fellow crying out for help;
 And Cassio following him with determin'd sword,
 To execute[89] upon him. Sir, this gentleman
 Steps in to Cassio, and entreats his pause:
 Myself the crying fellow did pursue,
 Lest by his clamour—as it so fell out—
 The town might fall in fright: he, swift of foot,
 Outran my purpose; and I return'd the rather 220
 For that I heard the clink and fall of swords,
 And Cassio high in oath; which till to-night
 I ne'er might say before. When I came back—
 For this was brief—I found them close together,
 At blow and thrust; even as again they were
 When you yourself did part them.
 More of this matter cannot I report:
 But men are men; the best sometimes forget:
 Though Cassio did some little wrong to him,
 As men in rage strike those that wish them best, 230
 Yet surely, Cassio, I believe, receiv'd
 From him that fled some strange indignity,
 Which patience could not pass.
OTHELLO.   I know, Iago,

---

85 **collied** darkened.
86 **approv'd in** found guilty of.
87 **court and guard** spot and guarding place, i.e., the main guardhouse.
88 **affin'd** bound by a tie.
89 **execute** give effect to (his anger).

Thy honesty and love doth mince this matter,
Making it light to Cassio. Cassio, I love thee;
But never more be officer of mine.

[*Enter* DESDEMONA, *attended.*]

Look, if my gentle love be not rais'd up!
I'll make thee an example.

DESDEMONA.   What's the matter?   240

OTHELLO. All's well now, sweeting; come away to bed.
Sir, for your hurts, myself will be your surgeon:
Lead him off.   [*To* MONTANO, *who is led off.*]
Iago, look with care about the town,
And silence those whom this vile brawl distracted.
Come, Desdemona: 'tis the soldiers' life
To have their balmy slumbers wak'd with strife.

[*Exit with all but* IAGO *and* CASSIO.]

IAGO. What, are you hurt, lieutenant?

CASSIO. Ay, past all surgery.

IAGO. Marry, God forbid!   250

CASSIO. Reputation, reputation, reputation! O, I have lost my reputation! I have
lost the immortal part of myself, and what remains is bestial. My reputation, Iago, my reputation!

IAGO. As I am an honest man, I thought you had received some bodily wound;
there is more sense in that than in reputation. Reputation is an idle and
most false imposition; oft got without merit, and lost without deserving:
you have lost no reputation at all, unless you repute yourself such a loser.
What, man! there are ways to recover the general again: you are but now
cast in his mood, a punishment more in policy than in malice; even so as
one would beat his offenseless dog to affright an imperious lion: sue to   260
him again, and he's yours.

CASSIO. I will rather sue to be despised than to deceive so good a commander
with so slight, so drunken, and so indiscreet an officer. Drunk? and speak
parrot?[90] and squabble? swagger? swear? and discourse fustian[91] with
one's own shadow? O thou invisible spirit of wine, if thou hast no name to
be known by, let us call thee devil!

IAGO. What was he that you followed with your sword? What had he done
to you?

CASSIO. I know not.

IAGO. Is 't possible?   270

CASSIO. I remember a mass of things, but nothing distinctly; a quarrel, but nothing wherefore. O God, that men should put an enemy in their mouths to
steal away their brains! that we should, with joy, pleasance, revel and applause, transform ourselves into beasts!

IAGO. Why, but you are now well enough. How came you thus recovered?

CASSIO. It hath pleased the devil drunkenness to give place to the devil wrath:
one unperfectness[92] shows me another, to make me frankly despise myself.

---

90 **speak parrot** talk nonsense.
91 **discourse fustian** talk nonsense.
92 **unperfectness** imperfection.

IAGO. Come, you are too severe a moraler: as the time, the place, and the condition of this country stands, I could heartily wish this had not befallen; but, since it is as it is, mend it for your own good.   280

CASSIO. I will ask him for my place again; he shall tell me I am a drunkard! Had I as many mouths as Hydra,[93] such an answer would stop them all. To be now a sensible man, by and by a fool, and presently a beast! O strange! Every inordinate cup is unblessed and the ingredient is a devil.

IAGO. Come, come, good wine is a good familiar creature, if it be well used: exclaim no more against it. And, good lieutenant, I think you think I love you.

CASSIO. I have well approved[94] it, sir. I drunk!

IAGO. You or any man living may be a drunk at a time, man. I'll tell you what you shall do. Our general's wife is now the general: I may say so in this respect, for that he hath devoted and given up himself to the contemplation, mark,   290 and denotement[95] of her parts and graces: confess yourself freely to her; importune her help to put you in your place again: she is of so free, so kind, so apt, so blessed a disposition, she holds it a vice in her goodness not to do more than she is requested: this broken joint between you and her husband entreat her to splinter;[96] and, my fortunes against any lay[97] worth naming, this crack of your love shall grow stronger than it was before.

CASSIO. You advise me well.

IAGO. I protest, in the sincerity of love and honest kindness.

CASSIO. I think it freely; and betimes in the morning I will beseech the virtuous Desdemona to undertake for me. I am desperate of my fortunes if they   300 check[98] me here.

IAGO. You are in the right. Good night, lieutenant; I must to the watch.

CASSIO. Good night, honest Iago.   [*Exit* CASSIO.]

IAGO. And what 's he then that says I play the villain?
When this advice is free I give and honest,
Probal[99] to thinking and indeed the course
To win the Moor again? For 'tis most easy
Th' inclining[100] Desdemona to subdue[101]
In any honest suit: she 's fram'd as fruitful
As the free elements. And then for her   310
To win the Moor—were 't to renounce his baptism,
All seals and symbols of redeemed sin,
His soul is so enfetter'd to her love,
That she may make, unmake, do what she list,
Even as her appetite shall play the god
With his weak function. How am I then a villain
To counsel Cassio to this parallel[102] course,

93 **Hydra** a monster with many heads, slain by Hercules as the second of his twelve labors.
94 **approved** proved.
95 **denotement** observation.
96 **splinter** bind with splints.
97 **lay** stake, wager.
98 **check** repulse.
99 **Probal** probable.
100 **inclining** favorably disposed.
101 **subdue** persuade.
102 **parallel** corresponding to his best interest.

Directly to his good? Divinity of hell!
When devils will the blackest sins put on,[103]
They do suggest[104] at first with heavenly shows,   320
As I do now: for whiles this honest fool
Plies Desdemona to repair his fortunes
And she for him pleads strongly to the Moor,
I'll pour this pestilence into his ear,
That she repeals him[105] for her body's lust;
And by how much she strives to do him good,
She shall undo her credit with the Moor.
So will I turn her virtue into pitch,
And out of her own goodness make the net
That shall enmesh them all.   330

[*Enter* Roderigo.]

How now, Roderigo!

Roderigo. I do not follow here in the chase, not like a hound that hunts, but one that fills up the cry.[106] My money is almost spent; I have been tonight exceedingly well cudgellèd; and I think the issue will be, I shall have so much experience for my pains, and so, with no money at all and a little more wit, return again to Venice.

Iago. How poor are they that have not patience!
What wound did ever heal but by degrees?
Thou know'st we work by wit, and not by witchcraft;
And wit depends on dilatory time.   340
Does 't not go well? Cassio hath beaten thee,
And thou, by that small hurt, hast cashier'd[107] Cassio.
Though other things grow fair against the sun,
Yet fruits that blossom first will first be ripe.
Content thyself awhile. By th' mass, 'tis morning;
Pleasure and action make the hours seem short.
Retire thee; go where thou art billeted.
Away, I say; thou shalt know more hereafter:
Nay, get thee gone.   [*Exit* Roderigo.]
Two things are to be done: 350
My wife must move for Cassio to her mistress;
I'll set her on;
Myself the while to draw the Moor apart,
And bring him jump[108] when he may Cassio find
Soliciting his wife: ay, that's the way:
Dull not device by coldness and delay.

     [*Exit.*]

---

103 **put on** further.
104 **suggest** tempt.
105 **repeals him** i.e., attempts to get him restored.
106 **cry** pack.
107 **cashier'd** dismissed from service.
108 **jump** precisely.

ACT III

SCENE I

Before the castle.

[*Enter* Cassio *and* Musicians.]

Cassio. Masters, play here; I will content[1] your pains;
 Something that 's brief; and bid "Good morrow, general."   [*They play.*]

[*Enter* Clown.]

Clown. Why, masters, have your instruments been in Naples, that they speak i'
 the nose[2] thus?

First Musician. How, sir, how!

Clown. Are these, I pray you, wind-instruments?

First Musician. Ay, marry, are they, sir.

Clown. O, thereby hangs a tail.

First Musician. Whereby hangs a tale,[3] sir?

Clown. Marry, sir, by many a wind-instrument that I know. But, masters, here's   10
 money for you: and the general so likes your music, that he desires you, for
 love's sake, to make no more noise with it.

First Musician. Well, sir, we will not.

Clown. If you have any music that may not be heard, to 't again: but, as they say,
 to hear music the general does not greatly care.

First Musician. We have none such, sir.

Clown. Then put up your pipes in your bag, for I'll away: go; vanish into
 air; away!   [*Exeunt* Musicians.]

Cassio. Dost thou hear, my honest friend?

Clown. No, I hear not your honest friend; I hear you.   20

Cassio. Prithee, keep up thy quillets. There 's a poor piece of gold for thee: if the
 gentlewoman that attends the general's wife be stirring, tell her there 's one
 Cassio entreats her a little favour of speech; wilt thou do this?

Clown. She is stirring, sir: if she will stir hither, I shall seem to notify unto her.

Cassio. Do, good my friend.   [*Exit* Clown.]

[*Enter* Iago.]

 In happy time, Iago.

Iago. You have not been a-bed, then?

Cassio. Why, no; the day had broke
 Before we parted. I have made bold, Iago,
 To send in to your wife: my suit to her   30
 Is, that she will to virtuous Desdemona
 Procure me some access.

Iago.   I'll send her to you presently;

---

 1 **content** reward.

 2 **speak i' the nose** i.e., like Neapolitans, who spoke a nasal dialect (with a joke on syphilis,
which attacks the nose).

 3 **tale** pun on *tail*, a wind instrument of sorts.

And I'll devise a means to draw the Moor
Out of the way, that your converse and business
May be more free.
CASSIO. I humbly thank you for 't.   [*Exit* IAGO.]
                          I never knew
A Florentine more kind and honest.

[*Enter* EMILIA.]

EMILIA. Good morrow, good lieutenant. I am sorry   40
    For your displeasure; but all will sure be well.
    The general and his wife are talking of it;
    And she speaks for you stoutly: the Moor replies,
    That he you hurt is of great fame in Cyprus
    And great affinity[4] and that in wholesome wisdom
    He might not but refuse you, but he protests he loves you
    And needs no other suitor but his likings
    To take the safest occasion by the front[5]
    To bring you in again.
CASSIO.   Yet, I beseech you,   50
    If you think fit, or that it may be done,
    Give me advantage of some brief discourse
    With Desdemona alone.
EMILIA.   Pray you, come in:
    I will bestow you where you shall have time
    To speak your bosom freely.
CASSIO. I am much bound to you.   [*Exeunt.*]

SCENE II

A room in the castle.

[*Enter* OTHELLO, IAGO, *and* GENTLEMEN.]

OTHELLO. These letters give, Iago, to the pilot;
    And by him do my duties to the senate.
    That done, I will be walking on the works.[6]
    Repair there to me.
IAGO.   Well, my good lord, I'll do 't.
OTHELLO. This fortification, gentlemen, shall we see 't?
GENTLEMEN. We'll wait upon your lordship.   [*Exeunt.*]

SCENE III

The garden of the castle.

[*Enter* DESDEMONA, CASSIO, *and* EMILIA.]

DESDEMONA. Be thou assur'd, good Cassio, I will do
    All my abilities in thy behalf.

---

4 **affinity** kindred, family connection.
5 **by the front** i.e., by the forelock.
6 **works** earthworks, fortifications.

EMILIA. Good madam, do. I warrant it grieves my husband,
    As if the case were his.
DESDEMONA. O, that 's an honest fellow. Do not doubt, Cassio,
    But I will have my lord and you again
    As friendly as you were.
CASSIO.   Bounteous madam,
    Whatever shall become of Michael Cassio,
    He's never any thing but your true servant.   10
DESDEMONA. I know 't; I thank you. You do love my lord:
    You have known him long; and be you well assur'd
    He shall in strangeness[7] stand no farther off
    Than in a politic distance.
CASSIO.   Ay, but lady,
    That policy may either last so long
    Or feed upon such nice and waterish diet,
    Or breed itself so out of circumstance,[8]
    That, I being absent and my place supplied,
    My general will forget my love and service.   20
DESDEMONA. Do not doubt[9] that; before Emilia here
    I give thee warrant of thy place: assure thee,
    If I do vow a friendship, I'll perform it
    To the last article: my lord shall never rest;
    I'll watch him tame[10] and talk him out of patience;
    His bed shall seem a school, his board a shrift;[11]
    I'll intermingle every thing he does
    With Cassio's suit: therefore be merry, Cassio;
    For thy solicitor shall rather die
    Than give thy cause away.[12]   30

[*Enter* OTHELLO *and* IAGO *at a distance.*]

EMILIA. Madam, here comes my lord.
CASSIO. Madam, I'll take my leave.
DESDEMONA. Why, stay, and hear me speak.
CASSIO. Madam, not now. I am very ill at ease,
    Unfit for mine own purposes.
DESDEMONA. Well, do your discretion.   [*Exit* CASSIO.]
IAGO. Ha! I like not that.
OTHELLO.   What dost thou say?
IAGO. Nothing, my lord or if—I know not what.
OTHELLO. Was not that Cassio parted from my wife?   40
IAGO. Cassio, my lord! No, sure, I cannot think it,
    That he would steal away so guilty-like,
    Seeing you coming.

---

7 **strangeness** distant behavior.
8 **breed . . . circumstance** increase itself so on account of accidents.
9 **doubt** fear.
10 **watch him tame** tame him by keeping him from sleeping (a term from falconry).
11 **shrift** confessional.
12 **away** up.

OTHELLO. I do believe 'twas he.
DESDEMONA. How now, my lord!
    I have been talking with a suitor here,
    A man that languishes in your displeasure.
OTHELLO. Who is 't you mean?
DESDEMONA. Why, your lieutenant, Cassio. Good my lord,
    If I have any grace or power to move you,   50
    His present reconciliation take;
    For if he be not one that truly loves you,
    That errs in ignorance and not in cunning,
    I have no judgment in an honest face:
    I prithee, call him back.
OTHELLO. Went he hence now?
DESDEMONA. Ay, sooth; so humbled
    That he hath left part of his grief with me,
    To suffer with him. Good love, call him back.
OTHELLO. Not now, sweet Desdemona; some other time.   60
DESDEMONA. But shall 't be shortly?
OTHELLO. The sooner, sweet, for you.
DESDEMONA. Shall 't be to-night at supper?
OTHELLO. No, not to-night.
DESDEMONA. To-morrow dinner, then?
OTHELLO. I shall not dine at home;
    I meet the captain at the citadel.
DESDEMONA. Why, then, to-morrow night; or Tuesday morn;
    On Tuesday noon, or night; on Wednesday morn:
    I prithee, name the time, but let it not   70
    Exceed three days: in faith, he's penitent;
    And yet his trespass, in our common reason[13]—
    Save that, they say, the wars must make examples
    Out of their best—is not almost a fault
    T' incur a private check. When shall he come?
    Tell me, Othello. I wonder in my soul,
    What you would ask me, that I should deny,
    Or stand so mamm'ring on.[14] What! Michael Cassio,
    That came a-wooing with you, and so many a time,
    When I have spoke of you dispraisingly,   80
    Hath ta'en your part; to have so much to do
    To bring him in! Trust me, I could do much,—
OTHELLO. Prithee, no more: let him come when he will;
    I will deny thee nothing.
DESDEMONA. Why, this is not a boon;
    'Tis as I should entreat you wear your gloves,
    Or feed on nourishing dishes, or keep you warm,
    Or sue to you to do a peculiar profit
    To your own person: nay, when I have a suit

---

13 **common reason** everyday judgments.
14 **mamm'ring on** wavering.

Wherein I mean to touch your love indeed, 90
It shall be full of poise[15] and difficult weight
And fearful to be granted.
OTHELLO.   I will deny thee nothing:
Whereon, I do beseech thee, grant me this,
To leave me but a little to myself.
DESDEMONA. Shall I deny you? No: farewell, my lord.
OTHELLO. Farewell, my Desdemona. I'll come to thee straight.
DESDEMONA. Emilia, come. Be as your fancies teach you;
Whate'er you be, I am obedient.   [*Exit with* EMILIA.]
OTHELLO. Excellent wretch![16] Perdition catch my soul, 100
But I do love thee! And when I love thee not,
Chaos is come again.
IAGO. My noble lord—
OTHELLO.   What dost thou say, Iago?
IAGO. Did Michael Cassio, when you woo'd my lady,
Know of your love?
OTHELLO. He did, from first to last: why dost thou ask?
IAGO. But for a satisfaction of my thought;
No further harm.
OTHELLO.   Why of thy thought, Iago? 110
IAGO. I did not think he had been acquainted with her.
OTHELLO. O, yes; and went between us very oft.
IAGO. Indeed!
OTHELLO. Indeed! Ay, indeed: discern'st thou aught in that?
Is he not honest?
IAGO.   Honest, my lord!
OTHELLO.   Honest! ay, honest.
IAGO. My lord, for aught I know.
OTHELLO. What dost thou think?
IAGO.   Think, my lord! 120
OTHELLO.   Think, my lord!
By heaven, he echoes me,
As if there were some monster in his thought
Too hideous to be shown. Thou dost mean something.
I heard thee say even now, thou lik'st not that,
When Cassio left my wife: what didst not like?
And when I told thee he was of my counsel
In my whole course of wooing, thou criedst "Indeed!"
And didst contract and purse thy brow together,
As if thou then hadst shut up in thy brain 130
Some horrible conceit: if thou dost love me,
Show me thy thought.
IAGO. My lord, you know I love you.
OTHELLO.   I think thou dost;
And, for I know thou 'rt full of love and honesty,

---

15 **poise** heaviness.
16 **wretch** term of affectionate endearment with a connotation of pity.

And weigh'st thy words before thou giv'st them breath,
Therefore these stops of thine fright me the more:
For such things in a false disloyal knave
Are tricks of custom, but in a man that's just
They 're close delations,[17] working from the heart   140
That passion cannot rule.

IAGO.   For Michael Cassio,
I dare be sworn I think that he is honest.

OTHELLO. I think so too.

IAGO.   Men should be what they seem;
Or those that be not, would they might seem none!

OTHELLO. Certain, men should be what they seem.

IAGO. Why, then, I think Cassio 's an honest man.

OTHELLO. Nay, yet there 's more in this.
I prithee, speak to me as to thy thinkings,   150
As thou dost ruminate, and give thy worst of thoughts
The worst of words.

IAGO.   Good my lord, pardon me:
Though I am bound to every act of duty,
I am not bound to that all slaves are free to.
Utter my thoughts? Why, say they are vile and false;
As where 's that palace whereinto foul things
Sometimes intrude not? Who has a breast so pure,
But some uncleanly apprehensions
Keep leets[18] and law-days[19] and in sessions sit   160
With meditations lawful?

OTHELLO. Thou dost conspire against thy friend, Iago,
If thou but think'st him wrong'd and mak'st his ear
A stranger to thy thoughts.

IAGO.   I do beseech you—
Though I perchance am vicious[20] in my guess,
As, I confess, it is my nature's plague
To spy into abuses, and oft my jealousy[21]
Shapes faults that are not—that your wisdom yet,
From one that so imperfectly conceits,[22]   170
Would take no notice, nor build yourself a trouble
Out of his scattering and unsure observance.
It were not for your quiet nor your good,
Nor for my manhood, honesty, or wisdom,
To let you know my thoughts.

OTHELLO.   What dost thou mean?

IAGO. Good name in man and woman, dear my lord,

---

17 **close delations** secret or involuntary accusations.
18 **Keep leets** hold courts.
19 **law-days** court days.
20 **vicious** wrong.
21 **jealousy** suspicion of evil.
22 **conceits** judges.

Is the immediate jewel of their souls.
Who steals my purse steals trash: 'tis something, nothing;
'Twas mine, 'tis his, and has been slave to thousands;   180
But he that filches from me my good name
Robs me of that which not enriches him
And makes me poor indeed.
Othello. By heaven, I'll know thy thoughts.
Iago. You cannot, if my heart were in your hand;
Nor shall not, whilst 'tis in my custody.
Othello. Ha!
Iago.   Oh, beware, my lord, of jealousy;
It is the green-ey'd monster which doth mock
The meat it feeds on: that cuckold lives in bliss   190
Who, certain of his fate, loves not his wronger;
But, O, what damned minutes tells he o'er
Who dotes, yet doubts, suspects, yet strongly loves!
Othello. O misery!
Iago. Poor and content is rich and rich enough,
But riches fineless[23] is as poor as winter
To him that ever fears he shall be poor.
Good God, the souls of all my tribe defend
From jealousy!
Othello.   Why, why is this?   200
Think'st thou I'd make a life of jealousy,
To follow still the changes of the moon
With fresh suspicions? No; to be once in doubt
Is once to be resolv'd: exchange me for a goat,
When I shall turn the business of my soul
To such exsufflicate and blown[24] surmises,
Matching thy inference. 'Tis not to make me jealous
To say my wife is fair, feeds well, loves company,
Is free of speech, sings, plays and dances well;
Where virtue is, these are more virtuous;   210
Nor from mine own weak merits will I draw
The smallest fear or doubt of her revolt:
For she had eyes, and chose me. No, Iago;
I'll see before I doubt; when I doubt, prove;
And on the proof, there is no more but this,—
Away at once with love or jealousy!
Iago. I am glad of this; for now I shall have reason
To show the love and duty that I bear you
With franker spirit: therefore, as I am bound,
Receive it from me. I speak not yet of proof.   220
Look to your wife; observe her well with Cassio;
Wear your eye thus, not jealous nor secure:[25]

---

23 **fineless** boundless.
24 **exsufflicate and blown** unsubstantial and inflated, flyblown.
25 **secure** free from uneasiness.

I would not have your free and noble nature,
Out of self-bounty,[26] be abus'd; look to 't.
I know our country disposition well;
In Venice they do let heaven see the pranks
They dare not show their husbands; their best conscience
Is not to leave 't undone, but keep 't unknown.

OTHELLO. Dost thou say so?

IAGO. She did deceive her father, marrying you;   230
And when she seem'd to shake and fear your looks,
She lov'd them most.

OTHELLO.   And so she did.

IAGO.   Why, go to then;
She that, so young, could give out such a seeming,[27]
To seel[28] her father's eyes up close as oak—
He thought 'twas witchcraft—but I am much to blame;
I humbly do beseech you of your pardon
For too much loving you.

OTHELLO.   I am bound to thee for ever.   240

IAGO. I see this hath a little dash'd your spirits.

OTHELLO. Not a jot, not a jot.

IAGO.   I' faith, I fear it has.
I hope you will consider what is spoke
Comes from my love. But I do see y' are mov'd.
I am to pray you not to strain my speech
To grosser issues nor to larger reach[29]
Than to suspicion.

OTHELLO. I will not.

IAGO.   Should you do so, my lord,   250
My speech should fall into such vile success
As my thoughts aim not at. Cassio 's my worthy friend—
My lord, I see y' are mov'd.

OTHELLO.   No, not much mov'd.
I do not think but Desdemona's honest.

IAGO. Long live she so! and long live you to think so!

OTHELLO. And yet, how nature erring from itself,—

IAGO. Ay, there's the point: as—to be bold with you—
Not to affect many proposed matches
Of her own clime, complexion, and degree,   260
Whereto we see in all things nature tends—
Foh! one may smell in such a will[30] most rank,
Foul disproportion,[31] thoughts unnatural.
But pardon me; I do not in position[32]

---

26 **self-bounty** inherent or natural goodness.
27 **seeming** false appearance.
28 **seel** blind (a term from falconry).
29 **reach** meaning.
30 **will** sensuality.
31 **disproportion** abnormality.
32 **position** general argument.

Distinctly speak of her; though I may fear
Her will, recoiling to[33] her better judgment,
May fall to match you with her country forms[34]
And happily repent.[35]
OTHELLO.   Farewell, farewell:
If more thou dost perceive, let me know more;   270
Set on thy wife to observe. Leave me, Iago.
IAGO [*going*]. My lord, I take my leave.
OTHELLO. Why did I marry? This honest creature doubtless
Sees and knows more, much more, than he unfolds.
IAGO [*returning*]. My Lord, I would I might entreat your honour
To scan this thing no farther; leave it to time:
Although 'tis fit that Cassio have his place,
For, sure, he fills it up with great ability,
Yet, if you please to hold him off awhile,
You shall by that perceive him and his means: 280
Note, if your lady strain his entertainment[36]
With any strong or vehement importunity;
Much will be seen in that. In the mean time,
Let me be thought too busy in my fears—
As worthy cause I have to fear I am—
And hold her free,[37] I do beseech your honour.
OTHELLO. Fear not my government.[38]
IAGO. I once more take my leave.   [*Exit.*]
OTHELLO. This fellow 's of exceeding honesty,
And knows all qualities; with a learned spirit,   290
Of human dealings. If I do prove her haggard,[39]
Though that her jesses[40] were my dear heartstrings,
I'd whistle her off and let her down the wind,
To prey at fortune.[41] Haply, for I am black
And have not those soft parts of conversation
That chamberers[42] have, or for I am declin'd
Into the vale of years,—yet that 's not much—
She 's gone. I am abus'd, and my relief
Must be to loathe her. O curse of marriage,
That we can call these delicate creatures ours,   300
And not their appetites! I had rather be a toad,
And live upon the vapour of a dungeon,
Than keep a corner in the thing I love

---

33 **recoiling to** falling back upon, or recoiling against.
34 **fall . . . forms** happen to compare you with Venetian norms of handsomeness.
35 **repent** i.e., of her marriage.
36 **strain his entertainment** urge his reinstatement.
37 **hold her free** regard her as innocent.
38 **government** self-control.
39 **haggard** a wild female duck.
40 **jesses** straps fastened around the legs of a trained hawk.
41 **at fortune** at random.
42 **chamberers** gallants.

For others' uses. Yet, 'tis the plague of great ones;
Prerogativ'd[43] are they less than the base;
'Tis destiny unshunnable, like death:
Even then this forked[44] plague is fated to us
When we do quicken.[45] Look where she comes:

[*Enter* DESDEMONA *and* EMILIA.]

If she be false, O, then heaven mocks itself!
I'll not believe 't.   310

DESDEMONA.   How now, my dear Othello!
Your dinner, and the generous[46] islanders
By you invited, do attend your presence.

OTHELLO. I am to blame.

DESDEMONA.   Why do you speak so faintly?
Are you not well?

OTHELLO. I have a pain upon my forehead here.

DESDEMONA. 'Faith, that 's with watching;[47] 'twill away again.
Let me but bind it hard, within this hour
It will be well.   320

OTHELLO.   Your napkin is too little

[*He puts the handkerchief from him; and it drops.*]

Let it alone. Come, I'll go in with you.

DESDEMONA. I am very sorry that you are not well.   [*Exit with* OTHELLO.]

EMILIA. I am glad I have found this napkin.
This was her first remembrance from the Moor.
My wayward husband hath a hundred times
Woo'd me to steal it; but she so loves the token,
For he conjur'd her she should ever keep it,
That she reserves it evermore about her   330
To kiss and talk to. I'll have the work ta'en out,[48]
And give 't Iago: what he will do with it
Heaven knows, not I;
I nothing but to please his fantasy.

[*Enter* IAGO.]

IAGO. How now! what do you here alone?

EMILIA. Do not you chide; I have a thing for you.

IAGO. A thing for me? it is a common thing[49]—

EMILIA. Ha!

IAGO. To have a foolish wife.

EMILIA. O, is that all? What will you give me now   340

---

43 **Prerogativ'd** privileged.
44 **forked** an allusion to the horns of the cuckold.
45 **quicken** receive life.
46 **generous** noble.
47 **watching** working late.
48 **work ta'en out** design copied.
49 **common thing** *common* suggests coarseness and availability to all, and *thing* is slang for
female sexual organs.

For that same handkerchief?
IAGO.   What handkerchief?
EMILIA. What handkerchief!
    Why, that the Moor first gave to Desdemona;
    That which so often you did bid me steal.
IAGO. Hast stol'n it from her?
EMILIA. No, 'faith; she let it drop by negligence,
    And, to th' advantage, I, being here, took 't up.
    Look, here it is.
IAGO.   A good wench; give it me.   350
EMILIA. What will you do with 't, that you have been so earnest
    To have me filch it?
IAGO.   [*Snatching it.*] Why, what is that to you?
EMILIA. If it be not for some purpose of import,
    Give 't me again: poor lady, she'll run mad
    When she shall lack it.
IAGO. Be not acknown on 't;[50] I have use for it.
    Go, leave me.   [*Exit* EMILIA.]
    I will in Cassio's lodging lose this napkin,
    And let him find it. Trifles light as air   360
    Are to the jealous confirmations strong
    As proofs of holy writ: this may do something.
    The Moor already changes with my poison:
    Dangerous conceits are, in their natures, poisons,
    Which at the first are scarce found to distaste,
    But with a little act[51] upon the blood,
    Burn like the mines of sulphur. I did say so.

[*Enter* OTHELLO.]

    Look, where he comes! Not poppy, nor mandragora,
    Nor all the drowsy syrups of the world,
    Shall ever medicine thee to that sweet sleep   370
    Which thou owedst yesterday.
OTHELLO.   Ha! ha! false to me?
IAGO. Why, how now, general! no more of that.
OTHELLO. Avaunt! be gone! thou has set me on the rack;
    I swear 'tis better to be much abus'd
    Than but to know 't a little.
IAGO.   How now, my lord!
OTHELLO. What sense had I of her stol'n hours of lust?
    I saw 't not, thought it not, it harm'd not me:
    I slept the next night well, fed well, was free and merry;   380
    I found not Cassio's kisses on her lips.
    He that is robb'd, not wanting what is stol'n,
    Let him not know 't, and he 's not robb'd at all.
IAGO. I am sorry to hear this.
OTHELLO. I had been happy, if the general camp,

---

50 **Be . . . on't** do not confess knowledge of it.
51 **act** action, working.

Pioners[52] and all, had tasted her sweet body,
So I had nothing known. O, now, for ever
Farewell the tranquil mind! farewell content!
Farewell the plumed troop, and the big wars,
That make ambition virtue! O, farewell!   390
Farewell the neighing steed, and the shrill trump,
The spirit-stirring drum, th' ear-piercing fife,
The royal banner, and all quality,
Pride, pomp and circumstance[53] of glorious war!
And, O you mortal engines,[54] whose rude throats
Th' immortal Jove's dread clamours counterfeit,
Farewell! Othello's occupation 's gone!

IAGO. Is 't possible, my lord?

OTHELLO. Villain, be sure thou prove my love a whore,
Be sure of it; give me the ocular proof;   400
Or, by the worth of mine eternal soul,
Thou hadst been better have been born a dog
Than answer my wak'd wrath!

IAGO.   Is 't come to this?

OTHELLO. Make me see 't; or, at the least, so prove it,
That the probation bear no hinge nor loop
To hang a doubt on; or woe upon thy life!

IAGO. My noble lord,—

OTHELLO. If thou dost slander her and torture me,
Never pray more; abandon all remorse;   410
On horror's head horrors[55] accumulate;
Do deeds to make heaven weep, all earth amaz'd;
For nothing canst thou to damnation add
Greater than that.

IAGO.   O grace! O heaven forgive me!
Are you a man? Have you a soul or sense?
God be wi' you; take mine office. O wretched fool,
That liv'st to make thine honesty a vice!
O monstrous world! Take note, take note, O world,
To be direct and honest is not safe.   420
I thank you for this profit; and from hence
I'll love no friend, sith love breeds such offense.

OTHELLO. Nay, stay: thou shouldst be honest.

IAGO. I should be wise, for honesty 's a fool
And loses that it works for.

OTHELLO.   By the world,
I think my wife be honest and think she is not;
I think that thou are just and think thou art not.
I'll have some proof. Her name, that was as fresh
As Dian's visage, is now begrim'd and black   430

---

52 **Pioners** sappers, a low grade of soldiers.
53 **circumstance** attendant fact; here, formal display.
54 **mortal engines** i.e., cannon.
55 **horrors** object of *accumulate*.

As mine own face. If there be cords, or knives,
Poison, or fire, or suffocating streams,
I'll not endure it. Would I were satisfied!
IAGO. I see, sir, you are eaten up with passion:
I do repent me that I put it to you.
You would be satisfied?
OTHELLO.   Would! nay, I will.
IAGO. And may: but, how? how satisfied, my lord?
Would you, the supervisor, grossly gape on—
Behold her topp'd?   440
OTHELLO.   Death and damnation! O!
IAGO. It were a tedious difficulty, I think,
To bring them to that prospect: damn them then,
If ever mortal eyes do see them bolster[56]
More than their own! What then? how then?
What shall I say? Where 's satisfaction?
It is impossible you should see this,
Were they as prime as goats, as hot as monkeys,
As salt[57] as wolves in pride, and fools as gross
As ignorance made drunk. But yet, I say,   450
If imputation[58] and strong circumstances,
Which lead directly to the door of truth,
Will give you satisfaction, you may have 't.
OTHELLO. Give me a living reason she 's disloyal.
IAGO. I do not like the office.
But, sith I am ent'red in this cause so far,
Prick'd to 't by foolish honesty and love,
I will go on. I lay with Cassio lately;
And, being troubled with a raging tooth,
I could not sleep.   460
There are a kind of men so loose of soul,
That in their sleeps will mutter their affairs.
One of this kind is Cassio.
In sleep I heard him say "Sweet Desdemona,
Let us be wary, let us hide our loves";
And then, sir, would he grip and wring my hand,
Cry "O sweet creature!" and then kiss me hard,
As if he pluck'd up kisses by the roots
That grew upon my lips: then laid his leg
Over my thigh, and sigh'd and kiss'd; and then   470
Cried "Cursed fate that gave thee to the Moor!"
OTHELLO. O monstrous! monstrous!
IAGO.   Nay, this was but his dream.
OTHELLO. But this denoted a foregone conclusion.[59]

---

56 **bolster** lie together.
57 **salt** wanton, sensual.
58 **imputation** i.e., opinion founded on strong circumstantial evidence.
59 **foregone conclusion** previous trial or experience (not used in our sense).

'Tis a shrewd doubt, though it be but a dream.

IAGO. And this may help to thicken other proofs
That do demonstrate thinly.

OTHELLO.   I'll tear her all to pieces.

IAGO. Nay, but be wise: yet we see nothing done;
    She may be honest yet. Tell me but this,   480
    Have you not sometimes seen a handkerchief
    Spotted with strawberries in your wife's hand?

OTHELLO. I gave her such a one; 'twas my first gift.

IAGO. I know not that: but such a handkerchief—
    I am sure it was your wife's—did I to-day
    See Cassio wipe his beard with.

OTHELLO.   If it be that,—

IAGO. If it be that, or any that was hers,
    It speaks against her with the other proofs.

OTHELLO. O, that the slave had forty thousand lives!   490
    One is too poor, too weak for my revenge.
    Now do I see 'tis true. Look here, Iago;
    All my fond love thus do I blow to heaven.
    'Tis gone.
    Arise, black vengeance, from the hollow hell!
    Yield up, O love, thy crown and hearted[60] throne
    To tyrannous hate! Swell, bosom, with thy fraught,[61]
    For 'tis of aspics'[62] tongues!

IAGO.   Yet be content.

OTHELLO. O, blood, blood, blood!   500

IAGO. Patience, I say; your mind perhaps may change.

OTHELLO. Never, Iago. Like to the Pontic sea,
    Whose icy current and compulsive course
    Ne'er feels retiring ebb, but keeps due on
    To the Propontic and the Hellespont,
    Even so my bloody thoughts, with violent pace,
    Shall ne'er look back, ne'er ebb to humble love,
    Till that a capable and wide revenge
    Swallow them up. Now, by yond marble[63] heaven,
    [*Kneels*] In the due reverence of a sacred vow   510
    I here engage my words.

IAGO.   Do not rise yet.
    [*Kneels.*] Witness, you ever-burning lights above,
    You elements that clip us round about,
    Witness that here Iago doth give up
    The execution[64] of his wit, hands, heart,
    To wrong'd Othello's service! Let him command,

---

60 **hearted** fixed in the heart.
61 **fraught** freight, burden.
62 **aspics'** venemous serpents'.
63 **marble** i.e., gleaming like marble.
64 **execution** exercise.

And to obey shall be in me remorse,⁶⁵
What bloody business ever. [*They rise.*]

OTHELLO.   I greet thy love,   520
Not with vain thanks, but with acceptance bounteous,
And will upon the instant put thee to 't.
Within these three days let me hear thee say
That Cassio 's not alive.

IAGO. My friend is dead; 'tis done at your request:
But let her live.

OTHELLO. Damn her, lewd minx! O, damn her! damn her!
Come, go with me apart; I will withdraw,
To furnish me with some swift means of death
For the fair devil. Now art thou my lieutenant.   530

IAGO. I am your own for ever.   [*Exeunt.*]

SCENE IV

Before the castle.

[*Enter* DESDEMONA, EMILIA, *and* CLOWN.]

DESDEMONA. Do you know, sirrah, where Lieutenant Cassio lies?

CLOWN. I dare not say he lies any where.

DESDEMONA. Why, man?

CLOWN. He's a soldier, and for one to say a soldier lies, is stabbing.

DESDEMONA. Go to: where lodges he?

CLOWN. To tell you where he lodges, is to tell you where I lie.

DESDEMONA. Can any thing be made of this?

CLOWN. I know not where he lodges, and for me to devise a lodging and say he
lies here or he lies there, were to lie in mine own throat.

DESDEMONA. Can you inquire him out, and be edified by report?   10

CLOWN. I will catechize the world for him; that is, make questions, and by them
answer.

DESDEMONA. Seek him, bid him come hither: tell him I have moved my lord on
his behalf, and hope all will be well.

CLOWN. To do this is within the compass of man's wit; and therefore I will attempt
the doing it.   [*Exit* CLOWN.]

DESDEMONA. Where should I lose that handkerchief, Emilia?

EMILIA. I know not, madam.

DESDEMONA. Believe me, I had rather have lost my purse
Full of crusadoes⁶⁶ and but my noble Moor
Is true of mind and made of no such baseness   20
As jealous creatures are, it were enough
To put him to ill thinking.

EMILIA.   Is he not jealous?

---

65 **remorse** pity for Othello's wrongs.
66 **crusadoes** Portuguese gold coins.

DESDEMONA. Who, he? I think the sun where he was born
    Drew all such humours from him.
EMILIA.   Look, where he comes.

    [*Enter* OTHELLO.]

DESDEMONA. I will not leave him now till Cassio
    Be call'd to him.—How is 't with you, my lord?
OTHELLO. Well, my good lady. [*Aside*] O, hardness to dissemble!—   30
    How do you, Desdemona?
DESDEMONA.   Well, my good lord.
OTHELLO. Give me your hand. This hand is moist, my lady.
DESDEMONA. It yet hath felt no age nor known no sorrow.
OTHELLO. This argues fruitfulness and liberal heart.
    Hot, hot, and moist this hand of yours requires
    A sequester[67] from liberty, fasting and prayer,
    Much castigation, exercise devout;
    For here 's a young and sweating devil here,
    That commonly rebels. 'Tis a good hand,   40
    A frank one.
DESDEMONA.   You may, indeed, say so,
    For 'twas that hand that gave away my heart.
OTHELLO. A liberal hand: the hearts of old gave hands;
    But our new heraldry is hands, not hearts.[68]
DESDEMONA. I cannot speak of this. Come now, your promise.
OTHELLO. What promise, chuck?
DESDEMONA. I have sent to bid Cassio come speak with you.
OTHELLO. I have a salt and sorry rheum[69] offends me;
    Lend me thy handkerchief.   50
DESDEMONA.   Here, my lord.
OTHELLO. That which I gave you.
DESDEMONA.   I have it not about me.
OTHELLO. Not?
DESDEMONA. No, indeed, my lord.
OTHELLO.   That 's a fault.
    That handkerchief
    Did an Egyptian[70] to my mother give;
    She was a charmer, and could almost read
    The thoughts of people. She told her, while she kept it,   60
    'Twould make her amiable and subdue my father
    Entirely to her love, but if she lost it
    Or made a gift of it, my father's eye
    Should hold her loathed and his spirits should hunt
    After new fancies: she, dying, gave it me;
    And bid me, when my fate would have me wive,
    To give it her. I did so: and take heed on 't;

---

67 **sequester** separation, sequestration.
68 **new . . . hearts** a current expression referring to marriages in which there is a joining of
hands without the giving of hearts.
69 **sorry rheum** distressful head cold.
70 **Egyptian** gypsy.

Make it a darling like your precious eye;
To lose 't or give 't away were such perdition
As nothing else could match.   70
DESDEMONA.   Is 't possible?
OTHELLO. 'Tis true. There 's magic in the web of it:
A sibyl, that had numb'red in the world
The sun to course two hundred compasses,
In her prophetic fury sew'd the work;
The worms were hallow'd that did breed the silk;
And it was dy'd in mummy[71] which the skilful
Conserv'd of[72] maidens' hearts.
DESDEMONA.   Indeed! is 't true?
OTHELLO. Most veritable; therefore look to 't well.   80
DESDEMONA. Then would to God that I had never seen 't!
OTHELLO. Ha! wherefore?
DESDEMONA. Why do you speak so startingly and rash?
OTHELLO. Is 't lost? is 't gone? speak, is it out o' th' way?
DESDEMONA. Heaven bless us!
OTHELLO. Say you?
DESDEMONA. It is not lost; but what an if it were?
OTHELLO. How!
DESDEMONA. I say, it is not lost.
OTHELLO.   Fetch 't, let me see 't.   90
DESDEMONA. Why, so I can, sir, but I will not now.
This is a trick to put me from my suit:
Pray you, let Cassio be receiv'd again.
OTHELLO. Fetch me the handkerchief: my mind misgives.
DESDEMONA. Come, come;
You'll never meet a more sufficient man.
OTHELLO. The handkerchief!
DESDEMONA.   I pray, talk me of Cassio.
OTHELLO. The handkerchief!
DESDEMONA.   A man that all his time   100
Hath founded his good fortunes on your love,
Shar'd dangers with you,—
OTHELLO. The handkerchief!
DESDEMONA. In sooth, you are to blame.
OTHELLO. Away!   [*Exit* OTHELLO.]

EMILIA. Is not this man jealous?
DESDEMONA. I ne'er saw this before.
Sure, there 's some wonder in this handkerchief:
I am most unhappy in the loss of it.
EMILIA. 'Tis not a year or two shows us a man: 110
They are all but stomachs, and we all but food;
They eat us hungerly, and when they are full,
They belch us.

---

71 **mummy** medicinal or magical preparation drained from the flesh of mummified bodies.
72 **Conserv'd of** preserved out

[*Enter* IAGO *and* CASSIO.]

               Look you, Cassio and my husband!

IAGO. There is no other way; 'tis she must do 't:
   And, lo, the happiness! go, and importune her.

DESDEMONA. How now, good Cassio! what 's the news with you?

CASSIO. Madam, my former suit. I do beseech you
   That by your virtuous means I may again
   Exist, and be a member of his love   120
   Whom I with all the office of my heart
   Entirely honour. I would not be delay'd.
   If my offense be of such mortal kind
   That nor my service past, nor present sorrows,
   Nor purpos'd merit in futurity,
   Can ransom me into his love again,
   But to know so much be my benefit;[73]
   So shall I clothe me in a forc'd content,
   And shut myself up in some other course,
   To fortune's alms.   130

DESDEMONA.   Alas, thrice-gentle Cassio!
   My advocation[74] is not now in tune;
   My lord is not my lord; nor should I know him,
   Were he in favour as in humour alter'd.
   So help me every spirit sanctified
   As I have spoken for you all my best
   And stood within the blank[75] of his displeasure
   For my free speech! You must awhile be patient.
   What I can do I will; and more I will
   Than for myself I dare: let that suffice you.   140

IAGO. Is my lord angry?

EMILIA.   He went hence but now,
   And certainly in strange unquietness.

IAGO. Can he be angry? I have seen the cannon,
   When it hath blown his ranks into the air,
   And, like the devil, from his very arm
   Puff'd his own brother:—and can he be angry?
   Something of moment then. I will go meet him:
   There 's matter in 't indeed, if he be angry.

DESDEMONA. I prithee, do so.   [*Exit* IAGO.]   150

   Something, sure, of state,
   Either from Venice, or some unhatch'd practice
   Made demonstrable here in Cyprus to him,
   Hath puddled[76] his clear spirit; and in such cases
   Men's natures wrangle with inferior things,
   Though great ones are their object. 'Tis even so;

---

73 **to know . . . benefit** to know that my case is hopeless will end my vain endeavor.
74 **advocation** advocacy.
75 **blank** white spot in the center of a target; here, range.
76 **puddled** sullied the purity of.

For let our finger ache, and it indues[77]
Our other healthful members even to a sense
Of pain. Nay, we must think men are not gods,
Nor of them look for such observancy   160
As fits the bridal. Beshrew me much, Emilia,
I was, unhandsome[78] warrior as I am,
Arraigning his unkindness with my soul;
But now I find I had suborn'd the witness,
And he 's indicted falsely.

EMILIA. Pray heaven it be state-matters, as you think,
And no conception[79] nor no jealous toy
Concerning you.

DESDEMONA. Alas the day! I never gave him cause.

EMILIA. But jealous souls will not be answer'd so;   170
They are not ever jealous for the cause,
But jealous for they are jealous: 'tis a monster
Begot upon itself, born on itself.

DESDEMONA. Heaven keep that monster from Othello's mind!

EMILIA. Lady, amen.

DESDEMONA. I will go seek him. Cassio, walk here about:
If I do find him fit, I'll move your suit
And seek to effect it to my uttermost.

CASSIO. I humbly thank your ladyship.   [*Exit* DESDEMONA *with* EMILIA.]

[*Enter* BIANCA.]

BIANCA. Save you, friend Cassio!   180

CASSIO.   What make you from home?
How is 't with you, my most fair Bianca?
I' faith, sweet love, I was coming to your house.

BIANCA. And I was going to your lodging, Cassio.
What, keep a week away? seven days and nights?
Eight score eight hours? and lovers' absent hours,
More tedious than the dial eight score times?
O weary reck'ning!

CASSIO.   Pardon me, Bianca.
I have this while with leaden thoughts been press'd;   190
But I shall, in a more continuate[80] time,
Strike off this score of absence. Sweet Bianca,

[*Giving her* DESDEMONA *'s handkerchief.*]

Take me this work out.[81]

BIANCA.   O Cassio, whence came this?
This is some token from a newer friend:
To the felt absence now I feel a cause:

---

77 **indues** brings to the same condition.
78 **unhandsome** unfair.
79 **conception** mere fancy.
80 **continuate** uninterrupted.
81 **Take . . . out** i.e., copy this embroidery for me.

Is 't come to this? Well, well.

CASSIO.   Go to, woman!
    Throw your vile guesses in the devil's teeth,
    From whence you have them. You are jealous now   200
    That this is from some mistress, some remembrance:
    No, in good troth, Bianca.

BIANCA.   Why, whose is it?

CASSIO. I know not, sweet. I found it in my chamber.
    I like the work well. Ere it be demanded—
    As like enough it will—I would have it copied:
    Take it, and do 't; and leave me for this time.

BIANCA. Leave you! wherefore?

CASSIO. I do attend here on the general;
    And think it no addition, nor my wish,   210
    To have him see me woman'd.

BIANCA.   Why, I pray you?

CASSIO. Not that I love you not.

BIANCA. But that you do not love me.
    I pray you, bring me on the way a little,
    And say if I shall see you soon at night.

CASSIO. 'Tis but a little way that I can bring you;
    For I attend here, but I'll see you soon.

BIANCA. 'Tis very good; I must be circumstance'd.[82]   *[Exeunt omnes.]*

---

82 **circumstance'd** governed by circumstances.

ACT IV

SCENE I

Cyprus. Before the castle.

[*Enter* OTHELLO *and* IAGO.]

IAGO. Will you think so?

OTHELLO.   Think so, Iago!

IAGO.   What,
    To kiss in private?

OTHELLO.   An unauthoriz'd kiss.

IAGO. Or to be naked with her friend in bed
    An hour or more, not meaning any harm?

OTHELLO. Naked in bed, Iago, and not mean harm!
    It is hypocrisy against the devil:
    They that mean virtuously, and yet do so,   10
    The devil their virtue tempts, and they tempt heaven.

IAGO. So[1] they do nothing, 'tis a venial slip:
    But if I give my wife a handkerchief,—

OTHELLO. What then?

IAGO. Why, then, 'tis hers, my lord: and, being hers,

---

1 **So** so long as.

She may, I think, bestow 't on any man.
OTHELLO. She is protectress of her honour too:
    May she give that?
IAGO. Her honour is an essence that 's not seen;
    They have it very oft that have it not: 20
    But, for the handkerchief,—
OTHELLO. By heaven, I would most gladly have forgot it.
    Thou said'st—O, it comes o'er my memory,
    As doth the raven o'er the infected house,[2]
    Boding to all—he had my handkerchief.
IAGO. Ay, what of that?
OTHELLO.   That 's not so good now.   30
IAGO.   What,
    If I had said I had seen him do you wrong?
    Or heard him say,—as knaves be such abroad,
    Who having, by their own importunate suit,
    Or voluntary dotage of some mistress,
    Convinced or supplied[3] them, cannot choose
    But they must blab—   Hath he said any thing?
OTHELLO.
IAGO. He hath, my lord; but be you well assur'd,
    No more than he'll unswear.
OTHELLO.   What hath he said?
IAGO. 'Faith, that he did—I know not what he did.
OTHELLO. What? what?   40
IAGO. Lie—
OTHELLO. With her?
IAGO.   With her, on her; what you will.
OTHELLO. Lie with her! lie on her! We say lie on her, when they belie her. Lie
    with her! that's fulsome.—Handkerchief—confessions—handkerchief—To
    confess, and be hanged for his labour;—first, to be hanged, and then to
    confess.—I tremble at it. Nature would not invest herself in such shadowing
    passion without some instruction.[4] It is not words that shakes me thus. Pish!
    Noses, ears, and lips.—Is 't possible? Confess—handkerchief—O devil!
                                                    [*Falls in a trance.*]
IAGO. Work on,   50
    My medicine, work! Thus credulous fools are caught;
    And many worthy and chaste dames even thus,
    All guiltless, meet reproach. What, ho! my lord!
    My lord, I say! Othello!

    [*Enter* CASSIO.]

                        How now, Cassio!
CASSIO. What 's the matter?
IAGO. My lord is fall'n into an epilepsy:

---

2 **raven . . . house** allusion to the belief that the raven hovered over a house of sickness or
infection.
    3 **Convinced or supplied** i.e., mistresses gained by importunity and those who doted voluntarily.
    4 **Nature . . . instruction** i.e., my jealousy cannot be merely the result of natural imagination,
but must have some foundation in fact.

This is his second fit; he had one yesterday.

CASSIO. Rub him about the temples.

IAGO.   No, forbear;   60
    The lethargy[5] must have his quiet course:
    If not, he foams at mouth and by and by
    Breaks out to savage madness. Look, he stirs:
    Do you withdraw yourself a little while,
    He will recover straight. When he is gone,
    I would on great occasion speak with you.

                                              [Exit CASSIO.]

    How is it, general? Have you not hurt your head?

OTHELLO. Dost thou mock me?

IAGO.   I mock you! no, by heaven.
    Would you would bear your fortune like a man!   70

OTHELLO. A horned man's a monster and a beast.

IAGO. There's many a beast then in a populous city,
    And many a civil[6] monster.

OTHELLO. Did he confess it?

IAGO.   Good sir, be a man;
    Think every bearded fellow that's but yok'd
    May draw with you.[7] There's millions now alive
    That nightly lie in those unproper[8] beds
    Which they dare swear peculiar:[9] your case is better.
    O, 'tis the spite of hell, the fiend's arch-mock,   80
    To lip a wanton in a secure couch,
    And to suppose her chaste! No, let me know;
    And knowing what I am, I know what she shall be.

OTHELLO. O, thou are wise; 'tis certain.

IAGO.   Stand you awhile apart;
    Confine yourself but in a patient list.[10]
    Whilst you were here o'erwhelmed with your grief—
    A passion most unsuiting such a man—
    Cassio came hither. I shifted him away,
    And laid good 'scuse upon your ecstasy,   90
    Bade him anon return and here speak with me;
    The which he promis'd. Do but encave[11] yourself,
    And mark the fleers,[12] the gibes, and notable scorns,
    That dwell in every region of his face;
    For I will make him tell the tale anew,
    Where, how, how oft, how long ago, and when
    He hath, and is again to cope your wife:
    I say, but mark his gesture. Marry, patience;

---

5 **lethargy** unconscious condition.
6 **civil** i.e., in civilized society.
7 **draw with you** i.e, share your fate as cuckold.
8 **unproper** not belonging exclusively to an individual.
9 **peculiar** private, one's own.
10 **patient list** within the bounds of patience.
11 **encave** conceal.
12 **fleers** sneers.

Or I shall say y' are all in all in spleen,
And nothing of a man.   100
OTHELLO.   Dost thou hear, Iago?
      I will be found most cunning in my patience;
      But—dost thou hear?—most bloody.
IAGO.   That 's not amiss;
      But yet keep time[13] in all. Will you withdraw?

                                                            [OTHELLO *retires*.]

      Now will I question Cassio of Bianca,
      A housewife that by selling her desires
      Buys herself bread and clothes: it is a creature
      That dotes on Cassio; as 'tis the strumpet's plague
      To beguile many and be beguil'd by one: 110
      He, when he hears of her, cannot refrain
      From the excess of laughter. Here he comes:

[*Enter* CASSIO.]

      As he shall smile, Othello shall go mad;
      And his unbookish[14] jealousy must conster[15]
      Poor Cassio's smiles, gestures and light behaviour,
      Quite in the wrong. How do you now, lieutenant?
CASSIO. The worser that you give me the addition[16]
      Whose want even kills me.
IAGO. Ply Desdemona well, and you are sure on 't.
      [*Speaking lower*] Now, if this suit lay in Bianca's power,   120
      How quickly should you speed!
CASSIO.   Alas, poor caitiff!
OTHELLO. Look, how he laughs already!
IAGO. I never knew woman love man so.
CASSIO. Alas, poor rogue! I think, i' faith, she loves me.
OTHELLO. Now he denies it faintly, and laughs it out.
IAGO. Do you hear, Cassio?
OTHELLO.   Now he importunes him
      To tell o'er: go to; well said, well said.
IAGO. She gives it out that you shall marry her: 130
      Do you intend it?
CASSIO. Ha, ha, ha!
OTHELLO. Do you triumph, Roman?[17] do you triumph?
CASSIO. I marry her! what? a customer![18] Prithee, bear some charity to my wit; do
      not think it so unwholesome. Ha, ha, ha!
OTHELLO. So, so, so, so they laugh that win.
IAGO. 'Faith, the cry goes that you shall marry her.
CASSIO. Prithee, say true.

---

13 **keep time** use judgment and order.
14 **unbookish** uninstructed.
15 **conster** construe.
16 **addition** title.
17 **Roman** epithet arising from the association of the Romans with the idea of triumph.
18 **customer** prostitute.

Iago. I am a very villain else.

Othello. Have you scored me?[19] Well.   140

Cassio. This is the monkey's own giving out: she is persuaded I will marry her, out of her own love and flattery, not out of my promise.

Othello. Iago beckons me; now he begins the story.

Cassio. She was here even now; she haunts me in every place. I was the other day talking on the seabank with certain Venetians; and thither comes the bauble,[20] and, by this hand, she falls me thus about my neck—

Othello. Crying, 'O dear Cassio!' as it were: his gesture imports it.

Cassio. So hangs, and lolls, and weeps upon me; so shakes, and pulls me ha, ha, ha!

Othello. Now he tells how she plucked him to my chamber. O, I see that nose of yours, but not that dog I shall throw it to.   150

Cassio. Well, I must leave her company.

Iago. Before me![21] look, where she comes.

[*Enter* Bianca.]

Cassio. 'Tis such another fitchew![22] marry, a perfumed one.—What do you mean by this haunting of me?

Bianca. Let the devil and his dam haunt you! What did you mean by that same handkerchief you gave me even now? I was a fine fool to take it. I must take out the work?—A likely piece of work, that you should find it in your chamber, and not know who left it there! This is some minx's token, and I must take out the work? There; give it your hobby-horse.[23] Wheresoever you had it, I'll take out no work on 't.   160

Cassio. How now, my sweet Bianca! how now! how now!

Othello. By heaven, that should be my handkerchief!

Bianca. If you'll come to supper to-night, you may; if you will not, come when you are next prepared for.   [*Exit.*]

Iago. After her, after her.

Cassio. 'Faith, I must; she'll rail in the street else.

Iago. Will you sup there?

Cassio. Yes, I intend so.

Iago. Well, I may chance to see you; for I would very fain speak with you.

Cassio. Prithee, come; will you?   170

Iago. Go to; say no more.   [*Exit* Cassio.]

Othello [*Advancing*]. How shall I murder him, Iago?

Iago. Did you perceive how he laughed at his vice?

Othello. O Iago!

Iago. And did you see the handkerchief?

Othello. Was that mine?

Iago. Yours, by this hand: and to see how he prizes the foolish woman your wife! She gave it him, and he hath given it his whore.

---

19 **scored me** made up my reckoning, or branded me.
20 **bauble** plaything.
21 **Before me!** On my soul!
22 **fitchew** polecat (because of her strong perfume; also, slang word for a prostitute).
23 **hobby-horse** harlot.

OTHELLO. I would have him nine years a-killing. A fine woman! a fair woman! a   180
    sweet woman!

IAGO. Nay, you must forget that.

OTHELLO. Ay, let her rot, and perish, and be damned to-night; for she shall not
    live: no, my heart is turned to stone; I strike it, and it hurts my hand. O,
    the world hath not a sweeter creature: she might lie by an emperor's side
    and command him tasks.

IAGO. Nay, that 's not your way.[24]

OTHELLO. Hang her! I do but say what she is: so delicate with her needle: an
    admirable musician: O! she will sing the savageness out of a bear: of so high
    and plenteous wit and invention:—

IAGO. She 's the worse for all this.   190

OTHELLO. O, a thousand thousand times: and then, of so gentle a condition!

IAGO. Ay, too gentle.

OTHELLO. Nay, that 's certain: but yet the pity of it, Iago! O Iago, the pity of it, Iago!

IAGO. If you are so fond over her iniquity, give her patent[25] to offend; for, if it
    touch not you, it comes near nobody.

OTHELLO. I will chop her into messes;[26] cuckold me!

IAGO. O, 'tis foul in her.

OTHELLO. With mine officer!

IAGO. That 's fouler.

OTHELLO. Get me some poison, Iago; this night I'll not expostulate with her, lest   200
    her body and beauty unprovide[27] my mind again: this night, Iago.

IAGO. Do it not with poison, strangle her in her bed, even the bed she hath
    contaminated.

OTHELLO. Good, good: the justice of it pleases: very good.

IAGO. And for Cassio, let me be his undertaker.[28] You shall hear more by midnight.

OTHELLO. Excellent good. [*A trumpet within.*] What trumpet is that same?

IAGO. I warrant something from Venice.

[*Enter* LODOVICO, DESDEMONA, *and* ATTENDANTS.]

                'Tis Lodovico.
    This comes from the duke: and, see, your wife's with him.

LODOVICO. God save you, worthy general!   210

OTHELLO.   With all my heart, sir.

LODOVICO. The duke and the senators of Venice greet you. [*Gives him a letter.*]

OTHELLO. I kiss the instrument of their pleasures. [*Opens the letter, and reads.*]

DESDEMONA. And what's the news, good cousin Lodovico?

IAGO. I am very glad to see you, signior;
Welcome to Cyprus.

LODOVICO. I thank you. How does Lieutenant Cassio?

IAGO. Lives, sir.

DESDEMONA. Cousin, there's fall'n between him and my lord
    An unkind breach, but you shall make all well.   220

---

24 **your way** i.e., the way you should think of her.
25 **patent** license.
26 **messes** dishes of food.
27 **unprovide** weaken, unfit.
28 **let . . . undertaker** i.e., let me settle with him.

OTHELLO. Are you sure of that?

DESDEMONA. My lord?

OTHELLO [*Reads*]. "This fail you not to do, as you will—"

LODOVICO. He did not call; he's busy in the paper.
     Is there division 'twixt my lord and Cassio?

DESDEMONA. A most unhappy one. I would do much
     T' atone them, for the love I bear to Cassio.

OTHELLO. Fire and brimstone!

DESDEMONA.   My lord?

OTHELLO.   Are you wise?   230

DESDEMONA. What, is he angry?

LODOVICO.   May be the letter mov'd him:
     For, as I think, they do command him home,
     Deputing Cassio in his government.[29]

DESDEMONA. Trust me, I am glad on 't.

OTHELLO.   Indeed!

DESDEMONA.   My lord?

OTHELLO. I am glad to see you mad.

DESDEMONA.   Why, sweet Othello,—

OTHELLO [*Striking her*]. Devil!   240

DESDEMONA. I have not deserv'd this.

LODOVICO. My lord, this would not be believ'd in Venice,
     Though I should swear I saw 't; 'tis very much.
     Make her amends; she weeps.

OTHELLO.   O devil, devil!
     If that the earth could teem with woman's tears,
     Each drop she falls would prove a crocodile.[30]
     Out of my sight!

DESDEMONA.   I will not stay to offend you.   [*Going.*]

LODOVICO. Truly, an obedient lady.   250
     I do beseech your lordship, call her back.

OTHELLO. Mistress!

DESDEMONA.   My lord?

OTHELLO.   What would you with her, sir?

LODOVICO. Who, I, my lord?

OTHELLO. Ay; you did wish that I would make her turn:
     Sir, she can turn, and turn, and yet go on,
     And turn again; and she can weep, sir, weep;
     And she 's obedient, as you say, obedient,
     Very obedient. Proceed you in your tears.   260
     Concerning this, sir,—O well-painted passion!—[31]
     I am commanded home. Get you away;
     I'll send for you anon. Sir, I obey the mandate,
     And will return to Venice. Hence, avaunt!

                                              [*Exit* DESDEMONA.]

-----

29 **government** office.

30 **prove a crocodile** i.e., by weeping crocodile tears; it was believed the crocodile shed tears
over the body of the person it was eating.

31 **well-painted passion** well-simulated emotion.

Cassio shall have my place. And, sir, to-night,
I do entreat that we may sup together.
You are welcome, sir, to Cyprus.—Goats and monkeys!   [*Exit.*]
Lodovico. Is this the noble Moor whom our full senate
  Call all in all sufficient? Is this the nature
  Whom passion could not shake? whose solid virtue   270
  The shot of accident, nor dart of chance,
  Could neither graze nor pierce?
Iago.   He is much chang'd.
Lodovico. Are his wits safe? Is he not light of brain?
Iago. He's that he is. I may not breathe my censure
  What he might be: if what he might he is not,
  I would to heaven he were!
Lodovico.   What, strike his wife!
Iago. 'Faith, that was not so well; yet would I knew
  That stroke would prove the worst!   280
Lodovico.   Is it his use?
  Or did the letters work upon his blood,
  And new-create this fault?
Iago.   Alas, alas!
  It is not honesty in me to speak
  What I have seen and known. You shall observe him,
  And his own courses will denote him so
  That I may save my speech: do but go after,
  And mark how he continues.
Lodovico. I am sorry that I am deceiv'd in him.   [*Exeunt.*]   290

SCENE II

A room in the castle.

[*Enter* Othello *and* Emilia.]

Othello. You have seen nothing then?
Emilia. Nor ever heard, nor ever did suspect.
Othello. Yes, you have seen Cassio and she together.
Emilia. But then I saw no harm, and then I heard
  Each syllable that breath made up between them.
Othello. What, did they never whisper?
Emilia.   Never, my lord.
Othello. Nor send you out 'o th' way?
Emilia. Never.
Othello. To fetch her fan, her gloves, her mask, nor nothing?
Emilia. Never, my lord.   10
Othello. That 's strange.
Emilia. I durst, my lord, to wager she is honest,
  Lay down my soul at stake: if you think other,
  Remove your thought; it doth abuse your bosom.
  If any wretch have put this in your head,
  Let heaven requite it with the serpent's curse!

For, if she be not honest, chaste, and true,
There's no man happy; the purest of their wives
Is foul as slander.
OTHELLO.   Bid her come hither: go.   [*Exit* EMILIA.]   20

She says enough; yet she's a simple bawd
That cannot say as much. This is a subtle whore,
A closet lock and key[32] of villainous secrets:
And yet she'll kneel and pray; I have seen her do't.

[*Enter* DESDEMONA *and* EMILIA.]

DESDEMONA. My lord, what is your will?
OTHELLO.   Pray, chuck, come hither.
DESDEMONA. What is your pleasure?
OTHELLO.   Let me see your eyes;
    Look in my face.
DESDEMONA.   What horrible fancy 's this?   30
OTHELLO [*to Emilia*]. Some of your function,[33] mistress;
    Leave procreants[34] alone and shut the door;
    Cough, or cry "hem," if any body come.
    Your mystery, your mystery:[35] nay, dispatch.   [*Exit* EMILIA.]
DESDEMONA. Upon my knees, what doth your speech import?
    I understand a fury in your words,
    But not the words.
OTHELLO. Why, what art thou?
DESDEMONA.   Your wife, my lord; your true
    And loyal wife.   40
OTHELLO.   Come, swear it, damn thyself;
    Lest, being like one of heaven, the devils themselves
    Should fear to seize thee: therefore be double damn'd:
    Swear thou are honest.
DESDEMONA.   Heaven doth truly know it.
OTHELLO. Heaven truly knows that thou are false as hell.
DESDEMONA. To whom, my lord? with whom? how am I false?
OTHELLO. O Desdemon! away! away! away!
DESDEMONA. Alas the heavy day! Why do you weep?
    Am I the motive of these tears, my lord?   50
    If haply you my father do suspect
    An instrument of this your calling back,
    Lay not your blame on me: if you have lost him,
    Why, I have lost him too.
OTHELLO.   Had it pleas'd heaven
    To try me with affliction; had they[36] rain'd
    All kinds of sores and shames on my bare head,

---

32 **closet lock and key** complete storeroom.
33 **Some . . . function** i.e., set to work in your chosen profession, that of bawd.
34 **procreants** mating couples.
35 **mystery** trade, occupation.
36 **they** heavenly powers.

Steep'd me in poverty to the very lips,
Given to captivity me and my utmost hopes,
I should have found in some place of my soul   60
A drop of patience: but, alas, to make me
A fixed figure for the time of scorn
To point his slow unmoving finger at![37]
Yet could I bear that too; well, very well.
But there, where I have garner'd up my heart,
Where either I must live, or bear no life;
The fountain from the which my current runs,
Or else dries up; to be discarded thence!
Or keep it as a cistern for foul toads
To knot and gender[38] in! Turn thy complexion [39] there,   70
Patience, thou young and rose-lipp'd cherubin,—
Ay, there, look grim as hell!
DESDEMONA. I hope my noble lord esteems me honest.
OTHELLO. O, ay; as summer flies are in the shambles,[40]
That quicken[41] even with blowing. O thou weed,
Who are so lovely fair and smell'st so sweet
That the sense aches at thee, would thou hads't ne'er been born!
DESDEMONA. Alas, what ignorant sin have I committed?   80
OTHELLO. Was this fair paper, this most goodly book,
Made to write "whore" upon? What committed!
Committed! O thou public commoner![42]
I should make very forges of my cheeks,
That would to cinders burn up modesty,
Did I but speak thy deeds. What committed!
Heaven stops the nose at it and the moon winks,
The bawdy wind that kisses all it meets
Is hush'd within the hollow mine of earth,
And will not hear it. What committed!
Impudent strumpet!
DESDEMONA.   By heaven, you do me wrong.   90
OTHELLO. Are not you a strumpet?
DESDEMONA.   No, as I am a Christian.
If to preserve this vessel[43] for my lord
From any other foul unlawful touch
Be not to be a strumpet, I am none.
OTHELLO. What, not a whore?
DESDEMONA.   No, as I shall be sav'd.
OTHELLO. Is't possible?

---

37 **A . . . at** Othello possibly thinks of himself as a man set in a pillory at whom the scornful world points in mockery. There seems to be a comparison with the sundial, whose gnomon, or indicator, becomes the finger of scornful time.
38 **gender** engender.
39 **Turn thy complexion** grow pale.
40 **shambles** slaughterhouse.
41 **quicken** come to life.
42 **commoner** prostitute.
43 **vessel** body.

DESDEMONA. O, heaven forgive us!

OTHELLO.   I cry you mercy, then.   100
>   I took you for the cunning whore of Venice
>   That married with Othello. [*Raising his voice*] You, mistress,
>   That have the office opposite to Saint Peter,
>   And keep the gate of hell!

[*Enter* EMILIA.]

>   You, you, ay, you!
>   We have done our course; there's money for your pains.
>   I pray you, turn the key and keep our counsel.   [*Exit.*]

EMILIA. Alas, what does this gentleman conceive?
>   How do you, madam? how do you, my good lady?

DESDEMONA. 'Faith, half asleep.   110

EMILIA. Good madam, what 's the matter with my lord?

DESDEMONA. With who?

EMILIA. Why, with my lord, madam.

DESDEMONA. Who is thy lord?

EMILIA.   He that is yours, sweet lady.

DESDEMONA. I have none: do not talk to me, Emilia;
>   I cannot weep; nor answers have I none,
>   But what should go by water.[44] Prithee, tonight
>   Lay on my bed my wedding sheets, remember;
>   And call thy husband hither.   120

EMILIA.   Here 's a change indeed!   [*Exit.*]

DESDEMONA. 'Tis meet I should be us'd so, very meet.
>   How have I been behav'd, that he might stick
>   The small'st opinion on my least misuse?[45]

[*Enter* IAGO *and* EMILIA.]

IAGO. What is your pleasure, madam? How is 't with you?

DESDEMONA. I cannot tell. Those that do teach young babes
>   Do it with gentle means and easy tasks:
>   He might have chid me so; for, in good faith,
>   I am a child to chiding.

IAGO.   What is the matter, lady?   130

EMILIA. Alas, Iago, my lord hath so bewhor'd her,
>   Thrown such despite[46] and heavy terms upon her,
>   As true hearts cannot bear.

DESDEMONA. Am I that name, Iago?

IAGO.   What name, fair lady?

DESDEMONA. Such as she said my lord did say I was.

EMILIA. He call'd her whore: a beggar in his drink
>   Could not have laid such terms upon his callet.[47]

IAGO. Why did he so?

DESDEMONA. I do not know; I am sure I am none such.   140

---

44 **go by water** be expressed by tears.
45 **misuse** evil conduct.
46 **despite** contempt, scorn.
47 **callet** lewd woman.

IAGO. Do not weep, do not weep. Alas the day!

EMILIA. Hath she forsook so many noble matches,
    Her father and her country and her friends,
    To be call'd whore? Would it not make one weep?

DESDEMONA. It is my wretched fortune.

IAGO.   Beshrew him for 't!
    How comes this trick upon him?

DESDEMONA.   Nay, heaven doth know.

EMILIA. I will be hang'd, if some eternal villain,
    Some busy and insinuating rogue,   150
    Some cogging,[48] cozening slave, to get some office,
    Have not devis'd this slander; I will be hang'd else.

IAGO. Fie, there is no such man; it is impossible.

DESDEMONA. If any such there be, heaven pardon him!

EMILIA. A halter pardon him! and hell gnaw his bones!
    Why should he call her whore? who keeps her company?
    What place? what time? what form? what likelihood?
    The Moor's abus'd by some most villainous knave,
    Some base notorious knave, some scurvy fellow.
    O heaven, that such companions thou 'dst unfold,   160
    And put in every honest hand a whip
    To lash the rascals naked through the world
    Even from the east to th' west!

IAGO.   Speak within door.[49]

EMILIA. O, fie upon them! Some such squire he was
    That turn'd your wit the seamy side without,
    And made you to suspect me with the Moor.

IAGO. You are a fool; go to.

DESDEMONA.   Alas, Iago.
    What shall I do to win my lord again?   170
    Good friend, go to him; for, by this light of heaven,
    I know not how I lost him. Here I kneel:
    If e'er my will did trespass 'gainst his love,
    Either in discourse of thought or actual deed,
    Or that mine eyes, mine ears, or any sense,
    Delighted them in any other form;
    Or that I do not yet, and ever did,
    And ever will—though he do shake me off
    To beggarly divorcement—love him dearly,
    Comfort forswear me! Unkindness may do much;   180
    And his unkindness may defeat my life,
    But never taint my love. I cannot say "whore":
    It doth abhor me now I speak the word;
    To do the act that might the addition[50] earn
    Not the world's mass of vanity could make me.

IAGO. I pray you, be content; 'tis but his humour:

---

48 **cogging** cheating.
49 **Speak . . . door** i.e., not so loud.
50 **addition** title.

The business of the state does him offense,
And he does chide with you.

DESDEMONA. If 'twere no other,—

IAGO.   'Tis but so, I warrant.   [*Trumpets within.*]   190
Hark, how these instruments summon to supper!
The messengers of Venice stay the meat;[51]
Go in, and weep not; all things shall be well.

                                    [*Exeunt* DESDEMONA *and* EMILIA.]

[*Enter* RODERIGO.]

How now, Roderigo!

RODERIGO. I do not find that thou dealest justly with me.

IAGO. What in the contrary?

RODERIGO. Every day thou daffest me[52] with some device, Iago; and rather, as it
seems to me now, keepest from me all conveniency[53] than suppliest me
with the least advantage of hope. I will indeed no longer endure it, nor am   200
I yet persuaded to put up[54] in peace what already I have foolishly suffered.

IAGO. Will you hear me, Roderigo?

RODERIGO. 'Faith, I have heard too much, for your words and performances are
no kin together.

IAGO. You charge me most unjustly.

RODERIGO. With nought but truth. I have wasted myself out of my means.
The jewels you have had from me to deliver to Desdemona would half
have corrupted a votarist.[55] You have told me she hath received them and
returned me expectations and comforts of sudden respect and acquaintance,
but I find none.   210

IAGO. Well; go to; very well.

RODERIGO. Very well! go to! I cannot go to, man; nor 'tis not very well: nay, I think
it is scurvy, and begin to find myself fopped[56] in it.

IAGO. Very well.

RODERIGO. I tell you 'tis not very well. I will make myself known to Desdemona:
if she will return me my jewels, I will give over my suit and repent my
unlawful solicitation; if not, assure yourself I will seek satisfaction of you.

IAGO. You have said now.[57]

RODERIGO. Ay, and said nothing but what I protest intendment[58] of doing.

IAGO. Why, now I see there's mettle in thee, and even from this instance do build   220
on thee a better opinion than ever before. Give me thy hand, Roderigo.
Thou hast taken against me a most just exception; but yet, I protest, I have
dealt most directly in thy affair.

RODERIGO. It hath not appeared.

IAGO. I grant indeed it hath not appeared, and your suspicion is not without wit
and judgment. But, Roderigo, if thou hast that in thee indeed, which I have

---

51 **stay the meat** are waiting for supper.
52 **daffest me** put me off with an excuse.
53 **conveniency** advantage, opportunity.
54 **put up** submit to.
55 **votarist** nun.
56 **fopped** fooled.
57 **You . . . now** well said, quite right.
58 **intendment** purpose, intention.

greater reason to believe now than ever, I mean purpose, courage and valour, this night show it; if thou the next night following enjoy not Desdemona, take me from this world with treachery and devise engines for[59] my life.

RODERIGO. Well, what is it? Is it within reason and compass?   230

IAGO. Sir, there is especial commission come from Venice to depute Cassio in Othello's place.

RODERIGO. Is that true? Why, then Othello and Desdemona return again to Venice.

IAGO. O, no; he goes into Mauritania[60] and takes away with him the fair Desdemona, unless his abode be lingered here by some accident: wherein none can be so determinate[61] as the removing of Cassio.

RODERIGO. How do you mean, removing of him?

IAGO. Why, by making him uncapable of Othello's place; knocking out his brains.

RODERIGO. And that you would have me to do?   240

IAGO. Ay, if you dare do yourself a profit and a right. He sups to-night with a harlotry,[62] and thither will I go to him: he knows not yet of his honourable fortune. If you will watch his going thence, which I will fashion to fall out between twelve and one, you may take him at your pleasure: I will be near to second your attempt, and he shall fall between us. Come, stand not amazed at it, but go along with me; I will show you such a necessity in his death that you shall think yourself bound to put it on him. It is now high[63] suppertime, and the night grows to waste: about it.

RODERIGO. I will hear further reason for this.

IAGO. And you shall be satisfied.   250

[Exeunt.]

SCENE III

Another room in the castle.

[*Enter* OTHELLO, LODOVICO, DESDEMONA, EMILIA, *and* ATTENDANTS.]

LODOVICO. I do beseech you, sir, trouble yourself no further.

OTHELLO. O, pardon me; 'twill do me good to walk.

LODOVICO. Madam, good night. I humbly thank your ladyship.

DESDEMONA. Your honour is most welcome.

OTHELLO.   Will you walk, sir?
O,—Desdemona,—

DESDEMONA. My lord?

OTHELLO. Get you to bed on th' instant; I will be returned forthwith. Dismiss your attendant there: look 't be done.

DESDEMONA. I will, my lord.   10

[*Exit* OTHELLO, *with* LODOVICO *and* ATTENDANTS.]

EMILIA. How goes it now? He looks gentler than he did.

DESDEMONA. He says he will return incontinent.[64]

---

59 **engines for** plots against.
60 **Mauritania** Roman name of northwest Africa, supposed land of the Moors.
61 **determinate** decisive.
62 **harlotry** courtesan.
63 **high** quite.
64 **incontinent** immediately.

He hath commanded me to go to bed,
And bade me to dismiss you.

EMILIA.   Dismiss me!

DESDEMONA. It was his bidding; therefore, good Emilia,
Give me my nightly wearing, and adieu.
We must not now displease him.

EMILIA. I would you had never seen him!

DESDEMONA. So would not I. My love doth so approve him,   20
That even his stubbornness,[65] his checks,[66] his frowns,—
Prithee, unpin me,—have grace and favour in them.

EMILIA. I have laid those sheets you bade me on the bed.

DESDEMONA. All's one. Good faith, how foolish are our minds!
If I do die before thee, prithee, shroud me
In one of these same sheets.

EMILIA.   Come, come, you talk.

DESDEMONA. My mother had a maid call'd Barbary.
She was in love, and he she lov'd prov'd mad
And did forsake her. She had a song of 'willow';   30
An old thing 'twas, but it express'd her fortune,
And she died singing it. That song to-night
Will not go from my mind; I have much to do,
But to[67] go hang my head all at one side,
And sing it like poor Barbary. Prithee, dispatch.

EMILIA. Shall I go fetch your night-gown?[68]

DESDEMONA.   No, unpin me here.
This Lodovico is a proper man.

EMILIA. A very handsome man.

DESDEMONA. He speaks well.   40

EMILIA. I know a lady in Venice would have walked barefoot to
Palestine for a touch of his nether lip.

DESDEMONA [*Singing*]. "The poor soul sat sighing by a sycamore tree,
        Sing all a green willow;
    Her hand on her bosom, her head on her knee,
        Sing willow, willow, willow.
    The fresh streams ran by her, and murmur'd her moans;
        Sing willow, willow, willow;
    Her salt tears fell from her, and soft'ned the stones;—"
Lay by these —   50
[*Singing*]. "Sing willow, willow, willow"
Prithee, hie thee; he'll come anon —
[*Singing*]. "Sing all a green willow must be my garland.
        Let nobody blame him; his scorn I approve,—"
Nay, that's not next.—Hark! who is 't that knocks?

EMILIA. It 's the wind.

---

65 **stubbornness** harshness.
66 **checks** rebukes.
67 **But to** not to.
68 **night-gown** dressing gown.

DESDEMONA [*Singing*]. "I call'd my love false love; but what said he then?
　　　Sing willow, willow, willow:
　　　If I court moe women, you'll couch with moe men.—"
So, get thee gone; good night. Mine eyes do itch;　　　　　　　60
Doth that bode weeping?
EMILIA.　　　　　　　　　'Tis neither here nor there.
DESDEMONA. I have heard it said so. O, these men, these men!
　　　Dost thou in conscience think,—tell me, Emilia,—
　　　That there be women do abuse their husbands
　　　In such gross kind?
EMILIA.　　　　　　There be some such, no question.
DESDEMONA. Wouldst thou do such a deed for all the world?
EMILIA. Why, would not you?
DESDEMONA.　　　　　No, by this heavenly light!　　　　　70
EMILIA. Nor I neither by this heavenly light; I might do 't as well i' the dark.
DESDEMONA. Wouldst thou do such a deed for all the world?
EMILIA. The world 's a huge thing: it is a great price
　　　For a small vice.
DESDEMONA. In troth, I think thou wouldst not.
EMILIA. In troth, I think I should; and undo 't when I had done. Marry, I would
　　　not do such a thing for a joint-ring,[69] nor for measures of lawn, nor for
　　　gowns, petticoats, nor caps, nor any petty exhibition;[70] for all the whole
　　　world,—why, who would not make her husband a cuckold to make him a
　　　monarch? I should venture purgatory for 't.
DESDEMONA. Beshrew me, if I would do such a wrong　　　　　80
　　　For the whole world.
EMILIA. Why, the wrong is but a wrong i' the world; and having the world for
　　　your labour, 'tis a wrong in your own world, and you might quickly make
　　　it right.
DESDEMONA. I do not think there is any such woman.
EMILIA. Yes, a dozen; and as many
　　　To the vantage[71] as would store the world they played for.
　　　But I do think it is their husband's faults
　　　If wives do fall. Say that they slack their duties,
　　　And pour our treasures into foreign laps,[72]　　　　　90
　　　Or else break out in peevish jealousies,
　　　Throwing restraint upon us; or say they strike us,
　　　Or scant our former having in despite;[73]
　　　Why, we have galls,[74] and though we have some grace,[75]
　　　Yet have we some revenge. Let husbands know
　　　Their wives have sense like them: they see and smell
　　　And have their palates both for sweet and sour,

---

69 **joint-ring** a ring made in separable halves as a lover's token.
70 **exhibition** gift, present.
71 **to the vantage** in addition.
72 **pour . . . laps** i.e., are unfaithful.
73 **scant . . . despite** reduce our allowance to spite us.
74 **have galls** are capable of resenting injury and insult.
75 **grace** i.e., to forgive.

As husbands have. What is it that they do
When they change us for others? Is it sport?
I think it is. And doth affection breed it? 100
I think it doth. Is 't frailty that thus errs?
It is so too. And have not we affections,
Desires for sport, and frailty, as men have?
Then let them use us well: else let them know,
The ills we do, their ills instruct us so.
DESDEMONA. Good night, good night: heaven me such uses send,
Not to pick bad from bad, but by bad mend! [*Exeunt.*]

ACT V

SCENE I

Cyprus. A street.

[*Enter* IAGO *and* RODERIGO.]

IAGO. Here stand behind this bulk;[1] straight will he come:
Wear thy good rapier bare, and put it home:
Quick, quick; fear nothing; I'll be at thy elbow:
It makes us, or it mars us; think on that,
And fix most firm thy resolution.
RODERIGO. Be near at hand; I may miscarry in 't.
IAGO. Here, at thy hand: be bold, and take thy stand. [*Retires.*]
RODERIGO. I have no great devotion to the deed;
And yet he hath given me satisfying reasons:
'Tis but a man gone. Forth, my sword: he dies. 10
IAGO. I have rubb'd this young quat[2] almost to the sense,[3]
And he grows angry. Now, whether he kill Cassio,
Or Cassio him, or each do kill the other,
Every way makes my gain. Live Roderigo,
He calls me to a restitution large
Of gold and jewels that I bobb'd[4] from him,
As gifts to Desdemona;
It must not be. If Cassio do remain,
He hath a daily beauty in his life
That makes me ugly; and, besides, the Moor 20
May unfold me to him; there stand I in much peril:
No, he must die. But so: I hear him coming.

[*Enter* CASSIO.]

RODERIGO. I know his gait, 'tis he.—Villain, thou diest!

[*Makes a pass at* CASSIO.]

CASSIO. That thrust had been mine enemy indeed,

---

1 **bulk** framework projecting from the front of a shop.
2 **quat** pimple, pustule; used contemptuously.
3 **to the sense** to the quick.
4 **bobb'd** filched cunningly.

But that my coat[5] is better than thou know'st.
I will make proof of thine. [*Draws, and wounds* RODERIGO.]
RODERIGO.   O, I am slain!
          [IAGO *from behind wounds* CASSIO *in the leg, and exits.*]
CASSIO. I am maim'd for ever. Help, ho! murder! murder!   [*Falls.*]

     [*Enter* OTHELLO.]

OTHELLO. The voice of Cassio. Iago keeps his word.
RODERIGO. O, villain that I am!
OTHELLO.   It is even so.   30
CASSIO. O, help, ho! light! a surgeon!
OTHELLO. 'Tis he: —O brave Iago, honest and just,
          That hast such noble sense of thy friend's wrong!
          Thou teachest me. Minion, your dear lies dead,
          And your unblest fate hies: strumpet, I come.
          Forth of my heart those charms, thine eyes, are blotted;
          Thy bed, lust-stain'd, shall with lust's blood be spotted.
                                                        [*Exit* OTHELLO.]

     [*Enter* LODOVICO *and* GRATIANO.]

CASSIO. What, ho! no watch? no passage?[6] murder! murder!
GRATIANO. 'Tis some mischance; the cry is very direful.
CASSIO. O, help!   40
LODOVICO. Hark!
RODERIGO. O wretched villain!
LODOVICO. Two or three groan. It is a heavy[7] night;
          These may be counterfeits. Let 's think 't unsafe
          To come in to the cry without more help.
RODERIGO. Nobody come? Then shall I bleed to death.
LODOVICO. Hark!

     [*Enter* IAGO with a light.]

GRATIANO. Here's one comes in his shirt, with light and weapons.
IAGO. Who's there? Whose noise is this that cries on[8] murder?
LODOVICO. We do not know.   50
IAGO.   Did not you hear a cry?
CASSIO. Here, here! for heaven's sake, help me!
IAGO.   What's the matter?
GRATIANO. This is Othello's ancient, as I take it.
LODOVICO. The same indeed; a very valiant fellow.
IAGO. What are you here that cry so grievously?
CASSIO. Iago? O, I am spoil'd, undone by villains!
          Give me some help.
IAGO. O me, lieutenant! what villains have done this?
CASSIO. I think that one of them is hereabout,
          And cannot make away.   60

---

5 **coat** coat of mail.
6 **passage** people passing.
7 **heavy** thick, cloudy.
8 **cries on** cries out.

IAGO.   O treacherous villains!
    What are you there? Come in, and give some help.
                                        [*To* LODOVICO *and* GRATIANO.]
RODERIGO. O, help me here!
CASSIO. That's one of them.
IAGO.   O murd'rous slave! O villain!
                                        [*Stabs* RODERIGO.]
RODERIGO. O damn'd Iago! O inhuman dog!
IAGO. Kill men i' th' dark!—Where be these bloody thieves?—
    How silent in this town!—Ho! murder! murder!—
    What[9] you be? Are you of good or evil?
LODOVICO. As you shall prove us, praise us.
IAGO. Signior Lodovico?   70
LODOVICO. He, sir.
IAGO. I cry you mercy. Here's Cassio hurt by villains.
GRATIANO. Cassio!
IAGO. How is 't, brother!
CASSIO. My leg is cut in two.
IAGO.   Marry, heaven forbid!
    Light, gentlemen. I'll bind it with my shirt.

    [*Enter* BIANCA.]

BIANCA. What is the matter, ho? Who is 't that cried?
IAGO. Who is 't that cried?
BIANCA. O my dear Cassio! my sweet Cassio!
    O Cassio, Cassio, Cassio!   80
IAGO. O notable strumpet! Cassio, may you suspect
    Who they should be that have thus mangled you?
CASSIO. No.
GRATIANO. I am sorry to find you thus: I have been to seek you.
IAGO. Lend me a garter. So. O, for a chair,[10]
    To bear him easily hence!
BIANCA. Alas, he faints! O Cassio, Cassio, Cassio!
IAGO. Gentlemen all, I do suspect this trash[11]
    To be a party in this injury.
    Patience awhile, good Cassio. Come, come;   90
    Lend me a light. Know we this face or no?
    Alas, my friend and my dear countryman
    Roderigo! no:—yes, sure:—O heaven! Roderigo.
GRATIANO. What, of Venice?
IAGO. Even he, sir: did you know him?
GRATIANO.   Know him! ay.
IAGO. Signior Gratiano? I cry your gentle pardon;
    These bloody accidents must excuse my manners,
    That so neglected you.
GRATIANO.   I am so glad to see you.   100
IAGO. How do you, Cassio? O, a chair, a chair!

---

9 **What** who.
10 **chair** sedan chair.
11 **trash** worthless thing—i.e., Bianca.

GRATIANO. Roderigo!

IAGO. He, he, 'tis he. [*A chair brought in.*] O, that's well said; the chair.
Some good man bear him carefully from hence;
I'll fetch the general's surgeon. [*To* BIANCA] For you, mistress,
Save you your labour. He that lies slain here, Cassio,
Was my dear friend: what malice was between you?

CASSIO. None in the world; nor do I know the man.

IAGO [*To* BIANCA]. What, look you pale? O, bear him out o' th' air.

[CASSIO *and* RODERIGO *are borne off.*]

Stay you, good gentlemen. Look you pale, mistress?   110
Do you perceive the gastness[12] of her eye?
Nay, if you stare, we shall hear more anon.
Behold her well; I pray you, look upon her:
Do you see, gentlemen? Nay, guiltiness will speak,
Though tongues were out of use.

[*Enter* EMILIA.]

EMILIA. 'Las, what's the matter? what's the matter, husband?

IAGO. Cassio hath here been set on in the dark
By Roderigo and fellows that are scap'd:
He's almost slain, and Roderigo dead.

EMILIA. Alas, good gentlemen! alas, good Cassio!   120

IAGO. This is the fruit of whoring. Prithee, Emilia,
Go know of Cassio where he supp'd to-night.
[*To* BIANCA] What, do you shake at that?

BIANCA. He supp'd at my house; but I therefore shake not.

IAGO. O, did he so? I charge you, go with me.

EMILIA. Fie, fie upon thee, strumpet!

BIANCA. I am no strumpet; but of life as honest
As you that thus abuse me.

EMILIA.   As I! foh! fie upon thee!

IAGO. Kind gentlemen, let's go see poor Cassio dress'd.
Come, mistress, you must tell's another tale.   130
Emilia, run you to the citadel,
And tell my lord and lady what hath happ'd.
Will you go on afore? [*Aside*] This is the night
That either makes me or fordoes[13] me quite.   [*Exeunt.*]

SCENE II

A bedchamber in the castle.

[*Enter* OTHELLO *with a light;* DESDEMONA *in her bed.*]

OTHELLO. It is the cause, it is the cause,[14] my soul,—
Let me not name it to you, you chaste stars!—

---

12 **gastness** terror, ghastliness.
13 **fordoes** undoes, ruins.
14 **It is the cause** i.e., the cause of justice on which Othello must act, Desdemona's deed, which is too unmentionable to be named to the chaste stars.

It is the cause. Yet I'll not shed her blood;
Nor scar that whiter skin of hers than snow,
And smooth as monumental alabaster.
Yet she must die, else she'll betray more men.
Put out the light, and then put out the light:
If I quench thee, thou flaming minister,
I can again thy former light restore,
Should I repent me: but once put out thy light,   10
Thou cunning'st pattern of excelling nature,
I know not where is that Promethean heat[15]
That can thy light relume.[16] When I have pluck'd the rose,
I cannot give it vital growth again,
It needs must wither: I'll smell thee on the tree.   [*Kissing her.*]
O balmy breath, that dost almost persuade
Justice to break her sword! One more, one more.
Be thus when thou art dead, and I will kill thee,
And love thee after. One more, and that's the last:
So sweet was ne'er so fatal. I must weep,   20
But they are cruel tears: this sorrow 's heavenly;[17]
It strikes where it doth love. She wakes.

DESDEMONA. Who's there? Othello?
OTHELLO.   Ay, Desdemona.
DESDEMONA. Will you come to bed, my lord?
OTHELLO. Have you pray'd to-night, Desdemon?
DESDEMONA.   Ay, my lord.
OTHELLO. If you bethink yourself of any crime
    Unreconcil'd as yet to heaven and grace,
    Solicit for it straight.   30
DESDEMONA. Alack, my lord, what may you mean by that?
OTHELLO. Well, do it, and be brief; I will walk by:
    I would not kill thy unprepared spirit;
    No; heaven forfend! I would not kill thy soul.
DESDEMONA. Talk you of killing?
OTHELLO.   Ay, I do.
DESDEMONA.   Then heaven
    Have mercy on me!
OTHELLO.   Amen, with all my heart!
DESDEMONA. If you say so, I hope you will not kill me.
OTHELLO. Hum!   40
DESDEMONA. And yet I fear you; for you're fatal then
    When your eyes roll so: why I should fear I know not,
    Since guiltiness I know not; but yet I feel I fear.
OTHELLO. Think on thy sins.
DESDEMONA.   They are loves I bear to you.

---

15 **Promethean heat** divine fire; allusion to the theft of fire from heaven by Prometheus.
16 **relume** rekindle.
17 **this . . . heavenly** this tenderness, with which I lament the punishment which justice compels me to inflict, is a holy passion.

OTHELLO. Ay, and for that thou diest.
DESDEMONA. That death 's unnatural that kills for loving.
 Alas, why gnaw you so your nether lip?
 Some bloody passion shakes your very frame: 50
 These are portents; but yet I hope, I hope,
 They do not point on me.
OTHELLO.   Peace, and be still!
DESDEMONA. I will so. What 's the matter?
OTHELLO. That handkerchief which I so lov'd and gave thee
 Thou gav'st to Cassio.
DESDEMONA.   No, by my life and soul!
 Send for the man, and ask him.
OTHELLO.   Sweet soul, take heed,
 Take heed of perjury; thou are on thy deathbed.   60
DESDEMONA. Ay, but not yet to die.
OTHELLO.   Yes, presently:
 Therefore confess thee freely of thy sin;
 For to deny each article with oath
 Cannot remove nor choke the strong conception[18]
 That I do groan withal. Thou art to die.
DESDEMONA. Then Lord have mercy on me!
OTHELLO.   I say, amen.
DESDEMONA. And have you mercy too! I never did
 Offend you in my life; never lov'd Cassio   70
 But with such general warranty of heaven
 As I might love; I never gave him token.
OTHELLO. By heaven, I saw my handkerchief in 's hand.
 O perjur'd woman! thou dost stone[19] my heart,
 And makes me call what I intend to do
 A murder, which I thought a sacrifice:
 I saw the handkerchief.
DESDEMONA.   He found it then;
 I never gave it him: send for him hither;
 Let him confess a truth.   80
OTHELLO.   He hath confess'd.
DESDEMONA. What, my Lord?
OTHELLO. That he hath us'd thee.
DESDEMONA.   How? unlawfully?
OTHELLO.   Ay.
DESDEMONA. He will not say so.
OTHELLO.   No, his mouth is stopp'd;
 Honest Iago hath ta'en order[20] for 't.
DESDEMONA. O! my fear interprets: what, is he dead?
OTHELLO. Had all his hairs been lives, my great revenge   90
 Had stomach for them all.

---

18 **conception** plan, intention.
19 **stone** turn to stone, harden; Othello means that he will be tempted to kill her in sheer anger because of her perjury.
20 **ta'en order** taken measures.

DESDEMONA. Alas! he is betray'd and I undone.

OTHELLO. Out, strumpet! weep'st thou for him to my face?

DESDEMONA. O, banish me, my lord, but kill me not!

OTHELLO. Down, strumpet!

DESDEMONA. Kill me to-morrow: let me live to-night!

OTHELLO. Nay, if you strive,—

DESDEMONA. But half an hour!

OTHELLO.   Being done, there is no pause.[21]

DESDEMONA. But while I say one prayer!   90

OTHELLO.   It is too late.   [*Smothers her.*]

EMILIA [*at the door*]. My lord, my lord! what, ho! my lord, my lord!

OTHELLO. What noise is this? Not dead? not yet quite dead?
    I that am cruel am yet merciful;
    I would not have thee linger in thy pain:
    So, so.

EMILIA [*within*]. What, ho! my lord, my lord!

OTHELLO.   Who's there?

EMILIA [*within*]. O, good my lord, I would speak a word with you!

OTHELLO. Yes: 'tis Emilia. By and by. She 's dead.   100
    'Tis like she comes to speak of Cassio's death.—
    The noise was here. Ha! no more moving?
    Still as the grave. Shall she come in? were 't good?—
    I think she stirs again:—no. What 's best to do?
    If she come in, she'll sure speak to my wife.
    My wife! my wife! what wife? I have no wife.
    O, insupportable! O heavy hour!
    Methinks it should be now a huge eclipse
    Of sun and moon, and that th' affrighted globe
    Should yawn[22] at alteration.[23]   110

EMILIA.   [*Within*] I do beseech you
    That I may speak with you, O, good my lord!

OTHELLO. I had forgot thee: O, come in, Emilia:
    Soft; by and by. Let me the curtains draw.
    Where art thou?   [*Closes bed-curtains and opens door.*]

[*Enter* EMILIA.]

                What's the matter with thee now?

EMILIA. O, my good lord, yonder's foul murders done!

OTHELLO. What, now?

EMILIA. But now, my lord.

OTHELLO. It is the very error[24] of the moon;   120
    She comes more nearer earth than she was wont,
    And makes men mad.

---

21 **Being . . . pause** i.e., when the execution of the deed has once begun, there is no stopping.

22 **yawn** gape in amazement.

23 **at alteration** at the change.

24 **error** irregularity.

EMILIA. Cassio, my lord, hath kill'd a young Venetian
    Call'd Roderigo.
OTHELLO.   Roderigo kill'd!
    And Cassio kill'd!
EMILIA.   No, Cassio is not kill'd.
OTHELLO. Not Cassio kill'd! Then murder 's out of tune,
    And sweet revenge grows harsh.
DESDEMONA. O, falsely, falsely murder'd!   130
EMILIA.   Alas, what cry is that?
OTHELLO. That! what?
EMILIA. Out, and alas! that was my lady's voice.
    Help, help, ho! help. O lady, speak again!
    Sweet Desdemona! O sweet mistress, speak!
DESDEMONA. A guiltless death I die.
EMILIA. O, who hath done this deed?
DESDEMONA. Nobody; I myself. Farewell:
    Commend me to my kind lord: O, farewell!   [*Dies.*]
OTHELLO. Why, how should she be murd'red?   140
EMILIA.   Alas, who knows?
OTHELLO. You heard her say herself, it was not I.
EMILIA. She said so: I must needs report the truth.
OTHELLO. She's, like a liar, gone to burning hell:
    'Twas I that kill'd her.
EMILIA.   O, the more angel she,
    And you the blacker devil!
OTHELLO. She turn'd to folly,[25] and she was a whore.
EMILIA. Thou dost belie her, and thou art a devil.
OTHELLO. She was false as water.   150
EMILIA.   Thou art rash as fire, to say
    That she was false: O, she was heavenly true!
OTHELLO. Cassio did top her; ask thy husband else.
    O, I were damned beneath all depth in hell,
    But that I did proceed upon just grounds
    To this extremity. Thy husband knew it all.
EMILIA. My husband!
OTHELLO. Thy husband.
EMILIA. That she was false to wedlock?
OTHELLO. Ay, with Cassio. Nay, had she been true,   160
    If heaven would make me such another world
    Of one entire and perfect chrysolite,[26]
    I'd not have sold her for it.
EMILIA. My husband!
OTHELLO.   Ay, 'twas he that told me first:
    An honest man he is, and hates the slime
    That sticks on filthy deeds.

---

25 **folly** unchastity.
26 **chrysolite** the golden stone; a name given to various precious stones of green color.

EMILIA.   My husband!

OTHELLO. What needs this iterance,[27] woman? I say thy husband.

EMILIA. O mistress, villainy hath made mocks with[28] love!   170
    My husband say that she was false!

OTHELLO.   He, woman;
    I say thy husband: dost understand the word?
    My friend, thy husband, honest, honest Iago.

EMILIA. If he say so, may his pernicious soul
    Rot half a grain a day! He lies to th' heart:
    She was too fond of her most filthy bargain.

OTHELLO. Ha!

EMILIA. Do thy worst:
    This deed of thine is no more worthy heaven   180
    Than thou wast worthy her.

OTHELLO.   Peace, you were best.

EMILIA. Thou hast not half that power to do me harm
    As I have to be hurt.[29] O gull! O dolt!
    As ignorant as dirt! thou has done a deed—
    I care not for thy sword; I'll make thee known,
    Though I lost twenty lives.—Help! help, ho! help!
    The Moor hath kill'd my mistress! Murder! murder!

[*Enter* MONTANO, GRATIANO, *and* IAGO *with others.*]

MONTANO. What is the matter? How now, general!

EMILIA. O, are you come, Iago? You have done well,   190
    That men must lay their murders on your neck.

GRATIANO. What is the matter?

EMILIA. Disprove this villain, if thou be'st a man:
    He says thou told'st him that his wife was false:
    I know thou didst not, thou'rt not such a villain:
    Speak, for my heart is full.

IAGO. I told him what I thought, and told no more
    Than what he found himself was apt[30] and true.

EMILIA. But did you ever tell him she was false?

IAGO. I did.   200

EMILIA. You told a lie; an odious, damned lie;
    Upon my soul, a lie, a wicked lie.
    She false with Cassio!—did you say with Cassio?

IAGO. With Cassio, mistress. Go to, charm[31] your tongue.

EMILIA. I will not charm my tongue; I am bound to speak:
    My mistress here lies murdered in her bed,—

ALL. O heavens forfend!

EMILIA. And your reports have set the murder on.

---

27 **iterance** iteration, repetition.
28 **made mocks with** derided, made sport of.
29 **to be hurt** i.e., to endure hurting.
30 **apt** natural, likely.
31 **charm** keep silent.

OTHELLO. Nay, stare not, masters: it is true, indeed.

GRATIANO. 'Tis a strange truth. 210

MONTANO. O monstrous act!

EMILIA.   Villainy, villainy, villainy!
 I think upon't, I think: I smell't: O villainy—
 I thought so then:[32] I'll kill myself for grief:—
 O villainy, villainy!

IAGO. What, are you mad? I charge you, get you home.

EMILIA. Good gentlemen, let me have leave to speak:
 'Tis proper I obey him, but not now.
 Perchance, Iago, I will ne'er go home.

OTHELLO. O! O! O!   [*He falls on the bed.*] 220

EMILIA.   Nay, lay thee down and roar;
 For thou hast kill'd the sweetest innocent
 That e'er did lift up eye.

OTHELLO.   [*Rising*] O, she was foul!
 I scarce did know you, uncle: there lies your niece,
 Whose breath, indeed, these hands have newly stopp'd:
 I know this act shows horrible and grim.

GRATIANO. Poor Desdemon! I am glad thy father's dead:
 Thy match was mortal to him, and pure grief
 Shore[33] his old thread in twain: did he live now, 230
 This sight would make him do a desperate turn,
 Yea, curse his better angel from his side,
 And fall to reprobation.[34]

OTHELLO. 'Tis pitiful; but yet Iago knows
 That she with Cassio hath the act of shame
 A thousand times committed; Cassio confess'd it:
 And she did gratify his amorous works
 With that recognizance[35] and pledge of love
 Which I first gave her; I saw it in his hand:
 It was a handkerchief, an antique token 240
 My father gave my mother.

EMILIA. O heaven! O heavenly pow'rs!

IAGO. Come, hold your peace.

EMILIA.   'Twill out, 'twill out: I peace?
 No, I will speak as liberal as the north:[36]
 Let heaven and men and devils, let them all,
 All, all, cry shame against me, yet I'll speak.

IAGO. Be wise, and get you home.

EMILIA.   I will not! [IAGO *offers to stab* EMILIA.]

GRATIANO.   Fie!
 Your sword upon a woman? 250

EMILIA. O thou dull Moor! that handkerchief thou speak'st of

---

32 **then** i.e., at some earlier time, probably IV, ii, when she suspected the machinations of *some eternal villain*; she did not, however, know that villain to be Iago until this moment.

33 **Shore** cut.

34 **reprobation** damnation, rejection by God.

35 **recognizance** token.

36 **liberal as the north** freely as the north wind.

I found by fortune[37] and did give my husband;
For often, with solemn earnestness,
More than indeed belong'd to such a trifle,
He begg'd me to steal it.

IAGO.   Villainous whore!

EMILIA. She give it Cassio! no, alas! I found it,
And I did give't my husband.

IAGO.   Filth, thou liest!

EMILIA. By heaven, I do not, I do not, gentlemen.   260
O murd'rous coxcomb![38] what should such a fool
Do with so good a wife!

OTHELLO.   Are there no stones in heaven[39]
But what serves for the thunder?—Precious villain!

                    [*He runs at* IAGO; IAGO, *from behind,*
                              stabs EMILIA, *and exits.*]

GRATIANO. The woman falls; sure, he hath kill'd his wife.

EMILIA. Ay, ay: O, lay me by my mistress' side.

GRATIANO. He 's gone, but his wife 's kill'd.

MONTANO. 'Tis a notorious villain. Take you this weapon,
Which I have here recover'd from the Moor:
Come, guard the door without; let him not pass,   270
But kill him rather. I'll after that same villain,
For 'tis a damned slave.   [*Exit with all but* OTHELLO *and* EMILIA.]

OTHELLO.   I am not valiant neither,
But every puny whipster[40] gets my sword:
But why should honour outlive honesty?[41]
Let it go all.

EMILIA.   What did thy song bode, lady?
Hark, canst thou hear me? I will play the swan,
And die in music. [*Singing*] "Willow, willow, willow.—"
Moor, she was chaste; she lov'd thee, cruel Moor;   280
So come my soul to bliss, as I speak true;
So speaking as I think, I die, I die.   [*Dies.*]

OTHELLO. I have another weapon in this chamber;
It is a sword of Spain, the ice-brook's temper[42]:—
O, here it is. Uncle, I must come forth.

GRATIANO [*within*]. If thou attempt it, it will cost thee dear:
Thou hast no weapon, and perforce must suffer.

OTHELLO. Look in upon me then and speak with me,
Or, naked[43] as I am, I will assault thee.

[*Enter* GRATIANO.]

---

37 **fortune** chance.

38 **coxcomb** fool; addressed to Othello.

39 **stones in heaven** thunderbolts. It was supposed that real stones fell with the thunder and caused the damage.

40 **whipster** contemptible fellow.

41 **honour outlive honesty** Othello realizes that he has done a shameful deed; he asks why his reputation for valor should endure.

42 **ice-brook's temper** usually defined as "tempered in ice-cold water."

43 **naked** unarmed.

GRATIANO. What is the matter?   290
OTHELLO.   Behold, I have a weapon;
 A better never did itself sustain
 Upon a soldier's thigh: I have seen the day,
 That, with this little arm and this good sword,
 I have made my way through more impediments
 Than twenty times your stop:[44] but, O vain boast!
 Who can control his fate? 'tis not so now.
 Be not afraid, though you do see me weapon'd;
 Here is my journey's end, here is my butt,[45]
 And very sea-mark[46] of my utmost sail.   300
 Do you go back dismay'd? 'tis a lost fear;
 Man[47] but a rush[48] against Othello's breast,
 And he retires. Where should Othello go?
 Now, how dost thou look now? O ill-starr'd wench!
 Pale as thy smock! when we shall meet at compt,[49]
 This look of thine will hurl my soul from heaven,
 And fiends will snatch at it. Cold, cold, my girl!
 Even like thy chastity. O cursed, cursed slave!
 Whip me, ye devils,
 From the possession of this heavenly sight!   310
 Blow me about in winds! roast me in sulphur!
 Wash me in steep-down gulfs of liquid fire!
 O Desdemona! Dead Desdemona! dead!
 Oh! Oh!

[*Enter* LODOVICO, CASSIO *carried in a chair*, MONTANO, *and* IAGO, *prisoner*,
with OFFICERS.]

LODOVICO. Where is this rash and most unfortunate man?
OTHELLO. That's he that was Othello: here I am.
LODOVICO. Where is that viper? Bring the villain forth.
OTHELLO. I look down towards his feet;[50] but that's a fable.
 If that thou be'st a devil, I cannot kill thee.   [*Wounds* IAGO.]
LODOVICO. Wrench his sword from him.   320
IAGO.   I bleed sir; but not kill'd.
OTHELLO. I am not sorry neither: I'd have thee live;
 For, in my sense, 'tis happiness to die.
LODOVICO. O thou Othello, that wert once so good,
 Fall'n in the practice of a damned slave,
 What shall be said to thee?
OTHELLO.   Why, any thing:
 An honourable murderer, if you will;
 For nought I did in hate, but all in honour.

---

44 **stop** power.
45 **butt** mark for archery, goal, limit.
46 **sea-mark** beacon (marking his destination or limit).
47 **Man** provide, as in manning a gun.
48 **rush** reed.
49 **compt** account, judgment day.
50 **towards his feet** i.e., to see if they were cloven like a devil's.

Lodovico. This wretch hath part confess'd his villainy: 330
    Did you and he consent in Cassio's death?
Othello. Ay.
Cassio. Dear general, I never gave you cause.
Othello. I do believe it, and I ask your pardon.
    Will you, I pray, demand that demi-devil
    Why he hath thus ensnar'd my soul and body?
Iago. Demand me nothing: what you know, you know:
    From this time forth I never will speak word.
Lodovico. What, not to pray?
Gratiano.   Torments will ope your lips.   340
Othello. Well, thou dost best.
Lodovico. Sir, you shall understand what hath befall'n,
    Which, as I think, you know not. Here is a letter
    Found in the pocket of the slain Roderigo;
    And here another: the one of them imports
    The death of Cassio to be undertook
    By Roderigo.
Othello. O villain!
Cassio.   Most heathenish and most gross!
Lodovico. Now here's another discontented[51] paper,   350
    Found in his pocket too; and this, it seems,
    Roderigo meant t' have sent this damned villain;
    But that belike Iago in the interim
    Came in and satisfied him.
Othello.   O thou pernicious caitiff[52]—
    How came you, Cassio, by that handkerchief
    That was my wife's?
Cassio.   I found it in my chamber:
    And he himself confess'd but even now
    That there he dropp'd it for a special purpose   360
    Which wrought to his desire.
Othello.   O fool! O fool! fool!
Cassio. There is besides in Roderigo's letter,
    How he upbraids Iago, that he made him
    Brave[53] me upon the watch; whereon it came
    That I was cast:[54] and even but now he spake,
    After long seeming dead, Iago hurt him,
    Iago set him on.
Lodovico. You must forsake this room, and go with us:
    Your power and your command is taken off,[55]   370
    And Cassio rules in Cyprus. For this slave,
    If there be any cunning cruelty
    That can torment him much and hold him long,

---

51 **discontented** expressing dissatisfaction.
52 **caitiff** wretch.
53 **Brave** defy.
54 **cast** dismissed.
55 **taken off** taken away.

It shall be his. You shall close prisoner rest,
Till that the nature of your fault be known
To the Venetian state. Come, bring him away.
OTHELLO. Soft you; a word or two before you go.
I have done the state some service, and they know 't.
No more of that. I pray you, in your letters,
When you shall these unlucky deeds relate,   380
Speak of me as I am; nothing extenuate,[56]
Nor set down aught in malice: then must you speak
Of one that lov'd not wisely but too well;
Of one not easily jealous, but being wrought,
Perplex'd[57] in the extreme; of one whose hand,
Like the base Judean,[58] threw a pearl away
Richer than all his tribe; of one whose subdu'd eyes,
Albeit unused to the melting mood,
Drop tears as fast as the Arabian trees
Their medicinable gum. Set you down this;   390
And say besides, that in Aleppo[59] once,
Where a malignant and a turban'd Turk
Beat a Venetian and traduc'd the state,
I took by th' throat the circumcised dog,
And smote him, thus.   [*Stabs himself.*]
LODOVICO. O bloody period![60]
GRATIANO. All that is spoke is marr'd.
OTHELLO. I kiss'd thee ere I kill'd thee: no way but this;
Killing myself, to die upon a kiss.   [*Falls on the bed, and dies.*]
CASSIO. This did I fear, but thought he had no weapon;   400
For he was great of heart.
LODOVICO.   [*To* IAGO] O Spartan dog,[61]
More fell than anguish, hunger, or the sea!
Look on the tragic loading of this bed;
This is thy work: the object poisons sight;
Let it be hid. Gratiano, keep the house,
And seize upon the fortunes of the Moor,
For they succeed on you. To you, lord governor,
Remains the censure of this hellish villain;
The time, the place, the torture: O, enforce it!   410
Myself will straight abroad; and to the state
This heavy act with heavy heart relate.   [*Exeunt.*]

(1604)

---

56 **extenuate** diminish, depreciate; the idea is contrasted with the thought of *malice* in the following line.

57 **Perplex'd** confounded, distracted.

58 **Judean** infidel or disbeliever.

59 **Aleppo** a Turkish city where the Venetians had special trading privileges. It is stated that it was immediate death for a Christian to strike a Turk in Aleppo; Othello risked his life for the honor of Venice.

60 **period** termination, conclusion.

61 **Spartan dog** Spartan dogs were noted for their savagery.

Questions for Discussion and Writing

1. How does Shakespeare establish the dignity, nobility, and heroism of Othello early in the play? Does Othello regain any of his lost stature in the end? How?
2. Analyze the relationship between Othello and Desdemona, and explain how tragedy enters their lives.
3. Why is Iago committed, above all else, to destroying Desdemona?
4. Explain Desdemona's behavior in the scene in which Othello accuses her of being a whore (Act IV, Scene II). Why can't Othello perceive her goodness and innocence?
5. How do race and racism contribute to Othello's downfall?
6. Professor Carol Neely maintains that "the play's central theme is love—especially marital love; its central conflict is between the men and the women." Write an essay in which you argue for or against these claims.
7. Some people think Othello acts with unjustified haste and violence, that it is inexcusable for him to suspect his wife and unbelievable that he would not suspect Iago. Write an essay in which you answer these charges.

Making Connections

Write an essay in which you compare the tragedy of Othello with the tragedy of Antigone (page 633).

Susan Glaspell 1882–1948

Born in Davenport, Iowa, Susan Glaspell took a degree in philosophy from Drake University before becoming a newspaper reporter in Des Moines. She turned her play *Trifles*, based on a murder case she covered on the job, into a widely anthologized short story, "A Jury of Her Peers." She married a freethinker who also believed in free love and unfettered drinking, making her life with him difficult. The couple moved to the East Coast, where they founded the Provincetown Players, an experimental theater group. Glaspell won the 1931 Pulitzer Prize for her play *Alison's House*, which depicted the life of Emily Dickinson. She said she promoted "all progressive movements, whether feminist, social, or economic."

Trifles

CHARACTERS

County Attorney	Hale
Mrs. Peters	Mrs. Hale
Sheriff	

SCENE

The kitchen in the now abandoned farmhouse of JOHN WRIGHT, *a gloomy kitchen, and left without having been put in order—the walls covered with a faded wallpaper. Down right is a door leading to the parlor. On the right wall above this door is a built-in kitchen cupboard with shelves in the upper portion and drawers below. In the rear wall at right, up two steps is a door opening onto stairs leading to the second floor. In the rear wall at left is a door to the shed and from there to the outside. Between these two doors is an old-fashioned black iron stove. Running along the left wall from the shed door is an old iron sink and sink shelf, in which is set a hand pump. Downstage of the sink is an uncurtained window. Near the window is an old wooden rocker. Center stage is an unpainted wooden kitchen table with straight chairs on either side. There is a small chair down right. Unwashed pans under the sink, a loaf of bread outside the breadbox, a dish towel on the table—other signs of incompleted work. At the rear the shed door opens and the* SHERIFF *comes in followed by the* COUNTY ATTORNEY *and* HALE. *The* SHERIFF *and* HALE *are men in middle life, the* COUNTY ATTORNEY *is a young man; all are much bundled up and go at once to the stove. They are followed by the two women—the* SHERIFF'S *wife,* MRS. PETERS, *first; she is a slight wiry woman, a thin nervous face.* MRS. HALE *is larger and would ordinarily be called more comfortable looking, but she is disturbed now and looks fearfully about as she enters. The women have come in slowly, and stand close together near the door.*

COUNTY ATTORNEY [*at the stove rubbing his hands*]. This feels good. Come up to the fire, ladies.

MRS. PETERS [*after taking a step forward*]. I'm not—cold.

SHERIFF [*unbuttoning his overcoat and stepping away from the stove to right of the table as if to mark the beginning of official business*]. Now, Mr. Hale, before we move things about, you explain to Mr. Henderson just what you saw when you came here yesterday morning.

COUNTY ATTORNEY [*crossing down to left of the table*]. By the way, has anything been moved? Are things just as you left them yesterday?

SHERIFF [*looking about*]. It's just the same. When it dropped below zero last night I thought I'd better send Frank out this morning to make a fire for us—[*sits right of center table*] no use getting pneumonia with a big case on, but I told him not to touch anything except the stove—and you know Frank.

COUNTY ATTORNEY. Somebody should have been left here yesterday.

SHERIFF. Oh—yesterday. When I had to send Frank to Morris Center for that man who went crazy—I want you to know I had my hands full yesterday. I knew you could get back from Omaha by today and as long as I went over everything here myself—

COUNTY ATTORNEY. Well, Mr. Hale, tell just what happened when you came here yesterday morning.

HALE [*crossing down to above table*]. Harry and I had started to town with a load of potatoes. We came along the road from my place and as I got here I said, "I'm going to see if I can't get John Wright to go in with me on a party telephone." I spoke to Wright about it once before and he put me off, saying folks talked too much anyway, and all he asked was peace and quiet—I guess you know about how much he talked himself; but I thought maybe if I went to the house and talked about it before his wife, though I said to Harry that I didn't know as what his wife wanted made much difference to John—

A photo of the original 1916 production of *Trifles*. (The New York Public Library, Billy Rose Theatre Collection/Art Resource, NY.)

COUNTY ATTORNEY. Let's talk about that later, Mr. Hale. I do want to talk about that, but tell now just what happened when you got to the house.

HALE. I didn't hear or see anything; I knocked at the door, and still it was all quiet inside. I knew they must be up, it was past eight o'clock. So I knocked again, and I thought I heard somebody say, "Come in." I wasn't sure, I'm not sure yet, but I opened the door—this door [*indicating the door by which the two women are still standing*] and there in that rocker—[*pointing to it*] sat Mrs. Wright. [*They all look at the rocker down left.*]

COUNTY ATTORNEY. What—what was she doing?

HALE. She was rockin' back and forth. She had her apron in her hand and was kind of—pleating it.

COUNTY ATTORNEY. And how did she—look?

HALE. Well, she looked queer.

COUNTY ATTORNEY. How do you mean—queer?

HALE. Well, as if she didn't know what she was going to do next. And kind of done up.

COUNTY ATTORNEY [*takes out notebook and pencil and sits left of center table*]. How did she seem to feel about your coming?

HALE. Why, I don't think she minded—one way or other. She didn't pay much attention. I said, "How do, Mrs. Wright, it's cold, ain't it?" And she said, "Is it?"—and went on kind of pleating at her apron. Well, I was surprised; she didn't ask me to come up to the stove, or to set down, but just sat there, not even look-ing at me, so I said, "I want to see John." And then she—laughed. I guess you would call it a laugh. I thought of Harry and the team outside, so I said a little sharp: "Can't I see John?" "No," she says, kind o' dull like. "Ain't he home?" says I. "Yes," says she, "he's home." "Then why can't I see him?" I asked her, out of patience. "'Cause he's dead," says she. "*Dead*?" says I. She just nodded her head, not getting a bit excited, but rockin' back and forth. "Why—where is he?" says I, not knowing what to say. She just pointed upstairs—like that. [*Himself pointing to the room above.*] I started for the stairs, with the idea of go-ing up there. I walked from there to here—then I says, "Why, what did he die of?" "He died of a rope round his neck," says she, and just went on pleatin' at her apron. Well, I went out and called Harry. I thought I might—need help. We went upstairs and there he was lyin'—

COUNTY ATTORNEY. I think I'd rather have you go into that upstairs, where you can point it all out. Just go on now with the rest of the story.

HALE. Well, my first thought was to get that rope off. It looked... [*stops, his face twitches*]...but Harry, he went up to him, and he said, "No, he's dead all right, and we'd better not touch anything." So we went back downstairs. She was still sitting that same way. "Has anybody been notified?" I asked. "No," says she, unconcerned. "Who did this, Mrs. Wright?" said Harry. He said it busi-ness-like—and she stopped pleatin' on her apron. "I don't *know*," she says. "You don't know?" says Harry. "No," says she. "Weren't you sleepin' in the bed with him?" says Harry. "Yes," says she, "but I was on the inside." "Some-body slipped a rope round his neck and strangled him and you didn't wake up?" says Harry. "I didn't wake up," she said after him. We musta looked as if we didn't see how that could be, for after a minute she said, "I sleep sound." Harry was going to ask her more questions but I said maybe we ought to let her tell her story first to the coroner, or the sheriff, so Harry went fast as he could to Rivers' place, where there's a telephone.

COUNTY ATTORNEY. And what did Mrs. Wright do when she knew that you had gone for the coroner?

HALE. She moved from the rocker to that chair over there [*pointing to a small chair in the down right corner*] and just sat there with her hands held together and looking down. I got a feeling that I ought to make some conversation, so I said I had come in to see if John wanted to put in a telephone, and at that she started to laugh, and then she stopped and looked at me—scared. [*The* COUNTY ATTORNEY, *who has had his notebook out, makes a note.*] I dunno, maybe it wasn't scared. I wouldn't like to say it was. Soon Harry got back, and then Dr. Lloyd came, and you, Mr. Peters, and so I guess that's all I know that you don't.

COUNTY ATTORNEY [*rising and looking around*]. I guess we'll go upstairs first—and then out to the barn and around there. [*To the* SHERIFF.] You're convinced that there was nothing important here—nothing that would point to any motive?

SHERIFF. Nothing here but kitchen things. [*The* COUNTY ATTORNEY, *after again looking around the kitchen, opens the door of a cupboard closet in right wall. He brings a small chair from right—gets up on it and looks on a shelf. Pulls his hand away, sticky.*]

COUNTY ATTORNEY. Here's a nice mess. [*The women draw nearer up center.*]

MRS. PETERS [*to the other woman*]. Oh, her fruit; it did freeze. [*To the* LAWYER.] She worried about that when it turned so cold. She said the fire'd go out and her jars would break.

SHERIFF [*rises*]. Well, can you beat the women! Held for murder and worryin' about her preserves.

COUNTY ATTORNEY [*getting down from chair*]. I guess before we're through she may have something more serious than preserves to worry about. [*Crosses down right center.*]

HALE. Well, women are used to worrying over trifles. [*The two women move a little closer together.*]

COUNTY ATTORNEY [*with the gallantry of a young politician*]. And yet, for all their worries, what would we do without the ladies? [*The women do not unbend. He goes below the center table to the sink, takes a dipperful of water from the pail and pouring it into a basin, washes his hands. While he is doing this the* SHERIFF *and* HALE *cross to cupboard, which they inspect. The* COUNTY ATTORNEY *starts to wipe his hands on the roller towel, turns it for a cleaner place.*] Dirty towels! [*Kicks his foot against the pans under the sink.*] Not much of a housekeeper, would you say, ladies?

MRS. HALE [*stiffly*]. There's a great deal of work to be done on a farm.

COUNTY ATTORNEY. To be sure. And yet [*with a little bow to her*] I know there are some Dickson County farmhouses which do not have such roller towels. [*He gives it a pull to expose its full length again.*]

MRS. HALE. Those towels get dirty awful quick. Men's hands aren't always as clean as they might be.

COUNTY ATTORNEY. Ah, loyal to your sex, I see. But you and Mrs. Wright were neighbors. I suppose you were friends, too.

MRS. HALE [*shaking her head*]. I've not seen much of her of late years. I've not been in this house—it's more than a year.

COUNTY ATTORNEY [*crossing to women up center*]. And why was that? You didn't like her?

MRS. HALE. I liked her all well enough. Farmers' wives have their hands full, Mr. Henderson. And then—

COUNTY ATTORNEY. Yes——?

MRS. HALE [*looking about*]. It never seemed a very cheerful place.

COUNTY ATTORNEY. No—it's not cheerful. I shouldn't say she had the homemaking instinct.

MRS. HALE. Well, I don't know as Wright had, either.

COUNTY ATTORNEY. You mean that they didn't get on very well?

MRS. HALE. No, I don't mean anything. But I don't think a place'd be any cheerfuller for John Wright's being in it.

COUNTY ATTORNEY. I'd like to talk more of that a little later. I want to get the lay of things upstairs now. [*He goes past the women to up right where steps lead to a stair door.*]

SHERIFF. I suppose anything Mrs. Peters does'll be all right. She was to take in some clothes for her, you know, and a few little things. We left in such a hurry yesterday.

COUNTY ATTORNEY. Yes, but I would like to see what you take, Mrs. Peters, and keep an eye out for anything that might be of use to us.

MRS. PETERS. Yes, Mr. Henderson.

[*The men leave by up right door to stairs. The women listen to the men's steps on the stairs, then look about the kitchen.*]

MRS. HALE [*crossing left to sink*]. I'd hate to have men coming into my kitchen, snooping around and criticizing. [*She arranges the pans under sink which the Lawyer had shoved out of place.*]

MRS. PETERS. Of course it's no more than their duty. [*Crosses to cupboard up right.*]

MRS. HALE. Duty's all right, but I guess that deputy sheriff that came out to make the fire might have got a little of this on. [*Gives the roller towel a pull.*] Wish I'd thought of that sooner. Seems mean to talk about her for not having things slicked up when she had to come away in such a hurry. [*Crosses right to Mrs. Peters at cupboard.*]

MRS. PETERS [*who has been looking through the cupboard, lifts one end of a towel that covers a pan*]. She had bread set. [*Stands still.*]

MRS. HALE [*eyes fixed on a loaf of bread beside the breadbox, which is on a low shelf of the cupboard*]. She was going to put this in there. [*Picks up loaf, then abruptly drops it. In a manner of returning to familiar things.*] It's a shame about her fruit. I wonder if it's all gone. [*Gets up on the chair and looks.*] I think there's some here that's all right, Mrs. Peters. Yes—here; [*holding it toward the window*] this is cherries, too. [*Looking again.*] I declare I believe that's the only one. [*Gets down, jar in her hand. Goes to the sink and wipes it off on the outside.*] She'll feel awful bad after all her hard work in the hot weather. I remember the afternoon I put up my cherries last summer. [*She puts the jar on the big kitchen table, center of the room. With a sigh, is about to sit down in the rocking chair. Before she is seated realizes what chair it is; with a slow look at it, steps back. The chair which she has touched rocks back and forth. Mrs. PETERS moves to center table and they both watch the chair rock for a moment or two.*]

MRS. PETERS [*shaking off the mood which the empty rocking chair has evoked. Now in a businesslike manner she speaks*]. Well, I must get those things from the front room closet. [*She goes to the door at the right, but, after looking into the other room, steps back.*] You coming with me, Mrs. Hale? You could help me carry them. [*They go in the other room; reappear, Mrs. PETERS carrying a dress, petticoat and skirt, Mrs. HALE following with a pair of shoes.*] My, it's cold in there. [*She puts the clothes on the big table, and hurries to the stove.*]

MRS. HALE [*right of center table examining the skirt*]. Wright was close. I think maybe that's why she kept so much to herself. She didn't even belong to the Ladies' Aid. I suppose she felt she couldn't do her part, and then you don't enjoy things when you feel shabby. I heard she used to wear pretty clothes and be lively, when she was Minnie Foster, one of the town girls singing in the choir. But that—oh, that was thirty years ago. This all you was to take in?

MRS. PETERS. She said she wanted an apron. Funny thing to want, for there isn't much to get you dirty in jail, goodness knows. But I suppose just to make her feel more natural. [*Crosses to cupboard.*] She said they was in the top drawer of this cupboard. Yes, here. And then her little shawl that always hung behind the door. [*Opens stair door and looks.*] Yes, here it is. [*Quickly shuts door leading upstairs.*]

MRS. HALE [*abruptly moving toward her*]. Mrs. Peters?

MRS. PETERS. Yes, Mrs. Hale? [*At up right door.*]

MRS. HALE. Do you think she did it?

MRS. PETERS [*in a frightened voice*]. Oh, I don't know.

MRS. HALE. Well, I don't think she did. Asking for an apron and her little shawl. Worrying about her fruit.

MRS. PETERS [*starts to speak, glances up, where footsteps are heard in the room above. In a low voice*]. Mr. Peters says it looks bad for her. Mr. Henderson is awful sarcastic in a speech and he'll make fun of her sayin' she didn't wake up.

MRS. HALE. Well, I guess John Wright didn't wake when they was slipping that rope under his neck.

MRS. PETERS [*crossing slowly to table and placing shawl and apron on table with other clothing*]. No, it's strange. It must have been done awful crafty and still. They say it was such a—funny way to kill a man, rigging it all up like that.

MRS. HALE [*crossing to left of* MRS. PETERS *at table*]. That's just what Mr. Hale said. There was a gun in the house. He says that's what he can't understand.

MRS. PETERS. Mr. Henderson said coming out that what was needed for the case was a motive; something to show anger, or—sudden feeling.

MRS. HALE [*who is standing by the table*]. Well, I don't see any signs of anger around here. [*She puts her hand on the dish towel which lies on the table, stands looking down at table, one-half of which is clean, the other half messy.*] It's wiped to here. [*Makes a move as if to finish work, then turns and looks at loaf of bread outside the breadbox. Drops towel. In that voice of coming back to familiar things.*] Wonder how they are finding things upstairs. [*Crossing below table to down right.*] I hope she had it a little more red-up[1] up there. You know, it seems kind of sneaking. Locking her up in town and then coming out here and trying to get her own house to turn against her!

MRS. PETERS. But, Mrs. Hale, the law is the law.

MRS. HALE. I s'pose 'tis. [*Unbuttoning her coat.*] Better loosen up your things, Mrs. Peters. You won't feel them when you go out. [MRS. PETERS *takes off her fur tippet,[2] goes to hang it on chair back left of table, stands looking at the work basket on floor near down left window.*]

MRS. PETERS. She was piecing a quilt. [*She brings the large sewing basket to the center table and they look at the bright pieces,* MRS. HALE *above the table and* MRS. PETERS *left of it.*]

MRS. HALE. It's a log cabin pattern. Pretty, isn't it? I wonder if she was goin' to quilt it or just knot it? [*Footsteps have been heard coming down the stairs. The* SHERIFF *enters followed by* HALE *and the* COUNTY ATTORNEY.]

SHERIFF. They wonder if she was going to quilt it or just knot it! [*The men laugh, the women look abashed.*]

COUNTY ATTORNEY [*rubbing his hands over the stove*]. Frank's fire didn't do much up there, did it? Well, let's go out to the barn and get that cleared up.

[*The men go outside by up left door.*]

MRS. HALE [*resentfully*]. I don't know as there's anything so strange, our takin' up our time with little things while we're waiting for them to get the evidence. [*She sits in chair right of table smoothing out a block with decision.*] I don't see as it's anything to laugh about.

MRS. PETERS [*apologetically*]. Of course they've got awful important things on their minds. [*Pulls up a chair and joins* MRS. HALE *at the left of the table.*]

MRS. HALE [*examining another block*]. Mrs. Peters, look at this one. Here, this is the one she was working on, and look at the sewing! All the rest of it has been so nice and even. And look at this! It's all over the place! Why, it looks as if she didn't know what she was about! [*After she has said this they look at each*

---

1 **red-up** cleaned up, neat.
2 **tippet** a scarf-like wrap.

other, then start to glance back at the door. After an instant Mrs. Hale has pulled at a knot and ripped the sewing.]

MRS. PETERS. Oh, what are you doing, Mrs. Hale?

MRS. HALE [*mildly*]. Just pulling out a stitch or two that's not sewed very good. [*Threading a needle.*] Bad sewing always made me fidgety.

MRS. PETERS [*with a glance at door, nervously*]. I don't think we ought to touch things.

MRS. HALE. I'll just finish up this end. [*Suddenly stopping and leaning forward.*] Mrs. Peters?

MRS. PETERS. Yes, Mrs. Hale?

MRS. HALE. What do you suppose she was so nervous about?

MRS. PETERS. Oh—I don't know. I don't know as she was nervous. I sometimes sew awful queer when I'm just tired. [*Mrs. Hale starts to say something, looks at Mrs. Peters, then goes on sewing.*] Well, I must get these things wrapped up. They may be through sooner than we think. [*Putting apron and other things together.*] I wonder where I can find a piece of paper, and string. [*Rises.*]

MRS. HALE. In that cupboard, maybe.

MRS. PETERS [*crosses right looking in cupboard*]. Why, here's a bird-cage. [*Holds it up.*] Did she have a bird, Mrs. Hale?

MRS. HALE. Why, I don't know whether she did or not—I've not been here for so long. There was a man around last year selling canaries cheap, but I don't know as she took one; maybe she did. She used to sing real pretty herself.

MRS. PETERS [*glancing around*]. Seems funny to think of a bird here. But she must have had one, or why would she have a cage? I wonder what happened to it?

MRS. HALE. I s'pose maybe the cat got it.

MRS. PETERS. No, she didn't have a cat. She's got that feeling some people have about cats—being afraid of them. My cat got in her room and she was real upset and asked me to take it out.

MRS. HALE. My sister Bessie was like that. Queer, ain't it?

MRS. PETERS [*examining the cage*]. Why, look at this door. It's broke. One hinge is pulled apart. [*Takes a step down to Mrs. Hale's right.*]

MRS. HALE [*looking too*]. Looks as if someone must have been rough with it.

MRS. PETERS. Why, yes. [*She brings the cage forward and puts it on the table.*]

MRS. HALE [*glancing toward up left door*]. I wish if they're going to find any evidence they'd be about it. I don't like this place.

MRS. PETERS. But I'm awful glad you came with me, Mrs. Hale. It would be lonesome for me setting here alone.

MRS. HALE. It would, wouldn't it? [*Dropping her sewing.*] But I tell you what I do wish, Mrs. Peters. I wish I had come over sometimes when *she* was here. I—[*looking around the room*]—wish I had.

MRS. PETERS. But of course you were awful busy, Mrs. Hale—your house and your children.

MRS. HALE [*rises and crosses left*]. I could've come. I stayed away because it weren't cheerful—and that's why I ought to have come. I—[*looking out left window*]—I've never liked this place. Maybe because it's down in a hollow and you don't see the road. I dunno what it is, but it's a lonesome place and always was. I wish I had come over to see Minnie Foster sometimes. I can see now—[*Shakes her head.*]

MRS. PETERS [*left of table and above it*]. Well, you mustn't reproach yourself, Mrs. Hale. Somehow we just don't see how it is with other folks until—something turns up.

MRS. HALE. Not having children makes less work—but it makes a quiet house, and Wright out to work all day, and no company when he did come in. [*Turning from window.*] Did you know John Wright, Mrs. Peters?

MRS. PETERS. Not to know him; I've seen him in town. They say he was a good man.

MRS. HALE. Yes—good; he didn't drink, and kept his word as well as most, I guess, and paid his debts. But he was a hard man, Mrs. Peters. Just to pass the time of day with him—[*Shivers.*] Like a raw wind that gets to the bone. [*Pauses, her eye falling on the cage.*] I should think she woulda wanted a bird. But what do you suppose went wrong with it?

MRS. PETERS. I don't know, unless it got sick and died. [*She reaches over and swings the broken door, swings it again; both women watch it.*]

MRS. HALE. You weren't raised round here, were you? [MRS. PETERS *shakes her head.*] You didn't know—her?

MRS. PETERS. Not till they brought her yesterday.

MRS. HALE. She—come to think of it, she was kind of like a bird herself—real sweet and pretty, but kind of timid and—fluttery. How—she—did—change. [*Silence; then as if struck by a happy thought and relieved to get back to everyday things. Crosses right above* MRS. PETERS *to cupboard, replaces small chair used to stand on to its original place down right.*] Tell you what, Mrs. Peters, why don't you take the quilt in with you? It might take up her mind.

MRS. PETERS. Why, I think that's a real nice idea, Mrs. Hale. There couldn't possibly be any objection to it, could there? Now, just what would I take? I wonder if her patches are in here—and her things. [*They look in the sewing basket.*]

MRS. HALE [*crosses to right of table*]. Here's some red. I expect this has got sewing things in it. [*Brings out a fancy box.*] What a pretty box. Looks like something somebody would give you. Maybe her scissors are in here. [*Opens box. Suddenly puts her hand to her nose.*] Why—[MRS. PETERS *bends nearer, then turns her face away.*] There's something wrapped up in this piece of silk.

MRS. PETERS. Why, this isn't her scissors.

MRS. HALE [*lifting the silk*]. Oh, Mrs. Peters—it's—[MRS. PETERS *bends closer.*]

MRS. PETERS. It's the bird.

MRS. HALE. But, Mrs. Peters—look at it! Its neck! Look at its neck! It's all—other side to.

MRS. PETERS. Somebody—wrung—its—neck. [*Their eyes meet. A look of growing comprehension, of horror. Steps are heard outside.* MRS. HALE *slips box under quilt pieces, and sinks into her chair. Enter* SHERIFF *and* COUNTY ATTORNEY. MRS. PETERS *steps down left and stands looking out of window.*]

COUNTY ATTORNEY [*as one turning from serious things to little pleasantries*]. Well, ladies, have you decided whether she was going to quilt it or knot it? [*Crosses to center above table.*]

MRS. PETERS. We think she was going to—knot it. [SHERIFF *crosses to right of stove, lifts stove lid and glances at fire, then stands warming hands at stove.*]

COUNTY ATTORNEY. Well, that's interesting, I'm sure. [*Seeing the bird-cage.*] Has the bird flown?

MRS. HALE [*putting more quilt pieces over the box*]. We think the—cat got it.

COUNTY ATTORNEY [*preoccupied*]. Is there a cat? [MRS. HALE *glances in a quick covert way at Mrs. Peters.*]

MRS. PETERS [*turning from window takes a step in*]. Well, not now. They're superstitious, you know. They leave.

COUNTY ATTORNEY [*to* SHERIFF PETERS, *continuing an interrupted conversation*]. No sign at all of anyone having come from the outside. Their own rope. Now let's go up again and go over it piece by piece. [*They start upstairs.*] It would have to have been someone who knew just the—[Mrs. PETERS *sits down left of table. The two women sit there not looking at one another, but as if peering into something and at the same time holding back. When they talk now it is in the manner of feeling their way over strange ground, as if afraid of what they are saying, but as if they cannot help saying it.*]

MRS. HALE [*hesitatively and in hushed voice*]. She liked the bird. She was going to bury it in that pretty box.

MRS. PETERS [*in a whisper*]. When I was a girl—my kitten—there was a boy took a hatchet, and before my eyes—and before I could get there—[*Covers her face an instant.*] If they hadn't held me back I would have—[*catches herself, looks upstairs where steps are heard, falters weakly*]—hurt him.

MRS. HALE [*with a slow look around her*]. I wonder how it would seem never to have had any children around. [*Pause.*] No, Wright wouldn't like the bird—a thing that sang. She used to sing. He killed that, too.

MRS. PETERS [*moving uneasily*]. We don't know who killed the bird.

MRS. HALE. I knew John Wright.

MRS. PETERS. It was an awful thing done in this house that night, Mrs. Hale. Killing a man while he slept, slipping a rope around his neck that choked the life out of him.

MRS. HALE. His neck. Choked the life out of him. [*Her hand goes out and rests on the bird-cage.*]

MRS. PETERS [*with rising voice*]. We don't know who killed him. We don't know.

MRS. HALE [*her own feeling not interrupted*]. If there'd been years and years of nothing, then a bird to sing to you, it would be awful—still, after the bird was still.

MRS. PETERS [*something within her speaking*]. I know what stillness is. When we homesteaded in Dakota, and my first baby died—after he was two years old, and me with no other then—

MRS. HALE [*moving*]. How soon do you suppose they'll be through looking for the evidence?

MRS. PETERS. I know what stillness is. [*Pulling herself back.*] The law has got to punish crime, Mrs. Hale.

MRS. HALE [*not as if answering that*]. I wish you'd seen Minnie Foster when she wore a white dress with blue ribbons and stood up there in the choir and sang. [*A look around the room.*] Oh, I wish I'd come over here once in a while! That was a crime! That was a crime! Who's going to punish that?

MRS. PETERS [*looking upstairs*]. We mustn't—take on.

MRS. HALE. I might have known she needed help! I know how things can be—for women. I tell you, it's queer, Mrs. Peters. We live close together and we live far apart. We all go through the same things—it's all just a different kind of the same thing. [*Brushes her eyes, noticing the jar of fruit, reaches out for it.*] If I was you I wouldn't tell her her fruit was gone. Tell her it ain't. Tell her it's all right. Take this in to prove it to her. She—she may never know whether it was broke or not.

MRS. PETERS [*takes the jar, looks about for something to wrap it in; takes petticoat from the clothes brought from the other room, very nervously begins winding this around the jar. In a false voice*]. My, it's a good thing the men couldn't hear us. Wouldn't they just laugh! Getting all stirred up over a little thing like a—dead canary. As if that could have anything to do with—with—wouldn't they *laugh*! [*The men are heard coming downstairs.*]

MRS. HALE [*under her breath*]. Maybe they would—maybe they wouldn't.

COUNTY ATTORNEY. No, Peters, it's all perfectly clear except a reason for doing it. But you know juries when it comes to women. If there was some definite thing. [*Crosses slowly to above table.* SHERIFF *crosses down right.* MRS. HALE *and* MRS. PETERS *remain seated at either side of table.*] Something to show—something to make a story about—a thing that would connect up with this strange way of doing it—[*The women's eyes meet for an instant. Enter* HALE *from outer door.*]

HALE [*remaining up left by door*]. Well, I've got the team around. Pretty cold out there.

COUNTY ATTORNEY. I'm going to stay awhile by myself. [*To the* SHERIFF.] You can send Frank out for me, can't you? I want to go over everything. I'm not satisfied that we can't do better.

SHERIFF. Do you want to see what Mrs. Peters is going to take in? [*The* LAWYER *picks up the apron, laughs.*]

COUNTY ATTORNEY. Oh, I guess they're not very dangerous things the ladies have picked out. [*Moves a few things about, disturbing the quilt pieces which cover the box. Steps back.*] No, Mrs. Peters doesn't need supervising. For that matter a sheriff's wife is married to the law. Ever think of it that way, Mrs. Peters?

MRS. PETERS. Not—just that way.

SHERIFF [*chuckling*]. Married to the law. [*Moves to down right door to the other room.*] I just want you to come in here a minute, George. We ought to take a look at these windows.

COUNTY ATTORNEY [*scoffingly*]. Oh, windows!

SHERIFF. We'll be right out, Mr. Hale. [HALE *goes outside. The* SHERIFF *follows the* COUNTY ATTORNEY *into the other room. Then* MRS. HALE *rises, hands tight together, looking intensely at* MRS. PETERS, *whose eyes make a slow turn, finally meeting* MRS. HALE's. *A moment* MRS. HALE *holds her, then her own eyes point the way to where the box is concealed. Suddenly* MRS. PETERS *throws back quilt pieces and tries to put the box in the bag she is carrying. It is too big. She opens box, starts to take bird out, cannot touch it, goes to pieces, stands there helpless. Sound of a knob turning in the other room.* MRS. HALE *snatches the box and puts it in the pocket of her big coat. Enter* COUNTY ATTORNEY *and* SHERIFF, *who remains down right.*]

COUNTY ATTORNEY [*crosses to up left door; facetiously*]. Well, Henry, at least we found out that she was not going to quilt it. She was going to—what is it you call it, ladies?

MRS. HALE [*standing center below table facing front, her hand against her pocket*]. We call it—knot it, Mr. Henderson.

CURTAIN.

(1916)

Questions for Discussion and Writing

1. Describe the atmosphere evoked by the play's setting.
2. How would you characterize the men in the play?
3. What is the point of the women's concern about the quilt and whether Mrs. Wright "was going to quilt it or knot it"?
4. What sort of person was Minnie Foster before she married? What do you think happened to her?

5. Describe your reaction to the decision made by Mrs. Peters and Mrs. Hale to hide the dead bird from the men. Did they do the right thing? Write an essay in which you explain your answer to this question.

Making Connections

Compare Mrs. Peters and Mrs. Hale with the women in *Othello* (page 730) and *A Doll's House* (which follows). Which women seem to have the most control over their lives?

Henrik Ibsen   1828–1906

Henrik Ibsen, a Norwegian dramatist, was one of the most influential figures in modern theater. He worked as a stage manager, playwright, and director and is best known for breaking away from the romantic tradition in drama in order to portray life realistically. His social plays, such as *A Doll's House* (1879), *Ghosts* (1881), and *Hedda Gabler* (1890), shocked audiences with subject matter (venereal disease, suicide, women's independence) that was considered unmentionable in public. In these and other plays, Ibsen explored the conflict between social restrictions and the psychological, often unconscious demands of individual freedom.

A Doll's House

Translated by R. Farquharson Sharp

CHARACTERS

TORVALD HELMER, *a lawyer and bank manager*
NORA, *his wife*
DOCTOR RANK
MRS. CHRISTINE LINDE
NILS KROGSTAD, *a lawyer and bank clerk*

IVAR, BOB, *and* EMMY, *the Helmers' three young children*
ANNE, *their nurse*
HELEN, *a housemaid*
A PORTER

The action takes place in HELMERS' *apartment*

ACT 1

SCENE

A room, furnished comfortably and tastefully, but not extravagantly. At the back, a door to the right leads to the entrance hall, another to the left leads to HELMER's *study. Between the doors stands a piano. In the middle of the left-hand wall is a door, and beyond it a window. Near the window are a round table, armchairs and a small sofa. In the right-hand wall, at the farther end, another door; and on the same side, nearer the footlights, a stove, two easy chairs and a rocking-chair; between the stove and the door, a small table. Engravings on the walls; a cabinet with china and other small objects, a small book case with well-bound books. The floors are carpeted, and a fire burns in the stove. It is winter.*

A bell rings in the hall; shortly afterwards the door is heard to open. Enter NORA, *humming a tune and in high spirits. She is in outdoor dress and carries a number of parcels; these she lays on the table to the right. She leaves the outer door open after her, and through it is seen a* PORTER *who is carrying a Christmas Tree and a basket, which he gives to the* MAID *who has opened the door.*

NORA. Hide the Christmas Tree away carefully, Helen. Be sure the children do not see it till this evening, when it is dressed. [*to the* PORTER, *taking out her purse*] How much?

PORTER. Sixpence.

NORA. There is a shilling. No, keep the change.

[*The* PORTER *thanks her, and goes out.* NORA *shuts the door. She is laughing to herself, as she takes off her hat and coat. She takes a packet of macaroons from her pocket and eats one or two; then goes cautiously to her husband's door and listens.*]

Yes, he is in.

[*Still humming, she goes to the table on the right.*]

HELMER. [*calls out from his room*] Is that my little lark twittering out there?

NORA. [*busy opening some of the parcels*] Yes, it is!

HELMER. Is my little squirrel bustling about?

NORA. Yes!

HELMER. When did my squirrel come home?

NORA. Just now. [*puts the bag of macaroons into her pocket and wipes her mouth*] Come in here, Torvald, and see what I have bought.

HELMER. Don't disturb me. [*A little later, he opens the door and looks into the room, pen in his hand.*] Bought, did you say? All these things? Has my little spend-thrift been wasting money again?

NORA. Yes, but, Torvald, this year we really can let ourselves go a little. This is the first Christmas that we have not needed to economise.

HELMER. Still, you know, we can't spend money recklessly.

NORA. Yes, Torvald, we may be a wee bit more reckless now, mayn't we? Just a tiny wee bit! You are going to have a big salary and earn lots and lots of money.

HELMER. Yes, after the New Year; but then it will be a whole quarter before the salary is due.

NORA. Pooh! We can borrow till then.

HELMER. Nora! [*goes up to her and takes her playfully by the ear*] The same little featherhead! Suppose, now, that I borrowed fifty pounds to-day, and you spent it all in the Christmas week, and then on New Year's Eve a slate fell on my head and killed me, and—

NORA. [*putting her hands over his mouth*] Oh! don't say such horrid things.

HELMER. Still, suppose that happened—what then?

NORA. If that were to happen, I don't suppose I should care whether I owed money or not.

HELMER. Yes, but what about the people who had lent it?

NORA. They? Who would bother about them? I should not know who they were.

HELMER. That is like a woman! But seriously, Nora, you know what I think about that. No debt, no borrowing. There can be no freedom or beauty about a home life that depends on borrowing and debt. We two have kept bravely on the straight road so far, and we will go on the same way for the short time longer that there need be any struggle.

NORA. [*moving towards the stove*] As you please, Torvald.

HELMER. [*following her*] Come, come, my little skylark must not droop her wings. What is this! Is my little squirrel out of temper? [*taking out his purse*] Nora, what do you think I have got here?

NORA. [*turning around quickly*] Money!

HELMER. There you are. [*gives her some money*] Do you think I don't know what a lot is wanted for housekeeping at Christmas-time?

NORA. [*counting*] Ten shillings—a pound—two pounds! Thank you, thank you, Torvald; that will keep me going for a long time.

HELMER. Indeed it must.

NORA. Yes, yes, it will. But come here and let me show you what I have bought. And all so cheap! Look, here is a new suit for Ivar, and a sword; and a horse and a trumpet for Bob; and a doll and dolly's bedstead for Emmy—they are very plain, but anyway she will soon break them in pieces. And here are dress-lengths and handkerchiefs for the maids; old Anne ought really to have something better.

HELMER. And what is in this parcel?

NORA. [*crying out*] No, no! You mustn't see that till this evening.

HELMER. Very well. But now tell me, you extravagant little person, what would you like for yourself?

NORA. For myself? Oh, I am sure I don't want anything.

HELMER. Yes, but you must. Tell me something reasonable that you would particularly like to have.

NORA. No, I really can't think of anything—unless, Torvald—

HELMER. Well?

NORA. [*playing with his coat buttons, and without raising her eyes to his*] If you really want to give me something, you might—you might—

HELMER. Well, out with it!

NORA. [*speaking quickly*] You might give me money, Torvald. Only just as much as you can afford; and then one of these days I will buy something with it.

HELMER. But, Nora—

NORA. Oh, do! dear Torvald; please, please do! Then I will wrap it up in beautiful gilt paper and hang it on the Christmas Tree. Wouldn't that be fun?

HELMER. What are little people called that are always wasting money?

NORA. Spendthrifts—I know. Let us do as you suggest, Torvald, and then I shall have time to think what I am most in want of. That is a very sensible plan, isn't it?

HELMER. [*smiling*] Indeed it is—that is to say, if you were really to save out of the money I give you, and then really buy something for yourself. But if you spend it all on the housekeeping and any number of unnecessary things, then I merely have to pay up again.

NORA. Oh but, Torvald—

HELMER. You can't deny it, my dear little Nora. [*puts his arm round her waist*] It's a sweet little spendthrift, but she uses up a deal of money. One would hardly believe how expensive such little persons are!

NORA. It's a shame to say that. I do really save all I can.

HELMER. [*laughing*] That's very true—all you can. But you can't save anything!

NORA. [*smiling quietly and happily*] You haven't any idea how many expenses we skylarks and squirrels have, Torvald.

HELMER. You are an odd little soul. Very like your father. You always find some new way of wheedling money out of me, and, as soon as you have got it, it seems to melt in your hands. You never know where it has gone. Still, one must take you as you are. It is in the blood; for indeed it is true that you can inherit these things, Nora.

Nora. Ah, I wish I had inherited many of papa's qualities.

Helmer. And I would not wish you to be anything but just what you are, my sweet little skylark. But, do you know, it strikes me that you are looking rather— what shall I say—rather uneasy to-day?

Nora. Do I?

Helmer. You do, really. Look straight at me.

Nora. [*looks at him*] Well?

Helmer. [*wagging his finger at her*] Hasn't Miss Sweet-Tooth been breaking rules in town to-day?

Nora. No; what makes you think that?

Helmer. Hasn't she paid a visit to the confectioner's?

Nora. No, I assure you, Torvald—

Helmer. Not been nibbling sweets?

Nora. No, certainly not.

Helmer. Not even taken a bite at a macaroon or two?

Nora. No, Torvald, I assure you really—

Helmer. There, there, of course I was only joking.

Nora. [*going to the table on the right*] I should not think of going against your wishes.

Helmer. No, I am sure of that! besides, you gave me your word—[*going up to her*] Keep your little Christmas secrets to yourself, my darling. They will all be revealed tonight when the Christmas Tree is lit, no doubt.

Nora. Did you remember to invite Doctor Rank?

Helmer. No. But there is no need; as a matter of course he will come to dinner with us. However, I will ask him when he comes in this morning. I have ordered some good wine. Nora, you can't think how I am looking forward to this evening.

Nora. So am I! And how the children will enjoy themselves, Torvald!

Helmer. It is splendid to feel that one has a perfectly safe appointment, and a big enough income. It's delightful to think of, isn't it?

Nora. It's wonderful!

Helmer. Do you remember last Christmas? For a full three weeks beforehand you shut yourself up every evening till long after midnight, making ornaments for the Christmas Tree and all the other fine things that were to be a surprise to us. It was the dullest three weeks I ever spent!

Nora. I didn't find it dull.

Helmer. [*smiling*] But there was precious little result, Nora.

Nora. Oh, you shouldn't tease me about that again. How could I help the cat's going in and tearing everything to pieces?

Helmer. Of course you couldn't, poor little girl. You had the best of intentions to please us all, and that's the main thing. But it is a good thing that our hard times are over.

Nora. Yes, it is really wonderful.

Helmer. This time I needn't sit here and be dull all alone, and you needn't ruin your dear eyes and your pretty little hands—

Nora. [*clapping her hands*] No, Torvald, I needn't any longer, need I! It's wonderfully lovely to hear you say so! [*taking his arm*] Now I will tell you how I have been thinking we ought to arrange things, Torvald. As soon as Christmas is over— [*A bell rings in the hall.*] There's the bell. [*She tidies the room a little.*] There's someone at the door. What a nuisance!

HELMER. If it is a caller, remember I am not at home.

MAID. [*in the doorway*] A lady to see you, ma'am—a stranger.

NORA. Ask her to come in.

MAID. [*to* HELMER] The doctor came at the same time, sir.

HELMER. Did he go straight into my room?

MAID. Yes sir.

[HELMER *goes into his room. The* MAID *ushers in* MRS. LINDE, *who is in travelling dress, and shuts the door.*]

MRS. LINDE. [*in a dejected and timid voice*] How do you do, Nora?

NORA. [*doubtfully*] How do you do—

MRS. LINDE. You don't recognize me, I suppose.

NORA. No, I don't know—yes, to be sure, I seem to—[*suddenly*] Yes! Christine! Is it really you?

MRS. LINDE. Yes, it is I.

NORA. Christine! To think of my not recognising you! And yet how could I—[*in a gentle voice*] How you have altered, Christine!

MRS. LINDE. Yes, I have indeed. In nine, ten long years—

NORA. Is it so long since we met? I suppose it is. The last eight years have been a happy time for me, I can tell you. And so now you have come into the town, and have taken this long journey in winter—that was plucky of you.

MRS. LINDE. I arrived by steamer this morning.

NORA. To have some fun at Christmas-time, of course. How delightful! We will have such fun together! But take off your things. You are not cold, I hope. [*helps her*] Now we will sit down by the stove, and be cosy. No, take this arm-chair; I will sit here in the rocking-chair. [*takes her hands*] Now you look like your old self again; it was only the first moment—You are a little paler, Christine, and perhaps a little thinner.

MRS. LINDE. And much, much older, Nora.

NORA. Perhaps a little older; very, very little; certainly not much. [*stops suddenly and speaks seriously*] What a thoughtless creature I am, chattering away like this. My poor, dear Christine, do forgive me.

MRS. LINDE. What do you mean, Nora?

NORA. [*gently*] Poor Christine, you are a widow.

MRS. LINDE. Yes; it is three years ago now.

NORA. Yes, I knew; I saw it in the papers. I assure you, Christine, I meant ever so often to write to you at the time, but I always put it off and something always prevented me.

MRS. LINDE. I quite understand, dear.

NORA. It was very bad of me, Christine. Poor thing, how you must have suffered. And he left you nothing?

MRS. LINDE. No.

NORA. And no children?

MRS. LINDE. No.

NORA. Nothing at all, then?

MRS. LINDE. Not even any sorrow or grief to live upon.

NORA. [*looking incredulously at her*] But, Christine, is that possible?

MRS. LINDE. [*smiles sadly and strokes her hair*] It sometimes happens, Nora.

NORA. So you are quite alone. How dreadfully sad that must be. I have three lovely children. You can't see them just now, for they are out with their nurse. But now you must tell me all about it.

MRS. LINDE. No, no; I want to hear you.

NORA. No, you must begin. I mustn't be selfish to-day; to-day I must only think of your affairs. But there is one thing I must tell you. Do you know we have just had a great piece of good luck?

MRS. LINDE. No, what is it?

NORA. Just fancy, my husband has been made manager of the Bank!

MRS. LINDE. Your husband? What good luck!

NORA. Yes, tremendous! A barrister's profession is such an uncertain thing, especially if he won't undertake unsavoury cases; and naturally Torvald has never been willing to do that, and I quite agree with him. You may imagine how pleased we are! He is to take up his work in the Bank at the New Year, and then he will have a big salary and lots of commissions. For the future we can live quite differently—we can do just as we like. I feel so relieved and so happy, Christine! It will be splendid to have heaps of money and not need to have any anxiety, won't it?

MRS. LINDE. Yes, anyhow I think it would be delightful to have what one needs.

NORA. No, not only what one needs, but heaps and heaps of money.

MRS. LINDE. [*smiling*] Nora, Nora haven't you learnt sense yet? In our schooldays you were a great spendthrift.

NORA. [*laughing*] Yes, that is what Torvald says now. [*wags her finger at her*] But "Nora, Nora" is not so silly as you think. We have not been in a position for me to waste money. We have both had to work.

MRS. LINDE. You too?

NORA. Yes; odds and ends, needlework, crochet-work, embroidery, and that kind of thing. [*dropping her voice*] And other things as well. You know Torvald left his office when we were married? There was no prospect of promotion there, and he had to try and earn more than before. But during the first year he overworked himself dreadfully. You see, he had to make money every way he could, and he worked early and late; but he couldn't stand it, and fell dreadfully ill, and the doctors said it was necessary for him to go south.

MRS. LINDE. You spent a whole year in Italy didn't you?

NORA. Yes. It was no easy matter to get away, I can tell you. It was just as Ivar was born; but naturally we had to go. It was a wonderfully beautiful journey, and it saved Torvald's life. But it cost a tremendous lot of money, Christine.

MRS. LINDE. So I should think.

NORA. It cost about two hundred and fifty pounds. That's a lot, isn't it?

MRS. LINDE. Yes, and in emergencies like that it is lucky to have the money.

NORA. I ought to tell you that we had it from papa.

MRS. LINDE. Oh, I see. It was just about that time that he died, wasn't it?

NORA. Yes; and, just think of it, I couldn't go and nurse him. I was expecting little Ivar's birth every day and I had my poor sick Torvald to look after. My dear, kind father—I never saw him again, Christine. That was the saddest time I have known since our marriage.

MRS. LINDE. I know how fond you were of him. And then you went off to Italy?

NORA. Yes; you see we had money then, and the doctors insisted on our going, so we started a month later.

MRS. LINDE. And your husband came back quite well?

Nora. As sound as a bell!

Mrs. Linde. But—the doctor?

Nora. What doctor?

Mrs. Linde. I thought your maid said the gentleman who arrived here just as I did was the doctor?

Nora. Yes, that was Doctor Rank, but he doesn't come here professionally. He is our greatest friend, and comes in at least once every day. No, Torvald has not had an hour's illness since then, and our children are strong and healthy and so am I. [*jumps up and claps her hands*] Christine! Christine! it's good to be alive and happy!—But how horrid of me; I am talking of nothing but my own affairs. [*sits on a stool near her, and rests her arms on her knees*] You mustn't be angry with me. Tell me, is it really true that you did not love your husband? Why did you marry him?

Mrs. Linde. My mother was alive then, and was bedridden and helpless, and I had to provide for my two younger brothers; so I did not think I was justified in refusing his offer.

Nora. No, perhaps you were quite right. He was rich at that time, then?

Mrs. Linde. I believe he was quite well off. But his business was a precarious one; and, when he died, it all went to pieces and there was nothing left.

Nora. And then?—

Mrs. Linde. Well, I had to turn my hand to anything I could find—first a small shop, then a small school, and so on. The last three years have seemed like one long working-day, with no rest. Now it is at an end, Nora. My poor mother needs me no more, for she is gone; and the boys do not need me either; they have got situations and can shift for themselves.

Nora. What a relief you must feel it—

Mrs. Linde. No, indeed; I only feel my life unspeakably empty. No one to live for any more. [*gets up restlessly*] That was why I could not stand the life in my little backwater any longer. I hope it may be easier here to find something which will busy me and occupy my thoughts. If only I could have the good luck to get some regular work—office work of some kind—

Nora. But, Christine, that is so frightfully tiring, and you look tired out now. You had far better go away to some watering-place.

Mrs. Linde. [*walking to the window*] I have no father to give me money for a journey, Nora.

Nora. [*rising*] Oh, don't be angry with me.

Mrs. Linde. [*going up to her*] It is you that must not be angry with me, dear. The worst of a position like mine is that it makes one so bitter. No one to work for, and yet obliged to be always on the look-out for chances. One must live, and so one becomes selfish. When you told me of the happy turn your fortunes have taken—you will hardly believe it—I was delighted not so much on your account as on my own.

Nora. How do you mean?—Oh, I understand. You mean that perhaps Torvald could get you something to do.

Mrs. Linde. Yes, that was what I was thinking of.

Nora. He must, Christine. Just leave it to me; I will broach the subject very cleverly—I will think of something that will please him very much. It will make me so happy to be of some use to you.

Mrs. Linde. How kind you are, Nora, to be so anxious to help me! It is doubly kind in you, for you know so little of the burdens and troubles of life.

NORA. I—? I know so little of them?

MRS. LINDE. [*smiling*] My dear! Small household cares and that sort of thing!—You are a child, Nora.

NORA. [*tosses her head and crosses the stage*] You ought not to be so superior.

MRS. LINDE. No?

NORA. You are just like the others. They all think that I am incapable of anything really serious—

MRS. LINDE. Come, come—

NORA. —that I have gone through nothing in this world of cares.

MRS. LINDE. But, my dear Nora, you have just told me all your troubles.

NORA. Pooh!—those were trifles. [*lowering her voice*] I have not told you the important thing.

MRS. LINDE. The important thing? What do you mean?

NORA. You look down upon me altogether, Christine—but you ought not to. You are proud, aren't you, of having worked so hard and so long for your mother?

MRS. LINDE. Indeed, I don't look down on any one. But it is true that I am both proud and glad to think that I was privileged to make the end of my mother's life almost free from care.

NORA. And you are proud to think of what you have done for your brothers.

MRS. LINDE. I think I have the right to be.

NORA. I think so, too. But now, listen to this; I too have something to be proud of and glad of.

MRS. LINDE. I have no doubt you have. But what do you refer to?

NORA. Speak low. Suppose Torvald were to hear! He mustn't on any account—no one in the world must know, Christine, except you.

MRS. LINDE. But what is it?

NORA. Come here. [*pulls her down on the sofa beside her*] Now I will show you that I too have something to be proud and glad of. It was I who saved Torvald's life.

MRS. LINDE. "Saved"? How?

NORA. I told you about our trip to Italy. Torvald would never have recovered if he had not gone there—

MRS. LINDE. Yes, but your father gave you the necessary funds.

NORA. [*smiling*] Yes, that is what Torvald and all the others think, but—

MRS. LINDE. But—

NORA. Papa didn't give us a shilling. It was I who procured the money.

MRS. LINDE. You? All that large sum?

NORA. Two hundred and fifty pounds. What do you think of that?

MRS. LINDE. But, Nora, how could you possibly do it? Did you win a prize in the Lottery?

NORA. [*contemptuously*] In the Lottery? There would have been no credit in that.

MRS. LINDE. But where did you get it from, then?

NORA. [*humming and smiling with an air of mystery*] Hm, hm! Aha!

MRS. LINDE. Because you couldn't have borrowed it.

NORA. Couldn't I? Why not?

MRS. LINDE. No, a wife cannot borrow without her husband's consent.

NORA. [*tossing her head*] Oh, if it is a wife who has any head for business—a wife who has the wit to be a little bit clever—

MRS. LINDE. I don't understand it at all, Nora.

NORA. There is no need you should. I never said I had borrowed the money. I may have got it some other way. [*lies back on the sofa*] Perhaps I got it from some other admirer. When anyone is as attractive as I am—

Mrs. Linde. You are a mad creature.

Nora. Now, you know you're full of curiosity, Christine.

Mrs. Linde. Listen to me, Nora dear. Haven't you been a little bit imprudent?

Nora. [*sits up straight*] Is it imprudent to save your husband's life?

Mrs. Linde. It seems to me imprudent, without his knowledge, to—

Nora. But it was absolutely necessary that he should not know! My goodness, can't you understand that? It was necessary he should have no idea what a dangerous condition he was in. It was to me that the doctors came and said that his life was in danger, and that the only thing to save him was to live in the south. Do you suppose I didn't try, first of all, to get what I wanted as if it were for myself? I told him how much I should love to travel abroad like other young wives; I tried tears and entreaties with him; I told him that he ought to remember the condition I was in, and that he ought to be kind and indulgent to me; I even hinted that he might raise a loan. That nearly made him angry, Christine. He said I was thoughtless, and that it was his duty as my husband not to indulge me in my whims and caprices—as I believe he called them. Very well I thought, you must be saved—and that was how I came to devise a way out of the difficulty—

Mrs. Linde. And did your husband never get to know from your father that the money had not come from him?

Nora. No, never. Papa died just at that time. I had meant to let him into the secret and beg him never to reveal it. But he was so ill then—alas, there never was any need to tell him.

Mrs. Linde. And since then have you never told your secret to your husband?

Nora. Good Heavens, no! How could you think so? A man who has such strong opinions about these things! And besides, how painful and humiliating it would be for Torvald, with his manly independence, to know that he owed me anything! It would upset our mutual relations altogether; our beautiful happy home would no longer be what it is now.

Mrs. Linde. Do you mean never to tell him about it?

Nora. [*meditatively, and with a half smile*] Yes—some day, perhaps, after many years, when I am no longer as nice-looking as I am now. Don't laugh at me! I mean of course, when Torvald is no longer as devoted to me as he is now; when my dancing and dressing-up and reciting have palled on him; then it may be a good thing to have something in reserve—[*breaking off*] What nonsense! That time will never come. Now, what do you think of my great secret, Christine? Do you still think I am of no use? I can tell you, too, that this affair has caused me a lot of worry. It has been by no means easy for me to meet my engagements punctually. I may tell you that there is something that is called, in business, quarterly interest, and another thing called payment in instalments, and it is always so dreadfully difficult to manage them. I have had to save a little here and there, where I could, you understand. I have not been able to put aside much from my housekeeping money, for Torvald must have a good table. I couldn't let my children be shabbily dressed; I have felt obliged to use up all he gave me for them, the sweet little darlings!

Mrs. Linde. So it has all had to come out of your own necessaries of life, poor Nora?

Nora. Of course. Besides, I was the one responsible for it. Whenever Torvald has given me the money for new dresses and such things, I have never spent more than half of it; I have always bought the simplest and cheapest things. Thank Heaven, any clothes look well on me, and so Torvald has never noticed it. But it was often very hard on me, Christine—because it is delightful to be really well dressed, isn't it?

MRS. LINDE. Quite so.

NORA. Well, then I have found other ways of earning money. Last winter I was lucky enough to get a lot of copying to do; so I locked myself up and sat writing every evening until quite late at night. Many a time I was desperately tired; but all the same it was a tremendous pleasure to sit there working and earning money. It was like being a man.

MRS. LINDE. How much have you been able to pay off in that way?

NORA. I can't tell you exactly. You see, it is very difficult to keep an account of a business matter of that kind. I only know that I have paid every penny that I could scrape together. Many a time I was at my wit's end. [*smiles*] Then I used to sit here and imagine that a rich old gentleman had fallen in love with me—

MRS. LINDE. What! Who was it?

NORA. Be quiet!—that he had died; and that when his will was opened it contained, written in big letters, the instruction "The lovely Mrs. Nora Helmer is to have all I possess paid over to her at once in cash."

MRS. LINDE. But, my dear Nora—who could the man be?

NORA. Good gracious, can't you understand? There was no old gentleman at all; it was only something that I used to sit here and imagine, when I couldn't think of any way of procuring money. But it's all the same now; the tiresome old person can stay where he is, as far as I am concerned; I don't care about him or his will either, for I am free from care now. [*jumps up*] My goodness, it's delightful to think of, Christine! Free from care! To be able to be free from care, quite free from care; to be able to play and romp with the children; to be able to keep the house beautifully and have everything just as Torvald likes it! And, think of it, soon the spring will come and the big blue sky! Perhaps we shall be able to take a little trip—perhaps I shall see the sea again! Oh, it's a wonderful thing to be alive and be happy. [*A bell is heard in the hall.*]

MRS. LINDE. [*rising*] There is the bell; perhaps I had better go.

NORA. No, don't go; no one will come in here; it is sure to be for Torvald.

SERVANT. [*at the hall door*] Excuse me, ma'am—there is a gentleman to see the master, and as the doctor is with him—

NORA. Who is it?

KROGSTAD. [*at the door*] It is I, Mrs. Helmer. [*Mrs. Linde starts, trembles, and turns to the window.*]

NORA. [*takes a step towards him, and speaks in a strained, low voice*] You? What is it? What do you want to see my husband about?

KROGSTAD. Bank business—in a way. I have a small post in the Bank, and I hear your husband is to be our chief now—

NORA. Then it is—

KROGSTAD. Nothing but dry business matters, Mrs. Helmer; absolutely nothing else.

NORA. Be so good as to go into the study, then. [*She bows indifferently to him and shuts the door into the hall; then comes back and makes up the fire in the stove.*]

MRS. LINDE. Nora—who was that man?

NORA. A lawyer, of the name of Krogstad.

MRS. LINDE. Then it really was he.

NORA. Do you know the man?

MRS. LINDE. I used to—many years ago. At one time he was a solicitor's clerk in our town.

NORA. Yes, he was.

MRS. LINDE. He is greatly altered.

NORA. He made a very unhappy marriage.

MRS. LINDE. He is a widower now, isn't he?

NORA. With several children. There now, it is burning up.

[*Shuts the door of the stove and moves the rocking-chair aside.*]

MRS. LINDE. They say he carries on various kinds of business.

NORA. Really! Perhaps he does; I don't know anything about it. But don't let us think of business; it is so tiresome.

DOCTOR RANK. [*comes out of* HELMER's *study. Before he shuts the door he calls to him.*] No, my dear fellow, I won't disturb you; I would rather go in to your wife for a little while. [*shuts the door and sees* MRS. LINDE] I beg your pardon; I am afraid I am disturbing you too.

NORA. No, not at all. [*introducing him*] Doctor Rank, Mrs. Linde.

RANK. I have often heard Mrs. Linde's name mentioned here. I think I passed you on the stairs when I arrived, Mrs. Linde?

MRS. LINDE. Yes, I go up very slowly; I can't manage stairs well.

RANK. Ah! some slight internal weakness?

MRS. LINDE. No, the fact is I have been overworking myself.

RANK. Nothing more than that? Then I suppose you have come to town to amuse yourself with our entertainments?

MRS. LINDE. I have come to look for work.

RANK. Is that a good cure for overwork?

MRS. LINDE. One must live, Doctor Rank.

RANK. Yes, the general opinion seems to be that it is necessary.

NORA. Look here, Doctor Rank—you know you want to live.

RANK. Certainly. However wretched I may feel, I want to prolong the agony as long as possible. All my patients are like that. And so are those who are morally diseased; one of them, and a bad case too, is at this very moment with Helmer—

MRS. LINDE. [*sadly*] Ah!

NORA. Whom do you mean?

RANK. A lawyer of the name of Krogstad, a fellow you don't know at all. He suffers from a diseased moral character, Mrs. Helmer; but even he began talking of its being highly important that he should live.

NORA. Did he? What did he want to speak to Torvald about?

RANK. I have no idea; I only heard that it was something about the Bank.

NORA. I didn't know this—what's his name—Krogstad had anything to do with the Bank.

RANK. Yes, he has some sort of appointment there. [*to* MRS. LINDE] I don't know whether you find also in your part of the world that there are certain people who go zealously snuffing about to smell out moral corruption, and, as soon as they have found some, put the person concerned into some lucrative position where they can keep their eye on him. Healthy natures are left out in the cold.

MRS. LINDE. Still I think the sick are those who most need taking care of.

RANK. [*shrugging his shoulders*] Yes, there you are. That is the sentiment that is turning Society into a sickhouse.

[NORA, *who has been absorbed in her thoughts, breaks out into smothered laughter and claps her hands.*]

RANK. Why do you laugh at that? Have you any notion what Society really is?

NORA. What do I care about tiresome Society? I am laughing at something quite different, something extremely amusing. Tell me, Doctor Rank, are all the people who are employed in the Bank dependent on Torvald now?

RANK. Is that what you find so extremely amusing?

NORA. [*smiling and humming*] That's my affair! [*walking about the room*] It's perfectly glorious to think that we have—that Torvald has so much power over so many people. [*takes the packet from her pocket*] Doctor Rank, what do you say to a macaroon?

RANK. What, macaroons? I thought they were forbidden here.

NORA. Yes, but these are some Christine gave me.

MRS. LINDE. What! I?—

NORA. Oh, well, don't be alarmed! You couldn't know that Torvald had forbidden them. I must tell you that he is afraid they will spoil my teeth. But, bah!—once in a while—That's so, isn't it, Doctor Rank? By your leave? [*puts a macaroon into his mouth*] You must have one too, Christine. And I shall have one, just a little one—or at most two. [*walking about*] I am tremendously happy. There is just one thing in the world now that I should dearly love to do.

RANK. Well, what is that?

NORA. It's something I should dearly love to say, if Torvald could hear me.

RANK. Well, why can't you say it?

NORA. No, I daren't; it's so shocking.

MRS. LINDE. Shocking?

RANK. Well, I should not advise you to say it. Still, with us you might. What is it you would so much like to say if Torvald could hear you?

NORA. I should just love to say—Well, I'm damned!

RANK. Are you mad?

MRS. LINDE. Nora, dear—

RANK. Say it, here he is!

NORA. [*hiding the packet*] Hush! Hush! Hush!

[HELMER *comes out of his room, with his coat over his arm and his hat in his hands.*]

NORA. Well, Torvald dear, have you got rid of him?

HELMER. Yes, he has just gone.

NORA. Let me introduce you—this is Christine, who has come to town.

HELMER. Christine—? Excuse me, but I don't know—

NORA. Mrs. Linde, dear; Christine Linde.

HELMER. Of course. A school friend of my wife's, I presume?

MRS. LINDE. Yes, we have known each other since then.

NORA. And just think, she has taken a long journey in order to see you.

HELMER. What do you mean?

MRS. LINDE. No, really, I—

NORA. Christine is tremendously clever at book-keeping, and she is frightfully anxious to work under some clever man, so as to perfect herself—

HELMER. Very sensible, Mrs. Linde.

NORA. And when she heard you had been appointed manager of the Bank—the news was telegraphed, you know—she travelled here as quick as she could. Torvald, I am sure you will be able to do something for Christine, for my sake, won't you?

HELMER. Well, it is not altogether impossible. I presume you are a widow, Mrs. Linde?

MRS. LINDE. Yes.

HELMER. And have had some experience of book-keeping?

MRS. LINDE. Yes, a fair amount.

HELMER. Ah! well, it's very likely I may be able to find something for you—

NORA. [*clapping her hands*] What did I tell you? What did I tell you?

HELMER. You have just come at a fortunate moment, Mrs. Linde.

MRS. LINDE. How am I to thank you?

HELMER. There is no need. [*puts on his coat*] But to-day you must excuse me—

RANK. Wait a minute; I will come with you.

[*Brings his fur coat from the hall and warms it at the fire.*]

NORA. Don't be long away, Torvald dear.

HELMER. About an hour, not more.

NORA. Are you going too, Christine?

MRS. LINDE. [*putting on her cloak*] Yes, I must go and look for a room.

HELMER. Oh, well then, we can walk down the street together.

NORA. [*helping her*] What a pity it is we are so short of space here: I am afraid it is impossible for us—

MRS. LINDE. Please don't think of it! Good-bye, Nora dear, and many thanks.

NORA. Good-bye for the present. Of course you will come back this evening. And you too, Dr. Rank. What do you say? If you are well enough? Oh, you must be! Wrap yourself up well.

[*They go to the door all talking together. Children's voices are heard on the staircase.*]

NORA. There they are. There they are! [*She runs to open the door: The* NURSE *comes in with the children.*] Come in! Come in! [*stoops and kisses them*] Oh, you sweet blessings! Look at them, Christine! Aren't they darlings?

RANK. Don't let us stand here in the draught.

HELMER. Come along, Mrs. Linde; the place will only be bearable for a mother now!

[RANK, HELMER *and* MRS. LINDE *go downstairs. The* NURSE *comes forward with the children;* NORA *shuts the hall door.*]

NORA. How fresh and well you look! Such red cheeks!—like apples and roses. [*The children all talk at once while she speaks to them.*] Have you had great fun? That's splendid! What, you pulled both Emmy and Bob along on the sledge?—both at once?—that *was* good. You are a clever boy, Ivar. Let me take her for a little, Anne. My sweet little baby doll! [*takes the baby from the* MAID *and dances it up and down*] Yes, yes, mother will dance with Bob too. What! Have you been snowballing? I wish I had been there too! No, no, I will take their things off, Anne; please let me do it, it is such fun. Go in now, you look half frozen. There is some coffee for you on the stove.

[*The* NURSE *goes into the room on the left.* NORA *takes off the children's things and throws them about, while they all talk to her at once.*]

NORA. Really! Did a big dog run after you? But it didn't bite you? No, dogs don't bite nice little dolly children. You mustn't look at the parcels, Ivar. What are they? Ah, I daresay you would like to know. No, no—it's something nasty!

Come, let us have a game! What shall we play at? Hide and Seek? Yes, we'll play Hide and Seek. Bob shall hide first. Must I hide? Very well, I'll hide first.

[*She and the children laugh and shout, and romp in and out of the room; at last* Nora *hides under the table, the children rush in and look for her, but do not see her; they hear her smothered laughter, run to the table, lift up the cloth and find her. Shouts of laughter. She crawls forward and pretends to frighten them. Fresh laughter. Meanwhile there has been a knock at the hall door, but none of them has noticed it. The door is half opened, and Krogstad appears. He waits a little; the game goes on.*]

Krogstad. Excuse me, Mrs. Helmer.

Nora. [*with a stifled cry, turns round and gets up on to her knees*] Ah! what do you want?

Krogstad. Excuse me, the outer door was ajar; I suppose someone forgot to shut it.

Nora. [*rising*] My husband is out, Mr. Krogstad.

Krogstad. I know that.

Nora. What do you want here, then?

Krogstad. A word with you.

Nora. With me?—[*to the children, gently*] Go in to nurse. What? No, the strange man won't do mother any harm. When he has gone we will have another game. [*She takes the children into the room on the left, and shuts the door after them.*] You want to speak to me?

Krogstad. Yes, I do.

Nora. To-day? It is not the first of the month yet.

Krogstad. No, it is Christmas Eve, and it will depend on yourself what sort of a Christmas you will spend.

Nora. What do you want? To-day it is absolutely impossible for me—

Krogstad. We won't talk about that till later on. This is something different. I presume you can give me a moment?

Nora. Yes—yes, I can—although—

Krogstad. Good. I was in Olsen's Restaurant and saw your husband going down the street—

Nora. Yes?

Krogstad. With a lady.

Nora. What then?

Krogstad. May I make so bold as to ask if it was a Mrs. Linde?

Nora. It was.

Krogstad. Just arrived in town?

Nora. Yes, to-day.

Krogstad. She is a great friend of yours, isn't she?

Nora. She is. But I don't see—

Krogstad. I knew her too, once upon a time.

Nora. I am aware of that.

Krogstad. Are you? So you know all about it; I thought as much. Then I can ask you, without beating about the bush—is Mrs. Linde to have an appointment in the Bank?

Nora. What right have you to question me, Mr. Krogstad?—You, one of my husband's subordinates! But since you ask, you shall know. Yes, Mrs. Linde *is* to have an appointment. And it was I who pleaded her cause, Mr. Krogstad, let me tell you that.

Krogstad. I was right in what I thought, then.

Nora. [*walking up and down the stage*] Sometimes one has a tiny little bit of influence, I should hope. Because one is a woman, it does not necessarily follow that—. When anyone is in a subordinate position, Mr. Krogstad, they should really be careful to avoid offending anyone who—who—

Krogstad. Who has influence?

Nora. Exactly.

Krogstad. [*changing his tone*] Mrs. Helmer, you will be so good as to use your influence on my behalf.

Nora. What? What do you mean?

Krogstad. You will be so kind as to see that I am allowed to keep my subordinate position in the Bank.

Nora. What do you mean by that? Who proposes to take your post away from you?

Krogstad. Oh, there is no necessity to keep up the pretence of ignorance. I can quite understand that your friend is not very anxious to expose herself to the chance of rubbing shoulders with me; and I quite understand, too, whom I have to thank for being turned out.

Nora. But I assure you—

Krogstad. Very likely; but, to come to the point, the time has come when I should advise you to use your influence to prevent that.

Nora. But, Mr. Krogstad, I *have* no influence.

Krogstad. Haven't you? I thought you said yourself just now—

Nora. Naturally I did not mean you to put that construction on it. I! What should make you think I have any influence of that kind with my husband?

Krogstad. Oh, I have known your husband from our student days. I don't suppose he is any more unassailable than other husbands.

Nora. If you speak slightingly of my husband, I shall turn you out of the house.

Krogstad. You are bold, Mrs. Helmer.

Nora. I am not afraid of you any longer. As soon as the New Year comes, I shall in a very short time be free of the whole thing.

Krogstad. [*controlling himself*] Listen to me, Mrs. Helmer. If necessary, I am prepared to fight for my small post in the Bank as if I were fighting for my life.

Nora. So it seems.

Krogstad. It is not only for the sake of the money; indeed, that weighs least with me in the matter. There is another reason—well, I may as well tell you. My position is this. I daresay you know, like everybody else, that once, many years ago, I was guilty of an indiscretion.

Nora. I think I have heard something of the kind.

Krogstad. The matter never came into court; but every way seemed to be closed to me after that. So I took to the business that you know of. I had to do something; and, honestly, I don't think I've been one of the worst. But now I must cut myself free from all that. My sons are growing up; for their sake I must try and win back as much respect as I can in the town. This post in the Bank was like the first step up for me—and now your husband is going to kick me downstairs again into the mud.

Nora. But you must believe me, Mr. Krogstad; it is not in my power to help you at all.

Krogstad. Then it is because you haven't the will; but I have means to compel you.

NORA. You don't mean that you will tell my husband that I owe you money?

KROGSTAD. Hm!—suppose I were to tell him?

NORA. It would be perfectly infamous of you. [*sobbing*] To think of his learning my secret, which has been my joy and pride, in such an ugly, clumsy way—that he should learn it from you! And it would put me in a horribly disagreeable position—

KROGSTAD. Only disagreeable?

NORA. [*impetuously*] Well, do it, then!—and it will be the worse for you. My husband will see for himself what a blackguard you are, and you certainly won't keep your post then.

KROGSTAD. I asked you if it was only a disagreeable scene at home that you were afraid of?

NORA. If my husband does get to know of it, of course he will at once pay you what is still owing, and we shall have nothing more to do with you.

KROGSTAD. [*coming a step nearer*] Listen to me, Mrs. Helmer. Either you have a very bad memory or you know very little of business. I shall be obliged to remind you of a few details.

NORA. What do you mean?

KROGSTAD. When your husband was ill, you came to me to borrow two hundred and fifty pounds.

NORA. I didn't know any one else to go to.

KROGSTAD. I promised to get you that amount—

NORA. Yes, and you did so.

KROGSTAD. I promised to get you that amount, on certain conditions. Your mind was so taken up with your husband's illness, and you were so anxious to get the money for your journey, that you seem to have paid no attention to the conditions of our bargain. Therefore it will not be amiss if I remind you of them. Now, I promised to get the money on the security of a bond which I drew up.

NORA. Yes, and which I signed.

KROGSTAD. Good. But below your signature there were a few lines constituting your father a surety for the money; those lines your father should have signed.

NORA. Should? He did sign them.

KROGSTAD. I had left the date blank; that is to say your father should himself have inserted the date on which he signed the paper. Do you remember that?

NORA. Yes, I think I remember—

KROGSTAD. Then I gave you the bond to send by post to your father. Is that not so?

NORA. Yes.

KROGSTAD. And you naturally did so at once, because five or six days afterwards you brought me the bond with your father's signature. And then I gave you the money.

NORA. Well, haven't I been paying it off regularly?

KROGSTAD. Fairly so, yes. But—to come back to the matter in hand—that must have been a very trying time for you, Mrs. Helmer?

NORA. It was, indeed.

KROGSTAD. Your father was very ill, wasn't he?

NORA. He was very near his end.

KROGSTAD. And died soon afterwards?

NORA. Yes.

KROGSTAD. Tell me, Mrs. Helmer, can you by any chance remember what day your father died?—on what day of the month, I mean.

NORA. Papa died on the 29th of September.

KROGSTAD. That is correct; I have ascertained it for myself. And, as that is so, there is a discrepancy [*taking a paper from his pocket*] which I cannot account for.

NORA. What discrepancy? I don't know—

KROGSTAD. The discrepancy consists, Mrs. Helmer, in the fact that your father signed this bond three days after his death.

NORA. What do you mean? I don't understand—

KROGSTAD. Your father died on the 29th of September. But, look here; your father has dated his signature the 2nd of October. It is a discrepancy, isn't it? [NORA *is silent*.] Can you explain it to me? [NORA *is still silent*.] It is a remarkable thing, too, that the words "2nd of October," as well as the year, are not written in your father's handwriting but in one that I think I know. Well, of course it can be explained; your father may have forgotten to date his signature, and someone else may have dated it haphazard before they knew of his death. There is no harm in that. It all depends on the signature of the name; and that is genuine, I suppose, Mrs. Helmer? It was your father himself who signed his name here?

NORA. [*after a short pause, throws her head up and looks defiantly at him*] No, it was not. It was I that wrote papa's name.

KROGSTAD. Are you aware that is a dangerous confession?

NORA. In what way? You shall have your money soon.

KROGSTAD. Let me ask you a question; why did you not send the paper to your father?

NORA. It was impossible; papa was so ill. If I had asked him for his signature, I should have had to tell him what the money was to be used for; and when he was so ill himself I couldn't tell him that my husband's life was in danger—it was impossible.

KROGSTAD. It would have been better for you if you had given up your trip abroad.

NORA. No, that was impossible. That trip was to save my husband's life; I couldn't give that up.

KROGSTAD. But did it never occur to you that you were committing a fraud on me?

NORA. I couldn't take that into account; I didn't trouble myself about you at all. I couldn't bear you, because you put so many heartless difficulties in my way, although you knew what a dangerous condition my husband was in.

KROGSTAD. Mrs. Helmer, you evidently do not realise clearly what it is that you have been guilty of. But I can assure you that my one false step, which lost me all my reputation, was nothing more or nothing worse than what you have done.

NORA. You? Do you ask me to believe that you were brave enough to run a risk to save your wife's life?

KROGSTAD. The law cares nothing about motives.

NORA. Then it must be a very foolish law.

KROGSTAD. Foolish or not, it is the law by which you will be judged, if I produce this paper in court.

NORA. I don't believe it. Is a daughter not to be allowed to spare her dying father anxiety and care? Is a wife not to be allowed to save her husband's life? I don't know much about law; but I am certain that there must be laws permitting such things as that. Have you no knowledge of such laws—you who are a lawyer? You must be a very poor lawyer, Mr. Krogstad.

KROGSTAD. Maybe. But matters of business—such business as you and I have had together—do you think I don't understand that? Very well. Do as you please. But let me tell you this—if I lose my position a second time, you shall lose yours with me.

[*He bows, and goes out through the hall.*]

NORA. [*appears buried in thought for a short time, then tosses her head*] Nonsense! Trying to frighten me like that!—I am not so silly as he thinks. [*begins to busy herself putting the children's things in order*] And yet—? No, it's impossible! I did it for love's sake.

THE CHILDREN. [*in the doorway on the left*] Mother, the stranger man has gone out through the gate.

NORA. Yes, dears, I know. But, don't tell anyone about the stranger man. Do you hear? Not even papa.

CHILDREN. No, mother; but will you come and play again?

NORA. No, no—not now.

CHILDREN. But, mother, you promised us.

NORA. Yes, but I can't now. Run away in; I have such a lot to do. Run away in, my sweet little darlings. [*She gets them into the room by degrees and shuts the door on them; then sits down on the sofa, takes up a piece of needlework and sews a few stitches, but soon stops.*] No! [*throws down the work, gets up, goes to the hall door and calls out*] Helen! bring the Tree in. [*goes to the table on the left, opens a drawer, and stops again*] No, no! it is quite impossible!

MAID. [*coming in with the Tree*] Where shall I put it, ma'am?

NORA. Here, in the middle of the floor.

MAID. Shall I get you anything else?

NORA. No, thank you. I have all I want.

[*Exit Maid.*]

NORA. [*begins dressing the tree*] A candle here—and flowers here—. The horrible man! It's all nonsense—there's nothing wrong. The Tree shall be splendid! I will do everything I can think of to please you, Torvald!—I will sing for you, dance for you—[HELMER *comes in with some papers under his arm*] Oh! are you back already?

HELMER. Yes. Has anyone been here?

NORA. Here? No.

HELMER. That is strange. I saw Krogstad going out of the gate.

NORA. Did you? Oh yes, I forgot, Krogstad was here for a moment.

HELMER. Nora, I can see from your manner that he has been here begging you to say a good word for him.

NORA. Yes.

HELMER. And you were to appear to do it of your own accord; you were to conceal from me the fact of his having been here; didn't he beg that of you too?

NORA. Yes, Torvald, but—

HELMER. Nora, Nora, and you would be a party to that sort of thing? To have any talk with a man like that, and give him any sort of promise? And to tell me a lie into the bargain?

NORA. A lie—?

HELMER. Didn't you tell me no one had been here? [*shakes his finger at her*] My little song-bird must never do that again. A song-bird must have a clean beak to chirp with—no false notes! [*puts his arm round her waist*] That is so, isn't it?

Yes, I am sure it is. [*lets her go*] We will say no more about it. [*sits down by the stove*] How warm and snug it is here!

[*Turns over his papers.*]

NORA. [*after a short pause, during which she busies herself with the Christmas Tree*] Torvald!

HELMER. Yes.

NORA. I am looking forward tremendously to the fancy dress ball at the Stenborgs' the day after to-morrow.

HELMER. And I am tremendously curious to see what you are going to surprise me with.

NORA. It was very silly of me to want to do that.

HELMER. What do you mean?

NORA. I can't hit upon anything that will do; everything I think of seems so silly and insignificant.

HELMER. Does my little Nora acknowledge that at last?

NORA. [*standing behind his chair with her arms on the back of it*] Are you very busy, Torvald?

HELMER. Well—

NORA. What are all those papers?

HELMER. Bank business.

NORA. Already?

HELMER. I have got authority from the retiring manager to undertake the necessary changes in the staff and in the rearrangement of the work; and I must make use of the Christmas week for that, so as to have everything in order for the new year.

NORA. Then that was why this poor Krogstad—

HELMER. Hm!

NORA. [*leans against the back of his chair and strokes his hair*] If you hadn't been so busy I should have asked you a tremendously big favour, Torvald.

HELMER. What is that? Tell me.

NORA. There is no one has such good taste as you. And I do so want to look nice at the fancy-dress ball. Torvald, couldn't you take me in hand and decide what I shall go as, and what sort of a dress I shall wear?

HELMER. Aha! so my obstinate little woman is obliged to get someone to come to her rescue?

NORA. Yes, Torvald, I can't get along a bit without your help.

HELMER. Very well, I will think it over, we shall manage to hit upon something.

NORA. That is nice of you. [*Goes to the Christmas Tree. A short pause.*] How pretty the red flowers look—. But, tell me, was it really something very bad that this Krogstad was guilty of?

HELMER. He forged someone's name. Have you any idea what that means?

NORA. Isn't it possible that he was driven to do it by necessity?

HELMER. Yes; or, as in so many cases, by imprudence. I am not so heartless as to condemn a man altogether because of a single false step of that kind.

NORA. No you wouldn't, would you, Torvald?

HELMER. Many a man has been able to retrieve his character, if he has openly confessed his fault and taken his punishment.

NORA. Punishment—?

HELMER. But Krogstad did nothing of that sort; he got himself out of it by a cunning trick, and that is why he has gone under altogether.

NORA. But do you think it would—?

HELMER. Just think how a guilty man like that has to lie and play the hypocrite with everyone, how he has to wear a mask in the presence of those near and dear to him, even before his own wife and children. And about the children—that is the most terrible part of it all, Nora.

NORA. How?

HELMER. Because such an atmosphere of lies infects and poisons the whole life of a home. Each breath the children take in such a house is full of the germs of evil.

NORA. [*coming nearer him*] Are you sure of that?

HELMER. My dear, I have often seen it in the course of my life as a lawyer. Almost everyone who has gone to the bad early in life has had a deceitful mother.

NORA. Why do you only say—mother?

HELMER. It seems most commonly to be the mother's influence, though naturally a bad father's would have the same result. Every lawyer is familiar with the fact. This Krogstad, now, has been persistently poisoning his own children with lies and dissimulation; that is why I say he has lost all moral character. [*holds out his hands to her*] That is why my sweet little Nora must promise me not to plead his cause. Give me your hand on it. Come, come, what is this? Give me your hand. There now, that's settled. I assure you it would be quite impossible for me to work with him; I literally feel physically ill when I am in the company of such people.

NORA. [*takes her hand out of his and goes to the opposite side of the Christmas Tree*] How hot it is in here; and I have such a lot to do.

HELMER. [*getting up and putting his papers in order*] Yes, and I must try and read through some of these before dinner; and I must think about your costume, too. And it is just possible I may have something ready in gold paper to hang up on the Tree. [*Puts his hand on her head.*] My precious little singing-bird!

[*He goes into his room and shuts the door after him.*]

NORA. [*after a pause, whispers*] No, no—it isn't true. It's impossible; it must be impossible.

[*The* NURSE *opens the door on the left.*]

NURSE. The little ones are begging so hard to be allowed to come in to mamma.

NORA. No, no, no! Don't let them come in to me! You stay with them, Anne.

NURSE. Very well, ma'am.

[*Shuts the door.*]

NORA. [*pale with terror*] Deprave my little children? Poison my home? [*a short pause. Then she tosses her head.*] It's not true. It can't possibly be true.

ACT 2

The Same Scene. The Christmas Tree is in the corner by the piano, stripped of its ornaments and with burnt-down candle-ends on its dishevelled branches. Nora's cloak and hat are lying on the sofa. She is alone in the room, walking about uneasily. She stops by the sofa and takes up her cloak.

NORA. [*drops the cloak*] Someone is coming now! [*goes to the door and listens*] No—it is no one. Of course, no one will come to-day, Christmas Day—nor tomorrow either. But, perhaps—[*opens the door and looks out*] No, nothing in the letter-box; it is quite empty. [*comes forward*] What rubbish! of course he can't be in earnest about it. Such a thing couldn't happen; it is impossible—I have three little children.

[*Enter the* NURSE *from the room on the left, carrying a big cardboard box.*]

NURSE. At last I have found the box with the fancy dress.
NORA. Thanks; put it on the table.
NURSE. [*doing so*] But it is very much in want of mending.
NORA. I should like to tear it into a hundred thousand pieces.
NURSE. What an idea! It can easily be put in order—just a little patience.
NORA. Yes, I will go and get Mrs. Linde to come and help me with it.
NURSE. What, out again? In this horrible weather? You will catch cold, ma'am, and make yourself ill.
NORA. Well, worse than that might happen. How are the children?
NURSE. The poor little souls are playing with their Christmas presents, but—
NORA. Do they ask much for me?
NURSE. You see, they are so accustomed to have their mamma with them.
NORA. Yes, but, nurse, I shall not be able to be so much with them now as I was before.
NURSE. Oh well, young children easily get accustomed to anything.
NORA. Do you think so? Do you think they would forget their mother if she went away altogether?
NURSE. Good heavens!—went away altogether?
NORA. Nurse, I want you to tell me something I have often wondered about—how could you have the heart to put your own child out among strangers?
NURSE. I was obliged to, if I wanted to be little Nora's nurse.
NORA. Yes, but how could you be willing to do it?
NURSE. What, when I was going to get such a good place by it? A poor girl who has got into trouble should be glad to. Besides, that wicked man didn't do a single thing for me.
NORA. But I suppose your daughter has quite forgotten you.
NURSE. No, indeed she hasn't. She wrote to me when she was confirmed, and when she was married.
NORA. [*putting her arms round her neck*] Dear old Anne, you were a good mother to me when I was little.
NURSE. Little Nora, poor dear, had no other mother but me.
NORA. And if my little ones had no other mother, I am sure you would—What nonsense I am talking! [*opens the box*] Go in to them. Now I must—. You will see tomorrow how charming I shall look.
NURSE. I am sure there will be no one at the ball so charming as you, ma'am.

[*Goes into the room on the left.*]

NORA. [*begins to unpack the box, but soon pushes it away from her*] If only I dared go out. If only no one would come. If only I could be sure nothing would happen here in the meantime. Stuff and nonsense! No one will come. Only I mustn't think about it. I will brush my muff. What lovely gloves! Out of my thoughts, out of my thoughts! One, two, three, four, five, six—[*Screams.*] Ah! there is someone coming—

[*Makes a movement towards the door, but stands irresolute.*]

[*Enter* MRS. LINDE *from the hall, where she has taken off her cloak and hat.*]

NORA. Oh, it's you, Christine. There is no one else out there, is there? How good of you to come!

MRS. LINDE. I heard you were up asking for me.

NORA. Yes, I was passing by. As a matter of fact, it is something you could help me with. Let us sit down here on the sofa. Look here. To-morrow evening there is to be a fancy-dress ball at the Stenborgs', who live above us; and Torvald wants me to go as a Neapolitan fisher-girl, and dance the Tarantella that I learnt at Capri.

MRS. LINDE. I see; you are going to keep up the character.

NORA. Yes, Torvald wants me to. Look, here is the dress; Torvald had it made for me there, but now it is all so torn, and I haven't any idea—

MRS. LINDE. We will easily put that right. It is only some of the trimming come unsewn here and there. Needle and thread? Now then, that's all we want.

NORA. It *is* nice of you.

MRS. LINDE. [*sewing*] So you are going to be dressed up to-morrow, Nora. I will tell you what—I shall come in for a moment and see you in your fine feathers. But I have completely forgotten to thank you for a delightful evening yesterday.

NORA. [*gets up, and crosses the stage*] Well I don't think yesterday was as pleasant as usual. You ought to have come to town a little earlier, Christine. Certainly Torvald does understand how to make a house dainty and attractive.

MRS. LINDE. And so do you, it seems to me; you are not your father's daughter for nothing. But tell me, is Doctor Rank always as depressed as he was yesterday?

NORA. No; yesterday it was very noticeable. I must tell you that he suffers from a very dangerous disease. He has consumption of the spine, poor creature. His father was a horrible man who committed all sorts of excesses; and that is why his son was sickly from childhood, do you understand?

MRS. LINDE. [*dropping her sewing*] But, my dearest Nora, how do you know anything about such things?

NORA. [*walking about*] Pooh! When you have three children, you get visits now and then from—from married women, who know something of medical matters, and they talk about one thing and another.

MRS. LINDE. [*goes on sewing. A short silence*] Does Doctor Rank come here every day?

NORA. Every day regularly. He is Torvald's most intimate friend, and a great friend of mine too. He is just like one of the family.

MRS. LINDE. But tell me this—is he perfectly sincere? I mean, isn't he the kind of man that is very anxious to make himself agreeable?

NORA. Not in the least. What makes you think that?

MRS. LINDE. When you introduced him to me yesterday, he declared he had often heard my name mentioned in this house; but afterwards I noticed that your husband hadn't the slightest idea who I was. So how could Doctor Rank—?

NORA. That is quite right, Christine. Torvald is so absurdly fond of me that he wants me absolutely to himself, as he says. At first he used to seem almost jealous if I mentioned any of the dear folk at home, so naturally I gave up doing so. But I often talk about such things with Doctor Rank, because he likes hearing about them.

Mrs. Linde. Listen to me, Nora. You are still very like a child in many things, and I am older than you in many ways and have a little more experience. Let me tell you this—you ought to make an end of it with Doctor Rank.

Nora. What ought I to make an end of?

Mrs. Linde. Of two things, I think. Yesterday you talked some nonsense about a rich admirer who was to leave you money—

Nora. An admirer who doesn't exist, unfortunately! But what then?

Mrs. Linde. Is Doctor Rank a man of means?

Nora. Yes, he is.

Mrs. Linde. And has no one to provide for?

Nora. No, no one; but—

Mrs. Linde. And comes here every day?

Nora. Yes, I told you so.

Mrs. Linde. But how can this well-bred man be so tactless?

Nora. I don't understand you at all.

Mrs. Linde. Don't prevaricate, Nora. Do you suppose I don't guess who lent you the two hundred and fifty pounds?

Nora. Are you out of your senses? How can you think of such a thing! A friend of ours, who comes here every day! Do you realise what a horribly painful position that would be?

Mrs. Linde. Then it really isn't he?

Nora. No, certainly not. It would never have entered into my head for a moment. Besides, he had no money to lend then; he came into his money afterwards.

Mrs. Linde. Well, I think that was lucky for you, my dear Nora.

Nora. No, it would never have come into my head to ask Doctor Rank. Although I am quite sure that if I had asked him—

Mrs. Linde. But of course you won't.

Nora. Of course not. I have no reason to think it could possibly be necessary. But I am quite sure that if I told Doctor Rank—

Mrs. Linde. Behind your husband's back?

Nora. I *must* make an end of it with the other one, and that will be behind his back too. I *must* make an end of it with him.

Mrs. Linde. Yes, that is what I told you yesterday, but—

Nora. [*walking up and down*] A man can put a thing like that straight much easier than a woman—

Mrs. Linde. One's husband, yes.

Nora. Nonsense! [*standing still*] When you pay off a debt you get your bond back, don't you?

Mrs. Linde. Yes, as a matter of course.

Nora. And can tear it into a hundred thousand pieces, and burn it up—the nasty dirty paper!

Mrs. Linde. [*looks hard at her, lays down her sewing and gets up slowly*] Nora, you are concealing something from me.

Nora. Do I look as if I were?

Mrs. Linde. Something has happened to you since yesterday morning. Nora, what is it?

Nora. [*going nearer to her*] Christine! [*listens*] Hush! there's Torvald come home. Do you mind going in to the children for the present? Torvald can't bear to see dressmaking going on. Let Anne help you.

MRS. LINDE. [*gathering some of the things together*] Certainly—but I am not going away from here till we have had it out with one another.

[*She goes into the room on the left, as* HELMER *comes in from the hall.*]

NORA. [*going up to* HELMER] I have wanted you so much, Torvald dear.

HELMER. Was that the dressmaker?

NORA. No, it was Christine; she is helping me to put my dress in order. You will see I shall look quite smart.

HELMER. Wasn't that a happy thought of mine, now?

NORA. Splendid! But don't you think it is nice of me, too, to do as you wish?

HELMER. Nice?—because you do as your husband wishes? Well, well, you little rogue, I am sure you did not mean it in that way. But I am not going to disturb you; you will want to be trying on your dress, I expect.

NORA. I suppose you are going to work.

HELMER. Yes. [*shows her a bundle of papers*] Look at that. I have just been into the bank. [*Turns to go into his room.*]

NORA. Torvald.

HELMER. Yes.

NORA. If your little squirrel were to ask you for something very, very prettily—?

HELMER. What then?

NORA. Would you do it?

HELMER. I should like to hear what it is, first.

NORA. Your squirrel would run about and do all her tricks if you would be nice, and do what she wants.

HELMER. Speak plainly.

NORA. Your skylark would chirp about in every room, with her song rising and falling—

HELMER. Well, my skylark does that anyhow.

NORA. I would play the fairy and dance for you in the moonlight, Torvald.

HELMER. Nora—you surely don't mean that request you made of me this morning?

NORA. [*going near him*] Yes, Torvald, I beg you so earnestly—

HELMER. Have you really the courage to open up that question again?

NORA. Yes, dear, you *must* do as I ask; you *must* let Krogstad keep his post in the Bank.

HELMER. My dear Nora, it is his post that I have arranged Mrs. Linde shall have.

NORA. Yes, you have been awfully kind about that; but you could just as well dismiss some other clerk instead of Krogstad.

HELMER. This is simply incredible obstinacy! Because you chose to give him a thoughtless promise that you would speak for him, I am expected to—

NORA. That isn't the reason, Torvald. It is for your own sake. This fellow writes in the most scurrilous newspapers; you have told me so yourself. He can do you an unspeakable amount of harm. I am frightened to death of him—

HELMER. Ah, I understand; it is recollections of the past that scare you.

NORA. What do you mean?

HELMER. Naturally you are thinking of your father.

NORA. Yes—yes, of course. Just recall to your mind what these malicious creatures wrote in the papers about papa, and how horribly they slandered him. I believe they would have procured his dismissal if the Department had not sent you over to inquire into it, and if you had not been so kindly disposed and helpful to him.

HELMER. My little Nora, there is an important difference between your father and me. Your father's reputation as a public official was not above suspicion. Mine is, and I hope it will continue to be so, as long as I hold my office.

NORA. You never can tell what mischief these men may contrive. We ought to be so well off, so snug and happy here in our peaceful home, and have no cares— you and I and the children. Torvald! That is why I beg you so earnestly—

HELMER. And it is just by interceding for him that you make it impossible for me to keep him. It is already known at the Bank that I mean to dismiss Krogstad. Is it to get about now that the new manager has changed his mind at his wife's bidding—

NORA. And what if it did?

HELMER. Of course!—if only this obstinate little person can get her way! Do you suppose I am going to make myself ridiculous before my whole staff, to let people think that I am a man to be swayed by all sorts of outside influence? I should very soon feel the consequences of it, I can tell you! And besides, there is one thing that makes it quite impossible for me to have Krogstad in the Bank as long as I am manager.

NORA. Whatever is that?

HELMER. His moral failings I might perhaps have overlooked, if necessary—

NORA. Yes, you could—couldn't you?

HELMER. And I hear he is a good worker, too. But I knew him when we were boys. It was one of those rash friendships that so often prove an incubus in after life. I may as well tell you plainly, we were once on very intimate terms with one another. But this tactless fellow lays no restraint on himself when other people are present. On the contrary, he thinks it gives him the right to adopt a familiar tone with me, and every minute it is "I say, Helmer, old fellow!" and that sort of thing. I assure you it is extremely painful for me. He would make my position in the Bank intolerable.

NORA. Torvald, I don't believe you mean that.

HELMER. Don't you? Why not?

NORA. Because it is such a narrow-minded way of looking at things.

HELMER. What are you saying? Narrow-minded? Do you think I am narrow-minded?

NORA. No, just the opposite, dear—and it is exactly for that reason.

HELMER. It's the same thing. You say my point of view is narrow-minded, so I must be so too. Narrow-minded! Very well—I must put an end to this. [*Goes to the hall-door and calls.*] Helen!

NORA. What are you going to do?

HELMER. [*looking among his papers*] Settle it. [*Enter* MAID.] Look here; take this letter and go downstairs with it at once. Find a messenger and tell him to deliver it, and be quick. The address is on it, and here is the money.

MAID. Very well, sir.

[*Exits with the letter.*]

HELMER. [*putting his papers together*] Now then, little Miss Obstinate.

NORA. [*breathlessly*] Torvald—what was that letter?

HELMER. Krogstad's dismissal.

NORA. Call her back, Torvald! There is still time. Oh Torvald, call her back! Do it for my sake—for your own sake—for the children's sake! Do you hear me, Torvald? Call her back!! You don't know what that letter can bring upon us.

HELMER. It's too late.

NORA. Yes, it's too late.

HELMER. My dear Nora, I can forgive the anxiety you are in, although really it is an insult to me. It is, indeed. Isn't it an insult to think that I should be afraid of a starving quill-driver's vengeance? But I forgive you nevertheless, because it is such eloquent witness to your great love for me. [*takes her in his arms*] And that is as it should be, my own darling Nora. Come what will, you may be sure I shall have both courage and strength if they be needed. You will see I am man enough to take everything upon myself.

NORA. [*in a horror-stricken voice*] What do you mean by that?

HELMER. Everything, I say—

NORA. [*recovering herself*] You will never have to do that.

HELMER. That's right. Well, we will share it, Nora, as man and wife should. That is how it shall be. [*caressing her*] Are you content now? There! there!—not these frightened dove's eyes! The whole thing is only the wildest fancy!— Now, you must go and play through the Tarantella and practise with your tambourine. I shall go into the inner office and shut the door, and I shall hear nothing; you can make as much noise as you please. [*turns back at the door*] And when Rank comes, tell him where he will find me.

[*Nods to her, takes his papers and goes into his room, and shuts the door after him.*]

NORA. [*bewildered with anxiety, stands as if rooted to the spot, and whispers*] He is capable of doing it. He will do it. He will do it in spite of everything.—No, not that! Never, never! Anything rather than that! Oh, for some help, some way out of it! [*The door-bell rings.*] Doctor Rank! Anything rather than that—anything, whatever it is!

[*She puts her hands over her face, pulls herself together, goes to the door and opens it. RANK is standing without, hanging up his coat. During the following dialogue it begins to grow dark.*]

NORA. Good-day, Doctor Rank. I knew your ring. But you mustn't go in to Torvald now; I think he is busy with something.

RANK. And you?

NORA. [*brings him in and shuts the door after him*] Oh, you know very well I always have time for you.

RANK. Thank you. I shall make use of as much of it as I can.

NORA. What do you mean by that? As much of it as you can?

RANK. Well, does that alarm you?

NORA. It was such a strange way of putting it. Is anything likely to happen?

RANK. Nothing but what I have long been prepared for. But I certainly didn't expect it to happen so soon.

NORA. [*gripping him by the arm*] What have you found out? Doctor Rank, you must tell me.

RANK. [*sitting down by the stove*] It is all up with me. And it can't be helped.

NORA. [*with a sigh of relief*] Is it about yourself?

RANK. Who else? It is no use lying to one's self. I am the most wretched of all my patients, Mrs. Helmer. Lately I have been taking stock of my internal economy. Bankrupt! Probably within a month I shall lie rotting in the churchyard.

NORA. What an ugly thing to say!

RANK. The thing itself is cursedly ugly, and the worst of it is that I shall have to face so much more that is ugly before that. I shall only make one more examination of myself; when I have done that, I shall know pretty certainly when it will be that the horrors of dissolution will begin. There is something I want to tell you. Helmer's refined nature gives him an unconquerable disgust at everything that is ugly; I won't have him in my sick-room.

NORA. Oh, but, Doctor Rank—

RANK. I won't have him there. Not on any account. I bar my door to him. As soon as I am quite certain that the worst has come, I shall send you my card with a black cross on it, and then you will know that the loathsome end has begun.

NORA. You are quite absurd to-day. And I wanted you so much to be in a really good humour.

RANK. With death stalking beside me?—To have to pay this penalty for another man's sin! Is there any justice in that? And in every single family, in one way or another, some such inexorable retribution is being exacted—

NORA. [*putting her hands over her ears*] Rubbish! Do talk of something cheerful.

RANK. Oh, it's a mere laughing matter, the whole thing. My poor innocent spine has to suffer for my father's youthful amusements.

NORA. [*sitting at the table on the left*] I suppose you mean that he was too partial to asparagus and pâté de foie gras, don't you.

RANK. Yes, and to truffles.

NORA. Truffles, yes. And oysters too, I suppose?

RANK. Oysters, of course, that goes without saying.

NORA. And heaps of port and champagne. It is sad that all these nice things should take their revenge on our bones.

RANK. Especially that they should revenge themselves on the unlucky bones of those who have not had the satisfaction of enjoying them.

NORA. Yes, that's the saddest part of it all.

RANK. [*with a searching look at her*] Hm!—

NORA. [*after a short pause*] Why did you smile?

RANK. No, it was you that laughed.

NORA. No, it was you that smiled, Doctor Rank!

RANK. [*rising*] You are a greater rascal than I thought.

NORA. I am in a silly mood to-day.

RANK. So it seems.

NORA. [*putting her hands on his shoulders*] Dear, dear Doctor Rank, death mustn't take you away from Torvald and me.

RANK. It is a loss you would easily recover from. Those who are gone are soon forgotten.

NORA. [*looking at him anxiously*] Do you believe that?

RANK. People form new ties, and then—

NORA. Who will form new ties?

RANK. Both you and Helmer, when I am gone. You yourself are already on the high road to it, I think. What did that Mrs. Linde want here last night?

NORA. Oho!—you don't mean to say you are jealous of poor Christine?

RANK. Yes, I am. She will be my successor in this house. When I am done for, this woman will—

NORA. Hush! don't speak so loud. She is in that room.

RANK. To-day again. There, you see.

NORA. She has only come to sew my dress for me. Bless my soul, how unreasonable you are! [*sits down on the sofa*] Be nice now, Doctor Rank, and tomorrow you will see how beautifully I shall dance, and you can imagine I am doing it all for you—and for Torvald too, of course. [*takes various things out of the box*] Doctor Rank, come and sit down here, and I will show you something.

RANK. [*sitting down*] What is it?

NORA. Just look at those!

RANK. Silk stockings.

NORA. Flesh-coloured. Aren't they lovely? It is so dark here now, but to-morrow—. No, no, no! you must only look at the feet. Oh well, you may have leave to look at the legs too.

RANK. Hm!—

NORA. Why are you looking so critical? Don't you think they will fit me?

RANK. I have no means of forming an opinion about that.

NORA. [*looks at him for a moment*] For shame! [*hits him lightly on the ear with the stockings*] That's to punish you. [*folds them up again*]

RANK. And what other nice things am I to be allowed to see?

NORA. Not a single thing more, for being so naughty. [*She looks among the things, humming to herself.*]

RANK. [*after a short silence*] When I am sitting here, talking to you as intimately as this, I cannot imagine for a moment what would have become of me if I had never come into this house.

NORA. [*smiling*] I believe you do feel thoroughly at home with us.

RANK. [*in a lower voice, looking straight in front of him*] And to be obliged to leave it all—

NORA. Nonsense, you are not going to leave it.

RANK. [*as before*] And not be able to leave behind one the slightest token of one's gratitude, scarcely even a fleeting regret—nothing but an empty place which the first comer can fill as well as any other.

NORA. And if I asked you now for a—? No!

RANK. For what?

NORA. For a big proof of your friendship—

RANK. Yes, yes!

NORA. I mean a tremendously big favour—

RANK. Would you really make me so happy for once?

NORA. Ah, but you don't know what it is yet.

RANK. No—but tell me.

NORA. I really can't, Doctor Rank. It is something out of all reason; it means advice, and help, and a favour—

RANK. The bigger a thing is, the better. I can't conceive what it is you mean. Do tell me. Haven't I your confidence?

NORA. More than anyone else. I know you are my truest and best friend, and so I will tell you what it is. Well, Doctor Rank, it is something you must help me to prevent. You know how devotedly, how inexpressibly deeply Torvald loves me; he would never for a moment hesitate to give his life for me.

RANK. [*leaning towards her*] Nora—do you think he is the only one—?

NORA. [*with a slight start*] The only one—?

RANK. The only one who would gladly give his life for your sake.

NORA. [*sadly*] Is that it?

RANK. I was determined you should know it before I went away, and there will
never be a better opportunity than this. Now you know it, Nora. And now you
know, too, that you can trust me as you would trust no one else.

NORA. [*rises, deliberately and quietly*] Let me pass.

RANK. [*makes room for her to pass him, but sits still*] Nora!

NORA. [*at the hall door*] Helen, bring in the lamp. [*goes over to the stove*] Dear Doctor Rank, that was really horrid of you.

RANK. To have loved you as much as anyone else does? Was that horrid?

NORA. No, but to go and tell me so. There was really no need—

RANK. What do you mean? Did you know—? [MAID *enters with lamp, puts it down on
the table, and goes out.*] Nora—Mrs. Helmer—tell me, had you any idea of this?

NORA. Oh, how do I know whether I had or whether I hadn't? I really can't tell
you—To think you could be so clumsy, Doctor Rank! We were getting on so
nicely.

RANK. Well, at all events you know now that you can command me, body and
soul. So won't you speak out?

NORA. [*looking at him*] After what happened?

RANK. I beg you to let me know what it is.

NORA. I can't tell you anything now.

RANK. Yes, yes. You mustn't punish me in that way. Let me have permission to do
for you whatever a man may do.

NORA. You can do nothing for me now. Besides, I really don't need any help at
all. You will find that the whole thing is merely fancy on my part. It really is
so—of course it is! [*Sits down in the rocking-chair, and looks at him with a smile.*]
You are a nice sort of man, Doctor Rank!—don't you feel ashamed of yourself,
now the lamp has come?

RANK. Not a bit. But perhaps I had better go—for ever?

NORA. No, indeed, you shall not. Of course you must come here just as before.
You know very well Torvald can't do without you.

RANK. Yes, but you?

NORA. Oh, I am always tremendously pleased when you come.

RANK. It is just that, that put me on the wrong track. You are a riddle to me. I
have often thought that you would almost as soon be in my company as in
Helmer's.

NORA. Yes—you see there are some people one loves best, and others whom one
would almost rather have as companions.

RANK. Yes, there is something in that.

NORA. When I was at home, of course I loved papa best. But I always thought it
tremendous fun if I could steal down into the maid's room, because they never
moralised at all, and talked to each other about such entertaining things.

RANK. I see—it is *their* place I have taken.

NORA. [*jumping up and going to him*] Oh, dear, nice Doctor Rank, I never meant
that at all. But surely you can understand that being with Torvald is a little
like being with papa—

[*Enter* MAID *from the hall.*]

MAID. If you please, ma'am. [*whispers and hands her a card*]

NORA. [*glancing at the card*] Oh! [*puts it in her pocket*]

RANK. Is there anything wrong?

NORA. No, no, not in the least. It is only something—it is my new dress—

RANK. What? Your dress is lying there.

NORA. Oh, yes, that one; but this is another. I ordered it. Torvald mustn't know about it—

RANK. Oho! Then that was the great secret.

NORA. Of course. Just go in to him; he is sitting in the inner room. Keep him as long as—

RANK. Make your mind easy; I won't let him escape. [*goes into* HELMER'S *room.*]

NORA. [*to the* MAID] And he is standing waiting in the kitchen?

MAID. Yes; he came up the back stairs.

NORA. But didn't you tell him no one was in?

MAID. Yes, but it was no good.

NORA. He won't go away?

MAID. No; he says he won't until he has seen you, ma'am.

NORA. Well, let him come in—but quietly. Helen, you mustn't say anything about it to anyone. It is a surprise for my husband.

MAID. Yes, ma'am, I quite understand.

NORA. This dreadful thing is going to happen! It will happen in spite of me! No, no, no, it can't happen—it shan't happen!

[*She bolts the door of* HELMER'S *room. The* MAID *opens the hall door for* KROGSTAD *and shuts it after him. He is wearing a fur coat, high boots and a fur cap.*]

NORA. [*advancing towards him*] Speak low—my husband is at home.

KROGSTAD. No matter about that.

NORA. What do you want of me?

KROGSTAD. An explanation of something.

NORA. Make haste then. What is it?

KROGSTAD. You know, I suppose, that I have got my dismissal.

NORA. I couldn't prevent it, Mr. Krogstad. I fought as hard as I could on your side, but it was no good.

KROGSTAD. Does your husband love you so little, then? He knows that what I can expose you to, and yet he ventures—

NORA. How can you suppose that he has any knowledge of the sort?

KROGSTAD. I didn't suppose so at all. It would not be the least like our dear Torvald Helmer to show so much courage—

NORA. Mr. Krogstad, a little respect for my husband, please.

KROGSTAD. Certainly—all the respect he deserves. But since you have kept the matter so carefully to yourself, I make bold to suppose that you have a little clearer idea, than you had yesterday, of what it actually is that you have done?

NORA. More than you could ever teach me.

KROGSTAD. Yes, such a bad lawyer as I am.

NORA. What is it you want of me?

KROGSTAD. Only to see how you were, Mrs. Helmer. I have been thinking about you all day long. A mere cashier, a quill-driver, a—well, a man like me—even he has a little of what is called feeling, you know.

NORA. Show it, then; think of my little children.

KROGSTAD. Have you and your husband thought of mine? But never mind about that. I only wanted to tell you that you need not take this matter too seriously. In the first place there will be no accusation made on my part.

NORA. No, of course not; I was sure of that.

KROGSTAD. The whole thing can be arranged amicably; there is no reason why anyone should know anything about it. It will remain a secret between us three.

NORA. My husband must never get to know anything about it.

KROGSTAD. How will you be able to prevent it? Am I to understand that you can pay the balance that is owing?

NORA. No, not just at present.

KROGSTAD. Or perhaps that you have some expedient for raising the money soon?

NORA. No expedient that I mean to make use of.

KROGSTAD. Well, in any case, it would have been of no use to you now. If you stood there with ever so much money in your hand, I would never part with your bond.

NORA. Tell me what purpose you mean to put it to.

KROGSTAD. I shall only preserve it—keep it in my possession. No one who is not concerned in the matter shall have the slightest hint of it. So that if the thought of it has driven you to any desperate resolution—

NORA. It has.

KROGSTAD. If you had it in your mind to run away from your home—

NORA. I had.

KROGSTAD. Or even something worse—

NORA. How could you know that?

KROGSTAD. Give up the idea.

NORA. How did you know I had thought of *that*?

KROGSTAD. Most of us think of that at first. I did, too—but I hadn't the courage.

NORA. [*faintly*] No more had I.

KROGSTAD. [*in a tone of relief*] No, that's it, isn't it—you hadn't the courage either?

NORA. No, I haven't—I haven't.

KROGSTAD. Besides, it would have been a great piece of folly. Once the first storm at home is over—. I have a letter for your husband in my pocket.

NORA. Telling him everything?

KROGSTAD. In as lenient a manner as I possibly could.

NORA. [*quickly*] He mustn't get the letter. Tear it up. I will find some means of getting money.

KROGSTAD. Excuse me, Mrs. Helmer, but I think I told you just now—

NORA. I am not speaking of what I owe you. Tell me what sum you are asking my husband for, and I will get the money.

KROGSTAD. I am not asking your husband for a penny.

NORA. What do you want, then?

KROGSTAD. I will tell you. I want to rehabilitate myself, Mrs. Helmer; I want to get on; and in that your husband must help me. For the last year and a half I have not had a hand in anything dishonourable, and all that time I have been struggling in most restricted circumstances. I was content to work my way up step by step. Now I am turned out, and I am not going to be satisfied with merely being taken into favour again. I want to get on, I tell you. I want to get into the Bank again, in a higher position. Your husband must make a place for me—

NORA. That he will never do!

KROGSTAD. He will; I know him; he dare not protest. And as soon as I am in there again with him, then you will see! Within a year I shall be the manager's right hand. It will be Nils Krogstad and not Torvald Helmer who manages the Bank.

NORA. That's a thing you will never see!

KROGSTAD. Do you mean that you will—?

NORA. I have courage enough for it now.

KROGSTAD. Oh, you can't frighten me. A fine, spoilt lady like you—

NORA. You will see, you will see.

KROGSTAD. Under the ice, perhaps? Down into the cold, coal-black water? And then, in the spring, to float up to the surface, all horrible and unrecognisable, with your hair fallen out—

NORA. You can't frighten me.

KROGSTAD. Nor you me. People don't do such things, Mrs. Helmer. Besides, what use would it be? I should have him completely in my power all the same.

NORA. Afterwards? When I am no longer—

KROGSTAD. Have you forgotten that it is I who have the keeping of your reputation? [NORA *stands speechlessly looking at him.*] Well, now, I have warned you. Do not do anything foolish. When Helmer has had my letter, I shall expect a message from him. And be sure you remember that it is your husband himself who has forced me into such ways as this again. I will never forgive him for that. Good-bye, Mrs. Helmer.

[*Exit through the hall.*]

NORA. [*goes to the hall door, opens it slightly and listens*] He is going. He is not putting the letter in the box. Oh no, no! that's impossible! [*opens the door by degrees*] What is that? He is standing outside. He is not going downstairs. Is he hesitating? Can he—

[*A letter drops into the box; then* KROGSTAD'S *footsteps are heard, till they die away as he goes downstairs.* NORA *utters a stifled cry and runs across the room to the table by the sofa. A short pause.*]

NORA. In the letter-box. [*steals across to the hall door*] There it lies—Torvald, Torvald, there is no hope for us now!

[MRS. LINDE *comes in from the room on the left, carrying the dress.*]

MRS. LINDE. There, I can't see anything more to mend now. Would you like to try it on—?

NORA. [*in a hoarse whisper*] Christine, come here.

MRS. LINDE. [*throwing the dress down on the sofa*] What is the matter with you? You look so agitated!

NORA. Come here. Do you see that letter? There, look—you can see it through the glass in the letter-box.

MRS. LINDE. Yes, I see it.

NORA. That letter is from Krogstad.

MRS. LINDE. Nora—it was Krogstad who lent you the money!

NORA. Yes, and now Torvald will know all about it.

MRS. LINDE. Believe me, Nora, that's the best thing for both of you.

NORA. You don't know all. I forged a name.

MRS. LINDE. Good heavens—!

NORA. I only want to say this to you, Christine—you must be my witness.

MRS. LINDE. Your witness? What do you mean? What am I to—?

NORA. If I should go out of my mind—and it might easily happen—

MRS. LINDE. Nora!

NORA. Or if anything else should happen to me—anything, for instance, that might prevent my being here—

MRS. LINDE. Nora! Nora! you are quite out of your mind.

NORA. And if it should happen that there were someone who wanted to take all the responsibility, all the blame, you understand—

MRS. LINDE. Yes, yes—but how can you suppose—?

NORA. Then you must be my witness, that it is not true, Christine. I am not out of my mind at all; I am in my right senses now, and I tell you no one else has known anything about it; I, and I alone, did the whole thing. Remember that.

MRS. LINDE. I will, indeed. But I don't understand all this.

NORA. How should you understand it? A wonderful thing is going to happen.

MRS. LINDE. A wonderful thing?

NORA. Yes a wonderful thing!—But it is so terrible, Christine; it *mustn't* happen, not for all the world.

MRS. LINDE. I will go at once and see Krogstad.

NORA. Don't go to him; he will do you some harm.

MRS. LINDE. There was a time when he would gladly do anything for my sake.

NORA. He?

MRS. LINDE. Where does he live?

NORA. How should I know—? Yes [*feeling in her pocket*] here is his card. But the letter, the letter—!

HELMER. [*calls from his room, knocking at the door*] Nora!

NORA. [*cries out anxiously*] Oh, what's that? What do you want?

HELMER. Don't be so frightened. We are not coming in; you have locked the door. Are you trying on your dress?

NORA. Yes, that's it. I look so nice, Torvald.

MRS. LINDE. [*who has read the card*] I see he lives at the corner here.

NORA. Yes but it's no use. It is hopeless. The letter is lying there in the box.

MRS. LINDE. And your husband keeps the key?

NORA. Yes, always.

MRS. LINDE. Krogstad must ask for his letter back unread, he must find some pretence—

NORA. But it is just at this time that Torvald generally—

MRS. LINDE. You must delay him. Go in to him in the meantime. I will come back as soon as I can.

[*She goes out hurriedly through the hall door.*]

NORA. [*goes to* HELMER'S *door, opens it and peeps in*] Torvald!

HELMER. [*from the inner room*] Well? May I venture at last to come into my own room again? Come along, Rank, now you will see—[*halting in the doorway*] But what is this?

NORA. What is what, dear?

HELMER. Rank led me to expect a splendid transformation.

RANK. [*in the doorway*] I understood so, but evidently I was mistaken.

NORA. Yes, nobody is to have the chance of admiring me in my dress until tomorrow.

HELMER. But, my dear Nora, you look so worn out. Have you been practising too much?

NORA. No, I have not practised at all.

HELMER. But you will need to—

NORA. Yes, indeed I shall, Torvald. But I can't get on a bit without you to help me; I have absolutely forgotten the whole thing.

HELMER. Oh, we will soon work it up again.

NORA. Yes, help me, Torvald. Promise that you will! I am so nervous about it—all the people—. You must give yourself up to me entirely this evening. Not the tiniest bit of business—you mustn't even take a pen in your hand. Will you promise, Torvald dear?

HELMER. I promise. This evening I will be wholly and absolutely at your service, you helpless little mortal. Ah, by the way, first of all I will just—

[*Goes towards the hall door.*]

NORA. What are you going to do there?

HELMER. Only see if any letters have come.

NORA. No, no! don't do that, Torvald!

HELMER. Why not?

NORA. Torvald, please don't. There is nothing there.

HELMER. Well, let me look. [*Turns to go to the letter-box.* NORA, *at the piano, plays the first bars of the Tarantella.* HELMER *stops in the doorway.*] Aha!

NORA. I can't dance to-morrow if I don't practise with you.

HELMER. [*going up to her*] Are you really so afraid of it, dear.

NORA. Yes, so dreadfully afraid of it. Let me practise at once; there is time now, before we go to dinner. Sit down and play for me, Torvald dear; criticise me, and correct me as you play.

HELMER. With great pleasure, if you wish me to.

[*Sits down at the piano.*]

NORA. [*takes out of the box a tambourine and a long variegated shawl. She hastily drapes the shawl round her. Then she springs to the front of the stage and calls out.*] Now play for me! I am going to dance!

[HELMER *plays and* NORA *dances.* RANK *stands by the piano behind* HELMER *and looks on.*]

HELMER. [*as he plays*] Slower, slower!

NORA. I can't do it any other way.

HELMER. Not so violently, Nora!

NORA. This is the way.

HELMER. [*stops playing*] No, no—that is not a bit right.

NORA. [*laughing and swinging the tambourine*] Didn't I tell you so?

RANK. Let me play for her.

HELMER. [*getting up*] Yes, do. I can correct her better then.

[RANK *sits down at the piano and plays.* NORA *dances more and more wildly.* HELMER *has taken up a position beside the stove, and during her dance gives her frequent instructions. She does not seem to hear him; her hair comes down and falls over her shoulders; she pays no attention to it, but goes on dancing. Enter* MRS. LINDE.]

MRS. LINDE. [*standing as if spell-bound in the doorway*] Oh!—

NORA. [*as she dances*] Such fun, Christine!

HELMER. My dear darling Nora, you are dancing as if your life depended on it.

NORA. So it does.

HELMER. Stop, Rank; this is sheer madness. Stop, I tell you! [RANK *stops playing, and* NORA *suddenly stands still.* HELMER *goes up to her.*] I could never have believed it. You have forgotten everything I taught you.

NORA. [*throwing away the tambourine*] There, you see.

HELMER. You will want a lot of coaching.

NORA. Yes, you see how much I need it. You must coach me up to the last minute. Promise me that, Torvald!

HELMER. You can depend on me.

NORA. You must not think of anything but me, either to-day or to-morrow; you mustn't open a single letter—not even open the letter-box—

HELMER. Ah, you are still afraid of that fellow—

NORA. Yes, indeed I am.

HELMER. Nora, I can tell from your looks that there is a letter from him lying there.

NORA. I don't know; I think there is; but you must not read anything of that kind now. Nothing horrid must come between us till this is all over.

RANK. [*whispers to Helmer*] You mustn't contradict her.

HELMER. [*taking her in his arms*] The child shall have her way. But to-morrow night, after you have danced—

NORA. Then you will be free.

[*Maid appears in the doorway to the right.*]

MAID. Dinner is served, ma'am.

NORA. We will have champagne, Helen.

MAID. Very good, ma'am.

[*Exit.*]

HELMER. Hullo!—are we going to have a banquet?

NORA. Yes a champagne banquet till the small hours. [*calls out*] And a few macaroons, Helen—lots, just for once!

HELMER. Come, come, don't be so wild and nervous. Be my own little skylark, as you used.

NORA. Yes, dear, I will. But go in now and you too, Doctor Rank. Christine, you must help me to do up my hair.

RANK. [*whispers to* HELMER *as they go out*] I suppose there is nothing—she is not expecting anything?

HELMER. Far from it, my dear fellow; it is simply nothing more than this childish nervousness I was telling you of.

[*They go into the right-hand room.*]

NORA. Well!

MRS. LINDE. Gone out of town.

NORA. I could tell from your face.

MRS. LINDE. He is coming home to-morrow evening. I wrote a note for him.

NORA. You should have let it alone; you must prevent nothing. After all, it is splendid to be waiting for a wonderful thing to happen.

MRS. LINDE. What is it that you are waiting for?

NORA. Oh you wouldn't understand. Go in to them, I will come in a moment. [MRS. LINDE *goes into the dining-room.* NORA *stands still for a little while, as if to compose herself. Then she looks at her watch.*] Five o'clock. Seven hours till midnight; and then four-and-twenty hours till the next midnight. Then the Tarantella will be over. Twenty-four and seven? Thirty-one hours to live.

HELMER. [*from the doorway on the right*] Where's my little skylark?

NORA. [*going to him with her arms outstretched*] Here she is!

ACT 3

The Same Scene. The table has been placed in the middle of the stage, with chairs round it. A lamp is burning on the table. The door into the hall stands open. Dance music is heard in the room above. Mrs. Linde is sitting at the table idly turning over the leaves of a book; she tries to read, but does not seem able to collect her thoughts. Every now and then she listens intently for a sound at the outer door.

MRS. LINDE. [*looking at her watch*] Not yet—and the time is nearly up. If only he does not—. [*listens again*] Ah, there he is. [*Goes into the hall and opens the outer door carefully. Light footsteps are heard on the stairs. She whispers.*] Come in. There is no one here.

KROGSTAD. [*in the doorway*] I found a note from you at home. What does this mean?

MRS. LINDE. It is absolutely necessary that I should have a talk with you.

KROGSTAD. Really? And is it absolutely necessary that it should be here?

MRS. LINDE. It is impossible where I live; there is no private entrance to my rooms. Come in; we are quite alone. The maid is asleep, and the Helmers are at the dance upstairs.

KROGSTAD. [*coming into the room*] Are the Helmers really at a dance to-night?

MRS. LINDE. Yes, why not?

KROGSTAD. Certainly—Why not?

MRS. LINDE. Now, Nils, let us have a talk.

KROGSTAD. Can we two have anything to talk about?

MRS. LINDE. We have a great deal to talk about.

KROGSTAD. I shouldn't have thought so.

MRS. LINDE. No, you have never properly understood me.

KROGSTAD. Was there anything else to understand except what was obvious to all the world—a heartless woman jilts a man when a more lucrative chance turns up?

MRS. LINDE. Do you believe I am as absolutely heartless as all that? And do you believe that I did it with a light heart?

KROGSTAD. Didn't you?

MRS. LINDE. Nils, did you really think that?

KROGSTAD. If it were as you say, why did you write to me as you did at the time?

MRS. LINDE. I could do nothing else. As I had to break with you, it was my duty also to put an end to all that you felt for me.

KROGSTAD. [*wringing his hands*] So that was it, and all this—only for the sake of money!

MRS. LINDE. You must not forget that I had a helpless mother and two little brothers. We couldn't wait for you, Nils; your prospects seemed hopeless then.

KROGSTAD. That may be so, but you had no right to throw me over for any one else's sake.

MRS. LINDE. Indeed I don't know. Many a time did I ask myself if I had the right to do it.

KROGSTAD. [*more gently*] When I lost you, it was as if all the solid ground went from under my feet. Look at me now—I am a shipwrecked man clinging to a bit of wreckage.

MRS. LINDE. But help may be near.

KROGSTAD. It *was* near; but then you came and stood in my way.

MRS. LINDE. Unintentionally, Nils. It was only to-day that I learnt it was your place I was going to take in the Bank.

KROGSTAD. I believe you, if you say so. But now that you know it, are you not going to give it up to me?

MRS. LINDE. No, because that would not benefit you in the least.

KROGSTAD. Oh, benefit, benefit—I would have done it whether or no.

MRS. LINDE. I have learnt to act prudently. Life, and hard, bitter necessity have taught me that.

KROGSTAD. And life has taught me not to believe in fine speeches.

MRS. LINDE. Then life has taught you something very reasonable. But deeds you must believe in.

KROGSTAD. What do you mean by that?

MRS. LINDE. You said you were like a shipwrecked man clinging to some wreckage.

KROGSTAD. I had good reason to say so.

MRS. LINDE. Well, I am like a shipwrecked woman clinging to some wreckage—no one to mourn for, no one to care for.

KROGSTAD. It was your own choice.

MRS. LINDE. There was no other choice—then.

KROGSTAD. Well, what now?

MRS. LINDE. Nils, how would it be if we two shipwrecked people could join forces?

KROGSTAD. What are you saying?

MRS. LINDE. Two on the same piece of wreckage would stand a better chance than each on their own.

KROGSTAD. Christine!

MRS. LINDE. What do you suppose brought me to town?

KROGSTAD. Do you mean that you gave me a thought?

MRS. LINDE. I could not endure life without work. All my life, as long as I can remember, I have worked, and it has been my greatest and only pleasure. But now I am quite alone in the world—my life is so dreadfully empty and I feel so forsaken. There is not the least pleasure in working for one's self. Nils, give me someone and something to work for.

KROGSTAD. I don't trust that. It is nothing but a woman's overstrained sense of generosity that prompts you to make such an offer of yourself.

MRS. LINDE. Have you ever noticed anything of the sort in me?

KROGSTAD. Could you really do it? Tell me—do you know all about my past life?

MRS. LINDE. Yes.

KROGSTAD. And do you know what they think of me here?

MRS. LINDE. You seemed to me to imply that with me you might have been quite another man.

KROGSTAD. I am certain of it.

MRS. LINDE. Is it too late now?

KROGSTAD. Christine, are you saying this deliberately? Yes, I am sure you are. I see it in your face. Have you really the courage, then—?

MRS. LINDE. I want to be a mother to someone, and your children need a mother. We two need each other. Nils, I have faith in your real character—I can dare anything together with you.

KROGSTAD. [*grasps her hands*] Thanks, thanks, Christine! Now I shall find a way to clear myself in the eyes of the world. Ah, but I forgot—

MRS. LINDE. [*listening*] Hush! The Tarantella! Go, go!

KROGSTAD. Why? What is it?

MRS. LINDE. Do you hear them up there? When that is over, we may expect them back.

KROGSTAD. Yes, yes—I will go. But it is all no use. Of course you are not aware what steps I have taken in the matter of the Helmers.

MRS. LINDE. Yes, I know all about that.

KROGSTAD. And in spite of that have you the courage to—?

MRS. LINDE. I understand very well to what lengths a man like you might be driven by despair.

KROGSTAD. If I could only undo what I have done!

MRS. LINDE. You can. Your letter is lying in the letter-box now.

KROGSTAD. Are you sure of that?

MRS. LINDE. Quite sure, but—

KROGSTAD. [*with a searching look at her*] Is that what it all means?—that you want to save your friend at any cost? Tell me frankly. Is that it?

MRS. LINDE. Nils, a woman who has once sold herself for another's sake, doesn't do it a second time.

KROGSTAD. I will ask for my letter back.

MRS. LINDE. No, no.

KROGSTAD. Yes, of course I will. I will wait here till Helmer comes; I will tell him he must give me my letter back—that it only concerns my dismissal—that he is not to read it—

MRS. LINDE. No, Nils, you must not recall your letter.

KROGSTAD. But, tell me, wasn't it for that very purpose that you asked me to meet you here?

MRS. LINDE. In my first moment of fright, it was. But twenty-four hours have elapsed since then, and in that time I have witnessed incredible things in this house. Helmer must know all about it. This unhappy secret must be disclosed; they must have a complete understanding between them, which is impossible with all this concealment and falsehood going on.

KROGSTAD. Very well, if you will take the responsibility. But there is one thing I can do in any case, and I shall do it at once.

MRS. LINDE. [*listening*] You must be quick and go! The dance is over; we are not safe a moment longer.

KROGSTAD. I will wait for you below.

MRS. LINDE. Yes, do. You must see me back to my door.

KROGSTAD. I have never had such an amazing piece of good fortune in my life.

[*Goes out through the outer door. The door between the room and the hall remains open.*]

MRS. LINDE. [*tidying up the room and laying her hat and cloak ready*] What a difference! what a difference! Someone to work for and live for—a home to bring

comfort into. That I will do, indeed. I wish they would be quick and come—
[*listens*] Ah, there they are now. I must put on my things.

[*Takes up her hat and cloak.* HELMER'*s and* NORA'*s voices are heard outside; a key is turned, and* HELMER *brings* NORA *almost by force into the hall. She is in an Italian costume with a large black shawl round her; he is in evening dress and a black domino which is flying open.*]

NORA. [*hanging back in the doorway, and struggling with him*] No, no, no!—don't take me in. I want to go upstairs again; I don't want to leave so early.
HELMER. But, my dearest Nora—
NORA. Please, Torvald dear—please, *please*—only an hour more.
HELMER. Not a single minute, my sweet Nora. You know that was our agreement. Come along into the room; you are catching cold standing there.

[*He brings her gently into the room, in spite of her resistance.*]

MRS. LINDE. Good evening.
NORA. Christine!
HELMER. You here, so late, Mrs. Linde?
MRS. LINDE. Yes, you must excuse me; I was so anxious to see Nora in her dress.
NORA. Have you been sitting here waiting for me?
MRS. LINDE. Yes, unfortunately I came too late, you had already gone upstairs; and I thought I couldn't go away without having seen you.
HELMER. [*taking off* Nora's *shawl*] Yes, take a good look at her. I think she is worth looking at. Isn't she charming, Mrs. Linde?
MRS. LINDE. Yes, indeed she is.
HELMER. Doesn't she look remarkably pretty? Everyone thought so at the dance. But she is terribly self-willed, this sweet little person. What are we to do with her? You will hardly believe that I had almost to bring her away by force.
NORA. Torvald, you will repent not having let me stay, even if it were only for half an hour.
HELMER. Listen to her, Mrs. Linde! She had danced her Tarantella, and it had been a tremendous success, as it deserved—although possibly the performance was a trifle too realistic—a little more so, I mean, than was strictly compatible with the limitations of art. But never mind about that! The chief thing is, she had made a success—she had made a tremendous success. Do you think I was going to let her remain there after that, and spoil the effect? No indeed! I took my charming little Capri maiden—my capricious little Capri maiden, I should say—on my arm; took one quick turn round the room; a curtsey on either side, and, as they say in novels, the beautiful apparition disappeared. An exit ought always to be effective, Mrs. Linde; but that is what I cannot make Nora understand. Pooh! this room is hot. [*throws his domino on a chair and opens the door of his room*] Hullo! it's all dark in here. Oh, of course—excuse me—.

[*He goes in and lights some candles.*]

NORA. [*in a hurried and breathless whisper*] Well?
MRS. LINDE. [*in a low voice*] I have had a talk with him.
NORA. Yes, and—
MRS. LINDE. Nora, you must tell your husband all about it.
NORA. [*in an expressionless voice*] I knew it.
MRS. LINDE. You have nothing to be afraid of as far as Krogstad is concerned; but you must tell him.

NORA. I won't tell him.

MRS. LINDE. Then the letter will.

NORA. Thank you, Christine. Now I know what I must do. Hush—!

HELMER. [*coming in again*] Well, Mrs. Linde, have you admired her?

MRS. LINDE. Yes, and now I will say good-night.

HELMER. What already? Is this yours, this knitting?

MRS. LINDE. [*taking it*] Yes, thank you, I had very nearly forgotten it.

HELMER. So you knit?

MRS. LINDE. Of course.

HELMER. Do you know, you ought to embroider.

MRS. LINDE. Really? Why?

HELMER. Yes, it's far more becoming. Let me show you. You hold the embroidery thus in your left hand, and use the needle with the right—like this—with a long, easy sweep. Do you see?

MRS. LINDE. Yes, perhaps—

HELMER. But in the case of knitting—that can never be anything but ungraceful; look here—the arms close together, the knitting-needles going up and down—it has a sort of Chinese effect—. That was really excellent champagne they gave us.

MRS. LINDE. Well,—good-night, Nora, and don't be self-willed any more.

HELMER. That's right, Mrs. Linde.

MRS. LINDE. Good-night, Mr. Helmer.

HELMER. [*accompanying her to the door*] Good-night, good-night. I hope you will get home all right. I should be very happy to—but you haven't any great distance to go. Good-night, good-night. [*She goes out; he shuts the door after her, and comes in again.*] Ah!—at last we have got rid of her. She is a frightful bore, that woman.

NORA. Aren't you very tired, Torvald?

HELMER. No, not in the least.

NORA. Nor sleepy?

HELMER. Not a bit. On the contrary, I feel extraordinarily lively. And you?—you really look both tired and sleepy.

NORA. Yes, I am very tired. I want to go to sleep at once.

HELMER. There, you see it was quite right of me not to let you stay there any longer.

NORA. Everything you do is quite right, Torvald.

HELMER. [*kissing her on the forehead*] Now my little skylark is speaking reasonably. Did you notice what good spirits Rank was in this evening?

NORA. Really? Was he? I didn't speak to him at all.

HELMER. And I very little, but I have not for a long time seen him in such good form. [*looks for a while at her and then goes nearer to her*] It is delightful to be at home by ourselves again, to be all alone with you—you fascinating, charming little darling!

NORA. Don't look at me like that, Torvald.

HELMER. Why shouldn't I look at my dearest treasure?—at all the beauty that is mine, all my very own?

NORA. [*going to the other side of the table*] You mustn't say things like that to me tonight.

HELMER. [*following her*] You have still got the Tarantella in your blood, I see. And it makes you more captivating than ever. Listen—the guests are beginning to go now. [*in a lower voice*] Nora—soon the whole house will be quiet.

NORA. Yes, I hope so.

HELMER. Yes, my own darling Nora. Do you know, when I am out at a party with you like this, why I speak so little to you, keep away from you, and only send a stolen glance in your direction now and then?—do you know why I do that? It is because I make believe to myself that we are secretly in love, and you are my secretly promised bride, and that no one suspects there is anything between us.

NORA. Yes, yes—I know very well your thoughts are with me all the time.

HELMER. And when we are leaving, and I am putting the shawl over your beautiful young shoulders—on your lovely neck—then I imagine that you are my young bride and that we have just come from the wedding, and I am bringing you for the first time into our home—to be alone with you for the first time—quite alone with my shy little darling! All this evening I have longed for nothing but you. When I watched the seductive figures of the Tarantella, my blood was on fire; I could endure it no longer, and that was why I brought you down so early—

NORA. Go away, Torvald! You must let me go. I won't—

HELMER. What's that? You're joking, my little, Nora! You won't? Am I not your husband—?

[*A knock is heard at the outer door.*]

NORA. [*starting*] Did you hear—?

HELMER. [*going into the hall*] Who is it?

RANK. [*outside*] It is I. May I come in for a moment?

HELMER. [*in a fretful whisper*] Oh, what does he want now? [*aloud*] Wait a minute! [*unlocks the door*] Come, that's kind of you not to pass by our door.

RANK. I thought I heard your voice, and felt as if I should like to look in. [*with a swift glance round*] Ah, yes!—these dear familiar rooms. You are very happy and cosy in here, you two.

HELMER. It seems to me that you looked after yourself pretty well upstairs too.

RANK. Excellently. Why shouldn't I? Why shouldn't one enjoy everything in this world?—at any rate as much as one can, and as long as one can. The wine was capital—

HELMER. Especially the champagne.

RANK. So you noticed that too? It is almost incredible how much I managed to put away!

NORA. Torvald drank a great deal of champagne tonight, too.

RANK. Did he?

NORA. Yes, and he is always in such good spirits afterwards.

RANK. Well, why should one not enjoy a merry evening after a well-spent day?

HELMER. Well spent? I am afraid I can't take credit for that.

RANK. [*clapping him on the back*] But I can, you know!

NORA. Doctor Rank, you must have been occupied with some scientific investigation to-day.

RANK. Exactly.

HELMER. Just listen!—little Nora talking about scientific investigations!

NORA. And may I congratulate you on the result?

RANK. Indeed you may.

NORA. Was it favourable, then?

RANK. The best possible, for both doctor and patient—certainty.

NORA. [*quickly and searchingly*] Certainty?

RANK. Absolute certainty. So wasn't I entitled to make a merry evening of it after that?

NORA. Yes, you certainly were, Doctor Rank.

HELMER. I think so too, so long as you don't have to pay for it in the morning.

RANK. Oh well, one can't have anything in this life without paying for it.

NORA. Doctor Rank—are you fond of fancy-dress balls?

RANK. Yes, if there is a fine lot of pretty costumes.

NORA. Tell me—what shall we two wear at the next?

HELMER. Little featherbrain!—are you thinking of the next already?

RANK. We two? Yes, I can tell you. You shall go as a good fairy—

HELMER. Yes, but what do you suggest as an appropriate costume for that?

RANK. Let your wife go dressed just as she is in everyday life.

HELMER. That was really very prettily turned. But can't you tell us what you will be?

RANK. Yes, my dear friend, I have quite made up my mind about that.

HELMER. Well?

RANK. At the next fancy dress ball I shall be invisible.

HELMER. That's a good joke!

RANK. There is a big black hat—have you never heard of hats that make you invisible? If you put one on, no one can see you.

HELMER. [*suppressing a smile*] Yes, you are quite right.

RANK. But I am clean forgetting what I came for. Helmer, give me a cigar—one of the dark Havanas.

HELMER. With the greatest pleasure. [*offers him his case*]

RANK. [*takes a cigar and cuts off the end*] Thanks.

NORA. [*striking a match*] Let me give you a light.

RANK. Thank you. [*she holds the match for him to light his cigar.*] And now good-bye!

HELMER. Good-bye, good-bye, dear old man!

NORA. Sleep well, Doctor Rank.

RANK. Thank you for that wish.

NORA. Wish me the same.

RANK. You? Well, if you want me to sleep well! And thanks for the light.

[*He nods to them both and goes out.*]

HELMER. [*in a subdued voice*] He has drunk more than he ought.

NORA. [*absently*] Maybe. [HELMER *takes a bunch of keys out of his pocket and goes into the hall.*] Torvald! what are you going to do there?

HELMER. Empty the letter-box; it is quite full; there will be no room to put the newspaper in to-morrow morning.

NORA. Are you going to work to-night?

HELMER. You know quite well I'm not. What is this? Some one has been at the lock.

NORA. At the lock—

HELMER. Yes, someone has. What can it mean? I should never have thought the maid—. Here is a broken hairpin. Nora, it is one of yours.

NORA. [*quickly*] Then it must have been the children—

HELMER. Then you must get them out of those ways. There, at last I have got it open. [*Takes out the contents of the letter-box, and calls to the kitchen.*] Helen!—Helen, put out the light over the front door. [*Goes back into the room and shuts the door into the hall. He holds out his hand full of letters.*] Look at that—look what a heap of them there are. [*turning them over*] What on earth is that?

Nora. [*at the window*] The letter—No! Torvald, no!

Helmer. Two cards—of Rank's.

Nora. Of Doctor Rank's?

Helmer. [*looking at them*] Doctor Rank. They were on the top. He must have put them in when he went out.

Nora. Is there anything written on them?

Helmer. There is a black cross over the name. Look there—what an uncomfortable idea! It looks as if he were announcing his own death.

Nora. It is just what he is doing.

Helmer. What? Do you know anything about it? Has he said anything to you?

Nora. Yes. He told me that when the cards came it would be his leave-taking from us. He means to shut himself up and die.

Helmer. My poor old friend. Certainly I knew we should not have him very long with us. But so soon! And so he hides himself away like a wounded animal.

Nora. If it has to happen, it is best it should be without a word—don't you think so, Torvald?

Helmer. [*walking up and down*] He had so grown into our lives. I can't think of him as having gone out of them. He, with his sufferings and his loneliness, was like a cloudy background to our sunlit happiness. Well, perhaps it is best so. For him, anyway. [*standing still*] And perhaps for us too, Nora. We two are thrown quite upon each other now. [*puts his arms round her*] My darling wife, I don't feel as if I could hold you tight enough. Do you know, Nora, I have often wished that you might be threatened by some great danger, so that I might risk my life's blood, and everything, for your sake.

Nora. [*disengages herself, and says firmly and decidedly*] Now you must read your letters Torvald.

Helmer. No, no; not to-night. I want to be with you, my darling wife.

Nora. With the thought of your friend's death—

Helmer. You are right, it has affected us both. Something ugly has come between us—the thought of the horrors of death. We must try and rid our minds of that. Until then—we will each go to our own room.

Nora. [*hanging on his neck*] Good-night, Torvald—Good-night!

Helmer. [*kissing her on the forehead.*] Good-night, my little singing-bird. Sleep sound, Nora. Now I will read my letters through.

> [*He takes his letters and goes into his room,*
> *shutting the door after him.*]

Nora. [*gropes distractedly about, seizes* Helmer's *domino, throws it round her, while she says in quick, hoarse, spasmodic whispers*] Never to see him again. Never! Never! [*puts her shawl over her head*] Never to see my children again either—never again. Never! Never!—Ah! the icy, black water—the unfathomable depths— If only it were over! He has got it now—now he is reading it. Good-bye, Torvald and my children!

> [*She is about to rush out through the hall, when* Helmer *opens his door hurriedly and stands with an open letter in his hand.*]

Helmer. Nora!

Nora. Ah!—

Helmer. What is this? Do you know what is in this letter?

NORA. Yes, I know. Let me go! Let me get out!

HELMER. [*holding her back*] Where are you going?

NORA. [*trying to get free*] You shan't save me, Torvald!

HELMER. [*reeling*] True? Is this true, that I read here? Horrible! No, no—it is impossible that it can be true.

NORA. It is true. I have loved you above everything else in the world.

HELMER. Oh, don't let us have any silly excuses.

NORA. [*taking a step towards him*] Torvald—!

HELMER. Miserable creature—what have you done?

NORA. Let me go. You shall not suffer for my sake. You shall not take it upon yourself.

HELMER. No tragedy airs, please. [*locks the hall door*] Here you shall stay and give me an explanation. Do you understand what you have done? Answer me? Do you understand what you have done?

NORA. [*looks steadily at him and says with a growing look of coldness in her face*] Yes, now I am beginning to understand thoroughly.

HELMER. [*walking about the room*] What a horrible awakening! All these eight years—she who was my joy and pride—a hypocrite, a liar—worse, worse—a criminal! The unutterable ugliness of it all! For shame! For shame! [*NORA is silent and looks steadily at him. He stops in front of her.*] I ought to have suspected that something of the sort would happen. I ought to have foreseen it. All your father's want of principle—be silent!—all your father's want of principle has come out in you. No religion, no morality, no sense of duty—. How I am punished for having winked at what he did! I did it for your sake, and this is how you repay me.

NORA. Yes, that's just it.

HELMER. Now you have destroyed all my happiness. You have ruined all my future. It is horrible to think of! I am in the power of an unscrupulous man; he can do what he likes with me, ask anything he likes of me, give me any orders he pleases—I dare not refuse. And I must sink to such miserable depths because of a thoughtless woman!

NORA. When I am out of the way, you will be free.

HELMER. No fine speeches, please. Your father had always plenty of those ready, too. What good would it be to me if you were out of the way, as you say? Not the slightest. He can make the affair known everywhere; and if he does, I may be falsely suspected of having been a party to your criminal action. Very likely people will think I was behind it all—that it was I who prompted you! And I have to thank you for all this—you whom I have cherished during the whole of our married life. Do you understand now what it is you have done for me?

NORA. [*coldly and quietly*] Yes.

HELMER. It is so incredible that I can't take it in. But we must come to some understanding. Take off that shawl. Take it off, I tell you. I must try and appease him some way or another. The matter must be hushed up at any cost. And as for you and me, it must appear as if everything between us were just as before—but naturally only in the eyes of the world. You will still remain in my house, that is a matter of course. But I shall not allow you to bring up the children; I dare not trust them to you. To think that I should be obliged to say so to one whom I have loved so dearly, and whom I still—. No, that is all over. From this moment happiness is not the question; all that concerns us is to save the remains, the fragments, the appearance—

[*A ring is heard at the front-door bell.*]

HELMER. [*with a start*] What is that? So late! Can the worst—? Can he—? Hide yourself, Nora. Say you are ill.

[NORA *stands motionless.* HELMER *goes and unlocks the hall door.*]

MAID. [*half-dressed, comes to the door*] A letter for the mistress.

HELMER. Give it to me. [*takes the letter, and shuts the door*] Yes, it is from him. You shall not have it; I will read it myself.

NORA. Yes, read it.

HELMER. [*standing by the lamp*] I scarcely have the courage to do it. It may mean ruin for both of us. No, I must know. [*tears open the letter, runs his eye over a few lines, looks at a paper enclosed and gives a shout of joy*] Nora! [*she looks at him questioningly.*] Nora!—No, I must read it once again—. Yes, it is true! I am saved! Nora, I am saved!

NORA. And I?

HELMER. You too, of course; we are both saved, both you and I. Look, he sends you your bond back. He says he regrets and repents—that a happy change in his life—never mind what he says! We are saved, Nora! No one can do anything to you. Oh, Nora, Nora!—no, first I must destroy these hateful things. Let me see—[*takes a look at the bond*] No, no, I won't look at it. The whole thing shall be nothing but a bad dream to me. [*tears up the bond and both letters, throws them all into the stove, and watches them burn*] There—now it doesn't exist any longer. He says that since Christmas Eve you—. These must have been three dreadful days for you, Nora.

NORA. I have fought a hard fight these three days.

HELMER. And suffered agonies, and seen no way out but—. No, we won't call any of the horrors to mind. We will only shout with joy, and keep saying "It's all over! It's all over!" Listen to me, Nora. You don't seem to realise that it is all over. What is this?—such a cold, set face! My poor little Nora, I quite understand; you don't feel as if you could believe that I have forgiven you. But it is true, Nora, I swear it; I have forgiven you everything. I know that what you did, you did out of love for me.

NORA. That is true.

HELMER. You have loved me as a wife ought to love her husband. Only you had not sufficient knowledge to judge of the means you used. But do you suppose you are any the less dear to me, because you don't understand how to act on your own responsibility? No, no; only lean on me; I will advise you and direct you. I should not be a man if this womanly helplessness did not just give you a double attractiveness in my eyes. You must not think any more about the hard things I said in my first moment of consternation, when I thought everything was going to overwhelm me. I have forgiven you, Nora; I swear to you I have forgiven you.

NORA. Thank you for your forgiveness.

[*She goes out through the door to the right.*]

HELMER. No, don't go—. [*looks in*] What are you doing in there?

NORA. [*from within*] Taking off my fancy dress.

HELMER. [*standing at the open door*] Yes, do. Try and calm yourself, and make your mind easy again, my frightened little singing-bird. Be at rest, and feel secure; I have broad wings to shelter you under. [*walks up and down by the door*] How warm and cosy our home is, Nora. Here is shelter for you; here I will protect you like a hunted dove that I have saved from a hawk's claws. I will bring peace to your poor beating heart. It will come, little by little, Nora, believe me. Tomorrow morning you will look upon it all quite differently; soon everything will be just as it was before. Very soon you won't need me to assure you that I have forgiven you; you will yourself feel the certainty that I have done so. Can you suppose I should ever think of such a thing as repudiating you, or even reproaching you? You have no idea what a true man's heart is like, Nora. There is something so indescribably sweet and satisfying, to a man, in the knowledge that he has forgiven his wife—forgiven her freely, and with all his heart. It seems as if that had made her, as it were, doubly his own; he has given her a new life, so to speak; and she has in a way become both wife and child to him. So you shall be for me after this, my little scared, helpless darling. Have no anxiety about anything, Nora; only be frank and open with me, and I will serve as will and conscience both to you—. What is this? Not gone to bed? Have you changed your things?

NORA. [*in everyday dress*] Yes, Torvald, I have changed my things now.

HELMER. But what for?—so late as this.

NORA. I shall not sleep to-night.

HELMER. But, my dear Nora—

NORA. [*looking at her watch*] It is not so very late. Sit down here, Torvald. You and I have much to say to one another.

[*She sits down at one side of the table.*]

HELMER. Nora—what is this?—this cold, set face?

NORA. Sit down, it will take some time; I have a lot to talk over with you.

HELMER. [*sits down at the opposite side of the table*] You alarm me, Nora!—and I don't understand you.

NORA. No, that is just it. You don't understand me, and I have never understood you either—before to-night. No, you mustn't interrupt me. You must simply listen to what I say. Torvald, this is a settling of accounts.

HELMER. What do you mean by that?

NORA. [*after a short silence*] Isn't there one thing that strikes you as strange in our sitting here like this?

HELMER. What is that?

NORA. We have been married now eight years. Does it not occur to you that this is the first time we two, you and I, husband and wife, have had a serious conversation?

HELMER. What do you mean by serious?

NORA. In all these eight years—longer than that—from the very beginning of our acquaintance, we have never exchanged a word on any serious subject.

HELMER. Was it likely that I would be continually and forever telling you about worries that you could not help me to bear?

NORA. I am not speaking about business matters. I say that we have never sat down in earnest together to try and get at the bottom of anything.

HELMER. But, dearest Nora, would it have been any good to you?

NORA. That is just it; you have never understood me. I have been greatly wronged, Torvald—first by papa and then by you.

HELMER. What! By us two—by us two, who have loved you better than anyone else in the world?

NORA. [*shaking her head*] You have never loved me. You have only thought it pleasant to be in love with me.

HELMER. Nora, what do I hear you saying?

NORA. It is perfectly true, Torvald. When I was at home with papa, he told me his opinion about everything, and so I had the same opinions; and if I differed from him I concealed the fact, because he would not have liked it. He called me his doll-child, and he played with me just as I used to play with my dolls. And when I came to live with you—

HELMER. What sort of an expression is that to use about our marriage?

NORA. [*undisturbed*] I mean that I was simply transferred from papa's hands into yours. You arranged everything according to your own taste, and so I got the same tastes as you—or else I pretended to, I am really not quite sure which—I think sometimes the one and sometimes the other. When I look back on it, it seems to me as if I had been living here like a poor woman—just from hand to mouth. I have existed merely to perform tricks for you, Torvald. But you would have it so. You and papa have committed a great sin against me. It is your fault that I have made nothing of my life.

HELMER. How unreasonable and how ungrateful you are, Nora! Have you not been happy here?

NORA. No, I have never been happy. I thought I was, but it has never really been so.

HELMER. Not—not happy!

NORA. No, only merry. And you have always been so kind to me. But our home has been nothing but a playroom. I have been your doll-wife, just as at home I was papa's doll-child; and here the children have been my dolls. I thought it great fun when you played with me, just as they thought it great fun when I played with them. That is what our marriage has been, Torvald.

HELMER. There is some truth in what you say—exaggerated and strained as your view of it is. But for the future it shall be different. Playtime shall be over, and lesson-time shall begin.

NORA. Whose lessons? Mine, or the children's?

HELMER. Both yours and the children's, my darling Nora.

NORA. Alas, Torvald, you are not the man to educate me into being a proper wife for you.

HELMER. And you can say that!

NORA. And I—how am I fitted to bring up the children?

HELMER. Nora!

NORA. Didn't you say so yourself a little while ago—that you dare not trust me to bring them up?

HELMER. In a moment of anger! Why do you pay any heed to that?

NORA. Indeed, you were perfectly right. I am not fit for the task. There is another task I must undertake first. I must try and educate myself—you are not the man to help me in that. I must do that for myself. And that is why I am going to leave you now.

HELMER. [*springing up*] What do you say?

NORA. I must stand quite alone, if I am to understand myself and everything about me. It is for that reason that I cannot remain with you any longer.

HELMER. Nora! Nora!

NORA. I am going away from here now, at once. I am sure Christine will take me in for the night—

HELMER. You are out of your mind! I won't allow it! I forbid you!

NORA. It is no use forbidding me anything any longer. I will take with me what belongs to myself. I will take nothing from you, either now or later.

HELMER. What sort of madness is this!

NORA. To-morrow I shall go home—I mean, to my old home. It will be easiest for me to find something to do there.

HELMER. You blind, foolish woman!

NORA. I must try and get some sense, Torvald.

HELMER. To desert your home, your husband and your children! And you don't consider what people will say!

NORA. I cannot consider that at all. I only know that it is necessary for me.

HELMER. It's shocking. This is how you would neglect your most sacred duties.

NORA. What do you consider my most sacred duties?

HELMER. Do I need to tell you that? Are they not your duties to your husband and your children?

NORA. I have other duties just as sacred.

HELMER. That you have not. What duties could those be?

NORA. Duties to myself.

HELMER. Before all else, you are a wife and a mother.

NORA. I don't believe that any longer. I believe that before all else I am a reasonable human being, just as you are—or, at all events, that I must try and become one. I know quite well, Torvald, that most people would think you right, and that views of that kind are to be found in books; but I can no longer content myself with what most people say, or with what is found in books. I must think over things for myself and get to understand them.

HELMER. Can you not understand your place in your own home? Have you not a reliable guide in such matters as that?—have you no religion?

NORA. I am afraid, Torvald, I do not exactly know what religion is.

HELMER. What are you saying?

NORA. I know nothing but what the clergyman said when I went to be confirmed. He told us that religion was this, and that, and the other. When I am away from all this, and am alone, I will look into that matter too. I will see if what the clergyman said is true, or at all events if it is true for me.

HELMER. This is unheard of in a girl of your age! But if religion cannot lead you aright, let me try and awaken your conscience. I suppose you have some moral sense? Or—answer me—am I to think you have none?

NORA. I assure you, Torvald, that is not an easy question to answer. I really don't know. The thing perplexes me altogether. I only know that you and I look at it in quite a different light. I am learning, too, that the law is quite another thing from what I supposed; but I find it impossible to convince myself that the law is right. According to it a woman has no right to spare her old dying father, or to save her husband's life. I can't believe that.

HELMER. You talk like a child. You don't understand the conditions of the world in which you live.

NORA. No, I don't. But now I am going to try. I am going to see if I can make out who is right, the world or I.

HELMER. You are ill, Nora; you are delirious; I almost think you are out of your mind.

NORA. I have never felt my mind so clear and certain as to-night.

HELMER. And is it with a clear and certain mind that you forsake your husband and your children?

NORA. Yes, it is.

HELMER. Then there is only one possible explanation.

NORA. What is that?

HELMER. You do not love me any more.

NORA. No, that is just it.

HELMER. Nora!—and you can say that?

NORA. It gives me great pain, Torvald, for you have always been so kind to me, but I cannot help it. I do not love you any more.

HELMER. [*regaining his composure*] Is that a clear and certain conviction too?

NORA. Yes, absolutely clear and certain. That is the reason why I will not stay here any longer.

HELMER. And can you tell me what I have done to forfeit your love?

NORA. Yes, indeed I can. It was to-night, when the wonderful thing did not happen; then I saw you were not the man I had thought you.

HELMER. Explain yourself better—I don't understand you.

NORA. I have waited so patiently for eight years; for, goodness knows, I knew very well that wonderful things don't happen every day. Then this horrible misfortune came upon me; and then I felt quite certain that the wonderful thing was going to happen at last. When Krogstad's letter was lying out there, never for a moment did I imagine that you would consent to accept this man's conditions. I was so absolutely certain that you would say to him: Publish the thing to the whole world. And when that was done—

HELMER. Yes, what then?—when I had exposed my wife to shame and disgrace?

NORA. When that was done, I was so absolutely certain, you would come forward and take everything upon yourself, and say I am the guilty one.

HELMER. Nora—!

NORA. You mean that I would never have accepted such a sacrifice on your part? No, of course not. But what would my assurances have been worth against yours? That was the wonderful thing which I hoped for and feared; and it was to prevent that, that I wanted to kill myself.

HELMER. I would gladly work night and day for you, Nora—bear sorrow and want for your sake. But no man would sacrifice his honour for the one he loves.

NORA. It is a thing hundreds of thousands of women have done.

HELMER. Oh, you think and talk like a heedless child.

NORA. Maybe. But you neither think nor talk like the man I could bind myself to. As soon as your fear was over—and it was not fear for what threatened me, but for what might happen to you—when the whole thing was past, as far as you were concerned it was exactly as if nothing at all had happened. Exactly as before, I was your little skylark, your doll, which you would in future treat with doubly gentle care, because it was so brittle and fragile. [*getting up*] Torvald—it was then it dawned upon me that for eight years I had been living here with a strange man, and had borne him three children—. Oh, I can't bear to think of it! I could tear myself into little bits!

HELMER. [*sadly*] I see, I see. An abyss has opened between us—there is no denying it. But, Nora, would it not be possible to fill it up?

NORA. As I am now, I am no wife for you.

HELMER. I have it in me to become a different man.

NORA. Perhaps—if your doll is taken away from you.

HELMER. But to part!—to part from you! No, no, Nora, I can't understand that idea.

NORA. [*going out to the right*] That makes it all the more certain that it must be done.

[*She comes back with her cloak and hat and a small bag which she puts on a chair by the table.*]

HELMER. Nora, Nora, not now! Wait till to-morrow.

NORA. [*putting on her cloak*] I cannot spend the night in a strange man's room.

HELMER. But can't we live here like brother and sister—?

NORA. [*putting on her hat*] You know very well that would not last long. [*puts the shawl round her*] Good-bye, Torvald. I won't see the little ones. I know they are in better hands than mine. As I am now, I can be of no use to them.

HELMER. But some day, Nora—some day?

NORA. How can I tell? I have no idea what is going to become of me.

HELMER. But you are my wife, whatever becomes of you.

NORA. Listen, Torvald. I have heard that when a wife deserts her husband's house, as I am doing now, he is legally freed from all obligations towards her. In any case I set you free from all your obligations. You are not to feel yourself bound in the slightest way, any more than I shall. There must be perfect freedom on both sides. See here is your ring back. Give me mine.

HELMER. That too?

NORA. That too.

HELMER. Here it is.

NORA. That's right. Now it is all over. I have put the keys here. The maids know all about everything in the house—better than I do. To-morrow, after I have left her, Christine will come here and pack up my own things that I brought with me from home. I will have them sent after me.

HELMER. All over! All over!—Nora, shall you never think of me again?

NORA. I know I shall often think of you and the children and this house.

HELMER. May I write to you, Nora?

NORA. No—never. You must not do that.

HELMER. But at least let me send you—

NORA. Nothing—nothing—

HELMER. Let me help you if you are in want.

NORA. No. I can receive nothing from a stranger.

HELMER. Nora—can I never be anything more than a stranger to you?

NORA. [*taking her bag*] Ah, Torvald, the most wonderful thing of all would have to happen.

HELMER. Tell me what that would be!

NORA. Both you and I would have to be so changed that—. Oh, Torvald, I don't believe any longer in wonderful things happening.

HELMER. But I will believe in it. Tell me? So changed that—?

NORA. That our life together would be a real wedlock. Good-bye.

[*She goes out through the hall.*]

HELMER. [*sinks down on a chair at the door and buries his face in his hands*] Nora! Nora! [*looks round, and rises*] Empty. She is gone. [*A hope flashes across his mind.*] The most wonderful thing of all—?

[*The sound of a door slamming is heard from below.*]

(1879)

Questions for Discussion and Writing

1. What do the early conversations between Nora and Torvald tell us about their relationship?
2. At what point did you realize that Nora was going to leave her husband?
3. How many scenes are between only two people? How does Ibsen use contrasting pairs of characters?
4. What is the function of Dr. Rank?
5. What or who is the main antagonist? Is it a person, an environment, or a social force? Is there more than one?
6. This play follows traditional dramatic structure rather closely. What point would you identify as the climax?
7. Why do Torvald's arguments against Nora's leaving fail?
8. Is Ibsen attacking marriage? What else may he be attacking?
9. What will become of Nora? Will she find happiness and fulfillment? Write an essay about Nora's future.
10. Write an essay in which you support this claim: "*A Doll's House* concerns the trouble caused by clinging to illusions."

Making Connections

Compare the use of setting in *A Doll's House* to the setting in *The Glass Menagerie* (page 677) and *Trifles* (page 816). In which play is the setting most important to the story? Explain your answer.

33 A Portfolio of Humorous and Satirical Plays

Chapter Preview

In this chapter, you will learn to do the following:

- Analyze plays that employ humor, especially satire.
- Compare what kinds of humor two different playwrights use, as well as how and why they each use humor.
- Write essays that reflect on and interpret humorous or satirical plays.

You watch humorous plays—in various types and sizes—all the time: skits on *Saturday Night Live* and *Key and Peele*, episodes of *The Big Bang Theory* and *Louie* and reruns of *30 Rock*, movies by Judd Apatow and Tyler Perry, musicals like *Hairspray* and *Grease*, school productions of *Arsenic and Old Lace* and community theater performances of *The Odd Couple*. Comedy is big business and always has been. Audiences like to laugh, and playwrights like to make money by making their audiences laugh. But the humor isn't always sunny and happy; it can also include anger, criticism, and ridicule. The plays in this portfolio use comedy to mock human folly or denounce social wrongs. *Beauty* combines irony with theatrical fantasy to comment on human vanity, and *Sure Thing* pokes witty fun at the vicissitudes of dating. You will enjoy reading and responding to these plays for both their humor and their satirical perspectives.

Jane Martin   1938?–

Jane Martin is a woman of mystery. She has never been seen, has given no interviews, and there are no pictures. Theater critics speculate that her spokesperson, Jon Jory, retired artistic director of the Actors Theatre of Louisville, wrote the plays in collaboration with his wife. He firmly denies it, saying simply, "I'm not going to talk about that." But he has been the first to produce all of her plays and has accepted all of her awards for her. When asked whether her identity would be disclosed after her death, Jory responded, "That's a press conference that no one will come to. By the time I die, no one will care anyway." So Jane Martin remains, as one critic attests, "The best-known unknown playwright in America."

Beauty

CHARACTERS

CARLA

BETHANY

An apartment. Minimalist set. A young woman, Carla, on the phone.

CARLA. In love with me? You're in love with me? Could you describe yourself again? Uh-huh. Uh-huh. And you spoke to me? [*A knock at the door.*] Listen, I always hate to interrupt a marriage proposal, but...could you possibly hold that thought? [*Puts phone down and goes to door. Bethany, the same age as Carla and a friend, is there. She carries the sort of Mideastern lamp we know of from Aladdin.*]

BETHANY. Thank God you were home. I mean, you're not going to believe this!

CARLA. Somebody on the phone. [*Goes back to it.*]

BETHANY. I mean, I just had a beach urge, so I told them at work my uncle was dying...

CARLA [*motions to Bethany for quiet*]. And you were the one in the leather jacket with the tattoo? What was the tatoo? [*Carla again asks Bethany, who is gesturing wildly that she should hang up, to cool it.*] Look, a screaming eagle from shoulder to shoulder, maybe. There were a lot of people in the bar.

BETHANY [*gesturing and mouthing*]. I have to get back to work.

CARLA [*on phone*]. See, the thing is, I'm probably not going to marry someone I can't remember...particularly when I don't drink. Sorry. Sorry. Sorry. [*She hangs up.*] Madness.

BETHANY. So I ran out to the beach...

CARLA. This was some guy I never met who apparently offered me a beer...

BETHANY. ...low tide and this...[*The lamp.*]...was just sitting there, lying there...

CARLA. ...and he tracks me down...

BETHANY. ...on the beach, and I lift this lid thing...

CARLA. ...and seriously proposes marriage.

BETHANY. ...and a genie comes out.

CARLA. I mean, that's twice in a...what?

BETHANY. A genie comes out of this thing.

CARLA. A genie?

BETHANY. I'm not kidding, the whole Disney kind of thing, swirling smoke, and then this twenty-foot-high, see-through guy in like an Arabian outfit.

CARLA. Very funny.

BETHANY. Yes, funny, but twenty feet high! I look up and down the beach, I'm alone. I don't have my pepper spray or my hand alarm. You know me, when I'm petrified I joke. I say his voice is too high for Robin Williams, and he says he's a castrati. Naturally. Who else would I meet?

CARLA. What's a castrati?

BETHANY. You know...

[*The appropriate gesture.*]

CARLA. Bethany, dear one, I have three modeling calls. I am meeting Ralph Lauren!

BETHANY. Okay, good. Ralph Lauren. Look, I am not kidding!

CARLA. You're not kidding what?!

BETHANY. There is a genie in this thingamajig.

CARLA. Uh-huh. I'll be back around eight.

BETHANY. And he offered me *wishes!*

CARLA. Is this some elaborate practical joke because it's my birthday?

BETHANY. No, happy birthday, but I'm like crazed because I'm on this deserted beach with a twenty-foot-high, see-through genie, so like sarcastically...you know how I need a new car...I said fine, gimme 25,000 dollars...

CARLA. On the beach with the genie?

BETHANY. Yeah, right, exactly, and it rains down out of the sky.

CARLA. Oh sure.

BETHANY [*pulling a wad out of her purse*]. Count it, those are thousands. I lost one in the surf.

[*Carla sees the top bill. Looks at Bethany, who nods encouragement. Carla thumbs through them.*]

CARLA. These look real.

BETHANY. Yeah.

CARLA. And they rained down out of the sky?

BETHANY. Yeah.

CARLA. You've been really strange lately, are you dealing?

BETHANY. Dealing what, I've even given up chocolate.

CARLA. Let me see the genie.

BETHANY. Wait, wait.

CARLA. Bethany, I don't have time to screw around. Let me see the genie or let me go on my appointments.

BETHANY. Wait! So I pick up the money...see, there's sand on the money...and I'm like nuts so I say, you know, "Okay, look, ummm, big guy, my uncle is in the hospital"...because as you know when I said to the people at work my uncle was dying, I was on one level telling the truth although it had nothing to do with the beach, but he was in Intensive Care after the accident, and that's on my mind, so I say, okay, Genie, heal my uncle...which is like impossible given he was hit by two trucks, and the genie says, "Yes, Master"...like they're supposed to say, and he goes into this like kind of whirlwind, kicking up sand and stuff, and I'm like, "Oh my God!" and the air clears, and he bows, you know, and says, "It is done, Master," and I say, "Okay, whatever-you-are, I'm calling on my cell phone," and I get it out and I get this doctor who is like dumbstruck who says my uncle came to, walked out of Intensive Care and left the hospital! I'm not kidding, Carla.

CARLA. On your mother's grave?

BETHANY. On my mother's grave.

[*They look at each other.*]

CARLA. Let me see the genie.

BETHANY. No, no, look, that's the whole thing...I was just, like, reacting, you know, responding, and that's already two wishes...although I'm really pleased about my uncle, the $25,000 thing, I could have asked for $10 million, and there is only one wish left.

CARLA. So ask for $10 million.

BETHANY. I don't think so. I don't think so. I mean, I gotta focus in here. Do you have a sparkling water?

CARLA. No. Bethany, I'm missing Ralph Lauren now. Very possibly my one chance to go from catalogue model to the very, very big time, so, if you are joking, stop joking.

BETHANY. Not joking. See, see, the thing is, I know what I want. In my guts. Yes. Underneath my entire bitch of a life is this unspoken, ferocious, all-consuming urge…

CARLA [*trying to get her to move this along*]. Ferocious, all-consuming urge…

BETHANY. I want to be like you.

CARLA. Me?

BETHANY. Yes.

CARLA. Half the time you don't even like me.

BETHANY. Jealous. The ogre of jealousy.

CARLA. You're the one with the $40,000 job straight out of school. You're the one who has published short stories. I'm the one hanging on by her fingernails in modeling. The one who has creeps calling her on the phone. The one who had to have a nose job.

BETHANY. I want to be beautiful.

CARLA. You are beautiful.

BETHANY. Carla, I'm not beautiful.

CARLA. You have charm. You have personality. You know perfectly well you're pretty.

BETHANY. "Pretty," see, that's it. Pretty is the minor leagues of beautiful. Pretty is what people discover about you after they know you. Beautiful is what knocks them out across the room. Pretty, you get called a couple of times a year; *beautiful* is twenty-four hours a day.

CARLA. Yeah? So?

BETHANY. So?! We're talking *beauty* here. Don't say "So?" Beauty is the real deal. You are the center of any moment of your life. People stare. Men flock. I've seen you get offered discounts on makeup for no reason. Parents treat beautiful children better. Studies show your income goes up. You can have sex anytime you want it. Men have to know me. That takes up to a year. I'm continually horny.

CARLA. Bethany, I don't even like sex. I can't have a conversation without men coming on to me. I have no privacy. I get hassled on the street. They start pressuring me from the beginning. Half the time, it never occurs to them to start with a conversation. Smart guys like you. You've had three long-term relationships, and you're only twenty-three. I haven't had one. The good guys, the smart guys are scared to death of me. I'm surrounded by male bimbos who think a preposition is when you go to school away from home. I have no woman friends except you. I don't even want to talk about this!

BETHANY. I knew you'd say something like this. See, you're "in the club" so you can say this. It's the way beauty functions as an elite. You're trying to keep it all for yourself.

CARLA. I'm trying to tell you it's no picnic.

BETHANY. But it's what everybody wants. It's the nasty secret at large in the world. It's the unspoken tidal desire in every room and on every street. It's the unspoken, the soundless whisper… millions upon millions of people longing hopelessly and forever to stop being whatever they are and be beautiful, but the difference between those ardent multitudes and me is that I have a goddamn genie and one more wish!

CARLA. Well, it's not what I want. This is me, Carla. I have never read a whole book. Page six, I can't remember page four. The last thing I read was *The Complete Idiot's Guide to WordPerfect*. I leave dinner parties right after the dessert because I'm out of conversation. You know the dumb blond joke about the application where it says, "Sign here," she put Sagittarius? I've done that. Only beautiful guys approach me, and that's because they want to borrow my eye shadow. I barely exist outside a mirror! You don't want to be me.

BETHANY. None of you tell the truth. That's why you have no friends. We can all see you're just trying to make us feel better because we aren't in your league. This only proves to me it should be my third wish. Money can only buy things. Beauty makes you the center of the universe.

[*Bethany picks up the lamp.*]

CARLA. Don't do it. Bethany, don't wish it! I am telling you you'll regret it.

[*Bethany lifts the lid. There is a tremendous crash, and the lights go out. Then they flicker and come back up, revealing Bethany and Carla on the floor where they have been thrown by the explosion. We don't realize it at first, but they have exchanged places.*]

CARLA/BETHANY. Oh God.

BETHANY/CARLA. Oh God.

CARLA/BETHANY. Am I bleeding? Am I dying?

BETHANY/CARLA. I'm so dizzy. You're not bleeding.

CARLA/BETHANY. Neither are you.

BETHANY/CARLA. I feel so weird.

CARLA/BETHANY. Me too. I feel… [*Looking at her hands.*] Oh, my God, I'm wearing your jewelry. I'm wearing your nail polish.

BETHANY/CARLA. I know I'm over here, but I can see myself over there.

CARLA/BETHANY. I'm wearing your dress. I have your legs!!

BETHANY/CARLA. These aren't my shoes. I can't meet Ralph Lauren wearing these shoes!

CARLA/BETHANY. I wanted to be beautiful, but I didn't want to be you.

BETHANY/CARLA. Thanks a lot!!

CARLA/BETHANY. I've got to go. I want to pick someone out and get laid.

BETHANY/CARLA. You can't just walk out of here in my body!

CARLA/BETHANY. Wait a minute. Wait a minute. What's eleven eighteenths of 1,726?

BETHANY/CARLA. Why?

CARLA/BETHANY. I'm a public accountant. I want to know if you have my brain.

BETHANY/CARLA. One hundred thirty-two and a half.

CARLA/BETHANY. You have my brain.

BETHANY/CARLA. What shade of Rubenstein lipstick does Cindy Crawford wear with teal blue?

CARLA/BETHANY. Raging Storm.

BETHANY/CARLA. You have my brain. You poor bastard.

CARLA/BETHANY. I don't care. Don't you see?

BETHANY/CARLA. See what?

CARLA/BETHANY. We both have the one thing, the one and only thing everybody wants.

BETHANY/CARLA. What is that?

CARLA/BETHANY. It's better than beauty for me; it's better than brains for you.
BETHANY/CARLA. What? What?!
CARLA/BETHANY. Different problems.

Blackout.

END OF PLAY

(2001)

Questions for Discussion and Writing

1. What values and obsessions does this play satirize?
2. What stereotype does each character represent? Are they both objects of derision? Do you think one of them gets a better deal in the end?
3. Why does Bethany not believe Carla when she (Carla) tries to explain the downside of beauty?
4. Does this play have to be about women? Write an essay explaining how you would adapt the play to satirize two young men.

David Ives 1950–

Born and raised on Chicago's south side, David Ives began his career in Hollywood writing scripts for TV movies. After moving to New York, he did humorous pieces for the *New York Times Magazine* and the *New Yorker* before turning to playwriting. He describes one of his short plays featuring a cross-dressing corporate executive as being about "the ontological problem of lingerie" and says that he's grateful for the shortness of his plays because "when the lights go down, at least the audience isn't thinking, 'Oh, God, two more hours of this.'" Asked by a reporter, "If you weren't a writer, what would you be?" he responded, "I'd be a hawk. Or maybe a seal in the waters off Alaska. Preferably with my wife Martha as my fellow hawk or fellow seal."

Sure Thing[1]

CHARACTERS

BILL, *in his late twenties*   BETTY, *in her late twenties*

SETTING

A café table, with a couple of chairs.

SCENE

[BETTY, *reading at the table. An empty chair opposite her.* BILL *enters.*]

BILL. Excuse me. Is this chair taken?
BETTY. Excuse me?
BILL. Is this taken?
BETTY. Yes, it is.
BILL. Oh. Sorry.
BETTY. Sure thing.

---

[1]Ives, David. "Sure Thing." (Dramatists Play Service, Inc.) Reprinted by permission of the author and Dramatists Play Service, Inc.

[*A bell rings softly*]

BILL. Excuse me. Is this chair taken?
BETTY. Excuse me?
BILL. Is this taken?
BETTY. No, but I'm expecting somebody in a minute.
BILL. Oh. Thanks anyway.
BETTY. Sure thing.

[*A bell rings softly*]

BILL. Excuse me. Is this chair taken?
BETTY. No, but I'm expecting somebody very shortly.
BILL. Would you mind if I sit here till he or she or it comes?
BETTY [*Glances at her watch*]. They seem to be pretty late...
BILL. You never know who you might be turning down.
BETTY. Sorry. Nice try, though.
BILL. Sure thing.

[*Bell*]

BILL. Is this seat taken?
BETTY. No, it's not.
BILL. Would you mind if I sit here?
BETTY. Yes, I would.
BILL. Oh.

[*Bell*]

BILL. Is this chair taken?
BETTY. No, it's not.
BILL. Would you mind if I sit here?
BETTY. No. Go ahead.
BILL. Thanks. [*He sits. She continues reading*] Everyplace else seems to be taken.
BETTY. Mm-hm.
BILL. Great place.
BETTY. Mm-hm.
BILL. What's the book?
BETTY. I just wanted to read in quiet, if you don't mind.
BILL. No. Sure thing.

[*Bell*]

BILL. Everyplace else seems to be taken.
BETTY. Mm-hm.
BILL. Great place for reading.
BETTY. Yes, I like it.
BILL. What's the book?
BETTY. *The Sound and the Fury.*
BILL. Oh. Hemingway.

[*Bell*]

BILL. What's the book?
BETTY. *The Sound and the Fury.*

BILL. Oh. Faulkner.
BETTY. Have you read it?
BILL. Not...actually. I've read *about* it, though. It's supposed to be great.
BETTY. It is great.
BILL. I hear it's great. [*Small pause*] Waiter?

   [*Bell*]

BILL. What's the book?
BETTY. *The Sound and the Fury*.
BILL. Oh. Faulkner.
BETTY. Have you read it?
BILL. I'm a Mets fan, myself.

   [*Bell*]

BETTY. Have you read it?
BILL. Yeah, I read it in college.
BETTY. Where was college?
BILL. I went to Oral Roberts University.

   [*Bell*]

BETTY. Where was college?
BILL. I was lying. I never really went to college. I just like to party.

   [*Bell*]

BETTY. Where was college?
BILL. Harvard.
BETTY. Do you like Faulkner?
BILL. I love Faulkner. I spent a whole winter reading him once.
BETTY. I've just started.
BILL. I was so excited after ten pages that I went out and bought everything else
   he wrote. One of the greatest reading experiences of my life. I mean, all that
   incredible psychological understanding. Page after page of gorgeous prose.
   His profound grasp of the mystery of time and human existence. The smells
   of the earth...What do you think?
BETTY. I think it's pretty boring.

   [*Bell*]

BILL. What's the book?
BETTY. *The Sound and the Fury*.
BILL. Oh! Faulkner!
BETTY. Do you like Faulkner?
BILL. I love Faulkner.
BETTY. He's incredible.
BILL. I spent a whole winter reading him once.
BETTY. I was so excited after ten pages that I went out and bought everything else
   he wrote.
BILL. All that incredible psychological understanding.
BETTY. And the prose is so gorgeous.
BILL. And the way he's grasped the mystery of time—
BETTY. —and human existence. I can't believe I've waited this long to read him.

BILL. You never know. You might not have liked him before.
BETTY. That's true.
BILL. You might not have been ready for him. You have to hit these things at the right moment or it's no good.
BETTY. That's happened to me.
BILL. It's all in the timing. [*Small pause*] My name's Bill, by the way.
BETTY. I'm Betty.
BILL. Hi.
BETTY. Hi.

> [*Small pause*]

BILL. Yes, I thought reading Faulkner was...a great experience.
BETTY. Yes.

> [*Small pause*]

BILL. *The Sound and the Fury...*

> [*Another small pause*]

BETTY. Well. Onwards and upwards. [*She goes back to her book*]
BILL. Waiter—?

> [*Bell*]

BILL. You have to hit these things at the right moment or it's no good.
BETTY. That's happened to me.
BILL. It's all in the timing. My name's Bill, by the way.
BETTY. I'm Betty.
BILL. Hi.
BETTY. Hi.
BILL. Do you come in here a lot?
BETTY. Actually I'm just in town for two days from Pakistan.
BILL. Oh. Pakistan.

> [*Bell*]

BILL. My name's Bill, by the way.
BETTY. I'm Betty.
BILL. Hi.
BETTY. Hi.
BILL. Do you come in here a lot?
BETTY. Every once in a while. Do you?
BILL. Not much anymore. Not as much as I used to. Before my nervous breakdown.

> [*Bell*]

BILL. Do you come in here a lot?
BETTY. Why are you asking?
BILL. Just interested.
BETTY. Are you really interested, or do you just want to pick me up?
BILL. No, I'm really interested.
BETTY. Why would you be interested in whether I come in here a lot?
BILL. Just... getting acquainted.
BETTY. Maybe you're only interested for the sake of making small talk long enough to ask me back to your place to listen to some music, or because

you've just rented some great tape for your VCR, or because you've got some terrific unknown Django Reinhardt record, only all you'll really want to do is fuck—which you won't do very well—after which you'll go into the bathroom and pee very loudly, then pad into the kitchen and get yourself a beer from the refrigerator without asking me whether I'd like anything, and then you'll proceed to lie back down beside me and confess that you've got a girlfriend named Stephanie who's away at medical school in Belgium for a year, and that you've been involved with her—*off and on*—in what you'll call a very intricate relationship, for about *seven* YEARS. None of which *interests* me, mister!

BILL. Okay.

[*Bell*]

BILL. Do you come in here a lot?

BETTY. Every other day, I think.

BILL. I come in here quite a lot and I don't remember seeing you.

BETTY. I guess we must be on different schedules.

BILL. Missed connections.

BETTY. Yes. Different time zones.

BILL. Amazing how you can live right next door to somebody in this town and never even know it.

BETTY. I know.

BILL. City life.

BETTY. It's crazy.

BILL. We probably pass each other in the street every day. Right in front of this place, probably.

BETTY. Yep.

BILL [*Looks around*]. Well, the waiters here sure seem to be in some different time zone. I don't see one anywhere... Waiter! [*He looks back*] So what do you...

[*He sees that she's gone back to her book*]

BETTY. I beg pardon?

BILL. Nothing. Sorry.

[*Bell*]

BETTY. I guess we must be on different schedules.

BILL. Missed connections.

BETTY. Yes. Different time zones.

BILL. Amazing how you can live right next door to somebody in this town and never even know it.

BETTY. I know.

BILL. City life.

BETTY. It's crazy.

BILL. You weren't waiting for somebody when I came in, were you?

BETTY. Actually I was.

BILL. Oh. Boyfriend?

BETTY. Sort of.

BILL. What's a sort-of boyfriend?

BETTY. My husband.

BILL. Ah-ha.

[*Bell*]

BILL. You weren't waiting for somebody when I came in, were you?
BETTY. Actually I was.
BILL. Oh. Boyfriend?
BETTY. Sort of.
BILL. What's a sort-of boyfriend?
BETTY. We were meeting here to break up.
BILL. Mm-hm...

[*Bell*]

BILL. What's a sort-of boyfriend?
BETTY. My lover. Here she comes right now!

[*Bell*]

BILL. You weren't waiting for somebody when I came in, were you?
BETTY. No, just reading.
BILL. Sort of a sad occupation for a Friday night, isn't it? Reading here, all by
  yourself?
BETTY. Do you think so?
BILL. Well sure. I mean, what's a good-looking woman like you doing out alone
  on a Friday night?
BETTY. Trying to keep away from lines like that.
BILL. No, listen—

[*Bell*]

BILL. You weren't waiting for somebody when I came in, were you?
BETTY. No, just reading.
BILL. Sort of a sad occupation for a Friday night, isn't it? Reading here all by
  yourself?
BETTY. I guess it is, in a way.
BILL. What's a good-looking woman like you doing out alone on a Friday night
  anyway? No offense, but...
BETTY. I'm out alone on a Friday night for the first time in a very long time.
BILL. Oh.
BETTY. You see, I just recently ended a relationship.
BILL. Oh.
BETTY. Of rather long standing.
BILL. I'm sorry—Well listen, since reading by yourself *is* such a sad occupation
  for a Friday night, would you like to go elsewhere?
BETTY. No...
BILL. Do something else?
BETTY. No thanks.
BILL. I was headed out to the movies in a while anyway.
BETTY. I don't think so.
BILL. Big chance to let Faulkner catch his breath. All those long sentences get
  him pretty tired.
BETTY. Thanks anyway.
BILL. Okay.
BETTY. I appreciate the invitation.
BILL. Sure thing.

[*Bell*]

BILL. You weren't waiting for somebody when I came in, were you?
BETTY. No, just reading.
BILL. Sort of a sad occupation for a Friday night, isn't it? Reading here all by yourself?
BETTY. I guess I was trying to think of it as existentially romantic. You know—capuccino, great literature, rainy night....
BILL. That only works in Paris. We *could* hop the late plane to Paris. Get on a Concorde. Find a café...
BETTY. I'm a little short on plane fare tonight.
BILL. Darn it, so am I.
BETTY. To tell you the truth, I was headed to the movies after I finished this section. Would you like to come along? Since you can't locate a waiter?
BILL. That's a very nice offer, but—I can't.
BETTY. Uh-huh. Girlfriend?
BILL. Two of them, actually. One of them's pregnant, and Stephanie—

[*Bell*]

BETTY. Girlfriend?
BILL. No, I don't have a girlfriend. Not if you mean the castrating bitch I dumped last night.

[*Bell*]

BETTY. Girlfriend?
BILL. Sort of. Sort of...
BETTY. What's a sort-of girlfriend?
BILL. My mother.

[*Bell*]

BILL. I just ended a relationship, actually.
BETTY. Oh.
BILL. Of rather long standing.
BETTY. I'm sorry to hear it.
BILL. This is my first night out alone in a long time. I feel a little bit at sea, to tell you the truth.
BETTY. So you didn't stop to talk because you're a Moonie, or you have some weird political affiliation—?
BILL. Nope. Straight-down-the-ticket Republican.

[*Bell*]

Straight-down-the-ticket Democrat.

[*Bell*]

Can I tell you something about politics?

[*Bell*]

I consider myself a citizen of the universe.

[*Bell*]

I'm unaffiliated.

BETTY. That's a relief. So am I.

BILL. I vote my beliefs.

BETTY. Labels are not important.

BILL. Labels are not important, exactly. Like me, for example. I mean, what does it matter if I had a two-point—

[*Bell*]

—three-point—

[*Bell*]

—four-point at college, or if I did come from Pittsburgh—

[*Bell*]

—Cleveland—

[*Bell*]

—Westchester County?

BETTY. Sure.

BILL. I believe that a man is what he is.

[*Bell*]

A person is what he is.

[*Bell*]

A person is what they are.

BETTY. I think so, too.

BILL. So what if I admire Trotsky?

[*Bell*]

So what if I once had a total body liposuction?

[*Bell*]

So what if I don't have a penis?

[*Bell*]

So what if I spent a year in the Peace Corps? I was acting on my convictions.

BETTY. Convictions are important.

BILL. You just can't hang a sign on a person.

BETTY. Absolutely. I'll bet you're a Scorpio.

[*Many bells ring*]

BETTY. Listen, I was headed to the movies after I finished this section. Would you like to come along?

BILL. That sounds like fun. What's playing?

BETTY. A couple of the really early Woody Allen movies.

BILL. Oh.

BETTY. Don't you like Woody Allen?

BILL. Sure, I like Woody Allen.
BETTY. But you're not crazy about Woody Allen.
BILL. Those early ones kind of get on my nerves.
BETTY. Uh-huh.

[*Bell*]

BILL.	[*Simultaneously*]	BETTY.
Y'know, I was headed to the…		I was thinking about…

BILL. I'm sorry.
BETTY. No, go ahead.
BILL. I was just going to say that I was headed to the movies in a little while, and…
BETTY. So was I.
BILL. The Woody Allen festival?
BETTY. Just up the street.
BILL. Do you like the early ones?
BETTY. I think anybody who doesn't ought to be run off the planet.
BILL. How many times have you seen *Bananas*?
BETTY. Eight times.
BILL. Twelve. So are you still interested?
BETTY. Do you like Entenmann's crumb cake?
BILL. I went out at two o'clock this morning to buy one. Did you have an Etch-a-Sketch as a child?
BETTY. Yes! Do you like brussel sprouts?
BILL. I think they're gross.
BETTY. They *are* gross!
BILL. Do you still believe in marriage in spite of current sentiments against it?
BETTY. Yes.
BILL. And children?
BETTY. Three of them.
BILL. Two girls and a boy.
BETTY. Harvard, Vassar, and Brown.
BILL. And will you love me?
BETTY. Yes.
BILL. And cherish me forever?
BETTY. Yes.
BILL. Do you still want to go to the movies?
BETTY. Sure thing.
BILL *and* BETTY [*Together*]. Waiter!

BLACKOUT

(1988)

Questions for Discussion and Writing

1. The play was originally set at a bus stop. What does its setting in a café say about the characters?

2. At one point Bill says, "You have to hit these things at the right moment or it's no good." Explain how this statement describes the play's basic dramatic premise.

3. What is the purpose of the ringing bell?

4. Describe the play's plot. What is its central conflict and how is it resolved? Where does the climax occur?

5. In 2001, a theater company in Denver put on *Sure Thing* by using three separate couples, each with the names Bill and Betty. The lines shifted from one couple to the next after each ring of the bell. Can you picture how this performance would work? Try reading the play this way out loud in class. You can make it easier to follow if you put numbers in the margin of the script to indicate which couple should read.

Ideas for Writing: Making Connections

1. How would you describe the tone of each play in this portfolio? Which is harshest in its satire? Which is the friendliest? Did the plays make you laugh? Write an essay comparing the humor in the two plays.

2. Examine the theatrical devices in both plays—the Aladdin's lamp and the bell. Compare their purposes and their effectiveness.

3. In what ways are the two sets of characters alike? In other words, are Martin and Ives satirizing the same essential qualities? Argue for or against this possibility.

4. Rewrite a key scene from another play using the bell device from *Sure Thing*. For example, you might write a sequence of possible drafts of Othello's dying words (in which he revises his assessment of what he did) or Amanda's repeated attempts to get Tom to bring home a gentleman caller (in *The Glass Menagerie*).

5. Alice Childress's play *Florence* (page 948) also exposes a social problem. Write an essay in which you argue that it could be included in this Portfolio of Humorous and Satirical Plays.

MultiModal Project

Write and perform a short two-character skit that satirizes some human foible, such as greed, laziness, procrastination, gullibility, or carelessness. With your instructor's permission, work with several classmates on both the writing and the production of the play. You might make a video (with a phone or camera) of your finished product.

Part V Critical Approaches to Literature

This final section brings together the various strands of our instruction in reading and writing about literature. After a concise review of the major schools of literary criticism, we present a casebook of stories, poems, and plays that challenge you to explore the issues of culture and identity.

34 Critical Approaches for Interpreting Literature

Chapter Preview

Literary critics can be loosely grouped according to what they look for in written works. They apply a systematic method to the interpretation of a piece and usually have a preferred method or combination of methods. For example, one critic may customarily think about a work in terms of how it reflects the historical period in which it was written, whereas another likes to focus on the images of femininity and masculinity depicted in the work. You can learn the various points of view that people use to interpret and judge literature. Probably some of them are the points of view you already use informally, but seeing them laid out in an orderly way will help you study and write about literature. You will want to be acquainted with all the standard approaches, because you need to match the critical point of view with the specific work you are studying.

After reading this chapter, you should be able to do the following:

* Identify the general goals and practices of literary criticism.
* Identify and understand the major schools of critical theory.
* Apply these various viewpoints to your own writing about literature.

Literary Criticism

We are all critics. That is, we find ourselves in conversations about books, movies, and TV shows, conversations in which we express our likes and dislikes, approval and disapproval, often disagreeing with one another. You may devour romance novels in your spare time, while your best friend thinks those same novels are silly and a waste of time. Meanwhile, that friend seeks out the latest in experimental science fiction, which you find confusing and pointless. The two of you are coming from different tastes, but you are also taking different critical stances about what makes a book good. You value emotional involvement and absorption, as well as a satisfying beginning–middle–happy-ending structure, and that's what you get in romance novels. Your friend doesn't care at all about a predictable structure and an absorbing love story but values mental playfulness, challenge, and the element of surprise in her leisure reading. No one can say that one or the other is right. The word *criticism*, in relation to the arts, does not mean faultfinding as it does in everyday conversation; literary criticism has to do with interpretation of a work. Some literary criticism does evaluate or judge a work as good or bad, but appraisal is not the main point in most cases.

Formalism

A formalist critic looks at a piece of literature as complete within itself. The formalist approach appreciates the way in which all the features of a piece work together in a unified, meaningful whole. These features are, for the most part, what you study in this textbook: structure, imagery, character development, setting, language, and so on. The term *formalist*, instead of being directly related to the idea of formality, is related to the idea of *form*. In this book we encourage you to perceive the form and content of literature as deeply entwined. For example, on page 443, rhythm and rhyme are considered for the way they enhance tone and meaning. A prominent technique of the formalist critic is *close reading*, which we have promoted in this textbook as essential in making a first attempt at interpreting literature.

A strictly formalist reading does not bring in outside sources. The main tools are imagination and skill in analyzing the various features of literature. Support for an interpretation comes from evidence within the poem, story, or play.

Historical Approaches

In contrast with formalism, several approaches emphasize that the writer was leading a life in a certain time in history and that events in personal life and in the world affect the literature produced. Historical critics examine a literary work in the context of its time. They try to see the work as people in the original audience would while also being aware of how the experiences of their own time and place influence their interpretations. For example, Henrik Ibsen's *A Doll's House*, first performed in 1879, shocked its audiences by rejecting socially sanctioned rules. Nothing could justify a wife's walking out on her marriage, away from her children. When actresses and theater companies refused to perform the play, Ibsen reluctantly rewrote the ending so that Nora gives her husband another chance. He later regretted his decision. But as women gained more rights and independence, the play also grew in popularity and importance. In 2006, *A Doll's House* was the world's most performed play for that year, and Nora's act of slamming the door as she leaves had become a symbol of women's liberation.

Several types of historical approach are possible, focusing on specialized aspects of the past. These aspects may be biographical, cultural, or political.

Biographical

Diaries, letters, journals, biographies, and autobiographies are tools of the critic who investigates how an author's life is reflected in his or her imaginative writing. Emily Dickinson's hermitlike seclusion in real life often serves to help illuminate her difficult poems, because we can speculate on how her unusual solitude gave her an extraordinary point of view on things others take for granted or do not see at all. Similarly, we can appreciate Wilfred Owen's "Dulce et Decorum Est" more fully when we know that he served in World War I, was wounded in 1917 (shortly before the poem was written), and died in action in 1918. The powerful, detailed imagery of the poem is rooted in real-life experience.

Cultural

Cultural critics use materials beyond the standard biographical information and history books to examine literature. They are likely to look at cultural artifacts like the period's advertisements, architecture, journalism, campaign speeches, political tracts, fads, and popular literature such as comic books when they set a work in historical context. A cultural critic would be more likely than a formalist to examine a work of literature in terms of its times. For example, Dudley Randall's poem "Ballad of Birmingham" derives from an incident during the U.S. Civil Rights movement when white supremacists bombed a church in Birmingham, Alabama, where African Americans were worshiping: four school children were killed. Rather than focus on the ballad format, as a formalist might do, a cultural critic would consult journalistic and historical writings about this 1963 event when interpreting the poems' themes and purposes. William Faulkner's "Barn Burning" must be understood in terms of the fierce class and racial strife in post–Civil War Mississippi. When Abner Snopes is enraged by his encounter with a well-dressed black servant who scolds him on the threshold of a white landowner's palatial home, readers should grasp the extra sting of losing a last, spurious claim of white superiority in the social order. Abner's vicious retaliation against this order is illuminated by the cultural setting of the story.

Marxist

Another historical point of view that may include judgment or evaluation of literature is the Marxist approach. Marxist critics take the stance that literature is an artifact of history, which is driven by economic forces and class struggle. They see the fine arts as frequently a reflection of the values of the privileged class, endorsing the status quo rather than challenging it. A Marxist critic would probably point out that Alice Walker's "Everyday Use" demonstrates the shift from a barter-based to a cash-based economy, in which a homemade quilt is detached from its natural purpose and instead elevated as a fetish, a work of folk art never to be used. Many works of literature do lend themselves to a fruitful Marxist analysis;

for example, the play *Los Vendidos* can be understood more clearly by considering the power relationships, both economic and political, between Chicano workers in the United States and their Anglo employers.

Psychological Approaches

John Steinbeck's "Chrysanthemums" is a story often approached from a psychological point of view. The sexual and aggressive impulses of Elisa Allen, the main character, are barely controlled and manifest themselves in her energetic work with plants, her fascination with the roving tinker's life, and her desires to see prize fighting and drink wine. Her sexual yearnings are thinly veiled in her description of viewing the sky at night: "Why, you rise up and up! Every pointed star gets driven into your body. It's like that. Hot and sharp and—lovely."

Because a grasp of human motivation is key to understanding so much literature, psychology comes into play continually, and many critics make a practice of looking at literature through the lenses of psychological theories. It is difficult to discuss a poem like Robert Browning's "My Last Duchess" without psychoanalyzing the speaker, the Duke, who seems narcissistic as well as paranoid. Freud's early twentieth-century theories inform much psychological literary criticism, so explorations of characters' subconscious motivations, defenses, inner conflicts, and symbolic acts are commonplace. In Joyce's "Eveline," the main character's psychological and finally physical paralysis, her desperate last-minute clutch at girlhood, can be interpreted as her fear of adult sexuality, as embodied in Frank's masculinity, the tumbling seas, and exotic Buenos Aires. Contemporary psychological research often comes into play as well, because literature so often entails emotional experience and its sequelae. Louis Erdrich's "The Red Convertible" involves a portrait of post-traumatic stress disorder (PTSD), a common syndrome among soldiers returning from the Vietnam War.

In attempting to interpret a literary work, sometimes psychological critics use their tools to analyze the author as well as the characters, and in such cases their pursuit combines the biographical and psychological approaches.

Mythological and Archetypal Approaches

Another approach is related to mass psychology rather than individual idiosyncrasies. Mythological or archetypal critics look at commonalities among dreams, myths, legends, religions, visual arts, and literature, and they see the same threads running through human imaginative work throughout the ages and across cultures. One such thread, for instance, is the quest or journey, during which the main character is challenged sorely (often three times), gaining wisdom and insight along the way to a heroic ending point (or not, having failed the challenge). Another thread is the hero who dies for the salvation of all humankind. Archetypal plots and characters are associated with the theories of the Swiss psychologist Carl Jung, who believed that every person is born equipped with a collective unconscious, a set of images including many universal fictional characters such as the wise old man, the fool, the trickster, the manly rescuer, the earth mother, and the mysterious stranger, as well as others. Our attraction to certain types of stories and characters comes from the way they appeal to our collective unconscious. Arnold Friend, the menacing yet magnetic visitor in Joyce Carol Oates's "Where Are You Going, Where Have You Been?" can be seen as a trickster archetype.

Gender Focus

Drawing from psychological, sociological, and political thought as well as from literary studies, many critics in the twentieth and twenty-first centuries look at art through the lenses of gender. They ponder how sex roles, sexual identity, and relationships between the sexes affect the way that a work is written and read. A gender-based reading of Tillie Olsen's "I Stand Here Ironing" would emphasize that all three main characters are female, with experiences different from those they would have if they were men. Within the fold of gender-focused critics are feminist critics, who would analyze the story in terms of women's strategies to cope with their powerlessness in the male-oriented world. Feminists explain the disparate experiences of the sexes by analyzing the effects of the differences in power, privilege, and expectations. Hisaye Yamamoto's "Seventeen Syllables" is ripe for a feminist approach, especially for understanding the mother's motivations. Feminist critics are interested in the images of women and men as presented in literature, often pointing out negative portrayals of women that might otherwise go unnoticed.

Another gender focus involves the lives and lifestyles of gay and lesbian authors, characters, and readers. As a minority culture, gays and lesbians have a distinctive experience that has often been ignored, despised, or treated as exotic. These attitudes frequently affect the way they write and are written about (or avoided). Sherwood Anderson's "Hands" would be baffling without the allusions to fear-ridden stereotypes of gay men, especially gay teachers.

Reader Response

The critical approaches discussed so far share the idea that a work of literature has a meaning, probably one that is stable and coherent. The last two we will take up do not share this idea but focus on the variety of interpretation that is possible. The reader response approach accepts that each person brings his or her own experiences and points of view to bear while reading. No one reads a work in exactly the same way as anyone else, as you have probably noticed in discussions with classmates and friends. In fact, you may have read the same work differently within your own life as you get older. One of our colleagues claims that no one can possibly understand *Macbeth* before the age of thirty! Although reader response critics will not allow totally far-fetched interpretations of a work, they are interested in individuals' different reactions to ambiguous clues. For example, when J. Alfred Prufrock asks, "Do I dare to eat a peach?" one reader may think that Prufrock is worried about the embarrassing messiness of consuming a ripe peach, another may think that he fears looking greedy, and another may decide that the peach is a feminine symbol and Prufrock fears the sex act. All of these thoughts are defensible using other evidence within the poem, and all are probably projections of the reader's own fears.

Deconstruction

Deconstructionists take a step beyond reader response critics by viewing a work of literature as unstable and therefore vulnerable to being taken apart (de-constructed). Whereas formalists look for the way that all the elements of a piece fit together, deconstructionists look for the way these elements contradict each other and undermine coherence. Their point of view is rooted in a philosophy of language which says that words are incapable of accurately expressing meaning, that every utterance contains a lie by omitting all other possible utterances at the moment. Other critical stances reject interpretations that cannot be supported by evidence within the work, but deconstructionists delight in bizarre and contradictory claims. For example, while most people view J. Alfred Prufrock as a timid, self-effacing, and fearful fellow, deconstructionists might ask why a timid person would present such a lengthy, detailed, self-absorbed introspection (the poem itself). They could argue that J. Alfred is a braggart and narcissist, enchanted with his own superhuman sensitivity.

Intertextual Approaches

The meaning of literature is frequently enriched by each work's interdependence with other texts and the way they cast light on each other. Thus, critics use an *intertextual approach* in interpreting meaning. Sometimes intertextuality is right there on the surface, as it is in Susan Ludvigson's "Inventing My Parents." The author imagines her parents in lively intellectual chat about modernist writers Ernest Hemingway, Sinclair Lewis, Kay Boyle, and F. Scott Fitzgerald, and her father quotes by heart from the seventeenth-century poet John Donne.

If you investigate these writers and their devotees, you will understand much about why Ludvigson wrote a charming, lighthearted response to the painting *Nighthawks*, which usually evokes feelings of isolation and hopelessness in its viewers (see page 469). You can create an intertextual approach even when it is not explicit, by noticing relationships among literary pieces. For example, student Ben Hardy noticed that both science fiction stories, "The Ones Who Walk Away from Omelas" and "Speech Sounds," have something to do with how the basic underpinnings of civilization are not obvious until they are violated. In "Omelas," the violators are people who quietly decide to leave a beautiful society instead of live with its cruel substructure; in "Speech Sounds," the taken-for-granted civilizing influence of language is lost. By thinking about this idea in terms of the philosophical concept of *social contract*, Hardy was able to write an essay of intertextual criticism (pages 352–54).

Where Do You Stand?

As you read our brief summaries of critical approaches, you probably recognized the ones that you most regularly use when you think and write about literature. You may find it illuminating to try out some different approaches, especially when your usual tools are not working. You may also find it mind-expanding to look up work by other critics who share your favorite stance, learning from them how to use it more consciously and effectively. You can begin by reading an example of a formalist interpretation of Robert Hayden's "Those Winter Sundays" that we have reprinted on pages 451–54 or by examining the critical interpretations in Chapter 12 regarding "Where Are You Going, Where Have You Been?" on pages 205–207.

35 Critical Casebook: Writing About Culture and Identity

Chapter Preview

In this chapter, you will learn how to do the following:

- Reflect on and analyze works of literature through the lens of cultural criticism (see pages 895-96).
- Compare works of literature across genres (poetry, fiction, and drama).
- Compose essays that examine literature from a cultural approach, using argument and, in some cases, research.

Works of literature that have been around for generations, yet still appeal to modern readers, are sometimes called *timeless*. But such works were created in a particular time and place, and the beliefs, attitudes, material conditions, and worldviews of that era influenced their creators. As a reader, you are similarly affected by the time and place in which you read a literary work. For example, Mark Twain's *Adventures of Huckleberry Finn* (1884) was a remarkably antiracist novel for its time; yet readers today cringe at the use of the word *nigger* in the novel. This outdated language does not diminish Twain's attack on slavery and racism—in fact, many critics claim that the realistic language exposes the true nature of these institutions. But the setting we read it in today influences our reaction.

What Is Cultural Analysis?

Culture is a broad term that includes habits of thought, feeling, and behavior that were invented by humans, taught to other humans, and passed down to descendants—but not practiced among all human groups. It is often entwined with racial identity, ethnic category, and geographical background. Because culture changes from time to time, place to place, and social category to social category, we can speak about American culture of the 1990s, lesbian culture, deaf culture, Apostolic Christian culture, traditional Japanese culture, Victorian upper-class culture, middle-class culture of the 1950s, and so forth.

A cultural approach to literature assumes that a work is part of its social context—both a product of its culture and a contribution to that culture. We may read *Antigone* as a way of understanding ancient Greek culture, or we may study the culture of ancient Greece as a way to understand *Antigone*. Many works unwittingly embody elements of the culture that engendered them. Others are specifically designed to question or support some cultural value or practice. As you read the stories, poems, and plays in this casebook, pay close attention to the cultural issues that each selection raises. Ask yourself what the authors are trying to say about race, class, gender, ethnicity, beliefs, and values—and how these ideas interact with your own observations and personal experiences. The Questions for Discussion and Writing following each selection will guide you in exploring the cultural issues in these works.

Short Stories

Kate Chopin 1851–1904

See page 234 for a biographical note about this author.

Désirée's Baby

As the day was pleasant, Madame Valmondé drove over to L'Abri to see Désirée and the baby.

It made her laugh to think of Désirée with a baby. Why, it seemed but yesterday that Désirée was little more than a baby herself; when Monsieur in riding through the gateway of Valmondé had found her lying asleep in the shadow of the big stone pillar.

The little one awoke in his arms and began to cry for "Dada." That was as much as she could do or say. Some people thought she might have strayed there of her own accord, for she was of the toddling age. The prevailing belief was that she had been purposely left by a party of Texans, whose canvas-covered wagon, late in the day, had crossed the ferry that Coton Maïs kept, just below the plantation. In time Madame Valmondé abandoned every speculation but the one that Désirée had been sent to her by a beneficent Providence to be the child of her affection, seeing that she was without child of the flesh. For the girl grew to be beautiful and gentle, affectionate and sincere,—the idol of Valmondé.

It was no wonder, when she stood one day against the stone pillar in whose shadow she had lain asleep, eighteen years before, that Armand Aubigny riding by and seeing her there, had fallen in love with her. That was the way all the Aubignys fell in love, as if struck by a pistol shot. The wonder was that he had not loved her before; for he had known her since his father brought him home from Paris, a boy of eight, after his mother died there. The passion that awoke in him that day, when he saw her at the gate, swept along like an avalanche, or like a prairie fire, or like anything that drives headlong over all obstacles.

Monsieur Valmondé grew practical and wanted things well considered; that is, the girl's obscure origin. Armand looked into her eyes and did not care. He was reminded that she was nameless. What did it matter about a name when 5 he could give her one of the oldest and proudest in Louisiana? He ordered the *corbeille*[1] from Paris, and contained himself with what patience he could until it arrived; then they were married.

Madame Valmondé had not seen Désirée and the baby for four weeks. When she reached L'Abri she shuddered at the first sight of it, as she always did. It was a sad looking place, which for many years had not known the gentle presence of a mistress, old Monsieur Aubigny having married and buried his wife in France, and she having loved her own land too well ever to leave it. The roof came down steep and black like a cowl, reaching out beyond the wide galleries that encircled the yellow stuccoed house. Big, solemn oaks grew close to it, and their thick-leaved, far-reaching branches shadowed it like a pall. Young Aubigny's rule was a strict one, too, and under it his negroes had forgotten how to be gay, as they had been during the old master's easy-going and indulgent lifetime.

The young mother was recovering slowly, and lay full length, in her soft white muslins and laces, upon a couch. The baby was beside her, upon her arm, where he had fallen asleep, at her breast. The yellow nurse woman sat beside a window fanning herself.

Madame Valmondé bent her portly figure over Désirée and kissed her, holding her an instant tenderly in her arms. Then she turned to the child.

"This is not the baby!" she exclaimed, in startled tones. French was the language spoken at Valmondé in those days.

"I knew you would be astonished," laughed Désirée, "at the way he has grown. The little *cochon de lait!*[2] Look at his legs, mamma, and his hands and finger-nails,—real finger-nails. Zandrine had to cut them this morning. Isn't it true, Zandrine?" 10

The woman bowed her turbaned head majestically, "Mais si, Madame."

"And the way he cries," went on Désirée, "is deafening. Armand heard him the other day as far away as La Blanche's cabin."

Madame Valmondé had never removed her eyes from the child. She lifted it and walked with it over to the window that was lightest. She scanned the baby narrowly, then looked as searchingly at Zandrine, whose face was turned to gaze across the fields.

"Yes, the child has grown, has changed," said Madame Valmondé, slowly, as she replaced it beside its mother. "What does Armand say?"

Désirée's face became suffused with a glow that was happiness itself. 15

"Oh, Armand is the proudest father in the parish, I believe, chiefly because it is a boy, to bear his name; though he says not,—that he would have loved a girl as well. But I know it isn't true. I know he says that to please me. And mamma," she added, drawing Madame Valmondé's head down to her, and speaking in a whisper, "he hasn't punished one of them—not one of them—since baby is born. Even Négrillon, who pretended to have burnt his leg that he might rest from work—he only laughed, and said Négrillon was a great scamp. Oh, mamma, I'm so happy; it frightens me."

What Désirée said was true. Marriage, and later the birth of his son, had softened Armand Aubigny's imperious and exacting nature greatly. This was what made the gentle Désirée so happy, for she loved him desperately. When he frowned she trembled, but loved him. When he smiled, she asked no greater

---

[1]Wedding presents given by the groom.
[2]Suckling pig.

blessing of God. But Armand's dark, handsome face had not often been disfigured by frowns since the day he fell in love with her.

When the baby was about three months old, Désirée awoke one day to the conviction that there was something in the air menacing her peace. It was at first too subtle to grasp. It had only been a disquieting suggestion; an air of mystery among the blacks; unexpected visits from far-off neighbors who could hardly account for their coming. Then a strange, an awful change in her husband's manner, which she dared not ask him to explain. When he spoke to her, it was with averted eyes, from which the old love-light seemed to have gone out. He absented himself from home; and when there, avoided her presence and that of her child, without excuse. And the very spirit of Satan seemed suddenly to take hold of him in his dealings with the slaves. Désirée was miserable enough to die.

She sat in her room, one hot afternoon, in her *peignoir*;[3] listlessly drawing through her fingers the strands of her long, silky brown hair that hung about her shoulders. The baby, half naked, lay asleep upon her own great mahogany bed, that was like a sumptuous throne, with its satin-lined half-canopy. One of La Blanche's little quadroon boys—half naked too—stood fanning the child slowly with a fan of peacock feathers. Désirée's eyes had been fixed absently and sadly upon the baby, while she was striving to penetrate the threatening mist that she felt closing about her. She looked from her child to the boy who stood beside him, and back again; over and over. "Ah!" It was a cry that she could not help; which she was not conscious of having uttered. The blood turned like ice in her veins, and a clammy moisture gathered upon her face.

She tried to speak to the little quadroon boy; but no sound would come, at first. When he heard his name uttered, he looked up, and his mistress was pointing to the door. He laid aside the great, soft fan, and obediently stole away, over the polished floor, on his bare tiptoes.

She stayed motionless, with gaze riveted upon her child, and her face the picture of fright.

Presently her husband entered the room, and without noticing her, went to a table and began to search among some papers which covered it.

"Armand," she called to him, in a voice which must have stabbed him, if he was human. But he did not notice. "Armand," she said again. Then she rose and tottered towards him. "Armand," she panted once more, clutching his arm, "look at our child. What does it mean? Tell me."

He coldly but gently loosened her fingers from about his arm and thrust the hand away from him. "Tell me what it means!" she cried despairingly.

"It means," he answered lightly, "that the child is not white; it means that you are not white."

A quick conception of all that this accusation meant for her nerved her with unwonted courage to deny it. "It is a lie; it is not true, I am white! Look at my hair, it is brown; and my eyes are gray, Armand, you know they are gray. And my skin is fair," seizing his wrist. "Look at my hand; whiter than yours, Armand," she laughed hysterically.

"As white as La Blanche's," he returned cruelly; and went away leaving her alone with their child.

When she could hold a pen in her hand, she sent a despairing letter to Madame Valmondé.

20

25

---

[3]Dressing gown.

"My mother, they tell me I am not white. Armand has told me I am not white. For God's sake tell them it is not true. You must know it is not true. I shall die. I must die. I cannot be so unhappy and live."

The answer that came was as brief: 30

"My own Désirée: Come home to Valmondé; back to your mother who loves you. Come with your child."

When the letter reached Désirée she went with it to her husband's study, and laid it open upon the desk before which he sat. She was like a stone image: silent, white, motionless after she placed it there.

In silence he ran his cold eyes over the written words. He said nothing. "Shall I go, Armand?" she asked in tones sharp with agonized suspense.

"Yes, go."

"Do you want me to go?" 35

"Yes, I want you to go."

He thought Almighty God had dealt cruelly and unjustly with him; and felt, somehow, that he was paying Him back in kind when he stabbed thus into his wife's soul. Moreover, he no longer loved her, because of the unconscious injury she had brought upon his home and his name.

She turned away like one stunned by a blow, and walked slowly towards the door, hoping he would call her back.

"Good-by, Armand," she moaned.

He did not answer her. That was his last blow at fate. 40

Désirée went in search of her child. Zandrine was pacing the sombre gallery with it. She took the little one from the nurse's arms with no word of explanation, and descending the steps, walked away, under the live-oak branches.

It was an October afternoon; the sun was just sinking. Out in the still fields the negroes were picking cotton.

Désirée had not changed the thin white garment nor the slippers she wore. Her hair was uncovered and the sun's rays brought a golden gleam from its brown meshes. She did not take the broad, beaten road which led to the far-off plantation of Valmondé. She walked across a deserted field, where the stubble bruised her tender feet, so delicately shod, and tore her thin gown to shreds.

She disappeared among the reeds and willows that grew thick along the banks of the deep, sluggish bayou; and she did not come back again.

Some weeks later there was a curious scene at L'Abri. In the centre of the 45 smoothly swept back yard was a great bonfire. Armand Aubigny sat in the wide hallway that commanded a view of the spectacle; and it was he who dealt out to a half dozen negroes the material which kept this fire ablaze.

A graceful cradle of willow, with all its dainty furbishings, was laid upon the pyre, which had already been fed with the richness of a priceless *layette*.[4] Then there were silk gowns, and velvet and satin ones added to these; laces, too, and embroideries; bonnets and gloves; for the *corbeille* had been of rare quality.

The last thing to go was a tiny bundle of letters; innocent little scribblings that Désirée had sent to him during the days of their espousal. There was the remnant of one back in the drawer from which he took them. But it was not Désirée's; it was part of an old letter from his mother to his father. He read it. She was thanking God for the blessing of her husband's love:—

---

[4] Baby clothes.

"But, above all," she wrote, "night and day, I thank God for having so arranged our lives that our dear Armand will never know that his mother, who adores him, belongs to the race that is cursed with the brand of slavery."

(1893)

Questions for Discussion and Writing

1. What sort of wife is Désirée? What sort of person is Armand? Cite examples from the text to support your judgments.
2. Why is it important to Armand that his family is "one of the oldest and proudest in Louisiana"? How does this patriarchal pride relate symbolically to the shadow cast over Désirée by the stone pillar? (Remember that phallic symbols can be associated with male potency and male privilege as well as with male sexuality.)
3. What themes does this story convey?
4. What do you think happens to Désirée and the baby? What evidence is there to support your conclusion?
5. How do you think Armand reacted to the letter from his mother?
6. Write an essay focusing on the role of Désirée as slave in the story.

Sherwood Anderson   1876–1941

Sherwood Anderson, who grew up poor in Clyde, Ohio, delved into the dark side of small-town American life, exposing the psychological deformity and frustration beneath the placid surface. At age thirty-six, he just walked out on his thriving paint business, abandoning his wife and three children, and went to Chicago to become a writer. After the 1919 publication of *Winesburg, Ohio*, a collection of twenty-three linked stories, Anderson became financially comfortable, but he did not achieve a happy marriage until his third try in 1933. While traveling to South America in 1941, he died from peritonitis after swallowing a toothpick in an hors d'oeuvre. His writing influenced Faulkner, Hemingway, and Steinbeck.

Hands

Upon the half decayed veranda of a small frame house that stood near the edge of a ravine near the town of Winesburg, Ohio, a fat little old man walked nervously up and down. Across a long field that had been seeded for clover but that had produced only a dense crop of yellow mustard weeds, he could see the public highway along which went a wagon filled with berry pickers returning from the fields. The berry pickers, youths and maidens, laughed and shouted boisterously. A boy, clad in a blue shirt, leaped from the wagon and attempted to drag after him one of the maidens who screamed and protested shrilly. The feet of the boy in the road kicked up a cloud of dust that floated across the face of the departing sun. Over the long field came a thin girlish voice. "Oh, you Wing Biddlebaum, comb your hair, it's falling into your eyes," commanded the voice to the man, who was bald and whose nervous little hands fiddled about the bare white forehead as though arranging a mass of tangled locks.

Wing Biddlebaum, forever frightened and beset by a ghostly band of doubts, did not think of himself as in any way a part of the life of the town where he had lived for twenty years. Among all the people of Winesburg but one had come close to him. With George Willard, son of Tom Willard, the proprietor of the New Willard House, he had formed something like a friendship. George Willard was the reporter on the *Winesburg Eagle* and sometimes in the evening he walked out along the highway to Wing Biddlebaum's house. Now, as the old man walked up and down on the veranda, his hands moving nervously about, he was hoping that George Willard would come and spend the evening with him. After the wagon containing the berry pickers had passed, he went across the field through the tall mustard weeds and climbing a rail fence peered anxiously along the road to the town. For a moment he stood thus, rubbing his hands together and looking up and down the road, and then, fear overcoming him, ran back to walk again upon the porch of his own house.

In the presence of George Willard, Wing Biddlebaum, who for twenty years had been the town mystery, lost something of his timidity, and his shadowy personality, submerged in a sea of doubts, came forth to look at the world. With the young reporter at his side, he ventured in the light of day into Main Street or strode up and down on the rickety front porch of his own house talking excitedly. The voice that had been low and trembling became shrill and loud. The bent figure straightened. With a kind of wriggle, like a fish returned to the brook by the fisherman, Biddlebaum the silent began to talk, striving to put into words the ideas that had been accumulated by his mind during long years of silence.

Wing Biddlebaum talked much with his hands. The slender expressive fingers, forever active, forever striving to conceal themselves in his pockets or behind his back, came forth and became the piston rods of his machinery of expression.

The story of Wing Biddlebaum is a story of hands. Their restless activity, like   5
unto the beating of the wings of an imprisoned bird, had given him his name. Some obscure "poet" of the town had thought of it. The hands alarmed their owner. He wanted to keep them hidden away and looked with amazement at the quiet inexpressive hands of other men who worked beside him in the fields, or passed driving sleepy teams on country roads.

When he talked to George Willard, Wing Biddlebaum closed his fists and beat with them upon a table or on the walls of his house. The action made him more comfortable. If the desire to talk came to him when the two were walking in the fields, he sought out a stump or the top board of a fence and with his hands pounding busily talked with renewed ease.

The story of Wing Biddlebaum's hands is worth a book in itself. Sympathetically set forth it would tap many strange, beautiful qualities in obscure men. It is a job for a poet. In Winesburg the hands had attracted attention merely because of their activity. With them Wing Biddlebaum had picked as high as a hundred and forty quarts of strawberries in a day. They became his distinguishing feature, the source of his fame. Also they made more grotesque an already grotesque and elusive individuality. Winesburg was proud of the hands of Wing Biddlebaum in the same spirit in which it was proud of Banker White's new stone house and Wesley Moyer's bay stallion, Tony Tip, that had won the two-fifteen trot at the fall races in Cleveland.

As for George Willard, he had many times wanted to ask about the hands. At times an almost overwhelming curiosity had taken hold of him. He felt that there must be a reason for their strange activity and their inclination to keep hidden away and only a growing respect for Wing Biddlebaum kept him from blurting out the questions that were often in his mind.

Once he had been on the point of asking. The two were walking in the fields on a summer afternoon and had stopped to sit upon a grassy bank. All afternoon Wing Biddlebaum had talked as one inspired. By a fence he had stopped and beating like a giant woodpecker upon the top board had shouted at George Willard, condemning his tendency to be too much influenced by the people about him. "You are destroying yourself," he cried. "You have the inclination to be alone and to dream and you are afraid of dreams. You want to be like others in town here. You hear them talk and you try to imitate them."

On the grassy bank Wing Biddlebaum had tried again to drive his point   10
home. His voice became soft and reminiscent, and with a sigh of contentment he launched into a long rambling talk, speaking as one lost in a dream.

Out of the dream Wing Biddlebaum made a picture for George Willard. In the picture men lived again in a kind of pastoral golden age. Across a green open country came clean-limbed young men, some afoot, some mounted upon horses. In crowds the young men came to gather about the feet of an old man who sat beneath a tree in a tiny garden and who talked to them.

Wing Biddlebaum became wholly inspired. For once he forgot the hands. Slowly they stole forth and lay upon George Willard's shoulders. Something new and bold came into the voice that talked. "You must try to forget all you have learned," said the old man. "You must begin to dream. From this time on you must shut your ears to the roaring of the voices."

Pausing in his speech, Wing Biddlebaum looked long and earnestly at George Willard. His eyes glowed. Again he raised the hands to caress the boy and then a look of horror swept over his face.

With a convulsive movement of his body Wing Biddlebaum sprang to his feet and thrust his hands deep into his trousers pockets. Tears came to his eyes. "I must be getting along home. I can talk no more with you," he said nervously.

Without looking back, the old man had hurried down the hillside and across a   15
meadow, leaving George Willard perplexed and frightened upon the grassy slope. With a shiver of dread the boy arose and went along the road toward town. "I'll not ask him about his hands," he thought, touched by the memory of the terror he had seen in the man's eyes. "There's something wrong, but I don't want to know what it is. His hands have something to do with his fear of me and of everyone."

And George Willard was right. Let us look briefly into the story of the hands. Perhaps our talking of them will arouse the poet who will tell the hidden wonder story of the influence for which the hands were but fluttering pennants of promise.

In his youth Wing Biddlebaum had been a school teacher in a town in Pennsylvania. He was not then known as Wing Biddlebaum but went by the less euphonic name of Adolph Myers. As Adolph Myers he was much loved by the boys of his school.

Adolph Myers was meant by nature to be a teacher of youth. He was one of those rare little-understood men who rule by a power so gentle that it passes as a lovable weakness. In their feeling for the boys under their charge such men are not unlike the finer sort of women in their love of men.

And yet that is but crudely stated. It needs the poet there. With the boys of his school, Adolph Myers had walked in the evening or had sat talking until dusk upon the school house steps, lost in a kind of dream. Here and there went his hands, caressing the shoulders of the boys, playing about the tousled heads. As he talked his voice became soft and musical. There was a caress in that also. In a way the voice and the hands, the stroking of the shoulders and the touching of the hair were a part of the school master's effort to carry a dream into the young minds. By the caress that was in his fingers he expressed himself. He was one of those men in whom the force that creates life is diffused, not centralized. Under the caress of his hands doubt and disbelief went out of the minds of the boys and they began also to dream.

And then the tragedy. A halfwitted boy of the school became enamored of   20
the young master. In his bed at night he imagined unspeakable things and in the morning went forth to tell his dreams as facts. Strange hideous accusations fell from his loose-hung lips. Through the Pennsylvania town went a shiver. Hidden shadowy doubts that had been in men's minds concerning Adolph Myers were galvanized into beliefs.

The tragedy did not linger. Trembling lads were jerked out of bed and questioned. "He put his arms about me," said one. "His fingers were always playing in my hair," said another.

One afternoon a man of the town, Henry Bradford, who kept a saloon, came to the school house door. Calling Adolph Myers into the school yard he began to beat him with his fists. As his hard knuckles beat down into the frightened face of the schoolmaster, his wrath became more and more terrible. Screaming with dismay, the children ran here and there like disturbed insects. "I'll teach you to put your hands on my boy, you beast," roared the saloon keeper, who, tired of beating the master, had begun to kick him about the yard.

Adolph Myers was driven from the Pennsylvania town in the night. With lanterns in their hands a dozen men came to the door of the house where he lived alone and commanded that he dress and come forth. It was raining and one of the men had a rope in his hands. They had intended to hang the school master, but something in his figure, so small, white, and pitiful, touched their hearts and they let him escape. As he ran away into the darkness they repented of their weakness and ran after him, swearing and throwing sticks and great balls of soft mud at the figure that screamed and ran faster and faster into the darkness.

For twenty years Adolph Myers had lived alone in Winesburg. He was but forty but looked sixty-five. The name of Biddlebaum he got from a box of goods seen at a freight station as he hurried through an eastern Ohio town. He had an aunt in Winesburg, a black-toothed old woman who raised chickens, and with her he lived until she died. He had been ill for a year after the experience in Pennsylvania, and after his recovery worked as a day laborer in the fields, going timidly about and striving to conceal his hands. Although he did not understand what had happened he felt that the hands must be to blame. Again and again the fathers of the boys talked of the hands. "Keep your hands to yourself," the saloon keeper had roared, dancing with fury in the school house yard.

Upon the veranda of his house by the ravine, Wing Biddlebaum continued to   25
walk up and down until the sun had disappeared and the road beyond the field was lost in the grey shadows. Going into his house he cut slices of bread and spread honey upon them. When the rumble of the evening train that took away the express cars loaded with the day's harvest of berries had passed and restored the silence of the summer night, he went again to walk upon the veranda. In the darkness he could not see the hands and they became quiet. Although he still

hungered for the presence of the boy, who was the medium through which he expressed his love of man, the hunger became again a part of his loneliness and his waiting. Lighting a lamp Wing Biddlebaum washed the few dishes soiled by his simple meal and, setting up a folding cot by the screen door that led to the porch, prepared to undress for the night. A few stray white bread crumbs lay on the cleanly washed floor by the table; putting the lamp upon a low stool he began to pick up the crumbs, carrying them to his mouth one by one with unbelievable rapidity. In the dense blotch of light beneath the table, the kneeling figure looked like a priest engaged in some service of his church. The nervous expressive fingers, flashing in and out of the light, might well have been mistaken for the fingers of the devotee going swiftly through decade after decade of his rosary.

(1919)

Questions for Discussion and Writing

1. Reread the first paragraph of the story closely. How does the imagery of the scene forecast themes developed later?
2. Why does the author say more than once that the story of Wing's hands is material for a poet? In what ways do you think a poem is different from a story?
3. What did the men of the Pennsylvania town decide about Adolph Myers? Why did they have such a rabid reaction? What is the significance of the source of the rumors? Why do you think the first confrontation came from the saloon keeper? Have you ever witnessed a situation like this?
4. Do you think Adolph Meyers's physical contact with his students was inappropriate? How would such contact be viewed in your community today?
5. How do you reconcile the final image of Wing with the rest of the story? What emotional tone does it convey to you?

Chinua Achebe   1930–2013

Chinua Achebe was born in Ogidi, Nigeria, the son of an African teacher in a missionary school. Although he was christened Albert, after Queen Victoria's husband, he later took his Nigerian name, Chinua. His fiction depicts the effects of European culture on African traditions. His best-known novel, *Things Fall Apart*, has sold more than 8 million copies and been translated into fifty languages. Achebe defines himself as a cultural nationalist with a revolutionary mission "to help my society regain belief in itself and put away the complexes of the years of denigration and self-abasement." In 1990 Achebe was paralyzed from the waist down in a serious automobile accident. A short time later, he moved to the United States to teach at Bard College in New York. From 2009 until his death, he served as Professor of Africana Studies at Brown University.

Dead Men's Path

Michael Obi's hopes were fulfilled much earlier than he expected. He was appointed headmaster of Ndume Central School in January 1949. It had always been an unprogressive school, so the Mission authorities decided to send a young and energetic man to run it. Obi accepted this responsibility with enthusiasm. He had many wonderful ideas and this was an opportunity to put them into practice. He had had sound secondary school education which designated him a "pivotal teacher" in the official records and set him apart from the other headmasters in the mission field. He was outspoken in his condemnation of the narrow views of these older and often less-educated ones.

"We shall make a good job of it, shan't we?" he asked his young wife when they first heard the joyful news of his promotion.

"We shall do our best," she replied. "We shall have such beautiful gardens and everything will be just *modern* and delightful...." In their two years of married life she had become completely infected by his passion for "modern methods" and his denigration of "these old and superannuated people in the teaching field who would be better employed as traders in the Onitsha market." She began to see herself already as the admired wife of the young headmaster, the queen of the school.

The wives of the other teachers would envy her position. She would set the fashion in everything.... Then, suddenly, it occurred to her that there might not be other wives. Wavering between hope and fear, she asked her husband, looking anxiously at him.

"All our colleagues are young and unmarried," he said with enthusiasm 5 which for once she did not share. "Which is a good thing," he continued.

"Why?"

"Why? They will give all their time and energy to the school."

Nancy was downcast. For a few minutes she became skeptical about the new school; but it was only for a few minutes. Her little personal misfortune could not blind her to her husband's happy prospects. She looked at him as he sat folded up in a chair. He was stoop-shouldered and looked frail. But he sometimes surprised people with sudden bursts of physical energy. In his present posture, however, all his bodily strength seemed to have retired behind his deep-set eyes, giving them an extraordinary power of penetration. He was only twenty-six, but looked thirty or more. On the whole, he was not unhandsome.

"A penny for your thoughts, Mike," said Nancy after a while, imitating the woman's magazine she read.

"I was thinking what a grand opportunity we've got at last to show these 10 people how a school should be run."

Ndume school was backward in every sense of the word. Mr. Obi put his whole life into the work, and his wife hers too. He had two aims. A high standard of teaching was insisted upon, and the school compound was to be turned into a place of beauty. Nancy's dream-gardens came to life with the coming of the rains, and blossomed. Beautiful hibiscus and allamanda hedges in brilliant red and yellow marked out the carefully tended school compound from the rank neighbourhood bushes.

One evening as Obi was admiring his work he was scandalized to see an old woman from the village hobble right across the compound, through a marigold flower-bed and the hedges. On going up there he found faint signs of an almost disused path from the village across the school compound to the bush on the other side.

"It amazes me," said Obi to one of his teachers who had been three years in the school, "that you people allowed the villagers to make use of this footpath. It is simply incredible." He shook his head.

"The path," said the teacher apologetically, "appears to be very important to them. Although it is hardly used, it connects the village shrine with their place of burial."

"And what has that got to do with the school?" asked the headmaster.   15

"Well, I don't know," replied the other with a shrug of the shoulders. "But I remember there was a big row some time ago when we attempted to close it."

"That was some time ago. But it will not be used now," said Obi as he walked away. "What will the Government Education Officer think of this when he comes to inspect the school next week? The villagers might, for all I know, decide to use the schoolroom for a pagan ritual during the inspection."

Heavy sticks were planted closely across the path at the two places where it entered and left the school premises. These were further strengthened with barbed wire.

Three days later the village priest of *Ani* called on the headmaster. He was an old man and walked with a slight stoop. He carried a stout walking-stick which he usually tapped on the floor, by way of emphasis, each time he made a new point in his argument.

"I have heard," he said after the usual exchange of cordialities, "that our   20 ancestral footpath has recently been closed...."

"Yes," replied Mr. Obi. "We cannot allow people to make a highway of our school compound."

"Look here, my son," said the priest bringing down his walking-stick, "this path was here before you were born and before your father was born. The whole life of this village depends on it. Our dead relatives depart by it and our ancestors visit us by it. But most important, it is the path of children coming in to be born...."

Mr. Obi listened with a satisfied smile on his face.

"The whole purpose of our school," he said finally, "is to eradicate just such beliefs as that. Dead men do not require footpaths. The whole idea is just fantastic. Our duty is to teach your children to laugh at such ideas."

"What you say may be true," replied the priest, "but we follow the practices   25 of our fathers. If you re-open the path we shall have nothing to quarrel about. What I always say is: let the hawk perch and let the eagle perch." He rose to go.

"I am sorry," said the young headmaster. "But the school compound cannot be a thoroughfare. It is against our regulations. I would suggest your constructing another path, skirting our premises. We can even get our boys to help in building it. I don't suppose the ancestors will find the little detour too burdensome."

"I have no more words to say," said the old priest, already outside.

Two days later, a young woman in the village died in childbed. A diviner was immediately consulted and he prescribed heavy sacrifices to propitiate ancestors insulted by the fence.

Obi woke up next morning among the ruins of his work. The beautiful hedges were torn up not just near the path but right round the school, the flowers trampled to death and one of the school buildings pulled down.... That day,

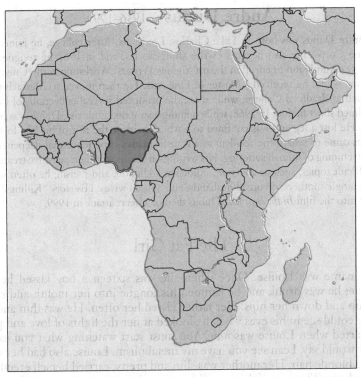

The most populous in Africa, Nigeria gained independence from Great Britain in 1960. It is the setting for Chinua Achebe's stories and novels.

the white Supervisor came to inspect the school and wrote a nasty report on the state of the premises but more seriously about the "tribal-war situation developing between the school and the village, arising in part from the misguided zeal of the new headmaster."

(1972)

Questions for Discussion and Writing

1. Reread the last sentence of the opening paragraph. What is ironic about that statement? Did you notice the irony the first time you read it?
2. What do you think of Michael Obi's wife? Why does the author include several paragraphs about her?
3. Why is Michael Obi unable to bring progress to Ndume School? Do you think he understands why he failed?
4. Achebe once wrote that the fundamental theme for all African writers must be "that African people did not hear of culture for the first time from Europeans; that [tribal societies] had a philosophy of great depth and value and beauty, that they had poetry and, above all, dignity." Write an essay explaining how this story illustrates Achebe's theme.

Andre Dubus   1936–1999

Andre Dubus was born in Lake Charles, Louisiana. After college, he joined the Marine Corps. He also began to write short stories, and in 1963 he resigned his military commission to enroll in the prestigious Writers' Workshop at the University of Iowa, where he received a Master of Fine Arts. He then moved to Massachusetts to teach at Bradford College; while there, he produced several collections of highly acclaimed short fiction. In 1968, while helping a stranded motorist, Dubus was hit by a car. He lost a leg and was confined to a wheelchair for the rest of his life. In time, Dubus came to regard the accident as a transformative experience that deepened his understanding of human suffering. His writings are noted for their sensitive treatment of difficult topics, such as abortion, infidelity, addiction, and racism; he often wrote about single mothers, divorced husbands, and abused wives. His story "Killings" was made into the film *In the Bedroom*. Dubus died of a heart attack in 1999.

The Fat Girl

Her name was Louise. Once when she was sixteen a boy kissed her at a barbecue; he was drunk and he jammed his tongue into her mouth and ran his hands up and down her hips. Her father kissed her often. He was thin and kind and she could see in his eyes when he looked at her the lights of love and pity.

It started when Louise was nine. You must start watching what you eat, her mother would say. I can see you have my metabolism. Louise also had her mother's pale blonde hair. Her mother was slim and pretty, carried herself erectly, and ate very little. The two of them would eat bare lunches, while her older brother ate sandwiches and potato chips, and then her mother would sit smoking while Louise eyed the bread box, the pantry, the refrigerator. Wasn't that good, her mother would say. In five years you'll be in high school and if you're fat the boys won't like you; they won't ask you out. Boys were as far away as five years, and she would go to her room and wait for nearly an hour until she knew her mother was no longer thinking of her, then she would creep into the kitchen and, listening to her mother talking on the phone, or her footsteps upstairs, she would open the bread box, the pantry, the jar of peanut butter. She would put the sandwich under her shirt and go outside or to the bathroom to eat it.

Her father was a lawyer and made a lot of money and came home looking pale and happy. Martinis put color back in his face, and at dinner he talked to his wife and two children. Oh give her a potato, he would say to Louise's mother. She's a growing girl. Her mother's voice then became tense: If she has a potato she shouldn't have dessert. She should have both, her father would say, and he would reach over and touch Louise's cheek or hand or arm.

In high school she had two girl friends and at night and on week-ends they rode in a car or went to movies. In movies she was fascinated by fat actresses. She wondered why they were fat. She knew why she was fat: she was fat because she was Louise. Because God had made her that way. Because she wasn't like her friends Joan and Marjorie, who drank milk shakes after school and were all bones and tight skin. But what about those actresses, with their talents, with their broad and profound faces? Did they eat as heedlessly as Bishop Humphries and his wife who sometimes came to dinner and, as Louise's mother said, gorged between amenities? Or did they try to lose weight, did they go about hungry and angry and thinking of food? She thought of them eating lean meats and salads with friends, and then going home and building strange large sandwiches with French bread. But mostly she believed they did not go through these failures; they were fat because they chose to be. And she was certain of something else too: she could see it in their faces: they did not eat secretly. Which she did: her creeping to the kitchen when she was nine became, in high school, a ritual of deceit and pleasure. She was a furtive eater of sweets. Even her two friends did not know her secret.

Joan was thin, gangling, and flat-chested; she was attractive enough and all   5 she needed was someone to take a second look at her face, but the school was large and there were pretty girls in every classroom and walking all the corridors, so no one ever needed to take a second look at Joan. Marjorie was thin too, an intense, heavy-smoking girl with brittle laughter. She was very intelligent, and with boys she was shy because she knew she made them uncomfortable, and because she was smarter than they were and so could not understand or could not believe the levels they lived on. She was to have a nervous breakdown before earning her Ph.D. in philosophy at the University of California, where she met and married a physicist and discovered within herself an untrammelled passion: she made love with her husband on the couch, the carpet, in the bathtub, and on the washing machine. By that time much had happened to her and she never thought of Louise. Joan would finally stop growing and begin moving with grace and confidence. In college she would have two lovers and then several more during the six years she spent in Boston before marrying a middle-aged editor who had two sons in their early teens, who drank too much, who was tenderly boyishly grateful for her love, and whose wife had been killed while rock-climbing in New Hampshire with her lover. She would not think of Louise either, except in an earlier time, when lovers were still new to her and she was ecstatically surprised each time one of them loved her and, sometimes at night, lying in a man's arms, she would tell how in high school no one dated her, she had been thin and plain (she would still believe that: that she had been plain; it had never been true) and so had been forced into the week-end and night-time company of a neurotic smart girl and a shy fat girl. She would say this with self-pity exaggerated by Scotch and her need to be more deeply loved by the man who held her.

She never eats, Joan and Marjorie said of Louise. They ate lunch with her at school, watched her refusing potatoes, ravioli, fried fish. Sometimes she got through the cafeteria line with only a salad. That is how they would remember her: a girl whose hapless body was destined to be fat. No one saw the sandwiches she made and took to her room when she came home from school. No one saw the store of Milky Ways, Butterfingers, Almond Joys, and Hersheys far back on her closet shelf, behind the stuffed animals of her childhood. She was not a hypocrite. When she was out of the house she truly believed she was dieting; she forgot about the candy, as a man speaking into his office dictaphone may forget the lewd photographs hidden in an old shoe in his closet. At other times, away from home, she thought of the waiting candy with near lust. One night driving home from a movie, Marjorie said: "You're lucky you don't smoke; it's incredible what I go through to hide it from my parents." Louise turned to her a smile which was elusive and mysterious; she yearned to be home in bed, eating chocolate in the dark. She did not need to smoke; she already had a vice that was insular and destructive.

She brought it with her to college. She thought she would leave it behind. A move from one place to another, a new room without the haunted closet shelf, would do for her what she could not do for herself. She packed her large dresses and went. For two weeks she was busy with registration, with shyness, with classes; then she began to feel at home. Her room was no longer like a motel. Its walls had stopped watching her, she felt they were her friends, and she gave them her secret. Away from her mother, she did not have to be as elaborate; she kept the candy in her drawer now.

The school was in Massachusetts, a girls' school. When she chose it, when she and her father and mother talked about it in the evenings, everyone so carefully avoided the word boys that sometimes the conversations seemed to be about nothing but boys. There are no boys there, the neuter words said; you will not have to contend with that. In her father's eyes were pity and encouragement; in her mother's was disappointment, and her voice was crisp. They spoke of courses, of small classes where Louise would get more attention. She imagined herself in those small classes; she saw herself as a teacher would see her, as the other girls would; she would get no attention.

The girls at the school were from wealthy families, but most of them wore the uniform of another class: blue jeans and work shirts, and many wore overalls. Louise bought some overalls, washed them until the dark blue faded, and wore them to classes. In the cafeteria she ate as she had in high school, not to lose weight nor even to sustain her lie, but because eating lightly in public had become as habitual as good manners. Everyone had to take gym, and in the locker room with the other girls, and wearing shorts on the volleyball and badminton courts, she hated her body. She liked her body most when she was unaware of it: in bed at night, as sleep gently took her out of her day, out of herself. And she liked parts of her body. She liked her brown eyes and sometimes looked at them in the mirror: they were not shallow eyes, she thought; they were indeed windows of a tender soul, a good heart. She liked her lips and nose, and her chin, finely shaped between her wide and sagging cheeks. Most of all she liked her long pale blonde hair, she liked washing and drying it and lying naked on her bed, smelling of shampoo, and feeling the soft hair at her neck and shoulders and back.

Her friend at college was Carrie, who was thin and wore thick glasses and   10
often at night she cried in Louise's room. She did not know why she was crying. She was crying, she said, because she was unhappy. She could say no more. Louise said she was unhappy too, and Carrie moved in with her. One night Carrie talked for hours, sadly and bitterly, about her parents and what they did to each other. When she finished she hugged Louise and they went to bed. Then in the dark Carrie spoke across the room: "Louise? I just wanted to tell you. One night last week I woke up and smelled chocolate. You were eating chocolate, in your bed. I wish you'd eat it in front of me, Louise, whenever you feel like it."

Stiffened in her bed, Louise could think of nothing to say. In the silence she was afraid Carrie would think she was asleep and would tell her again in the morning or tomorrow night. Finally she said Okay. Then after a moment she told Carrie if she ever wanted any she could feel free to help herself; the candy was in the top drawer. Then she said thank you.

They were roommates for four years and in the summers they exchanged letters. Each fall they greeted with embraces, laughter, tears, and moved into their old room, which had been stripped and cleansed of them for the summer. Neither girl enjoyed summer. Carrie did not like being at home because her parents did not love each other. Louise lived in a small city in Louisiana. She did not like summer because she had lost touch with Joan and Marjorie; they saw each other, but it was not the same. She liked being with her father but with no one else. The flicker of disappointment in her mother's eyes at the airport was a vanguard of the army of relatives and acquaintances who awaited her: they would see her on the streets, in stores, at the country club, in her home, and in theirs; in the first moments of greeting, their eyes would tell her she was still fat Louise, who had been fat as long as they could remember, who had gone to college and returned as fat as ever. Then their eyes dismissed her, and she longed for school and Carrie, and she wrote letters to her friend. But that saddened her too. It wasn't simply that Carrie was her only friend, and when they finished college they might never see each other again. It was that her existence in the world was so divided; it had begun when she was a child creeping to the kitchen; now that division was much sharper, and her friendship with Carrie seemed disproportionate and perilous. The world she was destined to live in had nothing to do with the intimate nights in their room at school.

In the summer before their senior year, Carrie fell in love. She wrote to Louise about him, but she did not write much, and this hurt Louise more than if Carrie had shown the joy her writing tried to conceal. That fall they returned to their room; they were still close and warm, Carrie still needed Louise's ears and heart at night as she spoke of her parents and her recurring malaise whose source the two friends never discovered. But on most week-ends Carrie left, and caught a bus to Boston where her boy friend studied music. During the week she often spoke hesitantly of sex; she was not sure if she liked it. But Louise, eating candy and listening, did not know whether Carrie was telling the truth or whether, as in her letters of the past summer, Carrie was keeping from her those delights she may never experience.

Then one Sunday night when Carrie had just returned from Boston and was unpacking her overnight bag, she looked at Louise and said: "I was thinking about you. On the bus coming home tonight." Looking at Carrie's concerned, determined face, Louise prepared herself for humiliation. "I was thinking about when we graduate. What you're going to do. What's to become of you. I want you to be loved the way I love you. Louise, if I help you, *really* help you, will you go on a diet?"

Louise entered a period of her life she would remember always, the way some people remember having endured poverty. Her diet did not begin the next day. Carrie told her to eat on Monday as though it were the last day of her life. So for the first time since grammar school Louise went into a school cafeteria and ate everything she wanted. At breakfast and lunch and dinner she glanced around the table to see if the other girls noticed the food on her tray. They did not. She felt there was a lesson in this, but it lay beyond her grasp. That night in their room she ate the four remaining candy bars. During the day Carrie rented a small refrigerator, bought an electric skillet, an electric broiler, and bathroom scales.

On Tuesday morning Louise stood on the scales, and Carrie wrote in her notebook: *October 14: 184 lbs.* Then she made Louise a cup of black coffee and scrambled one egg and sat with her while she ate. When Carrie went to the dining room for breakfast, Louise walked about the campus for thirty minutes. That was part of the plan. The campus was pretty, on its lawns grew at least one of every tree native to New England, and in the warm morning sun Louise felt a new hope. At noon they met in their room, and Carrie broiled her a piece of hamburger and served it with lettuce. Then while Carrie ate in the dining room Louise walked again. She was weak with hunger and she felt queasy. During her afternoon classes she was nervous and tense, and she chewed her pencil and tapped her heels on the floor and tightened her calves. When she returned to her room late that afternoon, she was so glad to see Carrie that she embraced her; she had felt she could not bear another minute of hunger, but now with Carrie she knew she could make it at least through tonight. Then she would sleep and face tomorrow when it came. Carrie broiled her a steak and served it with lettuce. Louise studied while Carrie ate dinner, then they went for a walk.

That was her ritual and her diet for the rest of the year, Carrie alternating fish and chicken breasts with the steaks for dinner, and every day was nearly as bad as the first. In the evenings she was irritable. In all her life she had never been afflicted by ill temper and she looked upon it now as a demon which, along with hunger, was taking possession of her soul. Often she spoke sharply to Carrie. One night during their after-dinner walk Carrie talked sadly of night, of how darkness made her more aware of herself, and at night she did not know why she was in college, why she studied, why she was walking the earth with other people. They were standing on a wooden foot bridge, looking down at a dark pond. Carrie kept talking; perhaps soon she would cry. Suddenly Louise said: "I'm sick of lettuce. I never want to see a piece of lettuce for the rest of my life. I hate it. We shouldn't even buy it, it's immoral."

Carrie was quiet. Louise glanced at her, and the pain and irritation in Carrie's face soothed her. Then she was ashamed. Before she could say she was sorry, Carrie turned to her and said gently: "I know. I know how terrible it is."

Carrie did all the shopping, telling Louise she knew how hard it was to go into a supermarket when you were hungry. And Louise was always hungry. She drank diet soft drinks and started smoking Carrie's cigarettes, learned to enjoy inhaling, thought of cancer and emphysema but they were as far away as those boys her mother had talked about when she was nine. By Thanksgiving she was smoking over a pack a day and her weight in Carrie's notebook was one hundred and sixty-two pounds. Carrie was afraid if Louise went home at Thanksgiving she would lapse from the diet, so Louise spent the vacation with Carrie, in Philadelphia. Carrie wrote her family about the diet, and told Louise that she had. On the phone to Philadelphia, Louise said: "I feel like a bedwetter. When I was a little girl I had a friend who used to come spend the night and Mother would put a rubber sheet on the bed and we all pretended there wasn't a rubber sheet and that she hadn't wet the bed. Even me, and I slept with her." At Thanksgiving dinner she lowered her eyes as Carrie's father put two slices of white meat on her plate and passed it to her over the bowls of steaming food.

When she went home at Christmas she weighed a hundred and fifty-five pounds; at the airport her mother marvelled. Her father laughed and hugged her and said: "But now there's less of you to love." He was troubled by her smoking but only mentioned it once; he told her she was beautiful and, as always, his eyes bathed her with love. During the long vacation her mother cooked for her as Carrie had, and Louise returned to school weighing a hundred and forty-six pounds.

20

Flying north on the plane she warmly recalled the surprised and congratulatory eyes of her relatives and acquaintances. She had not seen Joan or Marjorie. She thought of returning home in May, weighing the hundred and fifteen pounds which Carrie had in October set as their goal. Looking toward the stoic days ahead, she felt strong. She thought of those hungry days of fall and early winter (and now: she was hungry now: with almost a frown, almost a brusque shake of the head, she refused peanuts from the stewardess): those first weeks of the diet when she was the pawn of an irascibility which still, conditioned to her ritual as she was, could at any moment take command of her. She thought of the nights of trying to sleep while her stomach growled. She thought of her addiction to cigarettes. She thought of the people at school: not one teacher, not one girl, had spoken to her about her loss of weight, not even about her absence from meals. And without warning her spirit collapsed. She did not feel strong, she did not feel she was committed to and within reach of achieving a valuable goal. She felt that somehow she had lost more than pounds of fat; that some time during her dieting she had lost herself too. She tried to remember what it had felt like to be Louise before she had started living on meat and fish, as an unhappy adult may look sadly in the memory of childhood for lost virtues and hopes. She looked down at the earth far below, and it seemed to her that her soul, like her body aboard the plane, was in some rootless flight. She neither knew its destination nor where it had departed from; it was on some passage she could not even define.

During the next few weeks she lost weight more slowly and once for eight days Carrie's daily recording stayed at a hundred and thirty-six. Louise woke in the morning thinking of the one hundred and thirty-six and then she stood on the scales and they echoed her. She became obsessed with that number, and there wasn't a day when she didn't say it aloud, and through the days and nights the number stayed in her mind, and if a teacher had spoken those digits in a classroom she would have opened her mouth to speak. What if that's me, she said to Carrie. I mean what if a hundred and thirty-six is my real weight and I just can't lose anymore. Walking hand-in-hand with her despair was a longing for this to be true, and that longing angered her and wearied her, and every day she was gloomy. On the ninth day she weighed a hundred and thirty-five and a half pounds. She was not relieved; she thought bitterly of the months ahead, the shedding of the last twenty and a half pounds.

On Easter Sunday, which she spent at Carrie's, she weighed one hundred and twenty pounds, and she ate one slice of glazed pineapple with her ham and lettuce. She did not enjoy it: she felt she was being friendly with a recalcitrant enemy who had once tried to destroy her. Carrie's parents were laudative. She liked them and she wished they would touch sometimes, and look at each other when they spoke. She guessed they would divorce when Carrie left home, and she vowed that her own marriage would be one of affection and tenderness. She could think about that now: marriage. At school she had read in a Boston paper that this summer the cicadas would come out of their seventeen year hibernation on Cape Cod, for a month they would mate and then die, leaving their young to burrow into the ground where they would stay for seventeen years. That's me, she had said to Carrie. Only my hibernation lasted twenty-one years.

Often her mother asked in letters and on the phone about the diet, but Louise answered vaguely. When she flew home in late May she weighed a hundred thirteen pounds, and at the airport her mother cried and hugged her and said again and again: You're so *beautiful.* Her father blushed and bought her a martini. For days her relatives and acquaintances congratulated her, and the applause in their eyes lasted the entire summer, and she loved their eyes, and swam in the country club pool, the first time she had done this since she was a child.

She lived at home and ate the way her mother did and every morning she   25
weighed herself on the scales in her bathroom. Her mother liked to take her shopping and buy her dresses and they put her old ones in the Goodwill box at the shopping center; Louise thought of them existing on the body of a poor woman whose cheap meals kept her fat. Louise's mother had a photographer come to the house, and Louise posed on the couch and standing beneath a live oak and sitting in a wicker lawn chair next to an azalea bush. The new clothes and the photographer made her feel she was going to another country or becoming a citizen of a new one. In the fall she took a job of no consequence, to give herself something to do.

Also in the fall a young lawyer joined her father's firm, he came one night to dinner, and they started seeing each other. He was the first man outside her family to kiss her since the barbecue when she was sixteen. Louise celebrated Thanksgiving not with rice dressing and candied sweet potatoes and mince meat and pumpkin pies, but by giving Richard her virginity which she realized, at the very last moment of its existence, she had embarked on giving him over thirteen months ago, on that Tuesday in October when Carrie had made her a cup of black coffee and scrambled one egg. She wrote this to Carrie, who replied happily by return mail. She also, through glance and smile and innuendo, tried to tell her mother too. But finally she controlled that impulse, because Richard felt guilty about making love with the daughter of his partner and friend. In the spring they married. The wedding was a large one, in the Episcopal church, and Carrie flew from Boston to be maid of honor. Her parents had recently separated and she was living with the musician and was still victim of her unpredictable malaise. It overcame her on the night before the wedding, so Louise was up with her until past three and woke next morning from a sleep so heavy that she did not want to leave it.

Richard was a lean, tall, energetic man with the metabolism of a pencil sharpener. Louise fed him everything he wanted. He liked Italian food and she got recipes from her mother and watched him eating spaghetti with the sauce she had only tasted, and ravioli and lasagna, while she ate antipasto with her chianti. He made a lot of money and borrowed more and they bought a house whose lawn sloped down to the shore of a lake; they had a wharf and a boathouse, and Richard bought a boat and they took friends waterskiing. Richard bought her a car and they spent his vacations in Mexico, Canada, the Bahamas, and in the fifth year of their marriage they went to Europe and, according to their plan, she conceived a child in Paris. On the plane back, as she looked out the window and beyond the sparkling sea and saw her country, she felt that it was waiting for her, as her home by the lake was, and her parents, and her good friends who rode in the boat and waterskied; she thought of the accumulated warmth and pelf of her marriage, and how by slimming her body she had bought into the pleasures of the nation. She felt cunning, and she smiled to herself, and took Richard's hand.

But these moments of triumph were sparse. On most days she went about her routine of leisure with a sense of certainty about herself that came merely from not thinking. But there were times, with her friends, or with Richard, or alone in the house, when she was suddenly assaulted by the feeling that she had taken the wrong train and arrived at a place where no one knew her, and where she ought not to be. Often, in bed with Richard, she talked of being fat: "I was the one who started the friendship with Carrie, I chose her, I started the conversations. When I understood that she was my friend I understood something else: I had chosen her for the same reason I'd chosen Joan and Marjorie. They were all thin. I was always thinking about what people saw when they looked at me and I didn't want them to see two fat girls. When I was alone I didn't mind being fat but then I'd have to leave the house again and then I didn't want to look like me. But at home I didn't mind except when I was getting dressed to go out of the house and when Mother looked at me. But I stopped looking at her when she looked at me. And in college I felt good with Carrie; there weren't any boys and I didn't have any other friends and so when I wasn't with Carrie I thought about her and I tried to ignore the other people around me, I tried to make them not exist. A lot of the time I could do that. It was strange, and I felt like a spy."

If Richard was bored by her repetition he pretended not to be. But she knew the story meant very little to him. She could have been telling him of a childhood illness, or wearing braces, or a broken heart at sixteen. He could not see her as she was when she was fat. She felt as though she were trying to tell a foreign lover about her life in the United States, and if only she could command the language he would know and love all of her and she would feel complete. Some of the acquaintances of her childhood were her friends now, and even they did not seem to remember her when she was fat.

Now her body was growing again, and when she put on a maternity dress for 30 the first time she shivered with fear. Richard did not smoke and he asked her, in a voice just short of demand, to stop during her pregnancy. She did. She ate carrots and celery instead of smoking, and at cocktail parties she tried to eat nothing, but after her first drink she ate nuts and cheese and crackers and dips. Always at these parties Richard had talked with his friends and she had rarely spoken to him until they drove home. But now when he noticed her at the hors d'oeuvres table he crossed the room and, smiling, led her back to his group. His smile and his hand on her arm told her he was doing his clumsy, husbandly best to help her through a time of female mystery.

She was gaining weight but she told herself it was only the baby, and would leave with its birth. But at other times she knew quite clearly that she was losing the discipline she had fought so hard to gain during her last year with Carrie. She was hungry now as she had been in college, and she ate between meals and after dinner and tried to eat only carrots and celery, but she grew to hate them, and her desire for sweets was as vicious as it had been long ago. At home she ate bread and jam and when she shopped for groceries she bought a candy bar and ate it driving home and put the wrapper in her purse and then in the garbage can under the sink. Her cheeks had filled out, there was loose flesh under her chin, her arms and legs were plump, and her mother was concerned. So was Richard. One night when she brought pie and milk to the living room where they were watching television, he said: "You already had a piece. At dinner."

She did not look at him.

"You're gaining weight. It's not all water, either. It's fat. It'll be summertime. You'll want to get into your bathing suit."

The pie was cherry. She looked at it as her fork cut through it; she speared the piece and rubbed it in the red juice on the plate before lifting it to her mouth.

"You never used to eat pie," he said. "I just think you ought to watch it a bit.   35 It's going to be tough on you this summer."

In her seventh month, with a delight reminiscent of climbing the stairs to Richard's apartment before they were married, she returned to her world of secret gratification. She began hiding candy in her underwear drawer. She ate it during the day and at night while Richard slept, and at breakfast she was distracted, waiting for him to leave.

She gave birth to a son, brought him home, and nursed both him and her appetites. During this time of celibacy she enjoyed her body through her son's mouth; while he suckled she stroked his small head and back. She was hiding candy but she did not conceal her other indulgences: she was smoking again but still she ate between meals, and at dinner she ate what Richard did, and coldly he watched her, he grew petulant, and when the date marking the end of their celibacy came they let it pass. Often in the afternoons her mother visited and scolded her and Louise sat looking at the baby and said nothing until finally, to end it, she promised to diet. When her mother and father came for dinners, her father kissed her and held the baby and her mother said nothing about Louise's body, and her voice was tense. Returning from work in the evenings Richard looked at a soiled plate and glass on the table beside her chair as if detecting traces of infidelity, and at every dinner they fought.

"Look at you," he said. "Lasagna, for God's sake. When are you going to start? It's not simply that you haven't lost any weight. You're gaining. I can see it. I can feel it when you get in bed. Pretty soon you'll weigh more than I do and I'll be sleeping on a trampoline."

"You never touch me anymore."

"I don't want to touch you. Why should I? Have you *looked* at yourself?"   40

"You're cruel," she said. "I never knew how cruel you were."

She ate, watching him. He did not look at her. Glaring at his plate, he worked with fork and knife like a hurried man at a lunch counter.

"I bet you didn't either," she said.

That night when he was asleep she took a Milky Way to the bathroom. For a while she stood eating in the dark, then she turned on the light. Chewing, she looked at herself in the mirror; she looked at her eyes and hair. Then she stood on the scales and looking at the numbers between her feet, one hundred and sixty-two, she remembered when she had weighed a hundred and thirty-six pounds for eight days. Her memory of those eight days was fond and amusing, as though she were recalling an Easter egg hunt when she was six. She stepped off the scales and pushed them under the lavatory and did not stand on them again.

It was summer and she bought loose dresses and when Richard took friends   45 out on the boat she did not wear a bathing suit or shorts; her friends gave her mischievous glances, and Richard did not look at her. She stopped riding on the boat. She told them she wanted to stay with the baby, and she sat inside holding him until she heard the boat leave the wharf. Then she took him to the front lawn and walked with him in the shade of the trees and talked to him about the blue jays and mockingbirds and cardinals she saw on their branches. Sometimes she stopped and watched the boat out on the lake and the friend skiing behind it.

Every day Richard quarrelled, and because his rage went no further than her weight and shape, she felt excluded from it, and she remained calm within layers of flesh and spirit, and watched his frustration, his impotence. He truly believed they were arguing about her weight. She knew better: she knew that beneath the argument lay the question of who Richard was. She thought of him smiling at the wheel of his boat, and long ago courting his slender girl, the daughter of his partner and friend. She thought of Carrie telling her of smelling chocolate in the dark and, after that, watching her eat it night after night. She smiled at Richard, teasing his anger.

He is angry now. He stands in the center of the living room, raging at her, and he wakes the baby. Beneath Richard's voice she hears the soft crying, feels it in her heart, and quietly she rises from her chair and goes upstairs to the child's room and takes him from the crib. She brings him to the living room and sits holding him in her lap, pressing him gently against the folds of fat at her waist. Now Richard is pleading with her. Louise thinks tenderly of Carrie broiling meat and fish in their room, and walking with her in the evenings. She wonders if Carrie still has the malaise. Perhaps she will come for a visit. In Louise's arms now the boy sleeps.

"I'll help you," Richard says. "I'll eat the same things you eat."

But his face does not approach the compassion and determination and love she had seen in Carrie's during what she now recognizes as the worst year of her life. She can remember nothing about that year except hunger, and the meals in her room. She is hungry now. When she puts the boy to bed she will get a candy bar from her room. She will eat it here, in front of Richard. This room will be hers soon. She considers the possibilities: all these rooms and the lawn where she can do whatever she wishes. She knows he will leave soon. It has been in his eyes all summer. She stands, using one hand to pull herself out of the chair. She carries the boy to his crib, feels him against her large breasts, feels that his sleeping body touches her soul. With a surge of vindication and relief she holds him. Then she kisses his forehead and places him in the crib. She goes to the bedroom and in the dark takes a bar of candy from her drawer. Slowly she descends the stairs. She knows Richard is waiting but she feels his departure so happily that, when she enters the living room, unwrapping the candy, she is surprised to see him standing there.

(1975)

Questions for Discussion and Writing

1. Richard "truly believed" that he and Louise "were arguing about her weight." But Louise "knew better." What did she know? Do you agree with her?

2. What is the story's central conflict? How is it resolved?

3. Why does the author include Joan, Marjorie, and Carrie?

4. What view of obesity does this story seem to present? Is overeating a physical need, a psychological disorder, a moral issue, a social condition? Write an essay arguing your answer to these questions.

5. How does Louise feel about herself and her life when she is thin? How does she feel at the end of the story? Write another section that shows what happens to Louise in the next five years.

Toni Cade Bambara   1939–1995

Toni Cade Bambara wrote under the name Toni Cade until 1970, when she adopted the African name Bambara. Early on, she championed the civil rights struggle and the women's liberation movement and, in the 1970s, visited both Cuba and Vietnam to meet with women's groups there. In her fiction, her colorful characters speak in black dialect, which she spoke of as "riffs" or "be-bop." For a while, she said, writing seemed to her "rather frivolous, like something you did because you didn't feel like doing any work. But…I've come to appreciate that it is a perfectly legitimate way to participate in a struggle." She fought colon cancer but died in 1995 at age fifty-six.

The Lesson

Back in the days when everyone was old and stupid or young and foolish and me and Sugar were the only ones just right, this lady moved on our block with nappy hair and proper speech and no makeup. And quite naturally we laughed at her, laughed the way we did at the junk man who went about his business like he was some big-time president and his sorry-ass horse his secretary. And we kinda hated her too, hated the way we did the winos who cluttered up our parks and pissed on our handball walls and stank up our hallways and stairs so you couldn't halfway play hide-and-seek without a goddamn gas mask. Miss Moore was her name. The only woman on the block with no first name. And she was black as hell, cept for her feet, which were fish white and spooky. And she was always planning these boring-ass things for us to do, us being my cousin, mostly, who lived on the block cause we all moved North the same time and to the same apartment then spread out gradual to breathe. And our parents would yank our heads into some kinda shape and crisp up our clothes so we'd be presentable for travel with Miss Moore, who always looked like she was going to church, though she never did. Which is just one of the things the grownups talked about when they talked behind her back like a dog. But when she came calling with some sachet she'd sewed up or some gingerbread she'd made or some book, why then they'd all be too embarrassed to turn her down and we'd get handed over all spruced up. She'd been to college and said it was only right that she should take responsibility for the young ones' education, and she not even related by marriage or blood. So they'd go for it. Specially Aunt Gretchen. She was the main gofer in the family. You got some ole dumb shit foolishness you want somebody to go for, you send for Aunt Gretchen. She been screwed into the go-along for so long, it's a blood-deep natural thing with her. Which is how she got saddled with me and Sugar and Junior in the first place while our mothers were in a la-de-da apartment up the block having a good ole time.

So this one day Miss Moore rounds us all up at the mailbox and it's puredee hot and she's knockin herself out about arithmetic. And school suppose to let up in summer I heard, but she don't never let up. And the starch in my pinafore scratching the shit outta me and I'm really hating this nappy-head bitch and her goddamn college degree. I'd much rather go to the pool or to the show where it's cool. So me and Sugar leaning on the mailbox being surly, which is a Miss Moore word. And Flyboy checking out what everybody brought for lunch. And Fat Butt already wasting his peanut-butter-and-jelly sandwich like the pig he is.

And Junebug punchin on Q.T.'s arm for potato chips. And Rosie Giraffe shifting from one hip to the other waiting for somebody to step on her foot or ask her if she from Georgia so she can kick ass, preferably Mercedes'. And Miss Moore asking us do we know what money is, like we a bunch of retards. I mean real money, she say, like it's only poker chips or monopoly papers we lay on the grocer. So right away I'm tired of this and say so. And would much rather snatch Sugar and go to the Sunset and terrorize the West Indian kids and take their hair ribbons and their money too. And Miss Moore files that remark away for next week's lesson on brotherhood, I can tell. And finally I say we oughta get to the subway cause it's cooler and besides we might meet some cute boys. Sugar done swiped her mama's lipstick, so we ready.

So we heading down the street and she's boring us silly about what things cost and what our parents make and how much goes for rent and how money ain't divided up right in this country. And then she gets to the part about we all poor and live in the slums, which I don't feature. And I'm ready to speak on that, but she steps out in the street and hails two cabs just like that. Then she hustles half the crew in with her and hands me a five-dollar bill and tells me to calculate 10 percent tip for the driver. And we're off. Me and Sugar and Junebug and Flyboy hanging out the window and hollering to everybody, putting lipstick on each other cause Flyboy a faggot anyway, and making farts with our sweaty armpits. But I'm mostly trying to figure how to spend this money. But they all fascinated with the meter ticking and Junebug starts laying bets as to how much it'll read when Flyboy can't hold his breath no more. Then Sugar lays bets as to how much it'll be when we get there. So I'm stuck. Don't nobody want to go for my plan, which is to jump out at the next light and run off to the first bar-b-que we can find. Then the driver tells us to get the hell out cause we there already. And the meter reads eighty-five cents. And I'm stalling to figure out the tip and Sugar say give him a dime. And I decide he don't need it as bad as I do, so later for him. But then he tries to take off with Junebug still in the door so we talk about his mama something ferocious. Then we check out that we on Fifth Avenue and everybody dressed up in stockings. One lady in a fur coat, hot as it is. White folks crazy.

"This is the place," Miss Moore say, presenting it to us in the voice she uses at the museum. "Let's look in the windows before we go in."

"Can we steal?" Sugar asks very serious like she's getting the ground rules 5 squared away before she plays. "I beg your pardon," say Miss Moore, and we fall out. So she leads us around the windows of the toy store and me and Sugar screamin, "This is mine, that's mine. I gotta have that, that was made for me, I was born for that," till Big Butt drowns us out.

"Hey, I'm going to buy that there."

"That there? You don't even know what it is, stupid."

"I do so," he say punchin on Rosie Giraffe. "It's a microscope."

"Whatcha gonna do with a microscope, fool?"

"Look at things."

"Like what, Ronald?" asks Miss Moore. And Big Butt ain't got the first 10 notion. So here go Miss Moore gabbing about the thousands of bacteria in a drop of water and the somethinorother in a speck of blood and the million and one living things in the air around us is invisible to the naked eye. And what she say that for? Junebug go to town on that "naked" and we rolling. Then Miss Moore ask what it cost. So we all jam into the window smudgin it up and the price tag say $300. So then she ask how long'd take for Big Butt and Junebug to save up their allowances. "Too long," I say. "Yeh," adds Sugar, "outgrown it by that time." And Miss Moore say no, you never outgrow learning instruments. "Why, even medical students and interns and," blah, blah, blah. And we ready to choke Big Butt for bringing it up in the first damn place.

"This here costs four hundred eighty dollars," say Rosie Giraffe. So we pile up all over her to see what she pointin out. My eyes tell me it's a chunk of glass cracked with something heavy, and different-color inks dripped into the splits, then the whole thing put into a oven or something. But for $480 it don't make sense.

"That's a paperweight made of semi-precious stones fused together under tremendous pressure," she explains slowly, with her hands doing the mining and all the factory work.

"So what's a paperweight?" asks Rosie Giraffe.

"To weigh paper with, dumbbell," say Flyboy, the wise man from the East.   15

"Not exactly," say Miss Moore, which is what she say when you warm or way off too. "It's to weigh paper down so it won't scatter and make your desk untidy." So right away me and Sugar curtsey to each other and then to Mercedes who is more the tidy type.

"We don't keep paper on top of the desk in my class," say Junebug, figuring Miss Moore crazy or lyin one.

"At home, then," she say. "Don't you have a calendar and a pencil case and a blotter and a letter-opener on your desk at home where you do your home-work?" And she know damn well what our homes look like cause she nosys around in them every chance she gets.

"I don't even have a desk," say Junebug. "Do we?"

"No. And I don't get no homework neither," say Big Butt.   20

"And I don't even have a home," say Flyboy like he do at school to keep the white folks off his back and sorry for him. Send this poor kid to camp posters, is his specialty.

"I do," says Mercedes. "I have a box of stationery on my desk and a picture of my cat. My godmother bought the stationery and the desk. There's a big rose on each sheet and the envelopes smell like roses."

"Who wants to know about your smelly-ass stationery," say Rosie Giraffe fore I can get my two cents in.

"It's important to have a work area all your own so that...."

"Will you look at this sailboat, please," say Flyboy, cuttin her off and pointin   25
to the thing like it was his. So once again we tumble all over each other to gaze at this magnificent thing in the toy store which is just big enough to maybe sail two kittens across the pond if you strap them to the posts tight. We all start reciting the price tag like we in assembly. "Handcrafted sailboat of fiberglass at one thousand one hundred ninety-five dollars."

"Unbelievable," I hear myself say and am really stunned. I read it again for myself just in case the group recitation put me in a trance. Same thing. For some reason this pisses me off. We look at Miss Moore and she looking at us, waiting for I dunno what.

Who'd pay all that when you can buy a sailboat set for a quarter at Pop's, a tube of glue for a dime, and a ball of string for eight cents? "It must have a motor and a whole lot else besides," I say. "My sailboat cost me about fifty cents."

The interior of F.A.O. Schwartz, a glittering festival of toys that
overwhelms Sylvia and the other underprivileged children in
"The Lesson."

"But will it take water?" says Mercedes with her smart ass.

"Took mine to Alley Pond Park once," say Flyboy. "String broke. Lost it. Pity."

"Sailed mine in Central Park and it keeled over and sank. Had to ask my   30
father for another dollar."

"And you got the strap," laughs Big Butt. "The jerk didn't even have a string
on it. My old man wailed on his behind."

Little Q.T. was staring hard at the sailboat and you could see he wanted it
bad. But he too little and somebody'd just take it from him. So what the hell.
"This boat for kids, Miss Moore?"

"Parents silly to buy something like that just to get all broke up," say Rosie
Giraffe.

"That much money it should last forever," I figure.

"My father'd buy it for me if I wanted it."   35

"Your father, my ass," say Rosie Giraffe getting a chance to finally push
Mercedes.

"Must be rich people shop here," say Q.T.

"You are a very bright boy," say Flyboy. "What was your first clue?" And he
rap him on the head with the back of his knuckles, since Q.T. the only one he

could get away with. Though Q.T. liable to come up behind you years later and get his licks in when you half expect it.

"What I want to know is," I says to Miss Moore though I never talk to her, I wouldn't give the bitch that satisfaction, "is how much a real boat costs? I figure a thousand'd get you a yacht any day."

"Why don't you check that out," she says, "and report back to the group?" 40 Which really pains my ass. If you gonna mess up a perfectly good swim day least you could do is have some answers. "Let's go in," she say like she got something up her sleeve. Only she don't lead the way. So me and Sugar turn the corner to where the entrance is, but when we get there I kinda hang back. Not that I'm scared, what's there to be afraid of, just a toy store. But I feel funny, shame. But what I got to be shamed about? Got as much right to go in as anybody. But somehow I can't seem to get hold of the door, so I step away for Sugar to lead. But she hangs back too. And I look at her and she looks at me and this is ridiculous. I mean, damn, I have never ever been shy about doing nothing or going nowhere. But then Mercedes steps up and then Rosie Giraffe and Big Butt crowd in behind and shove, and next thing we all stuffed into the doorway with only Mercedes squeezing past us, smoothing out her jumper and walking right down the aisle. Then the rest of us tumble in like a glued-together jigsaw done all wrong. And people lookin at us. And it's like the time me and Sugar crashed into the Catholic church on a dare. But once we got in there and everything so hushed and holy and the candles and the bowin and the handkerchiefs on all the drooping heads, I just couldn't go through with the plan. Which was for me to run up to the altar and do a tap dance while Sugar played the nose flute and messed around in the holy water. And Sugar kept giving me the elbow. Then later teased me so bad I tied her up in the shower and turned it on and locked her in. And she'd be there till this day if Aunt Gretchen hadn't finally figured I was lyin about the boarder takin a shower.

Same thing in the store. We all walkin on tiptoe and hardly touchin the games and puzzles and things. And I watched Miss Moore who is steady watchin us like she waitin for a sign. Like Mama Drewery watches the sky and sniffs the air and takes note of just how much slant is in the bird formation. Then me and Sugar bump smack into each other, so busy gazing at the toys, 'specially the sailboat. But we don't laugh and go into our fat-lady bump-stomach routine. We just stare at that price tag. Then Sugar run a finger over the whole boat. And I'm jealous and want to hit her. Maybe not her, but I sure want to punch somebody in the mouth.

"Watcha bring us here for, Miss Moore?"

"You sound angry, Sylvia. Are you mad about something?" Givin me one of them grins like she tellin a grown-up joke that never turns out to be funny. And she's lookin very closely at me like maybe she plannin to do my portrait from memory. I'm mad, but I won't give her that satisfaction. So I slouch around the store bein very bored and say, "Let's go."

Me and Sugar at the back of the train watchin the tracks whizzin by large then small then gettin gobbled up in the dark. I'm thinkin about this tricky toy I saw in the store. A clown that somersaults on a bar then does chin-ups just cause you yank lightly at his leg. Cost $35. I could see me askin my mother for a $35 birthday clown. "You wanna who that costs what?" she'd say, cocking her head to the side to get a better view of the hole in my head. Thirty-five dollars could buy new bunk beds for Junior and Gretchen's boy. Thirty-five dollars and the whole household could go visit Granddaddy Nelson in the country. Thirty-five dollars would pay for the rent and the piano bill too. Who are these people that spend that much for performing clowns and $1,000 for toy sailboats? What kinda work they do and how they live and how come we ain't in on it? Where we are is who we are, Miss Moore always pointin out. But it don't necessarily have to be that way, she always adds then waits for somebody to say that poor people have to wake up and demand their share of the pie and don't one of us know what kind of pie she talkin about in the first damn place. But she ain't so smart cause I still got her four dollars from the taxi and she sure ain't gettin it. Messin up my day with this shit. Sugar nudges me in my pocket and winks.

Miss Moore lines us up in front of the mailbox where we started from, seem   45
like years ago, and I got a headache for thinkin so hard. And we lean all over each other so we can hold up under the draggy-ass lecture she always finishes us off with at the end before we thank her for borin us to tears. But she just looks at us like she readin tea leaves. Finally she say, "Well, what did you think of F.A.O. Schwartz?"

Rosie Giraffe mumbles, "White folks crazy."

"I'd like to go there again when I get my birthday money," says Mercedes, and we shove her out the pack so she has to lean on the mailbox by herself.

"I'd like a shower. Tiring day," say Flyboy.

Then Sugar surprises me by sayin, "You know, Miss Moore, I don't think all of us here put together eat in a year what that sailboat costs." And Miss Moore lights up like somebody goosed her. "And?" she say, urging Sugar on. Only I'm standin on her foot so she don't continue.

"Imagine for a minute what kind of society it is in which some people can   50
spend on a toy what it would cost to feed a family of six or seven. What do you think?"

"I think," say Sugar pushing me off her feet like she never done before, cause I whip her ass in a minute, "that this is not much of a democracy if you ask me. Equal chance to pursue happiness means an equal crack at the dough, don't it?" Miss Moore is besides herself and I am disgusted with Sugar's treachery. So I stand on her foot one more time to see if she'll shove me. She shuts up, and Miss Moore looks at me, sorrowfully I'm thinkin. And somethin weird is goin on, I can feel it in my chest.

"Anybody else learn anything today?" lookin dead at me. I walk away and Sugar has to run to catch up and don't even seem to notice when I shrug her arm off my shoulder.

"Well, we got four dollars anyway," she says.

"Uh hunh."

"We could go to Hascombs and get half a chocolate layer and then go to the   55
Sunset and still have plenty money for potato chips and ice-cream sodas."

"Uh hunh."

"Race you to Hascombs," she say.

We start down the block and she gets ahead which is O.K. by me cause I'm goin to the West End and then over to the Drive to think this day through. She can run if she want to and even run faster. But ain't nobody gonna beat me at nuthin.

(1972)

Questions for Discussion and Writing

1. How would you characterize Sylvia? What makes her first-person point of view effective? Is she a reliable narrator?

2. How would you characterize Miss Moore? Why doesn't Sylvia admire her, as the adults do? Why does Sugar not feel hostile toward Miss Moore, as Sylvia does?

3. Why doesn't Sylvia get the point of the lesson being taught by the visit to the expensive toy store? Why is she so angry that she wants "to punch somebody in the mouth"?

4. What is the significance of the last line of the story? How does it relate to the lesson Sylvia was supposed to learn?

5. In what ways is this a story about borders, both literal and figurative? Pick out several examples and explain them.

Sandra Cisneros   1954–

Sandra Cisneros, the daughter of a Mexican father and a Mexican-American mother, grew up with her six brothers in a barrio of Chicago that seemed to her "like France after World War II—empty lots and burned out buildings." Although the males in her family pressured her to adopt a subservient woman's role, she was determined to be "nobody's mother and nobody's wife." She achieved a higher education but has said, "If I had lived up to my teachers' expectations, I'd still be working in a factory." She has focused on the Latina experience in her sketches, short stories, novels, and poetry. In 1995 she was awarded a MacArthur "genius" grant of $500,000.

Geraldo No Last Name

She met him at a dance. Pretty too, and young. Said he worked in a restaurant, but she can't remember which one. Geraldo. That's all. Green pants and Saturday shirt. Geraldo. That's what he told her.

And how was she to know she'd be the last one to see him alive. An accident, don't you know. Hit and run. Marin, she goes to all those dances. Uptown. Logan. Embassy. Palmer. Aragon. Fontana. The Manor. She likes to dance. She knows how to do cumbias and salsas and rancheras even. And he was just someone she danced with. Somebody she met that night. That's right.

That's the story. That's what she said again and again. Once to the hospital people and twice to the police. No address. No name. Nothing in his pockets. Ain't it a shame.

Only Marin can't explain why it mattered, the hours and hours, for somebody she didn't even know. The hospital emergency room. Nobody but an intern working all alone. And maybe if the surgeon would've come, maybe if he hadn't lost so much blood, if the surgeon had only come, they would know who to notify and where.

But what difference does it make? He wasn't anything to her. He wasn't her   5
boyfriend or anything like that. Just another *brazer* who didn't speak English.

Just another wetback. You know the kind. The ones who always look ashamed. And what was she doing out at three A.M. anyway? Marin who was sent home with her coat and some aspirin. How does she explain?

She met him at a dance. Geraldo in his shiny shirt and green pants. Geraldo going to a dance.

What does it matter?

They never saw the kitchenettes. They never knew about the two-room flats and sleeping rooms he rented, the weekly money orders sent home, the currency exchange. How could they?

His name was Geraldo. And his home is in another country. The ones he left behind are far away, will wonder, shrug, remember. Geraldo—he went north ... we never heard from him again.

(1983)

Questions for Discussion and Writing

1. Why was only one intern working in the emergency room? Why didn't the surgeon come? Why are these facts included?
2. In the next-to-last paragraph, who is the "they" who never saw the kitchenettes and never knew about Geraldo's life? What is the point of this paragraph?
3. How would you describe the tone of the final paragraph? In what way does this paragraph sum up the story's main themes?
4. Write an essay from Geraldo's point of view. Let him speak for himself. What does he have to say about his life and what happened to him?

Celeste Ng 1981–

Celeste Ng's debut novel, *Everything I Never Told You*, was a *New York Times* bestseller, a *New York Times* Notable Book of 2014, and named Amazon's #1 Best Book of 2014. She was also named one of *BuzzFeed*'s "20 Under 40 Debut Writers You Need To Be Reading." Ng holds an MFA from the University of Michigan and lives in Cambridge, Massachusetts, where she is currently working on her second novel and a collection of short stories.

How To Be Chinese

Take pleasure in the surprise on people's faces when you say, "My name is Mackenzie Altman." When they ask, explain that yes, your mother adopted you from China; no, you don't know your birth parents; no, you don't speak the language. Smile politely when they say you have no accent.

At eighteen, accept a place at a small liberal arts school in Ohio, four hours away, just over the state border. According to the website, the incoming freshman class is 450. Its average Asian population is three percent. Do the math: thirteen and a half Asians in your class. Try not to think about who the half is. Announce to your mother that you want to get in touch with your heritage: make it a going-to-college resolution. She will be delighted. "Kenz," she will say, "Oh Kenz, I'm so proud." She has wanted this since you were an infant, since she carried you off the Beijing–Detroit flight swaddled in a Minnie Mouse blanket. She has taken you to a Chinese restaurant on your birthday every year; she has always bought you panda teddy bears, the Asian Barbie. Your mother will kiss you, her eyes glossy with tears.

Don't bring up the difficulties of learning to be Chinese in the middle of Michigan. Don't remind her that except for the waiters at The Pearl of the Orient, you have never met another Chinese person. Don't tell her you have no idea where to begin.

Begin with a false start. In your first week of college, join the Chinese Students Association. At the introductory meeting, in a conference room in the union, there are fourteen of you. Look around and think, "This is what China must be like." Then blush. Look around and think, "My god, we all *do* look alike." This meeting's get-acquainted activity is mahjong. The other students are all international, from Beijing and Shanghai, with vaguely British accents. Pull a chair up to the corner of a table. "Watch," one girl says. "We'll teach you how." It is glamorous, like *The Joy Luck Club*. Prop your elbows on the table and feel porous, ready to soak up culture.

Except you have no idea what's going on. In the middle of an English sentence a patch of Chinese will pop up, sudden as switching the station on the radio. "My boyfriend, you know, he *m-m-m-m*. And I said, you know, I don't think *m-m-m* really *m-mm*, but it's like *m-m-m*." Parts fall out of the conversation like paper snowflakes you cut out in kindergarten, mostly holes. You want to ask the girl next to you to translate, but you glance at her name tag and don't know how to pronounce what's there. *Xiaoxia*. She looks over at you and smiles.

"Do you get it?" she asks. Four pairs of hands stack mahjong tiles into brick walls. Suddenly the table is a tiny fortress with you on the outside. Nod and smile. Tell her you have to go. Forget to say thank you on your way out the door.

Begin again, in that most American of all places: McDonald's. October. You're at the register waiting for your Big Mac when a voice behind you says, "What would you recommend?"

"What?" you say, turning. This is a question you associate with steak houses, with restaurants that have specials. The boy behind you is Chinese too, hands tucked into pockets, a soft doglike expression in his eyes. Wonder if this boy is screwing with you. You get your order and the cashier turns to the boy, who points to your tray and says, "I'll have the same."

Ask him about himself as you peel the paper from your burgers. He tells you his name, Winston Liu; that his family moved to the U.S. a few months ago from Hong Kong and lives half an hour away; that he's a freshman too. Marvel in unison about how you haven't met until now. Listen to Winston's voice for a trace of an accent, but don't find one until he says the word *strawberry*. After that you can hear it everywhere: a faint Britishness in the vowels, a slight mingling of L and N, the hard *ch* when he says *Chicago*. It's sexy, the way the voice and the face don't match; like artfully clashing clothing, like mussed-up hair.

"Say something in Chinese," you tell him.

"Like what?"

"Like anything."

5

10

He thinks for a moment, then says something. English words lurk in the sounds: *Jaw, deem, naugahyde.*

"What does that mean?" you ask.

"'Pardon me, miss, my hotel room is full of monkeys.'" 15

Lean across the speckled plastic table and kiss him. His lips taste of salt and ketchup, which you find strangely exotic. Don't realize that this is the taste of your own mouth as well.

For your first date Winston takes you to dinner. There are two Chinese restaurants in town, in strip malls across the street from each other. Peking Garden is the one you know. It has tasteful, smoky watercolors of mountains on the walls, and each sugar packet teaches you the name of a Chinese boat: sampan, junk. But the food comes on pink and white Corningware; the waiters bring coffee after the meal without asking, and they're all students, white kids with the same flat midwestern tones as you and your mother and everyone you know. Winston takes you to the other one, Happy Buddha, which is tucked between Office Max and the Home Depot. Everyone says it's much more authentic and, as a result, when you go in on Saturday evening, you're the only customers there.

Look around to see what it's like in a *real* Chinese restaurant. The tablecloths are pink and the napkins maroon. The teacups don't have handles. Honeycomb balls of red paper and gold plastic bats dangle from joins in the ceiling tile. Worry that your people have bad taste. A woman croons in Chinese over the speaker system. Sit in a corner booth and imagine you're in China. In a minute you recognize the tune being piped in: it's the theme from *Titanic.*

The waiter at Happy Buddha is the age your father would be, if you had a father, with skin the deep tan of tea. He has an accent and needs a haircut. When he asks if you want ice water, his tone is almost an accusation, and it takes you a minute to understand what he's said. Say, "Yes please," and smile brightly. Try not to be disappointed when he doesn't smile back.

Winston skips the moo shu and the lo mein and the General Tso's chicken, 20
all the things you and your mother love, and orders dishes you've never heard of. "You sure?" the waiter says. He looks at you out of the corner of his eye. Then he says something to Winston in Chinese, and Winston looks at you and nods. Nod too, as if you understand. The waiter finally scrawls a few characters on his notepad. After he goes off to put in your order, ask,

"What did he say?"

"Oh," Winston says, "he wanted to know if you were Chinese."

The food, when it comes, isn't bad, but it's strange. Its textures unnerve you: blocks of tofu the consistency of your mother's flan; crispy yellow noodles and brown gravy and knuckles of spareribs that are mostly bone. The waiter watches you eat from across the room, sitting at another table and smoking a cigarette. Try not to catch his eye as you put sugar in your tea, as the spareribs slip from your chopsticks again and you reach for a fork.

When dinner's over, Winston pays with a fifty-dollar bill. Then he goes to the bathroom, and the waiter says something to you that you can't quite make out. Say, "Hmm?" and miss it again. You can't understand until he says, quite clearly, "Do you want to take this home?" and you realize it isn't the accent: he'd been speaking Chinese. Say, "Yes, please, wrap it up," and hope he doesn't notice how red you've become.

While you wait for your doggie bag, look at the placemat, now stained with   25
grease and drops of brown sauce. Find your birth year and learn that you are a
dragon. It makes you think of yourself as sleek and powerful and assured, not small
and traitorous. It says: *You are determined and passionate, a quick learner.* Look the
waiter in the eye when he returns and tell yourself that the look in his eyes isn't pity.

After Winston drives you back to your dorm, wait for him to leave, then slip
across the street to Pinocchio's and order two slices of pepperoni. Clap them
between two paper plates and smuggle them back to your room to eat alone,
with a rerun of *Friends* on.

A few weeks later, Winston calls and asks if you'd like to meet his mother for
Sunday brunch. She comes down to visit, he says, every couple of weeks. Hide
your surprise. You've gone out a few times—to a safe PG-13 comedy, and to the
first football game of the season, where you held his hand in the pocket of his
coat and tried to explain what a blitz was. You haven't even mentioned him to
your own mother yet. Is it time, you think, to meet parents?

"She really wants to meet you," Winston says. "She thinks it's wonderful that
I'm meeting other Chinese students." Feel a rush of warmth, like a deep hug.
Wonder about this woman: a Chinese mother. What does she look like? You can
picture only your mother with her hair dyed black. Say, "All right, what time?"

Winston decides on The Vineyard, the wood-paneled restaurant everyone
takes visiting parents to. By the time you get there, two minutes early, he and
his mother are already seated at a white-clothed table. Mrs. Liu wears a fur coat,
dark and sleek, and two gold necklaces. On her left index finger is a circle of jade
the size of a dime.

"Mackenzie," she says. She holds out her hand but doesn't shake yours, so   30
that you end up grasping the tips of her fingers like the corner of a wet dishcloth.
"You so thin," she says. For a moment you think she's going to pinch your cheek.

"Thank you," you say after a pause, and she smiles at you with her lipsticked
lips closed, as if you've made a mistake. She orders a cup of fruit salad and a
croissant, and you feel vaguely disappointed at the Europeanness of it, though
you and Winston have both ordered waffles, with bacon.

"What your mommy do?" Mrs. Liu asks.

"An architect," you tell her.

"And your daddy?"

You have a stock answer, a stock tone for this.   35

"Oh, it's just my mom and me," you say. "She adopted me as a single mom.
Just the two of us girls."

"Mm-*hm*," she says, as if you've said something fascinating.

Winston's mother is a feng shui expert. Feng shui, as far as you can tell, is
good luck through interior design. She doesn't work. His father is some kind
of businessman, in China a lot. This week he's in Shanghai. Mrs. Liu asks what
your major is, and you tell her you haven't decided yet. When she lifts her eyebrows, add, "But I'm thinking of East Asian Studies."

"You want to learn about your culture," Mrs. Liu says. "That's gooooood."
She draws out the last word like she's spinning a thread of silk. Then she smiles,
a real smile this time, and slices a chunk of cantaloupe with the side of her fork.

"You adopted?" At your nod, she says, "Very important, you learn about your   40
culture." The way she says it, like an edict, makes you feel entitled. *Culture* glistens in the distance, like the prize in a scavenger hunt.

After that, brunch follows a pattern. Mrs. Liu speaks to you in Chinese. You can pick out only your name, which comes out like three words: Ma. Ken. Zee. Smile blankly while Winston says, "Mom, remember? Mackenzie doesn't speak Chinese." Mrs. Liu apologizes, patting your hand with hers, which is pale and cool and soft, like a little satin cushion. "You keep listening, you pick it up," she says each time. "You born with it, inside you understand it. In here." She taps her chest.

Don't tell them about the package in your mailbox last month, the eight-CD set of *Introductory Chinese* from Barnes & Noble, the note from your mother saying, "Picked up one for myself too—we can learn together." Lesson One: "How are you? I am an American. I speak a little Chinese, but I don't speak well." In your mouth the words tasted strange as gravel. Don't tell them how Lesson Two bewildered you, how you forgot the word order, how you jumbled the words for "eat" and "is," the words for "buy" and "sell." How when your mother called last week, sounding like the woman on the tape, you understood nothing until she spoke in English. "*Do you want to have a drink at my place? Lesson Eight: Meeting People.*" After a moment: "Are you not there yet?" Try to forget the care package that arrived yesterday, chocolate-chunk cookies, hot cocoa mix, tortilla chips and salsa, a note from your mother that read, "I promise to stop propositioning you." Focus instead on Mrs. Liu's eyes, the same deep brown as yours. Chant her words in your mind: *you born with it, inside you understand it.*

After the meal, say goodbye in the parking lot. Mrs. Liu takes your hand and the jade in her ring presses into your fingers. She says, "Mackenzie, I buy a lot of art for our new house, Chinese art. Maybe you want to come and see it? Learn about your culture?"

"I'd love to," you say. Behind her, Winston beams.

"Good," she says, and gets into the car. Winston pecks you on the cheek and 45
whispers, "Call you later," and they're gone in a streak of pale gold Lexus.

That night, go over to Winston's room. Kick off your shoes and sink down onto the bed. Like you, like most other freshman, he has a single; the university believes it prevents rooming conflicts. But the rooms in his building are older, and awkwardly shaped: the desk has to go in the niche in the wall, the bed in the corner, with the closet at its foot.

"So that was my mother," he says, looking at you sideways from the chair.

"She's nice," you say.

"She likes you. She wants you to come by the house. Next weekend, maybe."

You feel a tingle in your shoulders and feel his eyes resting on you. Don't 50
meet them. Survey the built-in mirror on the closet door, the cinderblock walls painted dingy off-white.

Winston says, "So your mom adopted you alone?" Tell him yes. Tell him, "Nowadays that's not allowed. Nowadays there are more rules. You have to be married. You have to be straight. You can't be blind, or hard of hearing, or have a wooden leg or epilepsy or someone else's kidney. Nowadays they screen you to make sure you're not a criminal, or a crazy."

Don't explain that she'd always wanted a baby but never found the right man, that when she read that China was opening its orphanages she'd cried right there in the coffee shop, tears spotting the newspaper. That when she came to China to pick you up she had horrible stomach cramps all sixteen hours, threw up three times into one paper bag and another and another, as if her body were atoning for the lack of labor. Don't tell him that when she first picked you up in her arms, she whispered, *Hello beautiful, where have you been all my life?* These are private stories. Push them to the back of your mind and give Winston your biggest ironic smile. Say, "Good thing my mother acted fast."

Questions for Discussion and Writing

1. What is the point of view in this story? Who is the "you" being addressed?

2. A majority of the sentences are commands: "Take pleasure," "Smile politely," "Do the math," and so on. What is the effect of this unusual style? Why do you think the author chose this way to present the narrative?

3. Describe the relationship between Mackenzie and her mother. In what ways is Mackenzie's mother like Winston's mother? How are they different?

4. In the last paragraph, why does the narrator say "Don't explain" and "Don't tell him"? Why give Winston "your biggest ironic smile"?

5. Mrs. Liu tells Mackenzie that she will pick up Chinese just by listening to it because she is "born with it, inside you understand it" (para. 41). Do you agree? Is a person's culture inborn or acquired? Write a brief reflective statement discussing this question.

Poetry

William Blake   1757–1827

See page 494 for a biographical note about this author.

London

I wander through each chartered street,
Near where the chartered Thames does flow,
And mark in every face I meet
Marks of weakness, marks of woe.

In every cry of every man,   5
In every infant's cry of fear,
In every voice, in every ban,
The mind-forged manacles I hear.

How the chimney-sweeper's cry
Every black'ning church appalls;   10
And the hapless soldier's sigh
Runs in blood down palace walls.

But most through midnight streets I hear
How the youthful harlot's curse
Blasts the new-born infant's tear,   15
And blights with plagues the marriage hearse.
                            (1794)

Questions for Discussion and Writing

1. How does Blake convey the impression of pain and suffering?
2. "The youthful harlot's curse" is usually interpreted to mean venereal disease, which blinds the infant after birth. How does this information help you to understand Blake's metaphor in the final stanza? Why is this curse so important to the speaker?
3. What is the significance of the mention of a church, a soldier, and a palace?

Claude McKay 1890–1948

Claude McKay was born in Sunny Ville, Jamaica. At the age of twenty-three, he moved to the United States, where he encountered the strong racial prejudice prevalent during this period. A prominent figure in the Harlem Renaissance, McKay was a catalyst among African American writers, preaching black vitality and social reform. He wrote four volumes of poetry, including *If We Must Die* (1919); a novel, *Home to Harlem* (1928); and an autobiography, *A Long Way from Home* (1937).

America

Although she feeds me bread of bitterness,
And sinks into my throat her tiger's tooth,
Stealing my breath of life, I will confess
I love this cultured hell that tests my youth!
Her vigor flows like tides into my blood,
Giving me strength erect against her hate.
Her bigness sweeps my being like a flood,
Yet as a rebel fronts a king in state,
I stand within her walls with not a shred
Of terror, malice, not a word of jeer.
Darkly I gaze into the days ahead,
And see her might and granite wonders there,
Beneath the touch of Time's unerring hand,
Like priceless treasures sinking in the sand.

(1920)

Questions for Discussion and Writing

1. Who is speaking in this poem?
2. Explain the metaphors in the first three lines.
3. What does the speaker love about America? What does he regard as a threat to her strength?

Countee Cullen 1903–1946

Countee Cullen was adopted by a Methodist minister and raised in Harlem. His first volume of poems, *Color* (1925), was published when he was a student at New York University. His early work established him as a leader of the Harlem

Renaissance, but his collection *Copper Sun* (1927), which featured love poems, disappointed black nationalists. Cullen stopped writing poetry after he published *The Black Christ* in 1929. He taught school in New York City for the rest of his life.

Incident

(For Eric Walrond)

Once riding in old Baltimore,
    Heart-filled, head-filled with glee,
I saw a Baltimorean
    Keep looking straight at me.

Now I was eight and very small,   5
    And he was no whit bigger,
And so I smiled, but he poked out
    His tongue, and called me, "Nigger."

I saw the whole of Baltimore
    From May until December;   10
Of all the things that happened there
    That's all that I remember.

                    (1925)

Questions for Discussion and Writing

1. Though the main point of "Incident" is unstated, its theme is clear. How would you state it in a sentence?
2. "Incident" is very simple in form and language. Why do you think the author chose this simplicity?
3. Write an essay about your own introduction into a part of the adult world that you weren't aware of as a child or youth.

James Wright   1927–1980

James Wright was born in Martins Ferry, Ohio, a small city directly across the Ohio River from Wheeling, West Virginia. His father worked in a glass factory, and his mother quit school to work in a laundry. When in high school, Wright suffered a nervous breakdown and missed a year of school. After graduation in 1944 he joined the army and was stationed in Japan during the American occupation. He went to Kenyon College on the GI Bill, and did graduate work at the University of Washington. He went on to teach at Macalester College in Minnesota and Hunter College in New York City. His work dealt increasingly with a homeless, lonely persona confronted by an overwhelming, godless universe.

Autumn Begins in Martins Ferry, Ohio

In the Shreve High football stadium,
I think of Polacks nursing long beers in Tiltonsville,
And gray faces of Negroes in the blast furnace at Benwood,
And the ruptured night watchman of Wheeling Steel,
Dreaming of heroes.   5

All the proud fathers are ashamed to go home.
Their women cluck like starved pullets,
Dying for love.

Therefore,
Their sons grow suicidally beautiful   10
At the beginning of October,
And gallop terribly against each other's bodies.

(1962)

Questions for Discussion and Writing

1. Who is the "I" of the poem? What is he doing?
2. What do the men described in lines 2 through 4 have in common? What kind of lives do they lead? What kind of heroes are they dreaming of?
3. Why are the fathers "ashamed to go home"? Why are the women "dying for love"?
4. The third stanza begins with the word "Therefore," signaling a cause-and-effect relationship. What is the cause and what is the effect, according to the poem?
5. What do you make of the phrase "suicidally beautiful"? What does the speaker seem to believe about football?
6. Write an essay explaining the cultural importance of football in Martins Ferry, Ohio.

Audre Lorde   1934–1992

Audre Lorde was born of West Indian parents in New York City. She was educated at the National University of Mexico, Hunter College, and Columbia University. Her poetry is passionate about love, angry about race, and feminist. Her first major work of prose, *The Cancer Journals* (1980), depicts her struggle with breast cancer and mastectomy and carries her message of the strength of women. *The Black Unicorn* (1978) is a volume of her poems about Africa.

Hanging Fire

I am fourteen
and my skin has betrayed me
the boy I cannot live without
still sucks his thumb
in secret   5
how come my knees are
always so ashy
what if I die
before morning
and momma's in the bedroom   10
with the door closed.

I have to learn how to dance
in time for the next party
my room is too small for me
suppose I die before graduation   15
they will sing sad melodies
but finally
tell the truth about me
There is nothing I want to do
and too much   20
that has to be done
and momma's in the bedroom
with the door closed.

Nobody even stops to think
about my side of it   25
I should have been on Math Team
my marks were better than his
why do I have to be
the one
wearing braces   30
I have nothing to wear tomorrow
will I live long enough
to grow up
and momma's in the bedroom
with the door closed.

(1978)

Questions for Discussion and Writing

1. Do you think that the teenager's thoughts in this poem are true to life? Can
   you remember similar thoughts when you were around fourteen? What
   kinds of concerns does the speaker have?

2. Find out what the title means. How is it appropriate for the poem and the speaker?

3. What do you think of the refrain, "and momma's in the bedroom / with the
   door closed"? Is the speaker a victim of neglect?

Woman working in an apparel-industry sweatshop.

Gina Valdés   1943–

Gina Valdés was born in Los Angeles, spent her childhood in Mexico, and returned to Los Angeles during adolescence. She attended the University of California, San Diego, and still lives in San Diego today. Her stories and poetry often focus on the plight of undocumented workers, Chicano alienation in the United States, and the status of Chicanas. Her collection *Puentes y fronteras* [*Bridges and Frontiers*] (1982) takes the form of *coplas*, four-line stanzas from traditional Mexican folk poetry, with Valdés substituting a female for the conventional male narrator. In *Comiendo lumbre: Eating Fire* (1986), she experiments with alternating between Spanish and English in each poem.

My Mother Sews Blouses

My mother sews blouses
for a dollar a piece.
They must be working on
black cloth again, I see
her fingers sliding on   5
her eyelids.

Six months ago she went
to the old oculist, the
one who "knows all about
eyes," who turned her   10

eyelids inside out and
scraped them with a tiny
knife to get the black
lint out.

Her eyes were bright and   15
clear for a few months.
She's blinking now,
talking about night
school.

(1986)

Questions for Discussion and Writing

1. Why do you think the mother is so poorly paid for her sewing?
2. Consider possible symbolism in the poem. What do we usually associate with the inability to see? What could the black lint symbolize?
3. Why is the woman "thinking about night school"? What effect will her current job have on this goal? Does the poem suggest that she will succeed or fail? Explain.

Gregory Djanikian   1949–

Gregory Djanikian was born in Alexandria, Egypt, of Armenian parents. When he was eight years old, his family moved to Pennsylvania, where he still lives near Philadelphia. He has taught at the University of Pennsylvania since 1983 and is currently the Director of the Creative Writing Program there. The winner of numerous awards and fellowships, Djanikian has published six collections of poetry. His poems explore the legacies of family, history, and culture, particularly his own Armenian heritage and childhood emigration to the United States.

Immigrant Picnic

It's the Fourth of July, the flags
are painting the town,
the plastic forks and knives
are laid out like a parade.

And I'm grilling, I've got my apron,   5
I've got potato salad, macaroni, relish,
I've got a hat shaped
like the state of Pennsylvania.

I ask my father what's his pleasure
and he says, "Hot dog, medium rare,"   10
and then, "Hamburger, sure,

what's the big difference,"
as if he's really asking.

I put on hamburgers and hot dogs,
slice up the sour pickles and Bermudas,⁣ 15
uncap the condiments. The paper napkins
are fluttering away like lost messages.

"You're running around," my mother says,
"like a chicken with its head loose."

"Ma," I say, "you mean cut off,⁣ 20
loose and cut off being as far apart
as, say, son and daughter."

She gives me a quizzical look as though
I've been caught in some impropriety.
"I love you and your sister just the same," she says,⁣ 25
"Sure," my grandmother pipes in,
"you're both our children, so why worry?"

That's not the point I begin telling them,
and I'm comparing words to fish now,
like the ones in the sea at Port Said,
or like birds among the date palms by the Nile,⁣ 30
unrepentantly elusive, wild.

"Sonia," my father says to my mother,
"what the hell is he talking about?"
"He's on a ball," my mother says.

"That's roll!" I say, throwing up my hands,⁣ 35
"as in hot dog, hamburger, dinner roll ...."

"And what about roll out the barrels?" my mother asks,
and my father claps his hands, "Why sure," he says,
"let's have some fun," and launches
into a polka, twirling my mother⁣ 40
around and around like the happiest top,

and my uncle is shaking his head, saying
"You could grow nuts listening to us,"

and I'm thinking of pistachios in the Sinai⁣ 45
burgeoning without end,
pecans in the South, the jumbled
flavor of them suddenly in my mouth,
wordless, confusing,
crowding out everything else.⁣ 50

(1999)

Questions for Discussion and Writing

1. Djanikian says he is interested in how language is enriched or reinvented, especially "the unexpected syntactic constructions" and "surprising turns of phrase" that immigrants contribute to English. What examples of these reinventions does the poet include in "Immigrant Picnic"?
2. How would you describe the speaker and his relationship with his relatives? Is the speaker making fun of them?
3. Is it important that the poem is set on the Fourth of July?
4. Explicate the last stanza, especially the significance of the last two lines.

Essex Hemphill 1957–1995

The oldest of five children born into a working-class family in Chicago, Essex Hemphill took up writing as a teenager. "I was a skinny little 14-year-old black boy," he said, "growing up in a ghetto that had not yet suffered the fatal wounds and injuries caused by drugs and black-on-black crime." As an adult, he was an activist in the black gay rights movement, but he explained, "I love my race enough to know that I'm a Black man first and foremost and that my sexuality falls in line after that." He died at age thirty-eight from complications of AIDS.

Commitments

I will always be there.
When the silence is exhumed.
When the photographs are examined
I will be pictured smiling
among siblings, parents,   5
nieces and nephews.

In the background of the photographs
the hazy smoke of barbecue,
a checkered red-and-white tablecloth
laden with blackened chicken,   10
glistening ribs, paper plates,
bottles of beer, and pop.

In the photos
the smallest of children
are held by their parents.   15
My arms are empty, or around
the shoulders of unsuspecting aunts
expecting to throw rice at me someday.

Or picture tinsel, candles,
ornamented, imitation trees,   20

or another table, this one
set for Thanksgiving,
a turkey steaming the lens.

My arms are empty   25
in those photos, too,
so empty they would break around a lover.

I am always there
for critical emergencies,
graduations,
the middle of the night.   30
I am the invisible son.
In the family photos
nothing appears out of character.
I smile as I serve my duty.

                                              (1992)

Questions for Discussion and Writing

1. Why are the speaker's arms "empty or around the shoulders of unsuspecting aunts"? Why are the aunts "unsuspecting"? Unsuspecting of what?
2. Why does the speaker think of himself as "the invisible son"?
3. Explain the title. What commitments does the speaker fulfill? Does his family have any commitments to him? How does he feel about his place in the family?
4. Did you ever feel invisible even though you were plainly in sight? What was the social situation? Did you welcome the invisibility, or did you wish someone would take notice of you? In an essay, poem, or story, express how this invisibility affected you.

Richard Blanco   1968–

   Richard Blanco's parents left Cuba after the rise of Fidel Castro and traveled to Spain (where Richard was born); the family then emigrated to New York City and eventually moved to Miami, where Richard was raised and educated. He graduated from Florida International University in 1991 and worked as a civil engineer, but then returned to earn a master's degree in creative writing. He has taught at several universities, and he published his first book of poetry in 1999. In 2013, he was chosen to read at Barack Obama's second Presidential Inauguration, becoming the youngest, first Latino, first immigrant, and first gay writer to hold this honor. He currently lives and teaches in Maine. Blanco says that his work asks the questions we all ask: Where am I from? Where do I belong? Who am I in this world?

América

I.

Although Tía Miriam boasted she discovered
at least half-a-dozen uses for peanut butter—
topping for guava shells in syrup,
butter substitute for Cuban toast,
hair conditioner and relaxer—   5
Mamá never knew what to make
of the monthly five-pound jars
handed out by the immigration department
until my friend, Jeff, mentioned jelly.

II.

There was always pork though,   10
for every birthday and wedding,
whole ones on Christmas and New Year's Eves,
even on Thanksgiving Day—pork,
fried, broiled, or crispy skin roasted—
as well as cauldrons of black beans,   15
fried plantain chips and *yuca con mojito*.
These items required a special visit
to Antonio's Mercado on the corner of Eighth street
where men in *guayaberas* stood in senate
blaming Kennedy for everything—"*Ese hijo de puta!*"   20
the bile of Cuban coffee and cigar residue
filling the creases of their wrinkled lips;
clinging to one another's lies of lost wealth,
ashamed and empty as hollow trees.

III.

By seven I had grown suspicious—we were still here.   25
Overheard conversations about returning
had grown wistful and less frequent.
I spoke English; my parents didn't.
We didn't live in a two-story house
with a maid or a wood-panel station wagon   30
nor vacation camping in Colorado.
None of the girls had hair of gold;
none of my brothers or cousins
were named Greg, Peter, or Marcia;
we were not the Brady Bunch.   35
None of the black and white characters
on Donna Reed or on Dick Van Dyke Show
were named Guadalupe, Lázaro, or Mercedes.
Patty Duke's family wasn't like us either—
they didn't have pork on Thanksgiving,   40
they ate turkey with cranberry sauce;
they didn't have *yuca*, they had yams
like the dittos of Pilgrims I colored in class.

IV.

A week before Thanksgiving
I explained to my *abuelita*   45
about the Indians and the Mayflower,
how Lincoln set the slaves free;
I explained to my parents about
the purple mountain's majesty,
"one if by land, two if by sea,"   50
the cherry tree, the tea party,
the amber waves of grain,
the "masses yearning to be free,"
liberty and justice for all, until
finally they agreed: 55
this Thanksgiving we would have turkey,
as well as pork.

V.

Abuelita prepared the poor fowl
as if committing an act of treason,
faking her enthusiasm for my sake.   60
Mamá set a frozen pumpkin pie in the oven
and prepared candied yams following instructions
I translated from the marshmallow bag.
The table was arrayed with gladiolas,
the plattered turkey loomed at the center   65
on plastic silver from Woolworths.
Everyone sat in green velvet chairs
we had upholstered with clear vinyl,
except Tío Carlos and Toti, seated
in the folding chairs from the Salvation Army.   70
I uttered a bilingual blessing
and the turkey was passed around
like a game of Russian Roulette.
"DRY," Tío Berto complained, and proceeded
to drown the lean slices with pork fat drippings   75
and cranberry jelly—"*esa mierda roja*," he called it.
Faces fell when *Mamá* presented her ochre pie—
pumpkin was a home remedy for ulcers, not a dessert.
Tía María made three rounds of Cuban coffee
then *Abuelo* and Pepe cleared the living room furniture,   80
put on a Celia Cruz LP and the entire family
began to *merengue* over the linoleum of our apartment,
sweating rum and coffee until they remembered—
it was 1970 and 46 degrees—
in *América*.   85
After repositioning the furniture,
an appropriate darkness filled the room.
Tío Berto was the last to leave.

(1996)

Questions for Discussion and Writing

1. Richard Blanco said "My Cuban family never got Thanksgiving. It was one of those traditions without translation …. This poem ["América"] originates from one of my earliest memories of the clash between the two cultures that shaped me." Identify several specific clashes of culture in the poem.

2. Why is the poem divided into numbered sections? What is the theme or topic of each section?

3. Why does the poet include so many Spanish words and phrases? What point or theme does this practice emphasize?

4. Why does the speaker want so desperately to have a traditional American Thanksgiving dinner?

5. Describe the speaker's attitude toward his relatives. Is he ashamed of them or of his heritage?

Drama

Alice Childress   1916–1994

Alice Childress was the first African American woman to have a play produced professionally in New York, and she was one of the first black women to direct an Off-Broadway play. Born in Charleston, South Carolina, in 1916, she moved to Harlem to live with her grandmother in 1925. Dreaming of becoming an actress, she joined the American Negro Theatre in 1941, and in 1944 was nominated for a Tony as Best Supporting Actress for her role in the Broadway production of *Anna Lucasta*. Childress found little dramatic material that represented the lives of black women she knew, so she began writing it herself. In 1949, her first play, the one-act *Florence*, was produced at St. Mark's Church in Harlem. She wrote a dozen plays and several adult and children's novels.

Florence

CHARACTERS

MARGE   PORTER
MAMA   MRS. CARTER

PLACE

A very small town in the South.

TIME

The late 1940s.

SCENE

A railway station waiting room. The room is divided in two sections by a low railing. Upstage center is a double door which serves as an entrance to both sides of the room. Over the doorway stage right is a sign "Colored," over the doorway stage left is another sign "White." Stage right are two doors ... one marked "Colored men" ... the other "Colored women." Stage left two other doorways are "White ladies" and "White gentlemen." There are two benches, one on each side. The room is drab and empty looking. Through the double doors upstage center can be seen a gray lighting which gives the effect of an early evening and open platform.

At rise of curtain the stage remains empty for about twenty seconds ... A middle aged Negro woman enters, looks offstage ... then crosses to the "Colored" side and sits on the bench. A moment later she is followed by a young Negro woman about twenty-one years old. She is carrying a large new cardboard suitcase and a wrapped shoebox. She is wearing a shoulder strap bag and a newspaper protrudes from the flap. She crosses to the "Colored" side and rests the suitcase at her feet as she looks at her mother with mild annoyance.

MARGE. You didn't have to get here so early, Mama. Now you got to wait!

MAMA. If I'm goin' someplace ... I like to get there in plenty time. You don't have to stay.

MARGE. You shouldn't wait 'round here alone.

MAMA. I ain't scared. Ain't a soul going to bother me.

MARGE. I got to get back to Ted. He don't like to be in the house by himself. (*She picks up the bag and places it on the bench by* MAMA.)

MAMA. You'd best go back. (*smiles*) You know he misses Florence.

MARGE. He's just a little fellow. He needs his mother. You make her come home! She shouldn't be way up there in Harlem. She ain't got nobody there.

MAMA. You know Florence don't like the South.

MARGE. It ain't what we like in this world! You tell her that.

MAMA. If Mr. Jack ask about the rent, you tell him we gonna be a little late on account of the trip.

MARGE. I'll talk with him. Don't worry so about everything. (*places suitcase on floor*) What you carryin', Mama ... bricks?

MAMA. If Mr. Jack won't wait ... write to Rudley. He oughta send a little somethin'.

MARGE. Mama ... Rudley ain't got nothin' fo himself. I hate to ask him to give us.

MAMA. That's your brother! If push come to shove, we got to ask.

MARGE (*places box on bench*). Don't forget to eat your lunch ... and try to get a seat near the window so you can lean on your elbow and get a little rest.

MAMA. Hmmmm ... mmmph. Yes.

MARGE. Buy yourself some coffee when the man comes through. You'll need something hot and you can't go to the diner.

MAMA. I know that. You talk like I'm a northern greenhorn.

MARGE. You got handkerchiefs?

MAMA. I got everything, Marge.

MARGE (*wanders upstage to the railing division line*). I know Florence is real bad off or she wouldn't call on us for money. Make her come home. She ain't gonna get rich up there and we can't afford to do for her.

MAMA. We talked all of that before.

MARGE (*touches rail*). Well, you got to be strict on her. She got notions a Negro woman don't need.

MAMA. But she was in a real play. Didn't she send us twenty-five dollars a week?

MARGE. For two weeks.

MAMA. Well the play was over.

MARGE (*crosses to* MAMA *and sits beside her*). It's not money, Mama. Sarah wrote us about it. You know what she said Florence was doin'. Sweepin' the stage!

MAMA. She was *in* the play!

MARGE. Sure she was in it! Sweepin'! Them folks ain't gonna let her be no actress. You tell her to wake up.

MAMA. I ... I ... think.

MARGE. Listen, Mama ... She won't wanna come. We know that ... but she gotta!

MAMA. Maybe we shoulda told her to expect me. It's kind of mean to just walk in like this.

MARGE. I bet she's livin' terrible. What's the matter with her? Don't she know we're keepin' her son?

MAMA. Florence don't feel right 'bout down here since Jim got killed.

MARGE. Who does? I should be the one goin' to get her. You tell her she ain't gonna feel right in no place. Mama, honestly! She must think she's white!

MAMA. Florence is brownskin.

MARGE. I don't mean that. I'm talkin' about her attitude. Didn't she go to Strumley's down here and ask to be a salesgirl? (*rises*) Now ain't that somethin'? They don't hire no Colored folks.

MAMA. Others beside Florence been talkin' about their rights.

MARGE. I know it ... but there's things we can't do cause they ain't gonna let us. (*She wanders over to the "White" side of the stage.*) Don't feel a damn bit different over here than it does on our side. (*silence*)

MAMA. Maybe we shoulda just sent her the money this time. This one time.

MARGE (*coming back to the "Colored" side*). Mama! Don't you let her cash that check for nothin' but to bring her back home.

MAMA. I know.

MARGE (*restless ... fidgets with her hair ... patting it in place*). I oughta go now.

MAMA. You best get back to Ted. He might play with the lamp.

MARGE. He better not let me catch him! If you got to go to the ladies' room take your grip.

MAMA. I'll be alright. Make Ted get up on time for school.

MARGE (*kisses her quickly and gives her the newspaper*). Here's something to read. So long, Mama.

MAMA. G'bye, Margie baby.

MARGE (*goes to door ... stops and turns to her mother*). You got your smelling salts?

MAMA. In my pocketbook.

MARGE (*wistfully*). Tell Florence I love her and miss her too.

PORTER (*can be heard singing in the distance*).

MAMA. Sure.

MARGE (*reluctant to leave*). Pin that check in your bosom, Mama. You might fall
  asleep and somebody'll rob you.

MAMA. I got it pinned to me. (*feels for the check which is in her blouse*)

MARGE (*almost pathetic*). Bye, Ma.

MAMA (*sits for a moment looking at her surroundings. She opens the paper and begins
  to read*).

PORTER (*offstage*). Hello, Marge. What you doin' down here?

MARGE. I came to see Mama off.

PORTER. Where's she going?

MARGE. She's in there; she'll tell you. I got to get back to Ted.

PORTER. Bye now ... Say, wait a minute, Marge.

MARGE. Yes?

PORTER. I told Ted he could have some of my peaches and he brought all them
  Brandford boys and they picked 'em all. I wouldn't lay a hand on him but I
  told him I was gonna tell you.

MARGE. I'm gonna give it to him!

PORTER (*enters and crosses to white side of waiting room. He carries a pail of water and
  a mop. He is about fifty years old. He is obviously tired but not lazy*). Every peach
  off my tree!

MAMA. There wasn't but six peaches on that tree.

PORTER (*smiles ... glances at* MAMA *as he crosses to the "White" side and begins to mop*).
  How d'ye do, Mrs. Whitney ... you going on a trip?

MAMA. Fine, I thank you. I'm going to New York.

PORTER. Wish it was me. You gonna stay?

MAMA. No, Mr. Brown. I'm bringing Florence ... I'm visiting Florence.

PORTER. Tell her I said hello. She's a fine girl.

MAMA. Thank you.

PORTER. My brother Bynum's in Georgia now.

MAMA. Well now, that's nice.

PORTER. Atlanta.

MAMA. He goin' to school?

PORTER. Yes'm. He saw Florence in a Colored picture. A moving picture.

MAMA. Do tell! She didn't say a word about it.

PORTER. They got Colored moving picture theaters in Atlanta.

MAMA. Yes. Your brother going to be a doctor?

PORTER (*with pride*). No. He writes things.

MAMA. Oh.

PORTER. My son is goin' back to Howard next year.

MAMA. Takes an awful lot of goin' to school to be anything. Lot of money least-
  ways.

PORTER (*thoughtfully*). Yes'm, it sure do.

MAMA. That sure was a nice church sociable the other night.

PORTER. Yes'm. We raised 87 dollars.

MAMA. That's real nice.

PORTER. I won your cake at the bazaar.

MAMA. The chocolate one?

PORTER (*as he wrings mop*). Yes'm ... was light as a feather. That old train is gonna
  be late this evenin'. It's number 42.

MAMA. I don't mind waitin'.

Porter (*lifts pail, tucks mop handle under his arm. He looks about in order to make certain no one is around and leans over and addresses* Mama *in a confidential tone*). Did you buy your ticket from that Mr. Daly?

Mama (*in a low tone*). No. Marge bought it yesterday.

Porter (*leaning against railing*). That's good. That man is real mean. Especially if he thinks you're goin' north. (*He starts to leave … then turns back to* Mama) If you go to the rest room, use the Colored men's … the other one is out of order.

Mama. Thank you, sir.

Mrs. Carter (*A white woman … well dressed, wearing furs and carrying a small, expensive overnight bag breezes in … breathless … flustered and smiling. She addresses the* Porter *as she almost collides with him*). Boy! My bags are out there. There taxi driver just dropped them. Will they be safe?

Porter. Yes, mam. I'll see after them.

Mrs. Carter. I thought I'd missed the train.

Porter. It's late, mam.

Mrs. Carter (*crosses to bench on the "White" side and rests her bag*). Fine! You come back here and get me when it comes. There'll be a tip in it for you.

Porter. Thank you, mam. I'll be here. (*as he leaves*) Miss Whitney, I'll take care of your bag too.

Mama. Thank you, sir.

Mrs. Carter (*wheels around … notices* Mama). Oh … Hello there …

Mama. Howdy, mam. (*She opens her newspaper and begins to read.*)

Mrs. Carter (*paces up and down rather nervously. She takes a cigarette from her purse, lights it and takes a deep draw. She looks at her watch and then speaks to* Mama *across the railing*). Have you any idea how late the train will be?

Mama. No, mam. (*starts to read again*)

Mrs. Carter. I can't leave this place fast enough. Two days of it and I'm bored to tears. Do you live here?

Mama (*rests paper on her lap*). Yes, mam.

Mrs. Carter. Where are you going?

Mama. New York City, mam.

Mrs. Carter. Good for you! You can stop "maming" me. My name is Mrs. Carter. I'm not a southerner really. (*takes handkerchief from her purse and covers her nose for a moment*) My God! Disinfectant! This is a frightful place. My brother's here writing a book. Wants atmosphere. Well, he's got it. I'll never come back here ever.

Mama. That's too bad, mam … Mrs. Carter.

Mrs. Carter. That's good. I'd die in this place. Really die. Jeff … Mr. Wiley … my brother … He's tied in knots, a bundle of problems … positively in knots.

Mama (*amazed*). That so, mam?

Mrs. Carter. You don't have to call me mam. It's so southern. Mrs. Carter! These people are still fighting the Civil War. I'm really a New Yorker now. Of course, I was born here … in the South I mean. Memphis. Listen … am I annoying you? I've simply got to talk to someone.

Mama (*places her newspaper on the bench*). No, Mrs. Carter. It's perfectly alright.

Mrs. Carter. Fine! You see Jeff has ceased writing. Stopped! Just like that! (*snaps fingers*)

Mama (*turns to her*). That so?

Mrs. Carter. Yes. The reviews came out on his last book. Poor fellow.

Mama. I'm sorry, mam … Mrs. Carter. They didn't like his book?

MRS. CARTER. Well enough ... but Jeff's ... well, Mr. Wiley is a genius. He says they missed the point! Lost the whole message! Did you read ... do you ... have you heard of *Lost My Lonely Way*?

MAMA. No, mam. I can't say I have.

MRS. CARTER. Well, it doesn't matter. It's profound. Real ... you know. (*stands at the railing upstage*) It's about your people.

MAMA. That's nice.

MRS. CARTER. Jeff poured his complete self into it. Really delved into the heart of the problem, pulled no punches! He hardly stopped for his meals ... And of course I wasn't here to see that he didn't overdo. He suffers so with his characters.

MAMA. I guess he wants to do his best.

MRS. CARTER. Zelma! ... That's his heroine ... Zelma! A perfect character.

MAMA (*interested ... coming out of her shell eagerly*). She was colored, mam?

MRS. CARTER. Oh yes! ... But of course you don't know what it's about do you?

MAMA. No, miss ... Would you tell me?

MRS. CARTER (*leaning on the railing*). Well ... she's almost white, see? Really you can't tell except in small ways. She wants to be a lawyer ... and ... and ... well, there she is full of complexes and this deep shame you know.

MAMA (*excitedly but with curiosity*). Do tell! What shame has she got?

MRS. CARTER (*takes off her fur neckpiece and places it on bench with overnight bag*). It's obvious! This lovely creature ... intelligent, ambitious, and well ... she's a Negro!

MAMA (*waiting eagerly*). Yes'm, you said that ...

MRS. CARTER. Surely you understand? She's constantly hating herself. Just before she dies she says it! ... Right on the bridge ...

MAMA (*genuinely moved*). How sad. Ain't it a shame she had to die?

MRS. CARTER. It was inevitable ... couldn't be any other way!

MAMA. What did she say on the bridge?

MRS. CARTER. Well ... just before she jumped ...

MAMA (*slowly straightening*). You mean she killed *herself*?

MRS. CARTER. Of course. Close your eyes and picture it!

MAMA (*turns front and closes her eyes tightly with enthusiasm*). Yes'm.

MRS. CARTER (*center stage on "White" side*). Now ... ! She's standing on the bridge in the moonlight ... Our of her shabby purse she takes a mirror ... and by the light of the moon she looks at her reflection in the glass.

MAMA (*clasps her hands together gently*). I can see her just as plain.

MRS. CARTER (*sincerely*). Tears roll down her cheeks as she says ... almost! almost white ... but I'm a black! I'm a Negro! and then ... (*turns to* MAMA) she jumps and drowns herself!

MAMA (*opens her eyes and speaks quietly*). Why?

MRS. CARTER. She can't face it! Living in a world where she almost belongs but not quite. (*drifts upstage*) Oh it's so ... so ... tragic.

MAMA (*carried away by her convictions ... not anger ... she feels challenged. She rises*). That ain't so! Not one bit it ain't!

MRS. CARTER (*surprised*). But it is!

MAMA (*During the following she works her way around the railing until she crosses over about one foot to the "White" side and is face to face with* MRS. CARTER). I know it ain't! Don't my friend Essie Kitredge daughter look just like a German or somethin'? She didn't kill herself! She's teachin' the third grade in the colored school right here. Even the bus drivers ask her to sit in the front seats cause they think she's white! ... an' ... an' ... she just says as clear as you please ... "I'm sittin' where my people got to sit by law. I'm a Negro woman!"

MRS. CARTER (*uncomfortable and not knowing why*). ... But there you have it. The exception makes the rule. That's proof!

MAMA. No such thing! My cousin Hemsly's as white as you! ... an' ... an' he never ...

MRS. CARTER (*flushed with anger ... yet lost ... because she doesn't know why*). Are you losing your temper? (*weakly*) Are you angry with me?

MAMA (*stands silently trembling as she looks down and notices she is on the wrong side of the railing. She looks up at the "White Ladies room" sign and slowly works her way back to the "Colored" side. She feels completely lost*). No, *mam*. Excuse me please. (*with bitterness*) I just meant Hemsly works in the colored section of the shoe store ... He never once wanted to kill his self! (*She sits down on the bench and fumbles for her newspaper. Silence.*)

MRS. CARTER (*Caught between anger and reason ... she laughs nervously*). Well! Let's not be upset by this. It's entirely my fault you know. This whole thing is a completely controversial subject. (*silence*) If it's too much for Jeff ... well naturally I shouldn't discuss it with you. (*approaching railing*) I'm sorry. Let *me* apologize.

MAMA (*keeps her eyes on the paper*). No need for that, mam. (*silence*)

MRS. CARTER (*painfully uncomfortable*). I've drifted away from ... What started all of this?

MAMA (*no comedy intended or allowed on this line*). Your brother, mam.

MRS. CARTER (*trying valiantly to brush away the tension*). Yes ... Well, I had to come down and sort of hold his hand over the reviews. He just thinks too much ... and studies. He knows the Negro so well that sometimes our friends tease him and say he almost *seems* like ... well you know ...

MAMA (*tightly*). Yes'm.

MRS. CARTER (*slowly walks over the "Colored" side near the top of the rail*). You know I try but it's really difficult to understand you people. However ... I keep trying.

MAMA (*still tight*). Thank you, mam.

MRS. CARTER (*retreats back to "White" side and begins to prove herself*). Last week ... Why do you know what I did? I sent a thousand dollars to a Negro college for scholarships.

MAMA. That was right kind of you.

MRS. CARTER (*almost pleading*). I know what's going on in your mind ... and what you're thinking is wrong. I've ... I've ... eaten with Negroes.

MAMA. Yes, mam.

MRS. CARTER (*trying to find a straw*). ... And there's Malcolm! If it weren't for the guidance of Jeff he'd never written his poems. Malcolm is a Negro.

MAMA (*freezing*). Yes, mam.

MRS. CARTER (*gives up, crosses to her bench, opens her overnight bag and takes out a book and begins to read. She glances at* MAMA *from time to time.* MAMA *is deeply absorbed in her newspaper.* MRS. CARTER *closes her book with a bang ... determined to penetrate the wall* MAMA *has built around her*). Why are you going to New York?

MAMA (*almost accusingly*). I got a daughter there.

MRS. CARTER. I lost my son in the war. (*silence ...* MAMA *is ill at ease.*) Your daughter ... what is she doing ... studying?

MAMA. No'm, she's trying to get on stage.

MRS. CARTER (*pleasantly*). Oh ... a singer?

MAMA. No, mam. She's ...

MRS. CARTER (*warmly*). You people have such a gift. I love spirituals ... "Steal Away," "Swing Low, Sweet Chariot."

MAMA. They are right nice. But Florence wants to act. Just say things in plays.

MRS. CARTER. A dramatic actress?

MAMA. Yes, that's what it is. She been in a colored moving picture, and a big show for two weeks on Broadway.

MRS. CARTER. The dear, precious child! ... But this is funny ... no! it's pathetic. She must be bitter ... *really* bitter. Do you know what I do?

MAMA. I can't rightly say.

MRS. CARTER. I'm an actress! A dramatic actress ... And I haven't really worked in six months ... And I'm pretty well-known ... And everyone knows Jeff. I'd like to work. Of course, there are my committees, but you see, they don't need me. Not really ... not even Jeff.

MAMA. Now that's a shame.

MRS. CARTER. Now your daughter ... you must make her stop before she's completely unhappy. Make her stop!

MAMA. Yes'm ... why?

MRS. CARTER. I have the best of contacts and *I've* only done a few *broadcasts* lately. Of course, I'm not counting the things I just wouldn't do. Your daughter ... make her stop.

MAMA. A drama teacher told her she has real talent.

MRS. CARTER. A drama teacher! My dear woman, there are loads of unscrupulous whites up there that just hand out opinions for ...

MAMA. This was a colored gentleman down here.

MRS. CARTER. Oh well! ... And she went up there on the strength of that? This makes me very unhappy. (*puts book away in case, and snaps lock, silence*)

MAMA (*getting an idea*). Do you really, truly feel that way, mam?

MRS. CARTER. I do. Please ... I want you to believe me.

MAMA. Could I ask you something?

MRS. CARTER. Anything.

MAMA. You won't be angry, mam?

MRS. CARTER (*remembering*). I won't. I promise you.

MAMA (*gathering courage*). Florence is proud ... but she's having it hard.

MRS. CARTER. I'm sure she is.

MAMA. Could you help her out some, mam? Knowing all the folks you do ... maybe ...

MRS. CARTER (*rubs the outside of the case*). Well ... it isn't that simple ... but ... you're very sweet. If only I could ...

MAMA. Anything you did, I feel grateful. I don't like to tell it, but she can't even pay her rent and things. And she's used to my cooking for her ... I believe my girl goes hungry sometime up there ... and yet she'd like to stay so bad.

MRS. CARTER (*looks up, resting case on her knees*). How can I refuse? You seem like a good woman.

MAMA. Always lived as best I knew how and raised my children up right. We got a fine family, mam.

MRS. CARTER. And I've no family at all. I've got to! It's clearly my duty. Jeff's books ... guiding Malcolm's poetry ... It isn't enough ... oh I know it isn't. Have you ever heard of Melba Rugby?

MAMA. No, mam. I don't know anybody much ... except right here.

MRS. CARTER (*brightening*). She's in California, but she's moving East again ... hares California.

MAMA. Yes'm.

MRS. CARTER. A most versatile woman. Writes, directs, acts ... everything!

MAMA. That's nice, mam.

MRS. CARTER. Well, she's uprooting herself and coming back to her first home ... New York ... to direct "Love Flowers" ... it's a musical.

MAMA. Yes'm.

MRS. CARTER. She's grand ... helped so many people ... and I'm sure she'll help your ... what's her name.

MAMA. Florence.

MRS. CARTER (*turns back to bench, opens bag, takes out a pencil and an address book*). Yes, Florence. She'll have to *make* a place for her.

MAMA. Bless you, mam.

MRS. CARTER (*holds handbag steady on rail as she uses it to write on*). Now let's see ... the best thing to do would be to give you the telephone number ... since you're going there.

MAMA. Yes'm.

MRS. CARTER (*writing address on paper*). Your daughter will love her ... and if she's a deserving girl ...

MAMA (*looking down as* MRS. CARTER *writes*). She's a good child. Never a bit of trouble. Except about her husband, and neither one of them could help that.

MRS. CARTER (*stops writing, raises her head questioning*). Oh?

MAMA. He got killed at voting time. He was a good man.

MRS. CARTER (*embarrassed*). I guess that's worse than losing him in the war.

MAMA. We all got our troubles passing through here.

MRS. CARTER (*gives her the address*). Tell your dear girl to call this number about a week from now.

MAMA. Yes, mam.

MRS. CARTER. Her experience won't matter with Melba. I know she'll understand. I'll call her too.

MAMA. Thank you, mam.

MRS. CARTER. I'll just tell her ... no heavy washing or ironing ... just light cleaning and a little cooking ... does she cook?

MAMA. Mam? (*slowly backs away from* MRS. CARTER *and sits down on bench*)

MRS. CARTER. Don't worry, that won't matter to Melba. (*silence, moves around the rail to "Colored" side, leans over* MAMA) I'd take your daughter myself, but I've got Binnie. She's been with me for years, and I just can't let her go ... can I?

MAMA (*looks at* MRS. CARTER *closely*). No, mam.

MRS. CARTER. Of course she must be steady. I couldn't ask Melba to take a fly-by-night. (*touches Mama's arm*) But she'll have her own room and bath, and above all ... security.

MAMA (*reaches out, clutches* MRS. CARTER'S *wrist almost pulling her off balance*). Child!

MRS. CARTER (*frightened*). You're hurting my wrist.

MAMA (*looks down, realizes how tight she's clutching her, and releases her wrist*). I mustn't hurt you, must I.

MRS. CARTER (*backing away rubbing her wrist*). It's all right.

MAMA (*rises*). You better get over on the other side of that rail. It's against the law for you to be over here with me.

MRS. CARTER (*frightened and uncomfortable*). If you think so.

MAMA. I don't want to break the law.

MRS. CARTER (*keeps her eye on* MAMA *as she drifts around railing to bench on her side, gathers overnight bag*). I know I must look like a fright. The train should be along soon. When it comes, I won't see you until New York. These silly laws. (*silence*) I'm going to powder my nose. (*exits into "White ladies" room*)

PORTER (*singing offstage*).

MAMA (*sits quietly, staring in front of her ... then looks at the address for a moment ... tears the paper into little bits and lets them flutter to the floor. She opens the suitcase, takes out notebook, an envelope and a pencil. She writes a few words on the paper*).

PORTER (*enters with broom and dust pan*). Number 42 will be coming along in nine minutes. (*When* MAMA *doesn't answer him, he looks up and watches her. She reaches in her bosom, unpins the check, smooths it out, places it in the envelope with the letter. She closes the suitcase.*) I said the train's coming. Where's the lady?

MAMA. She's in the *ladies'* room. You got a stamp?

PORTER. No. But I can get one out of the machine. Three for a dime.

MAMA (*hands him the letter*). Put one on here and mail it for me.

PORTER (*looks at it*). Gee ... you writing Florence when you're going to see her?

MAMA (*picks up the shoebox and puts it back on the bench*). You want a good lunch? It's chicken and fruit.

PORTER. Sure ... thank you ... but you won't ...

MAMA (*rises, paces up and down*). I ain't gonna see Florence for a long time. Might be never.

PORTER. How's that, Mrs. Whitney?

MAMA. She can be anything in the world she wants to be! That's her right. Marge can't make her turn back, Mrs. Carter can't make her turn back. *Lost My Lonely Way!* That's a book! People killing theyselves 'cause they look white but be black. They just don't know do they, Mr. Brown?

PORTER. Whatever happened don't you fret none. Life is too short.

MAMA. Oh, I'm gonna fret plenty! You know what I wrote Florence?

PORTER. No, mam. But you don't have to tell me.

MAMA. I said "Keep trying." ... Oh, I'm going home.

PORTER. I'll take your bag. (*picks up bag and starts out*) Come on Mrs. Whitney. (PORTER *exits*)

> (MAMA *moves around to "White" side, stares at sign over door. She starts to knock on "White Ladies" door, but changes her mind. As she turns to leave, her eye catches the railing; she approaches it gently, touches it, turns, exits. Stage is empty for about six or seven seconds. Sound of train whistle is heard in the distance. Slow curtain.*)

CURTAIN.

(1950)

Questions of Discussion and Writing

1. Why is the play named after a character who never appears?
2. How would you describe Mrs. Carter? How would you characterize Mama? Why does she react to Mrs. Carter the way she does? Why does she grab Mrs. Carter's wrist and call her "Child!"?
3. How does Mama change in the course of the play? What causes her to change?
4. What is the significance of the divided stage and the separate restroom signs?
5. How would you update this play? Rewrite the encounter between Mama and Mrs. Carter (pages 952–56), placing it in a contemporary setting and using current language.

Luis Valdez   1940–

Born into a migrant farm-worker family in Delano, California, Luis Valdez often worked in the fields with his parents. After graduating from San Jose State in 1964 with a degree in drama, he formed a theater company of farm workers, El Teatro Campesino, to support the strikers at the Delano grape plantations by performing short, improvised, satirical skits in community centers and in the fields. By the 1980s, Valdez expanded his interests to film and television, in part to counter the broad ethnic stereotypes of Mexican Americans. His work included a film based on his widely successful play *Zoot Suit* (1978), and *La Bamba* (1987), a bio-pic of Chicano rock star Ritchie Valens. Critic John Leonard described Valdez's televised play *La Pastorela* (1991) as "the Nativity ... tricked up to look like a road-show amalgam of *The Wizard of Oz* and *Cats*."

Los Vendidos[1]

CHARACTERS

HONEST SANCHO	JOHNNY
SECRETARY	REVOLUCIONARIO
FARM WORKER	MEXICAN-AMERICAN

SCENE

HONEST SANCHO'S *Used Mexican Lot and Mexican Curio Shop. Three models are on display in* HONEST SANCHO'S *shop: to the right, there is a* REVOLUCIONARIO, *complete with sombrero, carrilleras[2] and carabina 30–30. At center, on the floor, there is the* FARM WORKER, *under a broad straw sombrero. At stage left is the* PACHUCO, *filero[3] in hand.*

[HONEST SANCHO *is moving among his models, dusting them off and preparing for another day of business.*]

---

[1]**Los Vendidos** The Sellouts.
[2]**carrilleras** cartridge belts.
[3]**Pachuco** Chicano slang for an urban tough guy; **filero** blade.

SANCHO. Bueno, bueno, mis monos, vamos a ver a quien vendemos ahora, ¿no?[4] [*To audience.*] ¡Quihubo! I'm Honest Sancho and this is my shop. Antes fui contratista pero ahora logré tener mi negocito.[5] All I need now is a customer. [*A bell rings offstage.*] Ay, a customer!

SECRETARY [*Entering*]. Good morning, I'm Miss Jiménez from—

SANCHO ¡Ah, una chicana! Welcome, welcome Señorita Jiménez.

SECRETARY [*Anglo pronunciation*]. JIM-enez.

SANCHO. ¿Qué?

SECRETARY. My name is Miss JIM-enez. Don't you speak English? What's wrong with you?

SANCHO. Oh, nothing, Señorita JIM-enez. I'm here to help you.

SECRETARY. That's better. As I was starting to say, I'm a secretary from Governor Reagan's office, and we're looking for a Mexican type for the administration.

SANCHO. Well, you come to the right place, lady. This is Honest Sancho's Used Mexican lot, and we got all types here. Any particular type you want?

SECRETARY. Yes, we were looking for somebody suave—

SANCHO. Suave.

SECRETARY. Debonair.

SANCHO. De buen aire.

SECRETARY. Dark.

SANCHO. Prieto.

SECRETARY. But of course not too dark.

SANCHO. No muy prieto.

SECRETARY. Perhaps, beige.

SANCHO. Beige, just the tone. Así como cafecito con leche,[6] ¿no?

SECRETARY. One more thing. He must be hard-working.

SANCHO. That could only be one model. Step right over here to the center of the shop, lady. [*They cross to the* FARM WORKER.] This is our standard farm worker model. As you can see, in the words of our beloved Senator George Murphy, he is "built close to the ground." Also take special notice of his four-ply Goodyear huaraches, made from the rain tire. This wide-brimmed sombrero is an extra added feature—keeps off the sun, rain, and dust.

SECRETARY. Yes, it does look durable.

SANCHO. And our farm worker model is friendly. Muy amable.[7] Watch. [*Snaps his fingers.*]

FARM Worker [*Lifts up head*]. Buenos días, señorita. [*His head drops.*]

SECRETARY. My, he's friendly.

SANCHO. Didn't I tell you? Loves his patrones! But his most attractive feature is that he's hard-working. Let me show you. [*Snaps fingers.* FARM WORKER *stands.*]

FARM WORKER. ¡El jale![8] [*He begins to work.*]

SANCHO. As you can see, he is cutting grapes.

SECRETARY. Oh, I wouldn't know.

SANCHO. He also picks cotton. [*Snap.* FARM WORKER *begins to pick cotton.*]

---

[4]**Bueno ... no?** Well, well, my cute ones, let's see who we can sell now, O.K?

[5]**Antes ... negocito** I used to be a contractor, but now I'm successful with my own little business.

[6]**Así ... leche** like coffee with milk.

[7]**Muy amable** very friendly.

[8]**El jale** the job.

SECRETARY. Versatile isn't he?

SANCHO. He also picks melons. [*Snap.* FARM WORKER *picks melons.*] That's his slow speed for late in the season. Here's his fast speed. [*Snap.* FARM WORKER *picks faster.*]

SECRETARY. ¡Chihuahua! ... I mean, goodness, he sure is a hard worker.

SANCHO [*Pulls the* FARM WORKER *to his feet*]. And that isn't the half of it. Do you see these little holes on his arms that appear to be pores? During those hot sluggish days in the field, when the vines or the branches get so entangled, it's almost impossible to move; these holes emit a certain grease that allows our model to slip and slide right through the crop with no trouble at all.

SECRETARY. Wonderful. But is he economical?

SANCHO. Economical? Señorita, you are looking at the Volkswagen of Mexicans. Pennies a day is all it takes. One plate of beans and tortillas will keep him going all day. That, and chile. Plenty of chile. Chile jalapenos, chile verde, chile colorado. But, of course, if you do give him chile [*Snap.* FARM WORKER *turns left face. Snap.* FARM WORKER *bends over.*] then you have to change his oil filter once a week.

SECRETARY. What about storage?

SANCHO. No problem. You know these new farm labor camps our Honorable Governor Reagan has built out by Parlier or Raisin City? They were designed with our model in mind. Five, six, seven, even ten in one of those shacks will give you no trouble at all. You can also put him in old barns, old cars, river banks. You can even leave him out in the field overnight with no worry!

SECRETARY. Remarkable.

SANCHO. And here's an added feature: Every year at the end of the season, this model goes back to Mexico and doesn't return, automatically, until next Spring.

SECRETARY. How about that. But tell me: does he speak English?

SANCHO. Another outstanding feature: is that last year this model was programmed to go out on STRIKE! [*Snap.*]

FARM WORKER. ¡HUELGA! ¡HUELGA! Hermanos, sálganse de esos files.[9] [*Snap. He stops.*]

SECRETARY. No! Oh no, we can't strike in the State Capitol.

SANCHO. Well, he also scabs. [*Snap.*]

FARM WORKER. Me vendo barato, ¿y qué?[10] [*Snap.*]

SECRETARY. That's much better, but you didn't answer my question. Does he speak English?

SANCHO. Bueno ... no, pero[11] he has other—

SECRETARY. No.

SANCHO. Other features.

SECRETARY. No! He just won't do!

SANCHO. Okay, okay pues. We have other models.

SECRETARY. I hope so. What we need is something a little more sophisticated.

SANCHO. Sophisti—¿qué?

SECRETARY. An urban model.

---

[9]**Huelga! ... files** Strike! Strike! Brothers, leave those rows.

[10]**Me ... qué?** I come cheap, so what?

[11]**Bueno ... no, pero** Well, no, but.

SANCHO. Ah, from the city! Step right back. Over here in this corner of the shop is exactly what you're looking for. Introducing our new 1969 JOHNNY PACHUCO model! This is our fast-back model. Streamlined. Built for speed, low-riding, city life. Take a look at some of these features. Mag shoes, dual exhausts, green chartreuse paint-job, dark-tint windshield, a little poof on top. Let me just turn him on. [*Snap.* JOHNNY *walks to stage center with a pachuco bounce.*]

SECRETARY. What was that?

SANCHO. That, señorita, was the Chicano shuffle.

SECRETARY. Okay, what does he do?

SANCHO. Anything and everything necessary for city life. For instance, survival: He knife fights. [*Snap.* JOHNNY *pulls out switch blade and swings at* SECRETARY.]

[SECRETARY *screams.*]

SANCHO. He dances. [*Snap.*]

JOHNNY [*Singing*]. "Angel Baby, my Angel Baby..." [*Snap.*]

SANCHO. And here's a feature no city model can be without. He gets arrested, but not without resisting, of course. [*Snap.*]

JOHNNY. ¡En la madre, la placa!¹² I didn't do it! I didn't do it! [JOHNNY *turns and stands up against an imaginary wall, legs spread out, arms behind his back.*]

SECRETARY. Oh no, we can't have arrests! We must maintain law and order.

SANCHO. But he's bilingual!

SECRETARY. Bilingual?

SANCHO. Simón que yes.¹³ He speaks English! Johnny, give us some English. [*Snap.*]

JOHNNY [*Comes downstage*]. Fuck-you!

SECRETARY [*Gasps*]. Oh! I've never been so insulted in my whole life!

SANCHO. Well, he learned it in your school.

SECRETARY. I don't care where he learned it.

SANCHO. But he's economical!

SECRETARY. Economical?

SANCHO. Nickels and dimes. You can keep Johnny running on hamburgers, Taco Bell tacos, Lucky Lager beer, Thunderbird wine, yesca—

SECRETARY. Yesca?

SANCHO. Mota.

SECRETARY. Mota?

SANCHO. Leños¹⁴... Marijuana. [*Snap;* JOHNNY *inhales on an imaginary joint.*]

SECRETARY. That's against the law!

JOHNNY [*Big smile, holding his breath*]. Yeah.

SANCHO. He also sniffs glue. [*Snap.* JOHNNY *inhales glue, big smile.*]

JOHNNY. Tha's too much man, ése.

SECRETARY. No, Mr. Sancho, I don't think this—

SANCHO. Wait a minute, he has other qualities I know you'll love. For example, an inferiority complex. [*Snap.*]

JOHNNY [*To* SANCHO]. You think you're better than me, huh ése?¹⁵ [*Swings switch blade.*]

---

¹²**En... la placa!** Wow, the cops!
¹³**Simón que yes** Yeah, sure.
¹⁴**Leños** joints (of marijuana).
¹⁵**ése** fellow, buddy.

SANCHO. He can also be beaten and he bruises, cut him and he bleeds; kick him
  and he—[*He beats, bruises and kicks* PACHUCO.] Would you like to try it?

SECRETARY. Oh, I couldn't.

SANCHO. Be my guest. He's a great scapegoat.

SECRETARY. No, really.

SANCHO. Please.

SECRETARY. Well, all right. Just once. [*She kicks* PACHUCO.] Oh, he's so soft.

SANCHO. Wasn't that good? Try again.

SECRETARY [*Kicks* PACHUCO]. Oh, he's so wonderful! [*She kicks him again.*]

SANCHO. Okay, that's enough, lady. You ruin the merchandise. Yes, our Johnny
  Pachuco model can give you many hours of pleasure. Why, the L.A.P.D. just
  bought twenty of these to train their rookie cops on. And talk about maintenance. Señorita, you are looking at an entirely self-supporting machine.
  You're never going to find our Johnny Pachuco model on the relief rolls. No,
  sir, this model knows how to liberate.

SECRETARY. Liberate?

SANCHO. He steals. [*Snap.* JOHNNY *rushes the* SECRETARY *and steals her purse.*]

JOHNNY. ¡Dame esa bolsa, vieja![16] [*He grabs the purse and runs. Snap by* SANCHO.
  He stops.]

[SECRETARY *runs after* JOHNNY *and grabs purse away from him, kicking him as
she goes.*]

SECRETARY. No, no, no! We can't have any *more* thieves in the State Administration. Put him back.

SANCHO. Okay, we still got other models. Come on, Johnny, we'll sell you to some
  old lady. [SANCHO *takes* JOHNNY *back to his place.*]

SECRETARY. Mr. Sancho, I don't think you quite understand what we need. What
  we need is something that will attract the women voters. Something more
  traditional, more romantic.

SANCHO. Ah, a lover. [*He smiles meaningfully.*] Step right over here, señorita.
  Introducing our standard Revolucionario and/or Early California Bandit
  type. As you can see he is well-built, sturdy, durable. This is the International
  Harvester of Mexicans.

SECRETARY. What does he do?

SANCHO. You name it, he does it. He rides horses, stays in the mountains, crosses deserts, plains, rivers, leads revolutions, follows revolutions, kills, can be
  killed, serves as a martyr, hero, movie star—did I say movie star? Did you ever
  see *Viva Zapata? Viva Villa? Villa Rides? Pancho Villa Returns? Pancho Villa Goes
  Back? Pancho Villa Meets Abbott and Costello—*

SECRETARY. I've never seen any of those.

SANCHO. Well, he was in all of them. Listen to this. [*Snap.*]

REVOLUCIONARIO [*Scream*]. ¡VIVA VILLAAAAA!

SECRETARY. That's awfully loud.

SANCHO. He has a volume control. [*He adjusts volume. Snap.*]

REVOLUCIONARIO [*Mousey voice*]. ¡Viva Villa!

SECRETARY. That's better.

SANCHO. And even if you didn't see him in the movies, perhaps you saw him on
  TV. He makes commercials. [*Snap.*]

---

[16]**Dame ... vieja!** Give me that bag, old lady.

REVOLUCIONARIO. Is there a Frito Bandito in your house?

SECRETARY. Oh yes, I've seen that one!

SANCHO. Another feature about this one is that he is economical. He runs on raw horsemeat and tequila!

SECRETARY. Isn't that rather savage?

SANCHO. Al contrario,[17] it makes him a lover. [*Snap.*]

REVOLUCIONARIO [*To* SECRETARY]. ¡Ay, mamasota, cochota, ven pa'ca.[18] [*He grabs* SECRETARY *and folds her back—Latin-lover style.*]

SANCHO [*Snap.* REVOLUCIONARIO *goes back upright*]. Now wasn't that nice?

SECRETARY. Well, it was rather nice.

SANCHO. And finally, there is one outstanding feature about this model I know the ladies are going to love: He's a GENUINE antique! He was made in Mexico in 1910!

SECRETARY. Made in Mexico?

SANCHO. That's right. Once in Tijuana, twice in Guadalajara, three times in Cuernavaca.

SECRETARY. Mr. Sancho, I thought he was an American product.

SANCHO. No, but—

SECRETARY. No, I'm sorry. We can't buy anything but American-made products. He just won't do.

SANCHO. But he's an antique!

SECRETARY. I don't care. You still don't understand what we need. It's true we need Mexican models such as these, but it's more important that he be *American.*

SANCHO. American?

SECRETARY. That's right, and judging from what you've shown me, I don't think you have what we want. Well, my lunch hour's almost over; I better—

SANCHO. Wait a minute! Mexican but American?

SECRETARY. That's correct.

SANCHO. Mexican but . . . [*A sudden flash.*] AMERICAN! Yeah, I think we've got exactly what you want. He just came in today! Give me a minute. [*He exits. Talks from backstage.*] Here he is in the shop. Let me just get some papers off. There. Introducing our new 1970 Mexican-American! Ta-ra-ra-ra-ra-ra-RA-RAAA!

[SANCHO *brings out the* MEXICAN-AMERICAN *model, a clean-shaven middle-class type in business suit, with glasses.*]

SECRETARY [*Impressed*]. Where have you been hiding this one?

SANCHO. He just came in this morning. Ain't he a beauty? Feast your eyes on him! Sturdy US STEEL frame, streamlined, modern. As a matter of fact, he is built exactly like our Anglo models except that he comes in a variety of darker shades: naugahyde, leather, or leatherette.

SECRETARY. Naugahyde.

SANCHO. Well, we'll just write that down. Yes, señorita, this model represents the apex of American engineering! He is bilingual, college educated, ambitious! Say the word "acculturate" and he accelerates. He is intelligent, well-mannered, clean—did I say clean? [*Snap.* MEXICAN-AMERICAN *raises his arm.*] Smell.

SECRETARY [*Smells*]. Old Sobaco, my favorite.

---

[17]**Al contrario** On the contrary.
[18]**Ay . . . pa'ca!** Get over here!

SANCHO [*Snap.* MEXICAN-AMERICAN *turns toward* SANCHO]. Eric! [*To* SECRETARY.] We call him Eric Garcia. [*To* ERIC.] I want you to meet Miss JIM-enez, Eric.

MEXICAN -AMERICAN. Miss JIM-enez, I am delighted to make your acquaintance. [*He kisses her hand.*]

SECRETARY. Oh, my, how charming!

SANCHO. Did you feel the suction? He has seven especially engineered suction cups right behind his lips. He's a charmer all right!

SECRETARY. How about boards? Does he function on boards?

SANCHO. You name them, he is on them. Parole boards, draft boards, school boards, taco quality control boards, surf boards, two-by-fours.

SECRETARY. Does he function in politics?

SANCHO. Señorita, you are looking at a political MACHINE. Have you ever heard of the OEO, EOC, COD, WAR ON POVERTY? That's our model! Not only that, he makes political speeches.

SECRETARY. May I hear one?

SANCHO. With pleasure. [*Snap.*] Eric, give us a speech.

MEXICAN-AMERICAN. Mr. Congressman, Mr. Chairman, members of the board, honored guests, ladies and gentlemen. [SANCHO *and* SECRETARY *applaud.*] Please, please, I come before you as a Mexican-American to tell you about the problems of the Mexican. The problems of the Mexican stem from one thing and one thing alone. He's stupid. He's uneducated. He needs to stay in school. He needs to be ambitious, forward-looking, harder-working. He needs to think American, American, American, AMERICAN, AMERICAN, AMERICAN. GOD BLESS AMERICA! GOD BLESS AMERICA! GOD BLESS AMERICA!! [*He goes out of control.*]

[SANCHO *snaps frantically and the* MEXICAN-AMERICAN *finally slumps forward, bending at the waist.*]

SECRETARY. Oh my, he's patriotic too!

SANCHO. Sí, señorita, he loves his country. Let me just make a little adjustment here. [*Stands* MEXICAN-AMERICAN *up.*]

SECRETARY. What about upkeep? Is he economical?

SANCHO. Well, no, I won't lie to you. The Mexican-American costs a little bit more, but you get what you pay for. He's worth every extra cent. You can keep him running on dry martinis, Langendorf bread.

SECRETARY. Apple pie?

SANCHO. Only Mom's. Of course, he's also programmed to eat Mexican food on ceremonial functions, but I must warn you an overdose of beans will plug up his exhaust.

SECRETARY. Fine! There's just one more question: HOW MUCH DO YOU WANT FOR HIM?

SANCHO. Well, I tell you what I'm gonna do. Today and today only, because you've been so sweet, I'm gonna let you steal this model from me! I'm gonna let you drive him off the lot for the simple price of—let's see taxes and license included—$15,000.

SECRETARY. Fifteen thousand DOLLARS? For a MEXICAN!

SANCHO. Mexican? What are you talking, lady? This is a Mexican-AMERICAN! We had to melt down two pachucos, a farm worker and three gabachos[19] to make this model! You want quality, but you gotta pay for it! This is no cheap run-about. He's got class!

---

[19]**gabachos** whites.

SECRETARY. Okay, I'll take him.

SANCHO. You will?

SECRETARY. Here's your money.

SANCHO. You mind if I count it?

SECRETARY. Go right ahead.

SANCHO. Well, you'll get your pink slip in the mail. Oh, do you want me to wrap him up for you? We have a box in the back.

SECRETARY. No, thank you. The Governor is having a luncheon this afternoon, and we need a brown face in the crowd. How do I drive him?

SANCHO. Just snap your fingers. He'll do anything you want.

[SECRETARY *Snaps.* MEXICAN–AMERICAN *steps forward.*]

MEXICAN-AMERICAN. RAZA QUERIDA, ¡VAMOS LEVANTANDO ARMAS PARA LIBERARNOS DE ESTOS DESGRACIADOS GABACHOS QUE NOS EXPLOTAN! VAMOS.[20]

SECRETARY. What did he say?

SANCHO. Something about lifting arms, killing white people, etc.

SECRETARY. But he's not supposed to say that!

SANCHO. Look, lady, don't blame me for bugs from the factory. He's your Mexican-American; you bought him, now drive him off the lot!

SECRETARY. But he's broken!

SANCHO. Try snapping another finger.

[SECRETARY *snaps.* MEXICAN-AMERICAN *comes to life again.*]

MEXICAN-AMERICAN. ¡ESTA GRAN HUMANIDAD HA DICHO BASTA! Y SE HA PUESTO EN MARCHA! ¡BASTA! ¡BASTA! ¡VIVA LA RAZA! ¡VIVA LA CAUSA! ¡VIVA LA HUELGA! ¡VIVAN LOS BROWN BERETS! ¡VIVAN LOS ESTUDIANTES! ¡CHICANO POWER![21]

[*The* MEXICAN-AMERICAN *turns toward the* SECRETARY, *who gasps and backs up. He keeps turning toward the* PACHUCO, FARM WORKER, *and* REVOLUCIONARIO, *snapping his fingers and turning each of them on, one by one.*]

PACHUCO [*Snap. To* SECRETARY]. I'm going to get you, baby! ¡Viva La Raza!

FARM WORKER [*Snap. To* SECRETARY]. ¡Viva la huelga! ¡Viva la Huelga! ¡VIVA LA HUELGA!

REVOLUCIONARIO [*Snap. To* SECRETARY] ¡Viva la revolución! ¡VIVA LA REVOLUCIÓN!

[*The three models join together and advance toward the* SECRETARY *who backs up and runs out of the shop screaming.* SANCHO *is at the other end of the shop holding his money in his hand. All freeze. After a few seconds of silence, the* PACHUCO *moves and stretches, shaking his arms and loosening up. The* FARM WORKER *and* REVOLUCIONARIO *do the same.* SANCHO *stays where he is, frozen to his spot.*]

JOHNNY. Man, that was a long one, ése. [*Others agree with him.*]

FARM WORKER. How did we do?

---

[20]RAZA ... VAMOS Beloved Raza [people of Mexican descent], let's take up arms to liberate ourselves from those damned whites who exploit us! Let's go.

[21]ESTA ... CHICANO POWER! This great mass of humanity has said enough! And it has begun to march! Enough! Enough! Long live La Raza! Long live the Cause! Long live the strike! Long live the Brown Berets! Long live the students! Chicano Power!

JOHNNY. Perty good, look at all that lana,[22] man! [*He goes over to* SANCHO *and removes the money from his hand.* SANCHO *stays where he is.*]

REVOLUCIONARIO. En la madre, look at all the money.

JOHNNY. We keep this up, we're going to be rich.

FARM WORKER. They think we're machines.

REVOLUCIONARIO. Burros.

JOHNNY. Puppets.

MEXICAN-AMERICAN. The only thing I don't like is—how come I always got to play the godamn Mexican-American?

JOHNNY. That's what you get for finishing high school.

FARM WORKER. How about our wages, ése?

JOHNNY. Here it comes right now. $3,000 for you, $3,000 for you, $3,000 for you, and $3,000 for me. The rest we put back into the business.

MEXICAN-AMERICAN. Too much, man–. Heh, where you vatos[23] going tonight?

FARM WORKER. I'm going over to Concha's. There's a party.

JOHNNY. Wait a minute, vatos. What about our salesman? I think he needs an oil job.

REVOLUCIONARIO. Leave him to me.

[*The* PACHUCO, FARM WORKER. *and* MEXICAN-AMERICAN *exit, talking loudly about their plans for the night. The* REVOLUCIONARIO *goes over to* SANCHO, *removes his derby hat and cigar, lifts him up and throws him over his shoulder.* SANCHO *hangs loose, lifeless.*]

REVOLUCIONARIO [*To audience*]. He's the best model we got! ¡Ajua! [*Exit.*]

(1967)

---

[22]**lana** money.
[23]**vatos** guys.

Questions for Discussion and Writing

1. What is the meaning of the play's title? Who are the "sellouts" that the title alludes to?

2. What stereotypes of Mexican-Americans does the play present? Are these stereotypes offensive? Why does Valdez use them?

3. What change occurs in the end of the play? Does this change clarify or explain the reason for using stereotypes?

4. What social or political messages does the play convey? Do the politics interfere with the play's dramatic effectiveness?

The Writing Process

Prewriting: Exploring Cultural Themes

You can develop your ideas for a cultural analysis of a literary work by considering themes and questions that commonly give form to this type of interpretation. The following list of points should stimulate your thinking:

1. What categories do the characters in the work belong to? Remember that the speaker or narrator in a story or poem is also a character. We classify people into groups based on attributes that we (or they) believe are meaningful in distinguishing them from other groups. Some of these attributes are visible, such as skin color, gender, age, and physical features; others are evident only when purposely communicated, such as social class, education level, religion, ethnic background, and sexual orientation. Each character or persona in a literary work may belong to more than one noteworthy category.

2. What stereotypes are held about the categories you have identified? Think about stereotypes held by people in the writer's time and setting, and the stereotypes held by the characters themselves.

3. Themes of power and oppression also prevail in cultural analysis, primarily because power and prestige are often culturally defined. Identify who in the literary work holds what kind of power over whom. What are the sources of this power: money, political clout, convention, ideology, physical force, status? Do the power relationships change over the course of the work? How and why do they change? Are any power relationships illusory or ambiguous?

You will write with greater engagement if you can develop a key question concerning one of the topics in the above list as it applies to your chosen literary work. For example, you may wonder, as many readers do, why Désirée ("Désirée's Baby," page 902) felt it necessary to end her life. The question you might try to answer would be this:

Is Désirée's suicide an understandable choice?

To answer this question you would need to focus on the historical period and the social setting of the story—namely, the gender and class roles that govern Désirée's life, as well as the racial prejudice that means her baby would never gain full acceptance. In other words, the key question will guide you in undertaking a cultural analysis of Chopin's story.

You will also find it helpful to discuss possible topics and share your writing plans with fellow classmates. Feedback from other readers can help you to answer questions about your analysis. Review the material on pages 47–48 about getting feedback from your peers.

Ideas for Writing: Making Connections

1. Compare the use of racial stereotypes in *Los Vendidos* (page 958) and "How To Be Chinese" (page 931), particularly in terms of theme, tone, and purpose.

2. Describe and compare the issues of social class that are raised by Toni Cade Bambara in "The Lesson" (page 924) and James Wright in "Autumn Begins in Martins Ferry, Ohio" (page 938).

3. Family gatherings and preparing food are key elements in Djanikian's "Immigrant Picnic" (page 942), Blanco's "América" (page 945), and Hemphill's "Commitments" (page 944). How do the three poets agree and differ in their feelings about these family occasions?

4. Compare the clash between old and new cultural practices in Achebe's "Dead Men's Path" (page 910) and Richard Blanco's "América" (page 945).

5. How do you think Sylvia in "The Lesson" (page 924) would respond to the poem "Hanging Fire" (page 939)? How would Louise in "The Fat Girl" (page 914) respond? Would Sylvia and Louise sympathize with the fears expressed by the speaker in Audre Lorde's poem? Write a letter from either Sylvia or Louise to the poem's speaker.

6. Compare Claude McKay's feelings about living in a racist society ("America," page 937) with those expressed by Countee Cullen ("Incident," page 937), Laurence Dunbar ("We Wear the Mask," page 521), and Langston Hughes ("Harlem: A Dream Deferred," page 460).

7. Compare "Geraldo No Last Name" (Cisneros, page 930) with "Hands" (Anderson, page 906). What do these stories have to say about the effects of alienation?

8. What details tell you that the play *Florence* (page 948) was written in 1950? Write an essay in which you argue that the cultural issues in this play are still relevant today.

9. Which selections in this casebook deal with the struggle for social acceptance? Select at least three works that explore this issue, and analyze how each one sets up and resolves the conflict.

10. Find a story or poem in this book that deals with one of the cultural issues of this casebook. Show how it is similar to one selection in the casebook and how it contrasts with a different selection in the casebook.

11. The selections in this casebook involve very different historical, social, and political contexts. Choose one or more works, and write a research essay that uses secondary source material about the cultural background to explain and interpret the literature. If you need to, review the discussion in Chapter 5 on how to conduct research for a literary analysis.

MultiModal Projects

1. Interview someone who immigrated to the United States. Prepare some questions ahead of time that will help you capture the person's immigration experience. Audiotape the interview, and find images, sound effects, and music that illustrate the person's story. Maybe your interviewee will provide photos you can scan. Create a digital story on your computer telling about your interviewee's immigration experience. Guides to digital storytelling can be found at http://courseweb.lis.illinois.edu/~jevogel2/lis506/howto.html, tinyurl.com/ps3yt, and tinyurl.com/imovieyt, as well as other websites.

2. Choose one of the selections in this casebook and find at least three images that set off, augment, or limit the selection. Write a statement that explains how the images are related thematically to the issues of identity and cultural conflict in the selection.

Glossary
Literary
and Rhetorical Terms

Allegory A form of symbolism in which ideas or abstract qualities are represented as characters or events in a story, novel, or play. For example, in the medieval drama *Everyman*, Fellowship, Kindred, and Goods, the friends of the title character, will not accompany him on his end-of-life journey, and he must depend on Good Works, whom he has previously neglected.

Alliteration Repetition of the same consonant sounds, usually at the beginning of words:

> Should the glee—glaze—
> In Death's—stiff—stare—
> —Emily Dickinson

Allusion An indirect reference to some character or event in literature, history, or mythology that enriches the meaning of the passage. For example, the title of W. H. Auden's poem "The Unknown Citizen" is an ironic allusion to the Tomb of the Unknown Soldier.

Ambiguity Something that may be validly interpreted in more than one way; double meaning.

Analysis A method of understanding the theme and structure of a literary work by examining its component parts, resulting in a relatively complete, consistent interpretation.

Anapest *See* Meter.

Antagonist The character (or a force such as war or poverty) in a drama, poem, or work of fiction whose actions oppose those of the protagonist (hero or heroine).

Anticlimax A trivial event following immediately after significant events.

Archetype A recurring character type, plot, symbol, or theme of seemingly universal significance: the blind prophet figure, the journey to the underworld, the sea as the source of life, the initiation theme.

Argument Writing that attempts to influence readers to accept an opinion or interpretation; a good argument includes a clear claim or stance, ample evidence, and sound reasoning that explains the claim and connects it to the evidence.

Assonance The repetition of similar vowel sounds within syllables:

> On desperate seas long wont to roam
>> —Edgar Allan Poe

Atmosphere *See* Mood.

Audience In composition, the readers for whom a piece of writing is intended.

Ballad A narrative poem in four-line stanzas, rhyming *xaxa*, often sung or recited as a folk tale. The *x* means that those two lines do not rhyme.

Blank Verse Unrhymed iambic pentameter, the line that most closely resembles speech in English:

> When I see birches bend to left and right
> Across the lines of straighter darker trees,
> I like to think some boy's been swinging them.
>> —Robert Frost

Carpe Diem Literally, seize the day, a phrase applicable to many lyric poems advocating lustful living:

> Gather ye rosebuds while ye may,
> Old time is still a-flying:
> And this same flower that smiles today
> Tomorrow will be dying.
>> —Robert Herrick

Catharsis In classical tragedy, the purging of pity and fear experienced by the audience at the end of the play; a "there but for the grace of the gods go I" sense of relief.

Chorus In Greek drama, a group (often led by an individual) who comments on or interprets the action of the play.

Claim A positive statement or assertion that requires support. Claims are the backbone of any interpretation of a literary work.

Climax The point toward which the action of a plot builds as the conflicts become increasingly intense or complex; the turning point.

Coherence In good writing, the orderly, logical relationship among the many parts—the smooth moving forward of ideas through clearly related sentences. *Also see* Unity.

Comedy A play, light in tone, designed to amuse and entertain, that usually ends happily, often with a marriage.

Comparative Argument A form of argument that examines the relative strengths and weaknesses of two views or interpretations.

Complication The rising action of a plot during which the conflicts build toward the climax.

Conceit A highly imaginative, often startling, figure of speech drawing an analogy between two unlike things in an ingenious way:

> In this sad state, God's tender bowels run
> Out streams of grace....
>
> —Edward Taylor

Concrete Poetry   Poems that convey meaning by the way they look on the page. Also called *shaped poetry.*

Conflict   The antagonism between opposing characters or forces that causes tension or suspense in the plot.

Connotation   The associations that attach themselves to many words, deeply affecting their literal meanings (e.g., *politician, statesman*).

Consonance   Close repetition of the same consonant sounds followed by different vowel sounds (*flesh/flash* or *breed/bread*). At the end of lines of poetry, this pattern produces half-rhyme.

Controlling Idea   *See* Thesis.

Controlling Image   In a short story, novel, play, or poem, an image that recurs and carries such symbolic significance that it embodies the theme of the work, as the quilts do in Walker's "Everyday Use," and as the grass does in Whitman's "Leaves of Grass."

Convention   An accepted improbability in a literary work, such as the dramatic aside, in which an actor turns from the stage and addresses the audience.

Counterargument   A form of argument organized as a point-by-point refutation of opposing views or interpretations.

Couplet   Two rhymed lines of poetry:

> For thy sweet love remembered such wealth brings
> That then I scorn to change my state with kings.
>
> —William Shakespeare

Crisis   *See* Climax.

Critical Reading and Thinking   The use of analysis, inference, synthesis, and evaluation to seek the meaning beneath the surface of any text, written or visual; the process of seeing and judging implications, connections, and assumptions that might otherwise go unnoticed.

Dactyl   *See* Meter.

Denotation   The literal dictionary meaning of a word.

Denouement   Literally, the "untying"; the resolution of the conflicts following the climax (or crisis) of a plot.

Diction   Words chosen in writing or speaking.

Double Entendre   A double meaning, one of which usually carries sexual suggestions, as in the country-western song about a truck driver who calls his wife long distance to say he is bringing his "big ol' engine" home to her.

Dramatic Irony   *See* Irony.

Dramatic Monologue A poem consisting of a self-revealing speech delivered by one person to a silent listener; for instance, Robert Browning's "My Last Duchess."

Dramatic Point of View *See* Point of View.

Elegy A poem commemorating someone's death but usually encompassing a larger issue as well.

Empathy Literally, "feeling in"; the emotional identification that a reader or an audience feels with a character.

English Sonnet *See* Sonnet.

Epigraph A quotation at the beginning of a poem, novel, play, or essay that suggests the theme of the work.

Epilogue The concluding section of a literary work, usually a play, in which loose threads are tied together or a moral is drawn.

Epiphany A moment of insight in which something simple and commonplace is seen in a new way and, as James Joyce said, "its soul, its whatness leaps to us from the vestment of its appearance."

Episode In a narrative, a unified sequence of events; in Greek drama, the action between choruses.

Evidence Facts, details, examples, reasoning, quotations, personal experiences, and the like, which are used to develop and explain the claims in an argument or interpretation.

Explication An explanation of a literary work developed by analyzing details, images, meanings, and comparisons derived from a close reading of the text.

Exposition That part of a plot devoted to supplying background information, explaining events that happened before the current action.

Fable A story, usually using symbolic characters and settings, designed to teach a lesson.

Falling Action In classical dramatic structure, the part of a play after the climax, in which the consequences of the conflict are revealed. *Also see* Denouement.

Figurative Language Words that carry suggestive or symbolic meaning beyond the literal level.

First-Person Point of View *See* Point of View.

Flashback Part of a narrative that interrupts the chronological flow by relating events from the past.

Flat Character In contrast to a well-developed round character, a flat one is stereotyped or shallow, not seeming as complex as real people; flat characters are often created deliberately to give them a symbolic role, like Old Man Warner in "The Lottery."

Foil A character, usually a minor one, who emphasizes the qualities of another one through implied contrast between the two.

Foot   A unit of poetic rhythm. *See* Meter.

Foreshadowing   Early clues about what will happen later in a narrative or play.

Formal Writing   The highest level of usage, in which no slang, contractions, or fragments are used.

Free Verse   Poetry that does not have regular rhythm, rhyme, or standard form.

Freewriting   Writing without regard to coherence or correctness, intended to relax the writer and produce ideas for further writing.

Genre   A classification of literature: drama, novel, short story, poem.

Hero/Heroine   The character intended to engage most fully the audience's or reader's sympathies and admiration. *Also see* Protagonist.

Hubris   Unmitigated pride, often the cause of the hero's downfall in Greek tragedy.

Hyperbole   A purposeful exaggeration.

Iamb   *See* Meter.

Image/Imagery   Passages or words that stir feelings or memories through an appeal to the senses.

Inductive Reasoning   The use of known facts and specific details to arrive at a general conclusion or interpretation.

Informal Writing (or Usage)   The familiar, everyday level of usage, which includes contractions and perhaps slang but precludes nonstandard grammar and punctuation.

Internal Rhyme   The occurrence of similar sounds within the lines of a poem rather than just at the ends of lines:

> Too bright for our infirm delight
>
> —Emily Dickinson

Intertextual Approach   A way of interpreting literature through exploring comparisons and contrasts with other works. The comparisons can be direct (one work intentionally refers to another one) or indirect (one work reminds you of another due to its language, imagery, theme, characters, or some other feature).

Invention   The process of generating subjects, topics, details, and plans for writing.

Irony   Lack of agreement between expectation and reality.

Verbal irony involves a major discrepancy between the words spoken or written and the intended meaning. For example, Stephen Crane writes, "War is kind," but he means—and the poem shows—that war is hell.

Situational irony can stem quite literally from irony of situation. For example, in Shirley Jackson's "The Lottery," the fact that the inhabitants of a small town get together on a beautiful summer day not for a picnic but to stone one of their neighbors to death is heavily ironic. Situational irony can also involve the contrast between the hopes, aspirations, or fears of a character and the outcome of that person's actions or eventual fate. For example, in Flannery O'Connor's "A Good Man Is Hard to Find," the grandmother's desire to see an historic sight leads instead to the family's fatal encounter with the Misfit.

Dramatic irony involves the difference between what a character knows or believes and what the better-informed reader or audience knows to be true. For example, in Susan Glaspell's *Trifles* the audience knows that the evidence to establish motive for the murder is right under the noses of the law enforcement officials, but the men overlook it because they consider the suspect's "women's work" not worthy of their notice.

Issue An important point or question that has more than one view or answer and provides the basis for the claims in an argument or interpretation.

Italian Sonnet *See* Sonnet.

Jargon The specialized words and expressions belonging to certain professions, sports, hobbies, or social groups. Sometimes any tangled and incomprehensible prose is called jargon.

Juxtaposition The simultaneous presentation of two conflicting images or ideas, designed to make a point of the contrast: for example, an elaborate and well-kept church surrounded by squalorous slums.

Limited Point of View *See* Point of View.

Lyric A poem that primarily expresses emotion.

Metaphor A figure of speech that makes an imaginative comparison between two literally unlike things:

> Sylvia's face was a pale star.

Metaphysical Poetry A style of poetry (usually associated with seventeenth-century poet John Donne) that boasts intellectual, complex, and even strained images (called *conceits*), which frequently link the personal and familiar to the cosmic and mysterious. *Also see* Conceit.

Meter Recurring patterns of stressed and unstressed syllables in poetry. A metrical unit is called a *foot*. There are four basic patterns of stress: an *iamb*, or *iambic foot*, which consists of an unstressed syllable followed by a stressed one (*before, return*); a *trochee*, or *trochaic foot*, which consists of a stressed syllable followed by an unstressed one (*funny, double*); an *anapest*, or *anapestic foot*, which consists of two unstressed syllables followed by a stressed one (*contradict*); and a *dactyl*, or *dactylic foot*, which consists of a stressed syllable followed by two unstressed ones (*merrily, syllable*). One common variation is the *spondee*, or *spondaic foot*, which consists of two stressed syllables (*moonshine, football*).

Lines are classified according to the number of metrical feet they contain: *monometer* (one foot), *dimeter* (two feet), *trimeter* (three feet), *tetrameter* (four feet), *pentameter* (five feet), *hexameter* (six feet), and so on.

Metonymy A figure of speech in which the name of one thing is substituted for that of something else closely associated with it—for example, *the White House* (meaning the president or the whole executive branch), or *the pen is mightier than the sword* (meaning written words are more powerful than military force).

Mood The emotional content of a scene or setting, usually described in terms of feeling: somber, gloomy, joyful, expectant. *Also see* Tone.

Motif A pattern of identical or similar images recurring throughout a passage or entire work.

Myth A traditional story involving deities and heroes, usually expressing and inculcating the established values of a culture.

Narrative A story line in prose or verse.

Narrator The person who tells the story to the audience or reader. *Also see* Unreliable Narrator.

Objective Point of View *See* Point of View.

Ode A long, serious lyric focusing on a stated theme: "Ode on a Grecian Urn."

Omniscient Point of View *See* Point of View.

Onomatopoeia A word that sounds like what it names: *whoosh, clang, babble.*

Oxymoron A single phrase that juxtaposes opposite terms:

> the lonely crowd, a roaring silence.

Parable A story designed to demonstrate a principle or lesson using symbolic characters, details, and plot lines.

Paradox An apparently contradictory statement that, upon examination, makes sense:

> In my end is my beginning.
> —Mary, Queen of Scots

The motto is intelligible only in the context of Christian theology, which promises renewed life after death.

Paraphrase In prose, a restatement in different words, usually briefer than the original version; in poetry, a statement of the literal meaning of the poem in everyday language.

Parody An imitation of a piece of writing, copying some features such as diction, style, and form, but changing or exaggerating other features for humorous effect.

Pentameter A line of poetry that contains five metrical feet. See Meter.

Persona The person created by the writer to be the speaker of the poem or story. The persona is not usually identical to the writer—for example, a personally optimistic writer could create a cynical persona to narrate a story.

Personification   Giving human qualities to nonhuman things:

> the passionate song of bullets and the banshee shrieks of shells
> —Stephen Crane

Phallic Symbol   An image shaped like the male sex organ; suggests male potency or male dominance (*towers, snakes, guns, spurs, jet planes, sleek cars*).

Plagiarism   Carelessly or deliberately presenting the words or ideas of another writer as your own; literary theft.

Plot   A series of causally related events or episodes that occur in a narrative or play. *Also see* Climax, Complication, Conflict, Denouement, Falling Action, Resolution, and Rising Action.

Point of Attack   The moment of the play at which the main action of the plot begins; it may occur in the first scene or after several scenes of exposition.

Point of View   The angle or perspective from which a story is reported and interpreted. There are a number of points of view that authors can use.

First person—someone, often the main character, tells the story as he or she experienced it (and uses the pronoun *I*).

Omniscient—the narrator knows everything about the characters and events and can move about in time and place and into the minds of all the characters.

Limited—the story is limited to the observations, thoughts, and feelings of a single character (not identified as *I*).

Shifting—a limited view which can shift to the perspective of more than one character.

Objective or *dramatic*—the actions and conversations are presented in detail as they occur, more or less objectively, without any comment from the author or a narrator.

Unreliable—narrated from the point of view of a character unable or perhaps unwilling to give a fully accurate account.

Prewriting   The process that writers use to gather ideas, consider audience, determine purpose, develop a thesis and tentative structure (plan), and generally prepare for the actual composing stage.

Primary Source   The literary work under consideration by the reader.

Prose Poem   A literary composition that contains many of the attributes of poetry—such as imagery, symbols, allusions, rhythm, internal rhyme, alliteration, assonance, and the like—but does not use line breaks or a regular metrical structure.

Protagonist   The main character in drama or fiction, sometimes called the hero or heroine.

Pun   A verbal joke based on the similarity of sound between words that have different meanings:

> They went and *told* the sexton and the sexton *tolled* the bell.
> —Thomas Hood

Quatrain   A four-line stanza of poetry, which can have any number of rhyme schemes.

Reasoning   The process of thinking carefully about something in order to make a judgment; drawing conclusions through the use of observations and explanations.

Resolution   The conclusion of the conflict in a fictional or dramatic plot. *Also see* Denouement *and* Falling Action.

Rhyme   Similar or identical sounds between words, usually the end sounds in lines of verse *(brain/strain; liquor/quicker)*.

Rhythm   The recurrence of stressed and unstressed syllables in a regular pattern. *Also see* Meter.

Rising Action   The complication and development of the conflict leading to the climax in a plot.

Round Character   A literary character with sufficient complexity to be convincing, true to life.

Sarcasm   A form of *verbal irony* that presents caustic and bitter disapproval in the guise of praise. *Also see* Irony.

Satire   Literary expression that uses humor and wit to attack and expose human folly and weakness. *Also see* Parody.

Secondary Source   Critical material from the library or the Internet (articles, reviews, books, sections of books).

Sentimentality   The attempt to produce an emotional response that exceeds the circumstances and to draw from the reader a stock response instead of a genuine emotional response.

Setting   The time and place in which a story, play, or novel occurs. *Also see* Mood.

Shakespearean Sonnet   *See* Sonnet.

Simile   A verbal comparison in which a similarity is expressed directly, using *like* or *as*:

> houses leaning together like conspirators.
> —James Joyce

Also see Metaphor.

Situational Irony   *See* Irony.

Soliloquy   A speech in which a dramatic character reveals what is going through his or her mind by talking aloud to herself or himself. *Also see* Dramatic Monologue.

Sonnet   A poem of fourteen ten-syllable lines, arranged in a pattern of rhyme schemes. The *English* or *Shakespearean sonnet* uses seven rhymes that divide the poem into three quatrains and a couplet: abab, cdcd, efef, gg. The *Italian sonnet* usually divides into an octave (eight lines) and a sestet (six lines) by using only five rhymes: abba, abba, cdecde. (The rhyme scheme of the sestet varies widely from sonnet to sonnet.)

Speaker The voice or person presenting a poem. *Also see* Persona.

Spondee *See* Meter.

Standard English The language that is written and spoken by most educated persons of English-speaking countries.

Stereotype An oversimplified, commonly held image or opinion about a person, a race, or an issue.

Stilted Language Words and expressions that are too formal for the writing situation; unnatural, artificial language.

Structure The general plan, framework, or form of a piece of writing.

Style Individuality of expression, achieved in writing through the selection and arrangement of words and punctuation.

Subplot Secondary plot in a novel or play, usually reinforcing the main theme but sometimes just providing interest, excitement, or comic relief.

Summary A short, objective restatement of the important ideas in a passage or a complete document, usually without analysis, explanation, paraphrasing, or personal comment.

Symbol Something that suggests or stands for an idea, quality, or concept larger than itself: the lion is a symbol of courage; a voyage or journey can symbolize life; water suggests spirituality, dryness the lack thereof.

Synecdoche A figure of speech in which some prominent feature is used to name the whole, or vice versa—for example, *a sail in the harbor* (meaning a ship), or *call the law* (meaning call the law enforcement officers).

Synesthesia Figurative language in which two or more sense impressions are combined:

> blue uncertain stumbling buzz
> —Emily Dickinson

Syntax Sentence structure; the relationship between words and among word groups in sentences.

Theater of the Absurd A form of drama that departs markedly from the realistic representation of events on stage, attempting to show that the human predicament is anguished, meaningless, and futile.

Theme The central or dominating idea advanced by a literary work, usually containing some insight into the human condition.

Thesis The main point or position that a writer develops and supports in a composition. *Also see* Claim.

Tone The attitude a writer conveys toward his or her subject and audience. In poetry this attitude is sometimes called *voice*.

Tragedy A serious drama that relates the events in the life of a protagonist, or *tragic hero*, whose error in judgment, dictated by a *tragic flaw*, results in the hero's downfall and culminates in catastrophe. In less classical terms, any serious drama, novel, or short story that ends with the death or defeat of the main character may be called tragic.

Trochee *See* Meter.

Type Character A literary character who embodies a number of traits that are common to a particular group or class of people (a rebellious daughter, a stern father, a jealous lover); all of the characters in Valdez's *Los Vendidos* are types.

Understatement A form of ironic expression that intentionally minimizes the importance of an idea or fact.

Unity The fitting together or harmony of all elements in a piece of writing. *Also see* Coherence.

Unreliable Narrator A viewpoint character who presents a biased or erroneous report that may mislead or distort a reader's judgments about other characters and actions; sometimes the unreliable narrator may be self–deceived.

Usage The accepted or customary way of using words in speaking and writing a language.

Verbal Irony *See* Irony.

Verisimilitude The appearance of truth or believability in a literary work.

Versification The mechanics of poetic composition, including such elements as rhyme, rhythm, meter, and stanza form.

Yonic Symbol An image shaped like the female breasts, uterus, or genitalia; suggests fecundity or female sexuality (*caves, pots, rooms, apples, full-blown roses*).

Credits

PHOTO CREDITS

Index of Authors, Titles, and First Lines of Poems

Note: Authors' names and first lines are set in roman type; all titles are italicized.

Subject Index

Resources for Writing about Literature